, docks, and railway stations four years after the Great Fire of 1871 (*Archives, Holland Historical Trus*

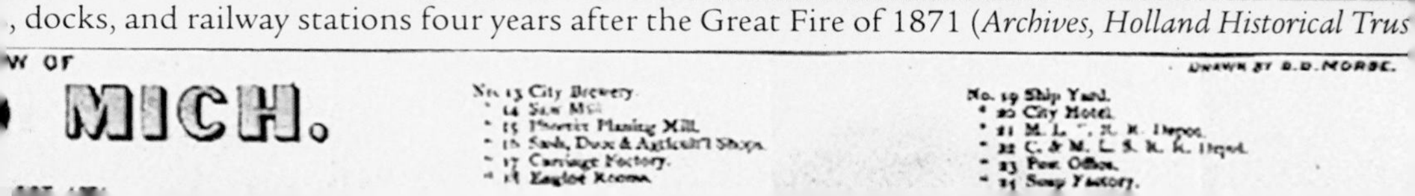

W OF

MICH.

DRAWN BY D.D. MORSE.

No. 13 City Brewery.
" 14 Saw Mill.
" 15 Phoenix Planing Mill.
" 16 Sash, Door & Agricult'l Shops.
" 17 Carriage Factory.
" 18 Engine Rooms.

No. 19 Ship Yard.
" 20 City Hotel.
" 21 M. L. S. R. R. Depot.
" 22 C. & M. L. S. R. R. Depot.
" 23 Post Office.
" 24 Soap Factory.

HOLLAND MICHIGAN

The Historical Series of the Reformed Church in America
In Cooperation with the
Van Raalte Institute
no. 80

HOLLAND MICHIGAN
From Dutch Colony to Dynamic City

Robert P. Swierenga

Van Raalte Press
Holland, Michigan

William B. Eerdmans Publishing Company
Grand Rapids, Michigan / Cambridge, UK

Van Raalte Press
Hope College
Theil Research Center
9 East 10th Street
Holland, Michigan 49423
www.hope.edu/vri

Wm. B. Eerdmans Publishing Co.
2140 Oak Industrial Drive SE, Grand Rapids, Michigan 49503
PO Box 163, Cambridge CB3 9PU UK
www.eerdmans.com

Printed in the United States of America

Library of Congress Cataloging-in-Publication Data

Swierenga, Robert P.
Holland Michigan : from Dutch colony to dynamic city / Robert P. Swierenga.
pages cm. -- (The historical series of the Reformed Church in America ; no. 80)
Includes bibliographical references and index.
ISBN 978-0-8028-7137-4 (cloth : alk. paper) 1. Holland (Mich.)--History. 2. Dutch Americans--Michigan--Holland--History. I. Title.
F574.H6S95 2013
977.4--dc23

2013046615

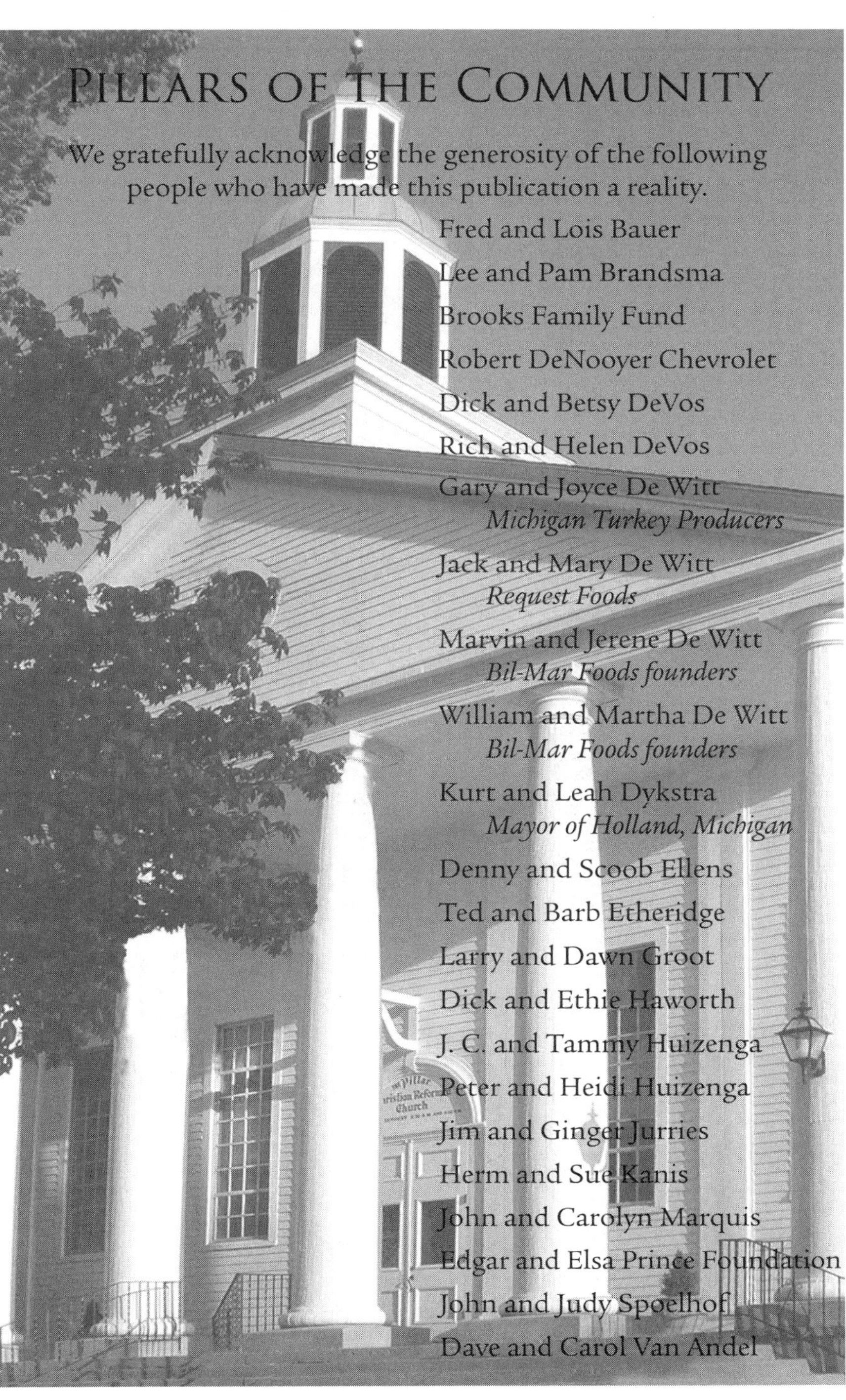

Pillars of the Community

We gratefully acknowledge the generosity of the following people who have made this publication a reality.

Fred and Lois Bauer

Lee and Pam Brandsma

Brooks Family Fund

Robert DeNooyer Chevrolet

Dick and Betsy DeVos

Rich and Helen DeVos

Gary and Joyce De Witt
Michigan Turkey Producers

Jack and Mary De Witt
Request Foods

Marvin and Jerene De Witt
Bil-Mar Foods founders

William and Martha De Witt
Bil-Mar Foods founders

Kurt and Leah Dykstra
Mayor of Holland, Michigan

Denny and Scoob Ellens

Ted and Barb Etheridge

Larry and Dawn Groot

Dick and Ethie Haworth

J. C. and Tammy Huizenga

Peter and Heidi Huizenga

Jim and Ginger Jurries

Herm and Sue Kanis

John and Carolyn Marquis

Edgar and Elsa Prince Foundation

John and Judy Spoelhof

Dave and Carol Van Andel

A. C. Van Raalte

To my grandchildren

Jacob Edward Groenhout
Trent Alan Groenhout
Jillanne Alyce Groenhout
Sydney Marie Swierenga
Henry Robert Breems
Louis Andrew Breems
Katherine Rebecca Breems

The Historical Series of the Reformed Church in America

The series was inaugurated in 1968 by the General Synod of the Reformed Church in America acting through the Commission on History to communicate the church's heritage and collective memory and to reflect on our identity and mission, encouraging historical scholarship which informs both church and academy.

www.rca.org/series

Contents

Figures

Tables

Acknowledgments

"Many hands make light work," the adage goes, and that has been my happy experience in the writing of this work during the past decade. Dozens of people helped in one way or another, and they will be acknowledged below. But I am especially indebted to two colleagues at the A. C. Van Raalte Institute—JoHannah (Mrs. Kraig) Smith and Elton J. Bruins—as well as my good friend Randall "Randy" P. Vande Water, author and former editor of the *Holland Sentinel*, and Michael J. Douma, my Hope College student assistant in the early days. JoHannah Smith, editorial assistant and office manager at the Van Raalte Institute, copy edited the manuscript with an eagle eye, bringing it into conformity with the sixteenth edition (2010) of the Chicago Manual of Style, which I swear, she has committed to memory.

Elton Bruins, founding director and Philip Phelps Jr. research professor emeritus at the Van Raalte Institute and the Blekkink professor emeritus of religion at Hope College, spent two months reading the completed manuscript with a sharp eye for errors of fact and "inconsistencies." He is the international authority on Rev. Albertus C. Van Raalte and of the religious history of Holland. His extensive knowledge of the city and region began in the 1960s, when he cataloged the manuscript collections of the Holland Historical Trust that are now safeguarded in the Holland Museum Archives. I "picked his brains" often about items that puzzled me, and he could always put his finger on the document I needed in his complete collection of Van Raalte manuscripts. His personal knowledge of people and events, especially concerning Hope College, Western Theological Seminary, and the Reformed Church in America over the past sixty years, is unique.

Randy Vande Water, a third-generation Hollander and renowned local historian, read every chapter, some more than once. He willingly shared his prodigious memory of people, places, and stories since the 1940s that only an insider could know. Nor did his editorial pen leave him; the early drafts came back marked liberally with missing words, commas, periods, and capital letters. He was equally generous in sharing his vast collection of historic photographs, some from his father and grandfather, and some of which he salvaged from the dumpster when a new regime came to power at the *Holland Sentinel* and did not appreciate their value. Michael Douma, author of *Veneklasen Brick* (2005), has a nose for finding historical "nuggets" in archival collections, and he found many to my advantage. Douma roughed out first drafts of chapters 10, 20, 22, and 29-31, and he later proofread several chapters. He gave me the boost that I needed early in the project. David Boeve of Audio Memories recorded lengthy interviews with seventeen Holland residents who were involved in major businesses, economic developments, and city administration, all of which Lori Trethewey, office manager at the Joint Archives of Holland, tediously transcribed. These interviews are now part of the permanent collection at the archives.

Fritz L. Kliphuis, Michael Lozon, Joel Lefever, and Paul A. Den Uyl, all authorities on Holland history and authors of books and articles on various aspects of it, read selected chapters. Kliphuis, a master of Holland's Sanborn Fire Insurance Maps and City Directories and a fount of knowledge about city history—especially the fascinating minutiae—read chapters 7, 10, 12, 15, and 19 with a meticulous eye. He saved me from numerous mistakes involving locations and postal addresses. Kliphuis graciously allowed me to publish in appendix 5 thirteen lists of businesses from auto dealers to saloons that he laboriously compiled from the Sanborn maps and the *Holland City Directories* from 1883 to 1950. These lists are an invaluable resource. Lozon, business reporter for the *Holland Sentinel* in the 1990s and author of company and community histories (Jack De Witt's Big Dutchman, Marvin De Witt's

Bil-Mar Foods, B. J. W. Berghorst & Sons, Patrick Thompson's Trans-Matic, and *Vision on Main Street*) read chapters 14, 15, 17, 19, and 33, and raised issues for me to consider. Lefever read the first six chapters and pointed me to photographs in the collections of the Holland Museum and the Joint Archives of Holland that might illuminate the text. Den Uyl, historian of Holland's fire department, in which his grandfather served, read chapter 25 on the fire department and helped me get the details correct. He indexed his book, *The Holland Fire Department: The First Fifty Years, 1867-1916*, partly for my benefit.

Robert "Bob" Vande Vusse, Holland city councilman and a specialist on Great Lakes shipping and Michigan railroads, read the sections on those topics in chapters 9 and 10. Philip Miller of the Howard Miller Clock Company read the chapter on industry and shared his keen interest in Holland business history. Huug van den Dool of the National Oceanic and Atmospheric Administration (NOAA) read the section on the Holland Fire of 1871 and provided historical weather information pertaining to the week of the fire. Michael Van Beek conducted research on the history of Holland Public Schools, work that prepared him for his present position as director of education policy at Michigan's Mackinac Center.

Earl Wm. (Bill) Kennedy and his wife, Nella, my associates at the Van Raalte Institute, shared their respective areas of expertise, Bill as a Reformed church historian and Nella as the institute's official Dutch-language translator. Nella translated countless Dutch-language documents and newspaper articles at my request and checked the English translations and the spelling of Dutch words and phrases.

Jacob (Jack) E. Nyenhuis, director of the Van Raalte Institute and provost emeritus and professor emeritus of classics at Hope College, graciously assigned student research assistants to support me in various ways. More important, he put the resources of the institute behind my research, without which this book would never have seen the light of day. Brigid Maniates assembled a preliminary bibliography, and Anthony Bednarz and Kara Robart assisted in indexing the book, checking quotations for accuracy, and other related tasks. Mark Cook, director of the Hope College bookstore and a graphics expert and historian, created all the maps and charts, notably the city ward maps and early Holland harbor maps, which required extensive research in original sources.

Librarians and archivists were always generous with their time and expertise. Geoffrey Reynolds, director of the Joint Archives of Holland, shared his knowledge of boats and the boating industry, connected me with people I needed to interview, and made available the electronic archives of photographs from the collections. Lori Trethewey located archival materials in the Joint Archives and patiently scanned photographs for me from numerous collections and from community members who lent me personal photos. Catherine "Caz" Jung, curator of archives and research at the Holland Museum, and former museum archivist Deborah Postema-George drew on their intimate knowledge of the collections to find information on request. Caz scanned dozens of photographs from the rich collections of the Holland Historical Trust and assisted me in identifying persons, places, and dates on photos lacking such crucial information. She proved to be an able detective with a nose for ferreting out the information I requested.

Mary VanderKooy, genealogy and reference librarian at Herrick District Library, instructed me in the use of the *Holland Sentinel* electronic files and facilitated the use of the Donald van Reken Collection, which she allowed to be moved for safekeeping to the Joint Archives of Holland. Ann Prins, former genealogy library assistant, compiled the Holland city federal population census of 1870 at my request and shared her detailed knowledge of local history. I thank Marlene (Mrs. Elmer) Veldheer and Kit Karsten of the Zeeland Historical Museum for photos from their collections. Marlene Veldheer passed away unexpectedly in June 2012 only weeks after assisting me. Jessica Hronchek, research and instruction librarian at the Gordon & Margaret Van Wylen Library at Hope College, searched web-based sources to track down information for me, and the inter-library loan staff obtained books that I needed from libraries across Michigan and beyond.

Unsung volunteers who patiently clipped articles from the *Holland Sentinel* over the years deserve special commendation. I made liberal use of the files of Elton Bruins at the Van Raalte Institute, of Sue Brandsen at the Joint Archives of Holland, and of the anonymous "clippers" at the Holland Museum archives and at Herrick District Library. Sue Brandsen also corrected information concerning Holland Christian School buildings in appendix 3.

Individuals who shared information and made historical records available include Hope professor Steve Vander Veen, David Koster (director of Holland Board of Public Works), Kay Walvoord, Eugene Westra, Calvin Langejans, Rev. Bob Terpstra of Immanuel Church of Holland, Mark Tucker (executive director of Community Action House), Janet De Young (president/CEO of Community Foundation of Holland/Zeeland), Maryam Komejan and Dwayne Baumgardner of Donnelly Corp., and former Hope College president Gordon Van Wylen and Greg Holcombe of Riverview Group in Holland. Other individuals whom I interviewed in person or by telephone are noted in the relevant footnotes. Myron "Mike" Van Ark generously made available his incomparable postcard collection of historic Holland. The numerous photo credits appended to the captions testify to the extensive use I made of his four-volume collection. Larry B. Massie allowed me to scan many photos in his vast photo archives, as did Randy Vande Water.

I thank Donald J. Bruggink, professor emeritus at Western Theological Seminary and the founding general editor of the Historical Series of the Reformed Church in America, for his and the editorial board's careful review of the manuscript and for his watchful shepherding of the project from idea to actuality. I also acknowledge other key links in the publication process: the staff at Wm B. Eerdmans Publishing Company and most essentially, the indefatigable Russell L. Gasero, archivist of the Reformed Church in America at the New Brunswick Seminary, who converted over 1,400 pages of single-spaced manuscript and nearly nine hundred images into the three-volume work that you hold in your hands. Tim Ellens, director of communications and marketing at Calvin College, designed the eye-catching dust jackets, taking care to make each cover unique. If the dust jacket sells the book, Tim did his part.

None of the dozens of specialists who assisted me in one way or another, particularly those who read and copy edited the manuscript, bear any responsibility for errors that remain. "The buck stops here," as any author will readily acknowledge.

Kudos to my wife, Joan Boomker Swierenga, for her support and understanding. When friends would ask her; "How's Bob doing?" Her reply often was, "His head's in the computer." How right she was. Many an evening she sat alone upstairs while I wrote in my study downstairs. The book is dedicated to my grandchildren. They are the best kind of children—all pleasure and no responsibility. Mine keep me young and bring pure joy.

My deepest appreciation also goes to Peter H. Huizenga, the "patron saint" of the Van Raalte Institute, for his unwavering support of and confidence in our research and publication and of this project in particular. He is not only a faithful benefactor but also a dear and trusted friend.

Finally, I cannot close without recalling the countless conversations with my colleagues at the Van Raalte Institute during our fabled morning coffee times, when I would raise issues concerning my research or ask questions about matters that stumped me. The collective knowledge of Dutch American history, especially regarding Albertus C. Van Raalte and associates of the founding generations, is unrivaled anywhere in the world. My gratitude and thanks go to Jack Nyenhuis, Elton Bruins, Don Bruggink, Bill Kennedy, Nella Kennedy, and Henk Aay for their patience for listening to more about the history of Holland then even they ever wanted to know.

Preface

When I moved to Holland in 1996 to join the A. C. Van Raalte Institute at Hope College, I looked for books to introduce me to the history of this dynamic city. I found a number of very readable popular histories by Larry Massie, Randall Vande Water, Donald van Reken, and Sara Michel, and more recently, newspaper articles by Steve Vander Veen, a professor of business at Hope College. Massie's histories, in particular, are lavishly illustrated with eye-catching photos and his writing style is unsurpassed. There is, however, no comprehensive history of Holland with citations of original sources that one trained in the discipline of history might come to expect.

This is surprising, given the annual Tulip Time historic tours and the marking of city milestones. Teachers at secondary schools and colleges have kept local history alive, and all the necessary documents and newspaper files that tell the story of Holland are available in libraries and archives. Even the language barrier was of little consequence until at least the 1950s, since many educators and amateur historians were fluent Dutch speakers.

This book is an attempt to provide a fresh and comprehensive history of Holland from its pre-history as an Indian colony to the increasingly diverse community of today. After telling the story of the Old Wing Mission and Chief Wakazoo's Ottawa Indian band, the topical chapters here recount the coming of the Dutch, the Americans who chose to live among them, and the history of religion, education, business, city services, politics, lake shipping, road and train transportation, industry and commerce, and social and cultural life. The complexity of this story after 1900 suggests an "historical period" format, that is, the Progressive Era, First World War, Interwar Years, Second World War and Korean War, downtown renewal, and the rise of a multi-ethnic community. The text is based mainly on original documents and newspaper files in the Joint Archives of Holland, the Holland Museum Archives, the Calvin College Archives, and Herrick Public Library. The primary sources are augmented with interviews, unpublished accounts, and secondary works of all kinds. Readers interested in the documentation on which the account is based will find extensive notes and a comprehensive bibliography. Numerous appendices provide statistical information on Holland's mayors and township officials, population trends, voting patterns, lists of businesses and other professions, and other data.

Those with ties to Holland and vicinity will find family members and friends among the thousands noted in the text or appendices. Most would be surprised to be publicly acknowledged. The Dutch are an unassuming lot, known for living quietly and avoiding the limelight. They follow the advice of King Solomon, "Let another man praise thee, and not thine own mouth" (Prov. 27:2, KJV). I am that man. My aim is to give praise where praise is due. Condemnation I leave to the judge of all the earth.

Robert P. Swierenga

Introduction

During the month of October 2011, the city of Holland commemorated the bicentennial of the birth of the city's founder, Rev. Albertus C. Van Raalte, with considerable public fanfare, special events, and an academic conference at Hope College, which continued early that November in the city of Ommen, province of Overijssel, where Rev. Van Raalte had nurtured a Separatist congregation from 1840 to 1844 and planted churches as the "apostle of Overijssel." To honor the founding father, whose impressive statue in bronze adorns Centennial Park, was fitting because the city was shaped in large measure by Van Raalte's vision and imprint.

The Dutch Calvinists who settled in 1847 on the shores of Lake Michigan at the mouth of Black Lake (renamed Lake Macatawa in 1935) considered themselves to be a people set apart by God for His glory. Like the English Pilgrims in the Netherlands, who set out on the *Mayflower* centuries ago, the Dutch Separatists, who had seceded in 1834 from the Netherlands *Hervormde Kerk* (Reformed Church), had a clear sense of destiny. God would do great things in their New Jerusalem, if they were faithful servants. This Providential vision led them to keep careful records of the life of the colony and to preserve key documents for posterity.

The colonists and their leader were intent on founding a Christian community guided by the Dutch Reformed faith and "salted" with a few Americans of Protestant persuasion. The freedom to establish churches and schools without government interference was a key goal. Within two years, every village in *De Kolonie* had a church, and Holland quickly earned a reputation as "a city of churches." Within ten years, Van Raalte had established a Christian preparatory school, the Holland Academy (1857), which soon evolved into Hope College (1866). More Americans came to the Holland colony than the pioneers expected; Americans, in fact, comprised one-third of the population by 1880. But all desired a community guided by Biblical principals, just like the Dutch Reformed. Most were Calvinists in the English Reformed tradition—Methodist, Congregational, Episcopal, and Presbyterian—besides a few Lutherans and Roman Catholics.

In the last fifty years, since the 1970s, Hispanics and Asians have settled in Holland in increasing numbers, and they now comprise more than one-third of the population. Most Hispanics are Roman Catholic, and most Asians are Buddhist. Despite the cultural differences, the newcomers share with the Dutch a strong work ethic, pride in homeownership, and conservative family values; some have joined Reformed and other Protestant churches.

Van Raalte was a man of letters and a careful administrator of the settlement. For the first decade or more, Van Raalte's quill pen and steady hand recorded the minutes of the key organizations—the consistory of the First Reformed Church of Holland; the regional church assembly known as the Classis of Holland; the People's Assembly, a type of town hall meeting that existed from 1847 to 1850; and the local school board. Van Raalte, the only university graduate in the colony, also kept meticulous ledgers of his lands, real estate mortgages, taxes, and business investments. And he helped start two local Dutch-language newspapers, *De Hollander* (in 1850) and *De Grondwet* (in 1860) to promote the colony and document its progress. With the demise of the *Sheboygan* (Wisconsin) *Nieuwsbode* (1849-61), the popular Dutch immigrant sheet, *De Grondwet*, dubbed the "Republican Bible," became the most influential Dutch-language newspaper in North America with more than 5,500 subscribers nationwide by 1892. The Holland Fire of 1871 destroyed countless records, including the back files of both newspapers, but church and college records survived.

Celebrating the story of the colony is a tradition in Holland. Beginning with the twenty-fifth anniversary in 1872, when Van Raalte and his fellow founders, the "old timers," recounted the pioneer days with pride, the city has marked every quarter century with parades, newspaper retrospectives, publications of histories and memoirs, and reunions where the original settlers recounted the "way it was." County judge and newspaper editor Gerrit Van Schelven in 1882 published the first "Historical Sketch of Holland City and Colony" as part of the first general history of Ottawa County. The semi-centennial of 1897 far surpassed the 1872 commemoration. City fathers generously spent tax dollars to stage elaborate parades and memorial events. That year saw the writing of a full-length history of the colony by Dingman Versteeg of Holland, entitled *Pelgrim vaders van het westen* (Pilgrim Fathers of the West). The manuscript, valuable as it is, has never been published, but an English translation by Clarence Jalving, is available in typescript.

The lavish semi-centennial of 1897 did not suffice, and ten years later, at the sixtieth anniversary in 1907, the leaders of Holland and Zeeland staged yet another celebration that was more flamboyant than all the others. Recognizing that the pioneers were dying off rapidly, Holland's first historian, Gerrit Van Schelven—a Civil War veteran, newspaper editor, justice of the peace, and postmaster (1899-1916)—invited the few surviving pioneers to write their memoirs. Dozens did so, and Van Schelven saved every one. Some he published in serial form in city newspapers. Van Schelven intended to publish all the pieces in a collected volume, but few readers submitted advance orders, and the plan had to be shelved (*Holland City News*, 11 Mar. 1902). Van Schelven, known by friends as "Van," knew more about early Holland history than anyone in the community. Following the sixtieth commemoration in 1907, he published in 1908 *Wat bracht U hier?* (What brought you here?), which explains the reasons for leaving the Netherlands and of the founding of Holland. But he never completed a history of the colony, despite compiling copious notes.

Van Schelven's efforts prompted the *Holland City News* editor Ben Mulder to begin publishing, as a regular feature, retrospective pieces entitled "Fifty Years Ago" and "Twenty-five Years Ago," that Mulder continued until his death in 1947. These snippets refreshed memories and served to keep alive the past, as did the lectures delivered by William O. Van Eyck, Van Schelven's intimate friend, successor as postmaster, and understudy as a local historian. Van Schelven joined the Republican Party after the Civil War, while Van Eyck, a second-generation Dutch

American, led the local Democratic Party. Van Eyck, a Hope College graduate with a law degree from the University of Michigan, was a highly regarded city clerk (1897-1909), Holland postmaster under Woodrow Wilson (1916-24), First Ward alderman (1909-11), and Ottawa County supervisor (1923-34). Van Eyck, a fastidious bachelor, was one of the most popular lawyers and politicians in the area.

Early in his career as a lawyer, Van Eyck determined to fulfill the goal of his mentor and write a comprehensive history of the first sixty years of the Holland colony. In 1909 Ben Mulder and Nicholas "Nick" J. Whelan, owners of the *Holland City News*, offered to any budding historian ready access to their back issues from 1872—thirty-seven years worth—so that this "wealth of local history" would not remain a "closed book to the general public for want of a historian." Van Eyck took them up on the offer and devoted a full year to indexing every issue of the city's first English-language paper. He also compiled notes for projected chapters—on the post office, mayors and elections, harbor improvements, businesses, industries, craftsmen, professional people, roads and bridges, Tulip Time, and many other topics. Perhaps he was looking to the seventy-fifth anniversary in 1922 to complete the work. But his thriving law practice, political activities, and public service stymied him, like it had for Van Schelven. Van Eyck died in 1934 at age sixty-four with not one chapter completed. The Tulip Time celebration, which began in a modest way in 1929, quickly developed into an annual commemoration of the history of the city.

Peter Theodore "Ted" Moerdyke of Zeeland picked up where Van Eyck left off. When Moerdyke's Zeeland haberdashery closed in the Great Depression, Willard C. Wichers, head of the Netherlands Museum, hired him under the WPA Historical Records Survey project to be the curator of the museum's historical records, which position he held from the mid-1930s until the early 1960s. With the detailed notes and writings of Van Schelven and Van Eyck at hand, Moerdyke meticulously compiled his own research notes on Holland's first century, including biographical sketches of nearly two hundred notables, dozens of businesses and industries, churches, wars, and many other subjects. His papers and hundreds of documents fill sixteen boxes in the Holland Museum archives. Although a master bibliophile and compiler, Moerdyke never wrote a narrative history of Holland.

In a sense, the history of Holland has been overdone, but not yet finished. The centennial spawned several major historical works. Albert Hyma was commissioned to write the first English-language biography of the colony's founder, titled *Albertus C. Van Raalte and His*

Dutch Settlements in the United States (1947). Hyma, professor of history at the University of Michigan, had previously acquired the Van Raalte Papers from the family and based his biography on this rich resource. In recent years the Van Raalte Institute and the continuing research of Dr. Elton J. Bruins, founding director of the institute, has led to three new biographies, a family genealogical history, and a collection of letters written by Van Raalte to Philip Phelps Jr., the founding president of Hope College. These books are: Jeanne Jacobsen, Elton Bruins, and Larry Wagenaar, *Albertus C. Van Raalte: Dutch Leader and American Patriot* (1996); Michael De Vries and Harry Boonstra, *Pillar Church in the Van Raalte Era* (2003), which focuses on the dominie more than the congregation; Elton Bruins, et al., *Albertus and Christina: The Van Raalte Family, Home, and Roots* (2004); and Elton Bruins and Karen Schakel, *Envisioning Hope College: Letters written by Albertus C. Van Raalte to Philip Phelps Jr., 1857-1875* (2011). Since Van Raalte played a central role in the life of the colony in the first decade or so, these books, "narrow-cast" as they are, help illuminate the general history.

The centennial celebration also prompted Henry Lucas, another native son and historian by training, to compile the best of the writings that Van Schelven had compiled a generation earlier and publish them in a two-volume work, *Dutch Immigrant Memoirs and Related Writings* (1955). Lucas also wrote a complete history of the Dutch immigration and settlement in North America, entitled *Netherlanders in America: Dutch Immigrants to the United States and Canada, 1789-1950*, which the University of Michigan Press published in 1955. This first comprehensive history of the immigration by a Dutch American complemented an older two-volume book under the same title, written in 1928 by a Netherlands socio-geographer and historian, Jacob Van Hinte, entitled *Nederlanders in Amerika: Een Studie over Landverhuizers en Volksplanting in de 19e en 20ste Eeuw in de Vereenigde Staten van Amerika* (*Netherlanders in America: A Study of Emigration and Settlement in the Nineteenth and Twentieth Centuries in the United States of America*). Baker Book House of Grand Rapids, Michigan, in 1985 republished this seminal work in English with translation by Adriaan de Wit under my general editorship. Wm. B. Eerdmans Publishing Co. reissued Lucas' *Netherlanders in America* in 1989, under the aegis of the Dutch American Historical Commission. Lucas and Van Hinte mastered the source materials of their subject, both in Dutch and English, and devoted considerable attention to the history of Holland in their comprehensive histories. But neither wrote a detailed history of the city.

The sesquicentennial in 1997 again revived the historical consciousness of the community. Hope College published a modern biography of the city founder: *Albertus C. Van Raalte: Dutch Leader and American Patriot* (cited above). The Peter H. Huizenga family and city council installed the first statue of Albertus C. Van Raalte in Centennial Park; it was a fitting fulfillment of the failed dream to erect a similar statue for the seventy-fifth anniversary in 1922. Pillar Church sponsored a lecture series by Elton J. Bruins and myself on the religious history of the colony, which was published under the title, *Family Quarrels in the Reformed Churches in the Nineteenth Century* (1999). The Dutch American Historical Commission commissioned a revised edition of Henry S. Lucas, *Dutch Immigrant Memoirs and Related Writings* (1997), first published in the Netherlands in 1955.

Larry B. Massie, Donald van Reken, Randall Vande Water, Mike Lozon, Paul Den Uyl, Elton Bruins, Michael De Vries and Harry Boonstra among others, have written histories of the city and region, or particular aspects of it—Albertus C. Van Raalte, Pillar Church, major companies, business leaders, railroads, Lake Michigan resorts, the fire department, Holland Christian Schools, and the like. These are the broad shoulders on which I was able to stand while writing this book. Hopefully, in the future, others will use these efforts to flesh out the many stories left untold or incomplete. If this book keeps alive the memory of Holland's history and inspires the next generation to dig into the history of this fascinating community, I will be fully rewarded for my efforts.

CHAPTER 13

Furnace Town

Holland had two specialized furnace companies—Holland Furnace and its junior rival, Home Furnace. The nationwide advertising and sales forces of these competitors put the city on the map as the Furnace Town of America.

Holland Furnace Company

Holland Furnace dominated local manufacturing in the first half of the twentieth century, as the Cappon & Bertsch leatherworks did in the nineteenth century. Both were the major companies of their era: they provided steady employment for many hundreds, and their executives led the business and civic community. Holland Furnace carried the city through the Great Depression, and its radio programs nurtured the nascent Tulip Time festival. Holland Furnace was connected in numerous ways to the community: in social clubs and societies like Kiwanis and the Holland Country Club, in churches and civic organizations like the chamber of commerce, in local radio and newspapers, and in state and local governments. Holland Furnace loomed large in the small Dutch community.[1]

Holland Furnace began humbly in 1906 and became the leading national brand of home furnaces, which were then rapidly replacing the traditional kitchen and parlor stoves to heat homes. It was also the first local company to have its stock listed on national stock exchanges, first on the American board and then the New York board. Holland Furnace exemplified the entrepreneurial genius of local businessmen and their successful quest of the American dream. The two founders were John P. Kolla, a native of France, and his son-in-law, August H. Landwehr, a German American raised in St. Louis, Missouri, who married Kolla's daughter Louise. Kolla's second daughter Kathryn "Katie" married Oscar Nystrom, an "inventive engineer" and tinsmith who had previously worked for an Akron, Ohio, furnace manufacturer. Nystrom was perfecting a warm-air furnace that would give a "maximum of heat for a minimum of fuel cost." The charismatic Landwehr, who had risen quickly through the ranks of an Akron publishing company to become head of its large sales force, saw great potential in Kolla's idea of a high-efficiency, cast iron furnace. Landwehr was a creative, dynamic person who motivated employees and salesmen alike. Kolla and Landwehr took Holland Furnace to unexpected heights and led the Holland business community for two decades.[2]

Kolla and Landwehr created a fiercely loyal workforce by providing steady work at fair wages and social activities for employees and their families that melded them into the Holland Furnace family. Its Relief Society stood ready to assist employees in times of need, and this nurtured the "family feel." So too the legendary company picnics and outings, notably the summer outing for factory employees and their families at Jenison Park, Tunnel Park, and from 1948 at Leisure Acres, the company's own grounds in Park Township (now a residential subdivision), which featured a rustic lodge where beer barrels could roll (beer was banned in public parks). The opposite extreme was the elegant Christmas banquet for officers and salesmen at the company gymnasium and, after 1925, at the firm's own Warm Friend Tavern, where expensive wines flowed freely in the staid Dutch city. The company's advertising

1 Donald L. van Reken and Randall P. Vande Water, *Holland Furnace Company, 1906-1966* (Holland, MI: privately printed, 1993), 1, 217, and passim. This book is the primary source for this section. See also William H. Boer, *The Holland Furnace Company Tragedy: An Insider's Lament* (Holland, MI: privately published, 1995); Doug Holm, "The History of the Holland Furnace Company," student paper, Hope College, 1986, Joint Archives of Holland (JAH).

2 Van Reken and Vande Water, *Holland Furnace*, 3-5 (quote 5), 77, 40.

Sisters Gertie Beek De Vries (*left*) and Abbie Beek Van Ark (*right*) frame the family woodpile used for home heating and cooking before coal and fuel oil (*courtesy Myron Van Ark*)

prowess was as legendary as its progressive labor policies. Americans nationwide knew that "Holland Furnaces make warm friends," and "Holland Furnaces are the heart of the home." Warm Friend became the name of the company newsletter and it flagship hotel.

Landwehr quickly became one of the city's prominent citizens, and his company supported countless amateur sport teams, sponsored radio broadcasts of high school and college football and basketball games, and contributed heavily to Tulip Time, especially by bringing Hollywood to Holland. In 1940, for example, Holland Furnace hosted

John P. Kolla (in suit) with Holland Furnace employees, 1920s (*Archives, Holland Historical Trust*)

Holland Furnace delivery wagon with slogan
"Holland Furnaces Make Warm Friends"
(*Archives, Calvin College*)

Dorothy Lamour, the leading lady of the silver screen. Landwehr served on the boards of several local companies, including Charles P. Limbert (president), Holland Maid (vice president), Holland City State Bank (president), and De Pree Chemical (director). A prominent Freemason, Landwehr helped finance the building of the Masonic Temple. He also golfed and dined regularly as a charter member of the Holland Country Club.[3]

Kolla moved his operations to Holland in large part because of the bonus committee (chapter 12), although the city's location made it accessible by rail and water for raw materials and shipping. The *Holland City News* reported that the bonus committee gave the firm the inducement of a three-acre site along the Pere Marquette Railway line north of East Twenty-Second Street, and the rail company agreed to run a siding to the factory. Company board minutes state: "It was decided to ask for a deed of the Company's grounds from the trustees of the bonus funds, giving in return a proper bond. That bond to be tendered to the Holland Improvement Company in exchange for the deed to the Furnace Company's grounds." In addition to the site, the members of the bonus committee and other boosters subscribed to $12,000 of the initial $50,000 in capital stock, and several prime investors became officers–Arend Visscher as president, William Beach as vice president, and Charles M. McLean as secretary. The board in 1907 gave Kolla $12,000 in shares, so that he had skin in the game, so to speak.[4]

3 Holm, "Holland Furnace," 12-13, 24-25.

4 Ibid., 3-6. Other Holland investors include Hope College professors John H. Kleinheksel and John W. Beardslee, Jacob G. Van Putten, pharmacist Heber Walsh,

August H. and Louise Kolla Landwehr being fetted at Holland Furnace branch office in Kokomo, Indiana (*Archives, Holland Historical Trust*)

The plant was up and running late in 1906 at a total cost of $10,000, under manager Guy Bowman, another Akron partner and the largest stockholder. Alderman James Arthur "Art" Drinkwater poured the first molten iron at the foundry to make sheet iron. Remarkably, Kolla chose to be the plant superintendent, and he walked the floor in "old dirty overalls." His men appreciated his personal touch, including placing a keg of beer on the foundry floor on a hot summer day and a ham for the family's Thanksgiving dinner. The foundry men worked ten-hour days to feed the furnace assembly teams. The fifty-five employees manufactured 1,500 furnaces the first year; thirty of which went into homes in Holland. Sales totaled almost $120,000. It was a stellar beginning. Kolla also patented the Holland Window Coal Chute for delivery of coal to basements of customers. It proved to be a hot item nationwide; the company sold six thousand coal chutes in 1908.[5]

---

attorney Philip H. McBride, physician Henry Kremers, realtor Isaac Marsilje and his son Thomas, Holland Foundry president Edward Muehlenbrock, Daniel G. Cook, Bastian Keppel, and merchant D. B. K. Van Raalte. Kleinheksel, Van Putten, and Keppel were all members of the Van Raalte family. Isaac Marsilje joined the board in 1910 and held the position of secretary until his death in 1922. Arend Visscher was president until his death in 1921.

5 Van Reken and Vande Water, *Holland Furnace*, 5-8; Holm, "Holland Furnace," 11.

Holland Furnace office building, 1920s, Columbia Avenue at Twentieth Street, erected 1906. On the left is the former YMCA building used as a gymnasium above and dock below (*courtesy Randall P. Vande Water*)

Within the year, the factory was too small, and the first of many expansions began. That year the company also began the direct distribution and installation of its furnaces to ensure quality, instead of selling through retail stores and relying on plumbers and handymen that merchants recommended to install them. Holland Furnace organized a system of branch offices throughout the Midwest, staffed with seven hundred salesmen, to give service from factory to consumer. The company could thus fully guarantee its products. By 1909 seventy-five workers were turning out fifteen furnaces a day, and sales surpassed $115,000 that year. Six plant additions in the first six years increased floor space six-fold. To finance the astounding growth, the capital stock was doubled to $100,000 within two years and to $800,000 within a decade. From 1907 until 1921, output doubled virtually every two years and business multiplied nearly five hundred-fold by 1928. Annual sales then topped forty-six thousand furnaces, and the company boasted that Holland Furnaces heated half the homes in the city.[6]

The key to its success was the branch system that Landwehr designed, so that the company was vertically integrated, from home office and some seven regional division headquarters, to hundreds of local branch offices, each with its own warehouse. Many of the branch

6 Van Reken and Vande Water, *Holland Furnace*, 9-12, 17.

Workmen assembling classic Holland Furnace boilers, 1908
(*Archives, Holland Historical Trust*)

managers were local men who were sent "out into the world" after proving themselves. Clarence "Kelley" Van Wieren and William "Bill" Sikkel (the businessman, not the mayor) were two Hollanders who became branch managers. Another, William H. "Bill" Boer, the long time corporate secretary and assistant treasurer, was the brains behind the office management.[7]

At the bottom of the pyramid stood the heating engineers who installed the furnaces. This eliminated middlemen–dealers and hardware stores–and ensured buyer satisfaction. Like Fuller Brush salesmen, Holland Furnace installers went door-to-door in their territories seeking homes that needed furnaces or existing furnaces that needed cleaning or repairs. The company had its own truck-mounted Sani-Vac cleaning system to suck dust out of the pipes, and any home found to have an old or defective furnace was marked for a visit by a salesman.

National sales conventions at company headquarters were called "Goat Conclaves," a name taken from the fourteen-carat gold and diamond pin Oscars, shaped liked a goat, first awarded to top salesmen in the 1920s, which elevated them to the "Exalted Order of the Goat." At its apex in 1948, the company had five hundred branches in forty-four states; sales reached $41 million, and net earnings surpassed $4

[7] Ibid., 79, 141, 144; Randall P. Vande Water, "Warm Friends," in *Holland: Happenings, Heroes & Hot Shots*, 1:47-50.

Oscar, the Holland Furnace "Goat" award to top salesmen, instituted in the 1920s (*Archives, Holland Historical Trust*)

million. Company teamsters operated twenty-two tractors and thirty-eight trailers to deliver furnaces to branch offices throughout the Midwest and eastern seaboard. Holland Furnace even had a company airplane and pilot Ernest "Ernie" Burns, who operated out of Holland's first airport at the former fairgrounds on Sixteenth Street.[8]

Landwehr, with the backing of the chamber of commerce, set about to change the city's character by building the Warm Friend Tavern to host salesmen, suppliers, and notables of all stripes, who came to company headquarters in a steady stream. The company's signature building opened in 1925 on the northeast corner of Eighth Street and Central Avenue. It was touted as the "finest hostelry on the entire west side of Michigan" (chapter 19). Some people objected to the word tavern in the name and on the marquee. Why not call it the Warm Friend Hotel, which indeed it was? The tavern occupied only one lavish room. But Landwehr presumably wanted to make a statement against the tee-totaling culture in the small ethnic enclave of his adopted home.

August and Louise Landwehr featured on Holland Furnace advertising card with a cute rhyme about goats (*courtesy Myron Van Ark*)

8 Van Reken and Vande Water, *Holland Furnace*, 146, 151; Holm, "Holland Furnace," 7-8, 28-37.

Holland Furnace salesmen on the road with their company cars, 1920s (*Archives, Holland Historical Trust*)

His tavern gave local elites a place to party and entertain. Most of the Holland Furnace executives and other business people, such as Thomas Venhuizen of Venhuizen Auto Garage, lived in the hotel with their families on a permanent basis. The hotel had a full house at least twice a year, for the Goat convention and Tulip Time. The Captains Room in the basement, adorned with a huge wall canvas in oil of the *North American* steamship, was reserved for steamship captains to "whet their whistles" in private before retiring for the night.[9]

The glory years of Holland Furnace were from 1910 to 1930, although the company enjoyed a long autumn period of another thirty years, until a financial scandal brought it down amid a flurry of law suits and court hearings. In 1930 Holland Furnace employed five thousand salesmen in five hundred branch offices, with four hundred workers in Holland itself. It was the largest employer and *the* company to work for. Its pay was the highest in town, and a job at Holland Furnace gave one status in the community; it was the epitome of success. There was no need whatsoever for a labor union at Holland Furnace. Shareholders also stood to gain handsomely. It was said that those who bought early and had the wisdom to sell before the 1929 market crash made $100 for every $1 invested.[10]

At least three things caused a turnabout. First was a tragedy on a fateful July day in 1928 when Landwehr's oldest son and heir apparent,

9 Van Reken and Vande Water, *Holland Furnace*, 34, 45-47; James Hoeksema interview by Donald van Reken, typescript, 7, JAH; Interview with Marj Vannette Wolters (chapter 19).

10 Van Reken and Vande Water, *Holland Furnace*, 79; *Holland City News*, 27 Jan. 1926.

Warm Friend Tavern, opened in 1925 by Holland Furnace Company to host its national sales force in style, 1940s (*Joint Archives of Holland*)

Paul, age twenty, died in a boating accident on Lake Macatawa, along with one of Kolla's two grandsons, John Kolla Nystrom, age fourteen, and two other men. Paul's reckless driving of the family speedboat caused it to be sucked into the side-paddle wheel of the *City of Holland*, a large pleasure boat bound for Chicago. The tragedy caused Landwehr, who blamed himself for pampering his son with expensive toys, to suffer a nervous breakdown that led to his being committed to various mental institutions until his death at age fifty-seven in 1937. [11]

Landwehr's brothers, Charles and Edgar G., salesmen for the company, took over temporarily and, in the midst of the Great Depression, built a new $250,000 company headquarters on Columbia Avenue between Twentieth and Twenty-First Streets (now Black River Public School). It was said about town that the building "up the hill" was paid for with Kolla's insurance settlement on the boating tragedy. The three-story, air-conditioned building, dedicated in 1931, provided forty-four thousand square feet of office space. The conservative John P. Kolla, who died of natural causes in 1933, objected to the "marble" extravagance. This likely set the stage for the management shakeup after his death, engineered, it is claimed, by his daughters Katie Cheff and Louise Landwehr, who ended up as majority stockholders. Katie, who had divorced Nystrom in 1926, at age forty-three, in 1931 married

11 Holm, "Holland Furnace," 13-21; August Landwehr obit., *Holland Sentinel*, 15, 21 July 1937.

Ornate foyer of Warm Friend Tavern (*courtesy Myron Van Ark*)

Paul Theodore "Ted" Cheff, the tall, handsome, twenty-seven-year-old son of Rev. Peter Paul Cheff of Hope Reformed Church. That Cheff, a contemporary of Katie's daughter Leona, married an "older woman," twenty-one years his senior, caused a major scandal in Holland. And he was a preacher's son at that![12]

The Great Depression was a second factor that hurt the company. Sales plummeted as the hard times forced homeowners to hold off on replacing their furnaces. Industrial employment, according to the chamber of commerce in 1934, had declined by 40 percent, and this squeezed families mercilessly. Furnace sales dropped off sharply and the company periodically furloughed workers and went to three-day workweeks, all without labor strife and strikes.

Third, Holland Furnace executives spurned new technologies. Cast-iron, coal furnaces were being replaced by fuel oil and natural gas furnaces that were smaller and more efficient, but company leaders refused to give up an "addiction" to the firm's signature coal furnace. In the end, however, it was not a lack of innovation, but ethical failings that proved fatal for the company. This was the fourth and final blow.[13]

Landwehr's mental collapse and Kolla's death were personal tragedies for the families, but the economic impact on the company

[12] John P. Kolla obit., *Holland Sentinel*, 30 Jan., 2 Feb. 1933; William Vogelzang interview by Robert P. Swierenga and David Boeve, 30 Sept. 2009, JAH; Cornelia Van Voorst interview by Abby Jewett, 7 June 1982, typescript, 14, JAH. The wedding took place in Los Angeles on 3 Nov. 1931 and is noted in the *Los Angeles Times*. Paul Cheff lived in the Holland area until the ripe age of 86; he died 14 Dec. 1991.

[13] Van Reken and Vande Water, *Holland Furnace*, 77-85, 87, 142-43; *Holland Sentinel*, 3 May 1934; Boer, *Holland Furnace*, 6.

Paul Theodore Cheff, late 1930s
(*Archives, Holland Historical Trust*)

and the city was far worse. Holland Furnace lost its leaders and driving forces, and the business community felt keenly the absence of its heavy hitters. In 1933 the board forced Landwehr's two brothers to resign in favor of a new executive team headed by Cheff as vice president and general manager, and after 1946, as president and chairman of the board. Why the board in 1933 named Cheff to head the company is difficult to comprehend. He had been Kolla's chauffeur and the foundry plant foreman. In a strange twist of fate, he had also helped John Kolla Nystrom climb into the speedboat that fateful day.[14]

Cheff had no selling or managerial experience; his standing derived from his fortuitous marriage and a dominating negative personality. He was the titular head, but Louise and Katie "called the shots." With Cheff as CEO and later as president for nearly three decades, from 1933 to 1961, Holland Furnace never recovered its past glory. Cheff lacked the vision of the founders, although he did ramp up output to full production again by 1939. During the Second World War, the Northside Plant No. 5 was converted exclusively to making armor plate for tanks and ship anchor chains, while the city factory made furnaces for the military. Military contracts ran into the millions of dollars. Holland Furnace held its own against the competing Home Furnace Co. of Holland (see below) and indeed against furnace companies everywhere. It ranked number one in the field of cast iron furnaces, which were high-end products with an excellent reputation.[15]

14 Van Reken and Vande Water, *Holland Furnace*, 103, 109, 131.

15 Boer, *Holland Furnace*, 9, 21, 21-22. Boer's first-person assessment of Cheff's character, personality, and moral values is noteworthy (23-27).

Rocky Marciano (*right*) spars with a local boxer at Holland Furnace's Leisure Acres clubhouse on November 3, 1952, his first training camp after winning the world heavyweight boxing crown on September 23, 1952 (*Archives, Holland Historical Trust*)

Chester Lokker, Holland Furnace truck fleet manager, with Diamond T tractor and trailer, 1953 (*Archives, Holland Historical Trust*)

Diligent office staff at Holland Furnace Co. Earl Van Lente is seated on the right (*Archives, Holland Historical Trust*)

On the surface all looked well, but there was rot on the inside. Cheff, who became company president in 1946 and was by then the boss in every respect, cut too many corners and condoned chicanery by salesmen. Historians Donald van Reken and Randall Vande Water refer to "shadows and shadowy events" that became "darker and more substantive" in the postwar decade. From 1942 on, the Better Business Bureau and city officials in Rochester, New York, Chicago, Detroit, St. Louis, and fourteen other cities filed complaints accusing Holland Furnace salesmen of using deceptive, high-pressure tactics and swindling homeowners. The Federal Trade Commission followed up in 1954 by charging the company with "unfair and deceptive acts and practices." It was the beginning of an unraveling over the next twelve years. After extensive hearings and 260 witnesses testifying under oath, the commission issued a cease and desist order, which is the equivalent of conviction in a court of law. A few bad apples spoiled the barrel. Many salesmen remained scandal free, such as Frank Kleinheksel in the Flint office. A direct descendant of A. C. Van Raalte, Kleinheksel was the "all-time super salesman" at Holland Furnace.[16]

Cheff and his board flatly denied the findings, believing that the anti-business rhetoric fostered by President Franklin Roosevelt

[16] Van Reken and Vande Water, *Holland Furnace*, 137, 173; Vogelzang interview, JAH; Van Voorst interview, 16-17 (Kleinheksel quote), JAH.

and his New Dealers had created a public bias against entrepreneurial enterprises. Holland Furnace began a series of appeals in the federal courts that went on for fifteen years, all the while trying to carry on business as usual. It was a "costly and very devastating battle" that was "hopeless from the beginning," said company insider Bill Boer.

Meanwhile, the company in Cheff's increasingly autocratic hands had sales of $36 million and profits of $3 million in 1950, down $5 million in sales from the apex in 1948. Its six thousand employees in 467 branches from coast to coast, plus seven hundred at headquarters, were working feverishly. Yet, sales declined slowly during the decade, to $30 million in 1960, with a slim profit of $76,000. The charges were damaging the company's reputation beyond repair. Profits plummeted, and key executives resigned or were fired, one after another. In 1953 alone, the company lost ninety years of management experience. To raise cash, Cheff in 1960 sold the Northside Plant No. 5 to Holland Color and Chemical Company. Holland Furnace's stock price that year plummeted from $75 to $16 a share.[17]

Cheff realized his predicament and got out in 1962. First he sold to Milton Stevens, a Chicago corporate raider, who fired some forty tainted salesmen and closed the Holland factory. But within two months, Stevens backed out and filed a lawsuit charging Cheff with fraud. Cheff counter-sued for $6 million for company losses incurred when Stevens backed out of the merger deal. The legal maneuverings showed that Holland Furnace was in deep trouble. In August 1962, Edward Groper, Jerome Jennings, and Henry Hafer of the Chamberlin Co. of New York took over the Holland company with the purchase of only 80,000 shares. Cheff and his wife still owned 275,000 shares, but he wanted no part of management. The Chamberlin group, as it was called, tried to salvage the company. They put assets on the block to raise cash, including the Warm Friend Tavern, Leisure Acres, Cheff's forty-foot Chris-Craft, and other items. They reopened the Holland factory briefly on a small scale with fifty employees, but shifted production to a New Jersey subsidiary, the Thatcher Furnace Company. By 1964 the local facilities were closed, and in September the New York Stock Exchange delisted Holland Furnace stock because it had fallen below its required minimum price of one dollar.[18]

After eleven years of fruitless litigation, in 1965 a three-judge panel of the US Court of Appeals for the Seventh Circuit found the

17 Holm, "Holland Furnace," 38-60, esp. 59.

18 Ibid., 61-78.

Holland Furnace Co. "guilty of criminal contempt of this Court" and fined it $100,000. More remarkable, company president and CEO Cheff was judged guilty personally and sentenced to six months in prison. After yet further appeals failed, he entered the Federal Correctional Institution at Milan, Michigan in June 1966. By that time, Althone Industries of New York, a holding company, had purchased controlling interest. They soon sold the company office building to Holland Suco Color Co. (formerly Holland Color and Chemical, now a subsidiary of Chemetron Corp.) and the patents and trademarks to Rybolt Heater Co. of Ashland, Ohio. By 1968 Holland Furnace was finished.[19]

Althone Industries successfully sued Cheff for the $100,000 fine and legal costs it had paid as a result of the trial. So, in the end Cheff served his time and also personally paid the company fine. How the mighty had fallen! Bernard Ebbers of WorldCom had nothing on Ted Cheff and his wife, with their yacht, private airplane, automobiles, stable of famous show horses, 176-acre hunting lodge, and the mansion at Hazelbank on Lake Macatawa's Pine Creek Bay, all purchased largely on the company tab.[20]

Home Furnace Company

Home Furnace always operated in the shadow of the behemoth Holland Furnace Company. Under manager Nicholas "Nick" Jonker, Home Furnace began operations in 1916 in a new factory on Sixth Street at Fairbanks Avenue near the Pere Marquette Railway and Holland Interurban stations, which allowed for shipping furnaces by rail. Jonker bought a new foundry outfit in Chicago, and the building contractors rushed the plant to completion to meet a backlog of more than one hundred furnace orders. Superior Foundry cast the mold for the furnace bodies. Before the year was out, the casting and smelting departments were running, and the first molten metal poured out. No longer would the company have to rely on the Superior Foundry for smelting.[21]

The upgrade could not have been more timely. The United States' entry into the First World War brought a bevy of government orders that pushed production to the limit. One order in late July 1917 required ten carloads of furnaces to be shipped within one month.

19 Van Reken and Vande Water, *Holland Furnace*, 212-13; Boer, *Holland Furnace*, 7. Cheff was granted an early release from prison to tend to his dying wife Katie (Van Voorst interview, 17, JAH).

20 Van Reken and Vande Water, *Holland Furnace*, 179-91, 203-4.

21 *Holland City News*, 8 June, 2, 23 Nov. 1916.

Army barracks required furnaces before winter set in. With maximum effort, the employees filled the order, with more to come. Home Furnace clearly had a superior product.

Despite the good times, management problems plagued the company and brought it close to insolvency by 1918. Then James De Young, former mayor of Holland, became manager, and he began a major turn-around. He had no knowledge of casting furnaces, but he brought proven management skills, business acumen, and a mechanical mind. De Young was the "Father of the Holland BPW" (board of public works), having served as the first superintendent from 1898 to 1910. Under his tutelage, Home Furnace flourished as never before. De Young, who also served as secretary-treasurer, slashed spending, retooled operations to raise efficiencies, and launched clever national advertising campaigns. One, in December 1922, depicted Santa Claus delivering furnaces as presents.[22]

Business volume increased 2,000 percent in five years and 72 percent in a single year, 1923. De Young increased the number of sales offices in Michigan alone to thirty-five, with more in other states. The common stock, which had fallen to junk status, appreciated handsomely. De Young earned kudos from business leaders for saving Home Furnace and helping make the city the world's greatest furnace center. In 1929 De Young stepped aside as manager in favor of an up-and-coming executive, John W. De Vries, but he stayed on as secretary-treasurer for another decade. In all, De Young remained with Home Furnace for twenty-one years, until 1939.[23]

Home Furnace survived the dark years of the Great Depression under the new president and secretary treasurer Clarence J. "Red" Becker, a Hope College alumnus and graduate of Harvard University's Graduate School of Business, who took over in 1935. De Vries continued as manager, followed by Clarence's father, Christian "Chris" E. Becker, who joined after twenty-five years with Holland Furnace as branch manager of the Grand Rapids office. Chris Becker left Holland Furnace due to the turmoil at the top and brought his management expertise to the rival firm. In 1937 Home Furnace faced a surging demand for its air conditioning units, powered by either fuel oil or natural gas, and began planning an expansion. Attorney Daniel Ten Cate was then board

22 Ibid., 2 Aug. 1917, 27 Jan. 1921, 9 Feb. 1922.

23 Ibid., 12 Dec. 1923, 16 May 1929. Home Furnace directors in 1921 were Otto P. Kramer, Henry J. Luidens, J. P. Huyser, John Y. and Tom Huizenga, and Henry Pelgrim Sr. In 1939 the list included Luidens, Kramer, Marinus C. Westrate, and John De Vries.

Attorney Daniel Ten Cate of the law firm of Diekema, Kollen, and Ten Cate (*courtesy Joan Ten Cate Bonnette*)

president and another former mayor, Abe Stephan, was vice president. In 1941 Home Furnace erected a modern factory on Fairbanks Avenue at Seventh Street.[24]

In the 1950s, Home Furnace needed a second resuscitation, and this came from a revolutionary invention by company engineer Lee Bauer and Jim Miller of Michigan State University. The breakthrough was a "gun" and fan that together forced fuel oil under high pressure into the furnace combustion chamber, which doubled the efficiency and made gun furnaces ideal for mobile homes. The "Miller Mobile Gun" saved the nation millions of gallons of oil and gave Home Furnace the edge in the growing vacation market. The company sold two hundred thousand units a year; it was a huge moneymaker. Another apt Red Becker move was to replace the standard cast iron furnace with a steel one. In 1965 and 1966, Home Furnace expanded by acquiring furnace companies in New York and Benton Harbor.[25]

In June 1966 Home Furnace suffered the loss of its East Sixth Street plant in a $3 million fire, which put its 250 employees out of work. At this low point, the Becker family in December sold the company to Lear Siegler Inc., the California automotive and aeronautics conglomerate, and the local plant became its Home Furnace Division. Becker stayed one year as president and another eight years as manager. His first task

24 Van Reken and Vande Water, *Holland Furnace*, 104; *Holland Sentinel*, 2 Dec. 1937, 23 Feb. 1939, 24 June 1941.

25 Steve Vander Veen, "How a 'gun' saved Home Furnace," *Holland Sentinel*, 6 Dec. 2006; "Company Originated with Furnace Patent," *Holland Sentinel*, 1968, Lear Siegler file, Herrick Library.

Christian "Chris" Becker (*left*) and Ben Timmer (*right*), as young office clerks, Home Furnace Company (*Archives, Holland Historical Trust*)

under Lear Siegler was to build a new factory; he chose a site on Brooks Avenue in the Northside Industrial Park. Dedicated in 1969, the plant stood near those of 7Up, Slick Craft, LaBarge Glass, and Holland Wire Products. The employees were recalled, and the $2 million annual payroll resumed. In 1972 an expansion doubled the floor space of the Home Division. The plant was upgraded again in 1976 to accommodate the Miller Gun—an oil-fired heat pump. That year, Lear Siegler also opened a plant for its Mammoth Division on the former Home Furnace site at 341 East Seventh Street. This facility made the Miller Guns to heat and cool mobile homes, a steadily growing market.[26]

Becker headed Lear Siegler's Holland plant until retiring in 1974. His job in the last years required a great deal of travel around the world. Tulip City Airport could only accommodate single engine planes on its half-mile runway. So Becker and other businessmen pushed to triple the runway length, sufficient for even a Boeing 727. This was only one of his many civic accomplishments that won for him the epitaph, "A dedicated public servant." Home Furnace became Miller Heating and Air Conditioning in 1980, and in 1986 the Rhode Island-based Nortek bought the firm and changed the name to Nordyne. This acquisition made Nortek one of the largest suppliers of heating and air-conditioning equipment for the mobile-home industry.[27]

26 *Holland Sentinel*, 8, 9 Aug. 1968, 29 Oct. 1969, 20 Sept. 1971, 16 Aug. 1972, 25 Sept., 10 Dec. 1976.

27 "Home is where the hearth is," Freedom Village *Crier*, June 1996; Clarence Becker obit., *Holland Sentinel*, 9 June 1996; Diane Wincour, "Lear Siegler has new

Hart & Cooley Inc.

The Hart & Cooley Co. had its roots in the Hart & Cooley Manufacturing Co. of Chicago, founded in 1892 by Howard S. Hart and Norman P. Cooley as the first cold-rolled steel plant west of Pittsburgh. In 1899 the pair sold the Chicago plant and returned to their home town of New Britain, Connecticut, where in 1901 they established the Hart & Cooley Co. with a capital of $50,000. The firm was the first to manufacture steel—instead of cast iron—furnace registers, regulators, and related heating parts. The steel registers found an immediate market, especially at the Holland Furnace Company headed by August Landwehr. He arranged in 1924 for Hart & Cooley to buy the Federal Manufacturing Co. of Holland, a subsidiary of Holland Furnace owned by Landwehr and Thomas Olinger, to supply the popular warm air registers.[28]

Federal Manufacturing began in 1901 as the Pneumatic Horse Collar Co. of veterinary surgeon Dr. L. L. Conkey to manufacture operating tables for horses and other large animals. The unique tables were in great demand in veterinary colleges everywhere and orders poured in from around the world. Conkey in 1902 hired Olinger to manage the factory and in 1914 he sold the business to him. The advent of automobiles depressed sales of the tables, and Olinger in 1919 sold the horse collar business and he and Landwehr formed Federal Stamping Works to manufacture small metal castings (chains, pulleys, and dampers) for Holland Furnace.[29] The payroll stood at twenty-five men and was projected to grow to eighty. Olinger continued as president and manager, and in 1928, supervised the construction of a one-story plant on fifteen acres just east of the city limits on Eighth Street. (This is part of the famed Van Raalte "cutout" of 1867, by which the Dutch dominie's home and surrounding lands were excluded from the city to meet his objection to its incorporation.)[30]

In 1929 the prosperous parent company, capitalized at $1.5 million, merged the Federal unit in Holland into its overall operations

---

Acquisition," ibid., 28 Jan. 1984, Wincour, "Nordyne has long Holland history," ibid., 5 Aug. 1988.

28 Larry B. Massie, Haven, Harbor, and Heritage: The Story of Holland, Michigan (Allegan Forest, MI: Priscilla Press, 1996), 158.

29 *Holland City News*, 11 July 1902. In 1917 Olinger also managed the Holland Light & Specialty Co. of H. J. Boone, a firm that manufactured electric generators (*Holland City News*, 3 May 1917).

30 *Holland City News*, 28 Mar., 5 July 1923, 5 Dec. 1929; *Holland Sentinel*, 9 Apr., 31 July 1923, 30 Mar. 1926, 11 Dec. 1936, 16 May 1956.

Hart & Cooley founders Howard S. Hart (*top*) and Norman P. Cooley (*bottom*) adorn cover of Fiftieth Anniversary book.

under the name Hart & Cooley, and Howard S. Hart came from Connecticut to replace Olinger. Hart's initial project was to supervise a $30,000 addition to double the factory floor; it was the first of several expansions that stretched the plant floor to three hundred thousand square feet, the biggest footprint of any firm in Holland. By the time Hart retired in 1935, he personally held the record for register patents. Hart & Cooley established itself as the world's largest manufacturer of furnace registers and grilles, and this reputation enabled the firm to maintain its three-hundred-employee payroll through the depression decade. By 1941 employment topped five hundred, and the next year, the firm purchased the former Hollander Inc. candy manufactory on Sixteenth Street just west of Van Raalte Avenue.[31]

During the war, Hart & Cooley shifted production from registers to 60mm mortar-shell casings, many of which were made by women who worked in shifts round the clock. In 1942, Hart & Cooley moved its Fafnir Bearings division from Connecticut to Holland and devoted half the factory floor to manufacturing ball bearings for the military. Until Fafnir closed at war's end in 1945, millions of bearings rolled off the assembly line. Employment peaked at one thousand. In 1951 Hart & Cooley marked fifty years in Holland by printing an anniversary booklet.[32]

31 *Holland City News*, 29 Aug., 1929; *Holland Sentinel*, 27 June 1941, 5 May 1942.

32 *Holland Sentinel*, 5 May 1942; *Holland City News*, 5 July 1951.

Dilligent workers in Hart & Cooley assembly room with Jieke Deur at front table (*Archives, Holland Historical Trust*)

When furnace manufacturers replaced gravity flow with forced air furnaces in the 1950s, Hart & Cooley designed a line of registers, grills, and diffusers for the new systems. The workforce held steady at four hundred in these years. In the 1960s the firm developed award-winning vents for gas-fired appliances, under the name Metelvent, which accounted for 16 percent of sales. In 1978 Hart & Cooley became a subsidiary of New Jersey-based Interspace Corp., a building and construction equipment conglomerate. In 1981 new president C. Jonathan Hauck determined to double sales in five years; he spent $250,000 for a new stamping machine in 1984 to boost production of its stamped steel grills, registers, and diffusers for the heating and cooling industry. The industrial complex at 500 East Eighth Street then had 14.5 acres under roof and its 760 employees produced seventy thousand finished products per day. A sixteen-day strike that summer by six hundred members of Local 1418, an affiliate of the International Association of Machinists (IAM), militated against those goals and led to a reduction in force of twenty-nine salaried workers. The previous year, 1983, Interspace had been sold to Clevepak Corporation of New York, and the Holland firm began its long downward path to extinction.[33]

In 1986 Hart & Cooley became part of Chicago-based Eagle Industries, which invested $1.5 million in new equipment in 1987 and another $2 million in 1988. Along with the infusion of new capital, Eagle demanded higher productivity and implemented cost control

33 *Holland Sentinel,* 16 May 1956, 30 Jan. 1982, 17 Aug., 13 Oct. 1983, 1, 17, 21 Aug., 10 Nov. 1984, 26 Jan. 1985, 8 Sept. 1986.

Patriotic Hart & Cooley employees march on River Avenue in a 1944 war bond drive. In the front rank (*left to right*) are Esther (Mrs. Harry D.) Smith, Margaret Michmerhuizen Schipper, Dick Smith (with sign), Cora Trap Doktor, Margaret O'Leary Adamitis, Harry D. Smith (*Holland Historical Trust*)

measures. The workers took umbrage at the changes, and in August 1990, the 460-member Holland IAM local, in a repeat of 1984, went on strike, again to the detriment of client relations and sales. This walkout lasted thirteen days and caused the distant owners to reassess their Holland operations. In the ensuing months, more than one hundred workers were laid off, and rumors of more to come unsettled workers, making local president Larry Lee's job all the harder.[34]

In the mid-1990s Eagle Industries, along with Hart & Cooley, became part of Falcon Industries, another Chicago firm, which in 1997 was absorbed by Investcorp. In 2000 Investcorp sold its Hart & Cooley division to London-based Tomkins PLC and walked away with $320 million in cash. Tomkins called Hart & Cooley an "excellent acquisition" and promised that "everyone will keep their jobs." Apparently, "everyone" did not include the top executives, because days later all five were fired, including President Lee. Few of the seven hundred production and salaried workers trusted the pledge, and rightly so. Seven years later, in late 2007, Tomkins announced the closing of the Holland facility, to take effect within a year. The vacant site is now being redeveloped for commercial and industrial use, but progress is slow.[35]

34 Ibid., 30 Jan. 1988, 1 Aug., 2, 19 Nov. 1989, 1, 14 Aug. 1990.

35 Ibid., 24 Dec. 1999, 4, 5, 6 Jan., 2 Dec. 2000; *Grand Rapids Press Lakeshore Edition*, 31 May 2001; *Holland Sentinel*, 12 Dec. 2007, 27 Mar. 2009; Larry B. Massie, *Haven, Harbor, and Heritage: The Holland Michigan Story* (Allegan Forest, MI: Priscilla Press, 1996), 158.

Holland Maid

The new electric and gasoline-powered products fed a rising consumerism in the 1920s, and one of the most coveted innovations was the washing machine, which relieved harried housewives of the laundry washboard. The Holland Maid Co. began manufacturing such labor saving machines in 1923 in the former Holland Gelatin factory on the north side. Landwehr of Holland Furnace again took the lead as company president, attorney Gerrit Diekema as vice president, Landwehr's brother-in-law Carl E. Gschwind (family name later changed to Swift) as treasurer and general manager, and Raymond M. Bosworth as secretary. Board members included the prominent businessmen Dirk B. K. Van Raalte Jr., Con De Pree of De Pree Chemical Co., and manager Dirk F. Boonstra of the F. Boonstra Mercantile Co. of Zeeland.[36]

The Holland Maid Electric Washer was touted as a "marvel of simplicity and efficiency." It was a cylinder-type machine, with wooden slats and aluminum sides, and the agitator was driven by a gear mechanism instead of a belt. Salesman Klaas Bulthuis recalled that it "did a fairly good job washing, but it did have a problem with the oil leak, because the main worm ran in a bath of oil, which oil was rather difficult to keep without having it leak." Soon the firm added a mangle iron to its product line, the Holland Maid Electric Ironer. Some twenty-eight branch stores in Michigan, Indiana, and Ohio sold the washers and ironers directly to housewives, all managed by head salesman E. R. Bronkema. Not surprisingly, this was the Holland Furnace business model. The firm's Eighth Street store in Holland served the local region and was a hot spot. Company packaging and advertising carried the imprint of a "clean, joyous Dutch maid's face," a slogan that played on the Dutch cleanliness motif. In 1925 the firm celebrated its overwhelming success with a parade of all fifty of its trucks, each tooting its horn and carrying a mechanical young lady, which were delivered around the city to banks, stores, and eateries for temporary display. Holland Maid, with nearly two hundred full-time employees, was the Maytag of its day.[37]

Holland Maid's success was short-lived, however, because its machines did not hold up, and many had to be shipped back to Holland for repairs. After only four years, in 1927, the board shook up the management and raised new capital to put the firm on a sound financial basis. Otto Szekely, the airplane manufacturer, was tapped

[36] *Holland City News*, 8, 22 Feb. 1923, 24 Jan. 1924.

[37] Klaas Bulthuis interview by Donald van Reken, 20 July 1977, typescript, 10. JAH; *Holland City News*, 4 June 1925, 18 Mar., 8, 28 Apr. 1926.

to re-engineer the washing machine; these were sold under a new company name, Vac-A-Tap. The name mimicked the workings of the washer, which combined a vacuum and tapping system of cleaning. Sears R. McLean (a son of Charles M.), who for many years managed the Holland-St. Louis Sugar Co., was appointed as general manager in place of Swift (Gschwind), and Herman Landwehr, August's younger brother and Swift's nephew, replaced Bronkema as sales manager.[38]

The strategy failed. Within a year Vac-A-Tap was in receivership, and in 1929, under the court's aegis, the plant was sold to satisfy creditors. Carl Swift bought it back for $35,000, including two buildings and all the machinery. In 1935 he and brother-in-law Landwehr again teamed up with Carl E. Swift & Co. to manufacture washing machines in their plant on Howard Avenue and the Pere Marquette Railway tracks. Swift began the company a year earlier to make steel pipe and asbestos in a plant at 208 Central Avenue. By 1939 Swift & Co. was making furnace cleaners as a subsidiary of Holland Furnace in a facility at 29 West Eighth Street.[39]

Crampton Manufacturing

Basel R. Crampton of Grand Rapids in late 1934 opened the Crampton Hardware Co. on West Thirteenth Street with thirty employees to manufacture stainless steel refrigerator hardware, but within three months, it became a branch of a Grandville firm. In 1937 the chamber of commerce lured a spin-off company, Crampton Manufacturing, back to Holland, under Alvin O. Shafer as vice president and general manager. The firm took over the vacant Szekely Aircraft factory (chapter 15) in the Bay View addition on West Twelfth Street and put thirty men to work manufacturing plumbing hardware and die castings. Shafer successfully petitioned the city to vacate an alley to allow for expansion of the factory. During the war, Crampton won many military contracts, and had to expand to fill the orders. The firm built a $25,000 addition in 1944 and increased the workforce to two hundred workers.[40]

In 1946 company president Herman E. Pleasant announced a $240,000 stock sale to raise working capital and capital for new equipment. The money, the company soon announced, was to acquire

38 *Holland City News*, 3 Mar. 1927.

39 *Holland City News*, 17 Jan. 1935; *Holland Sentinel*, 25 Oct. 1928, 29 Mar., 9, 24, 29 Apr. 1929; *Holland City Directories*, 1934, 1936, 1940.

40 *Holland Sentinel*, 10 Nov. 1934, 31 Jan. 1935; *Holland City News*, 15 Mar. 1937, 25 May 1944.

Crampton Manufacturing Company factory, 338 West Twelfth Street at Harrison Avenue (*Joint Archives of Holland*)

Grand Rapids Brass, a firm that manufactured refrigerator hardware. Crampton placed the Brass works under its Crampton Hardware division, which it revamped to make die castings for the automotive industry. The acquisition doubled Crampton's production capacity, and both plants increasingly supplied automotive dies. A $30,000 expansion in 1948 at 338 West Twelfth Street plant added much needed jobs, but fifty property owners turned out for a public hearing and demanded that the board of appeals reject the project anyway, so as not to further blight the residential neighborhood. Jobs came before ascetics, and Crampton Manufacturing received its permit. In 1957 the company acquired Conrad Inc. of Holland, a firm on Jefferson Street founded in 1954 by Charles F. Conrad to manufacture low temperature industrial testing equipment for everything from metal parts for aircraft to pharmaceuticals and rubber processing (see below). The Conrad subsidiary increased Crampton's floor space by 60 percent.[41]

Crampton Manufacturing's last year as an independent company was 1965, under president John H. Scott and vice president Clifford E. Thompson. The company was sold and became a division of Bay Casting, a transition that sparked labor troubles for new manager Lester Yott. The tool and die makers, the cream of the labor force, decided to organize under the United Auto Workers-CIO. The new owners fired seven employees for union-organizing activities and tried to block the union effort, but the National Labor Relations Board enjoined them from interfering. The NLRB also forced them to reinstate the employees with back pay. Essentially, the NLRB decision made Bay Casting a union shop, and every one of the 325 production workers had to sign up. But

41 *Holland City News*, 6 June 1946, 5 June 1947, 1 July 1948, 18 Apr. 1955; Charles Conrad, "A Recap of Career Development," typescript, 1991, JAH.

a year later, management balked at negotiating a new contract, and all 325 walked off the job, again charging the company with interfering with union activities.

The real issue was wages, as federal and state mediators soon found out. The company saw profits squeezed by cutbacks in auto production for several months and refused to accede to union demands. Indeed, they ratcheted up the pressure by announcing the closing of the plant, but salaried and supervisory personnel continued to come in. The company then called back one hundred strikers, but not one would cross the picket lines. With the company seemingly at a disadvantage, the strikers, led by Pat Nordhof, overplayed their hand by mass picketing and acts of vandalism that brought police on the scene. For this the company won an injunction in Ottawa County Circuit Court that placed tight limits on the strikers. This forced the workers to accept a settlement for less than they had demanded. Bitterness on both sides lingered, and within six years, in 1972, the plant was shut down and the factory sold to Thermotron Corporation.[42]

Thermotron Industries

Thermotron Industries was the brainchild of industrialist and inventor Charles F. "Chuck" Conrad, a refrigeration technician in Holland since 1948, who tinkered with low temperature refrigeration in his garage on West Twelfth Street and formed the Conrad Commercial and Industrial Refrigeration Company, later shortened to Conrad Inc. He built the actual test chambers at IXL Machine Shop on Seventh Street at Pine Avenue. In 1951 Conrad obtained his first patent on a refrigeration system for test chambers that could reduce temperatures to minus 100 degrees Fahrenheit, copyrighted as the Cascade system. Six years later, in 1957, he sold Conrad Inc. to Crampton Manufacturing (see above). In 1962 Conrad and his wife Elsie, risk-takers at heart, ventured $1,000 to begin a company to manufacture thermoelectric heating and cooling devices, which he appropriately named Thermotron Industries. Although the thermoelectric devices were a dead end, Conrad soon developed environmental simulation chambers that captured most of the world market, thanks to a marketing agreement signed about 1970 with a Japanese manufacturer.[43]

42 For this and the previous paragraph, see *Holland City News*, 23, 30 Mar., 20 Apr., 4 May 1967; *Holland Sentinel*, 5 Jan. 1966, 17, 23 Mar., 19, 22 Apr., 2, 3, 9, May 1967; *Holland City Directories*, 1965-72.

43 Charles Conrad, "A Recap of Career Development," typescript, 1991, JAH; Massie, *The Holland Area: Warm Friends and Wooden Shoes* (Northridge, CA: Windsor Publications, 1988), 112. I am indebted to Paul Den Uyl, a Thermotron division manager, for information in this and the following two paragraphs.

In 1980 Chuck Conrad purchased the former Hekman Rusk plant at 400 West Eighteenth Street to house a Thermotron subsidiary, Crusader Industries, which manufactured kilns, and another division making vibration units for the chambers. Conrad also purchased the old Sugar Beet Factory next door to the main plant and the empty West Side Christian elementary school south and adjacent to the Rusk plant. The school housed Automatic Control Systems, which made the electronic controllers for the chamber systems; the Defense Products Division, which made military cooling units used on the Trident Submarine; and a division that made a mercury detection module. In 1977 the federal Small Business Administration gave the Defense Products Division the Midwest subcontractor of the year award.

In 1980 Conrad sold Thermotron to Milwaukee-based Wehr Corporation for millions of dollars. Thermotron by then had grown to six local plants, five hundred employees, and a nationwide chain of offices. Within six months of the sale, Wehr released a number of executives and engineers, several of whom launched competing environmental companies: president John Sexton in Zeeland, vice president of sales Norm Rutgers in Grand Rapids, and several others in Byron Center.

In 1981 Wehr's Holland operations were consolidated into two large plants that manufactured an array of environmental control instruments. The primary plant is south of Thirty-Second Street near US-31 in the Southside Industrial Park (chapter 15), and the head offices are at 291 Kollen Park Drive. When Wehr sold the company to Milwaukee-based Venturedyne Ltd. in 1987, Thermotron was twice as large as any competitor and sold its testing devices around the world. In the 1990s company engineers developed vapor recovery systems demanded of factories by the 1990 Clean Air Act, and ultra-low-temperature freezers to store specimens for life sciences laboratories. In 2010 the company employed 350 people in its two Holland plants under president Ronald Lampen. Thermotron's knack for diversifying into new markets bodes well for its future.[44]

Hemco Gage

A company that fed off the metal-working industries is Hemco Gage, an arm of the H. E. Morse Co. that Henry Morse of Detroit

44 Massie, *Haven, Harbor, and Heritage*, 187; Charles Conrad obit., *Holland Sentinel*, 9, 10, 13 Feb. 1995; *Business Review West Michigan* 15, no. 43 (2010): 13. Conrad in 1991 revived Lake Michigan Car Ferry Service, a firm with three ships shuttling between his native Ludington and Manitowoc, WI. Conrad spent $1.5 million to refurbish the SS *Badger*, which is the only vessel still in service (*Grand Rapids Press*, 6 June 12011).

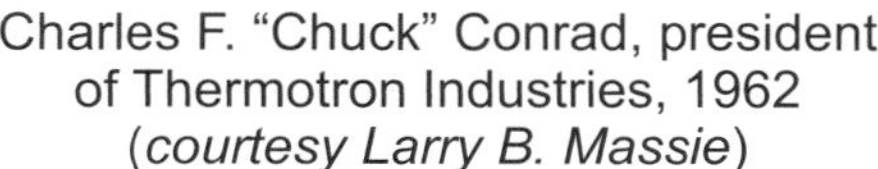
Charles F. "Chuck" Conrad, president of Thermotron Industries, 1962 (*courtesy Larry B. Massie*)

established in 1944 at 445 Douglas Avenue in Holland Township. The first Hemco products were gold-plated fountain pens for the luxury-brand Schaefer Pen Company. To make them, Hemco relied on a proprietary plating process that served the company well in the 1950s, when it began manufacturing chrome precision gages with the same unique plating process. This chrome increased the life of the gages by 400 percent, and customers clamored for the "longer lasting gauge," whose demand soon crowded out the manufacture of fountain pens. Hemco gages measure the accuracy of "anything with threads," such as fittings, pipes, and screws, explained Laurence "Larry" Wysong, who purchased H. E. Morse and its Hemco Gage brand from the Morse family in 1977. Wysong expanded its markets from the Midwest to the entire country and overseas. Morse & Hemco Gage in 1984 had a hundred employees and exports accounted for 25 percent of its sales volume. Today the workforce is down to seventy-five–mostly machinists–who can measure thread tolerances of one five-thousandths of an inch. Annual sales of the company, which usually ranks number one or number two in the industry worldwide, range from $6- to $8 million. Schlumberger, the oil-drilling giant, is a large buyer of Hemco specialty gages. The small company, led by Larry Wysong's son Christopher, thrives as a niche business and by cultivating participatory management on the shop floor.[45]

Conclusion

The Holland Furnace Co. brought Holland to the pinnacle of national fame and shame. The ride up was glorious and profitable for

[45] *Holland Sentinel*, 2 June 1984, 3 Sept. 2011; Steve Vanderveen, "Precision, craftsmanship drive Hemco," ibid., 6 Dec. 2006.

hundreds of local families, but the ride down was painful beyond belief. That the rival Home Furnace Co. never besmirched its reputation softened the blow to local pride and honor; Home Furnace was homegrown. Holland Furnace Co. failed because of an unethical chief executive officer and his cohorts, who were mostly outsiders who did not share the cultural mores of the community.

Spin offs from the furnace industry created a bevy of companies manufacturing related products, such as Hart & Cooley heat registers, Holland Maid electric washing machines, Crampton refrigerator parts, and Thermotron control devices and specialized freezers in the life sciences.

CHAPTER 14

Furniture for Home and Office

A rising demand for furniture at the turn of the century prompted the growth of this industry. The upper class made their lavish new homes into showplaces of fine furniture, preferably in Old World revival styles—Elizabethan, Victorian, Dutch, Colonial and Federal American—even Oriental. The rising middle class naturally wanted to emulate the wealthy, but on a lesser scale. This was a far cry from the first settlers, who resorted to crude, homemade furniture, such as tree stumps or hollow logs for chairs, boards for beds, and trunks and shipping crates for tables. Only a few had managed to carry a prized possession from the Netherlands.

Furniture was an ideal industry for a region rich in wood. In the 1870s Grand Rapids established its reputation as the nation's furniture city, and Holland was a cockboat in its wake, offering the advantages of skilled craftsmen; transportation by rail, lake steamer, and later trucks; and lower land prices, taxes, wage rates, and living costs. The key was the local labor force. Hollanders had a penchant for working with wood and the patience and desire to do it well. The craftsmen who turned out fine furniture with woodworking machines, specialized hand tools, and paints and varnishes were coveted. Local firms drew on their talents to produce furniture of the highest quality. For less-skilled jobs, the furniture factories hired farmers during the winter months, as did Heinz in its cooperage shop and Chris-Craft in its boat works (chapter 15).

For fifty years furniture was the mainstay of Holland's economy. Jan Kolvoord holds pride of place as the first manufacturer in the Holland colony. In 1849 he used his gristmill at Old Groningen, powered by an overshot waterwheel, to turn lathes and make carved furniture more readily accessible, including chairs, tables, bedsteads, and chests. It was a harbinger of things to come.[1]

By 1900 three of the four largest industries in Holland, based on number of employees and yearly wages, were West Michigan Furniture, Ottawa Furniture, and Holland Furniture. West Michigan Furniture's average payroll of 450 was double that of the Cappon & Bertsch tannery, the next largest employer. Yet, Cappon & Bertsch and also Holland Sugar had far more money invested in land and equipment, and their

Table 14.1 Holland Property Valuations, 1903

Assessed Property Valuation	**Realty**	**Personalty**
Holland Sugar Co.	$ 225,000	$ 3,880
Cappon & Bertsch Co.	86,000	240,380
West Michigan Furniture Co.	85,000	80,300
Holland Furniture Co.	49,000	35,330
Ottawa Furniture Co.	42,000	38,370
Walsh De Roo Co.	30,000	9,000
H. J. Heinz Co.	24,000	4,250
C. L. King & Co.	21,500	35,560
Guttman, Carpenter & Telling Co.	21,000	8,900
Bay View Furniture Co.	10,000	15,440
Scott-Lugers Co.	8,790	16,750
J. R. Kleyn	8,000	7,850
Western Machine Tool Works	6,000	10,500
DeKeyzer & Co.	6,500	1,000
Beach Milling Co.	5,000	1,400
Wolverine Motor Works	3,000	3,500
Buss Machine Works	n/a	9,100

1 Abraham Stegeman, "Historical Sketch of Groningen" (1897), in Lucas, *Dutch Immigrant Memoirs,* 1:160-61, 173; *De Hollander*, 20 Apr. 1854; Versteeg, *Pelgrim-Vaders van het Westen* (Grand Rapids: C. M. Loomis and Co., 1886), 60-61. English translation typescript by Rev. William K. Reinsma, Archives, Calvin College (ACC).

annual tax assessments were double that of West Michigan Furniture. This could be expected, because making furniture is a labor-intensive process. Of all the furniture companies, however, the assessed value of West Michigan Furniture's land and equipment was double that of the nearest competitor, Holland Furniture (table 14.1).[2]

Workers and unions

The first industry to face organized labor was furniture manufacturing, which employed at least one-third of the city's labor force in one of the most dangerous occupations, given the power tools—saws, chisels, and planers, and noxious paints and varnishes. In 1903 a state factory inspector reported that Holland factories employed nearly 2,400 people—1,670 men, 178 women, and 93 children of both sexes—who averaged eleven months of employment and earned total wages of $761,000, an average pay rate of 9.3¢ per hour. No factory workers had yet organized, in large part because the Reformed churches eschewed unions as socialistic secret societies and viewed strikes as anarchism. A few craftsmen were unionized, notably the masons, bricklayers, and carpenters; craftsmen enjoyed more leeway, given the historic nature of the guilds.[3]

In 1901 six local carpenters constructing the Ottawa Furniture factory under contractor John Oosting struck for an additional 5¢ an hour. They earned 35¢ but had learned that two Grand Rapids carpenters on the same job made 40¢, so they demanded the same pay. Oosting balked; the contract wage for Carpenters Local 1412 of Holland was 25¢ per hour. Factory workers in Holland at the time made from 8¢ to 15¢ an hour, with the leather workers at the top and food processors at the bottom. When trench diggers went on strike in 1903 for higher wages, contractors easily replaced all but the best workers, who were granted 17.5¢ per hour for a ten-hour day, "provided they did a certain amount of work."[4]

Labor unions in Grand Rapids and Holland in 1903 celebrated Labor Day for the first time. The Interurban carried to Jenison Park about twenty thousand people, where they listened to speeches by clerk

2 "Mayor's Office, Wm Brusse Mayor," in Holland City Records, Holland Museum Archives (HMA); *Holland City News*, 16 June 1903.

3 *Holland City News*, 10 Sept. 1892, 3 May 1901, 24 Apr. 1903. The average hourly wage was calculated by multiplying 11 months times 30 days times 9 hours per day, divided by total wages.

4 Ibid., 25 May 1903; Hope College *Anchor*, Feb. 1895; "Average Men Employed, Yearly Wages," by firm, Mayor's Office, Wm. Brusse, Mayor, 1900-1902, HMA.

Joseph Warnock and tanner Olef Hensen, and a Chicago organizer for the United Garment Workers of America.[5]

With socialism on the rise in the Progressive Era, including several socialist aldermen in Holland (chapters 20 and 24), the local carpenters union, twenty-five strong, went on strike in May 1913 for the second time, demanding 40¢ an hour. They were building the new Holland High School, which had to be ready by September. The contractors agreed in principle, but asked them to wait until business conditions improved. The strike generated little ill will. Local business and professional organizations organized the city's first official Labor Day commemoration, chaired by Peter Smith, replete with a parade with floats that featured each of the unions—masons and bricklayers, carpenters, ironworkers, furniture men, and barbers. So pleased were the union men, that they immediately laid plans for an annual parade. City leaders agreed; whatever affected the forces of labor, they reasoned, touched the entire community.[6]

The next strikes occurred in 1915 and 1916. The first involved ten laborers on the new post office building, who walked off the job for one afternoon after being refused a raise from 22½ to 25¢ per hour. Three labor battles took place in 1916. The freight checkers and truckers at the Pere Marquette depot walked out over unmet demands; the checkers wanted a raise from $50 to $55 a month and the truckers a raise from 17½ to 20¢ an hour. The strike tied up freight traffic at Holland for several weeks. About the same time, the carpenters and joiners struck the contractors for the raise from 35¢ to 40¢ that had been promised earlier. The contractors again protested that business conditions had not improved enough for them to comply, even though the wage rate had not changed in ten years, and food prices had risen sharply. A week later, workers on the city sewer system walked out in support of a demand to have their wages "adjusted." This forced employers to concede. The carpenters and joiners proved their bona fides in 1921, when in the face of a severe recession they voluntarily agreed to cut their hourly rate from 95¢ to 75¢. The 95¢ rate was just months old, and far above the 40¢ of six years earlier. So the union men had a mind to be magnanimous.[7]

When the furniture workers began agitating for a raise in 1918, all the West Michigan manufacturers agreed to hold the present wage

5 *Ottawa County Times*, 11 Sept. 1903; *De Grondwet*, 2 Feb. 1904.

6 *Holland City News*, 15 May, 7, 14, 28 Aug., 4, 11 Sept. 1913.

7 Ibid., 22 Apr. 1915, 4, 18 May 1916, 10 Feb. 1921. The Pere Marquette employees at the Waverly Yards went on strike again in 1922 as part of a general strike against the company (ibid., 3 July 1922).

scale, which was on par with the ironworkers and comparable skilled workers. In 1921 Cappon & Bertsch tannery had a brief walk-out when the firm cut wages in response to the postwar recession. More remarkable was the 1923 attempt by union men from St. Louis to organize iron molders at Holland Furnace Company. The molders sided with company president August Landwehr and literally rode the labor agitators out of town. They were put in a car, driven three miles from town, dumped out, and told to keep walking and never return.[8]

In 1919 an employment survey counted 5,100 men and women in the city labor force, which was almost 40 percent of the population. A 1920 tally of only the industrial labor force by Gerrit Van Schelven, secretary of the Holland Harbor Board, found 4,850 (20 percent women) employed in more than sixty factories, which had a total invested capital of $12.7 million and a total annual output of $46.4 million. The Committee on the Poor found very few families in want and distributed less than $100 a month on average, which was very low for a city of 12,000 population. Another tally in 1936, based on applications for Social Security cards, counted 5,000 employees residing in Holland and surroundings, which was down from the 1919 survey.[9]

The Christian Labor Association (CLA) is a labor movement founded in 1931 by Dutch immigrants of Reformed persuasion in West Michigan. The CLA is based on Christian social principles of dignity and respect and seeks a cooperative approach to labor-management relations. In 1934 Rev. Peter Jonker Jr. addressed the annual CLA meeting at the Sixteenth Street (later Providence) Christian Reformed Church. In 2012 the Zeeland-based CLA of Michigan served three locals in the construction trades. From the outset, hard-line AFL-CIO unions have challenged CLA locals and often picketed their job sites, especially in large cities, but this has not happened in the Holland area.[10]

Ottawa Furniture Company

Reinder E. "Ryn" Werkman was a prime mover in the first major furniture factory, Ottawa Furniture Co., which developed out of his factory on River Street. Werkman in 1888 began making furniture and cabinets with a workforce of eight men in leased space at the Phoenix Planing Mill. In 1887 he enlisted Hendrik "Heine" Te Roller, founder in 1880 of the Te Roller Manufacturing Co., creamery owner

8 *Holland City News*, 28 Nov. 1918, 31 Mar. 1921, 9 Aug. 1923.

9 Ibid., 18 Dec. 1919, 23 Dec. 1920, 21 May. 1921, 12 July 1923, 18 Dec. 1936.

10 Ibid., 13 Dec. 1934.

Ottawa Furniture factory, River at Fifth Streets, erected 1888, with two-story addition in 1891 (*Joint Archives of Holland*)

Matthew Notier, and Cornelius J. De Roo of the Standard Rolling Mills to join him in forming the Werkman Furniture Company. The object was to produce inexpensive furniture in the facilities of his Werkman Manufacturing Co., which had failed to thrive. His partner Abel Brink gladly sold his interest to the group. The three-story factory on River Avenue about Fifth Street went into production early in 1888 with from sixty to seventy workers, and the first successful product was a bird's-eye maple bedroom suite priced at only fourteen dollars (see chapter 12 for more details about Werkman's enterprises).[11]

A few years later, Werkman went bankrupt because of a faulty title on the property. Builder James Huntley, brother of the city's electricity pioneer, rescued the company with a large cash infusion and took over as manager. In 1891 an investment group of Jacob "Black Jake" Van Putten, Barteld "Bert" Slag, Cornelius Blom Sr., Cornelius Ver Schure, and several members of the Huntley and Herman Van Ark families, including Gradus Van Ark, put up $32,000 in capital, bought out Werkman's interest, and formed the Ottawa Furniture Company.[12]

Huntley's health failed within a year, and George W. Browning became manager; he enjoyed much success until his death in 1913. Ottawa Furniture paid a regular stock dividend of 10 percent, and its owners increased their paid-in capital to the authorized limit of $100,000.

11 *Holland City News*, 13 Aug. 1888, 2 Mar., 18 May 1889.

12 *Holland City News*, 11 Apr. 1891, 11 Aug. 1938; Arthur A. Visscher, "Early History of the Ottawa Furniture Company," ibid., 1 May 1926; "Ottawa Furniture Company," in *Holland, Michigan* 1892 (booklet); *Business and City Directory*, 1894; *American Graphic* (Chicago), 25 Aug. 1899; *Holland: The Gateway of Western Michigan*.

Cartoonist pictures George W. Browning, Ottawa Furniture Co. secretary and manager, with hammer in hand towering over his factory in this 1905 drawing (*courtesy Larry B. Massie*)

William Wing succeeded Browning and ran the factory until 1920, and Arthur Visscher followed him as president and general manager. Over the years, the firm targeted the medium-priced market, turning out dining room and bedroom sets, and breakfast and apartment suites under $1,000. The workforce increased gradually from eighty-five to two hundred, and the company practiced profit sharing. For the year 1915 the company distributed $1,500 in cash to the workers. In the mid-1920s, after a large addition, Ottawa Furniture occupied a three-story factory and an adjacent two-story warehouse, both served by a Chicago & West Michigan Railway siding.[13]

The firm marketed more than a million dollars' worth of furniture nationally under the slogan "Chief of Quality," with a sales force of twenty men. "Is it any wonder that where living conditions are ideal, labor is contented, and no strikes occur, workmanship is of the best?" declared a company brochure, which touted its "old time Dutch cabinet makers." To display its products, the company in 1928 opened a three-story retail store next door to the factory.

Skylights helped illuminate the third-floor merchandise. Only eighteen months after the auspicious store opening, the stock market crash of 1929 put a crimp in furniture sales, which consumers viewed largely as discretionary. In January 1930 Ottawa Furniture went into "friendly receivership." Three years later, in December 1933, the

13 *Holland City News*, 11 Apr. 1899, 27 Nov. 1913, 3 Feb. 1916, 7 Sept. 1922.

buildings were razed, leaving an empty lot for years. Holland's first major furniture company fell victim to the terrible depression that hit that industry especially hard.[14]

West Michigan Furniture

Ottawa Furniture held pride of place in its day, but the West Michigan Furniture Co. eclipsed it in importance, size, and longevity. George P. Hummer, superintendent of Holland Pubic Schools since 1882, resigned in 1889 to become manager of West Michigan Furniture, along with president Dirk Kruidenier (from Pella, Iowa), vice president Frederick Metz, and directors Frank Hadden, Jacob Schepers, E. W. Richmond, Adrian Ver Schure, and James Huntley. West Michigan Furniture grew out of the former School Seat Factory on land the Plugger family owned under the old flourmill. Hummer, a future mayor of Holland (1893-95) and prominent businessman and Democratic politician, had in 1885 married Marguerite "Maggie" Plugger, daughter of the late Aldert Plugger, who had died that year.

With his wife's inheritance in hand, Hummer risked $60,000 to launch West Michigan Furniture. He managed the operation and served as board secretary-treasurer for three decades, followed in 1920 by his son-in-law, Charles Kirchen. Kirchen bought the company in 1927 and managed it as sole owner for twenty-four years, until his death at age seventy-four in 1951. Kirchen cut a wide swath in Holland business, civic, and social circles, including serving as president of the National Furniture Manufacturers Association and director of the Grand Rapids Furniture Market Association. Theodore S. Yntema, Kirchen's son-in-law, worked in the firm briefly before pursuing a career in higher education and at the Ford Motor Company.[15]

West Michigan Furniture specialized in low- to mid-end bedroom suites. The factory on the waterfront north of Seventh Street was up and running early in 1890, with sixty workers producing from 1,200 to 1,500

14 Ibid., 28 June 1928, 2 Jan. 1930, 28 Dec. 1933, 30 June 1938.

15 For this and the next paragraphs, see *Holland City News*, 9 Feb. 1889, 26 Apr., 6 Sept. 1890, 3 June 1937, 3 May 1951; "West Michigan Furniture Company," ibid., 26 Apr. 1890; and *Holland, Michigan 1892* (booklet); *Business and City Directory*, 1894; *American Graphic*, 25 Aug. 1899; *Holland: Gateway of Western Michigan*; *Ottawa County Times*, 20 Jan. 1893; Steve Vander Veen, "Hummer served as school superintendent and mayor," *Holland Sentinel*, 26 Aug. 2007. Theodore S. Yntema (1900-185) was a professor in the University of Chicago, Booth School of Business, a director of the National Bureau of Economic Research, and a Ford Motor Company director and vice president of finance. See Cowles Commission, "A Twenty Year Research Report 1932-1952," accessed at cowles.econ.yale.edu/archive/people/directors/yntema.htm.

A caricaturist in 1905 lampoons George P. Hummer, secretary of West Michigan Furniture Co., for his ham-handedness. Hummer was superintendent of Holland Public Schools from 1882 to 1889, before becoming a venture capitalist (*courtesy Larry B. Massie*)

bedsteads a week, using the assembly line, mass production method that Henry Ford had perfected at his River Rouge plant for the Model A—the "peoples' car." Buss Machine Works furnished some thirty different machines for the factory, and the Chicago & West Michigan Railway ran tracks to the site to bring in some eight hundred thousand board feet of lumber a year and ship out finished furniture. The lumber came from a Louisiana land company in which West Michigan Furniture had wisely purchased a controlling interest in 1904. The Holland factory ran out of space almost immediately and expanded rapidly. After ten years, it employed 30 percent of the entire city workforce, far exceeding the payroll of the Cappon & Bertsch tannery.

When a financial panic in 1893 sparked a national economic crisis, West Michigan Furniture faced labor unrest. Three hundred workers, all members of the militant Knights of Labor, went on strike after President Hummer forced all employees to pay 1 percent toward their accident insurance. This had formerly been a free benefit. The workers charged Hummer with imposing taxation without representation. Their timing was perfect, since Hummer was running for mayor on the Democratic ticket, and presumably, he would not want to alienate working-class voters. Yet, Hummer refused to negotiate and won office anyway by thirty-six votes. Some former students backed him. The hard times hurt the Republican majority, and most local citizens condemned strikes, which they deemed confrontational, un-Christian, and even illegal.

Hummer claimed the election was a complete vindication of his hard-line stance. As he explained:

West Michigan Furniture, on waterfront between Seventh and Sixth Streets looking northwest (*Joint Archives of Holland*)

> There are two classes of laboring men. One class believes himself as good as any other man and no better, is willing to do an honest day's work for an honest day's pay, and who believes that his employer is worthy of some consideration. The other is the man who argues that capital is the sworn enemy of labor, necessarily so, the man who takes two-thirds of the sidewalk, and who feels himself above everyone else. The latter class is the one I blame for my trouble. I accepted the nomination for mayor because I would not be bluffed. I did not expect to be elected. . . . The agitators had a strong Knights of Labor organization and that was expected to work against me. . . . The businessmen, regardless of party, rallied to my support. [The election] has taught the labor organizations in Holland a lesson.

Meinardus G. Manting, editor of the Democratic *Ottawa County Times*, gloated: "The boys in the West Michigan Furniture factory as soon as the result was known, placed brooms on top of the building," warning the victor he might be swept away next time. But Hummer did win re-election the next time in 1894, albeit by an even slimmer margin of just twenty votes out of over one thousand cast.[16]

A bigger crisis came in 1896 when a huge fire, kindled in a drying kiln, destroyed the entire plant and threatened to engulf the nearby Cappon & Bertsch Tannery and West Michigan Seating Company, if not the entire downtown area. Fortunately, calm winds and a massive turnout of volunteers emptied a warehouse to save the inventory and

16 *Ottawa County Times*, 7 Apr. 1893.

snuff out the fire. City leaders considered the $125,000 fire the "most disastrous" since the Great Fire of 1871. Some four hundred employees were laid off until the plant was rebuilt on the same site. Newspaper editor Gerrit Van Schelven noted: "As a vision of disaster, nothing for a long time has wrought such dismay to the vast army of laborers who face the approaching winter with scanty storehouses and a small margin, if any, in their bank accounts. The condition of affairs will be universally felt by our merchants and other branches of trade."[17]

The company, with the help of many citizens, quickly rebuilt on a massive scale, with buildings covering five acres and equipped with the most modern machines. By 1898 West Michigan Furniture had 635 craftsmen turning out $700,000 worth of bedroom suites and bedsteads, with twelve salesmen on the road selling the furniture, mostly east of the Mississippi River. Craftsmen around 1900 took home an average of $1.68 for a standard ten-hour day, including Saturdays, or about 17¢ an hour. Unskilled workers earned less than 10¢ an hour. Hummer's expertise won him the first presidency of the National Furniture Association that was founded in Chicago in 1898. Sales declined somewhat after 1900, and the workforce under superintendent Frank Hadden fell to three hundred in 1912, but the firm continued to thrive for many decades, until 1975.[18]

In 1914, when sales declined sharply, management offered workers the choice of cutting hours by 20 percent or closing the plant until times improved. The older workers chose to keep working. "Whatever we can get at our old job is better than nothing," declared one. But the young men refused and stayed home for a time. Two years later, after good times returned, the employees received a surprise bonus averaging about one week's wages. One quarter had at least ten years of service and half at least five years. Labor's willingness to make concessions and management's willingness to reward industriousness, as at West Michigan Furniture, is one of the secrets of Holland's favorable labor climate over the years.[19]

In 1918 the company responded to an inquiry by Peoples State Bank relative to the security of its notes, by insisting that it was "prosperous and making money." The factory had just filled a United

17 Vande Water, "West Michigan Furniture Destroyed," in *Holland Happenings,* 3:53-55 (quotes); Paul A. Den Uyl, *The Holland Fire Department: The First Fifty Years* (Holland, MI: Flying Owl Publications, 2008), 121-23.

18 Larry B. Massie, *Haven, Harbor and Heritage: The Story of Holland, Michigan, Story* (Allegan Forest, MI: Priscilla Pres, 1996), 77; *Holland City News*, 26 Apr. 1890; Vande Water, "West Michigan Furniture Destroyed," 55.

19 *Holland City News*, 2 Apr. 1914 (quote); *De Grondwet*, 4 Jan. 1916.

Walter Verhoef displays his intricate workmanship at West Michigan Furniture, ca. 1905 (*Archives, Holland Historical Trust*)

States government order that brought a profit of $6,000. Overall profits had been above 10 percent every year since 1911, and the stock was worth $125 to $150 a share on the open market.[20]

West Michigan Furniture specialized in phonograph cabinets and hotel furniture in the 1920s and won contracts to furnish many first-class hotels. Its mahogany beds in colonial design, which featured heavily carved posts up to seven feet tall, were considered the "finest and highest grade" in the industry. During the Second World War, the factory turned to army bunk beds, and from the 1950s to the early 1970s, it produced beds for colleges, hospitals, and motel chains. W. Robert Fitzgerald directed the firm from 1955 to 1976, when the Louis Padnos Iron & Metal Co. purchased it. Mitchell and Doug Padnos managed West Michigan Furniture until 1984, when Padnos sold out to Mueller Furniture of Grand Rapids. Mueller retained the forty workers and promised more jobs in Holland. Instead of fine furniture, however, the factory would make office furniture and case goods, that is, tables and credenzas. The promised growth never came, and Mueller sold the company to Herman Miller. Eventually Padnos razed most of the factory to provide more space for their scrap yard. West

[20] George P. Hummer, President, to Peoples State Bank, 5 Sept. 1923 (T91-1508, box 1), HMA.

West Michigan Furniture workforce, ca. 1910; *left to right, row 1*: (* unidentified): Bert Wentzel, John Serier, John Wiebenga, Nicholas Fik, *, *, Albertus "Bert" Vande Water; *row 2*: *, Ben Veltman, *, Walter Ver Hoef, John Overweg, *, Harry Steffens, Henry Hyma, *, James B. Hadden; *row 3*: Gerrit De Vries, Henry Japinga, * teenager, Harry Coster, Albert Kraai (*up*), Herman Steggerda, *, *, *, Gerrit Vander Hill (*Archives, Holland Historical Trust*)

Michigan Furniture operated for a century and was by far the longest-running furniture maker in Holland. The red brick Padnos building on West Eighth Street is the lone remaining West Michigan Furniture structure.[21]

Holland Furniture

In 1893 John A. Vander Veen and partners built the Holland Furniture Co. on the southwest corner of River Avenue and Sixth Street, two blocks south of Ottawa Furniture. Herman Van Ark was plant superintendent, Jacob G. (White Jake) Van Putten was manager, and directors were Ed Vaupell, Roelof Veneklasen, Albert H. Meyer, Albertus Kolvoord, and Gradus Van Ark. Van Putten, a cousin of Black Jake, in 1890 had married a granddaughter of Van Raalte, Christina (Chris) Johanna Van Raalte, which linked Van Putten's important family with her powerful uncles, Dirk and Ben Van Raalte. Vander Veen, or "J. A."

21 *Holland City News*, 27 Jan. 1927, 4 July 1935; *Holland Sentinel*, 25 May 1984; Carron, *Grand Rapids Furniture*, 226. The Holland Museum Archives holds an extensive collection of West Michigan Furniture business records and catalogs.

Holland Furniture Co., Sixth Street and River Avenue, on fire at 2:00 a.m., March 15, 1901 (*Archives, Holland Historical Trust*)

to his friends, was the company president for forty-five years, until his death in 1937. He and Werkman were in the first rank of Holland industrialists. Holland Furniture was comparable in size to Ottawa Furniture, which Van Putten and Van Ark had also helped found. In 1901 the factory suffered a massive fire, but the brick walls remained intact, and the plant was rebuilt.[22]

Vander Veen's initial plan was to compete with West Michigan Furniture by making Golden Oak bedroom suites. He began strong with $50,000 of fully paid-in capital. In 1900 Holland Furniture had 170 workers, an annual payroll of $52,000, and national sales of $250,000. The firm suffered a devastating fire in 1901, with the loss of the building and equipment estmated at $50,000, of which insurance covered $35,000. Vander Veen and his partners promptly rebuilt. After manager Van Putten's death in 1909, Dr. Albert Knooihuizen ran the company until 1914, when he sold his majority shares and resigned as secretary-treasurer. Two years later, after an audit, the company filed suit against Knooihuizen for $40,000 on a charge of embezzlement. County Judge Orien S. Cross found the good doctor guilty on most charges and ordered him to repay $9,700, or about 25 percent of the

[22] For brief histories of the Holland Furniture Co., see "Mayor's Office, Wm Brusse Mayor"; "Holland Furniture Company," in *Holland, Michigan 1892* (booklet); *Business and City Directory*, 1894; *American Graphic*, 25 Aug. 1899, and *Holland: Gateway of Western Michigan*; Carron, *Grand Rapids Furniture*, 167; John A. Vander Veen obit., *Holland Sentinel*, 11 Oct. 1937. The fire is described in Den Uyl, *Holland Fire Department*, 127-29.

The rebuilt Holland Furniture Co. as seen looking southwest (*Archives, Holland Historical Trust*)

claim. George E. Kollen, Knooihuizen's attorney, argued the case on appeal before the state Supreme Court, but the high court upheld the lower court.[23]

Evert P. Stephan, who for twenty years was manager of the Jas. A. Brouwer Furniture store, bought Knooihuizen's shares, and Vander Veen, who had recruited him, hired Stephan as manager. He had learned furniture making as a young man and quickly won kudos from the employees and national recognition in the industry for his innovative leadership. At the behest of his workers, he allowed them in the summertime to begin work an hour earlier to have more family time in the evening. In 1920 Stephan and his crew petitioned the common council to make the practice uniform throughout the city, which led ultimately to daylight savings time in Holland.

In 1923, after a prosperous year, the company shared its good fortune with its 175 workmen by granting an average 10 percent raise. Holland Furniture under Stephan clearly had a progressive labor policy. In 1925 the Vander Veens–John A. and his brothers Jacob and Dirk, who held all the board offices–told Stephan to focus his energies

[23] *Holland City News*, 15 Oct. 1914, 24 Feb., 14 Sept. 1916, 4, 18 Jan., 19 Apr. 1917, 11 Mar. 1920. Van Putten served in local government (fourth ward alderman and mayor), on community boards (education, trade, police and fire commissioners, harbor, and Pilgrim Home Cemetery), and was connected with major companies–Ottawa Furniture, West Michigan Furniture, Holland Sugar, and Holland City Bank. See Elton J. Bruins, Karen G. Schakel, Sara Frederickson Simmons, and Marie N. Zingle, *Albertus and Christina Van Raalte: The Van Raalte Family, Home and Roots* (Grand Rapids: Eerdmans, 2006), 81-82.

Employees of Zeeland Furniture Company, ca. 1920
(*Zeeland Historical Museum*)

on plant efficiency, and Stephan hired John's brother-in-law John G. Van Leeuwen of Zeeland to direct the national sales force. In 1927 the National Furniture Men's Alliance elected Stephan as its head, giving him pride of place in the furniture world. Stephan took a hiatus from Holland Furniture in 1928, but returned as plant manager from 1935 until 1938, when he resigned a second time to lead the chamber of commerce, a vital organization in helping the city survive the Great Depression.[24]

In 1926 several Holland men, led by John A. Vander Veen, bought the bankrupt Zeeland Furniture Co. and reorganized it as the Dutch Woodcraft Shop. Zeeland Furniture, directed by Cornelius Van Loo, and then his son Benjamin, had been for most of its thirty-five years the largest employer in Zeeland. After twelve good years, in 1938, following Vander Veen's death, Holland Furniture closed the Dutch Woodcraft Shop, consolidated operations in the larger Holland plant, and put ninety men out of work.[25]

Stephan's deft touch in labor relations was sorely missed in 1948, when the entire workforce at Holland Furniture staged a wildcat walkout over a new wage incentive plan that they claimed would reduce take-home pay. During the war, the men had put in many hours of overtime to build wooden gliders for the D-Day invasion at Normandy, and they wanted their just rewards. After a one-week work stoppage, which union officials in Grand Rapids did not authorize, the company, claiming a misunderstanding by the men, rescinded the plan, and they went back to work. After a run of eighty years, Holland Furniture was sold to Baker Furniture (see below) in 1973. Under plant manager William Covert, Baker tried to salvage the company, but a huge backlog of defective pieces needing repair stymied their efforts. In 1975 Baker

24 *Holland City News*, 8 Mar. 1923, 11 Mar. 1925, 23 June 1927, 28 Mar. 1935, 14 Oct. 1937, 4 Aug. 1938.

25 *Holland City News*, 28 Oct., 9 Dec. 1926, 4 Apr. 1927, 20 Jan. 1938.

Bay View Furniture Co. on Black Lake at the foot of Fourteenth Street between Cleveland and Ottawa Avenues, with H. J. Heinz to the west. Note the waterlogged wooden storage buildings on the shore of Black Lake, ca. 1910 (*courtesy Myron Van Ark*)

gave up and closed the plant; a few profitable lines were moved to its North Carolina facilities. In 2008 Scott Bosgraaf turned the empty building into the upscale Scrap Yard Lofts condominium complex, on behalf of the owner and financier, Louis Padnos Iron & Metal Co.[26]

Bay View Furniture

Bay View Furniture was capitalized at $30,000 in 1898 by Herman Van Ark, Peter De Spelder, Cornelius Cook, and Henry Pelgrim Sr., with the goal of making tables of all kinds, from high-end dining room tables to end stands and extension and library tables. Extension tables became the company's exclusive item; it shipped one hundred per day across the United States. The factory stood along the railroad tracks at the end of Fourteenth Street and the lake between Cleveland and Ottawa Avenues, on the site of Paulus Den Bleyker's defunct Holland Carriage & Bending Works (now the eastern end of the Heinz Waterfront Walkway). The three-story building accommodated up to one hundred employees, and the annual payroll was $11,000. The business prospered with Van Ark as president and superintendent until his death in 1920, and Pelgrim as secretary-treasurer. After several building additions, the

26 Ibid., 12 Aug. 1948; *Grand Rapids Press*, 15 Sept. 2011; conversation with William Covert, 7 Mar. 2012.

workforce by 1912 ranged up to fifty, with a payroll of $70,000. Over the next decades, Bay View's workforce doubled to one hundred men, who turned out twenty thousand pieces of furniture annually, and the payroll topped $100,000. Pelgrim's son Henry Jr. succeeded him as director, and after his death in the mid-1930s, Henry's son George A. took over as president and manager. Bay View survived the Great Depression as the only family-owned furniture factory in Holland. It went out of business in 1954 after fifty-six years.[27]

Charles P. Limbert Furniture

The Charles P. Limbert Furniture Co., established in 1894 in Grand Rapids by the namesake, moved to Holland in 1906. Limbert named his furniture line "Limbert's Holland Dutch Arts and Crafts Furniture." As a marketing ploy, company advertising touted the "Holland Dutch craftsmen" who were "world famous as cabinet makers." The appeal to ethnic snobbery was an effective tactic. By 1912 Limbert kept 250 craftsmen busy in a modern three-story factory on Sixth Street at Columbia Avenue. Limbert in 1917 ranked first in volume of business among Holland's six furniture companies. Salesmen hawked the Arts and Craft line across the country. One of those five salesmen in 1917 was Dirk Van Raalte Jr. Despite his best efforts, Van Raalte found sales slipping because the big, heavy, and comfortable Limbert-style furniture, known as Period Revival, suffered from changing consumer tastes, and the company failed to react. Nevertheless, the firm survived the dismal sales volume during the First World War that bankrupted many other furniture companies. A few years later, an infusion of fresh capital saved the company in the "Dismal Twenties."[28]

In 1922 Van Raalte, August Landwehr of Holland Furnace, and two other Holland investors bought out Limbert and his Grand Rapids associate J. P. Homiller. In the $700,000 reorganization, Van Raalte became treasurer and manager and Landwehr president. This put the plant firmly in the hands of Holland businessmen, and none too soon,

27 "Bay View Furniture Company," in *Holland, Michigan 1892* (booklet); *American Graphic*, 25 Aug. 1899; and *Holland: The Gateway of Western Michigan*; *Holland City News*, 1 Jan. 1920, 3 June 1937, 1 Mar. 1929, 13 July 1944; "Fifty Years Ago Today," *Holland Sentinel*, 3 Mar. 1984, 28 Feb. 1948. Van Ark emigrated from Amsterdam in 1866 and arrived in Holland on Christmas Day. For 16 years he was a partner in the clothing store of Notier, Van Ark, and Winter. He also served as a city alderman and was prominent in Third Reformed Church.

28 *Holland: Gateway of Western Michigan*; Carron, *Grand Rapids Furniture*, 178-80; *Holland City News*, 4 July 1917; Joel Lefever, "Holland's Limbert least-known but influential furniture maker," *Holland Sentinel*, 30 Dec. 2001.

Charles P. Limbert Company, 1909 (now site of Freedom Village) (*Joint Archives of Holland*)

since Limbert died within a year. Van Raalte entirely redesigned the bedroom line in a lighter, innovative style, and launched an extensive national magazine advertising campaign in the *Saturday Evening Post* and *House and Garden*, to reach their three million readers with the message that the Limbert Company had reinvented itself under the [grand]son of the founder of the city of Holland and his men, who are the "finest craftsmen of the Netherlands . . . bred in the craft through many generations." Rev. Van Raalte would have been amazed that his descendants made fine furniture that is much coveted by connoisseurs today.[29]

Limbert furniture went bankrupt in 1942, and the Storm King Co. of Akron, Ohio, a maker of storm windows and doors, saw an opportunity to move into Michigan. In federal bankruptcy court in Grand Rapids, Storm King officials bought the vacant Limbert plant and equipment for a high bid of $63,000. The chamber of commerce labeled Storm King an essential industry and cheered the prospect of new jobs. The firm began production late in 1943 with seventy-five local workers, and quickly added thirty-five more. Norton Wisok of Ohio managed the Holland branch. After six months, Storm King Co. of Michigan reorganized itself as the Northern Wood Products Co.,

29 *Holland City News*, 26 Sept., 29 Dec. 1922, 13, 20 Jan. 1927.

and the new corporation issued $1 million in common stock to fund a building addition, double plant capacity, and boost production of the popular combination storm/screen windows. When the first truckload left the factory in January 1944, Mayor Henry Geerlings, Evert Stephan of the chamber of commerce, and company officials gathered at the gate to mark the occasion. Over the next few years, Northern Products was a leader in windows and doors. Despite the good times, in 1949 the company was sued successfully and forced into receivership and liquidation. The sudden end to a promising company left a hundred workers and many local stock investors "holding the bag." Baker Furniture bought the property for one of its plants and its famed furniture museum. In 1987 the building, then vacant, was razed to make way for Freedom Village.[30]

Bush & Lane

Bush & Lane originated in Chicago in 1901 under B. F. Bush and Walter Lane, the latter a renowned innovator in piano design. In 1905 Bush & Lane moved their operations to Holland, through the efforts of several leading local investors, led by William H. Beach, a former two-term Holland mayor. The next year Beach and his syndicate purchased Bush's interest in the business, which was capitalized at $300,000. Beach became the general manager and treasurer (and later vice president), his son Chester Beach the secretary, and Frank Congleton the vice president. It was a coup for the city. The firm very much became a local institution, and its national reputation added to the commercial prestige of Holland.[31]

Bush & Lane pianos held first place in the piano world, and by 1912 the company claimed to be the largest industry in Holland. The two-story plant on East Twenty-Fourth Street across from Prospect Park employed two hundred craftsmen making upright, baby grand, and player pianos. Self-playing pianos were a "hot" new product in 1910, and the firm shipped three hundred in the first two months. So popular were all the pianos that the factory was swamped with orders, especially in the banner year 1918. Bush & Lane expanded in 1919 with a $90,000 four-story addition, which relieved the cramped work floor and allowed the payroll to rise from 200 to 350 men. Bush & Lane brought a growth spurt to the entire southeastern section of town.

[30] Ibid., 23 Sept. 1943, 6 Jan., 29 June 1944, 2, 14, 21 Feb. 1946; *Holland Sentinel*, 23 Jan. 1942, 15 Aug. 1947, 21 Apr., 9 June 1949.

[31] *Holland City News*, 3 Aug. 1905, 12 July, 20 Dec. 1906.

Bricklayers interrupt their work on the Bush & Lane four-story addition to pose for the camera. Each bricklayer holds his trowel and level, and the hodcarriers stand behind. The man in the dress shirt (*top left*) is foreman Hyo Bos. John Dogger is the second person to his left in the top row (*courtesy Randall P. Vande Water*)

"Things industrially are looking up for Holland," the *City News* editor crowed. Holland Furnace, De Pree Chemical, Holland Canning, and P. S. Boter Clothiers also enlarged their facilities that year.[32]

The decade of the 1920s began on a high note for Bush & Lane but ended on a low one. Despite the sterling reputation of their pianos, sales began to decline, and by 1929, the company faced debts in the millions of dollars. The death in 1928 of Walter Lane, the driving force behind the firm, was a major blow. The week of his funeral saw the firm, under Chester Beach, the new president and treasurer, place its initial line of bedroom suites, featuring innovative woods and veneers, on display at the Grand Rapids Furniture Exposition. The plan was to focus on furniture and radio cabinets, not pianos. To push the new products, Beach lured Abe Stephan, manager for fourteen years of the Holland Furniture Co. and three-term ex-mayor of Holland, to take charge of the furniture division. Stephan would parlay his reputation as past president of the National Association of Furniture Manufacturers and an expert in fine furniture, and the ability of lead salesman James

[32] Ibid., 10 Oct. 1910, 20, 27 Mar. 1919.

De Pree to recruit the best sales force in the business, to make Bush & Lane one of the premier furniture lines in the country.[33]

The major decision to join the home entertainment revolution and manufacture cabinet radios for the parlors of the rising middle class did not go smoothly. In the spring of 1929, company salesmen from New York to California were called to the home office for a three-day conference, actually a pep rally, to build enthusiasm for the new products. This was just six months before the stock market crash, which undid the best-laid plans and pushed the company to the wall. That the able manager Stephan resigned in August 1929 further exacerbated the situation. Only the intervention of Arthur Morris of Detroit, a Bush & Lane distributor and retail storeowner, who brought in $750,000 of fresh capital and took over management, staved off disaster. Under Morris, Bush & Lane returned to its roots and signature product, the grand piano. The plan was to build monthly seventy-five grand pianos, six hundred radio sets, and two thousand radio cabinets. Stephan's bedroom furniture line ended with his departure from the company. It was hoped that the reorganization would save some 150 jobs (less than half the workforce in its heyday), but that was not to be. Within a year, in 1930, the plant went bankrupt.[34]

Furniture industry in the 1920s and 1930s

The furniture factories and related industries ran full tilt during the prosperous years of the First World War, but in 1920, the first postwar year, a severe slump hit many industries, including furniture. Wages had soared in Michigan, and the forests had been largely logged out. Furniture was destined to move south, notably to North Carolina, but West Michigan would not give up without a fight. When orders fell off sharply, and local companies announced layoffs or short weeks, the three hundred employees of West Michigan Furniture chose a 10-cent an hour wage reduction, in lieu of a temporary shut down or a two-day work week. Fortunately, the downturn was short-lived, mainly because increasing efficiencies from modern machinery and consolidations allowed firms to hold prices and wages down. The chamber of commerce also hit on the idea of highlighting local industries by staging in the armory an annual "Made-in-Holland Week," free to the public. In the first show in 1926, the armory was jammed with fifty booths displaying

[33] *Holland Sentinel*, 27 Feb., 5 Nov. 1928; *Holland City News*, 1 Mar., 11 Nov. 1928, 18 Apr. 1929.

[34] *Holland City News*, 11, 18 July 1929, 1 May 1930, 22 Oct. 1931; *Holland Sentinel*, 9 Apr. 1929.

local products from pianos and furniture to washing machines, and ten thousand people toured the exhibition.[35]

In 1930 an industrial survey of the city's twenty-seven factories with more than fifty employees showed the startling fact that furniture was fast losing its preeminence to the rising metal and machine industries, suppliers of the automotive industry. Furniture factories still employed 974 men in Holland, but this was only 16 percent more than the 837 employed in metals. All other factories together employed 1,200 workers. Holland could at last boast of a mature, diversified industrial base. This was critical to surviving the heavy blows of the Great Depression.[36]

The national economic collapse weeded out weaker furniture companies, including Ottawa, Limbert, and Bush & Lane, but West Michigan, Holland, and Bay View survived, and two new companies, Baker and Sligh, which focused on high-end furniture, joined their ranks. So Holland continued to be a furniture city.

Baker Furniture

Baker Furniture Co., Allegan's largest employer, relocated to Holland in 1933, the same year that Charles R. Sligh Jr. of the Sligh Furniture Co. of Grand Rapids moved his firm to Holland. Siebe Baker founded Baker Furniture in Hamilton, but in 1900 he shifted operations to Allegan, where he made the Baker name synonymous with the highest quality in fine furniture. In 1933, under son Hollis S. Baker, the firm purchased the vacant Bush & Lane Piano factory, renovated it, and moved all its machinery and equipment to Holland. The city fathers of Allegan never forgave Holland for crippling its economy in the midst of the depression.[37]

Recruiting Baker Furniture was a coup by the city industrial commission and chamber of commerce, who had worked long and hard to woo the famous firm and win some two hundred jobs. Hollis Baker had his eye on the skilled furniture craftsmen in Holland and its harbor, which would give his products ready access to national and even world

35 *Holland City News*, 18 Nov. 1920, 1, 8 Apr. 1926.

36 *Holland Sentinel*, 6 Feb. 1930.

37 *Holland City News*, 19, 26 Oct., 30 Nov., 14 Dec. 1933. In 1903, Cook, Baker & Co. became Baker & Co., and in 1927 Baker Furniture Factories. After Siebe Baker's death in 1925, son Hollis S. Baker took over. About 1929, the firm was sold to a national furniture wholesaler, Peck & Hills. But in 1933 after the distributor went bankrupt, Baker's son Hollis S. bought the company back (*Holland Sentinel*, 10, 11 Dec. 2003, 21 May, 29 Aug. 2004; Carron, *Grand Rapids Furniture*, 126-27).

Siebe Baker, founder of Baker Furniture Company (*Joint Archives of Holland*)

markets with the planned development of the St. Lawrence Seaway. The opportunity to consolidate all operations under one roof, instead of three as in Allegan, was also a consideration, as were the lower electric rates of the city-owned power plant. Allegan leaders lamented bitterly being dealt "the hardest commercial blow" the city "ever received." Baker Furniture began operations in the Prospect Park factory in early 1934, then added factories on Sixteenth Street at Van Raalte Avenue, and in 1950 took over the former Limbert plant on Sixth Street.[38]

The firm continued in Holland for seven decades, from 1933 to 2004. In its heyday, Baker had 450 on the payroll under plant managers Hollis S. Baker Jr., John De Wilde, and then ex-mayor Neal Berghoef. Frank Van Steenberg became president in 1953 and Hollis Baker Jr. in 1961. The Baker family sold the company in 1965, which ended local ownership and presaged its future demise. One factor in the decision was the unionized workforce, a local of the United Brotherhood of Carpenters and Joiners. Subsequently, Baker Furniture was sold three times: in 1969 to Magnavox of Chicago, in 1972 to Knapp & Tubbs of Grand Rapids, and in 1986 to the Kohler Co. of Wisconsin. From 1986 to 2004, as a Kohler subsidiary, Baker's main office was in its Grand Rapids factory and the Sixth Street plant was sold in 1985. It stood vacant until being demolished to make way for Freedom Village in 1990.[39]

Kohler closed the Twenty-Fourth Street plant in 2004 and moved the 135 jobs to Baker's North Carolina plant. About a dozen craftsmen

38 Ibid., 1 Jan. 1934, 30 Dec. 1937 (quote), 22 Dec. 1938, 22 Jan. 1948, 23 Mar. 1950, 7 June 1951.

39 *Holland Sentinel*, 26 July 1990, 31 July 2003; Carron, *Grand Rapids Furniture*, 127.

joined the exodus; the rest received severance pay from $500 to $3,000, based on longevity. Baker's custom designs and Old World hand-finished pieces made the Baker name one of the most respected in the furniture world. The closing marked the end of fine furniture making in Holland. Local entrepreneur Scott Bosgraaf bought the empty Twenty-Fourth Street building and renovated it into upscale housing and a commercial building, named Baker Lofts, which opened in 2005. Some $4 million in city and state tax breaks made the $17 million project feasible. The 101 residential units sold quickly to "empty-nesters," and six businesses rented the commercial space. After several successful years, the economic downturn and real estate crisis of 2008-9 and an ensuing bank squeeze, led in 2011 to Bosgraaf's default on the $5.3 million bank mortgage, followed in 2012 by his placing Baker Lofts and other property in bankruptcy. He owed $12 million at the time.[40]

Smaller furniture companies

Smaller furniture factories operated in the shadow of the "majors." One of the earliest was Westfield Bros. Furniture Co., founded by brothers John and William Westveld in 1889. That same year the Takken & De Spelder Wagon Works established the Lakeside Furniture Co. under the roof of their wagon and carriage factory on the northeast corner of River Avenue and Fourth Street. Lakeside specialized in oak tables, bookcases, and secretaries for libraries in offices and homes, and fifteen to twenty workers turned out several thousand items a year. The principals were Henry Takken, Peter De Spelder, J. Lafayette, and Cornelius Cook. Lakeside Furniture went defunct before 1906. De Spelder was a principal in Bay View Furniture, and in 1926, he had a hand briefly in the bankrupt Wolverine Furniture Co. of Zeeland, one of the town's oldest industries, dating from 1900. In 1923 De Spelder sold the business, then known as Michigan Star Furniture, to Dirk Jan (D. J.) De Pree, son-in-law of Herman Miller of the Colonial Clock Co. (see below).[41]

Larger furniture-related firms were Donnelly-Kelley Glass and Thompson Manufacturing. Donnelly began making mirrors for fine furniture in 1905 but sold that business to LaBarge Mirrors in 1962

40 *Holland Sentinel*, 10, 14 Dec. 2003, 31 July, 21 Dec. 2004, 29 Apr. 2007, 16 Sept. 2011, 12 Jan. 2012; *Grand Rapids Press Lakeshore Edition*, 10 Dec. 2003, 29 July, 22 Dec. 2004; *Grand Rapids Press*, 15 Sept. 2011, 7, 12 Jan. 2012.

41 Ibid., 25 Aug. 1888, 26 Apr. 1890, 18 Apr. 1896; "Lakeside Furniture Company," in *Holland, Michigan 1892* (booklet); Chicago *American Graphic*, 25 Aug. 1899; Massie, *Haven, Harbor, and Heritage*, 159.

Thompson Manufacturing Company, 167 East Twelfth Street, later the Hope College De Pree Art Center and Gallery (*Joint Archives of Holland*)

and focused on designing and manufacturing mirrors for automobiles (chapter 15).

Thompson Manufacturing evolved gradually from the Fitch & Thompson plumbing company, which began operations about 1903 at 4 West Eighth Street. Clifford E. Thompson was the principal of the firm. By 1906 Fitch & Thompson had moved into the former Lakeside Furniture building at Fourth Street and River Avenue, and the business changed from a plumbing shop to a manufacturing company producing wooden toilet closet tanks and seats under the name, Central Closet Manufacturing Company. In 1908 the firm was re-capitalized as the Thompson Manufacturing Co., with Charles M. McLean president, Cornelius Ver Schure vice president, and Thompson secretary-treasurer and general manager. George Kollen, Warren W. Hanchett, and later Louis J. Vanden Berg (in 1929 Vander Burg) were also identified with the firm. The plant produced bungalow furniture as well as toilets in the River Avenue factory until 1914, when the company moved to a new one-story facility at 167 East Twelfth Street adjacent to the Pere Marquette Railway tracks (now the De Pree Art Gallery of Hope College). There the firm also produced library furniture. Thompson products earned high marks with builders and consumers nationwide, and the firm turned a profit from the start and paid cash dividends within two years. "If it is made by Thompson, it must be right," was the proud advertising boast. But residential neighbors near the plant complained about the noisy sawing machines and the crude cursing of the operators.[42]

42 *Holland City News*, 2 Feb. 1911, 7 Jan. 1915; *Holland: The Gateway to Western Michigan* (Holland, MI, 1912) quote; *Directories*, 1903-4, 1906, 1908.

Workforce of Thompson Manufacturing Company, 1924
(*courtesy Randall P. Vande Water*)

In 1916, with adequate capital and a heavy order book, Thompson, the prime mover from the outset, resigned, and Louis J. Vanden Berg, the foreman, was elevated to manager. Gilbert T. Haan of Model Drug replaced Thompson as a director, and Otto P. Kramer became secretary-treasurer. Vanden Berg signed a five-year lease to display samples of company products in the Furniture Temple in Grand Rapids during the January and July furniture seasons. Vanden Berg managed the company until it closed in 1933 during the Great Depression. George Schurman was president during the latter years.[43]

In 1919 George Vande Riet and Henry Tuls founded the Holland Chair Co. in the former Lakeshore Furniture/Thompson building on Fourth and River, with Vande Riet as president and Tuls as vice president and plant superintendent. Orders came in so thick and fast for its solid mahogany chairs that the craftsmen could not keep up. Marshall Field & Co. of Chicago periodically ordered up to two thousand chairs at a time, for delivery within three months. After three years, rapid growth forced the partners to increase the capital stock from $25,000 to $100,000, erect a new $15,000 three-story factory, and double the workforce from thirty to sixty employees. This allowed the daily production rate of sixty chairs to more than double, and still customers had to wait for delivery.

[43] *Holland City News*, 15, 23 Mar. 1916, 5 Aug. 1920, 1 Dec. 1927; Charles M. McLean obit., *Holland Sentinel*, 29 Apr. 1931; *Holland City Directories*, 1921, 1931, 1934.

Despite the promising beginning, the company could not survive the difficult conditions in the industry in the 1920s. The business closed by 1928, and Vande Riet became a furniture designer. The site is today part of the Holland Waste Water Treatment plant.[44]

The Veit Manufacturing Co. of Grand Rapids, founded in 1902 and led by John Tazelaar, in 1916 moved its Grand Rapids plant, "lock, stock and barrel," to Holland, taking over and renewing the decrepit former Holland Veneer Works building at 301 West Sixteenth Street at Van Raalte Avenue. It was the only empty factory in the city. City officials and the chamber of commerce, after wooing the company mightily, were delighted to see the eyesore gone, and they were even more sanguine about gaining the sixty workers and their families, and a woodworking company with \$200,000 in annual sales and a \$60,000 payroll. As an inducement, the city gifted the building and three adjoining vacant lots, and paid for a spur from the Chicago & West Michigan Railway line. Veit made high-end retail furniture and office furniture for banks, public buildings, and hotels, such as the Pantlind Hotel in Grand Rapids. Soon after opening in Holland, the company announced winning an \$80,000 contract to furnish a bank in Newark, New Jersey. To expand the factory to meet the increasing orders, which they anticipated would reach \$500,000 annually, the company increased its capital stock by \$20,000 with a public offering to local investors, who fully subscribed the offering.[45]

By 1921 the company was renamed the American Cabinet Company, with John Stryker president, John A. Van Kley vice president, Henry R. Brink secretary, and Hyo F. Bos treasurer. The owners sold the company in 1928, and the name changed to Chippewa Cabinet, managed by Marvin Lambers. Chippewa was short lived, a victim of the Depression. By 1931 the 301 West Sixteenth Street building was vacant and remained so until 1942, when Hart & Cooley needed it for storage. After the war, the growing Baker Furniture bought the building for furniture making. After about five years, in 1951, Baker sold it to the W. J. Bradford Paper Co., a Chicago-based manufacturer of paperboard box partitions, which had relocated its Wedg-Loc Box Partition Division to Holland.[46]

44 Ibid., 2 Feb., 21 Sept. 1922; *Holland City Directory*, 1928.

45 *Holland City News*, 19 Nov. 1916, 25 Jan., 15 Feb., 15, 22 Mar. 1917; *Holland City Directory*, 1921. The building was the L. H. Hilsinger Shoe Factory before 1902 (*Sanborn Fire Insurance Maps*, 1902, 10).

46 This section relies heavily on Massie, *Haven, Harbor, and Heritage*, 139. See also *Holland City Directories*, 1929, 1947-2010.

After several decades on Sixteenth Street making cardboard partitions for boxes of candy, Bradford Paper in 1976 erected a new plant at 13500 Quincy Street in Holland Township and sold the old building to the West Michigan Canvas Co., which in 1996 sold the building to J. C. Huizenga for his Vanderbilt Charter Academy (chapter 7). Bradford's Quincy Street facility remains the corporate headquarters for the fifth-generation family- and employee-owned company, with presidents, in order, William J. Bradford; sons William J. Jr. and Charles L.; grandsons William J. III and Judson "Jud" T., and great grandsons Judson T. Jr. and Thomas R. Bradford. The company simplified its name in 1986 to Bradford Company, in recognition of its manufacture of packaging products, materials handling systems, and patented "Just-in-Time Packaging." This latter product, a system of customized reusable shipping containers for automobile parts, was a unique and highly successful solution to the industrial push for environmentally friendly packaging.[47]

Charles Zych started West Michigan Canvas Co. in 1959 at 157 Central Avenue, taking over the Edwin Raphael Draperies shop. Zych stitched awnings, sails, and coverings of all kinds and purposes for more than twenty years, until 1983. The business then passed briefly to Dorothy Carowitz and then to Karen De Jonge in 1986. The next year De Jonge moved the shop to 11037 Paw Paw Drive, and in 1992 she moved again to the former Bradford building at 301 West Sixteenth Street. Her advertising slogan was "One Call and You're Covered." When Huizenga bought the building for his school, Karen De Jonge relocated her canvas shop to Zeeland.[48]

Prison furniture

In the 1920s, for the first time, Holland furniture companies had to compete with prison-made furniture at the state-run Ionia Prison. The unfair competition so unnerved the for-profit firms that in 1926 the Grand Rapids Furniture Manufacturers Association, together with the Holland companies, sent a strong petition of protest to Governor Alex J. Groesbeck and state prison officials on behalf of the furniture companies of West Michigan and the thousands of craftsmen "hit by this prison competition." In the previous year, Ionia prison labor had made $200,000 worth of chairs, plus shirts and other products. Its "free labor" produced more than $1 million in sales.[49]

[47] *Holland Sentinel*, 28 Mar. 2004.
[48] *Holland City Directories*, 1958-97.
[49] *Holland City News*, 26 Aug. 1926.

The protest of Holland furniture men fell on deaf ears. Indeed, in 1937, Governor Frank Murphy, in a surprise move, named as warden Dr. Garret Heyns, superintendent of Holland Christian Schools. Heyns, a sociologist by profession, defended prison labor as essential to the rehabilitation of young men behind bars. The one hundred men at Ionia making furniture had no appreciable impact on the Michigan furniture industry, Heyns told members of the Kiwanis Club at the Pantlind Hotel. After two years, in 1939, the state corrections commission, in a split vote that was largely political, unceremoniously ousted Heyns. Prison labor continued unabated for another eighty years, until West Michigan Congressman Pete Hoekstra in 2005 managed to get Congress to curtail it greatly.[50]

Office and school furniture

Sligh Furniture

Sligh Furniture Co. of Grand Rapids, founded by Charles R. Sligh in 1880, was the largest furniture company in the world in the 1920s, and Sligh stood first among equals in the industry. Charles Sligh had transformed furniture production by bringing all the lines into one factory, instead of limiting a factory to a single line, for example, bed stands in one and dressers in another. The company employed 1,500 and was the largest maker of bedroom furniture in the world. Sligh, a Scotch American, taught his son and namesake Charles Jr., the making of chamber furniture. The Furniture Salesmen's Club of Grand Rapids later named Charles Jr. its president. Even a master salesman could not overcome the decline in home furniture sales that began in 1924-25, when southern furniture companies began to make inroads.[51]

The senior Sligh died aboard a transatlantic steamship in 1927, and two sons-in-law took over, since Charles Jr. at twenty-one years of age was not yet ready. The sudden death spared Sligh from seeing the company bearing his name liquidated in 1932 at the nadir of the Great Depression, a step soon followed by many other "great names" in West Michigan furniture. Most could not compete against southern wages and cheap lumber. Grand Rapids furniture workers in 1932 earned 35¢ to 40¢ per hour, compared with 10¢ in the South, and the South had

50 Ibid., 21 Aug. 1937, 20 July 1939.

51 Charles R. Sligh Jr. interview by Abby Jewett, 8 June 1982, typescript, Joint Archives of Holland (JAH); Francis X. Blouin and Thomas E. Powers, *A Furniture Family: The Slighs of Michigan*, Michigan Historical Collections Bulletin, no. 29 (May 1980), 10-14; *Holland Sentinel*, 25 Oct. 1992.

stands of timber nearby, while woodlands in the Grand Rapids area were depleted.[52]

In 1933, Charles R. Sligh Jr., then twenty-seven years old, and O. William "Bill" Lowry, the former Sligh plant manager, started a new company in Holland, the Charles R. Sligh Co., after purchasing the name of the Grand Rapids firm, some tools and materials, and hiring forty-five of its craftsmen. Operations began in the vacant Thompson Manufacturing Co. plant on East Twelfth Street. Secretary William Connelly of the chamber of commerce and Mayor Nicodemus Bosch recruited the partners and helped them secure a bank mortgage to buy the building. The banker, Don Matheson, also bought $6,000 of stock, as did Sligh and Lowry, making the paid up capital $18,000. For every $7 of payroll, the city gave the company $1 credit toward the mortgage. City leaders were desperate to fill empty factories and add jobs. In less than three years, the company owned the title free and clear. One of the first hires was bookkeeper George Lemmen, a veteran of the Ottawa Furniture Co., who worked for Sligh Furniture for forty years, rising to company treasurer, board member, and stockholder. Sligh was able to hire executives like Lemmen for $14 a week, and they were happy to have a job.[53]

Sligh and Lowry initially made maple bedroom furniture and mid-priced desks for the retail trade at $27.50 apiece. The desks sold well at a good profit, so the company turned the focus to desks, although it continued the bedroom line until 1957. The factory also made wall clocks. The bold moves by the "boy wonder" allowed the company to make money during the Depression. Sligh bought a house and moved his family from Grand Rapids to Holland in 1937. In 1940 he and Lowry opened the Sligh-Lowry Furniture Co. of Zeeland at 361 East Main Street, and were partners until 1968, when Sligh bought out Lowry and revived the original name of Sligh Furniture Company.[54]

To cope with the scarcity of raw materials during the Second World War, which adversely affected all furniture makers, Sligh-Lowry organized Holland Industries, an association of several large plants, to win war contracts on a wide variety of products, from gunners' seats and shell boxes to truck bodies. This shrewd strategy gave them priority for lumber supplies and kept the factories running and the skilled

52 For this and the next paragraph, see Sligh interview.

53 Cornelia Van Voorst interview by Abby Jewett, 7 June 1982, typescript, 12, JAH.

54 Sligh interview; *Holland City News*, 2 Nov. 1933, 4 Jan. 1934, 19 Nov. 1936, 21 July 1938, 18 Oct. 1939; *Holland Sentinel*, 25 Feb. 1996, 28 Jan. 1997; Massie, *Haven, Harbor, and Heritage*, 184.

workforce intact. After the war, the company caught the residential building boom by making casual furniture, especially tables they called the "Cross Country" line, for the small ranch-style homes in suburbia. In 1945 the company bought the Grand Rapids Chair Co., which was sold in 1957. This, together with Sligh Furniture Showrooms in New York City, gave the firm control of four companies, including Charles R. Sligh Co. of Holland and Sligh-Lowry Co. of Zeeland. In 1953 Charles Sligh at age forty-six was elected the youngest president of the National Association of Manufacturers since the organization's founding in 1896. Sligh was also the first association president from the furniture industry and from Michigan. The presidential term was one year, but Sligh was asked to stay on. He ran the New York-based association with four hundred employees from 1957 to 1963, when he returned to Holland.[55]

When a building boom in college and university dormitories in the 1960s created a market for dorm furniture, Sligh Furniture was well positioned to capitalize on it. Similarly, when personal computers became the rage in the 1970s, the company developed tables for them that hid the cords and wires. By this time, Charles Sligh Jr. had given day-to-day operations to his sons, Charles "Charlie" Sligh III and Robert "Bob" L. Sligh Jr. Bob had joined the family business in 1954 after a stint in the US Air Force, and in 1968 he became the third generation to lead the company. Sligh very perceptively foresaw a decline in dorm furniture and made the wise decision to diversify by buying the bankrupt Trend Clocks Co. of Zeeland for one dollar. Within a year, the company was back in the black, ready to ride the clock business boom of the 1970s. Trend Clocks in 1984 was renamed Sligh Clocks, but its craftsmen also manufactured high-end home and office furniture. In 1981 Sligh Furniture moved to Holland, at 1201 Industrial Drive on the south side near M-40. In 1993 the fourth-generation Sligh, Bob L. Jr., became president of the company that then employed 260 workers. Charles Sligh Jr. died in 1997, on the cusp of a sharp decline in the furniture industry that took Sligh Furniture down after 125 years and four generations.[56]

In 2005 Sligh Furniture sold the clock line to the Boliva Watch Co., shuttered the Holland factory, and moved most production

55 Sligh interview; *Holland City News*, 4 Dec. 1952.

56 Blouin and Powers, *Furniture Family*, 14-22; *Holland City News*, 4 Dec. 1952; *Holland Sentinel*, 3 Jan. 1993, 25 Feb. 1996, 28 Jan. 1997, Robert "Bob" Sligh obit., 27 May 2012. Gordon Van Tamelen and his father Garrett had started the Trend Clock Co. in 1937. After the war, they specialized in grandfather clocks.

overseas, keeping only the home offices in the Baker Lofts facility. Its workforce, which had dwindled to 150, was reduced to six in the office. The final shoe dropped in 2011 when Bob Sligh sold Sligh Furniture to Lexington Home Brands of High Point, North Carolina, and joined the firm as vice president of business development. After 131 years, the family-owned Sligh Furniture Co. was no more.[57]

The transition of Sligh into dorm furniture presaged the shift in the 1940s from home to office furniture that gave the West Michigan industry another golden era. In the 1940s office furniture stole the spotlight, with Herman Miller of Zeeland, Haworth of Holland, and Steelcase of Grand Rapids. Walter Idema, Peter Wege, and David Hunting Sr. founded Steelcase in 1912 as the Metal Office Furniture Company.[58]

Herman Miller Inc. (originally Herman Miller Furniture Company)

Herman Miller Inc. had its inception in 1923 when Dirk Jan "D. J." De Pree, the general manager of the Michigan Star Furniture Co. of Zeeland dating from 1905, convinced his father-in-law Herman Miller and C. J. Den Herder to buy the bedroom furniture company, which was in financial straits. De Pree had married Miller's daughter Nellie in 1914. Miller, a former shipping clerk for a Grand Rapids furniture company, had come to Zeeland in 1909 as general manager of the Colonial Manufacturing Co. (known in the vernacular as Colonial Clock Co.), since the main product was grandfather clocks. Five prominent Zeeland families owned Colonial: dry goods merchant Albert La Huis, physician Thomas G. Huizenga, merchant Henry De Kruif, banker Christian J. Den Herder, and brick maker Barend Veneklasen. The first four were the company officers; all served on the board of directors of the Zeeland State Bank owned by Den Herder's father Jacob. La Huis was Jacob's son-in-law. Herman Miller managed Colonial until he retired in 1939. Although Miller was raised in the Christian Reformed Church in Grand Rapids, his family affiliated with Zeeland's Second Reformed Church.[59]

57 *Holland Sentinel*, 17 Oct. 2004, 12 May, 27 Oct. 2005, 28 Sept. 2011; *Grand Rapids Press*, 27 Sept. 2011.

58 Carron, *West Michigan Furniture*, 212.

59 Hugh De Pree, *Business as Unusual: The People and Principles at Herman Miller* (Zeeland: Herman Miller, Inc., 1986), 11-12; Gordon L. Olson, "'Timeless Memories': The Story of Howard Miller and the Clock Company He Founded," typescript (Grand Rapids, 2007), 7-10; http://www.answers.com/topic/herman-miller-inc. Herman Miller was baptized as Harm Mulder in the village of Oldehove, province of Groningen, in 1867 and died in Zeeland on 18 Jan. 1948. He Americanized his name at about age twenty-five in 1892 (De Pree, "Business as Unusual," 4-5; Hugh De Pree obit., *Holland Sentinel*, 19 Jan. 1949).

Colonial Manufacturing (Colonial Clock) Co., Washington Avenue, 1912
(*Zeeland Historical Museum*)

As the new president of a company with a "corny" name—Michigan Star—De Pree decided to capitalize on the sterling reputation of his wife's father and major shareholder by renaming his company Herman Miller Furniture Company. (In retrospect, this proved to be an unfortunate decision, since it led to public confusion with the Herman Miller Clock Co. of Zeeland noted below.) The factory continued to turn out its ornate bedroom suites and added popular wall and mantel clocks. In all its products, De Pree emphasized quality over price. Zeeland at the time had two other smaller furniture companies, Wolverine and Zeeland Furniture. De Pree, a devout Baptist, applied Christian principles, adopted innovative office systems, and introduced employee-friendly labor practices. He gained an international reputation as an unconventional but very successful industrialist. The strong-willed yet humble man died in 1990 at ninety-nine years of age, full of wisdom and honor. A few months earlier he had been inducted into the American National Business Hall of Fame.

Meanwhile, Herman Miller founded the Herman Miller Clock Co. in 1926 under his son Howard to manufacture wall and mantel clocks. Howard, only twenty-one years of age, was fresh from an apprenticeship in Germany under master clockmakers and a two-year stint working for his brother-in-law, De Pree. The Millers intended to import German-made movements, but prohibitive United States tariffs on such products prompted them to form the Herman Miller Clock Movement Co. in partnership with the Winterhalder family of Germany. The partners imported the parts and assembled them in Zeeland. When the punitive tariff was abolished a few years later, Miller dissolved the partnership and again imported the complete movements. The Great

Herman Miller in his fifties, 1920s (*courtesy Philip D. Miller*)

Depression took a toll on the company, and with the workforce down to five in 1938, the company went bankrupt. Upon the judge's directive, Howard Miller continued to manage the firm until a Chicago company outbid him to buy it and move the assets to Illinois. By then Miller had married Martha Muller of Holland, daughter of Iete Muller, the owner of the Standard Grocery & Milling Company.[60]

While in receivership, Howard Miller managed to buy a small part of the company for $2,400 with money borrowed from his life insurance policy, plus delivery of two thousand clocks to a Chicago commission house. He began manufacturing wall clocks with German-made movements, as the renamed Howard Miller Clock Co., located on Washington Avenue. Howard Miller's sons Jack H. and younger brother Philip D. later joined the company, Jack as president and CEO and Phil as executive vice president. Since 1956, when Howard Miller Clock moved into a new building on Main Street across from Herman Miller Furniture, the two companies have faced each other, but do not directly compete. During Howard Miller's seventy-fifth anniversary in 2001, the company reported having crafted nearly fifteen million clocks of all shapes and sizes—many collectibles—and that it was the only company to build its own cabinets and movements.[61]

Howard Miller Clock and Colonial Manufacturing were two of five clock companies in the Holland-Zeeland area; it was a prime

60 *Holland City News*, 28 Oct., 9 Dec. 1926, 4 Apr. 1927, 27 Jan. 1938; Olson, "'Timeless Memories,'" 15.

61 Bill of sale, Howard Miller Co. to Herman Miller, 15 June 1938, on letterhead of Samuel L. Winternitz & Co., Chicago and New York Auctioneers and Commission Merchants, kindly provided by Philip D. Miller; Olsen, "'Timeless Memories,'" 38-39; *Holland Sentinel*, 18 Nov. 2001; *Grand Rapids Press*, 1 Jan. 2002.

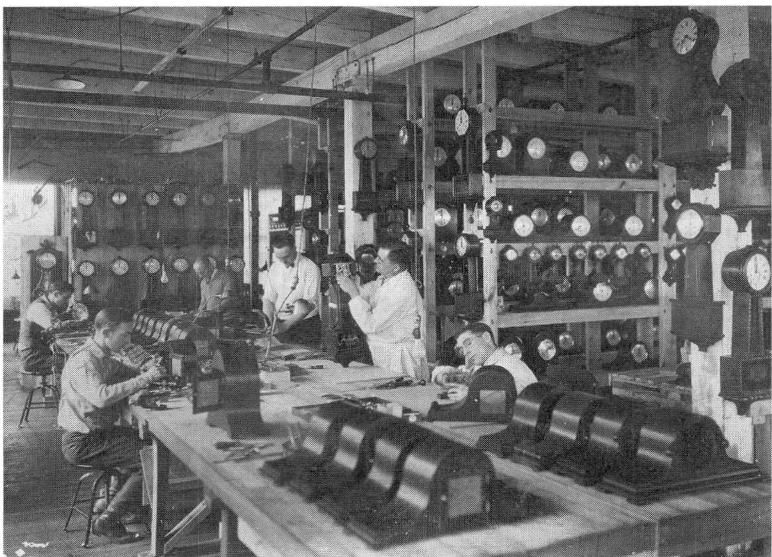

Howard Miller Clock Co. craftsmen making mantel clocks, 1927 (*courtesy Philip D. Miller*)

example of synergy. The others were Trend Clocks Co., later purchased by Sligh Furniture, and Hubbell Manufacturing, both of Zeeland, and Heritage Heirloom Clocks and Charter House in Holland. Heritage Clocks was located in the old Limbert plant on Sixth Street. To keep up with rising sales of its grandfather clocks, Howard Miller Clock in the 1970s had to expand its facilities nine-fold in a series of steps, including a new plant across Washington Avenue that was connected by a conveyor system. The workforce quintupled from 80 to 425 in that decade, and the growth continued. In 2010 Howard Miller Clock had 750 employees in Zeeland and another 1,100 in nine plants elsewhere in the United States and in Germany. Sales of $100 million was double that of the nearest competitor. The privately held company, renowned for its heirloom-quality clocks, is now in the hands Herman Miller's great-grandson Howard "Buzz" Miller.[62]

While Herman and Howard Miller were busy establishing their clock company in Zeeland, De Pree was desperately trying to keep the Herman Miller furniture company from bankruptcy in the early days of the Depression. The turning point came on a steamy July day in 1930

62 *Holland Sentinel*, 27 Dec. 1992, Howard Miller obit., 21 Sept. 1995, 18 Nov., 2 Dec. 2001; "Top 100 Companies," *Business Review West Michigan* 15, no. 43 (2010): 8. Herman Miller died in 1948 at age 80, and Howard Miller died in 1995 at age 85.

An elderly Howard Miller, Herman's son, enthralls Amanda with stories of his famous grandfather clocks, ca. 1990 (*courtesy Philip D. Miller*)

when Gilbert Rohde walked into the firm's Grand Rapids showroom unannounced and offered De Pree his innovative bedroom designs for a 3 percent royalty, to be paid *after* the suites were sold. "How could we lose on that?" De Pree reasoned. Rohde's designs were simple, functional, and durable, the very opposite of the high-end European styles that ruled supreme. Rohde led Herman Miller to see furniture as a lifestyle, rather than a dresser or dining room table. To make the radical change in the depth of the Great Depression took considerable courage.[63]

De Pree's openness to new designs distinguished him from the stodgy old-line family firms in Grand Rapids who settled into their comfortable niches and held to traditional designs, in seeming disregard of a changing marketplace that demanded innovation. Their lack of originality and even arrogance spelled trouble. Commissioned salesmen dictated to manufacturers what to make, but they often misread the market.[64]

Rohde's first designs were exhibited to great acclaim at the Chicago World's Fair in 1933. In 1936 Rohde persuaded Miller to drop

63 Massie, *Haven, Harbor, and Heritage*, 159; Dirk J. De Pree obit., *Holland Sentinel*, 12 Dec. 1990, 30 Apr. 1998; Olson, "'Timeless Memories,'" 16.

64 This is the conviction of De Pree, *Business as Unusual*, 12-14.

traditional lines altogether in favor of modern furniture. The country was on the cusp of an era of new materials, tools, and techniques, and Herman Miller must take full advantage. From then on, the De Prees allowed designers to rule the roost, not manufacturers or salesmen. Herman Miller became a "company designed by design."[65] De Pree's son Hugh graduated from Hope College in 1938 and went to New York as a low-paid "gofer" in the design studios of Rohde and Jim Eppinger. For six months Hugh did postgraduate studies in modern furniture design under experts, and the contacts and connections he made were priceless. In 1941 D. J. took the bold step of opening a Herman Miller showroom in New York City, with Jim Eppinger's nephew Gene as the salesman. It was a dramatic turning point for the fledgling Zeeland company. When Rohde died in 1944, D. J. and son Hugh were fortunate to find another influential modern designer in New York, the young George Nelson, who agreed to join the Herman Miller team in management. Nelson proved to be the most creative genius they ever knew, and his influence on Herman Miller was to be enormous.[66]

It was Nelson who in 1946 brought in the legendary husband-and-wife team Charles and Ray Eames, who experimented with molded plywood, fiberglass, aluminum, and wire. In 1956 the couple created the stunning Eames Swivel Lounge Chair and Ottoman and the relatively inexpensive Eames Lounge Chair. This "mid-century modern" furniture took the industry by storm. The iconic Lounge Chair and Ottoman later won a coveted display in Chicago's Art Museum and like venues.[67]

With the Rohde lines in their infancy, D. J. and Hugh De Pree made another far-reaching decision, to change radically their management practices by adopting the Scanlon Plan, a team-oriented philosophy rather than the usual top down structure. Joe Scanlon, a former prizefighter, labor leader, cost accountant, teacher, and theorist, developed the employee-driven, profit sharing system in cooperation with Professor Carl Frost at the Massachusetts Institute of Technology in the late 1940s. Frost, known affectionately as "Jack Frost," moved to Michigan State University in 1949 and tutored the De Prees in the plan and its ramifications for managing the shop floor. The plan required setting clear objectives and then enlisting employees to implement them and share in the resulting profits. The De Prees adopted the plan at Herman Miller in 1950, the first Michigan firm to do so. The concept

65 Ibid., 15-17, 41-42, 57 (quote).

66 Ibid., 17-21, 23-25, 46-47.

67 Ibid., 41-55.

jibed with their Christian ethics, to treat employees as partners and friends, almost family. On a practical level, employees are motivated to work harder and more efficiently when they are involved in setting goals and being rewarded for reaching them.[68]

Thanks to the De Prees, other company executives adopted the Scanlon Plan: John F. Donnelly of Donnelly Corp., Charles R. Sligh Jr. of Sligh Furniture, and Patrick "Pat" Thompson of Trans-Matic Manufacturing. Charles Conrad of Thermotron Corp., Ed Prince of Prince Corporation, Don Heeringa of Trendway, and Seymour Padnos of Padnos Iron & Metal adopted their own employee incentive plans. In a sense, nearly every local company was influenced by the Scanlon/Frost philosophy of participatory management, making the Holland area unique nationally in this regard.

The next major innovation in office furniture was the modular, or open-plan, office systems designed by Nelson and Robert "Bob" Propst. Nelson in 1945 had created the Storage Wall for office interiors that included drawers, cabinets, and closets. Propst called his design the Action Office. The open concept followed four years of field research among office workers, who disliked working in isolated cubicles. The open system provided the illusion of privacy while yet allowing easy communication with coworkers. The De Prees began moving into the office furniture market in the mid-1950s. The company was incorporated in 1960 as Herman Miller Inc. After Hugh De Pree became president and CEO in 1962, he followed Propst's leading and launched his cubicles concept. Glenn Walters successfully brought the "Action Office" system from development to market in 1967-68. Open-plan systems quickly became the industry standard, and the rows of little rooms or large "bullpens" with two hundred desks became obsolete. Herman Miller designers later introduced ergonomic office seating—the Ergon chair (1976), the Equa chair (1984), and the Aeron chair (1994).[69]

68 Ibid., 118-35; Ryan Harvey, "The Scanlon Plan: Holland's 'Work Ethic,'" (unpublished manuscript, 1994), JAH. Joseph N. Scanlon (1899-1956), president of a CIO steel-workers' union local in Ohio and lecturer at the Massachusetts Institute of Technology, in the 1930s and 1940s developed the plan bearing his name as a way to induce employers to share company profits with their workers, who in turn would work harder to increase company profits. See Daniel Wren, "Joseph N. Scanlon: the man and the plan," *Journal of Management History* 15, no. 1 (2009): 20-37. Herman Miller Inc. dropped the Scanlon Plan after 2000.

69 De Pree, *Business as Unusual*, 36, 39-40, 90-104, 138-39, 153; *Holland Sentinel*, 22 June 1979; Hugh De Pree obit., 9 July 2002, Glenn Walters obit., 22 Apr. 2010; Mark Schurman and Bruce Buursma, Herman Miller News Release, 5 Aug. 1999, www.hermanmiller.com; Ralph Caplan, *The Design of Herman Miller: Pioneered by Eames, Girard, Nelson, Propst, Rohde* (New York, 1976).

Herman Miller Inc. started their first foreign manufacturing plant in Bath, England in 1970, one of the first local firms to have international operations. The company had been manufacturing in western Europe since 1956, under licensing agreements with a number of furniture factories. Clarence "Con" Boeve was sent from Holland to Germany to oversee the international program. To raise the capital for expansion, Vernon Poest, the chief financial officer (CFO), led the way for Herman Miller to "go public" in 1970 and issue stock that traded on the NASDAQ exchange. Those who bought stock early and held on did very well, as sales skyrocketed from $49 million in 1975 to $865 million in 1990.[70]

By 1978 the De Prees had to revamp the company's Scanlon Plan. Herman Miller then employed 2,500 in the United States, Canada, and England, and half the jobs were off the shop floor, for which the bonus plan was designed. After surveying the entire workforce, the employees elected fifty-four people, representing every segment of the company, to revise the plan. After nine months of work, the employees approved the new plan by 96 percent. Carl Frost's philosophy had made a lasting impact on the company by bringing democracy into the workplace.[71]

In 1979 Herman Miller Inc. opened its first plant in Holland, an $8.5 million facility to manufacture office chairs and seats. It was located on West Forty-Eighth Street at Blue Star Highway near Tulip City Airport. The start-up workforce of two hundred was brought in from Zeeland, which greatly concerned city leaders. But company officials assured them that new hires would quickly replace those transferred to Holland. In 1980 Hugh De Pree retired, and his younger brother Max succeeded him as CEO. Max was equally committed to the Scanlon Plan, and he added an Employees Stock Ownership Plan (ESOP) that gave employees bonuses in company stock, which tied them even more to the enterprise. The company's labor-friendly policies earned it a place in 1984 in the prestigious listing, "The 100 Best Companies to Work for in America."

In the 1980s Max De Pree bought out the Hekman Furniture Co. of Grand Rapids and expanded into fine wood curio cabinets. In 1986 Herman Miller made the Fortune 500 list of America's largest companies. Two years later, under CEO Richard Ruch, the company bought Meridian, a Spring Lake manufacturer of office desks and file cabinets, headed by Michael Volkema. Other acquisitions included

70 De Pree, *Business as Unusual*, 71, 76-77.

71 Ibid., 118-35.

Max De Pree (*Joint Archives of Holland*)

Miltech, Integrated Metal Technology, and the German company General GmbH. Hugh De Pree explained his and his father's Christian management philosophy in *Business as Unusual* (1986). Max De Pree expanded on that philosophy in a series of best-selling books: *Leadership is an Art* (1987), *Leadership Jazz* (1992), *Leading Without Power* (1997), *Faith in Leadership* (2000), and *Called to Serve* (2001). In 1992 *Fortune* magazine inducted Max De Pree into the National Business Hall of Fame.[72]

The furniture industry, always cyclical in nature, suffered another downturn in the early 1990s, caused by a recession in commercial real estate. For the fiscal year 1992, Herman Miller reported its first loss in twenty-two years. J. Kermit Campbell, an industry outsider, replaced Ruch as CEO at that time, following Ruch's retirement. By 1994 profits dropped nearly 90 percent, Campbell was forced to restructure and close plants in California, Texas, and New Jersey, at a cost of $16 million. The result was unprecedented layoffs, including 180 white-collar positions. Board chair Max De Pree retired at this inauspicious time, and Campbell assumed his duties. Two months later, the board forced Campbell, the newly elected chair of Hope College's Board of Trustees, to resign and Volkema was named president and CEO. He replaced two-thirds of the top management team in a wholesale housecleaning. The next year, the company faced $12 million in damages and legal expenses to settle a four-year patent infringement suit filed by its larger competitor, privately held Haworth. The common stock of Herman Miller, the

72 Ibid., 138; *Holland Sentinel*, 22 Jan., 24 May 1979, *Grand Rapids Press Lakeshore Edition*, 5 Mar. 1992, 23 July 1996, 30 Sept. 1998; Herman Miller News Release; *Time*, 11 Sept. 1989, 56; *Fortune*, 14 Jan. 1991, 33.

largest publicly traded company in the area, fell on the red ink. On the brighter side, sales hit $1 billion, thanks to the acclaimed Aeron chair, introduced in 1994. The New York Museum of Modern Art added the ergonomic Aeron chair to its 20th Century Design Collection.[73]

In 1996 Volkema reveled in a sharp recovery in the industry and within his company. In the next thirteen quarters, Herman Miller had record sales and profits, which set the stage for the company's seventieth anniversary in 1998. Sales reached $1.7 billion that year. "God was in the business," declared retired chairman Hugh De Pree. The employees were also in the business; they owned 16 percent of outstanding shares in 1999.[74]

Volkema in 1999 moved his office and fifty employees to the company's Design Yard, affectionately called "the Farm" by employees, which had opened in 1987 at the Holland plant on West Forty-Eighth Street. He reassured jittery Zeeland employees and city leaders that the company's commitment to its headquarters remained strong. The boomlet was short-lived. The terrorist attack on the World Trade Center on September 11, 2001, set off a 40 percent decline in the furniture industry. Herman Miller's profits plunged by one-third, from $2.24 billion to $1.47 billion. Volkema closed several plants and cut the workforce by a third, nearly four thousand. Restructuring charges of $82 million sent the bottom line in fiscal 2002 to a minus $56 million. In 2003 Volkema after ten years at the helm "moved upstairs" as chairman of the board, and Brian Walker, president of the company's North American division, was named president and chief executive officer. The mid-priced Mirra chair, introduced in 2003, and the low-priced Cella chair offered in 2005, nicely complemented the high-end Aeron chair, and together these products returned the company to profitability. Profits more than quadrupled over the next three years, to $28.5 million in the third quarter of 2006. That year, the company opened a plant in China.[75]

In the Great Recession of 2008, office furniture sales again dropped by 30 percent. Herman Miller, faced with a 30 percent plunge in profits, laid off 1,100 employees (half its workforce), and the rest took cuts in pay and retirement benefits. The company turned to more

73 *Holland Sentinel*, 12 July 1995; *Grand Rapids Press Lakeshore Edition*, 12 July 1995; Herman Miller News Release.

74 *Holland Sentinel*, 28 July 1996, 30 Sept. 1998 (quote); *Grand Rapids Press Lakeshore Edition*, 8 Dec. 1998.

75 *Grand Rapids Press Lakeshore Edition*, 24 June 2004, 29 Sept., 6 Dec. 2006; *Holland Sentinel*, 21 Sept. 2006.

Herman Miller Corp. Design Yard dubbed "the Farm," 1987
(*courtesy Randall P. Vande Water*)

frugal designs and new healthcare products, such as infection-resistant wall panels and healthcare furniture. This required a $5.7 million plant expansion. The company also built a $5.3 million design center. Thanks to the new product lines and a reviving economy, sales and profits rebounded sharply in 2010, and were second only to Grand Rapids-based Steelcase. The 3,500 employees in West Michigan returned to full weeks in June 2010. This was little more than half the peak employment of 7,000 in West Michigan in 2008 (11,000 worldwide, now 5,600), but hiring was on the increase. Brian Walker in 2010 continued to run Herman Miller from its swank headquarters building at 10201 Adams Street in Zeeland Township, with plants in Holland, Grandville, and Spring Lake. Sales that year were $1.9 billion and rising sharply.[76]

Haworth Inc.

Gerrard "Gerry" or G. W. Haworth was born in 1911 in a sod house in Nebraska. Drought eventually drove the family off the land. The family moved to Benton Harbor around 1924, where his father made a meager living selling Watkins Products door-to-door there and in the sister city of St. Joseph. Gerry, the firstborn, earned a teaching degree at the Western Michigan Teachers College (now Western Michigan University) and a master's degree in school administration from the University of Michigan. Holland High School was pleased to hire such

[76] *Holland Sentinel*, 12 Nov. 2008, 19 Mar. 2009, 16 Dec. 2010; *Grand Rapids Press*, 16, 17 Dec. 2010, 22 Sept. 2011; *Business Review West Michigan* 15, no. 43 (2010): 64.

a qualified alumnus as the industrial arts teacher. He joined Hope Reformed Church. While Haworth taught from 1938 to 1948, he raised a family, built a home with his own hands, and started a woodworking business in his garage making retail furnishings, such as shoe and tie racks and display cases. He hoped the work would cover some of the college tuition for his four children. After selling his designs on special order for ten years, Haworth went to a local bank for financing in 1948 and was turned down. He then left teaching, mortgaged his home to the hilt, borrowed his parents' life savings of $10,000, and started Modern Products, which eventually became one of the three largest office furniture manufacturers in the world, along with Steelcase and Herman Miller.[77]

Haworth erected a shop at 339 East Sixteenth Street at Fairbanks Avenue just west of the Pilgrim Home Cemetery. With secondhand equipment and six employees, he started making RCA Victor television consoles and other products. His first big break came in 1958, when Grand Rapids furniture salesman Ray Murdock came to Haworth with a design for movable office partitions that the pair managed to sell to Walter P. Reuther, president of the United Auto Workers Union, for the new union headquarters in Detroit. The pair drove to see Reuther with several sample panels in the back of Murdock's station wagon. Reuther liked what he saw and placed an order for enough panels to fill the entire four-story building. Haworth recalled that the order "frightened" him because it was "bigger than anything I'd ever done before." Haworth continued: "I had to hire people right away—hired them just as fast as I could, and we worked day and night to get the job out." Haworth technician Lee Broekhouse recalls the next challenge: "Mr. Haworth and I went down there to install them. It was big, because we had never heard of movable office partitions before." Haworth speculated correctly that other companies might be interested in the innovative concept, so he shifted production from television consoles to moveable office wall partitions and checkout counters. This was a variation on the modular, or open-plan, office systems designed by George Nelson and Bob Propst in the 1940s (see above).[78]

Modern Products grew at a rate of 30 to 40 percent a year, and one day Gerry told Bill Vogelzang at his hardware store: "Bill, I'm so busy,

[77] G. W. Haworth interview by Anna Holt, 22 June 1999, typescript, JAH; Carron, *Grand Rapids Furniture*, 164-65, 185-88; www.fundinguniverse.com/company-histories/Haworth-Inc-Company-History.html.

[78] Haworth interview (quote, typescript, 6); Myron Kukla, "Haworth speaks at Meijer Lecture Series," *Grand Rapids Press*, 3 Nov. 2010.

I don't know which way is up," to which Bill replied, "I know just the man for you,"—Jerry Jonker of Holland Furnace. "He wants to get out of there. . . . He can't stand the heat anymore," said Bill in a classic pun. So Jerry Jonker joined Gerry Haworth in building the company in the early years.[79]

Modern Products had eighty-seven employees by 1959 when the company went national. To keep up with orders, Gerry Haworth dedicated a new plant at 545 East Thirty-Second Street in 1961, which had to be enlarged in six years to accommodate more than one hundred workers and a sales volume of $3 million. When Gerry took his aged father to see the original plant when it was still an empty shell, he asked his son: "Gerry, why do you want it so big?" to which Gerry replied: "Dad, I don't know how to control it. We have more customers that want our product. Unless we keep building, we can't satisfy them." When son Dick, who had started as an assistant sales manager in 1964, had fulfilled his army service in 1969, Gerry named him vice president for research and development, and assigned him the task of developing moveable office partitions covered in heavy fabric to reduce noise and provide privacy. The company sold the first padded partitions in 1971, and the two firms competed neck-in-neck. Sales went from an estimated $6 million in 1972 to $10 million in 1975. (As a private company, Haworth Inc. does not have to report sales or profits.)[80]

As Modern Products extended the reach of its wall partitions, the non-union company faced an unexpected problem. Carpenters affiliated with the American Federation of Labor damaged the partitions or they refused to install them altogether (such secondary boycotts were legal at that time). Haworth in desperation directed his employees to join the union, despite its inherent adversarial nature. As an inducement, he even paid the union dues. The decision was at odds with the prevailing anti-union views of workingmen in the Holland community, and it also grated with Haworth's practice of treating his employees and customers according to the Golden Rule. Haworth's decision to cozy up to the AFL Carpenters Union helped the company in the short run, but proved costly later.[81]

In 1973 the national union, frustrated by President Richard Nixon's wage and price controls to fend off hyperinflation, called a

79 *Grand Rapids Press*, 12 Oct. 1959; "Teacher at Heart: G. W. Haworth," *Focus 2009*, 15-16 (quote 16); William Vogelzang interview by author and David Boeve, 30 Sept. 2009 (quote), typescript, VRI.

80 *Holland Sentinel*, 28 Jan. 1967, Haworth interview (quote, typescript, 6); "G. W. Haworth," 9 Oct. 1986, 13 Dec. 1992.

81 Haworth interview.

G. W. "Jerry" Haworth (center with hat) and son Richard D. "Dick" (hatless) turn the ceremonial shovels for the new Haworth plant in the Southside Industrial Park in 1961. Mayor William A. Sikkel (*second from right*), a prime mover in the HEDCOR district, is proudly beaming. Three men with hats or caps to the left of G. W. are (*right to left*): Paul Winchestor, president of Hart & Cooley and a HEDCOR board member; William A. Sikkel (no relative of the mayor), a Haworth executive formerly at Holland Furnace and Big Dutchman; and Randall Dekker, president of First Michigan State Bank of Zeeland and another HEDCOR officer (photo Ted Jungblut Jr.) (*Archives, Holland Historical Trust*)

strike for higher wages. The job action put Modern Products workers on the picket lines for two weeks. Haworth recalled the crisis. "I told them very frankly that if I had to pay what the union was asking, that we would be out of business." The workers promptly voted by 76 percent to decertify their local.[82]

Gerry Haworth made some major decisions in 1975. He sold the wall partition division to Trendway Corp. (see below) in order to concentrate on pre-wired, moveable, floor-to-ceiling office panels, named Uni-Group, which Dick's shop had developed. These panels were made of metal and plastics, rather than wood, and they eliminated the need for a tangle of electrical cords running across the floor. Building inspectors applauded that innovation. The change in product lines required a change in the company name. After considerable discussion,

[82] Haworth interview (quote, typescript, 9); Stephen Kloosterman, "Haworth tells stories behind company story," *Holland Sentinel*, 3 Nov. 2010.

Jerry Haworth (*left*) with son Dick (*right*), keeping his eye on operations, 1980s (*Archives, Holland Historical Trust*)

Haworth Inc. was decided on, despite Dick's misgivings about how using the family name for the company might negatively impact his school-aged children. The next year Gerry named Dick president, because Gerry's wife was battling terminal cancer and required his undivided attention. He did, however, keep his hand in for another thirty years as chairman, until his death in 2006.

Under Dick Haworth, the company expanded its office product lines to include seating, desktop and computer tables, and storage systems (file cabinets). Employment grew from 156 in 1974 to 850 by 1980. The next year, Haworth opened a new plant in Allegan to manufacture seating and dedicated its new world headquarters and manufacturing plant on M-40 in Holland. The Allegan plant produced its one-millionth chair in less than ten years, by 1990. In 1986 Haworth opened plants in Germany and Switzerland, marking the first step in overseas production and marketing.[83]

To keep abreast of the industry leaders Herman Miller and Steelcase, Dick Haworth believed that Haworth must acquire key global companies. Building plants overseas was too costly and cumbersome. So Dick embarked on a global acquisitions tear, despite his father's misgivings about the risk involved. It was one of the few disagreements

83 *Holland Sentinel*, 23, 24 May 1979. Haworth closed the Allegan plant in 2009, and the Allegan County Sheriff's Department purchased the 22-acre site for a new corrections center, which opened in 2013 after a successful public referendum.

William "Bill" Calkins doing computer design work on the new CADvantage (computer-assisted design) system at Haworth, 1983 (*courtesy Randall P. Vande Water*)

between the two, Dick noted. In three years, 1990-93, Haworth bought eight office furniture companies in Europe, South America, and Asia. In 1993 sales increased by 20 percent over 1992, to $855 million. This required more help in the executive suite, so in 1994 Jerry Johanneson, the chief operating officer, was elevated to president. In 1997 he became chief executive officer, the first non-family member to be in top leadership.[84]

Just before Johanneson's promotion in 1994, CEO Dick Haworth faced another union threat when a group of disgruntled workers asked the United Auto Workers (UAW) to organize a union local at the company. That the non-union firm had furnished the wall partitions for their Detroit headquarters in 1959 had remained a sore point to union organizers. Some 2,450 of the 3,500 workers in Haworth's West Michigan plants were hourly workers, and many had signed union authorization cards. The father and son duo had always prided themselves on good employee relations, and the union move distressed them greatly. For Dick Haworth, it was a wake-up call to make employee relations his number one priority. He and G. W. met with the workers

84 Ibid., 13 Dec. 1992, 4 Jan. 1994, 25 Feb., 9 Oct. 1996, 6 July 1997, 3 Nov. 2010; *Forbes*, 17 Sept. 2007; "G. W. Haworth 1911-2006," memorial brochure.

and agreed to boost monthly retirement benefits and end any favoritism in job assignments, of which some workers had complained, but the pair rejected calls for bonuses.[85]

Fending off unions was the highest priority for the Haworths, and they breathed a sigh of relief when UAW officials announced that they had called off the drive. That close call shook up the management. "The biggest thing we learned is that our listening post and communications were not as good as we thought they were," said Johanneson. "I think there was a blind spot there." To this day, Haworth has seen no more unionizing efforts. Although Haworth did not institute a profit-sharing plan or bonuses, the company did try to elevate the status of employees by referring to them from then on as "members," and paying them one hour of overtime per week for sitting down and making suggestions to improve production systems and customer relations.[86]

During its time of rapid expansion in the 1980s, Haworth faced a second challenge, when industry giant Steelcase began manufacturing pre-wired panels very similar to those protected by Haworth's patent. Dick Haworth filed a civil lawsuit in 1985 that festered for twelve years. Steelcase won the first judgment, but Haworth prevailed on appeal in the US District Court, and Steelcase had to pay damages of $211.5 million; this was one of the largest patent infringement judgments in United States history. Haworth also filed a similar lawsuit against Herman Miller in 1992. "We have to protect what we invest in," Dick Haworth told *Forbes*, despite the ill will and high cost involved. The Steelcase suit cost Haworth $50 million, but the legal action "paid off handsomely," said Gerry Haworth, and so did the suits against Herman Miller and other competitors.[87]

In the 1990s Haworth introduced new products, especially adjustable-height tables. Then came movable raised floors that carried the open office equipment and created entire working environments. To gain market share, Haworth policy was to undersell any competitors. "If [Herman] Miller and Knoll are offering 65% off on a project, Haworth says 71%," reported *Forbes*. At the company's half-century celebration in 1998, "Haworth at 50" was nearing its apex of 10,000 employees worldwide, with 3,900 in Holland, Allegan, and Douglas, and sales

85 Haworth-Inc-Company-History.html.

86 *Grand Rapids Press Lakeshore Edition*, 1 Mar. 1997 (quote); *Holland Sentinel*, 6 July 1997, 23 Aug. 1998 (quote).

87 Haworth interview (quote, typescript, 10); Christopher Palmeri, "Smart Boy," *Forbes*, 11 May 1992, 146; Dick Haworth's presentation, Hope College's 2010 Meijer Lecture Series, 2 Nov. 2010.

totaling $1.54 billion. In 2000 sales peaked at $2.06 billion, which surpassed competitor Herman Miller's $1.34 billion in sales. Ten years later, after two downturns in the furniture market, Haworth's sales had climbed back to $1.21 billion and rising, but the workforce was down to 1,900 in West Michigan and 7,500 in ten countries worldwide.[88]

Sales pressure after 2000 caused some turbulence in Haworth's executive suites. Early in 2003, Robert Kruska, a long-time Dow Corning executive, succeeded Johanneson as CEO. But eighteen months later, in September 2004, Kruska abruptly resigned, and Dick Haworth had to resume those duties. He happily saw sales turn up. Haworth opened a new factory in India and began a $40 million redesign and expansion of its headquarters building. G. W. Haworth, who had continued to meet with customers and sales people and oversee special projects, took what was described as a "soft" retirement in April 2005. He died the next year, but not before the company promoted Franco Bianchi, chief operating officer for the North American plants, to CEO and president,[89]

The family-owned company in 2008 dedicated its new world headquarters, One Haworth Center, which fittingly marked the sixtieth anniversary. The roof was grass-covered, as part of a commitment to sustainable green technology. Haworth's Gulfstream jet that year was airborne for an incredible six hundred hours to bring in customers and keep the far-flung factories connected. In 2009 the company achieved its objective of zero landfill waste in all its United States facilities, down from 4.6 million pounds the year before. Dick Haworth in 2009 passed the torch to his son Matthew, Gerrard's forty-one-year-old grandson, who was named chairman of the board—the only third-generation family member in management.[90]

In the last decades, G. W. Haworth generously gave back to his community, including $1.1 million to the Holland Boys & Girls Club, $4 million for the Haworth Inn & Conference Center at Hope College, $5 million to Western Michigan University (his alma mater) for the Haworth School of Business, $1 million for the Midtown Campus of Jubilee Ministries, $300,000 in office furnishings for the Holland campus of Grand Valley State University, among other contributions.

88 Christie Brown, "You Say 65% Off, They Say 71%," *Forbes*, 20 May 1996, 164; *Holland Sentinel*, 10 Nov. 2008, 10 Feb. 2011; *Grand Rapids Press*, 9 Nov. 2011.

89 *Holland Sentinel*, 15 Sept. 2004, 25 Jan., 10, 22 Apr., 20 July 2005, 5 Nov. 2006, 7 Feb. 2008.

90 Ibid., 26 July 1998, 22 May 2005, 13 Feb., 23, 26 Apr., 19 Aug., 20 Dec. 2009; "G. W. Haworth 1911-2006"; *Grand Rapids Press Lakeshore Edition*, 31 May 2006, 13 Mar. 2007, 7 Feb., 10 Nov. 2008; *Business Review West Michigan* 15, no. 43 (2010): 10.

These gifts have impacted thousands of lives in West Michigan. A humble Nebraska farm boy and Holland High School shop teacher, Haworth has changed an industry and a city; it is a signal accomplishment.[91]

Worden Company

William I. Irwin started Worden in 1949 with thirty employees as the manufacturing division of Bolhuis Lumber & Manufacturing (chapter 12). The plant, which gradually shifted production from office and school desks to library furniture, still occupies its original site at 199 East Seventeenth Street at Lincoln Avenue. In the 1960s Worden became independent of Bolhuis Lumber. Irwin grew the business in 1983 by buying a small Grand Rapids furniture maker and moving the operations to an enlarged Holland plant. In 1985 William "Bill" Hendrick bought the business, and in 1989 he and newly-named Worden president Donald Wassink entered into a unique 50/50 venture with John Widdicomb Co. of Grand Rapids, one of the prestigious old-line firms, to manufacture office furniture. Worden's Holland factory then specialized in wood library furniture designed for computers rather than card catalogs. The next year, Worden transferred its Grand Rapids seating operations and twenty workers to Holland, which brought employment to 160. From 1990 to 2000 Wassink was Worden's president; he led the company in celebrating its fiftieth anniversary in 1999. The firm then employed two hundred, and its trucks delivered library furniture as far as the Gulf of Mexico and the East Coast.

That year, Worden Co. invested $1 million in new machinery and added fourteen workers. In 2001 Worden had $20 million in sales and was one of the few Holland furniture companies to see growth while others lagged. Bill Hendrick remains president and chief executive, and his son Javan and daughter Robin Hendrick Lane now manage the company, Javan as vice president of operations and Robin as vice president of sales and marketing. In 2010 the pair announced a strategy to diversify by spinning off a separate company, Sparkeology, to manufacture an innovative new product called "Flip," which is either a table, a stool, or storage, depending on whether it is flipped top-up or top-down. The offshoot shares space in the Worden facility. The workforce in 2011 was down to ninety employees.[92]

91 *Holland Sentinel*, 7 Mar. 1999, 11 Mar. 2008.

92 *Holland Sentinel*, 9 June 1989, 30 Jan. 1991, 4, 23 Feb. 1999, 6 Aug. 2000, 19 Aug. 2001, 22 June 2009, 6 June 2010; Holland Area Chamber of Commerce, *Business Magazine* (Fall 2011): 4.

ODL Inc.

Cy Mulder, a Chris-Craft employee, founded Art Craft Novelty Shop in 1945, making clothespins and other wood products from scraps left over at the boat company. The business evolved, and in 1950 Mulder began making glass inserts for front doors, called door lights. This called for a new company name, and in 1949 the company was renamed Zeeland Sash and Door Company until 1976, when it was again renamed ODL (Ottawa Door Lights) Inc. Besides door lights, the company added skylights, sidelights, and window grilles to its product line. In 1963 Larry Mulder joined the business as a salesman. The business grew, and in the 1970s, ODL began making windows for steel clad entrance doors and converted most of their production from wood to plastic.

In 1984 the company became a national firm through the purchase of a skylight company in California and distribution centers in Texas, Georgia, and Pennsylvania. ODL had 180 employees at its Zeeland facility by 1985 as it continued to grow, also adding a corporate center at 215 East Roosevelt Avenue in Zeeland.

In the late 1990s Dave Killoran became president, and Larry Mulder became chairman of the board. In 2000 the firm purchased its largest competitor, which doubled its workforce to 1,250. In 2011 Jeff Mulder, grandson of the founder, became president and CEO of the multinational firm, with facilities throughout North America as well as Mexico, England, and China.[93]

Fleetwood Group (formerly Fleetwood Furniture Company)

Norwood Hubbell founded Fleetwood Furniture Co. in 1955 in Grand Haven to manufacture school furniture and soon moved operations to Zeeland Township. Hubbell's purposes were two-fold, both idealistic, to tithe profits in support of Christian missionaries and to share ownership with the employees. In the fifty years from 1955 to 2005, the unique company contributed $4.7 million for mission endeavors and funded forty missionaries around the world. In 1975 then company president Frank Newcomb introduced an employee stock ownership plan, or ESOP, that made Fleetwood one of the first firms to take this risky step. In 2006, according to Steve Vander Veen, fewer than one in ten private-sector employees nationwide were covered

[93] *Holland Sentinel*, 26 Jan. 1985, 30 Jan. 1992, 25 June, 30 Jan. 2000; Holland Area Chamber of Commerce, *Business Magazine* (Fall 2011): 5.

by ESOPs. Fleetwood's 150 employees in 2006 owned 100 percent of the company, and total sales exceeded $20 million. Doug Rich, company president and CEO, said: "Employee ownership aligns perfectly with our Christ-centered business philosophy." During the busy summer months, the company hired one hundred teachers and college students as seasonal workers.[94]

Fleetwood Group, a furniture and electronics manufacturer, currently operates in a plant at 11832 James Street in Holland Township. Some 60 percent of sales consist of specialized school cabinetry for the storage of band and orchestra instruments, uniforms, and sheet music; the line is appropriately named Harmony. In 2012 Fleetwood Group celebrated a record-setting, five-year $3.5 million contract from a South Carolina school system. "We have a bell we ring when we get a sale over $25,000," said company official Jeff Pett. "We rang this one long and hard." Beating out the many competitors means dollars in the pockets of the 115 employee-owners.[95]

Trendway Corporation

Justin "Jud" Busscher and associates started Trendway Corporation in 1968 in a cornfield on Quincy Street near 136th Avenue in Holland Township that he bought from Irv Deur. Busscher and Deur were former Haworth employees. The firm initially offered a single product, floor-to-ceiling panels dubbed TrendWall. Deur joined the company and stayed on until his retirement a few years ago. When Busscher died, the company fell on hard times. George Heeringa, former president of Hart & Cooley, bought the near-bankrupt business in 1973, and recruited his sons Donald "Don" and James "Jim" to run it, Don as president and Jim as sales manager. The firm then had thirteen employees and annual sales of $1 million. In 1976 Haworth decided to end their floor-to-ceiling panel business and offered it to Trendway, which seized the opportunity. Trendway, with over one hundred employees, reached $5 million in sales in 1980 and was profitable. In 1981 the firm entered the rapidly growing open office furniture market with newly designed tables, chairs, and cubicles. They opened their first showroom at the Chicago Merchandise Mart in 1983. In the booming eighties, Trendway enlarged its plant five times and boosted the payroll to five hundred.

94 *Holland Sentinel,* 31 July 2005; Steve Vander Veen, "Area companies with employee ownership see success," 16 July 2006.

95 *Holland Sentinel,* 28 Aug. 2012.

From 24,000 square feet on ten acres in 1968, the company by 2005 had grown to 440,000 square feet on thirty-seven acres.[96]

Don Heeringa learned the importance of good employee relations early in his career while managing the night shift at Holland Hitch, a union shop where labor disputes were common (chapter 15). He implemented that team approach at Trendway, and it paid off handsomely. To give his company an edge on the competition, Heeringa in 1981 set about to shave several weeks off the twelve-week industry average of orders to delivery. With a keen mind for metrics, Heeringa's modus operandi was: "If you measure it, it will improve." The employees did give greater attention to detail and customers took notice. Rapid, timely, and accurate deliveries became a Trendway hallmark. The company grew steadily in the 1980s and 1990s. The company's profit-sharing plan, begun in 1980, gave employees a bonus check for eighty-four straight quarters until 2001, when the terrorist attack on the World Trade Center set off a 40 percent decline in the furniture industry. At the twenty-fifth anniversary in 1993, Heeringa boasted of its "Tribute to Teamwork" policy and honest dealings with employees, vendors, and customers. In 1995 Don bought the stock of his brother Jim and took sole ownership. Trendway's sales totaled $95 million in 1998 and were rising rapidly.[97]

When the office furniture industry struggled after 2000, Trendway beat the competition by focusing on small and medium-sized contracts, as it successfully downsized. Heeringa also took advantage of the talent available when the "majors" downsized, and he brought in a new team of seasoned managers. This allowed him to step back from the factory floor and focus on being chairman and CEO. In 2004 Trendway expanded its product line by acquiring CompuChair, an office-seating company, and it entered into a partnership with POSH, a private Hong Kong-based company like itself that was strong in designing filing and storage systems. The Asian company complemented Trendway's strengths in manufacturing and distribution. The Holland firm enjoyed record growth, thanks in part to a filing cabinet system designed with its Asian partner.[98]

During 2004 Trendway "closed" contracts with 88 percent of the customers it flew to Holland on the company airplane and hosted in

96 *Holland Sentinel*, 26 Jan. 1980, 25 Jan. 1994, 2 Aug. 1998, George Heeringa obit., ibid., 26 Mar. 1991; Don Heeringa, "Trendway's Corporation Profile, April 2005," compliments of Don Heeringa.

97 *Holland Sentinel*, 25 June 2010; Heeringa, "Trendway's Corporate Profile."

98 *Grand Rapids Press Lakeshore Edition*, 3 Feb. 2004, 8 Mar. 2005; Steve Vander Veen, "Area companies with employee ownership see success," *Holland Sentinel*, 16 July 2006.

its apartment adjacent to the Customer Center. The company in 2005 had a national sales force of 125, with showrooms in Washington, DC, Chicago, and Los Angeles, besides one in downtown Holland. In 2006 Trendway promised customers that it would cancel the entire bill if a shipment did not arrive when promised. "On time or on Trendway" was the motto. This bold guarantee again set the company apart from its peers. Not surprisingly, late shipments at Trendway dropped from eleven to four in 2007. Meeting the on-time guarantee became a "pride-thing."[99]

In 2007 Heeringa took an even riskier step: he made Trendway an ESOP company, giving his three hundred employees 25 percent of the company stock. "It's probably just a doorknob or something," production line coordinator Sue Bush quipped, "but it's special. It makes me feel good." That year Heeringa promoted vice president William Bundy to president and CEO, while retaining the office of board chairman. Sales totaled $100 million in 2007. Even a company with a sterling employee record could not survive the severe national depression of 2008, and in 2009, Trendway first asked forty of its 340 employees to take voluntary layoffs, and then it reluctantly cut twenty-five positions, 8 percent of the workforce. Heeringa never thought he would see the day he had to reduce his workforce so drastically. Sales in 2009 dropped by 25 percent, to an estimated $75 million. On the plus side, when the company makes a profit, so do the employees. The company resumed its growth trajectory in 2010.[100]

In the 1990s, office furniture companies in West Michigan employed twenty-five thousand people, and sales topped $6 billion in 1997. Steelcase, with seventy thousand different models of furniture, and 8,200 employees in ten plants in greater Grand Rapids in 1997, was then the largest firm of its kind in the world. Downturns in 2004 and the Great Recession of 2008-9 forced all the firms to downsize drastically. But the good times returned in this cyclical industry, and in 2010 West Michigan firms shipped almost half of all office furniture produced in the United States.[101]

Charter House Innovations (originally Charter House)

Holland Stitchcraft Inc. set off its former woodworking division to make booths for the restaurant industry under the name Charter

[99] *Holland Sentinel*, 5, 14 Nov. 2004, 26 Feb., 23 May (quote), 4 June 2006; Heeringa, "Trendway's Corporate Profile."

[100] *Holland Sentinel*, 18 Jan. 2007, 18 Apr. 2009, 25 June 2010; *Grand Rapids Press Lakeshore Edition*, 28 Sept. 2006, 24 Aug. 2007; *Grand Rapids Press*, 25 June 2010.

[101] Carron, *Grand Rapids Furniture; Grand Rapids Press Lakeshore Edition*, 23 Oct. 2005.

House in 1992. The new company operated in the same plant as the parent company at 4660 136th Avenue in the Northside Industrial Park (chapter 15). Charter House made restaurant furniture, while Stitchcraft concentrated on upholstery for the marine and restaurant industries. Total sales in 1987 were $1.5 million. Late that year, Stitchcraft sold its Charter House division to Detroit-based Stainless Inc., which allowed the latter company to sell complete restaurant interiors.

In the late 1990s, Charter House under manager Darrell Sult had ninety workers. In 2004 plant manager Charles "Chuck" Reid bought the struggling company that was bleeding staff and money, renamed it Charter House Innovations, and moved operations into leased space in the former Hart & Cooley plant at 500 East Eighth Street. Reid changed the focus to designing and manufacturing restaurant interiors for fast-food restaurants and quickly signed up McDonald's, Burger King, Wendy's, and Pizza Hut. The firm furnishes new eateries across the United States, Canada, the Caribbean, and as far away as Kuwait. Sales increased in the next five years by 450 percent, and they added 130 jobs.[102]

Reid hit on his next big thing, green design. Charter House developed environmentally friendly, recyclable interiors that his customers much desired. In fact, his company is the only one in the industry producing LEED-certified interiors. In 2006 Ried announced plans to build and operate a five-story hotel in downtown Holland on Seventh Street built largely with LEED products. The boutique City Flats Hotel opened in late 2007, the first LEED-certified hotel in the Midwest and one of only three worldwide at that time. The CityVU Bistro on the top floor is a popular dining place for business executives. Charter House also furnished Boatwerks Waterfront Restaurant adjacent to Kollen Park and in 2010 a refurbished McDonald's at 657 East Eighth Street at Coolidge Avenue. In 2009 the chamber of commerce gave Chuck Reid its Small Business Person of the Year award. The next year, the state chamber honored Reid as its Small Business Person of the Year.[103]

One of the newest furniture-related firms is the German-owned OMT-Veyhl USA Corp. at 11511 James Street in Holland Township, which opened in 2005 to manufacture height-adjustable bases for tables, desks, and workstations for the furniture industry. In 2011, in its sixth year of operation, the company projected $17 million in sales

102 *Holland Sentinel*, 30 Jan. 1988, 23 Oct. 1999, 13 Oct. 2009; Philip D. Miller interview by author, 7 July 2010.

103 *Holland Sentinel*, 25 Oct. 2006, 10 Jan. 2007, 27 Mar. 2009, 25 Feb., 7, 10, 27 Mar., 29 Apr., 20, 21 May 2010.

and a workforce of one hundred employees. This required a 50 percent expansion of the plant. Dan Shaw is vice president of operations for the Holland plant, which has earned a reputation for manufacturing "under the desktop" hardware for office furniture.[104]

Home furnishings

Mattresses and Bedding

Holland had a bedding industry beginning with the Holland Mattress & Supply Co. in the 1890s. In 1893 the company moved into larger quarters on River Avenue and Seventh Street to make mattresses and upholster furniture, but the shop was short-lived. Neither the city directories (1894-1908) nor the Sanborn fire maps (1883-1906) make mention of the company. Isaac Japinga, a laborer at West Michigan Furniture, in 1915 opened the Holland Mattress Company at 204 East Eighth Street, with Christian J. Lokker as a silent partner. This company was defunct by 1921.[105]

Buis Mattress

Gerbrand (Gerrit) Buis, a furniture upholsterer at Charles P. Limbert, in 1915 began the first successful mattress company, Holland Bedding and Upholstery Co. For fifteen years he labored in the garage behind his home at 139 East Fourteenth Street. Buis had mastered the craft as a teenage apprentice in the Netherlands. To raise capital in the boom times after World War One, he took in two partners, Louis J. Vanden Berg and George D. Albers, the superintendent and bookkeeper, respectively, at Thompson Manufacturing Co. The partnership, under the name Phoenix Upholstery Co., lasted several years at best, while Buis remained the sole proprietor of Holland Bedding & Upholstery. Both businesses were run out of his garage. In an advertisement in the *Holland City Directory* in 1921, Buis offered to recover auto tops, seat covers, cushions, and curtains; to do feather renovations; and to sell mattresses "made to order." By 1929 he added "overstuffed davenports and chairs" to mattresses and upholstery work for autos and boats. He prospered sufficiently to afford two automobiles in 1929, a Buick and Chevrolet, the latter likely the delivery vehicle.[106]

104 Ibid., 24 Sept. 2011; *Grand Rapids Press*, 24 Sept. 2011.

105 *Holland City Directories*, 1915-16, 1921.

106 *Holland Sentinel*, 18 July 1995; *Holland City Directories*, 1914-31. I am indebted to William G. Buis Jr. and Thomas E. Buis for information about the family history and businesses.

Brownstone Alley building on west side of Knickerbocker Theatre purchased by Gerbrand (Gerrit) Buis in 1930 (*Joint Archives of Holland*)

During the stock market boom of the 1920s, Buis acquired stock in General Motors and other major corporations, and fortuitously sold his holdings before the crash in October 1929. This gave him the cash to buy distressed East Eighth Street property in 1930, namely the "Brownstone Alley" building at 78-84 East, the Holland Theatre (now the Knickerbocker) at 86 East, and the Rokus Kanters building at 88 East. In 1931 Buis moved his upholstery shop downtown to the 88 East store.

In 1934 Gerbrand's son William "Bill" G. Buis began keeping the books. From his youth, Bill had worked at the shop, beginning at six or seven years of age looping buttons with string tied to one end. In a few years he helped make mattresses by threading the looped buttons with a long needle through the mattresses. By 1936 he was a full-fledged upholsterer. His father took him as a partner in 1938, and the firm became G. Buis & Son. The pair offered "guaranteed workmanship at reasonable prices," an advertisement designed to appeal to thrifty Hollanders. In 1942 G. Buis & Son moved a few doors west to 78 East Eighth Street, leaving the 88 East store vacant. This enticed Bill—an ambitious young man—in 1944 to strike out on his own in the vacant building by forming William G. Buis Mattress & Upholstery. His father Gerrit remained at 78 East for thirty years, until his death in 1958, and limited his trade to upholstery. The elder Buis also managed the rentals

Gerbrand Buis in his upholstery shop, 88 East Eighth Street, 1930s (*courtesy William "Bill" Buis*)

of his Eighth Street properties, including the Star Market & Grocery (78 East) until 1942, Dutch Maid Candy (80 East), J. Westenbroek & Co. metal shop (82 East), the Michigan State Liquor Control Commission (84 East), the Holland Theatre (86 East). Gerrit Buis prospered and returned to the Old Country several times, always taking aboard ship his black Cadillac, in order to drive around as the "rich uncle" who had realized the American dream.

In 1947 son Bill Buis moved his mattress shop to 174 Central Avenue on the corner of Seventh Street, where he remained until 1954, when he put up a building at 741 Chicago Drive east of Waverly Road between Holland and Zeeland. "We were way, way out of town." Bill recalled years later. But he was a master salesman, and locals drove out to the shop, drawn by his advertising slogan: "Buy Direct from Factory to You." In the old days, his shop turned out two to three mattresses a day, a far cry from the twenty to thirty he and several employees made daily in the 1990s. New sewing and stitching machines made the difference, as did faithful employees like Ray Lake, who stayed with him for decades. The mattress roll-edging machine in the early 1950s did in fifteen minutes what previously took a skilled stitcher half a day. Buis shipped products regionally but mostly sold to locals who became repeat customers due to the craftsmanship of the products. Buis was a farmer at heart and lived with his family on a quarter section of land

Gerbrand Buis at the wheel of his open top Ford. His wife Wilhelmina "Mina" is in the back seat with son Bill G. and daughter Wilhelmina "Mina." The couple on the passenger side front and back is unknown (*courtesy Bill Buis Jr.*)

on 168th Street between Ransom and New Holland Avenues, where Bill raised fox for the pelts, until mink supplanted fox fur in the fashion industry.[107]

When Bill Buis died in 1957, his wife Virginia took over the shop, with the help of sons William "Bill" G. Jr. and Thomas E., who worked full time after graduating from high school. Bill helped his mother run the shop, and Tom was the salesman and product designer. In 1968 the brothers bought out their mother, but she stayed in the store for another decade at least. At that time they changed the company name to Buis Mattress & Upholstery and opened a showroom at 230 River Avenue to display their wares in the city center. This was the former White's Market of Virginia's parents, Tom and Nellie White. In 1976 they added bedroom furniture and renamed the company Buis Mattress & Bedroom Furniture. In 1997 the company supplied all the mattresses for the Haworth Inn & Conference Center at Hope College.[108]

In 1995 the brothers parted ways. Bill Jr. took his son-in-law Marc Dozeman as a partner, and the two built a factory and showroom at

[107] *Holland City News*, 30 Mar. 1943; *Holland Sentinel*, 18 July 1995, *Holland City Directories*, 1934-58.

[108] *Holland Sentinel*, 26 Jan. 1980, 29 Mar. 1998; *Holland City Directories*, 1958-2004.

William "Bill" Buis operating his mattress roll-edging machine *(Grand Rapids Herald*, 25 Feb. 1951) (*courtesy Bill Buis Jr.*)

440 South Waverly Road for Buis Mattress Co. Dozeman has taken on increasing responsibilities to run the business, but Bill continues to spend every morning in the factory. Thomas E. Buis retired in 1995 and his son Thomas E. Jr., started his own business at 741 Chicago Drive under the name Spine Align Inc. He manufactures many types of mattresses, including "chirobedic" styles, and does a large business making non-standard sizes for the pleasure boat industry, notably Tiara Yachts. Spine Align is also a distributor of chiropractic supplies. Thus the Buis name in mattresses and upholstery is nearing the century mark in Holland across four generations.[109]

Spring Air Co.

In 1927 Charles Karr began a mattress factory at 12 West Fourth Street under the name Karr-Spring Air Co., to manufacture a unique bedspring designed by his father Francis Karr that was nationally marketed as the Spring-Air mattresses. Charles was a born promoter and launched an effective advertising campaign in leading magazines. Within one year, the workforce tripled to one hundred employees to meet the demand for the deluxe mattresses. The brand recognition

[109] *Holland Sentinel*, 29 Mar., 22 Nov. 1998.

was so high that the firm changed its name to the Karr Spring Air Co. Karr was a leader in the Master Bedding Makers of America, a trade association of forty manufacturers, and he led the group from his Holland factory. In the late 1930s, the employees voted to affiliate with the International Association of Machinists, and in 1946 they went on strike. Bastian Bouman headed the local strike bargaining committee. A. Bondy Gronberg led the sales force from 1937 to 1943, when he succeeded Karr as vice president. In 1946 Gronberg was promoted to president, taking the place of Charles J. McLean (a son of industrialist Charles M. McLean). The company built a $6,000 addition in 1949.[110]

Under Gronberg, Karr Spring Air thrived by making the latest innovation in bed innersprings, the "free-end" innerspring that varied the strength of the springs in the mattress. These mattresses could not be mass-produced, but had to be custom-made, vice president Bob Benzenberg explained. In 1979 the company could hardly keep up with the demand for the custom mattresses, even with a new plant in California purchased in 1978 to provide coast-to-coast distribution. In 1980 the Chicago-based Spring Air Co. bought the Holland firm and renamed it Karr Manufacturing. In 1986 Karr moved its operations to a new $1.35 million plant at 1455 Lincoln Avenue (then next door to Kandu Industries) that was twice the size of its Fourth Street plant, and pushed the workforce up to 125. But the heyday was over. The next year, Missouri-based Leggett & Platt Inc. bought Spring Air, and after another year, in 1988, it consolidated operations in Missouri, closed the Holland plant, and laid off its 120 employees. After more than sixty years, the Karr name disappeared from the local manufacturing scene.[111]

Holland Wire Products

In a real sense, Spring Air did not die. It continued at Holland Wire Products, a company that several Spring Air executives had formed in 1948 to manufacture innerspring mattresses in a factory on the southeast corner of Ninth Street and Maple Avenue. The founding partners were Henry Geerds of Geerds Electric and Company D fame, Howard Phillips, Herbert Thomas Jr., and Earl Ragains. Phillips and Ragains had been at Spring Air, as was the first hire, engineer and

110 *Ottawa County Times*, 28 Apr. 1893; *Holland City News*, 4, 18 Oct. 1928, 6 Nov. 1929, 30 Jan. 1930, 18 Apr. 1946, 2 June 1949; *Holland Sentinel*, 10 July 1941, 30 Mar. 1930, 18 July 1946.

111 *Holland Sentinel*, Jan. 1979 clipping (Karr Spring, Herrick Library vertical file, 15 May 1985, 25 Jan. 1986, 6 Oct. 1988.

designer Charles "Chuck" Wojohn, and James Seabright. Wojohn later invented and patented an automatic assembly machine to turn out innerspring mattresses. Holland Wire manufactured mattresses under the Holland Maid trademark for firms throughout the United States and in several foreign countries. They also sold to independent wholesalers who supplied motels, and to factory direct outlets such as Buis Mattress in Holland.[112]

By 1972 Holland Wire had more than fifty employees, who were unionized and went on strike sevaral times. Sometime in that decade, Geerds and his partners turned over day-to-day operations to Jack Feininger as vice president of operations. He was a friend of Geerds' son-in-law, William Beebe of Holland Hitch, who had assumed ownership of the Ninth Street plant. In the early 1980s Feininger relocated operations to 955 Brooks Avenue in the Southside Industrial Park (chapter 15). Over time, Holland Wire focused on commercial business, notably Serta, Spring Air, and in the late 1980s, Englander and Kingsdown. It also sold mattresses to the federal government and American Hospital Supply Company. In 1986 ten Hispanic employees, led by Hector Ruiz, filed a racial discrimination lawsuit against Holland Wire, claiming unsafe working conditions and an "unfair" wage cut. Jose Reyna, the Holland Human Relations Coordinator, offered to mediate, but a corporate spokesman refused. The company did respond to the complaints; they added safety devices to the machines and improved working conditions.[113]

In 1988 Geerds and his partners sold Holland Wire Products to the family-owned Hickory Springs Manufacturing Co. of North Carolina. Twenty-five years later, in 2012, after fifty-five years of operations in Holland, the parent company announced the closing of Holland Wire Products within six months, with the consolidation of all operations in its North Carolina facility. The decision costs the jobs of thirty-nine employees, although anyone willing to relocate was offered a job at Hickory Springs Manufacturing.[114]

Komforter Kotton Co.

Several soft goods factories developed in the city, notably the Komforter Kotton Co. The Van Duren family began Komforter Kotton

[112] *Holland Sentinel*, 26 Jan. 1980, 3, 7 Aug. 2012. I am indebted for information obtained in a phone interview with Charles Wojohn on 4 Aug. 2012.

[113] *Holland Sentinel*, 30 Jan. 1988.

[114] Ibid., 18 Oct. 1996, 3 Aug. 2012.

in 1916 to make a variety of cotton goods but mostly mattress pads. Business boomed, and the firm had to expand its facilities at Nineteenth Street and Columbia Avenue, despite the difficulty in getting building materials in wartime. In 1917 the Van Durens doubled the firm's capitalization to $20,000 in stock; president Arthur Van Duren owned two-thirds of the privately held shares, and his brother Alfred and his wife had the other one-third. Alfred served as secretary and manager. With the new capital, the brothers expanded the plant and bought a unique eighty-one-needle stitching machine in New York for $6,000 that promised to increase output by 300 percent. Komforter Kotton survived the Great Depression, and for twenty years, Arthur and Alfred Van Duren carried on the successful company.[115]

During the Second World War, the firm came under the wages and hours rules of the Federal Economic Recovery Act (FERA), but this gave it pricing power and sheltered it from market forces. In 1937 the brothers took the bold step of replacing their original building with a $20,000 fireproof factory and equipped it with the latest in stitching machinery for mattress pads. Four years later, local investors John and William Arendshorst bought the company from the Van Durens, with Alfred Van Duren continuing as manager. The Arendshorsts added fresh capital to upgrade the machinery and renamed the company Holland Cotton Products. Bernard Arendshorst took over management after he was mustered out of the service in 1946. In 1956 Holland Cotton erected a new $45,000 building at 462 Lincoln Avenue. Twelve years later, in 1968, the Louisville (Kentucky) Bedding Co. bought the Holland plant. It remained under local management for the next six years, until 1974, when the mother company consolidated operations in Louisville. The sixty-eight employees received their profit-sharing money, and the Lincoln Avenue building was sold.[116]

Conclusion

Furniture and its related industries flourished in the Holland/Zeeland area for several key reasons. First, employers could draw from a labor pool of conscientious workers who gave a full day's work for a full day's pay. The Dutch work ethic is legendary, and the Hispanics and Asian immigrants came with the same drive. Second, the cultural and social mores of the region produced a remarkable bevy of risk takers and

[115] *Holland Sentinel*, 19 Oct. 1916, 16 Nov. 1934; *Holland City News*, 1 Mar. 1917, 11 Nov. 1937.

[116] *Holland Sentinel*, 14 Nov. 1941, 17 May 1956, 26 Dec. 1968, 31 July 1974.

entrepreneurs. Dutchmen like to be their own boss. Third, beginning in the 1950s all the leading industrialists adopted cooperative labor practices in the wake of the De Prees, following the Scanlon Plan, ESOPS, or variants of these plans. Labor unions had trouble gaining traction in such an environment. Only a few companies had union workforces and experienced periodic strikes and work stoppages. These firms were the first to fail in economic downturns or to be sold to outside interests and eventually shuttered.

CHAPTER 15

Industrial Diversification: Automotive, Boats, Chemicals, Electricals

Holland's fine furniture companies have won acclaim in the United States and Canada, and its office furniture products enjoy global reach and status. But a manufacturing economy requires diversification, no matter how strong any single sector might be. Local manufacturers perceptively tapped new markets in automotive parts, boat building, chemicals, electric motors, and many other products. When the fine furniture industry moved south, the new industries took up the slack. The local companies first served a national market and then went global.

Automotive manufacturing

Early auto parts companies

Manufacturing automobiles was a logical progression in a city with foundries and machine tool works (chapter 12). That step seemed to be at hand late in 1913 when Charles A. Spenny of Chicago, president of the Spenny Motor Car Co. of Chicago and Dearborn, Michigan, announced the opening of a plant in Holland in January 1914 to build the $3,500 "Spenny 6." After setting back the start date several times, Spenny told the city fathers in July that unless local investors bought $25,000 in stock, the plant would remain in Chicago. They didn't, and Holland has never had an automobile assembly plant.[1]

Auto parts plants opened instead. One of the first was the newly formed Steelclad Auto Bow Co., which manufactured wooden front clips clad in reinforced steel. President Henry R. Schnaar of Chicago, an inventor of note, was persuaded to move the company to Holland in 1915, thanks to commitments by chamber of commerce members who bought $10,000 in company stock and joined Schnaar in the executive suite. Ex-alderman Dirk W. Jellema became vice president, treasurer, and manager, and the secretary was Henry Winter of the Peoples State Bank. With great difficulty obtaining machinery because of the war in Europe, the company finally opened its factory on East Eighth Street beyond Fairbanks Avenue along the Pere Marquette Railroad spur (now Lemon Fresh Laundry). By 1916 the company had 90 percent of its $50,000 capital stock in hand, and assets exceeded liabilities in 1918 by $20,000. It helped that Steelclad had ongoing contracts with Cadillac Motors and other car companies to supply the new front ends, or "bows," which were far stronger than all-wood bows.[2]

The firm built a new factory on the former site of the Holland Manufacturing Co., hired fifteen workmen, and shipped in thousands of dollars of sheet steel and the heavy machinery to bend the steel with steam or electricity. One large machine cost $1,800. The workforce quickly increased to forty, and the factory produced six hundred bows daily, with the expectation to quadruple that rate. One order from Canada for fifty thousand sets of bows had to be turned down for lack of capacity. The favorable business climate of the twenties disappeared after the stock market crash of 1929, and Steel-Clad Auto Bow closed its doors. By 1931 Peter VerPlanke's Royal Casket Co. of Zeeland was making caskets there for the Holland market. Zeeland's Royal Casket Co. in the early years faced Colonial Manufacturing (Colonial Clock) Co. across Washington Avenue, which locals dubbed the "intersection of time and eternity."[3]

1 *Holland City News*, 2 Oct., 20 Nov. 1913.

2 Ibid., 16 Sept. 1915, 17 Feb., 8 June, 6 Aug., 21 Dec. 1916; Steelclad Auto Bow Company, financial statement, 24 Aug. 1918 (T-91-1508, box 1), Holland Museum Archives (HMA).

3 *Holland Sentinel*, 6 Feb. 1931; quote per Phil Miller. In 1984 president Joel VerPlanke decided to phase out manufacturing and focus on sales and distribution. He sold Royal Casket to Batesville Casket of Indiana (*Holland Sentinel*, 7 Mar. 1984).

Wolverine Motor Works

Gasoline engines for boats and automobiles were in increasing demand after 1900, so entrepreneurs began manufacturing them. Wolverine Motor Works was Holland's first marine engine builder. In 1901 this Grand Rapids firm, which had come to dominate the marine and auto gas engine industry, decided to relocate to Holland's lake front in the former Anderson shipyard at the foot of Eighth Street just west of Austin Harrington's coal yard. Wolverine enjoyed much success under master craftsman George E. Clark, but after six years, in 1907, it relocated to Bridgeport, Connecticut, to tap the large East Coast market. With Wolverine's departure, a competitor, Holland Launch & Engine Co., moved from its Fifth Street location to the Wolverine building and manufactured small gas-powered launches until closing in 1911.[4]

Holland Automobile and Specialty Company

In 1913 Reinhard A. Vos opened the Holland Automobile and Specialty Co. for die work and gear cutting to repair gasoline motors for cars and boats. The company invested $20,000 in tools and machines and leased the former Holland Umbrella and Specialty Co. building on the southeast corner of River Avenue and Sixteenth Streets.[5]

Brownwall Engine & Pulley

In 1914 the Holland Businessmen's Association persuaded Frank Wall of the Brownwall Engine & Pulley Co. of Lansing to relocate to Holland. A $5,000 grant from the city's bonus committee helped, as did the purchase of $5,000 in stock by individual Holland businessmen. Brownwall was a two-year-old firm that made stationary gasoline and kerosene engines of all kinds and also a patented pulley system. The engines powered grindstones, washing machines, wringers, cream separators, and the like. The company built a factory immediately west of the Holland Canning Co. stretching from Fourth to Fifth Streets, and soon hundreds of homes and factories in Ottawa and Allegan Counties were "Brownwallized" with its engines. The Holland plant shipped hundreds of its large engines to factories, including those in Canada and England to power machines supplying war materials during the First World War.[6]

4 *Holland City News*, 12 June 1903; Geoffrey Reynolds, "Shipyard builds success in wooden vessels," *Holland Sentinel*, 4 Dec. 2005.

5 *Holland City News*, 28 Mar. 1912, 20 Mar. 1913.

6 Ibid., 2 Apr., 21 May 1914; *Holland Sentinel*, 15 Oct., 20 Nov. 1915.

Brownwall Engine & Pulley Co. teamster on a sled on Eighth Street delivering kerosene engines on a winter day (*Donald van Reken Collection, Joint Archives of Holland*)

Brownwall changed hands by 1920, and John Van Appledorn's Holland Engine Co. was manufacturing single and twin-cylinder gasoline engines in the former Brownwall plant. Local farmers especially preferred the light engines, and they also appreciated that parts were readily available at Ford dealers. The company at the beginning had to build its own foundry across Fourth Street to make castings, since few were available locally. By 1923 new manufacturing processes lessened the need for the foundry, and Van Appledorn sold the struggling Holland Engine Co. and its foundry to F. B. Parrish of Chicago, an experienced foundryman, who came to Holland to run the plant with some twenty-five workmen.[7]

In 1925 Holland Engine reinvented itself under the lead of August Landwehr of Holland Furnace, who arranged for the company to sell out to the Burke Furnace Co. of Chicago, which had built a solid reputation over three decades for its Burke Stokers. Landwehr became president of the revamped Burke Engineering Co. of Holland, which essentially made it a branch of Holland Furnace; Walter T. Pitter of Burke's Chicago office became treasurer and general manager and Emil W. Ritter president. Van Appledorn remained involved as secretary and John P. Kolla, also of Holland Furnace, as vice president. Burke Engineering supplied Holland Furnace and other furnace manufacturers with the highly regarded Burke Stokers. After 1927 the Burke name disappeared, and Holland Furnace craftsmen made the patented stokers.[8]

7 *Holland City News*, 16 Nov. 1922, 22 Feb. 1923.

8 Ibid., 15 Jan. 1925, 15 Apr. 1926; Sanborn [Fire] Insurance Map, Holland, Michigan, May 1925, 8 (microfilm copies at Joint Archives of Holland [JAH]); *Holland City Directories*, 1915-16, 1927.

Company brochure showing Brownwall engine (*courtesy Larry B. Massie*)

SAF-HOLLND S. A. (Holland Hitch)

In 1910 three Dutch immigrants in Corsica, South Dakota–Henry Ketel, Albert Hulsebos, and Gerrit Den Besten–developed a hitch for horse-drawn farm plows that would disengage when the plow struck a solid object, such as a rock or stump, and thus prevent injuries to man and beast, let alone to the plow itself.[9] The partners formed the Safety Release Clevis Co. to manufacture the popular hitches. The company thrived at first, but as farmers increasingly switched from horses to tractors, the partners realized that they needed to be nearer to the manufacturing hub for farm tractors and motor trucks, so they relocated to Michigan in 1920 and the next year adopted the company name Holland Hitch. Their initial location was the old Seif Brewery at 149-57 West Tenth Street at Maple Avenue. Tractors were taking over heavy farm work, and farmers needed all kinds of hitches, pulleys, and clevises to connect tractors and their power takeoffs with other machinery. By 1927 the company was debt free and paid a dividend of 14 percent. Den Besten was the key cog in the company; he invented and patented many of the hitches. Holland Hitch received its fifth patent in the early 1930s.[10]

9 The section relies on Massie, *Haven, Harbor, and Heritage*, 168; "The History of Holland Hitch, Part I (1910-1950) and Part II (1950-Present)," a brief company history.

10 *Holland City News*, 5 Dec. 1927.

Holland Hitch safety release hitch, 1920s
(*courtesy SAF-Holland S. A.*)

As the trucking industry developed, the company gradually shifted production from agricultural equipment to heavy duty transport: fifth wheels, kingpins, pintle hooks, and coupling gear—all critical technology to prevent the all-too-frequent uncoupling of tractor-trailers. Ketel invented a pintle hook for heavy-duty equipment. Holland Hitch went bankrupt during the Great Depression in 1935, but Ketel teamed up with Henry A. Geerds, a leading player in the local business community, to buy the firm's assets and nurse it back to health. Ketel ran the company, and Geerds raised investment capital by recruiting other local investors to join the board of directors, notably ex-mayor Henry Geerlings, John Y. Huizenga, Gerrit Vugteveen, and Gerrit Visser. By the end of 1935 the company had grown from three to ten employees, and orders from farm implement dealers were increasing. Ketel and Geerds saved the company, which had third-generation executives until 2011.[11]

As the Franklin Roosevelt administration boosted defense spending with war clouds gathering in Europe, Holland Hitch expected a flood of contracts from General Motors for pintle hooks to couple army trucks and field artillery. But no contracts were forthcoming until Geerds, a colonel in the Michigan National Guard, won GM's favor after he brought the Holland guard unit to Flint in 1937 on the governor's orders to keep the peace in the UAW Sit-Down strike. Holland Hitch won its first army contract in 1940 for 1,600 hooks. The firm at the time employed eighty-six and had sales of $1 million. So vital were these devices that the government in 1943 allocated "vital building materials"

11 *Holland Sentinel*, 14 Feb. 1993.

Pintle hook coupling, 1939 (*courtesy SAF-Holland S. A.*)

to the company for a new $40,000 plant at Eighteenth Street and Ottawa Avenue. Personnel manager William Vande Water succeeded in the difficult task of hiring enough workers to meet production deadlines. By war's end the firm had shipped one million hooks to the military.[12] In 1946 Geerds took over as director and restructured the management team.[13]

The postwar years were rocky on the labor front, because workers everywhere tried to catch up after Congress lifted wartime wage controls. To increase their clout, 105 Holland Hitch workers voted to affiliate as Local 284 of the United Auto Workers-CIO International Union. But company officials would not recognize the UAW, claiming that the contract with the plant Local took precedence. The company faced two strikes in 1946: one in May that lasted only one day and one in October that continued for 105 days. This was one of several strikes in Holland at that time. Col. Geerds, a decorated veteran turned industrialist, refused to meet with the strikers for more than two months, right through the Christmas holiday. His persistence wore down the strikers, who finally gave in. When the Korean War broke out in 1950, Holland industries again shifted from civilian to military production. Holland Hitch in 1951 won two contracts worth $14,500 for hooks and pintles. It was the first of several large military contracts.[14]

Holland Hitch became the world's leading manufacturer of fifth wheels for tractor-trailers, notably the world's first sliding fifth wheel, and the Holland-Apgar wheel, which was designed to reduce rollover and jackknife accidents. William Beebe, Geerds' son-in-law, who started as a production engineer, became president in 1976, having risen

12 *Holland City News*, "50 Years Ago 1943" 28 Mar. 1993.

13 *Holland Sentinel*, 25 Apr. 1945, 19 May 1948; Randall P. Vande Water, "Henry Geerds," WHTC radio talk, Oct. 2003.

14 *Holland City News*, 18 Apr., 29 May, 13 June, 5 Oct., 2 Dec. 1946, 18 Jan. 1951.

Machinists making Pintle hooks, 1940s
(*courtesy SAF-Holland S. A.*)

through the ranks after returning from World War Two with a "heroic conduct" medal. He was tested in 1978 when the 350-member UAW Local 284 under president Jim Holtgeerts again threw up picket lines at the two local plants. To diversify its operations and serve markets from coast to coast, Beebe led the family company into global markets. In 1983, when he retired as president and became chairman of the board, Holland Hitch had twenty-two manufacturing plants and distribution companies worldwide, including South Carolina, New Jersey, California, Texas, Arkansas, Canada, Australia, Japan, and western Europe. Beebe's son-in-law, Richard Muzzy Jr., succeeded him as president and kept control in family hands.[15]

The year 1985 was a banner year for Holland Hitch and a fitting way to celebrate its seventy-fifth anniversary. Muzzy moved the corporate headquarters from Eighteenth Street to the former Thermotron Corp. plant at 468 Cleveland Avenue (later changed to 467 Ottawa Avenue) at Twentieth Street. The building, originally the Westside Christian School, first had a $350,000 renovation and expansion. The next year the company bought the former Hekman Rusk Bakery to the north on Ottawa Avenue at Eighteenth Street to house its research and development departments. Also in 1986 the company invested $2.5 million to triple its forwarding plant at 1122 Industrial Drive in the Southside Industrial Park, to take the pressure off the Eighteenth Street plant. Holland Hitch that year had 650

[15] *Holland Sentinel*, 17 May 1950, 12, 16 June, 24 July 1978.

employees at its Holland facilities, and it was rated the number one manufacturer of truck fifth wheels and coupling devices in the world. In 1990 the company expanded and renovated its oldest plant on the southwest corner of Eighteenth Street and Ottawa Avenue. As long as the heavy-duty trucking industry continued to expand, Holland Hitch went along for the ride.[16]

By 1993 the company had four divisions—Holland Hitch, Holland Hitch Canada, Holland Hitch International, and the Binkley Company. The latter was a 1991 acquisition of a Missouri manufacturer of trailer supports (known as "landing gear" in the trucking industry), among other products. Holland Hitch in 1993 employed 1,200 worldwide, 250 in Holland. In 1997 Muzzy, still on a "global odyssey," acquired the Delphos Axle Division of the bankrupt Fruehauf Trailer Corp., deemed the "best in the industry," and added this to its product line. In 1999 Holland Hitch acquired Muskegon-based Neway Anchorlok International, adding air suspensions, brake chambers, and air control valves to the product offerings. Also in 1999 the Holland Group, a formerly passive holding company, became an active operating company as the parent to the four divisions, plus Holland Neway. Sam Martin, son-in-law of Geerds' son-in-law, Tom Thomas, joined the company in 1974 as a metallurgical engineer and rose though the ranks of management to become president in 2004.[17]

The company reached its zenith in 2000 with three thousand employees in twenty-two facilities. Then truck and trailer production plummeted, putting tremendous financial pressure on the expanded Holland Group. In response, the company closed three facilities in the United States, cut its workforce by a third, and consolidated the three United States divisions into one unit, named Holland USA, with headquarters in Muskegon. Holland Group, the parent company, maintained its headquarters in Holland. Slowly the economy and demand for heavy trucks improved, and by 2004 the company was again financially sound.[18]

In 2006 the Holland Group and all its subsidiaries were sold to Pamplona Capital of the United Kingdom and merged with another of its holdings, SAF, to form SAF-Holland S. A., based in Luxembourg.

16 Ibid., 11 Dec. 1984, Jan. 1985 clipping, 14 Dec. 1985, 1 Jan. 1986, 30 Jan. 1988, 14 Dec. 1993, 11 Dec. 1994, 17 Jan. 1990; William Beebe obit., ibid., 25 July 2000.

17 Ibid., 20 Feb. 1997, 9 Sept. 1998; *Grand Rapids Press Lakeshore Edition*, 23 Feb. 1997. I am indebted to former executives Sam Martin and Richard Muzzy for information about the company in recent decades.

18 *Holland City News*, 22 Dec. 2001.

Sam Martin continued as president and chief operating officer of US-based operations until retiring in 2011. The global recession of 2008 caused another significant decline in truck sales, and the company, faced with excess manufacturing capacity in West Michigan, closed the assembly plant on Industrial Avenue. Michigan-based manufacturing has continued at the Eighteenth Street and Muskegon facilities. SAF-Holland S. A., under president Jack Gisinger, has continued to maintain its world leadership position in the manufacture of heavy-duty components and systems for trucks, trailers, motor homes, and buses.[19]

Szekely Aircraft & Engine Co.

An unlikely gasoline-engine-related industry in Holland was aircraft manufacturing. Inventors of flying machines competed with automobiles after the Wright Brothers, Wilbur and Orville, proved in 1903 that propeller-driven craft powered by a small gasoline engines could fly. Only six years after the Wright Brothers' feat, a sixty-one-year-old Holland resident on Central Avenue, John Buchanan, an aeronautical buff for many years, built a model of an airship or "aeroplane" that the *Holland City News* featured in a news story. The full-scale version was to be a craft with rigid aluminum wings thirty-five feet in length, and a seven cylinder, fifty-horsepower gas engine with a unique reversible propeller. Enthusiastic businessmen talked of forming a company to "manufacture the ship on a large scale," believing the "Buchanan machine will be foremost of all." Buchanan displayed his model at the Detroit Aeroplane Club to enthusiastic acclaim, where "competent engineers" called his plane the "greatest airship of the age." Manufacturing companies in New York and St. Louis were said to be eager for the contract, and Buchanan and local investors formed the Flying Dutchman Aeroplane Co. of Holland to do the work. But aircraft designs were too fluid to begin production. In the next five years, Buchanan and his brother F. L. Buchanan of Valparaiso, Indiana, completely redesigned his model with dual propellers, a one hundred-horsepower engine, and a cabin underneath to carry forty passengers. Despite the excellent design work, the Buchanan brothers never built a full-scale model.[20]

19 Ibid., Dec. 2006 clipping (Herrick Library vertical file), 3 Apr., 13 Nov. 2008, 24 Jan. 2010.

20 *Holland City News*, 26 Aug. 1909, 24 Mar., 21 Sept. 1910, 9 Sept. 1915; Randall P. Vande Water, "'Flying Dutchman' Never Left Ground," in *Holland: Happenings, Heroes & Hot Shots*, 3:84-87.

The dream of a local aircraft industry became reality a dozen years later in the hands of another engineer with deeper pockets and a bevy of university-educated engineers. This was in 1926, when Landwehr and the chamber of commerce induced Otto E. Szekely (zay kī) of Moline, Illinois to relocate his mechanical and automotive engineering company to Michigan, to be in closer proximity to its Ford and General Motors accounts. The city only had to pay moving costs to woo the company. Szekely, a native of Budapest, Hungary, brought twenty of his top engineers to Holland and hired as many new ones. The firm, with an expected payroll of $2,000 a week, set up offices in the former Aniline Dye Works on the north shore of Black Lake (near the future Aniline Street), and built a new factory behind it. The firm made a variety of products, including air compressors, dynamometers, and electric dynamos. By 1928 business was booming, and to finance expansion plans, Szekely Aircraft & Engine Co. made its first stock offering at $45 per share. Enthusiastic local investors snapped up the beautifully engraved shares, which featured a vignette of an American eagle.[21]

Szekely decided to focus exclusively on his first love, racing aircraft and their engines. Placing Landwehr in charge of the northside industrial division, Szekely in 1928 opened an aircraft and motor division in a new factory at 338 West Twelfth Street between Harrison and Cleveland Avenues. For a trade name for his aircraft, Szekely wisely resurrected Buchanan's apt *Flying Dutchman*. To provide engine piston rings, Szekely purchased an Ohio company with a sterling product and brought the ring work to Holland. In the fall of 1928, Szekely exhibited a five-cylinder, two-seater for racing enthusiasts at the Los Angeles international air show, where the *Flying Dutchman* was "enthusiastically received" among 1,200 other planes. Three test pilots, including the one who flew Charles Lindbergh's *Spirit of St. Louis*, put the *Flying Dutchman* through its paces and praised it. Weeks later Szekely displayed two of his craft at the Chicago Coliseum air exhibition. Holland was gaining a reputation as an airplane city.[22]

The successful air shows prompted Szekely to focus exclusively on the *Flying Dutchman* airplanes. In December 1928, before embarking on a month-long trip to Europe and his homeland, he sold the Aniline operations to a Muskegon Heights firm, which relocated the work to its

21 Geoffrey Reynolds, "Plane Business," *Holland Sentinel*, 4 Jan. 2004; *Holland City News*, 4 Nov. 1926.

22 Reynolds, "Airplane maker's business fell to Great Depression," *Holland Sentinel*, 1 Feb. 2004; *Holland City News*, 22 Feb., 4 Oct., 29 Nov., 6 Dec. 1928.

Szekely famed *Flying Dutchman* airplane at Los Angeles air show, 1928 (*Archives, Holland Historical Trust*)

main plant. At the same time, the Hungarian announced a $1 million expansion of the aircraft factory, a production schedule of twenty-four planes and forty-two motors a week, and a nationwide sales force to market the craft. In actuality, the plant produced only a few Flying Dutchmen planes, although it continued to manufacture motors for another three years.[23]

In June 1929 Szekely arranged a lavish dedication ceremony for the city's first real airport that he had opened at Riley Street and 136th Avenue (chapter 10). Several thousand spectators came to watch renowned pilots race, compete in a dead-stick contest, and do flyovers in a Ford Tri-Motor powered by one of Szekely's three-cylinder Roamer (SR3) engines. The airport had four dirt runways, two of 2,200 feet and two of 1,500 feet. The sandy loam soil was drained by 4,400 feet of tile. All in all, it was splendid day, and the airfield was very adequate for its time, but it closed within three years.[24]

In 1931 Szekely Aircraft & Engine Co. expanded its plant yet again and doubled the workforce. That September the firm shipped four engine models to Washington for government testing, but only one, the SR3, passed the test before money ran out in Holland. The Great Depression was taking its toll. To maintain appearances, Szekely

23 Reynolds, "Airplane"; *Holland City News*, 20, 27 Sept. 1928, 14, 21 Feb. 1929.

24 Randall P. Vande Water, "Show at 'first real airport' draws thousands," *Holland Sentinel*, 17 June 2007.

Szekely personnel proudly show off a Ford Tri-Motor at Szekely Field. Otto Szekely (with open coat jacket) is likely standing in the center, ca. 1932 (*Archives, Holland Historical Trust*)

had a new brick residence built for his family on upscale State Street. In March 1932 the company declared bankruptcy, and the Szekely family left town abruptly for New York. Employees and creditors went unpaid, and stockholders were stuck with worthless certificates. Holland's only aircraft manufacturer and airport closed. The Great Depression ended Holland's day as an aviation center.[25]

In 1936 Michigan Bumper of Grand Rapids purchased part of Szekely's Twelfth Street plant to manufacture steam engines for trucks, busses, trains, and planes. The next year the Crampton Manufacturing Co. next door took over the vacant building for needed expansion and bought the remaining physical assets. Otto Szekely's last bit of fame came in the 1938 Hollywood film, "Men With Wings," in which aviators praised a plane with a Szekely engine.[26]

Holland Steel, Holland Chimney, and Holland Furnace Cleaning were other companies recruited or nurtured by the chamber of commerce in the 1920s and financed largely by local capital, Burke Furnace being an exception. Since local businessmen risked their own money only after careful investigation, these factories had a higher likelihood of

25 Reynolds, "Airplane"; *Holland City News*, 18 Mar. 1937; Fritz Kliphuis, "Szekely Aircraft & Engine Company," unpublished item; Lou Hallacy interview by author and Dave Boeve, 11 Nov. 2009, typescript, JAH.

26 Reynolds, "Airplane."

success than if outside interests came knocking, with hands out for bonus funds and suitcases crammed full of stock certificates for sale. Such firms faced a greater risk of failure, leaving worthless stock in their wake. Szekely Aircraft was exhibit one of the latter case.

Donnelly Corporation

Donnelly Corporation evolved out of Donnelly-Kelley Glass, which began as a branch of the Kinsella Glass Co. of Chicago, when employee Bernard P. Donnelly, then age twenty-four and newly married, was sent in 1905 to Holland to manufacture ornately engraved and beveled mirrors for the home-furniture industry centered in West Michigan. Donnelly's father managed the Armour & Cudahy Packing Co. of Chicago at the stockyards. Young Donnelly jumped at the chance to move his family across Lake Michigan and take charge of a company without the union problems so prevalent in Chicago.[27]

The Irish Catholic family joined the new St. Francis de Sales Catholic Church, and Bernard became an ardent lay leader. Kinsella Glass built their Holland factory on the northwest corner of River Avenue and Third Street, which remains the company headquarters a century later. In 1910 the parent company ran into financial difficulties and sold the Holland operations to Donnelly and partner John Kelley, the bookkeeper, for $64,000. In 1912 Donnelly-Kelley Glass had from forty to fifty craftsmen grinding and polishing beveled mirrors for china cabinets, buffets, oak sideboards, dressers, and walls. The mirrors were high quality works of art, engraved with woodland scenes or animals, notable Pegasus, the flying horse of Greek legend. Donnelly bought Kelley's interest in 1924, putting the company firmly in the hands of the Donnelly family until the present day. Donnelly-Kelley Glass produced these unique mirrors until the late 1950s, supplying all the local furniture companies—Bay View, Limbert, Ottawa, West Michigan, Colonial, and Star (forerunner of Herman Miller, see chapter 14).[28]

As the furniture industry in West Michigan went into decline in the 1920s and 1930s, so did the market for decorative mirrors. Already

[27] Margaret L. Karczewski, comp., *Our Heritage* (the Fenlon, Donnelly, and O'Keefe families in America) (privately printed, 1999), 212-13 (courtesy John F. Donnelly Jr.); Mike Lozon, *Reflections in the Mirror, 1905-2002: Magna Donnelly Corporation's Legacy of Product Innovation & Employee Participation* (Holland, MI: Magna Donnelly Corporation, 2002), 5 (quote).

[28] *Holland: The Gateway of Western Michigan*; *Holland City News*, 7 Dec. 1905, 15 Sept. 1910, 2 July 1915, 3 Feb. 1916; *Holland Sentinel*, 22 Nov. 1992; conversation with John Fenlon Donnelly Jr., 20 Aug. 2010; Maryam Komejan interview by Anna Holt, 1999, typescript, JAH; Donnelly interview.

in 1916 Donnelly sought to diversify by connecting to the young automobile industry, and he later manufactured rearview mirrors and windshields and side windows for the marine industry. This strategic decision allowed the company to grow with the automotive industry and the local Chris-Craft boat works (see below).

In 1921 Bernard P. Donnelly enlisted J. Frank Duffy, an engineer from Chicago, to head a subsidiary company, Duffy Manufacturing, to supply glass side windows and beveled rear windows for open touring cars. Donnelly was president, and Duffy managed the factory floor, which shared space in the River Avenue plant. The beveled glass was initially set in a wooden frame that was sewn onto the back of the car, but Donnelly developed a patented rubber frame for that window. This led to designing a wide variety of rubber car parts, which replaced the rear window business when touring cars became obsolete. Donnelly-Kelley also found a niche supplying replacement windows and windshields for sedans. The company barely survived the Great Depression on the strength of its high-quality, silver-coated mirrors for furniture and automobiles. Sales declined from $187,000 in 1929 to a depression low of $81,000 in 1932, and the workforce was cut from fifty to fifteen employees averaging only three-day work weeks.[29]

Bernard Donnelly died of a heart attack in 1932 at age fifty-four, while talking with Charles Landwehr in the office of Holland Furnace Company (now Black River Charter School), where Donnelly was a director. The sudden death shocked the company to the core and affected the entire business community of Holland. He was truly a leading citizen, serving as a director in the Holland City State Bank and De Pree Chemical; a stockholder in the Warm Friend Tavern, Holland Aniline Dye Co., and Grandview Poultry Farms Hatchery; president of the Rotary Club; and trustee of St. Francis de Sales Church.[30]

Fortunately for everyone, the family handled the transition is a superb way. Bernard's widow Mary Catherine (Fenlon) Donnelly and her five children inherited the company under a state trust. Mary Catherine and son John Fenlon took over the company, Mary as president and John, only twenty-one years old, as treasurer and day-to-day manager. In 1936 the family incorporated the business and dissolved the trust, with each family member eventually receiving stock and a seat on the board, which rights passed to their descendents. The company operated

29 Lozon, "Reflections in the Mirror," 8; *Holland Sentinel*, 23 July, 10 Aug. 1953.

30 Lozon, "Reflections in the Mirror," 8; John F. Donnelly interview by Abby Jewett, 21 June 1982, JAH; *Holland City Directories*, 1921, 1924, 1962.

Howard Diepenhorst etches a decorative mirror for the home-furniture industry, 1930s. Diepenhorst died at age eighty-seven in 2012 (*courtesy Donnelly Corp.*)

like a public corporation, with a newsletter and an annual meeting to keep the wider family informed. John left a chemical engineering major at the University of Notre Dame to join the family firm, but he resigned within four years to complete his baccalaureate degree at Catholic University. He then began studying for the priesthood but within a year determined that he was not truly called to the ministry and returned to Holland to manage the company.[31]

Duffy continued as president of Duffy Manufacturing until his death in 1953, when Riemer A. Boersma, an employee since 1927, who served as vice president and general manager since 1943, succeeded him, with Louis J. Hohmann named vice president.[32]

During the Second World War, Donnelly-Kelly Glass joined the war effort like every other major company. It formed the Glass Technics division and made optical parts for aircraft gun-sights, tank periscopes, and aerial cameras—all essentially prisms. This required the craftsmen to learn how to mass-produce the precision prisms, which were polished to a thickness of one ten-thousandth of an inch and comprised 65

31 Karczewski, *Our Heritage*, 223-25; Komejan interview; *Holland Sentinel*, 9 June 1935.

32 John F. Donnelly interview by Abby Jewett, 21 June 1982, JAH; *Holland City Directories*, 1921, 1924, 1962.

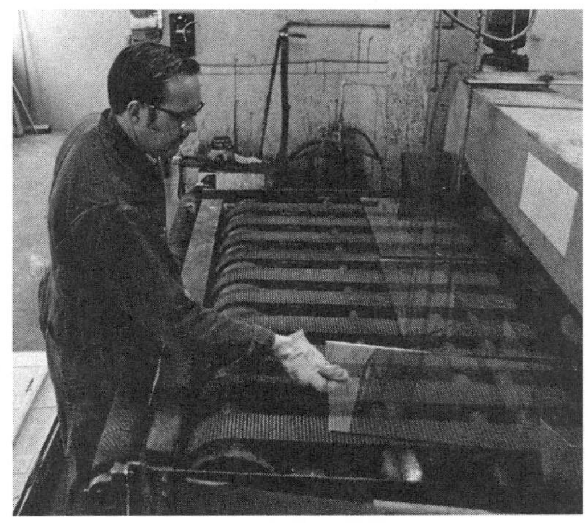

Stanley Kleis silver coats glass panels in a processing tank in the 1960s, his task for twenty-eight years. He then drove one of Donnelly's tractor trailer trucks for twelve years until retiring, thus completing forty years with the company (*courtesy Stanley Kleis*)

percent of the plant's production. War contracts fattened the bottom line; annual sales by 1945 reached $638,000.[33]

In the late 1930s, Donnelly heard that General Motors was looking for a rearview mirror that would stop glare at night by giving a dimmer image. He started designing such mirrors in 1939, but the war made other demands. When war production ended, Donnelly had his company capitalize on its prism expertise to make prismatic rearview mirrors for cars. General Motors in 1945 offered the first contract, and more followed; this sped the transition at Donnelly-Kelley from fine furniture to automotive products. At first the company only produced the rearview mirrors, but soon they made the frame and finally the entire assembly. Sales reached $1.2 million in 1951. An important adaptation in 1959 was to allow for dimming by manually "flipping" the mirror. After John Fenlon Donnelly became president in 1960, he renamed the firm Donnelly Mirrors Inc. In 1962 he sold the home-mirror business to William LaBarge Mirrors of Holland, and focused on automotive mirrors.[34]

In its first half century, 1910-60, the company had two core technologies–glass processing and glass coating. Processing glass involved cutting, grinding, shaping, and bending it; coating involved depositing metals onto the glass. Both of these core technologies became the nucleus for much more sophisticated applications in the automotive industry. John F. Donnelly led the way by making

33 Lozon, "Reflections in the Mirror," 10; *Holland Sentinel*, 16 Jan. 1943, 12 Apr. 1947; *Holland City News*, 30 Apr. 1942, 17 Apr. 1947; *Grand Rapids Press Lakeshore Edition*, 13 May 2001.

34 *Holland Sentinel*, 22 Nov. 1992; Donnelly interview.

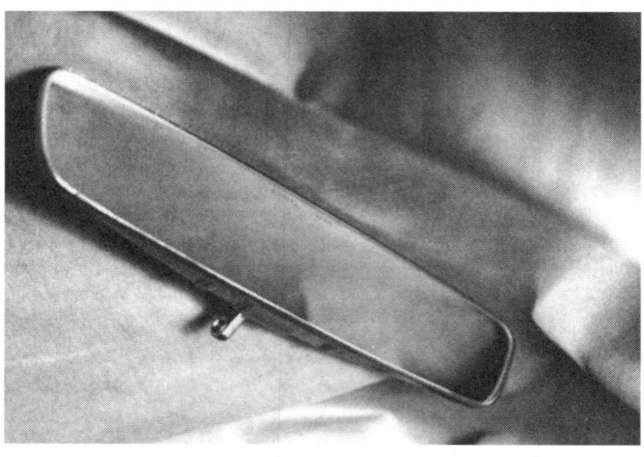

Donnelly Corp. prismatic rearview mirror that could be adjusted manually, 1965 (*courtesy Donnelly Corp.*)

technological innovation the engine of the company's growth. He invested 4-5 percent of sales revenue on research, compared to 1-2 percent by other auto suppliers, and it paid off handsomely. Donnelly pioneered the right-side exterior mirror that warns, "Objects in mirror are closer than they appear." This convex mirror greatly expanded the driver's field of view. Donnelly engineers also developed chrome coating for the exterior mirrors, because it was more resilient to weather and more reflective than silver coating. Chrome coating became universal on exterior mirrors, and this opened the way for other innovations, such as liquid crystal displays for watches.[35]

Glass coatings evolved into transparent coatings, beam splitter coatings, and anti-reflection coatings. These were used in the automotive industry, the early space program, and for computer touch screens. The automotive coatings were developed for self-dimming mirrors (electrochromic), sunroofs, interactive panels in offices (for privacy and data), and energy-saving architectural glass for major office buildings—a Donnelly project partially underwritten by Lawrence Livermore National Laboratories. All of these glass coatings were thinner than a human hair. The space program needed anti-glare coatings for spacecraft instrument panels and attitude indicators. Donnelly later spun off the touch-screen technology to a new company, Optera, which made 80-90 percent of the screens for the banking, retail, fast food, and gaming industries.

In the 1970s, Donnelly was the first to adapt plastic injection molding technology to make a plastic housing for interior rearview mirrors, replacing the early metal housings. In accidents, plastic was more forgiving than metal on passengers' faces. Taking the innovation

[35] Donnelly interview.

one step further, the company produced the bracket assembly for mounting the mirrors to the vehicle, thus allowing Donnelly to sell complete mirror assemblies. Donnelly rapidly expanded the plastics technology from making relatively simple interior and exterior automotive mirrors to providing a full assembly that was safer and could integrate an array of electronics.

As a result of an idea from an employee in the late 1970s, the plastic molding and coating technology was adapted to create the distinctive oval "opera" window for the rear panels of Lincoln Continentals and Ford Thunderbirds that glowed at night with the car's logo etched in the glass. The secret to that panel, which was housed in a polymer casing, was the transparent coating that conducted electricity in the floating logo. This was the genesis of a new product line, the coating group, which by the early 1990s had sales equal to those of the mirror group, some $400 million.

The ability to frame, or encapsulate, a window revolutionized car manufacturing. Instead of windows being manually assembled on the line, Donnelly introduced the idea of a window already framed and weather sealed before it arrived at the car company. This was a major quality breakthrough and greatly reduced the costs of manual assembly "on the line." Company engineers ultimately produced major window systems for a large portion of the automotive world, including fixed and vented side windows and rear windows. Donnelly also pioneered sleek minivan windows that involved innovative "single-sided" encapsulation, in which all attachments are made on only one side of the window.[36]

John F. Donnelly realized that mirrors were "valuable real estate . . . something we could do anything with," in the words of Maryam Komejan, Donnelly's secretary and confidant. Donnelly encouraged his engineers to add more technology to rearview mirrors. They designed "puddle lights" (tiny spotlights that illuminate the ground when the car door is opened), electronic compasses, heating elements, rain-sensors, and automatic dimming features. For exterior mirrors they added automatic dimming, de-icing, and electronic turn signal indicators. The assembly came with fully matched painted housings that would simply be attached as a complete unit at the car assembly plant. The consoles had to match a wide variety of interior color schemes, which required Donnelly to master the techniques of painting for the automotive industry.[37]

36 *Holland Sentinel*, 22 Nov. 1992.

37 Conversation with Maryam Komejan, 5 Nov. 2010; Tim Moran, "Your Mirror is Trying to Send Me a Message," *New York Times*, 10 Oct. 2001.

John F. Donnelly at his desk (*courtesy Donnelly Corp.*)

Immediately after the introduction of electronics to core products, Donnelly developed advanced optical and lighting systems that made use of unique miniature lenses that were molded directly onto optical grade plastics. These lenses, as fine as human fingerprints, focused light sharply inside a vehicle to reduce ambient light, direct light where needed, and increase privacy. The new lenses were first integrated into the housing of a rearview mirror to produce the first lighted interior mirrors during the 1980s. The integration of electronics and optics led to other breakthroughs, such as "heads-up" displays in vehicles (based on fighter jet instrumentation), liquid crystal instrument panels, and innovative electronic cameras and data chips that would be used in back-up systems and as sensors throughout the vehicle. These innovations added value that padded the bottom line; a $10 item was turned into a $100 to $200 item, which further fueled Donnelly's growth.[38]

Many Donnelly innovations spurred new industries; for example, window technology led to the development of the "spill-proof" refrigerator shelf, decorative engraved wall mirrors became beautiful furniture products, and glass coatings opened new opportunities in computers, hand-held electronics, and even sophisticated and safe welding helmets. From 1960 to 2000, the company received hundreds of patents to its innovations. The cumulative effect of these technological breakthroughs was to accelerate both output and sales. Donnelly's heavy investment in technological research paid off handsomely for its shareholders, employees, and the Holland community. The company expanded with plants on Ottawa Avenue and Fortieth Street in the

[38] Conversation with Komejan.

Southside HEDCOR (Holland Economic Development Corporation) Industrial Park (see below).

John F. Donnelly led the company for more than fifty years as CEO and president, and he operated from radical assumptions that made his company unique in terms of its management philosophy and investment strategy. His primary goal was to foster a culture of respect. He believed in hiring and promoting the best and brightest in every major discipline: technological innovation, market leadership in all major product groupings, strong financial performance, and globalization. He created an environment where innovative thinking was highly prized and merit was rewarded, irrespective of family or personal ties.[39]

Donnelly, a leader like his father at St. Francis de Sales Church, carried his Christian ethics into his plants. He told Konrad "Kon" Marcus, one of his chief engineers, more than once: "Kon, if you're aware of anyone in our organization that's having difficulty—financially or whatever the problem may be—by all means, bring that to my attention, and we'll take care of it." And Donnelly did so many times. In keeping with his principles, and in hopes of getting higher productivity, he sought to empower employees and share the company's success with them. He developed a unique corporate culture based on the principles of fairness, servant leadership, and team building. The policy even applied to the company parking lot, where executives—Donnelly included—had no designated spaces.[40]

Donnelly shared profits in the beginning, and later he shared power, which was quite rare in corporate management circles, but he also demanded excellence. When an employee came up with a new idea, that person's entire team received kudos. Donnelly based his hiring on character as much as knowledge. Being bright was not enough; his employees needed core beliefs that meshed with those of the company. Donnelly wanted his people to commit themselves and take emotional "ownership" of the company's success. He said more than once that the real purpose of profit was "to ensure that the resources exist in a society to raise the quality of life for everyone and that all investors would receive a fair return for their work." In other words, profit is not optional, but focusing on profit for its own sake is not enough. If an employee failed to meet his high ethical standards, he or she was at great risk of being

39 For this paragraph and the next, see Komejan interview; Conversations with Komejan, 7, 18 Nov. 2010.

40 Konrad Marcus interview by the author and Dave Boeve, 16 Oct. 2009, typescript, JAH; Conversation with Komejan; Donnelly interview.

Harold Lemmen, Donnelly truck driver, who informed John F. Donnelly about the Scanlon Plan, 1960s (*courtesy Donnelly Corp.*)

terminated. Stewardship was an equally strong moral imperative for himself and the company. Contrary to the business school axiom that profits are to increase shareholder wealth, Donnelly took the broader view that profits also must serve the needs of employees, customers, suppliers, and the local community. As a result, Donnelly did not have high absenteeism, work stoppages, or any labor problems in its first century of operations.

Donnelly was the second company in Holland to adopt the Scanlon Plan, a teamwork approach to management (chapter 14); this was a vital factor in the firm's success. John F. Donnelly was inspired by a report from Harald Lemmen, one of his truck drivers, that Herman Miller in Zeeland was "giving money away to his employees." Donnelly went over to talk with D. J. De Pree and learned about his profit-sharing system that was employee driven. Donnelly followed suit but tailored the plan to his company. He established the Donnelly Committee, a representative group of mostly shop floor workers, plus some managers and company executives.

This body met monthly, and one of its responsibilities was to determine annual cost-of-living raises and bonuses based on sales and profits. The committee established a standard cost for each product, and any savings that employees made by driving costs below the benchmark price were shared each month with the workforce. If production went up, the employees' pay went up by the same amount, up to 28 percent. The system policed itself because employees chastised sluggards who jeopardized their bonuses. So confident was Donnelly

Production manager Dick Arthur (*right*) wields sledge hammer in symbolic smashing of the factory time clock with (*l-r*): Art Van Dyke, Stanley Longworthy, Kelly South, and Art Phillipus looking on, 1960s (*courtesy Donnelly Corp.*)

in the system that he had a ceremonial smashing of the factory time clock; no longer did employees punch in and punch out on an hourly wage system. *Time Magazine* in its November 8, 1970, issue reported the remarkable self management program at the Donnelly Mirrors plant in Holland, Michigan.[41]

That many other corporations emulated this participative management system was a high compliment to De Pree and Donnelly. Harvard Business School used Donnelly's management system as a case study for its MBAs. In 1993 Donnelly was recognized as one of the "Top Ten" of the "100 Best Companies to Work for in America." Herman Miller and Haworth also made the "Top 100."[42]

In 1977 John F. Donnelly named Arlyn Lanting president–the first non-family member to run the company. At the same time, his son John F. Jr., a recent graduate of the University of Michigan, joined the company as manufacturing supervisor. He became senior vice president and general manager of the modular windows division in 1989, and chief operating officer of European operations, based in Germany,

41 Donnelly interview; Marcus interview; John Fenton Donnelly obit., *Holland Sentinel*, 9 June 1989; "John F. Donnelly," ibid., 17 June 1986, 22 Nov. 1992, 25 Jan. 1994; Lozon, *Reflections in the Mirror*, 16.

42 *Holland Sentinel*, 4 Oct. 1998; Levering and Moscovitz, *Top 100 Companies*.

in 1998.[43] Sales in 1979 were $30 million, and the company had six hundred employees. That year the worst recession hit since the 1930s. Donnelly's sales plunged 40 percent, and Lanting had to lay off one-third of the workforce. Rather than have management make the decision, the executives sat down with employees in small groups and explained the desperate situation. The teams of managers and workers together decided who would go and who would stay, regardless of seniority. Some older workers sacrificed their jobs for younger colleagues with small children. "We came out of that with people loving the company," Komejan recalled. And ten years later, the employees helped Donnelly win the coveted top-ten employer award.[44]

In 1980 Lanting left and joined Gentex (see below). Donnelly, who continued as CEO and chairman of the board, chose as president Dwane Baumgardner, the vice president of technology, who had joined the company in 1969 and had a doctoral degree in optics. Over the next twenty-five years, Baumgardner added the titles of CEO (1983) and chairman (1986); he led the company to globalize its operations, beginning with a Tokyo office in 1980. Back in 1968, Donnelly had opened a factory in Ireland, the first local company to go overseas. The factory served all of western Europe. Since the European business cycle at that time lagged the American economy by about eighteen months, and Asia had its own cycles, this balanced the business cycle for Donnelly and reduced risk.[45]

In 1984 Donnelly Mirrors became Donnelly Corporation in recognition of the fact that the mirrors group was rivaled in sales by the coated windows and lighting groups. John F. Donnelly Sr. died of a heart attack in 1986, soon after committing the company to build the first plant in the Northside Industrial Park, its fourth facility. He was greatly missed at St. Francis Church and in his many civic endeavors, notably as chair of the West Michigan Strategic Alliance, a collaborative effort to develop a twenty-five-year common vision for the region. Donnelly also endowed the Carl Frost Center for Social Science Research at Hope College, formed in 1990 and named after Michigan State Professor Carl "Jack" Frost, co-author of the Scanlon Plan and a pioneer in industrial psychology and participatory management in business. Baumgardner chaired the board of the Scanlon Leadership Foundation in the 1990s and received its annual leadership award in 1996.[46]

43 Conversation with John F. Donnelly Jr., 20 Aug. 2010.

44 Komejan interview.

45 Ibid.

46 Marcus interview; *Holland Sentinel*, 30 Jan. 1988, 13 May 2001, 25 Mar. 2002, 2 Feb. 2004.

To raise capital and provide liquidity to the family shareholders, the private corporation went public in 1988. Family members received B shares with ten votes per share, while A shares were sold to the public and carried one vote. This allowed the family to retain control. Donnelly shares traded on the New York Stock Exchange. The fresh capital funded new plants in Holland and Grand Haven, and spurred growth in Asian markets. Moira Donnelly, daughter of Bernard P. Donnelly, ran the Grand Haven start-up, until moving to the main office in 1990 as head of corporate training and development. In 1993 GM awarded Donnelly the "Mark of Excellence" for supplier performance and quality.[47] Besides Baumgardner and John F. Donnelly Jr., the team of senior executives included vice presidents Rich Cook, Niall Lynam, Paul Kalkman, Maryam Komejan, James Knister, and Ron Vanden Berg. Kalkman also served as president.

Modular auto windows were a major profit driver by the early 1990s, and automotive products made up 89 percent of total sales. This led the board to adopt a policy of focusing entirely on these products and spinning off non-automotive business, such as Optera. It was feared that the company might become too diverse and would dissipate too much of its energy trying to pursue so many avenues.[48]

By 1992 Donnelly was selling inside mirrors to ten foreign automakers operating in the United States. In 1996 Donnelly purchased the German company Hohe, built a factory in France, and opened joint ventures to manufacture automotive components in China, Brazil, and Malaysia. Donnelly-Hohe was the largest manufacturer of exterior mirrors in Europe. The 1996 Chrysler minivan contract brought in $60 million in annual revenue and the Ford Expedition another $50 million. In Baumgardner's first two decades at the helm, Donnelly Corp. saw sales double every five years on average, rising from $30 million in 1980 to $950 million in 2000. The firm literally spanned the globe, with operations in some thirty nations and foreign markets accounting for 30 percent of total sales.[49]

As Donnelly developed its mirror technologies, it came into conflict with Gentex, the Zeeland company that manufactured similar mirrors (see below). This rivalry set off a major patent dispute. In 1990 Gentex filed the first of several patent infringement lawsuits against Donnelly, who responded with several of its own. Litigation went against the grain of top executives in both companies, but the costly

47 *Holland Sentinel*, 22 Nov. 1992.
48 Ibid., 25 Jan. 1994.
49 Ibid., 22 Nov. 1992, 4 Oct. 1998.

"Mirror Wars" continued for six years. Finally, in 1996 both sides called a truce, and the legal war ended. Donnelly's technologies went well beyond automotive products, but the lawsuits over mirrors hindered its progress in the marketplace and resulted in lost profits over $1 billion. Company insiders believe that the lawsuits enabled Gentex to gain market share.[50]

In the middle of the legal fight, Chrysler in 1993 gave Donnelly its first multiyear contract for modular window systems, and Ford and Mazda signed contracts for exterior mirror systems. The same year, Donnelly engineers developed the Intelligent Window System that used a video camera and advanced processing program on a silicon chip to control its mirror system.[51]

Donnelly's exterior and interior mirror systems were in high demand, and its workforce grew to two thousand locally, plus another four thousand in nine foreign countries. In 1997 the company under CEO Baumgardner moved its corporate headquarters and one hundred executives and staff back to its original 1905 building on Third Street, after a $2 million "ground-up" renovation. In 2000 Milwaukee-based Johnson Controls Inc. (JCI), another large automotive parts supplier in Holland (see below), bought a 25 percent stake in Donnelly and became its largest stockholder. Two years later, JCI announced its intent to sell its shares, which had appreciated in value by $9.1 million. Donnelly sales in 2001 were nearly $1 billion, and the management team looked to expand even faster by exploring partnerships and acquisitions.

Baumgardner offered to buy the mirror business of Magna International of Toronto, which was a minor part of the automotive giant's sales. When Magna officials saw the obvious synergy between the two mirror operations, they decided instead to buy Donnelly Corporation. Magna offered its shares for Donnelly shares at a rate 20 percent above their all-time high price, or $320 million. Magna also assumed more than $80 million in debt, which made the total value above $400 million.[52]

50 *Holland Sentinel*, 28 Feb., 12 May 1990, 3, 4 Apr., 21 May, 8 June 1993, 27 Nov. 1994, 1 Apr. 1996; Robin Luymes, "Mirror Battles Reflect Change," *Grand Rapids Business Journal*, 24 Sept. 1990; Luymes, "Mirror Firms Show Mixed Results," *Grand Rapids Business Journal*, 21 Oct. 1991; Conversations with Komejan.

51 Maryam Komejan, "Donnelly looks forward to a bright 1994," *Holland Sentinel*, 25 Jan. 1994.

52 *Holland Sentinel*, 22 Nov. 1992, 25 Oct. 1997; *Grand Rapids Press Lakeshore Edition*, 23 Oct. 1997, 30 Apr. 2002; Massie, *Haven, Harbor, and Heritage*, 144; conversation with John F. Donnelly Jr., 20 Aug. 2010.

The Donnelly board accepted the offer, subject to approval by stockholders of at least two-thirds of the shares. "They simply made us an offer we couldn't refuse," said a Donnelly spokesperson. The Magna offer was on the table when the World Trade Center was attacked in September 2001, and the economy reeled under the blow. Donnelly sales also dropped sharply. In the end, 89 percent of the shares were tendered, and the merger became final in June 2002. So a conglomerate with $11 billion in sales bought a multi-national company with $848 million in sales after a run of ninety-seven years. "It was the natural evolution of a family-run business that gets to a certain size," explained Moira Donnelly, a company executive and granddaughter of the founder.[53]

For five years, per the sales agreement, the Holland firm was known as Magna Donnelly, and then it became Magna Mirrors in Holland, a division of Magna International, a $25 billion conglomerate in 2010. Dropping the Donnelly name in 2007 signaled a change in its traditional worker- and family-friendly business culture. The Holland division, with its administrative offices and five manufacturing facilities, had 1,200 employees in 2007, down from 2,000 in 2002. Donnelly-Kelley Glass went a long way in one hundred years in innovative glass technologies, and then, in a sense, it returned to its beginnings on Third Street.[54]

Gentex Corporation

Four technology geeks started an electronics company in 1974 that grew into the billion-dollar Gentex Corporation of today. Fred Bauer and his younger brother Dan, the first full-time officer, ran the company, with brother Larry and friend Arlyn Lanting as silent partners. Lanting, a top officer at Donnelly Corp., joined Gentex in 1980.

Fred Bauer was an electronics whiz and a driving force. A Michigan State University graduate with a degree in electrical engineering and a minor in business, Bauer first took his "EE" talents to the Fortune 500 Whirlpool Corp. in Benton Harbor, Michigan. But his entrepreneurial instincts soon led him in 1967 at age twenty-three to found his own company, Simicon, a manufacturer of electronic control units for furnaces. Bauer saw the need for more sophisticated controls while watching his father Lee Bauer invent and commercialize the Miller

53 *Holland Sentinel*, 6 Aug., 29 Sept., 1 Oct. 2002, 8 Jan. 2003; *Grand Rapids Press Lakeshore Edition*, 6 Aug. 2002.

54 *Holland Sentinel*, May 6, 2007.

Mobile Gun Furnace at Home Furnace Company (chapter 13). Fred invented a solid-state control using a photoelectric sensor. This was a seminal innovation at the core of his future business endeavors. Simicon began in an old building at 1601 Washington Avenue, which was later razed for the West Michigan Regional Airport. Within five years the firm had a hundred employees.[55]

Bauer's furnace control units caught the attention of Robertshaw Controls, another Fortune 500 company, which in 1972 purchased Simicon. This gave Bauer the capital in 1974 to launch Gentex, a company to market a second major invention, one of the first battery-powered smoke detectors, which used an LED (light emitting diode) light with a photoelectric sensor. To market this innovation of critical importance to the fire protection market, Bauer rented a building at 343 East Sixteenth Street and Fairbanks Avenue and placed his younger brother Dan in charge, while he continued to manage Robertshaw's Simicon Division until 1979.[56]

When Fred and several high-tech associates left Simicon to join Gentex in 1979, the start-up had only one customer and could not afford to pay its employees. Resolved to make the company profitable, the team invented one electronic product after another for the fire, security, and automotive industries. Gentex smoke detectors can still be found in US commercial airline lavatories.

Amway Corp. gave Gentex a major contract—a security device that was marketed broadly through Amway members. With the profits, Bauer and Lanting took Gentex public in 1981. Lanting went to Denver, then a venture capital hub, and sold 30 percent of the company stock to risk-taking investors at three dollars a share, thereby raising $4.3 million. The monies enabled Gentex to buy a building midway between Holland and Zeeland at 10985 Chicago Drive and grow the business. Early investors who bought and held on to Gentex stock have been handsomely rewarded.[57]

55 "Gentex Corporation History," *International Directory of Company Histories*, vol. 26 (St. James, MO: St. James Press, 1999), available at www:gentex.com; *Grand Rapids Press Lakeshore Edition*, 15 Nov. 1987; *Holland Sentinel*, 24 Jan. 1995; Katy Rent, "Bauer Tells Entrepreneurial Story," *Grand Rapids Business Journal*, 2 Jan. 2001. I am indebted to Fred Bauer for providing information about his career and companies.

56 "Bauer takes national entrepreneur title," *Shoreline Business Monthly*, Dec. 1998; Katy Rent, "Bauer tells entrepreneurial story," *Grand Rapids Business Journal*, 2 Jan. 2001. The Simicon Division moved in 1974 to 942 Brooks Avenue and in 1991 to 11768 James Street in Holland Township, where it continued as the Electric Controls Division and Ivensys Appliance Controls. Ivensys closed its James Street facility in 2010, and Gentex acquired the property for expansion.

57 *Holland Sentinel*, 29 June 1993, 23 Aug. 1994.

The biggest hit was auto-dimming rearview mirrors for automobiles. Fred Bauer and his fellow engineer Jon Bechtel, along with Dave Schmidt, a computer programmer, in 1979 entered into a partnership with Donnelly Corp. to develop self-dimming mirrors. Donnelly put up some funds and other assistance, and Gentex engineers focused on the mirror. They were seeking to solve a problem that had perplexed the automobile industry for twenty years—how to make a mirror that eliminated glare and made nighttime driving safer. By 1982 they had invented an electromechanical model—the first one that actually worked—and were ready to market it in conjunction with Donnelly. This first generation mirror utilized a pair of electronic sensors or "eyes" that sensed headlight glare and activated a small motor to "flip" the prismatic mirror up and down as needed. From a design perspective, it was practical but inelegant, because the motor made an annoying whirr, and it seemed to be "nervous;" its flipping back and forth in city traffic could be distracting. Nevertheless, auto companies wanted it for their luxury lines.[58]

The project was on the cusp of success when the national economy turned down sharply in what was dubbed "stagflation" (hyperinflation and high interest rates). Donnelly Corp. saw red flags and wanted to freeze the project. Bauer determined to press ahead on his own. He had invested too much time and money to give up. Using funding from its Denver IPO, Gentex acquired a partially complete mirror project and "trudged on." Bauer and his engineering team finished design work and put the mirror on the market. Beginning with a small volume order for the 1983 Lincoln Continental, Gentex sold 1.1 million units by 1991. Drivers generally liked the auto-dimming mirror, despite its shortcomings, which helped Gentex push the Big Three to move the product "down through the lines." Cadillac and Oldsmobile signed on in 1984, with others to follow. The mirrors graced three hundred thousand luxury cars by 1986, and Bauer and his team relished being named to the Michigan Tech 50, an elite group of leading technology firms in the state.[59]

It was 1985 before Gentex had the first profitable year, earning $570,000 on sales of $9 million. They had reported a net loss of $250,000 in 1983 and $527,000 in 1984. From 1985 on, sales increased steadily through the 1990s. Sales of the motorized mirrors peaked in

58 Conversation with Fred Bauer, 10 May 2013.

59 "Gentex Corporation History;" *Holland Sentinel*, 19 Jan. 1985.

1987 at 203,000 units, and net income peaked in 1989 at $2.1 million. The number of employees nearly quadrupled from 65 to 225.[60]

Not resting on their laurels, Bauer and his team in 1987 developed the world's first electrochromic mirror. These second-generation mirrors dimmed silently to match exactly the glare, much to the satisfaction of finicky customers. Harlan Byker was one of the creative geniuses behind this innovation. His father Gary Byker, a Gentex stockholder and former state representative from Hudsonville, brought Harlan to visit Gentex during the Christmas holidays in 1982. An electrochemist with Battelle Columbus Laboratories in Columbus, Ohio, Harlan had a passing familiarity with electrochromic technology. During the visit, according to *Sentinel* business editor Mike Lozon, Byker "openly mused" about the idea of turning Gentex's motorized unit into an electrochromic one, and Fred Bauer, who had seen an earlier unsuccessful electrochromic attempt, took him up on it.[61]

Gentex funded Byker to review the literature and work on electrochromic technology at Battelle. Two years later in 1985, Bauer wisely hired him. In a makeshift laboratory in the Chicago Drive building, Byker continued research on the next generation mirror, while colleagues Jon Bechtel and Bauer developed the circuitry. Byker, in reviewing some unsuccessful Russian technology, hit on the solution to the main problem, how to make the mirror darken over an infinite number of levels. The key was a thin gelatinous film sandwiched between two pieces of glass, which darkens when electrically charged and lightens when the electricity is switched off. Front and back light sensors control the electric current. When Gentex announced the invention in 1986, it was hailed as the first practical product based on electrochromic technology, a quest scientists had pursued for over forty years.[62]

Dan Bauer, Gentex's first president, stepped down in 1986. Fred then hired Kenneth LaGrand, his former associate at Simicon, as executive vice president. The pair made Gentex's first major acquisition, Larry Barrett's Vanguard Glass Fabricators of Zeeland, financed by $950,000 in Gentex common stock, which made Barrett a wealthy man. Vanguard's twelve precision glass craftsmen, including Barrett

60 "Gentex Corporation History;" *Holland Sentinel*, 10 Dec. 1987, 26 May 1988, 11 Oct. 1989.

61 Mike Lozon, "Looking at success in a rearview mirror," *Holland Sentinel*, 5 Nov. 1989.

62 "Gentex Corporation History," *Holland Sentinel*, 31 Jan. 1987, 11 Oct. 1989; *Grand Rapids Press Lakeshore Edition*, 15 Nov. 1987. I am indebted to Harlan Byker and Fred Bauer for details about the development of electrochromic mirrors.

and chief mechanical engineer Dan Suman, greatly enhanced Gentex's glass-working capabilities.[63]

In 1987 Ford Motor Company ordered the electrochromic mirrors in small volume for the 1988 Lincoln Continental. The first shipment went out in December 1987 at a cost of about forty dollars each or 40 percent more than the earlier motorized mirrors still in production. Ford had taken a similar leap of faith in 1983 when it ordered the first generation auto-mirrors. For the 1989 model year, GM bought the new mirrors for eight models, and Chrysler and BMW did the same in 1990.[64]

Gentex took an enormous risk to obsolete its proven electromechanical mirrors for an unproven technology. Fortunately the risk paid off. Mirror sales in 1989 totaled four hundred thousand units, with a million units projected in 1990. In three years, sales of mirrors completely surpassed fire-protection devices. In 1987 mirrors comprised 55 percent of annual sales and fire-protection devices 45 percent. Six years later the ratio was 75/25, and twelve years later it was 90/10. From a production rate in 1982 of from fifty to sixty electromechanical mirrors a day, the plant in 1988 produced one thousand electrochromic mirrors per day. It was a "blockbuster year," declared LaGrand.[65]

The innovative mirror business required rapid expansion of factory floor space. The former Vanguard Glass plant at 600 North Centennial Drive was expanded twice in 1988 at a cost of $5 million, both financed by industrial revenue bonds issued by the city of Zeeland. Sales that year totaled $24 million. "Gentex is like a rocket poised on the launching pad," Fred Bauer declared. "There is a world of possibilities out there, and we have just begun."[66]

With sales of Gentex electrochromic mirrors skyrocketing, Donnelly Corp. in 1989 announced its intention to market its own "polychromatic" mirrors and mirror assemblies. Upon investigation, Gentex was convinced Donnelly had copied its 1987 gel-based mirror and infringed on several of its patents. Gentex filed suit in May 1990, and Donnelly, aware of the move, counter-sued the same day, thus setting off the six-year Mirror Wars (see above). Both companies continued to work on electrochromic interior and exterior mirrors during the costly litigation. The mutually unpleasant litigation was finally settled in 1996.

63 *Holland Sentinel*, 29 Apr., 31 May 1986, 15 Nov. 1987.

64 "Gentex Corporation History," *Holland Sentinel*, 26 May 1988.

65 "Gentex Corporation History," *Holland Sentinel*, 31 Jan., 10 Dec. 1987.

66 *Grand Rapids Press Lakeshore Edition*, 15 Nov. 1987, 2 Sept. 1988 (quote); *Holland Sentinel*, 30 Jan. 1988 (quote), 31 Aug. 1988.

Woman working on the electrochromic mirror assembly line at Gentex plant in Zeeland, 1991 (*courtesy Randall P. Vande Water*)

So pleased were the auto giants with Gentex's night vision safety (NVS) mirrors that the company became a regular recipient of the number-one-supplier ratings. Gentex scientists and engineers next applied the technology to exterior mirrors, potentially a billion-dollar market. Exterior mirrors are subject to one thousand times more ultraviolet radiation than interior mirrors, which makes designing them more challenging. By 1991 Gentex had overcome the problem and marketed the first continuously variable, electrochromic, exterior mirror. In 1992 more than fifty domestic and foreign carmakers used the NSV mirrors, and the company had record net profits of $5 million on sales of $45 million. The next five years were even better, and by 1997 sales topped $186 million, a 200 percent increase over 1992. Sales were juiced by the introduction in 1993 of the NVS compass mirror with an electronic compass patented and licensed by Prince Corp. This started a successful partnership that extended to JCI and included "Homelink" garage door openers. Fred Bauer estimates that hundreds of engineers and scientists worked on the development of the various electrochromic mirrors and that it took hundreds of millions of dollars to bring the products to market. Ernst & Young, a national accounting firm, named Bauer its 1998 Master Entrepreneur of the Year.[67]

[67] Interview with Fred Bauer, 10 May 2013; "Gentex Corporation History," *Holland Sentinel*, 11 Oct. 1989, 26 Jan. 1993; *Shoreline Business Monthly*, Dec. 1998.

In 1996 Gentex opened a $12.5 million facility on Ninety-Sixth Avenue and Riley Street that doubled its floor space. The plant, located a quarter mile from the Centennial Street plant, boosted annual mirror production from 2.2 million to 4.5 million, with fully one-fourth exported to Asia and Europe. The company shipped its ten-millionth mirror in 1996, but only 10 percent of cars, mostly luxury models and light trucks, carried the popular product. The growth potential to equip mid-priced cars was great, provided Gentex could continue to cut its cost to the price-conscious automakers. The 1998 price range from $25 to $30 was half that of a decade earlier. *Forbes* business magazine included Gentex on its "200 Best Small Companies in America" list four times (1994 and 1996-98), which was a stunning achievement. The company had about 90 percent of the market for electrochromic mirrors and enjoyed record earnings. The net margin was among the best in the auto-parts industry. Investors in Gentex common stock saw the share price double in the second half of 1998.[68]

In 1998 the company built another plant off Riley Street between existing plants east of State Street in Zeeland, which was larger than any of its predecessors. The workforce grew to 1,750, and Gentex engineers kept the workers busy with new products. By 2001 they had wedded LED technology to its mirrors with LED map lights, which ushered in the third generation of Gentex mirror technology. LEDs generate little heat and never burn out. The mirrors also became the "gateway" for other electronic wireless, Internet, and navigation features car buyers wanted, including GM's OnStar system based on Global Positioning System (GPS) satellite technology. With Gentex's "telematic mirrors," one business reporter enthused that we were now "on the stars." Sales reached $310 million in 2001.[69]

In 2003 Gentex announced yet another $35 million expansion. Tax credits and other incentives from the Michigan Economic Development Corp. of $11.2 million induced the firm to build in Michigan rather than Georgia, where labor costs were lower. The state's deal was a harbinger of bad times to come among the Big Three automakers. Gentex and other suppliers had to continue to innovate and diversify or stagnate. In 2004 Gentex introduced its SmartBeam headlamps that

68 *Holland Sentinel*, 30 Sept., 20 Oct. 1994, 19 Sept., 12 Nov. 1995, 25 Feb., 23 Aug. 1996, 27 Jan. 1998; *Zeeland Record*, 14 Dec. 1989; Ted Knutson, "Gentex Stock Area's Hottest," *Grand Rapids Business Journal*, 18 Jan. 1999.

69 *Holland Sentinel*, 7 Apr. 1998, 19 Oct., 6, 20 Nov. 2002; Dan Calabrese, "Gentex Performance Reflects Expansion," *Grand Rapids Business Journal*, 17 May 1993, 8 Jan. 2001; Katy Rent, "Now—A Rearview Mirror on the Stars," *Grand Rapids Business Journal*, 16 Apr. 2001.

automatically switch between low and high beam. This was likely the first use of machine vision in the global automotive industry. Factory production was ramped up to meet the projected demand of a half-million such headlamps. A new Zeeland plant was dedicated in 2006, with a second in the Holland-Zeeland area in 2011. Zeeland's largest employer in 2005 landed a $15 million contract with Boeing to outfit its 787 Dreamliner passenger aircraft with the auto-dimming electrochromic windows, which eliminated the need for shades. But the first plane did not reach customers until 2012, because Boeing faced repeated production problems; the company, however, expects to ship dozens more 787s against their record backlog, and Gentex is ready.[70]

The latest innovation is the rear camera video display in the rearview mirror, which allows drivers to see objects or small children behind their vehicles. Gentex was the first to commercialize the rear camera display projected through the mirror surface, and it controls 95 percent of that market. Other companies market the display in the instrument panel. For several quarters in 2008 and early 2009, when the overall economy declined sharply and the new car market collapsed, Gentex posted small losses. But the company posted a record net profit of $135 million in 2010—double the 2009 figure—thanks to sales of auto-dimming mirrors, SmartBeam headlamps, and rear-camera display systems. Gentex emerged from the economic firestorm with an "amazing surge," led by exports to Europe and Asia that now exceed sales in the United States.[71]

Late in 2010, Gentex purchased the vacant Ivensys Appliance Controls plant at 11768 James Street to consolidate most circuit board and final assembly operations. It also increased facilities for the mass production of rear-camera displays to meet the demands of the reviving auto industry with a hiring binge in 2011 and a $160 million five-building expansion. Gentex, Zeeland's largest company, with 3,500 employees locally in 2013 (about 95 percent of the total workforce) and rising steadily, is one of the largest regional employers. Over the last twenty years, Gentex has experienced a growth rate of 19 percent compounded annually, which is unmatched by any other local industrial firm, and annual sales topped $1 billion for the first time in calendar year 2011. In 2013 Bauer remained at the helm of Gentex after

70 Mark Sanchez, "Gentex Ready to Launch SmartBeam Technology," *Grand Rapids Business Journal*, 5 May 2003; *Holland Sentinel*, 7 Jan. 2003, 17 Dec. 2005, 14 July 2006; *Grand Rapids Press*, 27 Sept. 2011.

71 *Grand Rapids Press Lakeshore Edition*, 29 Jan., 23 Apr. (quote), 24 Nov. 2010; *Holland Sentinel*, 2 Oct., 28 Nov. 2010.

nearly thirty years. He is the only Gentex engineer to hold more patents than Bechtel, who held 114 when he retired in 2012.[72]

Pleotint, LLC

Harlan Byker left Gentex in late 1997 and established his own company, Pleotint, LLC, based in West Olive, with the goal of using thermochromic technology to make a sunlight responsive film for use in windows. After years of experimentation, he invented self-tinting windows with a thermochromic film interlayer, aptly named "Suntuitive," made of polyvinyl butyral, which respond to temperature changes from sunlight. To successfully market the product, Byker and his team, including his brother David, had to create a neutral-colored film without troubling imperfections, develop the extrusion manufacturing process, and ensure its durability in a variety of buildings from homes to skyscrapers.[73]

In 2010 Pleotint received a $400,000 federal grant to help demonstrate the energy efficiency of the "dynamic windows." They found that they reduce heating and cooling costs up to 10 percent and minimize the need for window coverings. The next year Pleotint began manufacturing the high-tech windows in its plant in Jenison, under a joint marketing agreement with Pittsburgh-based PPG that combined its low-emissivity (low-e) glass with the thermochromic interlayer. In 2012 these unique windows were installed in some twenty buildings around the world. Byker has the unusual distinction as a scientist of making two significant inventions in his lifetime: electrochromic technology for self-dimming automobile mirrors and thermochromic technology for energy efficient windows in architectural settings.[74]

Prince Corporation (now Johnson Controls)

In December 1965, Ed Prince, chief engineer at Buss Machine Works for nearly ten years, left to found his own die-cast machinery company, which would become in the next thirty years the largest employer in Holland. The young entrepreneur, then only thirty-four

72 *Grand Rapids Press*, 12 Dec. 2010, 21 Oct., 1, 19 Dec. 2011, 4 Oct. 2012; *Holland Sentinel*, 1 Feb., 10 Aug. 2012.

73 I am indebted to Harlan Byker for this history of his company. See also John Rumery and Matthew Gryczan, "Easing the Pane of Energy Costs: Pleotint Launches Smart Window Film," 27 May 2010, www.rapidgrowmedia.com.

74 *Grand Rapid Press*, 19 June 2010; "PPG, Pleotint to co-market environmentally adaptive glazing technology with low-e glass," 19 Sept. 2011, www.ppg.com/en/newsroom/news/Pages/20220919P.aspx.

years of age, borrowed against his modest home for part of the start-up capital, and put up a small metal building on a dirt road east of US-31 near Thirty-Second Street. He hired as his chief engineer, Bill Van Appledorn, who like himself had "cut his teeth" in the trade at Buss. Prince brought two other key people from Buss: Wayne Alofs as his plant manager and Henry Vander Kolk as his head of assembly operations. Vander Kolk, although legally blind, was very adept at organizing production work. These four and several others left Buss Machine in the lurch, but the recent decision of Buss laborers to unionize did not sit well with Prince and the others. Bill Vogelzang, no mean businessman himself, considered Ed Prince "one of those genius guys—difficult to get along with, but a brilliant mind. He could see the end from the beginning."[75]

In the first years, Prince Machine operated on a shoestring, primarily rebuilding used die cast machines; every contract was precious and every piece of equipment a financing challenge. Frugality was inherent to Ed Prince, a "depression baby" who knew how to pinch a penny, especially after growing up without a father. (Peter Prince, a produce dealer, had died of a heart attack at age thirty-six in 1943, when Ed was only eleven years old.) The front office and the engineering and purchasing departments were in a concrete block addition to the plant. The water supply for the entire operation was a two-inch pvc pipe laid from the main at Thirty-Second Street. For drafting paper on which to sketch designs, Prince sent Van Appledorn to Peter Yff, a local butcher, to obtain meat-wrapping paper. They unrolled the paper on a card table and began drawing machinery layouts. The entire crew put in incredibly long hours, often starting at five o'clock in the morning and continuing late into the evening.[76]

Machinery salesman John Spoelhof of Wing & Jabaay Machine Tool Sales of Grand Rapids, who had been trained on the tool and die bench at the Fisher Body Plant in Grand Rapids, sold Prince the first two pieces of equipment, a used lathe and drill press. To clinch

[75] Massie, *Haven, Harbor and Heritage*, 198-99; William Van Appledorn phone conversation, 8 Aug. 2007; William Vogelzang interview by the author and Dave Boeve, 30 Sept. 2009, typescript, JAH. Buss employees joined the Christian Labor Association (CLA).

[76] Peter Prince obit., *Holland Sentinel*, 21 May 1943; Andrew Wierda, ed., *Edgar D. Prince Legacy Project*, "In His Words, Sept. 28, 1993 [Ed Prince]," Part I, 4; Insights, Part II. Employee recollections of Bill Van Appledorn, 22, used by permission of Emilie Prince Wierda. Peter Prince also grew up without a father. In 1908 when Peter was one year old, his father John Prince was struck and killed by an automobile on Eighth Street, according to great-granddaughter Emily Prince Wierda.

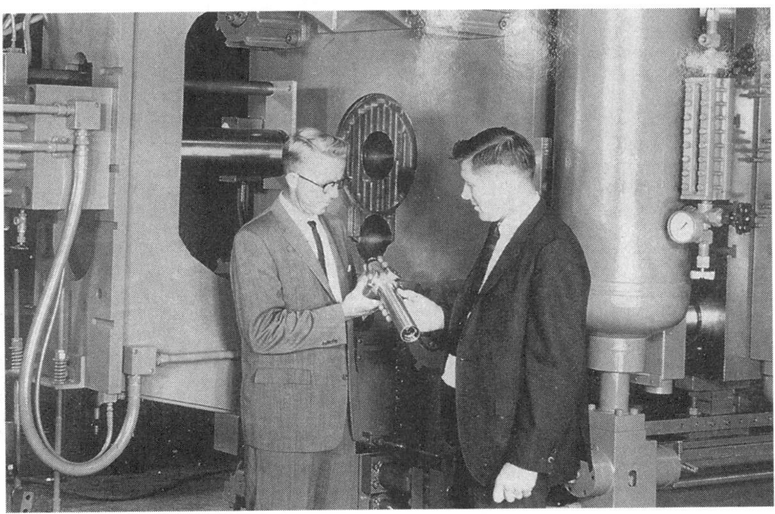

Ed Prince (*right*) confers with a customer, ca. 1968
(*courtesy Prince Corp. and Larry B. Massie*)

the deal, Spoelhof got his boss to back the Old Kent Bank loan. From this initial contact, Spoelhof, age twenty-five, and Prince, age thirty-four, developed a friendship that four years later, in late 1969, resulted in Spoelhof joining the Prince team. Both men were "cut from the same cloth" as machinists and members of the Christian Reformed Church. Teamwork was the hallmark of Prince operations–in the front offices and on the shop floor. Company operations reflected Ed Prince's character, which Spoelhof aptly described in a 2009 interview. Prince was "relentless in pursuit . . . absolutely the most intense guy for wanting to get things done. . . . It would be, 'let's do it,' . . . 'let's get a group together'. . . . He's a can-do guy . . . with lofty expectations [and] . . . a lot of passion and pursuit. But he was just tremendously fair and kind," Spoelhof concluded.[77]

The first two die cast machines went out the door within five months, in May 1966. Soon Prince had to scramble to build several dozen machines for Honeywell of Minneapolis; it was the first big contract. A General Motors contract soon followed. The workforce went from two to eighty within three years, and the capacity of the machines increased from 600-ton pressure to 1,600-ton pressure;

[77] This section relies on interviews by the author with Elsa Prince Broekhuizen, 18 Nov. 2009; Konrad Marcus, 16 Oct. 2009; John Spoelhof, 4 Dec. 2009 (quotes); and Robert Haveman, 20 Nov. 2009. Transcripts of Prince Broekhuizen, Marcus, and Spoelhof interviews are in JAH.

Busy shop floor at Prince Machine Co. ca. 1970
(*courtesy Prince Corp. and Larry B. Massie*)

the latter behemoth weighed 250,000 pounds and sold for $250,000. Chrysler bought it to form forty-pound aluminum transmission cases at its Kokomo, Indiana assembly plant at a rate of one case every two minutes. In 1967 Prince cheated death at Tulip City Airport when the company plane, piloted by twenty-year-old Ronald Ludema, ran out of gas on a flight from Syracuse, New York and made a belly landing in a cornfield three thousand feet short of the runway. Both men walked away unhurt.[78]

About 1969 Ed Prince's brother-in-law Ted Zwiep, also a skilled engineer in the plant, had an idea. "Let's build a machine to take the meat off a ham bone," he said to Ed. "That's kind of a strange business for a machine company," Ed replied. But he gave his approval, and assigned new engineer Kon Marcus to the project. Ed had recently recruited him from Donnelly Corp., where he had worked in management for fifteen years. Ted's machine reduced the time by one-third over manual de-boning. American meat processors very much wanted the machine, but their strongly unionized workforces resisted, because it made hand de-boning obsolete. Hormel did successfully use the machines in their Iowa meatpacking plants. European and Russian meat processors also bought several dozen machines, but the product line never flourished. After sinking several million dollars into the venture, Prince Corp. sold the rights to a Dutch company. In hindsight, the project was "dumb," Prince admitted later. But it provided work when the bottom fell out of the machinery business in 1970-71.

[78] *Holland Sentinel*, 22 May 1967, 5 June 1969.

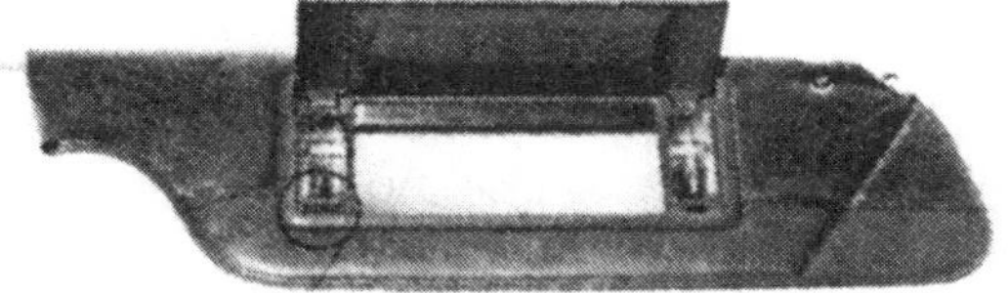

Lighted vanity visor for passenger side of 1972 Cadillac, designed by Prince Corp. engineer Konrad Marcus, was the firm's first automotive product (*Holland Sentinel*, 18 July 1996)

The secret to success at Prince Corporation, besides maintaining the highest ethical standards, was Ed Prince's decision to venture into the auto parts business, notably by designing and manufacturing the first lighted vanity visor that Cadillac, a luxury brand, ordered by the millions of dollars. Marcus, the vice president of product development and an inventive genius, devised the visor. Women loved the visor mirrors and automakers around the world signed on for them. It was their first big hit in the automotive parts venture, and it opened the door for Prince in the industry.

The idea came to Marcus one night in the late 1960s when his wife had difficulty applying lipstick in their darkened family car. Ed Prince thought the idea had possibilities and gave Kon the go-ahead, as he was wont to do with all his engineers. In 1971 Kon made a crude model by filing down a Tupperware dish and attaching a mirror and light to it. After the company filed a patent with the US Patent Office, they approached Ford Motor Company but were turned away. Prince, Marcus, and Spoelhof then visited the head of interior design at GM's Cadillac division, a man Marcus knew. The GM executive and his bosses "really liked the idea," and they asked to see a prototype. Weeks later as the trio was driving back to Detroit with the prototype, they discussed pricing. They roughly calculated the cost of materials and settled on a price per item that would provide a safe profit margin. At Ed's insistence, they also agreed that if Cadillac would not allow Prince to make the complete visor assembly, they would walk out of the meeting. When Cadillac executives demanded that very thing, the Holland men stood up to leave. At this, the executives readily backed down and ordered five hundred visors for the 1972 Cadillac.[79]

79 *Holland Sentinel*, 1 Jan. 2000.

The trio assured the executives that they could fill the order, but in truth they had no machine or production protocol to make the visors. The trick was to sew the plastic molding to the fabric, mirror, and light. The light had to be bright enough, but not cast a glare that might distract the driver. Since none of them knew how to sew, Ed told Kon to buy two commercial sewing machines, and over the weekend each dissembled and reassembled the machines to learn exactly how they functioned. They found that the sewing machine needles could not penetrate plastic with the desired exactness, given the uncontrollable speed of electric machines. Ed and his team drew on their expertise in hydraulic technology to devise a sewing machine powered by a hydraulic system that delivered slow-speed constant torque. For the next three months, Kon and a team of engineers sewed visors from dawn to dusk, making fifty a day. The assembly process also included plastic injection molding, sonic welding, and a host of other technical steps, including installing glass in such a shatter-resistant way, so as not to cut the faces of passengers in a crash. As Cadillac increased its orders by the week, the visor team designed a production system of a dozen sewing machines driven by one hydraulic system. Engineer Carl Flowerday headed up the project and became known as "Mr. Sun Visor." Prince Corp. was in the automotive business to stay, and as Spoelhof noted, "We created an enormous amount of value in a short period of time."[80]

Within a year, by 1973, the factory was producing thousands of the visors a day and ramping up production to the current sixty thousand per day, enough to supply forty-three automotive assembly plants around the world. Spoelhof and his team had all they could do to build more factory space to keep up with the demand. The company was on its ninth addition, a tenfold increase in floor space since 1965, which came online just as their engineers had developed an onboard computer that calculated gas mileage with every fill-up. It was in response to the first oil cartel embargo that put a premium on more efficient consumption. Prince suffered a heart attack in 1974 at the age of forty-two. This led him to reevaluate his priorities and devote more time to family and Christian causes.[81]

In 1978 Prince turned the presidency and day-to-day operations over to Spoelhof, retaining the title and role of chairman of the board. By this time, Prince engineers had designed map lights for the 1978 Ford Mustang and floor consoles for the 1979 Cadillac Seville. Prince

80 Spoelhof interview, JAH.

81 Wierda, "In His Words," 7; *Holland Sentinel*, 16 May 1973.

Ed Prince the year he retired from Prince Corp. (*Board of Public Works*, Annual Report, *1978*)

Corp., with 450 employees, was the fastest growing company in the Holland area, with a payroll of $6 million.[82]

To fill the orders, the company bought the former Roamer Boat facility off Lakewood Boulevard at a bargain price of $1 million. Five years later, they added a large addition to manufacture floor consoles. In 1983 Prince and his team brought together the sales, engineering, and purchasing departments in the new Corporate Center on South Waverly Avenue. Employment in 1984 reached one thousand, the majority women, and sales topped $100 million. Prince Corp. from the early days gave 5 percent of pretax earnings to non-profits, charities, and Christian schools. Ed Prince gave the money without strings attached. "If God's given me this money, and I've been directed to give it away this way," he said, "then he's going to make sure that its used in the right way. . . . And if it isn't, then they don't get any more money." His gifts include ten acres for Holland's Davenport College (later University) campus, donations to Hope and Calvin Colleges, James Dobson's Focus on the Family, Family Research Council, Haggai Institute, Hospice of Holland, $2.5 million to help found Evergreen Commons Senior Center (chapter 31), and $250,000 for the city snowmelt system (chapter 33), among others.[83]

The next big hit was the overhead console with a digital compass, mileage information, outside temperature reading, and map lights for the 1985 Chrysler New Yorker luxury sedan and the new and wildly

82 *Holland Sentinel*, 19 Jan. 1978, 26 Jan. 1980.

83 Spoelhof interview (quote), JAH; *Holland Sentinel*, 29 Jan. 1983, 3 Aug., 11 Sept. 1992, 27 Jan. 1993, 3 Mar. 1995.

Workers at Prince Corp. make a plastic mold for a sun visor base, 1980 (*courtesy Randall P. Vande Water*)

popular 1986 Dodge and Plymouth minivans. To fill these orders, Prince in 1987 built the Beechwood facility on the Roamer site. The year before, the firm had added the Southview Campus to produce door panels and handles, headliners, and overhead consoles, and paid for it with cash generated by the business. In 1988 Prince consolidated the design, engineering, modeling, and electronics departments in the Technology Center. During the tremendous growth spurt of the 1980s, the company workforce grew from six hundred to two thousand, and floor space increased tenfold to more than one million square feet. The key to growth for "first-tier" auto suppliers like Prince was to meet the changing demands of the assembly companies for suppliers to design products as well as make them. Prince Corporation excelled at this. They gave their word and kept it.[84]

From the outset, Ed Prince had determined to treat his employees as family, a goal that Spoelhof readily emulated. Bruce Los, vice president of human resources, saw to it that every plant was built with employee well being in mind, including brightly lit assembly floors, cafeterias, and fitness rooms. When the leadership team realized the financial benefits of healthier employees, they bought the Holland Tennis Club and turned it into the People's Center (now MVP), where employees were given financial incentives to work out. The company opened a $2 million

[84] *Holland Sentinel*, 11 Jan. 1986, 28 Jan., 29, 31 Aug. 1987, 21 Aug. 1994.

Prince Corp. Southview Campus, September 1987, looking south toward US-196 and M-40 interchange (*courtesy Randall P. Vande Water*)

medical center staffed by sixteen professionals—physicians, nurses, lab technicians, a pharmacist, and x-ray technicians—to treat employees on and off the job. Equally important, Prince gave annual bonuses based on individual performance and company profitability. The company in 1975 also instituted a defined-contribution, profit sharing plan that vested employees with company stock, known officially as an Employees Stock Ownership Trust, or ESOT. These policies stood the employees in good stead; teamwork was the modus operandi and the key to the company's success.[85]

Growth continued in the 1990s, with more state-of-the-art facilities, the People's Center, Interior Technology building, and two plants to produce door panels—Maplewood and Meadowbrook—behind the Tulip City Airport, which Prince facility also owned and developed to house company jets that kept executives and major customers connected. In 1990 Prince Corp. included nine buildings on three campuses, plus partnerships in Mexico City and England. The latter were harbingers of the future, since the team saw much growth potential in Europe and Asia. Bruce Los' staff could hardly hire enough employees; his office was processing twelve thousand job applications

85 Spoelhof interview, JAH; *Holland Sentinel*, 19 Jan. 1978, 11 Oct. 1988, 25 Jan. 1994, 25 Feb. 1996; Mike Lozon, "Prince brings the doctor to work," ibid., 16 Feb. 1997.

a year. They planned to hire three hundred engineers and thousands of assembly workers over the next few years. In the decade from 1986 to 1996, payroll went from three thousand to five thousand, and the company culture engendered a sense of community that knit them together.[86]

At the apex of success, Ed Prince died at age sixty-three on March 2, 1995, from a massive heart attack. The *Holland Sentinel* headline best voiced the community sentiments: "Holland loses a Prince." The *Grand Rapids Press Lakeshore Edition* declared him "A Christian man," a "giant," citing his spirit of giving. Being recognized as a Christian would have pleased Prince, but not the accolades for philanthropy; he was simply an obedient steward of the talents and monies God put in his hands. The eulogies at his funeral service focused on his Christian faith and its outworkings. The Reverend James Lont compared him to "an Old Testament prophet/warrior," and his wife Elsa described him as a "high-energy visionary" whose passion was to be of service to others.[87]

At his death, controlling ownership of the privately held corporation passed to his wife Elsa Zwiep Prince. Ed had been planning for a leadership transition that would keep the company private. Because of his sudden death, Elsa and her children felt compelled to sell the greater part of the company to Johnson Controls Inc. (JCI) of Milwaukee, a diverse multinational company that promised to carry on operations in Holland. Two years later, in 1998, JCI attached its name to the Holland plants, and the Prince name began to fade into history.[88]

After the JCI sale for $1.35 billion in 1997, the employees received a lump sum payout of their retirement accounts, totaling almost $300 million, and in addition, Elsa Prince gave bonuses of $80 million to some 4,500 employees based on longevity, as a token of appreciation for their part in making the company a success. With profit-sharing payouts and bonuses, some employees received checks of more than six-figures. Elsa Prince's decision to share the sale proceeds with employees was likely the most generous gesture by an owner ever witnessed in Michigan industrial history. But it was in keeping with her late husband's policy from the beginning of tithing company profits to

86 *Holland Sentinel*, 20, 21 June 1994, 19 July 1996; *Grand Rapids Press Lakeshore Edition*, 18, 21 July 1996.

87 Edgar D. Prince obit., *Holland Sentinel*, 3 Mar. 1995; Mike Lozon, "The man who shaped downtown Holland," ibid.; *Grand Rapids Press Lakeshore Edition*, 3, 6 Mar., 7 May 1995.

88 *Holland Sentinel*, 4 Mar. 1994, 19, 20 July 1996, 19 Aug. 1998; *Grand Rapids Press Lakeshore Edition*, 18 July, 28 Sept. 1996.

community organizations and charities. A wall plaque in the executive suite declared simply: "We tithe company profits."[89]

Two years later, in 1999, Elsa Prince sold the Prince Machine division, one of the largest producers of die casting equipment in the United States, to the Italian firm Idra, which renamed it IdraPrince. Idra in 2006 sold to the Swiss firm, Bühler, and it became BuhlerPrince. In 2008 Idra invested $2 million in the Windcrest Drive plant in Holland Township. BuhlerPrince with its one hundred employees was the largest producer of die casting equipment for the Big Three auto companies in North America.[90]

The sharp loss in market share of the Big Three, however, was a challenge for auto suppliers. JCI gradually cut its Holland workforce by more than one-third and closed the Meadowbrook and Zeeland facilities in favor of outsourcing visor assembly lines to Mexico. This again proved the adage, "When local owners sell, jobs leave." Seven hundred jobs in Holland were saved when JCI supplier Plastech Engineering Products of Dearborn in 2007 bought the Southview plant that made interior door panels and continued production there. When Plastech went bankrupt in 2008, JCI took over the operations.[91]

In 2009 Johnson Controls announced the formation of a joint venture with the French company, Saft Advanced Power Solutions, to be called Johnson Controls-Saft. JCI wanted to tap Saft's expertise in lithium-ion car batteries and bring production to its empty Meadowbrook building. The $299 million contract put Holland at the center of cutting-edge technology, which fact likely prompted the South Korean industrial giant LG Chem Ltd. to invest $303 million in a new plant to manufacture hybrid automotive batteries on Prince land on East Forty-Eighth Street. In 2010 LG Chem announced plans for an adjacent plant to produce electrolyte, a key component of batteries. With the battery plant under construction, JCI in 2010 began hiring again. The firm remains the largest employer in the Holland area with nine plants. In September 2011, three months after the Holland plant began production, Johnson Controls severed its partnership with Saft, upon paying $145 million in cash for access to the "li-ion" technology, because of disagreements over the "future direction of the joint venture."[92]

89 Mike Lozon, "New era begins at Prince," *Holland Sentinel*, 2 Oct. 1996. I am indebted to Elsa Prince Broekhuizen, Emily Prince Wierda, Robert Haveman, and John Spoelhof for information about the sale of Prince Corp.

90 *Holland Sentinel*, 4 Apr. 2004, 13 Dec. 2006.

91 Ibid., 1 Jan., 20, 25 Feb., 2 Dec. 2007, 5 Feb., 21 May 2008.

92 Ibid., 17 Nov. 2008, 28 Mar., 15, 16, 28 Apr., 6 Aug., 15 Oct., 27 Dec. 2009, 4 Feb., 14, 15 Sept., 6 Nov. 2010, 3 Sept. 2011 (quote); *Grand Rapids Press Lakeshore Edition*, 17 Oct. 2008, 5, 10 Jan. 2010; *Grand Rapids Press*, 5 Aug. 2011.

The two battery plants, which received 35 percent of all federal funding for these advanced technologies, promised to turn Holland into a national epicenter of green energy and hoped to spark ten thousand new jobs and $2 billion in new investment over the next ten years. President Obama made two visits to the Holland plants to tout the "green" technology. The "car battery start-ups," however, "have fizzled," according to a *Wall Street Journal* report in late May 2012, because of slow sales of electric vehicles. LG Chem's 220 workers have yet to begin production, and the Johnson Controls facility has been "nearly idle." In fact, LG Chem has put workers on "'rolling furloughs' . . . and plans to continue doing so until there's more demand for their product." The $1.26 billion in federal subsidies for nine American companies manufacturing car batteries promised 6,400 jobs, but they total only 2,000 employees after spending two-thirds of the money, said the report. In 2012 JCI attempted to purchase the automotive assets of the bankrupt Waltham, MA-based A123 Systems, a competitor in lithium-ion battery cell technology with in-state plants in Livonia and Romulus, but JCI lost out to a Chinese competitor.[93]

Recreational boat building

The invention of the steam and gas marine engines in the 1880s made possible a new dimension in boating, the manufacture of recreational boats. By 1920 two cottagers on Black Lake saw their steam yachts claim supremacy for speed. Ohioan A. J. Glanton, a Macatawa Park resident, boasted that his yacht *Amerigo* could go thirty-five miles per hour. Chicagoan Egbert H. Gold of Marigold Lodge took up the challenge with his steam yacht *Sundance*, which topped twenty-six miles per hour but could be "shoved up a notch." The racing yachts brought a friendly rivalry that put a "little pop in things" around the resorts. Yacht Clubs sprang up around Lake Michigan, notably the West Michigan Yachting Association, and members with sailing ships and motorboats challenged each other in regattas and processions, such as the Venetian Night Regatta every July, with the resorts at Macatawa Bay a regular stopping point. Thousands came out to witness the spectacle, complete with water shows and fireworks.[94]

The pleasure boat craze in the prosperous twenties spurred the boat-building industry, led by the Chris-Craft Boat Company of

93 *Wall Street Journal*, 31 May 2012; *Holland Sentinel*, 31 Aug., 27 Oct. 2012; A123 Systems, accessed 20 Mar. 2013.

94 *Holland City News*, 10 June 1920; 19, 26 July 1928, 23 Mar. 1939; Bernard P. Donnelly obit., *Holland Sentinel*, 3, 4 Mar. 2003.

Algonac, Michigan. In 1928 Chris-Craft sold 850 boats, Hacker Boat Company sold 250 boats, Gar Wood Company sold 300, and Dart Company 175. Profit margins ranged from 30 to 50 percent on the sleek wooden boats. Holland was an ideal locale for building, servicing, and storing speedboats and yachts; its inner lake provided safe anchorage, the work ethic was strong, and hundreds of skilled carpenters formerly employed in the furniture factories could readily be retooled to build pleasure craft. Indeed, it was the pleasure boat factories like Chris-Craft, Slick Craft, and later Tiara Yachts, S2 Yachts, and PowerQuest Boats, that looked to these craftsmen for their workforce. Holland has been home to some thirty-five boat manufacturing companies in the past century.[95]

North Star Marine, Gil-Boat, Campbell Boat

In October 1929, Holland entrepreneur Milo Bailey opened a new company, the North Star Marine Construction Company, to "Fordize" the industry by mass-producing speedboats in the $1,300 to $1,500 price range. This was one-third less than the cheapest price of competitors. The timing was bad; the New York stock market crashed that very month, and the economy went into the tank. Bailey responded by appealing to more snobbish customers, offering "really different" boats, "modern in the extreme," at prices up to $1,850, which although more pricey, still undercut competitors.[96]

The Great Depression crimped the pleasure boat industry, but some companies survived by appealing to niche markets. Mark L. Gilbert opened Gil-Boat Company in 1935 with a "better idea." Along with outboard motors, Gil-Boat made specialty craft—rowboats, unsinkable lifeboats, and futuristic cross-lake ferries—all constructed with rolled steel and aluminum. Business looked good at first, but in 1940, after five years, the company was insolvent amid charges of financial mismanagement, and two years later it was sold at liquidation.[97]

In 1937 Kenneth Campbell of Campbell Boat Company took another tack. A naval architect, he began building luxury sailboats in the fifty-foot class at dock facilities near Virginia Park, mostly for wealthy Chicago yachtsmen. This was the first company since the schooner era of the 1850s and 1860s to build sailing vessels in Holland. One of the

95 This and the next several paragraphs rely on Reynolds, "Boat Building in Holland," 99-104.

96 *Holland Sentinel*, 19 Oct. 1929, North Star advertising brochure, JAH.

97 *Holland City News*, 22 Nov. 1934, 3 July 1940, 23 Apr. 1942; Holland realtor John Arendshorst bought the real estate and personal property of the Gil-Boat concern.

premier vessels Campbell Boat christened with the traditional bottle of champagne broken against the hull was the *Batavia*, a speedy cutter designed for racing on Lake Michigan. Campbell Boat Works under master "boss" Edward Brown also built scows, cruisers, fishing tugs, and pile drivers. It flourished until 1953, when Campbell's health failed, and he sold to Beacon Boat Company. Beacon continued to build sailboats, yachts, and during the Korean War, wooden mine sweepers and navy utility boats. In 1960 Robert Dawson Sr. and his son Robert Jr. purchased Beacon Boat and renamed it South Shore Marine. They also made boats under the Great Lakes name from 1984 to 1986. The Dawsons carried on the marina and shipyard until 2003, when Robert Jr. died. In 1948 two protégés of Campbell's company, the furniture manufacturer Arthur Pelgrim and his son-in-law Jim White, established Mac Bay Boat Company. This was the first American manufacturer of inboard motorboats constructed of cheaper but more durable molded plywood. Mac Bay Boats was sold and production moved to Muskegon in 1956.[98]

Chris-Craft

The most important pleasure craft builder in Holland was Chris-Craft Corp. of Algonac. The Algonac firm, known for its speedboats with innovative hulls that "unzipped" the water, had been plagued by union labor conflicts, and the exasperated president Jay W. Smith, son of founder Christopher Columbus Smith, knew of Holland's reputation for Dutch Reformed wood craftsmen who eschewed unions. He opened a Holland plant in 1938. Many men were out of work at the time, and they welcomed the new company, which hired 240 and planned to add a hundred more.

First, however, city officials had to spike a rumor among workers that former mayor Abe Stephan, secretary of the chamber of commerce, had urged Smith to reduce the scheduled wages, so as to entice more such plants to Holland. Stephan vehemently denied the charge. Christopher Columbus Smith died before the factory opened on Aniline Avenue to the north of Ottawa Beach Road, but his sons Jay and Bernard, and grandson Harsen, carried the company to 1960. Jay and Bernard imbibed from their father the idea of copying Henry Ford's philosophy of manufacturing cheap cars for everyman with efficient assembly-line production. The Pere Marquette rail spurs connecting

98 Ibid., 26 Aug. 1937, 21 July, 18 Aug. 1938; *Holland Sentinel*, 11 July 1953; Lois Kayes, "Campbell Boat Company," Apr. 1994, one-page typescript, JAH.

Chris-Craft 15.5 foot "runabout," first production craft in Holland plant, 1939 (*Joint Archives of Holland*)

the plant to the national rail network were crucial in the 1930s, before interstate trucking supplanted rail shipments.[99]

The first product turned out in Holland in 1940 was a 15.5-foot mahogany "runabout" designed for speed. Its sixty-horsepower inboard motor and special hull design gave the hydroplane-type racing boat a top speed of thirty miles per hour. The boat sold for $475, the same price as a Model T, and quickly won a huge following. A decade later, in 1940, the factory was turning out thirty-one-footers. The firm so dominated its market that people commonly called all speedboats Chris-Crafts.

During the Second World War, the firm diverted production to marine landing craft, producing more than twelve thousand of the thirty-six-foot vessels. Shortly after V-J Day in September 1945, union members walked out in sympathy with fellow members at the Cadillac plant who were on strike (chapter 23). When production resumed, the Holland workers again crafted sleek wooden cruisers desired by newly prosperous Americans. Of the tens of thousands of boats manufactured in Holland at that time, the few that still survive are the pride of antique boat collectors. After the war, Chris-Craft also made cabin cruisers, ranging up to forty-two feet in length. So heavy was the demand that

99 *Holland City News*, 3, 10 Aug., 21 Sept., 16 Nov. 1939; *Holland Sentinel*, 20 Sept. 1939, 7 Nov. 1940; Mary Ann Sabo, "Boat Bonanza," *Grand Rapids Press Lakeshore Edition*, 8 Aug. 1999. Bernard Smith served for a time as vice-president. His son, Christopher John Smith, an engineer, worked in the Holland plant until 1985. Harsen, a vice president under his father Jay, was chairman of the board from 1958 to 1960.

Aerial view of sprawling Chris-Craft plant on Ottawa Beach Road at Aniline Drive, early 1940s (*Joint Archives of Holland*)

the company in 1953 added a new wing and boosted employment by 25 percent, to one thousand people.[100]

The Chris-Craft workers at the Algonac and Holland plants had organized into three craft unions (carpenters, machinists, and painters), and in 1954, the three AFL-affiliated locals struck the Michigan plants over wages and benefits. But the unions had signed up only one-quarter of the workers, which gave them a weak hand. The strike in Holland turned violent, and the company was forced to close the factory. One hundred out-of-town unionists joined in mass picketing at plant entrances, and when non-strikers drove cars in to work, strikers tried to block them, smashing windows, and physically assaulting some. County sheriffs had to intervene to maintain order. The company played hardball, withdrew its contract offer, and advised lower-seniority workers to "seek employment elsewhere."[101]

In 1955 the company added a new division by acquiring for $117,000 the rival Roamer Steel Boat Company of Robert Linn, whose firm had focused on steel-hulled cabin cruisers since its launch in 1946

[100] Sabo, "Boat Bonanza"; *Holland City News*, 7 Nov. 1940, 8 May 1953; *Holland Sentinel*, 29 Aug. 1945; Bob Vande Vusse, "Holland's Chris-Craft plant contributed to war effort," *Holland Sentinel*, 20 May 2001.

[101] *Holland Sentinel*, 25 Mar. 1954.

Chris-Craft plant in the 1950s, when trucks supplanted rail cars for shipments (*Joint Archives of Holland*)

on South Shore Drive. Ken Campbell of the Campbell Boat Company gave Linn his start and allowed him to use his facilities for several years. Linn completed his first all-welded steel boat in 1946, a thirty-two-foot express cruiser. Steel had the advantage of strength and durability. By 1950 Roamer Boat Co. occupied a factory at 961 Washington Avenue. During the Korean War, the firm made thirty-one tugs for the US Navy.[102]

For its new Roamer Division, Chris-Craft in 1956 built a new plant on Lakewood Boulevard and hired 350 workers to staff six production lines. At its height in 1960, the firm's seven hundred employees had as many as 120 boats in various stages of production on nine production lines in a half dozen buildings on twenty-two acres. An open house that year attracted 6,700 enthusiastic visitors. At the pinnacle of success in 1960, the Smith family, reportedly because of union activism, sold the company to National Automotive Fibers Inc. (NAFI), which named the division NAFI Chris-Craft. In 1962 Herb Siegel, a young venture capitalist, took over the company and combined the boat business with his other considerable interests, under the name Chris-Craft Industries. Siegel later drained the boat division's considerable cash reserves trying to gain control of Piper Aircraft. In the 1960s, aluminum replaced steel as the preferred "skin" for Roamer Division yachts. In 1966 the union

102 Geoffrey D. Reynolds, "Made of Steel: The History of the Roamer Boat Company," *Joint Archives Quarterly* 21, no. 1 (Spring 2011): 1-4.

Chris-Craft famed wooden speedboats on the water, with Chris Smith II and grandson in the foremost boat (*Joint Archives of Holland*)

locals struck the Holland plants and picketed them for more than three months.[103]

Boat technology was in flux at this time, with fiberglass threatening to undo wooden craft, the Chris-Craft cachet for more than a century. Chris-Craft Industries, the new company, built a prototype fiberglass boat in a top-secret, walled-off area in one of the Holland plants. The company switched entirely to fiberglass a few years later. The last wooden Chris-Craft, a fifty-seven-foot Constellation built for National Football League Commissioner Pete Rozelle, came off the line at Holland in 1972. Wooden boats were not selling in the volume needed to support a company as large as Chris-Craft. In 1975 Roamer left Holland for Florida and four years later closed the company.[104]

In 1989 the 450 union workers at Chris-Craft again went on strike, and this time some one hundred non-union employees honored the picket lines. The labor strife and ongoing financial issues compelled Chris-Craft Industries to sell the Boat Division in 1981 to G. Dale Murray and Associates of Murray Industries Inc. of Bradenton, Florida. The Murray Chris-Craft Cruisers Co. gradually shuttered its Holland plants between 1985 and 1989, when the last seventy-five of 350

[103] *Holland Sentinel*, 31 Mar., 1 Nov. 1955; *Holland City News*, 1, 8 Apr. 1954, 10 May 1956, 23 June 1960, 12 Apr. 1962.

[104] Michael Lozon, "Chris-Craft," *Holland Sentinel*, 26 Jan. 1989; Sabo, "Boat Bonanza."

Sanding a Chris-Craft 35-foot wooden speedboat in 1968
(*Archives, Holland Historical Trust*)

employees, down from seven hundred, in the Aniline Avenue plant were laid off. The final straw came in 1989 when some 220 members of the Christian Labor Association (CLA) local went on strike.[105]

By then Murray Industries had filed for bankruptcy and announced the closing of the last Holland plant at the end of January 1989. The skeleton crew rolled out the last boat on January 27, 1989. The storied Chris-Craft line came to an ignoble end after selling 250,000 boats in the fifty years since 1939. Outboard Marine Corp. purchased the valuable trade name and assets in bankruptcy court later in 1989 for $58 million.[106]

Chris-Craft had a final chapter under the name Grand-Craft Corp., which company Steve Northuis founded in 1984 to refurbish old Chris-Craft boats. Why let the talents of the local craftsmen go to waste? They worked out of a nondescript building just beyond the Heinz pickle plant at 430 West Twenty-First Street on the corner of Ottawa Avenue. The next year, when Chris Smith's career at Chris-Craft ended, he joined Northuis in the refinishing business. In 1989 Northuis and Smith convinced Outboard Marine to commission a

105 The CLA was founded on Christian principles modeled after a similar union founded by Calvinists in the Netherlands. See Respas, "Christian Labor Association."

106 Lozon, "Chris-Craft"; *Holland City News*, 30 June 1966; *Holland Sentinel*, 6, 28 Jan. 1989, 8 Mar., 8 Sept. 1999, 30 July 2007; *Grand Rapids Press Lakeshore Edition*, 8 Mar. 1999.

special commemorative series of Chris-Craft boats that Grand-Craft would build. Smith did the design and engineering work on the classic reproductions, which included the instrument panels detailed with black on silver.

In 1992 Northuis and Smith sold Grand-Craft to Richard (Dick) Sligh of the Sligh Furniture family. Northuis then launched Macatawa Bay Works in Saugatuck and continued restoring old Chris-Crafts. Sligh kept the restoration work as a sideline, but he ventured into building new luxury boats of Philippine mahogany, all made to order from twenty-one to forty-eight feet, with twelve coats of varnish and prices to match, ranging from $60,000 to $500,000. His twelve-man crew in 1999 could hardly keep up with the orders from mariners who coveted the sleek craft. In 2005 the seventy-five-year-old Sligh sold Grand-Craft to Chicago-based TMB Industries but continued as president. The factory turned out twelve custom craft that year. In 2007 Tim Masek of Grand Rapids, a former TMB managing director, purchased Grand-Craft Corp. Two years later, in the teeth of the "Great Recession" that hit the wealthy hard, Grand-Craft defaulted on a $400,000 mortgage and closed after twenty-five years of making classic wooden boats in the tradition of Chris-Craft.[107]

Jeff Cavanagh, president of Anchorage Marine Services at 1825 Ottawa Beach Road, in 2009 purchased the assets from Macatawa Bank, including the Grand-Craft name and two unfinished Mahogany boats. They hired a dozen craftsmen to finish them with retro Chris-Craft styling and modern engines. In the first three years, Grand-Craft completed four boats, one a forty footer. They also refurbish several boats a year over the winter. In 2012 they successfully water tested a thirty-six-foot "commuter" craft valued at $480,000 and built on "spec." Cavanagh expects in the future to build custom Mahogany boats primarily on order.[108]

S2 Yachts (Slick Craft Boats)

Leon Slikkers, a Chris-Craft worker since 1946, formed the competing Slick Craft Boat Company in 1954 to build molded plywood speedboats, called runabouts. He started in his garage on Thirty-Fifth Street, and when sales perked up, he sold his house to raise $5,000 of start-up capital for a plant at 791 Washington Avenue. Slikkers lured

[107] Sabo, "Boat Bonanza"; *Holland Sentinel*, 15 May, 25 Sept. 2005, 14 Oct. 2007, 13 June 2009, 20 Sept. 2010.

[108] *Holland Sentinel*, 6 Aug. 2012.

many of his former colleagues to Slick Craft by offering higher wages and a craftsman-centered environment. The men were frustrated by the constant conflict at the union shop. In fact, Slikkers himself quit during a strike. After Chris-Craft began using the new fiberglass technology in 1958, Slikkers followed suit. It was a risk for both companies, but paid off handsomely by attracting new customers who lacked the time or the desire to varnish and refinish their boats every winter. The prudent Slikkers hedged his bet initially by making mahogany boats until the 1961 model year, when he switched production completely to fiberglass.[109]

At first Slikkers bought fiberglass hulls from Poll Manufacturing, a Holland firm of Clyde Poll, who had developed the process of overlaying sheets of fiberglass chemically welded with resin. Soon Slikkers mastered the difficult skill himself. He succeeded beyond his wildest dreams as a designer and builder of speedboats, cabin cruisers, and yachts, first as Slick Craft and after 1974 as S2 Yachts, which specialized in sailboats. The manufacturing site then was at 725 East Fortieth Street. In 1977, S2 introduced Tiara powerboats, and in 1983 came the Pursuit division, to manufacture sport-fishing powerboats in Florida. The next year, S2 "sailed ahead" with a $2 million expansion of its Fortieth Street plant and added two hundred to the workforce. The Tiara Yacht division, launched in 1986, built the famed luxury yachts, which were a natural evolution of the early sailboats. S2 Yachts was one of the few major boat builders to manufacture both sailboats and powerboats.[110]

The rapid growth of the 1980s came to a sudden halt when a Democratic Congress in 1990 imposed a 10 percent luxury tax on new boats priced above $100,000. The effect of the law was like turning off a faucet, said S2 executive Jon Marcus. "It was pretty abrupt." Layoffs reduced the workforce from eight hundred to three hundred. When the lawmakers corrected their mistake in 1994, West Michigan builders enjoyed an unparalleled "boat bonanza" that lasted more than a decade.[111]

In 1996 Leon Slikkers was named Michigan Manufacturing Entrepreneur of the Year, a well-deserved recognition. The superb fit and

[109] Reynolds, "Fifty Years of Making Fun: The History of the Slikkers Family and Boat Building," *Joint Archives Quarterly* 15 (Winter/Fall 2005); Reynolds, "Boat builder started craft early," *Holland Sentinel*, 6 Feb. 2005; Reynolds, "Business built with quality at center," ibid., 3 July 2005.

[110] *Holland Sentinel*, 11 Aug. 1984, 8 Aug. 1999.

[111] Ibid., 27 Jan. 1994.

S2 Yachts plant in full production, 1987
(*courtesy Randall P. Vande Water*)

finish of Tiara Yachts was so impressive that customers with thirty-five-footers came back for fifty-footers, priced at $1 million. Making boats was very labor intensive; thirty to forty sets of hands made everything from the fiberglass hull and teak cabinets in the galley to the advanced electronics. S2 capitalized on the skilled craftsmen in the Holland area who took pride in their work and spoke of vessels moving through the plant as "my boat."[112]

The best years in the boating industry came to another halt in 2000, when the "dot-com bubble" of 1995-2000 burst, and stock prices plummeted. Sales rebounded in 2004, until the mini-crash of 2008 on Wall Street, which was accompanied by plunging home prices, the bankruptcy of GM and Chrysler, and wholesale layoffs in every industry. The Great Recession of 2008-9 wiped out luxury boat sales again. This time Tiara/S2, then under Slikkers' sons David and Robert, had to lay off seven hundred of its eight hundred employees over eighteen months, a painful 87 percent drop. In desperation, the brothers went green. S2 spun off Energetx Composites to manufacture giant wind turbine blades for the utility industry. The technology to make the 145-foot blades of advanced composite materials was similar to that of shaping

[112] Ibid., 24 June 1996, 8 Aug. 1999 (quote).

yachts. This "perfect and unprecedented marriage," as grandson Kelly Slikkers declared, promised one thousand jobs in a new $6.5 million plant in the Southside Industrial Park off Forty-Eighth Street. Given the prospect of new hires, the State of Michigan designated the Energetx plant a Renaissance Zone, freeing it from state and local taxes for fifteen years. In May 2011, with the plant in operation, Governor Rick Snyder selected Energetx Composites as the recipient of his first Reinventing Michigan award. Yacht sales also came back. In 2011, S2 secured a contract to manufacture forty-four-foot yachts costing up to $2 million for the world-wide manufacturer Zeelander Yachts of the Netherlands, which brought seventy new jobs to the S2 plant.[113]

PowerPlay (PowerQuest) Boats

Slikkers' only real competition in Holland boat building came from Kevin Hirdes and Todd Kamps, water skiing buddies, who in 1983 formed a partnership, with each contributing $3,500 to buy a mold and some tools and supplies. They started building their first fiberglass boat in space rented from William Mouw for $200 a month. Kamps nicknamed the first boat "PowerPlay," which became the company name. But the space was too small, and the young men decided to build their own building and complete the boat there. They raised $35,000 from family and friends, and Hirdes borrowed to the hilt against his home, in order to buy several acres of farmland on the corner of 112th and James Street. With the help of family members and friends, they put up a pole building in the dead of winter, 1983-84. The fledgling entrepreneurs were taking a huge risk before they had completed even the first boat. They managed to complete the craft just in time for the 1984 Chicago Boat Show, where a man bought it, but then backed out the next day. They came home with the boat and no orders for more. They displayed the model a month later at the Grand Rapids Boat Show and again came up empty.[114]

At this critical juncture, they got two breaks. A friend, insurance agent Len Miller, ordered a boat, and Eric Robinson and George Jelsma of Anchorage Yacht Sales offered to be their dealer and buy six boats. "You know, we're trying not to act like we're ecstatic, but that's like a year-and-a-half production," Kamps recalled. The Anchorage

113 *Holland Sentinel*, 29 Jan. 2010, 10 Oct. 2010, 12 May 2011; *Grand Rapids Press*, 30 Oct. 2010, 22 Sept. 2011.

114 This section relies on Kevin Hirdes' interview by Geoffrey Reynolds, 1 Dec. 2003, typescript; Todd Kamps interview by Geoffrey Reynolds, 17 Feb. 2004 (quotes), both in JAH.

connection soon opened a door to Detroit's best boat dealer, Greg Kruger of Jefferson Beach Marina, who showed boats at Cobo Hall, and orders began to come in as the firm captured the fancy of speed demons. Soon they had fifty dealers across North America and were on their way. Neither partner drew a paycheck for the first six months in 1984; then they took out $110 a week. Hirdes' wife Linda ran the office, such as it was. Larry Brouwer, a twenty-year employee of S2 Yachts, was the first hire after he solicited the job. Other S2 craftsmen followed Brouwer to PowerPlay, as did Chris-Craft workmen who were being laid off as the company phased out. "My formula" as Kamps explained company labor policy, "was to hire great people that work hard," and then to work hard as owners "hand in hand with them. [That way] you become part of who they are and part of their families." The three key words were: honesty, trust, and integrity. Within fifteen years, PowerPlay at 2385 112th Avenue had $15 million in sales and 105 employees.

PowerPlay's crafts were fast performance boats, dubbed "cigarette boats" by the industry, because of their long sleek shape. They were considered the Corvette of sport boats. From ten boats in 1984, the factory made fifty in 1985, 150 in 1986, and 2,250 in 1987, with the dollar volume going up even more with the ever larger boats. The initial eighteen-foot models handled amazing well at sixty miles an hour. By 1999 the standard model was a thirty-eight-foot, twin-engine craft that sold for up to $266,000. Ed Wennersten, who started at Chris-Craft and Roamer Yachts, was their first chief designer, followed by Mark Bonnette, another Tiara guy. After John Spoelhof, then president of Prince Corporation, purchased Kamps' interest in 1989, the firm restyled itself PowerQuest Boats, in response to a lawsuit by a Florida boat builder who claimed to have patented the PowerPlay name. Spoelhof mentored Hirdes in mastering financial statements and running a profitable business. "John played a very significant role in our success," Hirdes noted. In 1998 the plant reached full capacity and had to expand.

In 2001 Hirdes and Spoelhof sold the company at its apex to Jack Moll of Grand Rapids and Rick Koster of Holland. It proved to be a wise decision, since pleasure craft were on the cusp of a serious downturn; sales seemed to rebound in 2004, but PowerQuest shut its doors in 2005, after losing $3.5 million over four years. In 2007 Phil Hall of Muskegon-based Coastal Performance Marine bought the assets, but was unsuccessful in his attempt to relaunch the company. The assets went on the auction block in late 2011.[115]

[115] *Grand Rapids Press*, 3 Dec. 2011.

Powerboat owners organized the "Water Poke Run," an annual race on Lake Michigan from South Haven to Whitehall that attracted one hundred boats. The roar of the mighty engines could be heard for miles along the shoreline. Although the racers received special dispensation for exceeding the ninety-decibel sound limit, the Ottawa County Sheriff's Office Marine Patrol regularly monitored the powerboats with decibel meters, compliments of the Spring Lake Property Owners Association. In 2007 dozens of owners received tickets for sound violations. They took the fines in stride, satisfied that the superbly crafted boats had proved their worth.[116]

Out of forty pleasure craft companies in the past century, Grand-Craft and Tiara/S2 Yachts are the only ones still operating in Holland. S2 survived the downturn with a skeleton crew in its plant at 725 East Fortieth Street, until the Slikkers brothers ventured into turbine blades. Chris-Craft, S2 Yachts, Grand-Craft, and the other classic Holland boat lines were among the elite in their fields and enhanced the city's reputation as a Mecca for boat aficionados. Indeed, Geoffrey Reynolds, local historian and classic boat enthusiast, aptly noted that boats earned Holland a national reputation before tulips became the rage.[117]

Chemicals and pharmaceuticals

Since the early twentieth century, the Holland-Zeeland area has been a center for chemicals, dyes, paints, printers' inks, and pharmaceuticals, including De Pree Chemical, Aniline Dye Works, Renzleman Paints, RepcoLite Paints, Steketee-Van Huis Printing, Warner-Lambert, Parke-Davis, Pfizer, J. B. Laboratories, Welch Laboratories, and Zeeland Chemicals. In the 1990s companies producing chemicals for the food and pharmaceutical industries had been the fastest-growing segment of the region's economy, accounting for 20 percent of the total industrial workforce; they are more stable than the cyclical office furniture and automotive industries, which also employ 20 percent of the factory labor force.[118]

116 *Grand Rapids Press Lakeshore Edition*, 8 Aug. 1999; Geoffrey Reynolds, "Small companies could survive despite hardships," *Holland Sentinel*, 30 Nov. 2003.

117 *Grand Rapids Press Lakeshore Edition*, 8 Aug. 1999, 25 Aug. 2006; *Holland Sentinel*, 5 June 2003, 26 Aug. 2007, 7 Feb. 2008, 27 Feb., 13 June 2009; Steve Vander Veen, "Efficiency isn't everything for boat builders," ibid., 25 Sept. 2005; Reynolds, "Small companies.".

118 Mike Lozon, "Chemical producers play major role in area's economy," *Holland Sentinel*, 13 Aug. 1995.

De Pree Chemical

Con De Pree, a registered pharmacist, began the chemical industry in a small way in 1906 by inventing a formaldehyde fumigator that disinfected enclosed spaces. The timing was perfect. The general public was just becoming aware of the spread of contagious diseases through airborne germs. De Pree began manufacturing the fumigators in two rooms over a store on Eighth Street. Meanwhile, he rented Otto Breyman's jewelry store to start the De Pree Drug Store on the southwest corner of Eighth Street and Central Avenue. Demand for the little machines increased rapidly, and Con formed the De Pree Chemical Company with local attorney Gerrit Diekema, Rol Eisele, and medical doctors Abraham Leenhouts and John J. Mersen.

In 1907 the company erected a three-story brick factory on Sixth and Central with 7,200 square feet of floor space, which allowed for new specialties such as embalming fluid that morticians nationwide came to prefer. The fumigator continued to be the growth engine. Health departments nationwide raved about its effectiveness in disinfecting homes, offices, schools, and even Pullman sleeping cars. After launching the chemical company, Con De Pree turned the drug store over to his brother Robert De Pree.[119]

Over the next five years, De Pree Chemical increased its capitalization to $200,000 and expanded the factory several times. Solid profit margins gave the shares a golden glow for investors; the directors paid 8 percent dividends consistently for the first two decades. In 1912 the factory spanned four buildings and was one of the largest in Holland. Fifteen salesmen traveled the country pushing its products. By then De Pree had developed San-Tox, a successful line of pre-packaged drug products for sale by druggists. The company advertised in the *Saturday Evening Post* and other mass-circulation magazines, and the trademark San-Tox, picturing a registered nurse, became a household name across the country.[120]

Sales were so strong by 1919 that De Pree Chemical needed to expand in a big way. Business interests at the company headquarters in Chicago tried to lure the firm, but De Pree, Diekema, and the other major stockholders remained committed to Holland. Instead, the company in 1920 bought the ten-acre site of the former C. L. King Basket Co. along Black Lake west of Van Raalte Avenue to Twelfth Street,

[119] *Holland: The Gateway of Western Michigan*; *Holland City News*, 17 Feb. 1910, "Forty Years Ago Today," 30 Apr. 1939.

[120] *Holland City News*, 5 Jan. 1956.

with the intent to consolidate all operations there. But plans changed when De Pree was able to expand directly to the west of their existing plant by buying the former James Kole Implement Company property on River Avenue and Sixth Street and all the property in between. De Pree then relocated its Chicago general office to Holland, along with some stenographers and clerks, and it also hired more local office help. Since the chemical company had become a vertically integrated and diversified corporation, it dropped *Chemical* from its name, becoming simply the De Pree Company. The assets of the Holland plant at the end of the year exceeded $1 million.[121]

The next year De Pree launched two new businesses on the former Kole site, a printing plant the equal of Steketee-Van Huis (see below) that employed thirty men, and the city's first paper box factory to manufacture boxes and cartons for packaging and shipping its products. The box company alone was a $200,000 business, and the printing plant began marketing a beautiful line of stationery, with names like Holland Fabric Finish and De Pree Quality Linen, all featuring a Dutch windmill on each box. With its significant footprint in Holland and its national marketing, De Pree could boast of being the "finest pharmaceutical establishment in the world."[122]

The best was yet to come. Chemists James De Pree, Andrew M. Hyma, and John Van Zoeren (the latter formerly with Holland Aniline) kept the De Pree Company focused on medical drugs by perfecting an antibiotic compound first discovered in Germany during the First World War but acquired by the United States government, called Arsaphenamine. Hyma joined the company in its first year, 1912, and remained for sixty-three years, while continuing his education in biochemistry until completing a doctorate at age fifty-seven. The De Pree board, consisting of P. Henry De Pree president, Edward J. De Pree vice president, Con De Pree secretary-treasurer, and Gerrit Diekema and Charles M. McLean, in 1923 founded a new subsidiary, De Pree Laboratories Inc., capitalized at $36,000, to manufacture and market the breakthrough drug. Local investors snapped up the stock offering.[123] In the 1920s James De Pree pioneered in manufacturing vitamins derived from special formulations, which he marketed under the Wheatamin name. Shortly after the B vitamin was discovered, De Pree in 1927

[121] Ibid., 31 July 1919, 8 Jan., 16 Sept. 1920, 5 Jan. 1956; De Pree Company, financial statement, 31 Dec., 1920 (De Pree Company Papers, box 1, HMA).

[122] *Holland City News*, 8 Jan. (quote), 16 Sept. 1920, 19 Jan. 1922.

[123] Ibid., 12 Apr. 1923, "Fifteen Years Ago Today," 28 Jan. 1937; Andrew M. Hyma interview by Donald van Reken, 7 Aug. 1975, typescript, 9, JAH.

developed a vitamin B pill from wheat germ that national advertising puffed up into a best seller. It was the first of four hundred vitamins in the Wheatamin line of natural vitamins that De Pree produced, most famously Wheatamin Extract and Wheatamin Dried Yeast. James De Pree, who headed the vitamin division, earned national acclaim as a nutritionist and medical and pharmaceutical societies clamored for him to address them as the expert in the emerging field.[124]

Willis A. Diekema, Gerrit's eldest son, was the marketing genius behind De Pree for many years. To distribute its Wheatamin line, Diekema had the company grant exclusive franchises to druggists, one to a territory. Over the years, the franchise network grew to several thousand drug stores that carried the vitamin line, including the popular multi-vitamin pills. John P. Oggel was the well-traveled salesman who visited the franchise outlets regularly for three decades until his death in 1935. A few years before, in 1930, when Gerrit Diekema died while serving as the United States envoy and minister in the Netherlands, Con De Pree took his chair as president and continued as treasurer, while Willis Diekema, became vice president and general manager, and the next year president. Besides the vitamin line, Diekema promoted the San-Tox drugs and toiletries, including in 1929 a line of assorted Wilhelmina Chocolates, packaged in boxes wrapped in Delft blue ribbons and featuring small wooden shoes inside.[125]

Under Con De Pree, James' brother, the company went bankrupt in the early 1930's. Willis Diekema was selected by the bankruptcy court to take the company out of receivership.

In 1939 a $50,000 expansion to the Sixth Street plant was necessary to keep up with demand. After some years, the familiar San-Tox brand was dropped in favor of the more professional Nurse Brand. In 1950 the company added chlorophyll, a first full-strength deodorant tablet, which it marketed under the name Nullo. The tablet hit the market just as Zeeland native Paul de Kruif's article on the deodorant qualities of chlorophyll ran in the *Readers Digest*. Nullo sales skyrocketed for several years, until the chlorophyll craze ran its course. Today Nullo LLC, under the Monticello Drug Company of Jacksonville, Florida, continues to sell Nullo Tablets, mainly to retirement homes, hospitals, and hunters. De Pree in the mid-1950s produced more than four hundred items.[126]

In 1977 Chattanooga-based Chattem Drug Co. bought De Pree Co., removed many executives, and continued operations on a much-

124 Ibid., 5 Jan. 1956.

125 Massie, *Haven, Harbor, and Heritage*, 170; *Holland City News*, 1 Jan. 1931.

126 *Holland City News*, 25 Apr. 1929, 19 Dec. 1935, 4 May 1939; *Holland Sentinel*, 27 Dec. 1930, 14 Jan. 1931, 31 Dec. 1955, 26 Jan. 1980, 8 Jan. 1982.

reduced scale until 1982, when Chattem sold all remaining assets for a "song" to J. B. Laboratories of Holland (see below) after it was on the market for several years with no takers. John Otting and William "Bill" Baker Jr., both former De Pree employees, had founded the company in 1978 to manufacture a discontinued De Pree line of bulk vitamins and mineral additives for Kellogg's Pop-Tarts carried by retail chains like Kmart and Walmart. Soon company chemists, microbiologists, and research scientists expanded product lines in over-the-counter drugs and additives for companies such as Perrigo, Kellogg, and Keebler, among others. In 1984 Baker and Otting began offering stock to selected employees with at least five years' seniority, and by 1992, when Otting retired, the company was 100 percent employee owned, with Baker continuing as company president. In 1996 J. B. Laboratories opened a $7.7 million facility in HEDCOR's Northside Industrial Park in Holland Township. The firm sold the Central Avenue building to Lumir Corp., Ed Prince's downtown realty company (chapter 33), which eventually restored the yellow brick building to its original condition.[127]

In 2008 Allegan-based Perrigo, a generic drug company founded in 1887, acquired J. B. Laboratories for $44 million. Perrigo was expanding rapidly and shifted some of its production work to the new Holland plant, which was expected to add $70 million in annual sales. In the next two decades, Perrigo became the largest generic drug manufacturer in the United States, supplying Walmart, Kmart, Walgreens, Rite Aid, Meijer, and Perry Drugs.[128]

Bill Baker Jr., while working for De Pree, had a second career as manager of the Holland sales and accounting office of the Larchmont, New York-based Charles Bowman & Company. Bowman founded the company in 1946 as a raw material vitamin, mineral, and animal feed supplier. It grew quickly, eventually adding sales offices in Chicago, Los Angeles, Montreal, and Holland. After Charles Bowman passed away in 1970, his two children took over, but neither of them had his passion for the business. Baker bought the business from the Bowman children when De Pree was sold to Chattem Drug Company, and in 1975 he became the president of the company, then headquartered in Saugatuck, Michigan, with a warehouse in Holland. He moved the offices back to Holland, and since 1998 the firm has been located on John

127 This paragraph relies on Massie, *Haven, Harbor, and Heritage*, 170; *Holland Sentinel*, 26 Jan. 1980, 29 Jan. 1995.

128 *Holland Sentinel*, 6 Jan., 17 Sept. 2008; Mike Lozon, "A Prescription for success: Chemical producers play major role in area's economy"; *Holland Sentinel*, 13 Aug. 1995.

Andrew M. "Dixie" Hyma (*left*) and Marion Postma (*right*) in laboratory of De Pree Chemical Company, 1943 (*Joint Archives of Holland*)

F. Donnelly Drive in the Northside Industrial Park. Greg Christensen joined the company as vice president in 1980 and in 1988 was elevated to president. John Ripley came to the company in 1994 as vice president and in 2012 was president, with Christensen as CEO. Baker retired from Charles Bowman & Company in 1998 and continued to work at J. B. Laboratories until it was sold to Perrigo in 2008, a few days after his seventy-eighth birthday. Charles Bowman & Company continues to specialize in raw material vitamins, herbs, minerals, amino acids, and other nutritional supplements, and their customers include household names like GNC, Cargill, and Perrigo.[129]

Richard "Dick" Welch is another J. B. Laboratories and Perrigo executive who struck out on his own. He and his wife Linda founded Welch Laboratories in 1989 to process bulk powders into granulated ingredients for nutritional supplements and over-the-counter pharmaceuticals. The company expanded so fast that in six years it outgrew its original facility at 4414 136th Avenue in Holland Township. In 1995 the privately-held company erected a $2.8 million plant with triple the floor space in the Northside Industrial Park near Charles Bowman & Co.[130]

[129] I am indebted to Maggie Baker Conklin, Bill's daughter, for the history of Charles Bowman & Co.

[130] Lozon, "Prescription for success"; *Holland Sentinel*, 13 Aug. 1995.

Mead Johnson & Co., East Main Street, Zeeland, 1940
(*Zeeland Historical Museum*)

Mead Johnson

Mead Johnson is a New Jersey company that Edward Mead Johnson started in 1905 to make powdered infant formula. Johnson developed the formula to feed his infant son, who could not digest his mother's milk. Johnson moved the company to Evansville, Indiana in 1915, and business increased to the point that a second plant was needed. Lambert Johnson, Mead's second son, chose Zeeland because it was surrounded by dairy farms. In 1924 Mead Johnson & Company bought the Phenix Cheese Company plant on Main Street, a maker of Philadelphia Cream Cheese, and converted it to powdered milk production (chapter 17). Thirty-five employees were at work in 1925 dehydrating liquid milk brought in by horse and wagon in ten-gallon creamery cans. In the early decades, the company lent farmers money to buy cows and upgrade milking equipment.[131]

In 1967 Bristol-Myers Squibb Company acquired Mead Johnson, and the Zeeland plant became part of the $2 billion pharmaceutical conglomerate. In 1995 the parent company invested $110 million in a new Zeeland plant that tripled their size and production capacity. The production lines, which turn out fifteen specialty infant formulas, are fully automated and fill five hundred one-pound cans per minute, sixty-five thousand cases per day. Enfamil has been the most popular product. In 2012 the company employed 325 workers, many women, most with thirty years or more on the assembly lines. The work was steady and the pay good. In 2009 Bristol-Myers Squibb spun off Mead Johnson, and now the $3 billion global company stands alone again.

[131] *Holland Sentinel*, 12 Sept. 1999.

The Zeeland plant pays the city $500,000 in taxes annually. Mead Johnson has also been a good corporate citizen, generously supporting local institutions, such as the $100,000 donation for the Howard Miller Library and Community Center. In 1999 Zeeland mayor Les Hoogland ranked Mead Johnson's philanthropy "right up there" with Herman Miller, Howard Miller, Gentex, and the former Batts Corporation.[132]

Aniline Dye Works

The outbreak of the First World War in 1914, with German submarines torpedoing merchant ships, raised the risk of importing dyes from the primary manufacturers in Germany (BASF and Hoechst), England (British Dyes), and France. The superior foreign dyes became scarce and commanded high prices. Dye making was a strategic industry because it was the leading supplier of nitro compounds for explosives and for chemicals used in gas warfare. One answer was to move production to neutral countries, such as the United States. In 1915 the owner of the Franken and Danders Aniline Dye Works of Amsterdam, one of the largest dye works in the Netherlands with five thousand employees, decided to establish a branch in the United States. The Netherlands was also a neutral country in the Great War, and remained so, unlike the United States.

The son of the owner of Aniline Dye, Frans Franken, was traveling in the United States in 1914 and happened to cross paths in Minnesota with Vance Mape, an executive of the West Michigan Furniture Company. Mape learned of Aniline's anticipated move, and persuaded Franken to consider Holland for the American plant. The bonus committee of the chamber of commerce again played a crucial role by offering $5,000 to snag the Dutch company. The fact that more than 150 individuals and companies contributed the monies sent an unmistakable message to the Netherlands that Holland was a special place to do business. The bonus and the promised "regular" bonus of another $5,000 was a pittance compared to the $500,000 investment Aniline Dye made in Holland. It took $15,000 just to purchase a 160-acre parcel on the north side of Black Lake, let alone to construct three manufacturing buildings, an electric plant with steam boilers, a gas plant, a water pumping station and scores of wells to provide a million gallons a day, and three ten-thousand-gallon underground acid tanks. Making organic dyes consumed prodigious amounts of electricity, steam power, gas, water, and chemicals. The location on Black Lake was

132 *Holland Sentinel*, 12 Sept. 1999; *Grand Rapids Press*, 15 Jan. 2012.

an ideal site for the massive plant, due to its high need for water and a place to flush chemical pollutants.[133]

Aniline Dye promised to be one of the largest companies in Holland, with high paying jobs for skilled and unskilled workers. The firm, located at 492 Douglas Avenue, hired several leading chemists from the Netherlands, but the main contingent was University of Chicago graduates. Franken also offered to hire as many local craftsmen as would apply. He specifically appealed for "ambitious young men" trained as carpenters, electricians, steamfitters, and millwrights. "Intelligent, handy men have a wonderful chance," he declared, and added: "I prefer to use as much home talent and labor as possible." By January 1917 the Aniline Company was running full force with four hundred men, including eighty chemists and technicians. The first dyes, methyl violet and methyl blue, went to paper mills as whitening agents for fine stationery. When the operations were successfully underway, Franken announced a $200,000 stock offering to provide funds for further expansion, and he offered local citizens the first "opportunity to invest in this enterprise . . . [and] share in the profits." Many jumped at the chance, and the entire block was fully subscribed within thirty days. The timing was auspicious. In a few months Aniline won its first large war contract for brown dyes for soldiers' uniforms. Brown was one of ten dye colors made at the plant.[134]

A year after the Armistice, in late 1919, a chemical fire sparked by spontaneous combustion destroyed one of the main buildings, for a loss of $150,000. Insurance monies helped the firm to rebuild, and manager Bernard P. Donnelly had contractor Abel Postma stake out the new foundation before the ashes had cooled. "Work will be started at once," Donnelly declared, and Postma had the new building ready in one month. Shortly, Donnelly hosted two Japanese businessmen who came to place an "enormous order" for dyes to be sold throughout the Far East, Australia, and India. War destruction had disrupted the normal European sources for dyes in the Far East as it had in North America.[135]

Aniline Dye never seemed to recover from the fire, however, and the board of directors decided in 1923 to sell the company. Company chemist Cornelius (Neil) Tiesenga saw opportunity. In 1924 he formed Tiesenga & Co. and bought the Aniline buildings. He salvaged whatever equipment he could, and continued operations under the Aniline

133 *Holland City News*, 25 May, 12 Oct. 1916.

134 *Grand Rapids Press*, 8 Dec. 1916; *Holland City News*, 21 Dec. 1916, 18 Jan., 2 Aug. 1917.

135 *Holland City News*, 12 Oct. 1916, 2, 30 Oct. 1919, 1 Jan. 1920.

Dye name. Many of the former stockholders bought stock in the new company. One of the largest investors was Abraham Peters, owner of Holland's five-and-dime store and a prominent Christian Reformed lay leader, who became the company president and general manager. Tiesenga, general manager and secretary, developed heat-resistant furnace cement that Holland Furnace purchased by the railcar load. The profitable product enabled the company in 1928 to expand into the pigment business, after taking on as partner DuPont chemist Cecil R. Trueblood, who had worked with Tiesenga briefly in Aniline's former Chicago plant.[136]

The reorganized plant with only three employees, Trueblood and "two good Dutchmen" (chemists Tiesenga and Gerrit John Van Zoeren), sold its first batch of color pigment after eleven months of hard work. The company sold $35,000 the first year of 1929 and continued to grow during the Depression years. In 1935 Ralph Eash, another DuPont chemist, came as Trueblood's assistant to direct a new color research department. In 1940 Peters fell dead of a heart attack while walking to his office, and within two years Tiesenga died the same way. The executive team of Trueblood as president, Eash as vice president, and Genevieve (Mrs. Cornelius) Tiesenga as secretary-treasurer, carried on for several years. But the Second World War starved the color business of chemicals, and in 1943-44 the partners sold their stock to National Cylinder Gas Company, and Aniline became a subsidiary, under the name Holland Color & Chemical. In 1960 National Cylinder Gas became a subsidiary of the Chicago-based Chemetron Corporation.[137]

Chemetron Corporation

Chemetron was a stepchild of the Holland Aniline Dye Works, begun in 1924 as Tiesenga & Co. The dye works attracted as a neighbor the 1932 start-up Colorcrete Industries, under William E. and Harry Dunn and Benjamin Van Raalte Jr., to manufacture coloring for brick, block, and tile. Over the years, Tiesenga & Co. went through a number of name changes and permutations: Holland Color & Chemical (1943), Holland Color & Chemical, Division of Chemetron Corporation (1960), Holland-Suco Color, Division of Chemetron Corp. (1964), Chemetron Corp., Pigments Division (1968), Bayer (1978), BASF Wyandotte (1979),

[136] Ibid., 1 Jan. 1928; Cecil R. Trueblood, "Fifty Years in the Color Business," typed manuscript in Chemtron Corporation Collection, HMA; "The Story of Chemetron Pigments" (company booklet, ca. 1971); "The Story of the People of Chemetron Pigments," typescript, ca. 1974, both in Herrick Library, vertical file.

[137] Trueblood, "Fifty Years"; *Holland Sentinel*, 28 Mar. 1940.

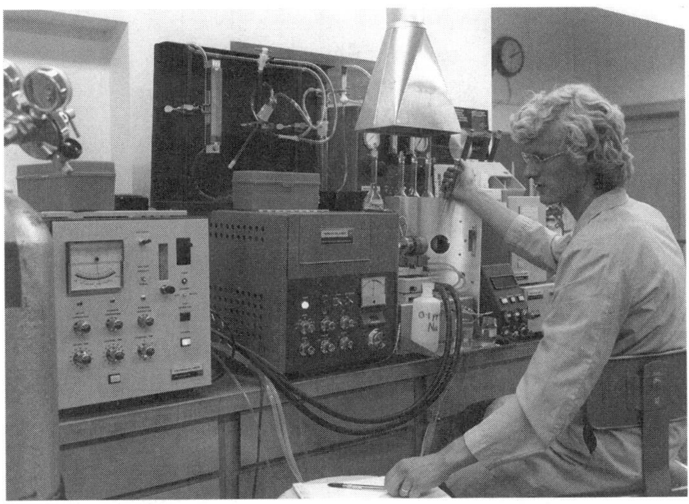

Jon Wood mixing colors at Chemetron Corporation plant, 1960s (photo Ted Jongblud Jr.) (*Archives, Holland Historical Trust*)

and finally Flint Ink Group (1996). From the 1950s through the 1970s, the firm was a leading producer of color pigments for paint, printing ink, plastics, and allied industries. Chemetron Pigments specialized in printing ink. The company expanded in 1965 by buying the Holland Furnace Howard Avenue Plant No. 5 and relocating a plastics division from Pennsylvania.[138]

In January 1978 a Pittsburgh steel producer (Allegheny Ludlum Industries) acquired Chemetron in another deal and immediately tried to divest itself of the Holland ink plant. The workers in Holland, members of the tough Teamsters Union, went on strike on October 1. After ten weeks of stalemate, with scattered rock throwing and fistfights on the picket lines, Chemetron made a "final" contract offer in mid-December and warned the strikers that it would begin hiring permanent replacements after a week. When the union rejected the final offer by three to one, the company acted on its threat. It had Ottawa County Sheriff deputies escort a convoy of new hires and a "significant number" of willing employees past the angry picketers, and police had to arrest a half-dozen strikers for acts of violence. It was a nasty scene.

[138] *Holland Sentinel*, 2 May 1932, *Holland City News*, 30 Apr. 1953, 31 Mar. 1960, 25 Aug. 1966, 5 Jan., 14, 16 Mar. 1967; *Grand Rapids Press*, 9 Apr. 1965; information courtesy of Marion Hoeve and David Vander Haar, both former employees of BASF Wyandotte and members of the company "25-year Club."

In the next weeks, the company hired several hundred replacements to work with several dozen strikebreakers.[139]

To safeguard the plants from sabotage, Chemetron hired the Wackenhut Security Company of Pittsburgh to provide armed guards around the clock. This led to an even greater tragedy. On the night of January 31, 1979, at least six Wackenhut guards, who had been staying at the Blue Mill Motel, abducted the night clerk, Hope College student Janet Chandler, gang raped and strangled her and dumped her body miles away along Interstate 196. The perpetrators kept a code of silence for nearly three decades, until finally one conscience-stricken culprit confessed, thanks to the work of a cold-case detective team that had been prodded by Hope College professor David Schock and his film arts students, who made a documentary on the tragedy. In 2006 and 2007, all six were convicted and sentenced to life in prison.[140]

Meanwhile, early in 1979 after fourteen weeks of picketing, the union asked to resume bargaining with a federal mediator, and the company agreed, but the talks were fruitless. The company then withdrew its final offer, and all of the striking workers lost their jobs, except for a few the company took back. Three months later, in March, Chemetron Pigment was sold to an American subsidiary of the German firm BASF-Wyandotte Corp. The union had overplayed its hand and lost. Negotiating with a Pennsylvania steel company that only wanted to sell its orphan chemical division gave the teamsters union no leverage. The union also faced an unsympathetic public, including the sheriff's department.

In 1984 BASF-Wyandotte dedicated a new pigments laboratory at its Columbia Avenue plant (also a former Holland Furnace facility) to keep up with the heavy orders. In 1986 BASF sold its Holland operations to Detroit-based Flint Ink Group, and the workers in the Columbia Avenue office and lab building, some one hundred or more, were laid off, and the Douglas Avenue workforce was downsized. Flint Ink declined to buy the Columbia Avenue building, and BASF in 1999, after unsuccessfully trying to sell it, donated the building to the Black River Charter School. Flint Ink closed in 2006 and laid off seventy of its eighty employees; ten workers continued in the Flint Group Ink division, which has since all but shut down.[141]

[139] *Holland Sentinel*, 1 Oct., 12, 13, 15, 18, 19, 21 Dec. 1978.

[140] Ibid., 30, 31 Jan. 1979, 29 Jan. 2007. Students involved in the 2006 film, "Who Killed Janey Chandler?" were Olim Alimov, Phil Blauw, Sarah Hartman, Wes Hollendonner, Jonathan Johnson, Amber Ross, Amy Schlusler, and Kyle Shepherd (*Holland Sentinel*, 10 Feb. 2006).

[141] Ibid., 29 Dec. 1978, 2, 3, 6, 13 Jan., 6, 9, 12, 22 Mar. 1979, 10 Nov. 1984, 11, 21 Jan., 22 Apr. 1996; *Grand Rapids Press Lakeshore Edition*, 28 Oct. 1998, 14 Apr. 1999, 4 Nov. 2006.

A thirty-year-old firm in the ink industry is Uniform Color Company, founded in 1981 by James Dewey in a large Zeeland garage on Harrison Street to mix custom dyes for use in plastics. From three employees in 1981, the company in 2011 had 225 employees in a large plant at 942 Brooks Avenue in the Southside Industrial Park. Bob Den Herder bought the business in 1994 and relocated it to 11395 Lakewood Boulevard, which the company had occupied since 1984. In 2012 Uniform Color received national recognition for its support of employees serving in the military during the wars in Iraq and Afghanistan. Tom Stevens, the chief executive officer, insists that this policy "is absolutely glued into the fabric of what we do" as a company because it is "the right thing to do."[142]

Zeeland Chemicals

Zeeland Chemicals, one of Zeeland's first high-tech firms, at 215 North Chestnut Street began as Chemical Specialties. Gerrit John Van Zoeren, the first Hope College graduate to earn a doctorate in chemistry, founded the company. Van Zoeren, who began making dyes at the Holland Aniline Company in 1919, joined with another Zeelander, Edward J. De Pree, to form De Pree Laboratories (see above). The Great Depression drove the company into bankruptcy in 1933, and Van Zoeren worked for several years researching embalming fluid in Indiana. In 1935 he returned to Michigan, and with the financial backing of De Pree, who was then working for Monsanto in St. Louis, Van Zoeren began manufacturing Carbromal (a mild sedative) for Upjohn in Kalamazoo. He made the drug in a rented room in the De Pree Chemical Company in Holland. Brisk sales encouraged Van Zoeren, De Pree, and Dr. Lucas Kyrides to create Chemical Specialties Inc. In 1940 the city of Zeeland gave the partners 3.5 acres for a factory in the expectation of creating good jobs. The city fathers were not disappointed. In six years, the trio developed several new drugs, erected additional buildings, and increased the workforce to twenty-eight. In 1947 the partners sold out to Miles Laboratories, who renamed the company Sumner Chemical Company. Under the Miles flag, the partners, who remained at the helm until their retirement, continued to develop new pharmaceutical products. By the mid-1950s, Sumner Chemical covered eight acres and employed 180.[143]

142 *Holland Sentinel*, 25 Sept. 2011; *Grand Rapids Press*, 29 May 2012 (quote); *Holland City Directories*, 1981-2011.

143 *Welcome to Hexcel Chemical Products* booklet, ca. 1980; Steve Vander Veen, "Zeeland's chemical footprint remains," *Holland Sentinel*, 7 Oct. 2007; Lozon, "Prescription for success," ibid., 13 Aug. 1995.

Zeeland (Sumner) Chemical Company laboratory, 1950s
(*Archives, Holland Historical Trust*)

In 1959 seventy-five-year-old Van Zoeren donated to his alma mater Hope College for a new library ten thousand shares of Miles Laboratories stock, worth $550,000, which he netted in the 1947 sale. The college, in recognition of this generous gift of the bulk of his estate, named the facility the Van Zoeren Library. Van Zoeren made the gift, the largest in the college's first century, in honor of his recently deceased wife Elizabeth.[144]

In 1977 Hexcel Corporation, a California-based international chemicals firm, bought Sumner Chemical and ran it as part of its Chemicals Division until 1992, when the New Jersey-based Cambrex Corporation acquired Sumner Chemical and brought in its own management team. Since 2006 Cambrex placed its Zeeland operations under the Indianapolis-based Vertellus Specialties. Over time Van Zoeren's company manufactured chemicals for the pharmaceutical industry to make mouthwash and cough suppressants. The next major products were chemical additives for the photographic and copier industries, including a special polymer used in Polaroid instant film.

[144] Vander Veen, "Zeeland's chemical footprint remains"; Wynand Wichers, *A Century of Hope, 1866-1966* (Grand Rapids: Eerdmans, 1968), 233-34. The contents of the Van Zoeren library were moved in 1988 into the new Van Wylen Library building. Van Zoeren Library became Van Zoeren Hall, in which education, sociology, and business courses are now taught.

Digital cameras made Polaroid film obsolete. Employment peaked in the late 1990s at about 170, and dropped sharply after that in response to poor economic conditions, to seventy-five by early 2001 and forty-five later in the year. The cuts represented a 40 percent reduction in all the departments based on seniority. In 2011 Zeeland Chemicals continued to make cetylpyridininum, an ammonium compound for the pharmaceutical industry used in mouthwash, nasal sprays, and antiseptic creams and lotions.[145]

Pfizer (Parke-Davis, Warner-Lambert)

Parke-Davis, a Detroit-based pharmaceutical company, opened a Holland plant in early 1952 to manufacture antibiotics in the vacant Armour Leather Company site encompassing thirty acres on the north shore of the Black River along Howard Avenue. They remodeled the buildings and installed the pharmaceutical equipment. Bringing this cutting-edge chemical technology to Holland was another coup by the chamber of commerce, headed by William "Bill" Vande Water from 1946 to 1965. The first blockbuster drug was chloromycetin, a miracle drug discovered in government labs during the Second World War and made available to the general public in 1949. With chloromycetin as its bestseller, Parke-Davis by 1952 captured 38 percent of the United States market for antibiotics, and the future looked bright. Then came a crisis that brought the company to its knees. The drug apparently had serious side effects. At least so claimed a physician in Los Angeles whose son had died after taking chloromycetin. Without awaiting case studies, the American Medical Association issued a warning to doctors nationwide, and the wire services picked up the story. Parke-Davis' market share of chloromycetin sales plunged to 5 percent, and the firm shut down production of the drug. Almost four hundred workers were furloughed or put on short weeks. Parke-Davis cooperated fully with the Federal Drug Administration, and soon the charges were cleared and sales picked up again.[146]

In 1975 Parke-Davis constructed chemical manufacturing and research buildings, the latter with seven laboratories. The entire complex in 1977 became part of Warner-Lambert of Morris Plains, New Jersey, another of the consolidations common among pharmaceutical giants at that time. The 350 employees, of which one-third were chemists,

145 *Welcome to Hexcel Chemical Products*; Vander Veen, "Zeeland's chemical footprint remains"; *Holland Sentinel*, 17 Dec. 1997, 7 June 1998, 24 Oct. 2001, 7 Oct. 2007.

146 Massie, *Haven, Harbor, and Heritage*, 121, 177; *Holland City News*, 15 Mar., 11 Oct. 1951.

Aerial view of Parke-Davis (Warner-Lambert) plant on Howard Street looking northwest, 1950s (*courtesy Larry B. Massie*)

discovered and produced many leading products, including the anti-convulsant drugs Dilantin and Neurontin, the cholesterol-lowering Lopid, the anti-histamine Benadryl, and the Alzheimer drug Cognex. These products were worth many millions of dollars in sales.[147]

In 2000 the facility changed hands again when Pfizer, a multinational pharmaceutical giant based in New York City since 1849, bought Warner-Lambert and committed $250 million for a research laboratory in Holland, which opened in 2002. The next year Pfizer began downsizing, first closing the laboratory in 2004 and laying off nearly one hundred chemists, and then in 2007 ending production in the adjacent manufacturing plant. Pfizer generously donated the $50 million laboratory to Michigan State University for biotechnology research, but razed the manufacturing plant after failing to find a buyer. Local lawmakers, notably Sen. Wayne Kuipers of Holland and Rep. Bill Huizenga of Zeeland, sought $20 million from Michigan's 21st Century Jobs Fund to develop the biotech lab, with local donors contributing $5 million. City leaders hoped the biotech facility would be "our breakthrough." In full operation, it would employ one hundred scientists with an annual budget of $7.5 million. Whether the MSU Biotech Research Lab will deliver on that promise only time will tell.[148]

147 Massie, *Haven, Harbor, and Heritage*, 177; *Holland Sentinel*, 30 Jan. 1991.

148 *Holland City News*, 9 May 2007; *Holland Sentinel*,13 May 2007; *Grand Rapids Press Lakeshore Edition*, 9, 10, 11 May, 16 Aug. 2007, 22 Jan. 2008.

RepcoLite Paints (formerly Renzleman Paint Company)

Holland has two paint companies: RepcoLite Paints (originally Renzleman Paint Company) and American Aerosols. RepcoLite Paints began in 1938 when Jacob Renzleman opened a plant in a former chicken hatchery on the corner of Columbia Avenue and Thirty-Second Street. There he began manufacturing his first brand, called Dutch Mill Paints. Paint was in Renzleman's blood; both his father and grandfather had been in the business. The company expanded rapidly after Benjamin "Ben" Altena came in 1945. The ambitious Altena had owned a barber and beauty shop in Washington Square, but "was tired of standing in the same place all the time," as he aptly put it. Renzleman and Altena manufactured its own line of paints during the day and peddled the product door-to-door in the evening. When Renzleman retired, Altena bought the business and moved operations to its present location at 473 West Seventeenth Street at Homewood Avenue. The building, which was originally a gas station and then a liquor store, has been expanded seven times and remains the flagship plant.[149]

Renzleman Paints survived a fire in 1952, and the next year the firm changed its name to RepcoLite Paints, because the larger Vogel Paint Company of Orange City, Iowa, complained that the Holland firm was infringing on its trade name, "Dutch Mill Paints." Thereafter, RepcoLite changed its focus from marketing a trade-name product to selling custom-mixed paints for commercial painters and architects who demanded unique customized batches. This specialization enabled the company to expand and prosper with five retail outlets in West Michigan. Ben Altena continued as president until his retirement in 1976; his son David and Fred Ver Schure succeeded him. When Ver Schure retired in 1983, Dave Altena's son Dan joined the firm, making it another example of a local multigenerational business. In 2004 RepcoLite had about fifty employees and manufactured 250,000 gallons of paint. In 2011 the company employed 181 in eight locations. Its home office and factory store remains on West Seventeenth Street, with a decorating center at 701 East Lakewood Boulevard. The company owns two decorating centers in Grand Rapids and one in Jenison, plus contract suppliers in Grand Haven, Muskegon, and Goshen, Indiana.[150]

[149] *Holland City News*, 16 Jan., 7 Nov. 1946, 1 May 1952; Steve Vander Veen, "Painters' Choice," *Holland Sentinel*, 7 Nov. 2004.

[150] Vander Veen, "Painters' Choice"; *Holland Sentinel*, 19 Dec. 1993; Benjamin Altena obit., ibid., 14 May 2002; RepcoLite Paints' Facebook page.

American Aerosols Inc.

American Aerosols, a pioneer in manufacturing paint in aerosol spray cans, began in 1961 at 182 East Twelfth Street. The principals were Herman Dirkse president, Robert J. Karr vice president, and Joseph Knoll secretary-treasurer. Knoll was president from the late 1960s into the 1980s, when Roger Scholten took over and Knoll became board chairman. The growing company moved in 1967 into a $350,000 plant in the Southside Industrial Park at 636 East Fortieth Street at Waverly Road, and the call went out for additional workers to increase output from twelve to fifty million cans annually. By the 1980s the company focused its business on contract packaging. Its patented aerosol cans were ubiquitous in the marketplace, and the local company was a prime acquisitions target. In 1990 Guardsman Products acquired it, with Gene Ivnik as operations manager. Within two years, the firm became Sprayon Packaging under Nick Dans. He stayed on for many years, even after Sherwin Williams in 1996 added the company to its Diversified Brands Division, where it continued in 2013.[151]

Printing houses

Newspaper publishers operated the first printeries to keep their machines busy between weekly editions and to utilize their expertise. Mulder Bros. (Charles and Berend), owners of the *Holland City News* and *De Grondwet*, ran a book and commercial printing business out of their printery (chapter 32) in the Vander Veen Block at 20 West Eighth Street in the 1890s.

A competitor since 1890 was the printery of John D. Kanters at 72 East Eighth Street. Quality local printing began with three sibling partnerships: Poole Bros., Klaasen Printing, and Steketee Bros. & Van Huis. Poole Bros. was a Chicago company that around 1901 opened a large printery in Holland at Thirteenth Street and Van Raalte Avenue (later the site of Kandu Industries). The inducement was that president George A. Poole owned a summer home on the Macatawa Park road (now South Shore Drive). Under the able management of George Clements, Poole Bros. outgrew their factory and in 1916 constructed a $15,000 addition and announced a hiring program to double their workforce. The J. Klaasen Book and Job Printery of Johannes and William Klaasen at 34 West Eighth Street had steady work printing

[151] *Holland Sentinel*, 7, 29 Oct., 3, 12 Nov. 1966; *Holland City Directories*, 1961-2010; http://careers.sherwin-williams.com/history, accessed 20 Mar. 2013.

Klaasen Bros. Book and Job Printing, 34 West Eighth Street, with Johannes (*left*) and William (*second from left*) (*Archives, Holland Historical Trust*)

the Christian Reformed Church weekly, *De Wachter*. Newton D. Askins was a partner in the 1890s. Later brothers Gerrit and Cornelius Klaasen joined the firm, and in 1916 the Klaasens built a new shop at 9 East Tenth Street.[152] Klaasen Printing developed into a first-class printery.[153] (For addresses of blocks, see appendix 5.13 Public Buildings and Private Blocks, 1921 and 2012.)

Chicago-based Dearborn Engraving Company opened a Holland branch in 1912 in a plant on the corner of Twenty-Fourth Street and Ottawa Avenue in the newly-platted Elmwood Addition of Benjamin L. and Charles B. Scott. The firm, financed entirely with $80,000 in outside capital, contracted with local builders for the construction work, but they had to bring in many skilled workers to staff the factory. Dearborn's one hundred employees, 75 percent male, did printing, designing, engraving, and commercial photography, but the main focus

152 Steketee-Van Huis owned this building from 1924 until 1956. Numerous businesses operated on this property until Hope College purchased the building in 2002, and in 2004 renovation began for the Theil Research Center, which now houses the Van Raalte Institute and the Joint Archives of Holland.

153 *Holland City News*, 13 July 1916, 10 June 1926, George A. Poole obit., 12 Sept. 1918.

was publishing high school yearbooks. The payroll in 1916 totaled $100,000. Holland counted nine printing plants at that time.[154]

In 1919 John L. Van Huis, Cornelius (C. Neal) Steketee Jr., and brother Louis Steketee entered the printing business by founding Steketee Bros. & Van Huis, with Van Huis president, Neal Steketee vice president, and brother Louis secretary-treasurer. The firm expanded through acquisitions, buying Brinks Bros. in 1920 and Gerrit Klaasen Printing in 1923. Klaasen sold out to take the more promising position of manager of the growing print shop of Holland Furnace Company. The renamed Steketee-Van Huis Printing House used the small Brinks Bros. second floor shop at 180 River Avenue briefly, until in 1924 they acquired the large Klaasen Tenth Street building, which could accommodate all their equipment. In 1928 the ten-employee firm was recapitalized for $50,000 and laid plans for further expansion. By 1941 the company employed nineteen master printers with a total experience of 385 years; they turned out advertising circulars and catalogs, broadsides, and booklets printed on high-speed, automated presses and folding and cutting machines. The firm outgrew the Tenth Street plant in 1954 and bought Holland Furnace's Plant No. 4 at Fourth Street and Central Avenue, the site it occupies today. By then, the founding partners were introducing the next generation to the business. Donald Van Huis was general manager and Neal Steketee's son Cornelius "Cornie" J. was Louis' understudy as secretary-treasurer. With a workforce of thirty-two and the best of modern equipment installed in the refurbished factory with twenty-two thousand square feet of floor space, Steketee-Van Huis became the premier printing house in Holland, a position they continue to hold.[155]

In 1978 Steketee-Van Huis acquired the Printery and ran it as a subsidiary. It was the former print shop of the *Holland City News*, which had been setting type there since 1871. When the newspaper closed in 1977, Herman Bos and Cyrus Vande Luyster bought the equipment, relocated from River Avenue to 74 West Eighth Street, and opened as Old News Printery. The linotype machine was already obsolete, so the pair sold out the next year. Steketee-Van Huis immediately modernized the Printery with computer-generated typesetting. In 1992 the Printery

[154] Ibid., 21, 28 Mar. (reprint from *Grand Rapids Herald*), 6, 20 June, 25 July 1912, 16 Mar. 1916. Other printing firms at the time were Edward Brouwer's Economy Printing, Holland Printing, Kamferbeek Bros., and Van Noord Book & Publishing.

[155] *Holland City News*, 8 Nov. 1923, 4 May 1928, 26 June 1841, 30 Sept. 1954, 28 Apr. 1955; Steketee-Van Huis financial statement, 31 Oct. 1923, HMA; Cornelius J. Steketee obit., *Holland Sentinel*, 31 July 2001.

moved into a fifteen-thousand-square-foot facility at 79 Clover Street, where it has continued.[156]

In 1999 the Steketee-Van Huis management team of president Robert Kapenga and vice presidents Dennis "Denny" Brewer and Michael "Mike" Elms sold the company to Holland residents Ted Etheridge and Bill Ockerlund, operating as SVH Group. Etheridge had owned Etheridge Co, a printing company in Grand Rapids prior to this acquisition. Kapenga, Brewer, and Elms agreed to stay on for three years, Kapenga as chief financial officer and treasurer until 2004 and then senior advisor from 2004 to 2006. Gary Kremers joined SVH in 2001 and assumed the role of COO. Denny Brewer retired in 2000, and Mike Elms stayed active at SVH until 2007. In 2000 and years following, the company won top honors in the industry. In fall 2001, SVH Group undertook a $4.1 million expansion of the 13 West Fourth Street plant, increasing the square footage by more than 25 percent, as well as adding four high speed printing presses and die cuttings, for which the state granted various tax incentives totaling $526,000.[157]

During the years from 1999 to 2006, the company almost tripled annual revenues. In 2006, SVH Group sold the company, including the Printery, to the New York-based Multi Packaging Solutions, and the key management, Gary Kremers, Scott Volkert, Peter Houlihan, as well as CEO Ted Etheridge, retained ownership as shareholders. In 2008 the Steketee-Van Huis name disappeared after seventy-eight years. In 2011 Multi Packaging Solutions, a company with twelve facilities in the United States and United Kingdom, chose the Holland plant for a major expansion, for which it received an $865 million, four-year tax abatement on the promise of adding 180 jobs. Since the 1999 sale of Steketee-Van Huis, more than 250 jobs have been added, and the Holland operations of Multi Packaging Solutions are still expanding. It is considered one of the top producers of high-end pharmaceutical, entertainment, and nutritional packaging in the country.[158]

Schreur Printing Company had its start in 1946 when George J. Schreur, a compositor at Steketee-Van Huis, quit to form his own company with John Vander Vliet. The partners set up shop at 177 College Avenue behind the Warm Friend Tavern at Seventh Street. In the early years, the firm was styled Schreur-Vander Vliet Printers. By 1956 George Schreur's brother Theodore "Ted" J. had replaced Vander

156 *Holland Sentinel*, 28 Feb. 1999.

157 Ibid., 22 Apr. 1999, 24 Sept. 2000.

158 Ibid., 10 June 2001, 21 Dec. 2005, 15 Mar., 19 Oct. 2011. I am indebted to Ted Etheridge for information in this and the previous paragraph.

Vliet as a partner. In 1961 the firm moved to 422 Diekema Avenue just south of South Shore Drive. A third brother, Donald W. Schreur, joined the family business in 1965. In 1972 George founded Holland Letter Service as an allied company; he retired the next year, leaving Ted and Donald to carry on. Hope College jobs kept the print shop and letter service humming for many years, even after the college opened its own print shop. Grandson Timothy "Tim" J. joined Schreur Printing in the early 1990s and became president in 1998. He orchestrated a move of the plant to 11287 James Street in Holland Township, where it boasts of being the oldest and last family-owned printery in Holland.[159]

Multinationals

General Electric

In 1953 the chamber of commerce, headed by William Vande Water and Clarence Klaasen, gained its biggest prize ever by snagging the $5 million General Electric (GE) motor plant from several competing cities. GE was the first "outside" multinational company with a union workforce—the International Union of Electrical Workers (IUE-CIO-AFL)—to locate in Holland, a provincial enclave of sixteen thousand residents. The impact on the quiet town was of seismic proportions, both on the business climate and wage rates. GE brought in seventy-five executives for the front offices, all college-educated "smart people," who sent their children to college and wanted a cultured community. On the shop floor, GE offered union-scale wages, with annual "escalator" increases pegged to the annual cost-of-living index, plus incentive wage increases and benefits. The starting wage of $1.30 per hour for welders attracted a plethora of applicants. The generous rates threatened all non-union shops, none more than the booming Holland Furnace, headed by the pompous Paul T. Cheff. GE's eventual payroll of twelve hundred surpassed that of Holland Furnace.[160]

The city sold the old airport to GE, twenty-two choice acres, a mile east of the city limits on the southwest corner of the new US-31 bypass and Sixteenth (Adams) Street. GE bought from private parties two adjacent parcels toward the south, running to Twenty-Fourth Street, to bring the total to thirty-five acres, all serviced by a Chesapeake

159 *Holland City Directories*, 1945-2011.

160 *Holland City News*, 3 Dec. 1953, 18 Mar., 1 May, 2 Dec. 1954; Marjorie J. Miller, "The Impact of General Electric on Holland," Holland Historical Trust *Review* 10 (Spring 1997): 4-6; Paul Van Kolken, "Arrival of General Electric shook up city," *Holland Sentinel*, 1 Jan. 2000; William Vogelzang interview.

General Electric employee assembling an electrical component (*Archives, Holland Historical Trust*)

& Ohio Railroad spur. John Van Dyke Jr. chairman of HEDCOR, the city's economic development arm, arranged for essential city services, for example, the railroad spur, extensions of roads, the Forty-Eighth Street water tower, and the Thirty-Second Street fire station.

GE constructed a large one-story building for its Hermetic Motor plant and began operations in 1955 under manager Willard Connor with four hundred workers, 40 percent of whom were women. For a unionized industrial plant in Holland to hire women for almost half its workforce was unprecedented. Only food processing plants like Heinz had previously hired large numbers of women. Eighty workers transferred from other GE plants and came with their families. Some were professionals and executives. All needed housing, and realtors and builders basked in the bonanza. One realtor, Roger MacLeod, sold eighty homes to GE people in a two-year period. More than five thousand residents heard GE president Harlow Curtis in his dedication speech call the plant a "good investment in tomorrow." Curtis did not mention the standard twenty-four/seven plant operations—including Sundays—another first for Holland, and a policy that threatened community values. On the other hand, GE families did join local congregations and provide leadership in churches and community organizations, thereby hastening the acculturation process.[161]

The GE plant served a growing market for hermetic motors for washing machines, dishwashers, air conditioners, and other small appliances. Ray Herrick of Tecumseh Products in eastern Michigan was one of the best customers, and this factor weighed heavily with the site

[161] Miller, "Impact of General Electric," 5.

selection committee. In a small city like Holland, GE's Holland Motor Division payroll of 1,200 workers in the 1960s had a huge impact. Over its thirty-six year run, the plant employed thousands. By the 1980s, GE was shifting its focus from manufacturing to finance, and the Holland plant—the tenth largest employer in the region—was rumored as closing. In 1984 as a first step, GE in a major consolidation, moved ninety management personnel from its Holland office to Fort Wayne, Indiana; sixty other white-collar workers were laid off or took early retirement. The second shoe dropped in 1988 with the announcement that GE's Holland plant was being consolidated into Kentucky and Singapore facilities. Five hundred workers, 93 percent IEU Local 931 members, lost their jobs when the plant finally closed in 1990. The building stood silent for fifteen years, until giant backhoes tore into it in 2005 to make way for a Menards superstore on the site in 2008. Locals are still heard to remark: "When GE came to town . . ." Such was the impact of the company on the community.[162]

Beech-Nut LifeSavers

In early 1965 HEDCOR enticed a second major corporation, Beech-Nut LifeSavers (later Planters LifeSavers) of New York, to select Holland for its third US manufacturing plant and the first in the Midwest. The company was considering a baby food plant in South Haven to tap the nearby fruit belt, but a declining birthrate dissuaded it, and Holland became the beneficiary. John Van Dyke Jr. went to New York to seal the deal. HEDCOR leased the seventy-five-year-old firm a one-hundred-acre site in the Southside Industrial Park at 635 East Forty-Eighth Street at Waverly Road for a $12 million plant to make its signature sweets—LifeSavers and Beech-Nut Gum—and other candies.[163]

With construction underway and 350 new jobs in prospect, the city in 1966 readily bowed to the company's demand to issue $12 million in industrial development bonds to cover construction and machinery costs. Floating bonds for such a purpose was a first for Holland but not for other Michigan cities, which had been quicker to exploit the Industrial Development Revenue Bond Act of 1963 that had just passed constitutional muster by the State Supreme Court in August 1966. The program also allowed companies to receive a 50 percent tax break for the twelve years. Some residents complained about the tax break, but

[162] *Holland City News*, 17 May 1956, 31 Jan. 1957, 5 Jan. 1959; *Holland Sentinel*, 17 Aug. 1984, 25 Oct. 1992, 29, 30 June 2005; *Grand Rapids Press Lakeshore Edition*, 30 June 2005.

[163] *Holland City News*, 10 Dec. 1964, 4 Feb., 28 May, 6 Sept. 1965.

Mayor Nelson Bosman (*third from right with hand on spade*) assists Beech-Nut LifeSavers officials in the ceremonial first shovel of dirt for the plant construction in the HEDCOR Southside Industrial Park, 1966 (photo Theodore Jungblut Jr.) (*Archives, Holland Historical Trust*)

city manager Herb Holt reminded them that taxpayers bore no bond risks, since rents covered the principal and interest. Chesapeake & Ohio Railroad ran a spur to the plant to provide access to its mainline track.[164]

The plant went into production in the fall of 1967, and for thirty-five years, it was one of the major employers, with a unionized workforce at its apex of eleven hundred, all represented by Retail, Wholesale, and Department Store Union Local 822. The plant saw its biggest expansion in 1978, when it began manufacturing the popular Bubble Yum Bubble Gum. In 1984 the Holland plant, then part of Squibb Corp., produced forty million pounds of sweets annually, according to plant manager John Tropilo. In 1988 it was the only one of seven nationally that manufactured roll candy and mints.[165]

In 2002 Kraft Foods, which had added Beech-Nut to its conglomerate, shocked the city by announcing the closing of the Holland plant within a year. LifeSavers was a Holland icon; it was the sole North American producer of the popular hard candy treats. The

164 Ibid., 9 June 1966; *Holland Sentinel*, 11 May 1966.

165 *Holland City News*, 19 Jan., 9 Mar., 27 July 1967, 22 Aug. 1968, 19 Mar. 1979; *Holland Sentinel*, 26 Jan. 1980, 30 Jan. 1988.

Worker on Beech-Nut LifeSavers production line
(*Archives, Holland Historical Trust*)

stated reason was that raw sugar was cheaper in Canada due to lower tariffs and so the company was moving production to its Canadian LifeSavers facility. The United States sugar lobby had cost another six hundred employees their jobs. But their anger was directed at Kraft and the "present corporate culture," rather than at Congress. Michigan Governor John Engler offered Kraft a $38 million incentive package to remain in Holland, but to no avail. The Holland area lost its fourth largest taxpayer; LifeSavers had a tax base of $40 million and added $2 million annually to public coffers.[166]

The facility is gradually being put back into productive use, after standing empty for several years. The timing of the Lifesavers closing could not have been worse. When Kraft made its plans public in 2002, furniture maker Herman Miller announced layoffs for six hundred employees, and when Lifesavers closed in 2004, Johnson Controls Inc. (JCI) revealed plans to eliminate 885 jobs at its Holland area plants and move production to Mexico. Despite the cutbacks and closings, manufacturing in 2009 accounted for 30 percent of employment in the Holland area, and Ottawa County counted thirty thousand manufacturing jobs.[167]

[166] *Holland Sentinel*, 19 Jan., 10 Feb., 10, 22 Mar. 2002, 6, 10, 11 Apr. 2003, 3 Apr. 2004.
[167] Ibid., 12 July, 19 Aug. 2009.

HEDCOR (Holland Economic Development Corporation)

The Holland Chamber of Commerce Planning and Economic Development Committee in 1957 became concerned with Holland's lagging industrial development and the need to provide better paying jobs for a growing population. Holland was known as a low-wage economy, with a relatively high level of employment and average wages below those in southeastern Michigan. The coming of Parke-Davis in 1952 and General Electric in 1955 showed the possibilities of recruiting other companies to Holland. Seeing an opportunity, William Vande Water, the chamber executive director, quietly had the chamber buy the former city airport site on East Sixteenth Street for future industrial growth. GE opened its Holland facility on the site in 1955, forever changing the city. Then came the bruising annexation fight in 1957-58, in which the city failed to persuade most residents of Laketown, Fillmore, Holland, and Park Townships, some thirty-nine square miles, with their twelve school districts, to annex to the city of Holland (chapter 7). In the end, residents in only five school districts—Maplewood, Apple Avenue, Montello Park, Van Raalte, and Lakeview—agreed to consolidate. Except for this ten-square-mile expansion, Holland was essentially landlocked for future industrial expansion.[168]

In 1957 the chamber named Marvin Lindeman to head up a ten-person committee of prominent business leaders to work with the Holland Planning Commission, Holland City Council, Michigan Department of Economic Development, and the Chesapeake & Ohio Railroad Industrial Department (successor of the Pere Marquette) to study the options. In July 1958, the chamber board transferred $1,000 from its building fund to a new industrial fund and in September the chamber discussed the possibility of forming an industrial development corporation. Clarence Jalving, president of Peoples State Bank, in 1959 and 1960 reported to the chamber on discussions with the Michigan Department of Economic Development.[169]

Mayor Robert Visscher was another leader in the campaign for Holland's future. "What do we want Holland to be?" he asked in a 1960 speech. The cozy "homogeneous town" was dying. The small town where

168 Massie, *Haven, Harbor, and Heritage*, 165; Randall P. Vande Water, "Us and Them," in Robert P. Swierenga, ed., *For Food and Faith: Dutch Immigration to Western Michigan, 1846-1960* (Holland, MI: JAH and Holland Museum, 2000), 99-102; Mike Lozon, "The History of HEDCOR: Holland Economic Development Corporation, Holland, Michigan," four-page booklet, ca. 1990.

169 Massie, *Haven, Harbor, and Heritage*, 165.

people knew who lived in every house and where everyone worked and went to church and where people relished hearing the familiar, "*Hoe is het met u*?" It was not enough, he declared, "to just sit back and say Holland is a good city and Providence will take care of us." City leaders had to be proactive and not be content to rest on their laurels of a rich heritage. The answer to the question of what we want Holland to be, Visscher concluded, "is not up to Rev. Van Raalte; it's up to us."[170]

In early 1961 the chamber executive director C. Neal Steketee, president of the Steketee-Van Huis Printing Co., induced Mayor Visscher to appoint an industrial coordinating committee with Henry Maentz of the board of public works and Alvin Cook of the board of education. Within weeks, Visscher and the city council allocated $20,000 for the Fantus Factory Locating Service to conduct an industrial survey of Holland in an effort to attract new industries. The board of public works and board of education, both of which had pushed annexation, shared in the study cost. Kenneth Berliant of Fantus' Chicago office, primary author of the Fantus Report (December 29, 1961), offered an outsider's perspective on Holland, along with numerous recommendations. The report noted that Holland was no longer a "religious-cultural-social island," but that mores were changing rapidly and that young people had a "more liberal outlook on life" than their parents; outsiders had to be accepted and integrated into the community, but without undermining the religious and moral foundation built upon a conservative Calvinist base. Berliant singled out the Christian Reformed congregations for reinforcing a "we" versus "they" mentality that looked on newcomers as "theys." But this denomination did not have a monopoly on exclusivity. A tight circle prevailed in most Dutch American congregations, including those in the more mainline Reformed Church in America.[171]

Arnold Mulder of Kalamazoo College, a Hope College graduate, author of several Dutch American historical novels, and former editor of the *Holland Sentinel*, published a guest editorial for his brother Ben Mulder's paper, titled "The Walls of Jericho," which reinforced Berliant's views, but in an iconoclastic, acerbic way that was guaranteed to offend traditionalists. Mulder declared that the walls keeping Holland isolated must come down for the city to prosper. The piece was written in support of the pro-annexation forces in the 1957-58 debate.[172]

The year 1962 was pivotal. The chamber that year responded to the Fantus Report and the prodding of Mayor Nelson Bosman and

[170] Vande Water, "Us and Them," 102.
[171] Ibid., 103-4, quotes the Fantus Report conclusion; *Holland City News*, 16 Feb. 1961.
[172] Randall P. Vande Water interview by John Maassen, 26 Oct. 1998, JAH.

the Mulders by forming a separate private non-profit corporation it called the Holland Economic Development Corporation (HEDCOR). The mission was to attract industry by acquiring open land in the city's southern and northern fringes and developing industrial parks. Michigan had an 11 percent unemployment rate at the time. To raise capital, the corporation issued 2,500 shares at a par value of $50 each, with no dividends. The chamber hired Roscoe Giles, a professional fundraiser from New York, as HEDCOR's administrator and salesman of the shares, and he raised an initial $1 million in seed money. HEDCOR officers and shareholders comprised a businessmen's "who's who," including banker Clarence Jalving, chamber of commerce president C. Neal Steketee, Jay Petter of Buss Machine, advertising executive Marvin Lindeman, realtor William De Roo, Stuart Padnos of Padnos Iron & Metal, George Heeringa of Hart & Cooley, Abe Martin of General Electric, Hope College treasurer Henry Steffens, Henry Maentz of First National Bank, *Holland Sentinel* publisher Wilford A. Butler, Jack Plewes of Post's Jewelry, and auto dealer Robert De Nooyer Sr. These men were willing to invest in the future of the community with no guarantee of a return on their money. It was another example of the cohesiveness and altruism of Holland area business leaders.[173]

Doug Rothwell, chief executive of the Michigan Jobs Commission, said it best: "The Holland area is blessed to have people with a vision of the future, who are willing to look around and identify the industrial needs of the community. If you were to plan an economy, you would do it just like Holland."[174]

With the stock sales and additional gifts from area businesses and individuals, realtor William C. De Roo in 1962 and 1963 acquired three hundred acres, beginning with the Boeve farm at Waverly Road and Forty-Eighth Street. The acreage was strategically located near M-40 and US-31 in recently annexed Fillmore Township (Allegan County), and was easily accessible to the Tulip City Airport. This was the nucleus of HEDCOR's Southside Industrial Park, founded in 1964. The first thing HEDCOR did was put in infrastructure—utilities and streets—which readied the site for industrial development and gave Holland a leg up on other cities. No industry in the HEDCOR district has ever been assessed for infrastructure.[175]

173 Vande Water, "Us and Them," 110-11; *Holland City News*, 26 July 1962; *Grand Rapids Press*, 8 Mar. 1987; Clarence Jalving interview by Donald L van Reken, 15 July 1976, typescript, JAH.

174 Quoted in Lozon, "History of HEDCOR," 1.

175 Hallacy interview.

Holland city and business leaders celebrate in front of HEDCOR sign, marking the opening of the Southside Industrial Park, 1964 (*Archives, Holland Historical Trust*)

Over the next decade, under president John Van Dyke Jr. of Rooks Transfer Lines, HEDCOR's southside park expanded to 615 acres and attracted sixteen industries. A major coup in 1967 was the addition of the Lifesavers plant, an affiliate of the international company Beech-Nut that was looking for a site in southwestern Michigan. The company president and a Consumers Power executive rejected a Kalamazoo site after a flyover, and the Consumers officer suggested a swing over the Holland area. When the Lifesavers executive saw the new industrial park, he "flipped," Giles recalled. "It was exactly what he wanted." HEDCOR later sold land to American Aerosols, S2 Yachts, 7Up Bottling, Haworth, Donnelly, Prince, Holiday Inn (later Best Western), Sligh Furniture, Seu-Tu-K Industries, Commercial Tool, Twin Lakes Manufacturing, Ram-Pac Engineering, Vanguard Glass Fabricators, and Holland Motor Express, among other companies. Holland voters approved sewer bonds, the board of public works laid sewer and water pipes, and the state granted tax abatements. Bosman considered the industrial park his greatest achievement as mayor. In 1974 Van Dyke after ten years stepped aside for George Heeringa to become the second president of HEDCOR. Jack De Roo joined the board that year and served eighteen years, culminating in the presidency in 1992.[176]

[176] *Holland Sentinel*, 12 May 1971, 16 Apr. 1974, 2 May 1986.

HEDCOR directors, 1963; *l-r, seated*: Clarence Jalving, Stuart Padnos, Nelson Bosman, and C. Neal Steketee; *standing*: William H. Vande Water, George Heeringa, Russell Klaasen, Abe Martin, Jay H. Petter, Henry S. Maentz, Henry Steffens, and Roger MacLeod (*courtesy Randall P. Vande Water*)

None of the new businesses were "oil on the floor" companies, such as the General Motors plant that opened in the Coopersville area, in keeping with the HEDCOR board's unwritten policy of keeping union labor at bay. Factory workers in the main union plants in the 1960s, which included Hart & Cooley, Holland Hitch, Lifesavers, GE, and Parke-Davis, earned up to 25¢ or more per hour more than non-union employees. Louis Hallacy, head of HEDCOR and the chamber of commerce in the 1970s and 1980s, thought that no more than one-quarter of factory workers in the Holland area were unionized. A larger proportion of "civil servants" were unionized, including public school teachers, police and firefighters, Herrick Library staff, nurses, employees of the board of public works, federal postal workers, and county roads crews. Most of the public locals were affiliated with the Service Employees International Union (SEIU). Some of the skilled trades were part of the Christian Labor Association, a Reformed group that for years rejected the strike weapon. Dutch Reformed workers eschewed unions for their adversarial nature and rigid seniority rules, and they abhorred strikes. They would rather have steady work at lower wages and avoid periodic layoffs and acrimony on the job.[177]

[177] Ibid., 2 Sept. 2001; Vande Water, "Us and Them," 111-12; Hallacy interview.

Michael "Mike" Lozon had it right in a 2003 presentation for the Holland Rotary Club, entitled "Like Oil and Water: Holland and Unions Don't Mix." He noted that less than 3 percent of the three hundred industrial plants in the Holland area were unionized, and only 1,500 of thirty thousand workers (5 percent) were covered by union contracts. Lozon attributed the union antipathy primarily to the Dutch Reformed churches, and secondarily to progressive employers who treated workers with respect and adopted participative management policies. These factors militated against union organizing.[178]

Before the coming of HEDCOR, industrial employment in the Holland area stood at 7,500; after only six years, in 1970, it had risen by 36 percent to 10,200. Of the 2,700 new jobs, 96 percent were in the Southside Industrial Park. The rest of the Holland area in these years saw seventeen industrial plants close with 1,100 jobs lost, twenty plants reduced their workforce by 756, while sixteen new plants created 193 jobs and thirty plants added 1,135 jobs, for a net loss of 528 jobs. This does not take into account the estimated seventy jobs created elsewhere for every one hundred new industrial jobs. So the 2,700 jobs created by HEDCOR added nearly 1,900 jobs in other endeavors. This was only after the first ten years; the best was still to come. At the twenty-fifth anniversary in 1987, the Southside Park had fifty-two companies employing more than 9,000 workers. The workforce jumped to 11,200 by 1992.[179]

By 1984 HEDCOR had sold the last lots in the Southside Industrial Park, and the board, led by Louis Hallacy, who also served as executive director of the chamber of commerce, looked to duplicate the success outside the city limits on the north side. In 1985 the non-profit agency purchased three hundred acres in Holland Township west of US-31 from Riley Street north to New Holland Street for the Northside Industrial Park. It was part of the aborted seven-hundred-acre Ottawa Industrial District formed in 1965 by Nick Yonker and Warner De Leeuw. Willis "Bill" Driesenga, Holland Township superintendent, convinced Hallacy and HEDCOR to undertake the project. A $400,000 federal grant for sewers, water mains, and roads financed the first phase of the project, which had two prospective tenants, one being Donnelly Corp., who expected to hire two hundred workers.[180]

178 Mike Lozon, untitled paper presented to the Holland Rotary Club, Jan. 2003, typescript kindly provided by the speaker.

179 *Holland Sentinel*, 16 Apr. 1974; *Grand Rapids Press*, 8 Mar. 1987; Mike Lozon, "HEDCOR: Thirty Years of Developing Things Right," [*Grand Rapids Press*] *Holland Market Gallery*, 1 May 1992.

180 *Holland Sentinel*, 27 Aug. 1965, 5 Apr., 19, 24 Sept., 12 Oct. 1985.

HEDCOR Southside Industrial Park after build out in 1987, looking east from US-31 with Thirty-Second Street on the left (*courtesy Randall P. Vande Water*)

HEDCOR also had in hand a $350,000 Small Cities Grant and a $300,000 state loan. But the board demurred when it learned that the state adhered to the federal Davis-Bacon Law, which required "prevailing" (union) wages for government-funded infrastructure work, and it also required the industries named in the loan application to pay union wages. President Dale Van Lente, secretary Louis Hallacy, and vice presidents Harvey Buter and Jack De Roo tried unsuccessfully to get the restriction waived. In the end, HEDCOR spurned the government grants in favor of private and township monies. The park was dedicated in 1986 and opened in 1987. Streets in the park were later named Driesenga Drive, Hallacy Drive, and John F. Donnelly Drive to honor the prime movers. Further land purchases increased the park to 535 acres. In the late 1990s, the industrial center had twenty businesses, including Donnelly, Request Foods, Dell Engineering, Fogg Filler Co., Russ' Commissary, and Agritek, employing 4,500 workers. More companies have moved in since, including Kandu Indistries (chapter 31).[181]

The East James Industrial Complex, a development by Lakewood Land Development, an arm of Lakewood Construction, opened the same year to the south of the HEDCOR complex, running east from 120th Avenue and south of James Street. Co-owners Maynard Miedema

[181] *Holland Sentinel*, 19, 20 Mar., 30 Apr., 2 May 1986, 5 Feb. 1987, 12 Mar. 1991, 6 July 2003; *Grand Rapids Press Lakeshore Edition*, 19 Dec. 1985, 8 Mar. 1987, 1 July 2003.

HEDCOR Northside Industrial Park before build out, looking northwest from intersection of US-31 and Quincy Street, 1987 (*courtesy Randall P. Vande Water*)

and James Stroop predicted that the $1.25 million complex, when fully built up with eleven buildings, would be worth $25 million. Tenants included Kenowa Tool & Die, B. J. W. Berghorst & Sons, Cardinal Bus Lines Holland garage, and various light industries and warehouses.[182]

In 1992, after thirty years, the sixty-eight firms in the two HEDCOR industrial parks had 14,700 workers. "The city has relied on them [HEDCOR's board] heavily to recruit and retain industry," conceded Soren Wolff, Holland's city manager. He credited the non-profit development corporation with fulfilling its mission of providing land for local manufacturers to expand and enticing out-of-town industries to locate in the Holland area. HEDCOR's efforts supplied the region with a diverse industrial base to tide it over tough economic times. This diversity, said Hallacy, a leader in industrial recruitment for twenty years, is the key to the region's industrial strength. Hallacy became president of HEDCOR in 1994, following a one-year stint by Harvey J. Buter, a board member since 1962. Buter was one of twenty-three board members. In 2000 the two industrial parks housed seventy-two companies with 16,500 workers.[183]

[182] Ibid., 3 May, 1 June 1985.

[183] Lozon, "HEDCOR"; *Holland Sentinel*, 12 Mar. 1991, 1 Jan. 2000.

In 1994 HEDCOR bought fifty acres near Tulip City Airport for another expansion of the Southside Industrial Park, but a group of neighbors mounted a vigorous protest against rezoning the land, in order to preserve their tranquil semi-rural lifestyle. After HEDCOR's "growing pains" tore at the South Side for two months, the Holland Planning Commission voted unanimously to approve the industrial park expansion. The only concession was a requirement to leave a three-hundred-foot buffer zone along Thirty-Second Street between the homes and industrial plants.[184]

In 1999 HEDCOR joined the chamber of commerce in a new strategic plan to "act as a champion for the development of human resources." Instead of recruiting industries to create jobs, the two organizations would provide money and advice to help companies retool workers for the high-tech jobs of the future. Some board members wanted to keep the focus on buying more land to add to the 535-acre northside park, but 133 acres were still standing vacant there in 2002, plus twenty-four acres in the southside park. But more companies, such as Beech-Nut Lifesavers, were closing than were new ones opening. HEDCOR's splendid run of successes was over. In 2007 the board voted unanimously to sell the last one hundred acres in the northside park to Holland Township for $2.3 million, which continues to sell the land for industrial use. After paying off mortgages and expenses, the board used the remaining $1.3 million in assets to create an endowment fund managed by the Community Foundation of the Holland/Zeeland Area to support future industrial expansion. The two parks in 2007 covered more than 1,200 acres and housed seventy-five companies employing fifteen thousand workers. HEDCOR in its forty-five-year history had accomplished far more than William "Bill" Vande Water, Mayor Visscher, and Roscoe Giles had dreamed possible.[185]

Conclusion

When Gordon Van Wylen assumed the presidency of Hope College in 1972, he was greatly surprised to find so many thriving and vibrant industries run by creative local owners who were willing to invest their time and money in the community. He was even more amazed to find a non-partisan city council that worked closely with business leaders in solving community problems. And the industries brought in educated

184 *Holland Sentinel*, 14, 19 Dec. 1994, 11 Jan., 1, 15 Feb., 2 Mar. 1995.

185 Ibid., 14 Feb. 1999, 9 Apr. 2002, 19 May 2007, 28 Sept. 2008, 17 Jan. 2009; *Grand Rapids Press Lakeshore Edition*, 18 May 2007.

and talented executives, who likewise came to share the local ethos of giving back to the community.[186]

The secret to Holland's industrial success was the skill and work ethic of the employees and the entrepreneurial talents of the many family-owned businesses, who passed their genes to succeeding generations in intergenerational companies. Already by the mid-1880s, Holland had twenty firms that employed up to five hundred workers, led by Cappon & Bertsch tannery, Standard Roller Mills, Werkman Manufacturing, West Michigan Furniture, and Seif Brewery. Zeeland had Veneklasen Brick. In the early 1890s, some twenty-five large firms in Holland employed over one thousand workmen and produced a total output exceeding $2 million. The workers, mainly Dutch American immigrants and their children and grandchildren, shared the Protestant work ethic and had a strong independent streak.[187]

In the twentieth century, names like Hollis Baker (Baker Furniture), Nicodemus Bosch (Western Machine Tool Works), August Landwehr (Holland Furnace), Earnest Brooks (Brooks Beverage), Buss Machine, Davis Die, Max De Pree of Herman Miller, Con De Pree of De Pree Chemical, Bill and Marvin De Witt of Bil-Mar Foods, Jack L. De Witt of Request Foods, the Donnellys, Hansen Machine, Otto Szekely (aircraft), G. W. Haworth, W. E. Dunn Manufacturing, Holland Hitch (Geerds), Jesiek Shipyard, Chris-Craft, Padnos, Trans-Matic (Thompson), Brown (Metal Flow), Heeringa (Trendway), Miller, Prince, Sligh Furniture, Chris Smith (Chris-Craft), Slikkers (S2 Yachts), RepcoLite Paints (Altena), Steketee-Van Huis Printing, and countless others, were synonymous with innovation, quality, design, efficiency, honesty, fairness, and community spirit. They made industry the engine of economic growth in Holland, and having succeeded, the owners and executives gave back to the community in remarkable ways. Augmenting the local entrepreneurial talent were top-flight executives of outside firms that relocated to Holland, such as Hart & Cooley, Chris-Craft, Chemetron, GE, and Beech-Nut LifeSavers. The outsiders caught the vision and joined the locals in promoting the city's welfare.

Some 30 percent of the economic base of the Holland-Zeeland area in 2012 was derived from manufacturing, according to Randy Thelen of Lakeshore Advantage, and that base has always been very

[186] Gordon Van Wylen interview with the author and David Boeve, 23 Sept. 2009, typescript, JAH.

[187] For the lists, see *Holland City News*, 26 May 1888, *Historical and Business Compendium of Ottawa County, Michigan, 1892-3*, 2 vols. (Grand Haven 1892), 1:180-81.

diverse. Holland and Zeeland were never "one company towns," he noted. The leading manufacturing industries until the Second World War were fine furniture, furnaces, and foodstuffs. Thereafter, office furniture, electronic components, and auto parts dominated. In retail and wholesale business, the list is equally long.

Inventions and products invented or developed by Holland and Zeeland companies are world-renowned. Automobile companies want to install the illuminated visors, self-dimming rearview mirrors with a digital compass, SmartBeam headlights, backup video cameras, and ever more sophisticated electronics developed by Donnelly, Prince Corp., and Gentex. In furniture, the mind focuses on the heirloom grandfather and mantel clocks from Howard Miller, the world's largest maker of fine clocks, and the celebrated Eames Chair designed at Herman Miller and featured in leading art museums.

In pharmaceuticals, Pfizer's blockbuster drugs Benadryl, Lipitor, Dilantin, and Neurontin were developed in their Holland laboratory. In pleasure boats, the sleek wooden Chris-Craft cruisers are the envy of boat aficionados, and Tiara yachts, Pursuit powerboats, and sailboats built by the Slikkers family are in demand around the world.

Renowned designers who worked their magic in local companies include Charles and Ray Eames, George Nelson, Raymond Loewy, Henry Dreyfuss, Hatley Earl, Gilbert Rohde, and Bill Stumpf. These geniuses started a tradition of designing cutting-edge products for international companies like General Electric, Ford, Chrysler, Chris-Craft, Tiara, Herman Miller, Haworth, Donnelly, Steelcase, Whirlpool, Tennant, Bissell, Brunswick, and Sears. In 2008 the Holland Area Arts Council mounted a display of products designed by these and other local designers under the acronym HIDDEN, or Holland Industrial Design Designing Everyday Necessities. The point of the exhibit was that local residents, completely unaware, rubbed shoulders while going about their daily business with designers of products they used everyday.[188]

Most of Holland's largest companies have been and remain non-union: GE, Chris-Craft, Hart & Coley, Holland Hitch, and Life Savers are exceptions. The United Auto Workers tried to organize Holland's JCI workers in 2005, but were unsuccessful. Many JCI plants around the country are unionized, and company officials had agreed in 2002 to a "neutrality agreement" for the six Holland plants, that is, they would

[188] *Holland Sentinel*, 9 Jan. 2008.

allow UAW organizers to enter the plants. Magna Donnelly signed the same agreement with the UAW, but its Holland plants also remain non-union.[189]

The faith dimension of leading business men and women is derived from their religious affiliation. Many of those of Dutch Reformed persuasion have embodied the Calvinist sense of stewardship and benevolence that has led to philanthropic endeavors. They strive to glorify God and use the resources He has entrusted to them wisely and responsibly. Business executives who came to Holland seemed to absorb the spirit of their counterparts to give back to the community and treat employees with respect.

189 Ibid., 6 Sept. 2005, 2 Sept. 2001.

CHAPTER 16

Pioneer Farming, Agricultural Fairs, and Colonization

"Holland City is a trade center in the midst of a thrifty farming community," boasted a local newspaper editor in 1892.[1] The local economy has always relied heavily on agriculture. The city's main function was to service the thousands of farms dotting the countryside. Farmers carted grains to city mills for processing, hides to tanneries, milk and butter to creameries, and fruits and vegetables to canneries. City processors and dealers shipped the products of the farm—grains, fruit, vegetables, poultry and eggs, beef and pork and hides—to regional and national markets, especially Chicago. Virtually every local farm product passed through Holland middlemen. Over time, as transportation improved with roads and railroads, local farmers learned the advantages of competition and took some of their business to neighboring towns and cities, especially Grand Rapids, but Holland remained the market center, and its merchants handled most of the business.

Even today, despite the impact of urbanization, food processing and farm equipment are major industries in Ottawa and Allegan

1 *Ottawa County Times*, 2 Mar. 1892.

Counties. These two counties have led the state in terms of market value of farm production. They rank in the top one hundred counties nationally in terms of fruit, nursery products, eggs, turkeys, and hogs. The market value of farm production in Allegan County grew 71 percent between 2002 and 2008 to $397 million. Market value in Ottawa County in the same six years grew 43 percent to $391 million. Allegan overtook Ottawa in this period.[2]

From the earliest days, farmers bought provisions and supplies, fertilizers, hardware goods, clothing and home furnishings, and farm implements from city businesses. Farmers hired veterinarians and medical doctors when necessary, and went to town on Saturday nights for shopping, recreation, entertainment, haircuts for the men, catching up on the local gossip, and enjoying small pleasures like ice cream. Holland hosted market days, fairs, farm institutes, and picnics for farmers and their organizations, such as the Holland Farmers Association, Holland Co-op, Holland Poultry Association, Ottawa County Farm Bureau, and the Holland Community Fair.

Language and ethnicity bound together *de Stad* and *de Kolonie*. Dutch farmers trusted those who shared their mother tongue, and they preferred to do business with fellow members of the "household of faith." Holland had its share of American merchants and businessmen, of course, but in the early decades, they had to master the rudiments of the Dutch language and culture in order to succeed. Many did so and put down deep roots, even intermarrying with the Dutch and joining their churches.

Early years

Most immigrants began in abject poverty. In the Old Country they had been field workers and laborers who suffered seasons of want. Their struggle did not cease in Michigan; it simply changed forms. The homeland had a surplus of workers and a shortage of land. In Michigan the reverse was true: laborers were at a premium, and land was cheap. The immigrants did not have to indenture themselves as laborers or apprentices, and they did not have to plow someone else's field or work the land as tenants of a *grote boer* (large farmer). They could become independent landowners. Within seven years of the first settlement of the Holland colony, most immigrants owned at least the fabled forty acres, and many had large farms, claimed Hermanus Doesburg, editor of *De Hollander*.[3] In the American frontier environment, the immigrants substituted self-reliance, entrepreneurship, and adaptability for the

2 *Holland Sentinel*, 8 Feb. 2009.

3 *De Hollander*, 16 Mar. 1854.

functions assumed by the community in the Old World patterns of village life.

Federal land records show that in 1847-49, Dutch immigrants in Holland and Zeeland Townships bought smaller farms than their compatriots in Fillmore Township in Allegan County. Ottawa County land entries averaged forty-six acres, compared to fifty-six acres in Allegan County. Three large purchasers at the Ionia Public Land Office dominated the market in Ottawa County: Jannes Vande Luyster, who platted the village of Zeeland, with 1,650 acres; A. C. Van Raalte, who platted the village of Holland, with 1,625 acres; and Jan Rabbers, who platted the village of Groningen, with 640 acres.[4]

Deprivation was a test to earn this New World freedom, and hunger, or the threat of it, encouraged hard work. One settler recalled that first year when "weeks passed that we did not even have Johnicake [*sic*], . . . but beans and water, morning, noon and night." (Johnnycake was an early type of pancake made from corn flour.) But the pioneer continued, more positively: "We had free fuel [firewood], free house, free beans, free water; I never had these things in the Netherlands."[5]

The Dutch at first had to change their traditional diet of potatoes, rye bread, cheese, and smoked sausage and bacon. Indian corn (or maize), a native grain, was one of the new staples for the Dutch. Once the Indians showed them how to prepare it, corn meal became the mainstay in their diet. The Dutch learned to cook and serve corn in every way imaginable, even burnt corn for a cheap coffee substitute, after it was ground in the coffee mill. As Douwe R. Drukker recalled, "Many ate Jonny-cake for breakfast, cornmeal mush for lunch, and mindful of the saying, 'variety is the spice of life,' they ate cornmeal pudding for supper." The tables in the log cabins were heaped with piles of this healthful gritty, thick, mash that would help settlers survive the winter. Most importantly, corn was cheap and readily available. The Indians maintained stockpiles of it, as did any grocer in the surrounding towns. Buckwheat and white beans were other staples. Pieter Van Anrooy remembered eating beans three times a day, including bean soup and baked beans. Some settlers suffered ill health from so limited a diet.[6]

4 Compilations by Richard Harms, as detailed in his "Fissures in the Fellowship: Graafschap as the Lightning Rod for Discontent within 'The Colony,'" unpublished paper, 2008, Archives, Calvin College (ACC).

5 Gerhard De Jonge Memoirs, Holland Museum Archives (HMA).

6 Marie De Young, "Old Settlers' Days," *Holland City News*, 13 Nov. 1913; Michael Duyser, "Memories of the Life of M. Duyser," undated, "Pioneer Memories," Gerrit Van Schelven Papers, box 9, HMA; D. R. Drukker, "Comparison of the Past and the Present," typescript, and Pieter Van Anrooy Memoir, both in P. T. Moerdyke Papers, box 15, HMA.

By 1848 the Dutch had learned from the Indians how to make maple sugar cakes by tapping the many maple groves in the area. Sugaring was the first communal activity of the late winter, and the procedure was simple. When the sap began to run, the people would go to the sugar camps carrying an ax to make troughs of logs, an auger to tap the trees, and a large iron kettle to boil the sap over a stone hearth until it was thick and would "grain" and slowly dry. The sugar cakes were their only sweetener until they could purchase honeybee hives from older states, or if they were extremely fortunate, they might find a queen and her hive in the wild. Teenagers recalled sugaring as a happy season of frolic and feastings.[7]

The first years were a time of disparity, of temporary but often-imagined abundance and of much more tangible and enduring want. Since few fields had been cleared of trees and plowed, and little could be grown, most provisions, including the inevitable sacks of cornmeal or buckwheat, had to be purchased elsewhere and shipped in. These imports included typical essentials like coffee, vinegar, tobacco, white beans, salted pork and bacon, tea, butter, and flour. By 1848 Johannes Vande Luyster, the financier of Zeeland, was importing large amounts of food from Grand Rapids, Grandville, and other points east. One purchase included one hundred barrels of flour, another, sixty bushels of potatoes.[8]

By 1849 when primitive road connections to Grand Rapids had been established, consumer goods, including heavy stoves, were also transported to Ottawa County. Nevertheless, the Dutch continued to maintain a simple lifestyle, even if "wealthy Americans may look with pity" on them, as Van Raalte declared. An official in the Michigan State Board of Agriculture noted that the Dutch farmers bought more land and built bigger barns, "but these results can only be accomplished by the most rigid economy in living, such as few American families would or could practice."[9]

Children of the settlers were sent to Grand Rapids and surrounding areas to find work with Americans as servants and farm hands. When they returned with their wages (in cash or food) and reported on the

7 Van Raalte to Karel de Moen, 11 Feb. 1849, in *Der Toestand der Hollandsche Kolonizatie in den Staat Michigan* (1849), translated by E. R. Post and D. F. Van Vliet, 1978, typescript, 7, ACC; "Spring Recalls Sugaring Times," *Holland City News* clipping, 1916, in Moerdyke Papers, box 15, HMA.

8 Johannes Vande Luyster, Vande Luyster Family Papers, box 3, HMA.

9 *Sheboygan Nieuwsbode*, 5 Feb. 1850; A. C. Van Raalte, 23 Sept. 1858, in *Detroit Daily Advertiser*, 19 Oct. 1858; Report, Sanford Howard, Member State Board of Agriculture, Lansing, 8 Sept. 1865, in *Grand Haven News*, 27 Sept. 1865.

abundance of food in the American towns, they initiated a "hunger migration" from the colony to the cities of Grand Rapids, Grand Haven, and Kalamazoo. This migration of 1847 and 1848 may have helped relieve some of the pressure on food stores.[10] It also helped scatter the Dutch, as farmers took up nearly all the valuable uplands, which thus protected the colony against an "invasion of speculators."[11]

While on the one hand, it seemed that anything of value had to be imported, on the other hand, the Black River watershed was fertile and promising—a "land of milk and honey." One could, in effect, live off the land, supplemented with the crops of corn, grain, and potatoes. In season, there were all sorts of wild berries and a plentiful supply of various nuts. The settlers, however poor marksmen at first, soon added meat to their diets from the plentiful wildlife. Game included rabbit, squirrel, deer, turkey, duck, passenger pigeons, fish, and (as late as 1874) the occasional bear. In this, there was little supply problem, and it was tempting to write home a "bacon letter," bragging about how much meat there was to go around. The Indians were glad to sell dressed venison to the settlers for from 1¢ to 3¢ a pound.[12]

The Dutch either bought animals on their way to the colony or they made special trips to purchase them. Although it was difficult to keep track of livestock in the woods, the land proved rich for grazing. It was a blessing that the cattle and hogs could roam freely.

Almost every family in Holland had a milk cow, and they allowed the animals to forage at will to save on feed and fencing costs. But the animals overran Market Square (later Centennial Park) and trampled picket fences, gardens, and shrubs. To end the general nuisance, in 1882 the city council enacted an ordinance that made it illegal for residents to allow their cows to roam the city at night. Fortunately, barbed wire had been invented by then, and residents could fence in their cows with this less expensive and more durable product. The issue resonated, because almost every homeowner had a garden plot and an orchard to supply the family table with potatoes, vegetables, greens, and fruit, though few were as entrepreneurial as the elderly market gardener Cornelius Van Herwynen. People from all over town came with their baskets to buy produce from his extensive garden, which covered nearly the entire block from River to Pine and from Thirteenth to Fourteenth Streets,

10 Robert P. Swierenga, "'Better Prospects for Work': Van Raalte's Holland Colony and Its Connections to Grand Rapids," *Grand River Valley History* 15 (1998): 14-22.

11 J. Kolvoord, Battle Creek, MI, to Gerrit Van Schelven, 14 Dec. 1916 (Van Schelven Papers, box 2, HMA).

12 "E. J. Harrington's Reminiscences," *De Grondwet*, 25 Jan. 1913.

all surrounded by a high board fence. Van Herwynen was the first to market sweet potatoes in 1878.[13]

Success in agriculture was not immediate. Farming was a process of trial and error until the Dutch learned the time-tested practices of Americans. The colonists first had to clear the land of trees, which were so dense as to be impenetrable. Unskilled in the ax, adze, and crosscut saw, the Dutch with minimal instructions from the few Americans and the Indians in the area quickly mastered these tools. An 1849 visitor described it well when he said the Dutch were "determined to shake off the problems and manners of the country they left, and become, as they termed it, 'Yankie,' as much and as soon as possible, particularly in the way of farming as Yankees do."[14]

In the first years, much of their time was spent with the axe clearing land, splitting fence rails, making barrel staves and shingles, and stripping hemlock bark for tannin. "We have many expert choppers among the Dutch," declared Doesburg, editor of *De Hollander*, "who will do as much work with the axe as their American neighbors." They felled trees by the thousands, leaving an equal number of three-foot stumps. Within the first year, most settlers had cleared five to ten acres for crops, but a few ambitious ones had twenty to forty acres planted. By January 1849, after eighteen months, the Dutch has cleared 1,744 acres, which by 1851 had grown to 3,000 acres, an average of one acre of tillable land per person.[15]

Hence, in the first years, the colonists were largely dependent for their livelihood on lumbering. And it was lucrative. Coopers or stave-makers earned from $4 to $6 per thousand for staves. Zeeland pastor Cornelius Vander Meulen felled seven pine trees and made $25, enough to buy twenty acres at the Ionia Land Office. When the Chicago market weakened and prices dropped for lumber, shingles, and staves, as it did briefly in 1857-58 during the national economic downturn, the Dutch suffered severely. "Lumber was their chief dependence," teacher Abraham Thompson of the Holland Academy wrote to friends in the East, and when that failed, "they are deprived of the necessities of life." A crop failure in 1858 added to the difficulties.[16]

13 *Holland City News*, 24 Oct. 1874, 20 May, 1 July 1876; "Fifty Years Ago Today" 4 June 1931, 11 Aug. 1932, 13 Oct. 1938; Adrian Van Koevering, *Legends of the Dutch* (Zeeland, MI: Zeeland Record Co., 1960), 354-70.

14 "Holland in Dutch Hands," *Grand River Eagle*, 9 Feb. 1849.

15 *De Hollander*, 16 Mar. 1854 (quote); Dingman Versteeg, *Pelgrim-Vaders of het Westen* (Grand Rapids: C. M. Loomis & Co., 1886), English translation typescript by William K. Reinsma (ACC), 143.

16 Jacob Den Herder, "Life Sketch of Jacob Den Herder," anonymous translation, typescript, 6, Dekker Huis Museum, Zeeland, MI; Report, Henry Griffin, Ottawa

Since wood was cheap and farm implements required cash, which was scarce, the Dutch used wood to fashion tools, shoes, and household items, including tables, chairs, chests, and beds. Tools included churns, troughs, axe-handles (which fetched 5¢ apiece at the market), and harrows with six or seven wooden pegs inserted into holes for teeth. The pegs gave way to steel teeth when money was available. Hayforks with handles twelve feet long were crafted of hickory or ironwood. The wooden tines on the bottom were said to be stronger than steel ones. The Dutch fabricated ox carts, wagons, and sleds entirely from wood, with not a single piece of iron.[17]

Wives and daughters helped on the farm as much as their regular housework would allow. They chopped trees, hoed and weeded crops, loaded produce on wagons, churned butter and collected eggs for the market, threshed wheat by beating the stalks with sticks, ground the grain into flour, and went along on hunting trips.[18]

The immigrants learned the hard way about soil quality, best cropping practices, and animal husbandry. Ottawa County contained every kind of soil imaginable. One quarter was prime farmland, heavy loam and well drained. Another quarter was lighter and suitable for horticulture. Forests and wetlands made up much of the remainder. The Dutch found that Old World farming methods did not work well in America. "The manner of cultivation has been bad, very bad," reported James Walker, a Yankee farmer and schoolteacher in early Zeeland. "Although informed of the folly of putting their potatoes so deep in the ground, they heeded it not, thinking they knew best. The result is, they have less than half a crop, some of very good quality and some rotten." And, Walker continued, "the corn was planted too thick, and consequently has not eared well; the stalks, which will be much needed here before next spring, have been permitted to waste upon the ground, or suffer damage by frost." Pumpkins, squash, turnips, and other new vegetables "they don't know what to do with," leaving the fruit to rot "while their cattle are Spring poor almost." The immigrants also failed to fertilize their fields, believing mistakenly that the ashes of burnt trees would nourish the soil for twenty years.[19]

County Clerk, 10 July 1848, in Grand Rapids *Grand River Eagle*, 14 July 1848; A. C. Van Raalte, "Census of the Colony, January 18, 1849," A. C. Van Raalte Papers, ACC; Isaac Wyckoff, "Report of Visit to Holland Colonies in Michigan and Wisconsin," 1849, Gerrit Van Schelven Collection, HMA; John Van Vleck, Holland, to Mr. and Mrs. Abner Hasbrouck, New York City, 22 July 1858, reprinted in *Holland Sentinel*, 29 Mar. 1979; *Christian Intelligencer*, 9 Sept. 1858 (quote).

17 Versteeg, *Pelgrim-Vaders*, English typescript, 135-36, 144.

18 Ibid., 144-45.

19 *Grand River Eagle*, 13 Oct. 1848; *Sheboygan Nieuwsbode*, 27 June 1850; *Holland Sentinel*, 12 Mar. 1983.

Lack of know-how was not the only obstacle to cultivation. Thick grasses and weeds covered the open ground, and it took two years after special breaking plows turned over the sod for the vegetation to rot. Teams of oxen provided the power for sodbusting and to pull out the stumps, which were burned. Before then, seed potatoes had to be planted in clusters of two or three between the stumps. With a piece of wood, the soil was mounded over the seedlings to form what looked like molehills. Only in the third year could regular plows pulled by a single ox cultivate the soil, but farmers still had to work around stumps and their root systems, which took many years to clear out. Horses were much less common, since they lacked the brute power of the ox, the true pioneer beast of burden. And old oxen could be eaten! As late as 1874, 107 work oxen still pulled the plow in Holland Township, compared to 366 horses.[20]

Not until 1851 or 1852 did the colony reach self-sufficiency in basic foodstuffs. New equipment brought marginal improvements. Gradually, through hard labor, patches of cleared land appeared in the forests, but trees still dominated the landscape. To maximize their yield without clearing yet more land, some farmers planted two separate crops in a field in the same year. The main crops included wheat, corn, oats, rye, potatoes, and hay. Dutch farms were smaller, on average, than their American neighbors, and they worked the land more intensively with their many children, as was customary in the land-starved Old Country. The scythe was the most efficient way to cut grain, and the new cradles obviated the need to bend over. Over time, the Dutch acquired the latest farm equipment, such as mowing machines, wheel horse-rakes, horse-pitchforks, and grain drills.[21]

Farming for the Dutch Reformed was a righteous calling. It brought a decent living through hard work and God's blessings, not through swindling, speculation, or profiting from another's want. Since outlots east of Holland were six acres and those south of town were five acres, city families there kept a dairy cow or two and a large vegetable garden. Many, including Van Raalte, bought grafted fruit trees in the 1850s from Harmon E. Hudson's Holland Nursery, which occupied the former farm of George N. Smith (chapter 1). In the core city, the lots

20 Jacob Harms Dunnink, 24 Jan. 1850, 9 Oct. 1853, translated by Jake Reedyk, Jacob Harms Dunnink Papers, HMA; *De Hollander*, 24 June 1874.

21 *Ottawa Register*, 16 Nov. 1857; *Allegan Journal*, 10 Aug. 1857; *Grand Haven News*, 27 Sept. 1865; Robert P. Swierenga and William Van Appledorn, eds., *Old Wing Mission: Cultural Interchange as Chronicled by George and Arvilla Smith in their Work with Chief Wakazoo's Ottawa Band on the West Western Frontier* (Grand Rapids: Eerdmans, 2008), 351-52.

Sod busting clay soil with a "three horsepower" plow
(*Joint Archives of Holland*)

ranged from a quarter to a full acre, which also allowed for a vegetable garden and some fruit trees. Canning fruits and vegetables was women's work. Self-sufficiency was the goal, with as much bartering as possible; only absolute necessities were store-bought.[22]

Because Holland was somewhat isolated and had little industry at first, the economy relied on farming. It would take years for specialists—bakers, butchers, and milkmen—to evolve. In 1858 Henry D. Post, the editor of the *Ottawa Register*, wrote: "The Farmer is the one upon whom all depend, and it is his produce which is indispensable for all."[23] One might well have added that the farmer, in turn, could rely on God alone for sun and rain in due time.

Post was partial to the farmer, but did little or no farming himself. Instead, he was for the first few years Holland's foremost grocer and provision merchant. Post & Co. began in 1848 by obtaining supplies from Allegan, Richmond, or Singapore via the Kalamazoo River, or from Chicago by lake schooner via Grand Haven. Henry's younger brother Hoyt, who turned twenty-one years old in 1848, was a traveling agent responsible for supplying the store. In the colony's third year, 1849, Hoyt became well aware of the precarious situation. By no means was it out of the question that the entire settlement could fall victim to famine or disease. He wrote:

22 Jacob Harms Dunnink, 20 May 1856, HMA; Versteeg, *Pelgrim-Vaders*, English typescript, 136-37; 1848 Holland City plat, HMA.

23 *Ottawa Register*, 19 Oct. 1858. Henry Post was involved in everything. "Henry is driving at me about some speculation or other all the time. He flies from one notion to the other, and would like to have me do as he is, running himself trying to do five times as much as a any man can do" (Hoyt Post Diary, 25 Feb, 1850, HMA).

> I tremble for the inhabitants of our settlement when the judgment comes, living as they do, paying little or no regard to cleanliness, regularity in diet and habits, houses half warmed or illy [*sic*] ventilated, sure to be one or the other; families living, sleeping and cooking in one room all their life, eating voraciously while food lasts and starving when it is gone. These I fear will form fit subjects for the cholera. But we shall hope for the best, and try to be prepared for the worst in case it comes.[24]

At Post & Co. one could purchase familiar imported items like tea, Dutch "Harlem Oil" (*Haarlemmer Olie*),[25] "Old Java Coffee," and brandy and port wine ("for medicinal purposes"). Also available were dry goods like nails, cotton, and calico. By 1852 medicines on hand included quinine to fight malaria and sulfate morphine, a pain-relieving narcotic. In regard to medicine and drugs, Post had no qualms selling any item that promised to put hair on your head or prevent stomach worms, so long as he saw a profit in it. But Post had not befriended the Hollanders to abuse them; he was in business for the long haul. He advertised that he would treat all customers equally, favoring none with lower prices, and that he would sell *goederen* (imported goods) for cash only. On this last point he had to be lenient to survive, and so in 1851 he advertised to buy ten thousand bushels of "good sound Corn in exchange for goods." *Waren* (domestic products) he exchanged for black salt, Indian corn, oats, potatoes, linen or cotton, gold, silver or copper, jewelry, or forest products.[26]

Post & Co. had to compete with specialized stores by 1852, including the bakery of Johannes "Jan" Vissers and the butter creamery of Klaas & William J. Mulder. In 1859 it was not uncommon for Pieter F. Pfanstiehl's general store to take in from three to four hundred pounds of fresh-made butter per day. His cool storage room sometimes held twice that amount.[27]

The detailed business records of Alderd Plugger, although difficult to decipher, shed light on the situation of food, particularly the staple grains. As early as 1853, Plugger owned a mill and a lake schooner and was shipping to Chicago a substantial amount of oats and buckwheat. These were his most profitable exports. Plugger did not

24 Hoyt Post Diary, 18 Feb. 1849, HMA.

25 Harlem Oil was castor oil developed in Haarlem, the Netherlands in 1696 and famous as a cure for intestinal ailments, notably as a laxative and to induce delivery.

26 *De Hollander*, 4, 25 Jan. 1851.

27 *De Hollander*, 21 July 1852; *Allegan Journal*, 14 Feb. 1859.

export flour (processed wheat) until 1858. Earlier he had occasionally imported flour, notably a two-hundred-barrel lot from Grand Haven in 1853. Since flour was not regularly imported, it can be assumed that Holland was growing just enough wheat for its own needs but with little or no surplus. The success of the oat crop, in comparison, may be attributed to its higher tolerance for wet weather and ability to grow in mild summers. Other locally grown grains included rye, barley, and timothy grass for animal feed; vegetables and legumes included peas, beets, potatoes, and turnips. Plugger's activities confirm editor Hermanus Doesburg's conclusion in *De Hollander* that the colony was becoming self-sufficient; merchants were importing less and exporting more.[28]

Although a primitive outpost itself, Holland served the surrounding area as a marketplace. It was a point of reference, the center of the world, except for colonists in Fillmore Township, who found Saugatuck an easier wagon route. Farmers came to Holland to buy tools and farming implements; already in 1852 two men were making corn husking machines and farm tools. Holland also held the largest cattle market in the colony. For a large part, the wealth of *de Stad* originated in the countryside. The *Holland City News* wrote: "The growth of a town is dependent in a great measure on that of the country about it. Holland is fortunately located in the midst of a fine farming country, and the trade of the farmer is an important part of the business of our merchants."[29]

One difficulty in buying or selling cattle was that farmers had little cash, and few could pay outright for their purchases. One solution was for the stores to serve as banks. It was not uncommon for a farmer to write out on a small piece of paper, "good for so many dollars on my store credit," and then sign his name. This was a primitive type of checking system, based on trust. In Zeeland, Vande Luyster employed a similar method. Since his brother-in-law and business partner, Herman De Kruif, owned a general store, he could offer payment either in cash, or a slightly higher amount in *stoorgoed* (store goods).[30] Bartering was common, and ministers and teachers often had to be content with payment in potatoes, chickens, or apples.

28 Aldred Plugger Account Book, 1853-69, Joint Archives of Holland (JAH), transcribed and translated by Michael J. Douma; *De Hollander*, 15 Dec. 1852, 8 Sept. 1859.

29 *Holland City News*, 5 Jan. 1889.

30 *De Hollander*, 28 June 1852, 1 Sept. 1859; Cornelius De Putter Papers, HMA; Jannes Vande Luyster Jr., to "Geliefde Broeder" [Dear Brother], 17 June 1851, Johannes Vande Luyster Family Collection, HMA.

Planting, harvesting, and attending church occupied the week; little time was left for leisure, and much thought was given to finding the most successful crops. Buckwheat continued to be an important cash crop. In 1859 *De Hollander* estimated that there were five hundred local farmers growing at least two acres of buckwheat each. With an expected yield of from thirty-five to forty bushels per acre at 50¢ a bushel, these few acres could bring in from $35 to $40 per farmer and up to $20,000 for the colony, unless an early September frost destroyed the grain, as happened in 1859. "The Lord makes rich and poor; He is sovereign," intoned the editor. Most crops grew well in the region's favorable climate, but farming was always a high-risk business.[31]

To cut the risk, farmers diversified. Farm wagons passing Eighth and River Streets carried live and dressed hogs, stave bolts, grain, wood, hay, and "almost everything else marketable." The various products helped farmers offset poor harvests. For example, in 1853, Plugger and Post exported pearlash, a refined wood ash product that when used in baking released carbon dioxide and helped bread to rise. By 1858 Plugger was also exporting small quantities of fish and cranberries. Suppliers were the commercial fishermen Nieterink, Vinke & Co. and the Woltman & Winter Bros., who launched their newly built schooner *Union* in 1857 to service their nets in Black Lake. Commercial fishing did not flourish in Holland, due to the frequent closing of the mouth of the harbor by siltation, but fruit growing did thrive. For excitement, the hard-at-work locals looked forward to the annual trading visits of Indians.[32]

Holland Community Fair

One way to promote the exchange of goods in the city was Market Day, a custom the Dutch brought from Europe. Holland's first Market Day was held in the fall of 1851. It brought farmers to town from far and near to barter and do business, and to learn about new agricultural techniques and equipment. The booths were short on fruits and flowers, but plenty of garden vegetables were for sale. Perhaps the most important aspect was the market for livestock, which could be traded or purchased outright. Jacob Quintus, editor of the Dutch-language

31 *Allegan Journal*, 22 June, 10 Aug. 1857; *De Hollander*, 8 Sept. 1859.

32 *De Hollander*, 7 Oct. 1857; *Holland City News*, 13 Jan. 1877; Plugger Account Book, JAH. The People's Assembly tried to start a fishery, but it failed (Van Koevering, *Legends of the Dutch*, 247).

Sheboygan (Wisconsin) *Nieuwsbode*, wrote that the Holland Market Day was an idea "deserving of imitation elsewhere."[33]

Although a local fair was first proposed in 1850, it took several decades to get the idea off the ground. Attorney Henry Post, the Holland Township supervisor and English editor of *De Hollander*, with the encouragement of Van Raalte, used his editorial pen to crusade for an annual fair with exhibits and prizes, and where the most enterprising farmers would "enlighten the whole" by precept and example, and thus "strengthen the bands that ought to bind us and our interests together." This would complement the market days in the spring and fall for "exchanges and purchases of cattle, sheep, hogs, horses, etc." Post invited interested people to assemble in Holland on January 31, 1851, "to plan a yearly fair." If ten or fifteen people got behind the idea, it could happen in time to feature a maple sugar exhibition, he noted hopefully.[34]

Two dozen men answered the call, including all of Van Raalte's ministerial colleagues—Marten Ypma at Friesland, Seine Bolks at Overisel, Cornelius Vander Meulen at Zeeland, and Hendrik Klyn at Graafschap—and leading farmers and businessmen in each settlement such as Jannes Vande Luyster of Zeeland and Aldert Plugger of Groningen. This group made up the general committee, chaired by Post, with Giles Vande Wall as secretary. Vande Wall, a teacher at the Holland Academy, was a bright young man who had mastered English and translated articles into Dutch for *De Hollander*. Annual fairs, the committee asserted, would promote husbandry and industry by bringing all the settlements together for 'friendly intercourse." Fairs would encourage new manufactures and industries, stimulate farmers and mechanics with the promise of "premiums and diplomas," and share the best techniques and farming practices. Everyone agreed that the exhibitions would "promote harmony and good feeling among the people, besides benefiting their pecuniary interests." Profit was the bottom line.[35]

33 *Allegan Journal*, 22 May 1875; *Sheboygan Nieuwsbode*, 14 Feb. 1851; *De Hollander*, 1 Feb. 1851; *Holland Sentinel*, 26 Sept. 1987.

34 Peter T. Moerdyke, "The Fair in the Holland Colony," Moerdyke Papers, HMA, citing *De Hollander*, 28 Dec. 1850; Randall P. Vande Water, "Holland Fairs Date Back to 1851," in *Holland: Happenings, Heroes & Hot Shots*, 4:47-55. Vande Wall in 1852 began publishing *De Nederlander* in Kalamazoo and then graduated from New Brunswick Theological Seminary and entered the Reformed Church ministry, including a stint as teacher at the Holland Academy and as a pastor in South Africa. See Henry S. Lucas, *Netherlanders in America* (Ann Arbor: University of Michigan Press, 1955, reprinted Grand Rapids: Eerdmans, 1989), 532.

35 *De Hollander*, 25 Jan., 1 Feb. 1851.

The idea seemed to catch on, and colonists came forward to offer articles for exhibit, including needlework, knitting, boots and shoes, fruits and vegetables, flowers, woodcrafts, and even the first hand loom made in the colony. Despite the push of the prominent leaders, plans for the fair stalled. In May 1851 Post published a plaintive letter in *De Hollander* urging, to no avail, that an agricultural fair be held yet that fall. Market Days, yes, but fairs, no. After the Dutch dropped the ball, the Americans stepped up, and in 1853 they organized the first Ottawa County Fair at Eastmanville in the northeastern part of the county. Hendrik Van Eyck, a lawyer, represented Holland Township on the organizing committee. But for many decades few Hollanders ever participated.[36]

Dutch farmers were content with periodic "free markets," which were essentially livestock auctions, modeled after those long familiar in the Netherlands. And Zeeland and Fillmore farmers took the lead, not Holland, which had no suitable market square for decades. The auctions created a market for livestock of all kinds and allowed farmers to trade among themselves at prices set in open competition. Soon hundreds of animals changed hands on these market days. In May 1856 the merchants Post and Pfanstiehl hosted the first livestock auction in Holland, which was held on Eighth Street near their stores. Only sixty cattle were brought for sale, which was half that in the Zeeland auctions. Post hosted a second auction in October, which was better organized and included a clerk of the market to record all transactions.[37]

For several decades, the Eighth Street market had a greater economic impact than agricultural fairs, which mainly offered entertainment. Farmers from far and near drove large herds of hogs, horses, cattle, and sheep along country roads to Holland. Horse "headquarters" was at Market Street (Central Avenue) around the livery barns of Hermanus Boone, E. J. Harrington, and Jacobus H. Nibbelink, with a smaller trading center at Gerrit Haverkate's livery at Fish Street (Columbia Avenue). Market Day scenes were chaotic: "[F]armers trading and selling and losing their tempers, and mixing forceful expletives with the bellowing of the sweltering cattle, the scene was a queer sight indeed." The livestock auctions were crucial to farmers' successful operations, but merchants and shopkeepers benefited too, despite the boisterous disruptions on Holland's main street, as farmers spent their money on food and goods. Market Day had a holiday atmosphere,

36 Moerdyke, "The Fair"; *De Hollander*, 16 Sept. 1853; *Ottawa Register*, 19, 26 Oct. 1958.

37 *De Hollander*, 31 Aug., 2, 9 Nov. 1853, 14 Nov. 1855, 21 May, 1 Oct. 1856.

Old fashioned Market Day on Eighth Street in 1879, with sidewalks lined with farmers and cattle brought in for the livestock auctions. Looking west (left to right) is Kuite's Meat Market, Peter "Dikke Piet" Brown's Saloon, Sprietsma's Shoe Store, Kenyon's Holland City Bank, Boot & Kramer's Grocery (in Vander Veen's original frame hardware store, which was moved from the southeast corner of River Street), vacant lot (later site of the Boston Restaurant), and Vander Veen's new brick hardware store erected on the River Street site (*Holland City News*, 23 Sept. 1909)

Holland Academy student J. H. Brown recalled, and "religion, politics, and business were talked on every corner."[38]

By the 1880s the old-fashioned Market Day wore out its welcome. Citizens complained about Eighth Street being overrun by farmers displaying their livestock, wares, poultry, and produce, and turning the city center into a veritable farm fair. "Lots of people but very little business. What a humbug these market days are," declared editor William Rogers of the *Holland City News*. Catching a greased pig was the highlight of the day for teenaged boys. The thirteen taverns in town "wet too many whistles," and fights broke out between city toughs and *Drenthe boeren* (Drenthe farm boys). Editor Rogers gave the scenario: "Holland had a bunch of 'young bloods' [the editor knew them well] who were aching for trouble and the farmer was their common enemy. They groomed for weeks, nursing for a coming Market Day. . . . The hardest fighting farmers came from around Drenthe. Overisel, too, had a few and honors were not always even in favor of the 'city bloods.' Holland had but one policeman, Dick Sakkers, and he could not begin

[38] *Holland City News*, 23 Sept. 1909, 29 Sept. 1910, 23 Aug. 1928; Vande Water, "Holland Fairs," in *Holland Happenings*, 4:49; "Recollections of Rev. J. H. Brown," box 15, Moerdyke Papers, HMA.

to cope with a half dozen fights going on at the same time." The troubles revealed a growing social and cultural distance between rural folk and city dwellers, between farmers and merchants. Market Day was weighed in the balance on Main Street and found wanting.[39]

To avoid the hullabaloo, civic leaders hit on the idea of moving the activities away from the central business district, and combining the livestock auctions with the typical fair activities–races, show animals, and handicraft prizes. In 1885 nearly thirty-five years after the initial attempt to organize an agricultural fair and at the invitation of Leendert Mulder, editor of *De Grondwet*, more than fifty leading merchants, progressive farmers, and fruit growers joined hands to form the South Ottawa & West Allegan Agricultural Fair, later renamed the Holland Community Fair. Oscar E. Yates, a prominent physician and surgeon in Holland, led the effort, along with attorney Arend Visscher, liveryman Hermanus Boone, dry goods merchant Dan Bertsch, editor Rogers of the *Holland City News*, Jacob Kuite Sr., John Pessink, Leendert Mulder, John Kramer, Otto Breyman, fire chief Leendert "Lane" T. Kanters, and Benjamin "Ben" Van Raalte of Holland Township. De Grondwet Hall, a popular meeting place on the corner of Seventh and Lake (River) Streets, hosted the group, and twenty men immediately paid membership fees, and the committee set about writing articles of incorporation, a constitution, and by-laws.

With advance sales of admission tickets up to ten years, the society raised sufficient funds to proceed. They obtained a ten-year lease from Hope College on forty-three choice acres a half-mile west of the city center along the waterfront from the banks of present-day Kollen Park westward to the foot of Sixteenth Street, where a harness-racing track was laid out. The grounds "cannot be excelled in the State," boasted Rogers. Wiepke Diekema was hired to supervise the construction of a half-mile oval, a thousand feet of stables, stalls, and pens, a grandstand, floral hall, and seven-foot fence around the entire perimeter, all in time for a planned opening in early October 1885. John Kleyn was contracted to build the grandstand and floral hall. The total cost was $4,000. Just before the fair opened, Diekema got up a building "bee" of volunteers to complete four hundred feet of cattle and horse stalls along the east fence.[40]

39 *Holland City News*, 11 Nov. 1882, 11 Nov. 1928, 30 Nov. 1933, 24 Oct. 1935. Nies singled out the Derk Fyte family of Drenthe, notably son Nick, for their pugnacious reputation (Ray Nies, *Autobiography*, ch. 12).

40 For this and the preceding paragraph, see *Holland City News*, 7, 21 Mar., 4 Apr., 23 May, 27 June 1885, 11 Nov. 1928; *De Grondwet*, 21 Apr., 1 Sept. 1885; Darlene Winter, "One Hundred Years Ago Today," *Holland Sentinel*, 7 Sept. 1985; *Ottawa County Times*, 1 May 1903.

The deadline was met, and the first annual Holland Fair was a smashing success. Ten thousand people attended, despite a wet week, which made four tents erected for the fair come in handy. Some thirteen hundred entries of animals, plants and flowers, and crafts and products of all kinds gave the visitors plenty to see. Local companies displayed their products, including Rokus Kanters & Sons hardware, Cappon & Bertsch tannery, the flour miller Walsh-De Roo & Co. of Standard Roller Mills, and the furniture store of Meyer, Brouwer & Co. Teunis Keppel was superintendent of grounds. Gate receipts totaled $1,500. "It is a success!" screamed the *News* headline, but the editor added the downer, "Rain the Only Drawback," which became a common refrain. Holland's first fair was better than the recent one at Grand Rapids, crowed Rogers. Ben Mulder of *De Grondwet* rejoiced that the rowdy market days were abolished and that the fair provided a community celebration without gambling and hard liquor to "bring shame" on the community.[41]

In 1886 the Holland fair grew bigger and better. The most popular feature was an authentic log cabin built by the Holland Historical Department, modeled after the original "log houses," and furnished with memorabilia, photos, furniture, and utensils from pioneer days. "In the midst of all these old curiosities stood the venerable Teunis Keppel, who was one of the band of Van Raalte's colonists, and it was indeed fitting to have him superintend those things he had lived with as a young 'trail blazer' in the Holland wilds." The cabin was "unique as well as antique," recalled editor Mulder.[42]

The third fair in 1887 attracted fifteen thousand visitors, despite several rainy days. The "magnificent" horses stole the show, as they did every year. Local bands and entertainers, such as high wire artists and hot air balloonists, stirred the crowds at the track prior to the horse races. "The Great De Boe" (Will De Boe), Holland's own high-wire performer, kept the crowd on edge for an hour as he walked the slack wire stretched across the racetrack. Church ladies societies sold food and crafts as fundraisers. A perennial problem was the conflicting interests and goals of fair organizers and fairgoers. The former wanted to balance the books and the latter to preserve community values against gambling, drinking, and bare skin. Devout church deacon and attorney Arend Visscher aptly stated the issue starkly:

> I shudder to think of the delicate balance that had to be maintained. The directors were all interested in making each

41 *Holland City News*, 5 Sept, 10 Oct. 1885; *De Grondwet*, 22 Sept. 1886.

42 *Holland City News*, "Fifty Years Ago Today," 22 Oct. 1936.

> fair a financial success; churchgoers, of which father was one, had puritanical scruples, which had to be respected and upheld; racing groups clamored for big appropriations for prizes and improvements in the track; townspeople as well as farmers wanted their money's worth; each application for sideshow entertainment had to be scrutinized separately with individual contracts signed—no booking agents for group entertainment in those days; the "girlie" shows had to be modest; the races honest. This was a Herculean task, but it was always a good show.[43]

The fourth fair in 1888 again faced "wretched weather" of wind, rain, and hail, but more than 1,600 entries filled the grounds. Thursday, the traditional big day, brought in eight thousand visitors (a thousand more than the year before), as schools, factories, and stores shut down for the day. The fifth fair in 1890 again operated at a profit, but it was the last one held on the college property. This choice tract along Lake Macatawa (now Kollen Park) was better suited to manufacturing companies, and soon the site was adorned with factories of the Holland Sugar, Holland Shoe, and Bay View Furniture Companies, and the C. L. King Basket Factory. Some saw a silver lining in the Holland fair getting away from the wintry winds coming off Black Lake, since every fair had been plagued by cold, stormy weather.[44]

For its new location, the fair board purchased the Frank Vanden Belt farm on East Sixteenth Street across from Pilgrim Home Cemetery. Most of the buildings were moved to the new site, including the covered grandstand, which continued to be the focal point for horse races and other events. The relocation was fortuitous, because with the ubiquitous family automobile in the 1920s, many acres were needed for parking up to 1,500 vehicles.[45]

Visitors were drawn to the September venue by the lure of big prizes and exciting entertainment. Beginning in 1920, on the Thursday "Farmers' Day" a Fordson tractor was given to the lucky ticket holder, and on the Friday "Holland Day" one patron won a "high-class automobile" and another won a Victrola or piano. The horse racing

43 Quoted in Vande Water, "Holland Fairs," in *Holland Happenings*, 4:52; "Fifty Years Ago Today," *Holland City News*, 28 Oct. 1937. Visscher was a son of Jan and Geesje Van der Haar Visscher.

44 *Holland City News*, 5 Feb., 27 Sept. 1887, 12 Oct. 1889, 14 Mar., 12 July 1890.

45 Vande Water, "Holland Fairs," in *Holland Happenings*, 4:50-51. When the fair closed in 1930, the grandstand was moved to Riverview Park and used for sporting events, beginning with the Holland-Kalamazoo Central football game on 8 Oct. 1932. The grandstand was used until 1979 and torn down in 1983 (ibid., 4:55).

purses were raised to $2,000, free attractions to $1,000, and music to $500. Attendance broke above twenty-two thousand, more than double the number of two years earlier, and gate receipts surpassed $15,000, more than $5,000 above expenses. In 1921, under president Austin Harrington and secretary John Arendshorst, the fair directors erected on the midway a $7,000 grandstand to seat two thousand, with a big bandstand and a dining hall underneath. This complemented the art hall and education building; the latter displayed thousands of exhibits from pupils in every school in the region. Education and pleasure were combined, but the latter gave the bigger boost. Each year the Holland Community Fair was bigger and better than ever. The grandstand was expanded from 3,000 seats in 1922 to 3,500 in 1925. A lighted arch greeted visitors at the entrance, aglow in the national colors. By this time the fair was billed as the Holland-Zeeland Community Fair, and the venue was advertised as the Big Ottawa County Fair. Clearly, Holland's fair had become the county's fair.[46]

The main attraction in 1919 was the chance to fly with the "daring" aviator Bert "Fish" Hassell of Rockford, Illinois in a Roseswift Airplane made in Grand Rapids. For $15 patrons could "take a flight in the upper regions" for fifteen minutes. Hassell did not lack for adventurous customers. In 1920 the main feature was Lil Kerslake's "The Farmer and his Pigs," whose ten pigs did "everything but talk." So popular was the act that fairs booked Kerslake's pigs five years in advance. In 1923 big time vaudeville, "amazing" fireworks, female trapeze artists, and airplane acrobats (Burns Flyers), entertained the crowds. Flyer Guy Burns crashed his plane and narrowly escaped death at the 1924 fair. The bandstand featured Fisher's Orchestra from Kalamazoo and the Holland American Legion Band. Business firms from as far as Detroit exhibited products and donated "special premiums" worth $1,560 to winning entries. Fifty horses, both trotters and pacers, competed for $300 in prize money. Each year the publication of a *Holland Fair Book* publicized the events and prizes.[47]

Attendance at the three-day event, which was moved up to August in 1923, climbed from 7,400 in 1918 to 19,700 by 1924. A rainy spell was the only threat to rising attendance. Mike Bos, a "dapper little man,"

46 *Holland City News*, 19 Feb. 1920, 3 Mar., 5 May, 16 June, 7 July, 8, 15 Sept., 24 Nov. 1921, 13 July, 3, 30 Aug. 1922, 26 July 1923, 7 May 1925; *Holland Sentinel*, 4 Jan. 1961. Arendshorst was a Holland insurance agent. Otto Schaap of Zeeland had served as director and then president during most of the 1910s, until his death in July 1920 (*Holland City News*, 22 July 1920).

47 *Holland City News*, 11 Sept. 1919, 23 Sept. 1920, 8 Feb., 26 July, 6, 13, 20 Sept. 1923.

Trotter races at the fair on Sixteenth Street, early 1920s
(*courtesy Myron Van Ark*)

was a familiar figure at the gate for thirty-nine years collecting entrance fees and John Murray took his seat in the judge's box for thirty years. Beginning in 1924, children under twelve years of age were admitted free if accompanied by a parent. This move was better late than never. Even so, less than 10 percent of attendees were children that year.[48]

Given the games of chance and special events, it is little wonder that Arendshorst and the board were criticized by religious leaders about the "class of amusements" staged at the fair. Horseracing, billiards, and Lotto were certainly in the cross hairs. In 1921 Classis Zeeland of the Christian Reformed Church forwarded a formal complaint. The executive committee of the fair board, all volunteers, shot back with a curt response: "Boost, don't knock, the fair." It is not a sin to attend. To emphasize the wholesomeness of the events, the board banned Lotto and offered cash prizes to the three largest families in attendance, with $15 in gold coins for the winning family, plus refunds of admission tickets. In 1923 the county sheriff banned games of chance and "gambling devices" throughout the county. This edict curtailed but apparently did not end the fair's experiments with such money-raisers. Classis Zeeland in 1925 again condemned "sideshows and all games of chance" as "detrimental to the public good," and advised church members to stay home. Secretary Arendshorst replied that he would "stand for no more kicks on his attractions and sideshows." To heed every objection would leave the fair with only "cows and chickens."[49]

This response riled Classis Holland of the Christian Reformed Church, which in 1927 not only condemned the sideshows and gaming

48 Ibid., 10 Apr., 28 Aug., 9 Oct. 1924.

49 *Holland City News*, 28 July 1928.

Children frame the sign for the Fourth of July celebration at the fairgrounds in the early 1920s featuring newfangled World War One Army "Air-Planes" (*Joint Archives of Holland*)

booths as Vanity Fair, but also published a lengthy statement warning members away from the fair so as not to become "partakers of its sins in giving it our financial as well as moral support." The next year the denomination's national synod advised members, on pain of discipline, not to participate at all in "worldly amusements," specifically, ballroom dancing, movie shows (silent screen), and "devil" cards. Given the thousands of Christian Reformed members in Holland and Zeeland, these pronouncements had a negative impact on the community fair.[50]

The fair board believed it could not curtail the sideshows, lotteries, carnival booths, and the horse races, because revenue from such activities supported the primary purpose of judging farm animals, products, and crafts. But the board did parry criticism by introducing some new attractions and raising the premiums for winning entries. Pitching "shoes," the "sport of the barnyard golf enthusiasts," proved to be a huge draw for men and boys. Even more appealing was an evening event called "auto polo," in which players flailed at a ball from cars instead of on horseback. Accidents came fast and furious, to the delight of all, and the "dangerous game" resulted in numerous broken wheels, gears, and other parts. Despite the hoopla at the grandstand and on the midway, the ideals of the fair remained the same, to inform

50 Ibid., 25 Aug. 1921, 3 Dec. 1925, 11 Apr. 1926, 21 July 1927.

farmers, poultrymen, and dairymen about the latest innovations and new products to improve the bottom line. Horses were always the biggest draw. In 1925 the largest poultry exhibits in the world, with five thousand prized birds, was the biggest feature of the fair, and the horse shows and racing cars became very popular. Gross revenues surpassed $22,000 in both 1924 and 1925, the highest ever. To accommodate the heavy traffic, the highway commission paved Sixteenth Street with concrete east of the fairgrounds past the Pilgrim Home and Holland Township Cemeteries (chapter 27).[51]

The 1926 fair exhibited items from the recently concluded Philadelphia sesquicentennial exposition, including a replica of the Liberty Bell and patriotic banners. Of course, it also had the usual horse races, fireworks, amusements, and agricultural exhibits. Purses for pacers and trotters enticed wealthy stable owners from Grand Rapids to enter their thoroughbreds in the competition. Following the races on "Holland Day," Governor Alex J. Groesbeck and Lieutenant Governor George Walsh of Grand Rapids addressed the three thousand patrons in the grandstands. Some fifty merchants of Holland and Zeeland donated prizes for the poultry exhibits and the largest ever pedigreed dog show. But the censors sent off a "girl show" as "too Hawaiian." Secretary Arendshorst explained lamely: "You cannot always tell in advance what you are to get when you make arrangements before the fair. Everything may look clean on the surface, but when business begins, it is another story." The race program doubled the prize money in 1927 to $600, which attracted more entrants. In 1928 the board added another popular feature, a draft horse-pulling contest, with two heats, for pairs over and under three thousand pounds. First prize was $10. That year the fair closed with a surplus of $2,600, or 11 percent of gross receipts. In 1928 John Arendshorst stepped down after eleven years, and Martin Vande Bunte, a clothier with Lokker Rutgers, was elected in his stead. Austin Harrington continued as president. They had two good years in 1928 and 1929, and then the bottom fell out.[52]

The Holland fair ran continuously for forty-six years and claimed to be among the very best in the state. In that time, the fair board spent $150,000 on improvements, premiums, utilities, and general expenses, and fairgoers spent many times more at the concession stands and in local stores and eateries. But the onset of the Great Depression, which

[51] Ibid., 20 July, 17, 31 Aug., 14 Sept. 1922, 21 Aug. 1924; 7, 28 May, 30 July, 13, 27 Aug., 1 Oct., 19 Nov. 1925.

[52] *Holland City News*, 22 July, 19, 26 Aug., 2 Sept. 1926, 6, 20 Oct., 10 Nov. 1927, 2 Feb., 19 July 1928, 3 Jan. 1929.

Trotters race at the Holland fair, with automobiles lined up facing the track, perhaps to illuminate the grandstand finish line with their headlights if necessary, late 1920s *(courtesy Myron Van Ark)*

brought a sharp decline in public support, especially from conservative Reformed believers, doomed the fair. The 1930 venue added $5,000 to an already large debt, and the directors saw no alternative but to dispose of the property. Harrington's announcement that the 1930 fair would be the last fell like a bombshell, especially among the merchants. For too long, the Holland Merchants Association had failed to put their shoulder to the wheel, Harrington charged bitterly, and now it was too late.[53]

The fair board and some seventy-five citizens met over the next months and wrestled with the question of what to do with the property. Donating it to the city was the best option. The city had been eyeing the site since 1926 for future expansion of Pilgrim Home Cemetery across the street (chapter 27), and the fair's demise now gave them the chance to buy the property for the total "encumbrance" of about $30,000. Hope College made the deal possible by putting up half the money in exchange for using part of the grounds for an athletic field. It was a good deal for both the city and the college. The next year the city moved the grandstand to Riverview Park, auctioned off the other buildings for $3,200, and cleared the site. The cemetery administrative building and the grave plots south of Sixteenth Street today occupy the former

53 Ibid., 9 Sept. 1926, 13 Mar., 10 Apr., 25 Sept., 9 Oct., 14 Nov., 18 Dec. 1930; *Holland Sentinel*, 13 Nov. 1930.

Holland Fair at its peak in the late 1920s, with fairgoers greeted by farm implements (lower right) at the entrance (*courtesy Myron Van Ark*)

fairgrounds. At the time and for years afterward, shortsighted critics complained that the city "will never need" the additional cemetery land.[54]

With the demise of the Holland fair, city officials and the chamber of commerce tried to keep the farmers coming by reviving the concept of the market day and hosting it at the Holland Armory, which was dedicated in 1925 (chapter 21). The first "Farmers' Day," as the event was billed, was held in December 1933. City officials and merchants gave the farmers a "royal welcome" and, according to Vande Water, "hearty handshakes will take the place of the black eye of yesteryear. No saloons to get 'fire water' to create false courage and bravado. [This was the Prohibition era.] Old amber brew will be served from the coffee bean, and there will be a clean wholesome fraternity between neighbors and friends." In 1937, 2,200 people from Ottawa and Allegan Counties came to the armory on Farmers' Day, despite heavy rains and the draw of the Allegan County Fair. The big attraction was the Prairie Farmer radio performers and a moving picture show run by the local movie houses. The free annual event clearly met a need during the hard times and nurtured a "friendly neighbor" spirit between city and farm folk.[55]

Holland had no fair for three decades after 1930, until a group of local and county leaders in 1959 organized the Ottawa County Fair

54 *Holland City News*, 5, 19 Nov. 1931, 14 Jan. 1932, 16 Jan. 1936.

55 Ibid., 6 Aug. 1925, 30 Nov. 1933, 23, 30 Sept. 1937.

to stage harness racing. The rest of the midway was incidental to the trotters. The fair opened on August 8 at the Park Township grounds on Ottawa Beach Road, across from the Park Township airfield, where it has continued to flourish, thanks to excellent leadership. The first manager was "sparkplug" Cliff Steketee; his board included president Al Looman, Cecil Terpstra, Nick Brouwer, John Pathuis, Oscar Bontekoe, John Huizenga, and John Van Wieren. Attendance quickly surpassed one hundred thousand. Steketee managed the fair for twenty-one years, until 1980. He and the board enlarged the grandstand, added a round exhibition building, extended the fair from four to six days, and booked such big name entertainers as Brenda Lee, Dolly Parton, Tex Ritter, and Roy Acuff. Earl Welling directed the fair for many years and retired from the executive board in 2012 after thirty-three years.[56]

Farming-related businesses

Since many students at Hope College were farm boys, their student newspaper, the *Excelsiora*, featured a regular column on agriculture, and the editors portrayed farmers as intelligent workers and businessmen. "The farmer" was also a focus group for advertisers, since farmers represented a large market. In the late 1870s William H. Deming began an iron foundry on Tenth Street. One application of his business was to forge iron plows, sometimes from scrap metal. Although his factory suffered at least two fires in 1883 and 1887, Deming's business remained strong.[57]

Farm implement dealers, wagon makers, and blacksmiths were also indispensable to farmers, who were increasingly substituting capital goods for labor, such as mowers, reapers, plows, cultivators, threshers, binders, drills, and harvesters. Most of these machines could be purchased in downtown Holland. The largest harvesting machines, more suited to large farms in the Great Plains, proved too expensive for the local farmer with his average eighty-acre farm.

Two of the earliest farm implement shops, founded in the 1860s, were Herman Verbeek's plow factory and Ben Van Raalte's shop. Van Raalte, the second son of the dominie, began dealing in agricultural implements at his farm on East Sixteenth Street in 1866. His business expanded to include stores in Zeeland and Drenthe. In the mid-1880s his average annual sales ranged from $25,000 to $35,000 to as much as $65,000 in the best year. Van Raalte regularly introduced the latest farm

56 Ibid., 30 Nov. 1933; *Holland Sentinel*, 22 Oct. 2012; Vande Water, "Holland Fairs," in *Holland Happenings*, 4:54-55.

57 Hope College *Excelsiora*, 3 Feb. 1871.

Ben Van Raalte & Son farm implement store, 221 River Avenue, 1899 (now the parking lot behind the Holland Museum) (*Joint Archives of Holland*)

equipment made by McCormick, Deering, Osborn, Oliver, and other manufacturers. Peter Wilms, a Van Raalte competitor on River Street, featured the "Egg" cultivator, a "spring tooth" device with sixteen steel coils shaped like eggs that broke plowed ground for planting. Wilms also manufactured drive well pumps to draw water, at a time when every home and business had its own pump handle on the porch or alongside the house. Another unique Wilms invention was a dog-powered treadmill.[58]

In the early 1890s, the teenaged Bert J. W. Berghorst of Zeeland began offering well-drilling services to area farmers, including installing windmills. Every farmer needed windmills to tap ground water for family use, for watering livestock, and to cool fresh milk. This was the beginning of B. J. W. Berghorst & Sons, a company still going strong under the fourth generation after one hundred years. In the 1920s Bert wisely transitioned his plumbing business into a wholesale house, which enabled him to survive the Great Depression. In 1992 the firm left its Main Street store in Zeeland for a new plant at 11430 East James Street in Holland Township.[59]

58 Henry S. Lucas, *Dutch Immigrant Memoirs and Related Writings*, 2 vols. (Assen: Van Gorcum, 1955, 2nd ed. Grand Rapids: Eerdmans, 1997), 2:497; *Holland City News*, 5 Feb. 1887, 1 Aug. 1896, "Fifty Years Ago Today" 16 Jan. 1936, "Sixty Years Ago Today" 21 Mar. 1940, Mary (Mrs. Peter) Wilms obit., 8 Sept. 1938; Chicago *American Graphic*, 25 Aug. 1899; *De Grondwet*, 29 June 1888.

59 Michael Lozon, *Selling Service: From Well Driller to Wholesaler of Plumbing Supplies—the 100-Year History of B.J.W. Berghorst & Sons* (Holland, 2001), 10-11, 59-72; *Holland Sentinel*, 30 Jan. 2000.

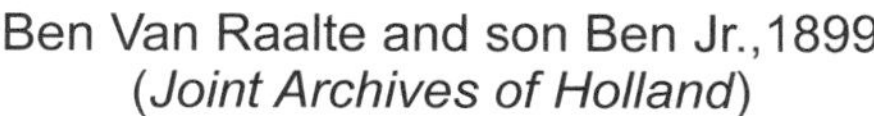
Ben Van Raalte and son Ben Jr., 1899
(*Joint Archives of Holland*)

In 1876 Richard K. Heald and Isaac Fairbanks formed a partnership and opened a farm implement store on the southeast corner of Eighth and Market (Central) Streets. This prompted Ben Van Raalte to move his business into the city, and he rented a two-story brick building near the prominent corner of Ninth and River Streets. Heald had been in business by himself at Tenth and River Streets since the 1850s. Andrew Thompson sold his farm machinery shop to Pieter E. Winters in 1874. Three flour and feed stores also lined Eighth Street in the 1870s, including Slooter & Higgins, Welton & Akley, and Walsh & Beach. Hardware storeowner William Melis began advertising "super-phosphate," a fertilizer applied on sandy soils to help grow clover, which in turn enriched the soil for other crops. Following in the spirit of Arbor Day, which was made a state holiday in 1881, local farmers in 1882 were allowed to pay up to one-fourth of their highway tax by planting trees at 20¢ each.[60]

In the 1880s Rokus and son Abraham M. Kanters of the Holland Manufacturing Company made hundreds of the Palmer Self-Regulating Windmills that farmers in West Michigan and northern Illinois found very desirable. The firm, located on Seventh Street between River and Market (Central) Streets, sold $10,000 worth in 1886. Holland's leading citizens founded Holland Manufacturing in 1881, including Mayor John Roost as president, John Kluite vice president, Heber Walsh

[60] *Holland City News*, 22 Apr. 1876, 22 Dec. 1877, 20 July 1878, 20 July 1878, 24 Apr. 1880, 30 Apr. 1881, 11 Mar. 1882.

B. J. W. Berghorst Plumbing Company, 51 East Main Street, 1910, with Bert Berghorst in front (*Zeeland Historical Museum*)

treasurer, and Henry D. Post secretary. "The best citizens of Holland are stockholders," reported the *City News*, and are pushing it for all there is in it." After flourishing for more than thirty years, the business went bankrupt in 1915, and workers received only 50¢ on the dollar in back wages.[61]

In 1887 Reinder E. Werkman formed the Werkman Agricultural Works in partnership with Graafschap capitalist Abel H. Brink, to manufacture various kinds of farm equipment—Vindicator Fanning Mills, milk cans, and the like—all powered by a huge steam engine. (Fanning mills removed the chaff from wheat seeds prior to being milled into flour.) The successful test of the engine in October 1887 brought a host of curious onlookers. The firm, which took up an entire city block west of River Street to the lake between Third and Fourth Streets, shipped carloads of milk cans to Iowa. By 1889 the renamed Werkman Manufacturing Company made all kinds of furniture, mainly bedroom suites (chapter 14).[62]

For farm wagons and buggies, and horseshoeing and blacksmithing, farmers turned to local craftsmen. The federal census

61 Ibid., 2, 23 July (quote) 1881, 11 Oct. 1885, 10 May, 18 Oct., 21 Dec. 1886.

62 Ibid., 5 Feb., 18 June, 22 Aug., 29 Oct., 19 Nov. 1887, 28 Sept. 1889, 26 Aug. 1898, 18 Mar., 14 Oct. 1915; *De Grondwet*, 19 Oct. 1886, 28 June, 13 Dec. 1887, 24 Jan. 1888; Van Reken and Kliphuis, *Werkman*, 29; *Sanborn [Fire] Insurance Maps*, 1883, 1889 (Sanborn Map Publishing Company).

marshal in 1850 registered five blacksmiths and two wagonmakers in the colony. The wagon shop of Roost & Vennema (engineer John Roost, the silent partner, and wheelwright Ame Vennema) opened in 1854. In 1857 Jacob Flieman began a wagon works on River Street that prospered for years.[63] Several smaller wagon works and blacksmith shops shared the iron trade with Flieman in the 1860s, including Hendrik Barendrecht and Marinus J. Oggel. Other pioneer blacksmiths were Jan Nagel, Hendrik Meengs, Albert Kroes, and Ryk Takken. In the 1870s Adrian Baert competed with Flieman by opening a shop on River Street to make wagon wheels. In 1881 Flieman's factory, then on Seventh Street two doors east of River Street, sold seventy-six wagons and buggies. Flieman's firm in 1887 made eighty wagons and forty cutters and sleighs, in addition to shop work and blacksmithing repairs.[64]

In 1886 the Holland Wagon Works of Henry Takken and Peter De Spelder on the southeast corner of Ninth and River Streets began to turn out carriages, wagons, top buggies, cutters, carts, and sleighs. By 1889 the renamed Holland Carriage & Wagon Works had moved to the northeast corner of Fourth and River Streets. The partners had twelve to thirty years of experience and competed with Flieman's long-established shop, which had a near monopoly in these conveyances. The Westveld brothers ran an old-fashioned smithy in a rookery on River Street just north of the new post office on Tenth Street until the First World War. Lampen Bros. (John and Benjamin) blacksmith shop continued into the late 1920s and was the last in the city to close.[65]

Grain elevators and flourmills encouraged farmers to raise wheat and other grains. In 1876 they harvested 27,000 bushels of winter wheat on 2,100 acres, an average yield of 13 bushels per acre. The four largest growers were Ben Van Raalte with 650 bushels, Berend Poest with 500, Cornelis J. De Koster with 460, and Kasper Lohuis with 400.[66]

By 1878 there were five active commission merchants and gristmills to process and market the locally-grown wheat—Plugger Mills, City Mills, Heber Walsh, Beach Bros. (William H. Beach), and James Higgins (chapter 12). In the first week of the wheat harvest that year, growers brought in more than ten thousand bushels and received from 85¢ to 97¢ per bushel, depending on quality, all cash. Output filled four

63 *Holland City News*, 5 Feb. 1887; *Holland Sentinel, Semi-Centennial Edition*, 1897.

64 *De Hollander*, 9 Jan. 1856; *Holland City News*, 22 May 1880, 7 Jan., 29 Apr. 1882.

65 *De Hollander*, 5 Dec. 1855, 9 Jan. 1856, 1 Aug. 1860; *De Hope*, 24 May 1866; *Holland City News*, 5 Feb. 1887, "Twenty Years Ago Today," 2 Mar. 1939.

66 Ibid., 22 May 1877, "Fifty Years Ago Today" 22 July 1937.

railcars daily, and Walsh and Beach Bros. built elevators on the railway "Y" to facilitate shipments. Competition kept the sale price of flour low, but since the mills paid up to 5¢ more than Grand Rapids and other regional markets, farmers came from twenty miles around to sell their grain in Holland. The city, it was claimed, offered the "best grain market on the Lake Shore." City merchants and local farmers alike benefited from the grain trade. To get in on the wheat craze, Walsh partnered with Cornelius J. De Roo and Isaac Cappon in 1882 to organize the Walsh-De Roo Standard Roller Mills, located on River Avenue at Fifth Street. Walsh-De Roo went head-to-head with Beach Bros. to dominate the city grain trade; its fifty-thousand-bushel elevator and cutting edge technology gave it the advantage, and it shipped large orders of specialty flours to England and Scotland. Walsh-De Roo's mammoth, four-story mill put Holland on the map as a manufacturing center (chapter 17).[67]

Wheat in the 1880s became an international commodity, with prices set daily by major world markets. At that time, farmers were breaking the sod of the world's great prairies—the American and Canadian Great Plains, the Argentine Pampas, the Russian Ukraine, and the Australian Outback—and cultivating wheat on a vast scale with gangplows pulled by teams of six or eight horses and later steam-powered tractors. The small-scale Dutch farmers of West Michigan faced competition not only from the Great Plains but also from around the world, and they could not survive on wheat. They had to raise other grains and diversify. They did this willingly, believing with presidents Calvin Coolidge and Herbert Hoover during the farm crisis of the 1920s, that the federal government had no business attempting to fix farm prices or control marketing. During the Great Depression, wheat growers received a brief reprieve, when in 1934 the federal government, under the Agricultural Adjustment Act (AAA), offered farmers the option of placing their wheat acreages in the allotment program in exchange for the parity price, which was double the market price in the middle 1930s. The government's goal was to reduce production and place a floor under farm income. But the resulting scarcity raised wheat prices for consumers. The Supreme Court struck down the AAA as unconstitutional in 1936, but local farmers continued to grow the king of grains, despite the comparative disadvantage.[68]

67 Ibid., 7 July, 3, 10, 17, 24 Aug., 7 Sept. 1878, 17 May 1879, 27 Nov. 1886, 19 Oct. 1889, 14 Nov. 1891, 1 Aug. 1896; *Holland Business and City Directory*, 1894.

68 *Holland City News*, 10 Dec. 1925; 25 Jan. 1934, 7 Nov. 1935. The Supreme Court in *U.S. v. Butler* (1936) invalidated the Agricultural Adjustment Act of 1933.

A changing economy

The year 1877 marked the end of the free land era in Ottawa County, but residents might have missed it. The newspaper noted in its "Jottings" column that "Mr. George S. Harrington took up the last piece of government land on Friday last in Ottawa County." While new immigrants were discouraged by the scarcity of farmland and high start-up costs, the established farmers, many now of the second and third generations, ran successful operations. Between 1850 and 1880, 86 percent of farm laborers in the Holland area had moved up to farm ownership. This rate of upward mobility was unthinkable in the Old Country. The relative wealth of farmers peaked in the 1870s and 1880s. While Holland struggled to rebuild from the 1871 fire, many farmers outside the city improved their farms and built expensive new brick homes. By 1897 Holland and Zeeland Townships led the county in improved farmlands, at 83 percent and 91 percent, respectively. In 1900 the city of Holland covered twenty-three thousand acres and counted 950 horses. This was the high point for horses; soon automobiles took over the streets.[69]

Holland served from the 1880s as the railhead to ship livestock from Allegan and Ottawa County farms to outside markets. Jan Kuite and John Lezman were the principal dealers in the 1880s. Large shipments of cattle, mainly yearlings, went by rail from Zeeland to western grasslands for fattening. Kuite in 1887 shipped 2,000 calves, 2,500 cattle, 2,000 sheep, and 1,500 swine, worth together $87,000. Horse dealers Hermanus Boone, William Kellogg, Ben Van Raalte, and E. J. Harrington shipped 300 horses and sold another 60 locally, with a total value of $70,000.[70]

Two auctions for deceased farmers' estates, printed in the *Ottawa County Times* in 1899, illustrate the variety of animals, tools, and machines that a farmer might have had. Both men seem to have been bachelors or widowers without heirs to claim the property. The first farmer, Johannes Hassevoort of New Holland, had one heavy mare, three cows, one heifer, two calves, one broad tire lumber wagon, one narrow tire wagon, one two-seat buggy, one road cart, four cultivators, one plow, one drag, one land roller, one mower, one horse rake, one dog

[69] *De Grondwet*, 30 Jan. 1900; *Holland City News*, 18 Dec.1897; Gordon W. Kirk Jr., *The Promise of American Life: Social Mobility in a Nineteenth-Century Immigrant Community, Holland, Michigan, 1847-1894* (Philadelphia: American Philosophical Society, 1978), 81; Michael J. Douma, *Veneklasen Brick: A Family, An Industry, and a Unique Nineteenth Century Dutch Architectural Movement in Michigan* (Grand Rapids: Eerdmans, 2005).

[70] *Holland City News*, 24 Jan. 1880, 5 Feb. 1887.

power churn, one fanning mill, one pair of bobs, one log chain, one harpoon with tackle, one set of harness, wood and hay rack, grindstone, corn with stalks, a quantity of straw, one cook stove, and more. The second farmer, John H. Willink, who lived on a forty-acre farm near Noordeloos, had one span of black mares, one gray horse, three cows, one heifer, one fat hog, eighty chickens, one lumber wagon, one top buggy, one two-seat buggy, one road coat, one scraper, three cutters, three pairs of bobs, one plow, three drags, three cultivators, one beet seeder and cultivator, one harpoon and rope, one fanning mill, one corn sheller, three tons of hay, straw and cornstalks, four hundred bushels of corn, one set of work harnesses, one buggy harness, one horse rake, one mower, one Deering binder, one iron kettle, forty bushels of carrots, 150 bushels of potatoes, milk utensils, and miscellaneous other items.[71]

The different possessions of the two farmers are notable. Both had a few milk cows, enough horses and machinery for sowing and reaping corn and wheat, buggies for general transportation, and all around useful tools like rakes and mowers. Beyond that, they had different priorities. The New Holland farmer, Hassevoort, had more equipment used in physical labor (lumber wagon, land roller) and may have subsidized his income with physical jobs on the side. He stored little food except what was needed for his horses and cows. Willink, on the other hand, grew and stored most kinds of available grains, tubers, and some vegetables. He was probably a` truck farmer who sold cash crops at the Holland market. He practiced diverse cropping and tended to a variety of animals, most of which were for his own use, except for marketing most of the eggs from his flock of chickens. His potato patch contributed to the fifty thousand bushels raised annually in Ottawa County at this time.[72] Willink also was experimenting with beets before most of his neighbors.

Different soils may have accounted for these contrasting patterns, but the real lesson is that both found a role and survived with their own type of farming. Since necessities and foodstuffs were available at the market, a farmer no longer needed to grow everything for himself, although he may still have chosen to do so to save money or to avoid extra outside labor. But specialization was the wave of the future.

Land prices climbed steadily. Isaac Kouw, one of the city's largest land agents, in 1912 advertised improved land containing "black sandy loam" within five miles of town for $40 an acre. With a home, barn, and

71 *Ottawa County Times*, 27 Oct. 1899.
72 *Holland City News*, 27 Sept. 1901.

Jan Laarman family farm, North Holland, 1890s
(*courtesy Peter Vander Wall*)

other outbuildings, neighboring farms fetched from $47 to $74 an acre, depending on soils and buildings.[73]

Colonization from the Holland area

The Dutch were a tight-knit group who placed a high value on close proximity. They willingly paid top dollar for farms on the fringes of the colony for their married children. Historian Jacob van Hinte painted the expansion of the Dutch in terms of "capture" and "conquest." Another metaphor is the outward seeping of a giant "oil slick." The prosperous Dutch bought out the Americans and took over their towns.[74] Within the first decade, the Holland colony expanded into virgin lands at Harderwyk, East Saugatuck, and Beaverdam, and into "American territory" at Jamestown and Byron Center.

By the 1870s, most fertile farmland in southern Ottawa and northern Allegan Counties was under cultivation and rising in value. The stream of immigrants from the Netherlands had never completely dried up, and as these newcomers, who were mostly farmers, arrived, they found that the only land left was either expensive, poor quality, or both. Fortunately, the United States had a seemingly inexhaustible supply of cheap land, primarily in the prairie states. Closer to home were the cutover lands of northern Michigan where the forests had been felled. New lands served as a "backdoor" or safety valve for the pressures of population growth in the Holland colony.

73 Ibid., 22 Feb. 1912.

74 Van Hinte, *Netherlanders in America*, 771-72.

Local newspapers supported out-migration. *De Grondwet*, in particular, lived off of it, since subscriptions for this thoroughly Dutch newspaper came from distant places. "We can not understate that making new immigrants out of old ones is not a delightful sign of the times, and is not wished by the early settlers here. Now that it has, however, become a necessity, we must rejoice that the great West still offers such openings." The *Holland City News* expressed similar sympathy: "Gradually some of our people pick up courage enough to launch out on the western prairies, on a more extended scale, and we wish them abundant success."[75]

The main direction the West Michigan Dutch turned was northward. Groningen immigrants, in particular, settled in the city of Muskegon and on truck farms on the outskirts. But the first "break-off" daughter colony was Vogel Center, founded by Jan Vogel, a Civil War veteran in Holland who purchased land in the pinewoods near Cadillac in Missaukee County in 1869. There he joined the Scotch Irish immigrants already involved in the lumber industry. Vogel's entrepreneurial drive and perhaps a bit of wanderlust were the primary reasons for his departure.[76]

Like the Holland of decades past, the Cadillac area promised wealth from wood products, and in the 1870s, more Hollanders, often with family connections, followed Vogel. Dutch settlements—Lucas in 1876 with a Christian Reformed Church in 1883, and Falmouth and Moddersville with Reformed congregations by 1891—sprouted up near Vogel Center, which earned its official name upon receiving a post office in 1878. That, coupled with a flourishing local lumber industry and rather successful farms and dairies, ensured the survival and long-term growth of this collection of colonies east of Cadillac. The relatively close proximity of this region to Holland, Grand Rapids, and Muskegon was a plus; it enabled the settlers to stay in contact with family and friends.[77]

Holland was not alone in forming Dutch daughter colonies in Michigan. Fremont, for example, was settled mainly by the overflow of Dutch from Muskegon. And New Era, a village north of Muskegon in Oceana County, counted by 1887 some fifty Dutch families, many of whom had been mill workers living in Montague.[78]

75 *De Grondwet*, 19 Mar. 1878, translation by Michael J. Douma; *Holland City News*, 27 Oct. 1877.

76 Huug van den Dool, "Jan Vogel and the Dutch Settlement of Missaukie County, Michigan," 179-96, in *Across Borders: Dutch Migration in North America and Australia*, eds. Jacob E. Nyenhhuis, Suzanne M. Sinke, and Robert P. Swierenga (Holland, MI: Van Raalte Press, 2010).

77 Lucas, *Dutch Immigrant Memoirs*, 2:262-63, 273-76.

78 *De Grondwet*, 16 Feb. 1887.

Holland's other daughter colony was founded in 1868 in Amelia County, Virginia by none other than the city's father, Albertus C. Van Raalte. But the venture in northern Virginia went against the national trend of westward expansion and was a failure. Civil War veterans spoke highly of the healthy climate in the Carolinas, Virginia, Alabama, and Tennessee. This prompted Van Raalte to scout out the region, where he found several "well-situated" areas for colonies, including North Carolina, whose state leaders tried to lure the "highly esteemed" Dutch immigrants. Amelia County, however, seemed to offer everything Van Raalte was looking for—a long growing season, accessible markets, and a shorter travel distance for emigrants from the Netherlands. Best of all, his old friend, Samuel B. Schieffelin of the Collegiate Reformed Church of New York City, owned a large tract of land there and offered it much below the going price of fifty dollars an acre in the Holland area. In 1868 Van Raalte wrote his son-in-law Peter Oggel: "When emigration will increase, new settlements are necessary." And Dutch emigration was indeed peaking again in the years following the American Civil War. So, unlike later daughter colonies that were formed from the overflow of the established Dutch settlements, Amelia was begun in anticipation of a resurgent immigrant stream from the Netherlands.[79]

Van Raalte took his family to Amelia in August of 1868 to help start the colony. Daughter Christina wrote home to her brother Ben, telling him how strange she found the place. In particular she noted the local agriculture. "Oh, Ben, how backward these southern people are compared to those in the north when it comes to farming. Father has a very good garden and a good hired man to work it. The garden and the land are being tilled in the northern manner and then when some of these southern gentlemen come to see them they are amazed. Yes, you would get a big laugh because you know a lot more about farming than Father. If you were to farm here they would probably think that you were a wonder from heaven."[80]

By 1869 the Amelia colony appeared to offer some promise, and as many as eighty Dutch, some from Michigan, others from the

79 Albertus C. Van Raalte to J. G. Van Heulen, 3 Aug. 1869, ACC; Albertus C. Van Raalte to Peter J. Oggel, 6 Oct. 1868, published in *De Hope*, 21 Oct. 1868; Lucas, *Netherlanders in America*, 308-12; Karry Ritter, "Albertus C. Van Raalte and his Settlement in Amelia County, Virginia," Hope College student paper, 1978, HMA; Janet Sjaarda Sheeres, "Ecumenicity in Amelia County, VA, 1868-1886," in *Diverse Destinies: Dutch* Kolonies *in Wisconsin and the East*, Nella Kennedy, Robert P. Swierenga, and Mary Risseeuw, eds. (Holland: Van Raalte Press, 2012), 105-27.

80 Christina Van Raalte to Benjamin Van Raalte, Amelia Court House, Virginia, 3 May 1869, translation by Clarence Jalving, HMA.

Netherlands, moved there. Within the year, Amelia had two organized churches and the beginnings of an educational institute. Yet the colony failed. Most of the Dutch left within two years, and those who remained worked as farm tenants or skilled laborers for Americans.

The downfall of the Amelia colony has been attributed to poor financing, both on the colonial and the individual levels, as well as the cultural incompatibility of the Dutch with former black slaves and southern whites. These problems, albeit in a different form, were nothing new; Dutch settlers elsewhere had overcome severe financial problems and divisive cultural differences. The third strike against the Amelia colony, and the one that ultimately led to its failure, was an inability to cultivate the land and reap a profit. Without the income from successful farming, the colony, with its weak infrastructure, collapsed under the weight of overhead costs and failed dreams, and the assemblage of largely unfamiliar faces that formed the colony had little time to become a cohesive social unit.

The colony's agricultural difficulties were manifold. First of all, the Dutch were unfamiliar with the southern climate, soil, and crops. The Amelia lands were best suited for tobacco, but the Dutch did not have enough of their own laborers (or monies to hire labor, however inexpensive) to run a productive cash crop enterprise. Instead, they attempted subsistence farming and found that without fertilizer little would grow in the red-clay soil that had been depleted by two centuries of tobacco culture.[81] The heavy soils also required sturdy horses to pull the plow, but these work animals were scarce, having been sacrificed in the losing war effort.

In 1870 a wave of settlers departed from the colony in disgust. Some may have paid too much for their land, all were poor, and some had begun to quarrel. Behind this mounting frustration was a severe drought that caused a crop failure in 1870. Those who had led Van Raalte and the settlers to believe the region was fertile were either misinformed or sharpies. Neither wheat nor corn grew very well, and the best choice of all was to let the fields lie fallow and abandon the area altogether until it could regain its fertility. By then the Dutch were turning west instead of south, although promoters later pushed several other southern colonies.[82]

In 1879 two men, one from Holland and the other from Zeeland, viewed a twenty-five-thousand-acre tract of land in eastern North

81 *De Hope*, 29 Mar. 1876.

82 Van Hinte, *Netherlanders in America*, 527-531.

Carolina, at Havelock near Beaufort harbor that Charles M. McLean was promoting as a Dutch colony. The landseekers found the people friendly and the politics Republican, and more important, potatoes and corn grew exceptionally well. They warned, however, that wages were low, and workers were lazy. Blacks lived and worked apart from whites, so Dutch farmers would have to work the soil with their own labor. By the next spring, six Holland families were tilling this southern soil, and twenty more families were expected by the fall. Several Grand Rapids Dutchmen also surveyed the Havelock colony, with mixed reviews. Gerrit Van Schelven, editor of the *Holland City News*, predicted that, "barring unforeseen accidents this Colony will be a success." John Vander Poel Sr., a postmaster in Chicago's West Side Dutch settlement and a columnist for *De Grondwet*, also wrote favorably about the colony. Despite these promotional efforts, the surge of new families at Havelock did not materialize. The 1880 federal census in June counted only twenty-three native-born Dutch in the entire state. Unfamiliarity with southern crops like cotton and tobacco, as well as cultural differences with southerners and a reluctance to live near blacks, made colonization south of the Mason-Dixon Line problematic for Hollanders.[83]

The "free states" of Iowa, Kansas, Nebraska, Minnesota, South Dakota, and Colorado beckoned, and vast areas of rolling prairies were free for the taking under the national Homestead Act of 1862, which offered 160 acres to any settler who would live on it and farm it for five years. Land pressures around the Dutch colony of Pella, Iowa led to the formation in 1870 of the daughter colony of Orange City in Sioux County in northwestern Iowa. Dutch farmers in West Michigan learned of the new venture in the pages of *De Grondwet*, and in the summer of 1875, Henry Hospers, one of the promoters of the Orange City settlement, visited Holland personally to tout his colony. Hospers was credible and convincing enough so that a month after his departure, Professor Hermanus Doesburg of Hope College and Johannes Dykema, traveled to Sioux County to survey the land. Others, including the brickyard business partners Berend J. Veneklasen and Albert Bolks, followed with a trip to the "new Northwest."[84]

Veneklasen and Bolks were impressed with Orange City's prospects, and they reported favorably on the fertility of the soil. They also knew that most settlers on the Great Plains had tried to grow and

83 *De Grondwet*, 11 Mar., 16 Dec. 1879, 12 Oct., 28 Dec. 1880; *Holland City News*, 13 Dec. 1879, 27 Mar. 1880; Van Hinte, *Netherlanders in America*, 525-26.

84 *Holland City News*, 14 Aug. 1875; *De Hollander* 11 Aug., 15 Sept. 1875.

export wheat before any other crop, regardless of the land's suitability for wheat culture. This had to change, the business partners said. "There are many who are of the opinion that wheat is and must remain the primary cultivation for the future. We are convinced, however, that this is not so. We think that within a few years, cattle and hogs will become the primary source of the existence and welfare of the agricultural class, and for that no better opportunity can be found." How right they were![85]

In the late 1870s, large groups of twenty to fifty people annually left Holland for Orange City. Despite a few grasshopper plagues in the early years, those who stuck it out thrived. Derk J. Werkman brought along wood products, like sashes and window frames, along with wooden shoes, and he quickly sold over one hundred pairs. His brother John D. Werkman, crippled financially by the 1871 fire, opened a general store near Hull. In 1878 Hospers offered farms in Orange City up to 160 acres from $400 to $2,200 an acre. As more settlers moved to northwest Iowa, land prices rose. Such steep prices drove the Dutch to stake out new colonies farther west across the Missouri River in Dakota Territory and Kansas and Nebraska, and northward in Minnesota. The Holland Brass Band stayed busy at the Holland station, playing sorrowful tunes of departure.[86]

The Dutch settlements in Dakota Territory were "granddaughter" colonies formed initially from the overflow into northwest Iowa and were fed with fresh immigration from the Netherlands, as well as from the colonies of Holland, Pella, and sister settlements in Wisconsin. In 1885 "Dakota fever" was at its height, and over one hundred fresh Netherlands immigrants and nearly as many migrants from Michigan left for the new territory. This movement prompted the editor of the *Holland City News* to make a trip there and check out the reports for himself. He painted a rosy picture of the new settlements and the rich organic black loam from "two to four feet deep." Waxing eloquent, the editor opined: "Beautiful and happy homes are springing into existence, as if by magic, all over the prairies, and everywhere we found the people intelligent, courteous and generous." All unemployed young men, he continued, should move to Dakota as soon as possible. But they had better move fast, declared Pieter Ellerbroek, a land agent in Campbell County, South Dakota, who warned that Russian (that is, Ukrainian) families were coming by the hundreds and taking the good land.[87]

85 *De Hollander*, 24 Nov. 1875, translation by Michael Douma.

86 *De Grondwet*, 5, 26 Mar., 3 Sept. 1878; *Holland City News*, 16 Mar., 28 Sept. 1878; John D. Werkman obit., *Holland City News*, 19 Mar. 1926.

87 *Holland City News*, 7 Apr. 1883, 21 Mar., 11, 18 (quote) Apr. 1885; *De Grondwet*, 17, 23 Mar. 1885.

Those who moved to Dakota typically bought relatively large farms of 160 to 320 acres. The soil was not quite as fertile as in Iowa, but one could successfully grow corn and wheat and raise cattle and hogs. Advertisements in *De Grondwet* in 1908 for Dakota lands at prices ranging from $20 to $45 an acre definitely caught the attention of Michigan farmers. In large letters, Holland realtor Isaac Kouw's block ad began: "*Boeren Attentie*!" (Farmers, Attention!). The ad of Kouw's competitor, John Rooks, went one better: "*Vrije heemsteden* [Free homesteads] in South Dakota" read the bold headline. Rooks touted the thousands of acres of rolling prairie land with "dark chocolate loam," all lying along the line of the Pacific Coast Extension of the Chicago, Milwaukee & St. Paul Railroad. "This is a land where a poor man can well hope to make a start," Rooks declared. Who could resist such alluring advertisements?[88]

Kansas and Nebraska also beckoned the Dutch. Once again, there was free or cheap land, fertile soil, and endless grasslands for grazing cattle. Two Reformed congregations formed in northern Kansas in 1871, as Dutch from around the Midwest relocated there. In 1877 an ad hoc Kansas Colony committee formed in Holland, Michigan, and sent John Van Landegend, Jan W. Garvelink, Cornelius J. Voorhorst, Pieter Van Anrooy, and Daniel Baert on an inspection trip to Kansas. The next spring, most of the twenty-five member families departed for Kansas. Reinder Werkman, one of Holland's strongest promoters of westward emigration, visited Kansas and Nebraska in 1879. Bonds between Holland and the new settlements built up a large Dutch American cultural network, and in Rotterdam, Kansas, Werkman happened to meet the oldest son of Holland's Pieter Zalsman.[89]

Other Dutch settlements formed at Holland and Firth in southern Lancaster County, Nebraska, in 1868, and Luctor and Prairie View in Phillips County, Kansas, in 1878. But none grew as quickly as those in Iowa. Still, the Lancaster Dutch had reason to boast. John W. Te Winkle, a Hope College and Western Theological Seminary graduate, accepted their call in 1871, thus ensuring the future of the settlement. Luctor also made its own way, declared a local resident. "No Prins & Zwanenburg [Netherlands land agents who sold over a million acres in Minnesota] or those of the same sort who had land to sell and made money from it, who made a lot of noise and used a lot of printer's ink to advertise the lands; no dear dominie who fled from a small district and

88 *De Grondwet*, 30 June, 7 July 1908.

89 *Holland City News*, 8, 15 Dec. 1877; *De Grondwet*, 4 Dec. 1877, 28 Jan. 1879.

sought a more spacious region; no shrewd businessman or selfish land agent; no enthusiast who sought a utopia; simple Luctor advertises for itself."[90]

In the 1890s the Dutch westward movement crossed the Rocky Mountains and reached the Pacific Northwest. In 1896 a dozen Ottawa County residents joined the new Dutch colony of Lynden, Washington in the Yakima Valley. They were drawn by Reinder Werkman, a former Holland industrialist who had become a land dealer in Seattle for a Netherlands banking house. He sent a carload of fruit, vegetables, and lumber to Michigan in 1894 and ran articles in *De Grondwet* to drum up interest in the Northwest among West Michigan farmers. They followed up by running special excursion trains from Chicago to Whidbey Island, where he had eighteen thousand acres of land for sale. Later, in 1899, Werkman moved to Billings, Montana, and sold Great Northern Railroad lands around the Dutch sister colonies of Amsterdam and Manhattan. Hendrik Essing of Zeeland was one who took up that offer. In 1900 Werkman moved his operations to St. Paul, Minnesota, and used the pages of the Orange City (Iowa) *Volksvriend*, the main rival to *De Grondwet* for Dutch-immigrant readers, to induce farmers to come West.[91]

The first colonization near the Gulf Coast of Texas from the Holland area took place in 1895, led by Hendrik De Kruif of Zeeland. In October and November, he took two large parties of farmers to the "charming and productive" southeastern Coastal Plain around Port Arthur. Peter Moerdyke, a Holland native and author of the column "Chicago Letter" in the *Christian Intelligencer*, the Reformed Church in America weekly, reported on the venture: "A company of Hollanders, who have bought a large tract of land in Southern Texas are making strenuous efforts to induce their countrymen to colonize in that region, so highly favored by nature and civilization and commerce, according to their account." Moerdyke very likely was referring to John Broekema, an executive in the Siegel, Cooper & Co. department store in Chicago, who recruited Dutch truck farmers for the Port Arthur Land Company. This was a venture of Netherlands capitalists who owned sixty-six thousand acres of prairie land near Port Arthur and the town

90 Van Hinte, *Netherlanders in America*, 542-45; *De Grondwet*, 1 Feb. 1887 (translation by Michael Douma); Donald van Reken and Frits L. Kliphuis, *Reinder Edward Werkman: The Gilded Hollander* (Holland, MI: privately printed, 2007), 42-52. One Werkman letter in the 8 Jan. 1985 issue of *De Grondwet* is published in English in van Reken and Kliphuis, *Werkman*, 46-47.

91 *Holland City News*, 14 Nov. 1896; *De Grondwet*, 7 Jan. 1900.

Reinder E. Werkman, "The Gilded Hollander" (*courtesy Fritz Kliphuis*)

of Nederland, where a Christian Reformed Church was established in 1898. Probably several dozen Michigan Dutch families settled around Nederland, but most returned after failing to adjust to the hot, humid climate and unfamiliar crops such as rice.[92]

From 1906 to 1913, a second Texas colonization attracted several families from Holland who were ensnared by advertisements in the *Banner* by the Theodore F. Koch Company of St. Paul, Minnesota. Koch, a railroad land promoter who sold a million acres in Minnesota alone, opened an office in Houston in 1906 for the purpose of planting a Dutch colony at Hampshire and Winnie in Jefferson County, some twenty miles from Port Arthur. Koch's modus operandi was to donate land and money for a Reformed church and manse, which he knew was essential to attracting Dutch buyers. Moerdyke noted in a "Chicago Letter" column in 1906 that "Rev. J[ohn] A. De Spelder, formerly of our [Maurice, Iowa, Reformed] Church, is active in promoting the settlement of Hollanders in a Texas colony." At Winnie, as in Nederland, neither the Reformed churches nor their farms thrived, and most settlers returned to the Midwest.[93]

In the 1920s a third Texas boom attracted dozens of Holland-area farmers to a development of the Stewart Land Company of Kansas City

92 *Holland City News*, 9 Nov. 1895; P. T. Moerdyke, "Chicago Letter," *Christian Intelligencer*, 14 Sept. 1895; Van Hinte, *Netherlanders in America*, 706-16; Robert P. Swierenga, *Dutch Chicago: A History of the Hollanders in the Windy City* (Grand Rapids: Eerdmans, 2002), 567-73.

93 Moerdyke, "Chicago Letter," *Christian Intelligencer*, 26 Sept. 1906; Lucas, *Netherlanders in America*, 435-37; Robert Schoone-Jongen, "Cheap Land and Community: Theodore F. Koch, Dutch Colonizer," *Minnesota History* 53 (Summer 1993): 214-24.

in the Rio Grande Valley along the Gulf Cost. In 1920 six men accepted the company offer for a free ten-day excursion to the Rio Grande to look over the area in which three hundred thousand northern farmers had already settled. In the end, few Holland-area farmers "took the bait." In 1932 four Holland men went to Mission, Texas and planted citrus groves. Henry Zwemer purchased ten acres of orange trees, Charles Van Zylen and Bert Gebben each bought five acres, and Albert C. Keppel planned to do the same. The four returned home in December "elated" over the fruit prospects and spread glowing reports about the excellent truck farming in the valley. In the end, no southern region and few western regions, other than northwest Iowa and southwetern Minnsota , could compete with West Michigan for successful farming and a satisfying religious and cultural life.[94]

[94] *Holland City News*, 11 Nov. 1920, 22 Dec. 1932.

CHAPTER 17

Farm Market Center

An agricultural revolution beginning in the 1880s coincided with Holland's industrial boom. Industries that no city could do without were flourmills, sawmills, blacksmith shops, breweries, and cooperages. Service industries like feed stores, implement dealers, hotels, and taverns were equally essential, but they did not require much capital, and they employed many men. Entrepreneurs seized opportunities, such as tanning hides and manufacturing windmills, which they perceived could succeed in the locale. The Cappon & Bertsch Leather Company was the only large employer (chapter 12). The tannery thrived because of the cheap and locally available hemlock bark used in the tanning process. After a few decades, however, when the surrounding forests had been chopped and burned, Holland could no longer rely on wood products to fuel its economic engine. Since the city was surrounded by farmland, the logical next step was to develop agricultural processing industries.

Much of Holland's initial industrial base was dedicated to the processing of agricultural products. The city had always been an agricultural market town serving most of the farmers of southern

Ottawa and northern Allegan Counties. But the coming of the railroad in the 1870s meant that farmers no longer had to sell their produce on the local market; instead, they could ship in volume to major population centers. Food processing factories arose in Holland to take advantage of the successful local farms. From these farms, horse teams with wagons brought a steady supply of wheat, corn, beets, and cucumbers to the city, and farmers made sure not to waste cowhide or pig skin, since both could fetch a good price at a tannery.

The very first tractor in Holland, a Fordson manufactured by the Ford Motor Company in Detroit, reached Holland in August 1918 aboard Ronald Rosie's specially-rigged flatbed, one-ton truck. The trip over two hundred miles of unimproved roads took eighteen hours, and upon inspection not a bolt in the truck or tractor was loosened, despite the truck being overloaded by one thousand pounds and the roads nearly impassable in places.[1] It was a portent of the future, when machines would obviate some of the backbreaking work of farming. In 1936 the national Rural Electrification program finally brought farm homes and milking parlors into the twentieth century.

Breweries

Farmers found a strong demand for barley and hops at local breweries. Brewing began in the earliest days because water was often tainted, just as in the Netherlands. Ale and beer were the alcoholic beverages of choice, but business and professional people also drank the costlier *jenever* (Dutch gin) and brandy. The People's Assembly, the first local government in the Holland colony, banned saloons and "hard liquor," although they allowed druggists to stock "pure wines and liquors" for "medicinal purposes." Typically, the common folk had a small keg of beer (usually five gallons) delivered to their homes on weekends for one dollar. Holland's founder, Albertus C. Van Raalte, reportedly received a free keg each Saturday. In the first years, the colonists imported beer and ale from Kalamazoo and Grand Rapids. Local brewing began in the 1860s. The ready supply of winter ice at Black Lake made the local industry possible. In a common scene, a small army of men went on the ice with bobsleds and large handsaws to cut slabs that horse teams dragged to icehouses and smothered in sawdust and straw to keep for the summer season (see below).[2]

1 *Holland City News*, 1 Aug. 1918.

2 Randall P. Vande Water, "Brewing Thrived in Holland," in *Holland: Happenings, Heroes & Hot Shots*, 2:38; Dave Cheadle, "Fifty Years of Brewing–Highlights from Holland, Michigan, 1863 to 1919," unpublished paper, 1985, Holland Museum Archives (HMA); *Holland City News*, 1 Mar. 1934.

The first brewery listed in a public record was Jannes (Jan) Aling & Co. in 1863. It was located on the "west side on River [Street]" (later the Ottawa Furniture Co. site); Simon Sluiter and Simon Baar owned and operated it at that time. In 1864 Aling & Co. produced only fifty barrels, or 1,550 gallons (31 gallons per barrel), but output by 1870 had increased to one thousand barrels, worth $10,000. Most of Aling's beer slaked local thirst and therefore kept some $6,000 to $8,000 circulating within the economy.[3]

The 1871 fire destroyed the Aling brewery, and this opened the door for Carl Zeeb, a German from Milwaukee, to come in and begin brewing in a small frame building on Tenth Street. Two years later, in 1873, Zeeb erected a new building on the northeast corner of Tenth Street and Maple Avenue and launched the Holland City Brewery. This firm for forty-seven years (1871-1917) dominated the local industry, but not under Zeeb. His first year's production was a paltry 450 barrels, which could not satisfy local demand, and city bottlers and saloons imported one hundred barrels a week during the "sickly season" (the summer months in those days, due to malaria and dysentery) to meet local demand. Zeeb sold to Xavier F. Sutton and John Steiner and left town late in 1874. Within a year, Sutton bought out Steiner and expanded the facilities; the company was debt-free in two years.[4]

Sutton claimed that his beer was the equal of the celebrated Cincinnati lager beer, and that it was "so light and palatable that hardly any intoxicating parts are left in it." To this improbable advertising hype, the local editor opined: "If his present brew proved to be as hinted above, it will take away one of the objectionable features to its use, to say the least." William Ten Hage, proprietor of the City Hotel Bar-Room, advertised Sutton's lager beer at 3¢ a glass. In 1879 Sutton launched another enterprise that unsettled the many prohibition advocates in Holland. He opened a bottling plant, named the City Bottling Works, located under the Germannia House on Eighth Street, complete with special bottles "blown with his name and business on it." In a newspaper advertisement, he offered free delivery of his "celebrated Lager Beer" to customers' homes at $1.20 per dozen quarts. "Come and try Samples at the Bar," Sutton urged readers in a large block ad. The saloon of "Dikke [Fat] Pete" Brown on West Eighth Street featured Sutton's Bock Beer, as did the Rose Bud saloon on River Avenue, and the saloons of August

3 Cheadle, "Fifty Years of Brewing."

4 Ibid.; Vande Water, "Brewing Thrived in Holland," in *Holland Happenings*, 2:38-41; *Holland City News*, 22 Feb. 1873, 31 Oct. 1874, 11 May 1878 (quote), *Holland Sentinel*, 12 Dec. 2005.

Lundblad and John Van Spyker.[5] (See appendix 5.12 for a list of saloons and taverns from 1874 to 1974.)

Soon after Sutton began the bottling works in 1879, he entered into a partnership with Anton Seif, another German from Milwaukee, who had learned the brewing art "from A to Z" in his native land and in the Cream City. Sutton continued his bottling works, adding soda pop to his inventory, and he opened a saloon complete with billiard tables. Seif, meanwhile, transformed the E. F. Sutton Brewery into one of the largest operations in the region, under the name Holland City Brewery. In 1886 Seif and his son Anton Jr. replaced the old frame building on the northeast corner of Tenth Street and Maple Avenue with a three-story brick plant, replete with tubs, boilers, cellars, and icehouses. The new facility allowed him to ramp up capacity from 1,500 barrels (46,500 gallons) to 4,000 barrels (124,000 gallons), worth $7 a barrel. Seif's biggest problem was getting enough "good Barley." He offered farmers the "highest market price" for the 3,000 bushels he needed to meet the annual demand.[6]

His second challenge was to entice customers to return empty kegs. Hollanders liked their beer, but many would not visit saloons, preferring to drink at home. "Please bring back the empty kegs," Seif pleaded in the local newspaper. "I need them for the 4th of July." Even then, he ran out of beer before the holiday. Are there "any prohibitionists and total abstainers" in the Holland area? he wondered out loud. His daily sales in the peak of summer suggested otherwise. Yet, Seif's annual sales throughout the 1880s remained flat at 1,500 barrels (about one-third of capacity), almost all of which was consumed locally. The editor of the *Holland City News* crowed that Seif can "boast of as good a brewery as there is in Western Michigan. . . . Holland will soon be a rival of Milwaukee in the beer trade," he added, in the overstatement of the century.[7]

In 1891 Seif built his own bottling works adjacent to his brewery and matched Sutton's long-standing offer of free delivery of bottled beer at 90¢ per dozen quarts and $1 per two-dozen pints. Seif's brewery bought from five- to six hundred cords of ice each winter and kept a large workforce busy on the ice and in his plants. Like Sutton, Seif in

5 *Holland City News*, 24 Apr., 1 May 1875, 11 May 1878, 17, 19 Apr. 1879, 30 Oct. 1919, 17 May 1923 "Forty Years Ago," 1 Mar. 1934, "Twenty-Five Years Ago," 15 Oct. 1936.

6 *Holland City News*, 21 Aug. 1880, 13 Aug. 1881, 29 Dec. 1883, 30 Jan., 9 Oct., 4 Dec. 1886, 30 Oct. 1919; Cheadle, "Fifty Years of Brewing."

7 *Holland City News*, 17 July 1886, 10 Jan. 1887, 23 June 1888.

1903 also opened a saloon in a building he erected at 180 River Avenue just north of Eighth Street, where he sold "The Beer without a Peer," ice cold and unadulterated, by the glass, pint, quart, or gallon. His was one of eleven local saloons at the time, most owned by local brewers. Seif's expansion pressured Sutton to lease his bottling works first to C. J. Richardson and then to Frank S. Underwood; both continued to bottle beer under the Sutton name until 1900, and to bottle soda pop, especially the favorite Orange Squeeze, until at least 1920, long after Sutton retired in 1910.[8]

The national depression of the mid-1890s drove Seif to the wall, and he was forced to sell temporarily in 1895 to George Schoenith. Three years later, Seif regained possession of A. Seif Brewery. His sons, Anton "Tony" F. and Peter, subsequently joined the company, which allowed it to pass seamlessly to the second generation and avoid the succession challenge that crippled many a family business. Stanley Curtis remembered hearing "some of the older fellas sing a song about Seif's beer; it went like this: 'We all drink Seif's beer, Johnny fill up my bowl.'" The Seif family gained wide respectability and integrated themselves successfully into the Dutch Reformed city, even though some townsfolk had a strong antipathy to their product. Anton Seif was a city fireman in the old days when the men pulled the two-wheeled pumper, and he belonged to the local chapters of the Masonic Order and Odd Fellows. Although baptized a Roman Catholic, he helped found Zion Evangelical Lutheran Church for the sake of his Lutheran wife, and he served as its trustee and a generous supporter for many years. Seif was buried by that church in 1934.[9]

In the end, it was not market forces, but prohibition laws, that put all local breweries out of business (chapter 20). The first shot across the bow came in 1908 with the passage in Holland of a local option law, which threatened to knock out the retail trade. But the saloonkeepers quickly hit on ways to get around the law. Customers simply drank their bottles outside in a practice known as "counting the stars." Francis E. Dulyea and Martin Vander Bie sold five-cent aluminum tokens that read on one side: "Good for 5 cents in trade." Customers simply exchanged a

8 Cheadle, "Fifty Years of Brewing," and "An Overview of Holland's Bottlers," both in HMA; Vande Water, "Brewery Thrived," 41; *Holland City News*, 5 Feb. 1887, 7 Jan. 1888, "Fifty Years Ago" 24 July 1930, 23 Feb. 1940.

9 Cheadle, "Fifty Years of Brewing"; Stanley Curtis interview by Donald van Reken, 29 June 1976, typescript, pt. 3, p. 3, Joint Archives of Holland (JAH); *Holland City News*, 7 May 1892, 30 Oct. 1919, Anton Seif obit., 1 Mar. 1934.

Seif name engraved on top of the 180 River Street building, housing the Seif Saloon (1903-4), Francis E. Dulyea's Union Saloon (1906-8), Union Bottling (1910), and in 2012 the Pioneer Club of Holland (*courtesy Fritz L. Kliphuis*)

token for a bottle of brew, and hence no sale took place. Thus, Seif and the other brewers kept their plants running.[10]

In 1916 the Michigan legislature enacted a prohibition law that barred the manufacture and sale of alcoholic beverages, as of December 31, 1917. "Soon the foaming brew that has bubbled and sizzled in the making at the Holland Brewery for the past fifty years will brew no more," lamented the editor of the *Holland City News*. Anton Seif & Sons converted their brewery to a cheese factory, named Holland Cheese Co. It was deemed a temporary measure, but the Eighteenth Amendment

Francis E. Dulyea, proprietor Union Saloon, 180 River Street (*Archives, Holland Historical Trust*)

10 *Holland City News*, 30 Apr. 1908; Steve Vander Veen and Greczek, "Hops in Holland," *Grand Rapids Press Lakeshore Edition*, 1 Oct. 2009.

THE UNION
Sample Rooms
F. E. DULYEA, Proprietor
OUR LEADING BRANDS
Holland Beer on Draught.
BOTTLED BEERS—Budweiser, Blatz Export, Blue Ribbon, Red, White and Blue, Grand Rapids Silver Foam.
WHISKEYS—Old Crow, Hermitage, Green River, Large, Gibson, Canadian Club, Seagram's, Golden Wedding, Guckenheimer, Old Overholt, Old Oscar Pepper, Old McBrayer, Tom Moore, I. W. Harper, Glymont, Hudson Rye, Hunter Rye, Wilson, Ringold, Jersey Rye
HOLLAND : MICH.
Citizens Phone 180 River Street

Union Saloon advertisement, 1908 (Holland City Directory, *1908*)

of 1919 fixed prohibition in the US Constitution, seemingly for good. When a shortage of raw milk stymied the cheese house, Seif finally sold the brewing equipment to junk dealer Morris Goldman of Holland Iron & Metal Co. on East Eighth Street (chapter 12).[11]

Seif had a near monopoly on the local beer trade, but the firm always had competitors. Besides Sutton's brewery, the new River Street Bottling Works of Cornelius Blom Sr. bottled seventy-five cases of Toledo Beer a day for the city trade in 1892. The saloon of Jacob Japinga and Nicholas Hofsteen on Central Avenue and Eighth Street sold bottled beer from 1897 to 1917 and delivered it to customers' homes for 60¢ a dozen. From 1901 Winslow N. Quackenbush's Atlas

Aluminum five-cent trade token issued in 1908 by Francis E. Dulyea of the Union Saloon (*courtesy Fritz L. Kliphuis*)

11 Cheadle, "Fifty Years of Brewing"; *Holland City News*, 18 Oct. 1917, 30 Oct. 1919, 19 Aug. 1920; *Holland Sentinel*, 28 Oct. 1919.

Bottling Works manufactured beer and soft drinks. The Union Bottling Works of Vander Bie and Dulyea operated from 1910 to 1917. Each of these bottlers and many others ran saloons to sell local and national beers, mostly along the main shopping fares of Eighth Street and River Avenue. David Blom's Crystal Palace Saloon, at 5 West Eighth Street from 1897 to 1917, was one of the longest running houses. Dulyea's saloon, the Union, located in the former Seif Saloon at 180 North River from 1906 to 1908, offered "Sample Rooms" for serving "our leading brands" of whiskey and "Holland Beer on draught." Dulyea also carried Bottled Beers—Budweiser; Pabst Blue Ribbon; Red, White, and Blue; and Grand Rapids Silver Foam—as well as twenty whiskeys. All breweries and saloons in Michigan closed with prohibition on January 1, 1918.[12]

Brooks Beverage

Soft drink bottlers fared better. Carbonated soda pop was a new drink that was wildly popular. And being non-alcoholic, the law never targeted it. Quackenbush of Atlas Bottling specialized in the registered Whistle pop and other flavors until he retired in 1927. In 1929 Nehi Bottling Co. at 323 W. Nineteenth Street began producing fruit flavors. In 1934 in the midst of the Great Depression, Phillips Brooks, brother of former mayor and future state senator Earnest Brooks, began bottling 7Up in the basement of his home, affixing paper labels on the bottles with a paintbrush, and making deliveries in the back seat of his 1929 Buick sedan, which he painted lime green with 7Up on each side.

Brooks had secured the 7Up franchise for seventeen counties in southwest Michigan and bottled part time while working in his brother's insurance agency. To raise capital for more bottles and cases, Brooks sold his home, but the fledgling business lost $600 the first year and showed a profit of only $600 the second year. Discouraged, he sold the business for $400 and contracted for bottling with Frank Underwood of the Holland City Bottling Works at 229 West Ninth Street. In 1937 Brooks bought the business back for the same price and was able to borrow enough money to make a down payment on the vacant Furniture Exhibition Building at 99 River Avenue. He ramped up production to sixty cases an hour, and the 7Up Bottling Company of Western Michigan became the premier wholesale distributor in Holland, with sales of three million bottles in 1938. By 1942 a fleet of thirty delivery trucks delivered ten million bottles to slack the thirst of

12 *Ottawa County Times*, 22 July 1892; Grand Haven *Ottawa Gazetteer*, 1908, cited in Vander Veen and Greczek, "Hops in Holland."

Brooks 7Up Bottling Company of Western Michigan, 99 River Avenue, 1938 (*courtesy Randall P. Vande Water*)

customers. Brooks managed to secure rationed sugar during the war, thanks to his political ties and position as chairman of the Ottawa County Rationing Board.[13]

James F. Brooks joined his father's company in 1945 after mustering out of the Air Corps, and in 1953 he succeeded him as president and chief operating officer. The River Avenue plant had to be enlarged to meet growing demand for 7Up and for new lines, such as the diet version of 7Up called Like, and Howdy, "the friendly drink." The business multiplied ten-fold, with the addition to its bottling operations of Dr. Pepper, RC Cola, Hires Root Beer, Vernors, Orange Crush, Schweppes, Squirt, Hawaiian Punch, Gatorade, and Lipton Tea. In 1969 James F. Brooks opened a new plant in the Southside Industrial Park at 777 Brooks Drive off Thirty-Second Street, which he had to enlarge several times in the next decade. Brooks Products Inc.—the new company name in 1969—also implemented self-directed employee work teams that shared decision-making and job responsibilities. This teamwork got them through the high demand summer months with many overtime hours. In 1977 James' son, James "Jim" W. F. Brooks,

13 The section relies heavily on Larry B. Massie, *Haven, Harbor, and Heritage: The Holland, Michigan Story* (Allegan Forest, MI: Priscilla Press, 1996), 136. See also *Holland Sentinel*, 18 Feb., 28 Mar., 23 Dec. 1937; Ollie Wierenga, Interview by Matthew Nickel, 8 July 2002, typescript, 8, JAH.

Loading "pop trucks" at the 7Up Bottling Company, 1930s
(*courtesy Larry B. Massie*)

joined the firm after graduating from Michigan State University, and within a decade he was ready to replace his father as president and CEO.[14]

In 1977 James F. Brooks made a bold move: he was the first bottler to purchase a franchised company—the Squirt Company of California. He transferred its offices to Holland and renamed his company Squirt & Co. The local operation, named SquirtPak Inc., was golden, and sales rose rapidly, fulfilling Brook's prediction of a "Squirt explosion." After his many triumphs, Brooks let up and named Bruce Van Dyke president and chief operating officer, while retaining the title of board chairman. In 1986 Brooks sold the US rights to Squirt for $30.5 million, and he fully retired. His son, Jim, who headed the Squirt operations, was ready to take over and bring the third generation into the executive suite. The Squirt acquisition rained cash, which Jim Brooks used to quadruple the size of his company, now renamed Brooks Beverage Management, by acquiring bottling plants in Detroit, Flint, and Columbus, Ohio, and distribution facilities in Michigan and Ohio.[15]

In 1992 Jim Brooks added "New Age" Snapple lines and a $4.5 million, PAK-PRO "hot-fill" technology that allowed beverages to be bottled without preservatives. The new technology was so thirsty for water and so overloaded the city's sewer system that the city council demanded that the company cut its hours of production, build a cooling

14 *Holland Sentinel*, 19 Jan., 21 Aug. 1978.

15 Ibid., 13 June 1977, 26 Jan. 1980 (quote), 2, 25 Jan., 11 Feb. 1988, 12 Jan. 1989.

tower to cut wastewater by 35 percent, and pay an even higher sewage surcharge. As Brooks aptly remarked, Brooks Beverage is "a David fighting two Goliaths" (the Philistine giant), to which *Grand Rapids Press* business editor Jim Harger quipped: the company is "no squirt either."[16]

In 1995 Brooks Beverage merged with Mid-Continent Bottlers of Des Moines, Iowa to create Beverage America, a $550 million company with three thousand employees, including three hundred in Holland. Jim Brooks remained chairman and chief operating officer for three years, until 1998, when the British soft-drink giant Cadbury Schweppes paid $724 million for Beverage America and merged it with Select Beverage of Chicago to form American Bottling Co. Brooks, believing that consolidation was necessary in the industry, stepped into retirement and philanthropic endeavors. He took satisfaction in building Beverage America into the largest independent soft-drink bottler in the United States. Since the sale, Brooks Capital Management, led increasingly by James' son Scott, has found new investment opportunities in apartment complexes and in a "pet project," Hopwood De Pree's Tic-Tock Studios, a Holland-based movie production company.[17]

How did Brooks Beverage thrive for three generations in the shadow of the giants Coca-Cola and Pepsi? James Brooks explained the strategy: "We decided we're not going to attack them where they're strong; we're going to be the kings of the flavor world." And they certainly won the crown. Innovation was another factor. Brooks Beverage introduced the thirty-two-ounce, family-sized bottle, and they were the first to use twist-off caps, first metal and then plastic.[18]

Zalsman & Co., owned by Peter J. Zalsman, in 1918 opened the first bottling plant to sell drinking water from an artesian well he sunk between Nineteenth and Twentieth Streets. Zalsman induced a Grand Rapids chemist to declare the water "No. 1 and entirely free from all pathogenic germs." He then hyped his product, sold by the quart and gallon, by claiming there was "as much difference between his artesian water and city water as between whiskey and beer." Zalsman was clearly the precursor of modern water merchandizing.[19]

Alcoholic beverage distributors

The end of Prohibition with the passage of the Eighteenth Amendment in 1933 opened the legal beer and wine market for the

16 Ibid., 23 Aug. 1988, 23 Jan., 19, 21 Oct., 4 Nov. 1993; *Grand Rapids Press*, 13 May 2001, 13 Dec. 1992 (quote).

17 *Holland Sentinel*, 24, 26 Feb. 1998, 13 May 2001, 13 Sept. 2011.

18 Meijer Lecture Series, Hope College, 12 Sept. 2011 (*Holland Sentinel*, 13 Sept. 2011).

19 *Holland City News*, 18 Sept. 1918.

first time since 1919, and several Holland businessmen seized the opportunity to slack the thirst of thousands. Theodore "Ted" Baker almost immediately began distributing beer at 23 West Ninth Street. He held the franchises for Budweiser, Pabst Blue Ribbon, and three Michigan brands—Goebel, Old Michigan, and Frankenmuth. Briefly in the mid-1930s, he rented space at 211 Central Avenue, and then relocated to 26 West Sixth Street, where he remained until 1952, when he sold his franchises to his sales manager, Arthur "Art" J. Mervenne, and switched product lines to plumbing fixtures, notably the prized "Peerless Water Softeners." Mervenne had in 1951 purchased part of the Brooks bottling business and began operations as Mervenne Beverage at 152 East Sixth Street at Columbia Avenue. He added Anheuser-Busch of St. Louis to his beer lines. A people-person par excellence, Art managed to gain 70 percent of the beer market in Holland. In 1958 Mervenne Beverage moved to 12611 James Street and in 1990 relocated again to a large facility at 4209 Lincoln Avenue (M-40) in Fillmore Township. By 1984 Art's son John A. joined him as vice president and is now president.[20]

Washington Square Beverage was the second distributor, which occupied various buildings in the 400 block of Washington Avenue for fifty-five years, from 1936 until 1991. Roy E. Young started the firm and then sold after two years to Benjamin Frens, who sold after another two years to Peter Raffenaud. Peter's brother Gerald joined him by 1949; the pair continued until Peter died in 1958, and his widow Martha continued as a partner. When Gerald died in 1969, Albert and Phyllis Klinge bought the business and carried on for almost two decades, until selling to Mark Tucker in 1986. The firm shuttered its doors in 1991. Over the years, the owners lived in the second floor flat above the shop.[21]

The third post-Prohibition wholesaler was Modern Beverage, begun in May 1937 by John and Janet Van Dam, Drenthe egg dealers who obtained exclusive West Michigan rights to sell Schlitz, Schmidt, Hamm's, and various brands of wine and champagne. The Van Dams determined to sell alcoholic beverages, despite the certain disapproval of their Christian Reformed church elders. By 1945 they operated from a warehouse at 1841 112th Avenue on the southwest corner of M-21 or Chicago Drive (now part of Crown Toyota). The business flourished, and they added property to the south up to Paw Paw Drive Bridge, including the 1851 Steketee House at 1811 112th Avenue. In the mid-

20 *Holland City Directories*, 1934-2011; *Holland Sentinel*, 16 May 1956, 25 Jan. 1994; Vander Veen and Greczek, "Hops in Holland."

21 *Holland City Directories*, 1934-1992.

1960s, John secured his realty license and associated with Tri-County realty.[22]

Son John H. Van Dam joined the firm as a salesman in 1959 after graduating from Hope College, and in the 1960s his parents began wintering in Florida and turned operations over to him. A fire destroyed the wooden warehouse on January 11, 1966, along with more than fifteen thousand cases of alcohol worth $65,000. Many bottles exploded in the heat, and the rest were unfit to drink. Employee Chris Hoogendoorn was overcome by smoke when he successfully went into the office to pick up $2,000 in cash. The bottles and debris were dumped in the backyard of the historic house on the bank of the Black River and covered with dirt, nicely leveling off the sloping backyard. Modern Beverage relocated temporarily to a warehouse across Chicago Drive on 112th Avenue at Lakewood Boulevard (across from the present Walgreens store) and then to another distributor's warehouse on Washington Avenue. Meanwhile, they secured property and erected a new warehouse in 1967 at 400 Center Street (essentially an extension of Ninth Street east of Fairbanks Avenue), which property adjoined a Pere Marquette Railroad siding. In the 1980s Van Dam hired James "Jim" F. Kaminski, also a Hope College graduate, as a laborer. Kaminski climbed the ranks to salesman and vice president. The firm has some twenty employees, plus additional help in the busy summer season.[23]

The Hollander Beverage Company of Harold J. Tanis was operating at 115 River Avenue by 1940. Tanis held franchises for Berghoff, Pabst Blue Ribbon, Frankenmuth, and Stroh's. By 1942 he relocated to 609 West Seventeenth Street and moved again by 1947 to 917 Washington Avenue, where the firm remained until closing in 1965. Another distributor in the 1970s was Isidore H. Sklansky's I. H. S. Beverage at 462 West 23rd Street, which relocated to Kalamazoo.[24]

Commercial bakeries

Another use for grain was to manufacture table foods such as the unique Dutch Rusk, a crisp biscuit that was typically eaten with butter and jam or soaked in coffee or tea. Berend Arendshorst's Holland Rusk Company became one of the leading industries in the city after 1897, when the home plant in Grand Rapids opened a branch factory. Arendshorst, a master baker, immigrated to West Michigan in 1890, bringing a recipe that his great grandfather had perfected. With one hundred years of rusk-baking experience in the family, it was no

22 I am indebted to John Van Dam for information about Modern Beverage.

23 *Holland City Directories*, 1935-2011; *Holland Sentinel*, 12 Jan. 1966.

24 Vander Veen and Greczek, "Hops in Holland;" *Holland City Directories*, 1938-1980.

Holland Rusk road sign with trademark windmill logo, touting "America's Finest Toast, At Grocers and Restaurants Everywhere," 1930s (*Donald van Reken Collection, Joint Archives of Holland*)

surprise that within five years Arendshorst began manufacturing the Dutch delicacy, first in Grand Rapids and then in Holland. This was in a three-story brick factory on East Eighth Street, which touted the name Arendshorst in the brick façade. The baking plant behind, which stretched to Ninth Street, featured special ovens imported from England. Within ten years, daily production was ramped up from ten thousand to two hundred thousand Holland Rusk biscuits. Each package featured a Dutch windmill—the company trademark and a symbol of quality. Hollanders, of course, desired this delicacy, but Americans also came to crave rusk for its tastiness.[25]

To keep up with the growing demand, Arendshorst recruited Dutch immigrants such as Melle Jan ten Hoor, a recent immigrant to New Era, who responded to a job offer letter in 1905 and moved to Holland to help raise production above the then sixteen thousand daily rate. By 1912 the bakery had a workforce of sixty, including many women. The war years were difficult. In 1917 the firm earned a net profit of only $718 on rusk and cookie sales of almost $100,000. In 1923 William "Will" Arendshorst, son of the company founder, took over management, aided by his brother John as vice-president. In 1921 the Arendshorsts took in Jelle Hekman of Grand Rapids-based

[25] *Holland: The Gateway of Western Michigan for Chicago and the Great West* (Chicago: Dearborn Corp., ca. 1912); *Holland City News*, 1 Jan. 1925; *Holland City Directories*, 1897, 1903-4, 1906, 1908.

Hekman Rusk bakery, 418 West Eighteenth Street at Cleveland Avenue (*Joint Archives of Holland*)

Hekman Rusk as a heavyweight partner, which linked them to the "rusk king" in Grand Rapids. Father Berend Arendshorst, another Horatio Alger type, came in every day until his death in 1928 at age eighty-nine just to keep his eye on things. His active baking career spanned seventy-five years. After a $10,000 upgrade of the baking machinery in 1926, daily production of the rusk "toasties" was ramped up to eight hundred thousand. In 1928 John Hekman and John Arendshorst sold out to the National Biscuit Company of New York, but Will Arendshorst continued to manage the local plant until Jerry Phillips replaced him in 1935. Phillips managed the plant thirty-one years, until 1966, when National Biscuit announced its closing; toasted biscuits no longer satisfied consumer tastes. Hope College bought the vacant plant in 1968 and converted the office building for use by the art department and the bakery for the maintenance building.[26]

A competitor of Holland Rusk was the Michigan (later Dutch) Tea Rusk Company, which Jacob Sr. and Edwin Heeringa, George and Gerrit Schurman, and William Beckman Sr. opened in 1905 at 170-74 East Eighth Street. Heeringa began as a salesman and rose to plant manager; master baker Beckman tended the ovens, and George Schurman kept

[26] Melle Jan ten Hoor to "Mom, Bro, and Sis," 9 Apr. 1905, translated by Henry ten Hoor and published in *Pillar Postscript* 19 (Jan./Feb. 2006): 3 (Newsletter of the Pillar Christian Reformed Church, Holland MI); *Holland City News*, 10 Feb. 1905, 14 Dec. 1916, 21 June 1923, 12 Nov. 1925, 25 Feb. 1926, 14 July 1927, 16 Feb., 8 Mar. 1928, 4 Aug. 1966; *Holland Sentinel*, 8 July 1935, 26 July 1955, 16 May 1956, 18 Aug. 1968; Holland Rusk Co., *Annual Report*, 1917, HMA.

the books as secretary-treasurer. John Arendshorst managed the plant. Jelle Hekman in 1928 invested in Michigan Tea Rusk, as he had with the Arendshorst bakery, and became company president, but he left his local partners in charge. The partners took in Hekman for the same reason as the Arendshorsts, to affiliate with the powerful Grand Rapids firm. With fresh capital from Hekman, the partners made three major changes: they renamed the company Dutch Tea Rusk; they sold the retail shop (which became the Royal Bakery); and in 1929 they built a new $20,000 bakery at 418 West Eighteenth Street at Cleveland Avenue, near the recently completed West Michigan Laundry. The ovens could turn out 350 loaves every forty minutes to supply independent grocers in West Michigan. Six trucks kept the stores supplied daily as the drivers ran their routes. After ten years the equipment had to be upgraded to keep up with the growing demand. Some thirty railcars a year brought fine flour to the bakery on a Pere Marquette Railroad spur to keep twenty-two employees busy at the ovens.[27]

In 1945 the company changed its name to Hekman Rusk, and Edgar Hekman, son of Jelle, came from Grand Rapids to serve as vice president and general manager, in place of William Beckman, who retired. In 1947 the Holland principals—Heerema, Schurman, and Beckman—after running the plant for more than four decades, sold their interest to Jelle and John Hekman. Heeringa and Schurman joined the Russell Klaasen real estate and insurance office. The Hekmans immediately built a new bakery on Columbia Avenue and Eleventh Street, where they continued operations until 1979, when they consolidated baking in Grand Rapids and sold the Holland plant to Charles Conrad of Thermotron for its purchasing department (later Hope College's De Pree Art Center and Gallery).[28]

Besides the rusk plants, Federal System of Bakeries, a national wholesaler, in 1921 opened a Holland branch to supply West Michigan with bread and other products. Local investors, led by Theodore "Ted" E. Sundstrom, Peter Knapp, and Richard "Dick" Oosting, began with a combined bakery and retail shop in the Steketee Building at 18 East Eighth Street. By 1924 master bakers Merrick Hanchett and Jacob De Bone were the joint proprietors, with Hanchett as manager. Hanchett bought out De Bone by 1927, and just before the stock market crash, he sold a controlling interest to William Arendshorst, who became president of the reorganized Holland Federal Baking Company. The partners built a new bakery at 400 West Seventeenth Street, one block

27 *Holland City News*, 17 Feb. 1921, 26 July, 16 Aug. 1928, 27 Aug. 1936, 21 Apr. 1938, 9 June 1939; *Holland City Directories*, 1906-1942.

28 *Holland City News*, 8 Jan. 1948; Heeringa obit., *Holland Sentinel*, 9 Nov. 1956; *Holland City Directories*, 1945-80.

north of Hekman's new bakery. Hanchett added the title of vice president to manager, and Henry P. Kleis was secretary. In 1931 Richard "Dick" Miles bought Arendshorst's interest and replaced him as president. John C. Welling also invested and was named vice president.[29]

In 1940 Holland Federal Baking Company became Federal Baking Company. In 1945 Miles, Hanchett, Kleis, and Rein Visscher bought another competitor, Dutch Boy Bakery, a "yeast food manufacturer," that Harry Winter, Sydney Jenckes, and Raymond J. and Theodore Kuiper had started in 1929 at 190-92 East Eleventh Street. In 1936 Dutch Boy fell to outside investors, although the Kuipers remained to fill the positions of secretary and treasurer. Federal Baking Company absorbed Dutch Boy in its Seventeenth Street plant and took its colorful name. Miles and his executive team owned Dutch Boy Baking Company for nearly twenty years. Hanchett managed the plant until he retired in 1947, and Melvin Groteler became manager. The major shake-up came in 1964, when the Hekmans added the Dutch Boy wholesale bakery to its Dutch Rusk plant a block away. Edgar Hekman became president-secretary and Henry J. Hekman vice president-treasurer. In 1973 the Hekmans sold Dutch Boy to Richard West, but his West Baking Company lasted only a year before closing.In the end, Hekman Rusk of Grand Rapids gained control of all the commercial bakeries in Holland, except Holland Honey Cake, which Henry Labotz of Chicago launched in 1940 in a new plant at 420 West Seventeenth Street. Its famed honey cakes and honey bread were distributed regionally by truck and nationally by parcel post. Garrett Pothoven, a Pella native and Labotz's brother-in-law, managed the firm from 1946 until retiring in 1972. Larry Bensink owned the firm from 1968 until 2001, when he converted the building to his current venture, the Holland Bar Stool Company. [30]

Cash crops

Beginning in the 1870s, local farmers thrived by raising cash crops of peaches, celery, sugar beets, pickles, and canned fruits and vegetables. The key was that the city of Holland provided processing facilities and markets for these crops. As the initial "majors" fizzled out, except for pickles, new industries came on line in cookies, ice cream, lunchmeats, frozen soups, and turkeys. In 2006 Ottawa County's thirty food processors employed 3,300 workers.[31]

29 *Holland City News*, 17 Feb. 1921, *Holland City Directories*, 1921-38.

30 *Holland City Directories*, 1940-73, 1940-2012. Estella Dahm Vis and Ronald Pothoven provided information on Holland Honey Cake Co.

31 *Grand Rapids Press*, 19 Apr. 2009.

Peaches and other fruit

If Holland merchants were to succeed in exporting agricultural products, they and the growers needed to determine the most profitable crops. Climate and soil conditions strongly influenced what would grow best. While the heavy clay soils east and south of the city favored agriculture, the sandy soils all along the lakeshore were best suited for horticulture. In the spring, cool winds off Lake Michigan prevented early budding of fruit trees, while warm winds in the fall would extend the growing season an extra few weeks. The regulating nature of the lake thus protected fruit trees and created a fruit belt that would eventually stretch from Oceana County in the north to Van Buren County in the south. It was only a matter of time before the fruit industry prospered along this favorable section of shoreline.

The fruit that first yielded a profit was the peach. Peaches were grown in the Saugatuck area quite early. In fact, by 1825, John Jacob Astor's American Fur Company was operating a trading post at a place called the Peach Orchard on the Kalamazoo River. These fur traders most likely brought peach pits along with them from the East.[32] Many settlers planted fruit trees for personal use in the 1850s, but local fruit cultivation did not become important commercially until the end of the 1860s.[33]

In the 1870s the fruit-growing industry in the area boomed. Ray Nies describes the frenzy of the new gold rush:

> The earlier crops of this fruit so free from attacks of insects were naturally of high quality and sold for such high prices that many people rushed to start a peach farm. It was something akin to an old time western "gold rush" after a strike of "color." Farmers, who had been growing other crops, changed at once to peaches. Merchants, boatmen, lawyers, doctors, school teachers, even preachers caught the excitement and planted orchards. Outsiders came in and started orchards. The whole cleared region went into fruit growing on such a vast scale that soon more fruit was produced than could be shipped and sold at profit.[34]

32 According to Gerrit Van Schelven, *De Grondwet*, 3 June 1913.

33 *History of Allegan & Barry Counties*. (Philadelphia: D. W. Ensign & Co., 1880), 329; Lee Lamberts, "Ottawa County Fair's roots in harness racing," *Holland Sentinel*, 28 July 2009.

34 Ray Nies Autobiography, typescript, ch. 5, p. 1, HMA.

The Great Fire of 1871 destroyed many young orchards, but the fruit trees were replanted, since peaches became increasingly more marketable, not only for home consumption but also as a cash crop. Van Raalte had this idea already in 1869 when he hoped that a recent financial contribution to Hope College would enable the cultivation of peach trees on college-owned lands at Point Superior (later site of the Gold Mansion at Waukazoo Woods). The agricultural produce of this farm was to help pay for the college's yearly expenses, or in Van Raalte's words, it would "be a noble basis for the security and growth of our young institutions."[35] Unfortunately, for Van Raalte and his dream of financial security for the school, the Hope Haven Farm never materialized (chapter 8).

Since fruit remained in high demand in the 1870s, many others scrambled to get a share of the market. In his inaugural address as mayor in 1872, E. J. Harrington urged citizens to buy and cultivate fruit lands along the lakeshore. Growers needed little prodding; they raised peaches, apples, strawberries, plums, and grapes. Special fruit trains and steamers began transporting fruit to Chicago. The largest shippers of peaches in 1874 were Jan Visscher, Charles A. Dutton, H. S. Eagle, C. Storing, John Coatsworth, Manly Howard, John Roost, and H. Bacon. Only Visscher and Roost were Dutch. By 1877 a market for selling the fruit trees themselves opened up, and trees could be contracted for and delivered. In the six years after the great fire, a quarter of a million fruit trees had been planted, and another two hundred thousand were planned for the shores of Black Lake. Owners of commercial and personal-use orchards began reading agricultural literature to apply scientific advancements to increase productivity and yields. In 1880 the Holland Farmers & Fruit Growers Association was formed to express "unity and harmony" among the farmers and fruit growers and to promote the industry. In 1882 Michigan peaches set a price record of 15¢ apiece. The *Grand Rapids Democrat* noted, "Nothing in nature that grows out of the ground in this latitude has such a capacity for coining money for its producer as the toothsome peach with its bedowned blushing cheek."[36]

35 Van Raalte to Phillip Phelps Jr., 5 Nov. 1869, in Elton J. Bruins and Karen G. Schakel, eds., *Envisioning Hope College: Letters written by Albertus C. Van Raalte to Philip Phelps Jr., 1857 to 1875* (Holland: Van Raalte Press; Grand Rapids: Eerdmans, 2011), 214-16; Van Raalte to Benjamin Van Raalte, 13 Nov. 1869 (quote), Archives, Calvin College (ACC).

36 *Holland City News*, 6 Apr. 1872, 12 Sept. 1874, 14 July, 10 Nov., 1 Dec. 1877, 3 Apr., 18 Dec. 1880, 16 Oct. 1897; *Holland City News*, 17 Sept. 1892 (citing *Grand Rapids Democrat*).

As the peach industry grew, commission houses from Chicago and other large cities came to the area to solicit consignments and put down deposits on future shipments. Banks in northern Allegan County in particular thrived. During harvest time, steamships and rail lines transported shipments of local fruit overnight to the Chicago wholesale market. In Ottawa County, the land devoted to peaches more than tripled in twenty years, from just under one thousand acres in 1884 to well over three thousand acres in 1904. Strawberry fields also multiplied. During the 1887 season, American Express shipped to Chicago on its fruit train more than thirteen thousand crates of strawberries weekly. Increased fruit production aided both railroads and steamships, and it also boosted supportive industries such as the C. L. King & Co. Basket Factory (chapter 12).[37]

Prosperity in the fruit industry was not ensured, and the market proved to be cyclical, like every other farm commodity. In the 1890s a peach glut led to drastically reduced prices and lower profits, which led to the eventual downfall of many orchards. Sometimes a shortage of pickers left some fruit to rot on the trees. The "full harshness" of the continental climate ruined many a year's crop with a late spring frost. Particularly feared in the locale was a peach disease called "the yellows," which caused considerable damage to the fruit. Some farmers took their trees for granted, not realizing that they required no less an investment of labor than did other crops. Since there were already too many growers in the market by the 1900s, only those who cultivated, pruned, and sprayed their trees survived in the long run. Because of these and other problems, some farmers found it unprofitable to keep orchards. But areas with well-suited soils, usually at raised elevation like lakeshore ridges and areas around Fennville and Saugatuck, continued successful operations. This led to an increased differentiation in the area, with agriculturalists generally found inland and horticulturists along the lakeshore.[38]

Nies elaborated on the bust that followed the boom:

> I have heard of whole steamship cargoes of choice peaches sold in the city market for less than the freight charges, which were low, and I have even heard of them being dumped overboard when there was no sale at any price. Then, right at the peak of

37 Henry F. Thomas (Comp.), *A Twentieth Century History of Allegan County* (Chicago: Lewis Publishing Co., 1907), 499; *De Grondwet*, 12 July 1887.

38 Van Hinte, *Netherlanders in America*, 772; *Holland City News*, 13 Apr. 1872; Thomas, *History of Allegan*, 500.

> the greatest production came a winter of unusual severity which destroyed many of the trees, and after that came a contagious disease which took many of the rest of them. The growers were disheartened by their losses, and many quit trying to raise more peaches, and either abandoned their farms or turned to other crops. Those that stayed had now to spend time and money on spraying, which formerly had not been necessary. And with little fruit to carry, the steamships gradually disappeared; likewise the factories making fruit packages, until at last there were little of either.[39]

In addition to all the natural challenges, fruit growers had to deal with high shipping costs that ate up profits. Transit to Chicago markets by lake steamer was cheap, but seasonal; railroads provided year-round service, but rates were higher. Thus, producers were very pleased when Congress in 1920 granted the post office the right to offer parcel post service. Holland-area fruit companies took advantage of the new service to ship fresh peaches, pears, apples, and muskmelons to Chicago and points west by rail. In the heyday of lake shipping, Graham & Morton ran two side-wheelers a day to Chicago from its Eighth Street dock, loaded with peaches, pears, and other fruit brought from the orchards by wagon and the Interurban.[40]

Celery

Holland's most innovative agriculturalist was nurseryman George H. Souter, who tried to capitalize on trends and stay ahead of the market. One of Souter's most promising attempts to introduce a new crop came in 1884, when he promoted the cultivation of celery. Since celery had become a widely planted and successful cash crop of the Dutch in Kalamazoo and Muskegon, Souter was convinced that it could also succeed in Holland. For fine celery Souter knew it must be planted on low, wet ground. One such place was the swamplands east of the city, where Souter in 1885 cultivated twenty-five thousand celery plants on five thousand acres. The *Holland City News* jumped on Souter's bandwagon. There were five hundred acres of muck land in the immediate vicinity of Holland ideal for celery, the editor asserted, and four hundred men could be put to work raising the tasty plant. John Huizenga and J. Regnerus, among others, answered the call and

39 Nies Autobiography, ch. 5, p. 1.

40 *Holland City News*, 18 Aug. 1921; Andrew M. Hyma interview by Donald van Reken, 7 Aug. 1975, typescript, 4, JAH.

marketed excellent celery. For years to come, celery promised to make its mark and be a successful crop. In 1889, for example, *De Grondwet* advertised the sale of a farm that had apple, cherry, and pear trees, grape vines, and more—all expensive crops. But it highlighted the fact that the farm had five acres of good celery ground.[41]

In the end, there was not enough muck land around Holland for commercial celery production. But the crop took hold farther east on the bottomlands between Vriesland and Hudsonville and south at Hamilton. By 1914 *De Grondwet* reported that celery production in the Hudsonville area surpassed that of Kalamazoo, although the two regions ran neck-in-neck for several decades. Kalamazoo celery had the cachet of premium quality, however, and Ottawa County celery growers marketed and sold their crops in Chicago as Kalamazoo Celery. Land prices in Hudsonville skyrocketed; in 1919 Jacob Dyke sold his forty acres of muck land for $1,000 per acre, and this was considered cheap, although it set a record for this region.[42]

Celery crops in 1922 covered nearly one thousand acres between Zeeland and Hudsonville, ranking Ottawa County third in the state behind Kalamazoo and Muskegon Counties. Farmers on some five hundred acres of muck soils in Hamilton formed the Hamilton Celery Growers Association and developed a sweet, crisp variety marketed as the Hamilton Golden Brittle brand. Typical was John Nevenzel, a laborer in Veneklasen's brickyard in Hamilton, who in 1926 bought a seventeen-acre tract of "worthless" swampland nearby and transformed it into a prime celery field. Thousands of cases of celery and other muck crops from Ottawa and Allegan Counties, totaling $1 million annually in the 1920s, were shipped overnight by truck and lake vessels to Chicago's South Water Market.[43]

Celery production had an industrial spin-off in 1927—the Holland Transplanter Company (Holland Celery Planter Co. before 1940)—founded by Louis "Lou" Poll and his younger twin-brothers Benjamin "Ben" and Henry, all Hamilton farm boys and tinkerers by nature. Louis got married and rented a farm on the muck soils south of Hamilton to raise the Golden Heart brand celery, a cash crop in high demand in fancy hotels. He found it very laborious to work on hands and knees planting the delicate young sprouts in rows only three to four inches apart—ten thousand plants to an acre—but good prices made it worth

41 *Holland City News*, 25 Oct. 1884, 27 June 1885, 3 Aug. 1889, "Forty Years Ago Today," 5 Jan. 1939; *De Grondwet*, 27 Jan. 1889.

42 *De Grondwet*, 6 Jan. 1914; *Holland City News*, 16 Nov. 1905, 2 July 1914, 16 Oct. 1919.

43 *Holland City News*, 24 Aug. 1922, 1 Feb., 12 Dec. 1923, 28 Oct., 23 Dec. 1926.

his while. Celery had to be planted close together to prevent the stalks from growing too big and becoming stringy.[44]

In 1920 Lou, Ben, and Henry began tinkering with mechanical ways to plant the new delicacy. Their first attempt was to rig up a winch and cable powered by a one-cylinder gas engine that pulled a "sled" (actually a two- by twelve-inch board with small wood "rudders" on the bottom to cut furrows in the soft muck soil), on which two men sat and set the celery sprouts. By mid-decade they had developed the first workable semi-automatic planter, with metal plant holders in place of hands, flat steel wheels to pack the soil around the plants, steel shoes in place of wood "rudders" to grove the furrows, and seats instead of sleds for the men. But the problem was that neither horse nor tractor could pull the prototype at the required slow and steady pace. So they invented a specially geared, self-propelled tractor that could run slow enough for the machine.[45]

The next step was to refine the transplanter to work at a faster pace. Soon they had a mechanical transplanter that was eight to ten times as fast as hand seeding, whether pulled by a team or a tractor. Moreover, the machine set every plant at a uniform depth for optimal growth. The machine helped the bottom line, and word spread quickly to Dutch celery farmers on the muck at Byron Center, Hudsonville, Kalamazoo, Celeryville (Ohio), and elsewhere.

By this time Ben was married and living at 151 Fairbanks Avenue between Fifth and Sixth Streets; he worked as a mechanic at the Packard Garage. Ben agreed to "kick the chickens out" of their coop and build transplanters there. The first year, 1927, the brothers and several part-time employees made forty machines, and sales tripled the next year. The brothers quit their "day jobs" and concentrated on making planters. But they faced an unexpected problem, a patent fight with George Schutmaat, head of Hamilton Manufacturing Co., who went to court in 1931 claiming to have invented the transplanter. Schutmaat won the first round, but Lou Poll won on appeal, and his patent was secure. In 1932 the Polls adapted their machines to plant cabbage, cauliflower, lettuce, onions, strawberries, tomatoes, and even spinach—as requested by the Gerber Foods Company of Fremont. Tomato growers in northern Indiana and Ohio requested machines for their crop and were happy to

44 This section relies on an interview with Howard Poll by the author, 8 June 2012; Poll's "History of Holland Transplanter Co." (2012); Poll's interview by Ellie Norden, 12 Jan. 1998, typescript, JAH; and articles in the *Holland City News*, 31 Dec. 1942, and *Holland Sentinel*, 15 Aug. 1947, 10 Jan. 1993.

45 *Holland City News*, 9 Apr. 1925.

First celery transplanter, late 1920s. The men faced backward to set the plants (*courtesy Howard Poll*)

pay $50 apiece when the Poll brothers devised one. When Appalachian tobacco farmers got word of this, they said: "If you can plant tomatoes, can't you plant tobacco too?"[46]

The Polls made slight modifications and were soon selling machines to tobacco growers. In the depths of the Great Depression in 1934, the brothers bought the former Standard Grocery Co. building at 341 East Seventh Street to meet the growing demand for their transplanters. In the late 1930s the Polls adapted the machines to plant tree seedlings for the lumber industry, notably in Norway, the British Isles, and Canada.

In 1940 Louis Poll sold his interest to his brothers and returned to his first love–farming. Ben and Henry carried on, renaming the company Holland Transplanter Co. They now had to meet new challenges brought on by the Second World War. In 1942 national war agencies asked them to manufacture special purpose transplanters, one to plant trees whose gum yielded artificial rubber, and a second to sow grass seed along runways on military airfields to suppress clouds of dust kicked up by planes on take-off that could damage the motors. The Polls ramped up production for the war effort, but a fire in 1943 caused $10,000 damage and interrupted the schedule. That year Raymond Kolk, a relative by marriage from Grand Rapids, joined the company to manage the office. The Polls preferred to get their hands dirty in the shop. In 1947 the twenty-five employees shipped machines to forty states and several foreign countries.

In 1953 Kolk left after ten years to form his own company, Mechanical Transplanters (see below), taking along his secretary and

[46] Poll interview, typescript, 22. For a compilation of press clippings on celery cultivation in Hamilton, see Mary Drenten, comp., "Celery Industry in Hamilton" (typescript, Herrick District Library, 2004).

Two-row, self-propelled celery transplanter, 1930s
(*courtesy Howard Poll*)

two key shop employees. He had earlier signed a non-compete clause, but Ben Poll graciously acquiesced. To fill the gap, Ben's son Howard and two of his sons-in-law, Charles "Chuck" Knooihuizen and Vern Kraai, joined the firm in 1954. Ben Poll that year developed a new plant holder, and the business grew five-fold. A few years earlier, the Polls had developed the first tractor-mounted transplanter that could plant up to twelve rows at a time. This was a far cry from the first self-propelled machines, followed by horse- and tractor-drawn machines that planted one or two rows. In 1963 the company relocated to their present location at 510 East Sixteenth Street, the vacant Super Foods building.

In the next decade Holland Transplanter outsold all other planter manufacturers combined.The forty employees in 1980 produced six thousand machines designed for a wide variety of crops; the company then controlled over half the market. The early 1980s were hard years for farmers, and the market for transplanters declined sharply. But business picked up when the company designed new machines that set potted greenhouse plants and penetrated plastic mulch that farmers (and later the transplanter itself) laid on the ground to eliminate weeds, warm the soil, and hasten the harvest by several weeks. In the 1990s Howard Poll invented a rotary planter that set plants twice as fast as by hand. At the request of the city parks department, Poll also devised a machine that digs up old tulip bulbs and plants new ones along the curbs of city streets. Holland Transplanter has continued operations as a third-generation family business under Poll and his son Ken and daughter Susan Brunsell, with sales of up to $5 million and a workforce of twenty. The company ships their specialized machines worldwide, including China, who buys transplanters for onion sets and tobacco.[47]

A second manufacturer supplying transplanters for Michigan farmers, and eventually for farmers and nurserymen across the country, is Mechanical Transplanters, founded in 1953 by Raymond G. Kolk (see above), who was a part-owner of Holland Transplanters since 1943. Kolk built a plant at 1150 Central Avenue on the south side of US-31 that has continued for nearly sixty years to design and make a wide variety of machines, including seed drills and attachments for a dozen garden crops and tobacco, spraying appliances, and hole diggers for planting Christmas trees and nursery stock. Kolk's first machine was a two-man planter pulled behind a farm tractor. In 1988 Kolk appointed two sons, Howard and Robert, as vice presidents, and in 1990, after thirty-seven years, he stepped down, and Robert became the president. In 2011 Robert Kolk retired and sold the company to employees Steven Van Loo and Daniel Timmer.[48]

Sugar beets—Holland-St. Louis Sugar Company

In the 1890s farmers in the Bay City and Saginaw area on cutover (logged) lands switched to sugar beet production and found it profitable. Local bankers and industrialists heard about the excitement over beets in eastern Michigan and met at the Opera House on Eighth Street to consider the possibilities, especially for farmers with heavy clay soils that were not ideal for vegetables or orchards. The timing was auspicious; it was the depths of a severe national depression. As Arend Visscher recalled: "Times were hard in Holland. Business was at a low ebb, and the thrifty Hollanders pricked up their ears when news came from Bay City that there was money to be made in beets." Beets could supply sugar for the nation's sweet tooth.[49]

The body sent a three-person delegation to Bay City to check out the beet craze there, made up of attorney and horticulturalist Visscher, Hope College chemistry professor Douwe Yntema, and Cornelius J. De

47 *Holland City News*, 26 Jan. 1980, 10 Jan. 1993; www.transplanter.com.

48 *Holland City Directories*, 1961-2010; www.mechanicaltransplanter.com.

49 For this and the next two paragraphs, see "The Holland Sugar Company," in Arthur A. Visscher, "Recollections [of Arend Visscher]," typescript, 1959, section "Holland-St. Louis Sugar Company," Visscher Family Papers, HMA. The state subsidy required beets to be of at least 90 percent purity, and processors had to pay growers at least $4 a ton for sugar content of 12 percent or better.

Roo. When the men returned, farmers from all around Holland came to the Opera House to hear their glowing report about a crop that netted growers from $25 to $30 an acre. Beets became the rage. That Professor Yntema endorsed the project gave local farmers the courage to try the new crop, and they pledged 1,500 acres. A larger committee laid plans for a processing factory in Holland, and investors on the spot subscribed to $160,000 in stock. Three weeks later, enthusiasm reached a fever pitch in another meeting at the Opera House, when farmers applied on a first-come, first-served basis for seed from a 65,000-pound order coming from Germany.

Growing beets was an easy decision for West Michigan farmers, who saw the risks of the cyclical fruit industry. Beet cultivation ran less chance of complete failure; beets could even withstand late spring frosts that proved fatal to other crops. Farmers hedged against a bad year with a few acres of beets. National sugar prices, however, were subject to big swings, due to changes in national tariff policy for cane sugar. So prices had to be watched carefully. Tariffs gave the sugar industry its start and later led to its demise. The Dingley Tariff of 1897 protected beets for the first time and stimulated the local industry. The Michigan legislature also did its part by offering processors a bounty of one cent per pound for homegrown beets. "Isn't it the function of government to aid the people?" insisted a Lansing newspaper editor, who pushed for the bounty. With these incentives, area farmers raised sugar beets in the tens of thousands of tons, and local companies converted the tubers into millions of pounds of sugar annually.

In 1899 a bevy of local bankers and industrialists established the Holland Sugar Company, led by president Arend Visscher and George P. Hummer of Peoples State Bank, Isaac Cappon and John C. Post of First State Bank of Holland, Fred C. Hall, Charles M. McLean, C. J. De Roo, Heber Walsh, and Mayor Germ Mokma, among others. The firm was capitalized at $350,000 in common stock, all but $40,000 local money. De Roo was the secretary and manager. In 1903 Holland Sugar's real property valuation exceeded that of Cappon & Bertsch, the city's first million dollar corporation, although the personal property of the leather giant was valued at one hundred times as much (table 15.1).[50]

"Sugar-beet Visscher," as locals dubbed him, hit on the novel idea of giving growers a stake in the plant by offering them, in lieu of cash, $25 in stock for every acre of beets they raised. Some 1,500 farmers

50 Cornelius J. De Roo, *Portrait and Biographical Record of Muskegon and Ottawa Counties* (Chicago: Biographical Record Co., 1893), 307-8.

Arend Visscher was president of Holland Sugar Co., Ottawa Furniture Co., and Peoples State Bank, and he practiced law. Under the pen of a 1905 caricaturist, Visscher holds up the burning torch of the bank in one hand, a sugar beet in the other, and stands atop the furniture company (mislabeled "Holland Furniture") (*courtesy Larry B. Massie*)

thus became stockholders. Manager Charles McLean, the former superintendent of Holland Public Schools, initially contracted with farmers in the spring for beets at $4.25 a ton delivered to the $300,000 plant, built on a twelve-acre site west of Harrison Street between Thirteenth and Fifteenth Streets near the docks and along the Chicago & West Michigan Railway spur. The Holland Sugar Company became one of the city's major industries under McLean, the long time manager and later president. The plant produced 190,000 pounds of granulated sugar in the first month, 1.3 million pounds the second month, and 920,000 pounds the third month, for a grand total of 2.4 million pounds the first season. This was an auspicious start, thanks in part to an excellent growing season. And it was all the sweeter because of the state bounty–Holland Sugar's bounty was $2,462! Unfortunately, it was the first and last payment, because the Michigan Supreme Court declared the bounty program unconstitutional.[51]

Holland residents watched excitedly as the old farm buckboards lined up by the hundreds at the beet bins south of Fourteenth Street. Each wagon had to be weighed, and an inspector took a half-bushel sample to measure the sugar content. Dump wagons were unheard of; unloading was by hand with large pitchforks. Farmers had to wait for

51 Visscher, "Recollections"; *Claims for Sugar Beet Production, Conservation* 29, State Archives of Michigan, Collection RG 57-31; *De Grondwet*, 21 Apr. 1899; *Holland City News*, 27 Jan., 3, 10 Feb., 3, 10 Mar., 20 Oct., 24 Nov. 1899; *Ottawa County Times*, 29 Oct. 1899, 16 Nov. 1900, 23 Oct. 1903. Holland Sugar occupied the square block between Harrison and Cleveland Avenues and 14th and 15th Streets.

hours to unload; the line stretched at times as far as Central Avenue. Waste products were dumped in the lake until 1904, when a chemist proved that the discharge was highly toxic to fish, and city game wardens ordered the practice stopped. In 1906 the fall harvest produced 5.3 million pounds of sugar. The company regularly contracted with some 1,800 farmers for four thousand acres of beets, which was expected to yield fifty thousand tons at twelve-and-a-half tons per acre. With beets consisting of 12 percent sugar, this produced more than a ton of sugar per acre. One Laketown grower cleared over $50 an acre. The yearly payments to farmers averaged between $150,000 and $200,000, and stockholders enjoyed healthy dividends of 7 percent or more. Hiring enough workers for the booming sugar mills was a challenge. It helped immensely when the C. L. King Basket factory went out of business in 1913 due to a scarcity of logs and a downturn in the fruit business, and some two to three hundred workers became available for processing the root crop.[52]

In 1911 Holland Sugar expanded by acquiring the St. Louis Sugar Company, with plants in St. Louis, Michigan (near Alma) and Decatur, Indiana. The renamed Holland-St. Louis Sugar Company was capitalized at $2.8 million, of which $2.1 million was in publicly offered stock. Charles McLean's sons, Charles J. and Sears R., joined the firm that year and remained in top management until 1926. From 1912 to 1916, the Holland plant paid beet farmers from $5 to $6 a ton and produced from six to nine million pounds of sugar annually. In 1916 the plant contracted with farmers for twenty-one thousand acres, which produced about thirty thousand tons of beets worth $1.1 million. The Holland plant was the smallest of the three factories at four hundred tons capacity, compared to six hundred tons at St. Louis and eight hundred tons at Decatur.[53]

The next year, after the United States entered the First World War, the company again set the contract price at $6 per acre, but the growers demanded $8 and struck to get it. The farmers yielded after Michigan Governor Albert Sleeper appealed to their patriotism. In the end, the farmers signed contracts for eighteen thousand acres on the company's terms both in 1917 and 1918, which was near capacity for its mills. But total acreage was down from 1916. The preferred German seed was no longer available, field labor was hard to find, and Congress capped

52 Visscher, "Recollections"; *Holland City News*, 6 Aug. 1904, 4 Jan. 1906, 9 Dec. 1915; *Holland Sentinel*, 31 Feb. 1905; *De Grondwet*, 31 May 1910, 14 Oct. 1913.

53 Holland-St. Louis Sugar Company, 1920 *Annual Report*, HMA.

Holland-St. Louis Sugar Company plant on present Kollen Park Drive, ca. 1915. Company office building on right is now Community Action House (*Joint Archives of Holland*)

sugar at 12¢ per pound under wartime price controls, thus weakening the industry's pricing power. Yet, the high demand for sugar during the war kept prices high, until the Armistice in 1918 brought an end to the market distortions. Employment in Holland sugar mills peaked in 1917 at 167 workers and dropped to only twenty-five the next year.[54]

The firm in 1918 added more rail spurs, bringing the total to eight, and purchased its own switch engine and a large twenty-two-ton crane to unload the cars loaded to the top with beets. Cars were also run up on a large trestle and their contents dumped into a "beet pit" that could hold 250 tons, ready for sluicing. The finished product, bagged in hundred-pound sacks, was shipped by rail to markets across the country. The north side of the plant was a veritable rail yard buzzing with activity; eleven cars could be switched at one time.[55]

After the war the economy grew rapidly, and the domestic sugar industry and related companies such as cooperages prospered, until 1921, when processors and growers had another brief tug of war. The Michigan Sugar Beet Growers Association, which was aligned with the Cuban Sugar Trust, contracted for fall delivery with hundreds of farmers and then offered to bargain collectively with the processing companies over prices. Every processor in the state, including the Holland-St. Louis Co., refused to recognize these contracts and demanded that

[54] US Department of Labor Factory Inspection Reports, 1917, 1918; *Holland City News*, 27 Nov. 1913, 11 Jan. 1914, 7 Jan. 1915, 13 Jan., 1 June 1916, 10 May 1917, 16 Feb. 1922; Sears McLean recollections, 31 Mar. 1926, P. T. Moerdyke Papers, HMA.

[55] *Holland City News*, 10 Oct. 1918.

Beets piled high awaiting sluicing, ca. 1915
(*courtesy Myron Van Ark*)

farmers negotiate individual contracts with them directly by mid-May. The mills had the upper hand, and the farmers had to play by their rules and accept lower prices. The Holland plant, under superintendent Sears McLean, contracted from twenty to twenty-five thousand acres annually in the 1920s.[56]

To harvest the beets, farmers needed extra field hands, and beginning during the war, they turned to migrants from Mexico and Texas, recruited by San Antonio labor agencies. This was the beginning of Hispanic migrant labor in the Holland area which soon became regular (chapter 34). By the hundreds, laborers came in the spring and then returned home in December after the beet harvest. Each worker had to sign a contract, and the Sugar Trust set the terms of hire. In 1914 and 1915, laborers earned $20 per acre for the harvest, plus free furnished housing. After the season ended, they were shipped back south by the carload like so many head of cattle.[57]

The Mexican Revolution of 1910 spurred even more of the rural poor to head north and take their chances in "Uncle Sam's dirt." The Mexicans proved to be more desirable than the "advancing horde" of European immigrants they replaced in the fields. Superintendent McLean even went to Texas specifically to recruit migrant laborers, whose praises he sang:

56 Ibid., 5 May, 13 Oct. 1921, 7 Dec. 1922.

57 Ibid., 13 Jan. 1916, 6 Dec. 1923.

> The Mexican is a good-natured, willing worker if he is well treated. He will do work that most other types of workers refuse. If I had a field of beets that had become overgrown with weeds and thistles, I would try to put Mexicans into it. They would go in and clean it out without complaint, while the average European worker would be likely to strike the next day.[58]

Dutch field hands were in short supply, because in 1921 Congress enacted the first national origins quota, which severely restricted the number of immigrants from the Netherlands to only 3,607 a year (reduced to 1,648 in 1924 and increased to 3,153 in 1929). Michigan state officials issued a call for Dutch immigrants in 1923 and even sent a recruitment agent to the Netherlands, but to little avail, given the federal quota law. Mexicans, who as citizens of a "contiguous country" were not subject to the law, were ideal substitutes in fields that required stoop labor. In the next years, the Holland-St. Louis Co. transported an army of five hundred Mexicans in fifteen buses to work its Michigan beet fields.[59]

The biggest challenge for beet farmers was federal tariff policy and wartime price controls, not labor. Sugar was a favorite political football in Washington between free traders and the Big Sugar Cartel of Cuban cane growers. The Underwood Tariff of 1913 placed a "temporary" duty of one-cent-per-pound on Cuban sugar, which gave domestic producers breathing room. During the war the cartel hoarded sugar and drove the price up to 30¢, while stateside producers, including Holland-area farmers, could get only 12¢ under federal price controls. The result was a "sugar famine" that pushed consumer prices to exorbitant levels. The federal income tax, enacted in 1913 and then increased to finance the war, also fell heavily on domestic sugar processors, confiscating more than half their profits, according to the editor of the *Holland City News*. In 1921 Congress threatened to end the one-cent duty, which action would ruin domestic producers.[60]

The year 1921 was a low point for sugar producers. After contracts with farmers were signed, the market price of sugar fell from $11 to $5 per ton, despite a sharp drop in crop yields and sugar content due to

58 *Holland City News*, 20 Jan. 1920.

59 Ibid., 10 Jan. 1924, 4 June 1925, 20 Feb. 1930. In a 1928 speech to the Social Progress Club in Holland, Sears McLean spoke disparagingly of the "advancing horde" of European immigrants and advocated continuing immigration restrictions (ibid., 5 Jan. 1928).

60 Ibid., 14 Apr., 15 Dec. 1921.

abnormally hot weather. The Holland plant alone lost $362,000. The company cut its contracts for the 1922 crop by one-third to reduce the inventory from the 1921 crop. That year the Holland plant had profits of $280,000. The three Holland-St. Louis plants turned 146,000 tons of beets into nearly thirty-three million pounds of granulated sugar. Farmers were paid $5 a ton, $1 less than in 1921, but their gross revenue still totaled $730,000. And the company offered farmers the wet pulp residue almost free for the taking as feed for their cattle. The 1923 crop was 50 percent larger, and the future was rosy. To increase its capacity to six hundred tons per day, the Holland-St. Louis factory in 1923 installed larger boilers and the tallest smokestack in Holland, at 125 feet. The brick chimney could be seen for miles around. In the 1924 slicing campaign, the Holland-St. Louis Sugar Co. manufactured thirty-five million pounds of sugar and earned gross profits of nearly $400,000.[61]

Sugar was a stable and dependable crop at a time when other crops failed, so farmers increasingly turned to beets. The market rewarded them handsomely. In 1923 the Holland-St. Louis firm contracted beets at $7.00 a ton, with a bonus of $2.29 a ton and $.75 for delivery to the plant. That year the farmers happily received the bonus and made $10.04 a ton. This represented a yield of about $110 an acre and was money that passed through the Holland economy in myriad ways, from implement dealers and distributors to retail merchants. During the fall processing campaign, which ran from October until January, the Waverly rail yard was choked with beet cars assigned to the Holland factory. Sears McLean went around the Midwest touting the "benefits of beet culture" in one community after another.[62]

Despite the rosy picture, sugar prices remained low and profit margins thin. In 1926 the directors of the Holland-St. Louis firm accepted a buyout offer—a dollar-for-dollar stock swap from the Continental Sugar Company of Toledo, Ohio, which operated three plants in Michigan. Shortly after the merger, superintendent McLean resigned after twelve years at the helm, and the handwriting was on the wall for the Holland plant, or so it seemed. After thirty-nine years, the company announced that the 1926 sluicing season would be its last. Sugar prices had fallen too low to make its cultivation pay for farmers. Over the years, the company had sliced and ground 1.2 million tons of beets and manufactured 2.7 million one-hundred-pound bags of sugar;

61 Ibid., 16 Feb., 9 Mar. 1922, 18 Jan., 25 Oct. 1923, 4 Jan. 1924, 8 Jan., 5 Mar. 1925; Holland-St. Louis Sugar Co., 1922 and 1923 *Annual Reports*, HMA.

62 *Holland City News*, 26 Sept. 1923, 13 Mar. 1924.

farmers had averaged about $5 a ton, which was more than most other crops paid.[63]

The loss of one of Holland's largest industries left a huge hole in the local economy, especially for farmers and plant workers. The onset of the Great Depression made people long again "to hear the toot of the sugar factory whistle." Farmers in the eastern part of the state were earning millions in beets, why not Holland? In 1931 Milton J. Cook, a local dentist, publicly urged merchant organizations and the chamber of commerce to push for reopening the old Holland-St. Louis Sugar mill. Nearly two full years passed with little but rumors and murmurings. Then in late 1932 the city council seized the initiative and appointed William C. Vandenberg to canvass farmers throughout Ottawa County about cultivating beets. The county agricultural agent and former officials of Holland Sugar joined him at seven regional meetings. Vandenberg found support everywhere he went; Holland Sugar would reopen under the Vandenberg brothers, William and John "Vaudie" Jr., as the Lake Shore Sugar Company. The city fathers greeted this wonderful news with applause and a "rising vote of thanks." Holland would have an economic reawakening; farmers could earn $200,000, and several hundred men on the welfare list might find work in the sluicing plant to support their families.[64]

Lake Shore Sugar signed farmers to contracts over the winter, and by spring 1933, they were in the field planting beet seeds. Throughout the summer the Vandenberg brothers refurbished the machinery that had stood largely unused for eight years, getting ready for the sluicing season to begin in October. They also had carloads of coal delivered by rail to heat the steam boilers. Farmers could hardly contain their excitement, and a thousand came to tour the refurbished plant on West Fourteenth Street at the invitation of management. The common council went one better: they passed a resolution urging citizens and businessmen in West Michigan to buy only Holland-made sugar so as "to keep our sugar factory going." The city fathers enlisted every civic organization—the Merchants Association, the Chamber of Commerce, the Exchange Club, the Woman's Literary Club, and the Rotary Club (chapter 29)—to get behind the "beets and sweets" campaign to buy only Lake Shore Sugar. The *Holland City News* gave page-one prominence to

63 Ibid., 18 Feb., 29 July, 5 Aug. 1926, 6 Jan. 1927, 13 Sept., 4 Oct. 1928, 7 Feb. 1929, 22 Mar. 1934; Darlene Winter, "Fifty Years Ago Today," *Holland Sentinel*, 7 Sept. 1985; Randall P. Vande Water, "Factory Brought Area Economic Security," ibid., 29 Sept. 1984.

64 *Holland City News*, 12 Feb. 1931 (quote), 16 Feb., 9 Mar., 6 Apr 1933.

Farm trucks line up to unload at the Lake Shore Sugar Company plant, 1938 (*courtesy Randall P. Vande Water*)

the slogan "Buy Holland Sugar." It is about time, declared the editor, "that Holland toots its own horn." The sugar was a home product raised by Holland farmers, made by Holland labor, sold by Holland salesmen, and carried by Holland merchants.[65]

The beet yield in 1933, due to bad weather, fell below the average of seven tons per acre, but Lake Shore Sugar for the 1934 season again offered farmers 50/50 contracts at $5 per ton, half on delivery and half after the firm sold the sugar and closed for the season. Vandenberg was enlisted to boost the contracted acreage to six thousand, in order fully to utilize the one-million-pound plant capacity. The 1933 crop had totaled only six hundred pounds of sugar, yet this kept 225 men busy day and night during the fall sluicing season and fifty men busy year round. The company in 1935 formed the Holland Factory District Association, which stretched across fifteen counties of West Michigan with 1,100 farm contracts. Ottawa County was the focal point with more than one-half the contracts; Allegan County had one-third.[66]

The federal government nudged farmers to participate by guaranteeing a $1.25 per ton subsidy to sugar growers under the Agricultural Adjustment Act (AAA), with higher subsidies if market prices did not reach the parity price (based on the 1910-14 average). In April 1935, even before the growing season began, the first checks from Washington, DC, hit the mailboxes of farmers under contract.

65 Ibid., 20 July, 5, 19, 26 Oct., 2, 9 Nov. 1933.

66 Ibid., 22, 29 Mar. 1934, 10 Jan. 1935.

Farm trucks being weighed at the Lake Shore Sugar Company plant, 1938 (*courtesy Randall P. Vande Water*)

This "cheering news" induced more to sign up, boosting beet acreage to the allocated 5,200 acres in Ottawa County. In the fall campaign, fully loaded trucks from farms within a forty-mile radius lined up for blocks to weigh and then unload their beets to form large pyramids in the beet yards. Lake Shore Sugar processed nineteen thousand tons that year, down from 1934, but still welcome.[67]

In 1936 the yield was up again, and 1937 came in even better at twenty-eight thousand tons. The mill paid out $100,000 to local beet growers, but the impact on trade was far greater. Vandenberg estimated that beets added $300,000 to the local economy, plus the additional city tax revenue. Most field hands at this time were Americans, with no more than twenty Mexicans from Texas at any one time in Ottawa County, according to local farmers. The US Supreme Court in 1937 nullified the AAA as unconstitutional, but local farmers continued to cultivate beets, and the federal government continued the allotment program. Locally, the Holland District Sugar Beet Allotment Committee signed growers to acreage contracts every spring.[68]

In 1940 field manager Cor F. Diekema signed 760 beet growers to contracts worth $213,000, and they delivered eleven million pounds for sluicing at $5.00 per ton, the standard price throughout the 1930s. In 1941 sugar prices advanced along with prices generally, with war in the offing, and some 850 growers and the company shared the increase.

[67] *Holland City News*, 11, 25 Apr., 30 May, 18 July, 1 Aug., 17 Oct., 26 Dec. 1935.

[68] Ibid., 1 Oct. 1936, 9 Dec. 1937, 20 Apr. 1939.

Tippler for unloading trucks at the Lake Shore Sugar Company plant, 1938 (*courtesy Randall P. Vande Water*)

Farmers received $5.50 a ton, worth $250,000; it was the first increase in nearly fifteen years, and the prospects for 1942 looked promising.[69]

But then, unexpectedly, the local beet industry was threatened by the return to Texas of many Mexican plant workers, who feared being stranded in Holland over the winter because of gasoline rationing with the onset of the Second World War. Just as unexpectedly, however, local women came to the rescue. Rosie the Riveter was not the only wife and mother to answer the call. "Sally the Sluicer" deserves equal billing. She and her cohorts staffed three shifts day and night and processed sixty thousand tons of beets in the 1942 sugar rush, which yielded fifteen million pounds for the war effort. This work allowed 869 local farmers to cash checks totaling $308,000, a 23 percent increase over 1941. Due to the war, the market price of sugar doubled, and farmers received $11.00 a ton (including a federal subsidy of $1.55 a ton). The next year prices shot up to $14.00 a ton. Good times had returned at last on the beet farms. But not so in town. Lake Shore Sugar was sold in 1942 to the Doughnut Corporation of America, and the new firm consolidated its beet processing in St. Louis instead of Holland, which became solely a distribution center. The 1943 sluicing season was the last, and one of the city's main seasonal industries was shut down forever. Farmers no longer planted the sweet tuber, but fortunately they had pickles as a replacement.[70]

69 *Holland City News*, 19 Dec. 1940, 27 Mar., 18 Dec. 1941.

70 Ibid., 1 Oct., 17 Dec. 1942, 16 Dec. 1843, 14 Dec. 1944, 11 Mar. 1948.

Pickles—H. J. Heinz Company

Pickles (actually cucumbers) were a choice complement to sugar beets, because pickles ripened in the summer and the tubers in the fall. Cultivating cucumbers fit well into farmers' work schedules, and the entire family could help in the harvest, although the children complained that the "lousy pickles" chafed and stained their hands.[71] Pickles were never subject to a powerful cartel and congressional tariff tinkering as was sugar. Cucumbers got a big boost in 1896 when the H. J. Heinz Co. of Pittsburgh, Pennsylvania sent an agent to West Michigan to find a suitable location for building another processing factory, as a companion to its successful Benton Harbor plant. Zeeland and Grand Rapids worked feverishly to secure the new plant, but in the end the company selected Holland, thanks to its ideal soils, a harbor with ready access to Chicago, and the masterful "selling job" by a local committee of leading citizens, which included William Beach, Walter Walsh, Gerrit J. Diekema, Arend Visscher, John Zwemer, Oscar E. Yates, and Jan W. Garvelink. For weeks, the joint venture between the business and agricultural interests of Holland was the topic of the day among the city's seven thousand residents and in every outlying village.[72]

Heinz, however, would build its new salting house in Holland, only if local farmers would pledge to plant three hundred acres of cucumbers and sell at 30¢ per bushel. By the second week of 1897, over two hundred farmers had pledged from one to ten acres each, for a total of over five hundred acres. The lure was the prospect that raising pickles would yield better profits than beets or cultivating grains, and the company would furnish the seeds. The plant would also call for tomatoes and cauliflower. Zwemer and George Souter, the celery king, led the effort, which far surpassed the minimum, and Heinz came to town. City leaders helped the firm find a suitable site on Wiepke Diekema's property at the city's southern border on Fifteenth Street along the south shore of Black Lake. And they obtained a commitment from the Chicago & West Michigan Railway to build a rail spur to the plant at no expense to Heinz. The company also demanded that the $800 cost of the two-acre parcel be donated. The local committee

71 Clarence Jalving called picking pickles a dirty job. "Your hands just got scaled with all the stuff from the pickles, and we'd sit there scouring our hands after we got through picking pickles." Clarence Jalving interview by Donald van Reken, 15 July 1976, typescript, 3, JAH.

72 Randall P. Vande Water, *Heinz in Holland: A Century of History* (Grand Rapids, MI: privately printed, 2001), 2-3, 9; *Holland City News*, 27 Jan. 1916. For the Indian colony, see chapter 1.

turned to the participating farmers, who stood to benefit, and made them take out personal bonds equal to $2.50 per acre under contract. Railroad companies used this same tactic to raise construction monies by forcing towns and cities along the projected right-of-way to take on bonded debt. No money, no railroad. The historic location of Salting House No. 16 was the famous Landing on Lake Macatawa at which Chief Joseph Wakazoo's Ottawa Indian band had built a village in the early 1840s, complete with a chapel and burial grounds (chapter 1).[73]

Within a year, in 1898, Heinz decided to expand its Holland operations and build a three-story factory. They demanded that participating farmers again bond themselves at $2.50 for every acre under contract to raise $2,500 for another three acres of land at the Sixteenth Street site and a suitable lake dock with five hundred feet frontage and extended into deep water. The farmers, who had quickly grown dependent on the Heinz payments, willingly complied. The plant expansion would allow processing of tomato ketchup, cauliflower, and vinegar from the abundant apple crop of the region. In the next decade, the company expanded south to Sixteenth Street with eight new buildings, all constructed at company expense. This was just the beginning. During the green season, farmers delivered up to 3,500 bushels of pickles a day and received checks for thousands of dollars. Every 3,000 bushels brought farmers $1,200, or 40¢ a bushel, but farmers every year clamored for more. By 1913 the firm agreed to pay the magic number of $1 per bushel; farmers got "dollar pickles" before "dollar wheat."[74]

In the 1920s Heinz opened salting stations in Zeeland, Hudsonville, Harlem, and West Olive. The entire region benefited from the initiative of Holland business leaders in landing the first "foreign" company. Heinz deserves full credit for developing the pickle industry in Holland. Without the firm's initiative, local farmers might never have considered cultivating cucumbers. The Holland plant became the second largest of sixteen in the Heinz system, and in 1913, the company concentrated all its brine pickling tanks there. The death of the company founder, H. J. Heinz, in 1919 did not alter the rising prospects of the Holland operations.[75]

By the 1920s West Michigan was the cucumber capitol of America, and Holland was the pickle capitol, since the Holland plant

73 Vande Water, *Heinz*, 3-12; *Holland City News*, 26 Dec. 1896, 9 Jan., 20 Feb. 1897.

74 Vande Water, *Heinz*, 13-19; *Holland City News*, 2 Dec. 1898.

75 Vande Water, *Heinz*, 20-36; *Holland City News*, 4, 11 Dec. 1913, 1 Jan. 1914, 15 May 1919, 23 Mar. 1929.

Original H. J. Heinz plant surrounded by farmers' buckboards delivering cucumbers. Each wagon had to be unloaded by hand, 1908 (*courtesy Larry B. Massie*)

was the largest pickle processor in the world. When agriculture fell on hard times, the company resumed an early practice of wooing farmers by treating them to a free luncheon, tours of the plant, and lectures by experts on raising pickles. The annual winter fete attracted over one thousand farmers and proved a very successful means to "build a bond of friendship" between farmers and the company. This winter dinner was in addition to the traditional summer picnic at Jenison Park for employees and contract farmers. In 1929 local farmers raised over five million bushels of pickles, a yield of $300 per acre. Heinz paid a going rate of $3.25 per 100 pounds for #1 pickles (5-12 inches) and $1.00 per 100 for the smaller #2 grade, delivered to the plant. Pickles proved to be among the most profitable cash crops locally for many decades. Best of all, consumers increasingly favored dill pickles and demand exceeded supply.[76]

Even the Great Depression did not stunt the steady expansion of the local Heinz plant, which operated at full capacity under the able management of James A. Hoover. Heinz provided steady work for two hundred employees, and pickles enabled many a local farmer to survive the hard years. In 1936 Heinz expanded across Lake Macatawa by buying a former gelatin factory for a distribution center and storage. The next year Heinz added a $100,000 building at its main plant, which was the biggest construction project in the city that year.[77]

76 *Holland City News*, 29 June 1922, 4 Oct. 1928, 28 Mar., 21 Nov. 1929.

77 Ibid., 8 May 1930, 10 Sept. 1936; Vande Water, *Heinz*, 39, 57-78.

H. J. Heinz Sr. personally honors two employees (one is Evelyn Zeiser) in front of the entire workforce in Factory No. 19, with women in front and men in back, about equal in number (*Archives, Holland Historical Trust)*

Besides the impact on the bottom line for farmers, the kraut factory and salting house provided year-round employment for around one hundred men, and up to eleven hundred (mostly young) women in the green season. During the Second World War the federal government allowed interstate companies to hire teens during the summer, and Heinz took advantage of the waiver. Even German prisoners of war from the camp in Allegan were put to work. Processing companies like Holland-St. Louis Sugar and Heinz provided blue-collar workers, including sons and daughters of farmers, with steady factory work in the city. The companies also spurred spin-off jobs in the construction trades, in the skilled crafts, such as coopers to make barrels and vats, and in cartage.

When the labor shortage continued after the war, Heinz hired white migrants, derisively dubbed "hillbillies," from Kentucky and other southern states. They had to work alongside Hispanics from Texas, who had traditionally picked sugar beets, pickles, fruits, tomatoes, and other vegetables. Holland counted nearly one hundred white migrant laborers in 1947 and many more Mexicans. In 1951 Heinz and its contract growers employed 2,800 Mexican laborers throughout Michigan; all came on six-month work visas. That year Heinz planned to erect an emergency housing camp for its migrant workers on 144th Avenue south of Riley Street, which was near its pickle fields. This riled up northside residents, who formed a committee to meet with the plant manager. After several meetings, Heinz scuttled the plan for its "employee city," much to the satisfaction of the locals.[78]

The same year, another citizens group demanded that migrants with tuberculosis be treated by their home state and not become a burden for local taxpayers. Migrants could pick their food crops, but not live near them or tap social services. Altogether, eighty-two thousand migrant laborers, including ten thousand Mexicans, worked Michigan fields in 1951, picking some fourteen farm crops valued at $80 million. Besides earnings spent locally for food and clothing, the Mexicans sent $15 million home to their families, which dollars their government took up and used to buy machinery and other products in the United States. The number of Mexican migrants in Holland declined in the 1950s, to seven thousand in 1954 and four thousand in 1957, but as farmers planted more cash crops such as blueberries and pickles, the demand for stoop labor rose again.[79]

Some of these Hispanics remained permanently in the area and changed the cultural landscape in significant ways (chapter 34). Ottawa County today leads the state with six thousand migrant and seasonal farm workers, and Hispanics, mostly Roman Catholic in religion, are the largest ethnic group in Holland after the Dutch Calvinists. Hispanics in 2012 comprised one-third of the city population (table 34.1) and 40 percent of public school students (chapter 7).[80]

The seventeen African American employees at Heinz in 1864 fared less well. Eleven members of the Black United Workers (BUW) union resigned, alleging unfair labor practices. The company, they claimed, discriminated in hiring and promotions, and assigned them the most difficult and tedious jobs. Company officials quickly arranged a meeting they described as "very useful," but it did not resolve the issue. With support from the Muskegon chapter of the National Association for the Advancement of Colored People (NAACP), the eleven picketed a Muskegon supermarket that carried Heinz products. Soon one hundred blacks joined the picketers, and the NAACP planned to expand the protest at supermarkets throughout the state and nation. Company officials instituted sensitivity training for supervisors and offered the eleven their jobs back, but only one accepted. The incident gave BUW officials a lever to cajole Heinz into adopting affirmative action policies.[81]

78 *Holland City News*, 27 Mar. 1947, 9 Aug., 13 Sept. 1951.

79 Ibid., 4 Oct. 1951, 16 Sept. 1954, 13 June 1957.

80 Vande Water, *Heinz*, 82-87, 102; *Holland Sentinel*, 22 Nov. 2006.

81 *Holland Sentinel*, 12, 13, 17 July 1964; *Holland City News*, 3 Nov. 1964.

Aerial view of H. J. Heinz "tank farm" of cypress wood brine vats that preserved millions of pickles during the "green season." All the tanks were removed when Kollen Park Drive was extended to Sixteenth Street in 2008 (*courtesy Larry B. Massie*)

Under Jerry Shoup, plant manager since 1984, Heinz has remained the only Holland company to continue for over a century with the same ownership and product line. Besides pickles, which in 1997 comprised 60 percent of production, the plant cans a variety of vegetables and fruits, including peppers, relishes, baby juices, and vinegar. Since the 1980s the workforce has slowly grown from 250 to 300. In 2008 Heinz North America in Holland donated sixteen feet of valuable lake frontage to the city of Holland for the Heinz Walkway that joins the Kollen Park walkway (chapter 27).[82]

Canning fruits and vegetables

Holland naturally became a canning center for fruits and vegetables, and the Holland Canning Co., directed by Charles L. Corey and then by ex-alderman William Vander Veen, dominated the business. In 1912 the firm built a two-story plant at Fifth Street and Central Avenue that could process up to twenty thousand cans daily. The company contracted with area farmers for strawberries,

82 Randall P. Vande Water, "Heinz Walkway provides access to Macatawa shoreline," *Holland Sentinel*, 21 Sept. 2008.

raspberries, gooseberries, cherries, peaches, plums, rhubarb, tomatoes, wax and baked beans, beets, peas, and crabapples. The firm employed several hundred workers, mostly women, during the harvest rush, and in the summer teenagers fifteen years and older to hull strawberries and snip beans. As products ripened, the processing crews moved like a well-trained army, in what was called a campaign, from one crop to another, beginning with rhubarb in May; strawberries, raspberries, and cherries in June; beans and beets in July; cherries, peaches, and pears in August; and ending with tomatoes and apples in September and October. Because the workers often could not keep up with the rush of perishables like strawberries, even with two shifts, the company installed large coolers at a cost of $20,000 to hold up to twenty tons of ripening fruit for a few days. Before the harvest was even underway, Holland Canning had sold much of its product to jobbers. In the next decades local growers also hired up to a thousand stoop laborers to harvest beans and fruits as they ripened.[83]

By 1916 Holland Canning continued to expand its facilities, adding a modern building with white tile walls and cement floors. Director William Vander Veen was said to be a "stickler for cleanliness in the factory." Outside the plant was a different matter, apparently. In 1918 city health officer Byron B. Godfrey found "decayed fruit, garbage, and apple pumace [*sic*]," and cited the company for violating public health laws. Vander Veen took umbrage in a public letter to the *City News*, in which he vowed to plead not guilty and to "fight the case to the last ditch to vindicate this company from the health officer's findings." It proved to be an empty threat, since the newspaper reported no further legal action by Vander Veen.[84]

The firm doubled its capital to $60,000 in 1919-20 and expanded the plant to double its capacity. In the strawberry rush, crates were piled to the ceiling as one hundred women in white caps and gowns sorted and hulled eight hundred crates daily, while rhubarb was stacked like cordwood to wait for processing until the fragile berries were all canned. Strawberry production set a record, and the bumper crop drew commission merchants, who contracted for the berries in the field and handled picking, crating, and shipping. Workers and farmers all benefited. Between 1918 and 1920, both total wages and payments to fruit growers doubled; wages rose from $30,000 to $60,000, and payments to growers increased from $63,000 to $134,000. In 1920

[83] *Holland City News*, 21 Mar. 1912, 25 Feb. 1915.
[84] Ibid., 5 Sept. 1918.

one farmer earned $2,000 on just two acres of strawberries; another harvested 150 crates off of one acre, with each crate worth $2.40, for a total of $3,600.[85]

Prices rose and fell depending on the bounty of the crop. In 1921 both workers' wages and growers' payments fell by one-third, and company profits rose by an equal proportion, to $279,000. Strawberries were so plentiful that Holland Canning paid only $1 a crate (sixteen quarts), and yet growers happily consigned all the firm would take—about fifteen thousand crates. The strawberry patch extended from Holland south to the Indiana line. Rhubarb paid somewhat less an acre, from $125 to $500, but it required far less labor. The company processed a million pounds of cherries and ten thousand cases of baked beans in 1922. Holland Canning that year shipped two million cans of fruits and vegetables and paid $35,000 in wages to several hundred employees and $60,000 to farmers for their produce. The value of the 1922 pack was nearly $2 million, and the next year's was even better.[86]

The publicly-owned company, with Luke Lugers as president, Henry Geerlings as treasurer, and Ben Brouwer as secretary in the 1920s, was a first-class operation that passed every inspection by the board of health. The thriving cannery made Holland a central marketing place for local fruit and vegetable growers. In 1926 Holland Canning plant manager Corey and Nick H. Hoffman, manager of the Zeeland Canning Company and owner of the Boston Restaurant in Holland, jointly purchased the Hartford Canning Company in Van Buren County for $15,000, and combined the three operations under one management in Hartford. In 1951 Holland Motor Express (chapter 19) bought the vacant Fifth Street site for its terminal and offices.[87]

Fred Bertsch in 1924 began a fruit juice processing plant on Macatawa Drive, which he marketed under the Old Dutch Farm label. His firm flourished beyond his wildest dreams, and within two years his cider mills were juicing twenty-five carloads of cherries from Michigan and Wisconsin. Chicago markets alone took a carload of cherry juice a week. In the fall, the plant pressed grapes and apples into cider. "Fruit juice products have a wonderful future," Bertsch asserted. He was following in the footsteps of Teunis Keppel, who fifty years earlier, in

85 Ibid., 14 June, 9 Aug. 1923, 8 May, 12 June, 3 July 1924; *Holland Sentinel*, 27 June 1927.

86 *Holland City News*, 29 June 1916, 16 Jan., 12 June 1919, 1, 20 July 1920, 8 June, 20 July, 10, 24 Aug., 12 Oct. 1922; Holland Canning Co., financial reports, 1918-1921, HMA.

87 *Holland City News*, 1 Feb., 17 May, 14 June, 23 Aug. 1923, 7 Feb., 10 July 1924, 6 July 1925, 27 May 1926.

the 1870s, had operated a cider mill that pressed apples on his farm on East Eighth Street (where Russ' Restaurant now stands.)[88]

In 1924 Peoples State Bank of Holland launched an annual exhibit, the apple show. Progressive banks in West Michigan had begun sponsoring such shows, and the bank officers thought it a sound idea to feature apple varieties grown in the Holland-Zeeland and Fillmore area. Come November the lobby of the bank was decked out with colorful trays of "the finest specimens of apples grown in the region." Impartial outside judges were brought in to determine the winners in the various varieties of fruit, and the bank funded the prizes. The hope was to increase farm income by encouraging the planting of apple orchards.[89]

Blueberries

Of all the bush fruit raised in the Holland area, blueberries emerged after the Second World War as the most enduring and profitable fruit industry. The acidic soils and moderate temperatures along the lakeshore were perfect for the cultivation of the plump sweet berries, and farmers devoted thousands of acres to them. For years, Hispanics provided the necessary stoop labor to harvest the tender fruit. But in recent years big growers like Reenders Blueberry Farm in West Olive have used $100,000 machines to automate harvesting. Today about three quarters of the fruit is picked mechanically, at a cost savings of 80 percent. A competitor of Reenders is Bowerman's Blueberry Farm on West James Street at 160th Avenue, started by William Bowerman in 1948 and owned in 2011 by son Randall "Randy" and grandson Kelly. Some 150 employees hand pick 80 percent of the berries on the 120-acre farm, and the rest is open for U-Pick. Thanks to Reenders, Bowerman's, and many other such farms, Ottawa County is the second largest blueberry producer in Michigan, behind Van Buren Country.[90]

Ice making

Ice from nearby Black Lake (Lake Macatawa) was a natural resource essential to the preservation of beer, meat, and milk products. These industries depended on ice for cooling, and in the case of ice cream, for actually making the treat. Harvesting ice, like commercial lumbering, was a winter job for hundreds of idle farmhands. Local newspapers first reported on the industry in 1877. The heavy crop that

88 Ibid., 2 Sept. 1926, 30 Sept. 1876, 2 June 1877.
89 Ibid., 15 Nov. 1924.
90 *Holland Sentinel*, 28 Aug. 2007, 19 July 2011.

year was destined for the mammoth icebox in George Van Duren's meat market and Leendert Kanters' ice cream parlor. From then on, every meat market and ice cream parlor was dependent on Black Lake ice until electric refrigeration made iceboxes obsolete. Anton Seif, the beer king, erected an icehouse in 1887 to preserve his malt and lager beer; he harvested his own ice.[91]

The winter ritual usually began in January when the ice was thick enough to cut into large blocks. Prized ice was clear and at least six or seven inches thick, but preferably from ten to fifteen inches. Unlike two-man crosscut saws in lumbering, the large ice saws had a single handle and the cutter stood and sliced the ice into blocks. It was as dangerous as working in the woods. Once harvested, the ice blocks were stacked on sleighs for transport by teams to ice houses, where they were stored between layers of sawdust to preserve them for the warm months of May to October. For weeks on end, a "continual train of teams" passed through the city with a thousand cords (a cord weighed 3.5 tons) or more. Some eight hundred cords were harvested in 1886. Ice peddlers delivered the ice to local homes, meat shops, stores, and milk and ice cream plants; some was shipped on lake vessels and railcars to distant markets. Families paid $2 a month or $6 a season for home delivery. Farmers sometimes harvested ice themselves and stored it in icehouses on the farm to keep milk chilled. Shortages of this essential commodity were common and could sharply drive up the price from 8¢ to 30¢ per pound for one-hundred-pound blocks, as in 1905.[92]

John De Boer opened one of the first icehouses in 1888 at the corner of Eighth Street and Pine Avenue, and he peddled ice all summer with his horse and wagon to dairies and farmers to safeguard their milk. George P. Hummer competed with De Boer by building a large icehouse on Lake (River) Street at Fifth Street. Later ice companies included Van Alsburg Brothers headed by John Van Alsburg, Crystal Ice Company of L. C. Bignall, Consumers Ice managed by Edward T. Bertsch, Bass & Plekke's, Superior Pure Ice & Machine Company, and Lakeside Ice Company, among others. The office of Van Alsburg Brothers in 1901 moved to (William) Van Dyke & (Gerrit) Sprietsma's hardware store on the northwest corner of Ninth and River Streets, where customers could conveniently leave their orders.[93]

91 *Holland City News*, 30 Jan., 28 Apr., 12 May 1877, 15 Feb. 1879, 31 Jan. 1880, 14 Jan., 28 Jan. 1882, 28 June 1884, 17 Jan. 1885, 28 Feb., 21 Apr. 1887.

92 Ibid., 17, 28 Jan. 1888, 2 Feb., 1 June 1889, 14 Feb. 1891, 14 Oct. 1895, 2 Nov. 1905; *Holland Sentinel*, 11 Jan., 28 Feb. 1912.

93 *Holland City News*, 13 Feb. 1886, 26 Feb. 1887, 19 Apr. 1901, 1 Jan., 1 Apr. 1904, 27 Feb. 1908.

Harvesting ice near Jenison Park on Black Lake in March 1921 for ice boxes in homes and businesses. The men handling primitive picks to load the blocks are; *left to right*: E. Lugers, Arend J. Neerken, and Adrian Heneveld (on wagon) (*courtesy Randall P. Vande Water*)

Superior Pure Ice & Machine Co., founded in 1909, harvested Black Lake ice for residential customers and made artificial ice for the commercial market by immersing water-filled cans in a large brine vats. From ten tons a day, the plant ramped up production of artificial ice to twenty-five tons. Superior, managed by Charles Fairbanks, stood on the lake shore at West Ninth Street and Van Raalte Avenue just west of the Western Machine Tool Works. To expand capacity, Superior in 1918 purchased two icehouses at the bend of West Sixteenth Street. Henry and Herman Prins of Prins Bros. had erected one in about 1896, and Ed Bertsch built the other in 1905. In February 1920 both of Superior's buildings burned to the ground. At the time, Alva J. Fairbanks was both president and manager, and Barton Naberhuis was secretary-treasurer. The Fairbanks family reopened the plant in 1922 with a twelve-thousand-ton capacity. Superior was the only local supplier of commercial ice until the 1920s. The Sixteenth Street plant was ravaged by fire a second time in 1936.[94]

Lakeside Ice on Douglas Avenue near Aniline Avenue, owned by John Van Wieren, also made ice in brine vats from 1922 until fire destroyed the plant in 1946. Van Wieren then bought Superior Ice and ran it with partners George Dykstra and Bert Cranmer, until selling out

94 Ibid., 31 Mar. 1910, 19 Feb. 1920, 30 Mar. 1926.

Superior Pure Ice & Machine Co. on the lakeshore at West Ninth Street and Van Raalte Avenue, ca. 1910 (*Archives, Holland Historical Trust*)

to Grand Rapids Ice & Fuel in 1954. The Grand Rapids firm closed the local plant and shipped ice to Holland for distribution. The closing of Superior Ice after forty-five years marked the end of an era. And men like Van Wieren, who began his career cutting natural ice on Black Lake, were the last of a breed. Electric refrigeration began replacing natural ice in the 1920s, and by the 1940s most businesses and homeowners had jettisoned their iceboxes.[95]

Milk, cheese, and butter

Besides canneries, companies that processed agricultural products included creameries, milk depots, and cheese and ice cream plants. All relied on ice harvested from Lake Macatawa for summer refrigeration. The Holland milk shed was extensive. An 1897 agricultural census counted 11,000 dairy cows in Ottawa County; the top three townships were Zeeland with 1,500, Jamestown 1,400, and Holland 1,100. Twenty years later Ottawa County counted 23,400 dairy cows, one for every two inhabitants, with 8,000 in the immediate vicinity of Holland. These were a sufficient number of "bossies" to keep local creameries and cheese factories humming steadily, although at times milk also became a glut on the market. This despite the fact that the people of Holland, according to the state director of dairying, were the "champion milk drinkers of the state." This should not have been surprising, given the historic role of dairying in the Netherlands, especially in Friesland.[96]

One by-product of milk is cheese. In the late 1880s Sikke Brouwers, Frank Boonstra, and other investors formed the Zeeland Cheese

95 Ibid., 20 Aug. 1936, 8 Dec. 1938, 3 June 1954.

96 *Ottawa County Times*, 17 Nov. 1893; *Holland City News*, 18 Dec. 1897, 12 Feb. 1904, 17 Dec. 1917.

Zeeland plant of Phenix Cheese Co., 725 Main Street, 1921
(*Zeeland Historical Museum*)

Company and built a plant where the Bristol-Myers Squibb plant is now located on East Main Street (chapter 16). Brouwers, the plant manager, and his son John gained fame for developing a new processing method to produce cream cheese. The new product was so successful that New York-based Phenix Cheese Company bought the Zeeland operation in 1921 to produce its famed five-pound Sandwich Loaf cheeses. Sikke Brouwers resigned to launch a produce business, and John remained as manager under the new regime. Phenix is thought to have renamed the cheese Philadelphia Cream Cheese. Phenix Cheese claimed to be the largest cheese house in the state. In 1924 Phenix Cheese sold the Zeeland plant to Mead Johnson, and four years later, in 1928, Phenix sold its entire operation to Kraft Foods, which continues to market Philadelphia Cream Cheese.[97]

Another milk by-product is butter. By 1904 several million pounds were produced annually in Ottawa County. One of the largest firms was Holland Crystal Creamery, which Graafschap shopkeeper Matthew Notier established in 1886 on the northwest corner of Sixth and Fish (Columbia) Streets. Local investors put up $500 to underwrite Notier and his partner Bakelaar. Notier & Bakelaar contracted for milk with local dairymen for fifteen miles around. Among the first to sign up were Overisel Township farmers with a total of five hundred cows, followed by dairies in West Olive, New Holland, East Saugatuck,

[97] *Holland City News*, 21 July 1921, 23 Feb. 1922; Steve Vanderveen, "Noted Kraft brand may have started in Zeeland," *Holland Sentinel*, 22 Oct. 2006.

Farmers delivering cans of milk to Holland Crystal Creamery, northwest corner of Columbia Avenue and Sixth Street, 1890s (*Archives, Holland Historical Trust*)

and Fillmore. All shipped their milk by rail to Holland. By 1888 the plant produced 5,000 pounds of butter a week, priced at 16¢ a pound, which was shipped principally to Chicago and eastern markets, notably Buffalo and New York City. Crystal Creamery's total production that year of 186,000 pounds (worth $30,000) exceeded by 20,000 pounds the next largest creamery in the state. The firm paid thousands of dollars to local dairymen and provided Holland with freshly churned butter and cream. All the grocery stores stocked it. "For quality it can't be beat," declared *City News* editor William Rogers. Hollanders could also buy buttermilk for only 8¢ per gallon to make the traditional *soep en brij* porridge.[98]

The creamery produced a million pounds of butter annually and delivered several thousand gallons of cream weekly to local restaurants and hotels. In 1891 Notier & Bakelaar sold the firm to Christian J. Lokker, and the Lokker family operated the Notier-Lokker Creamery for nearly four decades until Lokker's death in 1930. In 1924 the company was worth $55,000. It was then sold to the Wexford Company and later (in 1939) to Swift & Co. of Chicago, who upgraded the equipment. Crystal Creamery supplied dairy products for more than fifty years and outlasted every other creamery in town.[99]

98 *De Grondwet*, 21 Feb., 22 May 1888; *Holland City News*, 6 Mar., 24 Apr., 5, 19 June 1886, 5 Feb. 1887, 18 Feb., 9 June 1888, 28 Sept. 1889.

99 *Holland City News*, 26 May 1921, 1 Nov. 1928, 5 Mar., 2 July 1936; *Holland: The Gateway of Western Michigan*; Holland Crystal Creamery, financial report, 1924, T-9-1508, box 1, HMA.

Farmer with milk cans likely en route to Crystal Creamery. The farmer with his rig proudly posed in front of the Herman Prins Garage at 160 East Seventh Street at Lincoln Avenue, ca. 1905. The Dutch Tea Rusk plant on Eighth Street is seen in the background (*courtesy Randall P. Vande Water*)

In its next life, which began in 1948, the East Sixth Street plant made Reddi-wip, the original whipped cream dispensed in aerosol cans, a first for the can technology. The plant was part of Wisconsin-based Beatrice Foods until 2006, when ConAgra acquired Beatrice. In 2007 ConAgra closed the eighty-four-year-old Holland operation and laid off its sixty-two employees, despite offers by city leaders to find another food processor for the factory. In early 2011 Sixth Street Partners bought the empty building at 147 East Sixth Street from ConAgra Foods for $200,000 and leased it some months later to ITN Packaging, a company owned by Gene McClain that manufactures packaging for small parts shipped by automotive suppliers to assembly plants.[100]

The Holland Milk Products Company, founded in 1919 by August H. Landwehr of Holland Furnace, Dirk F. Boonstra of Zeeland, and other local businessmen, was another dairy-related company that provided a market for local farmers. Capitalized at $100,000, the firm purchased the last available factory building in town, the former Holland Gelatin Works (see below); they installed new machinery, hired twenty-five employees, and began operations in January 1920.[101]

[100] *Holland Sentinel*, 13 Apr. 2007, 20 Sept. 2011.
[101] *Holland City News*, 9 Oct. 1919.

A third creamery, the Holland Brand Butter Co., originated in 1869 when George Linn & Sons of Chicago shipped butter to the Chicago market under the trademark image of a Dutch boy and girl and the slogan, "Always fresh and sweet, try it." In 1920 Linn & Sons' successor company, Pioneer Creamery, sold Holland Brand Butter in cities from Chicago to New York and throughout the East Coast from Maine to Washington, DC. In 1928 Beatrice Creamery (later Beatrice Foods) swept up Holland Brand Butter when it bought out Pioneer Creamery. Beatrice continued to use the Holland trademark for many decades.[102]

The Hoekstra Ice Cream Co., a Grand Rapids firm from 1912, expanded into Holland in 1923 by purchasing the Timmer Ice Cream Co. on West Sixteenth Street. Manager Dewey Jaarsma upgraded the equipment in the plant to increase production. Hoekstra's refrigerated trucks carried the delicacy to retail shops throughout West Michigan. "Young and Old Demand It," boasted the advertising slogan. At the same time as Hoekstra's move into Holland, the Arctic Ice Cream Co. of Holland, a branch of the Detroit-based firm, was swept up in a massive $6 million dollar merger of seventeen factories in cities across the state, with a combined capacity of two million gallons. The craving for ice cream by affluent urban consumers pushed up sales and made the commodity an attractive play by entrepreneurs.[103]

Ottawa County in the early 1920s counted twelve creameries that produced thousands of pounds of butter, cheese, and ice cream for urban consumers in Grand Rapids, Muskegon, Grand Haven, and Holland. Ice cream required a steady supply of ice to manufacture, which proved problematic in Holland. In 1911 William Wagenaar and Benjamin Hamm opened the Wagenaar-Hamm Ice Cream Company in the Nibbelink Undertaking building on Ninth Street, and operated it for a decade until selling out to the Arctic Ice Cream Company of Detroit, one of the largest firms of its day, with plants in Grand Rapids and elsewhere. A shortage of ice in the mid-summer July heat of 1919, "terribly handicapped" the partners, and a more severe shortage in 1921, "simply floored them." "We can't make ice cream without ice," Hamm declared, "and as we ran out of ice the making stopped and many of our customers ran short." By 6:00 p.m. that hot July day, every ice cream store in town had sold out. Arctic Ice was immune from the local ice shortages; it shipped ice aplenty from its huge plant in Detroit.

102 Ibid., 23 Sept. 1948.

103 Ibid., 14 July 1921, 26 Sept., 6 Dec. 1923, 17 Jan. 1924, 1 Jan. 1925, 14 June 1928.

This advantage allowed Arctic to raise ice cream prices to retailers by 25 percent, from $1.00 to $1.25 a gallon. Customers with a craving had to pay the piper.[104]

Local merchants were adept at selling niche products to dairymen. Model Drug Store ran an advertisement in the *Holland City News* in 1921 that urged dairy farmers to "try Conkey's Fly Knocker," a disinfectant spray, to ensure a "full milk pail." The offer noted: "Cows stand quietly and give more milk when not pestered by insects." The ad also had a word for all farmers: "Horses do more work when free from torture." Piet Ver Lier, the local "hoss doctor," might have added to that torture, but he came cheap—often just a *slokje* (taste) of whisky. "Old Piet's" knowledge of animals came from experience, and his secret potion for treating a cow that had "lost its cud" went to the grave with him. Piet, who hardware merchant Ray Nies recalled as "a small, shriveled, querulous, spry, old man" with an "old horse and rickety buggy," was a fixture on Holland streets and farm roads for more than fifty years, from the 1880s to the 1930s.[105]

Holland often hosted meetings of dairymen and cattle breeders, such as the Michigan State Holstein-Frisian Association gathering in 1920, whose goal was to boost Holstein interests locally and statewide. Cattleman Cornelius Boven and banker Ray Knooihuizen of the First State Bank of Holland arranged the meeting, held at the town hall; it was one of the biggest livestock meetings ever. The association concentrated its efforts at the time on eradicating bovine tuberculosis, which had plagued the industry for years.[106]

To increase their pricing power, the dairy farmers in the Holland milk shed formed a cooperative exchange, which set the wholesale price for their milk that the dealers in town had to try to pass on to consumers. In 1917, for example, the dairy farmers co-op raised the wholesale price, arguing that feed costs had risen sharply, and the dealers in turn boosted the retail price by a penny, to 9¢ a quart. But the dealers soon gained the upper hand. The daily milk supply averaged about two thousand gallons. Government officials, such as city attorney Charles McBride, could not resist accusing the milk dealers of price gouging. In 1923 he urged the city council to "take some action that would help along the movement to put the milk price where it should be." Specifically, he demanded a 1 percent price cut. Several aldermen dismissed the idea out of hand: "The council has no power to interfere in a private business,"

104 *Holland City News*, 14 July 1921.
105 *Holland City News*, 27 Oct. 1921; Nies Autobiography, ch. 9, 1-2 (quotes).
106 Ibid., 26 Feb., 16 Dec. 1920.

they declared. The majority agreed, and Mc Bride's suggestion went nowhere. The Holland Milk Dealers Association continued to set milk prices. Like the cultural conflict that erupted during market days in pioneer times, marketing milk in the early twentieth century pitted dairymen against dealers and revealed the rift between rural producers and urban middlemen and consumers.[107]

In the early 1920s the common council first enacted "clean milk" regulations, and tasked the board of health with checking some ninety dairy farms in the immediate vicinity to ensure that "pure" milk reached consumers, especially the 3,800 school children in town who were heavy users. Diseases such as tuberculosis, typhoid fever, scarlet fever, diphtheria, and diarrhea were blamed on impure milk. So dairymen became a target for regulation. They had to hire veterinarians to test every cow for bovine tuberculosis and other diseases. Shockingly, more than 10 percent of the thirty-four thousand head of cattle in Ottawa County in 1922 had tuberculosis. Federal and state indemnities reimbursed farmers at 70 percent of the value of diseased animals put down. By 1924 the herds of all 120 farms in the Holland milk shed were disease-free, much to the relief of producers and consumers alike. The record was just as good for cleanliness. In 1923 only four of eighty-four dairy barns failed to pass inspection and were barred from selling their milk in Holland. In the 1930s some 130 farms supplied Holland consumers with several million quarts of milk a year, and inspectors ensured that they fulfilled the regulations for cleanliness.[108]

The twenty-two milk plants in Holland also came under greater scrutiny with new state licensing requirements. The fee was only $1, unless they received their milk from two or more dairy farms; then it was $5. At first the state was quite lax in enforcement, but in 1923 the hammer came down, and the state inspector fined several Holland dealers $5 for failure to have a license. Thereafter, all complied, prodded by the threat in 1925 of sharply increased fines of $100 and costs. The firms cleaned up their act by being careful and attentive, and by installing steam boilers and bottle sterilizers. As a result, all passed inspection. City health inspector Henry Bosch also began testing milk for butter fat content, which the state required to be at least 3 percent. In 1925 Bosch had the city purchase a new milk-testing machine to ensure that farmers, processors, and peddlers supplied consumers with "good wholesome milk." This was the story every year. In 1929, for

107 Ibid., 10 Mar. 1917, 16 Dec. 1920, 10 July 1924, 13 Dec. 1928.

108 Ibid., 17 May, 9 Aug. 1923, 10 July 1924; *Holland Sentinel*, 23 Apr. 1935.

example, Bosch tested all twenty-two dairies and declared the milk to be "exceptionally fine." Not one dairy was below par.[109]

In 1922 five veteran milkmen combined their forces and formed the Blue Valley Dairy to process and distribute milk products from a new plant on Lincoln Avenue and Thirty-Second Street.[110] Blue Valley Dairy, a precursor to some of Holland's thirty dairies, had the clout to set bulk prices paid to farmers. The consolidation shifted the balance of power between dairy farms and diary plants. The dairymen responded by forming Holland Milk Producers Inc., which set prices per hundredweight, and threatened to withhold supply if the dairy plants did not accept it. The processors then raised the price to consumers and hoped they would not balk. Regulation of the Holland milk market by city ordinance was standard by the 1930s, although milkmen chaffed under official policies to limit their supposed monopoly pricing power and nitpicking by inspectors over butterfat content and cleanliness standards. Another sticking point in the days before homogenizing and refrigeration was a city ordinance that required dairy farms supplying the city to be located within an eight-mile radius and milk plants within a three-mile radius, to ensure that fresh milk did not spoil in transit.[111]

By 1941 a quart of milk cost 11¢ in Holland, which, it was claimed, still was lower than in Grand Rapids, Grand Haven, and Muskegon. The next year it was 12¢. During the Second World War, the Office of Price Administration had the last word on milk prices, and the OPA forced dairy farmers and milkmen to lower the price from 12¢ to 11¢ a quart. In recent years, minimum wholesale milk prices have been set by an agency of the US Department of Agriculture.[112]

Holland dairies in the twentieth century which ringed the outskirts of town included Egbert "Bert" Bareman's milk shed on 132nd Street in Holland Township; Albert Speet's Hill Crest at 620 Michigan Avenue; Consumers of Arnold Hoek and Andrew Helder at 140 West Twenty-Seventh Street; Maple Grove of Harold Mannes at 876 Michigan Avenue; Dairy Maid of Kenneth Raak at 223 North River Avenue at Douglas Avenue; Elm Valley of Henry Grotenhuis at 788 Lincoln Avenue and Thirty-Second Street, which became Rivulet Hurst (formerly of Graafschap) of Harvey Scholten; Lake View of Fred De

109 *Holland City News*, 26 Mar., 9 Apr. 1925, 18 Feb., 8 July 1926, 6 Jan. 1927, 18 July 1929.

110 Ibid., 1, 29 June 1922. The five milkmen were Arthur, Jake, and John Schaap, John Jipping, and Edward Helder.

111 Ibid., 3 Aug., 19 Oct. 1922, 4, 11 Jan., 8 Mar., 24 May, 7 June, 27 Dec. 1923, 16, 23 Aug. 1934.

112 Ibid., 28 Aug., 4 Sept. 1941, 25 Nov. 1942, 10 Oct. 1946, 5 Feb. 1948.

Willis Mulder and family, all bundled up in the snow, proudly display his Lake Shore Dairy delivery truck at his home on the southwest corner of Diekema Avenue and Seventeenth Street, early 1940s (*Joint Archives of Holland*)

Boer at 16 East Eighteenth Street; Modern of Bert Arendsen at 110 East Thirty-Second Street; United of Robert Klomparens at 284 East Thirty-Second Street; Cloverdale of Harold Bussies at 784 Michigan Avenue at Thirty-Second; Lake Shore Diary of Willis Mulder, which became Lake Shore Creamery under Maurice Nienhuis at 422 Diekema Avenue in Montello Park; and Alf Hossink's Tulip City at 26 Waverly Road just south of Lakewood Boulevard, among others. Hossink ran his diary from 1949 to 1967, when he cleared the site for the Windmill Mobile Court, a move that proved more far profitable by far than dairying.[113]

Until the 1920s the dairies delivered door-to-door by horse and wagon beginning in the wee hours of the morning; later, one by one, they switched to trucks to cover their routes. By 1998 Al Van Den Berg was the only home-delivery milkman left; he had peddled for forty-eight years, since 1950, and sold Bareman's Dairy products.[114]

Bareman's Dairy became the "cream of the crop." Egbert "Bert" Bareman began peddling milk door-to-door in 1898 from his dairy farm on 132nd Street between James and Riley Avenues. He ladled the milk to customers from wooden barrels on a horse-drawn cart. The

113 *Holland City Directories*, 1906-70.

114 R. J. Brown-Essing, compiler, "Some Early Dairies in Zeeland and Holland," 5-page typescript, JAH; *Holland Sentinel*, 6 Sept. 1980; *Grand Rapids Press Lakeshore Edition*, 20 Aug. 1998.

dairy barn required the labor of the family of ten, including milking the cows, separating the cream and whipping it into butter, and in winter harvesting ice on Lake Macatawa for summer refrigeration. The ice was kept under straw in a shanty next to the milk house. In 1923 Bareman passed the business and its three routes to his sons John E. and Martin, and it became Bareman Bros., with the processing plant in 1930 at 253 North River Avenue at Lakewood Boulevard. In 1957 Stanley Bareman bought the processing business.

While in military service in Texas, Stanley Bareman was amazed to find gasoline stations selling milk. When he returned from service in 1961, he implemented the new business model, pushing milk at wholesale to convenience stores rather than retail home delivery. The timing was auspicious, since customers increasingly bought milk at supermarkets while big conglomerates were undermining small dairies. So successful was the idea that Bareman's Dairy could not keep up with the orders. Stanley became president in 1973. In 1977 he built a larger processing plant at 234 Charles Drive off East Lakewood Boulevard. From processing one million pounds of raw milk a month, the firm boosted production to twenty-two million pounds by 1998. Gradually, Bareman's bought out smaller competitors, notably Koning in 1981 and the Scholten family's Rivulet Hurst Dairy in 1985, in most cases giving the former owners executive positions at Bareman's. By 1998 Bareman's supplied some three thousand customers from its Holland plant and three regional distribution centers in West Michigan, and one in Hammond, Indiana, all supplied by a fleet of more than one hundred semi-trucks. The trucks deliver milk in gallon and half-gallon plastic jugs to gasoline stations of Bareman's, Westco, Essenburg's Quality, and other independents (chapter 18).[115]

Stanley Bareman, company president for many years, died in November 2011. Within four months, the family sold Bareman's brand and distribution center to Illinois-based Prairie Farms Dairy and Bareman's processing center to Meijer Inc., the supermarket chain with 101 stores in Michigan. Bareman's had supplied Meijer-brand milk for more than half a century, along with Dean Foods of Evart, Michigan. Meijer enfolded Bareman's into its own newly-formed dairy, Purple Cow Creamery, which has enabled it to profit at both the wholesale and retail levels and to use milk as a loss-leader in its stores.[116]

115 For this and the preceding paragraph, see *Grand Rapids Press Lakeshore Edition*, 29 Nov. 1998.

116 Stanley Bareman obit., *Holland Sentinel*, 22 July 2011; Shandra Martinez, "Meijer launching Purple Cow Creamery after buying Holland dairy company, 28 Mar. 2012; ibid., 12 July 2012.

Fogg Filler Co. bottling plant, plant manager Terry Rouwhorst (*left*) operates filler machine, while Mike (*right*) and brother John Fogg (*center*) look on (*courtesy Randall P. Vande Water*)

Hudsonville Creamery & Ice Cream Company is a modern creamery that buys five million pounds of milk annually from local dairy farms. Its roots go back to a farmers' cooperative from 1895. Dick Hoezee began the company in 1946 and was later joined by four of his sons. After fifty-five years, in 2001, the Hoezee family sold the creamery to the Landmark Group, a Holland-based investment company headed by Dennis "Denny" Ellens, a son-in-law of Elsa Prince Broekhuizen. Ellens in 2003 relocated operations from Burnips in Allegan County to the former Micromatic Textron plant along M-40 on Holland's south side. Long a leader in premium ice cream, Hudsonville Creamery and its growing workforce produces one hundred million servings annually. Most are sold in West Michigan stores, although Meijer Inc. carries the Hudsonville line in their tri-state region. In 2011 Hudsonville Creamery became the supplier of the TCBY (The Country's Best Yogurt) frozen yogurt chain, with 470 stores worldwide. In 2012 the company became the official ice cream vendor of the Detroit Tigers, and now its tasty treats, including the new "Tiger Tracks" ice cream, are sold at all home games.[117]

A local company that developed and manufactured automated systems to fill the plastic milk jugs at dairies and bottling plants in

[117] *Holland Sentinel*, 3 June, 5 Dec. 2003, 28 Oct. 2011, 21 Jan. 2012.

Holland, nationwide, and overseas, is Fogg Filler, a firm founded in 1956 by Clyde Fogg and today owned by his son Mike. Michigan's 450 dairies in the 1950s have dwindled to fewer than ten today due to consolidations, while Fogg's domestic competitors have increased from four to fifteen. Fogg's customers include Coca Cola and Pepsi. The company, located at 3455 John F. Donnelly Drive in the Northside Industrial Park, makes very complicated, custom-designed machines that sell for more than $1 million and can fill eight hundred bottles a minute. Technological innovations have kept Fogg Filler ahead of its competitors.[118]

Horticultural businesses

Horticultural businesses date from the early days with the Holland Nursery of Harmon E. Hudson, who in 1857 advertised ten thousand "choice grafted" fruit trees on his farm southeast of town, the former orchard of Indian missionary teacher George N. Smith (chapter 1). George Souter in 1877 purchased the nursery and stocked it with tens of thousands of seeds and saplings imported from Chicago. The Holland Nursery marketed primarily peaches and wheat, but Souter experimented with all sorts of other plants, including Osage Orange plants for hedging. In 1881 he advertised mulberry trees, the seeds of which were brought over by Mennonites from Russia. Two years later he was marketing the Catalpa shade tree. In 1885 Souter dug his own pond and began to raise German carp. In 1886 his nursery sold fifteen thousand grape vines and fifteen thousand trees– peach and others– amounting to $2,700. His advertisements promised "prices that defy competition" and trees of all kinds–ornamental, fruit, and others– "guaranteed in every particular." He also offered terra cotta vases for lawn ornaments.[119]

The second nurseryman was Charles A. Dutton, an ordained minister with degrees from Hope College and New Brunswick Theological Seminary, who was forced from the ministry by ill health in 1888. He began raising flowers in a greenhouse on the property of his father-in-law Henry Post, while his wife Mary was the city's first piano teacher and recitalist. Later Dutton moved his greenhouse to property owned by Ray Nies south of the city limits on present day Michigan Avenue at Holland Hospital. Dutton's former property became Post

118 Ibid., 18 Mar. 2007.

119 *Holland City News*, 10 Nov. 1877, "Fifty Years Ago Today" 26 Dec. 1929, 26 June 1880, 12 Nov. 1881, 16 Jan. 1883, 5 Feb. 1887, 11 Mar., 29 May 1893, 5 Dec. 1889; *Ottawa County Register*, 19 Nov. 1857.

Henry Ebelink's Central Park Greenhouses advertisement, *Holland City Directory*, 1910-11

Park, and the city greenhouses were constructed on the site (chapter 27). Dutton also kept a retail floral shop on West Eighth Street. In 1918 he moved his family to California in hopes of bettering his health.[120]

Ralson Jones in 1898 established the Central Park Greenhouses at 345 Myrtle Avenue in Central Park (Park Township). He took Henry Ebelink as partner in 1903, and the name became Jones & Ebelink Florists; they sold flowers at wholesale and retail. Ebelink bought out Jones by 1910 and made a success of the business by peddling flowers throughout the area. He is considered the father of Holland florists. Ebelink later added a retail floral shop at 238 River Avenue, which continued under various owners for almost ninety years, until 1997.[121]

Beginning with Ebelink, Dutch immigrants monopolized the bulb, flower, and seed business in the Holland until the present day, just like they did the bakeries (chapter 19). Ebelink's main competitor beginning in 1921 was Bert Vander Ploeg of Shady Lawn Florists at 281 East Sixteenth Street. Vander Ploeg got into the business because of his wife Johanna's hobby in plants; she had won countless gold ribbons at the Holland Fair and various county fairs. Johanna (Ten Cate) asked Bert, a furniture factory foreman, to build a greenhouse for her plants next door to the family home. He did, and then he caught the plant "bug." He quit his job, and the two opened a wholesale greenhouse

120 Charles Dutton obit., 17 Jan. 1935.
121 *Holland City Directories*, 1903-66; Ralson Jones obit., *Holland Sentinel*, 19 Feb. 1913.

operation and a retail floral shop on their five-acre lot down the hill from Fairbanks Avenue and Pilgrim Home Cemetery. Vander Ploeg erected three more greenhouses, bringing the total under glass to ten thousand square feet. Shady Lawn featured sprays for funerals and weddings but also offered complete floral service. The children, John B., Evelyn (later Mrs. Harold Gemmill), Bernice (later Mrs. Dennis Boer), Donald T. C., and Andrew all "grew up with it." Mother Johanna died in 1932.[122]

In 1923 Vander Ploeg became a member of the Detroit-based Florists Transworld Delivery (FTD) wire service. About this time oldest son John took over management and sister Evelyn ran a Shady Lawn Floral Shop that Bert opened on East Eighth Street. The downtown shop did not survive the Great Depression. In 1934 Bert incorporated the business; he was president-treasurer, son-in-law Dennis Boer vice-president, and daughter Evelyn Gemmill secretary. John, who had an advanced degree from Harvard University in architecture, left the business to work for the Works Progress Administration. John later operated a landscape business in Muskegon until 1959, during which time he served a term as Michigan state assemblyman (1964-65).

When Bert died in 1943, Bernice and Dennis assumed ownership, which entailed a heavy $10,000 mortgage. After the Boers paid off the mortgage in 1952 and stepped down, Donald became the owner for nearly thirty years, His son David, a vice president, managed the business throughout the 1970s and then started his own landscape business. Donald's oldest son Llewellyn "Lew," a school teacher for seventeen years, became the owner in 1980 and carried on for another seventeen years, until 1997, when he was forced to close. "Mom and pop" operations like Shady Lawn could no longer compete on price for large-scale orders from chain stores. Langeland-Sterenberg Funeral Homes purchased the property and razed the buildings for additional parking to serve their greatly expanded mortuary.

The Derick "Dick" Zwiep family was prominent in the seed and greenhouse business for more than fifty years, from 1936 until 1988. Zwiep and his wife Gertrude (Pott) opened Zwiep's Seed Store at 9 West Sixteenth Street in 1936. Daughter Elsa Prince Broekhuizen noted that her father, who had immigrated in 1922 at age twenty-one, learned the business working for a decade as the West Michigan salesman for Chicago-based N. Sluis Seed Company. Seeds and plants were in the

[122] *Holland City Directories*, 1921-98. I am indebted to Llewellyn Vander Ploeg for information about the family floral shop.

blood; the Zwiep family for three generations had practiced horticulture in the Netherlands. Zwiep's Seed Store carried seeds for truck farmers and gardeners, tulip bulbs, shrubs, fertilizers, pottery, birdseed, dog food (including frozen horsemeat during the Second World War), and canaries, parakeets, and goldfish. The plethora of products was dictated by the seasonal nature of the seed business—spring and summer; the other items carried them through the off-season. Zwiep obtained his seed supply from Detroit-based wholesaler Ferry-Morse Seed Company. The family lived in an apartment above the shop for five years, until 1941, when they bought a home on Lake Macatawa at 1789 South Shore Drive.[123]

For the first decade and more, Dick traveled throughout West Michigan in his Ford sedan selling seeds to truck gardeners from Hudsonville to Detroit and Imlay City, while Gertrude managed the store while raising three children, who also worked from an early age. Elsa recalled at age ten weighing seeds by hand and putting them in small packages, and Clare and Ted remembered planting seedlings in the greenhouses. Clare continued working part-time during high school and college years and joined the business full-time in 1952 after earning a degree in horticulture from Michigan State College (University in 1955).

Dick Zwiep expanded into greenhouse plantings in the early 1940s, raising flats of flowers and vegetables in a rented greenhouse at the former Getz farm. In 1944 he bought one of the greenhouses, a 25-by-100-foot structure, and re-assembled it on a three-acre plot he bought from truck gardener Gerrit Warmelink on Washington Avenue at Twenty-Fifth Street. Arnold Branderhorst of Branderhorst Construction handled the heavy work. Dick ran Zwiep's Greenhouses for several years and then hired Joseph "Joe" Romeyn to manage it, while he branched into wholesaling and "went on the road" selling seeds to truck gardeners and plants to chain stores such as Kmart and Woolworth. Romeyn ran the greenhouses for the next two decades until becoming city parks superintendent. For about five years, from 1947 to 1951, Zwiep set out a tulip garden on the corner of Twenty-Fifth Street and Washington Avenue for Tulip Time tourists to enjoy and order bulbs. In 1961 the board of education bought the property for the new Holland High School, and it now serves as the school parking lot.

In the 1950s the growing wholesale trade required more space under glass, and Dick Zwiep approached Henry Ebelink to rent

123 Elsa Prince Broekhuizen interview by the author and David Boeve, 18 Nov. 2009, typescript, JAH; *Holland City Directories*, 1938-66. I am indebted to Clare and Steve Zwiep for information about the family businesses.

a greenhouse. Ebelink declined, but he did offer to sell his entire operation, and Dick happily obliged. Son Clare and wife Elaine moved to the house on Myrtle Street and ran the operation for a decade, until assuming ownership in 1967. Dick sold the Sixteenth Street store to his brother John and wife Mary and his cousin Matt in 1958, which freed him to operate Ebelink's Florist Shop at 238 River Avenue, which he also purchased. When Dick Zwiep died in 1972, the family sold the floral shop to Harvey and Edward Dyk. About the same time, John and Mary Zwiep retired and closed the Sixteenth Street seed store, which had anchored the neighborhood shopping district for nearly forty years.[124]

Clare and Elaine Zwiep, meanwhile, converted one of the Myrtle Avenue greenhouses into a retail store in 1976, which Elaine ran very ably, and Clare concentrated on the growing wholesale trade in potted annuals (instead of flats), which he was the first to introduce. Sons Dave and Steven "Steve" came into the business at this time. Delivery trucks of Zwiep's Greenhouses serviced area florists on routes to Grand Rapids, Muskegon, Kalamazoo, and Lansing, and all points in between. In 1979 the booming Kmart account, which comprised 60 percent of the business, induced Clare to borrow heavily for a range of greenhouses of new design in Laketown Township on Beeline Road between 142nd and 143rd Avenues. This allowed the closing of the retail and wholesale businesses on Myrtle Avenue in 1985. Ed and Elsa Prince bought the property and later developed it for housing. Zwiep employed up to eighteen full time and dozens of part timers in the Beeline greenhouses, mostly high school students, during the spring and summer rush.

In 1980 the Zwieps bought another retail florist shop, Flowerland, at 1841 112th Avenue in Holland Township from Ken Michmerhuizen. Elaine again ably managed this shop that served the rapidly growing north end. But profits were slim, and after three years, the Zwieps sold the shop to Harold and Kent Merryman, who changed the name to Merryman's Nursery. In 1987 the Zwieps shuttered the Beeline Road greenhouses due to financial difficulties brought on by the loss of the Kmart account to large out-of-state competitors who undercut their pricing. Clare secured a real estate license and joined Greenridge Realty, while son Steve took his horticultural talents to the city parks department, where he became the director. Arie Mast of Grand Rapids-based Andy Mast Greenhouses bought the former Zwiep Greenhouses

124 In 1988 the Dyks sold the floral shop to Frank Rojek of Fennville and silent partner Bill Kujawa. Rojek was the sole owner during the final two years, 1996 and 1997.

at 4228 Beeline Road in 1990 and has raised annuals for chain stores like Meijer.

From 1936 to 1946, Dick Zwiep had a competitor in John Y. Huizenga, who since 1921 had operated a seed store in connection with his coal, wood, and feed store. Over time Huizenga also stocked coke, hay, straw, stock & poultry feed, and grain. First on East Eighth Street, Huizenga moved his shop in 1924 to 209 River Avenue. Huizenga was a Home Furnace executive, and the coal, feed, and seed business was an investment managed by his partners, John Van Dort and William Venhuizen. Huizenga's River Avenue store continued for twenty years, until closing about 1946. By then fuel oil had replaced coal, and the Zwieps dominated the seed business.[125]

Berend Hendrik Weller started the first Weller nursery in 1910 on East Eighth Street. He hailed from Boskoop in the province of Zuid Holland, which area counted more than eight hundred nurseries, making it the nursery center of the world. As the second son, he had no chance to inherit the family nursery, where he had worked all his life. He had immigrated in 1905 at age forty-two with a wife and eight children, drawn by an "America letter" from a cousin who had come a year or two earlier. Weller carried several cases of high-value nursery stock with him, which he planted around his rented house and tended in his spare time while working nights at a factory. He also raised vegetables that he peddled around town. Saving every penny, Weller in 1910 bought for $1,175 a narrow four-acre plot running south along present-day Hoover Boulevard, with a large two-story house fronting Eighth Street.[126]

Six years later, Berend's nephew, Peter Weller, also trained in the nursery business, immigrated as a newlywed. He came as a sales representative to the United States for a large Boskoop nursery and brought business savvy and fresh ideas. With his trade cut off by the German shipping blockade during the First World War, Peter was forced to fend for himself. With only $100 in capital, he started his own business, which he registered as the Weller Nurseries Company at the Ottawa County Courthouse in 1917. Leasing acreage and tools from his uncle Berend, Peter printed a small price list and began selling shrubbery house-to-house. The first day he sold $15.30 worth of shrubs, and after four months, he had $800 in the bank.

125 *Holland City Directories*, 1921-47.

126 I am indebted to Peter A. "Tony" Weller for making available his manuscript, tentatively titled "A Family Affair: The History of the Weller Nurseries Company," on which this section is based.

In 1919 Peter persuaded his cousin, Arie "Ira" Weller, a sharp salesman, to join him. The partners did $10,000 worth of business the first year. This success induced the elderly Berend Hendrik, "after a good deal of persuasion," to join the firm with his land and equipment. His skill at growing plants allowed the company to expand the wholesale trade, which proved to be even more profitable than retail sales. Peter was the general manager and landscape architect, and Arie was the sales manager. To raise much-needed capital for expansion, the company was incorporated and sold stock to family and friends. They also rented office space in the prestigious Peters Building on the corner of Eighth Street and Central Avenue, which they maintained for years, with Henry R. Brink as president by 1924. Brink, Peter's good friend and a substantial outside stockholder, owned Brink's Bookstore on Eighth Street.

The next phase came in 1921 when Peter's father, Pieter Anthonie Weller, age fifty-four and with a family of six, immigrated to Holland, followed the next year by Peter's younger brother Henry and new wife, in a classic example of "chain migration." Father and brothers joined the company, which had purchased twenty acres on the southeast corner of Lugers Road (Sixty-First Street) and Fortieth Street (147th Avenue per Allegan County), where they specialized in perennials and herbaceous plants, notably evergreens. The corporation raised its stated capital to $30,000 in 1922, and amalgamated with Nicholas "Nick" Kriek's Benton Harbor-based Standard Bulb Company. Kriek joined Weller Nurseries as sales manager for five years, with increased focus on wholesale marketing nationwide of hardy perennials and gladioli bulbs.[127]

By 1922 the firm grew three-and-a-half million plants for national distribution, and Holland had gained fame as a nursery center. Weller boasted of the "finest and largest perennial nurseries" in the country. The firm contracted with Orlando Reimold to raise twenty thousand peonies on the former Ben Van Raalte Farm on East Sixteenth Street. Sales increased 80 percent in 1923, and the value of the capital stock doubled to $60,000. The company rented and eventually purchased the Jacob "Jake" De Pree farm directly to the west and hired De Pree to plow, harrow, and drag the nursery fields with his team of horses. De Pree's son Andrew, "Deke," maintained the water supply system. With thirty employees working long days, plus ten Wellers in various management positions, the company still could not fill all the orders.[128]

[127] *Holland City News*, 15 June, 26 Oct. 1922, 12 Apr., 2 Aug. 1923.
[128] Ibid., 1 Apr. 1926.

Weller greenhouse, 1923, *l-r:* Pieter Anthonie Weller, grandson John, wife Alida, son Peter A. "Tony." Pieter and Alida's house is seen in the distance (*courtesy Peter A. "Tony" Weller*)

In 1929 Henry Weller entered a partnership with Peter De Vries of the Grandview Nursery at Zeeland, who had begun operations in 1922 with stock purchased from the Weller firm. De Vries, like Weller, ran an intensive operation modeled after the Boskoop system. Grandview Gardens the first year employed from fifteen to twenty men and shipped ten thousand evergreens and thirty-five thousand shrubs.

The 1920s were as good as the 1930s were bad. The hard times forced some family members to strike out on their own. By 1930 Berend Hendrik's son Arie and namesake, Berend Hendrik II, had left to form Regal Bulb Company, which continued until the late 1950s. Peter's brothers Henry and Ben later opened a short-lived seed store on River Avenue near Ebelink's Floral Shop. Pieter Anthonie II and Jack, another son of Berend Hendrik, each started their own nurseries, Pieter on Lakewood Boulevard west of Waverly Road and Jack on James Street in Holland Township. Berend Hendrik, the progenitor, died in 1938.

Peter, the true leader of the company, staved off bankruptcy by cutting the workforce to the bare minimum, forestalling creditors, and most importantly, by innovation. The Wellers realized that homeowners could not afford to buy plantings in standard large bunches, even at 50 cents apiece. So they hit on the novel idea of packaging plants in small bunches, individually wrapped. The plants had to be clean and able to survive shipping and handling. The key idea was to wrap the roots in peat, a very Dutch product used like coal for heating stoves. Kalamazoo paper plants developed sturdy yet thin wrapping paper. The brothers even invented a mechanical wrapping machine. Local chain stores—Woolworths, Kresge, McLellans, and Grants—jumped on the new packaging as did other major customers.

During the Second World War, Weller Nurseries, like Heinz, hired women and Hispanic laborers to meet their labor demands in a time of short supply. The company even built a small village of Quonset huts for the Texan and Mexican workers and employed German POWs from the nearby prison camp (chapter 23). Juke Van Oss assisted Peter Weller in managing the nursery for thirty months, from 1947 to 1949, until he caught the new-fangled "radio bug" at WHTC (chapter 19). The next turning point came in 1953 when Peter died. In the late 1930s, when the lean times ended, he had purchased most of the outstanding shares from siblings or heirs. His oldest son, John, an electrical engineer with Bell Laboratories in New York City, agreed to come and take over the company. In the next years, he gradually solidified ownership by purchasing the shares from his father's estate and those still held by other relatives.

After learning the business and evaluating the growing competition, John Weller designed new packaging machines that he successfully patented, which lowered the cost of production. He also added new bulb varieties, novelty plants, and even fruits and vegetables, but larger competitors continued to eat away at the basic perennial business. In 1980 John retired and sold the business to three executives, with operations vice president Gary Battaglia, a stepson, as majority stockholder and president. The buyers were fully aware of the challenges they faced. But they did not expect to lose their vital line of credit following a takeover of their long time Holland bank by a Kalamazoo bank. Battaglia suffered a heart attack from the stress. By about 1983 the famed Weller Nurseries Company was defunct, another victim of the risky transfer of ownership of small family-owned businesses from one generation to the next.[129]

Harry Nelis and John Zelenka were Weller's competitors. Harry Nelis immigrated in 1910 at age seventeen to Missouri, and a year later, his parents and eleven siblings followed. The Nelis family for generations cultivated bulbs in the "bulbstreek" (bulb region) of the province of Noord Holland. After several years, the staunch Catholic clan resettled in Roseland on the far south side of Chicago, joining St. Willebrord Roman Catholic Church, the only Dutch parish in greater Chicago.

[129] *Holland City News*, 29 Aug. 1929; *Holland Sentinel*, 5 July 1980, 15 Feb. 2008; *Grand Rapids Press*, 13 July 1980.

Nurseyman Frederick John Nelis (1867-1964) (*courtesy Nelis family*)

Frederick John Nelis moved his family to Holland after receiving a letter from Leonard Van Bragt, another multi-generation bulbstreek grower (see below), informing him of an eighty-acre farm for sale for $2,000 in Park Township. Nelis bought the farm and raised garden vegetables during the war and also nursery stock. The family joined St. Francis de Sales Church, and in 1922 they started Nelis Nurseries specializing in daffodil and tulip bulbs imported from the Netherlands. In 1923 son Harry married Wilhelmina "Minnie" Glass, whose family had also immigrated to Michigan via Missouri and Chicago, along with the Nelises. Harry soon took over running the farm at 1009 Alpena Road (later Lakewood Boulevard).[130]

In 1929 the Nelis firm first supplied the city with 250,000 tulip bulbs, and Tulip Time visitors by the thousands began flocking to the Nelis Tulip Farm every May to see a magnificent display of over five hundred varieties. But tulips were a seasonal item; daffodil bulbs for the Netherlands market kept the business afloat during the Great Depression, shipped overseas to Harry's cousin Charles "Charlie" van Bourgondien, also a horticulturalist. One large shipment brought in $3,000. Nelis added new tulip varieties, and by 1940 Nelis Tulip Farm had thirty-five distinct flower varieties. Harry Nelis, one of Holland's leading nurserymen, led in forming the Dutch Tulip Growers Association, serving as president of the trade group for a number of

130 Joe Nelis, "Outline Nelis Family History"; Joe Nelis' Power Point presentation for the Holland Historical Society, 2010. I am indebted to Joe Nelis for providing these documents. Antonia Van Bragt Mackay told me of the letter of her grandfather that brought the Nelis family to Holland.

Harry Nelis Sr., Fred Nelis, Harry Nelis Jr. (*right to left*) at Nelis Tulip Farm on Lakewood Boulevard, 1950s (*courtesy Nelis family*)

years. He also served on the Holland festival committee and helped organize the flower show at the armory. A renowned tulip expert, Harry traveled the country promoting the flower, and he published the book, *Tulips: Their Culture and Care*. During the Second World War, however, the farm raised onion sets, celery, and chickens, because it was impossible to import tulip bulbs. Nelis Nurseries also carried a full line of nursery stock.[131]

Harry Nelis Sr. retired in 1957, and his sons Harry Jr. and Fred took over Nelis Nurseries. A year later the pair constructed a building with a Dutch façade on US-31 at James Street as a retail bulb outlet, on land that father Harry had purchased in 1950 for its prime location. The Dutch Market opened for business during the Fourth of July holiday in 1958. Over the years, the Nelises added one building after another, including a Frisian farmhouse and barn and the Queen's Inn Restaurant, complete with Dutch roof tiles and a thatched roof. By 1962 the renamed Dutch Village had become a major tourist attraction, with Old Country antiques and an Amsterdam street organ, the "Golden Angel." Harry Jr. bought out his brother Fred's interest in the business in 1974. Nelis Tulip Farm on Lakewood Boulevard ran its last tulip display in 1979; it proved to be too difficult for Harry Jr. to manage two operations at the same time, especially after Harry Kolean, his right-hand man for fifty-four years, passed away in 1978. Later that same year, Harry Nelis Sr. and Wilhelmina both passed away. The three deaths marked the end of an era. In the 1980s the Nelis family sold the Lakewood farm, which became the Bay Meadows subdivision. In

131 *Holland City News*, 23 Aug. 1928, 14 May 1936, 6 Mar. 1941, 19 Aug. 1943, 10 Aug. 1944; Darlene Winter, "50 Years Ago Today," *Holland Sentinel*, 9 Feb. 1992.

Nelis Dutch Market opened 1958 at US-31 and James Street
(*courtesy Nelis family*)

2008 Nelis' Dutch Village celebrated its fiftieth anniversary with sixty thousand visitors to browse its shops and watch the colorful Klompen dancers. Harry Jr.'s son Joseph "Joe" and cousin Harry III continue to run the company, although son Steve and daughters Sue and Julie maintain ownership and a deep connection to the business.[132]

While Nelis' Dutch Village has focused on merchandizing Dutch-themed products and experiences in its miniature village, Veldheer's Tulip Gardens has emphasized the agricultural side—the cultivation of tulip gardens and the selling of bulbs and related products. Vernon Veldheer got into the bulb business as a hobby in the late 1940s. His business was based on his family farm on the east side of US-31 at Quincy Street, and beginning in 1926, he gradually expanded to eighty-three acres. Veldheer started with four hundred bulbs, three-quarters white and one-quarter red. Given his love of the bulbs and the very visible location of his farm, he saw opportunity in capitalizing on Holland's annual tulip festival. He linked up with Arie Le Feber, a Netherlands tulip specialist, to supply high-quality bulbs. Soon the Veldheer Tulip Farm was adorned in the spring with thousands of tulips of many varieties. His younger brother Elmer, a schoolteacher, worked for him in his spare time and during summer vacations. In 1984 Veldheer expanded his business by taking over De Klomp's wooden shoe and

132 *Holland Sentinel*, 16 May 1956, 4 May 2000, 26 Apr. 2008; *Grand Rapids Press Lakeshore Edition*, 20 Apr. 2008; *Holland Chamber News* 9 (April 1985).

Veldheer's Tulip Farm, US-31 at Qunicy Street, 1940s (*Archives, Holland Historical Trust*)

delftware trade. Son James (Jim) helped his father from his youth and became a co-owner in the early 1990s. Not one to retire, Vernon has continued to spend his days "on the farm," tending some 5.5 million bulbs in eight hundred varieties. In 2005 the Veldheers added a herd of American bison and began selling the lean meat to health-conscious customers. Combining the American West and Dutch tulips and pottery has been a winning combination at the Veldheer Tulip Gardens.[133]

Flanking the Nelis Tulip Farm on the west was Van Bragt Bros. Holland Tulip Farm, owned by Chris and William Van Bragt, sons of Leonard. The farm at 1024 Alpena Road (later Lakewood Boulevard) covered fifty-eight acres. The Van Bragt and Nelis families were fellow Dutch Catholics from the village of Heemskerke in the province of Noord Holland. The Van Bragt family brought a 150-year history of horticulture when they immigrated in 1911, but the men had to take work in local furniture and shoe factories. Leonard's brother John, who immigrated as a single man with the family, came to the attention of city parks superintendent Gerald Kooyers, who hired him in 1914. Van Bragt succeeded Kooyers in 1918 and served for nearly thirty years.[134]

[133] Phone interview with James Veldheer, 29 May 2012; *Grand Rapids Press Lakeshore Edition*, 21 Apr. 2005.

[134] *Holland City Directories*, 1910-58. I am indebted to Antoinette Van Bragt Mackay (Mrs. Willam) for information about the Van Bragt family and farm.

In the late 1920s, Leonard Van Bragt's sons, Chris and William, purchased land in Park Township for a truck garden and raised celery and vegetables. The site was a half mile west of the home Chris and Mary VandeKerkhoff had built at 878 Alpena Road when they married in 1927. Van Bragt Bros. soon turned to flower bulbs, notably tulips, and in the 1930s they had a half million blooms in two hundred varieties. But fewer tourists came to walk their gardens and order bulbs, because they came to the Nelis gardens first when heading west on Lakewood Boulevard. Harry Nelis Sr. also erected a fence along the ditch separating the two fields, thus keeping tourists from walking over to his competitor.

Mary Van Bragt's bachelor brothers-in-law, Aloysius "Wies" and Stephen Vande Kerkhoff joined Van Bragt Bros. in the late 1940s. Originally from Noord Brabant, the Vande Kerkhoffs had first settled in Ohio before coming to Holland, where sisters Mary and later Antonia lived. Antonia had married William Van Bragt in 1927, so sisters married brothers. The Vande Kerkhoffs joined St. Francis de Sales Church, along with the Nelis and Van Bragt families. In 1950 Van Bragt Bros. claimed in an advertisement to be "Holland's Largest Bulb Grower," but by 1957 the entire operation was closed down. The trigger was the decision of Wies and Stephen Vande Kerkhoff to leave the farm for Grand Rapids, which left Chris and William in the lurch. Chris and Mary's daughter Antonia "Toni" and her husband William Mackay, a Lansing attorney, bought the farm with his law partner Fred Newman to ward off a foreclosure. Ted Bosgraaf later bought the farm, together with the Nelis farm, for the Bay Meadows residential development.

In 1945 John Zelenka formed his nursery in Holland and Olive Townships, and over the next fifty years, John and his sons Paul and John Jr. built the company into a national powerhouse. Zelenka, like Weller, understood the power of aggressive advertising and the advantage of a trade name. He promoted his varied products under one name, Zelenka Nursery, and pioneered the concept of container-grown plants. This evolved naturally from his early practice of shipping plants in individual paper machè pots. His first hit was an autumnal evergreen, named "dark green spreader," which swept the market. Zelenka Nursery quickly became Michigan's largest wholesale stock grower. In the 1950s Zelenka and his competitor, Dennis Walters of Walters Gardens on Holland's south end, formed the Michigan West Shore Nursery Marketing Association. After John Zelenka retired in 1975, his sons continued to expand, until Zelenka Nursery became the

Costumed Van Bragt women in the Van Bragt Bros. Tulip Fields, 1024 West Lakewood Boulevard, ca. 1940. Mothers on left are, *l-r*: Dorothy (Mrs. Herman) Vande Kerkhoff, Clara (Mrs. Leo) Van Bragt, Mary (Mrs. Chris) Van Bragt; daughters on right are, *l-r*: Marie (of Mary), Antonia (of Mary), Dorothy (of Clara), Barbara (of Clara), and Margaret (of Mary) (DuSaar photo) (*courtesy Antoinette Van Bragt Mackay*)

sixth largest nursery in the nation. In 2000 they sold the company and its extensive lands for $58 million to a group of Chicago investors.[135]

Jonker's Gardens evolved out of a small fruit stand that John B. and Marie Jonker started in 1945 in front of their home at 816 Lincoln Avenue near Thirty-Seventh Street. John, a war veteran with very little capital, began peddling fruit and vegetables from the back of a truck in the alleys of Holland, ringing a bell to call housewives, while Marie staffed the stand and tended their young children. John bought the produce from Benton Harbor and Grand Rapids wholesale markets. Marie outsold John, and this convinced the couple in 1948 to borrow $50 from John's younger brother Andy and open a larger fruit and vegetable stand across the street at 897 Lincoln Avenue.[136]

Jonker's Produce Market carried plants in the spring and soon found that the mark-up was better on plants than produce, so they gradually shifted exclusively to plants. They built their first greenhouse in 1956 out of large window frames recycled from Louis Padnos

[135] *Holland Sentinel*, 15 Dec. 2005; *Grand Rapids Press, Lakeshore Edition*, 15 Dec. 2005.

[136] For the history of Jonker's Garden, see http://www.jonkersgarden.com/history.htm. I am also indebted to James S. Jonker for additional information.

junkyard, which they traded for plants. John began trucking in nursery stock from southern states and raising trees, shrubs, and perennials in the field behind the garden center, which was renamed Jonker's Garden Center by 1961.

To provide income during the off season, Jonker in 1962 built the Nuttin' But Puttin' miniature golf course in the field out back, which was so successful that in 1966 he sold off the remaining nursery stock and opened Gofer Golf, a pitch and putt nine-hole golf course. Jonker erected additional greenhouses along Lincoln Avenue and focused exclusively on raising flowers and plants under glass. Eventually they had five greenhouses.

In the early 1970s sons James "Jim" and David joined the business that they had worked in from an early age, and by 1974 they began to "buy in." About this time Mingo, a Texas-born monkey, became the mascot of the garden center. In 1979 Jonker's Gardens had the first telephone installed! It was to give peace of mind to Jim's wife Joy, who was pregnant with their first child. In 1981 the golf course gave way to more greenhouses, as Jonker's switched from buying nursery stock to growing their own. The sudden death of son Dave in 1994 from complications of a stroke required a major internal reorganization among children and grandchildren. John died in 2004 and Marie in 2009. Jonker's Gardens continues to thrive after nearly seventy years in the hands of son Jim and third-generation Jonkers.

Hollandia Gardens, founded in 1965 by brothers Nick and Karl (Karel) Ellerbroek, immigrants from Boskoop in the Netherlands, also developed into a major nursery and landscaping company. Nick came to Holland in 1951 and worked at Chris-Craft briefly before the army drafted him for the Korean War. After the war he returned to Chris-Craft, married a local woman, and bought four acres on Sixteenth Street just east of Country Club Road for the family home and the fledgling East End Nursery. The Ellerbroek family had been nurserymen for several generations. In 1960 Nick retuned to the Netherlands and induced his younger brother Karl, who had a degree in horticultural science, to help him in the nursery. Karl married a local woman and joined Nick at Chris-Craft. Together the brothers worked the nursery in off hours.

In 1965 the brothers launched Hollandia Gardens, and the business grew and prospered. After fifteen years, Karl wanted to expand into custom landscaping work, while Nick at age fifty wanted to kick back and limit his business to retail sales of perennials, bark, and other landscaping material. In 1980 Karl bought out Nick and relocated Hollandia Gardens to his extensive acreage at 13057 Quincy

Street. Nick continued at 1221 East Sixteenth Street under the name East End Nursery. After Nick retired in 2004, he sold his acreage to the Tendercare Health & Rehabilitation Center of Holland. His daughter Nancy moved the nursery to Stanton Street and changed the name to Zone 5 Perennials, while son Martin operated Ellerbroek Landscape Service. Hollandia Gardens continues under Karl Sr. and his son Kevin. Karl Jr. and Kelly also worked in the business as did Wayne Kuipers, Michigan state assemblyman and senator from 1998 to 2011, before launching his political career.[137]

Smaller farmers also cultivated flowers, fruit trees, and grape vines. Henry Deur's farm on East Twenty-Fourth Street, where East Middle School now stands, produced gladiolas, cherries, and grapes. Ken Beelen, Mike Van Ark, and countless other youngsters from ten to seventeen years old worked for Deur after school and during the summer, planting gladiola bulbs in the spring, weeding them in the summer, and in the fall digging them up and scraping off the old growth. They also harvested cherries and grapes. After six years on the job, Beelen earned 10¢ an hour in the 1930s. The money, and that of his three brothers, helped the family survive the Depression.[138]

Farmers cooperatives and the Farm Bureau

In the 1890s several hundred progressive farmers organized the Holland Farmers Association. They met at De Grondwet Hall to discuss common concerns. In 1903-4 president Gerrit J. Deur organized a discussion between the growers and the sugar beet factory owners, represented by attorney Arend Visscher and Professor Douwe Yntema, regarding the growers' complaints that the factory paid a low price of only six dollars a ton. These early efforts at organization remained weak and ineffective. The farmers had to learn to think like businessmen, not subsistence farmers. They began to view themselves as a separate interest group. This new mentality came from the Progressive Movement, with its emphasis on solidarity and cooperative enterprise, and then the First World War drove farm prices sharply higher and brought government price controls for the first time. Farmers competing in a regional economy like the Holland area realized they had to take account of international markets and prices. Locally, they organized cooperatives and exchanges to give them enough clout to deal with chambers of commerce dominated by local merchants and agribusiness interests.

137 Nick Ellerbroek, *A Bouquet for Family and Friends* (Holland, 2011).

138 Ken Beelen interview by Dave Boeve and the author, 30 Oct. 2009, typescript; Mike Van Ark interview by Ena Brooks, 25 Nov. 1997, JAH.

Agriculture changed drastically in the 1920s. Cars and trucks replaced horses, and supply lines lengthened ten-fold, so that what Hollanders consumed was less likely to have been grown in their backyard and more likely to be imported from another state. Holland became a commercial and industrial center, as well as an agricultural center.

The number of farmers peaked as well, because of the trend to consolidate smaller farms into larger and more efficient operations. For example, Albert P. Kleis, a rural mail carrier, in 1915 expanded his piggery a half-mile east of Holland to 125 animals, which was one of the largest operations for miles around.[139] This type of specialized, large-scale operation would today be called a factory farm. Higher-paying industrial jobs also drew farmers' sons into the cities. Between 1910 and 1920, the decline in the farm population became very pronounced, and the deep depression in the agricultural sector in the 1920s and 1930s further hastened the movement off the farm. By 1921 Michigan state officials considered sending an agent to the Netherlands to recruit experienced farm laborers. Ottawa County counted fewer than 4,500 farms at that time, and the number held steady through the 1940s. Tenancy was low in Ottawa County (12 percent) and Allegan County (15 percent); meaning that farmers tilled 88 percent and 85 percent, respectively, of their own land. A report in 1927 stated that the average value of farm lands in Ottawa County—$64 per acre for unimproved and $88 for improved land—was about the same as southwest Michigan generally, but local farmers shipped more products (wheat, oats, rye, potatoes, and apples) outside county boundaries than did farmers elsewhere.[140]

Despite their declining numbers, farmers' spending power exceeded that of city dwellers for many years, and Holland merchants went out of their way to capture those dollars. In 1917 the businessmen first coordinated one of their semi-annual Dollar Day promotions with the annual farm institute, in order to bring in hundreds of farmers. The institutes, called Round-Ups, were instigated by the Michigan Agricultural College (now Michigan State University) to educate farmers about the latest developments in agriculture and horticulture. Austin Fairbanks was the secretary of the Ottawa County Farm Institute of Holland. Local merchants, led by the mayor, had for several years hosted the farm institute at the city hall, where they treated their "rural neighbors" to a "warm dinner and social time." The royal reception,

139 *Holland City News*, 10 June 1915.

140 Ibid., 20 Jan. 1921, 9 Jan. 1922, 24 Mar. 1927, 27 Feb., 4 Mar. 1941.

it was noted with tongue in cheek, "offers an opportunity for local business men to get into close touch with the farmers of this vicinity in a social, not a business way." Despite their success during the Great War, farm institutes were not scheduled after 1918; merchants, however, continued the lucrative Dollar Days.[141]

By the fourth Dollar Day in 1920, nearly every merchant in Holland offered special bargains at "very low prices" to "make agricultural and urban districts alike feel there are mutual benefits to be derived by promoting a healthy and congenial feeling between farmers and city men." An additional attraction was the Free Farm School at the city hall, offered under the auspices of the Michigan Agricultural College, the Michigan Potato Growers Exchange, and corporations such as International Harvester and the Pere Marquette Railroad, which brought in experts on agricultural topics to give inspirational and informative lectures, illustrated with stereopticon slides and motion pictures. Some four hundred farmers attended the December 1920 institute. Throughout the twenties, the merchants staged annual farmers picnics, first at Jenison Park and then at Kollen Park.[142]

The close working relationship between farmers and merchants was also demonstrated that year when the farmers north of town wanted River Avenue improved from First Street to the Grand Haven (now North River Avenue) Bridge. The slippery surface threatened in wet and snowy weather to cause horses to slip and fall and motor vehicles to slide into the ditch. Instead of going to the city council directly, the farmers asked the Holland Retail Merchants Association to appeal to the city on their behalf. The merchants took the matter to the city council at its very next meeting, and the matter was referred to the Good Roads committee for action. The businessmen knew which side of the bread to butter.[143]

In 1919 a new national organization, the American Farm Bureau Federation, became the mouthpiece for the business of agriculture, and local farmers formed a branch, the Ottawa County Farm Bureau, centered in Grand Haven. The Farm Bureau encouraged members in every locale to organize cooperatives, so farmers could buy in bulk and deal on better terms with grain exporters, millers, city retailers, packers, and other middlemen. Since farmers had to learn to sell their products as well as produce them, the bureau also provided marketing,

141 Ibid., 20, 27 Jan. 1916, 25 Jan. 1917, 13 Jan., 1921, 5 Jan. 1922.
142 *Holland City News*, 18 Mar. 1920, 3 Mar. 1927.
143 Ibid., 9 Dec. 1920.

legislative, and transportation services to members. Throughout the next decades, the Farm Bureau defended the interests of farmers and lobbied for favorable farm legislation.[144]

Holland-area bureau members in November 1919 formed the first farmers' co-op, the Holland Co-operative Association. Within the first month some 175 farmers in Ottawa and Allegan Counties became members, putting down dues of $10 for the privilege. This gave them the right to buy supplies at a discount and share profits in marketing their produce. The Holland Co-op succeeded beyond anyone's expectations, despite a bitter fight at the end of the inaugural year over a decision to raise dues eleven fold, to $110. A number of members resigned over the steep increase, including president Simon Harkema, a Laketown Township poultryman, and general manager George Heneveld.[145]

In 1920 Ben Van Lente served on the executive committee that arranged the second annual Farm Bureau Festival in Holland, which featured exhibits of products from local farms and prizes for the best entries. For the exhibition Arend Visscher donated a recently vacant store on East Eighth Street below his law office. Another popular bureau event was the annual county picnic, which drew 1,200 people in 1921. The decision of the Ottawa County Farm Bureau in 1920 to establish a seed department with locally adapted seeds, met a real need of providing local farmers with quality seeds at reasonable prices and in a timely manner. The bureau that year organized a local unit in every township to increase attendance at monthly meetings. By 1923 the bureau had opened four other services besides seeds—namely, a purchasing department, wool pool (to market wool), a produce exchange, and a grain elevator. The Holland co-op, among all Ottawa County co-ops, proved to be the bureau's best customer. The bureau also held classes to instruct members on new methods, such as the best fertilizers for fruit trees and vegetables in the muck, both of which required special fertilization to be productive. Austin Harrington of Holland served as bureau president during the 1920s.[146]

In the 1920s the rural economy went down drastically, while cities prospered with rising factories and an influx of people off the farms. Falling farm prices cut into profits. Wheat brought a high of only 94¢ a bushel in 1923, and the average yield was a sparce forty bushels an acre. The tough times called for strong measures to keep farmers solvent.

144 *De Grondwet*, 27 Jan. 1903, 8 Feb. 1904, 10 May 1923.

145 *Holland Sentinel*, 15, 22 Jan. 1920; *Holland City News*, 13 Jan. 1921, 30 Nov. 1922.

146 *Holland City News*, 18 Mar., 7 Aug., 29 Oct., 4, 25 Nov. 1920, 4, 18 Aug. 1921, 1 Mar., 10 May 1923, 22 Jan. 1925, 7 June 1926.

Since farmers in Ottawa County put down more commercial fertilizer than any other county except one, given the demands of muck crop production and the thin sandy soils along the lakeshore, they turned to the Holland Farmers Co-op, as it was popularly called, to buy in bulk.[147]

To better finance its operations and take advantage of discount buying or cash, in 1925 the co-op reorganized from a membership basis to a stock company, capitalized at $100,000. Each member still had one vote, no matter the number of shares owned, but dividends were paid per share. That year, the co-op, managed by former teacher Frank Zonnebelt, counted over five hundred members and earned dividends of $7,000 on a sales volume of nearly $3 million. The grain elevator and gristmill stood at 88-90 East Seventh Street, while the supply yard on Fourteenth Street held coal, cement, lime, fertilizers, and other staples. The co-op also had branches in Harlem and West Olive. Zonnebelt ran the Holland Farmers Co-operative Elevator & Flour Mill (the official name) for twenty years, until 1948. Many farmers served on the board, including presidents Maurice Luidens in the 1930s and 1940s, Frank Kooyers in the 1950s, Nick Prins in the 1960s, and Harold Helder and Foster Kooyers in the 1970s. The co-op provided area farmers with fuel, feed, and farm supplies for six decades, until market forces rendered agricultural cooperatives obsolete.[148]

At the onset of the Depression, the need to tutor farmers in modern methods of agriculture was obvious, and the Holland Chamber of Commerce and the Merchants Association stepped forward to revive the annual farm institute day in Holland, in cooperation with the Ottawa County Farm Bureau and the Michigan State College of Agriculture. Some 1,500 farmers from Ottawa and Allegan Counties attended the 1930 event at the armory, the first in twelve years, and the next three institutes attracted two thousand farmers. More than one hundred merchants and manufacturers donated liberally to fund the free luncheons and cover the expenses of the day. The event fell by the wayside again after 1934, when economic conditions seemed to improve. In 1940 agricultural societies in West Michigan founded the annual Farm-To-Prosper Contest, a youth-oriented program for farm families and rural community organizations to advance rural life. The annual West Michigan Farm-To-Prosper round-up, with cash prizes for achievement, proved to be highly popular for several decades and

[147] Ibid., 10 June, 26 July 1923.

[148] Ibid., 5 Feb., 3 June 1925; Sanborn [Fire] Insurance Maps, Holland, 1902, 1908, 1916, 1925; *Holland City Directories*, 1915-90.

nurtured 4-H Clubs in the region. The events attracted more than a thousand farm folk and businessmen and more than one hundred organizations.[149]

Poultry

In the early twentieth century some local farmers, especially in Holland and Zeeland Townships, began to specialize in raising poultry, and this locale became the heart of the national poultry industry from the 1920s through the 1960s, with more than eighty hatcheries in the heyday. The business was second nature to the Dutch, and their large families were ideal for the labor-intensive work of tending incubators and feeding birds.

Henry De Pree, owner of the Meadow Brook Farm southwest of Holland on the Michigan Pike (today's Blue Star Highway, US-31), claimed to be *the* pioneer hatchery man in the state. He had raised chickens, mostly broilers, for the resort trade, but in 1902 an agent for an incubator company came by and convinced him to buy a lamp machine that could hatch 250 eggs at once and thus increase his flocks. De Pree took the risk and in twenty years owned machines with a 96,000-egg capacity. The operation was truly a family affair. His mother and siblings, both brothers and sisters, provided the twenty-four/seven labor required. In the 1920s brother Edward superintended the hatchery, and brother John was in charge of shipping, all under the direction of Henry as president and general manager.

The firm boasted of superior eggs imported directly from the Netherlands by a friend of De Pree, which strain they dubbed Holland Brown Leghorn. The Dutch birds were larger than the American White Leghorns and produced more eggs. Meadow Brook Farm produced 450,000 chicks annually by the 1920s and sent thousands of circulars throughout the United States and Canada, making the farm a major tourist destination. Hundreds of local farmers followed De Pree's path, and Ottawa County quickly became the chick hatchery capitol of the United States, and the Holland-Zeeland nexus rivaled the famous Petaluma, California district as a national poultry center.[150]

In the late 1890s the Holland Poultry and Pet Stock Association, led by Edward Brouwer, was the first in the state to form a promotional organization. The Zeeland Poultry Association, formed in 1907, also

149 *Holland City News*, 16 Oct., 11 Dec. 1930, 1, 8 Dec. 1932, 7, 14 Dec. 1933, 14 Feb. 1946, 24 Dec. 1953, 17 Nov. 1955; *Holland Sentinel*, 16 May 1956.

150 Ibid., 1 Jan. 1923.

claimed to be the seminal group. A third group, much smaller, was the Ottawa County Association based in Grand Haven. The Holland and Zeeland groups jointly sponsored exhibits of prized birds, arranged various educational programs, including an annual Holland poultry institute. This was modeled after the familiar "farm institutes" and featured professors from the poultry department of the Agricultural College of Michigan (now Michigan State University) and other experts, who introduced the latest methods of raising, feeding, fattening, and marketing chickens. Holland's city hall provided free space for the one-day schools, where experts touted large flocks of one thousand or more as a sure way to gain a "handsome net profit." The local associations also took the lead in forming the Michigan Chick Hatchers Association, which in 1923 joined the International Chick Hatchers Association. At the time, Louis Van Appledorn of Holland was president of the Michigan organization, and Clarence De Koster of Zeeland served as secretary.[151]

To encourage improved breeding among chicken fanciers, the Holland Poultry Association, as the organization was known, beginning in 1899 staged an annual show during Christmas week, with prizes for exhibitors from across the state. (The 1899 date gives the Holland association pride of place over Zeeland, which began annual shows in 1910.) The A. Harrington Coal & Feed Company, under president Austin Harrington, offered a specially engraved gold cup for the "best general display in the utility class," which would pass from winner to winner until a person won it for the third time; then it was his to keep. The Ancona breed was the favorite at the 1919 show, which featured six hundred birds, twice the previous number on exhibit. Tubergen Bros. captured the Harrington Cup in 1919 and 1920, but Lakewood Farm won the coveted trophy in 1922. Exhibitors entered more than a thousand prized birds that year.[152]

For years, the venue was the Vander Veen Block at 20 West Eighth Street (appendix 5.1 lists private blocks). The twenty-fifth-anniversary show in 1924, however, was held in the new Masonic Temple on Tenth Street. The spacious main hall and meeting rooms, covered in protective canvas sheeting, housed pens and cages featuring hundreds of prized strains. The music room rang with song from the hundreds of canaries on display, who regaled the feathered pet fanciers. Benjamin

[151] Ibid., 21 Nov. 1918, 10 Nov., 29 Dec. 1921, 2 Mar., 13 Apr., 24 June, 20 July 1922, 8 Feb., 19 Apr., 13 Sept. 1923, 18 Dec. 1924, 22 Jan. 1925.

[152] *Holland City News*, 27 Nov., 25 Dec. 1919, 1 Jan. 1920, 28 Dec. 1922, 4 Jan., 18 Nov., 6 Dec. 1923.

Poultry Show advertisement in *Holland City News*, December 1922 issues

"Ben" Van Raalte Jr., grandson of Holland's founder, was president of the Holland association, with Edward Brouwer secretary and James De Koster treasurer.[153]

In 1920 Simon Harkema, a county agricultural agent and poultry expert, and his foreman Luke Vredevelt, bought a forty-acre site on Castle Road (now 146th Street) in Laketown Township and built a giant, coal-fired incubator to hatch nine thousand chicks, and a brooder house and laying house with a capacity of three thousand "ready-to-lay pullets and breeding stock." The firm specialized in White Leghorns and touted as its trademark and marketing slogan: "Six Cylinder White Leghorns at Ford Prices," which mimicked Henry Ford's tin lizzie that sold for under $500. Harkema claimed his "modern" operation was the "only poultry plant of its kind in the middle west."[154]

The Star Hatchery at 666 Michigan Avenue was not to be outdone. The year-old firm of Lambertus "Bert" Tinholt built an incubator to hatch ten thousand eggs at a time, and the firm turned out fifty thousand chicks in the 1919-20 season. "It pays to advertise," declared Tinholt, after running a weekly one-inch ad in the *Holland City News*. "I've been swamped with orders ever since." Tinholt's business lasted barely one decade. Edward Brouwer, the company secretary, bought the Star Hatchery in 1926, but it closed within a year, and the property by 1929 sported the Nurses' Home of the new Holland Hospital a block to the north.[155]

153 Ibid., 18 Dec. 1924, 22 Jan., 24 Dec. 1925, 27 Jan. 1926.
154 Ibid., 1 (quote) Jan. 1920.
155 Ibid., 29 Jan. 1920 (quote); *Holland City Directories*, 1924-25, 1927-28, 1929.

Zeeland welcome sign "Visit our Hatcheries"
(*courtesy Jack Geerlings, Townline Poultry Farm*)

Ottawa County quickly took the lead in Michigan, and indeed nationally, in the chick-hatching business, producing one hundred thousand chicks a day during the 1922 season, with Tinholt's firm alone raising from eighty- to ninety thousand every three weeks. Local baby chick production made Ford's factory look like a piker. And this was only the beginning. A decade later, a welcome billboard in Zeeland read: "15 Million Chicks Produced Annually" and "Visit our Hatcheries." The sign could have added: "Three thousand employed."[156]

The new parcel post law of 1920 gave the chick industry a big boost by allowing producers conveniently to ship birds by rail as far as Pennsylvania and Kansas "almost as soon as they are out of the shell." Chicks required no food for seventy-two hours, because they ate the yolk of the egg just before hatching. During the spring hatching season, postal workers in Holland and Zeeland shipped out tens of thousands of chicks, packed one hundred to a box, and payments came back through the mail in the form of checks and money orders. To meet the increasing demand, incubator companies contracted up to six months in advance with local egg producers for ready-to-hatch eggs, which brought a premium of 5¢ over eggs for the consumer market.

[156] *Holland City News*, 12 Jan. 1922, 28 Oct. 1926; Randall P. Vande Water, *A Walk Through Time; A Pictorial History of Zeeland* (*Holland Sentinel*, 2005), 59-62 (quote 59).

Jake Overweg and Rufus Van Ommen pack boxes of chicks for shipment from the Zeeland railroad depot (*Zeeland Historical Museum*)

The symbiotic relationship between egg producers and chick hatcheries benefited both and pumped thousands of dollars into the local economy. Egg producers also used the new parcel post service to ship eggs packed in crated cartons to Chicago markets. In 1924 the Holland post office shipped two million chicks, at a rate of forty thousand per day, and the next year shipments rose to three million, with the single day record of one hundred thousand chicks in one thousand boxes. By 1929 shipments from the one hundred or more hatcheries in the Holland-Zeeland area totaled ten million chicks a year.[157]

In the next decades, the volume increased by a factor of ten. Until the 1950s Zeeland hatcheries alone produced three hundred thousand chicks a day, eighteen million per year. It was said that the "little peeps" gave casual visitors to the Zeeland and Holland post offices the "illusion of being in a bird store." Most went out by rail, but trucks by the 1920s took the short-haul routes, and by 1931 airplanes carried chicks across Lake Michigan to Milwaukee and parts beyond. To lower the extraordinary losses in the shipment of chicks, the post office assigned a trained crew of clerks to meet the special trains at Grand Rapids and Chicago to ensure that the chicks continued on without

157 *Holland City News*, 27 May 1920 (quote), 7 Apr. 1921, 8 Feb. 1923, 10 Apr. 1924, 16, 30 Apr. 1925, 4 Aug. 1927, 25 Apr., 1 Aug. 1929.

Shipping "peeps" (chicks) by parcel post from Zeeland railroad depot in cars equipped with heating and ventilation systems for shipment across the country, 1925 (*Zeeland Historical Museum*)

delay to their destinations. The Zeeland Poultry Association went one step further in 1926, hiring a "chick chaperon" to ride with the chicks in the climate-controlled boxcars from Holland to Chicago and monitor the six thermometers in each car.[158]

The egg industry was a natural extension of the chick industry, especially with the seemingly insatiable demand of the Chicago market. To succeed, producers needed to improve the quality of the laying hens. Henry Wiersma began culling his male birds in 1915 to safeguard the hybrid hens, and in 1921, the Holland Poultry Association, led by president Arend Siersma, had an expert come to town to advocate culling as standard practice. Under the colorful title, "Swat the Rooster, or America's $15,000,000 Yearly Egg Loss" K. A. Zimmerman, manager of Lakewood Farm of Holland, told producers that culling could save 45 percent on feed bills with almost no reduction in eggs. "You must get your birds culled," was the message. "Without culling them you cannot make a profit on your eggs." By 1922 the association mounted a major culling campaign, with seven or eight trained crews culling flocks of

[158] Ibid., 8 Mar. 1923 (quote), 25 Mar., 22 Apr. 1926, 16 Apr. 1931; Vande Water, *Pictorial History*, 59.

Japanese sexer Dave Miamoto at Townline Poultry Farm, Zeeland (*courtesy Jack Geerlings, Townline Poultry Farm*)

members for free, including under-producing hens. Local poultrymen sent one hundred thousand "lazy" birds to the butchers annually from then on. "Michigan eggs, like Michigan apples, are the best," was the claim. Culling naturally led to the next step in the evolution of the chick industry, certified hatcheries with superior birds and eggs stamped with a distinctive mark.[159]

"Sexing" the chicks also became a necessary skill, because buyers who specialized in boiler production wanted cockerels (males) and egg producers wanted pullets (females). Zeeland's first hatchery in 1906 was Townline Poultry Farm, owned by the Jacob Geerlings family and located north of Ransom Street on 96th Avenue (known locally as the Borculo Road). Geerlings hired Dwight (Douwe) "Whitey" Wyngarden, the first professional sexer in Zeeland, and Whitey trained a team of a dozen to work under him. He could sex up to one thousand day-old chicks an hour. He sorted more than 455,000 birds in the 1930s. Townline boasted innovative Newtown incubators, which won for the firm the distinction of being the first Zeeland hatchery approved by the US Department of Agriculture. By the 1940s Whitey and his team gave way to Japanese American sexers. The word on the street was that they were faster and more accurate. "Sitting on egg crates, the Japanese worked effortlessly with a rhythm that was 98 to 99 percent accurate," Jack L. De Witt recalled. They were also cheaper, since they worked by the season. During the Second World War, the Japanese Americans had

159 *Holland City News*, 2 June 1921, 23 Feb., 1, 22, 29 June 1922, 3 Apr. 1924, 6 Jan. 1938.

Jacob Geerlings (*shirt and tie*) with young son Henry, assisted by employees Elie (*center*) and Gert Zwagerman(*far right*) and a Mr. Roelofs (*on left*), inspecting newly hatched chicks in steam incubators, Townline Poultry Farm, Zeeland, ca. 1926 (*courtesy Jack Geerlings, Townline Poultry Farm*)

to contend with animosity toward the "enemy," even though they were native-born citizens.[160]

Zeeland became the "heart of chickendom" by the 1920s, and the Zeeland Poultry Association had 350 members and sixty-five hatcheries, compared to some thirty-five hatcheries in the Holland Poultry Association. "Zeeland is all Eggs! Eggs! Eggs! Pearly White," declared a newspaper headline. Quirinus De Vries' Grandview Poultry Farms northwest of Zeeland, with a 96,000-egg capacity, claimed to be the largest hatchery in the state, but Clarence De Koster and Gustav Romeyn of the nearby Superior Poultry Farm quickly outpaced Grandview with a 150,000-egg hatchery, the largest in Michigan. Superior required a full rail carload of eggs every three weeks to fill its incubators. Grandview Poultry increased its capacity to 200,000 chicks and shipped 750,000 in 1924, including 61,000 in a single day. Van Appledorn Brothers shipped 500,000 chicks that season, but their largest daily shipment was only 30,000. In 1927 Grandview bought out

160 Vande Water, *Pictorial History*, 60, 62; Mike Lozon, "Zeeland's Hatchery Heyday," *Michigan History* (Sept.-Oct., 2003): 9-16. I am indebted to Anthony Diekema, a Zeeland native and former president of Calvin College, for the information on Japanese sexers. He worked in the industry in his teenage years in the mid-1940s and early 1950s.

the smaller Forest Grove Hatchery, which made it the largest firm in Michigan with a capacity of 275,000 chicks. That year, Marinus Kole's Lakeview Poultry Farm, Holland's largest hatchery, shipped 200,000 chicks.[161]

In the early twenties poultry in the Holland area was a $3 million a year industry that doubled and tripled in the next years. Ottawa County stood at the top of the chicken business in the United States in the mid-1920s, with hundreds of producers; poultry had become the leading industry. Poultry brought many thousands of dollars to the Holland-Zeeland area and a small army of men and women handled the hen and its products. No wonder the Holland Common Council readily made its chambers available for the monthly meetings of the Holland Poultry Association, and the Holland Chamber of Commerce, Merchants Association, Exchange Club, Rotary, and Farm Bureau all strove to boost this key industry.[162]

The Holland Poultry Association's 1925 show, its red-letter twenty-fifth anniversary, featured five thousand birds on exhibit at the Holland Armory, the largest number ever. On the second floor, the association ran a poultry school, with the intent to encourage factory workers in town to raise chickens in the backyard. The *Holland City News* even published plans for the Michigan Type Poultry House. If managed carefully, each bird could bring a profit of five dollars a year, it was claimed. But the main push that year was a successful effort to ward off a threatened national boycott of Michigan poultry by pushing the state agricultural department and agricultural college to establish a poultry inspection system, as several other poultry states had done. To accomplish this, the local body helped launch a statewide organization, the Michigan State Poultry Improvement Association.[163]

By 1927 egg producers and hatcheries faced a growing dilemma that impacted profits. Every year in March and April, the hens laid fewer eggs, so the hatcheries had to contract for twice as many hens as they needed. But in the next months, the hatcheries could only take half as many fertile eggs as farmers could supply. And since the eggs were fertilized, they had to be sold at a discount for human consumption. The two groups convened a mass meeting in January to seek a solution. At the same time, some four hundred poultrymen from Holland to Hudsonville, led by Maurice Luidens of West Olive, organized the Ottawa

161 *Holland City News*, 20 July, 5 Oct., 16 Nov., 14, 28 Dec. 1922, 8 Feb., 1 Mar., 12, 19 Apr. 1923, 14 Feb., 15, 22 May 1924, 3 Mar., 28 July 1927, 30 Apr. 1931 (quote).

162 Ibid., 1 Apr. 1926.

163 Ibid., 12 Feb., 16 Apr., 14, 28 May, 10, 24 Dec. 1925, 15, 22 Apr. 1926.

Egg & Poultry Association, headquartered in Zeeland. It was the first cooperative egg-marketing organization in Michigan and quickly grew to 630 "henneries." The members, with 125,000 hens in total, pooled their operations in order to gain savings from bulk purchases, obtain better prices per carload of eggs shipped to market daily, and eliminate several layers of middlemen. The egg co-op also gave producers more clout with hatcheries. Under manager Al Otteman, the co-op proved that Ottawa hens were big moneymakers and the members divided the profits. The co-op did $200,000 worth of business the first year, shipping eggs to Grand Rapids, Detroit, Chicago, and New York City from its central warehouse in Zeeland. Dressed poultry shipments, which increased rapidly, reached a wider national market than the egg distribution network. Annual business meetings were held in the Zeeland city hall, and rightly so, since Zeeland had more hatcheries and produced six times as many chicks as Holland.[164]

The Ottawa Egg & Poultry Association experienced a leadership change in 1928 when Ed Brouwer resigned as secretary after eleven years. He had given excellent direction and the association prospered under his guidance. The group elected Dewey Jaarsma to succeed him. William Wilson continued as president and James De Koster as treasurer. Brouwer bent his energies for a larger goal, to unify the Holland and Zeeland associations in a new countywide body, the Ottawa County Greater Poultry Association. He succeeded and was elected secretary, with R. C. Jackson as president. The county association, soon renamed the Michigan Egg & Poultry Exchange, staged the first annual Poultry and Pet Show in conjunction with the 1928 Holland Community Fair. This replaced the annual one-day shows of the Holland and Zeeland Poultry Associations. The result was deemed the "finest exhibition of poultry ever seen" in Ottawa County and indeed in all of Michigan. Ottawa County was rightly known as the Petaluma of the Middle West, and Zeeland and Holland had earned their reputation as a national poultry center. Every year in December, the chamber of commerce hosted up to fourteen hundred local poultrymen at the armory for a free luncheon.[165]

164 Ibid., 1, 13 Jan., 10 Feb., 28 Apr., 20 Oct. 1927, 7, 14 Feb. 1929, 29 Mar. 1934.

165 *Holland City News*, 20 Oct., 3 Nov., 15, 22, 27 Dec. 1927, 29 Mar., 18 Oct. 1928, 3 Jan. 1929, 18 Jan., 17 Apr., 1 May 1930, 10 Dec. 1931. Ottawa County, it should be noted, ranked high in hatcheries and chicks but not poultry for meat. In this, Ottawa ranked ninth, behind Allegan in third place, based on the 1930 agricultural census (ibid., 22 Sept. 1932).

Zeeland Chick and Egg Association Tulip Time float in the late 1940s featured live chicks and an actual 1947 hatchery unit (*courtesy Jack Geerlings, Townline Poultry Farm*)

Bil-Mar Foods

But the best was yet to come for the Ottawa poultrymen, once they added turkeys to their production in the mid-1930s. It was just in time, because egg prices plummeted during the Depression to 13¢ a dozen. The Central Farms Hatchery of Lee Van Omman was one of the first to hatch poults (baby turkeys) and to ship hatching eggs. Johannes Janssen had the same idea; he converted his chick hatchery entirely to poults in 1937. Janssen Farms was about a mile from Townline Hatchery on the Borculo Road.[166]

While not the first to raise turkeys, the De Witt brothers, Marvin and his older brother William (Bill, as he was known), were pioneers in the industry. As boys growing up in Zeeland in the 1920s, they saw the booming chick hatcheries all around. Eight-year-old Marvin, already a risk-taker, asked for some culled chicks about to be destroyed, bought feed, and raised them for eggs and eventually the family dinner table. He quickly saw that one could make money in poultry. During the Depression Marvin found work at the Heinz plant in Holland; it was

166 Steve Vander Veen, "Switch to turkeys led to company's growth [Janssen Farms]," *Holland Sentinel*, 12 Aug. 2007.

Bill and Marv De Witt's turkey farm with a flock of "Broad Breasted Bronze Bourbon Reds," 1940s (*Archives, Holland Historical Society*)

better than milking cows and doing back-breaking farm work. Yet, Bill stayed in farming.[167]

In 1938 the brothers saw an ad in the *Holland Sentinel* for baby turkeys and bought fourteen hens and three toms for $60. Marvin borrowed $30 from his sister to raise the cash. The timing was impeccable. In three years the country was embroiled in World War Two, and consumers needed every possible source of cheap protein. Turkeys, a relatively new meat product, fit the bill perfectly. But none of the forty hatcheries in the area, which produced fifteen million chicks a year, would bother with a small quantity of turkey eggs. Marvin finally prevailed on De Witt's Zeeland Hatchery, owned by three other De Witt brothers–Ben, Jack H., and Dick (who, surprisingly, were not related to Marvin and Bill)–to hatch their few eggs. And in 1939 Bill and Marv's Turkey Farm, the initial name of the company, sold their first two hundred turkeys live to Holland butcher Bill McKay on Sixteenth Street for local Thanksgiving tables. In 1941 the brothers built their own brood house and quickly expanded production to six thousand birds.

The 1940s were good years, but not so good that five hundred poults that refused to eat could be wasted. The mystified De Witt brothers "borrowed" Anthony "Tony" Diekema, a teenager working for

[167] *Holland City News*, 28 Jan. 1932; Michael Lozon, *Mr. Turkey: A Biography of Bil-Mar Foods co-founder Marvin De Witt* (Zeeland, MI: De Witt Foundation, 1999), for this and the next two paragraphs; Vande Water, *Pictorial History*, 63.

Janssen Farms just up the road, to come and force feed the birds. It was a nearly impossible assignment to keep that many birds alive by hand feeding. But someone (Diekema does not remember who) came up with the idea of mixing something shiny or glittering in the mash to entice the poults to eat. Several attempts failed, but when they tried children's marbles (which were too large for the young turkeys to get in their beaks), they pecked at them and got a beak full of mash in the process. The birds actually competed to get at the marbles, so the hired hands seeded the mash with more. "Amazingly, it continued to work and the flock survived," Diekema recalled.[168]

Bill and Marv De Witt continued to expand in the postwar decades, until Bil-Mar Foods of Borculo became one of the largest producers of processed turkey products in the country. This breakthrough came in 1960 when Marvin took the risk to move beyond oven-ready birds and manufacture boneless breasts, hot dogs, luncheon meats, ham, and sausage. This is when the firm took the name Bil-Mar, taking the first three letters in each of their given names. The Bil-Mar processing plant on 96th Avenue in Olive Township was for many years one of the major employers in Ottawa County. A $4 million expansion was in the works in 1984 when an early morning fire destroyed the plant. Besides the $25 million loss, the blaze forced the temporary layoff of half the 1,100 employees. Those furloughed included many workers who three years earlier had staged a violent strike, including the lobbing of two Molotov cocktails—gasoline-filled Mason jars—into the company's retail store, causing $2,000 in damage. The strikers, who belonged to Teamsters Local 406 based in Grand Rapids, had also reported the company to federal officials for employing illegal immigrants, which resulted in a raid that snagged twenty-four Hispanics.[169]

When the brothers sold out to Sara Lee Corp. in 1987, they had a workforce of 1,200 and $170 million in annual sales. By 2011 sales had tripled to $600 million, and the number of employees had risen to two thousand, making the firm one of the largest employers in Ottawa County.[170]

After the sale to Sara Lee, Jack L. De Witt, son of Marvin, and Roger Draft, director of engineering at Bil Mar, led a group of investors in 1990 to buy the convenience frozen food division of Bil-Mar Foods and start Request Foods Inc. at 3460 John F. Donnelly Drive in the

168 Anthony Diekema recalled this incident in an email to the author on 30 June 2010.

169 *Holland Sentinel*, 25, 26 Sept. 8, 19 Oct. 1984.

170 Lozon, *Mr. Turkey*, 224-34, 251-55; Marvin De Witt obit., *Holland Sentinel*, 6 Aug. 2011.

former HEDCOR Northside Industrial Park. Sara Lee was willing to jettison a division that made up only 10 percent of Bil Mar's sales, even though the dollar amount was huge—$25 million. They launched Request Foods in November 1989, hired 240 employees, half former Bil Mar personnel, and moved production equipment to a new plant in the Northside Industrial Center. The sales team found new markets, and the plant ran double shifts every day except Sundays and holidays to keep up with orders. A key to the operation was a mammoth kitchen with a walk-in oven that could cook ten thousand steak patties at a time, a bevy of steam kettles, and mixers that could handle up to five thousand pounds. By 1990 airline meals comprised 20 percent of sales, and restaurant food service and contract packaging each 30 percent. Over time, airlines cut warm food in favor of soft drinks and snacks, while the military ordered more frozen food for troops in the field in Iraq and Afghanistan.[171]

Total sales of $240 million in 2010 surpassed those of Bil-Mar before its sale to Sara Lee. Request Foods shipped six million pounds of product per week in 2010, including lasagna, macaroni and cheese, and a variety of frozen soups. Its products are sold under various labels in retail grocery and club stores and in the food service industry generally. The workforce is currently more than 500 and is expected to reach 750 by 2015. The company has undergone several building expansions in its twenty-year history, the latest being a second manufacturing facility that opened in the summer of 2011 at 12875 Greenly Street. That plant can accommodate 250 employees.[172]

From the outset, Request Foods has been committed to a people-oriented workplace and the promulgation of conservative Christian social values. Periodically, Request Foods publishes its views in full-page advertisements in the *Holland Sentinel*. The corporate credo states: "We're devoted to offering people those opportunities that will enable them to fully develop their God-given skills so that they can enhance the quality of their lives as well as that of our customers, their fellow employees, and all mankind." With such a management ethic, Request Foods has a committed workforce with very low turnover.[173]

Today, only Janssen Farms and Townline Hatchery, which celebrated its centenary in 2006, remain of the one hundres hatcheries that once operated in the region. But "the legacy of the bustling egg-laying activity" continues; Ottawa and Allegan Counties still rank

171 *Massie, Haven, Harbor, and Heritage*, 182.

172 *Holland Sentinel*, 19 Feb., 15 Dec. 2010, 17 July 2011. I am indebted to Steve De Witt for information about Request Foods, Inc.

173 Quoted in *Massie, Haven, Harbor, and Heritage*, 182.

number one and number two in the state in egg-laying hens. Janssen Farms, a supplier of commercial poultry operations, hatches and ships six million poults annually; in 2012 the family sold its hatchery business. Townline remains in the Geerlings family under grandson Jack Geerlings and his children, making it a four-generation business. The hatchery operates seasonally and supplies "backyard" farmers.[174]

Big Dutchman

The other De Witt brothers—Ben, Jack H., and Dick—took local poultry to the next level through vertical integration of the industry from the hatchery to the dinner table. Ben had begun the De Witt Utility Hatchery (later Zeeland Hatchery) in 1935; Jack joined him right away, and Dick came two years later after four years in the Navy, bringing in $500 of his savings. Jack was the charismatic salesman whose mantra was "keep selling." Dick was the numbers cruncher. The partners hit on the idea of selling baby chicks direct to farmers. Over the winter months, Jack and Dick went to farmers throughout the state to sell contracts with a one dollar deposit per one hundred birds, with delivery promised during the spring hatching season. They capitalized on the good reputation of Zeeland-Holland area chicks, and farmers signed up in the thousands. De Witt's chick business grew rapidly. In 1938 the company was restructured, and a new hatchery and offices were built in Zeeland; this marked the beginning of the firm that became Big Dutchman. The next year the brothers began raising turkeys (De Witt Modern Feeds) and processing them (Zeeland Poultry Processing). Ben left the company in 1945 to begin a hatchery with his own sons.[175]

Chicken was in big demand during the Second World War, and the forty hatcheries in the Holland-Zeeland Chick Association made the region a leading national center for white meat production. They raised twelve million chicks in the 1943 season, and many hatcheries sold out for the season, so they geared up to increase production by 25 percent the next year. In one day in April, the peak time, the Zeeland post office shipped two hundred thousand chicks in 2,500 boxes by rail and truck. To meet the rush, the overburdened mail staff had to work nine- and ten-hour days and overtime on Saturday afternoons.[176]

174 Vanderveen, "Legacy of Big Dutchman"; Lozon, "Zeeland's Hatchery Heyday," 16 (quote). I am indebted to Jack Geerlings for information on today's Zeeland hatcheries.

175 Michael Lozon, *The Sun Never Sets on Big Dutchman* (Zeeland, MI: Jack De Witt Family, 2004), 95 and passim; Steve Vanderveen, "The Legacy of the Big Dutchman," *Holland Sentinel*, 27 Mar. 2005, Richard De Witt obit., ibid., 1 Aug. 2010.

176 *Holland City News*, 31 May 1945.

Jack H. (*left*) and Dick (*right*) De Witt inspect poults at their Zeeland Hatchery, late 1930s (*Archives, Holland Historical Trust*)

After the war, in 1947, Jack and Dick De Witt began raising broilers and hens for the table, to fill the void at the hatcheries in the off-season (Broiler Chick Producers). This coincided with the transition in food retailing from corner groceries to supermarkets, and the latter placed orders in the tens of thousands instead of the hundreds. Jack De Witt's vision was to feed the world with healthy poultry white meat. But the large groceries demanded lower prices, and this required more efficient production methods than was common in the smaller labor-intensive poultry farms. To gain the necessary efficiencies of scale, the De Witts devised an automatic feeding system that used a chain to push the feed through troughs to the birds. They formed the Automatic Poultry Feeder division in 1948 to produce and commercialize the feeders. Next came automatic watering, litter cleaning, and ventilation systems. In short, the De Witts vertically integrated poultry production by creating a half dozen specialized firms, all of which eventually became part of the Big Dutchman empire.

The De Witts adopted the name Big Dutchman as their trademark after customers so dubbed one of the company salesmen, because of his towering height and girth. By 1953 they were shipping poultry throughout the United States and for the first time to overseas markets. In 1958 Josef Meerpohl joined Big Dutchman in Germany. In 1959 the

Big Dutchman brochure featuring early poultry feeder, late 1940s
(*courtesy Big Dutchman*)

De Witts applied their business model in the Netherlands, which was the first of dozens of De Witt operations around the globe. Thus, Michael Lozon could aptly title his history of the company, *The Sun Never Sets on Big Dutchman*. In 1964 the Lyndon Johnson Administration awarded Big Dutchman the coveted E citation for "outstanding contributions to the export expansion of the United States."[177]

In these years Big Dutchman needed capital for expansion, especially to manufacture the automated feeding systems that poultry producers the world over were demanding. The only answer was to go public and issue shares on the New York Stock Exchange, but this put the company in play. In 1968 the brothers sold out to a New York-based conglomerate, US Industries, for $40 million in ISI stock, and they retired three years later.[178]

ISI eventually stumbled, and in 1981 sold out to another conglomerate, which in turn was acquired by a German firm headed by Josef Meerpohl, a former Big Dutchman distributor in northern Europe and longtime friend of the De Witt brothers. The Meerpohl family

177 Lozon, *Big Dutchman*, vi, 95.

178 Vanderveen, "Switch to turkeys." In 1968 Jack and Dick De Witt gave $600,000 to Hope College toward the $2.1 million Student Cultural and Social Center, the largest single gift in college history (Hope College *Anchor*, 13 Sept. 1968).

Bernd Meerpohl celebrating Jack H. De Witt's 100th birthday in January 2011. De Witt died a year later (*courtesy Big Dutchman*).

developed the business into a truly world-wide enterprise. The Holland plant was on East Fortieth Street at Waverly Road from 1989 to 2006, when it moved into spacious facilities at 3900 John F. Donnelly Drive in the Northside Industrial Park. For the last twelve years the business has been managed by Josef's eldest son, Bernd Meerpohl. In 2012 the Big Dutchman Group of companies included twenty-six companies around the world and nearly two-hundred distributors. They employ 2,500 globally—115 in the United States—and sales have surpassed $1 billion. The product line covers everything a chicken or hog producer might need to take care of his animals, including fully computerized feeding systems and other new technologies. Big Dutchman Inc., the group's unit responsible for the American continent, thrives at their location on the north side of Holland.[179]

Animal-related industries

Because of the general farming and livestock production of the region, meatpacking, rendering, fertilizer, and gelatin plants sprang up. In the 1880s the B. Wieck Glue Factory rendered carcasses in a plant on the lakefront at Howard Street. The Holland Gelatin Works, built

179 I am indebted to Clovis Rayzel, manager of Big Dutchman's Holland operations, for this recent history.

in 1908 north of the Black River on a rail spur, turned animal parts into a million pounds per year of pure food gelatin for the manufacture of jelly powders, confectionery, and ice cream, until it closed in 1914. The most prominent packing plant was the Holland Packing House, which at least once, in 1924, ran afoul of the state meat inspector for shipping tainted meat. The company blamed its Chicago shipper. In 1927 John Boone and Thomas Robinson of Holland and W. L. Eaton of Waukazoo and Chicago invested $25,000 to reorganize the company as a strictly wholesale operation. Its processing plant was located on West Fourteenth Street and a slaughtering plant on East Eighth Street. The West Michigan Packing Company, which began in 1925 in one of the buildings of Holland Aniline Company, in 1927 became a branch of a Kalamazoo firm, but remained under local management.[180]

Theodore "Ted" Everse and John Vredeveld in 1940 relocated Holland Meat Co. (Henry House after 1967) of Grandville to 700 Michigan Avenue (now Skip's Pharmacy). They slaughtered hogs there and processed the bellies into hams, bacon, and sausage. The clever plaque on the office wall in the shape of a pig said it best: "May your friends be many—your troubles few and all your sausages long." About 1965 the firm moved north of Black River to 300 Roost Street, and Everse's four sons took over, with Lyle as president. The firm, renamed Henry House, by 1980 had eighty-four employees, who turned pork bellies from slaughterhouses into trimmed, skinned, and cured hams and hot dogs. Some 60 percent of which went to food services and 40 percent to retailers.[181]

Subsequent owners, Holly Farms in 1987, Tyson Foods in 1989, and Boar's Head Provisions in 2000, processed pork products mainly for the restaurant and hospitality industries. Tyson Foods closed Henry House in 1995, idling 460 workers. Boar's Head, the New York-based meat processor, bought the defunct plant in 2000 and began operations with thirteen employees. Boar's Head made the plant a success, something that had eluded Henry House and Tyson Foods. In 2005 Boar's Head expanded its Holland plant into a national distribution center, boosting employment from 420 to 535 and increasing production from 1.5 to 2 million pounds a week. In 2008 the plant was expanded again, and the workforce increased to eight hundred, mostly Hispanics. Chris Antrup, the plant manager for many

180 Sanborn fire insurance map, Holland, 1883; *Holland: The Gateway of Western Michigan*; *Holland City News*, 4 Apr., 17 July, 29 Sept., 20 Nov. 1927, 27 June, 9 Oct. 1929, "Twenty Five Years Ago Today," 1 June 1933.

181 *Holland Sentinel*, 26 Jan. 1980.

years, successfully overcame the language barrier with workers by hiring bilingual overseers. Russ Rubley, the current manager, reported in 2010 that his six hundred employees processed fifty truckloads of raw meat and poultry per week and shipped out 105 truckloads of product.[182]

A pork processing company with a lower profile is Quincy Street Inc., located at 13350 Quincy Street. Since the founding by Douglas Hekman in 1994, Quincy Street has become one of Michigan's largest pork processing plants, producing from twenty-five to thirty million pounds annually of ham, sausages, and roasts. During the 2011 Christmas season alone, the firm shipped one million hams. Since 1996 CEO and president Hekman has led four plant expansions that quintupled the floor space, with another expansion planned for 2013. The workforce since 1996 has grown from 25 to 175, all with good benefit packages. The firm donates 10 percent of pre-tax profits to religious and community groups, as Ed Prince practiced at Prince Corp. in the 1970s and 1980s. Such tithing is rare and limited to privately-held companies.[183]

Rendering works

"The question has been for a long time what will you do with dead animals?" noted Bernard Wick in an 1877 advertisement in the *Holland City News*. Farmers needed a place to bring dead livestock, butchers needed a place to take meat scraps and bones, and housewives needed soap made from animal fat and lye. Rendering works transformed the offal into soap. Wick, who had a rendering plant near Metz Tannery across the Black River Bridge on Howard Street, offered "to remove all dead animals at his own expense." In the 1890s a soap factory on the northeast corner of Sixth Street and Central Avenue collected dead animals and meat scraps. Stanley Curtis, who was a boy then, recalled that the factory "made soap out of wood ashes and animal fats. They used to go around to the houses and collect the wood ashes, which everybody burnt in their stove, and in return for the wood ashes, they would leave a bar of this yellow laundry soap in payment. I don't remember who ran this soap factory, but I can remember we used to get this soap in our house for our wood ashes, which we saved."[184]

182 Ibid., 20 Aug. 1997, 10 Dec. 1998, 18 Feb., 27 Dec. 2005, 19 Mar. 2008, 15 Dec. 2010; *Grand Rapids Press Lakeshore Edition*, 18 Feb., 8 Apr. 2005.

183 *Grand Rapids Press*, 30 Nov. 2011; *Holland Sentinel*, 10 Oct. 2012.

184 *Holland City News*, 6 July 1877; Stanley Curtis interview by Donald van Reken, 23 June 1976, typescript, 26, JAH.

Peter A. Kleis, who owned a meat market on Ninth Street from the 1880s, slaughtered livestock on his ten-acre homesite at 225 Lincoln Avenue, which ran from Eighth to Ninth Streets and from east of Columbia to the present-day US-31 bypass. His son, Albert P. Kleis, who had worked for the Pere Marquette Railroad, joined his father by 1905 in operating the meat and hide processing and rendering plant, which became the Holland Rendering Works.[185] In 1918 the slaughterhouse of Kleis was one of ten caught in a surprise inspection by Byron B. Godfrey, Holland's health officer, and William Remus, the state food and drug inspector. Remus reported finding the Kleis plant in a "very dirty, filthy, and unsanitary" condition, where meat cattle were being butchered along with "old, decrepit and sick horses" for rendering. The officer banned Kleis from slaughtering livestock and limited his business to rendering and processing hides. Neighbor Fred Hieftje on East Sixteenth Street was found to be slaughtering tuberculous cattle in unsanitary conditions. The officer closed his plant and ordered him to clean and repair his building and sterilize his tools. Hieftje complied, and the ban was lifted a week later after a second visit by Godfrey found him in compliance.[186]

In 1929 Albert's son Russell Kleis joined the Holland Rendering Works, which remained in the family for four generations over eight decades. Kleis continued as president until his death in 1977 at age one hundred! Then his youngest son Albert P. Jr. moved up from vice president to president and son Russell moved from secretary treasurer to vice president. Albert Sr. served as a First Ward alderman for sixteen years between 1923 and 1941, and Albert Jr., a veteran of the US Army Air Corps in the Second World War, emulated him in the 1970s. Holland Rendering bought skins of deer, mink, raccoon, muskrat, and any other animals that could be rendered. In 1954 the company employed sixteen men. In the 1960s, when alewives washed up on Lake Michigan beaches by the thousands, Holland Rendering announced it could handle from five- to ten thousand pounds of fish per day. Over time, the plant converted animal by-products into fatty acid for paint, soap, cosmetics, and plastics and for protein for livestock feed.[187]

In the rerouting of US-31, Kleis and the State of Michigan had a legal tussle over the taking of his plant and land. The state in 1947

185 Albert P. Kleis Jr. interview by Donald van Reken, 3 June 1974, typescript, 3, JAH.

186 *Holland City News*, 18 Aug., 12 Sept. 1918; *Holland City Directories*, 1894, 1897-98, 1901-2; *Holland Sentinel*, 4 Jan. 1961, 17 May 2010.

187 *Holland City Directory*, 1929; *Holland Sentinel*, 4 Apr. 1954, 9 Dec. 1957, 4 Jan. 1964, "Twenty-five Years Ago Today" 11 Apr. 1966, 6 Apr. 1968, 27 Aug. 1970, 23 Nov. 1973, 14 Apr. 1976, 24 Jan. 1981.

offered Kleis $35,000 for his acreage, which he refused, believing $175,000 to be a fair price. The state played hardball by instituting condemnation proceedings, and a judge set the value at $80,000. Highway Commissioner Charles Ziegler appealed the ruling twice to the Michigan Supreme Court and lost both times. Albert Kleis told a *Sentinel* reporter that he and his sons had "always wanted to do what is right and honest and have tried to cooperate all the time. . . . We have served the community for almost fifty years and want to continue to serve." Holland Rendering used the proceeds to erect a plant on Primrose Street south of Chicago Drive, between the Black River and the C & O Railroad tracks.[188]

Fearing noxious odors, a coalition of local residents hired an attorney and sought to block the plan, but they failed in the absence of zoning ordinances. Seeing the predicament of the Holland Township trustees, the city council in 1953 enacted a "nuisance industries" ordinance to make certain that they had the last word concerning the more than fifty such companies operating in the city. The company offices were always located at the Kleis home at 225 Lincoln Avenue. In 1980 Holland Rendering's seven radio-dispatched trucks serviced slaughterhouses, supermarkets, restaurants, and farms within a one-hundred-mile radius and collected up to 350 tons a week. One recycled product was turkey feathers, which the company processed into "feather meal," a high-protein feed additive. A. James Kleis, who began as a truck driver, was the general manager for more than three decades, beginning in 1965 and until the mid-1990s when he left. Albert Jr. retired in 1980, and Russell became president. He continued as president until he retired in 1989 and sold the company to a firm that consolidated operations elsewhere. It was the end of another four-generation business in Holland.[189]

Fertilizer companies

Holland-area farmers in the 1920s used seven thousand tons of fertilizer a year, which kept two commercial fertilizer companies—Holland Fertilizer and Van's Fertilizer—busy, but only Van's survived the Depression. Holland's Waste Water treatment plant provided another source of fertilizer, namely sludge, which was free for the taking. The Holland Fertilizer mixing plant stood on Lake (later Pine)

188 *Holland Sentinel*, 1 Apr. 1953, 4 Jan., 4 Apr. 1954.

189 *Holland City News*, 21 Aug., 6 Nov. 1952, 23 Apr. 1953; *Holland Sentinel*, 24 Jan. 1981; *Holland City Directories*, 1965, 1988, 1990.

Avenue between Twelfth and Thirteenth Streets, opposite the sugar factory. Van's Fertilizer, the larger of the two, was owned by John "Vaudie" Vandenberg and his brothers, William and Ben, and managed by Peter Braamse, an expert with over twenty years' experience mixing fertilizers. In 1925 Van's Fertilizer, with a projected workforce of twenty men, opened a new plant on James Street along the Pere Marquette tracks. Van's gradually transformed itself into a chemical company, and in 1931, the Vandenbergs sold the company to the Smith Agricultural Chemical Company of Columbus, Ohio. Two years later Van's was given the Smith name, and Dick Miles took over general management of the Holland plant. Smith Agricultural Chemical doubled the capacity of its Holland subsidiary to twenty thousand tons a year by installing new machinery and a complete conveyor system. Smith Chemical was then Holland's sole fertilizer plant, and it had annual sales of $200,000 under the trade name Sacco, the initials of the company.[190]

Fox farming

One specialized national industry that came to Holland after the First World War was the raising of fox for the luxury fur trade. Muskegon entrepreneurs had demonstrated the profitability of fox farming during the war, and the Sawdust City with more than twenty fox farms was the national center of the business. In 1920 James H. Kelly, formerly of Holland, and E. F. Alberts brought the industry to Holland by organizing the Holland Silver & Black Fox Company, capitalized at $20,000. Lee De Feyter sold his farm near Pine Creek on the Grand Haven Pike for the operation and joined the company as treasurer and manager. Other local principals were Harry Hundley, hardware merchant Arend Siersma, and William Buis Sr. of Buis & Son Upholstery. The operation began with eight breeding pairs, valued at $2,000 each, that came originally from the prized Prince Edward Island stock, which was deemed the best strain in North America. The pelts brought an attractive price of $400 and more at the national St. Louis market, and the new venture enjoyed considerable success. The National Silver Fox Breeders Association in Muskegon promoted the industry in the Midwest. One issue the industry faced was taxes. Muskegon classed the animals as domestic and assessed them $100 per fox, but the ranchers refused to pay, claiming the animals were wild and

190 *Holland City News*, 4 Dec. 1924, 19 Feb. 1925, 28 Nov. 1929, *Holland Sentinel*, 19, 20 Feb. 1925, 20 Nov. 1929, 23 Jan. 1931, 2 Feb. 1933, 18 Nov. 1935, 15 Aug. 1947. Russell Kleis died in 2003 and Albert Jr. in 2010.

thus not subject to tax. But the tax courts ruled against the breeders. Fox farming had a relatively short run before fashions changed in favor of mink fur.[191]

Rabbits and goats

Some Holland residents raised rabbits for meat as a sideline to supplement their day jobs. The secretary of agriculture during the meat rationing of the First World War strongly recommended breeding rabbits for their tasty flesh. Edward Brouwer, director for seventeen years of the Holland Poultry Association, was the first to install a rabbitry and promote their breeding. In the 1920s Dewey Jaarsma, who worked in an ice cream plant, had the largest rabbitry with one hundred head in cages behind his East Twenty-First Street residence. He called rabbit breeding "interesting" and financially "gratifying." Other locals raised guinea pigs for laboratories. In 1928 Jaarsma and several dozen other breeders formed the Greater Holland Rabbit and Cavie Association (later the Holland Rabbit Breeders Association) to breed better stock and develop more efficient marketing. Brouwer served as secretary of the Michigan Rabbit Breeders Association, and he arranged for the rabbit breeders to show their animals in conjunction with the annual Holland poultry exhibitions.[192]

Arthur Hazzard was one of the last residents within the city limits to keep goats—and sometimes cows and calves—in his yard at Twenty-Eighth Street and Van Raalte Avenue. Since city ordinances forbade keeping such animals within 125 feet of neighbors, Hazzard's farm was closed in 1949 when eleven neighbors complained to the common council about odors and fly-infested manure piles.[193]

Confinement agriculture in the poultry industry led to similar enterprises in hogs and dairying. By the 1970s the countryside around Holland was dotted with barns housing a thousand sows, and milking parlors and feedlots with thousands of dairy cows. Given the high concentrations, manure management became a problem for farmers.

Microbreweries

In the 1990s small-scale brewing returned to Holland for the first time in eighty years with three microbreweries that made specialized

[191] *Holland City News*, 22 Jan., 11 Nov., 23 Dec. 1920, 15 June 1922; *Holland Sentinel*, 14 Jan. 1952.

[192] *Holland City News*, 22 Mar. 1928, 18 Dec. 1930, 1 Jan., 19 Mar. 1931, 5 Jan. 1933, 13 May 1954.

[193] Ibid., 4 Aug. 1949.

ales and retailed them in their own pubs. These were Roffey Brewing Co., Black River Bistro & Brewing Co., and New Holland Brewing Co. Jim Roffey's brewery at 697 Lincoln Avenue produced 250,000 gallons a year from 1996 to 2001, and one of his brands was declared the official beer of Holland's sesquicentennial in 1997, to the consternation of many. He sold his business in 2001 to a Grand Rapids brewery that shuttered the Holland plant. Doug Crank and Greg Alspach, co-owners of Black River Bistro & Brewing, in 1997 built a restaurant and brewpub at 13 West Seventh Street that became the Via Maria restaurant and pub. The next year, Jason Spaulding and Brett Vander Kamp of New Holland Brewing opened a brewery and taproom at 205 Fairbanks Avenue. Their 2004 production of five thousand barrels compares favorably with that of Anton Seif in the 1880s. In 2002 Spaulding and Vander Kamp bought the former Vogelzang Hardware store on Eighth Street at College Avenue. In this prime location they offer their specialty brews, notably Dragon's Milk Ale. Chicago in 2002 became the first expansion out of Michigan. In 2006 the partners built a new, larger brewery on Commerce Court in Holland Township, after the Fairbanks Avenue property was razed to make way for Hope College's De Vos Fieldhouse. In 2011 they spent $3 million expanding on Commerce Court to meet the demand for their brews, which have earned a national reputation. New Holland Brewing Co. in 2011 shipped 16,600 barrels of beer to thirteen states and distilled spirits to six states. The future looks bright for the innovative company.[194]

Holland Farmers Market

When the Holland Farmers Market opened in 1978, few would have predicted its success over the next three decades. Unlike its much older Grand Rapids counterpart, consumers, not farmers, launched the Holland market. The initiator was Judy Lukich, an active member of several local food co-ops. Rather than buying in bulk from the Grand Rapids market and divvying up the products among the members, she enlisted the support of the city manager Terry Hofmeyer as co-sponsor of a Saturday Holland market. The city's role was simply to provide free space in the Civic Center parking lot on West Eighth Street. Lukich tapped a growing interest in such a market. The previous summer, the city had sponsored a Farmers Market as part of its Old Fashioned Days

[194] *Grand Rapids Press Lakeshore Edition*, 8 Jan. 1997; *Holland Sentinel*, 26 July 2001, 12 Dec. 1905, 4 June 2006; Roel Garcia, "Tapping for Success" *Holland Sentinel* special New Holland Brewing Co. edition, 10 June 2012; Vander Veen and Greczek, "Hops in Holland"; email from Robert Vande Vusse, 30 July 2007.

downtown event. The Downtown Merchants Association donated $100 in 1979 as a token of their support. Under the hand of market master Brent Buursma, local farmers booked stalls for a $5 vendor's fee and $1 for a table, and sold their fresh produce to eager residents. Later, the market master acceded to the demand to add Wednesdays to the schedule.[195]

As early as 1990, the city mulled costs for a decorative canopy, but the low bid of $2 million in 2003 gave the city council pause. In place of metal, the council decided to substitute cheaper canvas material that resembled vinyl, which carried an eight-year warranty. This kept the total cost at the original bid, but also included resurfacing the Civic Center parking lot, installing a snowmelt system and brick sidewalk pavers on Eighth Street, a center market plaza, and decorative lighting. The canopy runs along both sides of Eighth Street west of Pine Avenue to Maple Avenue, and shelters more than one hundred vendors. Vendors rent stalls by the season, with fees from $300 to $475 in 2008, which helped cover the city's budget of $100,000 to operate the market. The Eighth Street Market Place, the official name, opened in April 2005 under market master Candy Todd, and ever since then eager shoppers have crowded the plaza on market days.[196]

Conclusion

Agricultural industries, from farms to food processors to retailers, are second only to industry as drivers of the local economy. West Michigan's big three food retailers—Meijer, Gordon Food Service (GFS Marketplace), and Spartan Stores (Family Fare, D & W Fresh Market, and Glen's Market)—have a $700 million a year impact on the region. They sell locally grown food and employ tens of thousands. Food processing industries have been mainstays of the economy for more than a century. In 2010 the five major companies—Heinz, Boar's Head Provisions, Sara Lee, Request Foods, and Hudsonville Creamery & Ice Cream—employed 1,500 workers and were looking to hire hundreds more. "People always need to eat," Jerry Shoup, long-time plant manager at Heinz, told a breakfast meeting of the Holland Area Chamber of Commerce. West Michigan's place on the map of the national food industry is solid and secure.[197]

195 *West Michigan Magazine* (Sept. 1980): 29-31.

196 *Holland Sentinel*, 12 Apr. 1990, 3, 12, 25 Sept. 2003, 4 Jan. 2004, 20, 28 Apr., 7, 11, 12 June 2005, 13 May 2008; *Grand Rapids Press Lakeshore Edition*, 25 Sept. 2003, 13 Oct., 14 Nov. 2004, 6 Jan. 2005, 20 May 2007, 1 June 2008; phone conversation with Candy Todd, 13 Feb. 2012.

197 *Grand Rapids Press*, 15 Dec. 2010 (quote), 8 May 2011.

Allegan and Ottawa Counties rank today in the top three agricultural counties in the state. They are among the first five producers of nursery crops, turkeys, blueberries, hogs, dairy, apples, and cattle. Local farmers in recent years have been among the largest beneficiaries of federal government subsidies for field crops. Some farms, such as the Kleinheksel Farm in Ottawa and the Drozd Farms in Allegan have received more than $2 million annually. Farmers in Allegan County were paid $72.5 million between 1995 and 2004 for wheat, corn, alfalfa, and soybeans, under federal farm programs. Ottawa County farmers have received $43 million in federal subsidies. Zeeland Farm Services, the state's largest soybean processor and a major exporter, turns soybean oil into gasohol. Many of those dollars have circulated throughout the local economy, boosting business of all kinds. The Holland area's role as an agricultural market center continues, since two-thirds of the Lake Macatawa watershed is devoted to agriculture. In 2007 total agricultural sales from the three thousand farms in Ottawa and Allegan Counties surpassed $675 million, and land in production actually increased in the previous decade. Over half of the agricultural sales came from livestock and poultry output. As new agricultural technology companies emerge, Holland continues to serve as an incubator for the farm economy.[198]

198 *Holland Sentinel*, 18 Oct. 2006, 3 Nov. 2009, 17 June 2010; *Grand Rapids Press*, 4 Dec. 2005, 2 Nov. 2009; Carl Van Fassen, Jennifer Soukhome, and Graham Peasley, *An Environmental History of the Lake Macatawa Watershed* (Holland, 2009), fig. 5.9.

CHAPTER 18

Shopkeepers City: Early Business and the Professions

Business is the lifeblood of a community, and early Holland had this vitality, thanks to the diligent efforts of its founder, Albertus C. Van Raalte, who was a businessman and entrepreneur at heart.[1] Van Raalte nurtured merchants, dealers, brokers, bankers, teachers, and physicians. Shopkeepers were especially welcome, but not lawyers; the colonists were averse to litigation and content to allow church consistories to settle civil cases. Many craftsmen were found among the immigrants, but few businessmen or professionals. Most were farmers or farm laborers. Americans such as Henry D. Post of Vermont by way of Allegan grasped the opportunities to serve the newcomers, since everyone needed basic foodstuffs. Post in 1847 shipped pork and flour to Holland via the Kalamazoo River to Singapore and Lake Michigan to the mouth of Black Lake, and then by scow into the village. Given the scarcity of cash, most trade was by barter.

From the beginning, the main business district was formed around Eighth and River Streets, the axis of the town. Eighth Street

1 Robert P. Swierenga, "Albertus C. Van Raalte as a Businessman," in Jacob E. Nyenhuis, ed., *A Goodly Heritage: Essays in Honor of the Reverend Dr. Elton J. Bruins at Eighty* (Grand Rapids: Eerdmans, 2007), 281-317.

Jan Binnekant's store (image from H. Lankheet, comp., *Map of Holland City 1870*) (*courtesy Randall P. Vande Water*)

linked Holland to Zeeland and eventually to Grand Rapids along the Chicago Road, and River Street became the main north-south artery and outlet for wharves at the neck of Black Lake. Hollanders opened their first businesses on River Street running north from Eighth toward Fourth Street. In mid-1847 Jan Binnekant opened the Holland Hotel on the northwest corner of Eighth and River Streets in a house moved from the failed town of Superior. Vander Veen recalled that Binnekant "asked grace before each meal, which was closed by all [the boarders] singing a psalm in chorus." Binnekant, a baker by trade, opened the first bakery in a building next door to the hotel, assisted by his wife Gerrigje, who was famous for her "freshly baked cookies." Binnekant later added a print shop and the first bookstore. He traveled the region buying provisions for the settlement and was the city's first provision merchant. He sold his hotel to William Baker (Bakker) in 1853.[2]

2 "Engbertus Vander Veen's Life Reminiscences" (pamphlet 1915), in Henry S. Lucas, *Dutch Immigrant Memoirs and Related Writings* 2 vols. (Assen: Van Gorkum, 1955, 2nd ed. Grand Rapids: Eerdmans, 1997), 1:501; "Edward Cahill's Old Colony Days in Holland [1853-54]," ibid., 1:376; Jan Binnekant obit., *Holland City News*, 19 Feb. 1876; *De Grondwet*, 15 Feb. 1876; *De Hollander*, 10 Sept. 1851, 4 May, 24 Aug. 1853; *De Sheboygan Nieuwsbode* 10 Oct. 1851 (first Holland Hotel ad). The earliest boarders included Arie Van Zoeren, Hendrik "Hein" Meengs, Geert Zalsman, Hendrik Geuring, Hein Van der Haar, and the millwright Bosdyke ("a gentleman of rank" who came from Amsterdam via Canada (Vander Veen, "Reminiscences," in Lucas, *Dutch Immigrant Memoirs* 1:510).

J. BINNEKANT,

Brood-, Beschuit- en Koekebakker. Ook kan men allerlei Suikergoed en alles, wat tot het vak behoort, bij hem verkrijgen. Men kan zich van eene eerlijke bediening verzekerd houden.

Holland, Mich.

Jan Binnekant advertisement in *De Hollander*, Mar. 1857

Colonial Store

A block north of Binnekant's hotel, on the southwest corner of Seventh and River Streets, the People's Assembly in the fall of 1847 opened the Colonial Store and bought a one-hundred-ton schooner in Chicago, renamed the *A. E. Knickerbocker* and piloted by Ale Steginga and his eldest son Menne, to stock it with Chicago goods. The communal venture aimed to buy goods at wholesale, on liberal credit, and sell them at cost. The assembly raised cash by a stock offering, and Jannes Vande Luyster, the wealthy farmer from Borssele, province of Zeeland and "banker of the forest" who platted the town of Zeeland, bought most of it. Van Raalte's right-hand man, Bernardus Grootenhuis, was named manager and Jannes Vande Luyster Jr., his assistant. The assembly commissioned Grootenhuis and Elias G. Young, a young man from the First Reformed Church of Grand Rapids, to travel to New York City and Albany to buy dry goods, groceries, shoes, Yankee notions, and many other articles. When their cash ran out, they charged the rest to "Dominie van Raalte and Company," a fictitious entity that the cleric later had to honor. Johannes Verhorst, a watchmaker, and Adrian Westveer also worked in the store.[3]

The communal endeavor proved the adage that a business owned by everyone is owned by no one. Immigrants carried on the *Knickerbocker* from Chicago to Holland even refused to pay for their voyage. When the goods from the East failed to arrive by the spring of 1848, the entire venture failed; the vessel was sold, and Van Raalte and Vande Luyster Sr. were left with the debt. That Chicago commission merchants

3 Henry S. Lucas, *Netherlanders in America: Dutch Immigration to the United States and Canada, 1789-1950* (Ann Arbor: University of Michigan Press, 1955; reprint, Grand Rapids: Eerdmans, 1989), 96, 99-100; Adrian Van Koevering, Legends of the Dutch: The Story of a Mass Movement of Nineteenth Century Pilgrims (Zeeland, MI: Zeeland Record, 1960), 248-49; "Pioneer Industry," clippings by A. Van Malsen, J. Vande Luyster Jr., Van Schelven Notes, and Wm O. Van Eyck in P. T. Moerdyke Papers, box 4; Vander Veen, "Life Reminiscences," 1:495-96; Young became the first schoolteacher at Zeeland in 1853 and was an accountant in Grand Haven by 1860.

subsequently advertised in *De Hollander*, Holland's first newspaper, shows the importance of the vessel in linking Holland to the region's major emporium. The local newspaper also regularly listed market prices in Chicago. Henry Griffin, a Grand Haven druggist, storekeeper, and provision merchant, ran his schooner *Pioneer* between Holland and Chicago monthly beginning in 1852 to pick up the growing volume of trade. Griffin in 1851 had come to Holland to take the citizenship oath of Holland men (chapter 24). Beginning in 1850, his Variety Cash Store in Grand Haven regularly advertised its $5,000 worth of merchandise in *De Hollander*. Holland merchants also joined together to buy goods in Chicago and chartered the *Pioneer* and other schooners to carry them back. Since Holland had no harbor, the vessels would have to anchor offshore, offload the cargo to "jawls" (scows) to cross the sandbar at the mouth, and then transfer the goods again to flatboats to traverse Black Lake. It was laborious process and fraught with risk of storms that could make offloading the scows impossible or damaging to the goods (chapter 10).[4]

Pioneer merchants

In 1848 Post opened a general store in Holland (Post & Co.) on Eighth Street, as did Aldert Plugger, one of the most successful early entrepreneurs, with his partners Binnekant and Willem Houtkamp. Post carried "groceries of all kinds" but advertised his high profit items–liquor "for medical purposes," coffee and tea, gold and silver jewelry, and patent medicines such as Harlem Oil and Bailey's Magical Pain Extractor. As was customary on the frontier where specie (gold or silver coins) was scarce, Post offered customers store goods in exchange for farm produce. One ad read: "10,000 bushels of good ground corn in exchange for goods." Merchants like Post offered to give suppliers 18¢ in gold or 20¢ in store goods for their merchandise. Post was a notary public and insurance, tax, and land agent. He even handled purchases at the federal land office in Ionia, which saved customers from making the onerous trip themselves. In 1855 Post gave his store the pretentious name, the New York Store, and began advertising in English. In 1859 he rented space to tailor Renze Postma. Post's younger brothers Hoyt and Charles F. clerked in his store. Henry Post was the premier merchant of early Holland; by 1870 he reported owning $41,000 in lands and goods to the US census marshal.[5]

4 *De Hollander*, 4 Jan. 1851, 15, 22 Sept., 13 Oct., 15 Dec. 1852; Vander Veen interview on his 87th birthday ("This is the day they celebrate," *Holland City News*, 1 Apr. 1915).

5 *De Hollander*, Dec. 1850, 4 (quote), 18, 25 Jan., 18 Sept. 1851, 15 Dec. 1853, 5 Mar., 30 May 1855, 23 Apr. 1859; Jannes van de Luyster Jr. (Holland) to Hendrik de Kruif

Jan Vissers started a bakery, but most housewives baked their own bread. To survive he sold beer by the glass on Saturdays to church-going folks who wanted to smoke, drink beer, and talk about Van Raalte's "sermons, the Bible, and Christian comfort." Critics castigated Vissers' "church saloon," as it was dubbed, and he finally closed it to keep the peace. Tinsmith Jacob Van Der Veen began the first hardware store with his son Engbertus. It was called Corner Hardware, because it stood on the southeast corner of River and Eighth Streets. Jacob Van Der Veen paid Van Raalte $43 for the lot. In his reminiscences, Engbertus recalled that upon his father's arrival in the colony, Jacob opened his box of tinsmith tools, started a fire to heat his solder irons, and began soldering tin, using a fallen tree as his workbench. Jacob died in 1849, and his wife and son carried on the store.[6]

Pieter F. Pfanstiehl sold leather goods, mirrors, shears, thread, and shoes in his general store on the southwest corner of River and Eighth Streets (now Reader's World). Jeweler Geert Albers carried clocks and jewelry in his store on Eighth Street, which continued under various owners into the twentieth century. Jan Nagel set up a smithy in 1850; blacksmith Hendrik (Hein) Meengs joined him in 1852, and the pair promised to make a machine before the 1853 harvest that could shuck a bushel of corn in five minutes. Willem Brouwer in 1853 opened a tailor shop in his home on Eighth and Cedar (College) Streets (the future site of Vogelzang Hardware). In 1860 he added a barber chair and also did "cupping" (*koppen zetting*), a folk procedure of drawing blood from a cut in the arm with a cupping glass, in order to remove "impure or surplus" blood. Brouwer lost his home and tailor shop in the Holland Fire of 1871, but he quickly rebuilt. The census marshals counted eight tailors in 1850 and ten in 1860. Jan Roest (John Roost) and Ame Vennema in 1853 built the first wagon shop, ending the need to buy wagons and wagon parts in Chicago. A year later, Roost sold out to his partner for other ventures. Gerrit Slink and Pieter Zalsman began

---

(Zeeland), 17 Jan. 1851, Jannes van de Luijster Papers, Holland Museum Archives (HMA); 1870 federal manuscript population census, Holland, Michigan.

6 This section relies on Jacob Van Hinte, *Netherlanders in America: A Study of Emigration and Settlement in the Nineteenth and Twentieth Centuries in the United States of America* (in Dutch, Groningen, 1928), Robert P. Swierenga, gen. ed., Adriaan de Wit, chief translator (Grand Rapids: Baker Book House, 1985), 235-36; Vander Veen, "Life Reminiscences," 1:492, 513; "A Contemporary Account of the Holland Fire," in Lucas, *Dutch Immigrant Memoirs,* 2:494; "Cahill's Old Colony Days in Holland," ibid., 1:375; *De Hollander*, 4, 18 Jan. 1851, 21 July, 1 Dec. 1852, 12 Dec. 1855; *Holland City News*, 16 Aug. 1943; Peter T. Moerdyke, "Pioneer Businesses," in P. T. Moerdyke Papers, box 4, HMA, citing advertisements in *De Hollander*, 1850-60.

a sash, blind, and door shop to supply carpenters and builders locally with these products.[7]

In the next few years, new stores appeared regularly, as seen in advertisements in *De Hollander*. In 1852 Jannes Vande Luyster Jr. and Leendert Schaddelee opened a general store opposite that of Binnekant & Houtkamp. Forty years later, Schaddelee's store, a landmark in the First Ward, was still going under Pieter (Peter) H. Prins & Gerrit Rooks. By 1853 Aldert Plugger was exporting oats and other products to Chicago on his own schooner. In 1855 he built a two-story building, with an adjoining large storeroom that was "well *filled* with goods when his fall stock first opened," according to a report on mercantile trade in *De Hollander*.[8]

Isaac B. Bailey opened a general store on River Street opposite Post's *saleratus* (baking soda) factory. Within a year, Bailey sold out to George Tarrey and lumberman Oswald Van der Sluis, another notary and one of the wealthiest colonists. In 1852 John Kerler's general store, among other items, carried pipes, eyeglasses, snuff boxes (*snijfdoozen*), children's toys, and even ice skates; he also dealt in furs and hides. By this point the village of Holland had seven stores, two hotels, a bakery, a hardware dealer, tailor shop, and jewelry store. In Zeeland, Klaas Smit and Jan Busquet began a general store, as Jan Rabbers did in Groningen.[9]

In 1852 E. J. Harrington started a clothing store next door to Henry Post's residence on River Street, and in 1853 the brothers Derk and Hendrik Te Roller, both merchant tailors, advertised the latest fashions and kept a number of tailors busy making suits. Albert Bakker opened a shoe store in 1854 opposite Schaddelee's store; he sold out the next year to Benjamin Ploeg. In 1855 Cornelius Vander Veere established the Grand Haven House on River and Sixth Streets, giving the village three hotels. Shoemaker Ernest Herold, German-born, started another boot and shoe store in 1856, and in 1857 Aaron Geerlings started a tin shop next door to Schaddelee, and shoemaker Lucas Sprietsma began selling foot ware out of his home. In 1859 in partnership with shoemaker Adrianus Verplanke, the pair built a store diagonally across from Post's store and post office. This was the start of the three-generation

7 "Century-Old Business Recalls Colorful History" (James A. Brouwer family history), *Holland Sentinel*, 22 Feb. 1986; *De Hollander*, 13 Apr., 3 Aug., 1853, 27 Dec. 1871. Willem Brouwer, obit., *De Grondwet*, 23 Apr. 1872, John Roost obit., ibid., 2 June 1885, translated by P. T. Moerdyke, P. T. Moerdyke Papers, box 2, HMA; 1850 and 1860 US population censuses for Holland Township.

8 *De Hollander*, 12 Dec. 1855, 23 Apr. 1859; *Holland City News*, 10 May 1890.

9 *De Hollander*, 9 Feb. 1853. The 1850 federal population census for Holland Township listed Oswald Van der Sluis with $2,000 in real estate, second only to Van Raalte with $2,600.

Sprietsma family shoe store that continued in the 1930s. Ryk Takken arrived from Grand Rapids to establish a blacksmith shop in 1858, the same year that Jacob Flieman began his wagon shop on River Street, which grew into the largest such shop in Holland (chapter 17). In 1859 Te Roller Bros. moved in above Plugger's store, while Jan W. Bosman, a tailor, broke ground for a new clothing store. He had arrived in Holland only two years before by way of Grand Rapids.[10]

In 1859 German-born Charles J. Pfaff began his *Duitsche stoor*, and his advertisements filled nearly an entire column of *De Hollander*. The same year Henry Vaupell of Livingston County, New York, a saddle and harness maker brought his trade to Holland. In 1860 implement dealer Richard K. Heald from New York announced his store and factory on River and Eleventh Streets; photographer I. I. Barker set up shop above Vander Veen's hardware store, and Joos De Koeyer, the first shoemaker in the colony, ran a boot and shoe store on the corner of Market and Eighth Streets for many years. These local merchants exercised great power by virtue of the poverty and dependency of the populace. Many immigrants with cash cut out the middlemen and went for provisions to Anton Schorno's store at Hamilton, and to Singapore, Newark, Allegan, and Grand Haven, where the merchants coveted their gold *willempjes*, a Dutch guilder coin worth from three to four dollars in trade. Tanner A. S. Wells of Newark offered the "highest market prices in cash" for "Hides!!! Hides!!! Hides!!!" In western Fillmore Township, everyone traded at Graafschap Hardware, founded in 1860 by the C. Mulder family. After more than 150 years in the family, it is now in the hands of Harlan Lubbers, a seventh-generation descendant.[11]

Merchants had to be creative in paying their bills from out-of-town companies in the era before Congress created the National Banking System in 1863. Absolute trust among businessmen was vital, and a man's word was his bond. This is evident in Pieter Pfanstiehl's letter of June 23, 1858, to a dealer on Chicago's South Water Street wholesale market:

> Dear Sir and Friend!
>
> In response to your letter of June 11, I would like to report to you that I have informed [Henry] Koningsberg [Koenigsberg, a

10 *De Hollander*, 13 Oct. 1852, 12 Dec. 1855, 23 Apr. 1859; *Holland City News*, 5 Feb. 1887. The Sprietsma store passed from father Lucas to son Simon in the late 1880s and to grandson Nicolas in 1908 (*Holland City News*, 4 Sept. 1913).

11 *De Hollander*, 23 Apr. 1859, De Koeyer obit., ibid., 21 Dec. 1886; *Holland Sentinel*, 5 Sept. 2010. Mulder's descendants, the Brink and Lubbers families, among others, operated the hardware store.

German saloonkeeper in Holland] of the contents of your letter. Would you please be so good and go with the enclosed to the indicated address. I still need to receive money for leather there that he has sent to Boston for me; subtract from that the $25.00 for Koningsberg and send me a receipt of that. Will you be so kind as to pay Mr. Bowen Brothers for me the balance of the money that you will receive; 72 Lake Street [Chicago]. Ask for Mr. Hurl who is clerk in the grocery store downstairs, and if he happens not to be at home go upstairs where the dry goods are stored. Say that I will be in Chicago soon myself, and will pay the balance. I would also appreciate it if you could order twelve pieces of mosquito mesh (preferably blue) and six pieces of Fremont sheeting. This week Plugger's ship will arrive and then I will send for it.

I am in the grocery business these days with Flanders McKinley & Co. Be so kind to ask for me there what is the lowest price of salt. I need 50 barrels soon. I can get it in Grand Haven for $1.85 per barrel, and freight to Holland per barrel cost 25 cent. Check for me whether you can find it cheaper, and be so kind as to report that to me as soon as possible.

I do not have specific news here that would warrant your attention. There are many complaints about the bad times, as is the case everywhere.

Greetings to you, and yours, and Mr. Pasdeloup
Your servant and friend,
P. F. Pfanstiehl

Ps. Flanders McKinley & Co.
Address: 79 South Water Street

Have you found any opportunity for schinkels [shingles]? I cannot use Schiedam gin, for I do not sell any liquor anymore. I was fined for that.[12]

The Dutch colony prospered. Already in 1849 the assessed valuation of real (realty) and personal property (personalty) in Holland Township surpassed that of Ottawa Township (including Grand Haven). Holland's valuation was $102,000 in realty and $71,000 in personalty, compared to Ottawa Township's $71,000 in realty and $23,000 in

12 P. F. Pfanstiehl, Holland, to "My Esteemed Friend," Chicago, 23 June 1858, H. J. Coster Papers, HMA. Schiedam was the center of the Netherlands distillery industry, particularly producing gin.

personalty. By 1864 the assessed valuation of real estate in Holland Township surpassed that of Grand Haven Township—$177,000 and $145,000—although the county seat reported more personalty—$69,000 and $32,500. Because Grand Haven was an older and more developed city, the township committee on equalization increased its realty assessment (by up to 30 percent) and reduced that of Holland Township (by up to 18 percent). In essence, Grand Haven residents bore a larger share of county expenses for many years, even though Holland was virtually its equal. The growing prosperity of Holland prompted the editor of the *Grand Haven News* to call his readers to "arouse from a state of indifference, if not stupidity, and earnestly engage to building up and improving the place of their homes and businesses."[13]

In June 1860, when the federal census marshal made his rounds and recorded the value of real and personal property for each family, nine men self-reported property worth at least $5,000. The land-rich Van Raalte topped the list at $14,800 in land and $1,300 in personalty. Lumber magnate Manly D. Howard came next with $11,500 in land and $2,000 in personalty, followed by merchant Henry D. Post and millwright William K. Flietstra with total wealth of $8,000, merchant Pieter Pfanstiehl $7,000, merchant Aldert Plugger $6,900, "gentleman" Jan Trimpe $5,7000, lumberman Nicholas Vyn $5,200, and miller Jan Pauels $5,000. Merchandizing and milling were the ways to gain a competence in early Holland.

Doctors in the colony

In the first years, Dutch clerics had to be doctor, dominie, and father to their flocks, just as George N. Smith did with his Black River Band of Ottawa Indians (chapter 1). Van Raalte at Holland, Cornelius Vander Meulen at Zeeland, Seine Bolks at Overisel, and Marten A. Ypma at Vriesland all dispensed medicines to the sick. Their followers praised them for their doctoring and life-saving care. Only Bolks had studied medicine in the Netherlands. The others had to learn on the job, mainly by asking advice of Smith, who had a decade of experience, and by consulting with Allegan and Grand Haven doctors when they infrequently came to the colony to tend the sick. The State of Michigan did not license doctors until 1883; before then, according to a Supreme Court ruling: "A doctor is any person calling himself such."[14]

13 *Grand Haven News*, 8 June, 26 Oct. 1864.

14 Jan Peter Verhave, *Disease and Death Among the Early Settlers in Holland, Michigan* (Lecture Series No. 4, Van Raalte Institute, Hope College, 2006), 33-44 (quote 38), gives a comprehensive history of doctors, diseases, and drugs; Van Koevering, *Legends*

Several settlers later recalled Van Raalte's doctoring. Grootenhuis saw him hold daily office hours, and go "night and day, in all kinds of weather . . . giving aid both spiritually and for the health of the body." During the "dying time" in the summer of 1847 from dysentery, malaria, smallpox, and other diseases, all brought on by overwork, poor hygiene, and inadequate food and shelter, "our never-to-be-forgotten Dominie van Raalte . . . comforted the sick. Every morning he received patients at his house, administering medicine with a tablespoon. Around him were bottles of quinine [for malaria], blue pills [mercury for consumption, etc.], and rhubarb root extract [a purgative for bowel complaints]. The log kitchen served as a waiting room; the sick sat on a long board bench." Once in the middle of a sermon that first summer, the exhausted dominie exclaimed: "Must we all die now?" The congregation took comfort in the assurance that sickness and death are in God's hands.[15]

The people trusted their dominies more than the so-called doctors who came and went in the first months. Engbertus Vander Veen recalled at least two quacks, a horse doctor who prescribed nothing but whiskey for humans, and a sheep herder who sold mutton "at a good price" as a cure-all. Their only purpose was "to fill their pockets."[16]

J. J. M. C. Van Nus, from the province of Zeeland, practiced medicine in the Dutch military before immigrating in the summer of 1847. He was the only trained physician among the Dutch immigrants and practiced for four years, until moving to Pella, Iowa in 1851. Chauncey B. Goodrich, a native of upstate New York who practiced in nearby Newark since 1843, was the first outsider to treat the Dutch. Van Raalte made recruiting a resident doctor his top priority. In October 1848 he advertised for a physician, and the next year Charles D. Shenick of Lockport, New York came with his wife and children and settled in New Groningen, midway between Holland and Zeeland. Shenick earned the trust of the Dutch and served them until moving farther west in 1854; N. R. Parsons of Connecticut continued his practice until he died in 1860. Isaac D. Bailey, a physician, surgeon and obstetrician, opened an office and apothecary in the Zeeland Hotel in 1851; he soon

of the Dutch, 349. See also "Mrs. J. H. [Grietje] Boone's Journey and Arrival of Tamme Vanden Bosch," in Lucas, *Dutch Immigrant Memoirs,* 1:257 (quote); "Cornelius van Loo's Zeeland Township and Village," in ibid., 1:249; "James de Pree's Reverend Seine Bolks," in ibid., 2:374, 381.

15 Bernardus Grootenhuis, *Our History*, trans. P. T. Moerdyke, HMA; Verhave, *Disease and Death*, 33-34, 37.

16 "Engbertus Vander Veen's Life Reminscences [1915]," in Lucas, *Dutch Immigrant Memoirs,* 1:497.

moved his office into the home of Groningen schoolteacher Anneus J. Hillebrands. Willem Van den Berg located in Groningen in 1854, and Daniel Baert apprenticed under him and opened his renowned practice in Zeeland in 1862. Van den Berg moved to Drenthe in 1857. Baert's mother Maatje (Aling) practiced midwifery in the colony, having trained in Middelburg, province of Zeeland.[17]

Van Raalte was greatly relieved when in early 1853 the doctor brothers, Wells R. and Charles P. Marsh of Kalamazoo, settled in Holland. This gave Shenick some relief in setting broken limbs and treating frontier diseases. The Marsh brothers graduated from Michigan University (later the University of Michigan) and practiced throughout the thinly settled colony, which then covered two hundred square miles. Apparently, their patients were slow to pay up, and the brothers ran advertisements in *De Hollander* demanding that all accounts be settled immediately. "No one can expect that we can live without being paid for past services," they declared. In 1855 Wells R. left for a professorship at the State University of Iowa, and in 1859, the elderly Charles P. retired and returned to Kalamazoo. He sold his "large and profitable" practice to two young Americans doctors, James Sutton of Pennsylvania and William Dowd of New York, who moved their apothecary and office above Plugger's store and Albert De Weerd's meat market. In March 1856, A. M. Smith established a practice at William Vander Veere's Hotel and continued for almost a year, leaving in February 1857.[18]

Bernardus Ledeboer, a graduate of the University of Groningen, settled in Holland in 1859, upon Van Raalte's invitation and a guarantee of two-years' salary. Ledeboer had immigrated already in 1834 and practiced in New York City until relocating to Grand Rapids in 1857. He bought Pfanstiehl's apothecary and took the business into his new home kitty-corner from the printery of *De Hollander*. He advertised the "cheapest prices" for patent and "genuine" medicines. Ledeboer, who also practiced surgery and obstetrics, became the most prominent Holland physician of the nineteenth century and gave leadership in medicine, politics, religion, and education. Almost immediately, he was elected to the school board and served with assiduity term after term for twenty years. After the Civil War, Ledeboer entered local politics as a Democrat. In 1867 he became the city health officer and in 1868 was

17 Verhave, *Disease and Death*, 40-41, 43; Van Koevering, *Legends of the Dutch*, 349; Lucas, *Netherlanders in America*, 115; *De Hollander*, 13 Mar., 1 May 1851; "Adriaan Keizer's Drenthe History to the Present [1911]," in Lucas, *Dutch Immigrant Memoirs*, 1:262.

18 *De Hollander*, 4 May 1853, 1 May 1854, 29 Aug., 24 Oct. 1855, 8 Sept., 20, 27 Oct. 1859; Verhave, *Disease and Death*, 41.

Physician Geert Manting of Overisel sporting a luxurious mutton chop beard, 1880s (*Archives, Holland Historical Trust*)

elected mayor for three terms and led the fire-ravaged city in 1871 to recovery. He also served as elder in the Hope Church consistory and on the board of trustees of Hope College, where he favored admitting women. His son, druggist Frank S., returned to Holland in 1873 as a physician and practiced in Gerrit Van Schelven's office on Eighth Street. At Ledeboer's death in 1879, he was mourned by all; he was the senior physician in the city and one of its foremost leaders.[19]

In the 1860s, besides Baert in Zeeland, Geert Manting began doctoring in Fillmore Township two miles south of Holland. (Manting's beautiful home, built in 1868, stood at what later became Fortieth Street and Michigan Avenue, the current site of John H. Arendshorst's Holland Eye Surgery and Laser Center.) A son of a doctor in the Netherlands, Manting worked in Overisel as a baker, while he resumed the study of medicine begun as a teenager under his father. He developed into a proficient country doctor of the old school—kindly and compassionate to all and charitable to the poor. R. B. Best began a long practice in Overisel in 1874, interrupted twice in the early years for further medical studies in New York.[20]

After the Civil War, Holland attracted three New York-born physicians, a dentist, and a midwife practitioner certified in the Netherlands. Dr. Thomas E. Annis, a graduate of Chicago's prestigious

19 Philip Phelps, "Bernardus Ledeboer," *The Anchor* 6 (Dec. 1892): 46-48; *De Hollander*, 18 Aug., 1 Sept. 1859, 25 Apr. 1860; *Holland City News*, 25 Jan. 1873, 25 Apr. 1874, Bernardus Ledeboer, obit., 15 Oct., 18 Oct. 1879.

20 Verhave, *Disease and Death*, 42; 1870 federal manuscript population census of Holland city; *History of Allegan and Barry Counties, Michigan, with Illustrations and Biographical Sketches of their Prominent Men and Pioneers* (Philadelphia, 1880), 308; *Holland City News*, 15 Dec. 1877, 6, 20 Mar. 1880; "Old Manting Home is 100 Years Old," *Holland Sentinel*, 28 Dec. 1948.

Rush Medical College in 1866, built up an extensive practice over the next eleven years, based in his drugstore on Eighth Street. He traveled to treat patients up to ten miles outside the city. Sylvester L. Morris, a Civil War-trained surgeon, combined medicine and journalism. From 1872 to early 1874, he edited both city newspapers, *De Hollander* and the *Holland City News* (chapter 32).[21] (See appendix 5.8 for a list of physicians and surgeons, dentists, and other doctors, 1870-1950.)

The midwife was Anna H. Sluyter (Sluiter), wife of Derk, who had immigrated to Holland after 1866. She carried a certificate from the Hooge School of Amsterdam, having successfully passed an examination in 1863. Derk Sluyter became a broom manufacturer. His wife bore him nine children, eight in Holland, and child-raising duties left her little time to practice her profession. But in 1886 her husband, then the custodian of the Ninth Street Christian Reformed Church, died and left her with nine mouths to feed and no income. That is when she advertised her services as a *vroedvrouw* (midwife) in *De Grondwet.* "I dare with complete confidence to present myself in this way," she declared. "My house is on Eleventh Street, behind the [Union] school."[22]

A third New Yorker, T. Delmar Powers, who trained in England as a homeopathic physician, practiced in the early 1870s over Kroon's Hardware Store on Eighth Street. William W. Nichols opened the first dental office in 1869. Two obstetricians in 1874 were Roelof A. Schouten on the corner of Ninth and Market (Central) Streets and N. Blank on Ninth and Cedar (College) Streets. The common council named Schouten the first city physician in 1875, under a new ordinance. Dentists were G. Sites, who sold his practice to Dallas M. Gee in 1873, and Benjamin Ferguson. In 1878 one of Gee's patients, Mrs. Francis Eagle, the oldest daughter of E. J. Harrington, took chloroform to ease the extraction of four teeth, over the strong objections of her parents and Dr. Morris, who was attending. But she insisted and died in the chair of Gee's "dental parlors," which were then upstairs in the Ame Vennema Building on Eighth Street. In 1879 Gee moved to an office just east of the First Reformed Church on Ninth and Market Streets.[23]

Albert Broek came to town in 1876; he died soon after, but not before performing the first surgery in Holland, the removal of a tumor from a young Steketee boy, with the help of Dr. Annis. By 1879 Frederick J. Schouten, Roelof's older brother, had joined him in the

21 *De Hollander*, 1 Sept. 1869, *Holland City News*, 25 Jan. 1873, 22 Dec. 1877.

22 *De Grondwet*, 19 Oct. 1886, translated by William Buursma.

23 *De Hollander*, 11 Apr., 27 May 1874, 5 May 1875; *Holland City News*, 14 Mar. 1874, 24 Apr., 12 June 1875, 31 Feb. 1877, 14 Sept. 1878.

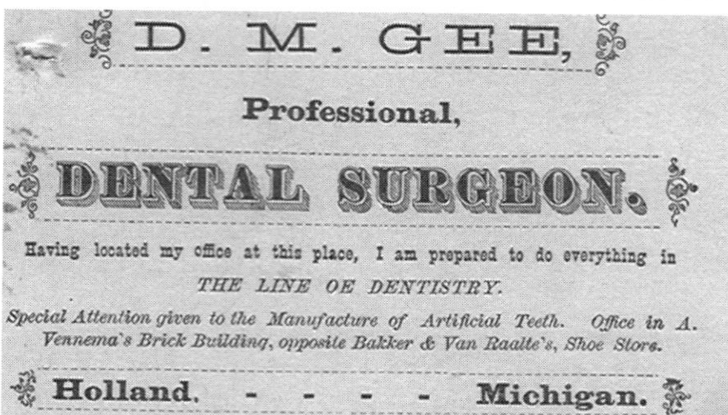

Dallas M. Gee's business card as "Professional, Dental Surgeon" with "Special Attention given to the Manufacture of Artificial Teeth" (*Archives, Holland Historical Trust*)

practice of medicine and surgery, with a room in the rear of Schouten's First Ward Drug Store on East Eighth Street. "The ghastly array of surgical instruments is not very inviting to the timid," opined editor Gerrit Van Schelven of the *Holland City News*, "but very necessary in emergencies." In 1880 Annis, the two Schoutens, and dentists Dallas and his brother Columbus L. Gee, were the only medical practitioners in the city. In 1881 Frederick Schouten and Henry Schepers partnered to manufacture patent medicines. They had to compete with peddlers such as Watkin's Remedies.[24]

Five druggists, several in partnership with doctors, supplied residents with the drugs and medicines touted to cure every ailment. On Eighth Street stood the drugstores of Heber Walsh, Jacob O. Doesburg (founded in 1864), Annis & Broek, and Meengs & Schouten; on River Street was William Van Putten's pharmacy. Doesburg promised "physician's prescriptions carefully put up." All the druggists carried toiletries and perfumes to augment their income. Several added paints and oils. In 1877 D. R. "Dirk" Meengs bought out Roelof Schouten's interest and opened a pharmacy in his father's grocery on River Street, opposite Van Putten's place. Meengs added books to his stock, mainly Bibles, catechism books, Dutch and English schoolbooks, and an assortment of Dutch literary and religious books.[25] (See appendix 5.5 for a list of drugstores, 1864-1950.)

24 *De Hollander*, 19 May 1877; *Holland City News*, 17 May (quote) 1879, 18 Oct. 1879, 31 Dec. 1881; *De Grondwet*, 6 Dec. 1881.

25 *Holland City News*, 14 Mar. 1874, 2 Sept. 1876, 31 Feb. 1877; *De Grondwet*, 17 Apr., 15 May 1877.

Frederick J. Schouten's First Ward Drug Store, 126 East Eighth Street, 1894-1913. The counter case on the left is well-stocked with cigars (*Archives, Holland Historical Trust*)

Watkin's Remedies, one of the ubiquitous patent medicine peddlers (*courtesy Myron Van Ark*)

Holland's first banker

Nathan Kenyon (1820-1908) opened the city's first bank in 1856 in the parlor of Aldert Plugger's house at 5 East Eighth Street (later site of Warm Friend Tavern). Kenyon's purpose was to facilitate local trade by enabling merchants to exchange notes issued by banks throughout the country. It was a private "exchange bank" established under the state "free banking" charter of 1837, which allowed any twelve landowners to form a banking association, if $50,000 in capital stock was subscribed and at least 30 percent was paid in specie (gold or silver coins). Before the creation of the National Banking System, private banks printed notes, much like banks today print checks, which circulated as paper money. Issuing banks had to redeem their own notes on demand at face value in gold or silver specie. Merchants discounted the banknotes, based on the financial solvency of each issuing bank, as determined by auditors of the *Thompson's Bank Note Reporter*, a New York City publication that was the bible of every merchant and stood next to the cash box. The merchant would look up a particular banknote in the *Reporter* and tell the customer the prevailing discount that week. The history of Kenyon's Bank is related below.[26]

Early lawyers

Lawyers first hung their shingles in Holland in the post-war years. In 1870 the city counted three lawyers, Dutch-born Cornelis Rot and the New Yorkers William Crouch and Cassius Wise. Rot had immigrated as a nineteen year old with his father Hendrik in 1855, along with several siblings. He was likely the first Dutchman to practice law in the city. Wise worked out of his East Eighth Street residence. In 1872, following the Great Fire, three other lawyers advertised in the *Holland City News*—Manly D. Howard, Patrick H. McBride, and F. W. Dunlap. Howard and McBride shared an office on the southwest corner of Eighth and River Streets. McBride's practice evolved into an insurance agency that had a run of more than sixty years. His son Charles H. joined the firm in 1894, after earning his law degree from the University of Michigan. In 1874 Felix J. Ort opened an office on Eighth Street at Market (Central), and

26 "Thirty Years Ago Today," *Holland City News*, 9 June 1938; "50 Years Ago," *Holland Sentinel*, 20 Dec. 1986; Willis Frederick Dunbar, *Michigan Through the Centuries*, 2 vols. (New York: Lewis 1955), 1:229-32; Randall P. Vande Water, "First Bank was in Home," in *Holland: Happenings, Heroes & Hot Shots*, 1:26-29; Robert P. Swierenga, *Pioneers and Profits: Land Speculation on the Iowa Frontier* (Ames: Iowa State University Press, 1968), 129-31.

Arend Visscher in his upstairs law office, Kenyon Block, early 1880s (*Joint Archives of Holland*)

the next year a Mr. Griswold partnered with him. Arend Visscher joined the fraternity in 1875 with an office in the Kenyon Block. Visscher, a Hope College graduate with a law degree from the University of Michigan, in 1877 shared his office with another young attorney, James Ten Eyck.[27]

So averse were Dutch Reformed businessmen to going to law with brothers in the faith that they used formal arbitration. On March 1, 1880, John Lezman, a cattle buyer, and butcher Louis De Kraker Jr. signed a formal agreement filed in the Holland city records, in which they agreed in their business dispute to abide by the decision of arbiters city clerk Isaac Marsilje and justice of the peace Gerrit Van Schelven.[28]

Dutch Reformed folk were also supposedly averse to insurance, although the antipathy had been overplayed in the popular press (chapter 2). Arend Visscher, the first insurance agent in Holland, found far greater reluctance to buy life policies than fire protection. Perhaps many had learned the hard way after experiencing major fires. Visscher

27 1870 federal manuscript population census of Holland City; *Holland City News*, 2 Mar. 1872, 30 May 1874, 24 Apr. 1875, 13 Oct. 1877; *Holland Sentinel*, 14 May 1938. Visscher served as prosecuting attorney for Ottawa County for many years, beginning in 1892.

28 "Arbitration Agreement," John Lezman and Louis De Kraker Jr., 1 Mar. 1880, Holland City Records, box 3, HMA.

was certainly convinced when his uninsured law office and $400 library were destroyed in the Kenyon Block fire in 1877; his fellow tenants, however, Gabriel Van Putten and Nathan Kenyon, had their property insured. As a lawyer, Visscher settled many estates and recognized the desirability of having cash on hand at death for final expenses. In 1873, after becoming a general agent of the Northwestern Mutual Life Insurance Co. office in Grand Rapids, he discovered that elderly people had a greater aversion to life insurance than to any other type of protection. Visscher convinced many otherwise and prospered as a result.[29]

Merchants suffer in the Holland Fire of 1871

The city experienced rapid growth after the Civil War, with the revival of pent-up immigration from the Netherlands. In 1864 E. J. Harrington erected a store and warehouse at the foot of Fifth Street, including the city's first substantial dock to service lake schooners.[30]

Grand Rapids-based Doornink & Steketee dry goods store in 1864 opened a branch on Eighth Street under Paul Steketee's brother Gilles. The city's first department store, Doornink, Steketee & Bro., carried dry goods, groceries, and provisions. The Grand Rapids store evolved into the flagship Steketee Department Stores, which grew to six stores and enjoyed a 139-year run in West Michigan. The Holland store was rebuilt immediately after the fire of 1871. A year later, Andries, the next brother in line, took over from Paul, and the store became A. Steketee & Sons. Younger brother Bastian started as a fourteen year old, delivering groceries in Holland with a two-wheeled pushcart. After fourteen years, in 1883, Bastian had accumulated $1,800 and opened a store with his brother Peter. Five years later he bought out his brother. The B. Steketee Grocery and Dry Goods Store was located in the Post Block on the northeast corner of Eighth and River Streets (now Model Drug Store). The store had two entrances, with general merchandize fronting on Eighth Street and groceries fronting on River Street. It prospered until the 1920s, when the national department stores came to Holland.[31]

29 Arthur A. Visscher, "Early Dutch Settlers Felt Insurance Was 'Worldly,'" newspaper clipping.

30 "E. J. Harrington," P. T. Moerdyke Papers, box 2, HMA.

31 "Bastian Steketee," *Portrait and Biographical Record of Muskegon and Ottawa Counties* (Chicago: Biographical Publishing Co., 1893), 287-88; *Holland City News*, 29 Apr., 12 Aug. 1876, 30 Oct., 22 Dec. 1877, 1 Aug. 1896, 25 June 1925, 28 Apr. 1926; *Holland Sentinel*, 12 Aug. 2001.

Ladies fabric department of A. Steketee Grocery & Dry Goods Store, 18-22 East Eighth Street (*clockwise from left*): unidentified female clerk, owner Andries Steketee, clerk Henry Van Ry, unidentified clerk, George Steketee, Gerrit Steketee, unidentified customer, clerk Anna Borgman, ca. 1895 (*Archives, Holland Historical Trust*)

The Dutch pram in the center isle seems to serve as a shopping cart in B. Steketee Grocery & Dry Goods Store, Post Block at Eighth and River Streets, ca. 1895. The counter on the right is where Model Drug Store later had its popular soda fountain (*Archives, Holland Historical Trust*)

CITY BAKERY,
ESTABLISHED 1866.
We keep a Full Line of Bakery Goods and make a Specialty of Fine Baking for parties.
Confectionery, Fruits and Canned Goods.
Ice Cream and Oysters in Season.
FINEST LINE OF CIGARS IN THE CITY.
JOHN PESSINK.
Chase Phone 42. ☆ ☆ ☆ ☆ 10 E. 8th Street.

Advertisement of John Pessink's City Bakery, established 1866 at 10 East Eighth Street, in the *Holland City Directory* 1897-98

Louis De Kraker Jr., a Civil War veteran, opened a small meat market in 1865 at 184 River Street and Lambert Pessink established his City Bakery at 10 East Eighth Street in 1866. Both firms continued into the twentieth century. De Kraker ran his meat market until he retired at age eighty-five, setting a state record for the longest continuous span in the meat business. De Kraker sold the business to his son Isaac and son-in-law James De Koster (see below). Pessink's son John took over the family bakery by 1894 and ran it until 1903, when he became a butter and cheese dealer and general insurance agent. M. C. De Graaf owned Home Bakery, a wholesale and retail shop on East Eighth Street in 1894, which his son John took over by 1897 and ran for several years.[32]

Two new hotels and two saloons opened in 1867, the City Hotel of Pieter F. Pfanstiehl on the northeast corner of Eighth and Market (Central) Streets and the Grand Haven Hotel of John Roost on the southwest corner of River and Sixth Streets. Together with the American House, Holland could finally accommodate traveling salesmen and businessmen. A Dutch American visitor direct from New York City in 1868, as he approached Holland by ship on Black Lake, described the hotels as "unpretentious, but comfortable wooden structures, standing fronting or close to the wharf. The last [the City Hotel] is the best, a well-appearing and well-kept house, the landlord being J. Meyers, a native of New Hampshire."[33]

32 "Pioneer Merchants of Holland, Michigan," P. T. Moerdyke Papers, box 4, HMA; *Holland City Directories*, 1894-1906.

33 Helen (Mrs. Hermanus) (Pfanstiehl) Boone obit., *Holland Sentinel*, 10 May 1921; Vande Water, "City Hotel Welcomed Visitors in 1872," in *Holland Happenings*, 4:31-

Three men petitioned the common council in 1867 for licenses to operate saloons: German-born Charles Brandt on the corner of Eighth and Market Streets, Sanford Helmer of New York in the American Hotel, and Edwin Westcott of New York on the east side of River Street between Sixth and Seventh Streets. Other saloonkeepers in 1870 were Henry Koenigsberg, Cornelius Blom Sr., Gerrit Doesburg, Peter Vanden Tak, and Robert Beukema.[34]

Six men were fabulously wealthy by 1870, according to property values reported to the federal census marshal, Willem Wakker of Holland. All were merchants and industrialists, except Van Raalte whose wealth was in undeveloped city lots and farmland. Tannery owner Isaac Cappon reported real and personal property worth $70,000, Henry D. Post $41,000, Jacob Van Putten $30,000, Manly Howard $29,000, Pieter Pfanstiehl $24,500, John Roost $21,000, and Van Raalte $16,100.[35]

The Holland Fire in October 1871 changed the face of the business district to such an extent that in January 1872 *De Hollander* published a listing of the stores and businesses along Eighth, River, and Ninth Streets that were rebuilt, under construction, or newly established. Many old businesses never reopened.

The economic impact of the fire was dire (chapter 2). Pieter Pfanstiehl lost $17,000 when his hotel, store, and two homes were destroyed, and he had not one dollar of insurance. The same held true for the Cappon & Bertsch leather works, valued at $65,000. E. J. Harrington lost his store, warehouses, wharves, and railroad, valued at $10,000; it cost him $7,000 to rebuild his store in brick, the first brick building on Eighth Street, known as the Harrington Block at 74 East. The fire set Roost on a downward spiral; it destroyed his fruit trees and cranberry marsh. Then his harbor investments failed. Within a short time, he lost $30,000. Gerrit Van Schelven, the future newspaperman, judge, and postmaster, lost the store he opened after returning from the Civil War, which broke him financially.[36]

34; *Holland Sentinel, Semi-Centennial Supplement, 1847-1897*; C. V. S., "Holland and the Hollanders," *Christian Intelligencer*, 8 Oct. 1868 (quote). The writer is likely Cornelius Van Zandvoort of New York City.

34 License applications, May 1867, in Holland City Clerk Records, box 1, HMA; 1870 Federal Census of Holland City, compiled by Delaney Ann Prins (Feb. 2007).

35 Prins, Federal Census of Holland City, 1870; Robert P. Swierenga, comp. *Dutch Households in U.S. Population Censuses, 1850, 1860, 1870: An Alphabetical Listing by Family Heads and Singles* (Wilmington, DE: Scholarly Resources, 1987).

36 John Roost obit., *De Grondwet*, 2 June 1885, translated by P. T. Moerdyke, P. T. Moerdyke Papers, box 2, HMA; *Holland City News*, 10 Feb. 1922.

Table 18.1. Stores and Businesses after the Great Fire of 1871

Eighth Street
P. Zalsman Hotel
E. J. Harrington Store and P. & A. Steketee Grocery and Dry Goods
William Brouwer Barber Shop
H. De Jong & Oggel Grocery
John Alberti Livery Stable
J. Van Landegend Hardware Store
P. Van Landegend Tobacco Shop
J. Albers Jewelry Store and C. B. Wynne Watchmakers Shop
Labarbe & Son Furniture Store
E. Herold Shoe Store
D. Bertsch Dry Goods Store
W. Joslin & O. Breyman Jewelry Store (corner of Market Street)
Hein Vander Haar Meat and Vegetable Market
Wm. Verbeek Post Office and J. O. Bakker Boots and Shoe Store
H. Koningsberg Saloon
A. Nibbelink Meat Market
L. Sprietsma & Son Shoe Store
E. Vander Veen Hardware Store
A. Verplanke Shoe Store
H. Koning Grocery
Jan Binnekant Pioneer Bakery
H. D. Post Drug Store
George Lauder Portrait Gallery
C. Brandt Saloon & Restaurant
Jan W. Bosman Clothing Store
G. J. Kroon Hardware Store
Heber Walsh Drug Store, Notary & Real Estate
U. De Vries Harness Shop and L. T. Kanters Stationery & Books
John Vanden Berg Fashions & Drapery Store
H. Vaupell Harness Shop

The fire forced Van Raalte to implement a bank plan that he had mulled over for some time. "A bank institution I seek; the National is what we need," the dominie wrote his friend Hope College president Philip Phelps Jr., then in New York City to raise money for the college. Phelps was a native of Albany, where his father was deputy comptroller of the State of New York. A bank could provide capital for Holland to rebuild, Van Raalte noted. Nathan Kenyon's private bank and Kommer

Table 18.1. (cont.)

River Street
H. W. Verbeek & Co., and S. Schaaf & Ploeg Woodworking
H. Meengs Grocery and W. Vorst Tailor Shop
John Aling's Store and Bakery (at Seventh Street)
M. P. Visser Grocery
D. Werkman Store
John Duursema & Co. General Store and Grocery (at Eighth Street)
Louis De Kraker Meat Market
Manly D. Howard Law Office (corner of Eighth Street)
Elferding & Co. Shoes and A. Cloetingh Bookbindery and Shop
Packard & Co. Feed Store (Pfanstiehl Bldg)
A. Dijkema & Bros Wagon and Blacksmith Shop
Ninth Street
Cappon Tannery (between Pine and Van Raalte Streets)
Boone (Hermanus) Livery Stable (at Market Street)
James Ryder's Phoenix Hotel (near Chicago Depot)

Source: *De Hollander*, 10 Jan. 1872

Schaddelee's exchange banks lacked credibility, and their bank notes (paper money) were worth no more than the reputation of the issuer. Van Raalte would take advantage of the National Banking System created by Congress during the Civil War and charter a bank under that charter. National banks could issue federal bank notes, dubbed Greenbacks. But the way to reach that goal was unclear to him. If he sought help to obtain a charter from Americans in Grand Haven, such as US Senator Thomas W. Ferry, the news would get out and "sharpers" and "society-enervating leeches or blood suckers" would try to take over.[37]

37 Van Raalte to Phelps, 23 Oct., 8 Nov. 1871, in Elton J. Bruins and Karen G. Schakel, eds., *Envisioning Hope College: Letters written by Albertus C. Van Raalte to Philip Phelps Jr., 1857 to 1875* (Holland: Van Raalte Press; Grand Rapids: Eerdmans, 2011), 267-70 (quote, 270), 283-84 (quote, 283); "Our Banking System," *Holland City News*, 26 Oct. 1872; Darlene Winter, "100 Years Ago Today," *Holland Sentinel*, 20 Dec. 1986; *Sheboygan* [WI] *Nieuwsbode*, 24 May 1871; Randall P. Vande Water, "First Bank Was a Home," *Holland: Happenings, Heroes and Hot Shots*, 4 vols. (Holland, MI, 1995-97), 3:26-29; Adrian Van Koevering, *Legends of the Dutch* (Zeeland, MI: Zeeland Historical Record, 1960), 475.

Van Raalte's "ripe plan," as he called it, was brilliant. The dominie would raise from $5,000 to $8,000 in seed money by mortgaging his farmlands. With this, he would partner with Arent Geerlings, a "practical miller" with a solid reputation, whose City Mills and feed store (Werkman, Geerlings & Co.) were both destroyed by the fire and would require $20,000 to rebuild. Van Raalte and Geerlings would found a national bank, capitalized from $50,000 to $100,000 and obtain the capital "in-house" from Hope College's endowment and from wealthy "eastern friends," that is, Dutch Reformed capitalists in New York whom Phelps knew personally. They could "take stock" in the bank by depositing government bonds, from which they would continue to clip 6 percent coupons. With the bonds as collateral, the bank would issue bank notes as loans to farmers and manufacturers. This would increase the local money supply and "bring business life back" after the fire. Hope College could also borrow from the bank to erect buildings.[38]

The bank would operate out of Geerlings' rebuilt feed store in Holland, and in his branch stores in outlying villages. Supplying feed and other necessities to farmers is "a safe and good business," Van Raalte reasoned, and the bank could piggyback on that cachet and expand into banking and investment services. "We could expect the first years more than barely to keep alive," but the business would expand "as fast as small deposits grow on the hands," Van Raalte told Phelps. "All my property is given to it, even self preservation compels me. . . . Most sickening will be our situation without capital." Van Raalte then came to the bottom line. "If you could effect a loan for me of 20 m [thousand] on ample security on real estate, this would perhaps provide matters. They tell me Life insurance companies are doing this sometimes." Despite the dominie's desperate tone and the bleak situation facing the city, his appeal to "eastern friends" went unheeded. No money for a charter bank in Holland was forthcoming, although relief funds for the townspeople did arrive. Hope College trustees also would not risk their endowment funds on such a risky venture.[39]

38 Van Raalte to Phelps, 8 Nov. 1871, in Bruins and Schakel, *Envisioning Hope College*, 283-84.

39 Henry S. Lucas, *Dutch Immigrant Memoirs and Related Writings*, rev. ed., 2 vols. (Assen, the Netherlands: Van Gorcum, 1955; reprint, Grand Rapids: Eerdmans, 1997), 2:495; Van Raalte to Phelps, 8 Nov. 1871, in Bruins and Schakel, *Envisioning Hope College*, 283-84 (quotes); Vande Water, "Holland Had State Bank in 1889," *Holland: Happenings, Heroes, and Hot Shots*, 2:62-64; "E. J. Harrington," *Holland City News*, 22 Dec, 1877; Wynand Wichers, *A Century of Hope, 1866-1966* (Holland, MI, 1966), 52. The *Holland City News* (10 Aug. 1872) gave some credence to Van Raalte's efforts; it

The Panic of 1873

The national financial panic in 1873 ended all hope for Van Raalte's bank project, but Nathan Kenyon, Holland's only private banker, was able to pay in currency all drafts drawn on him and to honor depositors' requests for withdrawals. Federal deposit insurance was unheard of at the time, and only a banker's solvency stood behind his operation. In May 1871, just months before the Great Fire, Kenyon had reorganized his bank under the new Michigan bank law that encouraged the formation of state banks by allowing them to maintain both savings and commercial departments. Kommer Schaddelee was his cashier. In the crisis, the enterprising Kenyon saw a future for local banking and laid plans to put up a new three-story building on the southwest corner of River and Eighth Streets (now the site of Reader's World). The upper two floors became Holland's first opera house. The new bank opened in 1876.[40]

Kenyon, Holland's first banker, did a general banking, an exchange, and a collection business. In an 1877 advertisement, he offered to make collections "on all points in the United States and Europe," especially from "banks and bankers," and to make remittances "on the day of payment," to buy and sell foreign exchange, and to pay interest on time deposits. Kenyon also sold Atlantic steamship tickets. The banker was a boon to Dutch American merchants and immigrants.[41]

Local leaders responded to the economic depression by forming the first businessmen's association. E. J. Harrington in April 1873 recruited George McBride, Heber Walsh, Sylvester Morris, and Kenyon to meet at the *Holland City News* office, where the group formed the Citizen's Association of Holland, with Kenyon as vice president, Heber Walsh treasurer, and Morris secretary. Other movers and shakers were Henry Post, John Roost, William H. Joslin, Richard Heald, Rokus Kanters, Dirk B. K. Van Raalte, and Gerrit Van Schelven. The stated purpose was to "invite immigration, promote manufacturing, and encourage every laudable enterprise. To develop our resources in mechanical arts, manufacturing, educational, and business prospects."[42]

The first projects were to develop an iron foundry to capitalize on the iron ore beds near the city, to develop the harbor and obtain

reported: "We learn that movements are being made toward establishing a National Bank in this city, and that it promises a success."

40 *Sheboygan Nieuwsbode*, 24 May 1871; Vande Water, "Tower Clock building originally housed Holland City State Bank," *Holland Sentinel*, 18 Jan. 2009; *Holland City News*, 4 Oct. 1873, 9 May 1874; Dunbar, *Michigan*, 231.

41 *Holland City News*, 16 June 1877.

42 *Holland City News*, 26 Apr., 3, 10, 31 May 1873.

Dirk B. K. Van Raalte at his cluttered desk, spittoon at the ready (*Archives, Holland Historical Trust*)

steamboat service to Chicago, and to encourage shipbuilding. But the group quickly expanded it horizons to push every kind of enterprise and set about to raise capital by a subscription campaign. Holland would pull itself up by its own bootstraps, despite the hard times caused by the depression from 1873 to 1877. Pushing a boulder uphill was harder than the boosters expected. Initially, the plan was to raise $25,000, and wealthier citizens had to put up only one-half of their pledges in cash. In 1881 the other half would be due within sixty days. That year Harrington, Post, Fairbanks, and Mayor John Roost transformed the Citizen's Association into the Holland Businessmen's Association. It was the first of several beginnings of this booster club.[43]

One who barely survived the fire financially was Jan Binnekant, the hotel keeper and merchant. The fire left him penniless, but he did manage to build the Pioneer Bakery in 1872. Almost immediately, a windstorm flattened the bakery, but he rebuilt it, only to die four years later, in 1876. The fire spurred the insurance business; in 1875 Isaac Marsilje opened his agency, which continues today under the fifth generation (chapter 19).[44]

Van Raalte's son Dirk, a one-armed Civil War veteran with "an eye for business," began his stellar career in 1872 by buying an interest in John O. Bakker's boot and shoe store on East Eighth Street. Then Van Raalte built a brick block on Eighth Street, the Central Block, all in white brick, with machinery that promised a new era in the local

43 *Holland City News*, 1 May 1881; *De Hollander*, 24, 31 May 1881.

44 Obituary in *Holland City News*, 12 Feb. 1876. Sons Herbert and grandsons Edward and Thomas Marsilje and granddaughter Louise Leestma carried on the Marsilje Insurance Agency (John Charles Robbins, "Local business leader Marsilje dies at 90," *Holland Sentinel*, 28 Nov. 2002).

Dirk and Kate Ledeboer Van Raalte at the family homestead send off their newly wed nephew Ben Van Raalte Jr. and bride Adeline (Addie) May Huntley, daughter of James and Julia Thorpe Huntley. The driver of the 1904-5 Ford Touring car and his companion (likely his wife) are unknown, as is the young man at the front door. The date of the wedding was 6 Feb. 1906 (*Joint Archives of Holland*)

manufacture of footware. Van Raalte's store was the largest of its kind in town, and in the era before macadamized streets, men bought boots rather than shoes. Dirk Van Raalte later went into lumbering and banking. Younger brother Ben operated an agricultural implement dealership in the Wakker Block at Ninth and River Streets for forty years, beginning about 1881. William Wakker rebuilt his building following a major fire in 1880. In 1886 Ben Van Raalte sold $65,000 worth of farm implements and earned accolades as one of the "solid businessmen of the city."[45]

Other new stores in the central district between 1872 and 1878 included Derk Te Roller & Jacob Labots' clothing store on the corner of Ninth and Market Streets, the groceries of Anne Flietstra and Gerrit Te Vaarwerk on Eighth Street, Werkman & Sons (John D. and Derk J. Werkman and later Henry D.) and Gabriel Van Putten on River Street, the meat markets of Jacob Kuite and Peter Kleis and Jan Bosman's clothing store just east of John Albers & C. Wynne's jewelry store. On River Street stood the department store of Peter and Andrew Steketee, the hardware store of John Van Landegend and William Melis, the harness shop of Edward Vaupell, and John Aling's grocery on the corner

45 *Holland City News*, 26 Oct. 1872, 28 Jan. 1873, Aug. 21, 1880.

Jan W. Bosman's rebuilt clothing store, 16 East Eighth Street
(*Archives, Holland Historical Trust*)

H[enry]. D. Werkman Dry Goods, Groceries, Flour, and Feed Store, 238-42 River Street, 1890s. One of the men is Werkman. The board in front advertises "Sunlight Daisy Hyperion," brand of flour
(*Archives, Holland Historical Trust*)

The dog poses obediently for the photographer along with the owners and staff of Gabriel Van Putten & Sons Dry Goods & Groceries, 202-4 River Street, 1890s. Gabriel and Anna Van Putten are standing at the front door (*Archives, Holland Historical Trust*)

of River and Seventh Streets. Melis stocked the first refrigerators ever seen in town. Peter Boot Jr. and A. I. Kramer started a grocery in 1879 on Eighth Street that evolved by 1906 under son John Kramer into Boot & Kramer Dry Goods & Notions, which became a landmark over the next three decades. But it did not equal Andrew Steketee's two-story, double-brick store.[46]

Four hardware stores fronted Eighth Street in 1874: Gerrit J. Haverkate near Columbia and Gerrit J. Kroon over William Verbeek's post office near Cedar (Central) Street, Engbertus Vander Veen on the southeast corner of River Street, and Van Landegend & Melis at 49 West (down the hill from River Street). Kroon hired Fred W. Beeuwkes to make hernia trusses and horns for the deaf. Vander Veen in 1878 replaced his 1872 store with a new three-story brick building on the same site, the "finest corner in the city." In 1877 Vander Veen's oldest

46 Ibid., 14 Mar. 1874, 29 Apr. 1876, 27 Apr. 1878, 13 Mar. 1880, 7 May 1881, 1 Aug. 1896, 3 May 1906, "Fifty Years Ago Today," 12 Mar. 1936. In 1878 John D. Werkman retired, and Derk J. Werkman and Derk Kamperman continued the firm under the name of Werkman & Son (*De Hollander*, 16, 1878). Peter Boot dissolved Boot & Kramer in 1918 due to ill health, after standing behind the counter for forty years cutting cheese, selling penny candy, and putting up sugar. His partner John Kramer had died already in 1911 (*Holland City News*, 6 June 1918).

Tyler Van Landegend whose dirty apron testifies to his hands-on service in his plumbing supply house, 49 West Eighth Street, ca. 1900 (*Archives, Holland Historical Trust*)

Boot & Kramer (Peter Boot Jr. and A. I. Kremar) Dry Goods, 22 West Eighth Street, 1890s (*Archives, Holland Historical Trust*)

son Jacob, only twenty-two years old, bought out Haverkate's store and began competing with his father. By that time, prime lots on Eighth Street sold for $30 a front foot![47]

Furniture stores were the new rage, in tandem with the emergence of the local furniture industry (chapter 14). The new showrooms were Hannes Meyer & Co. (with Jas A. Brouwer) on River Street, and Ame Vennema and Jan H. Reidsma & Son (Simon) on Eighth Street. Meyer and the Reidsmas stocked coffins, and Vennema carried carpeting. Vennema in 1874 sold out his entire stock to Reidsma & Son. Meyer, Brouwer & Company in 1876 advertised the "finest Coffins and Caskets ever exhibited in this city for sale at reasonable prices." Reidsmas offered the "finest Walnut Caskets in the market, and cheaper than in any other place." William Wakker's furniture showroom under *De Grondwet* office on the southeast corner of Ninth and River Streets went up in flames in 1880, but Wakker managed to save the most expensive pieces and coffins on the main floor. The rebuilt Wakker Block was considered one of the finest in town. These three furniture stores all sold and delivered coffins to homes for parlor viewing.[48]

The Jas. A. Brouwer Furniture store began in 1872 as Meyer, Brouwer & Company on East Eighth Street west of Lyceum Hall to serve residents needing to refurnish their homes after the 1871 fire. Brouwer also had an undertaking business until selling to Jacobus Nibbelink in 1890. In the early 1880s Brouwer erected a two-story frame building at 212-14 River Street. In 1899 he razed the store to make room for a modern three-story brick building. Brouwer was a progressive entrepreneur. He was one of the first retail merchants to sell furniture and carpeting on credit, especially to newlyweds short on cash, under his "Easy Payment Plan." In 1914 he published a 250-page furniture catalog, the "Home-Trade Price-Maker," which rivaled that of the largest mail order houses, and he fully guaranteed every purchase.

In 1924 Brouwer expanded again by buying the Van Dyke Block on the corner of Ninth Street, which had housed Van Dyke & Sprietsma Hardware and then Kraker Plumbing. Brouwer extensively remodeled the space for his furniture emporium, then in its fifty-second year. The oak woodwork, glass artwork, and massive eighty-five-foot copper

47 *Holland City News*, 14 Mar. 1874, 13 Jan. 1876, 31 Feb., 10 Mar., 22 Sept., 15 Dec. 1877, "Sixty Years Ago Today" 5 May and 11 Aug. 1938.

48 Ibid., 30 Dec. 1876 (quote), 8 Sept. 1877 (quote). In the 1880 Wakker Building fire, young Harry Verbeek daringly climbed to the rooftop to aid the firemen and became trapped by smoke and flames. He escaped by jumping to a lower adjoining roof, at the cost of broken leg (ibid., 10 May 1934).

James A. Brouwer in front of his two-story furniture and carpet store at 212-14 River Street. Note the wooden sidewalk and unpaved street early 1890s (*courtesy Randall P. Vande Water*)

canopy attracted 4,500 visitors for the open house in 1928. The four front-window displays made the façade one of the largest in West Michigan; Jas. A. Brouwer was the exclusive furniture house in Ottawa County.[49]

Jas. A. Brouwer Furniture Store, three-story brick building, ca. 1906, looking north from Ninth Street toward the Tower Clock Building (*courtesy Myron Van Ark*)

49 *De Grondwet*, 20 Jan. 1903; *Holland City News*, 9 Apr., 21 May 1914, 6 Mar., 23 Oct. 1924, 11 Mar. 1925, 15 Nov. 1928; *Sanborn Fire Insurance* maps, Holland, Michigan, 1883, 1889.

Jas. A. Brouwer Furniture Emporium, late 1930s. The curved, cast-iron façade on the corner of Ninth Street and River Avenue was a conspicuous part of the city's downtown (*courtesy Donald van Reken, Joint Archives of Holland*)

After Brouwer's son William J. and Fred Beeuwkes joined the firm as partners in 1918, Brouwer served for thirty years on the Holland school board and accepted the presidency of the Holland Merchants Association in 1932. The community showered James Brouwer with accolades on his eightieth birthday in 1934. He remained active another sixteen years, working at his desk at the store until age ninety-six, when he died in 1950 after an illness of only three days. James A. Brouwer was Holland's grand old man as a successful merchant and esteemed civic leader. His store anchored the intersection of River Avenue and Ninth Street for nearly a century.[50]

The rebuilt City Hotel, a three-story structure that replaced the fire-ravaged building, graced the northeast corner of Eighth and Market (Central) Streets in 1872, thanks to Hermanus Boone and John Duursma, who invested $25,000 in the luxury accommodations under lease to a Grand Rapids investor. John W. Minderhout served as the architect and contractor of the twenty-eight-room hotel, with a large dining hall and fully equipped kitchen. Each partner had a half interest. Both sold their shares, but Boone bought the building back in 1895. He

50 *Holland City News*, 7 Jan. 1932, 22 Feb. 1934, Jas. Brouwer obit., 21 Dec. 1950; *Holland Sentinel* obit., clippings, Dec. 1950, HMA.

Owners and guests of Scott's Hotel on the northeast corner of Ninth Street and Fish (Columbia) Street, 1880s. Hope College used the building for student housing in the early 1900s. The decrepit building was demolished in 1989 (*courtesy Randall P. Vande Water*)

took on partner E. O. Philips in 1897, and the pair renamed it the New City Hotel and fitted it with electric lights and steam heat, much to the delight of traveling salesmen. James Whelan, the manager, collected the $2 per night room rate.

Mary A. (Mrs. James) Ryder became the proprietor in 1898 and renamed it the Hotel Holland. This was the city's premier hostelry until 1924, when the Holland Furnace Company purchased the building and demolished it for the Warm Friend Tavern. In 1877 William J. Scott of Ohio and his wife Blanche opened Scott's Hotel in a private residence on the northwest corner of Ninth and Fish (Columbia) Streets. In 1879 came the Germania Hotel (later American and Commercial) at 20 West Eighth Street. These three newcomers gave Holland six hostelries, besides the Aetna House of Peter Zalsman, the City Hotel of the Canadian brothers Edward and George Williams, and the Phoenix Hotel of James Ryder (later Chas. Jacobus). The Aetna House (also called the Arbor Hotel) burned down in 1878. In 1882 James Ryder had his three-story wooden Phoenix Hotel moved from Ninth to Eighth Street just west of Land (Lincoln) Street near the Chicago Depot. The Phoenix catered to salesmen and railroad employees, since Holland was a switching point for the Chicago & West Michigan Railway (Pere Marquette in 1900). In the late 1880s, David L. Boyd operated the Park House at 1 West Tenth Street.[51] (See appendix 5.6 for a list of hotels, 1872-1966.)

In a sign of better times, an ice cream war broke out in 1877 between the parlors of Leendert T. Kanters and the brothers Gerrit and John Pessink. Kanters in newspaper ads touted Raymond's Root Beer as a "drink that does not knock you out!" Pessink Bros. countered with the first soda water fountain in town, and the young folks flocked to it. Pessink pleased the men by selling cigars of all grades from 2¢ to 10¢ apiece. Given the fact that a businessman counted ninety teams and wagons on Eighth Street on a Saturday in September 1877, there was considerable traffic to fight over. The next month, a spectacular fire destroyed the year-old Kenyon's Hall (chapter 30), taking with it the grocery stores of brothers William and Gabriel Van Putten and that of Kanters, and the law offices of Arend Visscher and James Ten Eyck. Only the heroic efforts of firemen and citizens saved the entire business district from being swept away just six years after the Great Fire.[52]

E. J. Harrington returned to the mercantile business in 1876. His general store at 74 East Eighth Street, known by the catchy name "Cheap John's Half Price Store," became the city's prime emporium, and bartering was the normal way of doing business. Harrington took in farm produce and wood products in exchange for groceries, ready-made clothing, boots and shoes, and sundries of all kinds "for such low prices and in such immense quantities that the purchaser doesn't think of going to other cities to do his trading." This newspaper "plug" certainly embellished the truth, but it tells much about the barter economy of early Holland. Harrington advertized his "Great Bargains" heavily in the *Holland City News* and held weekly Saturday public auctions at his store. "Come one, come all to the sale. . . . Terms cash. Cheap John," read one "Auction Sale!" block ad. An unusual ad read: "WANTED 2,000 Black Cats, immediately. I will pay the highest price in the market. Call at Cheap John." Cats were essential on every farm to control mice and rats.[53]

51 *Holland City News*, 26 Apr. 1873, 14 Mar. 1874, 27 Oct. 1877, 13 Feb. 1878, 16 June 1882, 30 Jan. 1886, 2 Feb. 1888, 28 Sept. 1889; *American Graphic* (Aug. 1899), in Moerdyke Papers, box 3, HMA; *Holland Sentinel*, 14 May 1938; *Holland Sentinel, Semi-Centennial Supplement, 1847-1897*; Randall P. Vande Water, "Holland Landmark Razed," 1 Mar. 1989. The Phoenix Hotel (1877-91) was formerly the Aniba (1891-92), Hemmingway (1893), and Alamo (1894-95) and became the St. Charles (1896-1904). See Fritz L. Kliphuis, comp., "Hotels of Holland," a listing compiled from *Holland City Directories*.

52 *De Grondwet*, 5 June 1877; *Holland City News*, 29 Sept., 13 Oct. 1877, "Sixty Years Ago Today," 19 Jan. 1939.

53 *Holland City News*, 23 Dec. 1876, 3 Mar., 7 Apr. 1877.

J. & H. De Jongh Grocery, first building, 16 East Tenth Street, ca. 1890. The owners and employees are unidentified, but surely John and Henry De Jongh are pictured. The horse is waiting to make a delivery (*Joint Archives of Holland*)

Another old-timer who recalled bartering was the banker Clarence Jalving, whose farming family brought eggs to the J. & H. De Jongh Grocery (John and Henry) at 16 East Tenth Street in the 1880s to pay for groceries. "Money was a scarce commodity back in those days," he recalled. Farmers also slaughtered their own animals for meat, and as Jalving noted, "very seldom purchased any meat from stores." Meat markets had to rely on city folk for customers. The John De Jongh family lived upstairs. About 1905, they replaced the frame building with a large two-story brick store directly across the street at 21 East Tenth Street.[54]

Holland businessmen demonstrated their acumen by expanding their reach far beyond the city limits. Hardware merchant Rokus Kanters in 1878 landed a contract from the Chicago Park Commission to build a breakwater of brush in the traditional Dutch way to protect the Lincoln Park roadway. Before his immigration in 1862, Kanters had established himself as an expert in the construction of dykes, harbors, breakwaters, and cribs, working under contracts from the Dutch government. His Chicago contract called for laying up to two thousand

[54] Ibid., 8 Dec. 1878, 21 June 1888; Clarence Jalving interview by Donald van Reken, 15 July 1976, typescript, 2, Joint Archives of Holland (JAH).

feet of brush at $8.50 a foot. Kanters and his son Abraham shipped the brush by schooner and took a ten-man construction crew from Holland to Chicago for the $17,000 job. When the brush withstood the waves and ice of winter, the Chicago Park District rewarded Kanters with contracts around South Thirty-Ninth Street to protect Burnham Park from the crashing waves. Eventually, he installed the brush breakwaters along much of Lake Shore Drive. Building on this success, R. Kanters & Sons landed contracts in Buffalo, New York, and on the Brazos River in Texas. Their novel and ingenious system was featured at the World Industrial and Cotton Centennial Exposition in New Orleans in 1884.[55]

Early photographers

We have George Lauder to thank for the earliest photographs of Holland, but all his negatives were lost when his Eighth Street studio went up in flames in 1871. About 1875 two excellent craftsmen, Azariah Burgess and Benjamin Higgins, joined Lauder in the photography business. Burgess had previously practiced his profession for nine years in Muskegon. Higgins, a Civil War veteran and Chicago photographer, came to Holland after suffering the loss of eight thousand negatives in the Chicago Fire of 1871, but he soon returned to Chicago. "Higgins had one of the first moving picture machines that ever was brought to Holland," Stanley Curtis recalled, "and he exhibited in the old wooden opera house building, that was located where Borr's Bootery now stands. . . . I saw *The Great Train Robbery* there, one of the earliest movies."[56] (See appendix 5.7 for a list of photographers and artists, 1860-1950.)

These photographers made their living taking portraits of the leading families, but they also provided the first photographic record of the city's development. Lauder's post-fire photos were in great demand. In 1874 he went to work again at the behest of the Dutch visitor, M. Cohen Stuart, who wrote a book about his travels in America. Lauder's stereoscopic photos included a view of Eighth Street looking east from River Street; the First, Second, and Third Reformed churches; Market Street (Central Avenue) Christian Reformed and Grace Episcopal Churches; Hope College buildings; Cappon & Bertsch tannery; and the Black Lake harbor. Lauder was the first chief of the Holland Fire Department, a leader in the local Republican Party, and a prominent

55 Ibid., 15 Dec. 1877, 6, 25 May, 29 June, 12 Oct., 30 Nov. 1878, 18 Dec. 1880, 13 Dec. 1884. Kanters' career is described in detail in the *Holland American Yearbook*, 1888, Part One, 225-62.

56 Ibid., 30 Mar. 1872; *De Grondwet*, 9 Apr. 1873; Stanley Curtis, interview by Donald van Reken, 29 June 1976, typescript, 3-4, JAH.

Benjamin P. Higgins Gallery, 79 East Eighth Street, 1876. Note the wooden sidewalks and unpaved street; the view looks north (*Archives, Holland Historical Trust*)

Worshipful Master Freemason. Lauder could not resist the lure of California and left for the West.[57]

In the 1880s William D. Hopkins began a photography shop in the Kanters Block at 17 (later 100) East Eighth Street, and in the 1890s J. C. Calhoun equipped a new studio in the same building in 1897; Calhoun moved to 243 West Tenth Street in 1900. All the photographers were up in arms when outside canvassers took portrait photos of residents and then skipped town with their money and never delivered the ordered photographs. The local men demanded that the city council enact an ordinance to prohibit canvassing, but the officials refused, citing a 1902 ordinance that allowed canvassing and selling, provided the sellers had a valid city license. *Caveat emptor* (Let the buyer beware).[58]

Joseph Warner was a professional portraitist in Holland, who like Lauder came from Chicago and revived his career. Joseph and his wife Francis were in their sixties when they came in 1895. From then until shortly before his death in 1924, Warner painted in oils and watercolor hundreds of local scenes and local people, working from a studio in his Ninth Street home. His best known canvases were portraits of Van

57 *Holland City News*, 20 May, 1 Aug., 19 Dec. 1874, 18 Sept., 27 Nov., 11 Dec. 1875, 22 Dec. 1877.

58 Ibid., 13 Aug. 1908, 29 Mar. 1927; *De Hollander*, 3 Apr. 1872; *Holland Sentinel, Semi-Centennial Supplement, 1847-1897*; *Holland Sentinel*, 4, 7 Apr. 1970.

Raalte based on old photographs and prints. He did the first for the 1897 semi-centennial, but when locals declared it not a good likeness, he painted another that was well received. This one hangs in the Van Raalte Institute of Hope College. (The photo is found in the conclusion of chapter 34). Warner painted large views of Black Lake and Black River, two of which the city council purchased and hung in the council chambers in 1914. Warner also painted "bird's-eye" views of Holland, Zeeland, Hamilton, Hope College, and Jenison Park. Warner died poor because few locals were willing to buy his works. His unsold paintings were auctioned off after his death for the benefit of his widow.[59]

Early banking

After the nation came out of the 1873 depression, banking flourished along with Holland's booming economy. Kenyon quickly rebuilt his bank building after the 1877 fire. He took as a partner the lumberman Jacob "Jaap" Van Putten, and with the capital injection, Kenyon & Van Putten put up a small frame building at 30 West Eighth Street to house their new Holland City Bank. It was dedicated on January 1, 1878. Later that spring Van Putten's son Lane (Leendert), "a first-class accountant," joined the firm, which became Kenyon & Van Putten & Son. Kenyon opened a hardware store in Ionia and later moved to Iowa. Van Putten's blind son Marinus was the teller. His skill at counting silver coins by fingering them amazed customers. Van Putten Sr., "a thorough Americanized Hollander," had a sterling reputation, and farmers trusted him with their savings, as well as the cashier, his son-in-law Cornelius Ver Schure, "one of the best businessmen in the county." To keep the money safe, Van Putten in 1885 bought a burglar-proof safe for $1,000—a princely sum. Even the machinist Alfred Huntley could not breach the safe with his best drills and chisels. The Holland City Bank "was a potent agency in the early growth and development of the town. Its founders and early officers were men of push and enterprise."[60]

The Michigan Banking Act of 1889 again liberalized state banking regulations, and the face of banking changed in Holland. The Holland

59 "The Warners: England, New York, Canada, Chicago," HMA; *Holland City News*, 21 Mar. 1896, 30 Nov. 1905, 11 Apr. 1907, 3 Sept. 1908; *Hamilton Herald*, April 2006.

60 *Holland City News*, 5 Jan., 13 Apr., 18 Oct. 1878, 20 Mar. 1880, 2 Jan. 1885, 18 Jan. 1890 (quote), 2 May 1892 (quote); *De Hollander*, 1 Jan. 1878; Vande Water, "First Bank Was in Home"; Vande Water, "Tower Clock building"; Steve Vanderveen, "Den Herders have long history in Zeeland area business," *Holland Sentinel*, 27 Aug. 2006. Jacob Den Herder opened a private bank in Zeeland in 1878, which in 1900 became the Zeeland State Bank. Later the bank affiliated with First Michigan Bank and much later Huntington Bank (*Holland City News*, 14 Dec. 1900).

City Bank was reorganized in February 1890 as the Holland City State Bank under a new charter, with paid-up capital of $30,000, assets of $88,000, and loans of $67,000. The $42,000 in deposits included the city accounts; the city treasurer trusted the Van Puttens. The directors were Jacob Van Putten, his sons Lane, Jacob Jr., Adrian, and Marinus, plus Cornelius Ver Schure and Cornelius Nyland. Principal stockholders included Holland's leading men: Isaac Cappon (first bank president), insurance man and realtor Isaac Marsilje, businessman John C. Post, and attorneys Gerrit J. Diekema and Patrick McBride.[61]

In 1892 the Van Puttens built the spectacular Tower Clock Building, costing $27,000, on the prominent northwest corner of River and Eighth Streets. The tower rose to seventy-three feet, making it the city's tallest building. It was constructed entirely of local Waverly sandstone. Samuel Lapish and Robert Warham, both English master stonemasons in Holland, cut the stone and carved the granite pillars. John Raven, a young jeweler from Hartford, Michigan, built the clock with a dial that was five feet in diameter and lighted at night, "so men wouldn't be late for work." Donations covered his $600 cost. The offices of the Waverly Stone Company were on the second floor, and the ornate bank lobby occupied an elevated main floor, accessed by a circular stone staircase.[62]

After the senior Van Putten's death in 1897, Dirk Van Raalte became president; deposits then totaled $270,000. Savings accounts and certificates of deposit with a $10 minimum paid 3 percent for three months and 4 percent for six months compounded. William Beach succeeded Van Raalte as president, and John Kollen, Gerrit's brother, held a directorship for twenty-five years (1906-32). By 1912 bank deposits surpassed $1 million, and the paid-in capital and cash surplus each stood at $50,000. The bank dealt in gold and silver coins and greenbacks, depending on customer preference. In 1919, after nearly three decades of use, the bank was updated in a $60,000 renovation that included a more secure vault. The raised floor was eliminated and the lobby made into the "last word in banking interiors."[63]

61 *Holland City News*, 18 Jan., 31 May 1890, 2 May 1892; Dunbar, *Michigan*, 231.

62 Vande Water, "Tower Clock building"; Vande Water, "Tower clock 'got men to work on time,'" *Holland Sentinel*, 1 Apr. 1988; Samuel Lapish obit., ibid., 2 Mar. 1939. Lapish and Warham also laid the stonework for Graves Hall and Winant's Chapel.

63 *Ottawa County Times*, 4 Mar. 1892; *American Graphic* (Chicago), Aug. 25, 1899; *Holland: The Gateway of Western Michigan for Chicago and the Great West* (Chicago: Dearborn Corp., ca. 1912); *Holland Sentinel*, 23. Jan., 26 Apr. 1932, "50 Years Ago Today" 24 Nov. 1984; *Holland City News*, 23 May 1892, 2 Apr. 1914, 20 Mar., 11 Sept. 1919.

Tower Clock Building, erected 1892 to house the Holland City State Bank, 1907. The Interurban waiting room was the second building on the right (*courtesy Myron Van Ark*)

The First State Bank of Holland and the Ottawa Building and Loan, a mortgage bank, were rivals of the Holland City State Bank. Both opened under the new state banking law. First State Bank, as the name implies, was the first state bank organized in Ottawa County, and it soon boasted of being the largest bank in West Michigan. It opened its doors right after Christmas in 1889 under the leadership of Marsilje, Diekema, and John C. Post, who announced their intention of serving the entire Dutch colony. The bank was capitalized at $50,000. In the first decade its profits totaled $15,000, and savings and commercial deposits reached $450,000. In 1899 the board of directors included president Isaac Cappon, Western Theological Seminary president John W. Beardslee as vice president, and directors Henry Kremers, Hope College president Gerrit J. Kollen, attorney Gerrit Diekema, Fillmore Township civic leader Jan W. Garvelink, Holland mayor Germ W. Mokma, clothier Jan Bosman, furniture magnate Henry Pelgrim Sr., and merchant Albert H. Meyer. The bank started in Bosman's clothing store at 52 East Eighth Street, with Marsilje as cashier and Mokma as assistant cashier and bookkeeper. Mokma later succeeded Marsilje as cashier in 1893, and Henry Luidens followed Mokma.[64]

In 1894 the First State Bank directors built an impressive three-story building a few doors to the west, at 2 East Eighth Street and Central Avenue (now the Alpen Rose Restaurant), complete with a "burglar-

64 Vande Water, "Holland Had State Bank in 1889," in *Holland Happenings*, 2:62-64.

First State Bank, with post office next door, southeast corner of Eighth Street and Central Avenue (*Joint Archives of Holland*)

proof money chest" and a tower to mimic the tower clock of its rival on River Street. Diekema moved his law office into a spacious second-floor suite. When Cappon died in 1902, Kollen became president, and at his death in 1915, Diekema succeeded him, with Isaac Marsilje as treasurer. At its twenty-fifth anniversary in 1914, the bank had more than 5,000 depositors, $1.6 million in deposits, and undivided profits of $125,000. In its first quarter century, the bank paid out $581,000 in interest on deposits. In 1915 the bank made a stunning move; it sold its building to Abraham Peters for an F. W. Woolworth's five-and-dime store, and then built the magnificent $50,000 bank building that now adorns the northwest corner of the intersection. In 1917 the bank announced that deposits reached the $2 million mark. That all three banks were thriving spoke volumes about the general prosperity of Holland and the thriftiness of the populace. Woolworth built its new building in 1923; it had three times the space of the original and employed fifty clerks.[65]

Ottawa County Building & Loan Association (later Holland Savings & Loan Association) was established in 1889 under the new Michigan Banking Law as a community cooperative to provide home mortgages. Jeweler C. A. Stevenson served as the first president, followed by Kremers, Holland's leading physician after Ledeboer. The association counted fewer than thirty members in the early years, and they were less prominent men than the principals of the banks. In a stockholders' meeting at Kenyon's Opera House, the founders bought seven hundred shares to finance the venture. The first offices were in the rear of the

65 *Ottawa County Times*, 13 Jan. 1905; *Holland City News*, 31 Dec. 1914, 2 Sept. 1915, 24 Aug., 29 Sept. 1916, 18 Jan. 1917, 14 June 1923.

Peoples State Bank, 36-38 East Eighth Street, erected 1905
(*Archives, Holland Historical Trust*)

Model Drug Store on the northeast corner of Eighth and River Streets, directly across from the Holland City Sate Bank. After a decade or two, more prominent men joined the board, including Michigan state representative and speaker of the House Gerrit Diekema, Isaac Marsilje, Van Raalte's son-in-law Gerrit J. Kollen, Jan Bosman, Cornelius Ver Schure, John J. "Jack" Rutgers, among others. Early loans were in the $100 to $1,000 range.[66]

Peoples State Bank (later Old Kent Bank, then Fifth Third Bank), the city's third bank, was established in 1905 by Arend Visscher, Bastian D. Keppel, John H. Kleinheksel, George P. Hummer, Walter C. Walsh, Cornelius ("C. J.") Lokker, Douwe B. Yntema, Lane Van Putten, and Derk Te Roller. The principals, a veritable Who's Who of Holland businessmen, raised the necessary $50,000 capital and erected a building at 29 East Eighth Street that opened two days before Christmas. The first officers of Peoples State Bank were Visscher as president; Keppel, vice president; John J. Rutgers, cashier, and Henry Winter, assistant cashier. Peoples Bank enjoyed steady growth in deposits, but it always stood in the shadow of its two bigger competitors. The bank deposits grew rapidly, from $87,000 in 1905 to $630,000 in 1915, and $3.3 million

66 *Ottawa County Times*, 31 Jan. 1902; Steve Vanderveen, "Ottawa County Building and Loan started as community cooperative," *Holland Sentinel*, 20 May 2007. In 1951 the Ottawa County Savings & Loan moved into a new building on the southeast corner of Central Avenue at Tenth Street (*Holland City News*, 8 Nov. 1951).

Ornate interior of the Peoples State Bank (*courtesy Myron Van Ark*)

in 1930. Alex Van Zanten worked his way up from janitor in 1911 to director in 1930. The capital stock was increased to $100,000 in 1925 and $150,000 in 1929, and in 1927 the directors erected a new facility on the south side of the street, at 36-38 East Eighth.[67] Control of all three banking institutions was in the same hands—the partners in the law office of Diekema, Kollen, & Ten Cate. Holland banking "resembled a plutocracy," according to local business historian Steve Vander Veen.[68]

The Federal Reserve Act of 1913, which created the Federal Reserve System, changed the industry from the bottom up, including the local banks. In 1918 the Holland City State Bank and the First State Bank of Holland joined the federal system, which required doubling the capital stock from $50,000 to $100,000. Both met the new standard. Being part of the "Fed" assured depositors and stockholders of the greater safety of their money. Member banks could borrow cash from the Federal Reserve, if needed, with their commercial paper and government bonds as collateral.[69]

Businessmen in the 1880s

The decade of the 1880s was one of unprecedented prosperity, and the local economy rode at high tide, thanks to new factories,

67 Clarence Jalving, "The Peoples State Bank of Holland," typescript, ca. 1970, HMA; *Holland City News*, 4 Mar. 1909, 2 Apr. 1914, 10 July 1930.

68 Vander Veen, "Ottawa County Building and Loan."

69 *Holland City News*, 25 July 1918.

fresh hiring, and the communications marvel—the telephone (chapter 25). New brick buildings dotted Eighth Street, thanks to Henry Post, Engbertus Vander Veen, and Hermanus Boone, and residents on the fashionable streets (Ninth, Tenth, and Eleventh) improved their homes or erected lavish new ones. Reinder Werkman laid the first concrete sidewalk in town in front of his new home on Ninth Street. Developers opened new subdivisions, and carpenters could not build houses fast enough. The town fathers funded numerous public improvement projects, notably a new city hall and firehouse on East Eighth Street (chapter 26). Twenty new buildings were under construction in 1885, and city leaders crowed about the biggest building boom ever.[70]

John C. Post published this ditty with his real estate ad:

> "What makes town lots go flying so?" the eager buyers cry.
> "Oh, Holland's on a boom, you know," the agents do reply.
> And so the owners mark them up, yet buyers do not squeal,
> but run impatiently about, for fear they'll lose a deal.[71]

Werkman alone in the late 1880s built thirty-five homes, stores, offices, and cottages for $36,000, and some forty other projects totaling $50,000. Another $36,000 was spent on cottages and improvements at Macatawa Park and Ottawa Beach. Many had the new-fangled coal furnace installed in place of a wood stove. In 1887 contractors built fifteen buildings costing $28,000. The aggregate wealth of the city that year was $2.5 million and the value of trade and industry was $2.2 million. Mercantile trade alone was estimated at $800,000.[72]

Merchants offered the full range of goods and services, and local newspaper editors urged citizens to show their public spirit and "buy everything at home." Commission merchants William Beech and Jan Pauels (Plugger's Mills) dealt in grain, flour and produce; Hermanus Boone, John Alberti, and Jacobus Nibbelink ran liveries and traded horses; hardware merchants Engbertus Vander Veen and Rokus Kanters & Sons carried everything from nails to appliances and furniture. Vander Veen's store was fifty years old in 1897; he was truly the pioneer hardware merchant. Ben Van Raalte, third son of Holland's founder, and Richard Heald competed in selling farm implements, carriages, and sleighs. Three butcher shops lined Eighth Street: those in Hein

70 Ibid., 25 Nov. 1882, 26 May, 20 Oct. 1883, 4 Oct. 1884, 11 Apr., 16 Sept., 7 Nov., 19 Dec. 1885.

71 *Holland City News*, 14 Mar. 1887.

72 Ibid., 9 Jan., 27 Mar., 24 Apr. 1886, 1 Jan. 5 Feb. 1887; *De Grondwet*, 16 Apr. 1889.

De Kraker & De Koster Meat Market, 184 River Street, ca. 1915, with hanging slabs of meat that butchers cut as customers requested (*Archives, Holland Historical Trust*)

Van der Haar's grocery, William Vander Veere's City Meat Market, and Gabriel Van Putten's general store and meat counter. The well-known meat market of De Kraker & De Koster at 184 North River Street also had a brisk trade. It was opened by two pairs of brothers, Louis and Isaac De Kracker and James and Jacob De Koster. Peter Prins' grocery, in partnership with John De Jonge and later Henry Geerlings, stood on East Eighth Street for forty-five years, from 1880 to 1925, before the Holland Theater was constructed on the site.[73]

John Kleyn, besides being a hardware merchant, was a self-taught architect who designed Third Reformed Church (1872), the Cappon & Bertsch tannery, the Isaac Cappon House (1874) and the John Coatsworth House (1863), which faced each other across First (Washington) Avenue on West Ninth Street, and the Boot & Kramer and Kiekinveld Blocks on East Eighth Street.[74]

Heber Welsh and William Van Putten, the city's first pharmacists, sold drugs, medicines, paints, and oils. Jan Bosman, the city's oldest

73 *De Grondwet*, 6 Dec. 1881, 28 Mar. 1882, 17 June, 13 Sept. 1884, 5 Feb. 1887 (quote); Peter H. Prins obit., *Holland Sentinel*, 13 May 1938. In 1888 Rokus Kanters turned his hardware store over to his three sons, Rokus, John, and Gerardus (*De Grondwet*, 17 Apr. 1888).

74 *Holland City News*, John R. Kleyn obit., 26 Oct. 1895; Joel Lefever, "Images of the past," *Grand Rapids Press*, 26 Nov. 2006.

Farmer Peter Middelhoek bringing in a load of split logs for firewood, early 1880s (*Archives, Holland Historical Trust*)

merchant tailor, clothed the locals, and shoemakers Ernest Herold, Joos De Koeyer, and George J. Van Duren handled all kinds of footware. Jas. A. Brouwer & Co. (formerly Meyer, Brouwer & Co.) was the leading furniture and carpet store. The pair later split up: James Brouwer took the furniture and Albert H. Meyer the music. This is the origin of Meyer Music House. Otto Breyman and later his son William ran one of the leading jewelry stores on Eighth Street at Market (Central) Street; they did engraving, repaired watches, and were opticians. Breyman first partnered with Joclin and in 1895 sold out to Henry W. "William" Hardie.[75]

In 1882 Leendert Mulder, owner and publisher of *De Grondwet*, installed the city's first steam printing press in his building. To fire up the press, Mulder had the Teunis Keppel Coal Co., founded in 1867, bring in the first carload of coal to the city. Keppel's ten-year-old son Albert delivered the coal in a two-wheeled cart that the firm proudly displayed in later years. Older son Bastian also joined the firm. Other merchants soon saw the advantage of coal over wood for fuel, especially since wood was increasingly scarce since the Great Fire.[76]

The city counted fourteen groceries in 1885, at least one in every neighborhood. Johannes Vissers & Son (Machiel) had two stores—on

75 *Holland City News*, 19 Aug. 1884, 1 Dec. 1888, 9 Apr. 1889, 1 Feb., 6 Dec. 1890, 1 Aug. 1896.

76 Ibid., 4 Feb. 1932, Bastian D. Keppel obit., 7 July 1932, Albert C. Keppel obit., 27 July 1939.

C. Steketee & Bos clothing store, northwest corner of Ninth and River Streets, 1880s. Cornelius Steketee in front of store and Cornelis Bos behind wagon, both in vests (*Archives, Holland Historical Trust*)

River near Eighth Street and on First (Washington) Avenue and Twelfth Street. On Eighth Street stood the stores of B. Wynhoff and A. Steketee & Sons, which by then had changed their stock from draperies and curtains to apparel. Cornelius Steketee and his father-in-law Cornelis Bos went into business as C. Steketee & Bos on the northwest corner of River and Ninth Streets, a corner shared by William G. Van Dyke's grocery. Daniel Bertsch's dry goods store rented space in Engbertus Vander Veen's new building on the southeast corner of Eighth and River Streets. Blacksmiths Johannes and Cornelius Dykema and H. Visser shod horses, welded iron, and made wagons. The job printer was William H. Rogers, editor of the *Holland City News*. Isaac Fairbanks, Henry Post, Derk Te Roller, and Arend Visscher were conveyancers and notaries who transferred property titles and validated documents.[77]

Reinder E. Werkman, Holland's leading industrialist, in 1887 opened his Phoenix Cheap Cash Store on the northwest corner of Tenth and River Streets. Werkman also purchased the stock of E. F. Metz & Co. and began the Werkman Millinery Emporium at 50 East Eighth Street, run by his sisters Hattie and Jennie, who trimmed first-class bonnets and hats for women. The sisters ran the store, known as Werkman Sisters, for twenty-five years. Their competition was the Vandenberg

[77] *Holland City News*, 5 Feb., 28 May, 8 Nov. 1887, 17 Apr., 15 Sept. 1888, "Forty Years Ago Today," 26 Jan. 1939; *De Grondwet*, 15 Sept. 1885, 25 June 1887; *The Anchor* (Hope College student newspaper), 6 (Nov. 1892), 35.

C. Blom Confectionery, 18 West Eighth Street, 1901. Owner Cornelius Blom Jr. is most likely at door on left. The store was obviously a magnet for children, but adults sought the "fresh bananas" hanging by the door (*courtesy Larry B. Massie*)

Sisters Millinery store at 72 East Eighth Street. Clara (Mrs. Dallas) Gee & Co. carried fashionable women's clothing. Leon Henderson's Chicago Clothing Store on River Street offered everyday clothing at prices "lower than Grand Rapids." R. Weertman's new Cookie Manufactory at Sixth and River Streets baked three hundred pounds of Dutch pastries a day to satisfy local cravings. His competitors, both on Eighth Street, were John Pessink's City Bakery and Peter Van Dommelen, who specialized in Dutch rusk (biscuits). Peter Steketee's grocery on Eighth and River Streets in season sold *nieuwe Hollansche haring* (new Dutch herring) direct from the Netherlands.[78]

The onyx soda fountain in fire chief Cornelius Blom Jr.'s Confectionery (later Boston Bakery) on Eighth Street featured milk shakes that were an instant hit with old and young. To make the shakes, two glasses of ice-cold milk and vanilla flavoring were fastened to a fast-moving teeter-totter device that was spun by a wheel with a hand crank.

78 Donald van Reken and Fritz L. Kliphuis, *Reinder Edward Werkman: "The Gilded Hollander"* (Holland, MI, 2007); *Holland City News*, 4 Apr., 8 Aug., 12, 26 Sept., 21 Nov. 1885, 25 Sept., 21 Dec. 1886, 19 Feb., 19 Mar., 27 Sept. 1887, Hattie Werkman obit., 29 June 1935.

This created a shaking movement that mixed the flavoring and left a head of frothy foam. The pretentious soda fountain was rivaled as a conversation piece by a large felt elephant in the corner with a clock mechanism that made the head nod. Blom advertised that his five-cent milk shakes were "One Step toward Temperance."[79]

A wandering soul who came to town in 1887 and stayed was Fred Griffin, an Italian-born chimney sweep with an assumed name, who quickly endeared himself to locals by his winsome ways. Griffin had lived so long in Mexico that locals at first called him "a Mick." Leendert Mulder of *De Grondwet* gave Griffin his first job, cleaning the building chimney. True to his trade, Griffin donned chimney sweep togs complete with a high pointed hat, and perched atop the chimney, he loudly sang the chimney sweep song as he dangled ropes down the flue. His act attracted up to five hundred curious onlookers, many of whom hired the Italian to clean their chimneys. The man, who was quite a character, to say the least, plied his trade here for forty-five years until his death in 1932. It was said that his lungs were filled with coal dust and soot. Editor Ben Mulder, Leendert's son, eulogized Griffin in a front-page obituary as "one of the best hearted Italians the city has ever known." On Sundays, Mulder added, Griffin never failed to attend high mass at St. Francis de Sales Church, always seated at the foot of the choir loft. During Griffin's funeral mass at the church, officiated by Father Fred Ryan, the school children's choir sang over his bier. Pallbearers were Tom Powers, Earl Francombe, Mike Fabiano, and Tom Halley. Griffin died in honor, loving and being loved by his adopted city.[80]

Mannes Kiekintveld, a retired Reformed Church pastor who served many Michigan congregations, opened a bookstore and stationary house in 1883. He also carried games, organs, musical instruments, and sewing machines. No one could make a living dealing strictly in books. The ex-dominie built the impressive Kiekintveld Block at 28-30 East Eighth Street out of Waverly stone for his retail and wholesale house. At his death in 1889, his oldest son Henry took over the business. When he put the building up for auction in 1902, the bidding was quite lively until attorney Arend Visscher quieted the crowd by raising the bid from $5,000 to $7,000.[81]

In medical services, several physicians and surgeons began practice in the 1880s. Frank S. Ledeboer doctored in Gee's former

79 *Holland City News*, 30 Dec. 1877, "Fifty Years Ago Today" 22 July, 16 Dec. 1937, "Fifty Years Ago Today" 27 Jan. 1938.

80 Ibid., 25 Feb. 1932.

81 Ibid., 20 Nov. 1886; 1 Aug. 1896, 31 Jan. 1902.

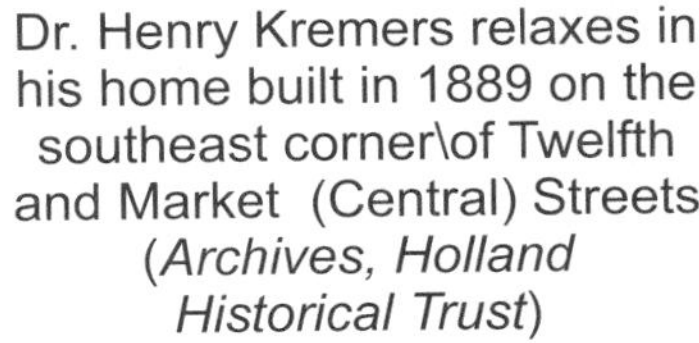

Dr. Henry Kremers relaxes in his home built in 1889 on the southeast corner\of Twelfth and Market (Central) Streets (*Archives, Holland Historical Trust*)

dentist office in Vennema's Building on Eighth Street. L. Schiphorst took over Frederick Schouten's practice and his First Ward Drug Store, in partnership with Henry Schepers. Schouten took patients at his East Ninth Street home until his death in 1919, which ended a practice of forty years. Druggist William Van Putten completed medical training and hung out his shingle as a physician. Doctors were often druggists and vise versa because both needed prescribed medicinal concoctions of the day.

Henry Kremers, born in Zeeland Township and educated at Hope College and the University of Michigan, began practicing medicine in Holland in 1882, after serving for six years in Drenthe and Zeeland. He built up a large practice in his own Kremers Block at 6 East Eighth Street just east of the post office. Later, he partnered briefly with William Z. Bangs in Kremers & Bangs Drug Store. In 1889 Kremers bought out Bangs and renamed it the Central Drug Store. Kremers practiced medicine for thirty-one years until he retired and sold his practice and building to Daniel G. Cook in 1913. Oscar E Yates, who had practiced several years in Overisel, opened an office on River Street opposite Market Square in 1883. He partnered with P. W. Kane in a drug store on the corner of River and Eighth Streets from 1885 to 1890, when Kane bought him out. Yates was elected mayor that year.[82]

82 "Henry Kremers," *Portrait and Biographical Record of Muskegon and Ottawa Counties* (Chicago: Biographical Record Co., 1893), 331-32; "Century Club Presidents, Holland, Michigan," typescript (Century Club: Holland, MI, 1994).

Yates displayed his surgical skills in 1888 when he operated on Sjoerd Jonker, who was badly wounded by a shotgun that blew up as he fired it, leaving his face mangled and full of metal fragments. Yates removed the bridge of the nose and one eye and cleaned out the debris in a delicate operation. Jonker survived, to the amazement of all. Yates was active in the city's social, industrial, political, religious, and educational life. He served one term as mayor (1890-91) and was a member of the board of education at his death in 1901. His large home with a sunken garden stood on the present site of the city hall. His entire family was musically inclined; daughter Grace Yates Brook was a prominent soloist, and daughter Amy Yates Kremers was a talented pianist. The family belonged to Hope Church.[83]

In 1891 Abraham Leenhouts, a graduate of the University of Michigan, opened his medical practice, and he quickly became one of the most prominent physicians, given his visible role as chair of school board. A unique pair were Dr. Jerred D. Wetmore and his wife Dr. Iantha Jane Wetmore, who took over her husband's practice in 1896 after his death. After fourteen years in Holland, she moved to Grand Rapids about 1912.[84]

There was little change in the practice of medicine in Holland until after 1900. Doctors saw patients in their offices and made house calls. No one thought a hospital was necessary; the wealthy went to Grand Rapids or Chicago for more complicated surgeries. Physicians and druggists seemed to be immune to the hard times in the mid-1890s. Dr. John G. Huizenga began his successful practice in an upstairs office near River Street, specializing in diseases of the eyes, ears, nose, and throat. In 1895 the good doctor was sued for malpractice after setting a fractured wrist, but the Circuit Court in Grand Haven ruled in his favor. Shortly thereafter, he accepted a faculty position in a medical college in Chicago.[85]

Milton J. Cook and Albertus C. Van Raalte Gilmore, the dominie's grandson, both with sheepskins from the University of Michigan Dental School, started their practices. So did Daniel G. Cook and J. R. McCracken. William R. Stevenson, a licensed optician, opened an office in his father's jewelry store, which allowed him to sell both jewelry and eye glasses. Van Putten sold his drug shop to Lawrence Kramer, his apprentice and assistant.[86]

83 *Holland City News*, 17 Mar. 1888, "Fifty Years Ago Today" 17 Apr. 1938; *Ottawa County Times*, 1 Nov. 1901.

84 Marie N. Zingle, *The Story of the Woman's Literary Club, 1898-1989* (Holland, 1898), photo caption of Bay View Reading Circle.

85 *Holland City News*, 20 Apr. 1890, 6 Nov. 1895, 27 Mar. 1897.

86 Ibid., 1 Jan. 1887.

Jacob O. Doesburg's Drug Store, Eighth Street between Central and College Avenues, ca. 1900. The people are thought to be Jacob O. (*on right*) and son Harry (Hermanus) (*on left*), mother Mrs. Harry Doesburg with baby in genuine Dutch pram and two children at her side, and Mrs. Jacob Doesburg with parasol (*Archives, Holland Historical Trust*)

In 1890, Miss Sue A. Martin and George H. Huizenga took over Yates & Kane's drugstore at 38 East Eighth Street. Martin bought out Huizenga in 1899 and started the Martin Drug Store. Her store in 1906 became the fabled Model Drug Store under Gilbert T. Haan (chapter 19).[87] James A. Mabbs opened an office in Walsh's drug store on East Eighth at Fish (Columbia) Streets. Bangs returned to Holland in 1889 and opened a drug store on Eighth Street where he manufactured his patented Pine Cones, Bangs' Magic Celery, and other elixirs. The Doesburg Drug Store at 32 East Eighth Street was thirty years old in 1894, having been rebuilt after the 1871 fire. Louis Lawrence was the pharmacist until starting his own drug store in 1921 (see below). Jacob O. Doesburg's son Harry clerked for his father in the 1890s and ran the pharmacy from 1901 to 1937. Fred Meppelink then owned it until it closed in 1960.[88]

87 *Holland City News*, 8 Sept. 1899, 23 July 1930; *Holland City News*, 4 Sept. 1913; *Holland City Directories*,

88 1894, 1901-2, 1913-14, 1915-16, 1960.

Jeweler C. A. Stevenson shared his store at 24 East Eighth Street with his optician son William R. Stevenson, 1890s (*courtesy Randall P. Vande Water*)

Jannetje (Mrs. Hendrik) Wykhuizen, the jeweler's wife, who had earned a medical degree in the Netherlands, practiced midwifery. Ben Mulder recalled fifty years later that she "had built up quite a patronage among the women of this town in the early days when women doctors were few and far between. In fact," he added, "her being announced as a physician created considerable comment in the city at the time." Mrs. Wykhuizen died at age fifty-four in 1889. The Wykhuizens immigrated in 1872 from Ablasserdam in the province of Zuid Holland and Henry joined John Albers in his jewelry store in 1876 and eventually took it over. He sold to C. A. Stevenson in 1887.[89]

Three attorneys advertised their services in the late 1880s: the old justice of the peace Isaac Fairbanks, Henry Post's son John C., and Gerrit J. Diekema, a graduate of Hope College and the University of Michigan, who put up his shingle in 1883. Three watering holes were Cornelius Blom Sr.'s Rose Bud Saloon on River Street, the Swede Peter Brown's establishment on Eighth Street near River, and Hunt & Hopkins Sample Room on Eighth at Market Street.[90]

89 *Holland City News*, 6 Dec. 1879, 21 Jan. 1882, 16 Sept. 1885, 5 Feb. 1887, 28 Sept., 7 Dec. 1889, 6 Dec. 1890, 1 Aug. 1896, 21 Aug. 1919, 22 Aug. 1935 (quote), "Fifty Years Ago Today" 2 Mar. 1939; Hope College *Anchor*, Nov. 1887.

90 *Holland City News*, 5 Feb. 1887.

Given the thriving trade among Holland's more than one hundred merchants in 1886, it was compelling for them to restart the Holland Businessmen's Association to promote the "social, moral, and business interests of its members." The twenty-five charter members met in October at Henry Post's office, under the auspices of the editor of the *Tradesman* of Grand Rapids. They listed ten objectives: to treat "honorable competitors" kindly and not to "berate and criminate" them, to strengthen their hand as employers, to encourage fair dealings, to limit store hours from seven o'clock in the morning to six o'clock in the evening six days a week and observe all national holidays, to limit credit sales in favor of "ready pay" in cash, to regulate weights and measures, to build a common list of blacklisted deadbeats, and to lobby politicians for laws favorable to business. The tenth rationale said it all: "To render the title 'Business Man' a synonym for honor, firmness, probity, justice, and high morals." To keep these ten principles was too much to expect; Holland never became a commercial utopia.[91]

The merchants' real objective, though unspoken, was to compile and enforce a debtors' blacklist, according to editor William Rogers of the *Holland City News*. The goal was "to protect merchants and business men generally doing a credit business in Holland and vicinity against defaulting, irresponsible, and delinquent debtors, and to report to the Association the names of such debtors with their address, occupation, amount of delinquency, etc., every member of the Association being pledged not to extend another dollar of credit to one so reported."[92]

Rogers on January 1, 1887, began publishing the *Holland Business Directory*, and he offered to list every one of the 135 mercantile and professional firms for a nominal fee of one dollar. During hard times in the 1890s, the association went defunct, only to be revived in 1907 when conditions improved. But apathy continued. In 1914 president John Vander Sluis complained that monthly meetings brought out only forty of the one hundred members. We need a "little more spirit," he cried—and a turnout of at least seventy-five members.[93]

Holland at fifty—hard times in the 1890s

The year 1890 began with an extremely harsh winter, and farmers talked of hard times. Yet the building boom in the city reached new heights; more than one hundred homes were constructed in 1891,

91 Ibid., 13 Nov. 1886.

92 Ibid., 23 Oct., 11 Dec. 1886 (quote).

93 *Holland City News*, 14 Feb. 1907, 19 Feb. 1914. The first extant city business directory is the 1892 edition.

amounting to over $100,000. In 1892 local factories, the backbone of the economy, kept on hiring and adding new machinery to boost production. The West Michigan Furniture Company alone added 125 jobs. Holland City State Bank erected its new Tower Clock building. The Chicago & West Michigan Railway reported that the increase in its Holland traffic was the greatest in its entire system. Holland also gained the first direct daily schooner service to Chicago with the creation of the Holland-Chicago Line by William Beach, Henry Post, and other local promoters. This promising scenario came to a sudden halt in 1893, when a financial crash on Wall Street set off the worst national depression of the nineteenth century.[94]

Siert (later Sears) Frederick Riepma, who was laid off, recalled the grim picture years later:

> In September 1894 the work in the lumberyard ceased, and many of us were laid off. I was among that number. My entreaties with Lou, the genial foreman, were of no avail. Times were slack, winter coming on and no work anywhere in sight. We tried hard enough but without avail, even entertaining the idea to "go way up North" to the lumber camps, but were persuaded to put that out of our minds. For days we walked the streets in search of something to do. It is tragic to have energy to sell and no takers at any price. My sympathy for the unemployed must have started there. . . . Nobody cared for us. No labor union looked after us. No WPA or other agency, governmental or private, seemed to care whether we lived or died. Walking the streets in search of work is physically exhausting, but it is hardest on a man's spirit. We were rather docile, I suppose, but there were elements of danger in such a situation—real dynamite. It belonged to the great American way of life.[95]

Riepma was mistaken about unions. In 1892 the mechanical trades in Holland had five unions—Carpenters and Joiners, Tanners and Curriers, Bricklayers and Masons, Industrials (undesignated trades), and Knights of Labor (unskilled). In 1903 the Painters and Paperhangers organized. All fought for "a fair and equitable scale of wages." The largest union was Assembly 441 of the United Brotherhood of Carpenters and Joiners, which met bi-monthly in Harrington's Hall,

94 Ibid., 11 Jan. 1890; *Holland Business Directory for1892*, 183; *Ottawa County Times*, 10 June 1892.

95 Sears Frederick Riepma, "Autobiography," typescript, 94, HMA.

led by Evert Takken, president; George Lawson, vice president; William F. Van Anrooy, secretary; and John Donahue, treasurer.[96]

Cigars were another popular consumer product made in Holland since the 1880s. Most men smoked stogies rather than cigarettes until the 1920s. The smoky haze in church consistory rooms around town testified to the custom. In the glory days of cigar making in Holland, deft-fingered workers, many teenagers, rolled hundreds of thousands of cigars every year. Holland was not a noted cigar center like New York's East Side with its Jewish rollers, but the local shops more than satisfied men in the "age of smoke." Henry Vander Weyden, one of the first cigar makers, reported in 1882 that his shop was "constantly growing" because of a "tremendous run" on his Little Hope and Little Fred cigars. James Vander Veen's six employees in 1886 rolled more than three hundred thousand cigars a year, priced at 3¢ apiece. The ORJ Cigar Company, founded in 1898 by O. R. Johnson and W. R. Reed, in the first three years turned out five hundred thousand cigars, sold under the Knights of the Grip label, known popularly as Grip. In 1895 two young men, Frank De Later and Albert Vegter, began the Snag Cigar Co. and rolled five-cent Havana and domestic cigars with colorful labels such as Country Girl, Little Cuban, and Lily Belle. Other cigar makers included Leonard De Loof and George and Charles Brownell.[97]

None made more cigars than Herman Van Tongeren, who opened a cigar factory on East Tenth Street in 1895, and within five years his workers were rolling eight hundred thousand Star Green brand cigars a year. Van Tongeren soon found larger quarters for his shop at 12 East Eighth Street. In 1917 he moved his factory, but not the retail store, to the third floor of the commodious A. C. Rinck Block at 58-60 East Eighth Street. Van Tongeren in 1919 advertised for "girls" to learn the cigar trade and promised the "best working conditions" and over $14 a week after ten weeks. His Dutch Novelty Shop was no sweatshop. Under his son Chester "Chet" Van Tongeren in the 1930s, the firm changed product lines from cigars to turning out millions of wooden shoes for Tulip Time tourists and klompen dancers (chapter 28).[98] (See appendix 5.3 for a list of cigar companies, 1887-1938.)

Hotels at the time included the St. Charles Hotel (formerly Aniba, Alamo, Hemmingway, and Phoenix), the City Hotel (later Hotel Holland), Scott's Hotel (First Ward Hotel in 1885), and the Sinclair

96 *Holland City News*, 6 Feb. 1892, 30 Jan. 1903.

97 Massie, *Haven, Harbor and Heritage*, 75-77; *Holland City News*, 28 Jan. 1882, 15 Jan. 1887,

98 *Holland City News*, 4 Jan. 1917, 2 Oct. 1919; *Holland Sentinel*, 13 May 1937.

Herman Van Tongeren's Cigar Manufactory, 12 East Eighth Street, ca. 1897, with six aficionados and a wooden Indian to tout his John Morgan 5¢ stogies (*Archives, Holland Historical Trust*)

Hotel, a large frame building on the south side of Eighth Street at the depot. In 1889 came the Williams Hotel (Hadden Hotel in 1896), and in 1902 the Bristol Hotel, which had a nearly fifty-year run, to 1949, under Urs F. and Inez Von Ins.

Hotel proprietors held an honored place in the community. In 1916 when Helene (Mrs. George) (Boone) Pardee, manager of the Hotel Holland, died at age thirty-five after a brief illness, the *Holland City News* proclaimed her the "most popular woman in Holland and possibly Ottawa County." Her father, Hermanus Boone, owned the hotel. She had previously owned and operated the leading millinery shop on West Eighth Street. A talented singer and outdoor enthusiast, Helene performed in countless churches and for society functions, and was an active member of both the Century Club and the Woman's Literary Club, the two most prestigious societies in town (chapter 29).[99]

Sophia Barnier opened one of the first restaurants on Eighth Street in 1877 next to Van Putten's grocery store on River Avenue. Her "Temperance Restaurant" appealed to "Red Ribbon Men!" and promised "meals at all hours," but traveling men who desired to "wet

[99] Kliphuis, "Hotels of Holland"; *Holland City News*, 2 Nov. 1916.

Herman Van Tongeren driving his mobile "Kum Bak" cigar store, September 1913 (*Archives, Holland Historical Trust*)

their whistles" would have to eat elsewhere. A popular Eighth Street restaurant since 1880 was that of Luman E. and Anna Van Drezer, Grand Haven natives. The eatery at 8 West Eighth had a lunch counter in front and an elegant dining parlor in back that seated sixty-five patrons. Their tables "are simply par excellence, and are always clean, neat, and inviting, with clean linens." The Van Drezers also catered weddings, banquets, receptions, and other special occasions. Anna Van Drezer baked fifty pies a day to go with the ever-ready cups of coffee. Van Drezers continued for thirty-five years, until 1915, the last five years as Van's Cafe under John and Anna Hoffman. Across the street from 1903 to 1931 stood the Boston Restaurant of Nicholas Hoffman at 32-34 West Eighth Street, replete with linen tablecloths and white-shirted waiters.[100] (See appendix 5.9 for a list of restuarants, 1897-1950.)

Eighth Street stores were in constant flux. Newcomers included the hardware stores of John Nies and J. B. Van Oort, Tyler Van Landegend's plumbing supply house, William Brusse & Co. men's clothing at Eighth and River below the offices of Dr. Abraham Leenhouts, John Vander Sluis dry goods, the grocery of Peter A. Kleis at Columbia Avenue, and Paul Tanis' Holland Tea Company in the City Hotel Block. Tanis

100 *Holland City News*, 9 June 1877, 11 Mar. 1893; Moerdyke, "Pioneer Merchants of Holland," P. T. Moerdyke Papers, box 4, HMA.

Van Drezer's Restaurant at 8 West Eighth Street, ca. 1910. The photo is likely of proprietors John and Anna Hoffman (*Archives, Holland Historical Trust*)

Anthony and Dena Romeyn's Alpena Restaurant at 70 East Eighth Street, ca. 1910, named after the steamship that in 1880 sank with all aboard off present-day Lakewood Boulevard (*courtesy Myron Van Ark*)

William Brusse men's clothing store, southwest corner of 194 River Avenue at Eighth Street (now Reader's World), with the office of Dr. Abraham Leenhouts upstairs (*courtesy Randall P. Vande Water*)

carried coffees, teas, spices, crockery, glassware, and silverware. Nies had operated a hardware store in Saugatuck for twenty-seven years before moving to Holland in the early 1890s. He built a modern building at 43-45 East Eighth Street with his name emblazoned above. Kanters' sons, Rokus A. and Gerardus, bought the John Van Landegend Hardware in 1883 and formed Kanters Bros. Hardware, which had a twenty-year run. Tyler Van Landegend's featured product was the Red Jacket Pump, an iron hand pump that every homeowner needed before city water became available. Merchant tailor Jan Bosman's custom tailoring shop, first opened in 1869, was passed to his sons, Adrian B. and John, and the firm became Bosman Bros. Abraham C. Rinck bought out the furniture, carpet, and home furnishings store of Walsh & Gilmore.[101]

In 1892 Lokker Rutgers clothing store began its 116-year run at 37-39 East Eighth Street, when Jacob Lokker (brother of Christian "Chris" J.) and John J. "Jack" Rutgers purchased the men's clothing store of Matthew Notier and John Verschure. Jacob Lokker had for ten years been a partner with his brother in the Holland Crystal Creamery (chapter 17), and prior to that he had clerked in mayor E. J. Harrington's general

[101] *Holland City News*, 5 Feb. 1887; William Brusse obit., 26 July 1956; *Holland City Directory*, 1896-97.

John Nies Sons Hardware store, 43-45 East Eighth Street, ca. 1912, decked out for a political campaign (*Archives, Calvin College*)

store on East Eighth Street near College Avenue. Lokker was "one of the wide awake business men" of Holland and a prominent member of Columbia Hose Company No. 2 (chapter 26). One of Lokker Rutgers' first hires in 1894 was fourteen-year-old Fred Beeuwkes, who rapidly advanced over the next twenty years. When the firm was incorporated in 1900, Beeuwkes became one of the stockholders, rising to secretary. At first, Lokker Rutgers sold men's and boy's clothing, blankets, bicycles, bicycle parts, and many other items. In 1902 the business needed more space very badly and was willing to pay the exorbitant price of $2,000 for Du Mez next door at 35 East Eighth, including all its furnishings.[102]

In 1907 the partners moved merchandize and the tailoring department to the second floor, making it one of the largest men's furnishing emporiums in Ottawa County. In 1910 Lokker rented the basement of his store to shoemaker William Kobes; this started a ninety-eight-year connection of the Kobes family to the store, most of the time as owners. In those days customers tied their horses to rails in

102 *Holland City News*, 14 Feb. 1907 (quote), 3 Apr. 1913, 5 Nov. 1914, 5 Apr. 1923, 10 Nov. 1927, Gerrit Du Mez obit., 24 Dec. 1931; *Holland Sentinel*, 6 Apr. 1973, 30 June 1989.

the street in front of the store, and the wax mannequins in the front display windows had real human hair. Fine china was given to loyal customers as premiums.

Beeuwkes in 1914 sold his stock to Lokker and took a position with the Jas. A. Brouwer Furniture Co. In 1915 Rutgers sold his interest to Lokker and launched a rival clothing store at 7 East Eighth Street. In 1929 John Kobes and friend John Sturing bought some stock from Lokker, and when Lokker retired in 1932, they bought him out. Sturing started as a clerk in 1913 and advanced to manager of the men's clothing department. John Kobes managed the store and kept it afloat during the Depression decade; after World War Two, he increased his ownership stake. When Jacob Lokker died in 1938, all the pallbearers were connected with the store, including Sturing, Kobes, Peter and Gelmer Boven, John Zoerman, and Ed Barkel.[103]

In 1955 John's son Ronald Kobes became the general manager of Lokker Rutgers, and in 1972 he assumed the presidency after becoming the majority stock owner. In 1969 Ronald's daughter Lynn took over management of the ladies department. Son Jerome, who began working at age twelve as a janitor and helper, joined the business in 1974, rising to general manager in the 1980s. In 1987 the Kobes clan embarked on a major expansion to add specialty departments, expanding into two adjacent businesses and more than doubling the floor space. The next year store traffic dropped precipitously for many months while the city tore up Eighth Street from sidewalk to sidewalk to install new utilities and the snowmelt system (chapter 33). In 1990 Ronald sold the business to his children, Jerome and Lynn, who experienced a "day of infamy" on March 27, 1992, when a small electrical fire was fanned by strong winds into an inferno that engulfed the store. Flames and smoke damage destroyed all the merchandise—90 percent of it new stock for the spring season. It was an awful way to mark the centennial of the business. After consulting with retail experts, the siblings hired Lakewood Construction to rebuild the store bigger and better than ever. It reopened within six months in September 1992. In the late 1990s, long time manager Ron Lugten became a part owner.[104]

After 2000 the store fell victim to a major shift in clothing styles from formal to casual wear and men bought fewer suits. Then in 2008

103 *Holland Sentinel*, 24 May 1917, William Kobes obit., 9 Aug. 1928, Jacob Lokker obit., 21 Apr. 1938; "Clothing business spans four generations," undated *Holland Sentinel* clipping, 1975-80, HMA.

104 *Holland City News*, 30 Jan. 1988; *Holland Sentinel*, 30 Jan. 1988, "Lokker Rutgers Chronicle," Nov. 1992 advertising supplement, 29 Sept. 1993, 20 Oct. 2003.

the national economy crashed and sales fell sharply; at the same time inflation sent clothing prices up 20 percent. These forces outside the control of the upscale clothiers forced Jerome and Lynn Kobes "to call it quits" and liquidate the merchandize. As a longtime city councilman, it was the last thing Jerome wished to do. Lokker Rutgers set the record in Holland for longevity in one location, closing in 2008 after a run of 116 years, as the oldest specialty store in the state.[105]

Du Mez Brothers (John, Gerrit, and Benjamin) dry goods and grocery opened in 1898 at 35 East Eighth Street. In 1902 they sold their building to Lokker Rutgers and used the money to buy the property of Matthew Notier to the west at 31-33 East Eighth and erected a three-story general department store, with Benjamin running the grocery out of the basement. The brick building had an ornamental stone façade and a new-fangled electric elevator. In its day it was the finest emporium in Holland. By 1913 the sales staff had grown from five to thirty-five, and Du Mez Brothers' boasted of being one of the largest stores in the region. Service was the brothers' mantra, as seen in their advertising slogan: "What we say we do, we do." John's son Andrew joined the firm in 1918 and became the manager after his father's death in 1927. During the difficult Depression years, the grocery gave way to dry goods, ready-to-wear clothes, sport and children's wear, and fashionable millinery. At its seventy-fifth anniversary in 1973, the store had forty employees under manager Ed Mosher. The De Mez store enjoyed a ninety-two-year run before closing in 1989.[106]

In 1929 Benjamin Du Mez converted his basement grocery store to an IGA (Independent Grocers Association) self-serve grocery, one of thirteen thousand IGA stores nationwide. Du Mez Grocery adopted the cash-and-carry policy, like the chain stores, and no longer sold on credit. This was in keeping with the strong recommendation of Austin Harrington, the new president of the Holland Merchants Association, who warned that losses on bad accounts drained even the best of businesses. The Depression undid the best of business plans. After four years, in 1933, Du Mez closed the Eighth Street store and opened a small IGA grocery at Nineteenth Street and Michigan Avenue, which he ran

105 *Holland Sentinel*, 17 June 2008; *Grand Rapids Press*, 18 June 2008.

106 *Holland City News*, 16 Apr. 1892, 1 Aug. 1896, 3 Apr. 1913, 5 Apr. 1923, 10 Nov. 1927, *Holland Sentinel*, 6 Apr. 1973, 30 June 1989; *Holland Business Directory for 1892*. Gerrit Du Mez retired from Du Mez Bros. in 1924; when Gerrit's son, John, died in 1927, John's son Andrew took over (*Holland City News*, John Du Mez obit., 13 Sept. 1927, Gerrit Du Mez obit., 24 Dec. 1931).

North side of Eighth Street looking east from Central Avenue in 1903 shows W. C. Walsh Drugs, Peoples State Bank, Du Mez Dry Goods, Lokker Rutgers store, and Nies Hardware (*courtesy Randall P. Vande Water*)

for twenty years until retiring in 1953. His career as a grocer spanned sixty-three years.[107]

John J. Rutgers opened his gentlemen's store at 7 East Eighth Street in 1915 with an inventory of men's clothing, hats, and furnishings. By 1921 he incorporated the John J. Rutgers Co., capitalized at $30,000 by a bevy of the "best known business men in Holland," and moved his inventory to the De Merrill Block (of Richard N. De Merrill) at 19 West Eighth Street, which he renovated and enlarged. The building featured a "tile front of the latest design," a Danzar lighting system featured in only two Chicago emporiums and the only such system in Holland, and mahogany fixtures. Company officers, besides president Rutgers, were Henry Geerlings vice president and Matthew Witvliet secretary treasurer. In 1924 son Gerrit J. Rutgers assumed Witvliet's office, and by 1929 he was the manager of "The House of New Ideas," the brash business motto. Despite the strong start, the Rutgers store had a short run, done in by the death of the founder and the Depression. It closed in 1933, and after the building stood vacant for several years, Gerald P. Houting and Harry Ten Cate took over the space in 1936 for their Houting & Ten Cate men's store.[108]

107 *Holland City News*, 13 Sept. 1928, 21 Feb., 7 Mar. 1929; *Holland Sentinel*, 31 Dec. 1952.
108 *Holland City News*, 24 May 1917; *Holland City Directories*, 1915-36.

Du Mez women's store with "unmentionables" on display, Gerrit and John Du Mez on right, 1920s. Note the all-female sales staff (*Archives, Holland Historical Trust*)

James Huntley, a civil engineer from England, was Holland's leading builder, contractor, manufacturer, and architect from 1870 to 1910. An entrepreneur with boundless energy, he took on big projects such as the First State Bank block, the Tower Clock Building, the City Hotel, Hotel Holland, and the Graves Library and Winants Chapel on Hope's campus. Huntley earned a reputation as the premier contractor and builder in West Michigan. No job was too large or complex. He manufactured machines and building components, such as sashes, windows, and doors, in his brick two-story factory powered by a seventy-five-horsepower steam engine. The plant burned down in 1888, but he rebuilt it better than ever. He kept fifty expert carpenters and machinists busy on both commercial and residential work, worth $100,000 a year. In 1891 alone, he built sixty homes and cottages at Macatawa Park and Ottawa Beach.[109]

Coal—the essential fuel

Coal heated most homes, stores, and shops and powered steam engines for many factories and generated electricity for city lighting. It was the essential fuel and this made it a lightning rod for criticism. "How would you like to be the ice man? How would you like to be the coal

[109] Huntley's business biography, *Ottawa County Times*, 24 June 1892; *Holland City News*, 1 Sept. 1889.

man?" went the popular ditty. The firms of Teunis J. Keppel and Austin Harrington controlled the Coal Combine of Holland, which became the object of public anger during the several "coal famines," when mine or rail strikes crippled production. Harrington, the "champion of the Combine," argued that it was "not an unmitigated evil, as so many people seem to think." Thanks to the combine, coal shortages that brought disaster to many other cities were not so severe in Holland. The combine should merit the citizen's gratitude, not condemnation, Harrington argued.[110]

The coal and coke business by the late 1920s had become far more competitive. Keppel and Harrington, the largest dealers, faced fourteen smaller operators, including Klomparens Coal (James Klomparens), Teerman & Van Dyke Coal (Ralph Teerman and Peter Van Dyke), Holland Co-Operative Association, and Holland Fuel Co.

Teerman & Van Dyke Coal Co. began in 1918 when Albert Teerman paid $1,000 for Rink Van Til's one-third interest in Peter Van Dyke's coal company and became his partner. The purchase included a yard along the Pere Marquette Railroad tracks at 121 East Seventh Street to store coal, coke, and wood. Teerman had been crippled as a youth by polio and was an adept bookkeeper. He worked out of the firm's downtown office at Eleventh Street and River Avenue. The company advertised the "very best grades of all kinds of coal" and delivered their products by horse and wagon. Al's brother Ralph joined the company, and the brothers also delivered fuel oil. In 1940 the Teerman brothers sold their interests to Peter Van Dyke, and the firm continued as the Van Dyke Coal Co.[111]

Brewer City Coal Docks, the successor company in 1948 of Neitring Coal Docks on Pine Avenue at Lake Macatawa, competed with the Harrington yards in the 1950s. Cornelius "Casey" Brewer, a laid-off furniture worker turned cinder hauler in the late 1930s, bought the Neitring operation in 1948, which put him in the coal business and gave him a dock for bringing in bulk shipments by ship. By the 1960s, coal furnaces were giving way to oil burners and natural gas furnaces, and Brewer wisely branched out into cement, gravel, and concrete. He developed the first ready-mix plant, with specially designed trucks to deliver on site. In the 1970s, Casey sold the company to his son Gary,

110 *Holland City News*, 14 Feb. 1907. Smaller coal dealers were Cecil Huntley, John De Boer, Henry P. Zwemer, Albert and Harry Klomparens, J. Van Huizen, and John Y. Huizenga (ibid., 4 Sept. 1913, 8 Feb. 1914).

111 Bill of Sale between Rink Van Til and Peter Van Dyke and Albert Teerman, 24 Sept. 1918, Teerman family records provided to the author by nephew Allen Teerman.

Ralph (holding horse) and Albert (holding reins) Teerman with their fuel oil wagon, 1920s (*courtesy Allan Teerman*)

who died young in 1981, leaving grandson Phil to take charge. In 1998 Phil Brewer moved the ready-mix operations to a new high-tech plant on Old M-21 (Chicago Drive) in Zeeland Township. The object was to tap the building and road construction business in the greater Grand Rapids area. The Pine Avenue yard focuses on sand and gravel.[112]

Teunis Keppel, one of the key merchants and civic leaders, dealt in coal, kerosene, fuel oil, lime, salt, wood, and bricks on East Seventh Street (now the city parking deck). In 1885 he erected a building on the northeast corner of Eighth Street at Cedar (College) Avenue that became his hardware store. Keppel was a son-in-law of Van Raalte, having married the dominie's widowed daughter, Wilhelmina "Mina" Van Raalte Oggel in 1896, just six months before his death. (The family home still stands on east side of College Avenue between Seventh and Eighth Streets.) As the first and only firm to handle Standard Oil products, he received more freight than anyone at the Chicago & West Michigan Railway (Pere Marquette in 1900) depot. Keppel's community roles were numerous: public school board member, treasurer of Hope College and Western Theological Seminary, highway commissioner, first city marshal, alderman, board member of Pilgrim Home Cemetery, philanthropist, churchman, and Sunday school teacher. One project was to hire Peter Oosting around 1893 to construct affordable brick homes

112 *Holland Sentinel*, 2 Oct. 1997, 27 July 1998, Cornelius Brewer obit., 2 Oct. 1997.

Teunis Keppel, prominent merchant and civic leader (*Archives, Holland Historical Trust*)

for working families between Thirteenth and Fourteenth Streets and Central Avenue. The homes, constructed of the distinctive Veneklasen red bricks with unique indented front corner windows, became known as Keppel's Village. In 2010 the city created Keppel's Village Historic District to safeguard six of the original seven historic houses that were still standing.[113]

When Keppel died in 1896, his shoes were impossible to fill. His sons Albert and Bastian carried on the business under the rubric T. Keppel's Sons. The company unloaded boxcars full of bricks at its Seventh Street rail yard, complete with a large truck scale to weigh trucks carrying the bricks to job sites. The firm provided bricks for many Hope College buildings. Bastian Keppel's wife, Anna Van Raalte, was a granddaughter of Van Raalte and a niece of his father's second wife Wilhelmina "Mina" Van Raalte. Long before the demand for coal waned, T. Keppel's Sons focused on their hardware store at 65 East Eighth Street, which Bastian, his son-in-law John Vander Broek Sr., and grandson John "Jack" Vander Broek Jr. operated. When Bastian Keppel died in 1932, the senior Vanden Broek bought the business, which junior later took over. T. Keppel's Sons Modern Hardware closed in the mid-1990s after nearly 130 years; it was then the city's longest running business. The firm actually continues as Keppel's Lock and Safe Company, which Ken Makepeace purchased from Keppel Hardware in 1986, but Makepeace has no Keppel family connection. Vogelzang Hardware bought the former Keppel Hardware building and used it for

113 Teunis Keppel, obit., ibid., 4 July 1896; Bastian D. Keppel, obit., ibid., 7 July 1932; Ruth Keppel, "Pioneer Merchants of Holland, Michigan," typescript, 1982; *Holland City News*, 25 July 1885; *Holland Sentinel*, 14 July 1991; 24 Oct. 2008, 27 Oct. 2009, 17 June 2010; Elton J. Bruins et al., *Albertus and Christina: The Van Raalte Family, Home, and Roots* (Grand Rapids: Eerdmans, 2004), 106-7.

Harrington Coal dock at foot of Eighth at First (Washington) Street, ca. 1900 (*courtesy Garnet Harrington VanderLeek*)

storage, until it was sold and razed in 2001 for the 85 East Center, the first new office building in the Superblock (chapter 33).[114]

Keppel's main competitor in the coal business was "Captain" Austin Harrington, a licensed lake captain and contractor who served as the Holland harbormaster for over fifty years and had a major hand in the development of the harbor. Harrington in 1888 opened a wood and coal yard on the corner of Eighth Street and First (Washington) Avenue, with a loading dock on Black Lake. Over the years, he expanded the yard and offices. In the early 1950s the firm completely remodeled its original building and added a large outdoor clock that every motorist relied on for the correct time. In the early years, wood sales predominated, hard coal ranked second, and soft coal third. Harrington was the first to sell soft Pocahontas coal in Holland. It is said that he practiced the art of treating competitors as friends, not enemies. In 1917 Harrington Coal tripled its operations by opening a branch office and coal yard on ten acres north of the Grand Haven Bridge on River Avenue at the Ottawa Beach spur of the Pere Marquette Railroad (the present-day sites of Burger King and McDonald's restaurants). The firm added kerosene and fuel oil tanks and sold animal feed by the carload. Austin Harrington's net worth in 1924 was a substantial $92,500.[115]

114 *Holland Sentinel, Semi-Centennial Supplement, 1847-1897*; Bruins, *Albertus and Christina*, 84-86; *Holland Sentinel*, 3 Sept. 1995, 14 Aug. 2001, John Keppel Vander Broek, obit., ibid., 24 Oct. 2008.

115 *Holland City News*, 14 May 1953. I benefited from conversations with Carl's daughter Garnet Harrington Vander Leek (Mrs. David) about her family. She also made available the Harrington Collection in her possession.

Austin Harrington and sons Harry and Carl clearing ten-acre lot on North River Avenue for new coal yard, 1917
(*courtesy Garnet Harrington VanderLeek*)

In the late 1920s Austin's sons Harry and Carl joined the company, which by then ran the largest coal yard in town. Harrington Coal never turned a needy customer away empty handed and even supplied competitors when supplies ran short due to the all-too frequent coal or rail strikes in the 1930s and 1940s. As young men, Carl and Harry practically "lived on the water." Before the red and green buoys marking the shipping channel in Lake Macatawa were wired for electricity in

Harrington Coal & Fuel Oil facility on North River Avenue, 1918
(*courtesy Garnet Harrington VanderLeek*)

Harrington Coal Co. office and dock on Lake Macatawa, Eighth Street at Washington Boulevard, with well-known clock, 1950s (*courtesy Garnet Harrington VanderLeek*)

1936, whenever freighters entered the harbor at night, the brothers willingly loaded their yacht with large oil lanterns and stuck them on poles where buoys ought to be, this enabled ship captains to bring their vessels in safely. Their father Austin died in 1939.[116]

In 1953 Harrington Coal celebrated its sixty-fifth anniversary, with Harry occupying the mayor's chair. (He served three terms, from 1949 to 1955.) In 1952 Harry had the pleasure to welcome Queen Juliana and Prince Bernhard of the Netherlands to Holland. It was barely a month after the Queen had knighted him in the Order of Orange Nassau, along with Hope College president Irwin Lubbers, Dr. Abraham Leenhouts, and municipal judge Cornelius Vander Meulen. With Harry's time consumed by political duties, Carl was the master of the coal yard and the Harrington Docks at the feet of Eighth and Ninth Streets. He drove the crane to unload coal freighters and doubled as a harbor pilot to guide freighters to the Holland docks. Carl rose to the presidency of the Michigan Coal Dealers Association. In the 1950s the firm serviced an area of fifty thousand inhabitants within a fifteen-mile radius.[117]

116 *Holland Sentinel*, 14 May 1938, "Let the Lower Lights be Burning" Apr. 1936 clipping, "Harbor Job Goes from Father to Son"(quote) June 1939 clipping, both in the Harrington Collection, Austin Harrington obit., 2 Aug. 1939, Carl Harrington obit., 30 Sept. 1991.

117 *Holland City News*, 8, 22 Mar. 1917; Harrington Coal financial statement, Jan. 11, 1924, filed with Peoples State Bank, Harrington Papers, HMA.

Harrington Coal Co. barge, crane, and pile driver all mastered by Carl Harrington (*courtesy Garnet Harrington VanderLeek*)

Conclusion

Business was in the blood of the Dutch immigrants; they relished owning their own stores and shops. Americans like Henry Post led the way at first, but Binnekant, Vander Veen, Plugger, Schaddalee, and other Hollanders emulated him, with Van Raalte's blessing. Eighth Street was the premier business address, with River Avenue close behind. Almost all the buildings had two floors, the first devoted to the retail trade and the second to offices for doctors, dentists, lawyers, and other services. Bernardus Ledeboer was first among his peers in the practice of medicine. Van Raalte's sons Dirk and Ben owned shops downtown for many years, Ben selling farm implements and Dirk boots and shoes. Family businesses such as the hardware stores of Vander Veen, Keppel, and Vogelzang, Du Mez dry goods, Lokker Rutgers clothing, and Model Drug were institutions in themselves, patronized by one generation after another. By 1900 almost every lot on the prime shopping street sported a store, many newly built in brick or stone, but half still the older wooden structures. Stores came and went with regularity, as proprietors failed to thrive, and others stepped up to try their hand. The retail scene saw a constant churning, with new businesses replacing older ones. Retail selling was a risky venture, and only the most able survived. The next chapter follows the retail trade in the twentieth century.

CHAPTER 19

Entrepreneurial City: Businesses and Professions in the Twentieth Century

A visiting businessman walked along Eighth Street in 1900 and gave the local merchants his impressions of their storefront appearances, window displays, and prices. It was a mixed review. The shopkeepers "do not have to feel inferior in comparison to inhabitants of other towns in the state," he observed. But "some are behind the times in many ways, especially in displaying merchandise attractively and in advertising their business by decorating the windows of the store in such a way that a pedestrian is compelled to stop." The lackadaisical approach to promotion and pricing was due to a lack of competition, the visitor reasoned. But that was about to change with the opening of the Interurban line linking Holland and Grand Rapids. This would bring competition and force the merchants to cut prices and "caress good taste" by modernizing their stores. If the locals did not accept the challenge, customers would take their business to Grand Rapids, the visitor warned. The critique of the outsider was on target as to local merchandising practices but not as to the threat of outside competition. He underestimated the loyalty of Hollanders to trade at home. Local consumers have always been willing to trade price for service and familiarity.[1]

Higher prices or not, local merchants did begin offering credit, something quite unheard of in earlier years. Furniture dealer James Brouwer sold his wares on credit, as did dealers in the new-fangled automobiles. Brouwer's advertisements in 1903 made the point: "In the old days courting couples had to save for years to fill their little house with the necessary items. It is different now. You only have to go to Brouwer's store and select from a large inventory what you would like, and everything is on credit. . . . Jas. A. Brouwer trusts you, and why should you not trust him?"[2]

Houses and vacant lots were also sold on credit. Attorney and developer John C. Post, president of the Holland Sugar Company, offered new homes for $100 down and $8 per month; he sold $10,000 worth in 1901. Frank and brother Jacob Essenburg Sr. began building homes in 1900 (see below). Lots in the new McBride Addition west of Van Raalte Avenue between Twentieth and Twenty-Second Streets went for $150 in 1903, with monthly mortgage payments of $4, with no interest. The principals were Philip McBride, Gerrit Diekema, and William Beach. Developer Richard H. Post offered houses in Post's Park Hill Addition between Twenty-Ninth and Thirty-First Streets from $25 to $100 down and from $7 to $11 a month, no interest. In 1912 lots in Sutton's Addition at Michigan Avenue between Thirty-Second and Thirty-Third Streets went for only $1 down and $1 a week, realty taxes included. Home prices in Holland in 1913 ranged from $900 for a five-room house to $3,200 for a ten-room mansion with all utilities, cement walkways, and large shade trees. Many of these developments were promoted by the Holland Improvement Company, a venture formed in 1905 by the city's fifty most prominent men, who wished to purchase, hold, deal, and improve local real estate. The Ottawa County Building & Loan Association of Holland provided much of the mortgage money, totaling $50,000 in 1917.[3]

1 *De Grondwet*, 30 Jan. 1900, translated by Nella Kennedy.
2 Ibid., 20 Jan. 1903, translated by Nella Kennedy.
3 *Holland City News*, 6 May 1902, 20 Jan., 14 July, 24 Nov. 1903, 23 June 1905, 4 Aug. 1908, 18 Sept. 1912, 6 May 1913, 2 Aug. 1917, 17 Jan. 1946.

Part One

Downtown shopkeepers and chain stores, 1900-1920

The Holland Merchants Association, headed by Richard "Dick" Boter, and the Holland Board of Trade, 114-members strong in 1912, promoted business and industry. The boosters had much to crow about. The city was enjoying another boom time. The Interurban Line between Grand Rapids and Jenison Park was humming with traffic; Graham & Morton had christened a new steamer for the Chicago-Holland route and improved their dock at the foot of Pine Avenue; stately homes and churches were under construction, as well as a new dormitory at Western Seminary and a new hospital. Building construction in 1914 exceeded $100,000, plus the new $75,000 post office. The Good Roads movement was connecting Holland to the state road network. It was an era of prosperity that far exceeded the booming 1880s. Holland property assessments in 1913 totaled $7 million—two and one-half times that of Grand Haven. In the five years from 1911 to 1916, aggregate savings accounts in Holland's three banks increased by more than 25 percent, from $1.8 to $2.2 million. Holland's population surpassed Grand Haven's in the 1890s and by 1910 it was nearly twice as large (5,856 to 10,490).[4]

Downtown Holland was a bustling place in 1910 as Stanley Curtis, who was born in 1884, recalled in his old age:

> There was a barber shop on the corner of 8th and College Avenue, southeast corner, which had a sign over the doorway which stated "Tomorrow we shave for nothing."
>
> Down the street in the middle of the block on the south side between College and Central, A. Steketee and Sons had a dry goods and grocery store; the sons helped their father run it. I remember going in there with my mother, and they would stand me on the counter and get me to sing one of the popular songs of the day, whose title was "Sweet Marie." So, if I sang it for them, I got a stick of candy.
>
> Down farther was Kuite's Meat Market, and that was where my father used to buy his meat for us. They made good hamburgers. They made hamburger with two parts of round steak, one part pork steak, and put it through the grounder once;

4 *De Grondwet*, 28 Oct. 1913, *Holland City News*, 19 Nov. 1914, 8 Feb. 1917; Dick Boter obit., *Holland Sentinel*, 2 Nov. 1965.

P. S. Boter & Co. men's clothier, 16 West Eighth Street (*Joint Archives of Holland*)

> then you put in some sage and salt and pepper and mixed it up good and put it through another time and that was real good hamburger. . . . I remember one [meat market] on the north side of the street between Central and River that had a peculiar name. It was known as Phernabucq's Meat Market. . . . I remember some of my friends used to like to go in there and get pigtails, the raw pigtails off of the butcher, who gave them away. They claimed they were nice, sweet eating, but I never tried them.[5]

In the 1910s Eighth Street had three dry goods stores: French Cloak (for women), Du Mez Bros., and A. Steketee & Sons; two groceries: A. Steketee & Sons and G. Van Putten; four hardware stores: Nies, De Pree, Vander Veen, and Van Dyke & Sprietsma; three furniture stores: Jas. A. Brouwer, Matthew Notier, and De Vries & Lokker; five jewelers and opticians: George H. Huizenga, William R. Stevenson, Wykhuizen & Karreman, C. Pieper & Son, and William Hardie; five clothiers: P. S. Boter, Lokker Rutgers, Notier-Van Ark & Winter, Nick Dykema, and Vander Linde & Visser; three shoe stores: George J. Van Duren, Simon Sprietsma & Son (Nicholas), and Enterprise Shoe; Meyer Music House,

5 Stanley Curtis interview by Donald van Reken, 23 June 1876, typescript, pt. 3, p. 2, Joint Archives of Holland (JAH).

Shoe boxes line the walls of Simon Sprietsma & Son Shoes & Rubbers store, 28 West Eighth Street, 1915. The sign advertises "The Giltedge Oil Shoe Dressing." The father-son duo carried on from founder Lucas Sprietsma, whose store had stood on East Eighth Street since 1872 (*courtesy Randall P. Vande Water*)

the photography studios of George A. Lacey and Edward J. O'Leary, Fris Book Store, and the Idea (later Royal) and Knickerbocker theaters.[6]

For thirty years (1897-1927) Herman Van Tongeren's cigar store on Eighth Street held pride of place as the hangout for sports talk. Men stopped by during baseball and football games to learn the latest scores. Nick Dykema opened his tailoring shop around 1900 in a room above the McBride Block. His sons Lewis and Claude joined him in the late 1940s. By the 1990s, when old age forced the brothers to close, they mainly did alterations, since tailor-made suits had given way to cheaper factory- and foreign-made suits.[7]

Lambertus Fris dealt in school supplies, books, Bibles, stationery, newspapers, notions, and confectionaries in a store he bought at 30 West Eighth Street in 1900. The building was originally the private bank of Jacob Van Putten. Tragedy befell the family in 1907 when Fris died,

6 *Holland City News* "Fifteen Years Ago Today" 15 Jan. 1931, 2 Mar., 9 Nov. 1911, 5 Feb. 1914; Andrew Steketee Sr. obit., 1 Mar. 1917. In 1920 A. Steketee & Son discontinued the grocery line in favor of dry goods (ibid., 22 Jan. 1920). Jeweler Geo. Huizenga began his business in 1900 and sold it in 1927 to his manager Joe Kuiker (ibid., 3 May 1927). Ray Nies bought the hardware from his father John in 1914 and sold to his sons William and James in 1947 (Ray Nies obit., *Holland Sentinel*, 5 Jan. 1950).

7 *Holland City News*, 15 Feb. 1927. *Holland Sentinel*, 12 July 1992.

Jacob Wolfert & Co. grocery store at 380-82 Eighth Street, featuring Kellogg's Toasted Corn Flakes, with Jacob (*in apron*), his wife Elizabeth (*far left*) and daughter and son holding the reins of their horse and wagon, early 1910s (*courtesy Myron Van Ark*)

Charles Harmon standing in door of his barbershop, 7 West Eighth Street, with two sleeping dogs blocking the entrance. His wife Mary Matilda (Ellis) stands in the door leading to their upstairs apartment and her hairdresser's room (*Archives, Holland Historical Trust*)

Lambertus Fris at the cash register of his first store at 30 West Eighth Street. He carried books, periodicals, office supplies, and stationery (*courtesy Fris Office Outfitters*)

leaving his oldest children, Henry, a salesman, and Christina, a clerk, to keep the store going for ten years until Jacob, the "baby brother" finished high school and could take over in 1917.

Already in 1910 the L. Fris News Depot specialized in selling five-cent postcards of area scenes and local and regional newspapers. Residents and resorters stopped in for newspapers and postcards, the latter being a popular way to pen brief messages to friends and family for a penny stamp, half the price of a letter. In 1920, with Jacob barely out of his teens, his mother Jenny died, which forced him to purchase the store to settle the estate. Local bankers, quite understandably, refused to make a loan to the young entrepreneur. But August Landwehr, co-founder of Holland Furnace and a rising entrepreneur himself, saw promise in the young man and lent him the needed funds. Later, Landwehr gave Fris a second loan to buy the building.[8]

Jacob Fris and his wife Sara worked long hours to build their business. They expanded the inventory to include "Everything for the Office," including typewriters and furniture and became wholesale distributors of magazines, newspapers, and paperback books. In the late

8 Larry B. Massie, *Haven, Harbor, and Heritage: The Holland Michigan Story* (Allegan Forest, MI: Priscilla Press, 1996), 150.

Fris delivery truck served a three-fold purpose in August 1915: advertising textbooks for Holland High School; advertising Arnold Mulder's new book, *The Dominie of Harlem*; and touting the *Grand Rapids Press* newsboys, who collected their papers at the store brought by the Interurban (*courtesy Fris Office Outfitters*)

1940s, they moved the Fris News Company division to a new building at 109 River Avenue, and son Dale, having served in the Army Air Force in World War Two, increasingly assumed day-to-day management. In 1956 Fris sold the news division to Chris De Vries, who relocated that business to the corner of Ninth Street and Columbia Avenue. At the same time, Fris moved the office supply and equipment business to the River Avenue store, which was restyled as Fris Office Outfitters. The original downtown store became Fris Stationers and then Fris Hallmark Shop, as Hallmark cards and products became the main inventory. Fris wisely became the sole local distributor of Steelcase office furniture and expanded the business to four locations and forty employees, including a second Hallmark store in the Cedar Village Plaza and a warehouse.[9]

In 1974 the fourth-generation entered the business; Mary and Dale's son J became a partner in Fris Stationers, and son John joined Fris Office Outfitters. In 1986 John was elected president of the corporation, and the next year all operations were consolidated under the Fris Office Outfitters rubric. Fris successfully fended off the category killers, Staples, Office Max, and Office Depot, by staying abreast of the latest product lines and offering prompt door-to-door delivery service.

9 Ibid.

Customers could also conveniently place their orders online. In 2010 John became the sole shareholder in Fris Office Outfitters. J's sons, Jonathon and Andrew, and John's daughter Elizabeth, started working in 2000, 2004, and 2011, respectively, thus making Fris another five-generation Holland company, like Marsilje Insurance (see below).[10]

A five-generation family store on Eighth Street is Fabiano's confectionary (now Holland Peanut Store), which Joseph "Joe" Fabiano, one of Holland's few Italian immigrants, started in 1902 after coming from Pittsburgh. As a typical Italian vendor, Fabiano began as a wholesale fruit and vegetable dealer at 196 River Avenue at Eighth Street, in a building purchased from veteran saloonkeeper Peter Brown. He soon added a confectionary store next door under sons Paul and Peter, while he and wife Mary opened a second confectionary at 9 East Eighth Street. In 1910 Joe Fabiano lost the fruit store when he defaulted on a chattel mortgage of $500. The store continued under new management, until 1914, when Joe regained control and placed son Charles in charge. This store continued until 1935, when Charles and son Michael, his partner, relocated the business to Lansing. Son Patsy, meanwhile, took over the Eighth Street store and moved it to 26 West Eighth Street; he sold confectionaries and had a soda fountain. A new concoction in 1931 was the Nutty Paddle Pop.[11]

In 1940 Patsy Fabiano divided his company: his son Joseph bought the wholesale business at 196 River Avenue and sons Sam and William "Bill" the retail store on Eighth Street. In 1954 Patsy helped younger son Paul open the Holland Peanut Store at 208 River Avenue. Paul moved his store in 1960 to 32 East Eighth Street and in 1972 to its present location at 46 East Eighth Street. Like his father and siblings, Paul and wife Ester willingly worked up to seventy hours a week in the store. In 1979 Sam and Bill closed the wholesale store on River Avenue. Paul's son Tom, representing the fourth generation, began managing the candy and peanut store in 1981. In 2012 he and his three sisters, Paula Fabiano, Mary Fabiano Stille, and Celeste Fabiano Porebski, ran the store. The display window filled with tasty treats and the aroma of peanuts roasting in the shell continues to entice regulars and visitors alike.[12]

Downtown storekeepers at the turn of the twentieth century agreed to keep regular hours and to close evenings, except Tuesday and

10 *Holland Sentinel*, Jan. 1986, 30 Oct. 1988, 18 July 1999, 2 Jan. 2000.

11 Mike Lozon, "Fabiano family continues confectionary tradition downtown," *Holland Sentinel*, 3 Aug. 1994; *Holland City News*, 27 Jan. 1910, "Thirty Years Ago Today" 25 May 1939; *Holland City Directories*, 1906-36.

12 Lozon, "Fabiano"; *Holland Sentinel*, 5 Feb. 1979, 22 Mar. 1996; *Grand Rapids Press Lakeshore Edition*, 16 June 1999, 29 Aug. 2009.

Saturday. Between 1900 and 1916, closing hours moved ever earlier, from seven thirty to six thirty to six o'clock, and starting in 1916, merchants stayed open only on Saturday evenings, except in the summer months. In 1919 the merchants adopted the nine-hour day—from 7:30 a.m. to 5:30 p.m. The nine saloonkeepers, understandably, remained open as late as the law allowed.[13]

The shopkeepers all learned of the consequences of dishonest business practices from the sad experience of clothier Harry Padnos, who obtained stock for his store on credit from a large New York City supplier, Endicotte-Johnson & Company, based on a falsified financial statement. His behavior was inconsistent with his weekly block advertisement in the Holland City News: "As we advertise, so do we conduct our business and when you see a statement above our name you may feel safe in taking it as a statement free from all exaggeration and untruth." Harry Padnos, a brother of Louis, the peddler and scrap dealer (chapter 12), opened his store on 188 River Avenue in January 1914 and advertised one "Big Sale" or "Clearance Sale" after another for men's suits and overcoats. But his store did not flourish, and in mid-1915 he declared bankruptcy, and a receiver sold the remaining stock at "unheard of sacrifice prices." Nineteen months later, Padnos was convicted in Ottawa County circuit court of fraudulent representation on a suit brought by Endicotte-Johnson for $428. Attorney Albert Van Duren represented the defendant.[14]

Padnos was convicted and sentenced to six months in jail on a "body execution," after Endicotte-Johnson paid the county sheriff the required 50¢ per day upkeep for the prisoner. After spending six weeks in jail and showing signs of failing health, friends of Padnos got up a petition drive among local businesses and factories asking the "millionaire firm" to "forget what is past and exercise mercy and order his release from jail, in order that he may redeem himself and work for the support and care of his family." The plea fell on deaf ears. Padnos completed his full sentence and then moved to Chicago with his family. Brother Louis, the co-signer, had to make good on the bad debts. Six years later, in 1923, Harry was back in his men's Bargain Store at 80 East Eighth Street near the Interurban depot, and running the following ad: "Padnos Adjusters Sale on men's clothing [that] will go down in history as the most Sensational Price Reduction and Price Slashing even held in Holland. Prices that will rock the foundations of the retail trade." At

13 *De Grondwet*, 17 July 1900; *Holland City News*, 28 Dec. 1916, 29 May 1919.

14 *Holland City News*, 14 Jan., 16 Apr. 25 Dec. 1914, 7 Jan., 17 June 1915, 1, 22 Feb. 1917.

Thanksgiving, he offered a free turkey with a purchase above $25. In 1925 he bought the entire stock in shoes of S. Sprietsma & Son, which was going out of business.[15]

Amazingly, Ida Cohen Padnos, Harry's wife, developed the Lady Esther line of cosmetics in Holland, and she convinced the Woolworth's chain to carry the line. Lady Esther cosmetics sales took off, and to meet the heavy demand, Ida Padnos opened a large factory in Chicago. When a major cosmetics firm later bought the company, the faltering "Uncle Harry" and wife Ida became far wealthier than brother Louis.[16]

Local merchants increasingly found themselves at a competitive disadvantage in the face of large mail order houses that were selling nationwide from catalogs and shipping by parcel post. Some ten thousand small town merchants fought back in 1914 by organizing a Chicago mail order cooperative with their own catalogs. Customers placed their orders with the merchants and prepaid, whether furniture, hardware, or groceries. They sent the order to the co-op, which forwarded them to the factories. The goods went directly to the purchaser by parcel post. Jas. A. Brouwer, Holland's largest retail furniture merchant, was the first to join the mail order co-op. Brouwer's store provided a 250-page furniture catalog, the "Home-Trade Price-Maker," which rivaled that of the largest mail order houses, and he fully guaranteed every purchase. Zoerman & Vereeke Hardware at 13 West Sixteenth Street was the second firm to join the co-op. The factory-to-home trade eliminated the middleman and allowed the merchants to compete with the big boys. Another cost-cutting tactic was the Self-Serve Grocery that Benjamin Du Mez began in 1914 at Du Mez Brothers—it was the first of its kind. The greatest advantage of the local shopkeepers was that almost everyone had clerks who still spoke Dutch. Many older customers had never learned English, and they traded where they could be understood.[17]

Dutch bakeries

In the twentieth century, Holland had a string of bakeries with long runs under Dutch master bakers. Johannes (John) Van Dyke was the first in 1913 with Just It Bakery at 21 West Seventh Street, which doubled as his store and his home. In 1928 Van Dyke sold to Hessel

15 Ibid., 1 Mar., 5 Apr.1917, 16 Sept., 22 Nov. 1923, 24 Sept. 1925.

16 Phone conversation with Seymour Padnos, 8 Jan. 2010.

17 *Holland City News*, 9, 16, 30 Apr., 14 Aug., 12 Nov. 1914; *Holland Sentinel*, 21 Dec. 1931; Clarence Jalving interview by Donald van Reken, 15 July 1976, typescript, JAH.

Turkstra, who operated Just It Bakery until it closed in 1945, and he went to work for Hekman Rusk. Turkstra's right hand man was Jacob "Jake" Visser, an immigrant baker who stayed with him from 1929 to 1945. (See appendix 5.2 for list of bakeries, 1894-1950.)

John Brieve founded Banner Bakery in 1928 at 200 River Avenue, and the shop continued in the same location for sixty-two years, until 1990, under a string of five owners: John A. Brieve (1928-42), William Gerritsen (1942-56), Cornelius "Neil" Bierling (1956-73), William R. Slagh (1973-78), Jack Hewitt (1978-85), and Ed Richardson (1985-90). In 1990 Banner morphed into Donutville at 676 Michigan Avenue, run by Neil Bierling.[18]

The French Pastry Shop was co-founded in 1929 by Arthur Bos and Leo Balfoort at 438 Washington Avenue. Within five years, they relocated downtown to 58 East Eighth Street. Balfoort then bought out Bos and carried on for twenty years, until selling out in about 1955 to Jannes (John) Elzinga. A few years later, Elzinga moved the shop across the street to 45 East Eighth Street. In 1973 Elzinga sold to John Meier, who turned the French Pastry Shop into a Dutch bakery that featured such delicacies as *krakelingen* (figure-eight-shaped butter cookies), *banket* (almond rolls), and "pigs in a blanket" (sausages wrapped in dough). In 1979 Meier became head chef in Hope College's dining service and sold the bakery to Mark Kaniff, who in 1985 sold it to Ralph Van Asperen of Zeeland Bakery (see below). Jacob Visser went to the French Pastry Shop in 1945, when Turkstra closed Just It Bakery, and remained until he retired at age seventy in 1978, his fiftieth year of baking in Holland. But he never ate sweets, his daughter noted at his one hundredth birthday celebration in 2005. Perhaps that was the secret of his longevity.[19]

William and Ardythe Du Mond opened the Triumph Bake Shop (later Du Mond Bakery) in 1938 on the northwest corner of Central Avenue and Sixteenth Street, which they operated for forty years until retiring in 1977. The Du Monds hired bakers John Elzinga from the Netherlands and John Meier from Graafschap (County) Bentheim, Kingdom of Hanover, and gave them a start. John Lokenburg opened Barbara Jean Bakery at 445 Washington Avenue in 1939, and the shop stayed in the family for thirty years, until 1968 under John and then his son Albertus and wife Francis.

Only two specialty bakeries have survived—Jakob de Boer's Bakerij on Ottawa Beach Road and Ralph Van Asperen's Dutch Delight Bakery on Butternut Road. De Boer's grew out of Hempel's Pastries at

18 For this and the next two paragraphs, see *Holland City Directories*, 1928-90.

19 *Holland City Directories*, 1913-78; *Holland Sentinel*, 26 June 2005.

French Pastry Shop, 58 East Eighth Street, late 1940s (*left to right*); Caroline Balfoort (Leo Balfoort's daughter), Arlyne Kraai, Leo Balfoort, Art Bos, Vinto Wright, Jacob "Jake" Visser (*Archives, Holland Historical Trust*)

170 West Thirteenth Street at Maple Avenue, which lasted nearly sixty years. Hempel's Pastries began in the mid-1930s as the E & T Bake Shop of Effie and Tony Last; Tony was a baker at Banner Bakery. The Lasts sold around 1952 to Jerry Hempel, who gave the bakery his name. In 1957 bakers Lammert de Boer and Fred "Fritz" Hoekstra, recent immigrants from the Netherlands, together bought Hempel's and retained the name. They had worked briefly at Elzinga's French Pastry Shop. In 1971 Lammert de Boer retired and sold his interest to John Van Munster, another Dutch immigrant baker at Hemple's since 1962. Elzinga and then de Boer also employed Van Munster's immigrant brother-in-law John Horsting for several years, until Horsting starting a home construction business. Fritz Hoekstra and Van Munster owned Hempel's for a decade, until Hoekstra retired and sold his interest to Lammert's son Jakob "Jake" de Boer, another Van Munster brother-in-law. The pair continued until 1988, when Van Munster sold his share to Jakob's brother Hendrik. Hempel's Pastries at Thirteenth and Maple was "all in the family" for over thirty years.[20]

20 Ibid., 24 Feb. 1989, 15 Mar. 1994, 24 Feb. 1995, 15 June 2008; Klaas de Boer, *Rough Seas: An Immigrant's Journey from Holland to Holland* (Holland, MI: Holland Litho, 2008), 121, 207, 211; Fred and Helen Hoekstra interview by Donna M. Rottier, 23 June 1992, JAH; *Holland City Directories*, 1928-90. I am indebted to John Van Munster for information about his business career. His wife Emma is Jake de Boer's sister, and he is the brother of Gesine (Mrs. John) Horsting. All these families joined the Central Avenue Christian Reformed Church.

Hempel's prospered until the neighborhood changed in the 1980s. Jake and Hendrik de Boer in 1991 sold the bakery to Byron and Susan Lamb. Within two years, the business went bankrupt. Six months later Julia Reed reopened it, to the delight of the neighborhood, but she could not sustain it, and the bakery closed for good in 1994. Meanwhile, in November 1998, Jake de Boer opened de Boer Bakerij at 360 Douglas Avenue. In December 2008, after his sons Samuel, Mitchel, and Jacob joined him, Jake added the Dutch Bros. Restaurant, which Mitchel manages. Both parts of the business are thriving.[21]

The Dutch Delight Bakery grew out of the Zeeland Bakery on East Main Street, which Ralph's father Arthur Van Asperen, another Dutch immigrant, established in 1954. Ralph took over in 1964, and after twenty years in Zeeland, in 1985 he bought the French Pastry Shop from Mark Kaniff at 45 East Eighth Street. With the rent becoming prohibitive, Van Asperen by 1993 relocated again to 501 Butternut Road in Holland Township.[22]

Rise of the chain stores

In 1916 the first national chain opened a store in Holland; Woolworth's five and dime occupied the first floor and basement of the former First State Bank on the southeast corner of Eighth Street and Central Avenue. Owner Abraham Peters accommodated the company by buying the former post office to the east—the post office having moved into its new building opposite Centennial Park. Peters, one of the city's most influential businessmen, also built an addition on the rear of the former bank building with frontage on Central Avenue for a bazaar and display area for higher-priced goods. This is now the Alpen Rose Restaurant. F. W. Woolworth's soon had two competitors—S. S. Kresge a few doors east and the McLellen Store (kitty-corner at later Alpen Rose). In 1922 a second major, J. C. Penney Co., opened at 40 East Eighth Street (later De Vries & Dornbos), as the 371st store in the nation-wide chain. The department store by 1927 had moved to the Walsh Block on the prime southeast corner of Eighth Street and River Avenue. In 1929 the prosperous J. C. Penney store almost doubled its floor space by taking out the upstairs apartments and opening the entire second floor for merchandize. The Walter Walsh interests, later managed by his son-in-law, Earnest Brooks, a Hope College alumnus

21 *Holland Sentinel*, 1 Jan. 2010. I am indebted to Jake de Boer for information about his business career.

22 *Holland City Directories*, 1954-1993.

F. W. Woolworth store, former First State Bank, 1949 (now Alpen Rose Restaurant), with Holland Business Institute on second floor, where many businessmen, clerks, and secretaries were trained (*courtesy Myron Van Ark*)

Interior of F. W. Woolworth Store, with managers and staff and customers (*Archives, Holland Historical Trust*)

Kroger Grocery & Baking Co., 23-25 West Eighth Street, ca. 1934. One of the men is undoubtedly manager Henry J. Kroll. Picnic hams sold for 23¢ per pound and round streak for 22¢ per pound (*Joint Archives of Holland*)

and World War One veteran, owned up to two-thirds of Eighth Street properties.[23]

The grocery chains followed the department stores in Holland—Great Atlantic and Pacific Tea (A & P) in 1924 and Kroger in 1929. A & P selected a choice downtown site at 52 East Eighth Street. An independent chain store grocery, the Grand Rapids-based C. Thomas Company, opened three Holland branches of its Yellow Front Store in 1924, at 7 West Eighth Street, at 376 Central Avenue, and 232 West Twelfth Street. The stores were easily identified by their façades. Kroger bought all three in 1929, plus George Heidema's Dry Goods and Clothing store at 407 Central Avenue. In the early 1930s Kroger relocated its Eighth Street store a few doors to the west, moving from 7 West to 23-25 West, and it erected its fifth store at 447 Washington Avenue, which gave Kroger the greatest footprint of the grocery chains.[24]

With the rise of chain stores, local merchants had their backs to the wall. They could talk for hours on "chain store evils," but they had to find a way to compete. To this end, one hundred independent

[23] *Holland City News*, 2 Sept. 1915, 22 Mar. 1923, 24 Jan. 1929; Joel Lefever, "Holland's economy has changed," *Holland Sentinel*, 23 Dec. 2007; Cornelia Van Voorst interview by Abby Jewett, 7 June 1982, typescript, 20; Klaas Bulthuis interview by Donald van Reken, 20 July 1977, typescript (both in JAH). Walter Walsh at one point owned seventeen buildings on Eighth Street.

[24] *Holland City Directories*, 1924-29.

Children line up for a "Bubble Gum Sale" after school on a Friday at Henry Van Ry's Store on the northeast corner of College Avenue and Fourteenth Street, 1940s. Note the tower of Dimnent Chapel in the distance (*Archives, Holland Historical Trust*)

grocers across the nation in 1926 formed the Independent Grocers Alliance (IGA), which allowed locally owned stores to buy in bulk at large distribution centers and advertise together. By 1926 some twenty-one independent grocers in Holland formed the distinctive Orange Front Stores that promised "Quick, Quality, Service."[25]

One advantage of local shops was that the chains did not sell on credit. In keeping with the Dutch adage, "In union there is strength," the Holland Businessmen's (formerly Merchants) Association and the board of trade voted in 1914 to consolidate in a new chamber of commerce. The combined organization began with two hundred members and grew to four hundred in three years. Officers included President J. Frank White, manager of the Beach Milling Company, attorney Thomas N. Robinson vice president, Bert Slagh secretary, and Alex Van Zanten of Peoples State Bank as treasurer. Directors included Gerrit Van Schelven, Andrew Klomparens, Simeon L. Henkle, Gerard Cook, and Cornelius J. Lokker.[26]

One of the first fruits of the new spirit of business harmony was an agreement by nearly all the merchants to emulate the big city stores

25 *Holland City News*, 7 Oct. 1926, 13 Oct. 1927, 19 Sept. 1929; http://en.wikipedia.org/wiki/IGA (supermarkets)#United_States.

26 *Holland City News*, 21 May 1914, 28 Jan. 1915, 1 Feb. 1917, 7 Feb. 1924.

and schedule their general spring opening days on the same date. On Saturday, March 20, 1915, almost all the stores "put on gala day dress" and kicked off the spring season with special sales and promotions. The event brought out large crowds and was a great success. Two years later, in 1917, the chamber induced almost every shopkeeper also to stage a Dollar Day promotion on a Saturday in the fall, running from seven o'clock in the morning to ten o'clock that evening, with many items bargain-priced at one dollar. Consumers caught the spirit of the day and came from miles around for the deep discounts. Under the crush of eager shoppers, Holland's Eighth Street resembled Chicago's State Street. Maybe the merchants were not so backward after all. Holland's semi-annual Dollar Days (the Spring Sale and the Harvest Sale) became a big picnic for young and old, and merchants promised a "square deal" for every customer. The term mimicked the beloved Teddy Roosevelt's 1912 presidential campaign theme under the Bull Moose banner.[27]

Wholesalers

Another way to increase profit margins in the food industry was to buy from a local wholesaler, the Standard Grocery & Milling Company. In 1908 John Leenhouts and Iete (Ite) Muller purchased at public auction the bankrupt Walsh-De Roo Mill (also called the Standard Rolling Mills) at 121-27 River Street, installed modern machinery, and formed Standard Grocery. It was a wholesaler for IGA-affiliated groceries, which is now headquartered in Chicago. Under manager Theodore Kuiper, Standard Grocery tripled its business in seven years, selling $3,200 in two days in early 1916, ranging from all-day lollipops to auto tires. The firm sent out trucks on regular routes to retail stores throughout the region, loaded with groceries, candy, and cereals mixed in its own elevators. The bookkeeping department kept track of every item shipped out and restocked promptly from large suppliers. The prosperous operation paid stockholders "fat dividends." Hence, in 1924, when the firm announced a $125,000 stock issue to open a second wholesale house, twenty citizens quickly invested $50,000, and the issue was soon fully subscribed. For a time, Standard Grocery manufactured breakfast cereals like the Kellogg Company of Battle Creek, but that did not prove successful.[28]

27 Ibid., 18 Mar. 1915, 23 Aug., 6, 13, 20 Sept. 1917, 29 Aug., 17 Oct. 1918, 30 Sept. 1920, 10, 17 Mar. 1921.

28 Ibid., 11 Oct. 1909, 16 Nov. 1916, 4 Dec. 1919, 10 Jan. 1924, "Twenty-five Years Ago Today" 12 Jan. 1933; *Holland: The Gateway of Western Michigan.*

After nearly thirty years of successful operations, Standard Grocery in 1936 remodeled the main office building, razed the landmark elevator, and put up a new one-story plant on the site. Ronald Johnson managed the firm in the 1940s and 1950s, with Muller's son Reindert as company president, son John E. as treasurer, and daughter Dena as secretary. When daughter Margaret joined the management team, locals referred to the company as the one "run by women." Dena kept the teamsters union out and was touted as the "woman who beat Jimmy Hoffa." In the early 1950s, the firm built a new facility at 516 East Sixteenth Street (now Holland Transplanters). The original site just south of the North River Avenue railroad tracks is now a parking lot behind the Holland Rescue Mission auto shop and used car lot.[29]

Milk wholesalers faced less sanguine market conditions, and they had to deal with angry dairymen who believed the dealers took advantage of them (see Creameries section of chapter 17). Typically, the Holland Milk Dealers Association allowed dairy farmers about 60 percent of the retail price of milk in the Holland market, which ranged from 11¢ to 13¢ per quart over the winter of 1916-17. But during this period, the dealers raised their margin to 60 percent, leaving producers with only 40 percent. The farmers complained that the dealers were earning excess profits at their expense. The dealers noted sharply higher prices on their end: bottle prices had doubled, bottle caps and fuel tripled, blacksmiths had doubled the charge of shoeing horses, and delivery wagons rose from $175 to $450. It was a classic case of the middlemen increasing their profits at the expense of the dairymen. In modern times, middlemen usually pass increased costs on to consumers, rather than squeeze suppliers. But in the early twentieth century, Holland and most local governments regulated retail prices of commodities like milk and coal in the interest of consumers, so it was easier to squeeze farmers than to raise the retail price of milk. Retail milk prices continued to hover between 12¢ and 13¢ through the mid-1920s.[30]

Upgrading downtown

The city's oldest hardware, Vander Veen's on the southeast corner of Eighth and River, changed hands in 1916, after being in the same family and location for three generations, since Jacob started it in 1847, followed by son Engbertus and then (in 1889) grandson John A.

29 *Holland City News*, 16 Apr. 1936, "Fifty Years Ago Today," 1 Dec. 1938; Phil Miller interview by the author, 20 May 2010.

30 *Holland City News*, 24 Feb. 1917, 24 Feb. 1924.

Two local men with hardware experience bought the business, John's clerk Arend Siersma and David Vereeke, a former partner in Zoerman & Vereeke. Vereeke's mother Gertrude of Zeeland put up some of the purchase price. Within two years, Vereeke & Siersma fell into bankruptcy, owing Mrs. Vereeke $4,000, John A. Vander Veen $1,250, and the Peoples State Bank $1,000. Fifty-four Holland businessmen filed various unsecured claims. Everyone breathed easier when Vander Veen repossessed the business and Siersma became the manager. Vander Veen by then was president of the Holland Furniture Company, where he devoted his energies.[31]

Dick Boter of P. S. Boter & Co. clothiers at 16 West Eighth Street spent $5,000 on a new oak interior, plate glass display cases, and lighting fixtures, making the men's store the equal of the best in Detroit. More mundane, however, was the newspaper report that barbers were raising their prices from 10¢ to 15¢ for a shave or a haircut; the 50 percent increase was the talk of the town.[32] It was quite amazing that the dozen barber shops in Holland acted in concert on the price increase. Traveling salesmen had far more trouble finding a bed than a drink. The city needed more hotel rooms, especially with plans to raze the old sixty-bed Hotel Holland. As it was, the "grip men" had to sleep in the train depot, on coaches in hotel lobbies, and in private homes.[33]

Arthur Visscher, son of Arend and a budding entrepreneur, gave a rousing talk to the Century Club in 1917 that breathed with the "do-it-for-Holland" spirit. He praised the "high standard Holland businessmen set in regard to wages, sanitary and cheerful buildings, excellence of productions, and fairness of methods," but the city had four unmet needs: a second railroad to compete with the Pere Marquette, more bonus fund money to attract industry, greater efficiency in manufacturing, and moderately priced housing.[34]

Visscher's accolades of city businessmen took a hit in 1919 when police chief Frank Van Ry's men checked the scales of grocers and meat markets and found forty-one to be inaccurate by from one-half to two ounces, with 75 percent registered against the customer. That local shoppers were being cheated by dishonest weights was a black mark, but the vast majority of merchants kept honest scales. Chief Van Ry

31 *Holland City News*, 7 Dec. 1916, 30 May, 27 June 1918, Vander Veen obit., ibid., 14 Oct. 1937; Randall P. Vande Water, "'Gasoline Carriage' Here in 1898," in *Holland: Happenings, Heroes & Hot Shots*, 3:66-69.

32 *Holland City News*, 29 Mar. 1917.

33 *Holland City News*, 31 Jan. 1924; *Holland City Directory*, 1924-25.

34 *Holland City News*, 8 Feb. 1917.

scolded the offenders and threatened to arrest any who were caught a second time.[35]

The state fire marshal changed the face of Eighth Street in 1918 by ordering the razing of one-half the buildings, all of wood, plus other wooden homes, sheds, and shops on crossing streets. Twelve structures on Zeeland's Main Street also were tagged. This was part of a statewide condemnation of urban wooden structures that raised fire insurance rates inordinately. The fifteen condemned fire traps on Eighth Street between River and Central Avenues included Luman Van Drezer's restaurant at 8 West, Jacob Kuite's meat market at 12 West, the Pieper Building (formerly Keefer's Lunch) at 24 West, and Fabiano's candy store at 26 West. Also condemned were Henry De Kraker's plumbing shop at 215 River, Toren's bowling alley on Ninth Street, John Lampen's blacksmith shop on Central Avenue, and all wooden shacks in the rear in the alleys. Three months later, the fire marshal returned and condemned virtually every wooden business block in the city. Fabiano invested $20,000 in a new fireproof store without a stick of wood in it.[36]

The wholesale condemnations, carried out by Fire Chief Cornelius Blom Jr., brought many financial hardships, especially since the First World War made building materials prohibitively expensive. The demolitions amid scarcity sparked brothers Hermanus Jr. "Hub" and John Boone to form the Holland Salvage Company, a firm that recovered every reusable part of the condemned structures—lumber (with all nails pulled), pipes, glass, bolts, sinks, and many other items. They used their Boone Bros. Livery on the northwest corner of Seventh Street at Central Avenue as a place to market the recycled materials. Chief Blom gave owners considerable leeway in replacing their buildings. Doede Du Saar's photo shop at 10 West Eighth and Herman Van Tongeren's cigar shop next door at 12 West Eighth were removed in 1922, and Kuite did not erect his new $30,000 building until 1923.[37]

35 Ibid., 14 Aug. 1919.

36 *Holland City News*, 9 May, 1 Aug. 1918, 20 Nov. 1919.

37 Ibid., 10 Apr. 1919, 3 Aug. 1922, 21 June 1923. Du Saar's shop moved to 10 East Tenth St.

Part Two

Automobile services—gas stations and fuel oil dealers

Automobiles were the leading national industry, and businessmen got on the bandwagon. Dealers sprang up locally to vie for customers. In 1915 Holland Auto Specialty Co. offered the five-passenger Dort for $650, or $665 with an electric starter and lights. Reinder A. Vos sold the high-class Chevrolet French lines—the Baby Grand for $750, the Royal Mail for $720, and the mid-priced Maxwell. H. H. Karsten & Bro. of Zeeland marketed Paige and Saxon; they sold eight cars in Holland in a single month in 1916. Owners, however, had trouble finding gasoline; Holland had no service stations until 1917. Drivers could either pay the retail price of 21¢ at local dealerships, go to one of the few service stations in Grand Rapids, or put in a fifty-gallon tank and buy at wholesale at 18¢ a gallon.[38]

In 1927 more than half of the families in Holland owned a car.[39] Auto ownership reflected the city's social structure and the auto dealerships selling the various makes and models. Eight hundred Holland residents, (32 percent) owned Fords—"everyman's car"—four hundred (16 percent) had Chevrolets, and 180 (7 percent) sported Buicks. The ratio was 4:2:1. The remaining forty-four makes ranged from Ajax to Velie. Auto manufacturers with fifty or more cars in Holland were Dodge, Essex, Hudson, Maxwell, Oakland, Overland, Roe, Star, and Studebaker. Less common were Auburn, Cadillac, Chrysler, Dort, Durant, Flint, Hupmobile, Jewett, Lincoln, Packard, Pontiac, Rollin, Rickenbacker, Olds, Stutz, Whippet, and Willys-Knight.

In a sign of the times, fifty-eight women owned cars, thirty-three were single professionals, and twenty-five were widows who inherited their husband's toys. Electric starters had been developed by the 1920s, making it possible for daring women to drive. Professional women with cars included teachers (seven), stenographers (seven), bookkeepers, (five), secretaries (three), clerks (three), and a nurse, millinery shop owner, housekeeper, and superintendent Nellie Churchford of the Holland City Mission. Most worked for the Holland Furnace Company, which testifies to the firm's progressive labor policies. Fourteen families owned two cars, and two families had three cars. The latter included Frank S. Underwood of the Holland Bottling Works and Arie Vos of

38 Ibid., 1 July 1915, 24 Feb., 23 Mar., 27 Apr., 24 Aug. 1916; *Holland Sentinel*, 29 Mar. 1919.

39 The 1924-25 and 1927 *Holland City Directories* are the only two that list the make of car owned by each householder.

Table 19.1. Auto Owners, 1927

Make	Number	Make	Number
Ajax	3	Lexington	1
Auburn	5	Lincoln	6
Buick	179	Marmon	2
Cadillac	10	Maxwell	49
Chalmers	6	Nash	91
Chandler	18	Oakland	54
Cleveland	4	Oldsmobile	28
Chevy	400	Overland	68
Chrysler	41	Packard	18
Cole	1	Paige	9
Columbia	1	Pearless	3
Dort	21	Pontiac	21
Dodge	111	Reo	52
Durant	13	Rickenbacker	1
Elcar	1	Rollin	1
Essex	150	Saxon	1
Flint	11	Scripps-Booth	1
Ford	797	Star	94
Franklin	1	Studebaker	84
Gray	4	Stutz	2
Hudson	73	Whippet	9
Hupmobile	10	Willys-Knight	16
Jewett	28	Viele	1
Jordan	5		

the Vos Electric Shop. The extra cars were clearly used in business by salesmen, factory executives, realtors, craftsmen, a veterinarian, a mail carrier, a milk dealer, and a landscape gardener.

Automobile services had an increasing economic impact on the economy, with filling stations and service garages lining the streets. All the "motors" needed gasoline for fuel. Service stations quickly replaced blacksmith shops, liveries, and stables, as multi-horsepower engines replaced horses. By 1923 some twenty-eight gas stations were operating in the city, with more on the way, besides several "curb pumps." One featured a "greasing service station" in back. The distinctive Windmill Station on West Seventeenth Street on the West Michigan Pike became a popular stop for tourists and truckers. Newspapers began to track the price of gasoline. The going price in the mid-1920s was under 20¢ per gallon, and it dipped to 12.5¢ in a price war. This included a new state gas tax of 2¢ per gallon to pay for road construction. For owners unwilling to wash their own cars, they could drive to the Holland Auto Laundry, where "skilled men" would "take care of the most costly finishes."

In 1924 three men began a bus line in Holland from the Graham & Morton boat dock down Eighth Street and then south on Columbia and East Streets to Twenty-Fourth Street. It attracted more than a thousand riders a day between Christmas and New Year's Day. To accommodate the growing demand for smooth roadways, the region experienced bouts of "paving fever." One such rush in the summer of 1922 covered five miles of roads with concrete (chapter 11).[40]

Oil companies opened distributorships as early as 1905, when the American Oil Co. erected a building "up the hill" from the Harrington Docks west of the H. J. Heinz plant. Vandenberg Bros. Oil Co., founded in 1919 with Benjamin as president, John Jr. as vice president, and William C. as secretary-treasurer, bought the Kremer building vacated by John Arendshorst as the headquarters for their three companies: Van's Gas (the Quality gas stations of that era), Van's Fertilizer, and Wolverine Advertising. One of the firm's major outlets was the Warm Friend Filling Station on River Avenue at Seventh Street. In 1927 Vandenberg Bros. "changed to Shell" by affiliating with the Royal Dutch Company of the Netherlands, and both grew apace with the automotive industry. Van's Gas service stations, "with a bunch of men ready to pounce on your car the minute you drive in," dominated the local area, including Zeeland, Hamilton, and Byron Center. The company owned some stations, such as the Warm Friend, but they leased others to tenants under tight conditions. Van's Gas had the advantage of owning all the billboard signs in the region, and they heavily advertised their products.[41]

The proliferation of corner gas stations became a major public issue. In 1934 residents along Ninth Street and surroundings raised strong complaints when the Standard Oil Company and Vandenberg Bros. Oil wanted to build gas stations at Ninth Street and Central Avenue. Opponents threatened to file injunctions, but the common council issued building permits anyway, believing that "no individual

40 *Holland City News*, 12 Apr., 3, 24 May, 16 Aug., 15 Nov. 1923; 17 Jan., 7 Feb., 7 Aug. 1924; 1 Jan., 5 Feb. 1925, 12 May 1927.

41 Ibid., 20 Feb., 7, 14 May, 18 June 1925, 18 Aug. 1927, 3 Mar. 1938, Ann Kiewel. "Even Holland's gas stations keep up city's clean image," ibid., 28 May 2000, citing a 1926 article in the *National Petroleum News* provided by Randall P. Vande Water.

American Oil Co. distributorship "up the hill" from the Harrington Docks west of the H. J. Heinz plant. Note the stacks of wooden barrels used to deliver kerosene and fuel oil to customers (*courtesy Myron Van Ark*)

or group could prevent progress." The upshot was three gas stations on this intersection–Standard Oil, Vandenberg Bros. Shell, and the Lievense Garage. John Knapp had no problem in 1936 obtaining a permit to build his Knapp's Mobil super-service station on the corner

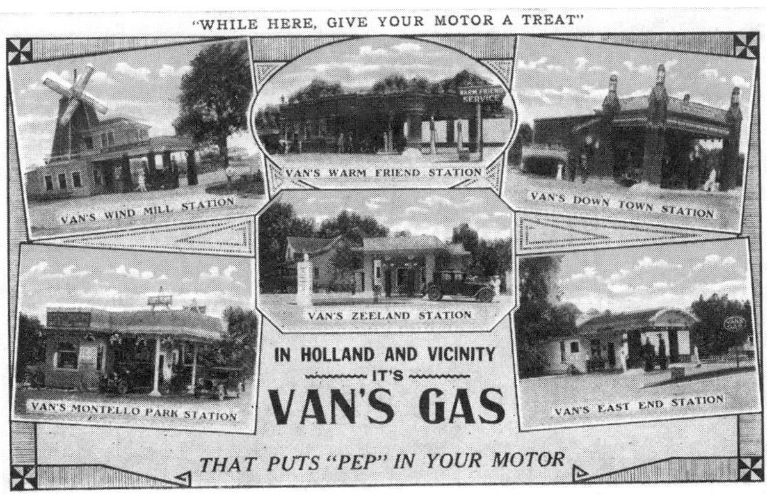

Van's Gas Stations in Holland and vicinity—Wind Mill, Warm Friend, Down Town, East End, Montello Park, and Zeeland (*courtesy Myron Van Ark*)

Van's Wind Mill Gas Station on the Michigan Pike (at 32nd Street and 160th Avenue), 1920s (*courtesy Larry B. Massie*)

of River Avenue and Eleventh Street, where he had for fifteen years run a tire and vulcanizing shop. Two years later, Vandenbergs razed their Ninth Street Shell station and sold the site to an "outsider" for a new station. This prompted First Reformed Church to sue to block the permit, on the grounds that pumping gas on Sunday was "annoying" the worshipers. The common council agreed and rejected the permit.[42] Local owners like Knapp and Lievense were given some slack, but not Big Oil outsiders.

Big Oil came to town in 1921when Standard Oil erected a gas station on the corner of Central Avenue and Ninth Street. The company was dotting Michigan, and indeed the entire country, with stations. First Reformed Church objected strongly to a retail business across the intersection that would be open on Sundays, as did nearby residents. But the common council gave its approval, and thereby caused a serious rift with the church. The drill was repeated a year later when Standard Oil applied to put up a station at River Avenue and Fourteenth Street. This time the council heeded the remonstrance of hundreds of residents and denied the company a permit. Property owner Peter Dornbos lost the sale of his choice corner lot for $6,000.[43]

Michigan in the early twentieth century ranked fifth among oil-producing states, and the Holland-Allegan area experienced an oil-drilling craze in the 1930s. The Holland oil pioneers were William C.

[42] *Holland Sentinel*, 22 Oct. 1936; *Holland City News*, 3 Mar., 2 June, 29 Dec. 1938.

[43] *Holland City News,* 17 Feb. 1921, 2 Jan., 4 May 1922.

Grand opening of Knapp's Super Service Mobil Oil Station, 260-64 River Avenue, 1937 (*Joint Archives of Holland*)

Vandenberg, William M. Connelly, and Gerrit Vander Leest. In 1937 the trio struck oil at the relatively shallow depth of 1,600 feet, known as "poor man's wells," in Salem Township. Within a year, seventy wells were producing more than one million barrels of the black gold, which was piped to refineries in Grand Rapids and Muskegon. Soon the men hit oil in the adjacent townships of Monterey and Door. This led to bold predictions that Ottawa and Allegan Counties would "have the greatest 'play' of any field in Michigan." They planned to lay a pipeline to Holland and build a refinery and storage tanks, but stiff protests by local residents gave the "boomers" pause.[44]

Bulk stations had to come first, supplied by truck. In 1927 Russell A. Boeve operated the Main Oil bulk station (Pure Oil by 1940, Mobil by 1965) at 715 Lincoln Avenue at Thirty-Second Street, which included a two-pump gas station and garage (recently razed). He launched the Main Oil Co. in 1926, with brothers Art and John and cousin Nick Dykema, by constructing a bulk storage tank on a Pere Marquette siding across the road from the family farm on Forty-Eighth Street and Waverly Road (near the later Life Savers plant). They delivered diesel fuel to farmers on dirt roads with a Model T Ford truck equipped with a four-hundred-gallon tank. To complete the delivery, they siphoned the fuel into five gallon buckets and carried the buckets to the farm tank or threshing machines. The partners survived the Depression by bartering gasoline for farm products—chickens, beef, potatoes, and the like. Gas rationing limited growth during the Second World War.[45]

44 *Holland Sentinel*, 14 May 1938.

45 For this paragraph and the next, see Massie, *Haven, Harbor, and Heritage*, 138.

Russell Boeve of Boeve Oil Co. delivering Puroil from his tank truck in five-gallon buckets, 1930s (*courtesy Larry B. Massie*)

After the war the Boeves erected a modern $20,000 gas station on the northwest corner of Eighth Street and Columbia Avenue and announced: "We Serve Cars from Bumper to Bumper." It was one of twenty in Holland and twenty in Kalamazoo, where they had branched out in 1931. But the Lincoln Avenue station remained the headquarters for Boeve Oil Co., which was incorporated in 1952 with five partners: Russell and John Boeve, Cornelius "Neil" Van Leeuwen, Myron Veldheer, and Dave Scripsema. Russell's son Paul joined the family business in the late 1940s and his Uncle John dropped out in 1954.

In the late 1950s Boeve Oil switched its affiliation from Pure Oil to Mobil Oil. Over the decades Boeve Oil purchased oil companies throughout West Michigan. Veldheer left the company in 1972 and

Boeve Pure Oil gas station, 715 Lincoln Avenue, late 1930s (*courtesy Larry B. Massie*)

A. Harrington Fuel-Feed office, North River Avenue, 1940s (*courtesy Garnet Harrington VanderLeek*)

Van Leeuwen in 1975. Paul Boeve Jr. joined the family business in 1975, managing the Allegan plant. Russell Boeve stepped out in 1988 after forty years, leaving his son Paul and partner Ronald Nykamp in charge. Paul Sr. retired in 1993 and Paul Jr. succeeded him as president. By 1996 the company had twenty seven employees and seven delivery trucks. It was downhill from there and by 2005 the company and the station at 715 Lincoln closed.[46]

Already by the 1910s, Austin Harrington of Harrington Coal and Wood carried kerosene and fuel oil at their coal yard and dock at the foot of Eighth Street and at their new coal yard on North River Avenue (chapter 18). As oil replaced coal in heating homes and businesses, Harrington switched its inventory and contracted with Shell Oil Co. to build a four-tank terminal alongside the Pere Marquette Railroad spur at its North River Avenue yard, and added a fleet of tank trucks to deliver the fuel oil.

In 1940 Egbert Boes, a driver for Standard Oil, became the giant company's Holland agent, and his son Merle J., an auto mechanic, began driving for him in 1956. In 1975 Merle J. Boes incorporated and opened a bulk plant at 11372 Lakewood Boulevard under the Amoco brand, the midwestern successor to Standard Oil, and now part of British Petroleum (BP). In 1968 Arlen L. Brenner opened Arlen's Maplewood Service at 881 Lincoln Avenue. In 1975 he sold out to Voss Boys (William and Jack Voss) and formed Brenner Oil Company, a wholesaler

[46] *Holland City Directories*, 1940-2005

Harrington tank truck at the Shell Oil Co. tank farm on North River Avenue just north of the Pere Marquette rail spur, 1940s (*courtesy Garnet Harrington VanderLeek*)

of petroleum products at 12948 Quincy Street in Holland Township. It was a family affair, with Arlen as president, Douglas and Jerry vice presidents, and Juliann E. secretary-treasurer. In recent years, Brenner Oil split into several businesses; Douglas and then Julie Brenner owned the Quincy Street facility, Paul Van Dyke had an office at 230 Central Avenue, and Leonard Brenner operates a station in Hopkins. By 2012, Michael Ethridge was the CEO of the Quincy Street operations.[47]

In the end, it was the Essenburg brothers–Julius and Jacob Jr. ("Junior" or "Jun")–who came to dominate the local petroleum market. In 1969 they opened their first gasoline station, at 435 West Seventeenth Street, and then a car wash on the southeast corner of River Avenue and Sixth Street, which was later donated to the Holland Rescue Mission. In 1972 the flagship Eastown station on East Eighth Street opened, followed by River Avenue at Lakewood Boulevard in 1988 and South Washington Avenue at Thirty-Third Street in 1990. A fourth station, in the planning stage in 2012, to be located on Chicago Drive at 112th Avenue. These stations cover the main roads leading into the city. The gasoline brands changed over the years, from Texaco to Amoco to Citgo. In 2005 they formed their own brand, Quality Oil, under the Quality Car Wash company. Son Tom and grandson Ryan Essenburg own Tommy's Car Wash Systems at 581 Ottawa Avenue, which markets car wash equipment nationally.[48]

47 *Holland City Directories*, 1938-2011.

48 *Holland Sentinel*, 29 Aug. 2012. I am indebted to Jacob Essenburg Jr. (known as Junior or "Jun") for information about the Essenburg family petroleum businesses in this and the following paragraph.

In 1987 the Essenburg's added the capstone, the twenty-acre Holland Terminal tank farm at 630 Ottawa Avenue that stretches from Twenty-Fourth to Twenty-Sixth Streets. Its tanks are fed by an eight-inch pipeline from Niles that taps into the main sixteen-inch Wolverine Pipeline running from refineries in Whiting, Indiana to Ferrrysburg.[49] The pipelines are owned by a consortium of big oil companies. The Texas Fuel Company, founded in 1901 in the Lone Star State, began the Holland tank farm on ten-acres in 1946, a year before the city annexed that area, and erected five tanks that each held seven million gallons. The terminal went into operation in 1947, fed by a pipeline from the oil terminal on Lake Macatawa west of the Heinz plant, which closed in the late 1960s with the opening of the Indiana pipeline. Texaco, the successor to Texas Fuel Co. in 1959, operated the tank farm until 1980, when it was closed. The Essenburg brothers bought the facility and reopened it in 1987, and the family continues to operate the facility that today has a capacity of eleven million gallons. Their terminal currently supplies local oil companies and gasoline stations, along with terminals in Muskegon and elsewhere.

A number of local gasoline stations are owned by outside corporations: Westco (Westgate Oil Co. of Norton Shores), Speedway (a Marathon subsidiary), Crystal Flash Petroleum of Indianapolis, Admiral Petroleum Co. of Greenville, J & H Oil (Mobil) of Wyoming, and the supermarkets Meijer and Spartan Foods (Family Fare Stores) of Grand Rapids.

49 Holland Sentinel, 3 Apr. 2013.

Part Three

Liveries and undertakers

Liveries were the car rental agencies of the horse and buggy days, and this inevitably involved them with funeral homes. Liveries rented rigs, and drivers if needed, to grieving families for the "last ride" to cemeteries, out-of-town traveling salesmen, advance men for circuses and other entertainers, visitors who arrived by train, and anyone else who needed transportation for the day or week. The old-timers were Hermanus Boone, Jacobus Nibbelink, and John Alberti. Boone's Livery was on both sides of Central Avenue south of Eighth Street, with the barn on one side and feedlot on the other side. Boone's son, P. Fred, took over the business in the mid-1890s. The stables of Nibbelink and Alberti faced each other across East Ninth Street. Luther Stratton began a livery in the mid-1890s on the northwest corner of Central Avenue and Seventh Street, which his wife Margaret and son Fred took over at his death about 1905; it became Mrs. L. A. Stratton & Son. The livery paid "special attention to Commercial Men." A one-horse buggy rental cost $3 per day.

P. Fred Boone's Bus & Baggage Line (209 Central Avenue) and Livery Feed & Sale Stable (231 Central Avenue), ca. 1906. Boone's stable for a quarter century was the largest wholesaler of horses on the east coast of Lake Michigan and shipped the animals to all parts of the United States (*Joint Archives of Holland*)

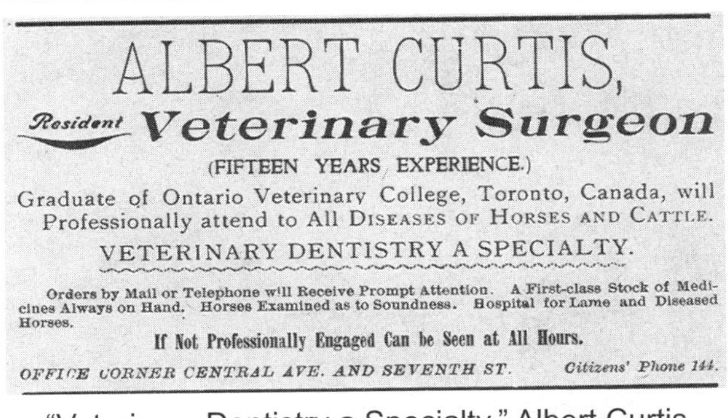

"Veterinary Dentistry a Specialty," Albert Curtis noted in his 1902 Holland City Directory advertisement

Liveries depended on horses and veterinarians kept the nags on the job. "Doc" Albert Curtis, Holland's first veterinary surgeon, had his office in Stratton's Livery Barn. Curtis gained the confidence of liverymen and farmers, who wanted "real" doctors rather than "hoss doctors," whose treatments were rooted in folklore and inflicted much misery. Curtis graduated in 1884 from the Ontario Veterinary College in Toronto, Canada, and came to Holland to practice. His son Stanley noted: "Mostly, he had a few remedies that were very popular amongst the farmers—tonics that he mixed up himself."[50]

Undertaking evolved from livery stables, hardware stores, and furniture stores—all businesses involved in serving families in bereavement. The stables provided horses and carriages, and the stores sold caskets. John Alberti is the first known undertaker in Holland; he went into the livery and undertaking business in 1865, a year after arriving in town. His home and barn on East Ninth Street stood next to the present Dykstra Funeral Home. Alberti moved to Chicago for a few years and established an undertaking business in the suburb of Englewood.[51]

In 1886 Alberti returned to Holland and carried on undertaking from his home at 19 East Ninth Street. He also erected the Alberti Block at 26 East Eighth Street (later De Vries & Dornbos furniture). It featured

50 Stanley Curtis interview by Donald van Reken, 23 June 1976, typescript, 18, JAH.

51 *Holland City News*, 23 May 1874, 5 May 1878, 25 Sept., 20 Nov. (quote), 21 Dec. 1886, 6, 13 Mar. 1897 (quote), "Sixty Years Ago Today" 5 May 1938, "Fifty Years Ago Today" 2 Mar. 1939, John Alberti obit., 24 Mar. 1920. John Alberti's nephew Jacob Alberti, who immigrated to Chicago in 1884, became an undertaker in Englewood, and John joined him there for a time after 1900 (Robert P. Swierenga, *Dutch Chicago: A History of the Hollanders in the Windy City* (Grand Rapids: Eerdmans, 2002), 518.

Livery stable of John Alberti, undertaker with fancy hearse, East Ninth Street, 1890s (*courtesy Larry B. Massie*)

an attractive plate glass front that suited a funeral parlor. The front of the store sported a large wooden horse's head. In newspaper ads, Alberti claimed to be experienced in "embalming and preserving dead bodies," he carried a "full line of caskets and coffins" at the "lowest prices

Committal service before an open grave at the Zeeland Cemetery, ca. 1910, with fancy horse-drawn hearse owned and driven by liveryman Dirk Van Eenenaam (*Joint Archives of Holland*)

Citizen's Transport coach doubling as a hearse, with coachman Evert Spykerman holding the reins of the matching whites on River Avenue with Centennial Park as a backdrop, 1912 (*courtesy Myron Van Ark*)

possible," and he would "attend to all funerals, and furnish everything, including hearse, hack, and carriages." Frank Slooter made the caskets and Alberti added the trimmings. He boasted that he did not belong to the undertakers' trust, and his prices were the same for "country" funerals as for those in the city, provided they were "in the vicinity." A solid clientele induced Alberti to enlarge his establishment in 1897.[52]

In 1900 John Alberti partnered with his assistant John S. Dykstra, and to augment his income, he added a bazaar to his business at 19 East Ninth Street. Two years later, Alberti retired and Dykstra bought the business. He operated as an undertaker and embalmer from his home at 37 (new numbering 29) East Ninth Street. For the first fifty years, undertakers laid out bodies and embalmed them in the homes of the deceased and brought coffins to churches for the funeral services and to the cemetery for interment. Preparation of bodies was time-consuming and could take all day. The state had no undertaker licensing requirements before 1901; most practitioners learned on the job. In 1904 Dykstra hired Gilbert Vande Water as his assistant, and Gil stayed for fifty-three years and eventually co-owned the business (see below). Dykstra, like Alberti, continued selling crockery and glassware from his home. By 1906 he had expanded by opening a store at 40 East Ninth Street that carried crockery, china, glassware, and household

52 *De Hollander*, 1 July 1879; *Holland City News*, John Alberti obit., 24 Mar. 1920; *Holland City Directories*, 1894, 1897-98, 1901-2.

J. H. NIBBELINK & SON,

PROPRIETORS

9th St. Livery, Board and Sale Stable.

The Best and most Extensive in the City.

First-class Horses and Carriages to Supply any Demand.

☆ ☆ ☆ ☆ Carryall to all Trains.

Undertaking a Specialty.

HOLLAND, - MICH.

Advertisement of J. H. Nibbelink & Son with pointed finger touting "Undertaking a Specialty" (*Holland City Directory, 1894*)

furnishings; John Miller was the first manager. By 1908 Dykstra had moved his funeral home to the remodeled home of Leo Best at 29 East Ninth Street, which was next door to the original Alberti Livery. This was the genesis of today's Dykstra Funeral Homes.[53]

In 1886 liveryman Jacobus "Koos" H. Nibbelink at 22 East Ninth Street added undertaking to his activities. His decision launched a mortuary that dominated the business for decades and has continued to serve after several ownership changes. His first advertisement in the *Holland City News* noted that he "kept constantly on hand CASKETS, COFFINS, ETC.," and provided "Good Horses and Carriages of all kinds and a first-class Hearse for funerals." In 1890 Nibbelink bought the undertaking business of Jas. A. Brouwer and took son Seth, then about twenty years old, as a partner. Their advertisement in the first *Holland City Directory* in 1894 boasted that J. H. Nibbelink & Son made undertaking a "Specialty," and their "9th St. Livery, Board and Sale Stable [was] the best and most extensive in the City."[54]

With profits rising, Koos Nibbelink built a substantial two-story house next to the livery barn, with a large driveway and storage rooms for vehicles, including a "handsome hearse" and a funeral car, horses, grain, and hay. If the deceased was a person of note, Nibbelink & Son would adorn the heads of their "first class horses" with large black plumes. When Koos died in 1913, Seth took over, assisted by his son

53 *Holland City News*, "Fifty Years Ago Today" 4 Feb. 1932; *Holland Sentinel, Semi-Centennial Supplement, 1847-1897*, 23 Sept. 1909; *Holland City Directories*, 1901-2, 1903-4, 1906, 1908; Mark T. Higgins, "The History of the Funeral Business in the Holland Michigan Area," Hope College student paper, 1976, JAH.

54 "Century-Old Business Recalls Colorful History," *Holland Sentinel*, 22 Feb. 1986 (quotes); *Holland City News*, 22 Jan. 1887, 3 Mar. 1888.

Nibbelink-Notier Funeral Home, 18 West Ninth Street, erected 1920 (*image from* Holland City News *clipping in Donald van Reken Collection, Joint Archives of Holland*)

Jacob (James), who fell victim to the 1918 flu epidemic at age 25. Seth sold mules by the dozen; in 1910 he sold eighty-eight, many shipped in from Missouri. In 1919 Seth formed a partnership with Peter Notier under the name Nibbelink-Notier. The pair dropped the livery business, and in 1920 they replaced the large livery stable at 18 West Ninth Street with an imposing two-story funeral chapel. The armory was built immediately to the west (chapter 21).[55]

Koos Notier had followed his father Matthew Notier in the undertaking profession. Matthew, a Civil War veteran and dry goods merchant at 22 East Ninth Street, often supplied clothing and helped dress the deceased for public viewing. Eventually, he put a sign as undertaker on the door of his Twelfth Street home and advertised his services as embalmer and undertaker. Son Peter worked for nearly two decades in the family store and learned embalming and undertaking from his father. When he joined Nibbelink in 1919, his father retired and sold the store to Herman Van Ark and Henry Winter, who carried on under the name Notier, Van Ark & Winter, clothiers and finishers. In the 1910s Nibbelink-Notier made the transition from horse-drawn carriages to automobiles, and Peter Notier, according to his son Robert, was "very proud of a gray, wooden carved hearse placed upon a Model-T chassis."[56]

55 *Holland City News*, 21 Aug. 1890, 1 Aug. 1896, 20 Jan. 1910.

56 Matthew Notier advertisement in *Holland City Directories*, 1906, 1908; *Holland City Directories*, 1894, 1897-98. 1901-2, 1903-4; Robert Notier interview by Donald van Reken, 21 July 1976, typescript, 3, JAH. Matthew Notier died in 1929.

M. Notier, Embalmer and Undertaker, bill for serving Herman Laarman, Feb. 2, 1910. Note the charges: casket $35, b[urial] box $3, embalming $5, service $5, hearse $5, *Holland Sentinel* obituary 25¢, for a total of $53.25. The family added a $2 contribution *voor de armen* (for the poor) (*Herman Laarman Family Papers, Joint Archives of Holland*)

Seth Nibbelink moved to Florida in the early 1930s, and his son James H. joined the family business upon completing mortuary school. In 1946 M. Robert Notier, a Hope College graduate and licensed mortician, also entered the family business after returning from military service. Robert had completed his two-year apprenticeship in the family business by 1934 and then worked for seven years in the General Motors plant in Grand Rapids until being drafted. James Nibbelink died in 1949, and the Notiers, father Peter and son Robert, carried on until Peter's death in 1959. Nibbelink-Notier Funeral Home continued at the prominent Ninth Street parlors for forty-five years, until 1965, when Robert Notier sold out (see below).[57]

Besides the established mortuaries there were three newcomers: Langeland in 1929, Kinkema in 1934, and Ver Lee in 1939. Henry Langeland opened H. Langeland & Sons Furniture, Shoes, and Undertaking in Overisel in 1911, which son James A. took over. In 1924 he and brother Fred L. branched out in Zeeland, with Fred running that business. Over the next century, Henry Langeland created a virtual funeral home dynasty; he and his offspring owned at least fourteen funeral homes. In the 1920s the village-agrarian society waned. In 1929 James sold his Zeeland interest to Fred and moved the Langeland Funeral Home from Overisel to the rising city of Holland, into a new building at 21 West Sixteenth Street between Central and River Avenues. Brother Fred moved to Kalamazoo to partner with brother

57 Higgins, "Funeral Business," 4-5; Notier interview.

Henry Langeland in 1930 (*courtesy Michael Langeland*)

Marvin in his funeral home there. In 1936 Fred sold the Zeeland parlor to C. J. "Kelly" Yntema and joined his brother James in Holland. James' son, Russell H. Langeland, joined the firm in 1940. Langeland Funeral Home remained at 21 West Sixteenth Street until 1965, but in 1956 the entire building was enlarged and rebuilt with a new brick façade and two second-floor apartments, all done without interrupting operations. This building today is the home of the Center for African American History (chapter 34).[58]

H. Langeland Furniture, Shoes, and Undertaking, Overisel, founded 1911 (*courtesy Michael Langeland*)

58 I am indebted to Michael Langeland for information about the Langeland dynasty and the West Sixteenth Street building.

Original 1929 Langeland Funeral Home, 21 West Sixteenth Street (*courtesy Michael Langeland*)

James Kinkema and partner Arend Smith set up business in a remodeled house at 66 West Tenth Street. Although Kinkema's chapel seated 250 people, along with a "slumber room" and reception room, the business did not thrive. Dykstra, on the other hand, grew to the point that in 1927 he hired a second assistant, Julius Kleinheksel, an auto mechanic and dealer in Overisel. Kleinheksel was a brother of Dykstra's son-in-law, Hope College professor Jay Harvey Kleinheksel. Julius Kleinheksel kept Dykstra's vehicles ship-shape, but he also earned a degree as a mortician. When Dykstra died in 1938, Kleinheksel and Gil Vande Water managed the business, and with Vande Water's death in 1966, the Kleinheksel family bought Dykstra Funeral Home.[59]

In 1939 John Ver Lee came to Holland from Zaagman's Funeral Home in Grand Rapids and started Ver Lee Funeral Home at 106 West Sixteenth Street on the southwest corner of Pine. Ver Lee took Adrian "Ade" Geenen as a partner in 1957, and the firm became Ver Lee-Geenen. In 1962 the pair opened a new chapel at 315 East Sixteenth Street at Fairbanks Avenue, across from Pilgrim Home Cemetery. The name then changed to Ver Lee-Geenen-Sterenberg, because Paul H. Sterenberg, Ver Lee's young mortician assistant, became licensed and joined the firm as a third partner.[60]

59 John Dykstra obit., *Holland City News*, 22 Dec. 1938.
60 *Holland Sentinel*, 2 Feb. 1934.

Russell Langeland with sons James R. and Jack (in arms) with their hearse, early 1950s (*courtesy Michael Langeland*)

With the transition from carriages to motor vehicles in the 1910s, funeral homes combined mortician and ambulance services. Hearses doubled as ambulances, often at little or no charge; funeral directors considered this a public service that engendered goodwill. It is thought that the need first arose to transport mothers and newborns home from the hospital, since new mothers were required to remain bedridden for a week.

Transporting accident victims was a natural extention, and funeral homes became "ambulance chasers." "Who could beat who" became the challenge after the emergency call went out. Since Gil Vande Water, Dykstra's hearse/ambulance driver, doubled as the coroner, he had the inside track during his tenure. Hearses had no first aid equipment, nor were the drivers trained in emergency medicine. It was "load and go" to the hospital. Over time, however, drivers acquired a modicum of emergency medical training; Randy Dykstra was one of the first EMTs in Holland. Many drivers developed bad backs from the heavy lifting.

Dykstra Funeral Home, 29 East Ninth Street, 1942. Julius Kleinheksel's home on the right was later razed for a parking lot (*courtesy Dykstra Funeral Homes*)

First automoble hearse in Holland, a 1911 Ford made by the Star Auto Company of Indianapolis, purchased by John S. Dykstra (*Holland Sentinel*, Dec. 7, 1911)

In the 1970s state regulations and liability insurance forced funeral homes to raise their fees substantially, which caused complaints and jeopardized reputations for little gain. When "Doc" Jerome Grysen in 1977 offered to buy the ambulance business from all the local funeral homes, the owners gladly accepted. Priority Ambulance was later followed by Grand Rapids-based Mercy Ambulance, and then American Medical Repsonse (AMR), the national chain that absorbed Mercy and other independents.[61]

The big merger came in 1965, when three funeral homes—Ver Lee-Geenen-Sterenberg, Nibbelink-Notier, and Langeland—combined to form Notier-Ver Lee-Langeland Funeral Home. The new partners erected a modern building on East Sixteenth Street across from Pilgrim Home Cemetery. The principals were Robert Notier, Adrian Geenen, Paul H. Sterenberg, and Russell H. Langeland. Geenen left in 1968 to go into property development and Ver Lee died in 1973. Langeland's son James R. joined the business in 1971 after receiving his mortuary license. Notier-Ver Lee-Langeland then went on an expansion tear. Within two years, they purchased the C. J. Yntema Funeral Home in Zeeland (1971), the Dykema Funeral Home in Hamilton (1972), and the Langeland Funeral Home (no relation) in Allendale (1973). The latter purchase was undone within two years by its sale to Harlan Throop. Yntema had taken John A. Hofman as a partner in 1970, and he, Hofman, and James R. Langeland, son of Russell, ran the Zeeland facility.[62]

In 2004 the next generation took over when Michael "Mike" and Steve Langeland and John and Paul Sterenberg bought out their fathers, James R. Langeland and Paul H. Sterenberg. In 2009 the younger generation adopted the name Langeland-Sterenberg Funeral Homes after completing a major building expansion that doubled the size of the facility, including a large parlor with moveable dividing

61 I am indebted to Paul H. Sterenberg and Craig Kleinheksel for information about the workings of the Holland funeral industry and the ambulance services.

62 Higgins, "Funeral Business," 5-7.

Dykstra Funeral Home ambulance on an accident call in the 1970s (*courtesy Dykstra Funeral Homes*)

walls, a dining room, and a children's room. Mergers in the funeral industry are less frequent now, and keeping the business in the family is more common. Local operators have become reluctant to sell, and children who grew up in the business and often lived in the funeral home want to carry on. Increasingly, funeral homes use websites to announce deaths and funerals, share memorials and condolences, and even conduct visitations and funerals via Skype for family and friends who cannot come in person due to illness or distance.[63]

As was common in Dutch Reformed communities across the United States, denominational ties often dictated the choice of a funeral home. This was because funerals were usually held in the church sanctuary of the deceased, and funeral directors had to work closely with pastors. Hence, the church affiliation of the morticians often determined their clientele. In Holland until recent decades, Reformed Church members generally patronized Dykstra, since the Dykstra and Kleinheksel families belong to that denomination, and Christian Reformed Church members usually went to Notier-Ver Lee-Langeland (Langeland-Sterenberg), since the Langeland and Sterenberg families belong to that denomination.[64]

63 *Holland Sentinel*, 26 June 2007, 7 Mar. 2009; *Grand Rapids Press Lakeshore Edition*, 24 Feb. 2008, 15 Mar., 20 Aug. 2009.

64 *Holland Sentinel*, 4 Feb. 2004.

Mulder Funeral Home stemmed from the Graafschap Hardware store of Johannes Mulder, who added undertaking to his trade; son Clarence later joined him to form Mulder & Son.[65] The Mulders handled almost every funeral in Graafschap. "They went straight to Hell otherwise," said wags among Holland undertakers. Clarence's two sons, James "Jim" and Vern, later entered the business, and it became Mulder & Sons. By then, the custom of embalming in private homes was going out of practice, and the Mulders began renting the funeral parlors of Nibbelink-Notier on Ninth Street. Their funeral announcements in the newspapers then read: "Mulder Funeral Home, Visitation at Nibbelink-Notier" In 1961 the family built the funeral home at 188 West Thirty-Second Street just east of Michigan Avenue. Vern died in 1975, and James carried on alone until 1980, when he sold to David Van Eck of Grand Rapids. In 1984 Van Eck sold to Dykstra, and the facility became their Mulder Chapel. James Mulder went to work for Notier-Ver Lee-Langeland until his death.

Julius Kleinheksel's sons Victor and Carrow, later joined by Victor's son Craig, directed Dykstra's Funeral Homes into the second and third generations, but "Pa" Kleinheksel, as Julius was known to many, came in almost every day until age ninety-two, three years before his death in 2000. Carrow operated the Northwood Chapel and lived on-site until his death in 1997. Dykstra also had a branch in Overisel. Son Victor similarly stayed on until he had to quit at age eighty, due to the onset of dementia. He died in 2012.[66]

Langeland and Dykstra faced a new competitor in 1997, Michael P. Dozeman of Lakeshore Memorial Services at 11939 James Street in Holland Township, who offered cut rates and simplified services, especially for cremation. Dozeman had previously worked for Langeland-Sterenberg. Karen (Mrs. Steven) Palmateer, whose husband is an associate of Dozeman, has been awaiting approval to open a crematorium in Holland Township. It is against Michigan law for a funeral director to own such a facility, but the law does not bar a wife from doing so.[67] In early 2013 Dozeman sold his business to Service Corporation International, the largest funeral home conglomerate in the world.

65 Mulder & Son statement, 2 Feb. 1916, Graafschap Christian Reformed Church Historical Archives, Holland, MI, compliments of William Sytsma.

66 *Holland Sentinel*, 20 June 1929, 1 Oct. 1997, Julius Kleinheksel obit., 23 May 2000, 7 Oct. 2002, 23 Aug. 2009, Victor Kleinheksel obit., 13 May 2012.

67 *Grand Rapids Press Lakeshore Edition*, 1 Oct. 1997, 23 May 2000.

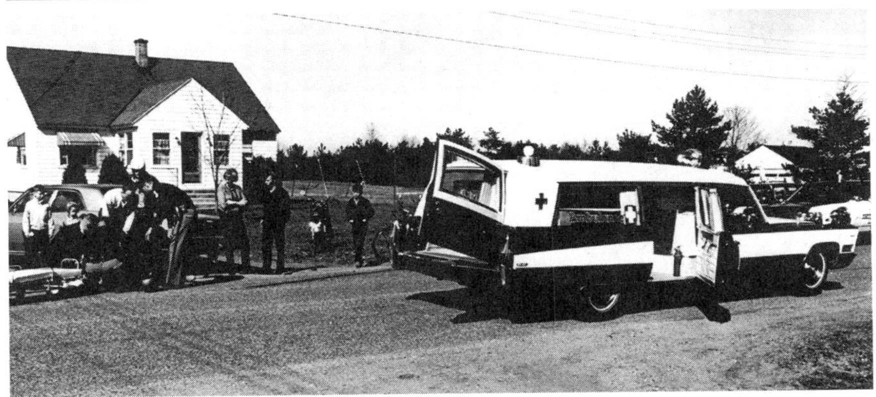

Carrow Kleinheksel and Lee Russcher (later a medical doctor) transport an accident victim in the Dykstra Funeral Home hearse/ambulance in the early 1960s. The location is likely Central Avenue at Thirteenth Street (*courtesy Dykstra Funeral Homes*)

Part Four

Business in the prosperous 1920s and depressed 1930s

The retail merchants in 1920 tried to form their own organization, believing that the decision of six years earlier to merge with the chamber of commerce was a mistake. The chamber had become largely defunct due a lack of financial support. Led by John Vander Sluis, G. John Kooiker, Henry R. Brink, John Rutgers, and Fred Beeuwkes, the merchants formed the Holland Retail Merchants Association, with Beeuwkes as secretary and Brink as treasurer. "Join and help boost business in our city and help boost our city," was the rallying cry. One of the first decisions was to close all stores on March 9, to observe the annual day of prayer for the crops in all Reformed and Christian Reformed congregations. One of the next decisions was to protest to the state legislature plans to implement an income tax.[68]

Six months later, the manufacturers determined to revive the chamber of commerce to represent their interests, which differed considerably from those of the shopkeepers. But it took four years and Mayor Evert P. Stephan's impetus to accomplish this. Some 160 members had paid their dues following the initial meeting chaired by the mayor at the city hall in April 1924. They elected Stephan the first president and Arendshorst, Beeuwkes, and William C. Vandenberg (of Vandenberg Bros. Oil Co.) to fill the other offices; Diekema and Landwehr were also on the board. The two organizations subsequently joined in the chamber's annual dinner, with four hundred or more in attendance. Cooperation was the theme of the day. Within a year the chamber reached its goal of five hundred members; the Merchants Association had 175 members in 1926. The chamber spent a large part of its monies promoting Holland as a spring and summer tourist destination by buying advertisements in leading dailies and magazines.[69]

If the national economy was in the doldrums, it was hardly noticeable among Holland consumers. The spring 1921 Dollar Day was the best ever, and goods literally jumped off the shelves and display cases. Henry Geerds Electric Co. did a brisk business selling to housewives General Electric appliances—washing machines, mangle irons, vacuum cleaners, and sewing machines. Gilbert T. Haan of Grand Rapids bought

68 *Holland City News*, 24 Mar., 21 Oct. 1920.

69 Ibid., 13, 27 Jan., 24 Feb., 3 Mar., 3 Apr. 1921, 19 Jan. 1922, 1 Mar., 12, 26 Apr., 3 May 1923, 7 Feb., 1 May 1924, 29 Oct. 1925, 4 Feb. 1926.

Model Drug Store and recouped his investment by selling old-stock cigars, originally priced from 10¢ to 15¢ apiece, or five for a quarter! Volume was the secret. In the first six months of 1921, he sold half a million cigars. On one Saturday he sold 9,400 cigars of one brand. Although not as fresh as newly rolled cigars, Hollanders jumped at the bargain. The men believed that for once they were getting their money's worth. Locals and tourists also lined up to buy copies of the Chicago *American* at the Jacob Fris Book Store. Beginning in 1922 the newspapers were flown in from Chicago on a seaplane that landed at the head of Black Lake. The flight took the plane only one hour and thirty-five minutes; truly, the news was hot off the press. Factories were running full or in overtime, and the purchasing power of the dollar was up 35 percent over two years. The banks in December 1921 distributed $80,000 in Christmas savings accounts; the merchants could hardly wait.[70]

So sanguine were conditions that some West Michigan investors took a flyer on the Texas oil boom. John Glupker of Holland and John De Pree and Jake Elenbaas of Zeeland went to Texas themselves to check out the Zee-Tex Syndicate, in which John B. Nykerk of Hope College and Cornelius J. Dregman, "two substantial men in Holland," and scores of other locals had already invested. Ben Mulder, editor of the *Holland City News*, warned his readers that "99 out of a hundred of these oil promoters are fakes and he who invests may just as well 'kiss his money goodbye.'"[71]

To help factories find workers and families hire domestic help, Russell Zalsman began the Manufacturers Employment Bureau in Holland. The bureau, modeled after one in Grand Rapids, was above the Vaupell Drug Store at 2 West Eighth Street.[72]

Model Drug changed hands when Henry Wilson and James Yonkman bought the popular store from Gilbert T. Haan in 1923. Wilson and Yonkman made $50,000 in renovations, which strengthened their hand against a competitor that opened in 1923 kitty-corner across River Avenue. It was Jacob "Jake" Haan's Drug Store, with new partner Nicholas Dykeman of Grand Rapids, which relocated from Eighth and Central to the McBride Block. In 1930 Haan Bros., then owned by Jake's sons John and Jacob, became part of Peck's Drug stores of Grand Rapids, a chain with twenty-five stores in Michigan and Ohio. Model Drug and Haan Bros. faced two venerable competitors on Eighth

70 *Holland City News*, 24 Mar., 28 July, 1 Dec. 1921, 6, 13 July 1922.

71 Ibid., 28 June 1923.

72 Ibid., 7 Dec. 1922.

Street, Walsh Drug and Doesburg Drug. Heber Walsh founded Walsh Drug way back in 1856, and his son Walter and pharmacist Albert J. Huizenga co-owned it for forty-five years until 1929, when they closed the business after seventy-five years. The old wooden landmark was torn down and replaced with a modern brick building. Harry Doesburg operated Doesburg's Drug store at 32 West Eighth Street until 1937, when he sold it to Fred Meppelink, who carried on for more than two decades, until he retired in 1960 and closed the business. In 1962 Model Drug passed into the hands of Keith Ditch, who took out the soda fountain in favor of the pharmacy. In 1998 Ditch's daughter Sharon Fisher bought Model Drug. The business, which still exists, outlasted every competitor, in large part due to its ideal location on the premier business corner of Holland.[73]

Ideally, each neighborhood had a drug store within walking distance. Smith's Drug Store on Central Avenue at Sixteenth Street served that neighborhood for several decades. Louis Lawrence's Drug Store at 166 West Thirteenth Street served the west side throughout the 1920s. Harold De Loof's Drug Store at 438 Washington Boulevard was a mainstay of Washington Square for more than four decades, until it closed in 1965. Jacob Haan in 1927 bought the East End Drug Store at 227 East Eighth Street from Prantic S. Woodall and R. Straight.[74]

James "Jim" E. Borr about 1926 tired of working at the Holland Shoe Company as a laster and opened his own store, the Holland Boot Shop at 232 River Avenue. His younger brother Matthew, who also worked in the shoe factory, joined the business in 1929, and the pair moved the store to 21 West Eighth Street and renamed it Borr's Bootery. Younger brother Simon waited on customers for a few years before going into the insurance business. Once the store survived the lean years of the Great Depression, it continued a run of eight decades and is still going strong. About 1963 the brothers sold the store to Thomas Muller, who kept the name because it had become something of a downtown landmark. Muller sold to Morris "Morrie" Tubergen in 1972, and Tubergen moved the store to 51 East Eighth Street, where it remains today. Tubergen sold the business to Roger Bergman in 1992, and he continues as the owner. The store carries the trendy Birkenstock line.[75]

73 *Holland City News*, 8, 15 Mar. 1923, 11 Feb. 1926, 10 Nov. 1927, 11 Apr. 1929, 23 July 1930, Jacob N. Haan obit., 23 Oct. 1947; *Holland City Directories*, 1924-65; Steve Vanderveen, three-part series, "Model Drug Store," *Holland Sentinel*, 15, 22, 29 June 2008.

74 *Holland City Directories*, 1924-27.

75 Ibid., 1921-2012; Warren Van Edmond, "The Descendents of Hendrik Bor and Bastiaantje Leenheer—The Second Generation, Twentieth Century Americans,"

French Cloak Store, with owners and female clerks, 26 East Eighth Street, 1920s (*Archives, Holland Historical Trust*)

John Vander Sluis closed his dry goods store in 1925 after more than twenty-five years and sold the double store to John Van Tatenhove, proprietor of the French Cloak Store next door, to expand his women's clothing store. Van Tatenhove had purchased the original store in 1919 from J. "Izzy" Altman, who had founded the French Cloak Store in 1909. Van Tatenhove's main competition, besides Du Mez, was the Rose Cloak women's store of Gerrit Rose (later Thaddeus Taft) located next door to Lokker Rutgers. Holland's music man, John Van Vyven, in 1926 purchased the Goodyke Music House and had to compete with the well-established Meyer Music House, with its display of pianos and pump organs. This prompted Albert H. Meyer to invest $30,000 in a new building next door to his old place at 15 West Eighth Street. The company, which became part of Meyer Music of Grand Rapids in 1999, relocated in 2001 to 675 East Lakewood Boulevard in Holland Township. Nearing its 140th year, Meyer may be the nation's oldest music house.[76]

A family business, now in its ninth decade, was founded by William Bos in 1921 after his marriage to Janet Van Tongeren, whose father Herman, a noted tobacconist at 12 East Eighth Street, rolled

http://www.angelfire.com/mi3/BorrFamily/borfam2.html, accessed 30 March 2013; Steve Vander Veen, "Borr's bootery continues to attract customers," *Holland Sentinel*, 13 Apr. 2008.

76 *Holland City News*, 8, 29 Jan., 20, 26 Feb., 1 Oct., 26 Nov. 1925, 28 Apr. 1926; *Holland Sentinel*, 10 Mar. 1919, 24 May 1926, 1 Oct. 2009; The Rose Cloak Store went out of business with the death of owner Thaddeus Taft in 1938 (Taft obit., *Holland City News*, 6 Jan. 1938).

Alvan D. Bos leaving Holland to service his customers in Grand Haven and Allegan (*courtesy Larry B. Massie*)

Knickerbocker brand cigars. William began selling the cigars but soon ventured out on his own as a tobacco and candy salesman, operating Bos Tobacco & Candy Co., first out of the basement of Van Tongeren's store and then in C. Blom's former saloon on River Avenue. Bos peddled his wares to retail tobacco and candy stores in the area in a Dodge panel truck. In 1928 he moved his wholesale operation to a house at 203 East Eighth Street near Lincoln Avenue. A year later his brother Alvin D. joined the company and took over the outlying territories of Grand Haven and Allegan. During Prohibition, Bos Tobacco & Candy added soda pop and near beer, and then with the repeal of Prohibition in 1933, they switched to beer. The business grew, and many family members joined the workforce which rose to fifteen and more with a dozen trucks. In 1939 Bos stopped distributing beer. The war years were more difficult than the Depression years, because the government rationed sugar and tobacco for the armed forces, but the company survived.[77]

In 1947 Bos sold out to Melvin Achterhof, but within a year or two, his brother Alvin purchased the firm and renamed it Alvin D. Bos Co. Supermarkets were decimating the local tobacco and candy shops, so Bos wisely focused on the increasingly popular vending machines, beginning in 1955 with cigarettes, and soon adding candy, pastries, coffee, pop, and chips in factories, businesses, and government buildings. In 1959 he placed a bank of his vending machines in the basement of Hope College's Kollen Hall, and in 1962 he added hot food vending machines in the new Holland High School stocked with hot dogs, hamburgers, and cold sandwiches. This innovative venture

[77] This section relies on Massie, *Haven, Harbor, and Heritage*, 133, and information provided by Thomas G. Bos.

required a student attendant to supply the food products to the coin-operated machines. Bos sold hot food in this way for sixteen years. In 1961 he renamed the firm Alvin D. Bos Co. Wholesale & Vending Co., and relocated to a warehouse at 704 Ottawa Avenue. At this time, Bos sold the wholesale and street vending business and began concentrating on commercial vending at factories, beginning with Holland Color and Home Furnace. In 1966 his son Thomas joined the company and helped in the relocation the next year to larger quarters at 424 West Twenty-Second Street. In 1981 the company secured the former offices and warehouse of De Pree Chemical at 1 West Fifth Street at Central Avenue, which comfortably house the offices and commissary.

The firm doubled its business every five years, and by the early 1990s under son Thomas G. Bos, two-thirds of the revenue came from 650 vending machines in industrial facilities. The rest was earned from catering, portable coffee dispensers, and city concession contracts at Windmill Island and the Thirty-Second Street recreation complex. Bos brought computers into the workplace, which allowed for up-to-date inventory control. A largely female staff marked a wide variety of fresh packaged foods, ranging from pizza slices and sandwiches to desserts and snacks. In 1993 A. D. Bos added more healthful items that qualified for the USDA Heart-Smart logo. Twenty deliverymen in large panel trucks stocked vending machines and kept workers in a wide variety of businesses happy with morning coffee and pastries and noon lunches. In 1996 the firm had eighty employees and catered daily to thirty thousand customers in Ottawa, Allegan, and Kent Counties, who quaffed a million cups of coffee a month. In 1999 some disgruntled employees induced the Christian Labor Association (CLA) of Zeeland to hold an election for a twenty-five-member bargaining unit of drivers, maintenance, and production workers; the organizing effort failed. Grandson Thomas J. Bos has led the company since 1999. He directed the move in 2005 to new facilities at 308 Garden Avenue in Holland Township, where the firm continues to thrive.[78]

Building boom in the 1920s

Holland had a severe housing shortage, and families could not afford the high prices. In 1921 the Associated Building Employers

[78] Mike Lozon, "A. D. Bos: One of areas largest vending-machine firms," *Grand Rapids Press*, 12 May 1991, 4 Oct. 1994; *Holland Sentinel*, 10 Feb., 24 Mar. 1993, 4 Oct. 1994. The CLA, a national union founded by Reformed Christians, represented 400 workers in West Michigan in 1999 and 1,800 nationwide, mostly in the skilled trades (ibid., 3 Nov. 1999).

of Michigan, the state trade group, recommended a 20 percent wage reduction in all the building trades to stimulate construction. The Holland Home Builders Association agreed and announced the cuts locally. This move had the desired effect of stimulating a building boom. The association started fifteen "spec" homes, and secretary John Arendshorst invited interested buyers to view colored drawings of the houses in the window of Du Saar's Photo shop on East Eighth Street. Jan Bosman, the former clothier turned real estate developer, built more than four hundred homes. It was said that he probably "built more houses for people of limited means than any other man in the city." His competitor, Bolhuis Lumber & Mfg., touted themselves as the "Builders of 'Expressive' Homes," ones that embody "your own ideals." The local builders had to compete with Sears, Roebuck & Co. mail order houses that customers could select from a catalog in all styles and price ranges—from the economy $629 Shelby model to the ritziest Glen Falls model for $4,909. Sears delivered the prefabricated kits by railcar in thirty thousand pieces on average, not counting nails and screws. At the factory each joist, stud, beam, and rafter was precut and numbered for assembly. Building a Sears home was truly a do-it-yourself project, but it is not known exactly how many Sears homes came to Holland.[79]

In 1926 Frank Essenburg of Essenburg Building & Lumber at Seventeenth Street and Ottawa Avenue, created an association of designers, contractors, and craftsmen, under the name Essenburg Building Service, to "serve the homebuilders of Holland and vicinity." His motto: "From Plans to Pass-Key—the Home of Your Heart's Desire." Hollanders were homeowners, not renters. "Renting of homes just isn't done in our city," declared a newspaper editor. Mayor Kammeraad declared: "About ninety percent of our people own their own homes and take pride in them. That is the reason for the well-kempt appearance of our city." Essenburg Building & Lumber was a leader in residential building construction for more than fifty years, and in 1947 it became De Leeuw Lumber, which has continued in business on Lakewood Boulevard. Jacob sold his interest to Frank and developed subdivisions in Holland Township—Rose Park, Maywood, and others. At one point he had an inventory of five hundred home sites. The two brothers and their three sisters also owned Northland Lanes bowling alley at 310 North River Avenue for thirty years, from 1956 to 1986.

[79] Ibid., 18 Mar., 10 June 1920, 17 Mar. 1921 (quote), 22 Mar. 1923 (quote); Cynthia Crossen, "Your Dream House by Mail, Assembled by Number," *Wall Street Journal*, 31 Oct. 2005.

Elberdene, Lillian, and May Rose Essenburg ran the operation and did so successfully without a bar.[80]

When a former resident returned for a visit in 1921 after being away eleven years, he remarked: "Gee, Holland looked good to me. When I left, my house was at the edge of the city. Now the edge of the city is a great deal further out. New things that I noticed are two new bank buildings, a new city hall, a new post office, lots of factories, and many enlarged ones. The skyline of Eighth Street and River Avenue has also changed a great deal. The old wooden buildings . . . have been replaced by fine stone ones. Holland surely looks good to me." One building no visitor could miss was the narrowest building in town, the nine-foot wide store with a copper front that the Colonial (now Park) Theater on River Avenue erected between the theater and the Arnold Confectionary store to the south to house Edward Zwemer's popcorn stand. The "popcorn king" leased the front part, and the back provided a restroom for musicians between performances.[81]

The torrid building pace continued downtown (fig. 19.1; see appendix 6 for actual dollar amounts per year). In 1925 the five-story De Vries & Dornbos "Furniture Emporium" on Eighth Street (now Riverview Building and Butch's) was opened. The ornate façade sported large show windows on every floor to display the merchandise in natural light. The new "skyscraper" was actually two floors built atop the three-story Visscher Block. Milo De Vries, a salesman for Jas. A. Brouwer, and William Lokker established the firm in 1915 in the Steketee Building. Two years later, Cornelius W. Dornbos, a salesman at Meyer Music House, assumed Lokker's interest, and the new partners purchased the original Rinck Block, which had housed his furniture store. They quickly filled the two floors and decided to create more floor space by building a third floor on top. In 1925 they moved west a few doors into the new skyscraper. Many thousands came for the grand opening. Years later the firm's product line changed from furniture to draperies, after they moved to smaller quarters at 26 East Eighth Street.[82]

In 1926 Thomas W. White of White's Market erected a two-story building next to the Tower Clock Building at 236 River Avenue. Joseph

80 Ibid., 1 Apr., 24 June 1926, 21 July 1927. I am indebted to Jacob Essenburg Jr. for information in this paragraph.

81 *Holland City News*, 25 Aug. 1921; *Holland Sentinel*, 24 May 1926.

82 *Holland City News*, 14 June 1917, 18 Dec. 1924, 9 May 1929. Milo De Vries remained with the firm until about 1935 (De Vries obit., ibid., 22 Nov. 1939). In 2009 De Vries & Dornbos, owned by Elizabeth Austin, relocated to 25 West Ninth Street and was renamed Elizabeth Austin Fine Linens & Interiors, but the store closed shortly thereafter.

White's Market at 236 River Avenue invites customers to buy their Thanksgiving chicken or turkey, but the hams were bound for Holland Furnace Co. employees, 1930s (*courtesy Randall P. Vande Water*)

White and his son Thomas W. sold fresh meat for forty-six years, from 1912 to 1958. De Kraker & De Koster did the same at 184 River; their meat market stood there for more than fifty years. This construction in 1926 cleaned up the last of the wooden shacks on River Avenue. The Holland Furniture Company joined the crusade in 1927 with a new $40,000, three-story office and warehouse building on River Avenue at Seventh Street. Peoples State Bank also erected a new $150,000 facility on Eighth Street, next door to De Vries & Dornbos. It was the first steel-skeleton building in Holland, and onlookers came to watch the riveters catch the white-hot bolts in pails, slip them into the I-beams, and tighten them with air hammers. The ultra-modern architecture was in the Italian cathedral style. (The building today houses Fifth Third Bank.)[83]

Benjamin Lievense, owner of Lievense Battery Co., induced the common council to amend the city ordinance to permit him to build a two-story brick building on the northeast corner of Central Avenue and Ninth Street, with a bowling alley on the second floor (later the Holland Bowling Center, now reconstructed by Lumir Corp.). The building permits in early 1927 totaled $212,000, which was far ahead of any similar-sized city in Michigan. That summer Henry Maatman

[83] *Holland City News*, 28 Apr., 13 May 1926, 17 Mar., 23 June 1927; "People's Bank celebrates anniversary," *Holland Sentinel*, 8 Aug. 1980.

built a $20,000, two-story brick building on the last open lot at 13 West Eighth Street, flanked by the Strand Theater (9 West) and Meyer Music House (17 West). Maatman's shoe store occupied the first floor.[84] (See appendix 5.11 for a list of shoe stores, 1872-1976.)

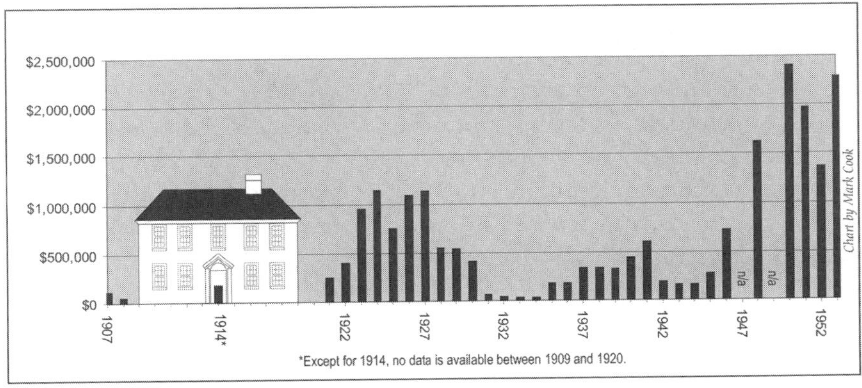

Fig. 19.1. New Building Construction Permits, 1907-1953

Warm Friend Tavern

Holland had a hotel boom in the 1920s. In 1921 William Van Asselt erected a three-story, forty-room hotel, the Asselton, on East Eighth Street across from the Pere Marquette station and immediately east of the tracks. The Asselton continued for forty-two years under various names, mainly the Hollander (1940-64). Alfred "Big Mike" Von Ins operated a tavern in the building from 1962 until he retired in 1994; Roger Reister reopened the tavern restaurant in 1995 with high hopes, but they were soon dashed. Henry Kraker in 1925 built the Hotel Kraker on River Avenue at Ninth Street, which in 1935 continued as the Netherlands Hotel until 1950 (see appendix 5.6 for a list of hotels, 1872-1966.)[85]

The new hotels downtown may have prompted the Holland Merchants Association to announce in 1921 that developers planned to raze the Hotel Holland on the choice northeast corner of Eighth Street and Central Avenue and erect a luxury four-story brick hotel with 110 rooms, more than double the old one. Local labor would have steady

84 *Holland City News*, 4 Apr., 5 May, 14 July 1927.

85 Ibid., 9 May, 10 Aug. 1922, 18 Jan., 26 Apr. 1923, 17 Oct. 1935, 16 Apr. 1995; Kliphuis, "Hotels of Holland." Lumir Corp. bought the decrepit Hollander Hotel at Eighth and Lincoln and razed it in 1998 (*Holland Sentinel*, 31 Dec. 1998).

work for several years. Unfortunately, the project languished until 1923, the same year that Hub Boone announced plans for a smaller $250,000 hotel nearby, but he too failed to deliver. His father Hermanus Boone had been the proprietor of the Holland Hotel since the mid 1890s.[86]

City leaders for years had decried the lack of a luxury hotel in Holland, with meeting rooms for local clubs and societies. In December 1923 August Landwehr took hold of the languishing luxury hotel project and announced plans for a $500,000 Warm Friend Tavern, to be built with local labor and financed by 6 percent realty bonds with a par value of $100. His company pledged to buy $200,000 worth, and a public subscription campaign would float the other $300,000, with an individual limit of five ($500) bonds, with every investor promised a listing by name on the framed Roll of Honor to be hung in the hotel lobby. This gave the chamber of commerce and the Merchants Association their first major project, and both rose to the occasion in a spirit of cooperation. Attorney Gerrit Diekema, Charles M. McLean of Holland-St. Louis Sugar Co., and William Beech of Bush & Lane Piano took the lead in making the project happen. The chamber formed thirty committees of two-men each, named Flying Squadrons, to canvass the city. Factory owners induced employees to invest by pledging to buy back at par any stock they might later wish to sell. Act fast, employees were advised, because "only the first one thousand signed applications will count." Other local residents also snapped up the bonds, which were considered as good as gold. The company paper could be purchased on the installment plan, 10 percent down, and the remainder spread over nine months. The campaign closed over the top by the final day, December 31, 1923, but no note holder ever received a penny back.[87]

The chamber named a committee of nine to supervise the project, with Landwehr, appropriately, the chairman. Their first success was the purchase of the Hotel Holland from the Boone family for $65,000. Next they hired an architectural firm to design the structure. Finally, they bid the contract and selected Frank Dyke as the general contractor. His men began by razing the old hotel in March 1924. The final plans were even more ambitious than the original; the brick building would stand six stories tall, plus a basement, with 144 rooms and six suites on the top floor, an ornate lobby, and a well-appointed restaurant supplied by a modern kitchen. The hotel was a Holland project from first to last. Its building permit helped push the total permits for the year above

86 *Holland City News*, 24 Feb., 3 Mar. 1921.

87 *Holland City News*, 13, 20, 27 Dec. 1923, 7 Feb. 1924.

INCORPORATED UNDER THE LAWS OF

The State of Michigan

No 387 Shares -2-

HOLLAND HOTEL COMPANY

HOLLAND, MICHIGAN

This Certifies That F. E. Dulyea, is the owner of Two Shares of One Hundred Dollars each of the Capital Stock of

HOLLAND HOTEL COMPANY

transferable only on the books of the Corporation by the holder hereof in person or by Attorney upon surrender of this Certificate properly endorsed.

In Witness Whereof, the said Corporation has caused this Certificate to be signed by its duly authorized officers and to be sealed with the Seal of the Corporation this 6th day of October A.D. 1924

Secretary President

SHARES $100.00 EACH

Holland Hotel Company, $100 stock certificate issued to Frank E. Dulyea, October 6, 1924 (*Donald van Reken Collection, Joint Archives of Holland*)

$1 million. Brickwork was completed in November 1924, and the hotel opened May 1, 1925, with a huge celebration.

Frank Dyke, a partner first with Peter Oosting and then briefly with Fred M. "Fritz" Jonkman (Yonkman), was the city's leading contractor in the interwar generation. Dyke constructed every major building: Holland High School (1914), Holland Christian High School (1923-24), Warm Friend Hotel (1925), Holland Hospital (1925), Holland Furnace office building (1925), the Memorial Chapel at Hope College (1929), and even the Franklin Street building of Calvin College in Grand Rapids (1917).[88]

The Warm Friend Tavern became the city's signature hotel, a $350,000 jewel that would rival the Pantlind Hotel of Grand Rapids, the Occidental of Muskegon, and the Burdick House of Battle Creek. The Warm Friend Tavern lodged and wined and dined company salesmen, visiting businessmen, and local leading families. It became the social hub of the city and the Dutch Grill the most exclusive restaurant in town. Old Dutch Cherry Elder Cider was the trademark aperitif. The bellboys wore the Old Dutch baggy pants and the waitresses colorful

[88] Ibid., 7 Apr. 1918, 4, 10, 17 Jan., 7 Feb., 13 Mar., 12 Apr., 1 Oct., 6 Nov. 1924, 30 Apr., 7, 14 May, 13 Aug., 8 Oct. 1925, Dyke obit., 12 Jan. 1939.

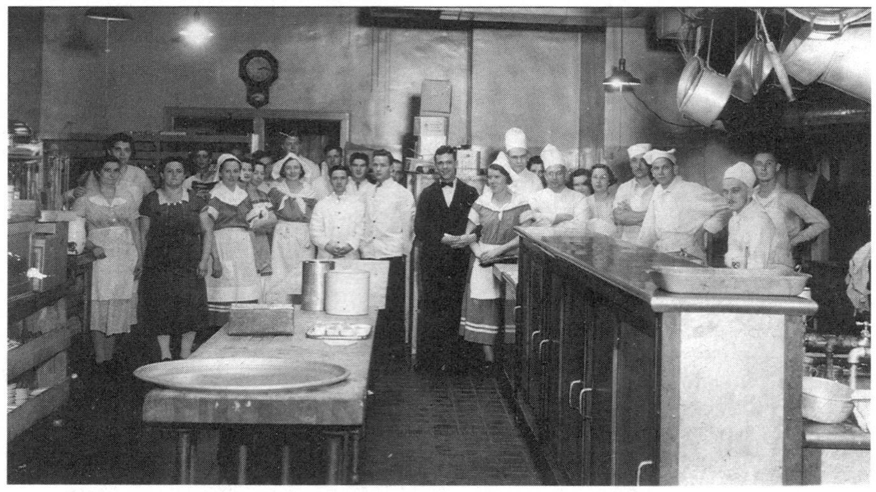

Warm Friend Tavern staff during Holland's first Tulip Time, 1929. Head chef Floyd C. Hansen is seventh from the right, together with his assistants, all in proper attire (*Archives, Holland Historical Trust*)

dress costumes. But the male guests flirted with the waitresses, and this forced the management to discard its Dutch Girl motif. Yet the Warm Friend, according to a Chicago newspaper report, remained "very Dutch and very clean." The hotel sparked a great deal of convention business over the next decades, and by 1929 Holland claimed to be a convention city. Left in the Warm Friend's wake were the Asselton Hotel, the Bristol Hotel (run by Hans A. and Ethel Von Ins), and the Kraker Hotel.[89] But in its forty years under Holland Furnace ownership, the hotel never turned a profit, and stockholders like Frank E. Dulyea never got their money back, unless they managed to sell their shares to third parties before the firm went bankrupt (see below).

The successful hotel financing received a boost from the unexpectedly rich payout on an earlier speculation, the 1906 investment in the American Newfoundland Pulp and Lumber Co., which held leases on 266,000 acres of virgin spruce and fir stands in Newfoundland. More than a dozen business and professional men in Holland, Zeeland, and Grand Rapids invested at least $150,000 in the venture, known as the Hanchett-Crittsinger deal. Nine locals included dentists Bernard J. De Vries and Milton J. Cook; industrialists Con De Pree, Charles M. McLean, and Henry Pelgrim Sr.; merchants James A. Brouwer, Jan Bosman, and Henry P. Zwemer; and Hope English professor John Nykerk. After "sweating blood for ten years" by throwing good money

89 Ibid., 4 Mar. 1926, 25 July 1929.

after bad to keep the operation going, the Newfoundland firm found an English buyer in 1923 who paid $450,000, with $126,000 down and 4.5 percent on the remainder over ten years. The investors' "long delayed ship came in loaded down with wealth." They were jubilant to be turned from sure losers into savvy investors.[90]

Professionals in the 1920s to 1940s

The ranks of professionals grew along with the buildings. In 1927 Holland had thirteen attorneys (out of 21 in Ottawa County), nine dentists, ten druggists (see appendix 5.5 for a list of drugstores, 1864-1950), two optometrists, fifteen physicians, eleven realtors, two morticians, a chiropractor, and a midwife–Johanna (Mrs. Gerrit) De Mots–who advertised her services as a *loskundige* (midwife) at 171 West Seventeenth Street. Singling out the most prominent in each field is problematic. Diekema, Kollen & Ten Cate (Gerrit J. Diekema, George E. Kollen, and Daniel Ten Cate) was clearly the most prestigious law firm. It is the direct predecessor of Cunningham Dalman, founded in 1959 and now located at 321 Settlers Road. President Andrew Mulder in recent years has led the firm with twelve partners and fourteen lawyers.[91]

Doctors' offices lined Eighth Street and River Avenue in the 1920s and 1930s. Physicians included Clifford Abbott, Arthur Brower, Seine De Pree, Cornelius J. Fisher (Visser), George H. Thomas, Harry C. Irvin, William C. Kools, Abraham Leenhouts, Rudolph H. Nichols, Charles Samson, Otto Vander Velde, William Westrate, and William G. Winter Sr. Dentists included John J. Brower, Milton Cook, Bernard J. De Vries, Rokus De Vries, Frank U. De Vries, George Stegeman, Chester Sulkers, George Van Vorst, and Ada C. Willis. Chiropractors were Ellis J. Bacheller, John de Jong, Morris Van Kolken, and Johanna Van Otterloo, the only female medical practitioner. When Fisher celebrated his ninety-first birthday in 1975, he had practiced for sixty-four years, the first seven in Hamilton, and he was the oldest doctor in town. Willis opened his office in the Tower Clock Building in 1921 and practiced there for several years.[92]

90 Ibid., 14 Feb. 1924.

91 Ibid., 1927-28; *Business Review West Michigan* 15, no. 43 (2010): 33.

92 *Holland City Directories*, 1921, 1924, 1927-1928; *Holland City News*, 10 Aug. 1922, 1 Jan. 1925; *Holland Sentinel*, 9 Feb. 1975. William G. Winter's sons continued his practice after his death in 1936, erecting a building at 10 East Tenth Street in 1941. Both retired in 1976 (William G. Winter Sr. obit., *Holland City News*, 13 Feb. 1936; John K. Winter obit., *Holland Sentinel*, 20 Apr. 1995, William G. Winter Jr. obit., ibid., 17 Nov. 2003).

Diekema, Kollen & Ten Cate, Holland's most prestigious legal firm, pose in one of their offices above First State Bank. The partners behind the desk are (*l-r*):Gerrit J. Diekema, George E. Kollen, and Daniel Ten Cate. The two women and man on right are unidentified (*courtesy Joan Ten Cate Bonnette*)

Holland Hospital by 1940 had seventeen physicians on staff from Holland and nine from neighboring cities. The staff doctors were Nelson Clark, Carl Cook, Harold De Vries, Marinus Hamelink, Cornelius Fisher, Herman Harms, William Kools, Abraham Leenhouts, Rudolph Nichols, Richard H. Schaftenaar, Edward Schrick, Chester Van Appledorn, Edwin Vander Berg, Otto Vander Velde, William Westrate, and the twin brothers John K. Winter and William G. Winter Jr. The Winter brothers, both graduates of Hope College, took over the medical practice of their father, William G. Winter Sr., in 1936 and touched the lives of thousands over the next forty years, including over five thousand babies they delivered. From 1942 until their retirement in 1976, they practiced in a building with a distinctive Dutch-gabled façade they erected at 10 East Tenth Street. Chester Van Appledorn was a product of Holland Christian, Calvin College, the University of Michigan, and Wayne State University Medical College. From 1941 until his unexpected death in 1967, he treated thousands, while also serving as a city health officer. As an expert on the wildflowers and Indians of Michigan, he lectured widely and joined the National Audubon Society. His photographs of wildflowers have won wide acclaim.[93] (See appendix

93 *Holland City News*, 24 June 1948, Chester Van Appledorn obit., 13 Apr. 1967; John Kools. Winter obit., *Holland Sentinel*, 20 Apr. 1995, William G. Winter Jr. obit., ibid., 17 Nov. 2003.

5.8 for a list of physicians and surgeons, dentists, and other doctors, 1870-1950.)

Laundries

The first hand laundry in Holland was Chinese. In 1899 Moy Chang and Lee Sing (or Wing) opened Hermitage Laundry at 182 River Street (the former Van Zanten Tea Co.). In mid-1909 Sing left hurriedly for Chicago's Chinatown when rival gangs began fighting in a "Tong war;" he never returned and was thought to have died in the fighting. This was the end of his Chinese laundry, leaving three Dutch or American firms, all on Eighth Street: John Dykema and Raymond Patrick's Model Laundry at 97-99 East Eighth, Henry Meengs and William Bosman's Holland Cleaners at 9 East Eighth, and William Swift and Nick Moes' West Michigan Steam Laundry, which opened in 1892 at 50 West Eighth. Swift and Moes charged 30¢ a dozen for "plain washing" and 50¢ a dozen for the same ironed. Martin Beukema bought West Michigan Laundry in 1893. He bore a $500 loss in 1908 when the engine room caught fire, placing in danger the entire line of wooden store buildings on the west side of River Avenue. Fortunately, Engine House No. 1 was right across the street, and the firemen kept the flames from spreading.[94]

Joseph Borgman in 1910 bought Patrick's interest in Model Laundry. In 1921 Gerrit Alderink and Herman Beukema launched Ideal Dry Cleaners at 75 East Sixth Street at College Avenue. The next year, three Chinese laundrymen from Chicago–Charlie Tan, Chin Chowe, and Chin Bew–bought West Michigan Laundry and renamed it Sam Lee Hand Laundry, but they sold it within a few years to First World War veteran Ray Tardiff and his younger brother Calvin "Cal," who brought back the West Michigan name. In 1927 the city had five laundries and dry cleaners–Model, Holland, West Michigan, Ideal, and C. H. Flickinger's Paris Dry Cleaners at 75 East Sixth Street. Customers apparently preferred Dutch or American proprietors, since the Chinese laundries were short-lived.[95]

The Tardiff brothers built West Michigan Laundry into the longest-lasting dry cleaning business in Holland; it has been in continuous operation since 1892. Their competitor for eighty years,

94 *Holland City News*, 5, 19 Mar., 20 Apr., 22 July, 5 Aug., 20 Oct. 1892, 6 Aug. 1908, 30 Dec. 1909; *Holland City Directory*, 1908.

95 *Holland City News*, 26 Oct. 1922, 1 Mar. 1923; *Holland Sentinel*, 10 July 1929. The spelling of the Chinese names is likely inaccurate.

Holland Cleaners, 9 East Eighth Street, ca. 1915
(*Archives, Holland Historical Trust*)

Model Laundry, closed in the mid-1970s. The Tardiff brothers in the early 1930s built a new plant at 407 West Seventeenth Street. To keep the machines humming, they sent out a fleet of five trucks to collect dirty laundry in resort towns from Ferrysburg to South Haven. Each driver plied his own territory and found business especially strong in the summer months. Ray Tardiff's French war bride Germaine ran the office, her mother Martha Billotte, who had accompanied the newlyweds back to Michigan, was the floor lady, and Ray and Cal managed operations at the "Home of Snow White Clothes," the company's advertising slogan. When Martha retired, Cal's wife Ann became the floor lady. As more housewives bought washing machines in the 1920s and 1930s, West Michigan Laundry added dry cleaning woolens to its service.[96]

In 1964 Cal and Germaine sold West Michigan Uniforms to Gordon Van Tuinen, who specialized in commercial work, cleaning and renting uniforms, replete with embroidered company logos, for a wide variety of occupations. Gordon's sons Ken and Tom took over the business in the 1980s, and their cousins Steve and Mitch Van Tuinen succeeded them in the 2000s.[97]

96 *Holland Sentinel*, Jan. 1986 clipping, vertical files, Herrick District Library. I am grateful to Germaine Tardiff, Bush's daughter Vivian (Mrs. Gerard) Cook, and to Calvin Tardiff's son Calvin for information about the company.

97 Holland Area Chamber of Commerce, *Business Magazine* (Fall 2011): 5-6.

A family-owned business now in its sixth decade is Maplewood Dry Cleaners, a neighborhood institution at 148 East Thirty-Second Street at Columbia Avenue. Vern and Leona Pathuis Houting, now with son John, have operated the store since 1951, when Vern bought out his partner of three years, his uncle Neal Jacobusse, who was the initiator. As the business grew, the Houtings expanded the building three times and upgraded the boiler and cleaning equipment. The high-tech $50,000 machine in an hour can wash and dry a large batch of clothes, renew the solvent, and water-cool itself. The secret of keeping its one thousand customers happy is personal service and quality work. Joyce Van Slooten, the store's expert presser for many decades, "is the best presser in the state," according to John Houting.[98]

In 1970 C. Edward Ralston of West Olive started Lemon Fresh as Thrifty Mat Laundry & Dry Cleaners at 402 East Eighth Street. In 1979 Roger and Kristi Lemmen bought the business and renamed it Lemon Fresh, a take-off on the family name. The new owners the same year opened a second plant at 22 River Avenue. In 1993 they added a third location on the north side at 983 Butternut Drive. This competes with nearby Lakewood Cleaners at 11539 East Lakewood Boulevard. In recent years Grand Rapids-based Sheldon Cleaners opened three Holland locations, at 118 Douglas Avenue, 15 South Waverly Avenue, and 777 Washington Avenue. South Shore Laundry at 513 West Seventeenth Street serves the southwest end of town.[99]

Downtown chain stores in the 1930s

The downtown added another chain store in 1930, Montgomery Ward's emporium at 25-27 East Eighth Street (later the Outpost), which advertised "Everything for Home and Farm." The Chicago-based company, with a large mail-order division and colorful catalogs, built Holland's largest downtown store after making an "exhaustive investigation proving that this city was one of the most progressive shopping centers in this section of the state." The management tried mightily to overcome its image as a foreign entity. The company president stated: "We are trying to make this store a real Holland institution [and] . . . local merchants need not fear the new store," which would bring new customers to town from a radius up to eighty miles. The first advertisement in the local press noted that it was company policy to hire local salespeople who "have a personal following of

98 Steve Vander Veen, "When a business is more than a business," ibid., 29 May 2005.

99 *Holland City Directories*, 1970-93.

acquaintances and friends who will prefer to buy from someone they know." Montgomery Ward also contracted with Rooks Transfer Line of Holland to handle all its freight.[100]

Montgomery Ward faced an uphill battle. Two months after the grand opening of its Holland store, the Holland Merchants Association invited as its luncheon speaker William H. Caslow, the self-described Main Street Crusader against the chain store "evils." Caslow had spoken to the association seven months earlier on the same subject to much applause from independent merchants. After lunch at the Warm Friend with the members, Caslow spoke to a large crowd at the armory. "Some will have it that big business is good," Caslow cried. But "I tell you that [big] business is not good. . . . The whole system of American syndication is creating an empire of big business, so called, that will make this a nation of clerks and hirelings." It is a "false economy," Caslow warned, to trade at the chain store to save a few dollars. A second Boston Tea Party is needed, he declared. The onset of the Great Depression gave the Main Street Crusader an ideal opportunity to play on the fears of his audience. In a short time, Franklin D. Roosevelt would be excoriating businessmen as "royalists in the temple," plutocrats that must be restrained by government. But the chain stores thrived, nonetheless, because of their lower pricing.[101]

National food chains came to Holland in 1924 when A & P opened its flagship store at 52 East Eighth Street, followed in 1938 by a second store on River Avenue at Tenth Street next door to the Colonial (now Park) Theater. By 1960 A & P was down to one store at 36 West Sixteenth Street, where it continued for a decade before closing in 1970.[102] The "depression decade" was hard on Kroger, which closed several of its stores. In 1940 Kroger consolidated operations of three nearby stores in a modern Park-N-Shop superstore at 224 River Avenue south of Ninth Street; it was a new building that featured a Dutch-gabled façade. For the grand opening, all employees dressed in Dutch costumes. Kroger's River and Washington Avenue stores continued until the 1950s; Washington Avenue closed in 1952, and River Avenue closed about 1955. In 1960 Kroger opened a new store at 182 West Thirty-First Street at Michigan Avenue, but it closed within nine years.[103]

The national department stores outlasted the national groceries in Holland. Montgomery Ward downsized in 1961 to a catalog and

[100] *Holland City News*, 30 Jan. 1930.

[101] Ibid., 19 Sept. 1929, 10 Apr. 1930 (quote).

[102] *Holland City Directories*, 1924-25, 1970.

[103] *Holland City News*, 13 Jan. 1938, 19 Oct., 22 Nov. 1939; *Holland City Directories*, 1938-70.

appliance store at 51 East Eighth Street and in 1971 to a catalog and auto service center on the southeast corner of Sixteenth Street and River Avenue. Montgomery Ward shut down its Holland store in 1973. The Kresge 5 & 10 at 12 East Eighth Street lasted until 1970, Woolworth's, JCPenney, and Sears Roebuck remained downtown until the late 1980s, when Woolworth's closed and Penney's and Sears relocated to Westshore Mall (chapter 33).[104]

Satellite shopping centers

As the city limits expanded southward, satellite shopping centers developed in the various neighborhoods, specifically on Sixteenth Street, Washington Avenue, Maple Avenue, Columbia Avenue, Maplewood, and South Shore. In 1927 one could find along Sixteenth Street between River and Central Avenues, Deur & Zwemer Hardware (William Deur and Jacob Zwemer), Service Tire Shop, Nash Sales & Service, and later, an A & P store. Deur had a law office there with Frank Lievense, and Du Mond Bakery graced the block for many years (see below). Around the corner on Central Avenue, locals traded at the Smith Drug Store, Kroger Grocery, Harold Boven & Co. Dry Goods (successor to Van Anrooy & Sons), Van Lente Grocery, and later, Consumers Cash Market. The successful Van Lente store changed hands in 1922; Harold Boven of Holland and Franklin Fazakerley of Muskegon jointly purchased it. Smith Drug Store was a fixture at 383 Central Avenue from 1929 to 1967.[105]

At Maple Avenue and Thirteenth Street Louis Lawrence's Drug Store opened in 1921; Lawrence "Larry" Wade purchased it in 1929. After more than twenty years, in 1951, Larry sold Wade Drug Store to Jack and Helen Jean Smith, both licensed pharmacists, who stocked sundries, filled prescriptions, and ran a busy soda fountain and a large photo department featuring Kodak film and Canon cameras. After forty years, in 1990, the Smiths closed the old-fashioned store. Steffens Market, owned by Len and Ann Steffens, stood on the corner of Van Raalte Avenue and Fourteenth Street. Henry Haveman's grocery, dry goods, and meats (later J. Hulst & Son) on the southeast corner of College Avenue at Twenty-Fourth Street served the Prospect Park area. The Maplewood district at Columbia Avenue and Thirty-Second also had the usual bevy of neighborhood businesses—a grocery, hardware store, barbershop, and a beauty shop. The nexus of College Avenue and

104 *Holland Sentinel*, 11 Apr. 1940; *Holland City Directories*, 1960-90.
105 *Holland City News*, 9 Feb. 1922; *Holland City Directories*, 1921, 1925-26, 1928.

Henry Haveman groceries, dry goods, and meats, 577-79 College Avenue, ca. 1908. Henry Haveman is on the far left and Marinus Van Ark, employee and later butcher, is second from the right (*courtesy Myron Van Ark*)

Twenty-Fourth Street in the 1930s hosted Bartel's Shoe Store, Buter's Grocery, Bert Koning's Barber Shop, and Van's Drug Store. Later came Hulst Grocery and Mannes Super Service. All the neighborhood groceries made home deliveries by bicycle and pickup truck.[106]

Along First Avenue (Washington Avenue after 1927) between Eighteenth and Nineteenth Streets in the 1920s stood De Loof's Drug Store, Dyke & Hornstra Grocery and Dry Goods (Gerrit Dyke and Frank Hornstra), Benjamin Vander Vliet's First Ave. Bicycle Shop, Benjamin Geerds' First Ave. Shoe Store, Harry Doornbos' First Ave. Market, Van Faasen & Marcus' First Ave. Confectionary, and on the corner of Eighteenth Street, John and son Leonard Vogelzang's hardware store. Later came Draper's Meat Market.[107]

Barber shops

No neighborhood was complete without a grocery and meat market, bakery, shoe store, drug store, hardware, gas station, and a barbershop. Koning, of East Saugatuck, opened at 572 College Avenue in 1929, and for a time partnered with brother-in-law Gilbert Rigterink under the name Bert & Gil's. In 1952 Bert's brother Willard "Bill,"

[106] Myron "Mike" Van Ark interview by Ena Brooks, 25 Nov. 1997, JAH; *Holland Sentinel*, 15 Oct. 1992, 24 June 1990.

[107] Various *Holland City Directories*, 1920s-30s.

Thirteenth and Maple Streets looking east, with the Interurban taking on passengers; Lawrence Drug Store (later Hempel's Pastries) occupied the corner building from 1921, and Blok Bros. Groceries and Dry Goods was next door (*courtesy Robert Vande Vusse*)

who previously had a shop in Grand Rapids, took Gil's place, and the signage changed to Bert & Bill's. When Bert retired in 1954, Bill carried on for another twenty-six years, before retiring in 1980 after barbering for forty-six years. The always popular Bill's Barber Shop relocated three times, in 1962 across the street to 567 College, in 1961 to 159 West Twenty-Ninth Street, and in 1973 to 726 Michigan Avenue.[108] Post Barber Shop was a fixture at 331 College Avenue at the corner of Fourteenth Street for fifty-six years, from 1936 until 1992. Cornelius "Casey" Huizenga opened the shop in 1931 but found the Depression years too tough and sold out to Edward Post in 1936. Post since 1929 had cut hair for Jacob "Jack" Vander Ploeg at 59 East Eighth Street. Post survived when Hope College students and professors started coming for the thirty-five-cent cuts. When Post's son Jim finished high school, he joined his father in 1940 at age eighteen and manned a second chair. The senior Post retired in 1961 and son Jim in 1973.

Randall L. "Randy" Driesenga replaced the elder Post in 1962 and bought the shop in 1972, allowing Jim to retire. Driesenga renamed the shop Stag Barber and Styling Salon. With long hair in vogue in the 1970s, the shop needed four barbers working seventy hours a week to keep up, and they still faced a dozen guys waiting on the bench.

108 *Holland City Directories*, 1929-80; Willard "Bill" Koning obit, *Holland Sentinel*, 23 Dec. 2012; phone conversation with Judy (Mrs. William) Koning Van Appledorn, Bill's daughter., 27 Dec. 2012.

A cut cost $1.50 in 1962, but it climbed to $11.00 by 1992. In 1990 Driesenga sold the shop to Tony and Micki Gamez, a husband and wife team, with Tony the barber and Micki the hairdresser, under the name Cutting Edge. In 1992 the couple moved the shop to 375 Columbia Avenue when Western Theological Seminary bought the 331 college property for a married student housing complex. Herman Meppelink had operated a barber shop there as early as 1928. After four years, in 1996, the Gamez couple left town, and the longest-operating barber shop in Holland closed without a whimper.[109]

Two other barbers on the east end were Harvey Bouwman at 198 East Fifth Street from 1954 to 1973 and William "Bill" Bruinsma, owner of the East Town Barber Shop at 401 East Eighth Street since 1969. Before opening his own place, Bruinsma cut hair for three years at Roger Plasman's Barber Shop at 545 West Seventeenth Street. Bruinsma in 2012 was still taking care of long-time customers.[110]

Vogelzang Hardware

Jan (John) Vogelzang and his bride Klaaskje (Clara) Nienhuis immigrated to Holland in 1907 with five dollars in their pocket. John was a farmhand, and Clara's family had wealth, but they lost it all. John found work at West Michigan Tool and then at Bush & Lane Piano under Walter Lane, but he had his heart set on the hardware business. Lane knew this, and one day he challenged John: "Either shut up, or quit your job and go out." John replied, "I quit." With this push out the door, John, at age forty-five in 1921, borrowed $500 from three friends and opened a hardware store in his home on Washington Street, moving the growing family upstairs. While Lane supported John's entrepreneurial ambitions, it was his wife Clara who really persuaded him to take the risk and go into business for himself. "She gave him the backbone," son William declared years later.[111]

In 1923 Vogelzang built a two-story brick building a little to the north of their home, fronting Eighteenth Street. Six years later, in

[109] *Holland City Directories*, 1928-97.

[110] Ibid., 1954-2011.

[111] William Vogelzang interview by the author and David Boeve, 30 Sept. 2009 (quote), typescript, JAH; Steve Vanderveen, "Vogelzang name has long history," *Holland Sentinel*, 7 Aug. 2005. John Vogelzang Sr. late in life wrote his memoirs in pencil on 52 rolls of shelf paper, each 25 feet long. The transcribed, typed text of 452 single-spaced pages, compliments of William Vogelzang, is available at the Archives, Calvin College. John Vogelzang Jr. also penned a short handwritten memoir of his momentous life in business and politics, which his widow, Jackie Swierenga Vogelzang, kindly provided to the author.

1929, he led his fellow merchants in getting the city fathers to create Washington Square on Washington Boulevard between Eighteenth and Nineteenth Streets. Washington Avenue itself had been recently renamed, in place of the nondescript First Avenue, at the suggestion of mail carrier and patriot Anthony Rosbach. Washington Avenue quickly became Washington Boulevard, given its wide expanse and tree-lined median. The merchants created a carnival atmosphere on that August Saturday to commemorate the establishment of the square. According the *Holland City News*, the highlight was a blackface skit by Arie Baumann and Henry Baker, who mimicked *Amos 'n' Andy*. Even the four Holland policemen took the "sun-tan cure" and walked around with faces as "black as the ace of spades." The participating merchants, beside Vogelzang, included a Kroger Grocery, contractor John Kampen, Dyke & Hornstra Dry Goods, milliner Anna (Mrs. Richard) Buursma's Snappy Hat Shop, John Ligtvoet's Barber Shop, Balfoort & Bos French Pastry Shop, Benjamin Geerds' Washington Square Shoe Store, Harry Dornbos' Washington Market, Van Fassen & Marcus' Washington Square Confectionary, William A. Thompson Plumbing & Heating, Earl Working's Barber Shop, Harry Fik's Holland Radio Shop, and John Spaman's Washington Square Tire & Battery Shop. Today, thankfully, such community revelry would be unthinkable.[112]

In 1930 Vogelzang expanded by adding another two-story building next door to the south, at 439 Washington Boulevard. The Depression years were difficult, but John survived by dint of hard work, frugality, and family labor. One by one, his four sons, John Jr., Leonard, Abraham "Abe," and William "Bill" joined the family business, as did sister Geraldine as bookkeeper. The Vogelzangs opened a second store in 1938 by buying Verburg Hardware at 7 East Eighth Street. Vogelzang Sr., a farmer at heart, about 1939 bought fifteen acres at 168 West Thirty-Second Street and erected the family home and several outbuildings that later served as warehouses. Vogelzang Sr. also became active in politics, serving two terms as a city councilman from 1936 to 1940 under mayors Nicodemus Bosch and Henry Geerlings. Later his son John Jr. followed in his footsteps, serving many terms as an Allegan County commissioner.

Tragedy struck the 210 West Eighteenth Street store in early May 1943 when Henry Borst, a new driver for Vandenberg Bros. Oil, whose tank farm was on Chicago Drive and Eighth Street (the present site of

112 *Holland City News*, 15 Aug. 1929. For more recent history, see Steve Vander Veen, "Washington Square held a business for every need," and "Life in Washington Square: A snapshot from 1975," *Holland Sentinel*, Oct. 23, 6 Nov. 2005.

Benjamin Geerds stands proudly in his new Washington Square shoe store (*Archives, Holland Historical Trust*)

Ver Hage-Mitsubishi of Holland), mistakenly delivered raw gasoline through a defunct pipe onto the basement floor, instead of using the active pipe nearby that fed the basement storage tank. After fifteen gallons of the five-hundred-gallon delivery lay on the floor, the sump pump kicked in, and a spark set off a violent explosion that killed Borst and Frank Volkema, age sixteen, a part-time store employee. John Vogelzang Jr. and five other employees in the store suffered less severe burns and cuts from flying glass, including Louis Van Hartesveld, who was blown six feet off the floor by the explosion. John Vogelzang carried Fanny Steketee out of the building. Off-duty police officer, Isaac De Kraker, who was shopping at the Dyke & Hoornstra Kroger Store across the street, prevented a worse tragedy by jumping into the gas truck and driving it more than a block away. Fire chief Andrew Klomparens counted at least thirty explosions, as his men fought the fire for more than three hours. Geraldine Vogelzang escaped, and her purse with $200 and business papers was recovered the next day. Both the original building and the 1923 addition were lost; only the 1930 addition survived. The reason for the gasoline delivery was that the store sold gasoline at retail for cars, delivered at the curb from a hand pump. Early gas stations consisted of pumps in front of other businesses, often auto garages.[113]

[113] *Holland City News*, 9 May 1943; John Vogelzang Sr. obit., ibid., 26 May 1966; Randall P. Vande Water, "Two Die in Vogelzang Fire," in *Holland Happenings*, 1:64-65; William Vogelzang interview.

Firemen fighting John Vogelzang Hardware store fire, May 5, 1943 (*Joint Archives of Holland*)

After the fire, John Vogelzang Sr. erected a variety store around the corner at 439 Washington Boulevard. In 1945 he sold the 7 East Eighth Street store and the Washington Square store to his four sons and daughter. Son Nicholas "Nick" bought the variety store, and John

Vogelzang Hardware, southeast corner of Eighth Street at College Avenue, 1989 (*Archives, Holland Historical Trust*)

Sr. helped him run it until 1952, when Nick decided to study for the Christian ministry at Calvin Theological Seminary. The variety store then became a warehouse for the downtown hardware business. The Eighth Street store meanwhile was under John Jr., who had been deferred from military service for being too tall, and Abe, who failed his physical. Leonard and Bill joined them after returning from military service. The four brothers then bought the store.

In 1946 the foursome moved from 7 East Eighth Street to 62-64 East Eighth Street, on the southwest corner of College Avenue (now Kilwin's), where they opened a store for furniture, house wares, and appliances. In 1947 the brothers erected the flagship hardware and sporting goods store across College Avenue at 64-66 East Eighth Street, a choice location on the southeast corner, where they remained for fifty years. Later, the Vogelzangs eliminated a competitor, buying and closing the Corner (formerly Vander Veen) Hardware store on River Avenue and Eighth Street.

In 1960 the Vogelzang brothers paired off. Abe and Len opened a furniture and appliance store at 51-53 East Eighth Street that, within the year, moved into the newly vacant store next door. John Jr. and kid brother Bill ran the flagship hardware and sporting goods store at College. Vogelzang Enterprises, the corporate umbrella entity, in 1960 sold the 62-64 East Eighth Street building and bought the three-story John Good Building at 23 West Eighth Street (now Talbots) for a warehouse. They rented part of the building to the army for a recruiting station.[114]

Bill chafed under the limited financial potential of small-scale retailing and left after several years to start Vogelzang International Corp., an import business that contracted with Asian factories to manufacture the Vogelzang brand of cast iron stoves and fireplaces, made to his specifications, for sale in the Holland store and in hardware and department stores across America. Bill started at 415 West Twenty-First Street. "Soon I was selling boatloads of stuff to all the major corporations," Vogelzang recalled, including seven thousand True Value stores, five thousand Ace Hardware stores, and Menards and Target Stores. In 1975 Bill convinced a Target executive to let him supply their thousands of stores with his products. "You have 52 categories to manage," he said. "You're a busy person. Let me pick out what to sell. I'll put the whole program together. At the end of the year, you'll have empty shelves and money in the bank." Two weeks later, Bill

[114] *Holland City News*, 16 Mar. 1961; Vander Veen, "Vogelzang."

had in hand an initial $650,000 order. The next year, he suffered a heart attack and decided to cut back. He offered 49 percent of the business to his son Steve, a Proctor & Gamble branch manager, who accepted and came home. By then the operations needed more space. So the pair bought the 400 West Seventeenth Street building and adjoining empty lot from Charles Conrad. In 1990 Steve purchased the remaining 51 percent, and Bill retired.[115]

In 1985 Len and Abe (John had left earlier for a political career) sold the Eighth Street store to their sons, David and Merrill, who carried on for fifteen years. The downtown location was handicapped by a lack of parking for building contractors, the primary customers. In 2001 the cousins closed the flagship store after fifty-five years, sold the building to New Holland Brewery, and opened Vogelzang Variety on Chicago Drive, but this venture failed within two years. After eighty-one years, Vogelzang Hardware was no more.[116]

Van Wieren Hardware on Douglas Avenue had its start in the late 1940s as a gas station, bait shop, and lunch room for sport fishermen headed for Lake Michigan. After a few years, owners Andrew "Andy" and Harriet Van Wieren sold the station and built a hardware store east of the station in its present location. Son Lester "Les" joined the business in 1968 and continued until failing health forced him to step down in about 2000 and turn his interests over to his daughter Deborah "Deb" Axce. Van Wieren competes with the big box stores, such as Lowes and Menards, by providing hands-on service. With the closing of the Vogelzang and Keppel stores, Van Wieren, Graafschap Hardware, and Holland Ace Hardware at 835 Lincoln Avenue are the last of their kind of old fashioned store. Lloyd Van Wieren began Holland Ace Hardware in 1993 at 100 Aniline Avenue under the umbrella of the national Ace chain. He increasingly specialized in hardwoods and in 2003 split the business in two: Holland Hardware Products moved to New Holland Street under his management, and Holland Ace Hardware moved to 835 Lincoln Avenue under manager Brian Glasser.[117]

115 William Vogelzang interview.

116 *Holland Sentinel*, 22 Jan. 1995; *Grand Rapids Press Lakeshore Edition*, 10 Dec. 2001, 14 Feb. 2003.

117 *Holland Sentinel*, 4 Sept. 2004; *Holland City Directories*, 1991-2003.

Part Five

Cartage, trucking, and cycling

Before the advent of trucks, draymen delivered freight by horse and wagon. Stanley Curtis recalled the draymen of the early twentieth century, who serviced the railroad freight house, the interurban freight house, and commercial and industrial customers.

> There was a group of draymen, as we called them, who delivered that stuff—people by the name of G[ysbert] Blom and Bill Mokma and Ollie Baker. I always remembered G. Blom. I was down at the interurban freight house one day, and he talked in sort of broken English. He was a short, fat, jolly Dutchman. He'd stop there, and they wanted him to take something away from there, but he was busy, he had to go somewhere else. So, he told the freight agent there, he says, "I come pretty soon back over." And Ollie Baker, he was another drayman. He used to get the job of hauling the old two-wheel hose reel to the fires. They'd give him a couple of dollars for doing that; otherwise it had to be pulled by hand.[118]

Two draymen with a penchant for posing for photographers with their team and wagon (or sled in winter) loaded to the brim with freight, were Albert De Weerd of De Weerd Contracting and Delivery Service and Henry P. Zwemer of Zwemer Express, Coal & Wood, 275 East Eighth Street.

After 1900 the railroad-affiliated American Express Company at 267 Central Avenue had agents Otto Breyman in 1903, Will Breyman in 1906, and William Hardie from 1908 to 1914. The rival United States Express Company (later Adams Express) in the Tower Clock Building at 121 River Avenue had agents J. A. Barron in 1908 and Bert Adams in 1915. By 1906 second-hand dealer Peter J. Zalsman started the Holland Storage and Transfer at 76 East Eighth Street. By 1908 horse trainer Albert A. (Albertus) Boone and William Nykamp operated Citizens Transfer & Storage Co. at 72 West Eighth Street, and Isaac Ver Schure had left farming to form Holland Parcel Express & Baggage at 204 West Eleventh Street. Holland Parcel had a short run; it closed by 1921. Nykamp sold his interest in 1910 to Baker. The firm handled baggage transfers at the docks and train depots and had carriages to wedding parties and funerals. Citizens Transfer enjoyed a long run of seventy

[118] Stanley Curtis interview by Donald van Reken, 23 June 1976, typescript, 7, JAH.

Albert De Weerd delivering a load of wood products, ca. 1916 (*Archives, Holland Historical Trust*)

years, moving operations in the early 1950s to 121 River Street and in 1966 to 68 West Eighth Street, until closing in 1979. Other teamsters after 1910 were John Verhoef, Albert Brinkman, Klaas Buurma, and William Mokma (of Mokma's Express at 91 East Nineteenth Street). By 1921 Verhoef was teaming for the Charles Limbert Furniture Company.[119]

Henry P. Zwemer at the reins of his Express, Coal and Wood delivery wagon and team, with a "load" of telephone linemen. The lineman on the far left with pole climbing spikes on his legs is Levinus Koeman, ca. 1906 (*Archives, Holland Historical Trust*).

119 *Holland City Directories*, 1910, 1913-14, 1915-16, 1921, 1966, 1979; *Holland City News*, 16 June 1910.

Citizen's Transfer rigs lined up at 72 West Eighth Street
(*Archives, Holland Historical Trust*)

Stanley Curtis, a fresh high school graduate, drove the wagon for American Express under Hardie, a jeweler who doubled as the resident agent. His experience about 1910 is typical.

> I collected express from around town from the different factories and shippers, and I delivered express. I billed it all out, made copies of all of the waybills I collected from the different people who paid on a credit basis—factories and so forth—and I practically ran the express end of it, except for monthly audits and so forth. For this I got paid $22.50 every two weeks. I had a horse by the name of Pete, a gentle old plodder; he could just go so fast. In the wintertime, we'd have to have a sleigh because there was sleighing around town and wagons didn't go good.[120]

By the 1920s motor freight was an integral part of Holland's transport system. Truckers offered advantages over railroads and lake shipping. Trucks provided door-to-door service to and from local stores and factories, and they ran all winter when lake ships were laid up. Boone's Citizens Transfer and Peter Boer of Boer's Transfer on East Eighth Street (485 Washington Avenue by 1940) handled local and long distance moving of household goods. Now in the hands of the third generation, Boer's Transfer & Storage under Andrew Boer and Boer's Republic Worldwide of Calvin Boer, who share offices and a storage building on East Riley Street, are going strong with a dozen trucks and thirty-five employees, including drivers and helpers, and many part-timers hired as needed.[121]

Paul and Gerrit Scholten owned the Grand Rapids-based Associated Truck Lines (later ATL), with a Holland terminal at 111-113

[120] Stanley Curtis interview by Donald van Reken, 23 June 1976, typescript, 14, JAH.
[121] *Holland City Directory*, 1929.

John Rooks with one of his trucks in the early 1930s loading boxes containing 18,000 chicks in a railroad baggage car for shipment across America (*courtesy Donald van Reken, Joint Archives of Holland*)

West Eighth Street. By 1925 the firm had fourteen routes serving eighty-five towns and cities. The Scholtens built a new $4,000 terminal in 1939 at 111 West Eighth Street at Pine Avenue. In 1981 the family sold the company, and it became a subsidiary of the ANR Freight System.[122]

John Rooks of Rooks Transfer Line began his freight, baggage, and trucking business in 1920 from his home base at 250 West Fourteenth Street. In 1928 the first specially designed trucks brought new automobiles directly from Detroit assembly plants, thereby keeping the speedometers at zero miles. The solid rubber truck tires, however, beat up the roads and led to the cry from William Connelly, chairman of the Ottawa County Road Commission: "Hard truck tires must go!" John Rooks moved his operations to 147 East Seventh Street by 1934, and by 1940 he had moved again to 13-15 West Seventh Street. Rooks Transfer added refrigerated service in the 1940s, and John Van Dyke Jr. replaced John Rooks as president by 1949. The company provided overnight delivery service from Holland, Zeeland, Grand Haven, Grand Rapids, Muskegon, and Allegan to Chicago. About 1953 James Rooks, brother of John and one of his drivers, split off Rooks Express as a local carrier. James retired in 1969 and his son Lester, who had driven for his father since 1961, took over. When Van Dyke sold Rooks Transfer in the early 1980s, it had 60 tractors, 150 trailers, and 180 employees. Lester Rooks closed Rooks Express in 1978.[123]

122 *Holland City News*, 4 July 1929; *Holland City Directory*, 1942.

123 *Holland City News*, 1 Feb. 1934, 19 Mar. 1942, 17 Dec. 1959; *Holland Sentinel*, 3 July 1934, 1, 4, 10 Apr. 1940, 20 May, 21 Oct. 1941; *Holland City Directories*, 1942, 1945-46, 1947-48; John Van Dyke Jr. obit., *Grand Rapids Press Lakeshore Edition*, 10 Nov. 1994.

Rooks Transfer Lines tractor-trailer, 1960s, advertising Tulip Time and De Zwaan Windmill, with the slogan "You'd like it in Holland Michigan—wish you were with us!" Rooks Transfer delivered the disassembled De Zwaan Windmill from the port of Grand Haven to Holland in 1964 (*Archives, Holland Historical Trust*)

George Heidema in 1929 began hauling berries grown on the West Michigan muck soils, when a fellow church member asked him to haul his blackberry crop to the Grand Rapids wholesale market. Other berry farmers sought his services, and George soon had a thriving company. His sons John and Gilbert began driving for their father. After George died in 1935, the sons purchased the business and named it Heidema Brothers. In 1947 they moved their operations to 166 East Lakewood Boulevard in Holland Township. In the 1970s John's sons George, Wesley, and John Robert joined the company. By that time, Heidema Bros. (later Heidema Logistics Services) had several dozen tractor-trailers hauling produce and food products from local packing houses to distribution centers in Michigan and surrounding states. John retired in 1993, and the next year the three brothers built a new warehouse and office at 5496 144th Street near I-96 and M-40 on Holland's south side. The timing was bad, since labor and fuel costs were rising faster than revenues; the company lost money five years running after 1995. John Robert died in 1998, leaving George and Wes to make the difficult decision in 2000 to close the doors after seventy years.[124]

Holland Motor Express

John Cooper, who grew up on the family farm in Talmadge Township, became disillusioned with farming, and in 1924 started

[124] *Holland Sentinel*, 26 Jan. 1994, 19 Nov. 2000, John Heidema obit., 29 Nov. 2001.

hauling farm products and freight for the Pere Marquette Railroad. His truck cab had no doors, and the body was made of wood. In 1928 he secured a contract to haul pulpwood in the Upper Peninsula and the entire family spent the summer up north. Interspersed with gravel and pulpwood, Cooper, a "big, gentle, cigar-smoking man," hauled general freight to Chicago for Grand Rapids Motor Express. In July 1929 he struck out on his own with two trucks, under the name Holland Motor Express, and offered overnight delivery to Chicago, shuttling a truck each way every night. His timing was poor; the stock market crash and depression cut freight shipments and the finance company repossessed his trucks. But Cooper leased other trucks and continued the Chicago run. It was a struggle for survival—ten hours at the wheel each way, sleeping in the cab, and hauling "anything that was offered us," as Gerald, the youngest son, recalled. But one lucrative load was turned down. It was to take liquor from Chicago to Grand Rapids during prohibition, when transporting "booze" was illegal. After refusing the tempting job with a firm "no," the man stuck out his hand to Cooper and said, "Stick to it, my boy. I'm Al Capone." Cooper, a son of the Christian Reformed Church, had remained true to his Christian principles.[125]

In 1931 Cooper somehow wrangled a bank loan of $5,200 to buy an old cannery on the northwest corner of Fifth Street and Central Avenue, which he transformed into a truck terminal with dry dockage and office space. In 1933 Cooper had two notable experiences: first, he hauled a rhinoceros from Getz Farm to Brookfield Zoo (chapter 28); and second, he opened a terminal in Indianapolis. His brother Peter was already running a small Grand Rapids terminal. Holland Motor Express was incorporated in 1934 and received a federal operating permit under the Motor Carrier Act of 1935 from the new Interstate Commerce Commission (ICC). The permit designated every city the company served, some seventeen in all, including Chicago, and the grandfather clause granted this authority in perpetuity. (In the 1970s an ICC permit for cartage between Chicago and Milwaukee was worth $1 million.) Holland Motor had twenty-six International tractors on the road in 1934, and by 1939 the company employed fifty-eight and grossed $300,000. In 1940 the Holland terminal was remodeled and expanded to provide inside truck docking, and a new terminal was built in Muskegon. John Cooper's three sons joined the firm—Charles in

125 Gerald Jay Cooper, *The History of a Company: Holland Motor Express, Inc. and the Founding Family, from the Years 1893 to 1984* (Holland, privately printed, 2010), 1-22 (quotes, 19). I am indebted to Gerald Cooper for information about his career, the Cooper family, and the company.

Holland Motor Express terminal, Fifth Street and Central Avenue, early 1940s, the former Holland Canning plant (*courtesy Holland Motor Express*)

1936, Robert in 1940, and Gerald in 1944.[126]

Times were good for trucking during the Second World War. The ICC regulated rates to ensure that small shippers were not disadvantaged at the expense of large shippers. But federal ratemaking also protected union wage rates and almost guaranteed that companies could operate at a profit. By 1942 fourteen local operators and ten intercity carriers were based in Holland or served the city. Besides Boer's Transfer, Citizens Transfer, Rooks Transfer, Holland Motor Express, and Gra-Bell, there was Allegan-Kalamazoo Truck Line on River Avenue, Blue Arrow Transport Lines on East Sixth Street, Grand Rapids Motor Express on Pine Avenue, Vyn Transportation on East Seventh, and Wolverine Express on River Avenue. Marinus Van Wyk bought Gra-Bell in 1939, and he and his brothers Paul and Jim hauled pickles for the H. J. Heinz plant in Holland. When Marinus' son Roger joined the firm in 1946, the company had five tractors and eight trailers. Vyn Transportation closed by 1947, and Alvan Motor Freight and Michigan Express joined the competition by 1952.[127]

Holland Motor Express (HMX) in 1943 acquired two interstate trucking companies and became one of the largest West Michigan haulers, with daily service to Louisville, Cincinnati, Kokomo, Indianapolis, Fort Wayne, South Bend, and Chicago. The downside was that its drivers had voted to join the AFL Teamsters Union, and this led to disputes and strikes. In 1944 the drivers participated in a slowdown by working only half days, due to a dispute between the union and the Federal War Labor Board over overtime pay.[128]

126 Cooper, *Holland Motor Express*, 23-32.

127 *Grand Rapids Press Lakeshore Edition*, 2 May 1995; *Holland City Directories*, 1942, 1945, 1947, 1952.

128 Cooper, *Holland Motor Express*, 35-43.

John Cooper (*second from left*) with sons Charles (*left*), Gerald (*second from right*), and Robert (*right*), with one of their Reo tractor-trailers with familiar wooden shoe logo, 1952 (*courtesy Gerald Cooper*)

This slowdown lasted only a few days, but it presaged a bitter strike the next December, when HMX was caught in a struggle between the Teamsters Union and one of its customers, Standard Grocery Company of Holland, whose employees had voted 100 percent not to affiliate with the Teamsters Union. Frustrated union organizers ordered picket lines at Standard Grocery. Since Holland Motor drivers refused to cross them, John Cooper arranged for Standard drivers to deliver their freight to Holland Motor's docks. At this, a Teamsters Union regional officer called a strike against Holland Motor, and its 140 drivers and dockworkers in Local 406 walked out. Cooper was so incensed by the "union dictatorship" that he threatened to liquidate the company. This got the attention of union president Dan Tobin, who ordered state boss Jimmy Hoffa of Detroit to intervene. The strike was settled within a week, and Cooper relented. From then on, he had his son Charles deal with the union.[129]

In 1949 the financial health of Holland Motor was threatened by an inside job. A trusted employee and family friend, Elmer J. Schepers, former mayor of Holland, was caught embezzling tens of thousands of dollars. In lieu of jail, the federal court allowed Schepers to sell his house, cottage, and automobiles, and make $38,000 in restitution, besides paying fines totaling $6,000. The Coopers tightened financial

[129] Ibid., *Holland Sentinel*, 4 Apr. 1940, 13 Dec. 1945.

Robert De Nooyer Sr. (*left*) of Robert De Nooyer Chevrolet and Charles Cooper (*right*) with 1955 Chevy Bellaire sedan to be given to an accident-free Holland Motor Express driver (*courtesy Robert De Nooyer Sr.*)

controls throughout the company in hopes of avoiding a repeat of this sad affair.[130]

In 1955 John Cooper and his wife Katherine (Kitty), always an active member of the management team, turned management over to their sons: Charles "Chuck" became president, Robert vice president, and youngest brother Gerald assistant vice president. Gerald had started as a dockworker in 1944 at age fourteen and was driving tractor-trailers by age sixteen. Later he managed terminal operations. The brothers embarked on a safe driving campaign to ratchet down insurance rates. They bought a 1955 Chevrolet Bellaire sedan from Robert De Nooyer Chevrolet and gave it to a driver chosen by lot from all those who had been accident-free the previous year.

In 1957, with the new generation in charge, John and Kitty sold the company to the "boys" for $304,000, its book value, and retired to Florida. The brothers in 1958 expanded the Holland terminal on former city property between Fourth and Fifth Streets. Charles Cooper implemented a profit-sharing plan for the 415 employees, and Les Walker implemented a cash award safe-driving program that saw the highway drivers log 1.5 million accident-free miles in 1961 and 1962.

In 1970 Chicago Teamsters Local 704 went on strike, and Holland Motor's city terminal, which generated one-third of total company

130 Cooper, "Holland Motor Express," 48-50.

revenue, was shuttered for three months. Charles took the drastic step of closing the Chicago terminal, and he returned the company to profitability after two months. In 1972 HMX built a new Holland terminal on forty-five acres at 750 East Fortieth Street, where the operation had plenty of room to expand. Some thirty drivers handled three million tons of freight out of that terminal in the next years. By 1980 annual revenue had increased by 350 percent, to $60 million, and the firm was a "life blood to business."[131]

President Jimmy Carter's deregulation of the trucking industry forced a total restructuring of the industry. The 1980 Motor Carrier Act abolished the ICC, and government bureaucrats no longer set freight rates or controlled operating permits. The coveted licenses—"grandfathered" or not—became worthless overnight. Non-union operators sprang up and drove out weaker companies and those under union contracts. Many closed or merged with larger carriers. In the first year under deregulation, Holland Motor lost one-third of its loads to non-union start-ups and had to lay off union drivers. The Cooper brothers responded by expanding; they bought "weak sisters" and opened several new terminals. The mechanized freight handling and efficient route structure also allowed the company to prosper at the expense of higher cost carriers. Robert Cooper died in 1981. HMX in 1984 had 1,100 employees operating out of thirty-seven terminals from Illinois to Ohio and Kentucky, and the company earned over $85 million. Not once since 1950 had the company had a losing year. In this sweet spot, Charles after thirty years at the helm, and younger brother Gerald, decided to sell to the Australian conglomerate TNT Limited, headed by Sir Peter Abeles, who had initiated the contact.[132]

Under the aegis of the Australian conglomerate, TNT Holland exploded on the transport scene. In ten years TNT Holland surpassed $1 billion in revenue and quadrupled in size to 4,600 employees, 4,000 trailers, and 2,500 tractors, plying sixteen Eastern states out of forty-four terminals. TNT Holland became the largest of six US subsidiaries of TNT Freightways Corp. of Illinois (later USF), part of TNT Limited's worldwide empire.[133]

By 1992 TNT Limited was drowning in debt, creditors were circling, and the company's demise seemed imminent. But Sir Peter, the

131 Cooper, "Holland Motor Express," 43, 53-79; *Holland Sentinel*, 22 Jan. 1972, 26 Jan. 1980 (quote).

132 Cooper, "Holland Motor Express," 77-81.

133 *Holland Sentinel*, 26 Jan. 1980, 30 Jan. 1982, 30 Jan. 1988, Charles Cooper obit., ibid., 27 Oct. 2002; Mike Lozon, "TNT on the road to expansion," ibid., 22 Mar. 1994; *Grand Rapids Business Journal*, 1991 clipping, vertical files, Herrick District Library.

titan at the helm in Sydney, held on until 2005, when he sold the entire American division, then known as USF Corp., for $1.37 billion to Yellow Roadway Freight Lines (now YRC Worldwide), a Fortune 500 company. The sale jeopardized the jobs of the twenty thousand employees and especially the Holland operations, which were the most profitable. Four years later, in 2009, USF Holland in a cost-cutting move closed eleven terminals, including Holland, which was consolidated with the Grand Rapids center. The seventy-five drivers and freight handlers were allowed to transfer. Company headquarters and billing operations, however, remain on Fortieth Street under president Jeff Rogers. In the end, consolidation spelled the end of the Cooper family's Holland Motor Express.[134]

Other trucking companies

Gra-Bell also continued to grow by concentrating on truckload freight, that is, complete loads brought from point to point, many from the Heinz plant in Holland. In 1982 the firm put fifteen new tractors and ten new trailers on the road, bringing the number of drivers to one hundred. In 1987 Gra-Bell opened warehouses in Charlotte and Fremont, the latter after buying Fremont-based Gilliland Transfer and its lucrative Gerber Baby Foods account. With the Gilliland acquisition of 70 tractors and 160 trailers, Gra-Bell had a total of 230 tractors and 600 trailers operating out of terminals in Holland, Fremont, Byron Center, and Charlotte. The company serves food-processing firms across America from its Allegan County warehouse on 144th Avenue near the intersection of I-196 and M-40. The building has has been enlarged three times. Roger retired in 1998 and turned the business over to his sons Mike and Tom Van Wyk. The drivers' ranks shrank drastically in the previous five years from 310 to 140 drivers and from 305 to 230 tractors, but the number of trailers held steady at 600. The decline can be explained in part by Mike Van Wyk's founding of Trans-Way Inc., which in 2010 employed thirty-five people on the same site at 931 Interchange Drive. Gra-Bell that year ranked fifth in sales and tenth in employees among the forty-six trucking companies operating in Holland.[135]

Total Logistics Control (TLC) Group moved to the Holland area in the 1930s and grew into five companies under one corporate

[134] *Wall Street Journal*, 20 Aug. 1991; *Holland Sentinel*, 1 Mar., 23, 26 Apr. 2009; *Grand Rapids Press Lakeshore Edition*, 23 Apr. 2009.

[135] *Holland Sentinel*, 29 Jan. 1983, 30 Jan. 1988, 17 Aug. 1993, 2 May 1995, 4 Jan. 1998, Marinus Van Wyk obit., 31 July 1996.

flag, including TLC Freight Services, TLC Warehousing Services, and TLC Logistic Management. George Taylor founded the company in Kalamazoo in 1902 as the Taylor Produce. In 1956 grandson Harold Taylor and Taylor's son-in-law Robert Hall reorganized the company as Taylor Produce and Storage Co. In the 1970s the firm became strictly a public warehouse, with cold storage facilities on Holland's north and south sides and in Kalamazoo; it was renamed Taylor Warehousing Services. When Robert Hall died in 1983, his son Craig and boyhood friend and partner Keith Klingenberg took over and formed the TLC Freight Services after buying a fleet of refrigerated trailers from Zeeland Farm Services. Craig Hall's innovation was to marry computers and warehousing for inventory control and on-time transport. In 1985 the firm employed twenty-six people and had only three tractor-trailers and two warehouses. Six years later, they had 230 people, 120 tractor-trailers, and eleven warehouses. The turning point came in 1988 when they formed a distribution partnership with New York-based Slim-Fast Foods, the popular diet drink, which led to an "almost fairy-tail-like story of mutual success and growth."[136]

By 1994 TLC Freight Services had 600 employees and a fleet of 100 refrigerated tractor-trailers servicing twenty-two warehouses around the country. Every truck was fitted with an onboard computer linked by a satellite beacon to central dispatch. Meijer of Grand Rapids, Perrigo of Hamilton, Bil-Mar Foods of Borculo, Brooks Beverage of Fillmore Township, Campbell Soup, and Proctor and Gamble were some of five hundred customers taking advantage of the high-tech logistics system. In 1997 TLC delivered 153,000 pieces of furniture to 209 Red Room Inn properties. In 2008 Supervalu Inc., a $38 billion grocery company, acquired TLC and moved the headquarters to 10717 Adams Street in Zeeland Township. Two years later, Supervalu sold TLC for cash to Ryder System Inc, which expected to add $250 million in annual sales. TLC in 2010 had 2,500 employees in thirty-four facilities in thirteen states, including huge temperature-controlled warehouses in Holland and Zeeland and the Adams Street headquarters. The CEO of TLC, Peter Westermann, continued to run operations from Zeeland under the Ryder name.[137]

Holland Special Delivery is a more recent trucking company that has become the largest locally owned carrier and the fourth largest in

136 Jim Harger, "TLC Trucking and Warehouse services under umbrella," *Grand Rapids Press*, 1985 clipping (vertical files, Herrick District Library); *Holland Sentinel*, 14 Oct. 1989, 31 Jan. 1991 (quote).

137 *Holland Sentinel*, 22 May 1994, 14 Dec. 1997, 9 Dec. 2010; *Holland Sentinel Focus*, 26 Jan. 1994; *Grand Rapids Press*, 9 Dec. 2010.

West Michigan. Jack Vannette, who with his wife Marjorie "Marj" owned the Warm Friend Hotel, entered the transportation business in 1970 when they purchased the Holland Cab Company from Jerry Horn and used the hotel as their base. During the Vietnam War, Western Union hired Holland Cab to deliver military telegrams informing families of injuries or deaths of loved ones. Jack took it upon himself to deliver such missives personally in hopes of offering Christian consolation and support to the shocked families. Besides carrying people and telegrams, the Vannettes began delivering packages on demand for local companies, such as the Prince and Donnelly Corporations. Jack and Marj were willing to take these time-critical shipments, even if it meant answering a call in the middle of the night at their farm at 120th Avenue and Ransom Street to carry a package to Grand Rapids or Detroit. "We would do what nobody else would do," son Jim recalled.[138]

In 1975 at the urging of the Holland Chamber of Commerce to provide public transit in Holland, Jack Vannette launched the Dial-A-Ride service. It was so successful that a year later the City of Holland took over the service and developed what later became Macatawa Area Express or MAX Transit (chapter 25). With the need for public transit largely met, Vannette in 1976 transitioned from carrying people to cartons of freight, using several cargo vans, one of which doubled as the family car on Sundays after reinstalling the back seats. Holland Cab thrived as an expediter for local companies needing time-critical deliveries within several hundred miles. Major customers included Prince, Donnelly, Trans-Matic, and Kent-Holland Die Casting. Kent-Holland called frequently in its last years, when its equipment wore out, and late shipments became endemic. Daughter Jacie served Holland Cab as receptionist, bookkeeper, and payroll clerk from the outset.

Holland Cab continued at the Warm Friend Hotel until the Vannettes sold the building in December 1981 to Resthaven Patrons as a Christian senior center. The cartage operations then moved to their farm. Vannette bought his truck in 1981, an International. Marj obtained her chauffeur's license, and she and Jack drove "semis" all over the Midwest. So did their sons as they came of age. Relatives, friends, and neighbors also stepped in as needed. The vehicles were linked to the office by two-way radios, until the company switched to satellite

138 I am indebted to Jim Vannette and Jim Albers, Holland Special Delivery executives, for the information in these paragraphs, obtained in an interview with them on 16 Feb. 2012. Jack Vannette died in 2002 (obit., *Holland Sentinel*, 26 July 2002) and Marjorie later married Rev. Lloyd Wolters, a widower and former classmate at Holland Christian High School.

Jack and Marjorie Vannette in their truck cab as they left for a delivery to Iowa in April 1984 (*courtesy Jim Vannette*)

communications about 1995. In 1997 the company bought an airplane, a twin-engine Piper Navaho based at the Grand Haven Airport, for airfreight. The craft today serves primarily to carry executives and customers.

In 1984 son Jim took over management. He changed the company name to Holland Special Delivery and moved operations from his parents' farm to his chicken farm on 128th Avenue at Van Buren Street. In 1987 Jim bought his father's share of the business, and the company was legally incorporated as a sole proprietorship; in 1995 it became a full-fledged corporation. Jack and Marj continued driving full time until 1997. Marvin Visser, the first non-family member to work in the office, joined the firm in 1991 as dispatcher, and Jim Albers came on as salesman in 1995. Holland Special Delivery then had seventeen employees and thirteen vehicles (only two tractor-trailers), all based in a new terminal building on Jim Vannette's property at 4600 128th Avenue. But the company was on the cusp of explosive growth servicing the booming automotive and furniture industries. In four years, by 1998, it had one hundred employees and forty-five vans, trucks, and semi-trailers, and the new terminal was too small. This necessitated moving into a 110,000 square foot terminal in Hudsonville near the I-196 interchange at Thirty-Second Street. This success led the Holland Area Chamber of Commerce to nominate Jack Vannette for the Northwood University award in 1997 as Small Business Person of the Year.[139]

The Holland facility serves as the maintenance shop and offices of the full truck load (FTL) division, while the Hudsonville facility

[139] *Holland Sentinel*, 3 Apr. 1998.

Holland Special Delivery owners and employees pose at a company picnic, summer 1984. Owner Jim Vannette is on the far right (*courtesy Jim Vannette*)

services logistics, warehousing, and less than truckload (LTL) and regional transportation services, and both locations focus on just-in-time deliveries within a 750-mile radius of West Michigan, including Canada. The company's Munster, Indiana terminal serves the greater Chicago area. In 2012 Holland Delivery Service had 200 tractors, 650 trailers, and 350 employees, to service some 1,500 active customers. To finance the 1995 building expansion and increase in tractor-trailers, Jim Vannette took in three partners: Marvin Visser, Jim Albers, and Richard Chandler. He died prematurely in 1997, but the others have continued as partners, with Vannette as chairman, Visser as chief operations officer, and Albers as president and chief executive officer.

Teddy's Transport began in 1982 as a mom and pop business (like Holland Special Delivery) of Ted "Teddy" and wife Mary Walters Gibbs of Bentheim near Hamilton. They offered local pickup and delivery services and nationwide expediting. They ran the business out of their home at 3986 Thirty-Eighth Street in Hamilton, with Teddy driving their one pickup truck, doing runs at ten o'clock in the morning and two o'clock in the afternoon from the Holland and Zeeland area into Grand Rapids, dropping off skids of material or packages, reloading, and bringing freight back into Holland for $15 per delivery. If a load filled the pickup, it was an "exclusive" run, and the charge was $50. As business grew, the couple bought pagers and hired an answering service. Whenever a pager sounded, Teddy or Mary had to find a pay phone and call in to find out the location of the next run. They answered the pagers at any hour of day or night and never turned down a request.

Ted and Mary Walters Gibbs of Teddy's Transport pose with their second pickup truck, ca. 1983 (*courtesy Helen Gibbs Zeerip*)

Teddy also hauled display materials, signage, and equipment for local companies to trade shows across the country, such as Detroit's Cobo Hall, Chicago's McCormick Place, and various sites in Las Vegas, where he would help set up and tear down the exhibits.[140]

After a few years Teddy added trucks to his fleet. Ted and Mary's daughters Helen and Carolyn and brother-in-law Jack Schrotenboer would drive when the company needed extra help. Daughter Helen began driving while in high school during school vacations. Prince Corporation became one of their major customers. Whenever an assembly line went down for lack of parts, Teddy or Mary would drive to Battle Creek, Greenville, or Cedar Springs, even if it was the middle of the night and they had worked all day. Helen recalls riding along on these nights to keep them awake. Teddy did not hire a sales person, relying instead on word-of-mouth recommendations. As volume increased, Helen's husband Craig Zeerip began driving full time in 1987. Shortly afterward they hired the first non-family members and promoted Craig to dispatcher. The fleet consisted of several "straight" trucks and several cargo vans.

Ted and Mary Gibbs ran the business out of their home from 1982 to 1994, when they purchased a building with some acreage at 4201

140 I am indebted to Helen Zeerip, company president, for the information about Teddy's Transport. A brief company history is available at www.teddystransport.com.

M-40 south of the I-196 interchange and moved all operations there, its present location. At this critical juncture with the added overhead costs, Prince Corporation decided to go to a "central dispatch system" and chose Holland Special Delivery as the carrier instead of Teddy's Transport. "It nearly put us out of business," Helen Gibbs Zeerip noted, because 80 percent of their work was for Prince. The Gibbs had to find new customers quickly. In desperation, Teddy hired the first sales person, who landed the Parke-Davis (later Pfizer) pharmaceutical account and other customers. Helen and Craig Zeerip took over day-to-day operations in 1996, and the next year Helen's parents sold them the business and retired.

The young couple was ambitious and expanded the business rapidly. With Helen as president and Craig as vice president, Teddy's bought its first tractor-trailers in 1998, hired up to sixty new drivers, and began full truck load (FTL) service to Chicago and cities across the country. Sales quickly passed $1 million on the way to $5 million, but without proper cost accounting systems in place, the business nearly floundered. In 2001 Teddy's was forced into reorganization, but the company pulled through with "battle scars and tough lessons learned," in Helen's words. The company received hazmat authority and Canadian/Ontario authority, and Teddy's gained certification as a Women-Owned Business. In 2000 Teddy's lost dispatcher David Leete in death, and in 2002 company founder Ted Gibbs passed away. He had been a volunteer fireman and ship captain and was an active member of the Bentheim Reformed Church and a former staff member of World Vision International.[141] .

In 2006 Teddy's began offering dedicated fleet services for manufacturing companies that decided to out-source their in-house fleets. This new revenue stream generated 25 percent of total sales. The good times came to an abrupt stop in late 2008 and 2009. Teddy's sales plummeted 50 percent as the national economy imploded, and two of the Big Three car companies, General Motors and Chrysler, went bankrupt. In desperation Teddy's launched a new service, less than truckload (LTL) cartage to the greater Chicago area for $60 per skid. This helped them succeed, and by the end of 2010, the company had recovered nearly all the decline in sales since 2008. In 2012 Helen Zeerip was recognized as one of the fifty most influential women in West Michigan by the *Grand Rapids Business Journal*. Teddy's Transport in 2011 was seventy-five employees strong, with trucking services to

[141] Ted Gibbs obit., *Holland Sentinel*, 2 Dec. 2002.

all forty-eight states and Canada and revenue of $7.2 million. In 2013 Teddy's Transport was named Michigan Family-Owned Small Business of the Year.[142]

Teddy's Transport and Holland Special Delivery are typical, locally-owned, small businesses on which the economic health of the region and the nation rests. In 2012 some twenty trucking companies were based in the greater Holland area, including Gra-Bell, Holland Special Delivery, Teddy's Transport, Art Mulder & Sons (AMST) with Philip, Hans, and Pete Mulder, and several of their grown children; Dina Knight's Zip Xpress; Brink Truck Lines of Les Brink; Hutt Trucking of James Hutt hauling food products; Supreme Transport, which carries liquid food products, and long-haul companies Grassmid Transport, Inontime, Western Logistics, and Black Hawk Express, among others. Together they have about 750 employees and are integral to local manufacturing and food industries.[143]

Truck leasing companies have a symbiotic relationship with trucking companies. Ryder Truck Rental started in 1983 at 870 South Waverly Road. In 1990 it merged with Atlas Truck Rental at 284 East Fortieth-Eighth Street to form Ryder-Atlas of West Michigan, which in 2004 became Ryder Truck Rental. Since 2004, a competitor, Penske Truck Rental, opened a large office, service garage, and dock a half-mile east on Forty-Eighth Street at Industrial Drive. Ryder has a small facility at 257 West Lakewood Boulevard, and Penske had one at 11298 Chicago Drive.[144]

Refuse hauling

The city council in 1903 appointed John Venhuizen, a Holland Township farmer, as the first city scavenger. This was the era when governments began legislating health and safety laws. Venhuizen could charge $1.25 to "clean vaults" (septic tanks) of residents and 50¢ a barrel for businesses, hotels, and boarding houses. He cleaned back yards and carted off rubbish "at a reasonable charge." Nicholas Bos replaced him in 1906.[145]

Until the 1960s most residents burned their refuse or took it to the city dump at the foot of Tenth Street (now Kollen Park), where they

142 *Holland Sentinel*, 26 Sept. 2011, 26 Apr. 2013; http://teddystransport.com/women-owned-busines-article.jpg.

143 Mike Lozon, "Gra-Bell Truck Line stays on the road to growth," *Holland Sentinel*, 17 Aug. 1993; www.hoovers.com/companyindex/Michigan/Holland/Trucking/1.html.

144 *Holland City Directories*, 1983-2011.

145 *Holland City News*, 11 Mar. 1893, 10 June 1909.

had free dumping privileges. Some businesses hired teamsters to haul it away. In the 1890s the valuable waterfront was converted into the city's first industrial district, and the dump was moved to the Black River marsh at the foot of College Avenue below Sixth Street. Both sites were eyesores, with open burning and flies and rodents swarming all over. In 1963 the city assumed ownership of the Sixth Street dump and placed it under the board of public works (BPW), which had bulldozers cover the refuse nightly with sand. Within a few years, the BPW closed the dump.[146]

It was 1962 before the *Holland City Directory* included a listing for "Trash Removal." Peter Jacobusse, a farmer in Park Township on Jacobusse Court off 168th Avenue, was the first trash man listed, but he had been picking up refuse since the early 1940s. Fred Vanden Brink, who owned a Standard Oil station at 611 West Lakewood Boulevard, carried Jacobusse's gasoline purchases on his books to help him get started. Jacobusse, a hard worker with a tall lean physique, slopped his hogs with food waste and dumped some non-food refuse on his farm, although he mainly used a 280-acre landfill off 160th Avenue north of James Street that the US government purchased in 1942 to take waste from Holland-area war industries.[147]

In 1956 Jacobusse bought forty acres at 2700 North 168th Avenue and created his own landfill and a lagoon for liquid industrial wastes on the east (back) half. In 1962 he and his son-in-law Hillis Timmer, one of his drivers, formed Jacobusse Garbage & Rubbish Removal, shortened to Jacobusse Refuse Service. They ran the business out of Timmer's home at 2150 Marlacoba Drive, a stub street off 168th Avenue south of James Street until 1968, when they erected an office-garage building and truck lot at the 2700 site. Geneva Vanden Brink, Fred's daughter, was the company dispatcher and office manager for twenty-five years. She recalled that in the 1960s residential customers paid 40¢ a week for garage service. Peter's son Marinus started driving at this time and seldom missed a day over several decades. In late 1968 Timmer bought the back forty acres from the US government for possible landfill expansion, but the company used the adjacent Ottawa County

146 Ibid., 21 Dec. 1964.

147 *Holland Sentinel*, 20 May 1998, 8 July 2011. EPA reports on the Waste Management of Michigan, Holland Lagoons Superfund Site (epa.gov/region5/cleanup/wm/holland), erroneously state that Jacobusse Refuse Service owned the site "from about 1945." but Ottawa County deed records show otherwise, as noted in the text. The two forty-acre tracts were deeded in 1969 and 1971 to Park Service Co., a Jacobusse entity.

landfill for solid wastes. That year they dumped in the lagoon forty-three 55-gallon drums of chloral hydrate, according to a later finding by the Environmental Protection Agency (EPA), a federal watchdog body formed in 1970.[148]

In 1970 the US Government in a land swap with Ottawa County deeded its Park Township landfill to the county and it became the Southwest Ottawa County Landfill, an open-burning dump managed by road commission employees. This site continued to accept industrial wastes, Contamination from the dump seeped downgradient and mixed with lagoon sludge. The first polluted well in a nearby home was discovered in 1970, but dumping continued until 1978, when Ottawa County on orders from the Michigan Department of Environmental Quality closed the landfill and capped the site with a layer of heavy clay. Dumping at the Jacobusse lagoon was stopped in 1980 and the forty-three drums were removed intact.[149]

In the early 1970s the De Boer brothers, James, Richard, and Edward, Dutch *garbios* from Chicago who owned summer homes nearby on Lake Michigan, became Jacobusse's silent partners, providing capital needed to buy packer trucks, tractors, roll-off rigs, and the containers themselves, which grew in size from one to forty and more yards. Chicago-based Waste Management Inc. (WMI) under acquisitions specialist H. Wayne Huizenga, who founded WMI in 1971 with his first cousin Peter H. Huizenga and Peter's brother-in-law Dean Buntrock, also extended its reach to the Holland area and in 1972 added Jacobusse's Refuse Service to its growing stable of garbage companies. The purchase included some twenty-five trucks and their commercial and residential routes, plus the office/garage facility on 168th Avenue and the lagoon with its potential liabilities. The contract called for Hillis Timmer to continue for three years to run the operation, and Geneva M. Vanden Brink continued as the dispatcher. Ron Baker took over day-to-day operations from Timmer, followed by Robert "Bob" A. De Boer in 1978.[150]

148 I am indebted to Geneva Vanden Brink and Marinus Jacobusse for information about the business, and Al Nykamp, Park Township assessor, for information about land ownership.

149 Michigan Department of Environmental Quality, "Five-Year Review Report for Waste Management Holland Lagoon," Sept. 2006, accessed epa.gov/region5/cleanup/wm/holland.

150 Timothy C. Jacobson, *Waste Management: An American Corporate Success Story* (Washington, DC, Gateway Business Books, 1993). See also Robert P. Swierenga, *Dutch Chicago: A History of the Hollanders in the Windy City* (Grand Rapids: Eerdmans, 2002), ch. 13.

In the early 1980s state and federal environmental agencies required remediation of the dump and lagoon. The cost, including purge wells and monitoring equipment, ultimately exceeded $5 million, which was shared by Ottawa County and the State of Michigan, with Waste Management paying $1 million in an out-of-court settlement. In 2006 the lagoon and county dump were recapped with hundreds of truckloads of clay. In 2012, after three decades, the EPA delisted the Superfund site as hazardous and the county took over monitoring groundwater.[151] Peter Jacobusse did not have to deal with these problems; he died of a heart attack while working his route in 1966. Waste Management continues to own the property.

The other national waste corporation in the early 1970s, besides Waste Management, was Browning Ferris Inc. (BFI), which went public in 1969 and also embarked on an acquisitions tear. The typical pattern of WMI and BFI was to buy family-owned trash businesses for a bit of cash and the rest in stock, which was golden. Sellers were always required to sign non-compete agreements, usually for five years. Some got back into the business after the agreements expired, and there were always ambitious newcomers who bought used equipment and started picking up. Both solicited customers by undercutting the monthly charges of established companies, and after building the business sufficiently, WMI or BFI would buy them out to cut the competition. As a result, garbage companies have come and gone with regularity since the 1980s.

Zeeland-based De Young Garbage & Refuse Company of James "Jim" De Young entered the business in 1966 and ran the full gamut, servicing residential, commercial, and industrial customers. The company opened a landfill off Adams Street at 76th Avenue west of Drenthe. In 1980 De Young decided to cut back; he sold his residential and commercial work to one of his former drivers, Larry Haveman, but kept the industrial "roll-off" accounts and formed De Young Industrial Disposal, which his sons Wayne and Bruce have continued to operate. The company hauls all kinds of materials, including sand and gravel, working from their office and garage on Harrison Street.

Haveman started his own company in 1976 with a used truck, under the unique company name of Larry's Leftovers. He ran the business from offices in the basement of his Zeeland home at 155 Jefferson Street and later purchased land for his trucks from Star Excavating Co. on East Lakewood Boulevard. In 1979 Haveman acquired Blok's Refuse Co. and Exit 41 Landfill in Saugatuck from John Blok. After buying

151 *Holland Sentinel*, 19 Apr. 1999, 13, 30 Jan., 25 May 2006, 8 July 2011, 12 Dec. 2012.

Larry Haveman, owner of Larry's Leftovers, activates the power packer on his garbage truck, 1978 (*courtesy Larry Haveman*)

the De Young accounts in 1980, Haveman hired another eager young man, Randy Dozeman as his general manager. In late 1981 Haveman constructed his own garage at 11558 East Lakewood Boulevard. In 1982 Rich Evenhouse, a vice president at Waste Management, persuaded Haveman to sell out and "join the team." The refuse giant valued the landfill as much as the accounts, because of the closing of the Southwest Ottawa County Landfill and the increasing public resistance to such eyesores. "Nimby" (Not in my back yard) was the hue and cry. Moreover, new federal regulations in 1983 forced small landfills to close, including Exit 41 and the De Young dump.[152]

Waste Management in 1982 consolidated the operations of Jacobusse's and Larry's Leftovers at 11558 East Lakewood Boulevard,

Larry Haveman's office and garage at 11558 East Lakewood Boulevard, with his fleet of twelve packer trucks lined up for an aerial photo, 1981 (*courtesy Larry Haveman*)

152 Larry B. Massie, *The Holland Area: Warm Friends and Wooden Shoes* (Northridge, CA: Windsor Publications, 1988), 120-21.

Waste Management employees, fifty in number, gather for a group photo at the office, 1987 (*courtesy Larry Haveman*)

with Haveman as the general manager and division president and Dozeman as operations manager. When Waste Management in December 1992 opened its Autumn Hills Landfill at 700 56th Avenue a mile east of Drenthe, Dozeman took charge of this operation. Haveman continued for eighteen years as West Michigan area president and regional vice president of acquisitions. A year after stepping down, in 1999, he started Arrowaste (see below). Tim Lucas took over running the area Waste Management operation. In 2004 the Lakewood Boulevard facilities were sold to Padnos Iron & Metal, and all of Waste Management's lakeshore operations were consolidated in Wyoming, Michigan.[153]

Larry Haveman left Waste Management shortly before the company was acquired in 1998 by USA Waste. The time seemed ripe, Haveman believed, for a local company to compete by offering personal service and recycling programs at reasonable prices. In 1999, he launched Arrowaste, and unlike his slow start with Larry's Leftovers, this time accounts increased rapidly. Within four months Arrowaste had three thousand customers, twelve trucks, and thirteen employees, all operating from a lot on 84th Street near Zeeland Farm Services. In 2001, after only three years, Haveman sold out again, this time to Tom Yonker of Chicago-based Homewood Disposal.[154]

Yonker bought a second Holland garbage company in 2001, Priority Waste Systems of Terry L. Nienhuis and his son Jeff. Terry

[153] I am indebted to Randy Dozeman and Larry Haveman for information in this and the previous paragraph.

[154] *Holland Sentinel*, 24 Apr., 9 Sept. 1999, 11 Dec. 2004.

Nienhuis had learned the garbage business from George Slater of Holland, first working for Slater in Benton Harbor and later in Traverse City. In 1984 Nienhuis went into business for himself by acquiring Northside Disposal from John "Red" and Jeff Kolean. The brothers had been in business since the late 1970s at 11269 Lakewood Boulevard. Nienhuis moved the operations south of Holland to 4392 M-40. After five years Nienhuis sold to William "Bill" Sterk of Jenison-based Able Sanitation and stayed on as the general manager for several years. In the mid-1990s Nienhuis and son Jeff started Priority Waste Systems, which they sold in 2001 to Yonker. The combined company was named Priority Arrowaste until 2007, and then it was simplified to Arrowaste.

Yonker's Arrowaste division faced a public relations disaster and almost inevitable lawsuit, when on January 5, 2006 one of the drivers servicing a regular customer—the Nortier-Ver Lee-Langeland Funeral Home at 315 East Sixteenth Street—mistakenly took from a gurney a six-foot cremation carton containing a body and loaded it on his truck. The carton had been placed temporarily in a locked, unheated garage near the recyclable containers that the driver picked up weekly. The funeral home's refrigerated units were full, so they resorted to the garage while waiting for the family's permission to proceed with cremation. The body was compacted at Waste Management's Autumn Hills landfill along with the day's refuse and covered with soil. State police with cadaver dogs tried unsuccessfully for two days to find the body but then called off the search, with the acquiescence of the family. The Michigan Department of Environmental Quality also declined to search, after concluding that no state landfill laws were broken.[155]

The Autumn Hills Landfill cordoned off the area and awaited developments, which involved the Ottawa County Circuit Court, because within ten weeks the family filed suit for "negligence, emotional stress, and breach of contract." The suit became a triangle, with the family suing both the funeral home and refuse hauler and the latter filing counter-suits. The legal wrangling went on for three years. Judge Jon Van Alburg ruled that the funeral home and refuse hauler were equally at fault, but the three-judge circuit court panel placed the blame on the funeral home and said the family could not sue the waste hauler. In the end, the insurance companies of the hauler and the funeral home quietly settled with the family, and the public relations nightmare ended. Yonker continues to own Arrowaste and Dan Loerop of Tinley Park

[155] Ibid., 10, 12, 13, Jan. 2006. I am indebted to Terry Nienhuis for information about Arrowaste and the local garbage industry in general.

supervises the business from afar, while Chris Groendyke comes from Chicago to handle day-to-day operations. In 2010 Arrowaste added the residential and commercial accounts of Dave Simmons' Hudsonville-based Macatawa Disposal, which Simmons founded in 2000.[156]

In 1986 William G. "Bill" Dryfhout started Lakeshore Disposal at 3310 Lincoln Road (M-40), which he sold in 2000 to Sunset Waste, an affiliate of Allied Waste, with his son Edward Dryfhout continuing as the manager. Not every scavenger sold out to WMI or BFI. A special character everyone remembers is Fred Stam, a typical rubbish man in old clothes and a rickety truck who picked up refuse from 1969 until his death in 1990, based at his home at 144 Fairbanks Avenue.[157]

In the 1990s, the number one and number two waste giants faltered. WMI, after acquiring 1,400 smaller companies, was forced to sell in 1998 to the number three company, USA Waste of Houston, which kept the familiar Waste Management name. The next year, BFI was forced to sell to the number four company, Allied Waste of Phoenix, and the BFI name was jettisoned. Republic Services (formerly Republic Waste) of Ft. Lauderdale, a company started by H. Wayne Huizenga with $6 billion in sales in 2008, bought Allied Waste in a $6.24 billion deal. The reshuffling was part of the continuing consolidation in the waste industry. Today Waste Management (green-colored trucks) and Republic Services (blue-colored trucks) dominate the industry.[158]

In recent years, cities and community associations let out on bid exclusive contracts with the company that offered the "best rate." Beginning in 1993 Waste Management won the city of Holland contract four times, the last time for $3 million per year. In 2005 Chef Container, a three-year-old company based in Laketown Township that serviced 1,500 customers in outlying townships, underbid the largest waste hauler in the world, offering to collect trash and recyclables from the city's nine thousand households for $2.6 million per year. The other contenders, besides Waste Management, were Reliable Disposal and Allied Waste. Chef Container president Sean Steele is a 1987 graduate of Holland High School who established Steele Enterprises, a lawn care business. City manager Soren Wolff and Mayor Albert McGeehan welcomed the local company with open arms, and the *Holland Sentinel* editorialized: "Chef is a small player in the refuse business, but it thinks big."[159]

156 *Holland Sentinel*, 29 Mar., 5 Apr. 2006, 29 Mar., 5 Dec. 2007, 14, 29 Nov. 2008.

157 *Holland City Directories*, 1969-1990; *Holland Sentinel*, Fred Stam obit., 28 Dec. 1990.

158 *Holland Sentinel*, 26 May 2002; *Wall Street Journal*, 9 Oct. 2001, 24 June 2008.

159 *Holland Sentinel*, 11 Dec. 2004, 10, 24 Mar., 5, 10 (quote), 26 June 2005.

Chef gained an edge by collecting recyclables and trash together and sorting them by hand at their Westshore Recycling and Transfer Station behind the offices and garage at 4376 Sixtieth Street. Chef does not own a landfill, and it paid dividends to recycle as much as possible. Chef also picks up yard waste containers for $100 a year and composts the grass clippings and leaves on their property. Winning the contract required Chef to ramp up quickly by buying several new trucks and thousands of containers and nearly doubling the ten-person workforce. In 2008 Chef Container again was the low bidder at $3.5 million, an 8 percent increase. In 2011 the city went to a seven-year contract to save some $164,000, and Chef again was the low bidder. This long-term contract gave company officials the confidence to triple the size of its recycling-sorting facility. By its tenth anniversary in 2012, Chef Containers served customers in eight counties, and owner Sean Steele was looking to expand statewide.[160]

Servicing septic tanks is another aspect of refuse removal. From 1972 to 1976 Jacobusse's nephew James W. Van Dyke operated a septic tank cleaning company, Holland Sanitary Service. Later Busscher's, Bosch, Kerkstra, T. Voss & Sons, City Sewer & Drain, and Van's (Tim Greving) provided septic tank cleaning.

Bicycle and motorcycle shops

From 1900 to 1940, the place to buy, rent, or repair bicycles was a shop on the southwest corner of Ninth Street and River Avenue. John F. Zalsman, who had a bicycle shop on East Eighth Street during the 1890s, moved to the corner of Ninth and River Avenue about 1900. In 1906 he sold it to Charles Hubbard, who introduced the popular Indian-brand motorbikes. Hubbard in 1910 sold to Marine Bishop and Gerrit Alofs, who continued to promote motorbikes, which appealed to daring young blades. In 1915 Peter Raffenaud replaced Alofs as Bishop's partner, and the two kept the shop for twenty-five years, right through the depression decade, until 1940. The shop featured a full line of bicycles and motorbikes and carried GoodYear tires.[161]

In 1932 Ed Vos established Vos Bike Shop on River Avenue at Tenth Street across from Centennial Park. Like Russ Bouws, Vos started on a shoestring in the middle of the Great Depression and soon

[160] Ibid., 12 June 2008, 4 Sept. 2010, 11 Nov. 2011, 19 May 2012.

[161] I am indebted to Fritz L. Kliphuis for the ownership information on the 38 West Ninth Street bicycle repair shop. In 1942 Raffenaud's Bicycle Shop moved to 176 West Ninth Street near Maple Avenue.

Bishop & Alofs Bicycle shop, southwest corner Ninth Street and River Avenue, ca. 1912-13. Note the patrolman standing behind the motorbikes, as if to warn the riders not to speed. The signage on the building notes the shop also sold lawn mowers, guns, locks, sewing machines, and graphophones (*courtesy Randall Vande Water*)

eclipsed Bishop's old shop one block to the north. Only fourteen years old, Vos began buying old bikes for a quarter and refurbishing them in a shed behind his family's home at 136 West Nineteenth Street. His only purpose was to help his parents put food on the table. He repainted the bikes by dipping them in an old acid vat that his father had used to clean street lamps. Ed first sprayed the frame with rust preventative, dipped it in either blue or maroon paint, and then applied a sharp pinstripe of white or ivory. By 1942 he had amassed more than 250 bikes. Then fortune smiled on him. Wartime rationing ended the manufacture of bicycles, as well as automobiles. So Ed opened Ed's Bike Rentals and brought his wheels to Holland State Park, Tunnel Park, Saugatuck Oval Park, Grand Haven State Park, and even Ramona Park on Reed's Lake in East Grand Rapids. The rental business proved to be profitable.[162]

After the war, Vos bought a vacant building at 254 River Avenue and opened the Reliable Cycle Shop, adding a profitable toy store

[162] The history of Reliable Sport is told by Steve Vander Veen in "When a business is more than a business," *Holland Sentinel*, 6 Dec. 2006; and the book by Ken Vos and Francis DeRoos Baron, *God is Reliable: A Small Storefront in God's Storehouse of Blessings* (Zeeland, MI, 2006).

upstairs at the suggestion of his wife Joyce (Wierenga). He soon added hunting and fishing gear, power lawnmowers, garden equipment, hardware items, ski and diving gear (Ski Haus was born), Cushman Scooters, Honda motorcycles (which outsold the scooters), Schwinn bicycles, billiard tables, trampolines, paddleboats, and other sporting equipment. Ed Vos and his son Ken, who succeeded him, had good instincts for taking a chance on new products, and the business grew. The store was enlarged in 1952 and 1955. On many products it was competing with Vogelzang and Teermans. By 1985 with Ken fully in charge, sales topped $3.5 million, and Reliable Sport & Ski Haus had thirty-five full-time employees.

Then the bottom dropped out, due to two trampoline lawsuits, a winter with very little snow, and a sharp drop in Honda sales, Vos found himself with $250,000 in excess inventory. He owed Honda $800,000 and local banks $400,000. Facing financial ruin, Ken, a devout Christian, asked God to "get him out of this mess." Almost miraculously, Schwinn offered Vos $300,000 for his bike business and Honda, wishing to reduce the number of dealerships, offered $800,000 for his cycle inventory. That money and a new mortgage on his house allowed Ken Vos to continue in business, although at only one-sixth the annual revenue. The current name, Reliable Sport and Billiards, conveys the new marketing niche.

In recent years, "wheels" have been supplied by Jack Koster's Holland Cycling and Fitness at 326 River Avenue, and on the north side by John Vander Ploeg's Cross County Cycle at 345 Douglas Road and Lakeshore Cycle & Fitness at 650 Riley Street, all of which carry a full line of bicycles, parts, and accessories. Vander Ploeg started from scratch in 1984 at the corner of North River Avenue at Howard Street and was forced to relocate in 2006 when the building was razed to make way for the widened intersection.

Part Six

Restaurants and drive-ins

In the early 1900s, Eighth Street was dotted with restaurants; most came and went with regularity. Fine restaurants included Van Drezer's, Thompson's, Alpena, Boston, and later Warm Friend Tavern with its Dutch Grill. Working class people patronized Allison House of A. C. Allison at 130 East Eighth, Mary Bouman's Restaurant at 45 West Eighth, Harry Tindell's Restaurant at 23 West Eighth Street, Patsy Fabiano's at 26 West Eighth from 1913 to 1940 and carried on several more decades by Nicholas Hoffman Jr. as Hoffman's Restaurant, Charles Fabiano's Restaurant at 196 River Avenue from 1910 to 1940, Covered Wagon Restaurant at 234 River Avenue from 1927 to 1961, Bernard Keefer's Restaurant from 1913 to 1936, and Ray and Estelle Skipper's Tavern at 124 East Eighth from 1947 (see appendix 5.9 for a list of restaurants, 1897-1950).

For one hundred years, 28 West Eighth Street has housed restaurants, and in 2013, Windmill Restaurant was the oldest in Holland, operating at that site since 1965. Many more opened after 1945. Pete's Barbecue on North River Avenue at Lakewood Boulevard was a "hot spot" for several decades. Llewellyn Michmerhuizen's Snack Shack drive-in at 219 East Eighth Street at Lincoln Avenue (now the parking lot of the train depot), attracted the young crowd from 1945 to

Hoffman's Restaurant, ca. 1950 (*courtesy Myron Van Ark*)

Skipper's Tavern, 134 East Eighth Street, established 1947 and called the "best spot in Holland" by one satisfied visitor (*courtesy Myron Van Ark*)

1957. Martin Japinga and Frederick "Fred" Schaafsma owned the eatery its last five years.[163]

The first restaurant chain in West Michigan was Russ'. In 1934, in the depths of the Great Depression, J. Russell "Russ" Bouws, a native of Noordeloos, Michigan, bought Doc's Barbeque stand for $147 from Carol "Doc" Hansen, who later founded Hansen Machine Co. (chapter 12). The diner, which stood on the bend of Chicago Drive (M-21) beyond the Eighth Street Y, was only a twelve-by-sixteen-foot wooden shack,

Snack Shack drive-in in its heyday in the 1950s (*courtesy Myron Van Ark*)

[163] *Holland City Directories*, 1938-58.

Russ Bouws in front of Russ' Place diner on M-21 (Chicago Drive), ca. 1937 (*courtesy Russ' Restaurants*)

but the strategic site on the highway to Grand Rapids was the eastern gateway to Holland. Father John Bouws and brother Rich helped buy the truck stop, and Russ paid them off within a year. John Zoerhof, who owned the property, along with his gas station next door, leased the site to Russ for the price of two meals a day. Rich's wife Metta helped him run the eatery for a wage of $4 a month, and his thirteen-year-old brother Gordon began coming in to help wash dishes and do odd jobs.[164]

Russ, with his father's assistance, soon added a six-by-sixteen-foot kitchen and a six-by-six-foot bedroom, where Russ slept at night after a series of break-ins. Two years later, he added a ten-by-twelve-foot addition with twenty more seats. Outdoor "tray-service" accommodated many more customers, with carhops, mainly young women, taking orders and bringing food to cars lined up under a string of lights along the graveled highway. This was the first tray service in Holland.

Russ Bouws admitted later that he "hardly knew what a hamburger looked like, and on second thought, we had only eaten one once before in our life." He "beefed-up" the menu with "all steak hamburgers" and offered a hearty breakfast of bacon and eggs. Hamburgers cost 10¢, beef and pork barbeque and fried ham, 15¢, and coffee, milk, or Coke, 5¢. Sales ranged from $3 to $6 a day, and by April 1935, Russ' Place was paid

164 *Russ' Review* (Russ' Restaurants, August 1974) 1; *Russ' Review: Published in celebration of Russ' 60th anniversary* (*Holland Sentinel*, 1994), 1-2; *Holland City News*, 3 Aug. 1950; Larry Wagenaar, "Russ' began with burner, skillet, and five chairs," undated *Holland Sentinel* clipping.

First Russ' Restaurant (now Eastown Russ'), featuring "all steak hamburgers," 1949. The carhop carrying a tray is Ada Bloemendal (later Mrs. Carl Van Dyke). (*courtesy Russ' Restaurants*)

for. Russ literally "lived" the business, putting in seventeen-hour days, from eight o'clock one morning until one o'clock the next morning. After his marriage in 1940, Russ had a home built across the street from the restaurant. His wife Julia worked alongside him until the 1960s; she took the laundry home and washed and ironed the aprons, shirts, and white blouses of the staff. After school and on Saturdays, their children also helped by clearing trays and washing dishes. They raised their own beef cattle on a farm in North Holland, and all the meat, including the steaks, went into the hamburgers, making them truly "all steak."[165]

As the business grew after the war, the property was simply too small for all the cars and customers. So Russ in 1946 moved the building two blocks west to property he purchased at the junction of Chicago Drive and Eighth Street. Despite two more additions, in 1949 Russ felt confident enough to raze the original building and erect a distinctive restaurant with a separate kitchen and bakery, and marked with a high pylon sign (now Eastown Russ'). The bakery featured Russ' pies and pigs-in-a-blanket (a Dutch delicacy of sausage wrapped in a crust). In 1950, as part of a coordinated move by all restaurant owners to counter sharp price hikes on provisions, Russ' raised the price of a cup of coffee to 7¢ and a plain hamburger to 23¢. The coffee "kletzers" were unhappy

165 *Russ' 20th Anniversary booklet, 1924-1954* (Holland, 1954), 4 (quote); *Holland Sentinel*, 15 Sept. 1984, 10 Sept. 1989, 18, 19 Aug. 1992.

Russ Bouws (*right*) working alongside employees in the kitchen of Russ' Restaurant. Note the overhead mirror that allowed customers to watch their food being prepared, 1950s. (photo Prince Studio Zeeland) (*courtesy Russ' Restaurants*)

to see the end of the nickel coffee. In 1958, in a now familiar ritual, Russ' remodeled and expanded to add thirty seats and a second drive-in canopy to serve sixty more cars.

In 1964 Russ' adopted the familiar logo of a costumed Dutch boy serving a hamburger at a drive-in, and since then every sign and menu has featured this logo. In 1965 Russ' Muskegon opened, and in 1969 Russ' Grand Rapids opened on Twenty-Eighth Street; it was the first of six Grand Rapids Russ' restaurants and the only franchise independent of ownership by the Bouws family. That same year Russ' Eastown was expanded to 110 seats, and the high pylon signage was removed. To maintain consistent food quality, in 1972 the company built a commissary behind the restaurant to supply the growing franchise. In 1989 Russ' erected a central office building across Eighth Street that continues to serve that purpose. The company thrived in spite of the local economy's ups an downs; its older clientele keep coming for the inexpensive, quality meals.[166]

Russ' Northtown opened in 1973 on North River Avenue, and Russ' Southtown in 1980 on Lincoln Avenue at US-31. In 1983 the

[166] John Bouws interview by author and David Boeve, 4 Nov. 2009, typescript, JAH; *Holland Sentinel*, 29 Jan. 1983.

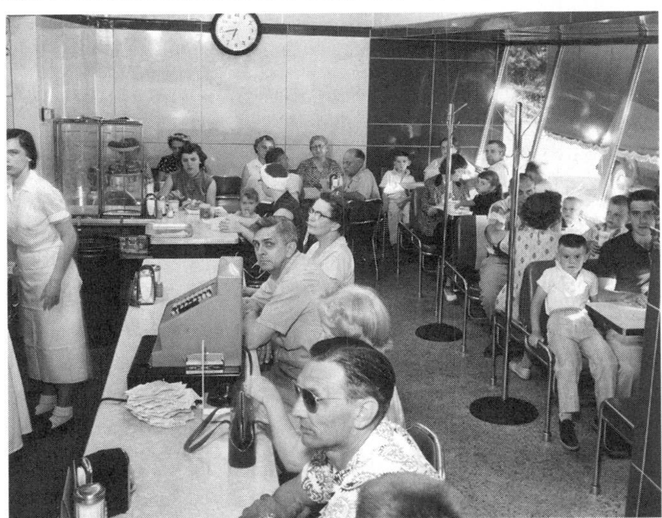

Hungry diners waited for seating at the popular Russ' Restaurant during lunch and dinner hours, 1950s (*courtesy Russ' Restaurants*)

original Eastown drive-in restaurant was razed to make way for the present structure with a solarium entrance and two dining rooms, one featuring *tele-dine*, a phone-ordering system, in each booth. Tight-fisted Hollanders appreciate not having to tip the waitresses, but many still miss the carhops, long a Russ' hallmark. Russ' younger brother Gordon ran the company in the 1980s, and Russ' sons John and Bryan took charge later. John Bouws attributed the success of the company first and foremost to its employees. "Character, values, work ethic of the employees is the critical factor," he declared. Russ' was "the only show in town," said Bouws, until the early 1980s when the first McDonalds opened several blocks down Eighth Street.[167]

By the time of Russ Bouws' death in 1992, a number of national restaurant chains had come to Holland, but his business thrived by appealing to the large retirement population. In death, Bouws was honored as a great patriarch. Today Russ' employs one thousand in its thirteen outlets, all supplied since 1998 from Russ' Commissary at 3440 128th Avenue in Holland Township. Russ' is one of the few remaining family eateries in West Michigan, along with Brann's Steakhouse. But no grandchild of Russ Bouws is waiting to take over the business, so someday it may be Russ' in name only.[168]

[167] Bouws interview, 8 (quote).

[168] Russ Bouws, obit., 20 Aug. 1992, Julia (Mrs. Russ) Bouws, obit., 16 Sept. 2010.

Restaurants followed the same trends as grocery stores. Locally-owned eateries gave way to national chains, but not until the 1980s, and even then local restaurants held their own, notably Russ', Dutch Mill Restaurant on US-31, Windmill Restaurant on Eighth Street, Hitching Post on River Avenue (housed in an old Interurban car), Point West at Macatawa Park, Alpen Rose, Butch's, Till Midnight (downtown and then at Prospect Park), and Smokey's Family Restaurant on East Sixteenth Street. Waleed "Wally" Karachy, a Jordanian immigrant (1955) and Hope College graduate (1960), opened Smokey's as a family diner in 1976 with his wife, Myra, and their four children who worked together cooking, serving, and cleaning. Smokey's motto was, "Where good friends meet to eat," and it proved true over the years as many of the same people visited the establishment on a daily basis drawn by Wally's warm hospitality and the good food. The Karachys sold the business to Burger King in 1984. Dave and Lois Johnson's Big Cheese pizzaria at 792 Lincoln Avenue is still going strong after thirty years, although national franchises and fast-food chains predominate, including McDonalds, Burger King, Wendy's, Taco Bell, Bob Evans, Applebee's, Ponderosa, and Perkins, among others.

Richard Den Uyl was the leading promoter of fine dining in Holland from 1963 until his death in 2011, after a forty-five-year career as Holland's leading hospitality entrepreneur.[169] He started first with the iconic restaurants: Point West in 1963 and the Hatch in 1972. Point West at the end of South Shore Drive at Macatawa Park was the place to go for wedding receptions, prom nights, birthdays, and anniversaries until it closed in 1986. With a view of Lake Macatawa, walls adorned with artwork, and fine china and silverware on the tables, it was the "height of elegance in Holland," said Gary Scholten, who recalled taking his prom date there in 1963—she in a formal gown, and he in a rented black tuxedo. The Hatch, a more casual, but still elegant restaurant on Ottawa Beach Road near the entrance to Holland State Park, catered to boaters, summer visitors, and residents for thirty years until it closed in 2002. Den Uyl also opened the 8th Street Grille and James Diesing the 84 East Pasta, also on Eighth Street, and the Crazy Horse Saloon on East Lakewood Boulevard. The 8th Street Grille has a noontime crush of business and professional people, 84 East attracts the evening theater crowd. Among his twenty eateries in West Michigan, Den Uyl also owned ten Mr. Steaks and four Great Lakes Shipping Company restaurants.

169 *Grand Rapids Press*, 16 Oct. 2011.

Other fine dining establishments are the Prince family's Alpen Rose Restaurant featuring a Bavarian décor and cuisine, Butch Ter Haar's Butch's (formerly Butch's Dry Dock) in the Riverview Building (formerly Waalkes Butcher Shop and then Filippini's Deli), the Piper (former Sandpiper) at the South Shore Marina that caters to boaters, and Boatwerks Waterfront Restaurant near Kollen Park. Specialty houses have also prospered, such as Pereddies Italian restaurant, Curragh Irish Pub, Mark Herman's Crazy Horse Saloon, and Greg Buter's Beechwood Inn. Among coffeehouses, Jack Groot's JP's Coffee and Espresso Bar on Eighth Street and Matt Scott's Lemonjello's Coffee on Ninth Street thrive, the former catering to the general public, and the latter, featuring local bands and Open Mic Night the first Wednesday of every month, catering to local students and Hope College faculty. Eighth Street boasts two ice cream stores—Kilwin's (formerly Ben & Jerry's), owned by Darl and Judy Dalman, and Cold Stone Creamery, owned by Tony Bilello.[170]

Oriental and Hispanic restaurants come and go. In 1995 the city counted ten Oriental eateries, including Peking House, the first to open in 1979 by Koreans Ben Han and wife Yung, Cau Dan Tran's China Inn and China Inn-South, Peter Nguyen's Imperial Garden, and Hy Quach's three Wok House restaurants. Among the few to survive the stiff competition are China Inn, Grand King Buffet, and China Kitchen at 777 Washington Avenue. Tres Lobos offered Mexican cuisine on Douglas Avenue for a decade before closing in 2011, but Margarita's Mexican Restaurant, with a live mariachi band on Saturday nights, and Don Miguel's Mexican Restaurant still prosper.[171]

170 *Holland Sentinel*, 1 Jan. 1986, 25 Sept. 1988, 18 Jan., 19 Apr., 10 May 1989, 20 Aug. 1993, 30 Apr. 1995, 6 Dec. 2009.

171 Ibid., 20 Aug. 1995.

Part Seven

Building boom 1940s

Economic conditions had improved markedly by 1940. The biggest building boom in ten years saw new construction surpass $450,000, a marked improvement from the low point in 1932 of $29,000 (fig. 19.1). New home construction in 1940 stood at eighty-nine. That year, 64 percent of Holland homes were owner-occupied (compared to 37 percent in cities nationally), with 55 percent free of a mortgage. The year 1941 set another construction record at $600,000, the highest since 1927. New homes totaled seventy-nine. Builders like the brothers-in-law, Henry Beelen & Bernard Wassink, rejoiced that the grim years had passed. They were happy to get the job of tearing down the Knoll & Knooihuizen building behind the Tower Clock Building; every piece of old lumber was salvaged. In the winter Beelen cut ice on Lake Macatawa for another brother-in-law, who sold it in the summer to resorters. When the nation went to war in 1941, building materials were rationed for military use. Home construction plummeted by two thirds in 1942, with further declines the next year. In the first post-war years, the demand for new housing caused a continuing shortage of lumber and cement. It took Beelen and his son Ken, a veteran who had just retuned home and joined the business, one full year to build a two-bedroom home because of delays over materials.[172]

The entire community was caught up in one building project, the restoration of the historic Tower Clock, which had stopped running after fifty years. The Junior Chamber of Commerce (JCC), called the Jaycees, kicked off a public fund drive in September 1947 to pay for an electric mechanism to replace the mechanical one. Within three months, the Jaycees, with Stuart Padnos in the forefront, had collected $500 in small donations. This was sufficient for the common council to solicit bids. Adrian Klaasen of City Sign Co. won the contract with the low bid of $1,360, which included re-bricking around the clock. A week before Christmas, Klaasen and employee Fred Vander Ploeg unveiled the city's most popular landmark. The clock sported four faces, each five feet across, made of heavy steel with a galvanized surface, in place of the original glass surface. Curved white fluorescent tubes illuminated

[172] *Holland Sentinel*, 31 Dec. 1940, 9 Jan. 1941, 1 Jan. 1942, 7 Jan., 25 June 1942, 13 Jan. 1943; Ken Beelen interview by David Boeve and the author, 30 Oct. 2009, typescript, JAH. In 1968 Beelen and a half dozen other contractors revived the Holland Home Builders Association, which had gone defunct in the Great Depression.

the clock at night. John Raven, who built the original, would have been pleased at the clock's new look.[173]

Forty years later, in 1987-88, Lumir Corporation, the downtown development arm of Ed and Elsa Prince, restored the Tower Clock Building to its former beauty. Lumir leased the first and second floors to the Tower Clock Gift store and turned the third floor into its swank corporate offices. The iconic structure was at risk of being demolished before Dale Wyngarden, the city's planner, lobbied to save it, and the Princes stepped forward. As Elsa Prince said, "It was a shame to see that beautiful building go downhill, and there was concern what a new owner might do—maybe even tear it down. So we bought it without any idea of what we were going to do with it."[174]

Teerman's store

A year after selling their coal business, Albert and Ralph Teerman in 1941 purchased the bankrupt De Pree Hardware store at 16 East Eighth Street and launched Teerman Hardware Co., the predecessor of today's department store. They took the plunge without knowing anything about running a hardware and paint store but everything about good customer care. The new owners completely remodeled the building and added fluorescent lighting. In a wise move, they hired two experienced clerks, Rena De Pree, who was associated with the former store, and Louis Jacobs, a friend who had worked more than two decades for Nies Hardware. "We aim to please," was their motto, and they matched the pledge with clever marketing. They passed out five-cent chits, called "checks," redeemable for merchandise "in appreciation of your valuable patronage." The checks, carried the slogan "Teerman Hardware Co., The Daylight Store," to highlight the modern interior lighting. The chits were a forerunner of Sperry and Hutchinson's S&H Green Stamps that Teerman's later offered, with double stamps on Tuesday.[175]

Over time, Teerman's changed locations twice along Eighth Street and also expanded three times. They moved from their original store in 1950 when their landlord, Earnest Brooks, leased the building

[173] *Holland City News*, 18 Sept. 6 Nov. 18 Dec. 1947.

[174] *Holland Sentinel*, 2 Dec. 1988; Michael Lozon, *Vision on Main Street: Downtown Holland's Resurgence as the Heart of the Community* (Holland: Lumir Corporation, 1994), 103 (quote).

[175] *Holland Sentinel*, 21, 24 Mar. 1941; James Teerman interview by the author and Dave Boeve, 5 Oct. 2009. I am indebted to James Teerman for providing access to Teerman family files.

Teerman Hardware store's five-cent "checks" (*courtesy Allan Teerman*)

to Kresge (predecessor of Kmart), who wanted to expand. Teerman's then moved a block west to the former Sears Roebuck catalog store at 19 West Eighth (on the north side of the street), after Sears opened a retail outlet on North River Street. In 1970 Teerman's returned to their original location at 16-20 East Eighth Street by buying Taylor's Men's Shop. It was a risky step, since the building was three times larger, but they cut the risk by leasing a part to Loker's Shoes for four years. Here they remain today, but in a much-expanded store. They added the Loker's space in 1974 and bought adjacent buildings to the west in 1980 (Clinton Store, formerly Kresge) and 1992 (Thomas Page's Toy Stop).[176]

Business grew slowly in the first twenty-five years, when the partners concentrated on hardware and paints. The first major breakthrough came in 1965 when Salome Teerman, James' wife, suggested starting a bridal registry. By then, Ralph's sons, James "Jim" and his brother Allen "Al," had taken over the business and they jumped on the idea. The registry was so successful that the store was renamed Teerman's Gift Shoppe, and its focus changed to Hallmark cards, house wares, and collectables such as Dutch delftware and pewter and German Hummels. Free gift wrapping and layaway added to the allure. Prior to this, only jewelry stores had wedding registries.

Salesmen instigated other product lines by stopping in at the store and telling the Teermans: "We have a product I think you can sell."

[176] Teerman interview; Teerman family files. Lokers Shoes, a Zeeland firm until the late 1960s, marked its 100th anniversary in 2013 (*Holland Sentinel*, 20 Oct. 2003, 9 Oct. 2008, 1 Nov. 2009).

This led to the opening of their clock store in 1970, which eventually featured more than one hundred wall and floor models from Zeeland's Howard Miller Clock Company, Holland's Sligh Furniture, and the New England and Hubbell manufacturing companies. Teerman's boasted of having one of the largest clock displays in Michigan, and they shipped pre-paid across the country. Al ran the clock shop and Jim the gift, card, and hardware/paint departments, but the latter was phased out by 1960. Jim preferred housewares to hardware. When stereo and television consoles became popular, Teerman's stocked them as well. Lee, another brother, joined the company and managed the electronics department. It was the only store in town that did in-house repair work on their TVs and stereos, which gave them an edge in customer service over the big box stores. Later Teerman's expanded their Samsonite line of card tables and chairs with patio furniture, another ideal product on the West Michigan lakeshore. Jim Teerman was leery of selling patio furniture at first, until the salesman offered to pay the freight and take back after ninety days any unsold items. The furniture was an immediate hit, and within a year Teerman's was ordering by the truckload. At every step, the brothers carved out unique marketing niches and kept on growing the business.[177]

The Teerman brothers knew marketing and how to win over customers by giving personal service. They had to beat out JCPenney, their main competitor. The sales staff grew to thirty employees in 1982, including in-laws Delia Timmer and her son Tom, and cousin Helen Teerman. They changed their slogan from the Daylight Store to the Willing Store to stress the commitment to customers. Only once, in 1983, did their policy of operating on trust fail them. That was when Grand Rapids' notorious swindler, James Robert Redican, owner of Computer Payroll & Accounting Service, left Teerman's and four hundred other businesses, churches, schools, and law firms throughout West Michigan in the lurch for $2 million. Redican ended up in the Milan (Michigan) federal prison after six years on the lam.[178]

In 1982 Teerman's opened Teerman's Hallmark Cards and Gifts Shop adjacent to a Family Fare store in Van Raalte Square on Washington Avenue and Fortieth Street, with Joyce Jacobs as manager. In 1996 the card and gift store moved, along with the supermarket, to the Family Fare Plaza on Washington Avenue at Fortieth-Eighth Street. The shop has since closed.[179]

177 *Holland Sentinel*, 16 Sept. 1982, 2 Oct. 1992; Teerman interview (quote); Teerman family files.

178 *Grand Rapids Press*, 29, 30 May 1983.

179 Teerman interview; Teerman family files; *Flashes*, 20 Nov. 1990.

In 1985 Al Teerman left the company, taking the import business and some clocks and opening a store in Zeeland. Within eighteen months, he joined Elhart Pontiac of Holland as a salesman and later became an independent mortgage broker. Jim Teerman doubtless wondered whether downtown retailers could survive the stiff competition from the new Westshore Mall (chapter 33). Both Model Drug, owned by Keith Ditch, and Teerman's under Jim and Lee, ran weekly newspaper ads in late 1989 to dispel rumors that their stores were closing. "Did you hear Teerman's was going out of business? Absolutely not!" declared the ad. "We want you to know that we are NOT moving to the mall and that we WILL remain in the downtown mall to serve you for many years to come."[180]

The year 1988 was the most difficult financially since the store's inception, as it was for every merchant on Eighth Street. That was because the Streetscape project required tearing up Eighth Street downtown in order to install new sewer and water pipes, and the innovative snowmelt system (chapter 33). From May until Thanksgiving, Teerman's had almost no foot traffic coming in the front door. Those with a back door off the alley, such as Teerman's, survived, but barely. Jim Teerman reported that business was down by one-third, and it took five or six year to recover. The popularity of a snow-free downtown helped the retailers recover, and it paid off big over time.[181]

Another test came in 1995, when an increasing number of downtown merchants opened on Sunday after nearly 150 years of deferring to the religious consciences of their customers. Facing the pressure to go along, Jim Teerman announced publicly, "My religious beliefs say that Sunday is a day of rest and time for family. Six days a week should be enough to shop and do business." In 2004 more shops and restaurants were opening on Sunday and advocates again leaned on Jim Teerman, who declared defiantly: "When I have to work on Sundays, I would quit." In 2005 when Jim Teerman announced his retirement on the fifty-fifth anniversary of the store, the city council recognized the milestone, and Mayor Albert McGeehan presented Teerman's with a council proclamation praising the family business for "unequalled customer service" and for being a "backbone of our downtown economy." Nephew Jeff Teerman, Lee's son, bought the store, and it remains closed on Sunday. In 2013, Jeff showed his entrepreneurial mettle by creating Teerman's Lofts, a boutique six-room hotel in renovated upstairs office space that opened for Tulip Time.[182]

180 Teerman family files; *Holland Sentinel*, 18 Nov. 1989 (quote).

181 Teerman interview.

182 *Holland Sentinel*, 28 May 1995 (quote), 26 May 2004 (quote), 28 Dec. 2005, 25 Apr. 2013.

Surprisingly, downtown family-owned businesses such as Vogelzang Hardware, Russ' Restaurants, Lokker Rutgers, Du Mez, Fris Hallmark Shop and Office Outfitters, and Fabiano's Peanut Store, among others, outlasted the chains. The three five and dime stores—Woolworth, Kresge, and McLellen—were all gone, the victims of discount outlets and malls. Kresge was the first to go. In 1976 Kresge held a grand opening for its Kmart superstore in the Cedar Village Plaza on Chicago Drive, where it joined a Family Fare supermarket. The mall developer was A. C. Geenen Construction, a company owned by Adrian "Ade" Geenen and son Charles "Chuck." The Kmart superstore replaced Kresge's smaller store in the East Town Plaza on Eighth Street at US-31. Both the Kmart and Family Fare stores in the Cedar Village Plaza have closed in recent years, leaving the mall a shadow of it former self. In 1989 Steketee's, JCPenney, and Sears Roebuck left the central city for Westshore Mall, and only JCPenney remains.[183]

Groceries and supermarkets

Holland had more than forty grocery stores in 1960, but the advent of the regional supermarkets— Foodlane, Meijer, Family Fare, D &W (both now owned by Spartan), Eberhard, Walmart and Sam's Club, Aldi Foods, and Gordon Food Service—cut the number in half, as the neighborhood family stores closed and the original chains could not compete and closed. The casualties included Sagger's Market in the Maplewood District, West Side Food Market and Montello Food Store in South Shore Village, Draper's Meat Market and Jerry's IGA in Washington Square, Buter's Grocery on College Avenue, Smitty's Grocery on East Twenty-Fourth Street, Holland Food Center on Central Avenue, Visscher Down Town at 35 East Eighth Street, Van's (became Town & Country) on Michigan Avenue, Yff's Food Fair in Holland Heights, Charley's Market on East Lakewood Boulevard, and Wilt's Food Center on North River Avenue.

One of the last locally-owned groceries is Central Park Market at 1158 South Shore Drive at Myrtle Avenue. Originally it was across Myrtle Avenue from the fire station, but Siebesma Auto Repairs has now been its neighbor for many years. This store has been an anchor of the Central Park community for more than one hundred years. Central Park incorporated as a village in 1927. The earliest known owner is Frank Mattison, who by 1904 was peddling fruits and vegetables to the resorts, such as Jenison Park and the Macatawa Park Association. The

183 *Holland Sentinel*, 16 Sept. 1976, 8 July, 29 Sept. 1987, 19 July 1997.

Central Park Grocery under Dick Miles, 1920s (*courtesy Nate Sankey*)

store was built by 1907, if not before. Dick Miles bought the business in 1917 and served resorters until 1930 when he joined the O. A. Wolbrink Insurance agency. The Central Park I. G. A. continued in the 1930s, but the ownership is unknown. In 1941 Joe Wiersma, a meat cutter at Naber's Market, bought the grocery store, along with a silent partner, James De Pree, who was a manager at the De Pree Chemical Company. The Wiersema family was connected with the store on and off for the next seventy years, from 1941 until 2011. Joe grew up nearby at 1174 South Shore Drive, and as a teenager he delivered groceries in a two-wheeled pushcart as far as Macatawa Park. Larry Vander Velde managed the store in 1949-50.[184]

From about 1952 until 1957, the Central Park grocery was part of Van's Department Food Stores headquartered at 694 Michigan Avenue, and it operated under the name Van's Central Park Supermarket. Gerrit Vander Hooning, another Central Park resident, and Robert Vander Hooning were the officers of Van's Food Stores. In 1956 Wiersma and De Pree started construction on a new "supermarket" on the parking lot of the store. On February 16, 1957, when the new store was almost ready for occupancy, a fire ruined the fifty-year-old landmark and much of the stock, except for the business records and cash box. The partners were able to reopen within a month.[185]

The Wiersmas sold the business outside the family up to five times, but they bought it back each time. Robert J. Kuiper owned

[184] Ibid., 12 Aug. 1904, Dick Miles obit., 11 Aug. 1969.

[185] Ibid., 18 Feb. 1957; *Holland City Directories*, 1952-69.

Interior of Central Park Grocery, 1920s, Dick Miles is likely pictured (*courtesy Nate Sankey*)

the store from 1959 to 1967, operating under the name Central Park Foodliner. Kuiper sold out to Joe's sons Max and Larry, both volunteer firemen at the Central Park Station. When the alarm rang, they left customers at the counter. Later, Max bought the Goodies Factory on South Washington Avenue, while Larry carried on at the grocery.[186]

In 1985 Larry Wiersma sold the business to the Grand Rapids-based Houseman's chain, and it became Houseman's Central Park Grocery. In 1994, however, Larry and son Michael "Mike" repurchased the store, and customers noticed two major changes at Wiersma's Central Park Foods: The new owners observed the Lord's Day, and they cleaned out the liquor shelf. But one thing did not change: Vivian Terpstra continued at the cash register, as she had for twenty-two years. Terpstra knew the customers and chatted while bagging their groceries. Wiersma's beat the chains handily in customer service and was able to compete on price by buying from a Wisconsin-based wholesale food distributor. In 2010 Mike Wiersma came to believe that the store was no longer viable, at least not without stocking alcoholic beverages and holding Sunday hours, so he announced its sale or closing. A young couple, Nate Sankey and Jamie DeJong, who had both grown up in the Central Park neighborhood, determined to keep the tradition alive. They bought the store in early 2011 and brought it back to a flourishing condition.[187]

186 *Holland Sentinel*, Max Wiersma obit., 30 June 2011; *Holland City Directory*, 1924-25.

187 *Holland Sentinel*, 28 Nov. 1993, 25 July 1994, 26 Feb. 1995, 11 Jan. 2011; *Grand Rapids Press Lakeshore Edition*, 24 May 1994; *Grand Rapids Press*, 12 Jan. 2011.

Two specialty meat stores have also bucked the big guys—Lamberts' Fresh Poultry and Seafood and Montello Meat Market—both on South Michigan Avenue. Julius Lamberts started his poultry business in 1945 while working at Hart & Cooley, raising chickens behind his home for the restaurant trade. When demand increased, he quit his day job in 1955 and opened Lamberts' Poultry in its present location at 689 Michigan Avenue. Jim Lamberts took up the butcher's knife in 1962 after graduating from high school. In the mid-1970s he and friend, Michael "Mike" Myrick, bought the business and later added fish and seafood. In 2011 Mike's son Marc bought out his father and Jim Lamberts, and the business passed to the third generation. Robert Kaashoek started Montello Meat Market in 1964 on South Shore Drive. Glenn "Tiny" Peters bought the shop in 1980 and later relocated to 746 Michigan Avenue. After Peters' death in 1997, Joel Nordyke and then David Kempers owned the business briefly until 2001, when the Tony Larson family of Ohio bought it, with the pledge to make Montello "an old-fashioned butcher shop" with the quality and cuts of meat that shoppers "can't get anywhere else." Both Lamberts' and Montello Market continue to cater to customers willing to pay a bit more for quality and service.[188]

The first of the regional grocery giants in Holland was Paul Baker's Hudsonville-based Foodlane Market, which opened a small grocery at Van Raalte Avenue and Nineteenth Street. Driven by his religious ideals, Baker operated on Christian principles: respect for the Sabbath Day and no alcoholic beverages, and customers responded in kind. Few would have predicted the future of this tiny store, which Baker enlarged twice before moving in 1962 to the corner of Lincoln Avenue and Thirty-Second Street. After a naming contest, Baker chose shopper Grace Prins' suggestion "Family Fare," a name that embodied his family-friendly policies. Baker sold Family Fare to the Byron Center-based Shop-Rite grocery, led by Don Koop and, for a brief time, Ron Kunnen. Shop-Rite operated on the same moral principles. In 1982 Family Fare, with headquarters in Hudsonville, moved to a new store in Van Raalte Square on South Washington Avenue at Fortieth Street. Subsequently, Family Fare stores were opened in the Cedar Village Plaza on Chicago Drive at 120th Avenue and in the Ottawa Village Mall on Butternut Drive at Riley Street. Robert and Jo Sluiter owned and operated the latter store until 1996. In 1995 Family Fare replaced the Van Raalte Square store with a superstore in the Family Fare Plaza farther south

[188] *Holland Sentinel*, 3 Apr. 1994, 15 Feb. 1995, 25 Apr. 2011; Steve Vander Veen, "Lamberts has remained despite larger and larger rivals," 12 Feb. 2006; Steve Vander Veen, "Customers share shop's history," 17 Apr. 2005.

on Washington Avenue at Forty-Eighth Street. Family Fare "rang up success" with its policy of no Sunday sales and no alcoholic beverage sales. But that changed after the Koop family in 1999 sold its thirteen Family Fare stores in West Michigan, including four in the Holland and Zeeland area, to Grand Rapids-based Spartan Foods.[189]

Within a year, in 2000, Spartan announced Sunday hours and devoted a full aisle to alcoholic beverages. The stated reason for the radical policy reversal was "changing lifestyles and customer convenience," but padding the bottom line was the real reason. The D&W Food Center in Zeeland was the last in the Grand Rapids-based chain of twenty-five stores to open on Sunday in August 2001. Some Christians objected, but most continued to trade at Spartan Food's Family Fare stores on weekdays. Over time, not a few also stopped on Sunday after church for needed items.[190]

Meijer came to town with a splash in 1968. The Grand Rapids-based chain, founded by Hendrik Meijer in 1934 in Greenville, opened a superstore on Douglas Avenue east of North River Avenue. Meijer initially observed the community norm and closed the store on Sundays, but before long the company "desecrated the Lord's Day" by opening all its stores seven days a week, twenty-four hours a day. Both were firsts for the conservative community. Meijer built a much larger store on East Sixteenth Street and Waverly Avenue in 1983. In 1992 Meijer sold the Douglas Avenue store to Zeeland-based Huizenga's Food Center, and two years later Huizenga sold the Douglas store and its mother store in Zeeland to Grand-Rapids-based D&W. In 2006 D&W sold out to Spartan Stores, which in 2003 had instituted all-night hours in all its stores. The Grand Rapids-based grocery Eberhard operated in the East Town Plaza on East Eighth Street at US-31 for a brief time, until Kmart moved to a new building in the Cedar Village Plaza.[191]

Walmart, which opened on the north side in 1993, soon began adding grocery aisles, besides selling food products in its adjacent Sam's Club membership warehouse. Illinois-based Aldi Foods erected its first local store in 1995 on Twenty-Fourth Street at US-31, and its second store along US-31 at Felch Street in 2011. They sell paper bags for a nickel and provide shopping carts that require a quarter to unlock; the coin is refunded when the cart is returned.

189 *Holland Sentinel*, 2 July 1995, 7, 30 Mar. 1999, 17 Sept. 2003; Mike Lozon, "Six-Day Operation," ibid., 17 Sept. 1995 (quote); Lozon, "Our Grocery Stores Through the Years," *Holland Chamber News* (Oct. 1997): 10, (Feb. 1998): 6.

190 *Grand Rapids Press*, 30 July 2000; *Holland Sentinel*, 30 Aug., 7 Oct. 2001; Lozon, "Our Grocery Stores."

191 Lozon, "Our Grocery Stores"; *Holland Sentinel*, 20 Dec. 2005.

Part Eight

Radio stations

Holland's first radio station WHBM began broadcasting on July 11, 1927, at 1490 kilocycles. This was barely seven years after KDKA Pittsburgh launched commercial radio, and not long after WOOD Grand Rapids went on the air. Radios were all the rage in the 1920s. Clyde Geerlings and Charles Sirrine, perhaps the most enthusiastic local fans, already in 1922 assembled a display of radio apparatus in the window of Van Tongeren's Cigar Store on Eighth Street, and many curious folks lingered to take a look. Hollanders bought battery-powered Franklin radios from $90 to $140 from Mark's Auto Store behind Model Drugs, and they strung antennas from the house to the garage to get maximum reception from Grand Rapid's WOOD, Chicago's WLS, Nashville's WSM, and even farther afield. Far costlier were the electric-powered RCA Victrola consoles that Meyer Music House carried.[192]

With radios came the need for repairmen, and Lewis De Kraker and Millard Westrate advertised their services in 1927. One moment of high radio drama occurred in December 1925, when every farmer and businessman rushed home to listen to President Calvin Coolidge on Chicago's WGN describe his administration's farm policy in the face of the severe agricultural depression. Coolidge addressed four thousand delegates of the American Farm Bureau in Chicago and declared to rousing applause that he did not "believe the government should go into the price fixing business or the marketing of the farmers' goods," since "the farmer would lose his independence."[193]

Henry Carley, owner of the Holland and Strand Theaters, was responsible for Station WHBM. The call letters signified **H**olland **B**uss **M**achine, a major financial backer of the station. Carley induced W. K. Pyle and radio engineer E. S. Adams to bring their equipment to Holland and broadcast from the stage of the Holland Theater and the Warm Friend Tavern in front of live audiences. Pyle made it clear from the outset that the station would remain as long as it could be financed. The *Holland Sentinel* gave the station top billing. Businessmen saw it as a big boost for the city, and Buss Machine Works, Holland Furnace, and other companies supported it. Even so, WHBM had a life span of only three months, from July 11 to September 14, 1927.

[192] Julius Van Oss, "Radio Holland began in 1920s," ibid., 30 Aug. 1998; Van Oss, "History of the WHTC Radio Station," typescript, talk given to Holland Historical Society, 9 Feb. 2010.

[193] *Holland City News*, 13 July 1922, 10 Dec. 1925 (quote).

The station broadcast every evening from eight to ten o'clock from the Masonic Temple on Tenth Street, which provided temporary space for a studio. The signal reached from Kansas City to the East Coast and featured the "best local talent" in music, such as the popular Trinity Reformed Church male quartet and the Weller Orchestra. The programs appealed to all ages and interests, including a children's hour and sports reports from the *Holland Sentinel*. The station even had its own jazz orchestra to play dance music, old-fashioned waltzes, hornpipes, and jigs.

Hope Church with Rev. John E. Kuizenga, a professor at Western Theological Seminary, preaching was the first church service to be broadcast. The biggest event turned out to be the last broadcast. It was a banquet for three hundred men in honor of George Getz, the founder of the "Getz Farm that was a Zoo," which featured addresses by Getz himself, Gerrit Diekema, Willard Wichers, Dick Boter, August Landwehr, Arthur Vandenberg of Grand Rapids, and former US Senator William Alden Smith. Days later, Pyle announced that he was transferring the station to Duluth, Minnesota. Apparently, too few residents owned radios to make the station viable. The final broadcast was the weekly Lions Club program on September 14, which featured Henry Karsten and the Melody Men, the Essenburg sisters (Elberdine, Lillian, and May Rose), and soloist Paul Nettinga accompanied by pianist James De Pree.[194]

Disappointed listeners had to wait twenty years before hearing another Holland radio broadcast, and that one proved to be enduring. WHTC (Holland Tulip City) went on the air on July 31, 1948, at 1450 kilocycles. Nelson "Nels" Bosman, an electrical engineer, began talking up a Holland station with *Holland Sentinel* publisher Wilford A. Butler in 1945. Butler saw an opportunity for his newspaper to broadcast the radio schedules and capitalize on the new medium. The two men recruited businessmen Isaac Herbert "Herb" Marsilje and Willard "Bill" Wichers, engineer Millard Westrate, and Holland Furnace Co. president P. T. "Ted" Cheff. The six men put in $4,000 to form the Holland Broadcasting Co. The partners labored long to obtain an operating license from the Federal Communications Commission (FCC). The 250-watt station reached a radius of about twenty-five miles, which easily covered the region.[195]

194 *Holland City News*, 7 July, 18 Aug., 1, 8, 15 Sept. 1927; Donald L. van Reken, *The Farm That Was a Zoo* (Holland: privately printed, 1983). The Federal Communications Commission required stations east of the Mississippi River to have call letters beginning with *W*.

195 *Holland City News*, 9 Oct. 1947, 22 Jan., 26 Feb., 20 May, 1 July, 5 Aug. 1948.

The studio and transmitter building, costing $2,900, was erected on an abandoned city dumpsite at Central Avenue and Fourth Street. The lease fee was reasonable, and the swampland underneath provided good grounding. Holland Furnace employees did much of the construction work, which required pilings for the foundation, and the company also donated office furniture. Locals dubbed it the "Little Green Shack in the Swamp." A second studio and offices were in the "penthouse" atop the Warm Friend Tavern, under a 160-foot tower mounted above. Butler served as the president and Bosman, Westrate, and Paul Hinkamp kept the transmitter and audio equipment in working order. Bosman stayed on more than thirty years, even while serving as Holland's mayor in the 1970s. Randall P. "Randy" Vande Water, a freshman at Hope College, snagged the job of doing the daily newscasts at 6:30 a.m., noon, and 6:05 p.m., which he continued all through college. Randy had been "weaned on journalism;" his father was a correspondent for the *Holland Sentinel*, *Grand Rapids Press*, and *Grand Rapids Herald*, and his mother wrote obituaries for the *Press*.[196]

Bill Wichers, WHTC's first program director, featured local talent and events, news every hour on the hour, sports reports, children's story hour, farm program, coffee kletz, western music, and especially Tulip Time, which merited full coverage. Listeners woke up to the voices of Robert "Bob" Greenhoe and Bill Wilson. Jean Hill led the children's program for many years. The most popular programs in the early days were *Trading Post*, started in 1954, and *Talk of the Town*, which Gargano started in 1959, after he returned from a job in Wisconsin. These programs were immediate successes.[197]

The strongest on-air personalities over the years were Julius "Juke" Van Oss and Ken Showers. Van Oss responded to an ad in the *Sentinel* for a "1st class engineer" in 1951 when the station was only three years old. One day when the early morning announcer came in twenty minutes late for his six o'clock program, Van Oss took over the microphone, and "the rest is history." In 1961 he became co-host of *Talk of the Town* and has soloed since 1980. He was going strong in 2012 at age eighty-nine—an amazing fifty-year stretch. Van Os also hosted the *Trading Post* for many decades. Showers, a disk jockey renowned for his humor, ran the early morning show and served as station manager for twenty-six years, from 1968 to 1994. Local history buffs tuned in

196 *Holland Sentinel*, 27 July 2003; Van Oss, "History of the WHTC Radio Station"; Vande Water interview, 18-20, 23-26.

197 *Holland Sentinel*, 30 July 1968.

Julius "Juke" Van Oss "on air" at the WHTC radio station
(*Joint Archives of Holland*)

to Randy Vande Water's Friday morning program, *Down History Lane*. Vande Water, a local boy, was managing editor of the *Holland Sentinel* and knew the secrets that lay under every rock in town. Hope College sports with college public relations director Tom Renner was another popular feature. For nine years, Renner appeared with Showers on the early program. WHTC also broadcast Detroit Tigers baseball since it went on the air in 1948, although not the Sunday games for a number of years. The station dropped the Tigers in 2004 after fifty-six years, due to a decline in listeners and sponsors. The Tigers had fallen on hard times, and a decade of futility took a toll on the faithful fans.[198]

When Greenhoe went into sales in the 1950s, Mike Baskett and later Larry Collins took his slot. Fred Merideth was the night announcer. Wichers soon gave way to Paul Naspar, an experienced station manager from Ohio. When Naspar resigned in 1950, the partners hired Sandy Meek, the veteran program director at WOOD-Grand Rapids with an appealing Scottish burr. Meek retired in 1964 after fourteen years. Wade Nykamp and Paul Van Kolken were two of his hires as announcers and engineers. Meek's costliest promotion came with the station's tenth anniversary celebration. WHTC encouraged listeners to bring in one dollar bills containing serial numerals 1, 4, 5, and 0 (the station's AM signal), and they would be given $2 in return, or $5, if the numbers

[198] Ibid., 23 July 1998, 5 Dec. 2007; Van Oss, "History of the WHTC Radio Station."

were in the proper sequence. "The response was overwhelming," Van Oss recalled, and WHTC lost $5,000 on the promotion.[199]

The move was spurred by new competition. In November 1956 the Ottawa Broadcasting Company obtained a license to send out a five-hundred-watt signal at 1250 kilocycles under the call letters WJBL (John, Bud, Len). It would be a Christian station. President Bernard Broekema of Grandville and partners John Klungle, Bernard "Bud" Grysen, and Len Ver Schure erected a building for the studio and offices, and a transmitter on the northwest corner of US-31 and James Street north of town. Klungle had worked with Van Oss at WHTC, and Grysen and Ver Schure were county deputies. Klungle was the chief engineer and program director, Grysen managed the station, and Ver Schure handled the business end. In 1964 the station moved into new studios at 5658 143rd Avenue in Fillmore Township two miles south of US-31 near M-40, and Peter J. Vanden Bosch, the new general manager, boasted that WJBL covered all of West Michigan.[200]

The Holland Broadcasting owners fiercely opposed WJBL at first, believing the local advertising market could not sustain two stations. But the FCC ignored the special pleading and licensed WJBL. In the end, both stations thrived. WHTC in 1961 erected a new two-story studio on its property at 87 Central Avenue at Fourth Street, with a one-thousand-watt transmitter, four times the power of the original, and a higher tower. The offices atop the Warm Friend Tavern were closed and all operations were moved to the $30,000 building. In 1966 the owners launched WHTC-FM at 96.1 megahertz with Thad Zeremba as manager; it went on the air at three o'clock in the afternoon and played contemporary light music. The FM station's call letters changed to WYXX in 1985, and the music was automated, so that it played for hours with little attention. In 2001 the call letters and place on the dial changed again to WYVN (the Van) at 92.7. The FM station has always shared offices with WHTC-AM.[201]

On its twentieth anniversary in 1968, WHTC proudly held an open house to show off the new facilities. Everyone wanted to see the nuclear-proof, emergency operating shelter designed to withstand a Soviet missile attack. By then, the staff had grown to sixteen, double the original number. Bill Gargano managed the station, assisted by Van

199 *Holland City News*, 6 Jan. 1949, 20 July, 3 Aug. 1950, 19 Aug. 1952, 2 Mar. 1961; Van Oss, "History of the WHTC Radio Station," *Holland Sentinel*, 23 July 1998.

200 *Holland City News*, 26 July, 9 Aug. 1956; *Holland Sentinel*, 13 Jan. 1964.

201 *Holland Sentinel*, 11 May 1966, 18 Mar. 1990.

Oss. Edward Ver Schure was the chief announcer, with Bosman and Ron Steenwyk as engineers.

In 1980 the aging WHTC owners sold the thriving station for $1 million to Michael Walton of Wisconsin-based Sheboygan Communications. Within days, Walton fired veteran staffers Gargano and a salesman, and appointed as operations manager Chris Marten, a "rock jock" from Wisconsin. Marten had little appreciation for the Holland community, and the local staff breathed a sight of relief when Walton fired him after several months. In 2000 WHTC changed hands a second time, when Duke Wright of Wisconsin-based Midwest Communications bought the station from the Walton group.[202]

Consistency in programming and a focus on the local area has always been the key to WHTC's success. Hiring ethnics to host programs also paid big dividends. In 1964 manager Bill Gargano hired Lupita Reyes, a leader in the city's growing Hispanic community, after she challenged him to give her the microphone. For more than four decades Reyes hosted the Sunday night program, *Algeria Latina*, that reaches out to her compatriots. In 2004 station manager Brent Allen hired Red Kingman, an Army veteran from San Diego, as a radio announcer. His *Red's Place* program quickly came to rival Van Oss' *Talk of the Town*. Kingman had such a gift of banter with listeners that most did not realize he was African American. Not being shy about his devout Christian faith also helped endear him. In 2008 WHTC celebrated its sixtieth anniversary. "Holland's Hometown Radio" remains the only AM station in Holland.[203]

Holland's Christian radio station WJBL-AM (1260) changed hands in 1983 when Les Lanser, owner of WJQ 99.3 FM, bought the station from Peter Vanden Bosch. In 1986 Lanser changed the call letters to WJQK-AM. He proved adept at keeping up with changing listener tastes. In 1993 he jettisoned traditional Christian hymns on the FM station in favor of talk radio, most notably the news commentary *Daybreak* program hosted by Dottie Barnes, and co-hosted by Mayor Al McGeehan for several years. In 2002 Lanser set up a remote WJQ-99 studio at Westshore Mall and broadcast there three days a week. In 2003 he changed the call letters of WJQK-1260 AM to WPNW (Praise and Worship Music), which became the new format. Dottie Barnes

202 Ibid.,18 Mar., 29 July 1990, 15 Aug. 1991, 29 Apr. 1994, 11 June 1997, 23 July 1998, 27 July 2003, 6 Mar. 2004, 20 July 2008; *Grand Rapids Press Lakeshore Edition*, 25 May 2005; Van Oss, "History of the WHTC Radio Station."

203 *Holland Sentinel*, 25 Oct. 2004, 19 Mar. 2006, 13, Jan. 2008.

was dropped, but not Charles Swindoll's *Insight for Living* and James Dobson's *Focus on the Family* from Colorado Springs. Dobson had faithful followers and strong financial backers in Holland, particularly the Edgar Prince family. In 2004 Lanser moved his AM and FM studios from Fillmore Township to new studios in Zeeland Township on Business I-196 west of State Street. The devotion of his listeners was evidenced when Lanser appealed for donations for the building project to help "1260 The Pledge" continue to offer Christian conservative programming. Lanser was amazed that $60,000 came in. When his son Brad took over as general manager, he returned the focus to talk radio, including popular psychologist Dr. Laura Schlesinger, Dave Ramsey of Financial Peace University, political commentator Janet Parshalls, and popular philospher Daniel Prager, among others.[204]

Hope College has had a student-run radio station on campus since 1956, operating for many years from a studio in the basement of the Kollen Hall dormitory. At first, WTAS reached only several campus buildings. In 1985 Anne Bakker Gras, director of student activities and a former student disk jockey, managed to obtain from the FCC an FM frequency to reach up to ten miles from campus. The call letters were changed to WTHS (The Hope Station), and the studios were moved to the first floor of the De Witt Center. Recently, the studio moved again to the Martha Miller Center, the communication arts building. As one would expect, the station reflects student tastes and interests.[205]

204 Ibid., 19 Mar. 1993, 4 Nov. 2002, 5 Jan. 2003; *Grand Rapids Press Lakeshore Edition*, 7 Jan. 2003, 9 Sept. 2004.

205 *Holland Sentinel*, 19 Sept. 1991, 19 May 1993.

Part Nine

Car dealers

Car dealers largely determined what makes of autos were seen on the streets. From 1908 to 1929, Holland had more than forty dealerships, including Teunis Prins (Buick) on Columbia Avenue, Fred W. Jackson's Auto Livery and Garage on West Seventh, Central Garage on Central Avenue owned by Harry Knipe, Overland Garage on West Seventh Street owned by Marinus Westrate, Venhuizen Auto (Studebacker) on East Seventh Street owned by Henry "Heinie" and Thomas Venhuizen, Wolverine Garage (Star, Durant, Flint) on the southeast corner of Tenth Street and River Avenue of Francis E. Dulyea and Martin Vander Bie, Holland Auto and Specialty Co. (Maxwell) of Reinder Vos on River Avenue, Westrate Bros. Auto (Overland, Willy-Knight, Maxwell, Chrysler) at 210 Central Avenue, H. P. Zwemer & Son owned by Henry P. and son Daniel on East Eighth Street (Willy-Knight, Overland), Edward Leeuw's Holland Hudson/Essex, People's Auto (Reo, Packard) of E. J. Bouwsma, Ter Haar & Timmer Motor Sales (Buick) of Arie Ter Haar and Zeelander Fred Timmer, and most lucrative of all, Holleman-De Weerd Auto (Ford) of John Holleman and Albert De Weerd at 25 West Seventh Street at River Avenue (see appendix 5.1 for a list of auto dealers, 1908-1940).[206]

Fred W. Jackson's Auto Livery and Garage, 25 West Seventh Street at River Avenue provided gasoline, tires, and parts, 1910 (*courtesy Larry B. Massie*)

[206] *Holland City News*, 10 May 1934; Frank E. Dulyea obit., ibid., 7 July 1938.

Venhuizen Studebacker Garage, 14-18 East Seventh Street
(*Joint Archives of Holland*)

In 1921 Holleman-De Weerd Auto sold in one month eighty-eight new Fords, thirty-two second-hand cars, and five Fordson tractors, worth nearly $62,000. This exceeded by 200 percent its monthly contract with Ford Motor Co. Over six months, the dealer sold 430 Lizzies, and monthly sales topped $75,000. In 1925 Holleman-De Weerd erected a $25,000 three-story building on its corner site to house the growing Ford and Lincoln dealership. It was one of the

Frank E. Dulyea and Martin Vander Bie opened the Wolverine Garage in 1921 on the southeast corner of River Avenue and Ninth Street as an Auburn, Cord, and Durant dealership; it later became a Chevrolet dealership. Note the two gasoline pumps on the roadside and the post office to the south (*Donald van Reken, Joint Archives of Holland*)

Holleman-De Weerd Ford dealership, 25 West Seventh Street, successor to Jackson's Auto Livery, with a full line of Fords for sale, 1920s (*courtesy Ed Bosch*)

largest garages and showrooms in western Michigan. The next year, the Holland Auto Dealers Association sponsored the first regional auto show at the new armory on Ninth Street. In 1929 Henry "Heinie" and brother Thomas Venhuizen built a new sales and service garage for their Dodge-Studebaker dealership at 14-18 East Seventh Street. Venhuizen Auto Co. had come far in eighteen years.[207]

The car business mirrored the general economy; sales rose and fell with the business cycle. In the 1930s cars became a product assembled largely by union labor in the plants of the Big Three–Ford, GM, and Chrysler. Big Labor gained the power to dictate wages and benefits. The symbiotic relationship between Big Labor and the Big Three led to ever-rising car prices. Automobile technology improved so rapidly that only the most nimble and innovative manufacturers survived. Car models went obsolete and new models appeared every year. With few exceptions, only models made by the Big Three survived the 1930s: Ford and Lincoln; Chevrolet, Buick, Oldsmobile, and Pontiac; and Chrysler, De Soto, Dodge, Plymouth, and Willys Jeep. The "minors" that managed to continue into the 1940s and 1950s were Hudson, Packard, Nash, and Studebaker.

The Great Depression tested the financial resources of car dealers, and many franchises in Holland changed hands or closed. By 1931 Westrate's dealership at 210 Central Avenue gave way to Edwin Owen's Oldsmobile dealership (Row Motor Sales), and Jesse C. Ridenour

207 *Holland City News*, 7 Apr. 1921, 21 May, 22 Oct. 1925, 11 Feb. 1926.

Holland Hudson-Essex garage of Edward Leeuw, 25 West Ninth Street, 1930s (*Archives, Holland Historical Trust*)

purchased E. J. Bouwsma's Peoples Auto Sales (Reo/Packard) directly across the street at 209 Central Avenue; Ridenour added Nash to his lineup and moved to 36 West Sixteenth Street by 1940. By 1934 Earl Bartholic's Auburn dealership, and Herman and son Daniel Zwemer's Rollin and Rickenbacker agency on East Eighth Street had closed, and Ralph Hayden and Dick Boter's Chevrolet dealership at 8-14 West Seventh Street had passed to C. E. McCleery. Herman Prins' City Garage (Buick) on 158 East Eighth Street had passed to sons Henry and Benjamin Ter Haar, with Henry as president and Ben as vice president. The brothers in 1931 opened a Chrysler/Plymouth dealership at 224 Central Avenue under the name Leeuw & Ter Haar. Henry Ter Haar and brother Arie of Ter Haar Auto at 150 East Eighth Street owned GM agencies until the early 1950s—Henry with Oldsmobile/Cadillac and Arie with Buick/Pontiac.

By 1936 Wynn Pemberton acquired McCleery's Chevrolet franchise and moved it to the former Wolverine Garage of Dulyea and Vander Bie on River Avenue and Ninth Street, which became Decker Chevrolet by 1940. Jack Decker put his name on the dealership but Dick Boter of P. S. Boter Clothiers owned 75 percent, as he had since the early 1930s. In 1938 Elmer Plaggemars and John Vrieling purchased the bankrupt Holleman-De Weerd Ford dealership on Seventh Street and River Avenue, and by 1940 Frank Brooks had purchased Edward Leeuw's Hudson/Terraplane agency at 25 West Ninth Street. Besides the Ter Haar brothers, only Thomas and Henry Venhuizen of Venhuizen Auto (Studebaker/Dodge) survived the 1930s.[208]

[208] *Holland City Directories*, 1929, 1931, 1934, 1936, 1938, 1940; conversation with Robert De Nooyer Sr. on 22 June 2012.

Decker Chevrolet, 217-27 River Avenue at Ninth Street, Tulip Time 1953, shortly before Robert De Nooyer Sr. bought the dealership. The building housed the Wolverine Garage from 1921 to 1936 (chapter 22), Wynn Pemberton's Chevrolet dealership from 1936 to 1938, and Jack Decker's dealership from 1938 to 1953. De Nooyer held this prime location from 1953 to 1965. It is now a parking lot behind the Holland Museum (*courtesy Robert De Nooyer Sr.*)

During the Second World War, all domestic auto plants were converted to turn out military vehicles; no American cars were manufactured in 1942, 1943, and 1944 (chapter 23). When production resumed in 1945, consumers were so eager to spend the extra dollars they had been forced to save under price controls and wartime scarcity that they flocked to car showrooms. The pre-war dealers who had managed to survive the lean years were busy again. They included Jack Decker Chevrolet on the southeast corner of River Avenue and Ninth Street, Willard "Bill" Haan's Hudson dealership at 211 Central Avenue (successor of Frank Brooks Motor Sales), Arie Ter Haar's Buick/Pontiac agency at 150 East Eighth Street (present site of Holland Area Arts Council), brother Henry Ter Haar's Oldsmobile/Cadillac agency at 224 Central Avenue, John Vrieling's Ford dealership at 159 River Avenue and Seventh Street, Henry Streur's Dodge/Plymouth agency (Ottawa Auto Sales) at 8 West Seventh Street, and facing them across the street, Bernard Deters Packard's garage at 23 West Seventh Street (having moved from the southeast corner of River Avenue and Sixteenth Street). Deters was the mechanic and salesman, and his wife Cleo kept the books; the couple lived upstairs, above the business. Haan Motors

Deters Auto Co., Packard sales and service, 23 West Seventh Street, 1945 (*Joint Archives of Holland*)

moved to 25 West Ninth Street at River Avenue by 1947, and dropped Hudson in favor of the Chrysler/Plymouth franchises.[209]

Four newcomers entered the car business in 1945, when auto production resumed after the war: William "Bill" C. Vandenberg Jr.'s Vandenberg Auto Sales at Sixteenth Street and River Avenue (Chrysler/Plymouth); Herman Dirkse's United Motor Sales (Kaiser/Frazier/Jeep) at 723 Michigan Avenue; Raymond Roelofs and Henry Strabing of Reliable Garage at 135 West Eighth Street, who carried the De Soto/Plymouth/Dodge lines from 1945 to 1969 after giving up the Dodge franchise to Iran "Ike" Huizenga of Zeeland; and Albert De Weerd of Down Town Nash at 224 Central Avenue–a building vacated by Henry Ter Haar when he erected a showroom and service building at 711 Michigan Avenue. In 1950 De Weerd sold the Nash dealership to Jim White and concentrated on his Down Town Service station at 77 East Eighth Street. Ike Huizenga erected a new building for his Dodge dealership at 1127 Central Avenue at the US-31 bypass. He sold in 1971 to Anthony "Tony" Jerome and Glen Reimink of Holland Dodge, who sold in 1975 to Jack Wyrick, who moved the Dodge franchise to Chicago Drive.[210]

209 Ibid., 1940, 1942, 1945.
210 Ibid., 1945.

Haan Motor Sales, Chrysler-Plymouth dealer, southeast corner of Ninth Street and River Avenue, 1950s (*Archives, Holland Historical Trust*)

Bill Vandenberg sold the Chrysler/Plymouth franchise to Haan in 1950 after buying the Buick franchise from Arie Ter Haar. General Motors had forced Ter Haar to sell either the Pontiac or Buick lines, because his dealership at 150 East Eighth Street was too small to accommodate both lines. Vandenberg then built a modern dealership on the southeast corner of River Avenue and Sixteenth Street (now a Dollar General store), after buying the old Deters property. Edgar Prince worked for Vandenberg Buick as a teenager in the 1950s, and found in Bill an apt teacher of the entrepreneurial skills demanded in the car business. In 1958 Vandenberg Buick (later Vandenberg Motors) erected a new building at 1185 Washington Avenue (now the site of a Family Fare Store), where the firm continued for twenty-seven years, until 1987, when Crown Motors (see below) bought the Buick franchise. Vandenberg added the Rambler line in 1960 and became Vandenberg Buick/Rambler.

Herman Dirkse's United Motor Sales began as a used car lot on Michigan Avenue south of the hospital, Holland's first "dealers' row" away from the city center, but by 1954 he moved to the second "dealers' row," on Chicago Drive, first at 540 and then 533. Fred's Car Lot, owned by Herman's brother Fred, was just up the road a block, at 675 Chicago Drive (present site of Quick Lube), from 1952 to 1980, when Fred sold it to Terry Wolters. For years Fred Dirkse sold pre-owned cars but added Toyota/Fiat in the 1970s. He unwisely gave up the Toyota franchise in favor of the Fiat line, which proved his undoing. Toyota awarded the franchise to Fred La Fontaine, who opened a dealership at 11260 Chicago Drive. Alvin Dirkse, Herman's brother, became manager

Vandenberg Auto Sales, southeast corner of Sixteenth Street and River Avenue, late 1940s (*Archives, Holland Historical Trust*)

of United Auto Sales in 1966, and Herman's son Richard joined the firm in 1972, when they added a Honda franchise to their Jeep lines. In 1979 Richard Dirkse moved United Auto (Jeep/Honda) to 1127 Central Avenue. In 1987 he sold to Alan Brockette, who renamed it Honda West. In its first full year, Brockette sold 1,500 Hondas and expected to sell 1,800 the next year, in tandem with the parent Japanese company's rising reputation for craftsmanship and reliability. Brochette sold Honda West to Jerry Timmer in 1990, and Timmer sold the Honda franchise to Crown Motors in 1993.[211]

When the Kaiser and Frazier car companies collapsed, Ter Haar Motor Sales at 711 Michigan Avenue in 1959 bought the Studebaker franchise of Venhuizen Auto, which became Ter Haar-Venhuizen, with Henry Ter Haar as president and William Venhuizen as vice president. The Oldsmobile/Cadillac dealer carried the Studebaker line until the storied company closed in 1966. Henry Ter Haar retired by 1964, and Don Hildebrands and Venhuizen served as co-vice presidents. In 1986 Crown Motors (see below) obtained the Oldsmobile/Cadillac franchises, and the Ter Haar name disappeared after more than fifty years. Robert De Nooyer Sr. had his OK Used Cars division just to the south, at 733 Michigan Avenue, from 1954 to 1964, when he brought it to his East Eighth Street property. The Michigan Avenue building in the late 1990s was razed for a Burger King and the southern portion of the lot became a city park.[212]

Arie Ter Haar hired Theodore "Ted" Elhart as a salesman in 1949. About five years later, Ter Haar sold the Pontiac brand to Don Michmerhuizen, which prompted Elhart to move to Vandenberg Buick.

[211] *Holland City Directories*, 1952-1980. Mrs. Edward Comstock of Grand Rapids, a Holland native, owned the property at 733 Michigan Avenue and built the building for Herman Dirske.

[212] Ibid., 1959, 1960, 1964, 1978.

Michmerhuizen sold the Pontiac franchise to Myron De Jonge about 1960, and De Jonge sold it again in 1965 to Ted's son Kenneth "Ken" Elhart. At this, Ted took his salesmanship to the new Elhart Pontiac/GMC dealership (see below). Ted Elhart was one of Vandenberg's salesmen for a decade, until he joined his son's new dealership in 1965.[213]

Other dealers who entered the auto business in the booming post-war years were Forrest Maycroft (Lincoln/Mercury), Robert "R. E." Barber (Ford), Robert De Nooyer Sr. (Chevrolet), Samuel "Sam" Dagen (Dodge/Plymouth), Philip Gordon's Volkswagen dealership next door to R. E. Barber Ford on Seventh Street, and Gordon Van Dyke and his son Kenneth, a mechanic, opened a used car lot, Van Dyke Auto Sales, in 1949 at 718 Michigan Avenue.[214] In 1945 B. Harold Westmoreland and Edwin Viehl purchased Henry Streur's Ottawa Auto Sales (Dodge/Plymouth) at 8-14 West Seventh Street. By 1947 Westmoreland sold his share to Samuel Dagen, the long time service manager at Decker Chevrolet. Dagen partnered briefly with Viehl, then Lawrence Milligan, and finally LaFern Kortering. Ottawa Auto Sales closed in 1953, and First National Bank bought the land for a parking lot.[215]

Forrest Maycroft in 1947 opened a Lincoln/Mercury agency at 16 West Seventh Street in partnership with Grand MacEacheron, a Grandville banker. Cornelius "Cornie" Versendaal began as a salesman with the new firm and advanced to general manager. In 1962 MacEacheron sold his share of the business to Maycroft, who then asked Versendaal to be a partner. The business, renamed Maycroft & Versendaal, relocated in 1960 to a new building at 124 East Eighth Street, next door to the historic Firehouse No. 2. When Maycroft died in 1974, Cornie became the sole owner. His son Cal joined the business in 1991, and the Maycroft name was then dropped. In 2005 Cornie and Cal sold Versendaal Lincoln/Mercury to Myron Molotky, who renamed the company Lincoln/Mercury of Holland. Molotky owned the Great Lakes Auto Group (Toyota/Volkswagen/Isuzu) at 11260 Chicago Drive for several years (1996-ca.1999) before selling it to Crown Motors. In 2005 Molotky moved Lincoln/Mercury of Holland—the only auto agency in the central city for thirty years—into a new building at 13001 New Holland Street at US-31, and added a Suzuki franchise.[216]

213 Ibid., 1947-48, 1949-50, 1952. I am indebted to Kenneth Elhart, who began his career in auto sales in 1949 at Ter Haar Auto, for sharing his rich knowledge of local dealers and dealerships during the past sixty years.

214 *Holland City Directories*, 1945, 1954, 1960, 1983.

215 Ibid., 1936-54.

216 Ibid., 1947-48, 1961, 1988-2004; *Holland Sentinel*, 21 Aug., 10 Nov. 2003, 11 Feb. 2004, 5 Oct., 17 Dec. 2005; Mike Lozon, "Auto Dealers," *Holland Chamber News* (Sept. 1997): 10.

Molotky lacked the staying power to survive the sharp downturn in auto sales. In late 2008 he sold his Holland Township dealership to Grand Rapids-based Fox Motors, owned by Dan De Vos, the second son of Richard De Vos, founder of Ada-based Amway Corporation. Dan had the deep pockets of that entrepreneurial family, but this did not deter him from closing the Holland franchise in 2010 in a preemptive strike, since Ford Motors had discontinued the popular Mercury brand and announced its intention to cut franchises. Instead, Fox Motors opened two new dealerships in the Grand Rapids area, bringing the total to nineteen.[217]

Robert Ellsworth "R. E." Barber, who had a dealership in Plainwell,, in 1949 bought John Vrieling's Ford franchise at 159 River Avenue and opened R. E. Barber Ford. R. E., as everyone knew him, grew the business and after sixteen years needed room to expand. His monthly sales were also lagging those of Robert De Nooyer Chevrolet, which stood a block south on the southeast corner of River Avenue and Ninth Street (now the parking lot behind the Holland Museum). In 1965, De Nooyer was the first dealership to move out of downtown, to five acres on East Eighth Street at the new US-31 by-pass (see below). In 1966 Barber bought five acres on Settlers Road across US-31 from De Nooyer and built a modern garage and showroom far larger than current sales warranted. But he had the foresight and determination to succeed.[218]

A member of Hope Church, Barber "walked the talk." He never asked his employees to do anything he would not do, including shoveling snow and sweeping the floors. Barber was always the first at work in the morning and the last to leave at night, until his health failed him. His younger brother Forrest "Forrey" Barber managed the body shop, and Louis Hallacy II, former owner of the Goodyear dealership in Holland, managed the leasing agency for eighteen years. Barber accommodated Hallacy's schedule when he served on the city council and then as mayor. Barber had an eye for entrepreneurial talent. Two of his understudies left to start their own dealerships–Ken Elhart in Holland and Dick Boyd of Boyd Ford of Ludington. Another, Tony Babinski of Hamilton Ford, came to R. E. Barber when the company closed his franchise. Barber was the "most tireless automobile dealer in Holland," declared Lloyd Ver Hage.[219]

217 *Holland Sentinel*, 30 Oct. 2010; *Grand Rapids Press*, 2 Nov. 2010.

218 I am indebted to Robert De Nooyer Sr. for information about his dealership and the local auto industry in general.

219 I am indebted to Ed Bosch for sharing his memories of R. E. Barber and the company, and the history of Holland dealerships generally (conversation with the author, 27 July 2011, and email exchanges).

R. E. Barber (*at table on right*) distributing bundles of "cold cash" to employees under the Barber Ford profit-sharing plan, ca. 1955 (*courtesy Ed Bosch*)

When Barber died of cancer in 1980, ownership passed to the family trust, controlled by his wife Wilda Barber, with William De Long as trustee. Two long time employees, Edward "Ed" Bosch and Douglas "Doug" Wierda, carried on with Bosch as general manager and Wierda as sales manager. Bosch began as the bookkeeper in 1964 and worked his way up to general manager. Wierda, sales manager at Dick Yerkey Ford of Zeeland, came in 1967 when R. E. Barber bought the Yerkey dealership. After Barber's death, Bosch and Wierda planned to buy the dealership, but they were stymied for two years after Ford Motor Company denied their application for funding under the Dealer Development Program. Finally, in frustration, Bosch and Wierda quit and "set up shop" in Smokey's Family Restaurant (see *Restaurants* above) on Sixteenth Street, a half mile south, to watch what would happen at the dealership. As expected, the business floundered, and within three weeks, trustee De Long called and agreed to a sale to the pair, who have been fifty-fifty partners since 1982. Ed Prince provided much-needed funding. It was another example of his desire to help family and friends get into business. Doug Wierda was the father-in-law of Prince's daughter Emilie, married to Craig Wierda.[220]

220 *Holland Sentinel*, 30 June 1992; Lou Hallacy interview by the author and Dave Boeve, 11 Nov. 2009, typescript, JAH.

Barber and team at Barber Ford pictured with a 1967 Ford Custom 500. This photo marks Barber's purchase in 1967 of Dick Yerkey Ford of Zeeland and his hiring of the four former Yerkey employees (*left to right*): technicians Garry Dykstra and Dan Buist, R. E. Barber, Douglas Wierda, and Dick Yerkey (*courtesy Ed Bosch*)

The second oil embargo following the Iranian Revolution in 1979 tested them immediately, and in 2000, they were impacted by the Firestone tire fiasco on Ford Explorers, when tread separation problems caused rollovers. The National Highway Transportation Safety Administration issued a recall notice that caused sales of the hot-selling Explorers to plummet for a brief period. The meltdown of the Big Three in 2008-9 was the greatest challenge, but Ford Motors was the only one to avoid bankruptcy. Barber Ford in 2011 had forty-nine employees, forty-one full-time, including Doug Wierda's sons Curt and Chuck. The brothers and colleague Ken Genzink purchased the business as of January 1, 2012.[221]

Robert "Bob" De Nooyer Sr. founded De Nooyer Chevrolet/Geo in 1953 after buying Decker Chevrolet from Jack Decker and Dick Boter. It was a natural step for the young man from Kalamazoo, whose family had owned dealerships in Kalamazoo and Battle Creek since the 1930s. In 1965 De Nooyer built a $400,000 dealership and service garage at 600 East Eighth Street. He bought the five acres from the City of Holland for

221 *Holland Sentinel*, 2 Dec. 2008, 5 Feb. 2010; Ed Bosch e-mail to author, 26 Dec. 2011.

Robert De Nooyer Sr. (*right*) at signing of the buy-sell agreement in May 1953 with Dick Boter (*second from right*) and Jack Decker (*second from left*). De Nooyer's father Jerry (*left*), a Kalamazoo Chevrolet dealer, is looking on (*courtesy Robert De Nooyer Sr.*)

$50,000. The site had contained three water pumping stations that the board of public works no longer needed. It was the largest auto sales-service in the Holland area and included an OK Used Cars division that was relocated from Michigan Avenue. He chose an auspicious time, since General Motors had close to 50 percent of the national car market and its many lines—a car for every taste and pocketbook—were the most coveted. De Nooyer's modus operandi was expressed in his dictum: "The speed of the boss is the speed of the gang." His sales shot up over 50 percent in 1965, thanks to his twelve salesmen under general manger Herman Miedema. Service managers Joe Schippers and Paul Vroon kept customers happy and sixteen mechanics busy. A few years later, union organizers from Detroit tried to organize De Nooyer's mechanics and body shop men, as the first step in organizing all the shops, but the election failed and the organizers gave up. In the late 1970s, De Nooyer Chevrolet won industry awards for selling one hundred or more trucks in a single month.[222]

After 1966, when Barber Ford opened at 640 East Eighth Street facing De Nooyer Chevrolet across US-31, the two competitors had the lion's share of the new car business in Holland. Yet, R. E. Barber and Bob De Nooyer maintained a warm personal relationship and

222 Interview with Robert De Nooyer Sr. on June 20, 2012; "Robert De Nooyer Chevrolet Grand Opening," *Holland Sentinel*, 29 May 1965, a twenty-four-page second section.

US-31 and Eighth Street interchange, with Barber Ford on upper right and De Nooyer Chevrolet on lower right with United States flag unfurled, 1983 (*courtesy Randall P. Vande Water*)

readily shared information. De Nooyer's business is readily identified by the thirty-six-by-sixty-foot United States flag that unfurls above the street on windy days, erected to honor the military and especially those missing in action. De Nooyer sold the first Corvettes in Holland, before handing management over to his son Bob Jr. in 1984. Later his grandchildren Dominique and Nicole De Nooyer joined the company, making it another three-generation business in Holland. Nicole, who began working in the dealership at age twelve, joined the firm after graduating from college and became the first female general manager of a Chevrolet dealership in Michigan.[223]

Lloyd Ver Hage started a Chrysler dealership at 343 East Eighth Street in 1963 for much the same reason as De Nooyer. It was an offshoot of his father's dealership, Henry Ver Hage Motors of Hudsonville, which since 1914 sold Chalmer, Overland, Maxwell, Star, and Durant autos, until becoming a Chrysler dealer in 1925. Lloyd Ver Hage, after graduating from the University of Michigan by way of Calvin College, worked for his older brothers Dick and Harold in the Hudsonville garage for seven years before starting his own Chrysler dealership in

223 Myron Kukla, "Family-owned DeNooyer Chevrolet celebrates 50 years in business," *Grand Rapids Press Lakeshore Edition*, 25 May 2008; Lozon, "Auto Dealers."

Holland. He bought the building from Elmer Nienhuis, founding owner for two years of Suburban Motors. Over time, Lloyd's sons Paul, Norman, and Blaine, joined the agency, and more recently Blaine's son Mitch. Paul, the heir apparent, died prematurely and Norm became general manager, with Blaine managing parts and service, and Mitch "learning the ropes" as a technician. Ver Hage carried Dodge lines from 1981 to 1985. Then in a strategic decision, Lloyd declined Chrysler Corporation's demand to expand his dealership to accommodate the new series of Dodge Ram pickup trucks just coming off the line. The decision seemed wise at the time, given the limited space to expand on the site, but it cost the dealership the opportunity to sell "Rams," which earned truck-of-the-year awards.[224]

After loyally representing Chrysler Corporation for forty-six years, in 2009 when Chrysler went bankrupt and was taken over by Fiat of Italy, the top executives decided to pare its dealerships by 25 percent. Ver Hage Chrysler of Holland was one of 789 dealers nationwide to lose its franchise. This left the greater Holland area, with a population of more than one hundred thousand, without a Chrysler dealer until the Italian company gave the franchise to Crown Motors (see below). Ver Hage Motors now represents Mitsubishi Motors and sells used cars and services all makes. The Ver Hage family has been in the auto business nearly ninety years over four generations, which is by far the longest run of any auto dealership in West Michigan. In 2011, Ver Hage acquired the Mitsubishi franchise from Crown Motors (see below). The rebranded company, Ver Hage Mitsubishi of Holland, expects to celebrate its fiftieth anniversary in 2013.[225]

Kenneth Elhart operated Elhart Pontiac/GMC at 150 East Eighth Street in 1965, but the limited space forced him to relocate in 1970 after just five years. He bought acreage on Chicago Drive east of Waverly Road, a site between Holland and Zeeland with plenty of room to expand, and he erected a new building at 822 Chicago Drive, which opened in January 1970. Later, Ken added American Motors to its GM lineup. In 1977 his son Wayne joined the family business after graduating from college, and six years later, in 1983, younger son Jeffrey "Jeff" became a partner after working five years as a district sales manager for GM in Detroit. In 1985 Ken and his sons jointly acquired the Dodge franchise and Chrysler Corporation then assigned them the popular Dodge Ram

[224] I am indebted to Lloyd and Norman Ver Hage for providing information of their dealership.

[225] Ben Beversluis, "End of the line," *Grand Rapids Press Lakeshore Edition*, 5 June 2009.

pickup line. But the new Yugo line (a small Yugoslav car) in the mid-1980s proved to be a flash in the pan; Yugo went bankrupt in 1989.[226]

By 1987 Wayne and Jeff held jointly owned dealerships on the "Elhart Automotive Campus," with Wayne directing Elhart Pontiac/AMC/GMC in the refurbished original building and Jeff running Elhart Dodge/Yugo in a new building at 870 Chicago Drive. Wayne had the Pontiac muscle cars and the hot American Motors Rambler. He lost AMC in 1987 when Chrysler Corporation acquired the company. Elhart Dodge secured the Nissan franchise in 1990, which more than filled the gap. In 2000 Elhart Dodge/Nissan added the Korean brand Hyundai, which stabilized the business when GM stopped building Pontiacs in 2009. That year, the Elharts were badly hurt again by the Chrysler and GM bankruptcies and the company's savaging of their dealerships. Elhart lost the Jeep and Dodge brands, including Rams. In 2010 Wayne retired, and Jeff bought his interest and continues to own Elhart GMC/Hyundai and Elhart Nissan, with some one hundred employees, on the Chicago Avenue dealers' row. In 2011 Jeff Elhart took another major step and broke ground for a new Hyundai showroom and major renovations of the GMC and Nissan showrooms to meet the manufacturer's branding and image.[227]

Crown Motors is a venture of Craig and Emilie Prince Wierda. In 1986 the young couple in their mid-twenties, with funding from Ed Prince, purchased the Oldsmobile/Cadillac franchises of Ter Haar-Venhuizen on Washington Avenue. Craig Wierda learned the business from his father Doug, who worked for R. E. Barber Ford, and from Barber himself after he hired Craig as a high school student. When Wierda obtained his General Motors franchises at the age of twenty-five, he was one of the youngest people ever to be granted a franchise by one of the majors. Within a year, the Wierdas relocated to a large campus off Blue Star Highway near Tulip City Airport, which Emilie's father Ed Prince had owned (chapter 10). Crown Motors built a service center with extensive showrooms at 196 Regent (originally Herman Miller) Boulevard. In 1989 the Wierdas bought Vandenberg Buick, and moved the franchise to the Regency Drive campus, selling the South Washington Avenue site at Forty-Eighth Street for a Family Fare store. Interestingly, Bill Vandenberg had given Ed Prince his first job at the dealership while he was in high school.[228]

[226] *Holland City Directories*, 1965, 1970. I thank Ken, Jeff, and Wayne Elhart for relating the history of their dealerships.

[227] *Holland Sentinel*, 30 Jan. 1988, 22 June 2009, 26 Sept., 2 Oct. 2011.

[228] *Holland Sentinel*, 30 Jan. 1988; Lozon, "Auto Dealers." I am indebted to Craig and Emilie Wierda for information concerning Crown Motors.

Crown Motors' focus from the beginning was customer service, typified by a well-furnished and inviting waiting room and courteous and knowledgeable service managers. The dealership set the standard in Holland for a first-class operation. The staff was increased by 50 percent to fifty mechanics, salesmen, and clerical staff. In 1992 the Wierdas purchased the Honda franchise from Jerry Timmer, and brought the popular line to its Regency Drive campus and converted the 1127 Central building to a body shop and the lot for selling pre-owned vehicles. The same year, Craig and Emilie Wierda acquired Hope Imports' Mazda and Volkswagen franchises from Willard Wolters. The next year, the Wierda's purchased the Toyota and Isuzu franchises from Myron Molotky. They also obtained a Mitsubishi franchise from Mitsubishi Motors, a Japanese newcomer in the American market in the 1980s, which they sold to Ver Hage in 2011. These brands are sold at the 11260 Chicago Drive campus. When GM discontinued the Oldsmobile line in 2004, Crown touted its Buick brand.

In 2010 Chrysler Corporation awarded to Crown Motors the Chrysler group of cars (Chrysler/Dodge/Jeep/Ram), after Crown presented a proposal for the franchises, in competition with numerous other dealers, including the former franchise holders. The Chrysler lines remain in local hands, and the new dealership opened in the Central Avenue facility after being refurbished and remodeled. Crown Motors then sold its Mitsubishi franchise to the Ver Hage family in 2011.[229]

In 1953 Bob De Nooyer organized the first Holland auto dealers organization. It started informally among men who shared a religious bond in the Christian Reformed Church, including Henry and Arie Ter Haar, Bill Vandenberg, Bill Venhuizen, and Bill Haan. The men first met on East Eighth Street (where the Holland Arts Council building now stands), and then at the Holliday Inn on US-31 and Thirty-Second Street. In the mid-1980s, R. E. Barber Ford, De Nooyer Chevrolet, and Elhart Pontiac instigated the Holland New Car Dealers Association (HNCDA), which was formally organized in 1989. In 1997 the association had eight members: R. E. Barber Ford, Crown Motors, De Nooyer Chevrolet, Elhart Dodge/Nissan, Elhart Pontiac/GMC/Jeep, Ver Hage Chrysler, Versendaal Lincoln/Mercury, and Great Lakes Toyota. In 2011 the trade association still represented eight dealerships: R. E. Barber Ford, Crown Motors, Crown Toyota, Crown Chrysler, De Nooyer Chevrolet, Elhart GMC/Hyundai, Elhart Nissan, and Ver Hage

229 *Holland Sentinel*, 30 Jan. 1988, 6 Oct. 2010, 8 Sept. 2011; Lozon, "Auto Dealers"; *Holland City Directories*, 1992, 1993, 1996, 2000, 2001.

Mitsubishi. The association under president Robert De Nooyer Sr. set common operating policies for the dealers. Evening hours were cut back, school yearbook donations were made collectively by the association buying full-page ads, the customary 10 percent discount to insurance companies on repairs was eliminated, cars were allocated for high school driver's training programs, and staff wages were surveyed. Bob De Nooyer tried to mimic Henry Ter Haar, who always had the highest paid mechanics in Holland. Dues were pro-rated according to sales, and the association never tried to control vehicle pricing, which would have been illegal.[230]

According to sales figures of the Holland New Car Dealers Association kept by Robert De Nooyer Sr., from 1953 to 2012 Chevrolet ranked first in total sales of new cars and trucks thirty-three times (60 percent), Ford was first twenty-one times (38 percent), and Toyota ranked first 1 time (2 percent).[231]

Since the 1970s, automobile and truck dealers have been one of the most heavily regulated industries. Although very few dealers employ more than five hundred associates, they are subject to the same regulations as big companies with thousands of employees.

Until the last decade, automotive dealers thrived with careful attention to the bottom line. Danger signs were already evident in 2001 when auto companies had to resort to zero percent financing, cash discounts, and fleet sales to move cars. The Big Three were bound by union contracts to pay workers whether they worked or not. That year, auto companies sold twenty-one million vehicles—an all-time high. GM was led by strong sales of its Chevy Impala and Monte Carlo, Chrysler had the hot Jeep Liberty and PT Cruiser, and the Focus and Explorer were top sellers for Ford, along with F-series pickups. After gasoline hit four dollars a gallon in 2007, the Toyota Prius, an electric-gas hybrid, had customers on wait lists up to six months. Honda, Nissan, and the other foreign makes also remained prosperous, but not the Big Three. Only Ford survived without a federal government takeover.[232]

The sharp downward spiral culminated in the unthinkable, the "managed" bankruptcy in 2009 of General Motors and Chrysler under government auspices. Under the federal courts' protection, officials appointed by the Obama administration arbitrarily and randomly selected thousands of dealerships nationwide for closing, in the belief

230 *Holland Sentinel*, 24 Aug. 1997.

231 Robert De Nooyer Sr. kindly provided for annual sales totals and overal first place percentages.

232 *Holland Sentinel*, 2 Nov. 2001, 29 June 2008.

that less competition would increase the pricing power of the remaining dealers. Locally, Chrysler cancelled the franchises, without any compensation, of Ver Hage Chrysler and Elhart Dodge and Elhart Jeep. General Motors presented a "wind-down agreement" to Crown Motors' Buick and Cadillac franchises. These unilateral actions prompted the Wierdas to join a small consortium of dealers, the Committee to Restore Dealer Rights, who pressed Congress for two years to pass legislation that would allow *all* dealers to arbitrate for their franchises. General Motors then returned nearly seven hundred franchises without arbitration procedures. Crown Motors was one of the first to have the wind-down agreement rescinded.[233]

Car sales in 2009-10 dropped on average 30 percent nationally and 28 percent regionally, but West Michigan dealers held their own. De Nooyer Chevrolet experienced no further decline from the abysmal 2007-8 base; in 2011 it happily announced selling the first GM electric car, the Chevy Volt, which is powered by ion-lithium batteries manufactured in Michigan. (chapter 15)[234]

233 Ibid., 22 June, 1 Aug. 2009; conversation with Craig and Emily Wierda on 23 Dec. 2011.

234 *Holland Sentinel*, 31 July, 3 Sept. 2011.

Part Ten

Insurance and real estate

In the nineteenth century, many land agents and attorneys sold insurance to augment their income in an age before specialization in financial affairs. Isaac Marsilje, who entered the insurance business in 1875, was the veteran agent (see below). Kommer Schaddelee's agency, founded in 1873, continued for more than 125 years under various names: Arend Visscher, Arthur A. Visscher, Raymond Visscher in 1913, Visscher-Brooks (with Raymond Visscher and Earnest Brooks) by 1925, Visscher-Marcusse (with Peter Marcusse) in 1945, and Visscher-Brooks-Van Lente (with Dale Van Lente) in 1958. The Visschers were all Northwestern Mutual Life Insurance agents, located in the Bosman Block at 84 East Eighth Street.

In 1929 Visscher-Brooks Insurance moved from the Warm Friend Tavern a half block east to the former Peoples State Bank at 29 East Eighth Street. Brooks at the time was mayor of Holland. By 1945 Visscher-Brooks erected its own building at 6 East Eighth Street. Brooks stepped down to concentrate on his political post as Democratic Party chairman from 1943 to 1945, and in 1944 he made an unsuccessful run for governor in the Democratic primary. Peter Marcusse, a Northwestern Mutual agent next door at 8 East Eighth Street, who had earlier joined the firm, replaced Brooks as a partner. The other partner, Arthur A. Visscher, also maintained his own firm at the same address until he retired in 1958 and sold his interest to Dale Van Lente. In 1969 Van Lente took in John Heyboer as partner and the pair renamed the firm the Holland Insurance Agency, thus ending the Visscher and Brooks names after many decades. By 1975 Lawrence Overbeek was the resident Northwestern Life agent.[235]

John C. Post's real estate agency had become Garrod and Post, headed by William J. Garrod and Richard H. Post, at 27 West Eighth Street. John C. Post died by his own hand in 1903 (chapter 3), and Garrod became the sole owner, having bought out the Post family interests by 1915. Other firms were the McBride Insurance Agency of brothers Philip and Charles McBride at Eighth and River Streets, Peter Brusse over the post office at 4 East Eighth Street, Walter Walsh at 73 East Tenth Street (later 25 East Eighth Street), and John Bosman at 38 East Ninth Street.

[235] *Holland City News*, 17 Feb. 1942, 11 Nov. 1943; *Holland Sentinel*, Earnest C. Brooks obit., 16 Apr. 1981, 16 Feb. 1993; *Holland City Directories*, 1929-85.

Isaac Marsilje, 1917 (*Holland High School* Boomerang, *1917*)

These agencies were joined after 1900 by Fred T. Miles, a future Ottawa County judge, with an office above 44 East Eighth Street, Arthur Van Duren worked above 14 West Eighth Street, and William J. Olive, a representative of Franklin Life, leased space at 33 West Eighth Street and later at 190 River Avenue. Attorney Cornelius Vander Meulen was above 8 East Eighth Street and John Weersing's agency was upstairs at 30 East Eighth Street. By 1915 more national firms had a local agent, including Ben H. Veneklasen for John Hancock Life Insurance and Nick Whelan for Equitable Life of New York.[236]

John Arendshorst of J. Arendshorst Inc., the most prominent real estate and insurance agency, was always on Eighth Street, beginning at 6 East from 1921 to 1924, then at 61 East until 1938, and finally

Arthur A. Visscher in his law office, Visscher-Brooks Building, 6 East Eighth Street, 1940s (*Archives, Holland Historical Trust*)

236 *Holland City Directories*, 1906-15.

in the Waverly Building at 29 East Eighth Street. Arendshorst bought the building, owned by the Henry Post family for fifty years, and incorporated his business for $100,000. The offices of the John Galien Agency and Thomas Marsilje and Egbertus Stegink were above the First State Bank, and the offices of Henry Oosting and C. C. Wood were above Peoples State Bank. Others on Eighth Street, often in second floor offices, included Nicholas Hoffman Jr., Russell Klaasen, Isaac Kouw, Maurice Kuite, Lucien Raven of Raven-Kramer & Raven, and Bessie R. Weersing, the first female agent, who practiced for four decades, until well into the 1960s. Cornelius De Kuyzer and Bessel Vande Bunte were on Tenth Street, and William Kooyers was on East Sixteenth Street.[237] Old line firms that continued into the 1960s were Galien Agency at 246 River Avenue and later 40 West Tenth Street, Klaasen Realty at 311 River Street, Isaac Kouw Realty (joined by son Robert) at 29 West Eighth Street, Henry Oosting at 222 River Avenue, Bessie Weersing at 127 West Tenth Street, and C. C. Wood (joined by son William) in the Peoples State Bank Building.

Marsilje Insurance Agency has the distinction of being the oldest Holland business with an ownership tie to the founding family—five generations over 136 years—since 1875. By 1906 Isaac Marsilje was partnered with attorney Gerrit W. Kooyers. Isaac's son Thomas joined the business in 1914 and became president by 1924, with son Edward vice president and treasurer. Grandson Isaac Herbert "Herb" Marsilje replaced Thomas in 1935, and in 1984 great-grandson Thomas Marsilje II became president. At his death in 2010, ownership passed to two of his children, Thomas Marsilje III and Anne Marsilje-Meyers. With fifth-generation owners, the firm is truly "Holland's Hometown Agency." The agency occupied a number of buildings over the decades, mostly around Central Avenue between Eighth and Seventh Streets. They were upstairs of First National Bank at 1 West Eighth Street and Central Avenue from 1875 to until 1955, when the bank needed the space for their new computer room. Marsilje then moved to the former Buis Mattress building at 174 Central Avenue on the northwest corner of Seventh Street. When the bank bought that building for a parking lot in 1969, Marsilje moved around the corner to the former Volkswagen Garage at 21 West Seventh Street, where they remained until moving in 1989 to the Visscher-Brooks Building at 6 East Eighth Street. In 1994 the firm erected their own building at 68 West Eighth Street. Kenneth Kleis was one of Herb's long-time agents from 1950 until 1986. Kleis

[237] Ibid., 1934, 1936, 1938.

remembers him as a friendly, outgoing man who was "very easy to work for," and he added, "We never had an argument."[238]

Herb Marsilje, quick to seize opportunities, in 1962 opened Holland's first travel agency, Marsilje Travel Association (later MTA), within the insurance office, in conjunction with his wife June and Willard C. "Bill" Wichers, the Netherlands consul general in West Michigan. The gregarious Wichers doubtless convinced Marsilje to capitalize on the increasing air travel to the Netherlands of Dutch Americans, especially the postwar generation who wished to return for family events. Wichers himself flew to Amsterdam almost every year. Marsilje expanded across West Michigan with ten offices. Marvin Lanser managed the Holland office for forty-one years (1955-96). Herb's son Thomas II took over the travel agency in 1984, as well as the insurance agency. When the insurance agency moved from 21 West Seventh Street in 1989, MTA took over that building. In 1999 Thomas Marsilje II sold MTA to Arlyn Lanting, who resold quickly to Larry Van Liere of Pathfinders Travel, Marsilje's competitor since 1975 at 8 West Eighth Street. In 2012 Marsilje relocated to Seventh Street east of River Avenue.[239]

The growth of the city and the increasing number of automobiles required more agents over the years. Newcomers in the 1920s included Cornelius De Kuyzer at 57 West Tenth Street, Frank Lievense Sr., Andrew Postma with an office above Model Drug, Charles McBride (later the McBride-Crawford Agency) with Donald Crawford at 194 River Avenue, Ben Van Lente at 177 College Avenue, and Orin Wolbrink's Citizens Mutual at 68 West Eighth Street. Lievense found space in the 215 Central Avenue building of Benjamin Lievense next to the Willard Car Storage Battery Service, which had a car ramp to the basement in the rear. Van Lente took in his son Paul as partner by 1942, and they represented State Farm Insurance for several decades. The Lemmen-Simmons Agency with Benjamin Lemmen and Fennville's Jack Simmons, took over their offices by 1970. Lievense started the agency bearing his name in 1922 by selling auto policies out of his home and then in an office at 216 River Street and by 1945 in the Temple Building (former Masonic Temple) at 17 West Tenth Street. In 1993, after seventy years, his grandson James D.

238 Mike Lozon, "Lenders and Insurers among Retail Community's Oldest Businesses," *Holland Chamber News* (Aug. 1997): 9; *Holland City Directories*, 1952-2007. Pathfinders was located at 6 East Eighth Street from 1975 to 1988. Phone conversation with Ken Kleis, 4 Oct. 2011. I am grateful to Tom VanderPlow, vice president of insurance and business operations at Marsilje Insurance Co., for information about the company.

239 *Holland City Directories*, 1996-2010; *Holland Sentinel*, 4 July 1999; conversation with Marvin Lanser, Sept. 26, 2011.

Lievense building at 215 Central Avenue on northeast corner of Ninth Street, housing Willard Car Storage Battery Service, Frank Lievense Insurance Agency, and the Holland Bowling Center upstairs (*courtesy Larry B. Massie*)

Lievense owned the Lievense Insurance Agency. In 1995 James Lievense bought the Wolbrink Agency to form Wolbrink-Lievense Insurance.[240]

Wolbrink Agency began in Ganges in 1917 under Orin A. Wolbrink, with his daughters, Evelyn and Irene, keeping the books. Son Irving joined the firm in 1933 as a salesman, and about 1937 A. O. Wolbrink & Son moved to 68 West Eighth Street. Irving's son Robert and daughter Evelyn Wolbrink-Allen were partners by the late 1950s. With Irving's retirement in 1968, Robert Wolbrink Sr. became president, and he switched the agency from Citizens Mutual to Outstanding Insurance. In 1980 Robert Wolbrink became chairman of the board, and John Marble joined the agency as president. The family regained executive control in 1984, when Robert Jr. became president. Robert Sr. continued as board chair until 1989, and Robert Jr. remained president until 1995. He then sold out to James Lievense of Lievense Insurance, to form Wolbrink-Lievense Insurance. Robert Jr. stayed on as an agent for a few years and then retired. After eighty years and four generations, the Wolbrink family was no longer connected with insurance in Ottawa and Allegan Counties. From 1996 until Wolbrink-Lievense was dissolved

240 *Holland City Directories*, 1920-96.

in 2006, the firm had a series of presidents—James Lievense, Robert Frieling, Thomas Helmstetter, and Harold Burrell.[241]

In 1945 the *Holland City Directory* listed over thirty agencies, with newcomers Russell Haight, Simon Borr, Herman Brower, Russell Burton, Gus De Vries, Charles Drew, Steph Karsten, Peter Klaver, Julia Kluite, Henry Streur, Albert Van Huis Jr., John Vinkemulder, Alex Van Zanten (Equitable Life), and Carl Zickler. With John Arendshorst's death, his agency by 1942 became Arendshorst Insurance, until it closed in 1966. By 1960 the number of agencies surpassed sixty. Arnold W. Hertel started in 1945 and occupied various offices on Eighth Street until 1973. Twenty-year-old Jay Keuning began selling insurance that year, working out of his father John Keuning's Realty office on East Sixteenth Street. In 1961 Jay started the Keuning Insurance Agency, located across the bridge on North River Avenue. In 1995 Keuning merged with the Lighthouse Insurance Agency to form the Lighthouse-Keuning Insurance Group, which within a year erected a new building at 877 East Sixteenth Street to accommodate its twenty-eight agents and staff. The Holland Area Chamber of Commerce chose Keuning for its 1998 Small Business Person of the Year Award. Two years later Keuning sold his portion of the agency and retired.[242]

More recently, State Farm Insurance has been represented by three agencies—Ken Johnson, Laurel Beukelman, and Coert Vander Hill. Farm Bureau has two agencies, Cal Timmer and Mark Hop; Wilk & Son represent Progressive Insurance. Other agencies with local offices are Allstate and Grand Rapids-based Berends Hendriks Stuit.[243]

Realtors in the old days doubled as insurance agents and often as lawyers, but the sustained housing boom after the Second World War gave rise to specialized realty companies. Anticipating the good times, and seeing the need for a cooperative effort, six brokers in 1944 founded the Holland Board of Realtors, which was changed in 1997 to the Holland Association of Realtors, to avoid comparisons to authoritative corporate boards. The association office was located at Fifteenth Street and River Avenue, in a building that was given a $100,000 facelift in 1997. In 2000 the Holland board merged with those of Muskegon, Grand Haven, and Saugatuck-Douglas to form the West Michigan Lakeshore Association of Realtors, based south of Grand Haven.[244]

241 *Holland City Directories*, 1929-99.

242 *Holland Sentinel*, 7 Oct. 1998, Jay Keuning obit., 25 June 2008.

243 *Holland Chamber News* (Sept. 1997): 9; *Holland City Directories*, 1960, 1964, 1970.

244 *Holland Sentinel*, 14 Dec. 1997. Presidents of the Holland Board of Realtors were: Lucien Raven (1944-45), Henry Oosting (1946-47), Isaac Kouw (1948-49), John

Members of the board in 1945 included the veterans John Galien, Jacob Grasmeyer, Klaasen, Kouw, Marsilje, Oosting, Raven, Vande Bunte, Weersing, and Wood, plus newcomers Herman Bos and Frank Lievense. In the 1950s board members were the veterans Arendshorst, Bos, Galien, Grasmeyer, Klaasen, Kooyers, Kouw, Kramer, Oosting, Percy Osborne, Henry Pieper, Raven, John P. Roels, Eugene Vande Vusse, Weersing, and William L. Wood. Newcomers were the second female realtor, May Kooyers, and John Keuning, both of Keuning Realty, and William C. De Roo of De Roo Realty.[245]

De Roo, an engineer, came to Holland from Cincinnati to work for Hart & Cooley. Seeing the postwar housing boom, De Roo in 1945 began selling real estate on the side. He enjoyed the work so much that after eleven years, in 1956, he went into the business full time, opening an office in a house at 327 River Avenue on the corner of Fourteenth Street. De Roo was one of the original organizers of HEDCOR (chapter 15) in 1961. In 1966 he was the first realtor to advertise listings on a daily basis in the *Holland Sentinel*. Soon he was buying full-page ads featuring new homes in subdivisions that the firm platted on Holland's south side.[246]

Realtors in the 1960s and early 1970s were Dennis Pieper (son of Henry) of Pieper Realty, the husband and wife team of LaRue "Rudy" and Francis Seats (L. & F. Real Estate), Hazen Van Kampen of Tulip City Realty, Bill Van Wieren of Van Wieren Realty, Tubergen Realty, Wilma Tuls of Tuls Realty, Gerald Van Noord of Van Noord Realty, Bessie Weersing, Leonard Westdale of Westdale Realty, Robert "Bob" Wiersma, and Nick Yonker of Yonker Realty. Female members of the Holland Board of Realtors in the early 1960s were Irene Steffens of

---

Galien (1950-51), Russell Klaasen (1952-53), C. C. Wood (1953-54), Robert J. Kouw (1956-58), Jack Galien (1959-60), William L. Wood (1961-62), William C. De Roo (1963-64), Hazen Van Kampen (1865-66), Harris D. Pieper, (1967-68), Gerald Van Noord (1969), Percy Nienhuis (1970), Jack De Roo (1971), Francis Seats (1972), Robert Tubergen (1973), Robert Piers (1974), LaRue Seats (1975), Roger MacLeod (1976), Nicholas Yonker (1977), William Sikkel (1978), Wilma Gebben (1979), John P. Tysse (1980), Harold Lampen (1981), Ron Boeve (1972, 1994), Graham Duryee (1983, 1998), Gordon Veurink (1984), Jack W. Bouman (1985), Jill C. Brown (1986), Wayne Boeve (1987), John J. Smith (1988), Richard Track (1989), Linda Scharlow (1990), Robert Piers (1991, 1996), Edwin Zehner (1992, 1999), Earl "Webb" Dalman and Gary VanLangeveld (1993), Hendrika "Henri" Paterson (1995), and Tom Speet (1997). See Holland Board of Realtors Records, HMA.

245 *Holland City Directories*, 1940, 1945, 1947-48, 1954.

246 "ReMax of Holland," in Larry B. Massie, *The Holland Area: Warm Friends and Wooden Shoes* (Northridge, CA: Windsor Publications, 1988), 116; *Holland Sentinel*, 23 Aug. 1963; Conversation with Jack De Roo, 16 May 2011.

Tulip City, Frances Seats of Vande Vusse Realty, Mary Medema of Van Wieren Realty, Jessie Nyland of Keuning Realty, and Norma Stroike of Wiersma Real Estate. They were soon joined by dozens more women in the profession.[247]

Jack De Roo began selling in his father's office at age twenty-one in 1962. Twelve years later, in 1974, William retired and Jack took over the business. Jack expanded the offices at 327 River Avenue and built up the business, but he had bigger ambitions. In 1984 he affiliated with Re/Max, an international realty franchise operation formed in 1976. His wife Henny, a former schoolteacher, joined the firm in 1986. Re/Max of Holland gained a reputation for innovation. For instance, the company bought a moving van to offer clients free local moving; one of his realtors, an ex-trucker, drove the tractor and handled the moves. The service gave a big boost to business at the firm, and soon twelve other Re/Max agencies in Michigan had moving vans. In 1998 De Roo sold his River Avenue office and built new offices at 593 Heritage Court near US-31 and East Twenty-Fourth Street. In 2009 Re/Max Lakeshore sold that building and rented the former Hub Insurance Building at 245 Central Avenue at Tenth Street. In 2012 Re/Max Lakeshore moved again a block north to 210 Central Avenue.[248]

The major local firms since the 1970s include Woodland Realty, Grand Rapids-based Westdale, Greenridge of Graham Duryee, Summit Properties of Tom Speet, David Gritter of Five Star Realty, Vogue, Roger MacLeod of MacLeod Realty, and Jack De Roo of Re/Max of Holland. In 1971 the Holland Board of Realtors under president Jack De Roo established the Million Dollar Club to recognize annually the highest performing realtors. The first year, only three qualified—Ernest Wehrmeyer and Roger Brower of the Galien Agency and John Tysse of Russell Klaasen Realtors. The next year, 1972, eight realtors went over the million dollar mark in total sales: Wehrmeyer and Brown repeated and were joined by Gerald Klein, Gary Jaarda, William A. Sikkel (the future mayor), Lou Hekman, Jill C. Brown, and Marge Miller.[249] MacLeod bought the Russell Klaasen Realty at 311 River Avenue and renamed the firm MacLeod's Gallery of Homes. He later sold to Greenridge Realty.

Woodland Realty, founded in December 1972 by Jaarda, Tysse, and James Jurries, grew in twelve years from an $8.5 million to a $33.8 million

247 *Holland City Directories*, 1960, 1964, 1970; *Holland Sentinel*, 24 Dec. 1962, 22 Apr. 1976.

248 "ReMax of Holland"; Conversation with Jack De Roo, 16 May 2011.

249 The Million Dollar Club program is outlined in a letter from Jack De Roo, president, to "Fellow Realtors," 12 Feb. 1971, Holland Board of Realtors Records, HMA.

William C. and Jack De Roo in front of De Roo Realty Co., 327 River Avenue, (now Lenk Transportation) in 1974, with William symbolically handing over the business to son Jack (*courtesy Jack De Roo and Larry B. Massie*)

business that dominates the market. Jurries bought out his partners before selling in 1981 to a group of six shareholders, including Jack W. Bouman, Ron Boeve, and Hendrika "Henri" Paterson. Woodland's large team of agents operated out of a brick building at 466 East Sixteenth Street across from Pilgrim Home Cemetery. The firm opened branch offices in Grand Haven, Saugatuck, Zeeland, Muskegon, and Fennville. In 2001 Woodland partnered with Chicago Title Company, the nation's largest title insurer, to form the Woodland Title Company.[250]

Following the stagflation of the late 1970s, home sales and average prices climbed steadily for twenty-five years, despite periodic downturns in the national economy. The top came in the first half of 2005. Almost two thousand homes sold in 2004, and the average price in the first half of 2005 reached $200,000, but the average selling time of the 1,700 listings stretched beyond one hundred days. This marked the beginning of the worst shakeout in the real estate market since the Great Depression.[251]

In 2006 the five Woodland Realty partners–Bouman, Paterson, Gary Beckman, Jeff Young, and William Vande Vusse–sold Woodland, the region's flagship realty with 190 agents, to Ken Schmidt of the Traverse City-based Coldwell Banker Schmidt agency. Schmidt's was

[250] *Holland Sentinel*, 29 Oct. 1984, 23 Sept. 2001, 25 May 2003.
[251] Ibid., 21 Aug. 2005.

the second largest realty company along the lakeshore, with $1 million in listings, twice the volume of Woodland. Schmidt was affiliated with Coldwell Banker, an international company based in New Jersey, with 132,000 realtors and 3,600 offices. Bouman stayed on as president of the new local agency, renamed Coldwell Banker Woodland Schmidt. When Bouman realized that the merger had changed the personality of the agency and disrupted relationships, he decided to sell his agency to Westdale Realty, which added the 150 Woodland agents to its West Michigan franchise. Less than two months later, Re/Max of Grand Rapids purchased from Jack De Roo and Doug Van Oss their Re/Max/Vogue agency in Holland with fifty agents, as well as the Grand Haven Re/Max agency with twenty-five agents. The combined company, with 150 agents, became Re/Max Lakeshore, based in Grand Haven, and affiliated with national Re/Max chain with 120,000 agents.[252]

The rational for each merger was to gain economies of scale, which allowed the companies to survive. In 2010 the Coldwell Banker Woodland Schmidt agency dominated the Western and Northern Michigan market and ranked in the Top 20 among Coldwell Banker affiliates nationally. But the ranks of individual realtors since 2006 have been cut by 40 percent, due to plunging property values and mortgage foreclosures. Agents in droves became "drops," that is, they gave up their licenses and left the profession. Some may live to regret it, since the market regained strength in 2011 and 2012.[253]

Contracting and engineering

Six contracting firms have dominated the Holland-Zeeland construction market: Elzinga & Volkers, founded in 1945 by Peter "Pete" Elzinga and John Volkers; Parkway Electric founded by Elton Achterhof in 1945; Lakewood Construction, formed in 1971 by Harold Branderhorst; GDK Construction, founded in 1982 by partners Chuck Geenen and Doug De Kock; Bouwens Construction of Zeeland founded by Glen J. Bouwens in 1956; and Lamar Construction, founded by Robert Lamar in 2002. Elzinga & Volkers began at 222 River Avenue until 1950 when the partners moved to their present location at 86 East Sixth Street. Elzinga had done architectural design work for almost twenty years, since 1931, and his construction company always provided this service. Elzinga bowed out in 1953, and Volkers carried on; the firm in the 1950s and 1960s employed up to 175 men and did jobs from

252 Ibid., 29, 30 Aug., 15 Sept., 1 Dec. 2006, 28 June 2007.

253 Ibid., 28 Feb. 2010.

Pete Elzinga in his office at 86 East Sixth Street
(*courtesy Elzinga & Volkers and Larry B. Massie.*)

Holland to Sault Ste. Marie. In 1967 his sons Paul and Martin "Marty" joined the firm. In the 1980s Paul became president and Marty the chief executive officer of Elzinga & Volkers, and Marty doubled as president of the construction subsidiary E & V Inc. The pair developed strong ties with the multimillion-dollar Japanese firm, Maeda Construction, and became Maeda's US partner. Since 1997 Elzinga & Volkers has been the general contractor for many major projects: rebuilding the fire-ravaged St. Francis de Sales Church, the ITW Drawform plant, expansion of the Zeeland-based Ottawa Door Light plant, the $50 million renewal of the Gerald R. Ford International Airport in Grand Rapids, the Paragon Bank building on East Eighth Street, the restoration of Hope Church, the Virginia Park Fire Station, the major renovation of Lubbers Hall and the $15 million Haworth Inn & Conference Center on the Hope College campus, and the $37 million Zeeland Community Hospital.[254]

One project that got away was the $10 million Holland police station and district court on West Eighth Street in 2002. When the city council in a split vote let the contract to an Ada-based firm, Peter Elzinga protested: "Our company needs this work to keep people employed in Holland." H. J. "Jim" Buter, Harvey's son, wrote a scathing letter to the *Sentinel* editor castigating city leaders for snubbing the leading local

[254] Larry B. Massie, *The Holland Area: Warm Friends and Wooden Shoes* (Northridge, CA: Windsor Publications, 1988), 112-13; *Holland City News*, 16 Nov. 1997, 8 Mar., 6 Dec. 1998, 21 Apr. 2002, 14 Sept. 2002, 14 Mar., 12 Oct. 2003, 6 Aug. 2004.

contractor at a time when LifeSavers was closing and Herman Miller was laying off six hundred employees. Paul Koop, another protesting letter writer, declared: "City bites the hand that feeds it." Despite the firestorm, the council held firm. In 2005 Paul Elzinga turned the company presidency over to Michael Novakoski, with Michael King continuing as CEO. The company had $38 million in revenue in 2010. In 2011 the firm achieved a safety milestone of 1,500 injury-free days on the part of its eighty to one hundred workers, thanks to strong safety guidelines, job training, and construction procedures. Elzinga & Volkers is clearly the "big boy" among local contractors.[255]

Elton Achterhof mastered the trade of electrician working for the venerable old firm, De Fouw's Electric Shop, founded by Herman De Fouw before 1913 at 28 East Eighth Street. In 1945 Achterhof struck out on his own, working from his home at 595 South Shore Drive. By 1952 he had taken Cornelius Oonk as a partner and by 1954 the newly named Parkway Electric moved to its own shop at 700 Ottawa Avenue, where it remained for thirty years. About 1974 Deane Lankheet joined the company as president and in 1983 Achterhof's son Robert G. became vice president and Ronald Kapenga was secretary treasurer. The next year, after three decades on Ottawa Avenue the firm relocated to 11952 James Street, where it continues. By 1991 the next generation of Achterhofs, Allen and James, were company officers, with Allen as president and James as vice president. About 1999 the Achterhof family sold the electrical and communications to the Grand Rapids-based Huizenga Group, owned by entrepreneur J. C. Huizenga, who also founded National Heritage Academies (chapter 7). Since 2005 Doug Mitchell has been the president of Parkway Electric.[256]

Lakewood Construction grew out of Branderhorst Construction, owned by brothers Arnold, Donald, and Harold Branderhorst. By 1949 Arnold was a building contractor with Harold as a mason and Donald and Harold as carpenters. The business was run out of Arnold's home at 486 Lakewood Boulevard. By 1962 Arnold and Donald ran Branderhorst Construction, and Harold had partnered with Earnest Vander Hulst, with both businesses run out of 486 Lakewood. Donald retired in 1965 and Arnold turned to a blueberry farm on Riley Street. By 1971 Harold had renamed the firm Lakewood Construction, and in 1973 he purchased land in Holland Township at 11395 Lakewood

255 *Business Review West Michigan* 15, no. 43 (2010): 19-20, 23; *Holland Sentinel*, 27 Nov. 1987, 27 Oct. 1997, 21 Feb. (quote), 23(Buter quote), 27 Mar. (Koop quote), 14 Apr. 2002, 10 July 2005, 6 May 2006, 8 Mar. 2007, 11 July 2010, 16 July 2011.

256 *Holland City Directories*, 1910-2012.

Boulevard and erected a building to house offices and equipment. His sons Terry and Chris joined him by 1976. Lakewood was incorporated by 1979 with Harold as president and Maynard Miedema as vice president. In recent years, Lakewood Construction under president James Stroop renovated Graves Hall at Hope College and erected Plaza Center on East Eighth Street. Earlier projects included the award-winning clubhouse at the Ravines Golf Course north of Holland, the United Manufacturing plant in the Northside Industrial Park, the Bank of Holland headquarters building on the northwest corner of Seventh Street and Central Avenue, the Holland High School gymnasium addition, and the $3 million Black River Public School. The firm, which relocated in 1996 to 11253 James Street, in 2010 had thirty-five employees and $35 million in revenue.[257]

GDK Construction is owned by Chuck Geenen and Doug De Kock. It was started by Geenen's father Ade (Adrian), a former funeral home director and real estate developer who died in February 2012. In 2000 GDK won top honors from the Associated Builders and Contractors for the historical renovation of its downtown offices at 12 West Eighth Street. GDK's major projects in the last decade include the development of Felch Plaza (the retail strip at US 31 and Riley), the renovation of JB Laboratories, and the construction of the corporate headquarters of Macatawa Bank on Eighth Street at Columbia Avenue and Boatwerks Waterfront Restaurant and City Flats Hotel. GDK Construction recently expanded and renovated both Holland Christian and Holland High Schools; erected the Van Andel Soccer Stadium at Hope College; developed Midtown Village, the former E. E. Fell Junior High; and built the Johnson Controls Lithium Ion Battery Plant. The firm's real estate arm, Geenen De Kock Properties, has managed thirty-one properties with more than 1.5 million square feet, notably Felch Plaza.[258]

Bouwens Construction had its origins with Glen J. Bouwens of Zeeland in 1956. His brother Howard joined the business in 1961, and it became Bouwens & Sons. In 1985 Glenn incorporated and son Joel joined him. In 1988 Glenn stepped back in favor of another son, John, who became president, while Glenn became vice president. The firm continued in Zeeland until 1996, when John's brother James (Jim) took over and relocated to 348 Waverly Road. From 1998 to 2003, the firm

[257] *Holland Sentinel*, 19 Aug., 25 Nov. 2001, 11, 17 Aug. 2002, 28 Nov. 2004, 20 Apr., 19 June 2006.

[258] Ibid., 30 Aug. 1998, 5 Nov. 2000, 27 Nov. 2001, 6 Jan. 2002, 2 June, 17 Sept. 2005, 3 July 2007, 29 Sept. 2009, 22 Sept. 2101.

renovated the Zeeland city hall, erected the Ottawa Kent-Koop Insurance building on Waverly Road and Chicago Drive, the Herman Miller plant in the North Holland Commerce Center, the Lake Michigan Credit Union building on Eighth Street and Waverly Road, the Rose Park Plaza strip mall at Butternut Drive and Riley Street north of Walgreen's Drug Store, and renovated the Macatawa Bank building in Zeeland. In 1999 the company moved into a new facility at 11379 Lakewood Boulevard in Holland Township. That year Bouwens Construction was named "Outstanding Builder of the Year" by the Star Building System organization for its construction of a new office building for ATLA Transportation Services, a locally-based trucking company. Mike Miedema became project manager of Bouwens & Sons in 2002.[259]

In the midst of the commercial and industrial building boom at the turn of the twenty-first century, Robert Lamar in 2002 launched Lamar Construction, located at A-4608 66th Street. The next year he sold the fledgling business to Carl Blauwkamp of Hudsonville, who in 2005 relocated the company to Hudsonville. Bruce and Carl Lamar, meanwhile, operated Lamar Bros. Construction at 15595 Ranson Street in Holland Township.[260]

Engineering and architectural companies that work closely with these construction contractors are GMB Architecture + Engineering, founded in 1968; Driesenga and Associates; Enviro-Clean Building Maintenance Services, launched in 1975; and Pennsylvania-based Environmental Resources Management, whose Holland branch was opened in 1978. Gordon M. Buitendorp founded GMB with the help of Peter Elzinga, who gave Buitendorp space in a corner of his basement shop on Sixth Street. The first major job was designing the Ex-Cell-O Corp. plant on Forty-Eighth Street. In the early 1970s GMB designed the new Brooks Products plant and new terminal for Holland Motor Express on Fortieth Street. In 1976 mechanical engineer Jim Vanderveen joined GMB's eight architects, and the engineering division was born. By the early 1980s, Buitendorp had his own building and a team of nearly fifty specialists. GMB had a hand in almost every major construction project in the Holland area since the 1980s. The firm designed the Macatawa Bank headquarters on Paw Paw Drive, the Plaza Center on East Eighth Street in 2002, and the Holland High School gymnasium in 2004. In 2010, under president Harm Perdok, GMB had twelve

259 Ibid., 6 Dec. 1998, 16 May, 5 Dec. 1999, 7, 21 May, 19 Oct. 2000, 25 Aug. 2002, 25 May 2003; *Holland City Directories*, 1960-88.

260 *Holland City Directories*, 2000-2012.

licensed engineers and fifty-six other staff in upstairs offices at 85 East Eighth Street. Recent projects include the Van Andel Soccer Stadium at Hope College, the Spoelhof Fieldhouse Complex at Calvin College, and the baseball stadium and student housing at Cornerstone University of Grand Rapids. In 2012 GMB acquired Grand Rapids-based Visbeen Associates, with which it had collaborated on the Cornerstone projects. GMB has eighty employees compared to Visbeen's nine.[261]

Dan Driesenga of Driesenga & Associates first secured major contracts between 1998 and 2000, such as the Waverly Road extension south of Forty-Eighth Street, the Ramada Inn, and the Old Navy store. In 2000 Driesenga purchased for the company's main office the former Federal School at 137 Walnut and East Eighth Street, which had served as Black River's first campus. In 2002 Dan Driesenga won a coveted Entrepreneur of the Year award from Ernst & Young, one of the Big Seven accounting firms. Driesenga & Associates gained contracts for the new North River Avenue bridge, the Macatawa Legends golf course, the Zeeland Ottawa Door Light expansion, and the Mercantile Bank of Holland banking center on Sixteenth Street; they are also heavily involved in designing the massive Park Drain project.[262]

Enviro-Clean Building Maintenance Services in 2010 had 750 employees in West Michigan under president Dan Koster with revenue of $15 million. Its Holland offices are at 2457 112th Avenue in Holland Township. Steve Koster, a partner and manager of the Environmental Resources Holland branch in 2010, supervised eight engineers and thirty-four other staff, who did risk consulting in environmental, health, and safety services. All three companies are among the Top Fifty private companies in West Michigan.[263]

261 "GMB Architects-Engineers," in Larry B. Massie, *Haven, Harbor, and Heritage, The Holland, Michigan Story* (Allegan Forest, MI: Priscilla Press, 1996), 151; *Holland Sentinel*, 6 Jan., 17 Aug., 29 Sept. 2002, 25 May 2003, 13 July 2012.

262 *Holland Sentinel*, 10 July, 15 Oct., 8 Nov. 1998, 5 Nov. 2000, 26 Apr. 2002, 4 Apr., 25 Nov. 2003, 6 Feb., 4 Aug., 14 Nov. 2004, 17 Apr. 2005, 18 Apr., 15 May 2009.

263 *Business Review West Michigan* 15, no. 43 (2010): 11, 22, 64; *Holland Sentinel*, 29 Sept. 2009, 16 Jan. 2011.

Part Eleven

Bank mergers since the 1930s

Holland's banks have merged into or been acquired by larger banks, first from Grand Rapids and Detroit, and then from Ohio and Pennsylvania.[264] In 1936 in the throes of the Great Depression, as noted earlier in this chapter, Holland City State Bank and First State Bank merged after losing half their deposits to form Holland State Bank. Ten years later, in 1946, Holland State Bank became First National Bank. In 1973 First National was bought by First of America Bank Corporation, which, in turn, was acquired in 1997 by Cleveland-based National City Bank. In 2009 Pittsburgh-based PNC purchased National City Bank. So Holland City Bank and First State Bank, since their founding in 1889 and 1890, respectively, went through four mergers and name changes and ended up in the hands of out-of-state banks. Its home since 1915 has remained the stately building at 1 West Eighth Street.

Peoples State Bank occupied prominent places on Eighth Street, first a Grecian-style building erected at 29 East Eighth Street and then in 1918 an emporium at 36-38 East Eighth Street. In 1973 the bank became a subsidiary of Grand Rapids-based Old Kent Bank. Ottawa County Building (later Savings) & Loan, founded in 1888, and located variously in the Tower Clock Building (1937-45), 9 East Eighth Street (1947-51), and 245 Central Avenue (1951-99), purchased Muskegon-based AmeriBank in 1995 and took its name. Within five years, in 2000, eight months after AmeriBank passed the $1 billion mark in assets, Fifth Third Bank of Cincinnati purchased Old Kent Bank for $160 million. Key bank executives for many years at Old Kent's Holland branch were Laverne "Curly" Dalman, Harvey Buter, Jerrald "Jerry" Redeker, and Clarence Klaasen.[265]

The out-of-state acquisitions led former bank officials to start three local banks: Macatawa Bank (by Benjamin Smith III of First Michigan and Phillip Koning of First of America) in Zeeland in 1997 and Holland in 1998; Bank of Holland (by Richard Lievense of Old Kent) in 1998; and a Holland branch of Grand Rapids-based Mercantile Bank (by Redeker of Old Kent) in 2004. In 2006 Fifth Third, Macatawa,

[264] This section relies heavily on Steve Vander Veen, "A History of Holland-area Banking," Power Point presentation for the Holland Historical Society, 31 Dec. 2007, kindly provided to the author.

[265] Phillip J. Koning, "First of America Bank," *Holland Sentinel*, 30 Jan. 1992, 30 June 1993, 25 Sept. 1994, 25 Nov., 2, 7 Dec. 1997, 13 Jan. 1998, 1 Sept. 2000.

and Bank of Holland each had either 21 or 22 percent of the Holland market, with Huntington at 11 percent and Mercantile below 1 percent. It is a classic "battle of the banks" in the "ultra-competitive" lakeshore banking market, said *Holland Sentinel* business editor Patrick Sanchez.[266]

Macatawa Bank started with $8 million in capital put up by forty-six investors. In the early years the community bank grew rapidly in tandem with local residential real estate, and it opened one branch after another. To raise capital for further expansion, the bank went public in 1998 with an initial common stock offering that yielded $12 million, followed in 1999 by a second sale that yielded $14.6 million. In 2003 "Mac Bank" built its headquarters building on Business I-196 and Paw Paw Drive in Holland Township. By then it had grown to seventeen branches and $1.2 billion in assets. In 2006 the bank opened its three-story downtown bank on East Eighth Street at Columbia Avenue. Ben Smith in 2006 sold his investment management firm to Macatawa Bank for $3.15 million in bank stock (137,000 shares). It proved to be a mistake. Since 2006 Macatawa's market share, assets, profits, and share price have plummeted on a raft of bad loans. Two local golf clubs went bankrupt—the Holland Country Club and Macatawa Legends—and two borrowers committed fraud. Non-performing loans rose to nearly $50 million, and the stock price fell from a high of $23 per share in 2006 to $1.50 in 2009. In early 2010 the Securities and Exchange Commission (SEC) auditor expressed "substantial doubt about the bank's ability to continue as a growing concern." The SEC demanded that the executives raise $31 million in additional capital, which they did. In 2009 the founding officers, Ben Smith, Phil Koning, and Robert Den Herder resigned, and Ronald Haan was named CEO and Richard Postma board chair. The smaller, leaner bank under new leadership returned to profitability in mid-2010 after two years of losses.[267]

The Bank of Holland prudently leased space in the first years and did not open branch offices. In 2002 the bank erected a two-story headquarters building on East Seventh Street at Central Avenue in 2002. It has weathered the financial crisis since 2007 far better than Macatawa Bank and seems to be winning the battle of the banks. This should not be surprising, since investors include the city's most influential business leaders: John Spoelhof of the former Prince Corp., Donald Heeringa of

[266] *Holland Sentinel*, 3 Dec. 2006 (quote), 16, 25 Nov. 1997, 1 Nov. 2004, 13 Mar. 2005.

[267] *Holland Sentinel*, 3 Apr. 1998, 31 Jan., 16 Apr., 20 June 1999, 18 May 2003, 24 Oct. 2004, 16 Oct., 19 Dec. 2007, 6, 8 Nov. 2008, 10 Feb., 12 Aug., 4 Nov. 2009, 7 Apr., 9 May, 3 Aug. 2010; *Grand Rapids Press Lakeshore Edition*, 15 June 2005, 13 Oct. 2006.

Trendway, Patrick Thompson of Trans-Matic, Dennis Ellens of Lumir Corp., and now Hudsonville Ice Cream, and others.[268]

In Zeeland, Den Herder's bank of 1878 became Zeeland State Bank in 1901, which acquired State Commercial Savings Bank of Holland in 1937 and opened branches across West Michigan in the 1950s and 1960s. In 1973 First Michigan Bank Corporation, a publicly traded holding company, bought Zeeland State Bank. Huntington National Bank of Columbus, Ohio, in turn, acquired First Michigan Bank Corp. in 1997. In 2006 Huntington Bank had 65 percent of the Zeeland market.[269]

268 *Holland Sentinel*, 9 May 1998, 13 Oct. 2002.

269 *Grand Rapids Press Lakeshore Edition*, 5 Oct. 1997.

Part Twelve

Physicians and medical groups

Physicians were a classic case of entrepreneurs who operated their own businesses as sole proprietors, perhaps with a partner or two. But in the last twenty-five years, government regulations, insurance company "red tape," and six-figure malpractice insurance rates, have forced many physicians to form ever-larger groups. Michigan Medical PC (MMPC) enrolled dozens of Holland/Zeeland-area physicians in the 1990s, and in 2010 the entire group merged with Spectrum Health Systems of Grand Rapids, the largest medical system in West Michigan. Now hundreds of local physicians are essentially employees of an outside medical conglomerate.

In 2012 Spectrum Health dedicated a new facility on East Lakewood Boulevard to consolidate five offices under one roof. Some physicians, particularly surgeons and specialists, continue to own their practices, for example, Holland Foot and Ankle Centers, Lakeshore Dermatology of Jack Dekkinga, West Michigan Heart, Lakeshore Internal Medicine & Pediatric Associates, OB/GYN Associates, Holland Eye Surgery & Laser Center of John H. Arendshorst and Eric Snyder, Sight Eye Clinic, Shoreline Orthopedics, and Shoreline Area Radiation Oncology Center. Plastic surgeons, dermatologists, fertility specialists, and dentists treat patients mostly on a self-pay, cash basis. Thus, they have been fortunate not to fall under the sway of insurance companies and government agencies and have remained independent businesses.

Conclusion

Henry ten Hoor, a native Hollander and long-time English professor at Hope College, when asked by an interviewer in 1996 what part the Dutch heritage plays in the community, replied that the Dutch were characteristically God-fearing, law-abiding, hardworking, and diligent in paying their bills on time. They hung together and built wealth slowly but inexorably by pinching pennies, saving religiously, and tithing faithfully.[270]

These are the ingredients in the strong tradition of entrepreneurship in Holland. Family-owned businesses are the hallmark of the city's retail and wholesale trade. The longest running, inter-generational businesses

[270] Henry ten Hoor interview by Tracy Bednarick, 27 June 1996, typescript, 18, 24, 26-27, JAH.

were (and are) the banker Van Putten, Vander Veen's Hardware, Teunis Keppel's Modern Hardware, Austin Harrington's coal yard, Muller's Standard Grocery, Loker's Shoes, Borr's Bootery, Vogelzang Hardware, Fabiano's Peanut Store, Fris Hallmark and Office Outfitters, Meyer Music House, Teermans, Jousma's Main Sport and Marine, funeral homes of Dykstra (Kleinheksel) and Langeland-Sterenberg (earlier Nibbelink, Notier, Ver Lee), insurance agencies Marsilje, Wolbrink, and Lievense, West Michigan and Ideal Laundries, Louis Padnos Iron & Metal, Brewer's Dry Dock, Haworth, Howard Miller, Donnelly, S-2 Yachts, De Vries & Dornbos, Model Drug, Wade Drug, A. D. Bos, Boer's Transfer, Gra-Bell Trucking (Van Wyk), Associated Truck Lines (Scholten), Heidema Bros. Trucking, Holland Motor (Cooper), Russ' Restaurant, Wiersma's Central Park Foods, Lambert's Poultry, Montello Meat Market, Family Fare, Hemple's Bakery (now de Boer Bakerij), De Nooyer Chevrolet, and Ver Hage Motors.

CHAPTER 20

The Progressive Era

Gerrit J. Diekema in a speech at the dedication of the new city hall in 1911 urged his hearers "of every occupation and profession, of every faith, creed, nationality and shade of political belief [to] work together with a unity of purpose for the common good" and to subordinate "personal ambition . . . to the public weal." As the motto, *Eendracht maakt macht* (In union is strength), produced the Golden Age of the Netherlands, so the same ideal would write the progressive history of Holland. "Our past is creditable and our future is full of promise," Diekema declared. His comparison with the Dutch Golden Age was nothing new, but his emphasis on unity in diversity was. The Progressive Era was birthed by a new worldview, one that put its faith in the unstoppable progress of humankind and the betterment of society through invention, adaptation, and reform. The future was bright, and Diekema had every reason to hope. "I see the great forces of today working into the future with resistless power and energy."[1]

1 Gerrit J. Diekema, 8 Apr. 1911, Diekema Papers, box 4, Holland Museum Archives (HMA). *Eendracht Maakt Macht* is also the motto of the Reformed Church in America.

Crowds attend the dedication of city hall, April 1911
(*courtesy Myron Van Ark*)

By 1900 someone born in the mid-nineteenth century could look back with amazement at what the past fifty years had brought. Diekema's "great forces" had been busy. Railroads and automobiles for transportation and the telegraph and the telephone for communication revolutionized daily life (chapter 25). Assembly lines, sewing machines, and a female workforce had forever altered manufacturing. Powered flight was on the horizon. In fact, everything seemed to be within grasp. The unstoppable belief in progress, humane values, open gender roles, and reformist politics demanded activism in every aspect of society. In the quarter century known as the Progressive Era, the social makeup of the United States changed in some fundamental ways. Governments at all levels began to take an active role in caring for the poor, aged, and disadvantaged. Rapid industrialization raised the issue of reconciling capital and labor, and urban social problems had to be faced with renewed enthusiasm.

Social divisions

A few years earlier, Diekema in another public address in Holland noted with pride that "members of all classes" were in attendance.[2] In previous decades, such a statement about class would have been unheard of, even insulting, but during the Progressive Era, social divisions became more accepted and more defined. At the top of Holland's social ladder was an established group that controlled most of the city's businesses, churches, and schools. These were factory owners, bankers,

2 *De Grondwet*, 21 July 1908.

shopkeepers, entrepreneurs, and educators. More than in past decades, these men—almost all were male—saw themselves as different from laborers and farmers. They were the caretakers of the city, responsible for ensuring its prosperity and growth. Duty demanded that they take a leading role on business and municipal committees, on school boards, and social clubs. It was their philanthropic responsibility to feed and clothe the poor. Few of the elite were fabulously rich. Few built mansions or lived extravagantly. In contrast to a city like Muskegon, which had some forty lumber baron millionaires in the early twentieth century, Holland had only a handful of millionaires. The Cappon home on West Ninth Street was one of the few mansions. Hollanders, especially of the Reformed faith, eschewed conspicuous consumption and stressed stewardship and equality of all before God. For religious and cultural reasons, therefore, the divide between the upper class and a strong middle class was not very obvious in Holland, apart from bank account ledgers.

The technological advances that led to the prosperity of the Progressive Era had the most effect on the middle class. A move away from subsistence farming and the introduction of labor-saving technology allowed time for recreation, and the growing number of merchants and skilled tradesmen could enjoy new-fangled, electric gadgets.

One result of increased free time was a marked rise in the number of social clubs and organizations. Clubs were formed to fit everyone's tastes (chapter 29). This included the Woman's Literary Club in 1894; the Century Club, a literary and musical circle, in 1897; and the Social Progress Club, a male-only organization in 1911. The YWCA was formed at Hope College in 1901, the Macatawa Bay Yacht Club was chartered in 1895, and the Holland Chapter of the Daughters of the American Revolution (DAR) was founded by a group of New England-descended women in 1907. For Republican Party activists, there was a Lincoln Club and a McKinley Club (originally called the Diekema Club), while the Democrats had their Wilson Club (chapter 24). A farmer's association formed to lobby for fair prices in selling, among other things, beets to the sugar factory and cucumbers to the pickle factory (chapter 17). In 1906 the Holland Businessmen's Association was formed to regulate store hours on Eighth Street. Gerrit Diekema, who spoke at the first association picnic at Jenison Park, aptly noted, "We are living in a day of organization. There was a day when a lawyer considered his brother lawyer his rival and personal enemy; now they all join in bar associations, have joint libraries, and work for the general good of the profession."

Lincoln Club dinner for Holland politicos, ca. 1900
(*Archives, Holland Historical Trust*)

Within eight months the association had 108 members, which was enough to underwrite the 1908 *Holland City Directory*.[3]

Car culture and Good Roads crusade

Characteristic of a rising standard of living was the love affair with the automobile. Compared to horses, cars were clean. In New York City around 1900, two hundred thousand horses produced up to twenty-five million pounds of manure every day, which in turn bred billions of flies that spread typhoid fever and other diseases. Horses were also expensive, thanks to rising prices for hay, oats, and carriages. Holland was not New York, of course, but it too had its manure piles and noxious flies. Cars also had therapeutic advantages; families could take joy rides, visit relatives in the country, and go to the beach or George Getz's Lakewood Farm, which morphed into a zoo (chapters 22 and 28).[4]

Automobiles had their downside, as with all new technologies. Cars could weaken the nuclear family by allowing members to flee family responsibilities and young people to escape parental supervision and act up. Entirely new industries arose around the tin lizzies: to manufacture them, market them through dealerships, fuel and service

3 *De Grondwet*, 9 Feb. 1907, 14 Jan. 1908; Diekema Papers, 16 July 1906 (quote), box 4, HMA.

4 www.ottawa.migenweb.net/holland/getzfarm/history.html.

McKinley Club, program of first annual banquet in commemoration of the assassinated president's birthday, January 29, 1909 (*Archives, Holland Historical Trust*)

them in gas stations and garages, and deal them second-hand for the less affluent.[5]

The first "gasoline carriage" seen on city streets was in 1898, two years after the birth of the automobile. A Chicagoan took the vehicle with him on the *Soo City* schooner with the hope of attracting investors and finding a site to manufacture automobiles. He found no takers in Holland. Two years later, in 1900, another car coming down Eighth Street caused quite a stir. Attorney Arend Visscher saw it out his window and excitedly called home; his two sons jumped on their bicycles to get a glimpse. They did not have to hurry, since the driver was trying to fix a mechanical problem.[6]

In 1901 George W. Browning, a Holland furniture manufacturer, bought a car, a chain-driven "locomobile steamer;" he was the first owner in town. Sam Miller, owner of the Holland depot restaurant, owned the second car, a chain-driven Monarch, with a top speed of fifteen miles per hour. In early spring 1903, Miller drove the length of Eighth Street, then a clay gravel quagmire, dodging heaps of snow and sloppy puddles. "Stores emptied to see what was coming down the line," he recalled. John J. Cappon, Isaac's son, owned the third car, a two-cylinder

5 James J. Flink, *The Automobile Age* (Cambridge, MA: MIT Press, 1988).

6 George S. May, "The Automobile's Impact on Holland," *Holland Historical Trust Review* 6 (Fall 1993): 4-6; Randall P. Vande Water, "The Automobile Comes to Holland," ibid., 9 (Summer 1996): 4-6.

Charles Sakkers Bertsch steers his 1903 Oldsmobile around town with a handle (*Archives, Holland Historical Trust*)

Ford, and stonecutter R. M. Merrill's two-cylinder Maxwell was the fourth. Visscher surprised his wife Annie with a Waverly electric car for Christmas in 1903; she appreciated not having to hand-crank the motor to start it. He treated himself to a Ford in 1908. Annie tooled around town for ten years, but Arend never learned to master his gas-powered Ford. His three sons and a daughter willingly drove him around town. By 1908 twenty-five residents had cars, including Rev. Evert J. Blekkink of Third Reformed Church, who in 1905 had his 1903 one-cylinder Phaeton shipped by rail from his previous charge in Kalamazoo.[7]

To support the demand for motoring, good roads were a must. In the city and on well-traveled routes, pavement began replacing gravel and sand. Improved roads were also called for at the county level, which included the rural districts. In 1912 Ottawa County passed a $600,000 Good Roads Initiative, which was well supported by the rural townships and even Grand Haven, but in Holland it met overwhelming opposition: 87 percent voted against the referendum. Before the vote, Engbertus Vander Veen of Holland pleaded with his fellow citizens, "Why should you so foolishly give money to the county good roads proponents to make beautiful roads where they are of no importance to you in the northwest and southeast of the county."[8]

Vander Veen had a legitimate complaint. Earlier that same year, the Special Committee on the Country Roads System argued that both Holland Township and city had paid their fair share for road

7 "Sam Miller gives Motor Car History," typescript, clipping file, Joint Archives of Holland (JAH).

8 *Holland City News,* 22 July 1915; *De Grondwet,* 26 Mar., 9 Apr. 1912, translated by Michael Douma.

James Brouwer's renowned 1925 Edison electric car that he drove daily from his home at 54 East Twelfth Street to his furniture store on River Avenue at Ninth Street, to church, and to run errands. The car had a handle for steering, a top speed of twenty-five miles per hour, and a range of sixty-five miles (*courtesy Randall P. Vande Water*)

construction but had been treated unfairly. Only a mile and a half of road had been cut west from the city toward Macatawa, only two miles led north along the lakeshore from Ottawa Beach, and only one and a half miles on Sixteenth Street, from the cemetery to the Ben Van Raalte property east of town, had been laid out. "These stub lines," the committee continued, "are of no value whatsoever to anybody. People living within a radius of two miles from Holland can easily reach the city without any difficulty regardless of weather or roads. It is the farmers living further [*sic*] away who need the stone roads."[9]

The debate on proper road construction continued, but progress itself was a given. New paved projects included trunk highways and other direct "escape" routes for the automobilist. Holland boasted the West Michigan Pike, a highway that by 1915 ran the length of the Michigan lakeshore as far north as Ludington (chapter 10). With the pike road (Butternut Road today), Grand Haven was only an hour away from Holland. Unlike modern highways that skirt the edges of a city, this highway passed right through Holland on River Avenue and Eighth Street.

9 Ottawa County Road Commission, HMA.

Also new in 1915 was a two mile addition to the Alpena Beach concrete road (Lakewood Boulevard) that led west to the Lakewood Farm[10]

City newspapers featured large automobile advertisements and news stories about who bought what make or style of car—touring, sport coupe, roadster, and the like. A newsworthy story in 1916 named three employees of De Kruif's Garage who had gone to Lansing to get a six-cylinder Reo Roadster, a "wonderful sensation" for Hope College Professor John B. Nykerk, a four-cylinder Reo for Mr. Heyboer of Jamestown, and a large three-quarter-ton truck. De Kruif, the local Ford dealer, had also recently sold six Fords "at the new price, which is now the same as a horse and buggy outfit." Little wonder that "the demand for Fords is very great." Curb pumps sprang up around the city to fuel the cars. In 1915 the common council received applications for four prospective businesses—Brouwer & Westrate, Fred W. Jackson, Henry Kraker, and Steffens Bros.—to install gas pumps on the street between the sidewalk and the curb line (chapter 19). The aldermen referred the applicants to the committee on streets and sidewalks and to the fire department.[11]

Homeownership

While the automobile was a status symbol, homeownership was the true mark of the middle class. In reference to Holland, Gerrit Diekema said in 1911, "We love the American home, are home owners and have no tenement district, no dens of vice." In large part, Diekema was correct. It was true that with mortgage credit, nearly any one who worked steadily could afford a house. In 1902 one of Holland's first true real estate agents, John C. Post, advertised houses at $100 down and just $8 per month. The next year, 1903, other land agents, Benjamin L. Scott and John H. Raven, advertised houses at $150 down and only $4 per month.[12]

Holland had no tenement district, but several price-specific residential districts contributed to social differentiation within the city. New additions south of Sixteenth Street attracted immigrants and young families, while the established wealthy held onto the historic district. Holland's poor, on the other hand, filed into a thickly settled four-square-block district along Fairbanks Avenue from Fourth to Eighth Street. This district, which lay outside the city boundaries near

10 *Holland City News*, 20 Jan. 1916, 17 Feb. 1916; Ottawa County Road Commission Report, 1912, HMA.

11 *Holland City News*, 10 Aug. 1916, 25 Mar. 1915.

12 Diekema Papers, box 4, HMA; *De Grondwet*, 6 May 1902, 14 July 1903.

the station and rail yards, was exempt from city taxes, but also lacked city amenities like electricity and gas, and was no stranger to poverty. Living here were over two hundred children who had to walk over a mile and a half to Holland Township schools, since few of their parents could afford to pay the extra cost to send them across the line to the closer Holland city schools. The location of these houses just outside the city limits enabled the city's promoters to maintain quite astutely that Holland had no slums.[13]

Protecting the poor

With few fallbacks to counter unemployment, the boundary between wage earners and the poor was easy to pass over. Progressive city legislation aimed to protect and care for the poor. Rather than hoping to receive charity from family or church, the poor in America now looked increasingly toward the government for aid. Welfare programs meant increased taxes and caused no little resentment. Hard-working Hollanders could take affront to these measures. In an editorial in *De Grondwet* in 1911, C. J. B. Vander Duys went on the offensive:

> There are the social poor, whose eyes are always turned toward the public. They think that society owns their lives. They want the state to release them of all their needs. Does a child in the public school complain about poor eyes, or does the state give glasses to every boy and girl? Does a child sometimes have hunger in the morning? Let the state open soup kitchens and give free breakfast in the morning for all such children. And in the evening let the state open a class which they can attend for free. These crazy thinkers appear to mean that the state is a magician: No, the individual must work. . . . The idle and worthless are the social parasites of the society. . . . It must be an honor for each person to personally make his way through life, and bring forth more than he uses.[14]

Social divisions were also evident in the choice of vacation spots. After the turn of the century a growing working class frequented Jenison Park while the socialites and tourists held sway at the lakeshore resorts. Increased leisure time all around meant more baseball and bicycling, more time to digest the written word or ponder the issues of the day, and larger numbers of wintertime shanties for ice fishing on Lake

13 *Holland City News*, 8 June 1915.
14 *De Grondwet*, 21 Mar. 1911, translation by Michael Douma.

Macatawa (chapter 28). Author William Schrier has pointed out that the Dutch (assumed to be the Protestant Dutch in America) accepted class distinctions as inevitable and part of divine will.[15] While this may be true to an extent, the image fails, however, to explain the social mobility that did exist in Holland. While a businessman or farmer may have had no desire to become "learned" or "high class," he usually had no problem with accumulating wealth.

American, yet Dutch

In many ways, Holland had become an American city by 1900, but there was an inescapable and obvious undercurrent of Dutch culture. Over one-third of the city's population had been born in the Netherlands; at least half spoke some Dutch, the language that was still holding on in the pulpit but not in the halls of commerce. On the fiftieth anniversary in 1897, the city celebrated by trumpeting its Dutch heritage and pioneer days. Gerrit Van Schelven, Holland's postmaster and premier amateur historian, recorded the memories of the old settlers. And like everyone else, these old-timers also had an organization, the Old Settlers, who since 1876 had gathered periodically, sometimes boarding a train to Grand Rapids to retell the old stories with other area pioneers. One side of the arch spanning Eighth Street listed the midwestern states with Dutch colonies. The other side recognized the American "melting pot" and proclaimed: "One in Origin, One in Aim, One in Destiny."[16]

The festivities and rather simple banter of Dutch cultural pride of 1897 gave way to a more serious cultural debate in the years to come as international wars and politics forced Hollanders to reinterpret their own place in the world. They were proud and patriotic Americans, as patriotic as any when the Spanish-American War broke out in 1898. Thirty young men from Holland volunteered and most served in the Thirty-Second and Thirty-Third Michigan Infantry Regiments. Three took part in the invasion of Cuba. All returned home safely, except engineer corporal James Lawyer, who was lost at sea. For Dutch Americans, this war had a dual significance: they were not only fighting for their country but also taking on the despised Spanish, who had scourged the Netherlands over three centuries ago in the Eighty Years' War. Spain was finally receiving its just desserts. Ray Nies recalled:

15 William Schrier, *Gerrit J. Diekema: Orator* (Grand Rapids: Eerdmans, 1950), 98.

16 *Holland City News*, 9, 23 Mar. 1878; *De Hollander*, 26 Mar. 1878. Henry S. Lucas published the best of the recollections in *Dutch Immigrant Memoirs and Related Writings*, 2 vols. (Assen, the Netherlands, 1955, revised ed., Grand Rapids: Eerdmans, 1997).

Semi-centennial arch on Eighth Street, 1897
(*Joint Archives of Holland*)

When the news came to town about the declaration of the Spanish-American War, I remember old grandmother (on my mother's side) who had come to America a young woman with the early settlers, and had lived most of her life here, and who was now past eighty, walking all morning up and down the main

Hope College semi-centennial parade float with female students with ribbons across their shoulders naming each state of the Union (*courtesy Randall P. Vande Water*)

Othelia "Tillie" Van Schelven with the Torch of Liberty, who represented the Goddess of Liberty (*Joint Archives of Holland*)

street, shaking hands excitedly and gladly with all she knew, telling them in Dutch, just as excitedly, "Now shall those devilish Spaniards catch it! Now they will be punished!"[17]

First State Bank draped in flags for the 1897 semi-centennial (*Joint Archives of Holland*)

17 Ray Nies Autobiography, typescript, ch. 6, p. 3 (quote), HMA; Joel Lefever, "Holland residents have always stepped up to serve," *Holland Sentinel*, 26 Aug. 2007; "Spanish-American War—Our Volunteers," P. T. Moerdyke Papers, box 16, HMA; "Holland, Michigan, May 30, 1963, Program at Pilgrim Home Cemetery," HMA.

Semi-centennial parade on Eighth Street with soldiers, bands, and floats (*Joint Archives of Holland*)

Replica log cabin (*blokhuis*) on the Hope College campus at Tenth Street and Columbia Avenue, with city leaders during Holland's semi-centennial in 1897. *Left to right*: Gerrit J. Diekema, Lane T. Kanters, Arend Visscher, Gerrit Van Schelven, Isaac Cappon, and Gerrit J. Kollen (*Joint Archives of Holland*)

Ray Nies, ca. 1898
(*Joint Archives of Holland*)

Upon returning home in November, Mayor Germ Mokma, himself a Civil War veteran, applauded the men for serving "without stain of honor on their record." More than one hundred civic leaders then feted them at a banquet at the City Hotel, with music provide by Breyman's Orchestra and a vocal quartet. Adjutant J. C. Haddock of the Van Raalte Grand Army of the Republic (GAR) Holland post spoke and several clergymen participated; Gerrit Diekema, as usual, gave one of his florid orations.[18]

As Hollanders struggled with the question of Americanization, they experienced a revival of Dutch ethnic consciousness during the South African Boer War of 1899 to 1902. This grueling war pitted the independent Boer republics of Transvaal and Orange Free State against the interests of British expansion and rule. Many Dutch Americans could relate to the underdog Boers who were, after all, descendents of an earlier immigrant stream from the Netherlands. Dislike for the English, America's assumed ally but practical opponent in many international issues, was also apparent. The few Boer victories brought rejoicing in Holland, while each successive British victory yielded sadness and frustration.

Fueled by sympathetic newspaper editors, literature from the Netherlands, and an historical consciousness of Dutch pride, the pro-Boer cause in Holland became a powerful movement that crossed party lines. At meetings and rallies, speakers addressed the outrage of British

[18] Randall P. Vande Water, "Local Men in Spanish-American War," in *Holland: Happenings, Heroes & Hot Shots,* 3:23; Vande Water, "War heroes welcomed home, *Holland Sentinel*, 25 Sept. 2011.

Charles Hiler, a Spanish-American War veteran, posed in full battle gear for a photograph at Edward J. O'Leary Studio. Hiler and his brother William served in the 33rd Regiment of the Michigan Infantry and saw action at the Battle of Santiago, Cuba, July 1-17, 1898 (*courtesy Randall P. Vande Water*)

atrocities against the Boers, atrocities that included the world's first concentration camps. Hollanders protested, petitioned the national government for intervention, and raised funds to aid war victims among their Boer "cousins." The anger about the destruction of the Boers was widespread and deep. As the war dragged on and the chances of Boer victory grew dim, supporters felt increasingly helpless, and Holland lost some of its motivation for protest and aid.

However strong these ethnic feelings may have been, Hollanders were unable to substantially affect the course of the war. Too many obstacles stood in their way. Faced with the difficulties of extending tangible support to a distant land, they could only hold meetings to vent their growing frustration with a distant, foreign war. The Boer War tested the patriotism of Dutch Americans, but they were no longer Dutchmen or Boers. They sent money and resolutions of sympathy but no soldiers.[19] As a testament to its Republicanism, Holland remained supportive of the Grand Old Party, despite the refusal of presidents William McKinley and Theodore Roosevelt to intervene in the war (chapter 24).

That there was an ethnic revival at all is indicative of the position in Holland of Dutch culture and language. America was a land of prosperity, but not everyone shared in it. Surely some Dutch were ashamed of their heritage, that their parents or grandparents were simple people of no status, farm laborers who wore wooden shoes and funny clothing. For many Americans, that is what the symbol of a

Dutchman had become: a *Volendammer*, a rural remnant of a bygone era, someone who had misplaced his inheritance of Rembrandt, Huygens, Vermeer, and Vondel. Ray Nies echoed the sentiment of many when he later remarked, "I do not know why a Hollander in America should ever be ashamed of his Dutch origin."[20]

It is true that many Dutch were proud of their origin, but success demanded Americanization. This is clearly shown in an event in 1907, when, years after the Boer War and with a continuing interest in the Dutch, Edward Bok, editor of the *Ladies' Home Journal* and a Dutch American himself, offered cash prizes up to $100 for Hope College students or graduates who would pen the best article on the history of Dutch colonists in midwestern America. The article had to be written in English.[21] One submission concluded, "The Hollander in the West today is an American first, and a Hollander afterwards, and is proud of being both." George Ford Huizenga of Zeeland, winner of the competition, spoke of the recent Dutch immigrants as of a "decidedly inferior type" than the pioneer immigrants of the late 1840s. Huizenga did admit, however, that the new immigrants "compare favorably with other contemporary immigrants" and that government officials have deemed them "intrinsically desirable." Bok was so enamored with Huizenga's article that he decided to print one hundred copies of it for distribution to historical societies.[22]

A new city library, which opened in 1901 in the old firehouse on East Eighth Street, was well stocked with journals and magazines so residents could keep up to date with world affairs. The library was so popular in its first year that, instead of the original plan to close at the end of the school year, it remained open all summer. In 1907 the library held over 4,500 books, with a Dutch language section that included traditional works by Isaac Da Costa, Hendrik Tollens, Willem Bilderdijk, and Anthony Brummelkamp, and more recent selections by the statesman Abraham Kuyper and nationalistic writer Louwrens Penning (chapter 27).[23] In addition to keeping up to date with foreign news, Dutch American Holland could now also keep up with the Netherlands Dutch, which for many had already become a foreign culture.

19 Michael Douma, "The Reaction of Holland, MI, to the Boer War," student paper, Hope College, 2003, JAH.

20 Nies Autobiography, ch. 6, p. 1.

21 *De Grondwet*, 29 Oct. 1907.

22 *Holland City News*, 19 Aug. 1909. The Bok Prize Essay Contest is detailed in Bok's biography by Hans Krabbendam, *The Model Man: A Life of Edward William Bok* (Amsterdam and Atlanta: Rodolpi, 2001), 185-94.

23 *De Grondwet*, 21 May 1901, 23 Apr. 1907.

"Foreigners" and immigration restrictions

After the turn of the century, eastern and southern Europe took over from western Europe as the primary source of emigration to the United States. How did Holland, with a population largely Dutch or of Dutch parentage, react to the general influx of these new immigrant groups? One editorial explained that the new immigrants, with a lion's share from Italy, were largely illiterate, but they helped to fuel the economy and contribute to America's progress by cultivating more land, constructing factories, and laying railroads. The newcomers, after all, wanted a better future for themselves and for America, just like the Dutch. Another editorial, however, argued that all sorts of undesirable immigrants were gaining entrance because they were not turned away at our ports. In particular, the editorial continued, officials at the port of departure must screen out the sick from coming to America. Gerrit Diekema may have summarized the ambiguous duality of popular opinion when in 1911 he added that America "must be a sifting as well as a melting pot."[24]

While the ethnic makeup of America underwent drastic changes, Holland's Dutchness remained firmly in place. From 1900 to 1920, the number of non-Dutch foreign-born in Holland remained low and relatively constant at 7 percent of the population. In 1900 this included mostly Canadians and Germans, a few Englishmen and Scandinavians, and only a handful of Irish and French. In the 1910s came the first Hungarians, Greeks, and Bulgarians. Between 1900 and 1920, however, only one non-Dutch foreign immigrant group—the Polish—significantly increased their numbers in the city.

The Polish immigrants who settled in Holland came in search of work. They found jobs at the pigskin tanneries, Cappon & Bertsch and Eagle-Ottawa Leather, the latter a Grand Haven company that opened a Holland plant in 1914. Working conditions were horrible; only the most desperate would accept the unsanitary, foul, and chemical-ridden conditions. Yet, tannery employment was all that was available for these Eastern Europeans caught in an uphill battle against the language barrier. The employment of the Poles indicates that Holland was seeking outside laborers for its worst jobs, that the Dutch were well beyond those desperate years when any good paying job was acceptable for survival. The Poles, however, would not let themselves be taken advantage of, and in 1916 the workers at Eagle-Ottawa, both in

[24] Ibid., 28 July, 24 Mar. 1903; Schrier, *Diekema*, 37.

Grand Army of the Republic parade on River Avenue, Memorial Day, 1912. Note the boy with the fishing rod in step with the veterans (*courtesy Randall P. Vande Water*)

Holland and Grand Haven, successfully went on strike for a nine-hour workday and a wage rate of 25¢ per hour. They circulated petitions in English and Polish, asking for public support. Enticed by improved wages and the reassurance of family and friends in the city, more Poles arrived. By 1920 there were some twenty-seven Polish-speaking heads of households and singles, in addition to their wives and children. Nearly all of them lived in the Second Ward, within a few minutes' walk from their largest employer, the Cappon & Bertsch tannery.[25]

A certain amount of suspicion was directed at these newcomers. When the first Pole came to town, his exotic looks made an impression on hardware storeowner Ray Nies, who described "Big John" as "a huge-framed, tall chap, not a bit of fat on him, who wore an enormous mustache, something of the cow horn, or handle bar variety, but much thicker, brushier, and bushier–the biggest I ever saw."[26] A Polish brawl in Holland in 1917 drew ample news coverage, including a headline that read, "POLOCKS BATHE IN BLOOD IN BATTLE RIOT." Participants in the melee were nine Polish men, described as "burly, raw-boned foreigners from the North River district," seven of whom received short-term jail sentences. One of the men, John Sodak, who had become well acquainted with the judge through past incidents, was chided: "We don't like your style, Sodak, of refusing to work but being willing to drink

25 *Holland City News*, 2 Mar. 1916; *De Grondwet*, 14 Mar. 1916.
26 Nies Autobiography, ch. 14, p. 1.

and fight. Holland can get along without you."[27] The following week, the editor of the *Holland City News* stood up for the Polish community and declared that most are "frugal, saving, law-abiding citizens, . . . the majority of which are highly religious and scrupulously honest."[28]

Prohibition

Alcohol was without a doubt one of the biggest and most discussed issues of the Progressive Era. In the Old Country, the Dutch Reformed had no problem with beer, wine, and the stronger *jenever* (gin) and brandy. These alcoholic beverages were part of everyday life and lubricated relations in families and in the community. American Protestants, mostly of English heritage, however, preached abstinence for themselves and strict legal regulation for others. The Dutch soon found themselves torn between their Old Country tradition of social drinking and the American Protestant prohibition crusade. The factor that made America different was that drinking hard liquor, notably whiskey, rum, and gin, had gotten out of hand in the 1820s and 1830s.

This is what prompted reformers in 1826 to found the American Temperance Society to combat this social evil that destroyed families and individuals. The goal of the society was to get drinkers to take the temperance pledge and forswear using alcohol. Many dismissed the tee-totalers as fanatics. Was it not hypocritical to be a temperance man? To rail against the misuse of alcohol only to come home and have a beer yourself? Why was it acceptable to be against hard liquor, when one could get drunk on other intoxicating beverages? Addressing these questions, the temperance movement, which had grown to become a national phenomenon by 1850, was divided into two camps: prohibitionists who would outlaw all alcohol, and moderates who stood for recreational drinking. The Dutch tended to be wary of government laws on moral matters, given the history of repression by the House of Orange.[29]

The Michigan Temperance Society was founded in 1833 and a state law prohibiting retail sales of alcohol was passed in 1855. But loopholes in this law were easily exploited, and it was repealed in 1875. To appease prohibitionist districts, a state local option law was first passed in 1887.[30] Although the Michigan Supreme Court declared this

27 *Holland City News*, 4 Jan. 1917.

28 Ibid., 11 Jan. 1917.

29 Hans Krabbendam, *Freedom on the Horizon: Dutch Immigration to America, 1840-1960* (Grand Rapids: Eerdmans, 2010), 309-10; Robert P. Swierenga, *Dutch Chicago: A History of the Hollanders in the Windy City* (Grand Rapids: Eerdmans, 2002), 699.

30 Willis F. Dunbar and George S. May, *Michigan: A History of the Wolverine State*, 3rd rev. ed. (Grand Rapids: Eerdmans, 1995), 299-300, 469-70.

law unconstitutional in 1888, the justices upheld a revised local option law in 1890, and counties and cities could then determine their own dry or wet status.

Alcohol was fairly well regulated in Holland before the 1870s, when the temperance cause came to the city in earnest. From the beginning, the *volksvergadering* had taken a strong position against selling liquor, although after considerable debate, alcohol sales were approved for "medicinal purposes."[31] The trafficking of liquor was strongly opposed, but drinking beer at home and serving communion wine in church were well established. Van Raalte's household accounts routinely listed beer. Koene Vanden Bosch of the Noordeloos Church had his own Bohemian beer stein (now in the Holland Museum collection). The Dutch also had no problem with alcohol producers.

In its 1866 general assembly, the Christian Reformed Church considered disciplining a brewery worker not for his choice of occupation, but for working on Sunday. The early settlers in Holland had little to say about saloons either, since the first saloons opened when the second generation—those born or raised in America and influenced by its drinking habits—came of age in the 1860s. By 1869 the common council felt it necessary to establish regulations for the alcohol industry, which outlawed selling to minors and known drunkards and prohibited Sunday sales. To operate a saloon one needed to buy a license and post a bond. Saloons also had to be closed from ten o'clock in the evening to six o'clock in the morning.[32] In the last quarter of the nineteenth century, these regulations were tested and solidified in a move toward more strictly controlling alcohol sales and consumption.

The temperance movement came to Holland by way of Methodist and Reformed social reformers with New England and New York roots, who hoped to usher in the Christian millennium by eliminating booze. Methodist idealists sought a booze-free America, the ultimate social gospel reform. Several Dutch immigrants on the fast track to assimilation joined the Methodist crusade, notably Dr. Bernardus Ledeboer and Jannis Vande Luyster Jr., who in early 1861 led in organizing the Temperance Society of Holland. The temperance cause was by no means an easy sell in Holland, even when the moral crusaders called alcohol abuse a danger to "soul, body, church, and society." In 1874 the white ribbon ladies organized a Holland chapter of the Women's Christian Temperance Union (WCTU), which thereafter carried the battle against alcoholic drinks. Sarah Annis of Hope Church was the

31 A. J. Pieters. *A Dutch Settlement in Michigan* (Grand Rapids: Eerdmans-Sevensma, 1923).

32 Adrian Van Koevering, *Legends of the Dutch* (Zeeland, MI: Zeeland Record, 1960), 401; Holland City Ordinances of 1869.

W. C. T. U.

The W. C. T. U. hold weekly meetings on Wednesday afternoon, of each week at 3 p. m., at Hope Church.

THE following arrangement of the words in Proverbs 23: 29-32, first appeared in the *Youth's Temperance Enterprise*, for April 1842.

A GLASS FOR THE INTEMPERATE.
Who hath woe? Who hath sorrow?
Who hath contentions? Who hath
babbling? Who hath wounds without
cause? Who hath redness of eyes?
They that tarry long at the
wine! They that go to seek
mixed wine! Look not
thou upon the wine
when it is red;
when it giveth
his color
in the
cup;
when it
moveth itself
aright.
At
the last
it biteth like a
serpent, and stingeth like an adder.

"A Glass for the Intemperate," Proverbs 23:29-32 in the shape of a wine glass, announcing weekly meetings of the Holland WCTU chapter at Hope Church (Holland City News, *7 September 1978*)

first president, and the church regularly hosted monthly meetings. In 1887 the church accommodated the WCTU county convention and, in 1924 and 1929, its state convention.[33]

A Methodist hymnbook published in 1880 and in use in Holland contained a "prayer for the intemperate." Two verses read:

What ruin hath intemperance wrought!
How widely roll its waves!
How many myriads hath it brought
To fill dishonoured graves!

Stretch forth thy hand, O God, our King,
And break the galling chain;
Deliverance to the captive bring,
And end the usurper's reign.[34]

33 *De Paarl*, 23 Jan. 1861 (Earl Wm. Kennedy provided this citation); Judy Tanis Parr, *Hope Church, Holland, Michigan, The First 150 Years, 1862-2012* (Grand Rapids: Dickenson Press, 2012), 102-3; P. T. Moerdyke, "Pioneer Organizations: WCTU," box 14, Moerdyke Papers, HMA.

34 *Methodist Hymnbook* (Toronto: Methodist Book and Publishing House, 1880); First Methodist Church, Holland, MI, Methodist Church Collection, HMA.

But how could these temperance advocates with their anti-alcohol hymns convince the already religious Hollanders that they needed deliverance?

Isaac Cappon, a Dutchman who co-founded Third Reformed Church, was convinced of the temperance cause and became a leading proponent. But when he tried to raise the liquor tax fee in the city, the ways and means committee of the common council rebuffed him. The committee reported that "the large majority of the inhabitants of Holland are sobre [*sic*] in the use of liquor, and don't need any guardianship. We have mostly been brought up where a moderate use of spirituous beverage is general, and no shame on it, and which [*sic*] has come customary with us." As this report indicates, complete abstinence of alcohol was a foreign concept to the Dutch settlers. That they eventually joined the cause of temperance was a marker of the process of Americanization.[35]

Holland's first anti-alcohol organization, the Holland Temperance Association (also known as the Holland City Temperance Society and later the Holland Reform Club) was founded in 1875 and held monthly meetings at Kenyon's Hall (chapter 30). When Kenyon's Hall burned down in 1877, the group moved its meetings to the First Methodist Church. The association's members saw alcohol as a major contributor to the city's problems. Public drunkenness and related crimes, they thought, was cause enough for prohibiting alcoholic drink. The society took a stance of total abstinence, a position lost on much of the city. Most Hollanders went on with their daily business and generally ignored this committed group of reformers. In 1877 high profile and exciting outside speakers began visiting the city to start a local temperance crusade. Those in attendance at the speeches were encouraged to sign abstinence pledges to "touch not, or handle not." As a direct result of these speeches, a Red-Ribbon Club of 210 members and a local chapter of the WCTU were formed in the city in 1877. Because alcohol was considered a threat to the home, it became a woman's issue.[36]

The WCTU was the "first women's mass movement," an organization that by 1892 had nearly 150,000 dues-paying members. The Holland chapter, like the national body, promoted total abstinence, sponsored community events, and educated the youth on the evils of alcohol. It also held weekly meetings at Hope Church, the "college church" and the most Americanized of the city's many Reformed

35 Elton J. Bruins, *The Americanization of a Congregation*, 2nd ed. (Grand Rapids: Eerdmans, 1995), 27.

36 *Holland City News*, 23 Dec. 1876, 5 May 1877.

Catarina De Boe (Mrs. Isaac) Cappon
(*Archives, Holland Historical Trust*)

congregations. The membership list of about thirty people reads like a roll call of Holland's most well-known and influential: Anna Coatsworth (Mrs. Henry D.) Post, Catarina (Mrs. Isaac) Cappon, Anna (Mrs. Daniel) Bertsch, Heiltje (Mrs. Aldert) Plugger, Mary (Mrs. Charles A.) Dutton, Mary (Mrs. Otto) Doesburg, Sara (Mrs. Frank) Ledeboer, Jane (Mrs. George) Deming, Martha (Mrs. George E.) Kollen, Mrs. Marsh, Mrs. Charles L. King, and Hendrika (Mrs. Derk) Te Roller, among others. These upper class women took seriously their role in promulgating the temperance cause and their determination outdistanced that of the men. In 1880 Daniel Van Pelt, the pastor of Hope Church, questioned what had happened to the men's Red-Ribbon Club. "Has it evaporated? Or have they fused with the WCTU, allowing the ladies to do the rough work, and keeping modestly back for fear of being seen."[37]

That the female crusaders had clout became clear in 1878 when the *Holland City News* dedicated a column directly under the masthead to the WTCU. "This space belongs to the Women's Christian Temperance Union," declared editor Otto Doesburg. The first announcement of the weekly meeting quoted Proverbs 23: 29-32, with the scriptural text cleverly indented in the shape of a wine glass.[38]

Another strength of the temperance movement came from its diverse field of supporters who could "evangelize" all the different sections of society. Proponents included reformed sailors, businessmen, and working men. Reinder E. Werkman, who fell into the latter two categories and who described himself as "no professional temperance

[37] Ruth Bordin, *Women and Temperance: The Quest for Power and Liberty, 1873-1900* (Philadelphia: Temple University Press, 1981), 3; *Holland City News*, 27 Nov. 1880.

[38] *Holland City News*, 7 Sept. 1878.

TEMPERANCE

CAUCUS.

A Temperance Caucus will be held at the law office of Justice ISAAC FAIRBANKS, on River Street, on

SATURDAY EVE., APRIL 2, '81

AT 7 O'CLOCK.

WCTU Temperance Caucus flyer announcing meeting in Justice Isaac Fairbanks' law office (*Isaac Fairbanks Papers, Joint Archives of Holland*)

talker," became enraged when a boarder that he had taken in and tried to set on a right course was sold alcohol at a local saloon. Werkman responded by distributing to the saloons a list of men who claimed to be drinking to the injury of themselves.[39] Years later, the police department printed a black list of people to whom it was punishable by fine or imprisonment to sell liquor.[40]

Hope College also had its share of temperance men, including President Charles Scott, who in 1884 petitioned to limit the operating hours of saloons. Professor Theodore Romeyn Beck, a New York-born Reformed Church cleric, was one of the more outspoken critics of alcohol. In a series of articles in the *Holland City News*, Beck decried the evils of alcohol. It was neither food nor strength, he said, but a drug that led to apoplexy, idiocy, delirium, and childhood disease. One German immigrant couple, John F. "Fritz" Hummel, former owner of three leather companies in Holland, notably Cappon & Bertsch, and who entertained lavishly and often, was so disgusted with the talk of prohibition that he and his wife packed up their belongings and returned to Germany.[41]

In the spring of 1885, the consistory of Hope Church warned that patronizing saloons was "inconsistent with the interests and advancement of the cause of Christ." On this point the Dutch American Christians could agree with the American Christians: the Sabbath must be protected. From this initial standpoint, the cause of Prohibition spread, and in the next two decades there was a rather noticeable change in the way many local Christians approached the alcohol issue. Many believed that alcohol and the Christian faith were incompatible. H. Bakker of Vriesland in 1885 asked rhetorically: "Drinking beer and

39 Ibid., 20, 27 Nov. 1886.

40 Ibid., 25 June 1914.

41 Ibid., "Fifty Years Ago Today" 30 Dec. 1937, 3 May 1884; Theodore Romeyn Beck Collection, JAH.

whisky and wanting to be a Christian, how does that go together?" Teunis Keppel asserted that saloons lie outside the path of a Christian.[42]

The temperance supporters pressured city lawmakers to increase the cost of a liquor license, which they did in 1877, to $300 a year for retailers, $500 for wholesalers, and $1,000 for druggists. Successive rises in the cost of both state and city licenses directly affected the number of saloons in the city, which dropped from a high of sixteen in 1877 to just three by 1887. All the while, it upset saloonkeepers greatly that druggists who sold liquor as medicine did not have to pay for a liquor license. The city tried to tax saloons to death, but it did not stop those who wanted alcohol from buying it, except on election days when all saloons were closed by law. Some argued that the loss of saloons negatively affected the city's budget, since half the license fee went to the city (the other half went to the county). Figures from 1888 put Holland's tax at $1,565, a figure substantially less than Grand Haven's $5,100. Others argued that the common council would not prohibit saloons, because it was greedy for the money that came to the city treasury through the licenses and bonds. While the saloon license fee remained high and was a mystery to no one, the number of druggists who sold alcohol increased.[43]

When Michigan put a prohibition amendment on the state ballot in 1887, schoolteacher Marietta Shuler (Mrs. Owen) Van Olinda of Hope Church, a leading crusader, had fifty thousand temperance tracts printed in the Dutch language to sway Holland voters. The WTCU held an enthusiastic meeting in the Dutch language at Ninth Street Church. Without a dissenting vote, the attendees passed a resolution that "We, Holland Christians . . . cast our vote in favor of this [prohibition] amendment." But *De Grondwet*, owned by the Leendert Mulder family who opposed prohibition, ridiculed the meeting and its one-sided vote and tried to paint some well-known participants as radicals. Mulder and his editor Isaac Verwey had their finger on the public pulse; Holland voted against prohibition 358 to 212. Van Olinda had taught in the First Reformed Church parochial school in 1860-61 (chapter 9), then in Union Public School, and from 1872 to 1878 in the Hope College grammar school and female department. She and Anna Post were leaders in the local temperance crusade.[44]

42 *Holland City News*, 2 May 1885; *De Grondwet*, 6, 13 Oct. 1885.

43 *Holland City News*, "Fifty Years Ago Today," 5 May 1932, 2, 23 June 1877, 26 May 1888, "Fifty Years Ago Today" 23 Mar. 1939; *De Grondwet*, 23 Jan. 1877, 13 Oct. 1885, 10 May 1887.

44 *Holland City News*, "Fifty Years Ago Today" 4 Mar. 1937, 5 Mar. 1887; *De Grondwet*, 8 Mar., 5 Apr. 1887; Parr, *Hope Church*, 102-3.

Marietta (Mary) Shuler Van Olinda, first female instructor at the Holland Academy and Hope College (*Joint Archives of Holland*)

By 1890 most churches in the city, including Reformed congregations, allowed temperance groups to meet on their premises. In a way, temperance, anti-saloon laws, and for some, even prohibition, had become unwritten church doctrine. Soon after the turn of the century, Hope Church, always in the lead of the anti-alcohol movements, allowed its name to be included on official petitions of the Anti-Saloon League. Mayor Germ Mokma considered it a "religious duty to absent himself from church occasionally to see if the saloons are closed." One Sunday in late 1899, Mokma caught "several prominent businessmen" imbibing in James Selby's liquor store on Eighth Street, and Selby was arrested. In 1908 the consistory of Central Avenue Christian Reformed Church resolved to censure any member "who to our knowledge frequents saloons." So devoted to temperance were Marietta Van Olinda and Kate Garrod (Mrs. John C.) Post, both members of Hope Church, that the WCTU honored them with a life membership, the only two in Holland so recognized.[45]

45 *Ottawa County Times*, 23 Feb. 1900; *Holland City News*, 14 Nov. 1899, 4 Feb. 1902, 24 Mar. 1908; Consistory minutes, Central Avenue Christian Reformed Church, 16 Mar. 1908, Art. 16, translated by Gerrit Sheeres; Mary L. Kansfield, "Francis Davis Beardslee and the Leading Ladies of Holland, Michigan, 1912-1917," in James Hart Brumm, ed., *Tools for Understanding: Essays in Honor of Donald J. Bruggink* (Grand Rapids: Eerdmans, 2008), 76.

Yet, for all the talk of temperance, prohibition itself had little support from the clergy. Ray Nies explained:

> Some of the colonists who loved their drink too much, and there were a few mighty drinkers among them, would sometimes be convinced by an earnest appeal from the dominie that they should stop, which sometimes they would do, but apparently the dominies rarely used their utmost influence in such cases. Perhaps the idea being that if a man was absolutely determined to drink, that was his affair to a certain extent, or perhaps because it was not strictly forbidden in the ten commandments, or perhaps the dominie felt that some were so far gone as to be beyond help.

Another contemporary Dutch American wrote: "The whole prohibition movement is anti-biblical and is therefore anti-Calvinistic."[46] This viewpoint is evidenced as well in voting patterns, since the Prohibition Party, even when it managed to field candidates for the municipal elections, failed to gather more than a handful of votes.

Since most Hollanders were more concerned with regulating alcohol and protecting the Sabbath than banning drink entirely, a reaction against the city's efforts to curb alcohol sales arose from the city's moderates. The editor of the *Holland City News*, Cornelius J. Doesburg wrote: "It is puritanism in the worst degree, hypocrisy, nonsense, and decidedly un-American to restrict trade because some people misuse the article of trade."[47]

In fact, the economic motive was perhaps the central reason for the city to keep up the sale of alcohol. K. Bendertegen, a Holland saloon owner, elaborated on the philosophy of the moderates in regard to the economics of alcohol sales:

> The less tee-totalers, the more moderate or respectable drinkers; the less red-ribbon boys, the more chance for them to become moderate drinkers; the more moderate drinkers, the more material for steady drinkers; the more steady drinkers, the more saloons, and the less of opposition to a general recognition of our claim as being the proper and suitable depositories of the earnings of the laborer and mechanic, the bark-peeler and the vessel-loader, the railroader and the factory hand, the wood-sawyer and the apprentice, the very men who at the close of a day's hard work in the sweat of their brow, invite us so kindly to share with them the

46 Nies Autobiography, ch. 7, pp. 3-4 (quote); Arnold Mulder, *Americans from Holland* (New York: J. B. Lippincott, 1947), 222 (quote).

47 *Holland City News*, 7 Aug. 1890.

> proceeds of their labor, and who for a valuable consideration on their part, look to us for their lager beer and their morals, their bitters, and their social standing.[48]

The opposition argued that saloons were profitable only for brewers and saloonkeepers, while the public taxpayer ended up paying for all the associated crime and poverty.[49]

If one did not agree with the economic justifications for drink, there were various other practical considerations for not restricting alcohol. Not the least of these was the need to keep alcohol on hand for medicinal purposes, liquor being an important nineteenth century cure for all sorts of ailments. Reijer Van Zwaluwenburg of Drenthe wrote that he did not want to appear as a regular drinker just because he had once bought a pint of brandy to treat a sick cow. Others argued that abstinence pledges were fine in theory but short-lived and insincere in practice. One anonymous editorial remarked that the temperance forces either played on people's fears of alcohol's evil effects, or they stressed "the mysterious attraction of secrecy and the more palpable one of pretty girls."[50]

Men were known to drink secretly, hiding the fact from their wives. Ray Nies tells the story of a Mr. D., who had established a routine of smuggling alcohol under the nose of his wife. "He never went into a store or saloon to buy his liquor, or never sent anyone after it. When his supply ran low he would just step over to the telephone, and call up W-'s [Wade's], the old pioneer drug store on the main street. When they answered by saying 'W-'s Drug Store,' he would simply say in reply, 'D-speaking—goodbye' and hang up. That was all." This simple code had long been arranged with the druggist, and meant that Mr. D. wanted his kind of liquor sent over at once. The druggist would wrap up a bottle of it, and send it over by the delivery boy, and charge it as "medicine."[51]

Others reacted against alcohol restrictions by simply ignoring or circumventing the laws. Mayor Rokus Kanters once found the deputy marshal playing cards and drinking in the back room of a saloon on Christmas day, a "flagrant violation of the police regulations" that quickly led to the deputy's dismissal. During the Kanters administration, the aldermen also decided that no pool room could be conducted in the same building in which a saloon was located. One clever proprietor responded by sawing "the rear end of his building from the front end,

48 Ibid., 23 June 1877.
49 *De Grondwet*, 28 Mar. 1911.
50 Ibid., 20 Oct. 1885; *Holland City News*, 11 Sept. 1875.
51 Nies Autobiography, ch. 8, p. 6.

moving it away about six inches, made a separate building of it, and that put the saloon and the pool room in two different locations – and the new ordinance was complied with." Another tactic was to sell alcohol from "bum-boats" anchored offshore in Macatawa Bay.[52]

As the reputations of the saloons were called into question, more citizens bought their alcohol quietly through wholesalers. Men at the 1888 Fourth of July celebration consumed one hundred barrels of beer. Ordinances in 1908, 1910, and 1912 required wholesalers to sell at one time no less that two dozen pints of beer or three gallons of whiskey.[53]

To continue their production, breweries sought compromises with the temperance crowd. In 1877 Xavier F. Sutton, the city brewer (chapter 16), produced a beer "so light and palatable that hardly any intoxicating parts [were] left in it." It is uncertain whether he had any success in marketing this product, but in 1885, Sutton had expanded his variety of non-alcoholic drinks to include "pop, birch beer, mead, lemon foam, root beer, Buffalo mead, Belfast ginger ale." An attempt at brewing light or even alcohol-free beers was tried again in 1908. Members of the police department, after testing this new brew, decided against it, probably on the grounds that it was in fact an alcoholic beverage. The police notified all dealers in "temperance beers" to cease selling.[54] The number of city saloons held steady; in the 1890s at least eight were in operation. The temperance faction agitated for an anti-saloon ordinance to put an end to these "dens of vice."

In the 1908 spring election, an anti-saloon referendum passed with a five-hundred-vote majority. All alcohol retailers had to close, but wholesale houses were not subject to the law. Before the ordinance took effect on May 1, 1908, the Holland Hotel bar on Eighth Street disposed of its alcohol at "half off" prices. The law required druggists to keep a record of every person who bought liquor, subject to inspection at will by the police board.[55] (See appendix 5.12 for a list of Holland saloons and taverns, 1874-1974.) The saloon prohibition was not set in stone; it had to be renewed or rewritten almost every year. A 1910 law banned all "games of chance, music, or other amusement or attractions," and required "no selling to or permitting in the place of minors, habitual drunkards, females, or any other persons prohibited by law; no

52 *Holland City News*, 9 Jan. 1886, 19 May 1938.

53 Ibid., 30 July 1887; 7 July 1888.

54 *Holland City News*, 16 May 1885, 5 May 1877, 11 May 1878; Board of Police and Fire, 1907-11, HMA.

55 *Holland City News*, 23, 30 Apr. 1908, 15 Apr. 1909, "Twenty Years Ago Today" 8 Mar. 1923, "Thirty Years Ago Today" 28 Apr. 1938.

screens preventing an unobstructed view of the place; no lunches or refreshments; no signs or anything to attract the attention of passersby." A flier of the anti-saloon faction declared that the exclusion of saloons was neither a question of local option prohibition nor even personal liberty, but a desire to have a civilized and moral community free from undesirable places.[56]

This atmosphere helps to explain why the Holland City Brewery, a practical landmark in the city built by Carl Zeeb in 1873, continued production throughout the period of anti-saloon fervor. Anton Seif, the owner of the brewery, had to apply for a license every year but was never rejected. The brewery typically employed five or six people, and as long as the brewery maintained a positive moral reputation, these jobs were secure. In addition, the German-Lutheran Seif family was well respected in the city (chapter 16).[57]

The alcohol question again took center stage at the common council meetings in 1911, when the merits of the previous year's legislation were questioned. The 1910 ordinance prohibited the consumption of alcohol by the glass at the place of purchase, but it did allow beer to be sold by the bottle and whiskey by the half pint. While the saloons had all but disappeared, wholesalers were selling more than ever. Men, admittedly decent as well as notorious, were known to pack cases of beer in baskets and congregate in open city lots where they held high carnival. Social clubs, known as "drinking dispensaries," such as the Marquette Club, circumvented prohibition laws by installing a "locker system," whereby each member was assigned a locker as his personal liquor cabinet.[58]

The frustrated drys set about to slice off the liquor trade with a thousand cuts. They pushed the common council to raise the minimum purchase to two-dozen pints of beer or three gallons of whiskey, with an annual $500 beer license and a second $500 liquor license. The profit margin was so thin that it only paid for merchants to sell beer and not spirits in that quantity. Moreover, the twelve drug stores in town could dispense whiskey, wine, gin, and malt liquor in any quantities as medicine at all hours and even on Sundays, under only a $25 license fee. The wholesalers chafed under the limitations and found creative ways to blunt them. Most effective was to hold the customers' bulk purchases in-house, the so-called locker system, and allow them to draw down small quantities from their lockers as they wished, by

56 Common Council Minutes, 7 Apr. 1910; Holland City Records, box 1, HMA.
57 *Holland City News*, 30 Oct. 1919.
58 Ibid., 20 July 1911, 20 Feb. 1913.

punching a "drink ticket" that the wholesalers issued. The customers then repaired to some forty drinking places, known as "the jungles," that sprang up behind billboards, in alleys, stairways of downtown buildings, and along the river north of the train station at Columbia Avenue where hobos gathered. Societies and clubs of the well-to-do, such as the Elks, Moose, and Marquette, all bore the added expense of installing the locker system, but clubs of the workingmen, such as the Eagles and Pyramids, could not afford lockers and needed all their funds to provide sick benefits and burial expenses.[59]

These subterfuges infuriated the drys, who got up another petition with a thousand signatures to ban the sale of alcohol, period. But the liquor interests had the upper hand at city hall, and they persuaded the council to table the proposition. The county prosecutor then stepped into the fray in 1913 and issued a sweeping order that every society and club in the county must close the lockers "at once." This prompted the dealers in Holland to "go for broke;" they got the council to put on the ballot a proposal to re-license saloons and saloonkeepers. If passed, saloons would be back in business with minimal regulation. Mayor Nicodemus Bosch vetoed the ballot act, but the council had no difficulty overriding his veto and sending it to the voters. One hundred prominent businessmen and citizens had stiffened the spines of the aldermen by submitting a petition asking for the public vote. The tide seemed to be turning in favor of saloons. The wets even managed to get the flamboyant New York attorney Clarence Darrow to come to Holland to speak in front of a packed house at James S. Price's Opera House. (Years later, Darrow capped his career by humiliating William Jennings Bryan in the 1925 Scopes "Monkey" trial.) But sixty businessmen disavowed the rationale of the pro-saloon petition and endorsed the prohibition referendum. In the April 1913 poll, the drys won again, although by a mere twenty-three votes. The city was evenly divided; Wards One, Two and Four had a slight majority for saloons, and Wards Three and Five had a slight majority against them.[60]

This poll threw the hot potato back to the council. Were the residents for "no saloon" or for "no local option"? Would druggists and the Seif Brewery also have to close? or did the vote mean a return to the previous system of lockers and the "jungle"? The committee on licenses, chaired by Frank Congleton, took the vote to be absolute and would shut them all down, including the druggists. All selling of

59 Ibid., 25 Apr., 7 Nov. 1912; 20 Feb. 1913, "Fifty Years Ago Today" 6 Jan. 1938; *De Grondwet*, 5 May 1908, 26 Apr. 1910.

60 *Holland City News*, 5, 27 Mar., 3, 10, Apr., 8 May 1913.

"spirituous, fermented, or intoxicating liquors" would stop. This set off a heated debate. Alderman Art Drinkwater, a wet, favored giving licenses to Seif Brewery and the druggists. L. Edward Van Drezer, like Congleton, wanted Holland to become so "blooming dry that College Avenue would crack open." Mayor Bosch and several others thought it unfair to close the wholesalers but not the druggists. In the end, when put to a vote, the council approved the committee recommendation unanimously! Holland would be bone dry. The police cracked down on club bars, which, due to the expense of liquor licenses, had formed as underground drinking establishments. But the saloonkeepers always managed to find new loopholes, and by 1914 there were nine saloons in operation, nearly as many as the high number of eleven prior to the first anti-saloon law of 1908.[61]

In 1914 Bosch and the city fathers had to face the "wet and dry" issue again, when saloonkeepers and liquor wholesalers got up a petition with 913 signatures that required a public referendum. The petition called for an end to all restrictions on the wholesale trade, in exchange for certain minimal controls on saloons. The wets were exercising with a vengeance the right of initiative granted in the 1913 city charter. The proposed law would only prohibit gambling, music, and prostitution in saloons, none of which saloonkeepers favored in the first place. Mayor Bosch issued a press release strongly urging the defeat of the referendum, which would revive the "old fashioned saloon." The Businessmen's Association backed him with a resolution of its own. Reformed and Christian Reformed church leaders, with help from the Methodists, also mobilized their congregants to defeat the initiative. If the effort succeeded, said an alderman, drinkers in Holland "will be so dry they can spit cotton." Prior to the June election, fearful customers stocked up before the coming "famine." Some bought thirty to forty cases of beer at a time. But the concern of the wets was needless; the pro-alcohol referendum passed by 222 votes (55 percent). It carried handily in Wards One, Two, and Four and lost in Wards Three and Five.[62]

Saloons were back in business again, but only for two years, until 1916, when another anti-saloon measure was on the ballot, this time an amendment to the state constitution. Wet and dry forces took out half-page advertisements in the *Holland Sentinel* in an attempt to win over last minute votes. One wet advertisement included a diagram of how to make a home distillery in case of prohibition, while another

[61] Ibid., 24 Apr. (quote), 30 Apr. 1913.
[62] Ibid., 7, 14, 21 May, 18 June 1914.

HOLLAND WILL NOT GO BACKWARD!

Lest it should be inferred from Saturday's issue of the Daily Sentinel that in the opinion of the Business men of Holland, the future trade and prosperity of the City will be greatly damaged by the closing of the saloons, we take this opportunity as the only way left us, at this late hour to state in the most emphatic way possible:

I. That no self-constituted "Business Men's Committee" has been authorized to represent us in the columns of the Sentinel.

II. That we repudiate all allegations, expressed or implied, of entertaining any fears that the closed saloon will curtail the growth of the city, paralyze its trade or blight its prosperity.

III. That we heartily endorse the present movement for the closing of all the saloons in the city, firmly believing that in the end it will result in the welfare and happiness of all.

C. J. Lokker Co.
Lokker Rutgers Co.
Notier. Van Ark & Winter
Cook Bros.
Du Mez Bros.
P. Brusse.
E. J. Harrington.
A. H. Meyer.
John De Boer.
Van Ark Furn. Co.
B. Steketee.
Wm. Brusse.
Frank Dyke.
A. Postma.
H. R. Brink.
T. Keppel's Sons.
E. J. Fairbanks.
Jas. A. Brouwer.
Sluyter & Dykema.
Holland Rusk Co.
G. W. Mokma
J. B. Mulder
Zanting & Tubergen.
Vinkemuller & Essenburg.
E. Nykerk.
R. Mulder.
F. J. White,
C. J. Dregman.
H. Van Ry.
S. Piers.
Steffens Bros.
A. De Groot.
A. Steketee.
Van Lente Bros.
Westing & Warner.
Henry Geerlings.
Lugers & Miles.
A. C. Rinck.
Henry Holkeboer.
Molenaar & De Goede.
Jacob G. Van Putten.
John Van der Sluis.
Frank Bolhuis.
C. M. McLaen.
H. Pelgrim.
A. Visscher.
Nickodemus Bosch.
John Arendshorst.
George Browning.
N. Yonker.
B. P. Donnelly.
John Nies.
A. Peters.
B. Slagh.
H. Van der Ploeg.
John S. Dykstra.
De Pree Hardware Co.
Geo. Huizenga.
E. S. Holkeboer.
Fred Steketee.

Pro-prohibition businessmen declare: "Holland will not go backward!" in campaign against saloons (Holland Sentinel, *May 1914*)

advertisement showed as a replacement for the respectable saloon a shady character on the street selling alcohol to anyone who wanted it, including the underage. Almost every Reformed and Christian Reformed pastor in the region signed public petitions urging a *yes* vote, and the national synods of both denominations meeting in West Michigan adopted resolutions in favor of the amendment. The churchmen even staged a "monstrous" Saturday parade led by the Holland Drum Corps, followed by many hundreds of children and adults.[63]

This time Holland voted *dry* by an overwhelming 577-vote majority (62 percent); the referendum also passed statewide. The Second Ward went against the grain as usual and voted *no*. The defeat of demon rum closed the dozen or so licensed saloons and four bottling works in Holland, as it did saloons statewide, beginning May 1, 1918, a year before the Volstead Act and Eighteenth Amendment began the experiment in national prohibition in 1919. Even the druggists in Holland stopped all liquor sales. "Today Holland is more nearly dry than it has ever been in the city's history," crowed the *City News* editor approvingly. "Not a single drunk was observed last evening, and not

[63] Ibid., 27 Apr., 25 May, 26 Oct. 1916.

a single arrest was made by the police for drunkenness."[64] The era of "near beer" had begun, when the patrons of the "ex-bar anti-Volstead association" of Holland bemoaned having to drink "kiss your sister" beer that had no "kick." Police now had the unenviable task of ferreting out bootleggers and moonshine stills.[65]

Ray Nies, son of a Dutch immigrant, who as an adolescent in the 1890s moved from Saugatuck to Holland, recalled the years before prohibition. "I was always told when young that one of the main reasons for the Hollanders leaving their home land so long ago, and coming to "the promised land" – America – was to enjoy 'free' religion, but when I recall how continually and chronically some very few of those old timers still left got drunk, I sometimes wonder if some of them at least didn't come over for 'free whisky' as well, or in place of free religion. Many of the pioneers did not drink at all, at least not to excess, but were sober, industrious, and really sincerely religious men."[66]

Curiously, smoking never came under the strictures of alcohol in the Progressive Era. Men puffed cigars in boardrooms, consistory rooms, and restaurants. Cigarettes were ubiquitous, except on the railroads, where they were banned to prevent fire.

Women's suffrage and workforce

The Dutch were traditionally opposed to women's suffrage, believing it to be contrary to scripture (chapter 24). The Christian Reformed Church in particular held to this position. While the Reformed Church by the 1910s did allow individual congregations to determine the voting status of women for church matters, the Christian Reformed Church opposed suffrage in congregational meetings until after 1920.[67]

The fight for women's suffrage, like the temperance movement, began well before the Progressive Era. In the 1870s and 1880s, western states and territories were experimenting with universal suffrage, and the movement began to spread. Theodore Roosevelt later remarked, "I think civilization is coming Eastward gradually."[68] Certainly in the

64 *Holland City News*, 2, 9 Nov. 1916; *Holland Sentinel*, 30 Oct., 1, 3, 7 Nov. 1916.

65 *Holland City News*, 2 May 1918, "Twenty Years Ago Today" 29 July 1938; 6 Feb., 3 Mar. 1919, 9 Feb. 1922.

66 Nies Autobiography, ch. 7, p. 1.

67 Suzanne Sinke, *Dutch Immigrant Women in the United States, 1880-1920* (Urbana and Chicago: University of Illinois Press, 2002), 54.

68 Quoted in Rebecca J. Mead, *How the Vote was Won: Woman Suffrage in the Western United States, 1868-1914* (New York: New York University Press, 2004), 1.

western, sparsely populated states, woman had to play a more complex role, often involving work outside the home. In Michigan, this was less the case, although the settler life often meant new challenges and new roles for women. In 1884 Byron Markam from neighboring Laketown Township editorialized that it was fine that women could vote, and some have been given the ability at school district meetings, but few actually want the vote. "The good wives, the motherly daughters, and affectionate sensible daughters have already as heavy a burthen as they can comfortably carry without meddling with the affairs of the state." [69]

The changing roles of women led to the gradual breakdown of separate spheres or the "cult of domesticity," the idea that women should be barred from the public arena to care for home life. Historian Suzanne Sinke notes that the "ideal of separate spheres had not carried much currency in the Dutch immigrant context, though it did make some inroads among later generations."[70] Under the guise of the temperance movement, women stepped over the boundary into the public sphere. Historian Eric Burns writes, "If there had been no temperance movement in the United States, the campaign for suffrage would have been delayed, perhaps by a matter of decades, and it might not have been accepted so equably. Suffrage's foundation was temperance, and no structure remains standing for long unless the foundation is solid."[71] Prohibition and suffrage became further intertwined in Michigan since the wets, or those who supported alcohol consumption, voted in accordance with their fear that woman's suffrage would give the drys all the votes they needed to pass prohibition laws.[72] In other words, if they wanted to keep their alcohol, they had to keep women out of politics.

In addition to their role in fighting against alcohol, women became more active and powerful in the public sphere through involvement in aiding foreign mission work. The RCA's Women's Board of Foreign Missions was organized in 1875 and the Woman's Board of Domestic Missions in 1882. Mary L. Kansfield writes, "For most women, involvement with other women to advance the cause of foreign missions brought affirmation and value to their individual lives and roles within the church. . . . Women's understanding of God's world was broadened, and women were changed because of it."[73] Women also

69 *Holland City News*, 19 Apr. 1884.

70 Sinke, *Dutch Immigrant Women*, 54.

71 Eric Burns, *The Spirits of America: A Social History of Alcohol* (Philadelphia: Temple University Press, 2004), 122.

72 *Holland City News*, 5 Dec. 1912.

73 Mary L. Kansfield, *Letters to Hazel: Ministry within the Woman's Board of Foreign Missions of the Reformed Church in America* (Grand Rapids: Eerdmans, 2004), 13.

learned public speaking and organizational skills. Christina Van Raalte (Mrs. William B.) Gilmore, the daughter of Albertus C. Van Raalte and "lady principal" (dean in 1907) of women at Hope College, was a key organizer for the western branch of the RCA Board of Missions. She also founded the Federation of Women's Societies in Holland in 1919. Such societies in every congregation provided social outlets for women.[74]

The case for women's suffrage also found its strength through a rise in female employment, which in Holland saw a dramatic change in employed women from 86 in 1901 to 250 in 1904. This growth correlates with expansion at H. J. Heinz Co. and the Holland Shoe Co., both of which employed many women, since only certain jobs were yet considered appropriate for the finer sex. Many women also worked for Poole Bros., a printery that produced and sold railroad tickets, and in the second decade of the twentieth century, still more women found employment with Holland Canning Co. and Holland Rusk Co., both of which generally employed more women than men. Women were also employed in significant numbers at C. L. King & Co., West Michigan Steam Laundry, and H. Van Tongeren's cigar factory, as well as in clerical positions at a few other factories. In the period from 1895 to 1919, female employment in Holland grew tenfold, from 61 in 1895 to 656 in 1919.[75]

Women were new to voting and could feel out of place, especially when put down by the men. In 1909, for example, the Woman's Literary Club was successful in getting one of its own, Alice (Mrs. Henry) Kremers, appointed as a member of the park board. The *Holland City News* noted, "The truth is that the ladies are not in any sense of the term 'in politics.' The club is composed of women who are housekeepers banded together for 'self-improvement and for the dissemination of useful information'—women who have no desire to conduct municipal affairs so long as they are, as now, so well administered by men."[76] In 1910 women were allowed to register for a vote on raising the pay of the aldermen. The problem for many, ridiculed *De Grondwet*, was that to register, the women had to answer the "brutal question" of "How old are you?" They had to write their exact age and were not allowed to write "elderly" or "young." The women also had to be sure to write their own full name, and not, for example, "Mrs. Klaas Smit."[77]

74 Sinke, *Dutch Immigrant Women*, 206; Ruth Keppel, interview by Carol Bechtel, 1980, typescript, 5, JAH.

75 Compiled from figures of Michigan Department of Labor Reports.

76 *Holland City News*, 6 Apr. 1909.

77 *De Grondwet*, 8 Nov. 1910, translation by Michael Douma.

Women Suffrage parade on River Avenue (*courtesy Myron Van Ark*)

In the general election of 1912, Michigan dealt with the suffrage question at the ballot box. The Holland Equal Suffrage Club, which Francis Davis (Mrs. John W.) Beardslee of Hope Church and other New Women chartered in 1912 under the Michigan Equal Suffrage Association, trumpeted the cry: "Let Women Vote: They Will Know How to Use the Ballot for Civic Housekeeping." The women dared to believe that men would come to agree. "There are several local pastors who are ardent supporters of equal suffrage, and this is expected to help the cause considerably, since in Holland a minister's judgment carries a great deal of weight." This axiom held true on the other side as well. When Calvin College professor Jacob G. Vanden Bosch published an article in the denominational weekly, the *Banner*, urging members to vote *no*, he carried considerable clout. "We cannot afford to vote for a measure which, if carried and enacted into law, will destroy love, harmony, and intimacy, and thus strike a blow at the very foundations of their ideal home." He had a better grasp of grassroots sentiment than the progressive clerics. Ottawa County voted against suffrage 4,613 to 2,717, and the amendment failed statewide by a wide margin. Women's suffrage was a dead issue locally. When Rev. Johannes Groen of the Eastern Avenue Christian Reformed Church in Grand Rapids spoke in Holland in 1913 against a prohibition amendment, he drew a large crowd, but when he returned the next year to speak in favor of women's suffrage, a small crowd of mostly women turned out. The *Holland*

"The New Suffragist Martyrs," Walt McDougall cartoon in *Holland City News*, March 16, 1913

City News noted after the speech that Hollanders "are much averse to women's suffrage."[78]

Progress for women's voting rights, however, was evident. Since a state law of 1908, women were allowed to vote on local bond issues and in school elections, and fifty did so in the 1913 vote on the purchase of the fairgrounds. Women could also run for the school board. Mrs. Kate Garrod Post was nominated for a seat in 1913, and although she garnered 160 votes, she fell short of a win. The next year Martha (Mrs. George) Kollen won a seat and was re-elected time and again. Emily (Mrs. Charles) McBride of the Woman's Literary Club and Dena (Mrs. Fred T.) Miles of the WCTU chapter added their voices to the cause. It was 1919 before the state constitution permitted women to vote for county school commissioners.[79]

Growth in the number of educated women in the city led to more female organizations and consequently a stronger female voice in community affairs. The Woman's Literary Club took on an extended role with a Civic Health Committee, which in 1914 raised money to

78 J. G. Vanden Bosch, "A Burning Question: The Equal Suffrage Question," *Banner*, 31 Oct. 1912, 684; *Holland City News*, 3 Oct., 28 Nov. 1912, 4 June 1914; Kansfield, "Francis Davis Beardslee," 87-91.

79 *Holland City News*, 17 July 1913; Kansfield, "Francis Davis Beardslee," 94; Vande Water, "Kollen Park Was Basket Factory," in *Holland Happenings*, 1:113; Vande Water, "First Woman Jury Tries 'Chicken Case,'" in *Holland Happenings*, 3:88-92.

Martha (Mrs. George E.) Kollen
(*Holland High School* Boomerang, *1915*)

fight tuberculosis. The conservative Gerrit J. Diekema, among others, befriended women's organizations by introducing petitions in the legislature on behalf of women's suffrage. And the Holland Equal Suffrage Club soldiered on under Iantha Aldrich (Mrs. Richard N.) De Merrill and Katherine Post, daughter of Kate Garrod and John C. Post. All were cheered that opposition was diminishing from Reformed and Christian Reformed churches.[80]

President Post induced Hope College female students to form the Susan B. Anthony chapter of the Collegiate Suffrage League. Throughout 1916 and 1917, the Equal Suffrage Club met weekly to study the issues, plot campaign strategy, and design block ads for the city newspapers. "Good Cooks Want Good Votes," declared one ad which included several recipes. Another cried: "Protect Your Home with Two Votes Instead of One." A successful ploy was to link suffrage to the prohibition cause, which had widespread male support. The Michigan legislature in April 1917 approved women's suffrage in state elections, but an amendment to the US Constitution was needed to guarantee the vote in national elections. This amendment, the Nineteenth, passed in Michigan in the November 1918 election (although it lost in Holland by a margin of more than two to one!) and secured the necessary three-fourths majority of the states in 1920. The women crowed: "Holland women will yet be able to vote in spite of their husbands, who did their best to keep them from the ballot." Women in Michigan voted for the first time in the state general election in March 1919 and in the presidential election of November 1920 (chapter 24).[81]

Women first served on a local jury in March 1919. It was the infamous "Chicken Case" heard in Judge Gerrit Van Schelven's

[80] *Holland City News*, 25 June 1914; Schrier, *Diekema*, 97.

[81] *Holland Sentinel*, 13 Mar. 1917; *Holland City News*, 3 May 1917, 6 Nov. 1918; Kansfield, "Francis Davis Beardslee," 92-104, (quotes 98).

courtroom, which involved a trivial slander dispute between two women, Mamie (Mrs. Erwin) O'Connor and Mrs. Elizabeth Gilmore (Widow Noul). The fact that women comprised six of eleven in the jury box made headlines such as, "More interest in jury than in the case." The six who took their seats in front of the "largest crowds ever assembled to listen to a mere justice case" in the city hall courtroom were Miss Jeanette Mulder, Margaret (Mrs. William J.) Olive, Elizabeth (Mrs. Egbert) Fell, Helen (Mrs. William) Wing, Mrs. Anna Aldworth, and Elizabeth (Mrs. Charles) Drew. That only one was of obvious Dutch ancestry was due, in part, to the fact that 40 percent of eligible women had not registered to vote, and thus they were not in the jury pool. Even those in the pool may well have given excuses to avoid fulfilling their new patriotic duty. Most of those opposed to women's suffrage were from Reformed and Christian Reformed congregations. The Chicken Case jury was hardly representative of the community, but it was historic nonetheless. Very likely, the same jury bias persisted in Holland throughout the 1920s and perhaps into the 1930s.[82]

Another social taboo was homosexual practices, especially among women. In 1927 Ottawa County Judge Thomas N. Robinson presided over a jury trial involving a lesbian encounter between a "pretty" Zeeland seventeen year old and a girl from Holland. The Zeeland teen, who was in the dock for "contributing to the delinquency of a minor," had her case dismissed midway through the trial, after testimony revealed that the Holland teen "has fallen low in the moral scale and is now involved in a bad case at Muskegon, Mich." The editor added: "The case developed so many lewd situations that this paper refrains from publishing the many statements made at the trial." He did not refrain, however, from publishing the names of both parties.[83]

Immigrants and factory work

In a citywide vote in 1900, $50,000 was approved for use in attracting businesses to the city.[84] Holland's industry was growing and diversifying. From twenty-seven factories employing 1,748 people in 1900, Holland's industry expanded to eighty-one factories with 2,754 employees in 1915. At the same time, real estate prices in West Michigan were on the increase, and little good land was left for new immigrants to become farmers. South Dakota, Montana, Iowa, even the Canadian

82 Vande Water, "First Woman Jury Tries 'Chicken Case.'"
83 *Holland City News*, 19 Apr. 1917.
84 *De Grondwet*, 29 Jan. 1900.

plains offered an alternative for Dutch immigrants who sought farm land. In 1908 the Holland-based insurance agency Isaac Kouw offered farms in South Dakota of 160 acres or more, which people could purchase outright or trade for their smaller farms in West Michigan (chapter 16). New immigrants (sometimes called *Groene Hollanders* or "Green Dutch") had a choice to stay in Holland and work at a factory, or move west and buy land. Factory work was not the most preferable, but to remain near family in the area, and for general wealth and well-being, many put up with it as a necessary evil.[85]

Holland held a reputation of being neat, organized, quiet, and safe, with a low crime rate. *Eigen Haard*, a periodical in the Netherlands, reported on the city in 1908: "One sees it not as a dingy, sooty place, where slow-rising smoke almost obscures all sun and life. On the contrary, I would call Holland a garden, a large garden of broad cool lanes, where wooden houses stand in the shadow of the beautiful row trees." The city, however, was not always so kind to newcomers.

In his autobiography, Siert F. Riepma recalled his first year as a Dutch immigrant in Holland (1894):

> Nobody cared for us. No labor union looked after us. No WPA or other agency, governmental or private seemed to care whether we lived or died. Walking the streets in search of work is physically exhausting, but it is the hardest on a man's spirit. We were rather docile, I suppose, but there were elements of danger in such a situation—real dynamite. However, we rather took it for granted. It belonged to the great American way of life. Personally, I think it did not do as much damage to our spirits and morale as the present procedure. In spite of my difficult experience I still believe in it.[86]

There were many in the area that could still speak Dutch, so the immigrants could get by without learning English. But if one wanted to succeed in a business that required contacts with Americans, one needed to learn English. New immigrants, even if they were of higher social standing, found themselves in the factories, associating with other Dutch-speaking immigrants. Because factory work was often unhealthy, many immigrants desired work on farms, if they could find a willing employer or comparable wages. The rise of industry created more

85 Ibid., 7 July 1908.

86 "Dutch in West Michigan," *Eigen Haard* [Haarlem (Netherlands) religious weekly], 29 Aug. 1908, translation by Michael Douma; Sears F. Riepma, *My Ancestry, Life and Ministry, 1878-1977* (New York, 1979).

jobs for skilled labor as well as unskilled labor. The Holland Business College, founded in 1896, prepared students for the new white-collar positions in industry and commerce. By 1908 some 800 students had attended the college, with 237 graduates who became accountants, stenographers, advertisers, secretaries, and the like (chapter 7).[87]

Health issues

Like other American cities coping with new industry, new regulations and standards, and advanced understanding of diseases, Holland had health issues of its own to address. Some problems were finite and easily remedied. For example, in 1911 the board of health prohibited swimming in Black Lake near the Bay View Furniture Factory, because sewage from the factory, as well as city sewage, had contaminated the water.[88]

Most of the health scares of the day, however, where those that filtered in from outside; sicknesses like smallpox, scarlet fever, and tuberculosis were ubiquitous. In 1904 Holland reported forty-one cases of smallpox, although none were fatal. Houses of the contagious were quarantined, and special lanterns placed on the porches warned passersby to stay away. Some houses were fumigated in an attempt to rid the city of the pox.[89]

Vaccination, however, met resistance from some citizens who still refused the procedure despite the orders of their physicians. Fortunately, the city had on its board of health a qualified director, Dr. Henry Kremers, who assured the city that vaccination was but a "slight annoyance" in preventing a horrible disease. Compared to the national death rate in 1900 of 17.2 deaths per thousand inhabitants, the rate in Holland was lower at 15.3. A scarlet fever epidemic in 1909 forced the health officer to close for a week all churches, Sunday schools, day schools, nickel theaters, and all such public places. In 1908 the short-lived Holland Sanitarium provided a place for TB sufferers to convalesce in rooms above 42 East Eighth Street.[90]

When death occurred, Hollanders followed the Old World custom of the death watch in the home of the deceased, where the body lay in repose. Two close friends would come at ten o'clock the night before

87 *De Grondwet*, 8 Sept. 1908.

88 Common Council Minutes, 26 May 1911, HMA.

89 *Ottawa County Times*, 21 Apr. 1905; *Holland City News*, 18 Nov. 1904.

90 *Holland City News*, 9, 16 Dec. 1909; one-page advertisement in *Holland City Directory*, 1908, 256; Edward M. Iams, "Changing Death in Holland, Michigan: The Nineteenth to the Twentieth Century," unpublished paper, Hope College, JAH. The Holland Sanitarium is not listed in any other city directory, nor was it mentioned in any newspapers.

the funeral and stay awake with the family until morning. During the night, it was expected to serve the friends coffee and cake. The front door was draped in black crepe to show a family in sorrow. For the funeral, the women would pin black crepe veils around their hats. A shining black hearse with curtained windows would come for the casket and take it to church for the funeral service. Behind the hearse came a carriage carrying the pallbearers, followed by a carriage for the immediate family. All were drawn by horses fittingly bedecked in black. The rubber-tired carriages made no sound except for the clop, clop of the horses.[91]

For the procession, the funeral director, dressed in mourning trousers and swallow-tailed coat, and with a list in hand provided by the family, would call the names of the family members in the descending order of age. The pallbearers then carried the casket into the church in a stately procession, followed by the family. "Dignity and protocol were important in a Dutch funeral." This was the scenario that Janet De Graaf Van Alsburg described in 1975 about the funeral of her grandfather in 1910, which was handled by Peter Notier of the Notier Funeral Home. The funeral service was in the Fourth Reformed Church. After the service, everyone passed before the open casket for the "last look," with the family going first, and then the carriages processed to the cemetery in the same order, with the church bell solemnly tolling the age of the deceased. After the committal service and lowering of the coffin into the grave, everyone returned to the house for refreshments served by the neighbors.

With advancements in science there also grew an awareness—although not a thorough understanding—of germs and contagions. Works like Upton Sinclair's shocking portrayal of the Chicago meatpacking industry in *The Jungle* (1906) led to increased fears of the possibility of unhealthy, and even dangerous, food and drugs. In 1907 the common council appointed Dr. Abraham Leenhouts as city health officer. Educated at Hope College and the University of Michigan, Leenhouts had spent time living around the Midwest and was up to date with national sanitation standards. He determined to raise local health standards. He raised concerns about sewage disposal, the public water supply, food merchants, and the milk supply. A test of city water found high levels of bacteria. A survey of merchants, particularly meat markets, uncovered "a careless lack of personal cleanliness."[92]

91 For this and the next paragraph, see Janet De Graaf Van Alsburg, interview by Donald van Reken, 31 Dec. 1975, typescript, 24-25, JAH.

92 Abraham Leenhouts, *From the Crest of the Hill* (Holland, MI: Denny-Lindenmuth-Hierta, n.d.), 110.

Leenhouts' most militant crusade was for safe milk. This was a serious health issue. Some fifteen to twenty infant deaths per year in the city were blamed on contagions in milk. One particular worry was cows with tuberculosis. In 1904 rumors circulated that a high number of cases of tuberculosis had occurred in Overisel Township, and that the sickness was in cows and was being passed through their milk to humans. Official reports showed the milk to be safe.[93] A later survey of the local dairy industry revealed what Leenhouts had feared. He reported:

> The majority of the premises where the cows were kept were dirty; the utensils in which the milk was placed were for the most part open, unsterilized wooden buckets and pails; the storage of the milk before delivery was often in a room at ordinary temperatures; [and] the delivery to the homes was by dipping the milk from the dealer's containers into the customer's pan or dish. The whole procedure from start to finish was most highly favorable for contamination and fermentation.[94]

As Leenhouts tried to initiate changes, he faced a divided public, with one faction strongly averse to regulating milk. In accordance with his wishes, however, the common council passed a milk ordinance in 1912. Mayor Evert Stephan had vetoed a previous attempt a year earlier. Some considered the new ordinance drastic and radical. Dairymen had to test milk for home delivery for tuberculosis, and cows whose milk failed the test could be destroyed without compensation. Leenhouts recalled: "Day after day, I was interviewed and accosted by people on the street, in the stores, and in my office condemning the action of the health board as new-fangled nonsense." Farmers who furnished the city with milk were especially angry. One objected to having his cattle tested because, he argued, defective equipment might lead to testing mistakes and cost him a lot of money. Leenhouts, the man behind the milk ordinance, claimed to have lost business as a medical doctor because of his stance. But laboratory tests proved that the city's measures did much to clean up the milk supply and that infant mortality rates went down.[95] These figures could comfort the doctor.

Nicholas Kammeraad, the only alderman to object to the ordinance, argued that milk prices would soar because of the cost of testing. Others worried about a "milk famine" in the city. Socialist alderman Vernon King (see below) added that if milk prices got too

93 *Ottawa County Times*, 20 May 1904.

94 Leenhouts, *From the Crest of the Hill*, 109.

95 Ibid., 110-11; *Holland Sentinel*, 3, 10 Aug. 1911, 22 Feb., 12 Mar. 1912.

high, the city could step in and take over the milk business. Due to testing costs, milk prices in 1913 did indeed rise by a penny a quart, from 6¢ to 7¢, and to 7½¢ in 1917.[96]

Regulations led to opposition in another way: cows with TB-tainted milk were unfit to eat. That was veterinarian Fred Brouwer's contention. He angrily denounced dairyman H. E. Van Kampen for selling beef in Holland that had been condemned by state agriculture inspectors for being infected with tuberculosis. If the animal "is not well enough to live, it is not good enough to eat," cried Brouwer. "Who wants to consume meat injected with tuberculin just days before being slaughtered?" Brouwer's fiery letter in the *Holland City News* echoed Sinclair's muckraking novel.[97]

City beautification

Beautification was a by-word of the era and a concept always on the minds of city administrators. The *Holland City News* regularly printed statements like, "the character of the owners is reflected in their homes," and "cleanliness in streets, backyards and alleys is essential in the attainment of the ideal state." In entering the modern era, Holland had to address issues with which it still struggles today. In a speech in 1913, city engineer Henry Naberhuis argued that Holland did not properly take advantage of its lakefront, which should have a park, and not so many factories. He also addressed the problem of housing and automobile traffic flow. He stressed that a city must be a place where "men, women and children can live, work, and play."[98]

Civic pride and city beautification ran hand in hand. A civic league was organized in 1914 and helped raise awareness and support for improvement and beautification projects, including filling in a "frog pond" at Eighth and Pine Streets and the addition of boulevard (street) lights. Public restrooms were considered for the downtown area, especially for out-of-town woman who came to shop. Bold declarations were made to the effect that "every citizen ought to be interested in city affairs." In one particular effort to clean the streets of a nuisance, Peter Ver Wey, Holland's overwhelmingly successful dogcatcher, killed three thousand dogs during the first fifteen years of the century. To some, the ruthless Ver Wey was the most-hated man in Holland, but every time he retired, a desperate common council hired him back. Ver Wey simply

96 *De Grondwet*, 26 Aug. 1913; *Holland Sentinel*, 1 Feb. 1917.

97 *Holland City News*, 23 Oct. 1913.

98 Ibid., 27 Feb. 1913.

stuck to the rules; he made no distinction as to the value or owner of the dog (chapter 26).[99] The strict dog ordinance, among others, was written not to be bothersome, but to maintain a high level of civility. Ordinances were, after all, not forced upon the city, but passed by public vote. They included the "Peace and Good Order" ordinance of 1909, and a proposed anti-smoking ordinance of the same year. Democracy, it was said, would determine the city's proper course. Holland's Forward Movement Club (chapter 29), for one, declared the citizen's first duty to the community was to vote.[100] The law reigned, and the most proper form of dissention was the ballot box.

Child labor and leisure

Official statistics of child labor (ages fourteen to sixteen) in Holland from 1895 to 1919 report large fluctuations in the number of children employed in city factories. These fluctuations were primarily due to seasonal employment trends and irregular reporting. In 1919, for instance, most of the Holland factories were inspected in August when many children would be free from school and able to work, while in 1914 the same inspections took place mainly in October when school was in session. The results were that in 1919 a high number of 129 children were reported in the workforce, while in 1914 the number was only four. When children did come to the factories, it was during the summer season or winter breaks. Most of them worked in handcrafts at C. L. King & Co. basket factory, H. J. Heinz Co. pickle factory, or Holland Shoe Co. Few worked year round. Factory pay could be enticing for a young worker, but an ideal persisted that it was healthier to have a farm job. Jantje Sloothaak Hooijer wrote to her siblings in the Netherlands, "You ask if we have children, do we have to send them to the factories too. Now, we don't have any children yet, but if they come, we will put a pair of wooden shoes on them and send them to a farmer."[101]

Increased time for leisure and recreation illustrated the rise of the middle class (chapter 28). For many the leisure sport of choice was baseball. Although some baseball had been played locally since the early 1870's, the sport did not reach widespread popularity until the turn of the century. Most teams consisted of teenage boys who met at the fairgrounds or on the Hope College campus. Local baseball found

99 Ibid., 3 June 1937.

100 Ibid., 16 Apr. 1906, 5 Aug., 8 July, 4 Nov. 1909, 1, 22 June 1911, 13 Jan., 10 Feb. 1916.

101 Jantje Sloothaak Hooijer to brother C. Warmels and sister (Hoogeveen, Drenthe), 26 June 1908, Heritage Hall Immigrant Letter Collection, Archives, Calvin College (ACC).

its greatest supporter in Nicholas J. Whelan, editor of the *Holland City News*, who regularly printed schedules, rosters, and results of local contests. Amateur teams were formed, and with attendance at the ballparks on the rise, Holland formed a semi-professional team in 1901. Baseball also grew as a company sport, as one company, factory, or association faced off against another. In joking fashion, the *Holland City News* reported on the regularity of business baseball: "The fat men have challenged the lean men, the police officials have challenged the city officials, the Eighth Street business men have challenged the River Street business men, the letter carriers have challenged the printers and some interesting games will very likely be arranged."[102]

Baseball, like religion, formed the community. It gave boys role models and heroes; it offered recreation and supported a feeling of commonality, of "us" versus "them." Such was the case with Holland playing against African American teams from Chicago and House of David teams from Benton Harbor. While it is interesting to note that Hollanders had no issue in playing against African Americans, these games "were viewed by the fans as some sort of mysterious and exotic showcase, rather than a statement of any sort of progressive or liberal position in Holland." The *Holland City News* referred to black teams as "Euthopians [*sic*]" and "real darkies of Africa." The newspaper also ridiculed the speech of the African American ballplayers, quoting one as having said, "We smuver you to death next Saturday shure as I's blacker than you."[103]

Labor unions and organizations

Organized labor came to Holland in the 1870s and 1880s. With only a fraction of the workingmen employed in industry in these years, there was a small pool of possible unionists from which to recruit. The United Sons of Industry, a secret society, was founded in 1877 to promote industries in the country. The Knights of Maccabees (Knights of Labor) established a cooperative wood yard in 1885, and in 1887 the Land and Labor Club was founded. By 1892 Holland had five unions, including the Tanners and Curriers, Bricklayers and Masons, Knights of Labor, Carpenters and Joiners, and the Industrialists. These early organizations held little power and exercised that power infrequently;

[102] *Holland City News*, 6 Sept. 1901 (quote); Michael Van Beek, "Baseball Arrives in Holland: A History of the Origins of Baseball in Holland, MI," Senior Thesis, Hope College, 2003, JAH.

[103] Van Beek, quoting *Holland City News*, 29 May 1903, 1 Aug. 1902.

they rarely demonstrated and held few strikes. Those who did strike in Holland were generally considered agitators and troublemakers. In 1884 the editor of *De Grondwet* called labor unions, "one part unneeded, the other part damaging."[104] This negative rhetoric is not surprising. An industrial survey by the Immigration Commission in 1911 found that only 2 percent of Dutch workers nationwide belonged to unions; it was the lowest percentage by far among any immigrant group.[105]

Farmers got in the act, too. In 1890 some Graafschap farmers proposed organizing a local branch of the Patrons of Husbandry, commonly called the Grange, but religious opposition against secret societies condemned the whole idea. The hope was for several hundred families to organize under the Grange and then entice local merchants to sell at a 10 percent discount. Among farmers at West Olive, in the Groenewold and New Holland districts, and two miles north of Zeeland, the Patrons gained a footing and successfully organized. They, too, had the idea of getting stores to sell at discount.

The traditional anti-union stance in the Holland-Zeeland area arose from the doctrines of the Reformed churches to which many residents ascribed. Most opposed unions due to their socialistic principles and the biblical ban on being "unequally joked with unbelievers." This was especially true of Christian Reformed churches. Some churches gave tacit approval, in order for members to obtain or keep jobs in union factories. A few gave complete approval on the grounds of justice, solidarity, and being a witness. Eventually, the middle view of tacit approval won out, largely on practical grounds. Between 1881 and 1914, twelve Christian Reformed synods dealt with the union issue, and every one warned strongly against joining unions and threatened those who did with censure and possible excommunication.[106] But there was sympathy for those who honestly and quietly earned their bread. The Dutch Americans, after all, were hard working, respectful people. They should not forget, warned *De Grondwet*, that they are civilized Americans and must not resort to picket lines and violence like Germans, Bohemians, Poles, and some Englishmen. For those who needed more warning, the local newspapers assessed the total damages caused by a recent strike, outlining the loss of pay, number of arrests,

[104] Ibid., 23 June 1877, 19 Dec. 1885, 6 Feb. 1892; *De Grondwet*, 16 Dec. 1884.

[105] Report of the Immigration Commission (Washington, DC, 1911-12), vol. 1, summary, 419.

[106] Harry Boonstra, "Johannes Groen: Groen in West Michigan," *Origins* 13, no. 1 (2005): 31-32.

number of wounded, and the effect of the work-stoppage on other industries.[107]

For many, the purpose of a union was not always defined or understood. When employees at the West Michigan Furniture Company went on strike in 1893, they did so to oppose a required accident insurance policy that cost them one cent for each dollar earned. That is, the strikers were arguing for individual rights. They wanted to earn what they deserved, but they also wanted to keep what they earned. Neither the union, nor strikers' rights, were much respected. In 1909 dockworkers at the Macatawa Park resort went on strike for a raise from 40¢ to 50¢ an hour. While on their "vacation," as the *Holland City News* called it, the workers were upset to see that student laborers had filled some of their places.[108]

John T. Bergen, a former minister at Hope Church, pointed to Holland as a model city of labor relations. He wrote, "If there exists a reason for the workers to stand up for their rights, then they raise a meeting, lay out clearly their case, and the righteousness of it is immediately recognized by the employer. There is no leader who decrees a strike; no salary is paid to a leader of the labor party, no annual contributions, no cold-blooded demagogue to tyrannize them."[109] Holland did maintain a rather clean record in labor relations, but not all were satisfied with the course of local events.

Populism

The historian Richard Hofstadter described Progressivism as "that broader impulse toward criticism and change that was everywhere so conspicuous after 1900, when the already forceful stream of agrarian discontent was enlarged and redirected by the growing enthusiasm of middle-class people for reform."[110] The agrarian discontent of which Hofstadter spoke came to expression in the Populist movement of the 1890s. The Populists believed that the true wealth of the nation rested in the hands of the "producers," that is, farmers and craftsman. The party's leader, William Jennings Bryan, found support in the rural South and in the West where his support of free silver, or the unlimited coinage of silver, was praised. The Populists opposed industrialization and espoused Jefferson's ideal of a nation of small farmers and

107 *De Grondwet*, 11 May 1886.
108 Ibid., 11 May 1886; *Holland City News*, 22 July 1909.
109 *De Grondwet*, 7 Jan. 1908, translation by Michael Douma.
110 Richard Hofstadter, *Age of Reform: From Bryan to F.D.R.* (New York: Knopf, 1955), 11.

shopkeepers. In Holland, the Populist Party was active, but small, and consisted mostly of Americans and non-Dutch immigrants. The Dutch largely rejected Populism, partly because they opposed its socialistic principles, and partly because it was fused with the Democratic Party. Uncharacteristic of the party at large, Populism in Holland appealed primarily to factory workers rather than farmers.[111]

Socialism

The Marxist ideal of a classless society was more closely approximated in the American Midwest than in any other locale in the early twentieth century. But in the minds of many in Holland, this economic equality was brought about by democracy, respect for the law, and charity. Threats to general stability were scorned. The editor of the *Ottawa County Times* summed up this position when he said, "We are opposed to those who preach agitation and discord." *De Grondwet* added that America was "no place for socialism with its impossible, unworkable demands, nor less for anarchism with its wild dreams and unholy vessels." Professor Nicholas M. Steffens of Western Theological Seminary in an 1885 Thanksgiving Day sermon preached at First and Third Reformed churches on the topic "The Foundation of a Healthy National Life," singled out the socialists for driving a wedge between rich and poor and for breaking down property rights, marriage, and religion.[112]

The 1886 Chicago Haymarket Riot, in which anarchists killed police with a bomb during a May Day rally for the eight-hour workday, and the assassination of President William McKinley in 1901 by an East European anarchist immigrant, did much to damage the reputation of the Socialist Party, both nationally and locally. This is best displayed in the story of Hendrik Meijer, a radical socialist who emigrated from the Netherlands to Holland, Michigan in 1907. When Meijer asked an American of Dutch descent if he knew about anarchy, the man responded simplistically that those people "throw bombs." The local Socialist Party, however, thought little of violent revolution, and few members had anarchist leanings. Rather, the local party was an outgrowth of earlier labor organizations, and to a lesser extent, an adaptation of the Populist ideal of cooperation. The Socialist Party

111 Howard Lubbers, "The History of the Populist Party in the City of Holland and the Dutch Reaction to It," paper, 1968, Calvin College, JAH.

112 *De Grondwet*, 8 Dec. 1885; *Ottawa County Times*, 22 Feb. 1912; *De Grondwet*, 1907, quoted in Hank Meijer, "Coming to Holland in 1907: Life in a City of Immigrants as Seen Through its Newspapers," Hendrik Meijer Papers, JAH.

sought change through the ballot box, and it attempted to convince the working class that they were being abused by capitalist business owners. The party's position was sometimes difficult to understand. New to the Holland scene, Meijer wrote, "the Socialist Dem[ocrats] preach on the streets sometimes. I don't know what the purpose is of that society. How they want to come to Socialism, I don't know. I hope they will all explain that to us."[113]

The Socialist Party in Holland, formed in 1897, was one of the first such organizations in the state. Reformed Church thinking disapproved of secret societies and pledges, and like the Freemasons and labor unions, the Socialists met opposition from the Reformed pulpits. Many believed that it was a contradiction to be both a practicing Christian and a Socialist. Thus, the latter tended to come from the ranks of the secular or unchurched who often lived on the cultural periphery. They included Americans born in other cities, new Dutch immigrants, and people who for one reason or another did not completely fit in. Among the Socialists themselves there was considerable debate on the party's platform and goals. Some of the new immigrants, being influenced by the socialist-anarchist ideologies of Ferdinand Domela Nieuwenhuis, known as the pioneer of socialism in the Netherlands, were of a more radical and utopian disposition and were called Free Socialists. Fifteen of these radicals, according to Hendrik Meijer, formed a Dutch-speaking wing of the local Socialist Party. The English-speaking American Socialists tended to support the more moderate ideologies of the Socialist Labor Party leader Eugene V. Debs. Debs made his presence felt locally, addressing a large audience when he spoke in Holland in 1905. Two years later, a committee of the local Socialist Party attempted, this time without success, to secure Debs as a speaker for Holland's Fourth of July festival.[114]

Because the Socialists were, in a sense, a separate and eventually faltering pillar of society, their story has been largely neglected. Historian Henry S. Lucas dismissed their presence when he wrote, "Neither among the Dutch farmers in Michigan, Illinois, Wisconsin, Iowa, and the Dakotas, who are as determinedly independent and individualistic

[113] Hendrik Meijer, Hengelo, the Netherlands, to Zientje Mantel, 17 Sept. 1907, 11 Aug. 1907, Hendrik Meijer Papers, JAH.

[114] Pieter Stokvis, "Socialist Immigrants and the American Dream," 98, in *The Dutch-American Experience: Essays in Honor of Robert P. Swierenga* (Free University of Amsterdam, 2000), eds. Hans Krabbendam and Larry J. Wagenaar; *Holland City News*, 9 May 1907. *De Grondwet*, 4 Feb. 1908, reports that another well-known figure, John C. Chase, a utopian socialist who later ran for governor of New York State, gave a speech in Holland in early 1908.

as farmers can be, nor among the Dutch factory workers in Grand Rapids and Holland, Michigan, were there any socialists." The voice of Holland's established citizenry has been predominant. These Hollanders were more likely to side politically with the Republican Party first, and they considered the Democratic Party as the only legitimate alternative. A sympathizer in *De Gereformeerde Amerikaan* declared that many of the periodical's readers knew as much about words like communism and socialism as a cow knows about the Spanish language![115]

Changing economic tides elevated the Socialist Party. In 1907 a financial panic disrupted the national markets, and socialists blamed the panic on a few very powerful men, like the industrialists J. Pierpont Morgan, John D. Rockefeller, and Cornelius Vanderbilt, who controlled large shares of the economy and had allegedly manipulated the banks for their own gain. Socialist sympathies in Holland reached their peak following this economic downturn. Several socialist newspapers appeared on the local scene, the *Volksstem* in 1908 and the *Holland Progressive Worker* in 1910. In 1914 the Dutch Socialists broke off from the latter newspaper to publish *Voorwaarts*, then the only Dutch-language Socialist newspaper in North America (the *Volksstem* having ceased publication).[116]

More telling was the clean sweep in the spring 1911 municipal elections, when every alderman was turned out of office. Their replacements believed that voters wanted to follow more progressive lines. The Second Ward elected a Socialist, Vernon F. King, who worked at a local furniture factory. King benefited from a three-way race, and with eighty-five votes, he slipped past Gerrit Van Zanten (seventy-seven votes) and Jacob De Peyter (thirty-seven votes) to claim the office. It was rare indeed that Holland would vote for a Socialist, but this had much to do with the demographics of the Second Ward, which had a population of largely native-born blue collar workers. Vernon King had been associated with the local Socialist scene for at least a decade.

[115] Henry S. Lucas, *Netherlanders in America: Dutch Immigration to the United States and Canada, 1789-1950* (Ann Arbor: University of Michigan Press, 1955; reprinted, Grand Rapids: Eerdmans, 1989), 573; Meijer, "Young Radical in Holland," 4 Aug. 1980, Hendrik Meijer Papers, JAH; Henry Holkeboer, "De Christen Werkman in den Socialen Strijd," *De Gereformeerde Amerikaan* (May 1904): 193-210 (from Christian Workers Association in Patterson, NJ).

[116] *Holland City News*, 15 Dec. 1910, 30 Apr. 1914; *De Grondwet*, 14 Apr. 1908, 15 Dec. 1910. *De Volkstem* was a monthly periodical under director Arie van Doesburg of Holland and editor J. Hoogerheide of Grand Rapids. *Der Anarchist: Anarchistisch-Communistisches Organ*, a German-language paper printed in New York, was also read among the Dutch Socialists in Holland, MI (Stokvis, "Socialist Immigrants," 91-101).

He had long endured threats and name-calling like "Shorty King, the Anarchist." But King rejected this label and actually considered anarchism to be in conflict with socialism.[117]

At the 1902 Socialist County Convention, King, then twenty-eight years old, made his politics known, when he proclaimed:

> The slavish wageworker, in submitting to being robbed of the meat from his table, may be assured that he may soon eat husks with the swine unless he asserts his manhood and stands for his birthright with the organization of his class, the Socialist labor party. The preachers of the Christian Reformed Church may assert the brotherhood of capital and labor, but the fact of the miners' and teamsters' strikes proves the class struggle in big broad facts.[118]

By 1911 citizens were curious and a bit concerned about how alderman-elect King would vote. The Holland Socialists tried to set their minds at ease. "If he thinks it is against the interests of the working class of Holland, then Alderman King will vote against it. If it is for the best interests of the workers of Holland, then Alderman King is for it." King tried to stay true to this maxim. In one council meeting, he argued that the city was favoring large consumers in electricity and water rates. King also became involved in the issue of the city gas plant, a dispute that had been drawn out over many years. The problem was that while Hollanders wanted to see a city-run gas plant, none of them wanted to pay the higher taxes to support it. On the other hand, a private gas company might gouge the consumer. When the common council finally decided in 1911 to let a private gas company operate in the city, King was the sole holdout for a public plant (chapter 25).[119]

Coal was the other fuel for home heating and firing steam boilers, and King and other trustbusters in 1912 charged that Holland was in the grips of the Coal Trust, a consortium of local dealers who kept supplies tight and prices high. Perhaps it was time for the city to open a municipal coal yard, they suggested. Commissioner John Vandenberg, chair of the city's Charter Review Commission, scotched that idea. Holland had plenty of competition among coal dealers, he declared, and no price-fixing took place. Coal mine barons fixed prices, not local dealers, Vander Berg declared, thereby deflecting the issue

117 *Holland City News*, 27 Apr. 1911; *De Grondwet*, 1 Oct. 1901. King failed in his bid for Justice of the Peace on the Labor Party ticket in 1901.

118 *Ottawa County Times*, 5 Sept. 1902.

119 *Holland City News*, 27 Apr., 21 Sept., 19, 26 Oct. 1911.

locally. Progressives also drew a bead on a so-called "plumbers' trust" in Holland that presumably set artificially high prices.[120]

King's major battle, however, was to reduce the workday from ten to eight hours for city employees, with *no* reduction in wages. In the first common council meeting of 1912, he made this proposal, thereby setting off a fiery debate that continued into the next few council meetings. Alderman Drinkwater supported a nine-hour day, given the "strenuous nature" of the work. Others did not think it fair to pay city workers for ten hours if they were to work less, and they argued that most other men in the city worked a full ten hours. King jumped in, "What's the matter with Holland. We are too conservative, always following, never leading. Let us lead in this 8-hour movement." Alderman Dirk W. Jellema moved to table King's motion, which passed six to four. The council then resolved, with only one dissenting vote, that the city sewer diggers, due to the heavy work and hot summer weather, be given ten hours pay for nine hours of work. King settled for the nine-hour workday as a small victory. This decision gave King some confidence, but when this decision was rescinded at a later meeting, "Rocket" King, speaking in a louder voice than usual, protested vigorously. Alderman Clarence J. Lokker took offense at King's rampage and said he would not "be hollered deaf, and be made a boy by a socialist agitator." Convinced by Mayor Stephan to lower his voice, King continued, and spoke honestly about the grievances of the laborers, pleading for an eight-hour day. To sufficiently appease, or at least temporarily quiet, alderman King, the council resolved to set up a committee to investigate labor conditions and to ask factories to cooperate with a nine-hour workday.[121]

While outwardly King appeared to be accepted as a fellow member of the city council, inwardly many feared his position of power. The *Holland City News* often portrayed him as a "loose cannon" and ridiculed him for having more passion than brains. It reported that he often "jumped" from his chair and roared like "the King of beasts." They also derided his speeches as "spiels." In 1913 King proposed, tongue in cheek, to rename Fifth Street near his home "Manhattan Boulevard." It was a "dig" at capitalists. His colleagues, editor Ben Mulder recalled, "laughed this off, fearing that this resourceful 'city father' would later demand that River Avenue be named 'Coney Island.'" Despite the editorial ridicule, King considered the newspaper to be a friend that stood up for him on labor issues even if it would not stand for socialism.

120 *Holland Sentinel*, 6 Aug. 1912.
121 *Holland City News*, 4, 18 Jan., 8 Feb. 1912.

In 1912, with the fiery council debates as impetus, King ran for mayor of Holland. He finished last in a three-way race, gaining less than 25 percent of the vote, but he held on to his council seat in 1913 and again in 1914. That year, Holland's Socialist Party asked for his resignation due to his alleged abuse of power while in office. King unsuccessfully appealed to the state organization but apparently left Holland after his fall-out with the party. He had been the leader of the local Socialists and their number one champion for four years.[122]

Other socialists began to make their mark as well. Olaf J. Hansen, who had worked at a tannery and later as a mail carrier, was ideologically rooted in the Labor Party of the 1880s. Hansen failed numerous times in his pursuit of political office: for alderman in 1905, 1909, 1914, 1915, and 1916; for constable in 1908, for coroner in 1910, for mayor in 1906, 1910, 1911, and 1913; and for state representative in 1914. But once, in 1912, Hansen won election as alderman in the Fourth Ward, while another socialist, Leonard DeWitt, who had also endured many electoral defeats, was elected constable for the Second Ward. This was the peak of socialist officeholders in city government.

In 1914, when Holland initiated non-partisan municipal elections, a candidate's political affiliation became secondary in importance to his personal character, if it had not been so already, and the Socialist Party faded into obscurity. Socialism in local politics was an undercurrent with a substantial following at the polls. Socialist policies appealed to factory workers, but political progressives tolerated this ideology only if it buttressed their agenda. For many new immigrants, socialism was simply not as attractive as capitalism. As Alexis De Tocqueville noted in his early nineteenth century political analysis of America, when a nation is democratic and a majority of the people feel they have more to lose than to gain by a revolution, they will generally oppose any threat to the social order. Hank Meijer, in his history of his grandfather Hendrik, agreed that Hollanders "felt that they had a stake in a great democracy and thus had little patience for rabble-rousers."[123] They thought the French Revolution, with its anti-religious enlightenment character and great display of violence, was no model to emulate.

Struggles were certain for the worker, but if one worked hard, one could succeed. Jantje Sloothaak Hooijer, a Dutch immigrant who arrived in Holland with her husband in 1904, wrote family in the Old Country that "the men earn good money here in the factories, so that

122 Ibid., 7 July 1911, 22 Oct. 1914, "Twenty-five Years Ago Today" 18 Nov. 1937.

123 Hank Meijer, *Thrifty Years: The Life of Hendrik Meijer* (Grand Rapids: Eerdmans, 1984), 32.

we can have a good life here if we are healthy. But you must not think, as you wrote in your last letter, that someone here can get rich all at once." Ten years later, in 1914, Jantje continued on the same theme, that although there were difficulties, they were mitigated by opportunity. "It is also not very busy nowadays with work. Some factories don't run a couple days a week, and a worker who has a household with children needs to work every day. Food is not as cheap as when we first came here." In comparison to workers in the Netherlands, Jantje noted, "local laborers are doing well. Here in America a worker can do as he wants and put on a white collar, and there are also those that don't have it so bad. America is a free country."[124]

Immigrant Hendrik Meijer was amazed at the flexibility in the job market. In the Netherlands he needed official papers to be released from one job and begin another. The process and the search for a new job could take months. In America, during a good year, one could literally quit a job in the morning and find employment somewhere else in the afternoon. Even Meijer, an anarchist-leaning radical Socialist, was won over by the tide of progressivism. As his grandson Hank Meijer wrote, "In the Old Country such radicalism seemed to a factory youth like the one hope for altering the oppressive status quo. . . . [But the radicals] found themselves swept up in the tolerant tide of the Progressive Era. Radicalism . . . [was] never a match for the American Dream."[125]

Problems of the laboring class were also difficult to pin on the local capitalists. Holland had no super-rich for workers to be jealous of or to blame for abuse. If the workers were being exploited, then who was doing the exploiting? Where were lavish mansions and flashy cars? Workers struggled, but they were content. This is perhaps best displayed in an August 1907 news report, which reads: "There was a strike Saturday in the ranks of the men employed by the city to build a sewer on West Fifteenth Street. A number of Hollanders, claiming that they did not get their share in the American Square Deal, refused to work and became so violent that it nearly came to blows. They were, however, soon appeased and sent to work."[126]

Influence of Abraham Kuyper

Mainstream Hollanders and especially the new wave of immigrants from the Netherlands were likely to be influenced by the thoughts of

124 Jantje Slothaak Hooijer letters, 1904, 23 Oct. 1914, ACC.

125 Hank Meijer, "Coming to Holland in 1907," 32; Meijer, *Thrifty Years*, 45.

126 *Holland City News*, Aug. 1907, quoted in Hendrik Meijer, "Young Radical in Holland" (1980), 9.

the Neo-Calvinist theologian and politician Abraham Kuyper, and particularly so after his 1898 tour of America and the subsequent 1899 publication of his Stone Lectures on Calvinism. Kuyper (1837-1920) was trained in history and theology, and this helped form his worldview, which he trumpeted in his newspaper, *De Standaard*, launched in Amsterdam in 1872. While the popular historian John Lothrop Motley attributed the Dutch Golden Age to a victory of reason and humanism, Kuyper credited Calvinism as its central force. Turning to politics in church and state, Kuyper advocated Christian schools and founded the Free University of Amsterdam in 1880. He became a political force in his own right and served as prime minister of the Netherlands from 1901 to 1905.

Religiously, Kuyper called for a reformation in the Dutch Reformed Church that, as in 1834, was rejected, and the dissenting congregations were forced to leave in 1886. The movement, called the *Doleantie*—from the Latin infinitive verb *doleren*, to sorrow—after several years of struggle, joined forces in 1892 with the main line of 1834 Seceders, the *Christelijke Gereformeerde Kerk*, to form the *Gereformeerde Kerk Nederland* (GKN).[127]

Kuyper was a powerful opponent of anarchism and revolution; he rejected all monolithic and utopian systems. Yet he also condemned overly conservative or laissez-faire governments. Kuyper therefore took a middle ground politically and advocated that Christians must become involved in political life. They were to shun conservative apathy and have a social conscience. He called for a pluralistic society, divided into segmented cultural "pillars" of Calvinists, Catholics, and Socialists/ Secularists, each with its own schools, newspapers, labor unions, political parties, and societies. The Calvinist ideal was to claim "every square inch of the culture" for King Jesus, who rules the world at the right hand of God the Father.[128]

Many Dutch emigrants in the decades before the First World War carried to America Kuyper's religious beliefs and cultural ideals, which were more socially active than the inward pietism of the Seceder emigrants of the 1840s. But both groups shared a commitment to Reformed Christian orthodoxy and a spirit-filled life.

In late October 1898 Kuyper visited Holland for the first and only time to repeat the last of his six Stone Lectures, entitled "Calvinism and

127 Hendrik Bouma, *Secession, Doleatie, and Union: 1834-1892* (in Dutch, Groningen, 1892, trans. Theodore Plantinga, Neerlandia, Alberta: Inheritance Publications, 1995).

128 James D. Bratt, *Dutch Calvinism in Modern America: A History of a Conservative Subculture* (Grand Rapids: Eerdmans, 1984), 14-33.

the Future," at Third Reformed Church before a "magnificent turnout." In a letter to his wife, Kuyper reported that two hundred students met him at the train station with "hurrahs," together with Mayor Germ Mokma and other dignitaries. His popularity can be attributed in part to his optimism. He praised the role that the Dutch played in founding and shaping early America into a Calvinistic nation. He then hailed this Calvinistic America as the future of humankind. Kuyper's Neo-Calvinism reinforced American patriotism by stressing the unique role that America, through Calvinism, would play in changing the world. Unfortunately, he chose for whatever reason to deliver the lecture in Dutch, rather than English, and not even one-third of the audience could understand him. Kuyper's strongest local proponent was Nicholas Steffens, professor of theology at Western Theological Seminary from 1884 to 1895. Steffens wrote Kuyper already in 1894: "I recognize your political persuasion—I hardly need say it—as the only proper one. We may or may not approve of Democratic principles, but the world *is becoming* democratic. And luckily our Calvinistic world-and-life-view is sufficiently elastic to exhibit its perfections in the new forms."[129]

Kuyper spent two days in Holland. Following his evening address at Third Church on the twenty-seventh, Professor Henry Dosker of Western Theological Seminary and his wife hosted him at a reception in their home. The next morning he gave a speech to a "chock-full" room of Hope College professors and students on campus, likely the gymnasium/chapel. Then he was taken on a tour of Vriesland, Zeeland, Drenthe, and Overisel, including lunch at a farmer's home. On the evening of the twenty-eighth, city leaders honored him at an exquisite banquet at the New City Hotel, complete with a printed menu card. "Toasts without end," the honoree told his wife. He slipped off his wedding ring after the first hundred hardy handshakes, because he "couldn't stand the pain. And then they say that many hands make light work," he quipped.[130]

Both Reformed and Christian Reformed leaders claimed Kuyper as their own, in hopes that he could help save Reformed tradition and theology in the struggle against modernism. Netherlands historian George Harinck explains, "It was to many of them as if a second apostle Paul had been sent to the Gentiles in darkened Europe and America. Kuyper's ideas gave the Reformed people the feeling they were delivered

129 George Harinck, ed., *Kuyper in America* (Sioux Center, IA: Dort College Press, 2012), 45-46 (quotes); *Holland City News*, 28 Oct. 1898; Nicholas Steffens to Abraham Kuyper, 1894 (quote), Heritage Hall Dutch Immigrant Letter Collection, ACC.

130 Harinck, *Kuyper in America*, 46-47 (quote 47).

Menu card of banquet at the New City Hotel honoring Dr. Abraham Kuyper, October 28, 1898 (*courtesy Kuyper Archive, Historical Documentation Centre for Dutch Protestantism, 1800 to the present day, VU University*)

from their dead alleys in church life and were overcoming their intellectual setbacks. Kuyper united and strengthened them by giving them a worldview as strong and cohesive as evolutionist or socialist theories." Hope College recognized Kuyper's accomplishments in 1908 by conferring on him an honorary doctorate in absentia.[131]

Kuyper's influence became readily apparent in the Dutch American press and helped form opinions on the role of labor and capital. *De Gereformeerde Amerikaan*, a Kuyperian sheet published in Grand Rapids, ran an article in 1904 on the role of the Christian worker in the battle of the social classes. The author used biblical passages to show that the struggle between rich and poor was age old and that selfishness was at the root of the problem. God wanted men to be equal, not in riches, but in sight, so that all could be taken care of by their fellow man. Both capital and workers were to blame for society's ills, although capital held the larger responsibility for easing tensions. Both sides had to continue in Christian ways. The unions and workers' groups most often ran antithetical to Christian virtues because they brought enmity between the two sides and even divided their own members into bitter and selfish camps.[132]

The Dutch in Grand Rapids started a new national political party based on neo-Calvinism, and in Holland in 1912, the Dutch organized the Puritan Club, a Christian political association. Kuyperian beliefs

131 George Harinck, "Henry Dosker, the man in between Albertus C. Van Raalte and Abraham Kuyper," lecture given at Hope College, 29 Mar. 2001, JAH.

132 Henry Holkeboer, "De Christen Werkman," *De Gereformeerde Amerikaan* (1904): 193.

also led to the Christian Labor Association, a labor union that tried to mediate between owners and workers and promote Christian ethics to prevent the exploitation of workers. It also eschewed the strike as a weapon. For some a Christian labor union was an oxymoron; for others it was an answer to class conflict.[133]

Changing lifestyles

The quickening pace of life, the Americanization of the culture, and new social mores were all issues of concern for the generation of pioneers now reaching their dotage. In 1897, the last year of the 1890s depression, Gezina Van der Haar-Visscher related many of her concerns in her diary.

> Things aren't getting any better in our city. There is so much sin evident. Not nearly as many people go to church any more but the saloons are patronized heavily. Three more saloons are opening up, so they say. There is also an Interurban train which now runs to Macatawa Park on Sunday. Oh, that Christians might be more faithful within their own family circles to combat sin. The preachers are denouncing the trend but apparently their hearers are merely giving lip service and not doing anything about it. I wish that more would take heed to what is said in the Bible—'Righteousness exalteth a nation but sins destroys it always.'[134]

Arnold Mulder, the editor of the *Holland Sentinel* from 1912 to 1929, published a few works of fiction set in West Michigan.[135] More than anyone else, Mulder was able to capture the feel of the Holland *Kolonie* as it wrestled with the changing of the times. Three of his books take up a similar setting, a conservative Dutch village lying outside the *De Stad*, and all with a similar protagonist, a college or seminary student from the village. *The Dominie of Harlem* (1913) relates the story of a young Christian Reformed minister, a man in sympathy with the social gospel, who accepts a call to the Harlem Christian Reformed Church. There he encounters prejudice and criticism over his preaching and free ways of living. In the end, he manages in sincerity and honesty to reclaim the community from prejudice and intolerance. Despite, or perhaps because of, the book's tendency to be critical of conservative

133 *De Grondwet*, 2 Apr. 1912; Mulder, *Americans from Holland*, 222; Christian Labor Association, http://cla.usa.com, accessed 12 Feb. 2010.

134 Geesje Van der Haar-Visscher Diary, May 1897, HMA.

135 Mulder was a Hope College graduate of 1907.

culture, reviewers lavishly praised Mulder for his "honest" portrayal of Holland and its surrounding villages. With this initial success, Mulder continued in the local genre.[136]

In *Bram of the Five Corners* (1915), Mulder used the fictitious Five Corners as the hometown of Bram, a student at Christian College (Hope College Preparatory Department). The book is principally a story of the love life of young Bram, which runs the gauntlet of issues surrounding relationships. As in his first book, readers could easily take offense at some of Mulder's more descriptive passages that were rife with barbs aimed at his local audience. "Practically all who graduated each spring from the theological seminary in *De Stad* rather perversely insisted on entering holy wedlock a few days after commencement." Church members abhorred "evollootion [evolution], . . . this woman votin' and them revival meetin's." Higher education was abhorrent, except for the local seminary. Bram's mother warns him in typical Dutch-speak, "You mustn't learn too hard Bram, *mijn jongen*." About Mulder's first two books, the *Holland City News* editor observed: "There has been a great deal of controversy, some alleging that the pictures Mr. Mulder drew are caricatures, others contending that they are drawn with absolute fidelity."[137]

Mulder waited five years before completing his trilogy with the *Outbound Road* (1919). Once again he drew a distinction between a conservative rural Dutch community, "East Nassau" and De Stad. In the story, a country couple, the stereotypical Dutch Foppe and Sarah Spykhoven, adopt a Polish child, name him Teunis, and try to raise him as a responsible, obedient youth. Teunis' frequent misbehavior is met by Foppe's strict punishment and Sarah's sympathy. The Spykhovens have their work cut out for them in raising Teunis. They disapprove of his attending the County Fair because of the *schandalig* (scandalous) horse races and "opra-houses," and they consider Shakespeare and Dickens *verderfelijk* (pernicious). When Teunis becomes a student at Christian College (Hope College), he struggles between his strict upbringing and now loose surroundings, becoming something of a hybrid of the two. In the final scene, an older, wiser, and changed Teunis returns to the Spykhoven home where he sees Foppe, worn thin in his later years, still at the family table, clutching his large Dutch Bible. Father and son shake hands, knowing that while their ideals will never be the same,

136 Arnold Mulder, *The Dominie of Harlem* (Chicago: A. C. McClurg, 1915).

137 Arnold Mulder, *Bram of the Five Corners* (Chicago: A. C. McClurg, 1915), 7, 39, 215; *Holland City News*, 27 May 1915.

their love for one another and the bond of friendship can never be broken. Mulder, an iconoclast in his younger days, in middle life came to appreciate his heritage.[138]

Paul de Kruif, son of Zeeland implement dealer and banker Hendrik De Kruif and his wife Hendrika—the Netherlands-born daughter of a Reformed Church minister—also turned against his faith and upbringing, although some traits persisted. "Raised in the narrowest little town in the USA," as he would say, De Kruif wiped the dust off his shoes when he left Zeeland to study medicine and bacteriology at the University of Michigan, earning a doctoral degree in 1916. During several years at the prestigious Rockefeller Institute (for Medical Research) in New York City, De Kruif made the acquaintance of the acerbic literary critic Henry L. Menken and the budding novelist Sinclair Lewis. He collaborated with Lewis in the Pulitzer Prize-winning "doctor's novel," *Arrowsmith* (1925). De Kruif, the "small town hick from the Dutch bible belt," as Menken first derided him, had already set himself to writing on medical subjects.

In 1926 De Kruif achieved international fame in his own right with the publication of *Microbe Hunters*, a history of medical discoveries from the invention of the simple microscope in the seventeenth century to the conquest of germs such as diphtheria, malaria, yellow fever, and syphilis in the early twentieth century. A flood of articles on science and medicine soon appeared in *Ladies' Home Journal*, *Country Gentlemen*, and *Reader's Digest*. Over time De Kruif became an advocate for American health care for the poor, improved hospital practices, and progressive politics. In the late 1920s, De Kruif and his wife Rhea moved to a cottage they named "Wake Robin" nestled in the dunes between Holland and Saugatuck. Here he lived out his years writing books with countless references to lakeshore flora and fauna, which enlightened readers nationwide about the natural beauty of the Holland area. Once De Kruif hosted novelist Ernest Hemingway at Wake Robin, but he shunned the locals as too religious and conservative for his secular humanist beliefs and socialist politics. Nevertheless, he was proud of his Dutch roots and chose to be buried in the De Kruif family plot in Zeeland Cemetery, where his grave is marked with a tall obelisk engraved simply "Paul."[139]

138 Arnold Mulder, *The Outbound Road* (Boston and New York: Houghton Mifflin, 1919); Michael Douma, "The Evolution of Dutch American Identities, 1847-2011" (PhD diss., Florida State University, 2011).

139 Jan Peter Verhave, "Paul de Kruif: Medical Conscience of America," 191-202, in *Dutch-American Arts and Letters in Historical Persepctive*, eds. Robert P. Swierenga, Jacob E. Nyenhuis, and Nella Kennedy (Holland, MI: Van Raalte Press, 2008); and

Paul de Kruif (1890-1971) in his later years, with his home in the dunes south of Holland (*courtesy Larry B. Massie*)

Movies and censorship

In 1910 Nick J. Whelan, editor of the *Holland City News*, was pleased that the city's new movie house, the Knickerbocker Theatre, did not have a generic name or one associated with frivolity. Knickerbocker is a term "that suggests all that is most dignified and cultivated in Dutch life in America," said Whelan, especially the "matchless literary art of [Washington] Irving." Hollanders hoped that the theater would provide amusement for the youth and keep them away from alcohol. "We must have amusements in order to make Holland loved by those who live here. The day of narrowness in these matters is passed," declared Whelan. "We believe that a theatre is what the people make it, so is a club house, pool-room, YMCA, or church."[140]

But theatres faced a tough task to gain acceptance. In 1914 the board of education became involved in a debate over letting children attend theaters. Movies, the board claimed, play an important role in education, but they also often give a false sense of morality or ideals. The board then recommended that the common council establish a committee (a censor board) to view and pass judgment on any show before its public release in Holland.[141]

Mayor Nicodemus Bosch noted: "The City of Holland is a cosmopolitan city, and yet it is also a religious city, as is well evidenced by the number of churches in our midst, and the regularity with which

---

"The Dutchness in Paul de Kruif: Different, but not Indifferent," in *Diverse Destinies: Dutch* Kolonies *in Wisconsin and the East*, Nella Kennedy, Robert P. Swierenga, and Mary Risseeuw, eds. (Holland: Van Raalte Press, 2012), 189-204.

140 *Holland City News*, 4 Aug. 1910, 30 Mar. 1911. Mulder seems to have been unaware of the critical image that Washington Irving had drawn of the Dutch.

141 Common Council Minutes, 19 Aug. 1914, HMA.

the people attend religious services. . . . In view of this fact and that our people are so largely religious in their views, sentiments and tendencies, it would seem to me that it particularly behooves us for that reason among many others, to see to it that our amusements are kept within pure and moral bounds." While admitting the usefulness of movies, Bosch would proscribe any "pictures of crimes, indecency, debauchery, and any suggestive pictures."[142]

The common council responded to public pressure and established the Board of Motion Picture Censors, with a badge that read "Censor—Special Police Arrangements." The ten-member board (soon raised to sixteen) was tasked to attend the movie houses and review new films for immorality and indecency. Censors had the power to reject a film or delete objectionable scenes. During the first six months, the censors banned fourteen films, four of which portrayed crime and ten deemed "indecent, immoral, vulgar, or suggestive." Another twenty-three films had scenes cut out that showed or suggested murder, burglary, and suicide. Patrons tried to outwit the censors by flocking to the first showings of films that reportedly "pushed the envelope." Little wonder that the "entire town was gotten by the ears on this matter."[143]

A flash point was the screenings by James W. Himebaugh of the Royal Theatre of six "indecent" Charlie Chaplin films, which so infuriated the censors that the common council nearly revoked his license. In 1916 the board screened "Trilby," a Parisian romance movie to be run by the Apollo Theater, and deemed it "not wholly in harmony with the standard of Morals and Decency." To maintain the movie's plot, the board recommended the omission of two scenes in which "women lift skirts immodestly." The interplay between theater managers and censors seemed like a game of "cat and mouse." One incident at the Strand Theater in 1919 almost caused a riot. After the feature film had ended and the trailer, a comedy, had the crowd in stitches, the screen went dark. Manager Himebaugh announced that the censors had banned the second and third reels. The crowd of shop and factory workers, who had put down good money for their one pleasure, "went wild" and threatened to "boycott the town."[144]

It did not help that the morals police were sometimes double-minded. The line between decency and indecency was in the eye of the beholder, and board members could not always agree. One time, eight

[142] Ibid., 7 Oct. 1914, HMA.

[143] *Holland City News*, 22 Apr., 6 May 1915.

[144] Ibid., 6 Apr., 1 June, 16 Nov. 1916, 18 Dec. 1919; Common Council Minutes, 5 Apr. 1916, HMA.

censors viewed a movie, and only two agreed to ban it; the other six disagreed and stuck to their guns. Being a censor board volunteer was time consuming and frustrating. It would have helped if the common council had passed the proposal of the board of education that was brought to the table in 1915, to require the censor board to screen all films *before* they were shown, not after. But the aldermen never could bring themselves to do this.[145]

The issue came to a head in early 1920, when the censor board resigned en masse after they could not agree on banning a controversial Strand movie. The aldermen read Himebaugh the riot act and threatened to revoke the Strand's license. Himebaugh, Holland's "pioneer 'movie' man," appeared with his attorney Daniel Ten Cate. Such a huge crowd packed the council chambers and the overflow room and lobby as to give the city fathers pause; they decided not to pull the permit. This spelled the end of the censor board. The morals police were not saddened when their nemesis, James Himebaugh, died suddenly in 1925.[146]

Several theaters in 1928 began running midnight shows on Sunday, and this led several churches to charge that the movie houses were planning to open their doors on Sunday. Although manager Henry Carley denied any such intentions, a coalition of Reformed churches called for the city to pass a law against Sunday shows. It failed to do so, and by 1931, the theaters did indeed open on Sundays. A pastors committee organized a petition drive and quickly amassed several thousand signatures asking the common council to legislate against Sunday movies. Another fight over "blue laws" was avoided only because the Butterfield Company, owner all of three city theaters, acquiesced to the will of the majority. "Theatre Folks 'Come Clean' on Sunday Movies," heralded the headline in the *Holland City News*.[147]

The growing power and commercialization of the Hollywood motion picture industry also crippled community censorship efforts. Film companies contracted with theater companies to screen all the latest pictures, and films were passed along from Holland to Grand Haven to Muskegon, and down the line. Holland was fortunate to get a first release of all new films. Censors that arbitrarily rejected certain films forced theaters to break contracts and to jeopardize their access to first-run films. The film industry went one better. They encouraged the creation of state and national boards to set standards, which took control out of local hands, and gave Hollywood the chance to help write

145 *Holland City News*, 21, 28 Oct. 1915, 18 May 1933.

146 Ibid., 8, 15 Jan., 5 Feb. 1920, 12 Nov. 1925.

147 Ibid., 2 Feb. 1928, 10, 17, 24 Sept. 1931.

the codes. Holland city attorney Clarence J. Lokker in 1933 admitted that local efforts were rendered moot, and Holland should simply trust the judgment of these greater bodies. Yet, efforts by city leaders to uphold public decency persisted. In 1950, because of citizen complaints about Ingrid Bergman's film "Stromboli," the city council by a six-to-five vote banned all Bergman and Rossellini films in Holland theaters.[148]

Conclusion

In 1916 the students at Hope College put on a pageant, retelling the major events in the history of Holland from 1847. Befitting the age, the story ended with words from "The Spirit of Progress," which proclaimed in the production's final breath:

> The past is great,
> The present greater still,
> but we shall see,
> The grander, nobler, future, yet to be.[149]

148 Ibid., 18 May 1933, 16 Feb. 1950.

149 "Pageant of Hope," Teunis Keppel Family Papers, box 1, HMA.

CHAPTER 21

The First World War

"President Wilson declared war against Germany today, Good Friday—the day that Christ died to bring peace into the world."

Diary of Hope College student Elizabeth Van Burk, April 6, 1917.[1]

On April 6, 1917, the United States declared war on Germany, and while the country mobilized for war, Holland organized patriotic drives for wartime support. Community action and cooperation were critical to coping with the demands of war. Fittingly, the theme of cooperation emerged at the first wartime patriotic rally held April 16 at Carnegie Hall on the campus of Hope College. When a Holland citizen asked if women could attend the meeting, the editor of the *Holland Sentinel* wrote, "YES. Their part in the war is recognized as well as the men's role. Without them, this country could do nothing. Every woman in Holland who is able to leave her home for the evening should be found at Carnegie tonight." Indeed the auditorium that evening was filled to capacity, and women were well represented.[2]

1 Elizabeth Van Burk Diary, Holland Museum Archives (HMA).
2 *Holland Sentinel*, 13, 16, 17, 18 Apr. 1917.

The rally began with local bands leading the citizens in renditions of standard tunes like "The Star Spangled Banner," "The Battle Hymn of the Republic," and "America." Speakers followed. The organizers could hardly have chosen more apt men to address the crowd. First, there was Civil War veteran Gerrit Van Schelven, a respected old-timer who had served as alderman, postmaster, and justice of the peace, as well as in a number of other positions. As the accepted local authority on all matters historical, Van Schelven chose to speak about the patriotism and courage of the boys of '61. A. P. Johnson, *Grand Rapids News* editor, arose next. While speaking in favor of the war aims, Johnson could little anticipate that three months hence, his brother Carl, one of the most popular students at the Preparatory School of Hope College in 1915, would be killed in France. That Carl had moved to Grand Rapids and was a lieutenant in a Grand Rapids battalion did little to lessen the shock of the tragedy, and the mayor ordered Holland's city hall flag lowered to half staff.[3]

The third speaker for the evening, and the main event, was the political face of Holland himself, the Honorable Gerrit J. Diekema, whose son Willis was then a pilot in the Ninety-First American Aviation Squadron and would later see action in France. Diekema began his speech with a tribute to Holland's brave Civil War veterans, then transitioned into a history lesson of America's great sacrifices for freedom and finished with a flurry of patriotic rhetoric. Nearing the end of his speech, Diekema looked into the eyes of the young women in the crowd, and with quivering lips, uttered a stern warning to any girl who would marry a young man to save him from conscription. She would be "guilty of treason and should thereafter wear dresses of yellow," he cried.[4]

With the rally nearing an end, the young men in attendance were asked to remain in the auditorium while the crowd dispersed and headed home. Major John H. Schouten, a recruiting officer for the Michigan National Guard, then addressed the men. When he finished the stirring speeches, 125 men volunteered within ten minutes, and many more followed suit later.[5]

Following the rally, Holland was pulsing with patriotism. Local retailers soon sold out of American flags, and when new shipments arrived a week later, nearly every factory in Holland purchased a new

3 Ibid., 12, 14, 16, 17 Apr., 10, 31 May 1917.

4 *De Grondwet*, 24 Apr. 1917.

5 *Holland Sentinel*, 16 Apr. 1917; *De Grondwet*, 24 Apr. 1917; *Anchor*, 25 Apr.1917; *De Hope*, 24 Apr. 1917; Speeches, Diekema Papers, box 5, HMA.

Holland Furniture Co. workers rally in support of Democratic President Woodrow Wilson's "America First" re-election campaign slogan in 1916 (*courtesy Larry B. Massie*)

flag to fly. The Limbert Company furniture factory, with a twenty-by-thirty-foot flag waving 135 feet in the air, stole the show. But patriotic displays were not enough. An anonymous contributor to *De Grondwet* argued that America needed a rallying call. Perhaps something like "*Allen voor Amerika, Alles for Amerika*" (Everyone for America, Everything for America), he thought, could be our "*Vive la France*." Also, in early May the chamber of commerce sent a resolution to President Woodrow Wilson, pledging its support in this difficult time. Soon thereafter, a patriotic society was founded, with Emory P. Davis as president. Early

Soldiers from Central Avenue Christian Reformed Church assemble for a group photo with the pastor, Rev. Bernard H. Einink, and two other leaders, perhaps leaders of the Young Men's Society (in suits seated on chairs in the middle). Every congregation had such an ensemble, and pastors prayed fervently every Sunday for the soldiers' safe return (*Central Avenue Christian Reformed Church Archives*)

War service banner at the entrance of First Reformed Church, with ninety-two stars representing service members formed into "USA." The banner was likely hung in 1918 under the pastorate of Rev. Henry J. Veldman (*courtesy Myron Van Ark*)

excitement culminated in a well-attended Memorial Day parade on May 31, 1917.[6]

By then Holland's wartime support organizations had begun in earnest. The most important organization was the Holland chapter of the Ottawa County Red Cross, with Diekema as president and widow Katherine (Mrs. George J.) Van Duren as executive secretary. Although the Red Cross nationally had been founded in 1881, and a Grand Haven chapter began in 1909, Holland did not join until 1917. The Red Cross set the standard for organizational work. The Holland chapter grew rapidly, both in members and resources, taking donations from churches, businesses, and individuals. Material donations included boxes of clothing items and hospital supplies. Red Cross membership was simple, and in an age of organizations, everyone wanted to be involved. To become a member, all one had to do was pay one dollar to purchase a membership card; there were no required meetings or further contributions. Unlike earlier gendered societies, like the A. C. Van Raalte Woman's Relief Corps No. 231, which the Red Cross replaced, both men and women were eligible to participate.[7]

Within two months of its organization, the Red Cross in Holland had over nine hundred members; by September, this number had ballooned to two thousand, a figure nearly in accordance with President Wilson's call for one-fifth of all Americans to be members. City businesses competed to reach a goal of 100 percent membership,

6 *Holland Sentinel* 14, 28 Apr., 31 May 1917; *De Grondwet*, 24 Apr., 8, 15 May 1917.

7 *De Grondwet*, 15 May 1917; Wallace K. Ewing, "The American Red Cross in Ottawa County: The Beginnings," 1988, HMA.

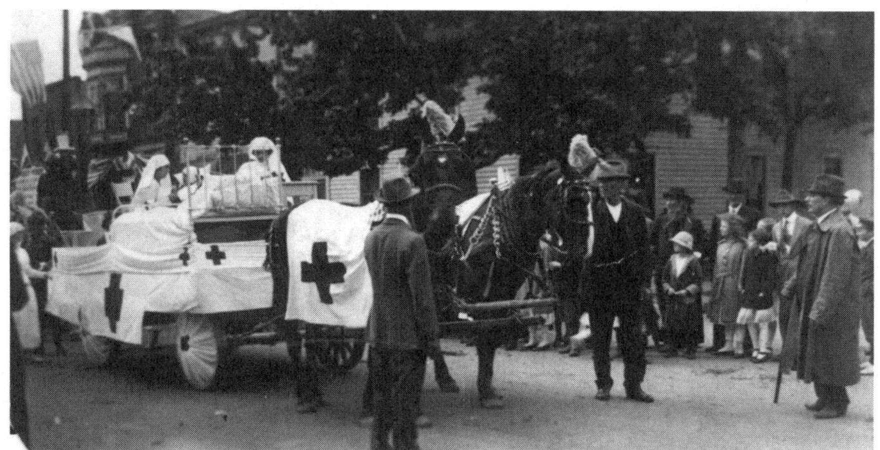

Red Cross wagon in parade, late 1917. Nurse on wagon (*right*) is Margaret Den Herder Van Der Velde and the "patient" is her husband Dr. Otto Van Der Velde (*courtesy Larry B. Massie*)

meaning that all of one's employees had joined the Red Cross. By the end of the year, nearly one hundred Holland companies had reported that they had reached the goal. Superior Foundry was the first, having purchased membership cards for all its employees.[8] City hall offered a room for the Red Cross headquarters, which became a center of activity, primarily for women. So active was the participation of local women in the Red Cross that, as *De Grondwet* noted, "It appears that the Red Cross work has become part of their daily work." Widow Van Duren ably directed the day-to-day activities for thirteen years, until she resigned at age seventy-eight in 1930.[9]

In November 1917 Holland Red Cross president Diekema was re-elected, and he continued the group's crusade. When a noted Chicago preacher failed to appear to address a crowd at Hope Church in May 1918, Diekema took the opportunity to give a history of the work of the Red Cross in the 1906 San Francisco earthquake, in Northern Michigan during forest fires, and in Europe during the ongoing war. He then sketched the workings of the German autocratic system, describing its pitfalls and evils. The Red Cross posted information about the war on a giant tack board, twelve by twenty feet, set up near the post office at the corner of River Avenue and Tenth Street. Privations and sacrifice were

8 *Holland City News*, 10 May, 21 June, 20 Sept., 27 Dec. 1917; *Holland Sentinel*, 26 Apr., 21 July 1917.

9 *De Grondwet*, 15 Jan. 1918, translation by Michael Douma; *Holland Sentinel*, 3, 8 July 1930.

United War Charities parade, 1918, with banner: "Throw your Money or Pledges on the Flag" (*Donald van Reken Collection, Joint Archives of Holland*)

worth it to defeat the Huns. In October 1918 Mayor Bosch declared Holland an official member of the "Unconditional Surrender Club" movement.[10]

Draft registration

Compulsory registration took place in early June 1917, and 989 men lined up at their respective booths to get their draft cards and lottery numbers. Low numbers went in the draft pool first. Subsequently, in answer to President Wilson's call, the draft board would draw names randomly for induction. In August a motley crew of inductees–farm boys, factory workers, and students from Holland and as far east as Georgetown Township–gathered at the city hall for physical examinations. The streets were lined with automobiles. Similar scenes followed with each call for induction. Dentists were warned not to pull teeth of "slackers" and help them avoid the draft. Soldiers' pay was thirty dollars a month, plus food, clothing, and shelter.[11]

The first soldiers to leave Holland, a group of seventy-six local men, departed on trains for Camp Custer in September 1917. The send-off included a luncheon at city hall, followed by a parade. Factories

10 *Holland City News*, 29 Nov. 1917, 16 May, 27 Aug., 10 Oct. 1918.

11 *Holland Sentinel*, 5 June 1917; *Holland City News*, 12 July, 2, 9 Aug. 1917; 12 Sept. 1918; Ray Nies Autobiography, typescript, ch. 17, p. 9, HMA.

Young recruits go off to war in suits and ties, September 19, 1917 (*courtesy Myron Van Ark*)

closed so employees could attend the farewell ceremony, where Diekema, never short of words, addressed the crowd.[12] The adventures of the departed soldiers made front-page news in the local press. Editors published letters from soldiers regularly, which helped keep the war alive in the minds of the folks back home. In the first six months, most of the Holland boys remained in Michigan, although a few officers and enlisted men were sent to camps outside the state.

An exception was Henry A. "Heinie" Geerds, who as a boy believed ardently in God and country, having listened intently to stories related by veterans of the Civil War and the Spanish-American War. In 1914 already, as a high school student, he had enlisted in the National Guard and rose to the rank of sergeant in 1917. In February 1918 Geerds found himself in charge of a platoon of fifty-four men in the trenches of France. He had to gird himself and his men for mortal combat. As part of the Red Arrow Division in the battle of the Argonne forest, his platoon suffered nearly 100 percent casualties; only he and one other man were not killed or wounded. One day while lying in a shell hole during a fierce firefight, watching new arrivals become cannon fodder, he lamented their inadequate training for combat and resolved to do something about it when he returned home.[13]

12 *Holland City News*, 20 Sept. 1917.

13 Vande Water, "Col. Henry Geerds," radio talk, WHTC, Oct. 2003.

Family and friends send the "boys" off on the train at Holland depot, September 19, 1917 (*courtesy Myron Van Ark*)

Another exception was the flamboyant Cornelius Van Putten,[14] grandson of pioneer settler Jacob Van Putten. Cornelius Van Putten swapped his Germanic name for the Gaelic "Patrick Terrance McCoy" when he enlisted with a Scottish regiment in 1914. For Van Putten, the war was an adventure. "The quietness of Holland irked me," he wrote. "I longed for action, and action I could not get among the good folks of my city." Van Putten was working in New Orleans in 1914 when an English friend and colleague asked Van Putten to join him on a business trip to England. There a woman pinned a white feather to Van Putten's left shoulder, marking him as a slacker. Because he had no other commitments, and since he felt that the war was a battle of ideologies, Van Putten took the challenge. But his British acquaintances convinced him to change his name to Patrick McCoy. Full of bravado, Van Putten boldly announced his true nationality when trying to enlist at a recruiting office near Glasgow. The officer looked him over and responded, "Go take a walk around the block and come back here a Canadian."

When Van Putten came home in January 1918, he had been at war against "Fritz" for three-and-a-half years, survived the Battle of

14 Not to be confused with Holland's Cornelius G. Van Putten, a clerk at the city hall and an insurance agent, who volunteered for military service in early 1918 (*Holland City News*, 17 Jan. 1918).

Doughboy Henry A. "Heinie" Geerds
(*Archives, Holland Historical Trust*)

the Somme, and with nearly as much agony, had grown accustomed to wearing a Scottish kilt. In that time, he claimed to have grown rather fond of his adopted pseudonym and never once heard his real name. He apparently kept his name a secret even when conversing in Dutch with a Flemish family whom he had befriended along the way.

And so it was that Patrick McCoy was the first Holland soldier to return from the trenches. With his left arm impaired by war wounds, McCoy related tales of allied courage and success against the barbarous Huns. He praised the work of the Red Cross and assured his listeners than the Germans were losing the will to fight. McCoy's story, which was serialized (and sensationalized) in the *Grand Rapids Herald*, was published as *Kiltie McCoy: An American Boy with a Irish Name Fighting in France as a Scotch Soldier*. While the war continued, McCoy's fame grew as a patriotic orator, and he became somewhat of a spectacle. He gave speeches in Chicago and New York City, and was a featured presenter at Holland's War Benefit Program on April 4, 1918. While he had not fought under the American flag, McCoy was a great aid in the recruitment of soldiers. The brash, adventurous, but patriotic and sentimental McCoy provided the perfect example of what an American soldier should be. Except that, of course, he was not one.[15]

Holland's first soldier to die was reported in April 1918. A short paragraph in the *Holland City News* informed the city that Ernest Voland of Holland, a seaman second class, had died of diphtheria in a Massachusetts camp. Voland was born in 1896 in Indiana of a Swiss German father and a Swiss French mother. The Volands, with their six

15 *Holland City News*, 17 Jan., 6 June, 10 Oct. 1918; *Holland Sentinel*, 16 Jan. 1918. Van Putten's book was published by Bobbs-Merrill, Indianapolis, in 1918.

Willard G. Leenhouts, killed in action in France, 3 July 1918 (*Archives, Holland Historical Trust*)

children, moved to Michigan by the turn of the century and settled down as farmers in Holland Township. At some point between 1910 and 1915, the parents divorced, and the older children went their own ways, while the youngest daughter, Margaret, stayed with her mother so that she could finish her studies and graduate from Holland High School in 1917. Perhaps because of the nature of Ernest's death, or perhaps because the family was not well established in the city, the story received no more notice.[16]

The first combat death made larger headlines. On August 15, 1918, Abraham and Elizabeth Leenhouts received a military telegram, informing them that their eldest son Private Willard G., not quite twenty years old, had died on the battlefield in France after being hit by artillery shrapnel. Like all parents of servicemen, the Leenhouts had read every issue of the newspaper, prayed daily for a letter from their son, and hoped to hear that he was well. Gerrit Diekema, a friend of the family and superintendent of Hope Church's Sunday school, delivered the bad news. In his memoirs, Leenhouts remembered the particulars of the dreadful occasion. He and his wife were sitting alone on the porch one afternoon, when they saw Diekema walking over from his house just a half block away. He led the couple inside, took a yellow envelope from his pocket, and cautiously, tenderly read the awful message. Later that day Mayor Nicodemus Bosch ordered flags flown at half-mast.[17]

16 *Holland City News*, 4 Apr. 1918; US Census, 1910 and 1920; *Holland City Directory*, 1915-1916. Voland's actual date of death was 29 Mar. 1918.

17 Abraham Leenhouts, *From the Crest of the Hill*, (n.p., n.d.), 121; Randall P. Vande Water, "Willard Leenhouts Was First to Fall," in *Holland: Happenings, Heroes & Hot Shots* (Holland, MI, 1996), 3:128-35.

Private Leenhouts was still a high school student when he volunteered for the service on April 17, 1917. He was also a member of the "Go-class," an entire Sunday school class at Hope Church that volunteered for the Marines. The church held memorial services for their hero. Following a sermon by Rev. Peter P. Cheff, Diekema gave an address in which he related that Will Leenhouts had been a friend of his son John. Diekema praised Leenhouts for his idealism, courage, and faith. He was slain by the "hand of the cruel Hun." And to make sure that he did not die in vain, Diekema insisted, all must join together so that "Freedom will defeat Oppression and the Cross of Christ will triumph over the Iron Cross." Another early casualty in France was Henry Wolters. The Holland GVFW Post (Grand Veterans of Foreign Wars) took Wolters' name for its own. By war's end, twenty-six Holland doughboys had made the supreme sacrifice. Ray Nies remembered seeing day after day at the Holland train station a "pile of rough coffins, containing the bodies of fine young men, who died of the 'flu' in the training camps." Why were the dead always privates, not officers, Nies noted laconically.[18]

Slackers and loafers

Fight, work, or go to jail, the military authorities said when they made loafing a misdemeanor. The American Patriotic League, city police, the draft board, and city justices all promised to find loafers and put them to work. "Persons knowing the whereabouts of loafers in the city are requested to notify these authorities at once," the *Holland City News* declared. In July 1918, nineteen-year-old John McCarthy was arrested under the new law. A judge put him on probation, and ordered him to stay out of pool halls for fifty-two weeks, to provide financial support to his parents, and save money in the bank.[19] A month later, police chief Frank Van Ry caught a "slacker," Conrad Burghoff, a Russian-born immigrant and employee at the Superior Foundry, who had lied about his age to avoid service. Despite being captured and found out, Burghoff was relieved to be sent to Camp Custer, rather than to the county jail in Grand Haven.[20]

18 Diekema Papers, HMA; Joel Lefever, "Holland residents have always stepped up to serve," *Holland Sentinel*, 26 Aug. 2007; Nies Autobiography, ch. 17, p. 3.

19 *Holland City News*, 4 July 1918.

20 Ibid., 1 Aug. 1918.

Hope College booth on campus in support of the American Patriotic League (*Donald van Reken Collection, Joint Archives of Holland*)

Hope College at war

In the beginning of the war in Europe in 1914, the Hope College student newspaper, *The Anchor*, took on a decidedly patriotic tone, promising total support for the war. The editors, having caught "war fever," called for the cancellation of baseball and track contests and all social events, and urged the introduction of obligatory military training for male students. "If the dark day should ever dawn when American troops shall be compelled to take an active part in the conflict," said *the Anchor*, "the Orange and Blue will be found flying beneath the Stars and Stripes."[21] Many college events and activities were indeed cancelled that academic year and the next, and military training began in due time. Scheduled events took on a war tone or theme: Oratory contests dealt with the evils of autocracy and Kaiserism; news articles focused on Northern France and conscription; and inauguration and commencement speakers cited German atrocities and the need to aid war victims.

Many male students were quick to enlist in the military, the majority having been assured of an officer's commission. In May 1917, with the semester and school year nearing an end, Hope already had six men accepted for officer's reserve training; five entered the Coast Artillery or Marines, six prepared to enlist in the active service, one went into hospital work, and twenty set to work on farms to help alleviate a labor crisis.

[21] *Anchor*, 18, 25 Apr. 1917.

Hope College President Ame Vennema, after consulting with the commissioner of education in Washington, proceeded to alter the school year. By holding classes six days per week and foregoing spring break, rural students were able to return home a month early and still receive full academic credit for the semester. Some students were allowed to go home even earlier, in time for spring planting, provided they were in good academic standing and had a note from a parent, or if over twenty-one years of age, an employer, stating that the student was a valued laborer and not a slacker. This would serve as evidence of employment and proof of legitimacy for being excused from class. These parental postcards and letters, some written in Dutch, the others in various levels of educated and uneducated English, came from as far away as Orange City, Iowa, and Randolph, Wisconsin, as well as from local hamlets like Overisel and East Saugatuck. All had a message to the same effect, "This year Johnny is needed on the farm."[22]

During the academic year of 1917-18, the number of Hope students at war continued to climb, and by June 1918, sixty-four had signed up for military service. In the fall semester of 1918, the *Anchor* listed over ninety young men who had enlisted since April 1917. The exodus of male students caused a sharp shift in the college's demographics. In the first year of war, enrollment fell by 20 percent, while the male student body fell by a remarkable 40 percent. By graduation in 1918, the senior class, which numbered fifty-seven in its junior year, had withered to thirty-seven students: seventeen men and nineteen women. For the first time in the college's history, coeds equaled men, and this at a school where, according to figures published in 1916, over 85 percent of living alumni were men! When the students in military training began eating at their own designated cafeteria, the women on campus saw even less of the men. "You can imagine how lonesome it has been in Voorhees Commons," one female student wrote. "There are only fourteen or fifteen boys who still eat with us—'little kids, cripples, and bums,' as one boy said to me." In 1918-19 the dominant ratio of males to females returned. With the war nearing an end, gender ratios and total enrollments returned to pre-war levels.[23]

22 Ibid., 9 May 1917; 27 Feb. 1918; Hope College Student Correspondence, Joint Archives of Holland (JAH); Debbie Dolph, "Dr. Ame Vennema: A Biography Focusing on his Years as President," 1974, in Ame Vennema Papers, JAH; Hope Faculty Minutes, 15 May 1917, JAH.

23 Betty Ann (likely Hope College student Elizabeth Renskers) to Mr. and Mrs. George Kollen, Rochester, MN, 9 Oct. 1918, JAH; *Anchor*, 9 Oct. 1918; *De Grondwet*, 28 May 1918, *Holland City News*, 23 May 1918.

Table 21.1. Hope College Student Enrollment during First World War (male/female)

Years	Freshmen	Sophomores	Juniors	Seniors	Totals
1916-17	55/26	43/16	35/19	25/15	158/76
1917-18	26/35	37/22	14/13	19/19	96/89
1918-19	54/19	25/25	31/19	30/28	150/81

Source: Enrollment figures from Hope College Alumni Bulletins, vols. 54-56 (1916-19).

Although the college administration was supportive of the war, the loss of so many students dealt an unexpected financial blow. To boost enrollment, tuition was not raised in 1918. For the college generation, war was a new experience, and the demands of the war often conflicted with the desires of their hearts. First of all, most students wanted to finish their education, which, despite its rigors, was more attractive than digging trenches in France. There had to be a middle way, they thought, to prepare for war and offer service to the country without joining the military. The solution the college devised was the Student Army Training Corps (SATC), an early type of ROTC (Reserve Officers Training Center) program, which would train and drill students in a military fashion right on campus, allowing its members to continue taking classes.

The Hope College SATC was organized on October 1, 1918 with federal funding. The men who joined SATC were formally inducted in the United States Army and were in uniform and under military discipline. Carnegie Gymnasium was converted into a barracks; an infirmary and dispensary were placed in Van Vleck Hall, and a mess hall was set up on the third floor of Van Raalte Memorial Hall.

SATC inductees continued to take classes at the college, but were also given classes on military subjects from the officers of the program. To the call of the bugle, these men drilled every weekday. On October 3, 1917, sixty-two men were inducted into the organization. At the ceremony, President Dimnent called Holland's own Pat McCoy, who was in the audience, to say a few words about America's inevitable victory. For male students under eighteen years old who could not yet apply for military service, "The Kollen Cadet Corps" named after the late college president, Gerrit J. Kollen, was organized at the Preparatory School. The corps drilled ten hours per week.[24]

24 *Holland City News*, 3, 17 Oct. 1918.

Such a program was seen as breaking all precedent and tradition of the liberal arts college. A female student, identifying herself only as Betty Ann, described the situation in a letter to George E. and Martha Kollen, former Holland residents who had recently moved to Rochester, Minnesota:

> The museum looks very un-civilian, to say the least, with its long rows of tables bearing their granite plates and cups. . . . We have three "lieuts," as the boys call them, and a sergeant. Goodness knows what *they* all find to do, but I suppose *they* know. It is very un-Hope-skollegy, to see them breezing about the campus receiving and giving salutes. They salute Dimmie [President Edward Dimnent] just for fun.[25]

Some alumni were even more alarmed, believing that military training on campus was misguided. Rev. John W. Brink of the Marion (North Dakota) Reformed Church wrote President Dimnent that SATC "was a step towards Universal Military Training, which I could never endorse for our beloved country." Brink noted that some members of his congregation refused to contribute financially to the college until the war ended and SATC had pulled out.[26]

Home front

Americans believed the war would be won on the home front. Through labor, conservation, and sacrifice, the country would be able to supply the foodstuffs to nourish the Allies and all the materials the soldiers needed to get the job done. To organize conservation measures, President Wilson appointed Herbert Hoover as head of the US Food Administration. Measures to conserve food were thereafter known as "Hooverizing."

Mayor John Vander Sluis, in one of his first official actions after America's declaration of war, proclaimed a city conservation week, and Superintendent Egbert E. Fell asked Holland school pupils to join the war effort. Boys could help in gardening, and girls could help Red Cross volunteers make socks and bandages for the soldiers. In the summer of 1918, Fell also systematically investigated textbooks at local schools, making sure none carried any German propaganda or were anti-America. "All teaching would be one hundred per cent American,"

25 Betty Ann to Mr. and Mrs. George Kollen.

26 John W. Brink to Edward Dimnent, 10 June 1919, Edward Dimnent Papers, JAH.

reported the *Holland City News*. For the coming year, Fell also planned to institute compulsory military training for all high school boys.[27]

"War gardens" became so popular that that local vegetable sellers found few customers. In the summer of 1917, William Brusse of the committee on city gardens reported that 125 to 150 acres were being tilled With wartime prices on the rise, the *Holland Sentinel* editor joked that people could use garden products for currency: "Two Lima beans equals one turnip; two turnips, one rutabaga; three rutabagas, one head of cabbage; two heads of cabbage, one sweet potato; two sweet potatoes, one onion; ten onions, one Irish potato, etc."[28] In the summer of 1918 Lida Rogers, a biology teacher at Holland High School, supervised a garden club movement that encouraged youngsters between the ages of ten and eighteen to raise vegetables, keep account of their expenses and profits, and prepare for a special prize contest at the Ottawa County Fair. Over the next decade, Rogers organized Arbor Day activities for students.[29]

Meat, sugar, and wheat were all regulated. Members of a food commission went door to door asking residents to designate days for abstaining from meat and bread, and to be *zuinig* (frugal) in their use of sugar and other scarce materials listed by the government. Some local restaurants observed "meatless Tuesdays" and "wheatless Wednesdays," and homemakers learned wheatless recipes. To prevent wheat shortages, milling companies mixed other cereal grains with standard wheat flour, and merchants were restricted from selling wheat flour without also selling the customer flour from other grains. In the months before the declaration of war, a bushel of wheat in Holland cost about $1.65. In May, the price shot up to $2.90, before settling at just over $2.00 for the duration of the war. Rye, the poor man's grain, at $1.25 before the war, rose steadily, peaking at $2.20 in the spring of 1918.[30]

Despite the high prices, a shortage of wheat seemed unlikely in the area, and rationing was difficult to take seriously. Rev. J. F. Bowerman of First Methodist Church chastized Hollanders for ignoring the wheatless and meatless days. They think, said Bowerman, that "patriotism is a fine thing to practice, providing [one's] neighbor does the practicing."[31]

Food prices, which had generally plateaued by early 1918, began coming down by summer. Sugar, however, was a commodity

27 *Holland Sentinel*, 11, 13 Apr. 1917; *Holland City News*, 29 Aug. 1918.

28 *De Grondwet*, 7 Aug. 1917; *Holland Sentinel*, 2 June, 13 Sept. 1917.

29 *Holland City News*, 28 Mar. 1918.

30 *De Grondwet*, 30 Oct. 1917; *Holland City News*, 25 Oct. 1917.

31 *Holland City News*, 7 Feb. 1918.

more susceptible to shortages. In late 1917 grocers called for a sugar rationing system to stave off shortages. In December of 1917, the city administration issued ration cards that limited people to one pound of sugar per week. The rationing regimin allegedly caused sugar hoarding, which stoked tempers. "The sugar situation in Holland is causing more discussion and more dissatisfaction to the square inch than any other question (outside of the gas question) could possibly be capable of," reported the *Holland City News*. In June 1918 Fred Kempker and George Ver Hage were arrested for stealing sugar sacks from the Holland Sugar Company factory. The sugar beet harvest that year was the best on record, but sugar prices rose anyway to 12½¢ a pound, while the federal government had fixed the retail price at 11¢. Holland merchants refused to buy sugar if they lost money on the product.[32]

Sugar was also needed for canning fruit. The Holland Canning Co. employed up to 175 women to process and can fruit. Many, according to *De Grondwet*, worked only for patriotic reasons, to provide fruit for soldiers and for domestic consumption. With suffrage on the national ballot in 1918, some women saw the work as a way to boost the chances of passage.[33]

A US Department of Agriculture emergency war survey at Hope College in February 1918 illustrates the complexities of sugar rationing. The survey showed that the college had eight hundred pounds of sugar in stock, but normally it stocked from eight- to nine thousand pounds. Thus, the cafeteria was under-stocked and the students underfed. Frankly, Dimnent wrote the chief of the Bureau of Markets in Washington, because of wartime prices, the cafeteria was operating at a loss and considering closing but for the poor students who could not afford meals otherwise.[34]

College coeds, who made bandages, pillows, and other items for the soldiers, took wartime shortages in stride according to Prof. Frank N. Patterson. "The girls especially try to look like the much abused heroines of the movies. . . . Of course you are aware that we, as patriots and your loving friends, have heatless, wheatless, meatless, and sweetless periods, but we are not visibly suffering."[35]

Rationing of commodities affected all merchants. Nies Hardware was allowed to buy only five kegs of nails at a time, and the cost was fifteen times higher than before the war. "I wondered, jokingly, if

32 *De Grondwet*, 18 Dec. 1917; *Holland City News*, 11 July, 27 Dec. 1917; 3 Jan., 20 June 1918.

33 *Holland Sentinel*, 11 June 1917; *De Grondwet*, 5 Nov. 1918.

34 *De Grondwet*, 6 Nov. 1917; *Holland Sentinel*, 25 Apr. 1918; Edward Dimnent Papers, JAH.

35 Frank N. Patterson, 18 Feb. 1918, correspondence in Teunis Baker Papers, HMA.

they were shooting nails at the Germans," Nies opined. Any kind of metal, even scrap, was golden. In October 1918 city food commissioner William Brusse published in the *Holland City News* regulations of the US Food Administration detailing what prices retailers were allowed to charge for necessary goods. The biggest temptation for merchants was to sell on the black market at sky-high prices.[36]

"Coal famine"

Coal, not oil, powered electric generators and homes, and shortages were greatly feared. A "coal famine" meant no heat and no electricity for lighting. In March 1917 coal merchant Austin Harrington bought from Katharine Vander Veen, heiress of the Manly D. Howard estate, ten acres north of the River Avenue Bridge to develop another coal yard and triple the capacity of his coal business. Harrington thought that if he could build a sufficient surplus of coal at the new site, which was on the Pere Marquette rail line to Ottawa Beach, then Holland would be able to overcome any short-term shortages.[37]

Circumstances conspired to bring about a coal shortage in the winter of 1917-18. In December 1917 Emory P. Davis, manager of the Holland Gas Company, reported that the plant had only a five-day supply of coal, and if a new shipment did not arrive, Holland could be without gas. The crisis was averted when two carloads of coal arrived from Grand Rapids. The situation was still critical, Davis asserted, and the company was not in the clear until it could receive regular shipments. The city decided to leave some street lights off at night and save coal. But the lights were left on near the lakefront between the West Michigan Furniture factory and the boat dock for fear of German spies and arsonists. Security came before frugality. In early January of 1918, the city initiated "lightless nights" on Thursday and Sunday, when all lighted signs, displays, and advertisements had to be turned off, and residents must limit the use of lights.[38]

Throughout the winter, Holland took measures to conserve energy and avoid the impending coal shortage. Local stores, with the exception of cigar dealers, candy stores, saloons, and poolrooms, were limited to nine hours of operation per day. Frank Ogden, manager of the Knickerbocker Theatre, used old-fashioned kerosene lamps as an

36 Nies Autobiography, ch. 17, p. 1; *Holland City News*, 17 Oct. 1918; 11 Sept. 1919. *De Grondwet*, 29 Oct. 1918.

37 *Holland City News*, 8 Mar. 1917.

38 Ibid., 20, 27 Dec. 1917; 3 Jan. 1918; *De Grondwet*, 25 Dec. 1917; 8 Jan. 1918.

alternative light source. Mayor John Vander Sluis requested churches to conserve fuel by heating smaller meeting rooms and leaving larger rooms unheated. On the college campus, Van Raalte Hall was kept at a chilly fifty-six degrees. With the cold winter weather and calls for conservation, some churches even cancelled services. On a bitter January day, Hope Church cancelled both worship services. During the cold months, First Reformed Church held morning services in their basement and canceled the evening services. The other churches all agreed to meet in smaller rooms. On Monday January 21, 1918, Holland had a "heatless day," following an order from the National Fuel Administration to most cities in the Midwest to shut down industries and stores to save fuel. Houses remained heated. Hope began holding chapel services in the YMCA room to conserve coal, and in late January all Holland schools, both public and private, were closed for a time.[39]

Despite conservation efforts, Holland was quickly running out of coal. Shipments were late in coming or did not arrive at all, having been confiscated by towns along the route. In January 1918, Holland Furnace, Limbert Furniture, Thompson Manufacturing, De Pree Chemical, and Bush & Lane Piano all shut down due to lack of coal. Two weeks later, Percy Reed, manager at Limbert, brought a grievance against the city, saying not enough had been done to provide coal and that the company had lost $6,000 because of it. Then a three-day snowstorm dumped four feet of snow over most of the city and effectively closed businesses anyway. While the roads remained impassable for automobiles, a shoveling crew of some two hundred men cleared the sidewalks and turned Holland into a canyon city. Residents along the sidewalks were encouraged to pay the men for their troubles. To relieve the temporary unemployment, 250 men were put to work shoveling sidewalks.[40]

Although the situation was serious, Holland was not yet in the dark, and the *Holland City News* editor ridiculed an article from a Benton Harbor paper that said people in Ottawa Country were chopping down shade trees and burning them to heat their houses. Holland averted a coal shortage through foresight, a tough policy, and public-mindedness. Former Mayor Nicodemus Bosch urged anyone with extra coal to turn it over to the coal dealers for redistribution. Local dealers also received instructions from the US Fuel Administration to prevent coal hoarding. No homeowner was allowed to have more than one ton of coal in his basement, but some residents ordered deliveries

39 *Holland City News*, 10, 17, 24 Jan. 1918; *Anchor*, 30 Jan. 1918.

40 *Holland City News*, 17, 24, 31 Jan. 1918; 18 Jan. 1923; *Holland Sentinel*, 29 Dec. 1951.

from multiple dealers and had more coal in storage than they could use during the whole winter. The mayor of Zeeland confiscated coal from a house whose inhabitants had gone to Florida for the winter. Charles M. McLean, president of the Holland Sugar Company, when learning of the possible future shortage, offered his company's four-hundred-ton coal surplus to local dealers. Holland Shoe Company did the same.[41]

For the winter of 1918-19, the city sought alternative fuel sources and other methods of conservation. The board of public works advertised electric heaters for sale, while manufacturers made oil heaters and wood stoves. To spare paper, *De Grondwet* reduced its page count from twelve to eight. Still, Holland could do more, some argued. In September 1918 Evert P. Stephan, manager of the Holland Furniture Company, after returning from an East Coast business trip, declared that Holland had not felt the war like the eastern cities. "Talk about sacrifices," he said, "we don't know what it is in Holland. Out East, everything is parceled out, and that very sparingly."[42]

Coal shortages continued after the war in the winter of 1919-20 due to miner strikes. The state fuel administrator named Austin Harrington as Holland's fuel director. He had the unanimous endorsement of the coal dealers, businessmen, and industrialists. Fortunately, the city of Holland had built a new coal shed and stockpiled the vital fuel during the summer of 1919, so the local hospital and power plant did not face a serious pinch. The board of education, however, was not so fortunate; it would run out by February 1, 1920, without new shipments. The Strand Theater cut back to one matinee daily, and several local factories risked shutting down.[43]

War regulations and taxes

Hollanders also had to deal with new automobile regulations and taxes. In March 1918 the common council organized a small war commission, known at the war board. Ten months before, in May 1917, they had instituted a broad-based war committee to inspire patriotism with parades and rallies and to aid families of soldiers. The war board, which apparently had little power to enforce its regulations, met every Tuesday evening to review wartime efforts. In May 1918 the board required automobile owners to register their vehicles with the city so that they might, if needed, be requisitioned for use in patriotic parades.

41 *Holland City News*, 24 Jan. 1918; *De Grondwet*, 22, 29 Jan. 1918.
42 *Holland City News*, 12 Sept. 1918; *De Grondwet*, 24 Sept., 8, 29 Oct. 1918.
43 *Holland City News*, 11, 18 Dec. 1919.

Only 114 automobiles, perhaps half of the city's total, were registered. The following October, the board decreed that all automobile users on Sundays needed to get an "O.K." stamp on their windshields. Automobiles could only be used for "legitimate" purposes, like going to church, and not for a holiday jaunt to the beach.[44]

Congress levied new war taxes on milk, bread, and ice cream. The price of butter steadily rose during the war, from 36¢ per pound in April 1917 to 55¢ in November 1918. Due to the high price of milk, milk taxes, and competition with manufacturers of condensed milk, local creameries went out of business.[45]

Motorboats and pleasure sailing craft, steamer berths, and railroad freight were also taxed. Congress raised the price of postage stamps from 2¢ to 3¢, and postcards from 1¢ to 2¢. Uncle Sam taxed long distance phone calls and collected 8¢ for every Interurban round trip ticket to Grand Rapids. Congress also reinstated an income tax for the first time since the Civil War, and personal and business income tax statements had to be delivered to the Holland post office each year between February 15 and March 1, beginning in 1918. Only married persons with net incomes of $2,000 or more, and single persons with net incomes at $1,000 or more, had to file.[46]

On top of the shortages and new taxes, for three weeks, beginning in late October 1918, Spanish influenza hit Holland hard. Because the flu was contagious and spread on contact, city officials discouraged large meetings and put the city under a nearly full quarantine. They closed the reading room at the city hall, although the library remained open so books could be checked for reading at home, where citizens waited out the epidemic. By October 29 the city health officer, city nurse, and school superintendent agreed to close the schools. Hope College also complied, as did all ice cream parlors. To limit crowds, the health officer asked stores to allow no more than ten people inside at one time. Only restaurants and drug stores could remain open after six o'clock in the evening. Although an election was coming up, no candidates held political meetings. The secretary of the state board of health asked churches to remain closed on the same basis as schools. "Spanish Influenza may be a bad disease, but what's bothering the Huns most now is the good old Yankee grip," joked the *Holland City News*. Fortunately, Holland had few cases of the flu, and as reports around

44 Ibid., 10 May 1917, 16, 23 May 1918, 10 Oct. 1918; *De Grondwet*, 2 Apr. 1918.

45 *Holland City News*, 24 Jan. 1918; 8 Feb. 1917; *De Grondwet*, 10 Apr. 1917; 5 Nov. 1918.

46 *Holland City News*, 1 Nov., 27 Dec. 1917.

the state dried up, local flu bans were lifted on November 7, 1918. The two-week scare was over.[47]

Economic impact

During the war some Hollanders left the city to find war contract work in Grand Rapids, Muskegon, and other large cities. Bert and Alfred Huntley, for example, decided, after forty years in Holland, to relocate their machine shop to Muskegon, where they hoped to get government work.[48] According to population estimates from the board of public works, Holland had the same number of citizens in 1919 as it had in 1914. Taking into account natural population growth, there was presumably a net out-migration from Holland during the war years.

Holland's industries had varied success in obtaining government war contracts. Dye and furnace companies thrived, while the furniture industry suffered. Holland Aniline Company, established in 1916, won a government contract in 1917 to provide olive-colored dye for military clothes. Holland Furnace Company doubled its business volume during the war years. Ray Nies tells how the "best furniture factory, long established, with a country-wide reputation for making the finest upholstered and other furniture," was taken over to manufacture army wagons. Tons and tons of iron bolts and carloads of lumber from western mills were rushed to the plant, but not a single wagon was completed because motor trucks had rendered army wagons obsolete." Looking back in 1919, Arthur Visscher noted that the war had been the salvation of some companies and the ruin of others.[49]

Liberty Loans

The best way to help America rid the world of the Hun and bring the boys back was to purchase Liberty Loans. These federal government bonds could be purchased at local banks at a minimum of $50 and would earn between 3½ and 4½ percent interest per annum; the later series of bonds offering higher interest than the earlier ones. In the first Liberty Loan campaign in June 1917, Holland's quota, as set by the government based on population figures, was $300,000. Although the energetic Diekema headed the local Liberty Loan Commission, Holland fell short of its quota by $100,000.[50]

47 Ibid., 26 Sept., 24, 31 Oct. 1918; *De Grondwet*, 29 Oct. 1918.

48 *Holland City News*, 15 Aug. 1918.

49 Ibid., 2 Aug. 1917, 17 Jan. 1918; Nies Autobiography, ch. 17, p. 5 (quote); *Holland Sentinel*, 5 Mar. 1919.

50 *Holland City News*, 31 May, 14, 21 June 1917. The government set interest rates as follows: 1st bond 3.5 percent, 2nd 4 percent, 3rd 4.5 percent, and 4th 4.25 percent.

Holland Shoe Company Liberty Bond advertisement (*Holland City News*, October 1917)

For the second Liberty Loan drive, begun in October, city leaders redoubled their efforts. The commission solicited door to door and called an evening gathering at Carnegie Hall to explain the program. Every major company and retail business, including Holland Furnace, Holland Aniline, Holland Shoe, Cappon & Bertsch, Graham & Morton Transportation, First State Bank of Holland, and Lokker Rutgers, paid for Liberty Loan advertisements in the city newspapers. Lokker Rutgers used the bonds as an advertising method, offering $52.50 worth of goods for $50. This was 50¢ more than the 4 percent bond was worth upon redemption. Merchants and organizations also accepted liberty bonds as a form of payment or donation. Even the City of Holland budgeted $10,000 from board of public works earnings to purchase Liberty Loans. On November 1, the *Holland City News* proudly reported that the city had exceeded its quota by $150,000, more than making up for the earlier shortfall.[51]

Like the drives for Red Cross membership, companies competed to be the first to reach "one hundred percent," that is, every employee had purchased a bond. In May 1918, for the third Liberty Loan drive, H. J. Heinz Co. was the first to reach the goal. For a second time the common council took $10,000 from its treasury to purchase Liberty bonds. Once again, the Liberty Loan drive was a success, and Holland exceeded its quota by 50 percent. In late September of 1918, the fourth Liberty Loan campaign began, and Holland again met its quota. The

51 *De Grondwet*, 9, 16 Oct. 1917; *Holland City News*, 18 Oct., 1 Nov. 1917.

Boys admire soldiers on parade and try to join the march
(*courtesy Myron Van Ark*)

campaign was aided by a war exhibit train filled with German military artifacts, which brought over six thousand curious citizens. By war's end, Hollanders had purchased over $1.5 million in war bonds. They were "bloated bond holders," boasted the press, "a thrifty people." In addition to bond holdings, the accumulated savings in the city's three banks by its twelve thousand inhabitants totaled $2.2 million. A fifth Liberty Loan drive, scheduled to begin on November 11, 1918, was cancelled when the armistice was declared that very day.[52]

German spies and anti-American activities

In contrast to the bright patriotic fervor of the bond campaigns, there was a genuine fear of German activity in America and a hatred of Kaiser Wilhelm and his German autocratic government, which many blamed for the war. The Wilson administration set off the nativist campaign by having Congress create the War Propaganda Committee, whose purpose was to arouse patriotism in the citizenry and ferret out "traitors" with pro-German sympathies. This led to efforts, even in Holland, to protect America from German spies, sympathizers, and "alien enemies" (non-naturalized German immigrants). The bridge connecting Grand Haven to Ferrysburg, for example, was put under special watch, and to the chagrin of Grand Haven citizens who worked

52 *Holland City News*, 2, 9 May, 26 Sept., 3, 17, 31 Oct. 1918, 2, 16 Jan. 1919.

Women march in Liberty Loan parade in 1918
(*courtesy Myron Van Ark*)

on the other side of the river, foot traffic on the bridge was forbidden. Rumors that local piers were also restricted territory turned out to be false. But in 1918 the government did require all local freight carriers, Interurban conductors, and dockworkers to provide a photograph to be put on file at the Graham & Morton Company. The government also placed two watchmen at the docks to keep an eye out for German spies, explosive materials, and suspicious people.

Hollanders also took their own measures to protect their city. In April 1917 the common council placed lights around every water and light plant in the city, and a number of young men considered organizing a Home Protection League of from twenty-five to fifty volunteers, armed with revolvers, to watch and protect homes and businesses not already guarded. While it appears that the Home Protection League never materialized as such, in nearby Zeeland, citizens formed a vigilance corps, supported by Mayor Isaac Van Dyke, which was tasked to root out German propaganda and enemy activity. Membership in the corps was kept secret. To defend the state from other agitators, notably the IWW (International Workers of the World, a socialist, anarchist labor union), the Ordnance Department in Washington required the Holland Rifle Club to relinquish all but five of its rifles to be used for public safety by the State of Michigan.[53]

53 *De Grondwet*, 22 May 1917, 16 Apr. 1918; *Holland City News*, 16 Aug., 27 Dec. 1917; *Holland Sentinel*, 14, 17 Apr. 1917.

Army howitzer attracts curious onlookers in Holland
(*courtesy Myron Van Ark*)

The official word was that non-naturalized German immigrants were "alien enemies," who might harbor sympathy for the Fatherland. They had to be watched to prevent any attempts of sabotage. Of course, many local German families had arrived in the area already in the 1840s and 1850s; they were Calvinists or Lutherans, spoke a familiar dialect, and had never caused any problems. Recent German immigrants were naturally more suspect, but they were so few in number as to hardly merit mention. As Ray Nies remembered:

> There was a great clamor back then in our little city from certain of our more hysterical citizens to have armed guards stationed at the city light and water plant, the bridges, and the railroad depot, to prevent them from being blown up by the Germans or their sympathizers. Now, we only had a few people of German extraction. They were well known and highly respected citizens, and had lived here many years. None of them [was] of the kind to blow up anything. We were a thousand miles inland, and there was another two thousand miles or more of ocean between our shores and Germany. In spite of this, the clamor persisted, but nothing was done about placing the guards.[54]

Enemy aliens were barred from filing their final papers during the war. Thus, while Orrie J. Sluiter, the Ottawa County Clerk, received

[54] Nies Autobiography, ch. 17, p. 6.

Army tank demonstrates its prowess for locals
(*courtesy Myron Van Ark*)

a number of requests from local German residents who wanted to renounce their natural citizenship and swear allegiance to the United States, he could only let them file their first papers. German nationals were also prohibited from coming within a half mile of the post office or any other government building. One could receive special exemption by providing for official files three "mug shot" photographs. The "half-mile law" was likely not enforced in Holland, since no offender was ever prosecuted. In any case, the law was nullified in February 1918 when all German nationals were ordered to register with police chief Frank Van Ry at the city hall, supply a recent photo, and be fingerprinted. In total, forty-six people registered in Holland. Some of these, it turned out, were established citizens, immigrants who came from Germany as children decades ago and who had assumed their American nationality without ever having gone through the process of naturalization. In the summer of 1918, they found out that because they were not citizens, they could not even get a fishing license.[55]

John F. "Fritz" and Anna Hummel, both American citizens, fell afoul of the federal government. In the late 1870s, the couple moved from Chicago to Holland. John became president of Cappon & Bertsch and bought a home near the plant at 151-59 West Eighth Street. In 1910 they decided to visit relatives in Germany. Before leaving town, they deeded their home to niece Tenna Hummel Zylman, effective upon their deaths. While John and Anna were abroad, Tenna could

[55] *De Grondwet*, 20 Nov. 1917; 22 Jan. 1918; *Holland Sentinel*, 18 Apr. 1917; *Holland City News*, 21 Mar., 22 Aug. 1918.

live in the home. John Hummel became ill in Germany and was unable to travel back to Michigan before war broke out in 1914. The German government then required the couple to leave the country or again become citizens. They had no choice but to do the latter. Then American authorities, believing that the Hummels had gone back so John could fight for the Fatherland, seized their home in Holland as alien property. (The postscript took many years to be written. In 1922, after both Anna and John had died in Germany, Tenna Zylman, then a widow with several children, asserted her claim to the house. The next year she died, and her children became heirs-in-law. Fifteen years passed before federal authorities in 1935 restored the home to the rightful heir, local tailor William Zylman.)[56]

Excitement and tension ran high in the first months of war, and it is not difficult to understand how Holland experienced a few alarms of suspicious activity. In the first event, which took place over a number of nights in mid-April 1917, a suspicious man was seen near the Holland Gas Company's tanks. Even more ominous, he was supposedly carrying a package, presumably a bomb, tucked under his arm. But when approached by a company guard, the man fled, leaving behind his "mysterious bundle," a chicken in a sack. The fowl was just one of many that had gone missing from local coops over the preceding nights.[57]

A more serious false alarm followed in May when, late one evening, a few unidentified Hope College students exploded some nitroglycerin on campus, blowing out seventeen windows of Carnegie Hall, and frightening many in the neighborhood who heard the blast. Student detectives were put on the case, but presumably they never solved the crime.[58] In his memoirs, hardware store owner Ray Nies explained that the perpetrator was a young student who had bought dynamite at Nies' store, claiming that his father in Groningen needed it for removing tree stumps from his yard. Instead of employing it for said purpose, the student had set off the dynamite on campus as a practical joke, without realizing the power of the explosion.

Nies described how an acquaintance of his reacted to the incident on campus, and suspected the worst:

> About the time of the highest pitch of hysteria, my wife and I were at the home of a young, newly-wed dentist friend and neighbor—the same young dentist who was now doing a wholesale job on

56 *Holland Sentinel*, "50 Years Ago," 4 Mar. 1939.

57 *Holland Sentinel*, 14 Apr. 1917.

58 *Anchor*, 9 May 1917; *Holland City News*, 3 May 1917.

young students' teeth for the government—one stormy, rainy evening playing cards. He had just dealt the cards, and as we picked up our hands to see what we had, a tremendous explosion came that shook the house, and it did not sound so close by either.

"It's the Germans!" cried our young host. "Now they have done it. Those guards should have been posted. That must have been the light plant." "But the electric lights are still burning," I objected, "so it could not have been the light plant." "But what else could such a terrific explosion be?" cried the young doctor; "It must be the Germans. They must have blown up something big."

"Maybe they have," I said, "but I can't believe it. Why should they bother with such a small, far off place, wasting their efforts here, when there are other places of so much more importance to them? It was not the light plant; we can be sure of that."

We sat quietly and anxiously for a while, waiting for another explosion we somehow felt was coming, but none came, and finally the tension relaxed and we began to investigate. We got police headquarters on the phone only after several attempts and were informed that the explosion took place on the college campus, right close to the side of a large, quite new, brick hall, in which a crowd of students were holding some kind of a mass meeting. No one had been hurt, but many windows on that side of the building were broken and the building jarred, and the students greatly excited. The police were at a loss to explain it. They thought that perhaps some inconsistent or fanatical "pacifist" had done it on account of some of those students being listed for "reserve service," or perhaps it was even done by Germans or their sympathizers.

It turned out to be a dimwitted college senior pulling off a fraternity prank with dynamite, thinking it would explode like a "good-sized fire cracker."[59]

Another case of suspicious activity came when alderman Frank Brieve, while on a business trip in Grand Rapids, was mistaken for a German spy. Brieve had missed his train out of the city and so decided to get a haircut while waiting for the next train. After paying the barber and exiting the shop, Brieve began pacing back and forth on the road, growing impatient for the train's arrival. The barber naturally grew suspicious, watching this stranger with a Dutch accent make multiple

59 Nies Autobiography, ch. 17, 8-9.

passes by his shop, and called the Grand Rapids police. When a policeman arrived and questioned Brieve, he showed his city of Holland alderman badge and was released.[60]

Alderman Jake DeWitt of the Second Ward was not as fortunate in dealing with the political pressures of patriotism. DeWitt, a well-known Socialist, resigned from the common council after being indicted for unpatriotic actions. Instead of investing public monies in war savings stamps, a measure that the rest of the council supported, DeWitt voted to keep the money in a sinking fund for the city's needs. He soon regretted this action, which citizens deemed contrary to the sacrificial and patriotic spirit of the war effort. DeWitt then admitted that he entertained doubts about the war, was ignorant of the war effort, and was incompetent to be an alderman. Pressured by Percy Ray, chief of the Ottawa County American Patriotic League, DeWitt tearfully tendered his resignation, which the council accepted unanimously. In the end, the locals forgave him, since throughout the proceedings he had shown every indication of wanting to be a good, loyal, and patriotic citizen.[61]

One-hundred-percent-Americanism demanded its pound of flesh. When Klaas Zuidewind failed to remove his hat during a playing of the "Star Spangled Banner," Justice of the Peace Thomas N. Robinson fined him ten dollars and would not accept Zuidewind's explanation that he did not immediately recognize the tune of the national anthem.[62] John Van Lente, who lived on a farm five miles south of Holland on the West Michigan Pike, refused to contribute in the fourth Liberty Loan campaign in 1918. When hauled before the board of review to defend himself, he unwisely uttered unpatriotic comments that "received the worst scoring that has come from anyone in all the campaigns that have been held in Holland during the war." A night or two later, vigilantes arranged a "painting bee" and gave his farmhouse and outbuildings a coat of yellow paint, a badge of disloyalty.[63]

Anti-German feelings abate

After an initial wave of hysteria had washed over, most realized that the local German population was benign, too small, and too Americanized to pose any real threat. Still, German immigrants were suspected of pro-Germanism if they did not contribute wholeheartedly

60 *Holland City News*, 31 Jan. 1918.
61 Ibid., 13 June 1918.
62 Ibid., 24 Oct. 1918.
63 *Holland Sentinel*, 5 Nov. 1918.

to Liberty Loan drives or Red Cross funds. Conversely, when the German enclaves of Graafschap Bentheim and Drenthe purchased their fair share of Liberty bonds, it was seen as proof of their commitment to America.

Hollanders knew deep down that their German neighbors were decent human beings. But pro-American advertisements in local newspapers served as anti-German propaganda, reinforcing the temptation to demonize the enemy. In one example in *De Grondwet*, Germans were labeled "Potsdam's Pirates" for sinking American shipping on the open seas. Germans who followed the Kaiser were "Huns" and rapacious barbarians bent on world domination, no doubt, but as Gerrit J. Diekema wrote for a speech in 1917, "no better people live upon all the earth than the German people, but they must lose to win."[64]

Despite the seriousness of the situation, some found fun in ridiculing the Germans and particularly the German language. The *Holland City News* noted that the word "heinous," meaning "hate; hateful; flagrant; odious, atrocious; giving great offense," was of German origin. In the *Anchor*, a Hope College student submitted the following German language joke. "Miss Brusse: '*Wie Kommst du Herr*?' Student Steininger: 'Nobody. I comb it myself.'"[65]

During the war, the use of the German language was strongly disapproved. For example, the Woman's Literary Club altered its German motto *Mehr Licht* into the English "More Light," and the Elks Lodge participated in its organization's nationwide movement to ban the German language at meetings.[66] German classes continued, however, at Hope College and its preparatory school, although with sharply lower enrollments. In 1917 the college had appointed a new chair of German and French languages, the Hanover-born, but patriotic American, Ludwig Eyme.[67] Dutch language studies also suffered, since so many students of the Dutch language, typically male students considering the ministry, had gone to war. In the fall semester of 1918, no Dutch classes were offered at all. Demand for French, on the other hand, was at an all-time high. After the war, the Dutch program was revived, but it took some time for the German courses to recover.

In 1921 college president Ame Vennema wrote about the situation of German language education at Hope:

64 *De Grondwet*, 18 June 1918; Diekema Papers, box 5, HMA.

65 *Holland City News*, 26 Sept. 1918; *Anchor*, 23 May 1917.

66 *Holland City News*, 11 July 1918; Marie Zingle: *The Story of the Woman's Literary Club* (Holland, MI, 1989), 29.

67 *Hope College Alumni Bulletin* 54, no. 4 (Feb. 1917); ibid. 57, no. 1 (May 1919).

> To what extent the national propaganda will succeed in restoring the German to its former place in the curricula one cannot say, but that there is a large probability for rapid increase in demand for this subject is beyond question. It will be our policy to restore it gradually in such degree as seems wise to meet the university requirements for graduate work, professional or research, and to make it possible for our students to minister to the German churches of our denomination.[68]

Herman Hoeksema and the "Flag in Church" controversy

Dutch Americans were often painted with the same brush of nativism as German Americans. And this was not without reason. After all, the Dutch tongue, a Low German dialect, sounded to Americans indistinguishable from High German (*Duits* or *Deutsch*). In addition, the Netherlands government chose to remain neutral during the war, and this led some Americans to conclude that the Dutch were sympathetic to Germany. Dutch Americans were also known to harbor anti-British sentiments lingering from the Anglo-Boer War (1899-1902). Further, many Dutch in Holland came in the last big wave before the war, and were not yet American citizens, which made them exempt from the military draft. That they prospered in the booming war economy while neighbors went off to fight aroused considerable animosity.

In Holland, the issue that embroiled the Dutch community came up suddenly and unexpectedly; it pertained to flying the American flag in church. During the war it became customary throughout the United States to display both the American and the Christian flags in the front of church sanctuaries. The influential Third Reformed Church, the congregation of many educators, was first to unfurl a flag in May 1917. As the *Holland City News* reported warmly, "Worshippers Sunday in the Third Reformed church saw an unusual sight upon entering the edifice. Moved by the patriotic spirit that is rampant in the country, the Sunday school of the Third Reformed church also felt this spirit, and for that reason, purchased a most beautiful flag measuring twelve by eighteen feet which occupies the top most peak in the organ loft, directly above the pulpit."[69]

Grace Episcopal Church went Third Reformed one better; it dedicated its "beautiful silk flag" during the regular morning worship

[68] Ibid. 56, no. 1 (May 1921).

[69] *Holland City News*, 17 May 1917. Unfurled flags in Third Reformed Church are pictured in Elton J. Bruins, *The Americanization of a Congregation*, 2nd ed. (Grand Rapids: Eerdmans, 1995), 49.

service with a special litany, including the national anthem, "sung in procession after the benediction of the flag." That same morning, Hope Church, the "College church," unfurled its flag above the pulpit and promised to display it for the duration of the war. Trinity Reformed, First Reformed, and St. Francis Catholic churches similarly hung flags and service banners in impressive ceremonies of national blessing.[70]

At St. Francis Church, the Right Reverend Michael J. Gallagher of Grand Rapids, bishop of the diocese of western Michigan, came to preach "an appropriate sermon, bless the flag, and give a solemn benediction" at a special Sunday evening service. Religion and patriotism are intimately bound together, said Gallagher, and "patriotism is far higher if it finds its source and inspiration in religion." Father Gallagher stressed the hyper-patriotism of Catholics, who "sent to the colors double their proportionate share." Catholics totaled only one-sixth of the American population, but made up 35 percent of the army, 40 percent of the marines, and over 50 percent of the navy, he reported proudly. "If necessary," Gallagher concluded in a spirit of frenzied emotion, "the church would give its all, and would even sell its churches and its plate[s] to give to the government the means to be used 'that this nation of the people, for the people, and by the people would not perish from the earth.'" What better way to close than to quote Abraham Lincoln's Gettysburg Address—America's sacred text.[71]

Amid the competition to hold flag ceremonies in Holland churches, one pastor, Rev. Herman Hoeksema of the Fourteenth Street Christian Reformed Church, stirred up a hornet's nest when he refused to follow the crowd. The congregation was the first English-speaking body of that denomination in town and proud of its Americanizing ways. But for Hoeksema, a strict Calvinist, unfurling the nation's banner in church was conceding too much to Caesar's realm. To honor the nation more than God smacked of civil religion, not Christianity.[72]

The issue was joined on Sunday morning February 10, 1918, when Hoeksema entered his pulpit and saw an American flag on a pole standing in the front corner of the sanctuary. He said nothing until after the service, when he asked the consistory to have it removed before the evening service. They complied, and that evening in the course of his

70 *Holland City News*, 28 June 1917, 7, 14, 21 Mar., 30 May 1918.

71 Ibid., 14 May 1918.

72 Robert P. Swierenga, "Disloyal Dutch? Herman Hoeksema and the Flag in Church Controversy during World War I," *Origins* 25, no. 2 (2007): 28-35; Jacob E. Nyenhuis, *Centennial History of the Fourteenth Street Christian Reformed Church, Holland, Michigan 1902-2002* (Holland, MI, 2002), 13-14; *Holland City News*, 14 Feb. 1918; *Holland Sentinel*, 13 Feb. 1918; *Michigan Tradesman*, 6 Mar. 1918.

Rev. Herman Hoeksema, pastor of the Fourteenth Street Christian Reformed Church (*Archives, Calvin College*)

sermon the pastor explained that the flag "had no place in a church and that the national anthem should not be sung there." Some congregants did not agree, and they broadcast their preacher's views about town.

Understandably, in the charged atmosphere of the war, this brought an immediate and unwanted public outcry. Three local men, Dr. Frank Ledeboer, a physician, Jacob Geerlings, a mail carrier, and Bert Slagh, a storekeeper, appointed themselves a committee of three, and within two days they went to Hoeksema to "discuss" his beliefs and let him know that "some indignation had been aroused" around town by his presumed remarks. The trio took a reporter for the *Holland Sentinel* along to splash Hoeksema's words on the front page of the paper, under the headline "Pastor Asked to Explain by Committee."[73]

According to the newspaper, "a spirited discussion ensued," and the dominie would not yield an inch. Though he was a native-born American, the son of immigrant parents, and entirely loyal to the American government, Hoeksema insisted that the Christian church, "as the manifestation of Christ's body on earth, is universal in character; hence the church as an institution could not raise the American flag nor sing the national hymns." The flag could be flown in the church edifice during choir concerts, Christian school graduation exercises, and similar events, but not during worship services. Members should also raise the flag at home, on the streets, and on all public and Christian school buildings. Hoeksema declared that his congregants, as Christian citizens, "are duty bound to be loyal to their country" and to answer the call when needed for military service. Finally, he declared, "anyone who

73 Gertrude Hoeksema, *Therefore Have I Spoken: A Biography of Herman Hoeksema* (Grand Rapids: Reformed Free Publishing Association, 1969), 81-82, which extensively quotes the *Holland Sentinel* articles of 13, 14, 15, 16, 18 Feb. 1918.

is pro-German in our time has no right to the name of Calvinist and is a rebel and traitor to his government."[74]

One would think that this strong statement of national loyalty would have satisfied the critics, but it only fanned the flames. Rev. Peter Cheff of Hope Church jumped into the fray immediately by penning a piece for the newspaper that challenged his colleague's contention that the universal nature of the church precluded honoring the American flag. Hoeksema's "proposition is illogical and wrong," Cheff declared. "Does this universality exclude nationalism? Cannot a man love humanity and be a patriot just the same? Isn't it perfectly proper to show one's colors and not at all clash with the universal character of the church? If theology makes a man 'neutral' while in the house of prayer on the Sabbath, God deliver us from such theology." Cheff continued: "The life of the church is interwoven with the life of the world so that you cannot separate the universal aspect of Christianity from the local colors."

Having dismissed Hoeksema's argument, Cheff would not lay down his pen before levying one more broadside that charged the Dutch dominie with poisoning the "minds of men" by raising the "adder of disloyalty." He concluded: "I believe I voice the sentiment correctly when I claim that the best element feel aggrieved and somewhat humiliated by the acute situation which has developed in our midst."

Within the week, the Honorable Gerrit J. Diekema, former Fifth District US Congressman and Holland's leading citizen, took his best shot at the Christian Reformed cleric. Diekema told a large assembly at Winants Chapel at Hope College that Hoeksema's rationale was not only "theological hair-splitting," but it bordered on treason. That Diekema used the *T* word in his "thrilling address" raised the ante considerably, especially when the crowd, which had gathered to witness the unveiling of the Hope Service Flag and the reading of the Hope Honor Roll of servicemen, greeted his remarks "with a loud and prolonged applause." Diekema, who had two sons in the military, reverenced the flag. In his eulogy, he declared: "If the flag stands for all that is pure and noble and good, it is worthy of being unfurled in any building on the face of the earth. The very portals of heaven would welcome such an emblem."[75]

The attacks on his patriotism forced Hoeksema to respond with a long letter, which the *Holland City News* editor published in its entirety alongside Cheff's letter. "Every citizen has a right to absolutely fair treatment," he declared sanctimoniously, although he gave Diekema

74 *Holland City News*, 14 Feb. 1918.

75 Ibid., 21 Feb. 1918, for this and the next six paragraphs.

Gerrit J. Diekema, 1910s
(*courtesy Joan Ten Cate Bonnette*)

equal space for a refutation that immediately followed Hoeksema's self defense. So it was two against one. Doubtless, the editor saw the newspaper war of words as a boon to sales.

Hoeksema responded with three main points, modeling his sermonizing, and he insisted he was speaking in defense of both himself and his entire denomination. In his first point, Hoeksema took the typical debater's tactic of insisting that his critics misunderstood the distinction he made between posting the flag during divine worship and at other times. He only opposed the former, not the latter. "You may be surprised to [find] Old Glory even in my own church building sometimes." Not only did he honor the flag; but he was also willing even to die for his country. "I am fully prepared to give my life for the country," said the dominie, but "I am no less prepared to do the same for the truth of the word of God." The war was just, Hoeksema noted, and he fully supported the president. He had never supported German tactics of sinking merchant ships and mercilessly marching through Belgium. These views are well known in the community, the cleric insisted. "How the gossip could spread that I was pro-German I fail to understand, unless for ecclesiastical differences, the 'wish was father to the thought.' No, Mr. Diekema, you are hopelessly mistaken if you call my attitude one of approximate treason: and mistaken you are again . . . if you try to present matters as if a certain college and a certain church had a monopoly of patriotism." Christian Reformed folk are "not the people that raise riots and insurrections, we are not the people that perform the work of spies, but we are loyal, obedient people on whom our country can rely!"

Having stated his personal views on the country and war, and hopefully disarmed his critics, Hoeksema developed his second point on the Biblical and doctrinal necessity of citizens to support and pray for their government, referring to historic Calvinism and the Heidelberg Catechism, which Diekema and Cheff, as Reformed adherents, are duty bound to uphold. In the third and final part of his statement, Hoeksema asserted his beliefs about the universal nature of the church. "In the church of Jesus Christ, we raise no flag, and sing no national anthems. . . . The church and state are separate, must be separate, and if you do not keep them separate, it is you who stab at the heart of all true liberty. Then you will either come to the domination of church over state, as is the ideal of Roman Catholicism, or to the subjugation of the church to the state, as was the condition in Old England, at the time of our Pilgrim Fathers." Hoeksema thus cleverly appealed to the anti-Catholicism of his readers and tied his wagon to the revered Pilgrims, whom Diekema himself held up as precursors to the Dutch Seceders who had founded Holland in 1847. Both groups had been driven out of their homeland under persecution.

In his rebuttal, Diekema declared that the "self-delusional" Hoeksema had displayed an "utter hopeless lack of good sense." During war is no time for community leaders to waffle on patriotism. Everyone must together fight the Kaiser and his master, the devil. The German "beast, armed with the greatest and cruelest military machine the world has ever seen," is bent on "world domination through terrorizing humanity with murder and rape." This beast had already devoured millions, Diekema continued as he warmed to his work; "the very earth is trembling under our feet" and the "fate of humanity hangs in the balance." At a time when "our sons and daughters are sinking to the bottom of the sea, are dropping from airships, crushed to earth, and are baring their breasts to German bombs and shrapnel, anyone [who] wastes his time in theological hair-splitting, rather than sincere patriotic effort . . . is guilty of conduct which is next to treason. . . . If the shoe fits," Hoeksema must "wear it."

Diekema then "hit below the belt" by quoting members of Hoeksema's own congregation in reaction to their pastor's sermon. "My blood ran cold," said one, and "I wanted to leave the church but seemed frozen to my pew." Another averred that his pastor was "such a good preacher but seems to be such a poor American." A third was more nuanced in his reaction. "I do not believe he is so wrong at heart but he is unfortunate in his expressions." That Hoeksema caused his parishioners pain and distress was bad enough, said Diekema, but that he gave comfort to the enemy was totally unacceptable. Moreover, Hoeksema wrongly asserted that he spoke for his entire denomination when his fellow Christian Reformed pastors, Marinus Van Vessum of First Zeeland, John H. Geerlings of North Street Zeeland, and US Chaplain Leonard Trap at Camp Custer near Battle Creek, all had recently delivered "wonderful patriotic addresses" in a Zeeland church.

Diekema concluded with a ringing endorsement of unbridled patriotism. "This is a Christian nation. Our flag represents God and Country. It is the emblem of Purity, Truth, Loyalty, Sacrifice, Liberty, and Justice. You cannot banish it from a church building, for although you may carry it out, it remains in all its glory engraved in the hearts of the people." Although Diekema had vented his spleen and displayed his debating skills, he missed Hoeksema's point entirely. The dominie welcomed the flag in church, just not during worship services.

Within a month of Hoeksema's "flag in church" sermon, he declined letters of call from three congregations, two in Grand Rapids and one in Paterson, New Jersey. For a strong-willed man who relished a fight and was determined to defend the integrity of the Christian faith, this was no time to cut and run. Even Rev. Henry Beets, the influential editor of the denominational weekly, *The Banner*, felt it necessary to criticize Hoeksema for placing "Our People's Loyalty Under a Cloud," as he titled his editorial on March 14, 1918. Hoeksema spoke for himself on this issue and not for "our entire people," Beets insisted. Beets them addressed the broader issue. The apparent pro-Germanism is "in reality nothing but anti-British sentiment, created by historical conditions, some of them going back to the days of Cromwell and Charles II, and some of it dating from the Boer War." Give the Dutch a little time "to get their bearings on the changing sea of world politics," and they will overcome their psychological inertia and "change their mind," Beets declared confidently.[76]

That the Christian Reformed Church hierarchy in Grand Rapids would not want to risk public opprobrium by backing the young cleric in Holland was understandable, but little did Hoeksema expect that some members of his own congregation would embarrass him publicly and undermine his crusade. In the wee hours of a Sunday morning in mid-July 1918, some congregants rifled the keys, sneaked into the church through the basement door, and hung a huge American flag behind

[76] *Holland City News*, 28 Feb., 14 Mar., 11 Apr. 1918. The call letters were from Twelfth Street and Franklin Street Christian Reformed Churches of Grand Rapids and Second Paterson Christian Reformed Church; Beets, "Our People's Loyalty Under a Cloud," 180-81. Beets also published a lecture of R. B. Kuiper of the Sherman Street CRC of Grand Rapids, entitled "Christian Patriotism," which he had delivered at Calvin College on 11 April 1918. Kuiper, the future president of Calvin College (1930-33), had "standing," and his views set forth the "official" position of the denominational establishment (*Banner*, 6, 13, 20 June 1918, 418-19, 432-33, 452-53.

the pulpit. When the dominie and consistory entered the sanctuary, they were shocked to find "Old Glory" filling the alcove from floor to ceiling. The sight "created no unusual stir during the services," the *City News* editor noted in the understatement of the year, but he went on to report that Hoeksema, amazingly, carried on the service as usual, but only after informing the body that the deed was done without his knowledge or that of the consistory. In the congregational prayer, the dominie "made a fervent prayer for the soldiers" and he also asked God to forgive those who committed "an act of rowdyism."[77] Having made their point, or perhaps in pangs of guilt, the culprits just as secretly re-entered the church that Sunday afternoon and removed the national emblem before the evening service.

The newspaper report failed to note that atop the pulpit Bible that morning, Hoeksema had found a note, signed by the American Protective League; it read: "This flag must and shall remain in this place." It is reported that the "ensuing uproar, especially among the better folk in town, prompted [Hoeksema] to carry a pistol, which he threatened to use one night on some vigilantes near his home."[78]

Hoeksema's principled position against civil religion was further undermined when a sister congregation, the Maple Avenue Christian Reformed Church, at a congregational meeting voted "with a great deal of enthusiasm" to place the American flag in their sanctuary, along with a congregational service flag. The decision clearly had the approbation of the consistory and the pastor, Rev. John P. Battema. The Christian Reformed churches of West Michigan did not present a united front behind Hoeksema.[79] The dominie lost the propaganda war. In the time of national crisis, most Americans, including Christian Reformed members, equated God and country and saw Christianity and patriotism to be one and the same holy crusade against German totalitarianism and militarism.

One of the remarkable aspects of the controversy was the contrasting views of Reformed and Christian Reformed believers on the flag question. The two churches shared a common ethnic and religious heritage, yet the differing rate of Americanization kept them apart. The

77 *Holland City News*, 18 July 1918. Whether due to the flag "break-in" or not, the consistory of the Fourteenth Street Church did not renew janitor Kroeze's contract in 1919, and he was "asked to resign" as of May 1 (consistory minutes, 10 Mar. 1919, quoted in Nyenhuis, *Centennial History*, 73).

78 James D. Bratt and Christopher H. Meehan, *Gathered at the River: Grand Rapids, Michigan and Its People of Faith* (Grand Rapids: Eerdmans, 1993), 119. The Bratts were long-time Holland residents.

79 *Holland City News*, 18 July 1918.

"Dutchy" Christian Reformed Church, which had gathered in most of the new immigrants since the 1880s and sought to hold American cultural influences at bay, was better able to hold the line against the worship of national icons.

The Reformed Church in America, on the other hand, was largely acculturated by 1917 and saw no conflict between American Christianity and America as a Christian nation. Indeed, it is a common practice to the present day for Reformed churches to hold special patriotic worship services on the Sundays around Memorial Day and the Fourth of July. Worshipers find the American flag and other red, white, and blue banners prominently displayed, they sing patriotic "God and country" songs, veterans rise and receive ovations, children's sermons celebrate the blessings of freedom, and church bulletins boldly display the national colors. Some pastors even sport a stars-and-stripes tie.[80]

Armistice Day

Holland twice celebrated the end of the war, once during the "false armistice," when Germany declared its intentions for an armistice, and four days later for the real armistice, when the armistice papers were actually signed. The first celebration featured a parade and a few speakers, but many spectators were not prepared for a peace celebration; they had no whistles or fireworks. When the armistice finally came on November 11, the people were ready for a true celebration.

The renowned day fell on a Monday. At 2:25 a.m. Holland's war board chairman, Thomas Robinson, was the first to learn of the German surrender. He hesitated to wake the city, but once he relayed the news, it spread quickly. In the wee hours, at ten minutes to three, Bert Slagh, like a town crier from a past age, stood on Eighth Street ringing a hand-bell and announcing the news. By three o'clock many citizens had begun celebrating. At 5:30 a train engineer at the depot blew the morning's first whistle, and half an hour later, at 6:00, the city's siren atop the power plant, dubbed the Mockingbird, sent its high-pitched squeal throughout the town. The siren was sounded for an hour, by which time hardly a soul was still asleep.

Other bells and whistles followed in course, and Hollanders rushed downtown with noisemakers in hand, filling Eighth Street as a "seething mass of joy-mad people." At seven o'clock, a mob of workers, beginning with those from the Western Machine Tool Works and gathering numbers from the Cappon & Bertsch Leather Co., marched

80 Brian Brooks, Hudsonville, letter to the editor, *Church Herald*, Jan. 2006, 6.

Hope College Student Army Training Corps (SATC) members march in "false armistice" parade, November 7, 1918 (*Joint Archives of Holland*)

toward downtown, calling on others to join in the celebrations. The Kaiser was hung in effigy and laid in coffins. A ten-block long parade of automobiles, floats mounted on truck beds, bands, businessmen, mail carriers, and schoolchildren, all carrying American flags and improvised

Fire truck and cars process down Eighth Street in the Armistice Day parade, November 11, 1918 (*courtesy Myron Van Ark*)

Doughboys carry the flag in the parade (*courtesy Myron Van Ark*)

slogans and pulling the wheeled coffins, continued until three in the afternoon, when organized speeches began at Centennial Park. Written in soap on many store windows was the phrase, "Closed, gone to the Kaiser's funeral."

At Centennial Park Gerrit Diekema won over the crowd with a well-crafted, patriotic speech. He memorialized the Holland-area soldiers who had died in the conflict. After a few more speeches, the exhausted residents returned to their homes for dinner around 6:00, and at 7:30 that evening, the festivities recommenced, with a huge bonfire in a grease-barrel (donated by the North Side Tannery) at River Avenue and Fifteenth Street. Fireworks followed. The war was over, the soldiers would be coming home, and shortages and wartime inflation would end.[81]

Waiting for the Polar Bears

Although most American soldiers stationed in France returned within a few months after the armistice, American soldiers in revolutionary Russia were not so lucky. Twenty-four of Holland's best in the 339th Infantry were secretly sent to Archangel under British command to counter the Bolsheviks in Russia's civil war. The United States and England had a strategic purpose for keeping the soldiers in Russia, but no political or military leaders explained it. Several men kept diaries or sent letters home that were preserved, including Levi Bartels

[81] *Holland City News*, 14 Nov. 1918; 17 June 1920; Vande Water, "Armistice Roused Celebrants in 1918," in *Holland: Happenings, Heroes & Hot Shots* 3:136-40.

The Holland City Gas Co. Brass Band piles into a vehicle with horns, bass drum, symbols, and a wash tub to add to the clamor. The two men in the middle of the group are brothers Tien and William Vande Water (*courtesy Randall P. Vande Water*)

and August Postmus. They often called the place Siberia, although technically it was not. Yet, the winter weather was extreme. By February 1919 it became clear that something strange was going on. They had heard via the Red Cross that the war with Germany was over, and most American boys were coming home. They were ordered to fight "Bolos," as the American soldiers called the Bolsheviks, seemingly forgotten by military superiors and without basic supplies or medical care.[82]

On February 13, 1919, Mayor Bosch called a meeting to discuss the situation. In six weeks Holland had written up an official petition to send to Washington, demanding either their soldiers or answers. For five long months, they received neither. Wives and families throughout Michigan joined the campaign, but President Wilson and his military brass stood firm. The president had unilaterally made the decision to commit American troops on the side of the White Army against the "Reds." Finally, California Congressman Hiram Johnson took up the cause, and Wilson and the military brass relented.[83]

In July 1919 Holland finally received word that all forty-three Ottawa County Polar Bears were coming home from what the *Holland City News* called "the most God-forsaken spot on the earth blessed with the angelic name of Archangel." The soldiers arrived on July 17, and city officials did their best to let the "boys" know they had not been forgotten. To bring them home they chartered a special Interurban car decorated with polar bear flags, bunting, and a large sign reading "Holland Polar Bear Special."

82 "Voices of a Never Ending Dawn," a 2009 video documentary of Michigan's Polar Bears by Pamela Peak of Pamela Peak Productions. A list of the twenty-four Polar Bears from Holland was published in the *Holland City News*, 24 July 1919.

83 *Holland City News*, 6, 13 Feb., 22 May, 17, 24 July 1919.

The Polar Bears missed the July 4, 1919, "Welcome Home" parade, including the Cappon & Bertsch Leather Co. float on which women, flanked by children, wear red crosses on their caps (*courtesy Randall P. Vande Water*)

The soldiers mustered out of Battle Creek's Camp Custer a few hours later than expected, but the welcome committee, consisting of ex-mayor John Vander Sluis, police board chairman Jack Schouten, and businessmen Peter Lievense and Jake Fris, remained on hand to treat the Polar Bears to dinner, cigarettes, candy, and ice cream. When the special car arrived in Holland, again the Mockingbird whistled the the good news to one and all. A crowd quickly filled Eighth Street from the Tower Clock Building to the train station, where families of the soldiers greeted their sons, grandsons, nephews, and brothers. The celebration was spontaneous and heartfelt, but polar bear signs were already on hand. The loquacious Diekema, who had sent the men off to war with torrid rhetoric, was there again to greet them with congratulatory words and expressions of gratitude for their grit in fighting Bolshevism. An auto caravan carried the men home.[84]

Beginning with the first anniversary of the armistice on Nov. 11, 1919, and continuing for years until the day became a national holiday, Holland observed Armistice Day with festivities. Many stores and factories closed, along with the city hall and post office, businesses and homes unfurled flags, children in school held special exercises, the Boy Scouts and American Legionnaires staged a parade, and young men played softball at Riverview Park. Hollanders were nothing, if not patriotic.[85]

84 Ibid., 29 July 1919.
85 Ibid., 11 Nov. 1932.

William Brusse family adorn their car with flags and join an Armistice Day Parade. Brusse owned a clothing store and served a term as mayor of Holland (1900-1902) (*Archives, Holland Historical Trust*)

Conclusion

The war hastened the pace of Americanization in immigrant communities like Holland. The Dutch Reformed churches and their pastors were almost forced by public opinion, if not by law, to drop Dutch language services in favor of English, due to anti-German propaganda that often failed to distinguish Dutch from Duits. That many Dutch still blamed the British for brutalizing their kinfolk in the South African Boer War (1899-1902) added to the untrue perception that they did not fully support a war to save Great Britain from Germany, a people with whom the Dutch had intermarried, inter-worshiped, and exchanged labor across a porous border.

The war also broke down the cultural isolation of the Dutch immigrant churches. For the first time, their young men left a tight little ethnic enclave to fight alongside of—and often bond with—men of other faiths and ethnic heritages. The Hollanders were inevitably changed by the experience and became more open to the American culture. Christian Reformed soldiers especially were affected. They went off to war believing in the long held church motto: "In isolation is our strength," but they found themselves worshiping in military chapels with Protestants of all stripes and fighting in foxholes alongside the same Protestants and also Catholics and Jews. The old saying rang true: "How can you keep a man down once he has seen Paree?"

Opening the Dutch immigrant churches to the wider culture soon brought theological conflict, especially within the Christian Reformed Church. All the professors of Calvin Theological Seminary were purged in 1922, except one who was about to retire, and the denomination suffered a painful split at the 1924 synodical assembly that led to the formation of the Protestant Reformed Church. Although the debate was couched in theological terms, the underlying issues were cultural and revolved around the pace of Americanization. In an attempt to turn back the clock, the denomination in 1929 adopted the infamous ban on dancing, devil cards, and Hollywood movies. James Bratt in his classic study of Dutch Calvinism in America titled the story of the postwar decade, "Wars Without and Within, 1917-1928."[86]

[86] James D. Bratt, *Dutch Calvinsism in Modern America: A History of a Conservative Subculture* (Grand Rapids: Eerdmans, 1984), 83-122.

CHAPTER 22

The Roaring Twenties and the Great Depression

Although the Great War was over and the excitement surrounding it was gone, life for many in Holland did not slow down and return to normal. Indeed, in the 1920s, modernization and Americanization continued to be the primary forces shaping the cultural life of the city. Holland between the wars was searching for its identity. Facing outside cultural pressures and motivated by a desire to escape the Great Depression of the 1930s, Holland promoted its Tulip Time festival as a symbol of the city's unique Dutch heritage. After decades of busily becoming Americans, it was time for many to look back and think about what it meant to be Dutch. The Depression tested the community as never before, and it was not found wanting. The Dutch virtues of thrift, hard work, and sturdiness in the face of adversity carried the day.

Be prepared!

Some months after First Lieutenant Henry Geerds was mustered out of the army in 1919, he determined to fulfill his pledge to train properly and equip young Americans to fight for their country, should that ever be necessary again. He would establish a National Guard unit in Holland.[1]

The opportunity came when Geerds learned of a vacancy in the 126th Infantry, and he worked with a will to establish a company in Holland, which became Company D, a machine gun battery. Almost a year before Co. D gained official recognition on March 22, 1921, he began signing up volunteers, and soon he had one hundred guardsmen. At twenty-five years of age, the grizzled soldier would pass his skills to the next generation. To do this Holland needed an armory, and Geerds determined to get one. As city treasurer in 1920-21, he pushed the armory at every opportunity, especially to organizations like the Rotary Club, which fully backed the project. Holland, Geerds insisted, needed to do its part in the National Guard to train a cadre of citizen soldiers "ready to answer the country's call." Best of all, should Holland act, the state government would provide most of the $55,000 needed for a building and maintain it. In the end, the state contributed $40,000, the city donated the site at 16 West Ninth Street worth $15,000, and private donations covered the remaining $15,000. The state appropriations bill was passed by a single vote in 1923, thanks to Holland-area representative Gerrit W. Kooyers. The Holland Armory was dedicated in 1925, complete with a drill floor that doubled as a gymnasium or a 1,200-seat auditorium and an office for Geerds off the lobby. The building was enlarged in 1933 and the kitchen upgraded. The armory served the National Guard, the American Legion, and its Women's Auxiliary for seventy-five years and filled the role of a public auditorium and a basketball arena for Holland High School and Hope College until the Civic Center was dedicated in 1954.[2]

Co. D and the Holland Armory quickly became a prestigious institution that gave a valued cache to the guardsmen. Men from the best families and Hope College students enlisted. In 1928 Co. D won the coveted Badger Cup for military proficiency, the highest honor awarded to guard units in Michigan and Wisconsin. Co. D captured the trophy again the next two years. This signal achievement won for Geerds a promotion to major.

The men of Co. D paid a price for their commitment. In the 1937 Detroit sit down strikes at Chevrolet, staged by Walter P. Reuther's

1 Randall P. Vande Water, "Co. D 126th Infantry Leaves Holland," Holland Historical Trust *Review* 3, no. 3 (Sept. 1990).

2 Vande Water, "Henry Geerds"; "Holland Armory," radio program on WHTC, 27 Oct. 2000; *Holland City News*, 16 Feb. 1922, 15, 22 Mar., 10 May 1923, 15 May 1924, 7 May 1925, 21 Dec. 1933. The city had initially purchased for the proposed armory the lot to the east, on the southwest corner of Ninth and Central. Despite calls by citizens to retain the lot, the city sold it in 1926 (ibid., 9 Sept., 7 Oct., 2 Dec. 1926).

United Auto Workers Union, the governor mobilized the sixty-four-man unit for riot duty that stretched out to thirty-six tense days. Three years later, in 1940, the president called Co. D to its greatest mission, to train for deployment in the South Pacific. Geerds at forty-six years of age re-entered active duty and was promoted to lieutenant colonel. He eventually led Co. D into the jungles of New Guinea, where they suffered a nearly 100 percent casualty rate.[3]

Company D 126th Infantry shared the local military spotlight with American Legion Post No. 6, which was formed in 1919, and the Henry Walters Post of the Veterans of Foreign Wars (VFW), which was founded in 1931 under John Bremer as first commander. The Holland American Legion post was the sixth nationally. The VFW, founded nationally in 1899, was open to all military who served on foreign soil or in foreign wars. It also sponsored orphans and soldiers' widows. The local VFW grew after the Second World War under commander Russell Huyser from 97 to 456 members, which overwhelmed its small rented building. The VFW in 1946 built a modern headquarters at 28 W. Seventh Street.[4]

Transition to a peacetime economy

In the immediate postwar years, everyone, and particularly veterans, had to deal with deflation and depression, which economic ills always followed the dismantling of a command economy necessitated by war. To help workingmen, the city established a community store on the third floor of the city hall to sell government war surplus goods at deep discounts on a cash-and-carry basis. The common council appointed Peter Brusse to manage the store, which carried everything from blankets to boots and canned food to camp buckets. He did a rousing business, and the first shipment was gone within two days. More shipments followed, but soon the nation-wide surplus goods sale was over. The *Holland City News* in 1921 offered free space to companies and veterans to advertise for jobs. The American Legion chapter also sprang into action and found employment for its more than three hundred members. Business, fortunately, had revived by 1922. The Pere Marquette Railroad agent in Holland reported billing 184 more rail cars out in January 1922 than in the January previous.[5]

3 Vande Water, "Co. D 126th Infantry," 9.

4 *Holland City News*, 10 Jan. 1946.

5 Ibid., 29 Jan., 12, 26 Feb. 1920, 30 June 1921, 9, 16 Feb., 11 Oct. 1922; Cynthia Crossen, "Veterans of World War I Ridiculed as Beggars for Seeking a Bonus," *Wall Street Journal*, 7 Nov. 2005.

The people of Holland also caught the "paving fever" that summer and five miles of city streets were macadamized. In 1924 the federal government offered veterans a "bonus plan" that provided life insurance at the rate of $1.00 per day of service and $1.50 per day for service overseas. Compounding would double the payout in twenty years. More than seven hundred men in Holland applied within the three-year deadline. Four years later, in the depths of the Great Depression, the desperate vets demanded the government pay off on their policies. This riled up fiscal conservatives, who decried a $2.4 billion payout for 4 percent of the population that would eat up more than half the federal budget for 1932. They labeled the veterans "bonus racketeers" and "treasury raiders." One wonders what Holland's last two surviving Civil War veterans, Gerrit S. Doesburg, age ninety, and John R. Douma, age eighty-six, who were honored on Memorial Day in 1933, thought about the bonus their recent comrades in arms were demanding.[6]

World peace

Holland seemed far removed from international movements to create the League of Nations, limit naval armaments, outlaw war, and enact protective tariffs. Locals were patriotic and duly nationalistic, but also very ready "to make war no more." The "war to ends all wars" cost enough bloodshed for one lifetime. On July 26, 1923, the ninth anniversary of the beginning of the Great War, Holland pacifists joined with idealists in cities around the world and demonstrated for world peace under the banner of the Fellowship of Reconciliation Society. "Brotherhood is the pressing need of the world today," declared Father D. D. Douglas to the American Legion at an Armistice Day celebration at the armory in 1927. International cooperation is the essence of One Hundred Percent Americanism, declared Hope President Wynand Wichers in 1928. That year virtually every nation on earth signed the Kellogg-Briand Pact that outlawed war as an instrument of national policy. Rev. J. C. Willits of the Methodist Episcopal Church and chaplain of the Holland American Legion, called Kellogg's Pact the "most glorious accomplishment in a decade" in his 1931 Memorial Day sermon. All Christians must "enlist in a real army to combat sin," he declared.[7]

6 *Holland City News*, 8 Dec. 1927, 4 May 1933. Douma was honored at the 1936 Memorial Day ceremony at the Hope Memorial Chapel as the "last man" of the Civil War veterans (22 May 1936).

7 Ibid., 17 Nov. 1927, 12 Jan. 1928.

That same year Raymond Drukker, a graduate of Holland High School and a veteran, described his war experiences for the Holland Exchange Club. Hope College Coach Milton "Bud" Hinga introduced him. "War is hell," Drukker declared, quoting Civil War General William Tecumseh Sherman; it should be a "punishable crime with a heavy penalty. . . . I feel that peace is the new patriotism, and the Christianization of nations will mean peace and will mean no empty chairs, no broken homes, the terrible scars that wars leave."[8] The yearning for peace was overwhelming.

The early 1920s

Holland, the largest city in Ottawa County with fourteen thousand inhabitants, had much about which to boast. Its water, rail, and road systems were more than adequate, and its city-owned water and electric utilities had the cheapest rates in Michigan. The fire and police departments were well equipped, yet the tax rate was "far below" neighboring cities. The three banks had more than $6 million in deposits. The educational system was excellent, with both public and Christian schools K-12, all capped by Hope College, a Christian liberal arts college, with five hundred students, Western Theological Seminary, and the Holland Business College. Twenty-one churches and a new YMCA provided for the religious needs. Nine newspapers and periodicals, both secular and religious, were published in Holland and had a combined circulation of twenty-six thousand. Three theaters provided popular entertainment.[9]

Holland continued to be the chief farm market center of the region, processing fruits and vegetables, cereal, sugar, dairy products, and poultry. Its diversified industries included the largest tannery and shoe factory in the state, the largest furnace company in the world, one of the largest sugar beet factories in the state, the largest pickle plant other than one near Pittsburgh, and the largest production of "chicks" in the state. Seven furniture factories employed one thousand workers, one-fifth of the city-wide workforce of five thousand.

The city was adorned with neat and well-kept homes and city parks, Centennial Park being the jewel (chapter 27). The city installed a modern "boulevard" lighting system throughout the downtown business district in 1921. Home ownership was high at 75 percent, including most laboring men, and no "shanty town" could be found.

8 Ibid., 28 May, 12 Nov. 1931.

9 Ibid., 15 June 1922 for this section.

"Holland is a unique city," Mayor Stephan told convention delegates. "We have no idle rich here, neither have we any paupers in our midst." The city had no millionaires and no large mansions, Stephan asserted. In the six years from 1921 to 1927, home building permits totaled more than $1 million and commercial building permits several times that amount. Property tax delinquency was consistently below 3 percent. Holland is a "City of Homes, Stephan boasted, but also a "Home City," with 90 percent of homes owner occupied. This reflected the high value Hollanders placed on their homes, he added. The pride of ownership shows in houses "freshly painted, tidy, and well-kept."[10] (See appendix 5.4 for a list of contractors and builders, 1897-1929.)

Cultural life

In 1922, in a welcome message to the Municipal League of Michigan, Mayor Stephan welcomed other city leaders to his hometown, calling it "the Plymouth of the Middle West."[11] But this familiar analogy to the early Pilgrims was no longer entirely valid. Yes, Holland's culture was rooted in Calvinism with a dash of Puritanism, but by 1920 it was thoroughly shaped by Americanization and modernization. And few new immigrants arrived to nourish the Dutch culture, due to several immigration quota laws based on "national origins." These fixed limits for each country, based on the number by birth or descent counted in various decennial population censuses. The Netherlands quota was 3,607 from 1921 to 1924, 1,648 from 1924 to 1929, and 3,153 from 1929 to 1956. The virtual cutoff of fresh immigrants after the war prompted many pioneer Holland-area families to organize family reunions to keep the memories and traditions alive in the third and succeeding generations, less they forget. Between 1925 and 1929, the *Holland City News* regularly reported on family reunions during the summer months.[12]

Contrary to Van Raalte's dream, Holland did not necessarily become an example for the world; rather, the world was an example for

10 Ibid., 30 Nov. 1922, 17 May, 7 June, 12 July, 30 Aug. 1923, 1 Apr. 1926 (quote), 5 Jan. 1928.

11 Ibid., 15 June 1922.

12 Jacob Van Hinte, *Netherlanders in America: A Study of Emigration and Settlement in the Nineteenth and Twentieth Centuries in the United States of America* (2 vols., Groningen, 1928; English edition, Grand Rapids: Baker, 1985), 618; Robert P. Swierenga, "Dutch," in *Harvard Encyclopedia of American Ethnic Groups*, Stephan Thernstrom and Ann Orlov, eds. (London and Cambridge, MA: Harvard University Press, 1980), 286. Examples of annual reunions, attended by 100 or more relatives, are the Hofmeyer, Albert Wolcott, Cornelius Schaap, Van Til, and Veneklasen families (*Holland City News*, 11 July 22, 29 Aug. 1929).

Holland. Despite the efforts of a few well-meaning cultural conservatives, Holland could not and did not close itself off from outside influences in American culture. The Hollywood silent screen, the flapper era of short skirts and bobbed hair, jazz music, speakeasies (illegal saloons) and the hip flask, and other hedonist movements penetrated western Michigan as everywhere else. The tension between the new trends that Hollanders generally deemed acceptable and those that they generally rejected contributed to Holland's unique character. So what were these trends and how did Holland receive them?

First of all, there were new technological advancements that were too beneficial to reject. The electric grid linked every home, and housewives could buy vacuum cleaners, washing machines, mangle irons, toasters, and other electric appliances to ease daily chores. A city sewer system allowed for indoor plumbing. Automobiles were within the financial reach of the common worker. Other inventions were just as important for opening minds to the wider world. Every home had a telephone by 1930 (chapter 25). Radios, first seen in Holland on display at Herman Van Tongeren's cigar store in 1922, were equally ubiquitous a decade later. Holland's Bush & Lane Piano Company, known primarily for manufacturing grand pianos, also by 1930 made radio sets and automobile radios.[13]

Holland's first radio station, WHBM, hit the airwaves in the summer of 1927, thanks to a push by Henry Carley, manager of the Holland and Strand Theaters, and generous funding from Holland Furnace and Buss Machine companies (chapter 19). The station ran its own programs, often with local musical talent, from eight to ten o'clock in the evening. The schedule also included jazz, children's stories, and a sports report, with Saturday night reserved for "old-timers music."[14]

National culture now emanated from local garage radios and hardware store speakers. One could hardly avoid all the music and noise, Alderman Peter Huyser reasoned in 1933 when he helped pass a city ordinance against playing radios on business streets.[15] Some proposed that radio did more than alter culture; it affected the weather as well. Newspaper editor Arnold Mulder rejected the absurd notion that radio waves could be the root cause of the "unusually heavy rainfall" and that the only way to "obviate this trouble [of radio's effect on the skies] is a reduction of the use of electricity." Indeed, the skies did deserve a second look. Americans were looking upward in the figurative sense of

13 *Holland City News*, 3 July 1922, 1 May 1930.
14 Ibid., 7 July, 1 Sept. 1927.
15 Ibid., 8, 22 June, 20 July 1933.

progress and improvement, but they were looking upward in the literal sense too. For the first time dreams of airborne travel seemed plausible. In fact, in the early 1920s airplanes in the Holland skies had "become so common . . . that people have ceased to sky gaze when a plane is approaching."[16]

Holland was also being shaped by a spirit of consumerism and increasing complexity. In the nineteenth century, the word "consumption" was a synonym for tuberculosis. The word had a negative connotation, and it meant to use up, or destroy, in contrast to the prized virtues of thrift and stewardship. In the new consumer society of the twenties, however, large retailers and their advertising agencies tried to break those traditional values. Manufacturers began producing products for a mass market—washing machines, electric refrigerators, watches, razor blades, jeans, toys, and even automobiles—and they needed consumers to buy, not save. A popular big-ticket item was a bungalow style house, with its cozy front porch that well suited the rising middle class. Nearly every house displayed a Christmas tree during the holidays; even the poor could afford to celebrate. This was a classic throwaway product, one of a bevy of disposable goods.[17]

Holland witnessed a sustained construction boom, and developers platted new subdivisions on every side. To accommodate this growth, the aldermen in 1929 extended the city boundaries, which increased the population to twenty thousand. The city was growing and prospering. At both the local and national levels, the economy ran full steam ahead. Farms reached to the corners of nearby agricultural lands, and local food processing plants and furniture-makers were profitable. This prosperity permitted the Holland County Club, an association of business and professional people, in 1922 to build a new $35,000 clubhouse and sports center for golf, tennis, and crochet (chapter 29). The entire project, costing its nearly one hundred members $80,000, lay east of Zeeland Road (now Paw Paw Drive) along present-day Country Club Road. The choice property straddled the winding Black River and Frenchman's Creek tributary.[18]

The nearby beach resorts and Lakewood Farm also gained national fame and drew millions of visitors (chapter 28). The Black Lake summer resorts began in the 1880s when Holland and Grand Rapids investors platted both sides of the channel at Lake Michigan. The pride of the Macatawa Park Association was the Macatawa Hotel

16 Ibid., 27 Nov. 1924, 13 July 1922.

17 Katherine Reynolds Lewis, "Is consumption good?" *Grand Rapids Press*, 29 Jan. 2008; *Holland City News*, 29 Dec. 1927.

18 *Holland City News*, 27 July, 3, 17 Aug. 1922, 11 Apr., 3, 24 June 1926, 5 Jan. 1928.

Yocum's Place grocery and gas station (now Raman Party Store, 394 Chicago Drive) under construction on unpaved Chicago Drive by George Woldring & Sons (Franklin and Kenneth), a plumbing and heating contractor, late 1930s. John Woldring founded the business, and by 1949 his son Lester had taken over (*courtesy Randall P. Vande Water*)

on the south channel, which faced the rival Ottawa Beach Association's Ottawa Hotel on the north side. Both featured docks for Chicago excursion boats and Black Lake ferries and connecting terminals for the Pere Marquette Railroad (Chicago & West Michigan Railway before 1900) from Chicago and the Interurban from Grand Rapids, both via Holland. Other promoters fed off the initial developments and opened the nearby resort communities of Jenison Park, Virginia Park, Waukazoo Park and Inn, Castle Park, and Alpena Beach. The Ottawa Beach resort did not thrive at first, and in 1891 the Chicago & West Michigan Railway bought it, invested thousands in improvements, and leased it to Charles Heald, a Grand Rapids banker, who later bought the resort. In 1901 Heald spent $50,000 to upgrade the hotel and hired J. Boyd Pantlind as manager. National organizations, such as the Automotive Engineers of America and the Michigan Bankers Association, came one thousand strong to the Holland resorts for their annual conventions.[19]

[19] Larry B. Massie, *Haven, Harbor, and Heritage: The Holland, Michigan Story* (Allegan Forest, MI: Priscilla Press, 1996), 78-89; Donald L. van Reken, *Macatawa Park: A Chronicle* (Holland, MI: privately printed, 1991); Donald L. van Reken, *Ottawa Beach & Waukazoo: A History* (Holland, MI, privately printed, 1987); *Grand Rapids Press*, 23 Mar. 1901; *Holland City News*, 12 Sept. 1891, 15 Feb. 1917, 24 June 1920, 8 Nov. 1923. Holland investors, who bought the "worthless sand dunes" from the federal government for a "song" and developed it into a million dollar property, included Henry D. Post and his son John C. (Jack), E. C. Westerveld, Rudolph F. Doornink, Austin Harrington, Heber Walsh, John Bertsch, Hermanus Boone, and James H. Purdy (*Holland City News*, 9 Apr. 1914). Doornink, a Grand Rapids businessman, was the only non-Holland partner.

Cars jam the parking lot at Ottawa Beach resort in the 1920s
(*Donald van Reken Collection, Joint Archives of Holland*)

In the next decades, these resorts became increasingly popular vacation destinations for Chicago and West Michigan elites. In the 1910s, with the advent of automobiles, the resorters built their own cottages along the big lake as access roads were cut through the dunes. One of the biggest estates was that of Chicago industrialist George Getz, who in 1910, bought a large tract on Lake Michigan two miles north of Ottawa Beach near Alpena Beach, where he developed Lakewood Farm into a showcase and then a zoo. To shunt beachgoers away from his farm, Getz purchased a choice lakefront tract a mile south and donated it to Park Township for the present Tunnel Park. After the Ottawa Hotel burned to the ground in 1923, Ottawa County bought the land for the Ottawa Beach State Park, which opened under the management of the state park board in 1926. The state appropriated $30,000 to complete a concrete road to the beach and build a parking oval to hold a thousand cars. For the first time, the middle class could enjoy the beach and tent there overnight. The next year, new management at Macatawa Park invested $1 million to upgrade the rundown resort across the channel, with the hope of making it the "future Atlantic City of the Great Lakes." Two million visitors hit the Holland beaches in 1929, but the good times ended with the stock market crash. By October, Macatawa Park resort was in foreclosure; it would never be another Atlantic City. The tourist trade, however, continued to sustain Holland during the hard times.[20]

20 Massie, *Haven, Harbor, and Heritage*, 103-5; *Holland City News*, 24 Dec. 1925, 17 Feb., 14 July, 4, 18 Aug. 1927, 3 Oct. 1929, 14 Oct. 1937; Donald L. van Reken, *Getz Farm Lakewood: The Farm That Was a Zoo* (Holland, MI, privately printed, 1983).

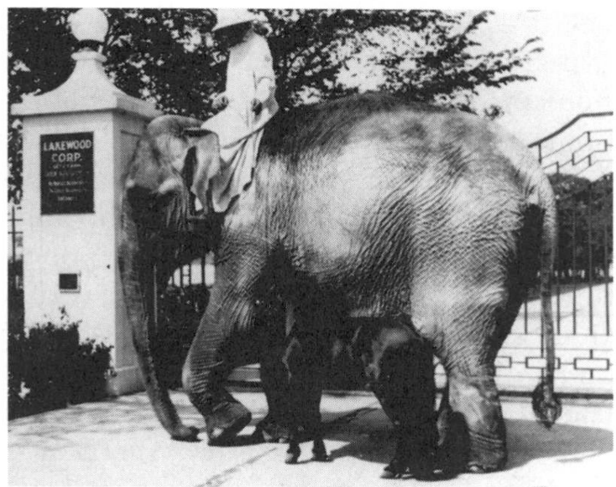
Nancy the elephant and Tiny Mite the miniature horse at entrance to Lakewood Farm, the zoo of George Getz at the end of Alpena Road (now Lakewood Boulevard) at Lakeshore Drive (*courtesy Myron Van Ark*)

The nearby Getz Zoo was another popular attraction. Since Getz graciously charged no entrance fee until 1931, local families who watched their pennies came in droves to see the animals, including an elephant, camels, monkeys, bears, lions and tigers, and many kinds of birds. In 1926 eight hundred thousand visitors walked the grounds, and in the early 1930s as many as seventy-five thousand a day came on holiday weekends. Unfortunately, the Great Depression put a dent in Getz's fortune, and he had to close the zoo in 1933. He donated most of the animals and birds to Chicago's Brookfield Zoo. The state wished to buy the property but lacked the funds. Getz died five years later, and his farm was platted and sold to developers for cottages.[21]

As with any change, there was bound to be some opposition. On numerous occasions city health officers chided "anti-Modern" Hollanders for ignoring quarantine or refusing vaccinations. In one example in 1923, a smallpox warning put the entire city on temporary quarantine. The churches and schools closed down, and organizers cancelled a much-anticipated concert at Carnegie Gymnasium. But then, hundreds of Hollanders were reported attending church in Zeeland, much to the frustration of the editor of the *Zeeland Record*. In 1924, with a push from the Exchange Club and other movers and shakers, the common council hired the first full-time health officer for Holland.[22]

National prohibition came with the adoption of the Eighteenth Amendment in 1919, and Holland went "dry" along with the rest of the country for fourteen years, until 1933 (chapter 20). When the Supreme

[21] *Holland City News*, 7 Nov. 1929, 26 Oct. 1933; Massie, *Haven, Harbor and Heritage*, 103-4.

[22] *Holland City News*, 11, 18, 25 Oct., 8 Nov. 1923, 15 May 1924.

Court upheld the constitutionality of the amendment in 1920, the Synod of the Reformed Church in America rejoiced. The law allowed homemade beer and wine for personal consumption but not for sale. Some in Holland sold "bathtub gin" anyway and were caught from time to time. When they did, the newspapers were sure to report it on page one.[23] The Women's Christian Temperance Union (WCTU) remained ever vigilant against a tendency by police and prosecutors to wink at illicit booze, and the blatant hypocrisy of public officials infuriated the "blue ribbon" reformers. Scofflaws made and drank alcohol illegally and with reckless abandon. A local judge told the Holland Exchange Club in 1930 that in his opinion prohibition had proven to be a failure. Nevertheless, in the last few years of prohibition, Holland police confiscated and poured down the sewers five hundred gallons of illegal liquor.[24]

Local businesses that thrived were the hardware stores; they sold the accessories for bathtub gin and home brews—every kind of jug, crock, and stone jar, bottle caps and funnels, tubs and tubbing. Hardware man Ray Nies noted that customers came with the same story, they "wanted the jugs for 'vinegar,' the crocks for 'butter,' the big jars for 'pickles' and 'salted meat,' the bottle caps for 'ketchup,' and so on. All wore the same sickly, half guilty grin on their faces. . . . None told the real reason."[25]

President Herbert Hoover declared that the liquor industry had no redeeming value and resisted the mounting public pressure for repeal, even though the law was almost impossible to enforce consistently. But not so in Holland and Ottawa County, where temperance had a long history. The local WCTU chapter, led by Mrs. Henry Vander Ark and Hattie (Mrs. Evert J.) Blekkink, held the feet of public officials to the fire. They induced a number of Reformed churches in Holland to pass resolutions demanding strict enforcement, and they pledged to vote only for candidates known to do the same. With men like Justice Gerrit Van Schelven and Mayor Nicholas Kammeraad, they need not worry. After the repeal of the Eighteenth Amendment by the Twenty-First Amendment in 1933, however, the common council in April 1934 voted nine to three to approve a state liquor store under the aegis of

23 For example, Margaret "Maggie" Arendsma (ibid., 20 Oct. 1921, 23 Nov. 1923, 26 Oct. 1926); J. J. Vander Veen (ibid., 31 Mar. 1921); Peter Arendsma (ibid., 19 Oct. 1922); John Tinholt of Zeeland (ibid., 23 Nov. 1923); Frank Chrispell, Chris Hoogendoorn, James Verona, Martin De Ridder, Lewis De Young (ibid., 7 Jan. 1932).

24 *Holland City News*, 10 June 1920, 24 Aug., 19 Sept. 1922, 4 Oct. 1923, 15 Jan. 1925, 27 Jan. 1927, 20 Mar. 1930.

25 Ray Nies Autobiography, typescript, ch. 17, p. 15, Holland Museum Archives (HMA).

the State Liquor Control Commission. The commission and all store employees were political appointees of the governor. The common council in 1937 approved a liquor license for the Warm Friend Tavern, which allowed the sale of liquor by the glass for hotel patrons only. Otherwise, residents had to drink hard liquor at home.[26]

Blacks and bigotry

The first black to live in the Holland area was likely the New Jersey-born Silas (or Siras) Sill, who the US census marshal in June 1880 recorded as a servant and farmhand, age thirty-five, in the Manly Howard household. This man is legendary in the annals of the city. After arriving in Holland "broke" in June 1873, Silas became the popular coachman at the City Hotel (predecessor of the Warm Friend), driving the team and hotel "buss" that conveyed guests to and from the train depot for fifty years, until after World War One. Ben Mulder, former editor of the *Holland City News*, recalled in 1939: "Old Silas was quite a character. He was never known to get angry. His big bass voice could be heard a block away when he started his team to the depot. Being polite and helpful was popular with the traveling public." Even more amazing, Silas startled many an arriving immigrant by greeting them in the Dutch tongue. It is safe to say that Silas Sill was the first black businessman in Holland.[27]

Silas Sill's life before coming to Holland is clouded in mystery. The census of 1880 says he was born in New Jersey, and the birthplaces of his parents are listed as "don't know."[28] Hardware merchant Ray Nies, in his autobiography written in the 1930s, claims Silas was brought home to Holland by a Civil War soldier. Rumors circulated that the veteran was sodomizing the boy, but these died quickly when the veteran married a local woman, and the couple adopted the boy. Nies recounted the story as it was passed from mouth to mouth and became part of the city's lore:

> There was another young soldier living near *De Stadt* who, when the war was over, came home with a small colored boy, just a child.

26 *Holland City News*, 12 Apr. 1934, 6 May, 2 Sept. 1937.

27 Ibid., "Fifty Years Ago Today" 15 June 1939 [8 June 1889]; Vande Water, "City Hotel," in *Holland Happenings*, 4:31; Vande Water, "Silas drove 'his bus' from hotel to depot," *Holland Sentinel*, 19 June 2100. Michael Douma, "The History of a Black Hollander," unpublished paper, 2009, tells the story of Silas (or Siras) with considerable conjecture. His sources are Michigan Civil War Centennial Observance Commission, *Negroes in Michigan in the Civil War* (Lansing, MI, 1966), 20-21, and *Census Report of Michigan* (1864), 606, 633.

28 Federal Population Census of 1880, Holland city.

City Hotel, erected by William Kellogg in 1872, with guests waiting to board the hotel bus of coachman Silas Sill (*courtesy Randall Vande Water*)

> No, it was not as some gossips insinuated. The boy really was, as the soldier said, a homeless, little stray, picked up on the field after a battle. The little fellow did not know where he belonged, and the war being now over, the soldier managed to bring him home to his house in the north. The soldier married soon after he got home, and settled in a village near De Stadt. The couple kept the little colored fellow . . . and raised him with their own children, teaching him the Dutch language along with their own children, and sending him to school with them where he learned English. When he grew up, he obtained a job at the railway station as a porter, which he kept all his life, representing in his person almost the whole colored population of the place."[29]

To reconcile Nies' oral history with the 1880 census information is impossible, unless we allow that Sill's age was mistakenly recorded as thirty-five, when it should have been twenty-five. Then Silas would have been ten in 1865. The 1870 census is of no help, since Silas is not listed there. If we assume the 1880 census information to be correct, then the story of Sill's origins was romanticized beyond recognition. But one fact is clear; Silas won the hearts and minds of Hollanders and visitors alike.[30]

Blacks gathered at Macatawa Park from time to time in the 1880s for "colored camp meetings" of the African Methodist Episcopal Church, but no attendees lived in Holland, nor were they welcomed in town. Interracial dating was strongly condemned and miscegenation

[29] Nies Autobiography, typescript, ch. 15, pp. 1-2 (quote p. 1), HMA.

[30] Silas Sill is not listed in any *Holland City Directory* from 1894 to 1930, nor in the Holland City decennial censuses of 1900 through 1920.

Business card of John W. Minderhout, New City Hotel proprietor as of May 1, 1875, offering "Livery connected with the Hotel" (*Joint Archives of Holland*)

absolutely forbidden. In 1913 Ottawa County Clerk Jacob Glerum refused to issue a marriage license to a black man and a white woman. "I believe it is best for society," Glerum opined. Most county clerks in the state agreed with him and followed the same policy.[31]

The screening of the controversial silent film, "The Birth of a Nation," in 1918 triggered the next racist "event" in Holland. Crowds flocked to theaters nationwide, including Grand Rapids, to see the blockbuster film that promoted white supremacy and portrayed KKK "Knights" as heroes. When Frank Ogden, owner of the Knickerbocker Theatre, announced the screening of the film, tongues wagged: "No one ever had the nerve to bring it here." Ogden ran a large announcement on the front page of the *Holland Sentinel* under the heading "WARNING!" Yes, indeed, the film was scheduled for showings that very Friday afternoon matinee and evening; "35¢ Seats Now On Sale." *Sentinel* editor Arnold Mulder, true to his progressive worldview, dismissed the enthused viewers as an "unthinking mob" stirred up by the Great War, much like the Russian peasants who had a "far-fetched" fear of the Bolsheviks. The *Holland City News* editor noted that Holland, being a "'Coonless' Town," did not have to worry about Negroes trying to censor the film. The local military draft board, which had recently registered every adult male, reported finding "not a colored citizen within the city limits; no not even one with a yellow shade or with crinkly hair." The next year the paper reported finding one Negro in town, probably Old Silas.[32]

Other blacks came into the city regularly as deckhands and maids on the various Lake Michigan passenger ships. When one young man drowned at the King dock at the foot of Harrison Street, and no one claimed the body, the Nibbelink-Notier Funeral Home

31 *Holland City News*, 22 Aug., 5 Sept. 1885, 7 Aug. 1886, 30 Jan. 1913.

32 *Holland Sentinel*, 2, 7, 8 Mar. 1918. "The Birth of a Nation" premiered with the title "The Clansman," based on a novel with that title by D. W. Griffith. It was the highest-grossing film of the silent film era.

opened its parlors, Guy B. Fleming of the Methodist Episcopal Church performed the service, and the city provided a plot at Pilgrim Home Cemetery, complete with a "suitable marker." Fellow crewmen acted as pallbearers, and the maids sang spirituals in the "southern fashion." It was a "respectable funeral," the newspaper concluded, and "enough funds were gotten together to make this possible."[33]

In 1921 Henry Flake, another "colored man," took up residence in a shack between Waverly Road and the Pere Marquette Railroad Bridge over the Black River, according to Ruth Keppel, a granddaughter of Teunis Keppel, as related in the *Holland Sentinel* in December that year. "Mr. Flake is a one-armed man, but in spite of that handicap, he can do a lot of kinds of work that would stump a two-armed man. . . . Mr. Flake came to Holland last July, and he has lived in his shack ever since. He declares that he likes Holland and that he expects to make this his permanent home." Five years later, in 1927, Flake exchanged his shack for a cell in the Jackson State Prison after pleading guilty in the Ottawa County Circuit Court to statutory rape of a fifteen year-old white girl who "came to clean his shack." Judge Cross sentenced Flake to four to fifteen years, while the young woman was taken to a state mental institution for treatment.[34]

That same year, members of the Century Club, painted in faces "blacker than the proverbial ace of spades," regaled the group in a skit at the annual "winter picnic" that impersonated the "happy-go-lucky colored race 'from Alabama.'" A year later, many of the same people flocked to hear a touring choir from the Southern Normal and Industrial School, a Negro high school in Alabama founded by the Reformed Church in America, which gave a series of concerts in local churches and schools, the free will offerings going to support the school. Both were socially acceptable forms of entertainment in the 1920s.[35]

Hollanders generally opposed the Ku Klux Klan (KKK), a nativist organization that preached hatred of Negroes, Catholics, and Jews. Except for a few hundred Catholics and one Jewish family (the Padnos family), one had to go to Saugatuck and southward to find pockets of blacks. City folk heard a distinct rumbling of the Klan in 1923, when an oil-soaked cross was found burning in Kollen Park. In an apparent propaganda blitz of the city, the Klan also distributed its *Fiery Cross*

33 *Holland City News*, 10 June 1926; *Grand Haven Tribune*, 30 Sept. 1920.

34 *Holland Sentinel*, 18 Dec. 1921; *Holland City News*, 26 Aug. 1926, 13 Mar. 1927.

35 *Holland City News*, 3 Feb. 1921, 8 Dec. 1922. Ruth Keppel, who related this story, was the granddaughter of Teunis Keppel, whose second wife, Wilhelmina, was the widow of Peter Oggel, a daughter of A. C. Van Raalte.

newspaper, which the Indianapolis-based organization proudly publicized. "It has been believed here by many that the Klan was secretly active in Holland, but the burning of the cross was the first visible evidence that the American organization was actually in existence in that place." In the weeks after the initial incident, more burning crosses were lit around town, including one in Centennial Park near the fountain. Holland, like Grand Haven, at first blamed adventurous youth for the "pranks" and dismissed the threat of a local KKK presence. Some residents apparently purchased the Klan newspaper out of curiosity. Months later, the Klan presence was felt more acutely when the city saw its ninth cross burning, this one at the west end of Eighth Street. In the Klan estimate of its membership, each cross meant one hundred members, so the Holland area had nine hundred members.[36]

In the spring of 1924, a Klansman from Indiana was invited to address the Holland and Zeeland ministerial associations at the Fourteenth Street Christian Reformed Church. The speaker tried to attract members by claiming that the Klan was not anti-Catholic, anti-Jewish, or anti-Negro, but simply a Protestant organization fighting for American values. This dalliance with bigotry riled Clarence Bouma, professor of systematic theology at Calvin Theological Seminary, who addressed a large crowd at the Central Avenue Christian Reformed Church on a Thursday evening in November. Bouma made himself very clear, according to the *Holland Sentinel* report, that he "was opposed to the Klan" as a "separate little dictatorship" that spread a message of "racial and religious hatred." Wherever the Klan is active, Bouma asserted, comes "unrest, rioting, and disturbance."[37]

It is unclear whether the KKK had much success in their local campaign. Mayor Evert Stephan and city editor Arnold Mulder of the *City News* and the *Sentinel* did their best to belittle Klan rhetoric. Southern blacks, however, were coming north into Michigan in record numbers, and the Klan fed off that situation. Mulder's *Holland Sentinel* editorial in August 1924 warned voters to beware of candidates for "one or more offices in Ottawa County during the coming primary and election" who might be affiliated with the Klan or have Klan sympathies. Mulder admitted that "there is no direct evidence to this effect, so that a positive statement cannot be made in cold print, but there are murmurings here and there to the effect that the hooded empire is trying to insinuate

36 Ibid., 5 July, 23, 30 Aug., 6 (quote), 26 Sept., 8, 15 Nov., 12 [13] Dec. 1923, 13 Mar., 22 May 1924; *Holland Sentinel*, 14 Aug. 1923; *Grand Haven Tribune*, 21, 25 Aug., 2 Oct. 1923.

37 *Holland Sentinel*, 7 Nov. 1924.

itself into office here as elsewhere." One Dutch American, who had lived in Holland for all of his seventy-five years, said he personally knew of Klansmen in local churches as late as the 1950s.[38]

The Klan did not single them out, but gypsies stood even lower in the social "pecking order" than blacks and Jews. Holland newspapers often warned about traveling bands of gypsies, and the police made sure their stay in town was very brief. "Gypsies seldom make a long stay in Holland," the newspaper reported in 1920. "Chief Van Ry is a kind-hearted officer, but he has a decided antipathy towards gypsies and fortune tellers." When a band of six families in cars with Tennessee license plates "disgorged" their "gypsy load" on Eighth Street, and "began to ply their wily tricks upon the business men of this city," Van Ry and the patrolmen ran them out of town within twenty minutes, and they headed for Muskegon. The next year, a caravan of seventy-five gypsies came to Holland, intending to camp overnight on the school lot at Fifteenth and River Avenue, and again, Van Ry and his men ordered them out and they headed for Chicago. In 1924 Van Ry's policemen similarly expelled five carloads of gypsies. Three years later, some twenty gypsies driving expensive Cadillacs managed to take $400 from Henry Nienhuis' cash register, after they distracted him under the pretense of buying candy at his store. Deputy Lamper gave chase and recovered the money, and ordered the gypsies to leave town for good.[39]

Bobbed hair and women's rights

Despite opposition from older folks, Holland's women followed new trends in fashion and public life. Women founded and ran their own societies and organizations, and increasingly sought employment outside the home. With the Nineteenth Amendment in 1919, women won the right to vote, and that year saw the first all-female jury in a Holland courtroom; it was the famous "stolen chicken case" (chapter 20).[40]

Women's fashions and the uproar they caused were perhaps the most tangible symbol of the broader changes in gender roles. "Knee-breeches" were most alarming. The "knickerbockers girls" created a sensation when the pants became popular about 1912. *City News* editor Ben Mulder remembered "one daring woman photographer

38 Ibid., 7 Aug. 1924; interview by the author, 25 Aug. 2010, of a person who wished to remain anonymous.

39 *Holland City News*, 3 June 1920 (quotes), 26 May 1921, 1 May 1924, 15 Sept. 1927.

40 Ibid., 7 Mar. 1918, 18 Sept. 1919; Vande Water, "First Woman Jury Tries 'Chicken Case,'" in *Holland Happenings* 3:88-92. An all-woman jury sat in Holland again in 1925 (*Holland City News*, 19 Feb. 1925).

who ventured to appear in public here in wide bloomers, shirtwaist, stockings, and a cap, much like an old-fashioned 'all cover' bathing suit—riding a man's wheel. The natives were rather shocked," Mulder noted dryly, "and Holland's 'femininity' continued to ride ladies 'bikes' without the cross bar—more like a swan's neck, as it were. Today," Mulder concluded, "the girl 'bikesters' dress—well, we can't begin to describe it, for there is nothing to describe. By the mid-1920s it was common to see women at the golf club and at Camp Fire Girls meetings in bloomers. Some were even smoking cigarettes, which was a far greater indiscretion than wearing pants. Men who dared to criticize were sure to get their "fingers burned," Mulder warned. "The ladies will have their last word."[41]

Like Mulder's "indescribable" clothing styles, the "bobbed" or short hairstyles were alarmingly radical. The trend seemed to arrive almost overnight, as such trends often do. To follow her peers, all a girl needed was a pair of scissors and her imagination. Others chose a more professional cut. In 1924 Ohmer Renck opened the "Bob Shop" downtown for women who were hard-pressed to find a barber knowledgeable enough or willing to give the proper "bob." He made certain to hire a "woman attendant." Meanwhile, Hope College's student newspaper, *The Anchor*, tabulated the bobbed-hair craze among female students and printed this interesting chart.[42]

The bobbed co-eds on the campus hold forth the following percentage.

Class	Bobbed	Unb.	%
Senior	3	18	14.28
Junior	13	39	25.
Soph.	23	18	56.1
Fresh.	22	30	42.346
Faculty	1	9	10.
"	2 ingrown Pompadours		
Total Bobbed			62
Total of Girls			176
% of Bobbed Heads			35.2%

On the surface, the radical nature of women's changing styles may seem laughable, but for many it was a serious issue that reflected the abandonment of moral values for a modern, irresponsible lifestyle. "Flappers," who sported the shapely dresses were, after all, anti-authority. The *Holland City News* reported that in the Netherlands village of Putten (province of Gelderland) the local *Hervormde Kerk* (Reformed Church) refused to marry girls with bobbed hair. Whether

41 *Holland City News*, 8 June 1922, 3 Apr. 1924, 19 Feb. 1925, 7 Apr. 1938.

42 Ibid., 8 June 1922; 3 Apr. 1924; Hope College *Anchor*, 26 Mar. 1924.

the story checked out or not, it was meant to contrast righteous Old Country norms with degenerate American behavior. One newspaper "short" read: "A 'chicken' is considered the weakest-minded vertebrate. A 'flapper' is a devolution from the former 'chicken,' having lost the little brain it did have." By late 1934, Knooihuizen Shoppe advertised its newest womens undergarment, a Vassarette girdle, to "make your sleek fall clothes even sleeker." The risqué ad, with a young female modeling the garment, declared: "They say, 'No Nice Girl Swears.' Be That as it may, 'no smart-looking girl wiggles!'"[43]

A sharp contrast with this anti-authority lifestyle was the Christian Endeavor movement, a nationwide, non-confessional Christian youth organization that the Reformed Church in America adopted as its youth program (chapter 5).[44]

What time is it? The Daylight Saving Time debate

National Daylight Saving Time started as a war measure in 1918, but remained an issue of local and regional contention for decades to follow.[45] In Holland the recurring debate was essentially an issue of local versus regional or state control. In the end, stubborn Holland had little choice but to give way to national efforts of standardized timekeeping.

The time debate began in Holland in 1922 when the common council gave up its prerogative and put the question to the citizens in a "straw vote." It passed by a two-thirds majority. Beginning on April 15, all clocks "sprang forward" one hour until October 15. Merchants wanted the start date moved up, but the council decided to abide by the referendum. Yet, Holland's proper operating time was far from settled. Each spring and fall, the issue resurfaced, and debate began anew or continued from where it had left off the previous season. Both sides of the debate, those for and those against daylight saving time, complained that the schedule was a strain on schoolchildren who, depending on one's view, either had to wake up too late or too early, and saw too little sunshine either in the morning or in the evening. Grand Rapids, the largest city in West Michigan, generally set the standard for the year, and Holland and other smaller municipalities felt compelled to follow. Those who disobeyed the "Furniture City" in this regard risked utter confusion within the regional transportation network. Throughout much of the 1920s, Holland seemingly followed Grand Rapids.[46]

43 *Holland City News*, 16 Feb. (quote), 13 Apr. 1922; 7 July 1927, 22 Nov. 1934.
44 Ibid., 7 July 1927.
45 *Holland City News*, 6 Mar. 1919.
46 Ibid., 12 Apr. 1922, 22 Mar., 5, 12 Apr. 1923; 6 Mar. 1924; 8 Oct. 1925.

The time issue was further complicated in 1931 when the state legislature strongly urged all of Michigan to adopt Eastern Standard Time. Holland had for years followed Central Time, primarily because the city's myriad business connections were with the premier midwestern *entrepot* of Chicago. In an act of defiance, Holland stayed on Central Time for 1931, thus rejecting the state's request and refusing to follow the example of Grand Rapids. In other words, Holland by staying on Central Time made the decision to "fall back" for the four winter months of 1931-32 (November through February), when Grand Rapids, by switching from Central to Eastern Time, maintained its summer daylight saving schedule. Now the debate was doubly complicated. Holland not only had to decide for or against daylight saving time, but it also had to choose a time zone.[47]

Like a groundhog, the debate resurfaced in March 1932. Holland went ahead with daylight saving time and came into line with other West Michigan communities that stayed on Eastern Time, but did not "spring forward." In the fall of 1932, however, Grand Rapids, Grand Haven, and Muskegon all lined up in opposition to Holland by maintaining Eastern Time year round without resorting to daylight saving time. At first, Holland remained stubborn, holding on to its position from the past year. The common council voted seven to five in favor of matching Chicago time, and a city referendum reinforced this decision by a 573-vote majority. So, in November, Holland took the step back to Central Time. Naturally, by now the citizens of Holland and the visitors to the city were as confused as the reader. What time was it? To help answer this question and to repeal Holland's mid-October vote, a two-thousand-signature petition was in the works. Whether the petition carried the names of enough respected people to raise the alarm, or whether the common council merely discovered the error of its way, is unclear. But, on November 17, 1932, just five days after the city had set it clocks back, the council declared that Holland would forgo its recent chronological adjustment, set its clocks forward once again, and stay on summer (Eastern) time just like everyone else. It was a decision few would regret.[48]

The car culture

Perhaps the most influential and irresistible trend of the 1920s was the new car culture (chapter 19). Automobiles promoted the divide between traditional and modern lifestyles and brought about a cultural revolution. The Grand Rapids Auto Show in 1923 displayed a "flock of

[47] Ibid., 10, 24 Sept., 22 Oct. 1931; 3 Mar. 1932.

[48] Ibid., 6, 20 Oct., 17 Nov. 1932.

Holland Automobile License Bureau "rush" on December 31, 1929, at Peoples State Bank as procrastinators lined up to buy new plates required the next day (*Archives, Holland Historical Trust*)

beauties" that attracted thousands. The top-of-the-line seven-passenger Lincoln sedan carried a price tag of $4,900, a prince's ransom. In 1924 Hollanders owned some three thousand automobiles, mostly cheap "flivvers" or "tin lizzies," that is, Ford Model Ts that had to be cranked to a coughing start. The flivvers came in only one color–black–and looked so alike that owners frequently tried cranking the wrong car. In a day when financing a car was unthinkable, dealers offered "weekly purchase plans," akin to local bank's Christmas savings club plans. Prospective buyers put $5 a week in local bank accounts at interest until they had enough to pay cash for the car of their choice. In 1927 the new Model A sedan and coupe sold for under $500 apiece. The city had its first automobile club in 1925, and the police began systematic safety inspections in 1927. The police also had to check if the required car licenses were current every January first. This set off a tremendous rush by procrastinators at the first Holland Auto License Bureau in the Peoples State Bank on the last day of the year.[49]

The automobile revolution changed the way Holland interacted with the outside world. Farmers and their families could more easily

[49] James Flink, *The Car Culture* (Boston: MIT Press, 1976); *Holland City News*, 9, 16 Feb. 1922, 22 Feb., 6 Sept., 20 Dec. 1923, 28 Feb. 1924, 23 July 1925, 8 Dec. 1927.

Downtown Holland jammed with parked cars of shoppers along Eighth Street looking east from River Avenue, late 1920s (*Archives, Calvin College)*

and more readily come to the city to shop and transact business and travel to visit friends or relatives. Cars made it more convenient for traveling salesmen to cover their territory. Hope College students from places like Vriesland, Overisel, and Grand Rapids benefited from this greater mobility by making more frequent trips home. Three days a week, Professor Gerrit E. Boer traveled twenty-five miles each way to and from his Grand Rapids home. Cars gradually replaced trains. While the Interurban remained popular through the early 1920s, the company ended service west of Jenison in 1926, and in 1932 even the link to Grand Rapids was ended. No public transportation could compete with private cars. Over the 1927 Easter weekend an estimated ten thousand cars passed through Holland on US-31 and M-21, mostly going to the beach resorts.[50]

No wonder that the police had to deal with a parking problem around churches, theaters, and public halls. On Sunday mornings, Central Avenue became so clogged with cars parked on both sides of the street that it presented a danger to pedestrians and traffic. "This is a hard nut to crack," declared the city fathers.[51]

50 Donald van Reken, *The Interurban Era* (Holland: privately printed, 1981); *Holland City News*, 18 Oct. 1917, 13 Aug. 1924, 21 Apr. 1927.

51 *Holland City News*, 7 Dec. 1927.

For traffic control and to reduce fender-benders at busy intersections, traffic police were stationed in the center of the crossing, whistle in hand and arms waving, to give motorists stop and go signals. As more and more intersections needed active controlling, the police department could not staff them all. In 1925 the city hung the first "stop and go lights" at Eighth and River and other principal intersections. "The system is as simple as can be, unless one is colorblind," declared a newspaper editor, but making left hand turns against traffic proved to be a difficult maneuver for motorists to master.[52]

Cars changed dating rituals. They provided privacy for romance to the point that the common council unanimously passed "spooning laws." "One arm" drivers would face a date in traffic court if caught by the police, and no more than three people over twelve years of age may occupy the front seat. "Necking" in out-of-the-way places in suburbia was another matter entirely.[53]

Another downside of cars was advertising signage. Storekeepers and promoters nailed advertising signs to trees along city streets and country roads to catch the eye of motorists. The common council in 1923 made the unsightly practice illegal. The Ottawa County Road Commission announced that it would enforce a law already on the books against signs, and road crews would trash every sign they spotted.[54]

Cars also enhanced the habit of chasing fire engines, which fire marshal Cornelius Blom Jr. and police chief Frank Van Ry lamented was all too common on "Main Street." In larger cities, said the chiefs, "every Tom, Dick, and Harry does not need to hasten to a fire the moment the fire whistle blows." In Holland, the "fire whistle usually is a signal for a large number of people to back their cars out of the garage in a great hurry and follow the fire trucks. Sometimes these goers-to-fires are in fact ahead of the fire truck or try to get ahead of them. . . . They are an all-around nuisance," the officials declared, and they interfered with fire fighters. The next time, the chiefs warned, motorists should leave their flivvers in the garage or risk fines.[55]

Automobiles contributed to tourism in many ways. One vacationer drove from Holland to Jacksonville, Florida in eight days in January 1923. Most townsfolk took short jaunts to the beach, out in the country, or to the Lakewood Farm of George Getz along the lakeshore north of Holland. A new car lot at Ottawa Beach promised to

52 *Holland City News*, 26 Feb., 16 Apr., 25 June 1925.
53 Ibid., 16 Aug., 13 Sept. 1923, 5 Aug. 1926, 24 June 1937.
54 Ibid., 23 Aug. 1923.
55 Ibid., 4 Jan. 1923.

Henry F. Tuurling made a living painting and installing signs from his shop at 63 West Ninth Street. His wife Sophia, son Henry F. Jr., and daughter Angeline G. pose proudly with his truck, which he entered from the passenger door rather than the driver's door, which was blocked by a ladder, ca. 1928 (*Joint Archives of Holland*)

hold one thousand cars. Until 1933 Getz ran one of the most popular amusements in the area, a zoo with large beasts of the African savannas. But too many visitors could bring trouble. In 1924 he threatened to close or severely limit entry to his estate because the public had routinely mistreated the grounds. He noted with disdain that one of his monkeys nearly died after visitors gave the animal cigarettes.[56]

One unexpected result of this use of private automobiles was the shift in the relationship between farmers and consumers. Whereas previously farmers had always carried their produce into the city to be sold to a processing plant or at the retail market, now city dwellers were also driving into the country to buy fresh from the farm. Others naturally went exploring at greater distances. It was newsworthy but not completely uncommon to hear that two married couples from Holland had made a 1,300-mile automobile trip around the Midwest or ventured even farther to Florida. And it was a sign of the times that when Arnold Mulder visited the East Coast, he found Henry Thoreau's Walden Pond "lined with Fords."[57]

Holland's streets were also jammed with cars. On a busy day in 1929, an estimated 225 cars passed through the central intersection

[56] *Holland City News*, 18 Jan. 1923, 17 Feb. 1927.

[57] Ibid., 7 Aug. 1922 (quote); 25 Oct. 1923.

of River Avenue and Eighth Street every ten minutes. The next year in August the chamber of commerce and car dealers staged the first annual Holland automobile parade, with 250 cars covering six city blocks. The new Chevrolets, Fords, Buicks, Chryslers, Studebakers, and Dodges each vied for the title of "best decorated" or "best polished." Some old "tin cans" took part as well. When the depression hit, the Holleman-De Weerd Auto Company, Holland's Ford dealership, brought the first "talking motion picture" to town for a free show, in order to promote the new 1930 line.[58]

With the increasing traffic around town, parking became a contentious issue. In 1929 downtown merchants addressed the matter with business-like seriousness. They complained that some people parked on Eighth Street all day, from nine to five, and suggested that the common council consider enforcing time limits on downtown parking. But there were obstacles to any parking laws, and the alderman appealed to a system of courtesy and personal responsibility. What about Saturday evening theatergoers, who must sometimes leave their autos for two or three hours? Parking problems, of course, turned particularly acute during the tourist season and especially at Tulip Time. The automobile did, however, make Tulip Time possible. Trains could feasibly have carried the large number of Tulip Time visitors, but they could never have offered the freedom that automobiles provided to drive the Tulip Lane, visit the Getz Farm, and come and go at will. Automobiles caused huge traffic jams in Holland. Locals were encouraged to leave their vehicles at home and walk or bike to work. If a car was absolutely necessary, they should park in an alley.[59]

The parking problem was most intense in the summer of 1937. Tulip Time that year brought a record number of visitors to Holland, and then the state highway department requested the city to replace diagonal with parallel parking along the major arteries of Eighth Street and River Avenue. Diagonal parking was easier for motorists, particularly women, and for this reason merchants favored it, but state road engineers and the local police department instituted parallel parking to speed the traffic flow by widening traffic lanes. The change had the exact opposite effect, however, and car bumpers took a beating as well. Ben Mulder reported: "It takes a very expert driver to park in small quarters, and from the window of the *News* office, where plain sight of the street can be seen for a block, the struggling to get cars in and out is evident hourly. Often cars are so close together that the

58 Ibid., 3 May 1923, 18 July 1929, 7 Aug. 1930, 19 Feb. 1931.

59 *Holland City News*, 7 Nov. 1929; 15 June 1933.

Parked cars line both sides of River Avenue in the late 1930s, looking south from Eighth Street. Peck's Cut Rate Drugs is now Reader's World (*courtesy Myron Van Ark*)

driver, who wants to get away, must first back up to move the rear car and then move up a little to advance the car ahead. A car with the brakes on stands an awful jolt."[60]

One had to admit that the streets in the city center were not built to accommodate cars, let alone diagonal parking. But the common council, reflecting the views of merchants and shoppers, "knocked in the head" parallel parking as "an unpopular and an impractical method." Every time the police changed parking from diagonal to parallel on a given block or two, protesters flocked to council meetings, and the police would back off. Finally, the two bodies compromised. One side of the street was designated for diagonal parking and the other side for parallel parking. At the same time, parking time limits were reduced from one hour to a half hour. After a two-week barrage of complaints, both whispered and open, the common council rescinded the half-hour parking law. But parking space had to be maximized, nonetheless, and the hour rule was difficult to enforce. Parking meters seemed to be the answer. The fire and police board first raised the issue in 1939 "to solve the parking problem" and to "raise additional revenue for the city," but a ten-year fight ensued. The common council contracted with the National Park-o-Meter Corporation of Chicago to install parking

[60] Ibid., 3 June 1937.

meters, with profits split fifty-fifty between the company and the city's treasury. But then the aldermen balked, because the chamber of commerce was "not sold on the idea."[61]

The war shelved any further thought of parking meters. After peace returned, however, city revenue needs led the common council in 1946 to install two hundred meters throughout the business district for a "trial period" of six months. The object was to control parking and raise revenue for policing, signage, and other traffic costs. Profit, not parking, was the real motive. The decision aroused a firestorm of opposition to the new "tax" and the inconvenience, so the aldermen batted the issue around for several months and then referred the question for "further study" to the public safety commission. Several council roll calls for meters failed by a single vote. The commission recommended meters as a way to pay for free off-street parking lots. Three years later, the council brought up the meter proposal again, and this time it passed, based on the commission rationale. Meters went up in 1949 with the fee set at one cent for twelve minutes with a one-hour limit. Violators faced fines and towing charges. Motorists had no choice but to pay the "nominal fee" by feeding the meters, but they voted with their feet when Westshore Mall opened in 1988, and the city council had to end the misguided tax.[62]

In the late 1950s the city bought several large lots along Seventh and Ninth Streets for off-street parking. Meter revenue paid for some small lots, but big projects required voter-approved revenue bonds or assessments on merchants. After voters rejected a $600,000 bond proposal in 1959 by a two-to-one margin, the city assessed downtown merchants, over the strong objections of their spokesperson John Arendshorst. Free parking was essential for the downtown to thrive. But it was 1988 before the last of the parking meters were scrapped.[63]

Tulip Time

Tulip Time would never have developed into one of the nation's premier cultural festivals without cars. Tourists could easily drive to Holland for a day trip and then meander along the miles of tulip lanes lined with colorful blooms. It was the magic appeal of the tulip that kept visitors coming, even during the depression decade.

61 Ibid., 3, 24 June, 8, 20 July, 12 Aug. 1937, 20 July 1939.

62 *Holland City News*, 9, 16 May, 5 June, 18 July 1946, 16 Dec. 1948, 20 Jan., 21 July 1949.

63 Ibid., 5 Feb., 9 Apr. 1959, 4 Feb. 1960.

Lida Rogers, a Holland High biology teacher, first suggested a tulip festival in a talk for the Woman's Literary Club in 1927.[64] The timing was perfect, because Mayor Earnest Brooks, the common council, and the chamber of commerce were looking for ways to promote tourism in Holland as a complement to the flourishing beach resorts. Tulip Time was thus part of a greater movement for Holland to market itself to the outside world. It was a new kind of boosterism, far beyond sports competitions, debate and oratory leagues, religious conferences, and church assemblies. Along with exporting industrial products such as furnaces and furniture, the city would sell its unique cultural heritage—its Dutchness. Mayor Brooks, though without a drop of Dutch blood, planted ten thousand tulips in the large gardens of the family home, which convinced the city fathers to initiate the tulip lanes along the curbsides.[65]

The city fathers in 1928 allocated funds to import one hundred thousand tulip bulbs from the Netherlands for citizens to plant in city parks around the city. The flowers attracted visitors like bees to honey, and city leaders set about planning a flower festival for May 1930. Merchants kept it a leisurely, non-commercialized celebration, with the tulip reigning as queen in lieu of a pretty girl. Holland High students performed a "Tulip Time operetta." Afterward everyone agreed that "Tulip Time in Holland" hit the spot. "Holland must have a "Tulip Week" each year. It brings a fine class of people who love the beautiful. A celebration such as Holland had, devoid of brass bands and expensive paradise and milling mobs is more desirable that these nerve-racking one day celebrations that are so often staged."[66] Given the onset of the depression, this low-key approach seemed wise, but it did not last long.

In the 1930s, as times became more desperate, luring visitors and their dollars became equally desperate. Tulip Time morphed into a major festival stretching to ten days. To keep people coming, the organizers developed new themes and attractions: street scrubbing to tout the Dutch stereotype of cleanliness; klompen dancers in Dutch costumes and wooden shoes no one wore any more, with a dance routine unknown in the Old Country; a children's costume parade; school marching bands; and floats sponsored by businesses and organizations, including Holland Community Chest, "Holland Shares and Cares" Red Cross, the City Mission, the Boy Scouts and Campfire Girls, the Civic

64 Vande Water, "Tulip Time Tales," in *Holland Happenings* 1:53-58.

65 *Holland Sentinel*, Earnest Brooks obit., 16 Apr. 1981.

66 *Holland City News*, 19 May 1978, 8, 22 May 1930, 23 Apr. 1931.

Tulip Time dancers had a precursor a generation earlier in this Wooden Shoe Drill Team that entertained old Civil War Veterans in town for a convention in 1910 (*courtesy Myron Van Ark*)

Health League, and others. The festival added beer sales and Dutch Psalm singing in 1933, and the *Klein Nederland* exhibit was set up in the Holland Armory (chapter 28). The return of good times in 1937 brought out a generously estimated crowd of 750,000. The next year, local charm took second place to Hollywood movie stars, thanks to Holland Furnace company sponsorship, and the "big names" attracted tourists for several years.[67]

A complimentary editorial in the *Grand Rapids Press* in 1933 noted: "Holland has retained the charm of its old country traditions without any sacrifice of the progressive spirit which has stamped it as one of the most aggressive cities. . . . Too often communities seek to import attractions that are less desirable than those on their own doorsteps. Holland has not made such a mistake." An added attraction in 1934 was the first windmill in Holland, in Windmill Park just south of the River Avenue Bridge, surrounded by colorful tulip beds. The mill and its white picket fence provided the backdrop for the 1938 Tulip Time brochures and became a popular tourist stop (chapter 27 and photo).[68]

67 Ibid., 22 Oct., 12 May 1932, 4 May 1933, 27 May 1937, 17 May 1978; Vande Water, "Tulip Time Attracts 'Stars' in Late 30s," in *Holland Happenings*, 4:113-19; Vande Water, "'41 Tulip Time Hosts Hollywood Stars," in ibid., 2:91-95.

68 *Grand Rapids Press*, 11 May 1933; Vande Water, "Windmill (Van Bragt) Park Began in 1934," in *Holland Happenings*, 4:99-102.

The Great Depression, 1929-33

After a decade of growth and prosperity, Holland was unprepared for the massive economic downturn of the 1930s. The city even had its own full-fledged stock exchange, after J. D. Forsythe in 1927 opened shop on the second floor of De Grondwet building on Eighth Street with a direct wire link to the big board on Wall Street. When the stock market crashed in October 1929, the residents remained optimistic; local banks continued to serve their customers, and plants kept up production. Hardship would not come immediately. The Holland City State Bank boasted that in the stock market crash, it did not have "to 'sell out' a single customer." Gilbert Daane, president of the Grand Rapids Savings Bank, reassured Holland that the national economy was sound, and the depression was mostly a mental malady. Forty thousand visitors came to the first advertised Tulip Time festival in 1930, and promoters deemed it "a wonderful success" (chapter 28).[69]

At a meeting of the Holland Exchange Club, former Hope president Edward Dimnent noted that national per capita wealth had never been higher, and Holland's three banks together held $10 million in savings. They carried mortgages on two-thirds of the homes in the city; three-fourths of that money came from savings accounts and was being re-circulated locally. The banks also paid out $175,000 of those deposits to Christmas Club savers in December 1931, which gave a brief boost to the local economy. There would be enough wealth to weather the storm. The "Holland spirit" will bring "real prosperity," Con De Pree reassured the chamber of commerce banquet crowd. Holland meat dealer and grocer, Leonard Knoll, unfortunately saw no way out but to help rob a Hudsonville bank. It was standing room only at his trial; the jury found him guilty, and the judge sentenced him to prison, but his appeal to the Michigan Supreme Court was successful.[70]

Gradually, however, these illusions faded. At first, the depression was not as threatening as it was inconvenient. The slowing economy meant fewer dollars were in circulation, and businesses had to reduce production to match the lowered demand for their products. City tax revenue fell, and the administration in 1931 had to cut the budget by layoffs or wage reductions, or both. The council considered asking all employees to take a 10 percent cut in wages, but backed away. Power plant employees volunteered to cut back six hours per week, from forty-eight to forty-two, and to donate 5 percent of their wages to the city

69 *Holland City News*, 10 Mar. 1927, 6 Nov. 1929; 22 May, 24 Sept., 12 Nov. 1931.

70 Ibid., 12 Feb., 28 May, 15, 22 Oct., 26 Nov. 1931, 9 Feb. 1933.

welfare fund. The aldermen, who received only a $50 honorarium per year, likewise cut their stipends 10 percent.

Holland's police and fire departments opposed the cuts and chose instead to decrease vacation time. As a token of good will, however, they voluntarily gave 5 percent of their income to the stressed city welfare department. Faculty at Western Theological Seminary suffered more, taking a voluntary 20 percent salary reduction beginning in 1932. In January 1932 the common council was forced to cut wages of city employees 10 percent across the board, except for the police and fire chiefs. In April a second round of cuts was in the offing. At the same time, the school board reduced teacher's salaries by 12.5 percent, and the next year they cut nine positions. In 1932 the city health officer, William Westrate, and Ottawa County farm agent, C. P. Milham, were both released from their duties, but the aldermen rehired Westrate the next year. Westrate had survived an "alienation of affections" lawsuit in the meantime.[71]

By 1932 it became clear that the city had fallen on hard times and the bleeding was not about to stop. Still, steadfast Republican Holland held firm, believing that the economy would soon right itself and needed but little interference from the federal government. The majority of the city had voted for the Republican Herbert Hoover in 1928 and was disappointed at his re-election loss in 1932. Henry Japinga, who supported Hoover in this election, made a creative wager with Democrat B. L. Davis. After the national election results were announced, Japinga rode Davis in a wheelbarrow on River Avenue from Fifteenth Street to Eighth Street, where he had to finish paying his bet by fishing with a rod and line in a water pail at the corner of Eighth and River, holding an umbrella over his head. Across his shoulders he wore the sign "I bet on Hoover. Where are the other fish?"[72] It was a dark day to be a Republican in Holland.

As the city struggled to keep its finances in the black, state loans and state and national funding for local welfare projects (up to 70 percent) helped carry the local economy. But the number of unemployed continued to rise and the welfare rolls grew apace. Mayor Brooks noted that the welfare fund was stretched to the limit and would have to be capped. By early 1932 some six hundred families relied on city support. In the summer, welfare payments reached as high as $2,000 per week. This was not pure charity. To receive a welfare check, the male head of

71 Ibid., 5 Mar., 7, 14 May, 17 Dec. 1931; 7 Jan., 11 Feb., 12 Mar., 19 May, 20 Oct., 17 Nov. 1932; 4 May, 14 Sept. 1933; *Holland Daily Sentinel*, 19 Jan. 1932.

72 *Holland City News*, 22 Oct. 1931, 17 Nov. 1932.

the household had to put in his time laboring for the city. Men were primarily employed in road construction, but could be seen in less strenuous occupations such as school crossing guards. In Zeeland, men were put to work on farms.[73]

The Community Chest, the Red Cross, and church deaconates stepped up charity giving, and needy residents helped one another by bartering goods and labor. The city ran a rescue mission, which by the end of 1932 had fallen into debt to the tune of over $10,000. Since the mission cost an estimated $2,200 annually, Holland wanted to release itself of the burden and have the Salvation Army take over. Even family dogs made the ultimate sacrifice; dog wardens shot two hundred dogs in 1932 when owners could not afford licenses fees. The animals received a reprieve in 1933 when the legislature cut the license fee in half, from $4 to $2 for females and from $2 to $1 for males. In 1938 owners licensed 714 dogs in Holland.[74]

The welfare recipients were rewarded for their labor in cash, but often they had to accept "orders" drawn on local merchants. This ensured that Holland's wealth was re-circulated locally rather than flee the area. Holland merchants also endeavored to protect their businesses by fighting "fly-by-night merchants" and "transient stores."[75] When Holland passed an ordinance requiring the payment of a fee for new businesses run by outsiders, Attorney Clarence J. Lokker informed the council that this kind of privilege and protectionism was against the state commerce law. In 1933 the board of education printed $54,000 in "floral scrip" as a local currency. The colorful paper, backed by tax anticipation warrants, went into teachers' pay envelopes in late April, their first pay in nearly three months. The scrip earned interest at 2.5 percent, redeemable in twelve months. One reason for the school budget shortfall was the failure of outlying school districts to pay the state-required tuition for their students attending Holland High.[76]

To continue providing relief work over the winter of 1932-33 for those on the dole, the Salvation Army distributed flour, often through the churches. Third Reformed Church, for example, distributed two thousand pounds in 1932 to poor and needy families. The city also borrowed $50,000 from the national Reconstruction Finance Corporation (RFC). Emergency assistance for food and housing

73 Ibid., 28 July, 25 Aug. 1932.

74 Ibid., 1, 29 Dec. 1932, 10 Jan., 30 July 1933, 7 Apr. 1938.

75 Ibid., 3 Dec. 1931; 28 July 1932.

76 *Holland City News*, 3, 24 Dec. 1931, 2 Feb., 2, 16 June, 8 Sept., 22 Dec. 1932, 5 Jan., 9 Mar., 6, 13, 20, 27 Apr., 18 May 1933.

Bert Kruiswyk's Jobbers Super Market at 139-41 River Avenue offered bargain-priced staples during the Depression—large loaves of bread for 6¢ and potatoes for a penny a pound (*courtesy Larry B. Massie*)

fell under the jurisdiction of the Ottawa County Emergency Relief Administrator, Deborah Veneklasen, RN, a daughter of the Zeeland brick manufacturer Albertus Veneklasen. Hope College treasurer Cornelius "C. J." Dregman, named head of the city welfare board in 1932, pressed to lower the cost to the poor for coal, medical services, prescriptions, milk, and rent. Local providers and landlords generally cooperated. If the city paid rent for welfare families, landlords had no choice but to accept reductions. Even so, not all the needy could be helped. The board of public works did its part by slashing electric rates by 10 percent, but the state government worked against recovery by instituting a 3 percent sales tax on all retail commerce. Despite the economic extremity, some sixteen saloons in Holland sold beer on the premises, including the Bier Kelder in the Warm Friend Tavern. Sipping a cold brew was one of the last pleasures to go.[77]

Banks in the Depression

The travails of the three banks tell the tale. In the late 1920s, all had built imposing new edifices, raised fresh capital, enjoyed bulging deposits, and relished surplus earnings. First State Bank promised "Miracles with Money" and a "Harvest of Savings" with its 4 percent

77 Ibid., 8 June, 20 July, 3, 17 Aug., 14, 21 Sept. 1933; Steve Vanderveen, "Local Holland brewers felt pinch of competition," *Holland Sentinel*, 28 Sept. 1908; Bruins, *Americanization of a Congregation*, 70; Deborah Veneklasen obit., *Holland Sentinel*, 22 Nov. 1939; C. J. Dregman obit., ibid., 14 Dec. 1937.

passbook savings accounts. Only weeks before the crash, bank president Gerrit Diekema announced the sale of a large block of First State Bank stock to the larger Industrial Bank of Grand Rapids, which affiliation helped it survive. The Holland banks, at first, seemed to weather the stock market crash without a sign of weakness. In 1930 both the First State Bank, under cashier Wynand Wichers, and the Peoples State Bank, under president William Beach and cashier Otto P. Kramer, had savings deposits over $3 million. Holland City State Bank, the city's first, had deposits over $1 million, under president Bastian Keppel and cashier Henry Winter. Combined deposits were $7.7 million. Fifteen months later, in January 1931, total savings deposits had slipped to $6.6 million, but the banks still had combined resources of $10 million. "Every one of them are being conducted by well-known, conservative Holland men, whose unswerving policy has always been 'Safety First,'" the editor asserted reassuringly.[78]

By July 1931 savings deposits had fallen to 6.4 million, with Peoples State Bank suffering the worst decline, from $3.3 to $1.7 million in one year. All three banks cut passbook interest rates to 3.5 percent. On January 11, 1932, Peoples State Bank closed its doors because of "runs on the bank" and it remained closed for a year under Clarence Jalving, the government-appointed receiver. After liquidating assets and selling mortgages to the Reconstruction Finance Corp. (RFC) to raise cash, Peoples State Bank was ready to open in early 1933. First State Bank and Holland City State Bank held the public confidence and suffered less severe "runs." On 14 February 1933, however, these two banks also had to close, under orders of Michigan Governor William Comstock, who declared a statewide nine-day "bank holiday" to protect several tottering Detroit banks. The move caught people off guard and those short of cash could not withdraw any money from their accounts. Jacob Bos, a city employee, recalled seeing "people who had lots of savings, and they were crying, and crying, and crying that they lost the money."

Following President Franklin Roosevelt's proclamation of a "holiday" for national banks on March 5, 1933, the Michigan legislature on March 21 again closed all state-chartered banks.[79] The boards of the three Holland institutions had to scramble to reorganize under

78 *Holland City News*, 27 Mar. 1921, 11 May 1922, 9 Aug. 1928, 12 Sept. 1929, 10 July 1930, 31 Jan., 23 July, 6 Aug. 1931.

79 *Holland City News*, 16, 23 Feb., 1 Mar., 15, 29 June, 16 July, 17, 24 Aug. 1933; Clarence Jalving interview by Donald van Reken, 15 July 1976, typescript; Jacob Bos interview by Donald van Reken, 3 Aug. 1976, typescript, 7 (quote), both at Joint Archives of Holland (JAH).

new and more stringent regulations. The Holland City State Bank remained closed for thirteen months, until March 1934, when it raised more capital in a subscription campaign. First State Bank reopened on 17 August 1934, and the other two followed, but none allowed cash withdrawals until 4 March 1934, when partial withdrawals were permitted at 50¢ on the dollar. For the remaining savings deposits, First State Bank issued "certificates of participation," essentially IOUs bearing no interest. Meanwhile, in January 1933, the Federal Deposit Insurance Act insured all bank savings deposits up to $2,500 ($5,000 by 1935), which gave future savers some comfort. The bankers also induced the Holland Ministerial Association to reassure their parishioners as to the soundness of the local institutions.[80]

In July 1935, the banks were again in "fine condition," but total saving deposits had dwindled to $2.2 million, one-third of the 1930 total. On 1 December 1936, Holland City State Bank and First State Bank merged as equals to form the Holland State Bank (later First National Bank of Holland), under the Allegan financier Henry Maentz as president and Henry Idema of Old Kent Bank of Grand Rapids as a major shareholder and director. The merged bank, which occupied the former First State Bank Bank on Eighth Street at Central Avenue (now Alpen Rose Restaurant), paid out by 1940 only 70 percent of its original deposits. John Arendshorst bought the former Holland City State Bank. Jalving appointed Laverne Dalman cashier at Peoples State Bank in 1933, and he remained for forty-four years, the last six as president. Gradually, the three banks liquidated the "certificates of participation" that they had given to passbook savers in lieu of cash, which they euphemistically called "dividends." By January 1, 1938, First State Bank had paid holders of the certificates 60 percent of the original amount, and by July 31, 1941, repayments reached 75 percent. The remaining certificates were redeemed over the next few years.[81]

In the meantime, there were bills to pay. The Holland Civic Orchestra put a notice in the paper that concertgoers without cash could leave an IOU and pay later, if and when the banks reopened. The *Holland City News* in June 1933 listed seven individuals who had defaulted on

80 *Holland City News*, 22 Feb., 22 Mar., 14 June 1934, 18 Apr. 1935; Phil Koning, "First of America Bank," *Holland Sentinel*, 30 Jan. 1992.

81 *Holland City News*, 25 July 1935, 16 Jan., 16 July, 19 Nov., 3 Dec. 1936, 9 Dec. 1937, 29 Sept. 1938, 5 Dec. 1940, 31 July 1941. The Holland State Bank in 1946 joined the national banking system and became the First National Bank of Holland (ibid., 25 July 1946). Dalman succeeded Jalving as president in 1968 and retired in 1974, when Old Kent Bank of Grand Rapids bought out Peoples State Bank (Laverne C. Dalman obit., *Holland Sentinel*, 10 May 2009).

Holland State Bank, northwest corner of Eighth Street and Central Avenue, late 1930s after merger (*Joint Archives of Holland*)

their mortgages and whose property was put up at auction. For years, the threat of foreclosure loomed. In 1932 Uke Wiersma requested a deal with the common council; he would turn over to the city his house and property, in return for the support of his basic needs for the remainder of his life. The council kindly informed Wiersma that the city already owned enough delinquent real estate. Real estate taxes were another obligation of homeowners. The state legislature in 1932 allowed delinquents to combine all back taxes and pay on a ten-year installment plan, with all penalties and back interest waived if paid in full by certain deadlines. A similar "tax drive" in 1935 for 1933 and 1934 delinquencies brought more millions of dollars into county coffers. These "hard-nosed" government measures induced some Holland residents to join the militant "taxpayer leagues" that sprang up around the country. Peter J. Zalsman, who ran unsuccessfully for a school board seat in 1933, was described as a "protégé of the Taxpayers League." Presumably, this did not help his candidacy, although Hollanders were tame compared to Chicagoans, where property owners went on a strike that forced Mayor Anton Cermak to threaten to cut off city water unless taxes were paid up.[82]

82 Helen Louise Sisson Wiegmink, "Hetchen Remembers," typescript, Nov. 1995, JAH; *Holland City News*, 8 Sept. 1932, 1, 29 June, 13 July (quote) 1933, 1, 29 Aug., 24 Oct. 1935, 5 Aug. 1937; David Beito, "The Forgotten Tax Revolt of the 1930s," *Wall Street Journal*, 15 Apr. 2011.

The Holland bank robbery

As the Depression deepened in the fall of 1932, six "desperate highwaymen" led by gangster Edward Bentz, visited Holland, intent on leaving the city with a fortune that they had no right to claim. It was nine fifteen on a usual downtown morning when the gangsters robbed the First State Bank. Nine customers and fourteen bank employees found themselves caught in the middle. When the bandits demanded access to the vault, the bank manager delayed. The gunmen ordered customers in the lobby to lie down. But one, Benjamin Hamm, slipped out the main door and "gave the alarm that the bank was being robbed." The message rang up and down Eighth Street, and soon Chief Peter Lievense came to the bank door. One of the gangsters spotted the chief and opened fire with his submachine gun. One bullet pierced the bank window and another deflected off a steel clip on Lievense's holster and entered his left side. Enraged, the chief drew his gun and began to fight back. He took cover behind a car and then worked his way around to the back of the bank. Meanwhile, three other officers, David "Dave" O'Connor, Ben Kalkman, and Peter Bontekoe, arrived and set up at the front door.[83]

Brandishing machine guns, the gangsters escaped through a side window with some $75,000 in cash and bonds and jumped into a stolen Studebaker.[84] They tried to escape down an alley that led to River Street, but were blocked after ramming their car into that of Mrs. Vance Bailey, the manager of the Budget Dress Shop, who had entered the alley unawares from the opposite direction at the very time. The gangsters tried to back up but hit a fire hydrant. In true civil action, another downtown merchant, Dick Claman, hearing the commotion—the bandits swearing at Mrs. Bailey and the crash of metal on metal—grabbed his shotgun, loaded it, and "let them have it," reportedly hitting one of the robbers in the face and another in the side. Lievense, now joined by National Guard sergeant, Henry Rowan, continued to exchange fire with the gang from behind a car parked at the Warm Friend Tavern.

The gang then hopped into another car and speed away, except for the wounded man, who had apparently fled on foot in the opposite direction. After running through a store, gun in hand, he was

83 *Holland City News*, 29 Sept., 6 Oct. 1932; Vande Water, "$73,000 Grabbed in Bank Robbery," in *Holland Happenings*, 1:59-62.

84 Original estimates put this figure at $12,000. Of the $73,000, $47,000 in cash was covered by insurance.

picked up on Seventh Street. The getaway car sped out of town, out Sixteenth Street toward the village of Drenthe, with the police in hot pursuit. The posse from Holland caught up with them and a second gunfight ensued—the robbers firing first and the pursuers returning fire. The gangsters continued to flee and dropped roofing nails on the roadway, puncturing the tires of the police cars. This was not the final confrontation, however. Near Drenthe the gang stopped and ordered George Boerman, a gravel truck driver, to block the road with his truck. Just then the police arrived and both sides again unloaded their weapons, apparently without hitting any flesh. Boerman escaped the hail of bullets by flinging himself on the ground in front of his vehicle. The bandits fled again and outran the police. They continued through Burnips Corners and, it was assumed, back to their "lair" in Chicago.[85]

The gangsters shattered First State Bank's front window, riddled several automobiles with bullet holes, and forever after, the Warm Friend Tavern across the street bore marks in the stone façade where bullets had ricocheted off the wall. Shattered glass lay everywhere in the vicinity. But when the police inventoried the damage from the melee, they were relieved that there had been no loss of life. Besides Chief Lievense, Peter De Jongh had also been hit by a bullet. De Jongh, an employee of Kuite's grocery market, ran out onto Eighth Street to check on the commotion surrounding the bank heist and a bullet pierced his chest above the heart. Both recovered from their wounds.

Mayor Nicodemus Bosch rightfully called the incident an example of the most shocking "lawlessness." The ruthless greed of the gangsters had caused much destruction and put many innocents in harm's way. But the citizens had shown "unselfish bravery." In addition to the participants already mentioned, Andrew Klomparens had his double-barreled shotgun aimed at the bandits but failed to get off a good shot, and Joe Kardux of the St. Clair Oil station managed to get off a "pot shot" at the bandits. For Mayor Bosch, the police were an armed, prepared extension of a larger society capable and willing to defend itself. "I wish to pay my tribute to all those who so fearlessly fought these outlaws and risked their own lives to register protest against such banditry."[86] So Holland had learned a lesson to be prepared to protect itself. The citizens hoped that news of their resolute defense would spread, discouraging any more gangsters from coming to the city.

Legal proceedings culminated four years later, in 1936, when the Ottawa County Circuit Court issued warrants for four of the robbers,

85 *Holland City News*, 6 Oct., 17 Nov. 1932, 6 Apr. 1933, 8 Feb. 1934.

86 Ibid., 6 Oct. 1932.

including Bentz and Charles Fitzgerald, who were serving time for other crimes in Atlanta and St. Paul federal prisons, respectively. A fifth man had died by then, and the sixth was still at large. Quite likely, the culprits were part of the Chicago-Northern Indiana organized crime syndicate, along with Al Capone and other notables.[87]

Anti-Big Government

Hollanders typically prized self-reliance and eschewed socialistic government welfare programs, as their stalwart Republican voting record shows. How would their traditional socio-economic philosophy fare in the unprecedented crisis of the 1930s? President Franklin Roosevelt's cure for the Great Depression was big government, as evidenced in the dozens of alphabet agencies spawned by his "New Deal" program that forever changed American life. Did Hollanders resonate with his "progressive" agenda, backed by alliances with special interests such as leftist unions and labor lawyers to save the "forgotten man" at the bottom of the economic pyramid?

The true test was the reaction to the National Industrial Recovery Act enacted in 1933 as the linchpin of Roosevelt's New Deal. The National Recovery Administration (NRA), created to implement the law, set about to put five million people back to work with "fair and adequate" wages (a federal minimum wage), a shorter workweek (a 10-20 percent cut in hours for the same pay), improved "standards of labor" (unionization of workers), and elimination of "unfair trade practices" (businesses may collude to fix prices). Companies that complied were allowed to display the "Blue Eagle" emblem on their products, office doors, store windows, letterheads, mastheads, or wherever, as a symbol of cooperation.[88]

While only a minority of Hollanders voted for Roosevelt in 1932, 1936, 1940, and 1944, city leaders, including the common council, chamber of commerce, women's clubs, American Legion, and other bodies, readily took to the Blue Eagle and its slogan: "We Do Our Part." In August 1933 the city fathers adopted a resolution of Third Ward alderman Al Van Zoeren, chair of the ways and means committee, putting the city on record as supporting the NRA and committing it to push local employers "at once and altogether to submit and scrupulously comply" with all the provisions of the act. Although Henry Ford in Dearborn declared that he would never put "that Roosevelt buzzard"

87 Ibid., 7 May 1936.

88 Stephen Schwartz, "Unhappy Days," *Weekly Standard* (July 30, 2007): 37-39.

American Legion toy drive headquarters on Eighth Street in the early 1930s (*courtesy Myron Van Ark*)

on his cars, Hollanders apparently had few such qualms. The Holland Woman's Club, under the leadership of Letitia (Mrs. John J.) Good, launched a campaign under the slogan "Never Retreat, America" to place the Blue Eagle in every home, thereby committing the household to trade only with stores and businesses displaying the insignia. William Connelly, head of the chamber of commerce, suggested the slogan and commended the women for their efforts. It was the NRA, he declared, that enabled the banks to reopen, factories to boom, and the welfare load to fade away.[89]

The Holland Merchants Association, Rotary Club, Exchange Club, and kindred bodies, all backed the NRA, including clergymen. The Exchange Club held a four-day NRA campaign in schools and societies, culminating in a mass rally at the armory, replete with a color guard under Captain Henry Geerds. Henry Ter Keurst of the progressive Trinity Reformed Church insisted that the campaign was not one of coercion, but it was to "point out the patriotic duty of every true-blooded American citizen." Ex-mayor Evert Stephan even paraphrased Scripture at a merchant's association meeting. It was "not enough," he said, "to simply display the Blue Eagle 'We Do Our Part,' but [we must] live up to it 'in spirit and in truth.'"[90] Jobs might be scarce in Holland, but florid rhetoric on behalf of a top-down, managed economy was not. Hollanders opposed big government in theory, but they were all too eager to share in the "free money."

89 *Holland City News*, 3, 17, 31 Aug. 1933.
90 Ibid., 5, 12 Oct., 2 Nov. 1933.

City leaders were determined to get NRA funds for civic projects that put local men to work, and the federal government paid 30 percent of the cost and provided credit for the remainder, with amortization over thirty years. A committee of the common council, headed by James De Young, developed a wish list of six projects, all labor intensive and costing more than $600,000. The list included upgrades of the water system, a new building at the power plant, completion of the sewage plant, improvements at the cemetery and fairgrounds, and a $350,000 city dock. The city fathers approved all the projects except the city dock, which expense Mayor Bosch called "too heavy" to bear, given the desperate times.[91]

William Connelly: an Irishman among the Dutch

After the notorious bank robbery and another year of recession, Holland saw a ray of hope in the person of William Connelly, an Irishman who was the city's savior during the Great Depression. An outsider to the city, Connelly became head of the Holland Chamber of Commerce on August 1, 1933, and he held the position for the next six years. Connelly is credited with saving the local economy by directly confronting the economic crisis. First, he developed a public relations campaign to boost the city by making Tulip Time a nationally known festival. Next, he fought for state and national funds for local highway construction projects. Third, he recruited new industry. By the end of 1936, Connelly's formula "transformed a town badly crippled by depression into one of the busiest industrial centers in Michigan."[92] By 1938, twelve new industries had come to Holland, bringing over $2 million in payrolls and four million man-hours of labor.[93]

Connelly, then in his fifties, parlayed his charisma and statewide political connections to build an overwhelmingly positive reputation for Holland. He was a successful businessman and an equally adroit politician. While yet in his thirties, he had developed a resort in his hometown of Spring Lake, and he later served a term as a state senator. His political connections were widespread. From 1915 on, he was an influential member of the State Road Commission, and in 1920 had served as a delegate to the Republican National Convention.[94] By the time he took the chamber of commerce position in Holland, he was known as "Concrete Connelly," the president of the Michigan Good

91 Ibid., 7 Sept. 1933.

92 *Holland City News*, 3 Dec. 1936.

93 Ibid., 19 Nov. 1936; 28 July 1938.

94 Wallace Ewing, *A Directory of People in Northwest Ottawa County* (Grand Haven: Tri-Cities Historical Museum, 1999).

William "Bill" Connelly in white suit honored by the state commissioner of highways during Tulip Time 1938 (*Archives, Holland Historical Trust*)

Roads Association, who promoted concrete over asphalt as the most suitable material for improving the state's expanding network of paved roads.[95]

One of Connelly's earliest actions as director or executive secretary (he was given various titles) of the chamber of commerce was to call the Good Roads Association to a meeting in Holland. Two hundred people heeded his call. In the same week in August, Connelly served as toastmaster at a sheriffs convention in Holland. Through his good humor and quick wit, he quickly built rapport with the Dutch. He even managed a successful joke about Lievense, who since his shootout with the bank robbers the previous year, had become a local celebrity. "Chief Lievense is here tonight," Connelly smiled, "with the whole board of police commissioners. Pete has talked of quitting the force, but he says he's been a policeman so long he hates to go to work."[96] Within weeks, Connelly presided at a meeting of the Holland Harbor Committee. Like a proto-city manager, he did more than promote the community. He became the "industrial director" who mastered the ins and outs of city development. Although he continued to live in Spring Lake, he spent most of his time in Holland, where the industrialists, merchants, and bankers enthused over him.[97]

95 *Holland City News*, 13 Jan. 1938.
96 Ibid., 3 Aug. 1933.
97 Ibid., 20 July, 3, 17, 24 Aug. 1933; 22 Mar., 3 May 1934.

Perhaps more than anyone else, Connelly found a supporter in Ben Mulder, the editor of the *Holland City News*, who hailed from a family of editors. Ben's father Leendert had been an editor of *De Grondwet*, and his relative, Professor Arnold Mulder, was his forerunner at the *Holland Sentinel*. Mulder, like Connelly, was a steadfast promoter of the city. He was also an informal amateur historian, filling in the history of the city from his own remembrances. Ben Mulder's writing technique was easily identifiable. First, he often referred to himself as "your editor," a position in which he prided himself. His style was to begin an article with some reminiscing, then insert the word "anyway" and continue to the story at hand. He also featured extensive historical sections in "his" newspaper and commented liberally about how the times had changed. As a respected elder and an influential voice, Mulder was just the right ally for Connelly.

Not only was Connelly an outsider by birth, but he was also an outsider by ethnicity in the Dutch community. Much was made of his Irish ancestry, but in an approving way. In 1934 Mulder reprinted a line about Tulip Time that had appeared in a newspaper in the Netherlands: "*Hollandsche meisjes in 'nationaal' costuum bij het bloemenfest in de Americaansche stad Holland.*" "Connelly, please translate," Mulder quipped.[98] Later, when the *News* received a Tulip Time clipping from a St. Louis German-language newspaper, Mulder lamented that Connelly was unable to read it because of all the gutturals; the exercise left his throat sore. This kind of ethnic banter, however blatant, was all in good humor. What made these jokes acceptable was that they spoofed fellow Americans. Like most in Holland by the 1930s, Connelly was native born and had American habits. He was as Irish as any third or fourth generation Hollander was Dutch. But his ethnicity still made a good headline. In 1934 cartoonist Robert L. Ripley's nationally syndicated column "Believe it or Not" featured Connelly as "the only Irishman" in a Dutch immigrant city.[99] Ripley's research was faulty. The 1934 *Holland City Directory* lists a dozen residents with obvious Irish names—Kelly, Murphy, O'Connor, and O'Leary.

Connelly was as attracted to Dutch culture as any American, and he keenly recognized the potential of ethnic tourism. His first big plan, and the most ambitious one, was to bring Holland out of the Depression by capitalizing on the city's unique ethnic heritage and its popular ethnic festival. Connelly and his supporters reasoned that the Black

98 *Holland City News*, 12 Apr. 1934.

99 Ibid., 5 Apr., 17 May 1934; 17 Oct. 1935, 24 Mar. 1938.

River was essentially useless as it was. He proposed to tap New Deal relief programs, such as the National Relief Administration (NRA), to put hundreds of unemployed men to work building a tourist attraction at Windmill Island to be called *Klein Nederland* (Little Netherlands). The plan called for cleaning up the swamp on the north end of town and creating an island with canals, dykes, a windmill, and even houses and barns reflecting the Dutch style. It would be a miniature "Little Netherlands," an American version of Vollendam, the famous tourist town on the Zuider Zee.[100]

"Reclaiming" the river would be a massive undertaking, but that is exactly what Holland needed. Initial cost estimates were $600,000, but Connelly assured the city that the NRA would grant funds for one-third of the amount. The city would have to borrow the remainder by selling bonds. The project promised to keep from three to four hundred men busy for two years, long enough to ride out the Depression and begin to reap the reward of tourism.[101]

A skeptical common council first voted seven to five against the project. It was too big a risk, they said. Some questioned whether construction of dykes along the Black River was even feasible. After all, were there not sinkholes in the area? and did not the Black River experience spring freshets? In addition, the river was rife with mosquitoes and shrouded in fog much of the time. Given the lukewarm local support, the NRA, not surprisingly, turned down the project. John Hyma joked: "It looks like NRA funds now stand for "No River Appropriation."[102]

But the idea of *Klein Nederland* refused to die. Connelly enlisted president Paul T. Cheff of Holland Furnace in the cause. In September the council voted eleven to one for a more modest version of the project. When the mayor vetoed the measure, fearful of the $350,000 loan the project required, the council still voted ten to two and overrode the veto. Over the next three months, however, reality set in as they discussed funding the project, and the aldermen rescinded their vote. *Klein Nederland* was no more.[103]

One part of the plan did come to fruition. In 1964-65 the city was able to buy De Zwaan, an authentic Netherlands windmill, disassemble and ship it across the Atlantic and St. Lawrence Seaway to Grand

100 Randall P. Vande Water, "City would not fund mini village in 1933," *Holland Sentinel*, 19 Aug. 2012.
101 *Holland City News*, 17 Aug., 21 Sept. 1933.
102 Ibid., 24 Aug. 1933, 31 Aug. 1933.
103 *Holland City News*, 28 Sept. 1933; 8 Feb. 1934.

Haven harbor, truck it to Holland, and reassemble it on the island as a working mill. Then, in the late 1990s, the council again came very close to building a replica Dutch village on the island, but the high cost dissuaded them at the last moment (see chapter 33). The city fathers are risk averse, if nothing else.

Connelly proposed a second massive, albeit shortsighted, project to resurrect Holland. This was a project first touted fifty years earlier, to build a canal linking Holland and Grand Rapids. Connelly found support from two Michigan congressmen, Representative Carl E. Mapes and Senator Arthur Vandenberg. In May 1934 Connelly pushed for a survey of the canal route. When the Army Corps of Engineers finally responded two years later, they rejected the project as too expensive to have merit. This was Connelly's last big idea, but his "little" ideas fared better. Most effective was to push the Bonus Plan that business leaders and the city fathers had implemented in the 1880s, which had attracted many new factories and created jobs. Connelly worked with the manufacturing committee of the chamber of commerce and common council in the recruitment effort, and snared the Baker Furniture Company from Allegan and Hekman's Holland Tea Rusk from Grand Rapids, among others. The Bonus program brought long-term benefits almost too large to measure.[104]

In early 1938 Connelly resigned as executive secretary manager of the chamber of commerce, despite a Rotary Club resolution urging him to stay on. He had carried Holland through the hard times and left the community ready to capitalize on the coming war boom. The old warhorse, former mayor Evert P. Stephan, succeeded him. A year later Connelly became the director of public relations for the Grand Rapids Furniture Exposition.[105]

The New Deal impacts Holland, 1933-36

Even before Connelly arrived in 1933, there had been some positive news about the local economy. In April 1933 the Holland Sugar mill reopened, and the Lake Shore Sugar Co. promised to start up again in October. Also, in June 1933, Holland Furnace was running at full capacity for the first time in nearly three years. As a marketing agent of Tulip Time, Holland Furnace continued to prosper throughout the 1930s. Hart & Cooley and the furniture manufacturers Baker and Sligh were all running full time again. Between April and July 1934,

104 Ibid., 11 Jan. 1934; 3 May 1934; 20 Feb. 1936; 3 Mar., 23 June 1938.
105 Ibid., 12 Jan. 1939, 11 Jan. 1940.

employment increased 20 percent.[106] Although the city budget remained tight, the common council had reason to be heartened. Alderman Henry Prins joked that if the city could afford a new streetlight on Thirteenth Street between Lincoln and Fairbanks, then surely it could afford a light over a certain unnamed alderman's favorite horseshoe court at Fifth Street and Columbia Avenue.[107]

The common council in the fall of 1933 launched $250,000 in public improvement projects, to be funded 75 percent by the RFC and Civil Works Administration (CWA), which included water projects, a new sewer disposal plant, a warehouse for the board of public works, a new firehouse and police station, and street and road upgrades. Nicodemus Bosch, in the annual "state of the city" address in 1934, noted that after four hard years things were looking up. His message was in sync with the national mood, but the optimism was premature. The New Deal stalled in 1934. The Supreme Court declared unconstitutional the NRA, the Agricultural Adjustment Act, and several other major programs. Independent-minded citizens began to realize that FDR's programs made people more, rather than less, dependent on government. Government, specifically democratic politicians, would take care of them in perpetuity through Social Security, farm subsidies, special favors for unions, and the like. In Michigan a $28 million bond issue for public works was rejected five to one statewide and twenty to one in Holland![108]

The 1934 Tulip Time committee tellingly invited Norman Thomas, three-time socialist candidate for president, to open the festival. Thomas predictably condemned capitalism for its cyclical nature and periodic depressions, all obviated by socialist command economies, such as that in the Soviet Union. Democratic Governor Comstock flew in by airplane for the occasion.[109]

The Federal Housing Administration, created in 1934, provided federal funds for delinquent homeowners to refinance their mortgages up to $14,000. Locally, Dick Boter, Frank Essenburg, John Post, G. John Kooiker, William Deur, John Rutgers, and Andrew Klomparens helped found the Holland Home Owners League (HOLC) to tap federal funds on behalf of hundreds of homeowners. Henry Beelen, a builder in partnership with Ben Wassink, his brother-in-law, was one who

106 *Holland City News*, 6 Apr. 1933; 8 June 1933, 3 Jan., 29 Mar., 26 July 1934.

107 Ibid., 26 June 1934.

108 Ibid., 7, 21 Sept. 1933, 18 Jan., 3 May 1934. Killing of the AAA program in 1935 cost Ottawa County farmers $20,000 that year (ibid., 16 Jan. 1936).

109 *Holland City News*, 17 May 1934.

benefited. He obtained an interest-only home loan, but his wife worried incessantly that a government agent would come and take the house. The family of eight, plus a grandmother, went without an icebox, milk for the children, and a gas heater; they warmed the whole house with a kerosene cook stove.[110]

To finance the federal alphabet agencies and their massive programs, taxes had to increase. In 1935 Congress increased income tax rates to 4 percent of net incomes over $2,000 for singles and $4,000 for married couples, with a surtax on incomes above $4,000. Congress soon provided for employers to withhold the tax and forward it to Washington, ending the temptation to underreport wages.[111]

In 1935 the city fathers' list of work relief projects included a city airport, merging the Fairlawn (Holland Township) Cemetery with Pilgrim Home Cemetery to the east, building a new playground on Pine Avenue at Twenty-Second Street, refurbishing several city parks, and clearing the old fairgrounds. To cover the $65,000 cost with federal matching funds, the city had to pay $15,000 (23 percent), which it planned to raise by a bond issue. Voters approved all the projects except the airport, which gained a simple majority but not the required three-fifths margin. A bevy of plant expansions and industrial newcomers that showed Holland was getting ahead made voters more sanguine, but Holland still had about one-third of the entire county welfare caseload of unemployables at an annual cost of $50,000. Many others got by on $48 a month in "make work" jobs under the Works Progress Administration (WPA), such as raking leaves, sweeping streets, planting red pine seedlings in the dunes to lessen erosion in cut-over areas, and whatever else local officials could find. The demeaning work prompted some five hundred WPA men in Holland to go on strike for a week in 1936, especially after they learned that their counterparts in Kent County received $60 a month to their $48. That they begrudged their pay, rather than be grateful for public assistance to feed their families, testifies to the fact that the worst of the hard times had passed.[112]

The veterans of the Great War felt like they won the lottery in 1936 when the federal government acceded to their request for the bonus

110 Ibid., 12 Apr. 1934; Ken Beelen interview by David Boeve and the author, 30 Oct. 2009, typescript, JAH.

111 *Holland City News*, 7 Feb. 1935.

112 Ibid., 8 Aug., 5, 12 Sept., 17, 24 Oct., 7 Nov. 1935, 20 Feb., 5, 12 Mar. 1936, 27 May 1937. After seventy-five years, these trees have become infested with pine bark beetles, and owners are harvesting them before they die and become worthless (*Holland Sentinel*, 15 Feb. 2008).

money. Ottawa County veterans collectively received $870,000, the largest part coming to Holland. Everyone eagerly awaited the mailman on June 15 when the checks arrived. For months the lucky families discussed how best to use the bonanza; some paid bills, spent a little, and saved a little. Men had the gleam of a new car in their eye, while wives wanted new furniture or an electric appliance. Some used the bonus as a down payment on a new home. No wonder that home building enjoyed a spurt in the next months, which pleased Frank Bolhuis of Bolhuis Lumber & Mfg., who built well-designed tract homes, much like Bosgraaf Homes in recent times. After the years of depression, it was time again to remodel, paint the trim, and so on—all the while reading newspaper reports of a new threat growing in Europe.[113]

The heroes of the 1930s were city leaders and officials, especially chamber head Connelly and Mayor Nicodemus Bosch. His Honor bore the brunt of the hard times from 1932 to 1936. In his farewell message before the aldermen in the council chambers, Bosch reflected on the past. "You and I took office when the days were darkest. . . . Methods were devised by this body to meet trying situations and imperative needs—matters that never came up before in a common council." Local, state, and federal programs had to be coordinated and the ins and outs of "welfare and works relief" mastered, often without knowing the specifics.[114] If FDR often "flew by the seat of his pants," imagine how confusing Washington policies were for local officials.

Thanksgiving Day in 1936 gave Mayor Henry Geerlings the opportunity in the customary mayor's proclamation to reflect on the meaning of being an American. "We are painfully aware that all our national problems are not yet solved. The way to complete recovery may be long and hard, but we are living under the Stars and Stripes," he noted. "Ours is a republic dedicated to cooperation, to love, to kindness. We live in a land where the government recognizes that its first duty is to protect the weak, feed the hungry, cloth the naked, and shelter the homeless." President Roosevelt would have approved these Messianic themes.[115]

War clouds bring economic recovery

Geerlings found it far easier to feed and house the needy than did his predecessor. Economic conditions in Holland and the nation

[113] *Holland City News*, 4 June, 1 Oct. 1936, 3 June, 23 Sept. 1937.
[114] Ibid., 16 Apr. 1936.
[115] *Holland City News*, 19 Nov. 1936.

improved markedly in 1937. City welfare costs by 1939 fell to $400 a week, which was a far cry from $2,000 in 1932. New industries, notably Chris-Craft and Holland Precision Parts, opened plants, with the promise of several thousand new hires to add to the 4,700 already employed. The Works Progress Administration (WPA) did its part by providing $675,000 from the US treasury toward construction of the city power plant at the neck of Lake Macatawa.[116]

War clouds gathering in Europe began to crowd out local economic concerns in the news. *The Anchor*, Hope College's newspaper, took a "peace poll" of the student body in 1935 and found that 80 percent would answer the call should the nation be attacked. Sixty percent believed the United States should stay out of war, and only 22 percent would fight if the United States started it. As to a United States military buildup as a way to ward off potential enemies, 40 percent of Hope students were opposed. The majority also would keep the United States out of the League of Nations.[117] The interwar era was marked by international disarmament conferences and arms control agreements that required the United States to scrap hundreds of naval vessels. Isolationist sentiment was so strong that Congress passed a series of Neutrality Acts in 1935, 1936, and 1937 that tied the hands of the president in any European war.

Hope student attitudes reflected those of their professors. Paul Hinkamp, college chaplain and professor of Bible, told a 1937 Memorial Day crowd at Centennial Park that he strictly opposed war and backed world peace at all costs. "The last war failed to end wars . . . failed in bringing about prosperity, and 'failed to make the world safe for democracy.'" Any future war would be more terrible than the last, awful as it was, Hinkamp concluded. At the 1938 Memorial Day exercises at Hope Memorial Chapel, William Van 't Hof of the Third Reformed Church spoke on the topic, "Lest We Forget." He bemoaned past wars and lack of preparedness for future ones. The real causes are always concealed beforehand, he insisted, and he blamed the First World War on "propaganda" and "super-patriotism." He asked, "Have we a right to kill, whatever the cause?" and answered by quoting the commandment, "Thou shalt not kill." Warming to his task, Van 't Hof concluded: "'Love your enemies' is the new way. War is the old way." One wonders how his large audience of veterans and their auxiliaries accepted this pacifist message.[118]

[116] Ibid., 2 Nov. 1939, 4, 11 Jan., 2 May 1940.
[117] Ibid., 28 Feb. 1935.
[118] *Holland City News*, 2 June 1938.

On September 1, 1939, German panzer divisions invaded Poland, and Europe was at war. The German *blitzkrieg* quickly overran Poland and then turned west into the Low Countries and France. The Roosevelt administration, with the help of Senator Arthur H. Vandenberg of Grand Rapids, induced Congress in November to lift the arms embargo in favor of a "cash and carry" policy, which allowed the United States to supply the beleaguered British, provided her ships carried the munitions and supplies. Bruce Raymond, chair of the Hope College history department, very much opposed this decision and predicted that the United States would be drawn into the war within three years. He was off by only one year. Off campus, Charles Karr, president of the Spring Air Company of Holland, a mattress manufacturer, sounded a similar theme in a speech that attracted national news coverage. "Please keep our business free from war-talk," he cried. "Unless we can help someone by talking of the war, may I suggest that we refrain from discussing it anywhere."[119]

This proved impossible. Army recruiters arrived in Holland within weeks at President Roosevelt's behest to sign up an additional 227,000 men in the "greatest peacetime recruiting campaign in the history of the army." Within eight months, German forces had conquered all of Western Europe, leaving only the British Isles free of Nazi occupation. The United States began selling war material on credit to Great Britain under the Lend-Lease Act, and the nation became the "arsenal of democracy."[120]

[119] Ibid., 3 June 1937, 14, 28 Sept. 1939.
[120] Ibid., 28 Sept., 28 Oct. 1939.

CHAPTER 23

The Second World War and the Korean War

In contrast to the Great War, nativism did not rear its ugly head in Holland in the 1940s. The Dutch Reformed churches were English speaking and Hollanders were fully acculturated to conservative Midwest norms and mores. This time, the Dutch as good Americans joined in the antipathy for Germans, Italians, and Japanese. Living through the Great War, however, was in many ways a preview of the same scenario twenty-five years later. For those old enough to remember, the similarities were easy to draw. A hesitant, isolationist foreign policy initially kept the United States at arm's length from the terrible bloodshed, but in self-interest and catalyzed by an attack—the sinking of the Lusitania in 1917 and the bombing of Pearl Harbor in 1941—America went to war, banking on the strength of its industrial heartland to support a long-term offensive in distant territory.

Holland, an industrial city in 1941 and becoming even more so during the war, had a crucial part to play as a cog in America's home front machine. As democratic and patriotic citizens, Dutch Americans worked overtime in local factories; gave liberally to relief agencies; subscribed heavily to war bonds; and sacrificed their goods, monies, and even their lives for the war effort. With hundreds of service men and women serving abroad, Holland had to broaden its horizons and face tough social and economic issues. The war also shook the social foundations of the city. Women saw greater employment, and children assisted in the war effort in any way they could. All the while, there remained looming in the background the question of what the soldiers would do for employment upon their return. Having endured four years of privations and tragedy, Holland emerged from the war a changed city.

Netherlands relief aid

The war began in Europe in September 1939, but it came a giant step closer to home in May 1940 with the German invasion of the Netherlands. For those in West Michigan who still had relatives, friends, and correspondents in the Netherlands, it was most unnerving to hear that the traditionally neutral country had been overrun by the totalitarian regime of the hated Nazis. By the time the United States joined the global conflict, the Netherlands had already suffered almost two years of German occupation. The position of Dutch Americans vis-à-vis the war was similar to what they had faced during the Boer War at the turn of the century. Once again, Dutch Americans had someone to cheer for, or rather another circumstance to lament, as their cousins in the Netherlands, like the Boers before them, struggled alone under the weight of a superior foe. Once again, Dutch Americans raised money and watched helplessly from afar.

The Dutch military resistance lasted only four days. After the Nazi aerial bombardment of Rotterdam on April 14, 1940, the Dutch, fearing the destruction of their other major cities, signaled surrender. When the invasion came, Arnold Mulder noted, "many [Hollanders] who had never given a thought to the land of their fathers discovered that they had a consciousness of '*land en volk*.' In attacking a 'foreign' country on the edge of the North Sea, Hitler had somehow attacked them."[1]

Almost immediately after hearing news of the surrender, Holland's mayor Henry Geerlings, and a second-generation immigrant, appointed a committee to work in conjunction with the Red Cross to raise funds for victims of war in the Netherlands.[2] For Geerlings, time was of the essence. He hastened to organize the committee before the opening day

1 Arnold Mulder, *Americans from Holland* (Philadelphia: J. B. Lippincott, 1947), 289.

2 *Holland City News*, 2, 16, 23 May 1940.

of the annual Tulip Time celebration, scheduled to begin on May 18, so that he could use the festival as a staging point for relief work. The committee also organized a Holland American "Netherlands Day" rally at Centennial Park on May 22, featuring speakers Alexander Loudon, Netherlands ambassador to the United States, and Hendrik Willem Van Loon of New York, noted historian and publicist. Tulip Time in 1940 brought in over 650,000 visitors, the second largest turnout since the crowd of 750,000 in 1937. The festival committee raised $3,700 and the aid rally $475 for Netherlands Relief. The mayor's Dutch relief fund netted $1,100 by late May and surpassed the $5,000 mark by the end of June.[3]

Successful as the relief efforts may have been, the monies raised were modest compared to those collected for the Boers. No one doubted that the Netherlands was in trouble, but there was little sense of urgency to do anything about it. There were no calls for "volunteers" as in the Spanish Civil War (1936-39), and no one staged anti-Nazi or pro-Dutch rallies. Dutch Americans could find no reason to protest American policy, which was one of strict neutrality. While the Netherlands relief effort was thoughtful, it seemed that it would make little impact. For the time being, the nation was firmly isolated behind the curtain of German expansion. Some in Holland had even raised doubts about whether the contributions to the Red Cross would be designated for the Dutch or if they would end up in the Red Cross general fund.

In 1940 a new relief agency, the Queen Wilhelmina fund, was organized through the work of Willard C. Wichers, curator of the Netherlands Museum (chapter 27). Wichers ensured through arrangements with the Red Cross that contributions to the new fund would be earmarked specifically for a free Netherlands after the war. He stated that the fund was to complement, not compete with, Mayor Geerlings' appeal for Red Cross aid. Despite Wichers' call, the Queen Wilhelmina fund took over fundraising to the point of being the exclusive Dutch relief concern. Geerlings was supportive, however, since the fund, by inviting speakers to the city, helped keep relief efforts active and in the public spotlight. In early October 1940, for example, the well-known Dutch writer, Adriaan J. Barnouw, who since 1921 held the chair of Dutch language and literature at Columbia University in New York City, came to Holland specifically to help raise funds for Netherlands relief. Later that month, US Senator Arthur Vandenberg of Michigan, a Grand Rapids resident, spoke at the Holland Armory

[3] Ibid., 29 May, 27 June 1940.

Women of the Salvation Army Home League sew clothing for refugee children displaced by the Nazi conquest, late 1940. The first shipments went to London, but the league also sent clothing to the Netherlands (photo Phillip A. Harrington) (*courtesy Randall P. Vande Water*)

during a rally for presidential candidate Wendell Wilkie. Vandenberg illustrated that he understood the concerns of his constituency. The evil Nazi dictatorship now ruled, but in time, he hoped, "there will be some justice in store for our Little Holland across the ocean."[4]

In early January 1941 Netherlands ambassador Loudon returned to Holland to drum up support for the Queen Wilhelmina fund. As part of his relief aid tour of the Midwest, Loudon's stop included a speech at the Warm Friend Tavern where he answered tough questions about why the Dutch royal family had fled to England upon the invasion of the Netherlands. His answer: "I have the proof that the Germans came with the intention of shooting the queen, to destroy Princess Juliana, her husband and two children and to kill all members of the Dutch government." He also told the audience that the Germans had forbidden the Dutch any display of patriotism, such as posting pictures of the queen or flying an orange flag. Loudon's appeal was on two levels: Not only did the audience sympathize with Dutch patriotism, but they also saw in the German regulations an affront to democratic principles.[5]

4 *Holland City News*, 20 June, 3, 31 Oct. (quote), 19 Dec. 1940.

5 Ibid., 9, 16 Jan. 1941.

In 1941, with no more speakers on the docket, and looking for an excuse to keep the Queen Wilhelmina fund alive, Wichers promoted February 8 as the ninety-fourth anniversary of Van Raalte's arrival in Holland. (The founding date was actually February 9, which fell on a Sunday in 1941, and to celebrate on the Lord's Day was unthinkable.) For the special day, the local pioneer and historical societies sent letters to churches asking for donations. The letters told of Van Raalte and the settlers' struggles for religious freedom. Further, the letters cited the Christian duty to aid war sufferers. The fund remained active throughout the war, but was incorporated in May 1942 under a local umbrella agency, the Community Chest. Wichers remained its leading proponent and the strongest link between the two Hollands.[6]

A royal visit

In early May 1941 the City of Holland sent invitations, signed by Henry Geerlings, its *burgomeester*, asking for the appearance of Crown Princess Juliana of the Netherlands at the Tulip Time festival, which she happily accepted. Juliana, the heir to the Dutch throne, and her two children (including future Queen Beatrix) had been living in Ontario, Canada since June of the previous year. They had arrived in Canada after fleeing the bombardment in England. Juliana's husband, German-born Prince Bernhard, remained in England, and for two years flew in the Royal Air Force, taking his vacations all the while in Canada.

During the visit of the princess to Holland, there was some mention about providing Netherlands relief aid, but other feelings took center stage. In this difficult time, amid serious conversations between war hawks and peace doves, the visit of the royal princess provided the local Dutch a catharsis and a sense of awe. This was the first time Netherlands royalty had ever visited the city, and naturally, many wanted to catch a glimpse. Holland had further cause to boast, since the princess came direct, without a stopover in Grand Rapids.[7]

The official reason for Juliana's visit was to celebrate the seventy-fifth anniversary of the founding of Hope College on June 10, 1941. College president, Wynand Wichers, Willard's uncle, organized a standing-room only reception at the Hope Memorial (Dimnent) Chapel, which began with an introduction and the presentation to the princess of an honorary degree. After the ceremony, the princess had a special dinner prepared for her at the Warm Friend Tavern and took an

6 *Holland City News*, 21 May 1942.

7 Ibid., 5 June, 3 Apr., 5 June 1941.

Crown Princess Juliana at Hope College to receive an honorary doctorate from President Wynand Wichers, May 1941 (*Joint Archives of Holland)*

automobile tour of the city. She also made a thirty-five minute visit to the Netherlands Museum, where she signed the registration book, met curator Wichers, and received a custom pair of wooden shoes addressed "To her Royal Highness, Princess Juliana." The princess also met August F. Breytspraak of Chicago, who wanted to show Juliana signed papers signifying that his grandfather, a cabinetmaker, had in 1828 designed the throne upon which the Queen sat before Nazi occupation.[8]

Throughout the war, the city of Holland hosted many visiting Netherlanders. Some were soldiers and sailors displaced by the war who came to the United States by way of England or the Japanese-occupied Netherlands East Indies. Some came seeking relatives, and sought out Willard Wichers to help locate them. A few of these visitors gave speeches about their war experiences. Captain Barteld van Dijk, for example, told a crowd at the Warm Friend Tavern, about losing his merchant ship in a battle against a German U-boat and his subsequent rescue by an allied ship. In another case, B. H. Sajet of Amsterdam, who had escaped from the Netherlands in 1941, stopped during a speaking tour to address conditions in the occupied Netherlands. "I should like people to understand," Sajet declared, "what it means to lose liberties of which we were proud–of which you are proud." Also in 1943 Captain Henry De Kuyper of Rotterdam came as a representative for registering

8 Ibid., 12 June 1941.

Willard C. Wichers' office in the Netherlands Information Service at city hall during the Second World War. Note the Dutch war posters on the wall: "Dutch Sailor—This man is your FRIEND. He fights for FREEDOM" (*Archives, Holland Historical Trust*)

individuals for the Dutch military. Indeed, De Kuyper found a few willing recruits among the non-naturalized Dutch immigrants in West Michigan.[9]

Pacifism

War in Europe is turning the "hands of the clock back to savagery," Joseph R. Sizoo, distinguished pastor of St. Nicholas Collegiate Reformed Church in New York City, told the Hope College graduating class in 1941. "There is no tomorrow in this type of world." Sizoo's pessimistic speech captured the mood of the day. A significant number of Americans, Hollanders included, were attracted to the peace movement that opposed American involvement in the war. A popular position early on was that American intervention was neither necessary nor likely to bring any positive lasting benefit.[10]

Mirroring the non-interventionist position of the First World War, John R. Dethmers, former Ottawa County prosecutor, the main speaker at the Netherlands Day aid rally, noted America's special role in the world: "We are all Americans regardless of where our forefathers, or we, ourselves, migrated from. We don't want any part in the old

9 *Holland City News*, 2, 23 July, 6 Aug. 1942, 1 Apr. 1943, 15 Nov. 1945.

10 Ibid., 19 June 1941.

world problems or their wars because America is the only citadel for the preservation of liberty, freedom, and peace. We can best serve posterity and the future by preserving these 'ideals.'" C. Wayland Brooks, Republican senatorial nominee from Illinois, explained his peace philosophy before a luncheon of assembled local associations. Brooks put it bluntly: "We [the United States] can't settle their [Europe's] differences." A month later, at Memorial Day services at Pilgrim Home Cemetery, attorney Cornelius Vander Meulen reminded the crowd of the blood in the fields of Flanders, and declared: "No, my friends, wars do not end wars; war breeds wars." Neither of Holland's two remaining Civil War veterans, Swan Miller and Madison Richards, could attend the ceremonies. In September the Holland Ministerial Association drew a capacity crowd to a special "Prayer for Peace" service in Hope's Memorial Chapel. A few weeks later, when the national board of the American Legion endorsed sending American troops abroad, local Legionnaires protested, finding the endorsement "contrary to a 23-year-old stand of the American Legion in opposing another American expeditionary force."[11]

As the European war continued, others in Holland promoted peace from religious conviction. In a move reminiscent of the "flag-in-church" controversy in 1918, Hope Church minister Marion de Velder preached against war by saying that we must not "let nationalism invade the church." But de Velder did allow a veiled ideology to enter by opening his church's doors for a "Prayer for Peace" service.[12] Local congregations, however, were far from unanimous in their support for the peace movement—a movement that had no central organization or official doctrine. Indeed, a "peace" stance was an ambiguous position: it was either blanket pacifism or opposition to this war based on contingency and circumstance.

A leading pacifist and voice of the anti-war movement, Abraham J. Muste, a 1905 Hope College graduate, clearly opposed the war from both positions. Muste was one of two pacifist speakers at a peace program held at Hope Memorial Chapel in November 1941, sponsored by the Reformed Church in America and the Committee of International Justice. The other speaker, Frederick Olert, a Western Theological Seminary graduate and pastor of Detroit's First Presbyterian Church, preached that the church's role was to support world peace through liberating individual souls. He warned that war could lead to the collapse of civilization. Muste's speech also hit on Christian themes,

11 Ibid., 23, 29 May, 6 June, 12 Sept. 1940, 9 Oct. 1941.
12 *Holland City News*, 29 May 1940.

but it betrayed his Socialist beliefs. All wars had economic causes, Muste said, related to the competition between national productions and their inherent inequalities. For Muste, the solution to war was to blend Calvinism and Socialism into a non-violent Christian socialism.[13]

On the other side of the war debate were those who thought America would inevitably join the war, and therefore reasoned that the country might as well get busy preparing for the impending conflict. The war preparedness faction used American history and Americanism as its rallying call. In July the local American Legion resolved to begin an ROTC (Reserve Officers Training Corps) program at Ottawa County high schools. The organization also ordered one hundred license plates that read, "No Isms but Americanisms." Speakers to rally the preparedness camp included Howard Heinz, president of H. J. Heinz Co., who gladly followed his visit to the local pickle plant with a speech at Hope College. At Hope, Heinz gave a chest-pounding speech of America's rise to greatness, promoting war preparedness and marking American democracy as the only hope for civilization. Bernard Ranger, a foreign correspondent in France, also spoke before a sizeable crowd in 1941 at the first annual Americanism program of the American Legion at the Holland Armory. Ranger mentioned the role that Dutch fighters were playing in the war. He said that Americans must live patriotism, not just talk about it.[14]

The crucial figure in the war preparedness faction, and indeed perhaps the most important figure for Holland during wartime, was the city's mayor, Henry Geerlings, who was appointed defense coordinator for the Holland area. Born in 1868, Geerlings had served as mayor from 1904 to 1906, and returned to that office with a victory in the municipal election of 1936, and re-elected in 1939 and 1942. Geerlings was a small-scale, Republican version of the term-limit testing Franklin D. Roosevelt. Geerlings was a champion of democracy, a promoter of civic projects who spoke in absolutes, and one to rally the city to action by rousing speeches, which few could understand because he talked much too fast. In his mayoral message in April 1941, Geerlings spoke candidly about the international situation: "Today as never before the very foundations upon which we have felt secure are being shaken. The whole civilized world is torn apart not only by guns and bombs and other implements of war, although these, too, are doing their share, but by an ideal. This is the ideal of force."[15]

13 *Holland City News*, 12 Sept. 1940, 22 May, 19 Nov. 1941.

14 Ibid., 25 July, 1, 15 Aug. 1940, 3 Apr. 1941.

15 Ibid., 17 Apr., 24 Dec. 1941. Henry Geerlings graduated from Hope College and McCormick Theological Seminary (Chicago), served briefly in a Presbyterian

Geerlings challenged the city to fight for American democracy by filling war bond quotas, working overtime, and making sacrifices in every aspect of life. At times his concessions to the war effort seemed excessive or irritating, but he lived his words, gave his share, and was as hard on himself and on his colleagues as anyone. His 1943 annual message pointed out the city's wartime responsibilities, under the theme: "democracy begins at home." For the mayor, the war was a war of civilization. There were shades of Winston Churchill in his language and demeanor: "If we fail, we go back to the dark ages, all of us. If we win, as I believe we will, there will be stability and plenty and happiness for every individual." Holland could be assured that during the war, its mayor would contribute as much as he could to ensure victory.[16]

Alien registration and the draft

By late 1940 war preparation was a nationwide phenomenon. The first step was to require all aliens to register with local postmasters, on pain of a $1,000 fine and possible six- month jail term. Aliens in Holland registered with postmaster Louis J. Vanderburg. In four months, over 500 came forward, plus another 250 in Zeeland. Holland High School offered a citizenship course, called a "class in Americanism," for aliens who wanted to prove their patriotism. When the war began, all enemy aliens (Germans, Japanese, and Italians) had two months to re-register. Paul Fried and Paul Gottwald, Austrian students at Hope College since escaping Europe in 1939, assured Hollanders that America was still the land of freedom and opportunity, unlike Germany where elections were mostly rigged. After completing his sophomore year, Fried enlisted in the army and was assigned to intelligence work in the European theater. After the war, he interrupted his studies at Hope to be a translator for the American delegation at the Nuremberg war trials. He joined Hope's history faculty in 1953.[17]

In September 1940 the Roosevelt administration won congressional authorization to reinstate the selective service system. All male citizens between the ages of eighteen and forty-five had to register for the draft. National conscription began on October 16, 1940, and Holland had 1,879 registrants, including 94 Hope College students

---

Church pastorate, and then became a banker and editor of the *Leader*, a Christian weekly in the interest of Hope College (Hope College *Milestone*, 1930, 293).

16 *Holland City News*, 15 Jan., 25 June 1942, 22 Apr. 1943.

17 Ibid., 5 Sept., 31 Dec. 1940, 14 Nov. 1941; 12 Feb., 24 Sept., 15 Oct., 14 Nov. 1942; Eileen Nordstrom and George D. Zuidema, eds., *Hope at the Crossroads: The War Years* (Holland, MI, 2008), 195-99.

and as many high school seniors. The first two selectees, John Golds and Gerald Sligh, left for boot camp in late November 1940, after being guests of honor at the weekly Kiwanis Club meeting. They were the vanguard of several thousand to follow in the next four years. Holland did not draft married men until March 1943. Men age twenty-six to thirty-seven who became fathers before the bombing of Pearl Harbor in 1941 remained exempt until February 1944, after which time they made up most of the selectees. Only those employed in essential "war work" remained exempt.[18]

Before the draft, local National Guard enlistments were on the rise. New recruits received inoculations and vaccinations and a new set of clothes, before being sent for training in Wisconsin. On the morning of October 15, after just eight weeks of training, eighty men of Holland's Company D 126th Infantry mobilized for active duty at the Holland Armory, in preparation for shipping out to Camp Beauregard in Louisiana (chapter 22). For their send-off ten days later, members of the Willard G. Leenhouts Post paraded with the recruits, led by the Holland American Legion color guard and band, down Central Avenue and Eighth Street to the train depot. In a scene reminiscent of 1917, some five thousand people came to the depot to see the men off. Unlike 1917, this time they were only going off to prepare to fight, in case of war. All but two of the men left by train. Corporal George Zietlow and Pfc. William Sikkel (who would later become mayor of Holland) received permission to travel south in their private automobiles. Major Henry Geerds, Company D's commanding officer, joined his men after three months for training at Fort Benning, Georgia. For the next year, community "soldier send offs" were common, but inductees let it be known that they preferred low-key family farewells. The city fathers then decided to save community celebrations until the boys came home.[19]

In April 1942 members of Company D 126th Infantry were sent to Detroit to protect "Negroes" moving into the Sojourner Truth housing project, where rioting had occurred the previous winter. A month later, the president called Company D into active duty in the Pacific war theater, and by October the unit was fighting in the jungles

[18] *Holland City News*, 1, 15 Aug., 14, 28 Nov., 12 Dec. 1940, 2 July 1942, 14 Jan. 1943, 17 Feb., 16 Mar., 21 Dec. 1944.

[19] Ibid., 19, 26 Sept., 2, 17, 31 Oct. 1940, 27 Aug. 1942; Randall P. Vande Water, "Company D Answered Call," in *Holland: Happenings, Heroes & Hot Shots* 1:126-28; Vande Water, "Co. D 126th Infantry Leaves Holland," Holland Historical Trust *Review* 3, no. 3 (1990): 5-8; Vande Water, "Company D cheered on by excited crowd," *Holland Sentinel*, 23 Oct. 2012.

of New Guinea. The men of Company D saw 654 days of combat in World War II, and suffered casualties of 27 percent, with ten dead and eleven wounded. After the Korean War, Company D 126th Infantry again demonstrated their special role in civil defense. In a national drill in 1955, known as Operation Minutemen, at a given signal, Company D mobilized 94 percent of its total manpower, 114 out of 128 men. Within minutes, they ringed every vital area around Holland to which they had been assigned. Company D's aging veterans disbanded in 1995 after a long and illustrious history.[20]

Several women in Holland also volunteered for military service. In the first nine months of war, four stepped forward: Alyda De Wilde, Hazel Ver Hey, Berdina Klomparens, and Hazel Steggerda. All signed up for the Women's Auxiliary Air Corps, known colloquially as the WAACS. De Wilde and Ver Hey were graduates of Holland High School and Klomparens and Steggerda of Holland Christian High. Two already in the nursing corps were Lyda Mae Helder in the Pacific and Coral Bremer in Italy. Bremer and Ver Hey rose to the rank of major.[21]

For the most part, civilian Holland was on amicable terms with the local service draft board, but a controversial decision by the common council in October 1940 to allow the board to use a particular room at the city hall sent the relationship into a temporary tailspin. The room was the domain of the GAR (Grand Army of the Republic), an organization of war veterans, who were summarily evicted and left with no place to hold meetings. The GAR also accused the draft board of changing the locks on the doors, thus preventing any joint use. By August 1941, six alderman had called for the draft board to vacate the room. When the draft board gave up its universal claim on the room and proposed sharing the premises, GAR spokesman Benjamin Hamm refused on behalf of his organization. On August 23 the draft board vacated on its own initiative and moved into a room on the second floor of the Masonic Temple. The quarrel between the GAR and the draft board remained civil, but it lasted for months. The GAR's claim to its organizational rights and its challenge of a national wartime agency would have been deemed "un-patriotic" had it occurred in 1917.[22]

By October 1943 a staggering 9 percent of Holland's population, well above the national average, was in military service, according to the chairman of the local selective service board, Vaudie Vandenberg.

20 *Holland City News*, 30 Apr., 28 May, 27 Aug. 1942, 21 Apr. 1955; Vande Water, "Co. D," 5.

21 *Holland City News*, 24 Sept. 1942, 1 June, 20 July 1944.

22 Ibid., 24 Oct. 1940; 7, 21, 28 Aug. 1941.

Every aspect of life was affected, particularly in the high schools and colleges. Young men (and their sweethearts) put their lives on hold while awaiting Uncle Sam's "Greetings" letter. On Hope's campus most of the males, even some teachers, were gone. A weekly column, "Serving under the Stars and Stripes," informed the city of the exploits of its young warriors. Stories from around the globe presented Holland with a taste of the exotic. "Yes, the War has been brought close to Holland," said an advertisement of the chamber of commerce, "Arawe, Kiska, Cassino, and the other strange names of distant places hold a very real and direct interest to us."[23]

In November 1943 the city fathers in a ceremony at Centennial Park dedicated a plaque bearing the names of the 1,275 local men and women in the service. The weather was cold, blustery, and wet, but a crowd of 250 strong came to hear the main speaker, attorney Cornelius Vander Meulen, praise the patriotism of those in service, and pay tribute to the thankfulness and spirit of Holland. Vander Meulen's address is worth quoting at length.

> When the historian shall record the events of this tragic chapter of human history, it may well be that not one of these names upon our panel will appear upon the printed page. Yet you and I and the future generations of our citizens should never forget that it is these boys and millions like them from all over our country who have for us and our posterity perpetuated the blessings of liberty. . . .
>
> These men are our own flesh and blood, our sons, our brothers. Yesterday they were carefree youngsters vying in friendly competition in our playgrounds. Now around the globe in every land and on every sea, in tropic jungles and in the frozen reaches of the Arctic circle—on the ground and in the skies, on the surface of the ocean and beneath its water, they are the champions of freedom, ready to fight and ready to die in the grim battle to save our civilization.[24]

And many did die in grim battle. The casualty list for Holland grew quickly in the summer of 1944, following the invasion of Normandy. By December of that year, sixteen from the Holland area had been killed, eleven were missing, fifteen were prisoners, and at least sixty-eight had been wounded. The *Holland City News* printed a full

23 Ibid., 7 Oct., 9, 30 Dec. 1943.

24 Ibid., 11 Nov. 1943, 20 July 1944.

list of local casualties. By December 1945 the confirmed casualties for Holland totaled forty-two, out of some eighteen hundred in military service (2.3 percent). Another seventy-six soldiers from other parts of Ottawa County died.[25] There was little cause for softening the realities of war and little censorship in the reprinted letters from soldiers. Pfc. Grafbofski, in an article entitled, "Writes Letter on Jap Stationary," declared in dark humor: "This stationary came from Tinian. The Jap that had it won't be writing letters for quite a while." Corporal Bernard Voss of Holland sent home the wristwatch and a photograph of the German who shot him. "I guess I'm one of the few fellows who know[s] the identity of the enemy who shot them," he said. "But this German is done for–I killed him. . . . I plugged him up with a German Luger I'd picked up earlier. . . . It was either kill or be killed and I won."[26]

Everyone hankered for news during the war, and no one received enough. It came belatedly and was serious and scary. Few missed the reports of the national news anchors Edward R. Morrow and Gabriel Heater. Wives, sweethearts, and parents often went weeks without letters from loved ones, and when they came, they had words and sentences literally cut out by military censors. Some soldiers devised codes to get key information about location or battles past censors. Sylvia Stielstra of Holland received a letter from a family member in the fierce Battle of the Bulge with the single word "Psalm 91" and his signature. He was claiming God's promise of protection in verse 7: "A thousand may fall at your side, ten thousand at your right hand, but it will not come near you."[27]

Defense contracts

In early 1940, after all the European democracies had crumbled under Hitler's blitzkrieg, President Roosevelt faced the greatest foreign policy crisis since the birth of the nation. The United States and Great Britain stood alone against the mighty German armed forces, soon to be joined by Italy and Japan. In this extremity Roosevelt did an about face in his economic policy, from bashing big business to allying with corporate America. "Mr. New Deal," he told the press, must give way to "Dr. Win the War." He tapped his nemeses, General Motors head William Knudsen, to make America the "arsenal of democracy" (a phrase Knudsen coined), and the president gave Knudsen a free hand to

25 *Holland City News*, 13 Dec. 1945. The memorial plaque in Centennial Park lists 118 World War Two dead.

26 Ibid., 21 Sept., 12 Oct., 7 Dec. 1944, 13 Dec. 1945.

27 "The War Years," Holland Christian High School Centennial video.

enlist businesses large and small to convert their plants to make planes, tanks, ships, and munitions. The industrialists responded to the war production "czar," including those in Holland.[28]

In January 1941 the national defense commission asked chambers of commerce nationwide to survey manufacturing facilities regarding machinery adaptable for war production. The Holland chamber coordinated the local census. Secretary-manager Evert P. Stephan urged local industries to be proactive and inform government contractors of sub-contract work they could do. Soon factories were humming with new work. In the first three years of war, 1942-44, Holland's industries secured more than $39 million in war contracts—the lion's share in Ottawa County. The resulting rise in demand for workers in Holland meant that no one had idle hands. In 1940 alone local industries added 1,000 employees, and the total number of factory workers rose from 4,500 to 5,500. While women took up a fair share of the newly created war jobs, in-migrating laborers filled the other positions, which caused a severe housing shortage. In 1940 and 1941 the city had tremendous growth in the housing sector. New home applications totaled eighty-eight in 1940, up from sixty-five and forty-seven respectively, in the previous two years, and there were seventy-nine applications in 1942, totaling over $600,000 worth of labor and materials. This kind of growth had not been seen since the 1920s.[29]

Because Holland was deemed an essential wartime production city, it received a defense housing priority rating, meaning that the city would be eligible to receive building materials that otherwise would have been restricted to the war effort. Despite the access to building materials, the run up in prices deterred many, and new housing construction actually declined in 1942; six months into the year, only fourteen building permits had been filed. To attract and keep workers, a congressional rent-freeze took effect on December 1, 1942, for urban areas deemed essential to the war effort, such as the Muskegon-Grand Rapids-Holland region. Landlords could no longer raise rents and, indeed, they had to reduce rents raised in the previous eight months. Holland was a city of immigrants, not a city of in-migrants, and it was not ready to host transitory workers. In June 1942 the US Department of Commerce released a report on Holland's housing situation, which found that 64 percent of dwellings were owner occupied, a rate nearly twice the national average of 38 percent. A citywide housing survey in

28 Quotes from Arthur Herman, "The FDR Lesson Obama Should Follow," *Wall Street Journal*, 10 May 2012.

29 *Holland City News*, 31 Dec. 1940, 30 Jan., 6, 27 Feb. 1941, 1 Jan. 1942, 31 May 1945.

1945 found only three available apartments in the entire city and only twenty-two homeowners willing to rent rooms.[30]

One way to address the labor shortage was to recruit African American laborers. But Kenneth R. Kemp, manager of the Holland Precision Parts Corporation, saw this as a "last resort." The chamber of commerce also "frown[ed] upon importation of Negroes and [was] doing everything possible to assist in lining up local labor." Chairman of the war manpower commission in Detroit, Montague A. Clark, explained in a speech in Holland in May 1943 that Holland's growing industries would need one thousand additional workers within the year, but the city, he averred, could never meet that need. Clark proposed that women and the handicapped should fill in where needed.[31]

Women were recruited for specific jobs that were thought to be suitable for their gender. In an advertisement titled, "Mary gets a war job," the Michigan Bell Telephone Company in Holland appealed to young women to apply as telephone operators. The comic strip style advertisement pictured eighteen-year-old "Mary" being interviewed and learning about her new job. The last strip read, "Mary is proud of her work, proud of the War Bonds she buys out of her pay. She has found the place she wanted—an interesting job where her abilities will count for victory." Such targeted job advertising proved effective. In the summer of 1942, the civil defense team opened a "day nursery" for mothers employed in defense plants.[32]

The Fafnir Co., which manufactured ball bearings for military aircraft, was a local firm that employed many women. It was one of three local companies to earn an Army-Navy "E" pennant for production excellence. At the award ceremony in 1944, some nine hundred employees received special "E" pins. One recipient, Fanna (Mrs. Clarence Jr.) Doktor, a serviceman's wife and the first woman to work at Fafnir, declared: "I am happy to note . . . that many of the women who started with me are in this audience today. We have worked together for a long time and will continue to work, gladly and willingly, as long as our husbands and sons must be instruments of war. We hope this will not be long; yet, if we must, we will stay on our jobs as faithfully and as long as our soldiers must stay on theirs."[33]

Students were also encouraged to seek employment. Students at the junior high and high school did not quit school for work, but

30 Ibid., 2 Apr., 11, 25 June, 16 July, 8 Oct. 1942, 28 Jan. 1943, 6, 27 Sept. 1945.
31 Ibid., 29 Apr., 13 May 1943.
32 Ibid., 25 June 1942.
33 *Holland City News*, 4 Feb. 1943, 27 Apr. 1944, 31 May 1945.

Hart & Cooley's Holland division of Fafnir Bearing won the coveted "E Award" for exemplary production in 1944. Holding the banner is general manager Harold S. Covell (*left*) and war veteran and employee John Flieman Jr. (*right*) (*Joint Archives of Holland*)

an estimated two hundred of the six hundred held part-time jobs in the summer of 1943. In the fall of 1943, the public schools opened a week later than normal to give students an extra workweek during the agricultural harvest and for the high season at the Heinz pickle factory.[34]

One of the primary wartime employers in Holland, and an employer of women and students, was the Holland-Racine Shoe Co., which received its first defense order for 50,000 pairs of shoes in December 1940. To meet the new demand, and to process the order within the stipulated 150 days, the company ordered special production machinery. By July 1941 the company had filled four defense contracts, each one for between 40,000 and 88,000 pairs of shoes. Although the military production for the first four contracts was carried out exclusively at the company's Racine, Wisconsin plant, all the civilian production was shifted to Holland, and the plant ran at peak capacity. For the fifth contract, which came in January 1942 and required 131,200 pairs, the Holland plant dedicated half of its production to fulfilling it. Employment at the Holland plant was 318 at the beginning of the war, but the company had already been growing for two years. At the peak, Holland-Racine employed 375. In August 1944 the company appealed

[34] Ibid., 17 June, 15 July, 26 Aug. 1943.

for even more workers to fill an order for 60,000 pairs to go directly to the front lines. They were packaged in watertight cases for air drops on the beaches, if necessary. By the end of the war, Holland-Racine Shoe tallied over 1,750,000 pairs of shoes, including more than 150,000 pairs of combat boots.[35]

The employment rolls at local machine works, furniture factories, and shipbuilding industries continued to be filled primarily by adult males. Seeking to take advantage of their skill and experience in the furniture industry, seventeen furniture companies, mostly in Holland and Zeeland, but also at least one each in Lowell, Hastings, Charlotte, and Grand Ledge, united under the title of Holland Industries Inc., to lobby for war contracts as one body. The partners then had to decide how best to divide the contract between them. Holland's Baker Furniture made ribs for gliders, and the Charles R. Sligh Company manufactured desks for the army. In 1943 a military contract of $250,000 and another of $500,000 allowed local furniture industries to manufacture beds, chests, mirrors, occasional chairs, and dinette chairs and tables. Local lumber companies also made pallets for the government, while the Dutch Novelty Shop produced boxes.[36]

Manufactured goods from the heavy industrial plants and shipbuilding industries were more likely to find their way into a combat zone. Holland Furnace shifted to military production in 1942, first making parts for anti-aircraft guns, then armor plating for tanks, which, when finished, was sent to plants in Detroit for welding assembly. In 1943 the company won several contracts for building heavy anchor chains for the navy. The contracts, which stretched over three years, totaled $5 million and required the company to hire several hundred workers. Military representatives were satisfied with the product. Just a month after the first anchor chain contract, the company signed a second contract for $4 million. This required running three shifts round the clock and expanding the northside plant. Employment peaked at 950, which was almost double the pre-war levels. In all, Holland Furnace shipped out twenty-five million tons of tank armor and thirty million tons of anchor chain.[37]

Chris-Craft Corporation also switched in 1942 from producing pleasure craft to military service ships. Employment at Chris-Craft in

35 Ibid., 19 Dec. 1940, 24 Apr., 2 July 1941, 22 Jan. 1942, 4 Feb. 1943, 31 May 1945.

36 Ibid., 1 Oct 1942, 18 Mar., 16 Dec. 1943, 31 May 1945.

37 *Holland City News*, 2 Apr. 1942, 27 May 1943.

Chris-Craft's 8,000th Navy landing craft, ready for shipment to Algonac for final water testing before shipping to the Marines in 1944 (photo Gerald Vande Vusse Sr.) (*courtesy Robert "Bob" Vande Vusse*)

Holland rose from pre-war figures of 350 to a peak of 690, and in June 1942, the company won a Navy "E" award. By war's end, the local plant had manufactured for the Pacific theater nearly one half of the ten thousand thirty-six-foot landing craft, known as LSTs and LCTs, made at its plants in Algonac, Cadillac, and Holland. All three plants were awarded the Navy E-award. Campbell Boat and Romer Boat also made landing craft, while Beacon Boat built minesweepers.

Jesiek Brothers, which specialized in large gasoline launches and cruisers, was the second major shipbuilder for the navy. The Jesiek family, Adolph, Joseph, Harold, and Donald, built navy submarine chasers under defense contract with the Chicago-based Victory Shipbuilding Company. With a workforce of 130 employees, many with no experience in shipbuilding, the Jesieks set about to construct the 110-foot, wooden-hulled chasers used for coastal patrol along the Atlantic shore. Some thirty-eight armed coastguardsmen protected the plant day and night from sabotage. The christening ceremony for the first historic launching in November 1942, marked by the traditional smashing of a bottle of champagne over the bow, brought out 1,200 curious onlookers, who were serenaded with a medley of sea songs by the Holland American Legion Band. It had taken one hundred men one hundred days to complete the craft. To train new boat builders, Holland Junior High School established a vocational program that bussed student workers to the dockyards. A second sub-chaser was

Beacon Boat Co. minesweeper ready for launch in Lake Macatawa
(*Joint Archives of Holland*)

launched with much less fanfare in the dead of winter in January 1943; the thick ice on the lake had to be dynamited to get the vessel into the water. These were the first (and last) major naval vessels ever built in Holland. Thereafter, Jesiek built harbor tugs for the navy. Roamer Boat also made tug boats.[38]

After the war, the second generation of Jesieks, Otto's sons Harold, Donald, and William "Bill", took over the shipyard and converted it to servicing pleasure craft and selling gasoline and fishing bait. Jesiek Brothers Shipyard was also a Chris-Craft dealer and repaired runabouts and ran a livery service. Kid-brother Bill "lived and breathed for sailing" and was Commodore of the Macatawa Bay Yacht Club in 1977 (chapter 28).[39]

Low unemployment rates and the influx of government money into the private sector did not eliminate labor issues. Western Machine Tool Works, with its commendable production record of drills, tappers, shapers, and lathes, won the Army-Navy "E" award an unprecedented three times between 1942 and 1944. Throughout this period, however,

[38] Ibid., 2, 23 Apr., 14, 28 May, 11 June, 19 Nov., 3 Dec. 1942, 8 Apr., 24 June 1943, 31 May 1945; *Holland Sentinel*, 29 Nov. 1941; *Holland City News*, 19 Nov. 1942, 21 Jan. 1943; Vande Water, "Jesiek's Builds Submarine Chasers," in *Holland Happenings* 4:123-26; Chris Hamlin, "Holland's Contribution to World War II," Hope College student paper, April 1986, Joint Archives of Holland (JAH).

[39] George Elliott, "From Minnows to Marina," *Motor News* (1954): 24-26; William Jesiek obit., *Holland Sentinel*, 14 Aug. 2012; Geoffrey Reynolds, "Jesiek Brothers Shipyard: From Minnows to Marina," *Joint Archives Quarterly* 22, no. 2 (Summer 2012).

Submarine chaser built at Jesiek Bros. shipyard during the Second World War (*Joint Archives of Holland*)

the company's relations with its workers were shaky. On January 20, 1942, 130 employees walked out of the plant, but two days later voted to return, following a request by the Federal War Labor Board (WLB). The board was instrumental in facilitating the negotiations that followed the strike. Within a week, a compromise was reached, and the workers received a pay increase of 12.5 percent. The new contract also guaranteed a minimum wage of 55¢ per hour for new hires; a differential pay scale between first, second, and third shift workers; and two weeks paid vacation for employees with five years' seniority, and one week for the rest. Again, on May 9, 1945, some eighty-five workers went on strike because they were upset about job reclassifications that required more work for the same pay. In 1944 Chris-Craft AFL members, led by Ralph Doktor, also went on strike, frustrated that the WLB had not acted fast enough on an appeal of a wage increase that the union deemed inadequate. The next year, the Chris-Craft local walked out again, this time in sympathy with fellow unionists at the firm's Cadillac plant. The strike lasted for six weeks. Air force officers came in to settle strikes at Precision Parts to keep production on schedule.[40]

There was a legitimate threat that consumers could fall victim to wartime price gouging, but government price ceilings could inflict damage on the producers as well. When Leon Henderson, director of the Office of Price Administration (OPA), in mid-1941 asked the automobile and furniture industries voluntarily to hold down prices,

[40] *Holland City News*, 29 Jan. 1942, 24 June 1943, 27 Apr., 3 Aug. 1944, 10 May, 30 Aug., 4 Oct. 1945.

Charles R. Sligh Jr., president of the Grand Rapids Furniture Exposition, responded: "Of course, we want to cooperate, but it is foolish to ask the industry as a whole not to raise prices when materials costs, labor costs, and taxes all are rising." Sligh had a point; business had to operate under the competitive rules of business. The implied threat was that the government would impose price controls, if industries did not discipline themselves. One local furniture company, after receiving the request to hold the line, raised prices 5 percent anyway. Most companies chose to comply. Local milk dealers encountered a similar situation. Feeling the squeeze from rising wartime costs, dealers tried to raise the price of milk, but first they had to get permission from the OPA. Once they raised the price from 11¢ to 12¢ per quart without prior permission, and the OPA ordered a price rollback and required dealers to issue refunds to consumers. By May 1943 the OPA controlled all restaurant menus and entrée prices. Every proprietor had to file a copy of the complete menu or price list with John Good's war price and rationing board, and woe to the one caught overcharging. The board actually sent out "checkers."[41]

Holland's factories bustled during the war, their whistles signaling the beginning and end of the workday, as well as the success of the industry. Factories involved in the war effort were making small fortunes. H. L. Friedlen & Co., with Louis Horwich as president and Herman L. Friedlen (Friedlund) as secretary-treasurer, made mackinaw and field jackets, more than half a million in total; Holland Precision Parts produced a half-million motor bearings; Holland Hitch made millions of pintle hooks for military jeeps and in 1942 gave out $20,000 in Christmas bonuses. Hart & Cooley switched from making heaters and cooling units to mortar shells, and its employment jumped from five- to seven hundred. Donnelly-Kelly Glass made optical gun sights. After a Holland lab discovered how to make dextrose from wheat, the Doughnut Corp. of America moved into the Lake Shore Sugar Co. plant and began preparing ingredients for military mixes. Doughnut Corp.'s employment rose from 20 to 250 at its peak. Parke-Davis contributed synthetic materials and chemicals, and Holland Color and Chemical made printing inks and zinc chromate, the latter used to repair airplane fuselages.[42]

Workers had their say in late 1942 when sixty businesses bought a full-page of the local newspaper for the "Soldiers of Production" to

41 Ibid., 2 July 1941, 25 Nov. 1942, 22 Apr. 1943.

42 Ibid., 24 Dec. 1942, 25 Mar. 1943, 31 May 1945; Hamlin, "Holland's Contribution."

declare in bold headlines: "Come On, Let's Show Adolf Where He Made His Biggest Mistake." Seven paragraphs of bombastic rhetoric followed:

> Maybe you didn't know it, Adolf, but you led with your chin when you and your sneaking pals started swinging at Uncle Sam. You see, Adolf, this is a war of production. Behind our boys in the armed forces is another army, 50 million strong . . . and I mean *strong*. We call them soldiers of production. . . . We're building planes and tanks and ships to smash you once and for all—and we're paying for them too—10% of our pay every pay day. . . . Yes, the American worker is doing his part. You kind of forgot us, Adolf, and whether you know it or not, sooner or later you'll agree *that was your biggest mistake*.[43]

Holland industries were successful during the war, but when the war ended, the local economy had a serious problem to deal with. Employment had peaked during the war at ten thousand, with barely two hundred filing unemployment claims.[44] The war's end brought massive layoffs, especially for women, as military contracts dried up. Where would the many hundreds of veterans coming home find employment?

Protecting the city

As soon as the news of the Pearl Harbor bombing reached Holland, local factories engaged in defense work asked for overnight police protection. Home Guards soon took over the duty, and later also watched the municipal power plant. Homeland defense during the war focused on prevention of enemy espionage and sabotage and preparedness for air raids. "America's greatest danger is not from without, but from within through the penetration of the fifth column," newsman Ranger told the Americanism forum at the armory.[45]

Even before the United States joined the war, Holland was increasing its security forces. Captain Henry Rowan, a member of the National Guard Armory advisory board, helped organize a local Home Guard unit in Holland. The unit's main purpose was to fill any security void created when Holland's National Guard troops were called away from the city. To qualify for the guard, one had to be an American citizen, eighteen to forty-five years of age, and unlikely to be drafted by the military. It was an assumed pre-requisite that applicants were

43 *Holland City News*, 29 Oct. 1942.
44 Ibid., 6 Apr. 1950.
45 *Holland City News*, 3 Apr., 11 Dec. 1941, 15 Jan. 1942.

Home Guards force protecting Fafnir Bearing Co. from theft, sabotage, and work stoppages (*Joint Archives of Holland*)

men. When a call went out for volunteers (they were unpaid positions, after all) in January 1941, fifty men responded, signed on for one year of service, and began to drill. In April the unit had forty-six men, but was looking to expand to fifty-seven. To meet the demand, the unit raised its maximum age requirement from forty-five to fifty years of age. Forty-one of the forty-six initial members were convinced to sign on for two additional years, in anticipation of being issued the forest-green uniforms, black pants, and government rifles and revolvers. When the war began, the guard sought an additional ten members, because it was stretched to provide security at all the local industrial and utility plants.[46]

Michigan industries were the backbone of the war effort; fully 30 percent of the nation's war effort was concentrated in the state. Strange as it might seem now, civil defense officials in Lansing feared the possibility of German bombing raids. In January 1942 Mayor Geerlings formed an auxiliary firefighting force, with a proposed corps of 425 men, in case of an attack. The mayor also appointed some thirty volunteers from the VFW (Veterans of Foreign Wars) as air raid wardens under commander Bert Andrus. As part of the Holland civil defense team, they received training in first aid, fire and police protection, handling bombs, and evacuation of civilians. Air raid drills were a regular part of daily life at work and school.[47]

46 Ibid., 31 Dec. 1940, 19 Jan., 24 Apr. 1941.

47 Ibid., 29 Jan., 26 Mar., 9, 23 Apr. 1942.

Civilian defense was not an organization limited to policemen and firefighters, but a war preparation movement in which everyone could contribute. In Holland, five thousand citizens enrolled in civilian defense. This number included eighty-five nurses (thirty-nine of whom were student nurses), who were busy leading the popular courses in first aid; approximately nine hundred school children, capable of driving trucks for farm help; all teachers, clerks, and janitors of the public school system; and nearly "one hundred percent" of the members of social organizations and churches. Mayor Geerlings thanked the citizens for their support of the nation, and stressed the patriotic duty of defense. "Today, we are engaged in another war. We did not choose this conflict. We were forced into it. It is a world war in the fullest sense. Our men have left their homes and friends to engage in a fierce battle. But they already have given a good account of themselves. . . . We all have a duty to perform. . . . Much remains to be done, it is true, but we already have done a great deal. The forces already trained can give a good account of themselves, even if a bomb dropped tonight."[48]

The only enemy action anywhere close to Holland occurred in the summer of 1944, when two German prisoners of war escaped from the Allegan prison camp, W. K. Kellogg Pine Point Camp. Heinz Stange was found three miles east of Holland on M-21 (Chicago Drive) at the Fish & Game Club camp. Arthur Lampen, assistant to Zeeland Police Chief Fred Bosma, readily identified the nineteen-year-old deserter who was "wearing a German uniform with swastikas." According to the newspaper report, Bosma "went to the conservation park on the tip of an unidentified tourist who reported a suspicious character in the bushes. At that time, Zeeland officers had not been notified of the escape." The scared German POW, it turned out, was harmless. The same was true of a prisoner named Kunz, who beset with homesickness for his wife and young son in Germany, walked away from camp on a Sunday afternoon and stopped at a nearby a farmhouse to ask for food in barely understandable English. They notified the Allegan County sheriff, who "captured" him and held him in jail for transfer to Fort Custer.[49]

At the time, the former Civilian Conservation Corps (CCC) camp, which was opened in May 1944, housed 250 German prisoners, who the federal government sent there to assist local farmers during the 1944

48 *Holland City News*, 29 Jan., 9 Apr. 1942.

49 Steve Ralph, "Former POW camp site will get informational sign," *Holland Sentinel*, 29 Aug. 2007; Vande Water, "German POWs Worked at Heinz," in *Holland: Happenings, Heroes & Hot Shots*, 3:108-12.

harvest. Several dozen, clad in blue uniforms with the initials "PW" stenciled on the back, were trucked under guard to the H. J. Heinz Pickle Works in Holland to process pickles during the "green season" six days a week. They made an indelible impression on everyone in the plant. When the prisoners hinted to fellow workers that a Heinz rotating onion peeler would ease the drudgery of peeling potatoes by hand, the employees informed company officials, who graciously donated a peeling machine to the camp and eased the duty of the kitchen police (KP).[50]

In late 1941 and early 1942, as America geared up for war, Holland began running through its security checklist to make sure its vital utilities were protected against any secret attack. Holland's new power plant was considered the likeliest enemy target. To be certain that the city could operate in case of an emergency, the old power plant on Fifth Street was tested in June 1941. The new power plant was shut down completely, and the old five-thousand-kilowatt plant was fired up; it could serve in a pinch. To protect the city's maritime interests, Captain Charles Bontekoe, chief of Holland's Coast Guard, issued regulations governing shippers and skippers. All yacht owners, officers, crews, and longshoremen had to file applications with Bontekoe and carry identification cards with photos issued by the government. In 1943 even fishermen had to register with the Coast Guard to fish off the piers at Big Red. Local doctors also organized for the war, designating emergency casualty centers at Holland Hospital, Warm Friend Tavern, the high school gymnasium, Washington and Lincoln Schools, and the armory.[51]

To protect the city and its inhabitants from possible German air raids, Mayor Geerlings established the position of chief air raid warden, with headquarters at the police station. He appointed Bert Andrus as the first officer. In March 1942 Geerlings and a city delegation attended an "industrial protection institute" in Detroit to learn about air raids. Then in August and October, Holland tested its air raid system. From ten o'clock until ten thirty on Wednesday evening, August 13, county administrators orchestrated a complete, countywide blackout test. When residents heard the Mockingbird whistle at the power plant sound off for three minutes, they shut off all lights or blackened their windows. No cars were allowed to enter or leave the city. "There is no doubt about it—it certainly was 'black,'" reported the newspaper about the practice "alert," and there were very few violations.[52]

50 *Holland City News*, 13 May, 6 July, 31 Aug. 1944.
51 Ibid., 1, 15 Jan., 5 Feb. 1942; 29 Apr., 18 May 1943.
52 Ibid., 26 Mar., 13 Aug. 1942.

In October 1942 there was a surprise, daylight alert to test business preparedness. To measure the reaction time of the fire department, fake reports of "bombs," "accidents," and "fires," were intentionally called in. A few weeks later, civil defense ran a daylight mock alert that required all cars to stop and all pedestrians to keep off the streets. A second blackout test followed in December and a third the next June. So sophisticated did the state civil defense office become, that in 1943, it developed three distinct warning signals, much like current tornado warnings–steady signal (raid is probable), undulating (raid is imminent), and intermittent (all-clear). The Boy Scouts were also enlisted in civil defense; they engaged in mock war games at Ottawa Beach to repel an enemy invasion of Holland. Even schoolboys did their part by making models of German and Japanese airplanes to help "spotters" identify them in the air.[53]

Hope College also had a role in the war effort. In late 1941 President Wynand Wichers returned to campus brimming with ideas gathered at a meeting of the American Association of Universities and Colleges. Wichers instituted no major changes in the college's curriculum in the spring of 1942, but he spoke of coming sacrifices that the students would have to make. The first sacrifice was to see most of the males go off to war as their numbers came up, except for pre-seminary and pre-engineering majors who were exempt and those who had failed their physicals. The exodus put an end to intercollegiate athletics and fraternities for the duration. Wichers found support for the college from the chamber of commerce, which gave $1,000 for the cause, while Park Township voted to pay for security costs. In March 1942 the college organized the Student Defense Council, a body of fraternity men to take training as firemen, policemen, and air raid wardens.[54]

The idea of a flying school and a civil air patrol found a warm reception, and over one hundred men turned out at a meeting to recruit pilots. In June 1942 Hope opened its training school for pilots. For the off-campus program, the college leased a building near the airport to use as barracks. The federal government paid the costs of the eight-week, summer course for thirty-nine trainees. One was a woman, Marguerite (Peggy) Hadden, whose father was a fighter ace in the First World War,

53 *Holland City News*, 1, 8 Oct., 24 Dec. 1942, 29 Apr., 10 June 1943, 22 June 1944; World War II scrapbook with clippings about school-related war activities, Holland Museum Archives (HMA).

54 *Holland City News*, 24 Dec. 1941, 8, 29 Jan., 18 June, 9, 23 July, 27 Aug., 24 Sept. 1942; Nordstrom and Zuidema, *Hope at the Crossroads*; 33.

Army Specialized Training Program soldiers on Hope College campus, 1943-44 (*Joint Archives of Holland*)

and whose brother was flying in the Navy Air Corps. By late September, ten trainees had logged 240 class hours and thirty-five flight hours each, and had left for New Mexico to join the military's active-duty gliders. For the school year of 1943-44, Hope College also hosted 268 soldiers from thirty-six states, many in the South, as the college participated in the Army Specialized Training Program, which was designed to ensure a steady supply of college-trained men. The military programs helped to offset the nearly 50 percent drop in college enrollments, from 555 in 1941 to 288 in 1943. Coeds were especially thrilled to see more young men on campus. They outnumbered men by four to one. At least three Hope women met their future mates among the soldiers, but the college did not allow any to marry before graduation. Following the war, so many married veterans wanted to enroll that the college had to change the rule barring married students.[55]

The military environment was contagious and affected student life at the college. "It was exciting; the uniforms, the passionate goodbyes, the promises to wait for our heroes' return," recalled Pinks Mulder Dudley. "But it was also scary. We saw the newsreels. We knew that

[55] *Holland City News*, 18 Mar., 23 Sept. 1943, 9 Mar., 30 Nov. 1944; Wynand Wichers, *A Century of Hope, 1866-1966* (Grand Rapids: Eerdmans, 1968), 219-25; Nordstrom and Zuidema, *Hope at the Crossroads*, 37, 45-49, 51, 53-54, 69-70, 171.

Army Specialized Training Program soldiers entertain Hope College coeds, 1943-44 (*Joint Archives of Holland*)

some of those we hugged goodbye would be wounded, and some would not be coming back at all." Beginning in the fall of 1942, Hope's male students were required to have three hours a week of "war conditioning" run by athletic trainer John (Jack) Schouten, coach Milton "Bud" Hinga's assistant. The gymnastics included "body building exercises such as calisthenics, broad jumping, wall scaling, football, basketball, military drill, and baseball throw, the latter in preparation for hand grenade throwing." In an interview with the *Holland City News*, Schouten declared that "discipline in [the] program will be strict, but the youths at the college are enthusiastic about the rigid schedule." The newspaper gave no student response to Schouten's statement. Nor did the paper note the disappointment on campus when the Michigan Intercollegiate Athletic Association (MIAA) cancelled the 1943 football season and the 1943-44 basketball season. The member schools all suffered a serious shortage of athletes, and in Hope's case the army needed to use Carnegie Gymnasium, Hope's practice facility, and the armory, its home court.[56]

Rationing and conservation

Civil defense was a serious issue, but war raids and sabotage, of course, never came to Holland. But when rationing and conservation

56 Nordstrom and Zuidema, *Hope at the Crossroads*, 65, 106-7; *Holland City News*, 29 Oct. 1942, 4 Nov. 1943.

measures did come—and with a vengeance—they changed one's whole life. Although sacrifice cleaned out the cupboards, one could argue that it also cleansed the soul. Rationing was a duty, and the common council passed laws to prevent abuse. Conservation, on the other hand, was voluntary. All of the sacrifices, however, built a sense of community. The operating principle in Congress was that defense needs took priority over non-defense needs. The first commodities the OPA rationed in 1941 were steel and iron. Local manufacturers with large military contracts had no problem, but those producing civilian goods were hurting for the duration. At Holland Hitch and Buss Machine, for example, 85 and 90 percent, respectively, of the work was defense projects and they got all the raw materials they needed. Holland Furnace and Hart & Cooley, however, expected shortages until they too could land defense contracts. Manufacturers sought the coveted designation for Holland of being declared a "defense area" by the Office of Production Mobilization (OPM), which would guarantee priority on defense materials.[57]

The conservation efforts that began in the summer of 1941 focused on collecting materials that would most likely be reserved for military purposes, including iron, tin, steel, aluminum, waste paper, and rubber. To coordinate scrap collection, the common council created a "Salvage for Victory" committee headed by L. Phillip Van Hartesveldt. Every Friday was curbside scrap pickup day, and city trucks fanned out across town to collect the precious cargo, which they dumped at the old tannery lot at Eighth Street and Pine Avenue (later site of the Civic Center). Tin can drives in 1941 and 1942 collected an estimated 90 percent of the available scrap, although by 1944 only half that percentage was collected. Yet Holland's 45 percent surpassed the national average by five points. Housewives did their part by scrounging in their cupboards and closets for aluminum kitchen utensils. The Aluminum Defense Drive netted 3,095 pounds, all piled at Riverview Park, where Boy Scouts removed the iron, steel, and wooden handles. High school girls collected old silk and nylon hosiery; one drive in 1943 yielded two hundred pounds. In early 1942 tire dealers and wholesalers contributed forty tons of old tires and inner tubes, which helped place Ottawa County second in the state in a rubber drive. Companies that manufactured food products had to be creative in finding substitutes for their usual containers, which were seldom as good and upset customers. When tin rationing began in March 1942 and grocery stores

57 *Holland City News*, 14 Aug., 4, 11 Dec. 1941.

Russell Boeve of Boeve Oil Co. collected scrap tires and inner tubes "to lick the Japs" (*courtesy Larry B. Massie*)

stocked ketchup in glass containers, the H. J. Heinz Company told irate consumers to "Blame Hitler, Hirohito, and Benito!"[58]

As the war continued, and much of the ready scrap was donated, the collection agencies had to find innovative measures to ferret out new sources to meet their quotas. Farms were an especially rich place to find old metal lying around, and many appeals were targeted at farmers. The city fathers decided to donate some relics in Centennial Park, namely, two Civil War cannons weighing 2,575 pounds each and thirty cannon balls at eighty pounds each, which added another 2,400 pounds. Gerrit Diekema had acquired the ordinance from the government when he served in Congress. Not to be outdone, the armory added to the scrap pile a collection of German weapons that it had received as a gift from the federal government after the Great War. City workers dug up 6,000 pounds of old Interurban tracks at Fourteenth Street and Harrison Avenue for a scrap drive. The city also collected old license plates in 1942 and asked for used wrapping paper after Christmas in 1943. Nothing was too insignificant to go to waste.[59]

In 1942 the federal government urged states and municipalities to push clocks ahead one hour all year long to save on electricity. Holland and Grand Rapids adopted what was dubbed "war time," and all the schools and businesses complied. The Ottawa County Farmers Union protested the "irregular" hours and fired off a resolution to their

58 Ibid., 24, 31 July, 7, 14 Aug., 27 Nov. 1941, 26 Feb., 23 Apr., 18 June, 9, 16 July, 4 Aug., 22 Oct. 1942, 9 Dec. 1943, 7 Sept. 1944; Vande Water, "Scrap Drives, Home Front Response," in *Holland Happenings,* 3:104-7.

59 *Holland City News,* 3 Sept., 22 Oct. 1942.

Holland High School students collect scrap metal. The truck driver is unidentified. (*Joint Archives of Holland*)

state representatives and the governor to repeal the measure. Zeeland initially refused to adopt war time, but eventually the common council agreed to follow the lead of the neighboring cities.[60]

After the United States entered the war, the Red Cross set a $50 million goal to fund services to the troops and aid civilian victims. The Ottawa County Red Cross chapter, headed by Mrs. John F. Telling, pledged to do "its utmost" to raise its quota of $15,000 for war relief. Red Cross volunteers and relief nurses also helped out at Holland Hospital, where the nursing staff of twenty four was reduced to eleven, less than half.[61]

Another major financial sacrifice was the decision of the city fathers in June 1942 to suspend Tulip Time for the duration of war (chapter 28). The 1941 festival had been a smashing success with its bevy of Hollywood movie stars brought in by Holland Furnace Company. The 1942 May festival ostensibly was needed to "boost morale," but attendance was barely half that of previous years. It was the last until 1946. People were not "festival minded," given the gravity of the war and the shortage of gasoline. Sacrifice took precedence, and all efforts went toward fighting the war on the home front. Even Fourth of July celebrations were muted by a ban on fireworks, which made for a quiet day. When Tulip Time 1943 came around, the chamber of commerce responded by letter to queries from potential visitors: "When the clouds of war have lifted, we intend to resume our festival and you, with us, will then have more reason than ever for rejoicing amidst the beauties of nature's grandest flower of spring—the tulip." Locally, however, the

60 Ibid., 5, 12 Feb. 1942.

61 Ibid., 11 Dec. 1941, Hamlin, "Holland's Contribution."

city still maintained the tulip lanes, and homeowners displayed tulips in their gardens and lawns, which made them eligible for $625 in prize money—paid in war stamps—for the best flower displays. In 1943 two men were arrested on charges of disorderly conduct and fined $14 each for mowing down a stretch of tulips with an open car door as they drove along.[62]

The collection campaigns and conservation efforts owed their success to community action and to participation of women and young people. Housewives, for example, were responsible for washing cans, removing the ends, flattening them, and then placing them in containers for pick-up. They also saved cooking grease for its glycerin, used in soap and bullets. Holland Rendering Works contributed 50,000 pounds of grease. The Boy Scouts and Camp Fire Girls were particularly active in door-to-door materials solicitation. The girls collected ninety pounds of grease in one summer month. Dozens of youngsters pitched in on the first day of the aluminum drive in 1941. Of the 3,200 pounds of aluminum collected, they carried the bulk of it by themselves to a large wire cage set up in Centennial Park directly across from the city hall. In 1943 one rail shipment of tin cans totaled 38,000 pounds, or an estimated 175,000 cans. The Boy Scouts collected over 38,000 pounds of waste paper in 1943, and forty-two tons more during the first half of 1945. The War Board at the same time had penalized the *Holland Sentinel* for using too much paper (perhaps a partial source of the Boy Scouts' success?). Nevertheless, the troop that collected the most paper was treated to a pancake supper. Elementary schools volunteered as general collection stations, and young students were often seen carrying scrap to school in their little red wagons. Schools competed to collect the most tins cans or the most paper. Indeed, competition was a consistent theme of conservation, as it was in the liberty bond campaigns. Women volunteers also rolled bandages for the troops.[63]

Victory Gardens again made their appearance. Henry P. Zwemer, owner of the later Country Club property, in a patriotic gesture offered twenty large plots for gardens. Children were also involved in planting gardens; over three hundred signed up in the summer of 1942. Naturally, gardening turned into a contest, the "Victory Garden Contest." Winners in 1942 included the Mokma brothers—Alvin (fourteen), Irvin

62 *Holland City News*, 18 Dec. 1941, 5 Feb., 11 June 1942, 18 Mar., 29 Apr., 27 May 1943; Vande Water, "'41 Tulip Time Hosted Hollywood Stars," in *Holland Happenings*, 2:91-95.

63 *Holland City News*, 24, 31 July, 27 Nov. 1941, 22 Jan., 2, 9 Apr. 1942, 11, 18 Mar., 3 May, 2 Sept., 24 Nov. 1943, 9 Apr. 1945; *Holland Sentinel*, 17 Jan. 1943; Hamlin, "Holland's Contribution."

(thirteen), and Paul (eleven)—who together cultivated two large city lots. On the minus side, youngsters under sixteen years of age faced a curfew for the first time since the late 1920s. It was deemed a "safety measure." The Mockingbird whistled at 8:55 p.m. to warn them that they had five minutes to leave the streets and public places for home. Teenager Ron Boeve recalled: "When that whistle blew, we left the tennis courts, got on our bikes, and got home by 9 o'clock."[64]

During the "Jalopy Roundup Campaign," conservationists tried to convince owners of run-down "junkers" to donate their old cars to the scrap collection. To speed the process and identify possible contributors to the campaign, the *Holland City News* printed in consecutive weeks of November and December 1942 a "Junk Car Report" that could be cut out and filled in.[65] Participants had to fill in lines following these statements:

(1) There is an automobile which I believe should be scrapped at ___________.
(2) Owner, if known, is ___________.
(3) His address is ___________.
(4) Signed ___________.
(5) Address ___________.

While conservation was a voluntary measure, rationing was compulsory, in order to conserve food, fuel, and rubber. Late in the war, even electricity was rationed to save on coal, at least for retail merchants who were not allowed any lighted displays or signage. In May 1942 the OPA froze the price of staples, starting with sugar and coffee, and then meat, butter, cheese, and many other everyday foods, but not bread. The coffee limit was one pound per week per adult, and restaurants refills were on the tab. One rural resident, desperate for coffee, asked the ration board for extra coffee stamps to treat his horse with colic. Secretary John Good denied the request but said he would ask a veterinarian about the veracity of the treatment. Housewives had only so many coupon points per month for rationed foods and had to spend them carefully. A pound of butter or cheese required eight points; sirloin steak was six points, a jar of peaches twenty-four points, and a can of green beans fourteen points.[66]

The threat of a sugar shortage was perhaps not as severe as in the First World War, but the restrictions continued until the end of the war.

64 *Holland City News*, 9 Apr., 14 May, 13 Aug., 8, 22 Oct., 5 Nov. 1942; Ron and Sonja Boeve interview, by the author and Dave Boeve, 9 Oct. 2009, typescript, 4, (JAH).

65 Ibid., 25 Nov., 3 Dec. 1942.

66 Ibid., 26 Feb., 4, 11 June, 30 July, 6 Aug. 1942; Hamlin, "Holland's Contribution."

Registration for sugar ration cards took place at local schools, where schoolteachers gave their free time to take charge of the registration procedures. Places like restaurants, bakeries, dormitories, and hospitals had to register separately from individual consumers. In June 1942 there was a special registration for those who wanted sugar for canning and making preserves. For this, each person was allowed only one pound per year. Over three thousand families applied under the "sugar for canning" program. In August the rationing board began to allow registration through the mail, which process they hoped would alleviate the pressure of long lines at the school registration sites. But when the 1943 allotment came around, local residents again swarmed the canning registration centers in the local elementary schools. Rumors of a shortage had panicked everyone.[67]

Leo Peters of Grand Rapids, a son of Abraham Peters, a leading Holland businessman and Christian Reformed Church elder, made a fortune inventing a way to color oleo (margarine) yellow to make it look like butter. His simple invention was a bag in which housewives could squeeze and mash oleo sticks, which had the appearance of gray paste, with a coloring powder until the ingredients were evenly mixed. Most Americans had to make do with margarine, since butter was scarce and expensive.

Nylon and silk hosiery were especially scarce, because the military needed nylon yarn for parachutes. Women mobbed stores on hearing rumors that nylons were in stock; these were the most sought-after clothing item of all. Norma and Elizabeth Baarman developed quite a little business repairing tears in nylons for local women. Andrew Steketee chaired a local committee to salvage women's discarded silk and nylon hosiery. He contacted women's clothing and dry goods stores to collect old hosiery, and he recruited school children to raid their mother's dresser drawers for torn items. Not until late 1947 did women find nylons readily available in the stores.[68]

Rubber tires and gasoline were more serious concerns, especially rubber that became scarce after Japan seized the plantations in the Dutch East Indies that supplied 90 percent of America's raw rubber. In January 1942 the government announced its Idle Tire Purchase Plan, under which no one could own more than five passenger tires, and anyone with extra tires or any not in use must sell them to the government on pain of losing gas coupons. Mayor Geerlings named Phillips Brooks to head a five-person committee to carry out tires and

67 *Holland City News*, 30 May 1943, 25 Jan. 1945.
68 Ibid., 22 Jan., 23 Apr., 22 Oct., 19 Nov. 1942.

tubes rationing in Holland. Voluntary gas rationing was tried first, but when that failed, the OPA in the spring of 1942 enacted mandatory rationing. Congress did its part by implementing the national "Victory Speed" of thirty-five miles per hour.[69]

The Holland Chamber of Commerce and local oil companies paid for advertisements protesting gas rationing, which they judged harsh, unnecessary, and counterproductive to economic growth. In some sense, these worries were justified. Gas rationing, coupled with high gas prices, forced hundreds of Mexican migrant workers to leave West Michigan and head for home, consequently causing a shortage of stoop labor in the vegetable fields. The government promised migrants that if they continued to work they would be provided with enough gasoline to return home when the harvest was over, but this reassurance had little effect.[70]

Gasoline regulations also disrupted businesses that relied heavily on motor vehicles. For example, according to wartime regulations, milkmen could deliver milk only three days per week instead of the traditional six, and consumers were always provided with a two-day supply of milk. This schedule was designed to preserve gasoline, but the every-other-day schedule meant that twice a month there had to be Sunday deliveries. For weeks in the fall of 1943, milk dealers corresponded with the Office of Defense Transportation (ODT) to establish a delivery schedule. Milk dealers opposed Sunday work and eventually the ODT gave in to their demand to deliver on Saturday night instead. After all the trouble, however, the milk distributors relented, concluding that Saturday night deliveries had too many complications. They would continue to deliver on Sunday.[71]

Vehicle owners had to register with the rationing board each year and prove that they needed gas for "nonessential" use, such as commuting to work (no pleasure driving allowed) and owned no more than five tires. By December 1942, over 3,500 automobiles of an estimated six thousand in Holland were registered and received a Mileage Ration Book with coupons. Owners were issued a colored letter "sticker" in one of five categories, depending on their essentiality to the war effort. Nonessential driving received a black "A" sticker for four gallons a week (cut to eight gallons a month in 1944). Workers in war industries received a green "B" sticker for eight gallons a week.

69 Ibid., 1 Jan. 1942; www.ameshistoricalsociety.org/exhibits/events/rationing.html, accessed 3 Feb. 2010.

70 *Holland City News*, 11 June 1942.

71 Ibid., 1, 8 Oct. 1942; 14 Oct. 1943.

Railroad workers, physicians, clergy, newspaper editors, mail carriers, and other categories integral to the war effort received a red "C" sticker, truckers a buff "T" sticker, and farmers a pink "R" sticker. The C, T, and R categories allowed as much gas as needed. Lucky was the family with a member holding one of these favored stickers; they might even have extra gas for family and friends. Holland police hit on the ultimate penalty for speeding in 1943—the loss of the driver's gas ration card. They simply reported speeders to the OPA, and the federal agency did the rest.[72]

Gasoline dealers had to take care not to sell to drivers without coupons; the penalties were severe. In 1943 Vandenberg Bros. Oil Co. of Holland was found guilty of selling oil without exchanging coupons. All company business had to be halted for ninety days. Unregistered automobiles, those without tags, were subject to fines of $25. Those found pooling rations together for hunting trips or other recreational activities were also punished. Since tires were also rationed, vehicle owners had to apply for permits to buy new tires or inner tubes. The limit was five. Only certain repair shops were designated to inspect tires and sign for the strict necessity of replacement, and the rationing board required proof of inspection before issuing purchase permits.[73]

In 1943 the federal government implemented a need-based "point system" of ration books for sugar (red book) and meat (blue book), ninety-six stamps to a book. The ration books were numbered seriatim: Book No. 1, Book No. 2, and so on, each covering several months. Distribution of Book No. 4 began November 1, 1943. Government functionaries assigned points to scarce commodities. For example, a scarce ham bone for pea soup might need eight stamps, but a shank bone or pig's feet might need only two stamps. To lessen the confusion, the government issued an "Official Table of Consumer Point Values for Meat, Fats, Fish, and Cheese," with points per pound for everything from bacon to sausage. Newspapers published the list for shoppers. The system was still a nightmare for housewives, who had to evaluate both the monetary and stamp values of a purchase.[74]

As ration coupons changed hands between consumers, retail merchants, and wholesalers, the government in 1943 asked banks to serve as transfer agents. The system, known as "ration coupon banking," required retailers to deposit stamps taken from consumers in

72 Ibid., 6, 19, 25 Nov., 3 Dec. 1942, 14, 21 Jan. 1943.

73 *Holland City News*, 17 June, 12 Aug., 21 Oct., 11 Nov. 1943, 24 Aug., 28 Dec. 1944.

74 Ibid., 14 Jan., 25 Mar., 3 June 1943.

special accounts at the banks, from which they could draw when buying rationed commodities from wholesalers. Banks thus had to handle stamp "currency" alongside legal tender, and track both through their exchange system. Bankers found the system almost as complicated as housewives.[75]

To lessen the need for private cars and preserve precious gasoline, the common council considered offering car ferry service across Lake Macatawa, and they also listened carefully to a proposal for citywide bus service, but neither idea came to fruition. Bus service won approval in 1945 (chapter 10). The aldermen also asked merchants to adopt a cash-and-carry policy to save on gas, including grocers, furniture stores, and others merchants who customarily made home deliveries. State basketball tournaments were canceled for the duration; only area tournaments were scheduled. Local furniture merchant James Brouwer had the last laugh. His electric car, the only one in Holland, used no gasoline, and its odd-sized tires were exempt from tire rationing. He was twice blessed and did not mind the limited capabilities of his glorified golf cart. The forty-two batteries generated a maximum speed of twenty miles per hour.[76]

War bonds and stamps

Hollanders supported the war effort by purchasing war bonds and defense stamps, just as in the First World War. Billions of dollars worth of bonds financed the war, with future generations left to pay off the principal and interest. Purchasing bonds was patriotic. "WHOSE BOY WILL DIE BECAUSE YOU FAILED?" declared the newspapers, thereby laying a heavy load of guilt on slackers. Ervin D. Hanson, the bond drive chairman, asserted in 1944 that "the first army is our fighting front, the second army is our production front, and the third army is our bond selling front."[77]

Bond sales were two kinds: workers purchased Series F bonds through a payroll savings plan, and the government announced periodic bond campaigns in which citizens purchased Treasury bonds and notes. The government held seven "bond campaigns" during the war. Each community was assigned a "quota" based on assessed property value. Purchasing bonds, of course, was voluntary. One citizen was a "100 percent patriot"; Anna (Mrs. Richard) Ellison in 1943 devoted all her

75 Ibid., 31 Jan. 1943.

76 Ibid., 19 Feb., 28 May, 8 Oct. 1942, 21 Oct. 1943, 24 Aug., 28 Dec. 1944, 9 Aug. 1945; Vande Water, "Brouwer Electric Car Holland Fixture," in *Holland Happenings,* 3:99-100.

77 *Holland City News,* 24 Sept. 1942, 16 Nov. 1944.

pay to war bonds. The *Holland City News* made sure to run a story with her photo. Holland fell behind on its quota, but usually it far exceeded expectations.[78]

When sales lagged, Frank M. Lievense, executive chair of the committee for selling war bonds and stamps, stepped in and turned up the heat. One government gimmick in 1943 was the "buy a bomber" campaign, which would paint the name "City of Holland" on a B-25 or B-29 bomber if local businesses and industries met a $175,000 quota. The "buy a bomber" bond campaign quickly exceeded its goal. Holland purchased $1.6 million in bonds in the first drive in 1942, $2 million in the second campaign in 1943—$350,000 over the quota—$1 million in the third, fourth and fifth drives in 1943 and 1944, $1.9 million in the sixth drive in 1944, and $1.3 million in the seventh in 1945. The outstanding display of patriotism in the second drive was due to one company—Holland Furnace—whose employees purchased $1 million! In addition, Holland residents that month purchased five thousand Series E bonds for $250,000, which was the largest monthly amount for the duration. The next two months, however, the city fell short of its quota, but the special display of a captured two-man Japanese suicide submarine brought out five thousand spectators. The price of admission was $1 in war stamps for adults and 25¢ for children. Bonds sales jumped $17,000 during that visit. After the war, in late 1945, the government ran yet another bond campaign, dubbed the "Victory Loan Drive," and Holland's share was $1.2 million. Representative Henry Geerlings was put in charge.[79]

In 1944 Lievense gave a typical appeal: "Right now more Americans are being killed all over the world than ever before. Yet America is buying fewer bonds than a year ago. It is up to the Americans to back the attack with everything they have. The good patriotic Americans need to make up for the profiteers, strikers, revelers, and shirkers." The difficulty was not in convincing citizens to subscribe, but in convincing them to continue subscribing when the extra money could be used at home. Organizations like the Lions Club helped canvass the city for pledges. As in the Great War, the common council purchased bonds with municipal funds. Special patriotic days, like Washington's Birthday and anniversaries of the bombing of Pearl Harbor, helped spur additional giving.[80]

78 Ibid., 13 May, 26 Aug., 2, 30 Sept,. 1943.

79 Ibid., 30 Apr., 16 July, 10 Dec. 1942, 7 Jan., 18, 25 Feb., 25 Mar., 1, 29 Apr., 8, 22, 29 July, 16 Sept. 1943, 13 Jan., 10 Feb., 25 May, 29 June, 9, 22 Nov. 1944, 17, 31 May, 21, 28 June, 5 July, 25 Oct., 1 Nov. 1945.

80 *Holland City News*, 16 Sept. 1943, 10 Feb. 1944.

Companies competed to win the "Bulls-eye Flag" award, which required a 99 percent employee participation rate in buying bonds and stamps, totaling at least 10 percent of the payroll. Holland Racine won the first flag. Donnelly-Kelly Glass also won a flag; the firm devoted 80 percent of factory hours to war work. Spring Air workers committed one day's wages per month to buy defense bonds and stamps.[81]

Perhaps the most difficult bond campaign came late in the war, when citizens were exhausted from years of rationing, working overtime, and sending their money to Uncle Sam. This seventh bond drive was turned into a competition between various segments of society—merchants, industries, schools, and residences—all were assigned a specific goal. The progress of the bond drive was charted in each weekly issue of the *Holland City News* in a symbolic horse race cartoon. The schools took first place, residences came in second, followed by industries, and the "stingy" merchants in last place. Hollanders were encouraged to hold on to the bonds they already had and buy more. The competitive atmosphere aided the drive, and Holland greatly oversubscribed this final wartime bond campaign. When the war ended, Lievense resigned as bond chairman and ex-mayor Geerlings took his seat.[82]

For those who could not afford war bonds, war savings stamps were a cheaper means of expressing patriotism. Stamps were available in denominations of 10¢, 25¢, and 50¢, and $1 and $5. Stamps did not earn interest like bonds, but they gave schoolchildren, in particular, the ability to participate in the patriotic movement and learn the value of saving money. City merchants sold stamps in the summer of 1941, long before the United States entered the war. In early 1942 employees at the Spring Air Co. volunteered one day's pay each month to purchase defense stamps and bonds. By the end of January 1942, the Holland club had sold $1,600 worth of stamps, in addition to $3,200 in bonds. High school students also sold stamps; the janitors built a booth that was set up in the city hall and staffed by students.[83]

Sacrifice and honor

The Pearl Harbor attack that claimed 2,400 lives left three Holland-area servicemen in the battle unscathed. Glenn Nyhuis cabled his parents that he had been stationed some twenty-five miles from Pearl Harbor. Ensign Fred Bertsch's parents had to wait ten days for

81 Hamlin, "Holland's Contribution."
82 *Holland City News*, 15 Feb., 22 Mar., 31 May, 21 June, 5 July, 1 Nov. 1945.
83 Ibid., 24 July 1941, 8, 29 Jan. 1942.

his letter to come. Fred survived the bombing of his destroyer in the harbor. Radioman Frank Varano's parents also had to wait for a letter to learn that he too was unharmed while serving as a deck "lookout" on his ship and directing return fire at enemy planes. Marine Jay Nevenzel, an enlisted officer stationed on Wake Island in the western Pacific Ocean, was the first Holland POW held by the Japanese. Thankfully, casualties of Holland men remained low in 1942 and 1943, as most had yet to see action. As of Memorial Day in 1942, Holland only had one casualty, twenty-year-old seaman George Stegenga, who was lost as sea when a German submarine sank his destroyer off the New Jersey coast. The Frank Stegengas were the first of hundreds to display the gold star banner in the front window of their East Ninth Street home. Thousands more displayed silver stars for a wounded son.[84]

It was the turn of the year 1942 before the second, third, fourth, and fifth Holland servicemen made the ultimate sacrifice. Marine fighter pilot Wallace Riemersma died in a training exercise when his plane went into the Pacific Ocean off the California coast. In November 1942 Paul Henagin of Company D was killed in the jungles of New Guinea in the capture of Burma, a strategic city. In the next seven weeks, seven more comrades fell to Japanese mortar fire: Henry Wehrmeyer, John Van Til, George "Blackie" Bruursema, Richard Overkamp, James Sullivan, Emil Brown, and Jess Nichol. Louis Van Slooten, was reported missing in action in the North Africa campaign. He ended up in a German prison in Rome, but escaped and made his way to liberated Algiers. By March 1943 nine families in Holland had received the feared "knock on the door" by a military officer. The sacrifices made it all the sweeter when in the 1943 Memorial Day parade all service personnel home on furlough or leave were given the place of honor at the head of the line.[85]

On Armistice Day 1943 the city dedicated a new "soldiers plot" at Pilgrim Home Cemetery, sponsored by the American Legion, for the heroes of the Second World War. Arthur Alverson was the first to be interred with honors by a legion color guard, bugler, and pallbearers on December 2, 1943. Soon two comrades joined him. By this date, sixteen Holland-area servicemen had been killed in action, out of 1,275 men and women then named on the service panel in Centennial Park

84 *Holland City News*, 18 Dec. 1941, 16 Jan., 5 Mar., 21, 28 May, 30 July 1942; Vande Water, "Stegenga First to Perish in WWII," in *Holland Happenings,* 4:150-52.

85 *Holland City News*, 24, 31 Dec. 1942, 7, 28 Jan., 4 Feb., 18 Mar., 20 May 1943, 20 July 1944; Vande Water, "New Guinea Jungles Claimed Guards," in *Holland Happenings,* 4:166-70. Bruursema was the first employee of any Heinz plant nationwide to die in the war, and the company made much of it.

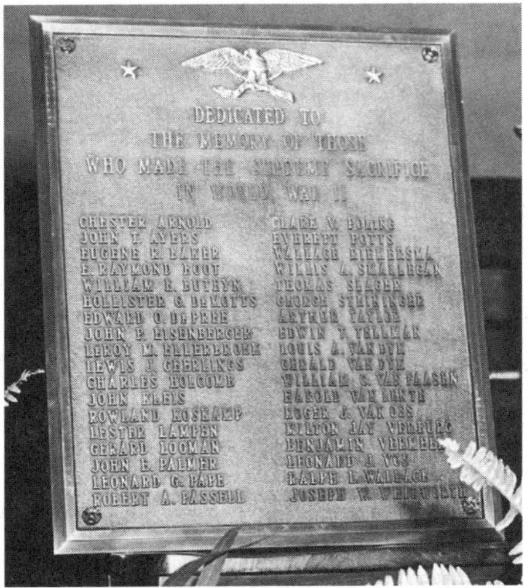

Hope College memorial plaque "Dedicated to the memory of those who made the ultimate sacrifice in World War II." The plaque lists forty-one men (*Joint Archives of Holland*)

sponsored by the Lions Club. Their families displayed blue star service banners. Memorial Day ceremonies in 1944 at the cemetery brought out more than one thousand people to pay their respects. None were prouder than Ralph N. and Emma Wagner of West Tenth Street, who had six sons in the armed forces.[86]

In the final year of the war, casualties mounted, and Holland papers carried several stories a week of soldiers killed in action, usually with a photo. The grim news had almost become routine. By the third anniversary of Pearl Harbor in 1944, ninety-six men from Ottawa County, including forty-five from Holland, had died in action. Holland also counted eleven soldiers missing, fifteen prisoners, and at least sixty-eight wounded—some more than once. On Pearl Harbor Day 1944, the *Holland City News* published a full-page "Roll of Honor," which listed by date all the dead, missing, and prisoners in each West Michigan community, based on official War Departments records. Five months later, in May 1945, the death toll for Holland had nearly doubled, to eighty-five. The last year of the war was the bloodiest by far. Before the guns went silent in August, the death tally for Holland men had risen to ninety-three—nine from Company D—out of an estimated 1,800 who served. For the larger Holland-area, the death toll was 118, including forty-one Hope College students and alumni. The war continued for the many who came home seriously wounded and emotionally scarred.[87]

86 *Holland City News*, 2, 9 Dec. 1943, 1 June 1944, 3 Feb. 1945.

87 Ibid., 21, 28 Sept., 12 Oct. (three death reports each), 7 Dec. 1944, 24 May, 21 Nov., 13 Dec. 1945 (lists complete Roll of Honor); Wichers, *Century of Hope*, 288.

President Jimmy Carter placing Congressional Medal of Honor around the neck of Lt. Colonel Matt Urban on July 19, 1980, thirty-six years to the day after his release from an English hospital to rejoin his comrades on the Normandy front. Urban's wife Amy and daughter look on proudly (army photo) (*Archives, Holland Historical Trust*)

Lt. Colonel Matt Urban was the only Holland-area soldier in the Second World War to be awarded the Congressional Medal of Honor. But he did not live in Holland until thirty years later, when in 1974 he became the city recreation and Civic Center director. Urban's heroics took place in the North African, Italian, and Normandy campaigns. Wounded seven times, each time he rejoined his men and continued to fight, earning twenty-nine metals in twenty months of combat. President Jimmy Carter draped the nation's highest medal around his neck in a Washington ceremony in 1980, making Urban the most-decorated soldier in the war. In recognition of his valor, the city council gave the name Matt Urban Drive to the new street off South Washington Avenue that leads past the Disabled American Veterans (DAV) Hall to West Forty-Eighth Street. Urban retired in 1989, and at his death at age seventy-five in 1995, his remains were interred with high honors in Arlington National Cemetery.[88]

88 Matt Urban with Charles Conrad, *The Matt Urban Story* (Holland, MI, 2004), 483-92; Randall P. Vande Water, *Holland: The Tulip Town* (Chicago: Arcadia Publishing, 2002), 80; Matt Urban obit., *Holland Sentinel*, 5 Mar. 1995.

The soldiers return

The penultimate victory in the war was D-Day June 6, 1944, and Holland noted it with the peals of church bells, services of prayer, and many hours of anxious listening for news on the family radio. Everyone knew the invasion of Europe across the English Channel was coming, and they awaited the official word. Holland police received the word from Michigan Governor Harry Kelly at six o'clock in the morning, and by arrangement, at nine o'clock, sirens, bells, and whistles were to sound briefly, followed by a moment of silent prayer. People then gathered at their churches for services of prayer. Marion de Velder timed his service at Hope Church for everyone to listen to President Roosevelt's prayer broadcast to the nation, ending with the benediction: "Thy will be done, almighty God, Amen."[89] When it became apparent that the invasion had succeeded, and Allied Forces were moving toward Germany, Americans knew that victory was assured. It was only a matter of time.

By the time of the spring mayoral elections of 1944, Holland was a well-tuned wartime manufacturing center. Henry Geerlings ran for a fifth term but was defeated in all but one ward by Elmer J. Schepers. Geerlings had been as active in the war effort as could possibly be asked of a public figure, but Schepers actually ran and won in a campaign that promised even more active participation in the war effort. Schepers also called for a youth center, retirement packages for city employees, and more youth involvement in city government. Geerlings was well liked, and he left the city in "excellent condition financially," as Schepers put it. In 1945 Geerlings became a state representative, his supporters boasting that he had devoted about "300 years" to public service in his various capacities in city government and on local school boards.[90]

In his farewell message as mayor, Geerlings identified the most serious issue that his successor would have to face. "When the veterans come home they can't eat medals," he said, "and the only way to enable them to eat properly, to work properly, to repair their disabilities, and to put them back into useful places in our social system is by preparing now to do these things." Indeed, Geerlings and the common council had been concerned with this issue for several years. In August of 1943 Geerlings named Clarence Jalving to head an economic development committee to help plan for post-war jobs in conjunction with the American Legion. Although Geerlings was interested in civic projects to provide employment, he hoped that private industries would take

89 Vande Water, "Holland Prays on D-Day," in *Holland Happenings,* 1:68-69.

90 *Holland City News*, 3, 24 Feb., 20 Apr., 9 Nov. 1944.

on most of the returnees. Mayor Schepers shared these concerns; he established a committee in June 1944 to look into ways to provide for veterans upon their return, including a counseling center.[91]

Peace celebrations

The war in Europe ended on May 8, 1945, with the fall of Berlin and Hitler's suicide in his bunker. V-E—Victory in Europe—Day had finally come, and the churches quickly filled for prayer services that had been planned for several months, since the fall of Germany was clearly in view. But the celebrations were muted, because the United States was still at war with Japan. The somber 1945 Memorial Day ceremony at Pilgrim Home Cemetery brought out two thousand people to hear Hope College professor Egbert Winter speak of the high price of freedom "paid in sacrifice and blood."

Attention turned to Japan in early August, when B-52 bombers firebombed Tokyo and then dropped the first A-Bomb on Hiroshima on August 5, followed by a second on Nagasaki on August 9.The two bombs had the blasting power of 2.4 million B-52 bombers dropping conventional TNT ordinance. Yet Emperor Hirohito held firm. The display of American might prompted a rare editorial comment from the *Holland Sentinel* editor, that even when the choice is total annihilation or unconditional surrender, Japanese leaders prefer war. President Harry Truman revealed that German scientists had also been on a quest to develop uranium-fueled bombs, but America won the "battle of the laboratories." The bomb's "new and revolutionary increase in destruction," Truman averred, could be a "powerful and forceful influence toward maintaining world peace." Readers later learned from Tokyo broadcasts that the two bombs cost half a million casualties and leveled buildings up to a ten-mile radius.[92]

Only when news came on August 10 that Emperor Hirohito wished to quit did Hollanders prepare to celebrate V-J Day. Everyone had their ears glued to their radios to hear President Harry Truman's announcement of Japan's surrender on Wednesday August 15. "Truman brings home the bacon," declared the editor.[93]

Unlike the pedestrian parades of World War One, the celebrations that August Wednesday were dominated by automobiles, caught in a downtown traffic jam with horns blaring in a discordant frenzy. "*Right away* there was noise just terrible," wrote Carrie Bielfield of Holland to her children. "We went downtown because everybody did. There was no

91 Ibid., 19 Aug., 7 Oct. 1943; 3 Feb., 20 Apr., 22 June, 3 Aug. 1944.

92 *Holland Sentinel*, 6, 7, 8, 9 (quote), 10 (quote), 11, 13 Aug. 1945.

93 Ibid., 14, 15 Aug. 1945.

Vehicles hurriedly decked out join an impromptu parade to celebrate V-J Day, August 15, 1945 (*courtesy Randall P. Vande Water*)

parade but cars, cars, cars with bells & whistles & noise. Everybody went wild. . . . What good news we have had, haven't we? Can hardly believe the war is over." "More gas was probably burned in a few hours in Holland's downtown section Tuesday night and more gears shifted, than during a corresponding period of the last big Tulip Time festival," declared the *Holland City News* happily. No matter; gas rationing happily ended that day. Business came to a virtual standstill, as stores and factories closed for the day, as did the post office and all government offices. Churches opened their doors for evening services of thanksgiving.[94]

Many stores closed for two days, but most factories resumed operations the next day, except for Holland-Racine Shoes and Armour Leather. They had been in danger of closing because of a severe shortage of leather, and the celebration gave them an excuse to suspend operations for a longer time.[95]

The next day ten thousand people assembled at Kollen Park to kick off a real parade, led by the cast of actors that had played important roles in the four-year struggle. The American Legion, Boy Scouts, doctors and nurses, and many other groups joined in the mile-long curtain call, accompanied by floats, one carrying a sign reading

94 Carrie Bielfield, Holland, MI, to "Dear Children," Sept. 1945, Mouw Family Papers, JAH; *Holland City News*, 22 Aug. 1945.

95 *Holland City News*, 16 Aug. 1945; *Holland Sentinel*, 16 Aug. 1945.

Boy Scouts march down Eighth Street past the Center Theatre in the V-J Day parade (*Archives, Holland Historical Trust*)

"One, Two, Three and Out," with effigies of Hitler, Mussolini, and Hirohito. After the parade, ex-mayor Geerlings gave a short speech, as did Hinkamp, a religion professor at Hope College, who noted that the development of atomic bombs cost $2 billion, but America had been spending $2 billion every nine days in war costs. The bomb was money well spent. In five years, V-J Day was all but forgotten.[96]

Postwar problems

With the war's end in sight, President Truman called for "orderly changes to civilian output." Government war procurement agencies canceled war contracts and freed metals and materials for industrial use. Federal labor control ended, and Congress readied a bill to end the draft. The biggest news was OPA's announcement of the end of gas rationing and the easing of meat rations.[97]

The return of several million veterans had consequences economically, socially, and culturally. The lifting of wage and price controls set off an inflationary spiral, as manufacturers raised prices and workers demanded "catch-up" wage increases, and went on strike,

96 Vande Water, "V-E Day Remembered in Holland," in *Holland Happenings,* 2:14-18; Vande Water, "Noisy V-J Day Celebrated Here," in ibid., 3:9-13; *Holland City News*, 8 Aug. 1948, 14 Aug. 1952.

97 *Holland Sentinel*, 9, 11, 15, 18 Aug. 1945.

Nine young men, including a veteran, join the V-J Day parade in and on Henry De Visser's souped up 1928 Chevrolet convertible. De Visser and brothers Herman and Harry were co-owners of A. (Arie) De Visser & Sons, an International truck dealership on Chicago Drive at Spruce Avenue. Contrary to impressions, Henry De Visser was married. (*Archives, Holland Historical Trust*)

if necessary, to get them. Finding jobs for the tens of thousands of veterans roiled labor markets, new marriages caused a housing shortage of epic proportions, and veterans flooded college campuses under the GI Bill that paid tuition and expenses. Hope College was approved for the program already in August 1944. Hope's enrollment jumped from 250 in 1943 to 1,200 in 1946. They erected Quonset huts across Columbia Avenue to house the rush of students and fed them in the Masonic Temple building.[98]

Housing needs in the city itself were even more acute. To compile a list of accommodations for hundreds of returning veterans, Bert Selles of the Veterans Housing Committee in September 1945 enlisted the Junior Chamber of Commerce and Office of Civil Defense "block mothers" to canvass every homeowner in greater Holland. The first six months were especially critical, Selles noted, and he urged homeowners who had never rented rooms before to consider doing so. Three hundred homes were needed, and the survey found only three apartments and twenty-two "possibilities." Although home building

[98] *Holland City News*, 10 Aug. 1944; Wichers, *Century of Hope*, 229; Henry ten Hoor interview by Tracy Bednarick, 27 June 1996, typescript, JAH.

permits in 1945 and 1946 were at an all-time high, contractors were stymied by OPA price controls on building materials. Six local cement block manufacturers, for example, suspended deliveries in May 1946 after OPA officials refused their request for a new ceiling price of 13¢ per block. All prices were going up, and government bureaucrats made it difficult for businesses to earn profits.[99]

In February 1946 a group of fifty veterans packed the common council chambers to demand action, and a "rather heated discussion" ensued, according to press reports. The common council promised action, and in desperation applied to the Federal Public Housing Authority (FPHA) for one hundred housing units. President Irwin Lubbers of Hope College also applied to FPHA for twenty-five family units and dormitories for fifty people. He and the City received positive responses and entered the temporary housing business. Hope received $20,000 to build a dormitory on campus, and the City obtained $56,000 for thirteen steel-framed duplexes that they placed on the site of the old Cappon & Bertsch tannery where the Civic Center now stands.[100]

The veterans' housing complex was named "Pine Court," but it was much too rustic. Wives complained to the common council that roofs leaked, window casings were flimsy, the carpeting had not arrived, and electric bills were exorbitant. This did not sit well with alderman Bernard De Pree, an officer of the Holland Color and Chemical Company. "Here we tried to do something for the veterans at their insistence and now we appear to be on trial because all is not well." Blame the federal government, not us, De Pree implied. The next year a child died in a fire at the city-operated complex, and residents continued to complain about high rents, peeling paint, open garbage containers, the lack of a children's playground, and flooded grounds in heavy rains. In desperation, the common council asked the federal government to turn over ownership so they could tear it down. Fewer than half the units were occupied by late 1949. The feds complied, and as units became empty, the city tore them down. Soon Pine Court again was a parking lot.[101]

Veterans pushed Hope College enrollment up from 400 in 1945 to 1,200 in 1946; 550 of the 700-student increase were vets studying under the GI Bill. The college, in conjunction with the Holland Air Service, re-opened flight training at the Park Township Airport for veterans who wanted to learn to fly and pilots wishing to keep up their

99 *Holland City News*, 6, 13, 27 Sept. 1945, 3, 31 Jan., 7 Feb., 2 May 1946.

100 Ibid., 14 Feb., 9 May, 11 July, 1 Aug., 26 Sept. 1946.

101 Ibid., 6 Feb. 1947, 19 Feb., 8 Apr., 15 Sept. 1948, 20 Oct. 1949.

skills. More than eighty veterans were taking training by April 1947, two-thirds as Hope College students. Hope was one of only a few colleges nationwide to offer courses in flight. The Holland Board of Education in 1946 launched a Veterans Institute to provide on-the-job training for veterans. It ran until 1951 and helped 438 veterans retool for civilian employment, at a total cost of only $8,000. The parallel adult education program also swelled, with 145 students signing up for hands-on learning.[102]

Tulip Time 1945 was pitched to local residents, in hopes of "maintaining the spirit of Tulip Time during the war-imposed cessation." The next year, however, the city went all out. They allotted $5,000 to buy one hundred thousand tulip bulbs, and they extended the event to four days.[103]

Auto factories in Michigan shifted back to domestic production in time for the 1946 models. Unionized workers resorted to strikes over unmet wage demands. Holland had more than its share of labor disputes as workers tried to catch up after years of wage controls, including a work stoppage by city employees. Workers at Holland Hitch, Bell Telephone, and Bohn Aluminum walked off the job. Some 80 percent of Holland Furniture workers also staged a spontaneous "walkout" to protest a new "incentive wage system" that threatened to reduce their take-home pay. The company refuted the charge, but almost immediately rescinded the new wage rates. The Holland Hitch and Bohn Aluminum strikes, however, were ugly and dragged on for months. Both involved more than one hundred workers who were affiliated with the same AFL-CIO local. The companies refused to sign contracts that included the International CIO union and generally opposed collective bargaining with employees. Holland Hitch had two strikes in 1946, one in May that lasted only one day and one in October that continued for 105 days. The Bohn strike lasted 127 days in 1947—the longest in the state that year.[104]

Standard Grocery suffered from a secondary strike in 1945. AFL Grocery Workers Local 406 set up pickets in front of the local store, even though six weeks earlier 100 percent of that store's employees had voted not to join the union. Picketing by the outsiders tied up delivery trucks and resulted in a union strike call at Holland Motor Express, which so infuriated president John Cooper that he announced he would liquidate

[102] *Holland City News*, 3, 24 Jan., 11 Apr., 19 Dec. 1946, 3 Apr. 1947, 16 Aug. 1951.

[103] Ibid., 12 Apr., 20 Sept., 4 Oct., 8 Nov. 1945, 10 May 1946.

[104] Ibid., 10 Jan., 7 Mar., 9 May, 3, 24 Oct., 5 Dec. 1946, 16 Jan., 2 Apr., 7 Aug. 1947; *Holland Sentinel*, 4 Aug. 1948.

his $350,000 firm. Fortunately, Circuit Judge Fred Miles in Grand Haven ruled that the grocers union had no right to picket the Holland grocer, and he enjoined them from doing so. This ended the trouble, and Cooper did not have to carry through on his threat (chapter 19). The Bell strike began in Detroit and spread across the state, including Holland. "Unless we do something to end industrial strife," Army Major Charles Estes of the Federal Mediation and Conciliation Service in Washington, DC, told the Holland Junior Chamber of Commerce, we may not continue to enjoy all that democracy now means to us."[105]

Even city workers—fire and police, board of public works crews, cemetery, and streets—went on strike in 1946. With staples like coal and milk going up in price, workers needed to keep up with the rising cost of living. Jacob De Graaf and Neal Houtman, president and secretary, respectively, of the Municipal Employees Union AFL Local 515, led the walkout after the common council rejected demands for a ten-cent-an-hour raise. (Tellingly, only half of the two hundred city employees joined the strike. Given that the city had an open shop policy, this meant that only half of the employees belonged to the union.) Joseph "Joe" E. Geerds of the board of public works quickly negotiated a separate agreement with his workers to get essential city services restored. Soon after, Governor Harry Kelly appointed a three-man commission to mediate the wage dispute. At this, the workers went back to work. City officials, meanwhile, reclassified all jobs and raised the minimum wage to 86¢ an hour. Rather than satisfy the union, this action infuriated them. De Graff set another strike date, charging the city with "fighting the union" rather than implementing the agreement. There was likely some truth to the complaint. City attorney Vernon Ten Cate stated the city's view quite clearly: "Unionization has been creeping in where it has no place. . . . When the legislature tells cities to recognize unions, Holland will recognize unions," and not a day earlier. The two sides settled and narrowly avoided a second strike, but the settlement boosted the city's costs by $17,000, or nearly 10 percent. To balance the budget, the council raised the assessed millage on real estate by the maximum allowed under the city charter.[106]

For years after V-J Day, Americans commemorated August 14 with far more emotion than Armistice Day on November 11, which paled in comparison. The Great War did not look as great after the Second World

105 *Holland City News*, 6, 13, 20 Dec. 1945, 4, 11 Apr., 3 July, 29 Aug., 5, 12 Sept. 1946, 20 Mar., 25 Sept. 1947; *Holland Sentinel*, 6, 10, 13 Dec. 1945.

106 *Holland City News*, 25 Apr., 16 May, 27 June, 11, 18 July 1946.

City attorney Vernon Ten Cate (*courtesy Joan Ten Cate Bonnette*)

War. The American Legion organized the massive V-J Day celebrations in Holland. In 1946 businesses, factories, and schools closed for the day. Activities began in the morning with a community worship service at the Fourteenth Street Christian Reformed Church, followed by a soapbox derby, an amateur contest at Kollen Park thronged by five thousand children and their parents, softball and donkey ball games at Riverview Park, and an American Legion band concert in the evening. John G. Swieringa served as master of ceremonies of the amateur instrumental musical contest. The Kiwanis club staged the annual soapbox derby on the Columbia Avenue hill at Twentieth Street. Thousands lined the runway to see David Ramsey win the race and pocket the $75 prize. The 1947 commemoration coincided with the city's centennial and included a three-hundred-pound birthday cake.[107]

The 1947 Holland centennial rivaled the 1897 semi-centennial, but it focused on history rather than memoirs and reminiscences. Several dozen pioneers were yet alive in 1897 to recount the "old days"; historians had to do the heavy lifting in 1947, notably two native sons, Albert Hyma and Henry Lucas. A pageant written for the occasion offered a folkloric portrayal of the history, with an emphasis on the founder and the travails and triumphs of the pioneers. The highlight for the community was the traditional parade, topped with fireworks after dark. Willard Wichers, the city historian, went to the Netherlands to enlist officialdom in the local centenary. He succeeded to such an extent that Marvin Lindeman, a non-Dutch advertising executive

[107] Ibid., 12 Sept., 10 Oct. 1946, 14 Aug. 1947.

Holland Centennial parade, August 14, 1947, with 1922 Oldsmobile passing in front of Montgomery Ward store, Eighth Street (*Archives, Holland Historical Trust*)

who came to Holland in 1921, charged that the Dutch invested the event with "a mantle of importance far out of proportion to our own local concept of the anniversary. . . . As it turned out," he continued, "the Dutch did dominate the show, and it somewhat irked the local populace," who received the guests "with a party amounting to almost a passive rebellion. The townspeople . . . would have preferred a nice homey centennial with the Dutch tie-ups left out." Nevertheless, the local Hollanders reveled in their heritage and were proud of their Dutch family names, so much so that Lindeman charged them with snobbishness and an immodest air of superiority.[108]

The membership of the Henry Walters Post of the VFW increased more than fourfold during the war, from 97 to 456, and the post outgrew its headquarters on River Avenue. In 1944 they bought the Bowmaster Building on West Seventh Street for $20,000, and when building materials again became available after the war, they renovated the building and added a large auditorium, commercial kitchen, and basement recreation center.[109]

Peace was wonderful after five long years of war, but the Cold War had already begun with Winston Churchill's "Iron Curtain" speech in

108 Ibid., 1, 15 Aug. 1946, 21 Aug. 1947, 1 Jan., 11 Nov. 1948; Albert Hyma, *Albertus C. Van Raalte and His Dutch Settlements in the United States* (Grand Rapids: Eerdmans, 1947); Henry S. Lucas, *Ebenezer, 1847-1947, Memorial Souvenir of the Centennial Commemoration of Dutch Immigration to the United States, Held in Holland, Michigan 13-16 August 1947* (New York: Netherlands Information Bureau, Booklet 15, 1947); Marvin Lindeman, "A Non-Hollander Looks at Holland," *Michigan History* 37 (Dec. 1947): 405-16.

109 *Holland City News*, 10 Jan. 1946.

March 1946, and in four years the nation would again be at war in the Korean peninsula. The closing of the Holland Selective Service local board No. 1 in May 1947 was obviously premature. In fact, President Harry Truman's administration re-instituted the draft within fifteen months, in August 1948.[110]

A capstone of the postwar period was the return visit in 1952 of Queen Juliana to thank the city for its generous assistance during and after the German occupation. The Queen and Prince Bernhard spent three days being "wined and dined." Ten thousand Hollanders thronged at Eighth Street and River Avenue to catch a glimpse of her motorcade. Another thousand waved along Chicago Drive from Grand Rapids via Grandville, Hudsonville, and Zeeland. Mayor Harry Harrington had the privilege of accompanying the entourage around town, including a ceremonial address at Hope Memorial Chapel before 1,300 invitees. Faces glowed and hearts warmed to hear Her Majesty say: "All of you in America and especially you of Dutch descent did so much to help us during the war, your young men during the war, and your citizens after the war. The bonds of friendship between our two counties are an ever present reminder, and I hope they remain alive forever."[111]

Korean conflict

The Second World War ended with Korea divided at the thirty-eighth parallel between a communist North and a democratic South. For five years there were border skirmishes but nothing major. Then, on June 25, 1950, the Democratic People's Republic of Korea, armed by the Soviets and sheltered in Red China, launched a sneak attack on the Republic of Korea. They "struck like a cobra," said the American General Douglas McArthur, who President Truman put in charge of United Nations expeditionary forces—90 percent American—after the UN Security Council voted to assist South Korea. The cold war had become a hot war that many believed would be World War III, especially when China entered the war in 1951, just as North Korea was on the verge of defeat. The UN "Police Action" would last three years and end in a stalemate that continues to this day. Several million Americans fought in Korea and casualties totaled 34,000 dead and 103,000 wounded.

Within thirty days of the outbreak of war, the first eight men from Holland, part of an active reserve Marine unit, were ordered into

110 Ibid., 15 May 1947, 26 Aug. 1948.

111 Vande Water, "Queen Juliana Visited Holland in 1952," in *Holland Happenings,* 2:96-100 (quote, 100).

Mayor Harry Harrington (*right*) welcomes Netherlands Queen Juliana and Prince Bernhard (*left*) in front of city hall, May 1952 (*courtesy Garnet Harrington VanderLeek*)

uniform. A month later, shortly after dawn, the first contingent of Ottawa County inductees boarded buses bound for Detroit; this became a distressing monthly event. By the end of November, 107 county men had answered the call, the first of many hundreds. The draft initially included only single men ages nineteen to twenty-three years, with the oldest called up first. A Holland dentist was swept up in the so-called "doctor's draft" in August, which applied to men trained at government expense during World War Two who were either deferred or served less than twenty-one months. In December 1950 Charles H. Hendricks of Zeeland was killed in action. A month later Leon Barbour of Holland, a technician on a Navy minesweeper was killed when his vessel struck a mine and sank. These were the first of ten local men to make the ultimate sacrifice. One, Army reservist Corporal John Essebagger Jr., a graduate of Holland High and former Hope College student, in April 1951 received posthumously the Congressional Medal of Honor for walking into murderous gunfire and single-handedly inflicting heavy losses on the enemy and disrupting their advance before falling mortally wounded. He was the first of four men from Holland to receive the highest honor the country can bestow.[112]

[112] *Holland City News*, 27 July, 31 Aug., 14 Sept., 12, 19, 26 Oct., 30 Nov., 7, 28 Dec. 1950, 8 Feb. 1951, 15 May 1952; Vande Water, "Essebagger's Efforts Exalted," in *Holland Happenings*, 1:130-32; "2 Holland Sergeants Honored," in *Holland Happenings*, 1:133-

Cpl. John Essebagger Jr., Congressional Medal of Honor posthumous recipient, April 1951 (*courtesy Randall P. Vande Water*)

Nine months into the war, the Selective Service decided to grant deferments to college students eighteen years and older who passed a three-hour aptitude exam and remained in good standing in school. President Lubbers of Hope College had strongly advocated this policy and the college gladly agreed to be one of the main exam sites. The new deferment did not sit well with the Grand Haven-area commissioners on the Ottawa County draft board. They sent a public letter to the state director opposing the policy as "unjust and unfair" to those "who do not have the means for a four or six year college course." The lone Holland board member, O. William Lowry, was "out of town" and did not sign the letter; he likely favored the policy. Lubbers answered the draft board by reminding them that military and civilian commissions had both concluded "after long study" that deferring college students was in the national interest because of the contributions they could make to the military after completing their studies. The argument sounded good, but few expected the war to run more than a few years, and students could wait it out by staying in school. In late 1951, some eighteen months into the war, the Selective Service expanded the draft pool to include young married men without children. The net was gradually widened as the war dragged on. In the end, seventy-seven thousand Michigan men were drafted.[113]

34; Vande Water, "Four Holland men have been Medal of Honor recipients," *Holland Sentinel*, 17 May 2009. Matt Urban also served in the Second World War; Gordon Yntema and Paul Lambers served in the Vietnam conflict. The total number from Holland and vicinity who served in the Korean War remains untallied from War Department records.

113 *Holland City News*, 18 Jan., 5, 12, 19 Apr., 29 Nov. 1951, 30 July 1953.

The military draft was controversial, in part, because the Korean conflict lacked the wholehearted national support of the Second World War. President Truman also feared provoking World War Three, so he barred the Air Force from pursuing the Chinese "Mig" fighter jets to their bases and supply depots across the Yalu River. General McArthur was so frustrated with the "limited war" policy that he publicly criticized the president, who fired the military hero unceremoniously in April 1951. Congress and the public gave McArthur an overwhelming homecoming. The Ottawa County draft board again went public by protesting President Truman's "tying the hands" of his military leaders. This time commissioner Lowry signed the letter. The board reflected the incredulity of the nation in Truman's dismissal of McArthur, but for an arm of the Selective Service to openly criticize the commander-in-chief was quite remarkable. The board suffered no repercussions for its act of insubordination. Two weeks later, Corporal Russell Van Dyke came home on furlough after nine months in the war zone and reported: "The GI's in Korea really thought a lot of McArthur and were quite upset when he was fired."[114]

As the massive scope of the Korean War became more apparent, cities began preparing for homeland defense, as in previous conflicts. Mayor Harry Harrington appointed A. E. Rackes as civil defense director, and he, in cooperation with Harold Klaassen, disaster chair of the local Red Cross, ordered a survey of local buildings suitable for air raid shelters and the number of people each could hold. Many saw the exercise as a waste of time, since Holland was hardly likely to be bombed by the enemy. Colonel Rackes pointed out in rebuttal that should Chicago or Detroit be hit, Holland might well have to house evacuees. As part of civil defense preparedness, the Red Cross offered instruction in home nursing and first aid for civil defense workers. Major Martin Japinga and his wife, who had manned an airplane observation post in California during the Second World War, volunteered their services again and set up a spotter's post at their home on West Twentieth Street to "watch for enemy airplanes" and report sightings by telephone to military authorities. Japinga later was awarded the Distinguished Military Service Medal for "exceptionally meritorious conduct."[115]

In 1953 the local civil defense moved its headquarters into the historic Van Raalte homestead on Fairbanks Avenue, at the behest of Hope College, which owned the property. The Ground Observers

[114] Ibid., 10, 24 May 1951.

[115] Ibid., 4 Jan., 24 May 1951, 31 Jan. 1952, 30 July 1953, 14 Apr. 1954.

Corps, some fifty strong in Holland, continued to watch the skies until 1959, when the government commended the volunteers and ended the program. Given the Russian A-bomb menace, a federally funded program of disaster control centers, defense-warning systems, and bomb shelters became necessary. Under federal direction, the city council formed a civil defense department with the city manager as director. Civil defense fell under the direct aegis of the executive department.[116]

Holland industries shifted from civilian to military production. Holland Hitch in 1951 won two contracts worth $14,500 for hooks and pintles. Hart & Cooley secured two defense contracts in 1952 for 856,000 mortar shells over nine months. The firm committed space for the jobs and hired an additional two hundred workers. Roamer Boats won the largest contracts from the US Navy, worth $1.5 million. The first, in 1951, was for ten steel-hulled harbor tugs, and a second in 1952 called for another twenty-one tugs. The firm expanded its plant south of Holland on US-31 and nearly doubled its workforce from twenty-three to forty in order to meet the schedule of one tug a month for thirty-six months. Clarence Jalving of Peoples Bank assisted in providing the needed working capital for the building addition and equipment. The tugs went by rail to Jesiek Bros. shipyards, where an honored female officially christened each one as it slid into Lake Macatawa. After passing rigorous trial runs in Lakes Macatawa and Michigan, the tugs sailed to Joliet, Illinois via the Chicago River, where they were hoisted on barges bound for New Orleans. In early 1954, after the active phase of the war, Beacon Boat (formerly Campbell Boat) Company on South Shore Drive won a $365,000 navy contract for twenty-six landing craft, LSTs, for ship to shore deployment of marines. Owner Orville Munkwitz also had to hire more workers to build the vessels, which underwent the same lake testing as the tugs before shipment by rail and truck to the East Coast.[117]

Six months before the signing of the armistice in July 1953, twenty-five men who had served together from the time of their induction in Detroit in January 1951 returned home and celebrated with a banquet in Holland. Only one of their number had been killed, a man from Nunica. Soon after the armistice, First Lt. Anne Norman, daughter of George and Jenny Zuverink and a flight nurse in Japan, helped in the repatriation of American prisoners-of-war from Korea. For months, family and friends welcomed back their men at the

[116] *Holland City News*, 9 Apr. 1953, 29 Jan. 1959, 19 May, 7 July 1960.
[117] Ibid., 18 Jan. 1951, 13, 27 Mar., 17 July, 14 Aug. 1952, 4 Mar. 1954.

Holland train depot. A special homecoming was that of airman Edward "Ted" Stickels, who had been shot down over Korea earlier that year and taken prisoner without any word to American officials or his family until after the armistice. When Lt. Stickels and his family arrived at the Holland train depot, Mayor Harrington welcomed him, and a color guard of the American Legion and a Veteran of Foreign Wars (VFW) drill team escorted the hero in an open car down Eighth Street to the city hall. The Legion band played several numbers and Harrington made a short speech, all broadcast on WHTC. Joyous homecomings were happy bookends to the tearful farewells of years earlier. For several more years, however, fresh draftees continued to answer the call and say their goodbyes. The Michigan voters approved the Korean Bonus Amendment, initiated by the VFW and modeled after the Second World War bonus, which provided every veteran with a bonus up to $500. It was a fitting way to mark the first Veterans Day on November 11, 1954, that replaced Armistice Day.[118]

Conquering polio

During the Korean War, scientists won another war, that against the dread disease of polio (poliomyelitis), called at the time "infantile paralysis," because it disproportionately struck youngsters with high fevers, leaving some crippled for life. Most serious were those whose pulmonary muscles were atrophied by the virus; they had to live the rest of their lives encased in a bulky "iron lung" machine that breathed for them. The late President Franklin Roosevelt was exhibit number one. He had been crippled by polio at age twenty-eight, while serving as governor of New York. Sulfa, the wonder drug of the 1930s, was helpless against the polio virus. Doctors had no cure, and parents feared for their children's lives. Local newspapers tracked the course of the outbreak, which seemed to peak in August and September. Health officials tried to limit polio outbreaks, which spread from person to person, by closing public swimming pools where youngsters congregated. Those Reformed churches that still used the common cup in the sacrament of Holy Communion switched to individual cups out of fear of contagion.[119]

On September 21, 1949, Ottawa County recorded its forty-third case, one of whom was a young mother. Three of the victims died. Statewide, Michigan counted 1,264 cases with 72 fatalities. The 1953 polio tally in Ottawa County dropped slightly to thirty-six cases, with

[118] Ibid., 20 Aug., 24 Sept. 1953, 7 Oct., 11 Nov. 1954.

[119] *Holland City News*, 8 Aug. 1946, 5 Aug. 1948, 25 Aug. 1949.

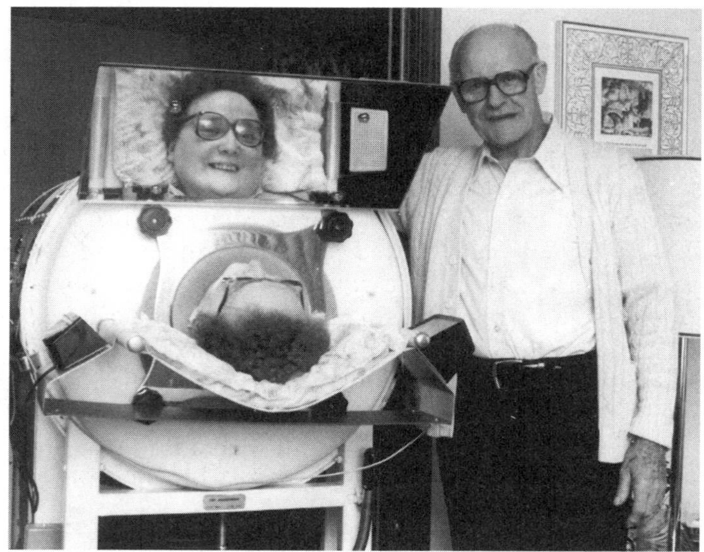

Marjorie and John Cooper, she in the iron lung in which she lived for forty years (*courtesy Dale Cooper*)

three deaths. Given the county population of 74,000 in 1950, the likelihood of contracting polio was only two per thousand. But parents worried–any cold or fever could be polio. The fear of the unknown made the disease all the more worrisome.[120]

Polio victims often required orthopedic surgery and long-term physical therapy at Mary Free Bed Hospital in Grand Rapids. In 1949 John F. Donnelly spearheaded a project to use local talent and materials to make a "homespun iron lung" machine for Holland Hospital. Donnelly-Kelley Glass Co. technicians made the machine, with the Elks Club providing $1,600 for the respirator, the most expensive part, which breathed for paralyzed patients. It was the first iron lung in the county. Polio paralyzed Marjorie (Mrs. John) Cooper (not the same family as the Holland Motor Coopers) from the neck down only a few weeks after the birth of her second son Jerry (son Dale was three), and she was confined to an iron lung in hospitals and in the living room of the family home for the remaining forty years of her life. The Holland Rotary Chapter stepped in to help victims like Marjorie pay for iron lungs, operations, and therapy. Rotary later adopted Polio Plus, a campaign to eradicate this plague worldwide by 2000.[121]

120 Ibid., 22 Sept. 1949, 22 Oct. 1953.

121 Ibid., 25 Aug. 1949; Vernon Boersma interview by Matthew Nickel, 22 May 2003, typescript, JAH.

To mitigate the economic impact on those who were hospitalized, or worse, crippled for life, the National Polio Foundation organized chapters in every county to hold an annual March of Dimes "polio drive." Half the money went to victims, and half went into research to conquer the disease. Ottawa County residents donated from $34,000 to $50,000 per year in the early 1950s. The city of Holland's goal was $22,000, and every social service club did its part, guided by the Inter-Club Council's polio committee. The Mother's March Against Polio, some 350 women strong, rang doorbells for donations. The two US factories that manufactured iron lungs ran their assembly lines twenty-four hours a day and yet could not keep up with demand by the National Foundation for Infantile Paralysis. This non-profit agency pledged to pay all expenses of polio victims not covered by medical insurance.[122]

In November 1953 the medical director of the National Foundation announced the amazing news that Jonas E. Salk of the University of Pittsburgh had developed a permanent polio vaccine. In a clinical trial the previous year, not one of 637 people inoculated with the "killed-virus" serum had contracted the disease. All were found to be immune to the three strains of polio. Plans were immediately implemented to inoculate up to one million children. Salk had shifted the fight against polio from defense to offense, but he had to wait some time to enjoy the national acclaim that was his due.

Instead of jubilation came controversy. Some doctors expressed "deep concern" about deliberately injecting children with the virus, even if it was dead. A report by Walter Winchell, national radio commentator that some batches of the Salk vaccine contained *live* viruses fanned the flames. Mothers swamped doctors with phone calls, who were equally dubious about the "highly experimental vaccine." As one doctor put it, "The 'yes' was so near to 'no' that you hardly knew what they mean." Before doctors would take up the needle, the Michigan State Medical Society had to declare the vaccine "absolutely safe."

In April 1954 Ottawa County teachers prepared for the "go ahead," pending word from the State Medical Society that the vaccine was "safe and sound." But only one thousand out of five thousand pupils showed up with their parental permission slips marked *yes*. Parents in the city of Holland and the outlying townships were particularly averse. Of the number of eligible children in Holland Public Schools, parents gave permission for only ten of fifty-one in Van Raalte, two

[122] *Holland City News*, 9 Oct. 1952, 8 Jan., 5 Nov. 1953, 28 Jan. 1954. The Inter-Club Council was composed of the five service clubs (Rotary, Kiwanis, Lions, Exchange, and Optimist) and the Junior Chamber of Commerce.

of fourteen in Apple Avenue, six of forty-five in Federal, five of ten in North Holland, and sixteen of sixty-two in Lakewood (Park Township). In the rural townships, the proportion was even lower: nine of thirty-two in Vriesland, two of twenty-five in Drenthe, none cooperating in West Drenthe and South Olive Christian, twelve of forty-eight in New Groningen, one of thirty-seven in Borculo, six of thirteen in Noordeloos, and seven of seventeen in South Blendon. In the end, only first and second graders received the vaccine, while third and fourth graders received a placebo.[123]

The next spring, plans were made to vaccinate the thousands not pricked the year before. But doctors assured fearful parents that they would wait until the 1954 "trial" inoculation of 440,000 children nationwide (half given a placebo) had proven to be effective. As Ralph Ten Have, county health officer remarked, "We do not know yet whether it [the Salk vaccine] really prevents polio." As late as September 1955, few doctors in Holland were willing to push for mass inoculations. As a result, polio continued to find its victims in Ottawa County—nineteen in 1955 and thirteen in 1956.[124]

The first big vaccination day in Holland was April 26, 1955. Some 1,200 youngsters came by school bus and parents' cars to the armory, where Drs. Warren Westrate, Walter Kuipers, and Vernon Boersma, assisted by a team of nurses, administered shots at a rate of 150 to 200 an hour, as the lines of youngsters came forward. The bravest ones stifled their cries, but most let loose in the bedlam of the moment. For the consenting parents, allowing the anti-polio shots took considerable courage and trust in the medical profession. It was no easy decision, although the alternative, being struck by polio, was deemed to be the greater risk. [125]

By January 1957, 80 percent of youngsters ages one through fourteen in Ottawa County had received at least one inoculation, but three "booster" shots were recommended for complete immunity. Very few people age fifteen and up had received any shots. This was disturbing, since one-fourth of all polio victims were between twenty and fifty years of age. The March of Dimes polio drives had to continue, with Holland and Park Townships together asked to raise $22,000 annually. The mothers drives brought in a quarter of that quota. By 1958 polio was conquered; the county had only four new cases. But 330 polio victims

123 Ibid., 12 Nov. 1953, 3, 15 (quote), 29 (statistics) Apr. 1954, 21 Apr. 1955.

124 Ibid., 17 Mar. (quote) 1955, 31 Jan. 1957.

125 *Holland City News*, 14, 21 Apr., 15 Sept. 1955.

in the county still needed medical treatment, and seventeen required major surgery. The 1960 March of Dimes polio drive in Holland and Park Townships raised $25,000 for their continuing care. In 1961 only 161 cases of polio were reported in the United States. By then, Albert Sabin's oral live vaccine had replaced Salk's inactivated vaccine. It was easier to administer, and it went directly to the intestinal tract where the virus normally resided. The oral vaccine gave lifetime immunity, and no boosters were needed. Medical science had conquered the scourge of polio.[126]

[126] Ibid., 31 Jan., 12 Dec. 1957, 26 Feb. 1959. Matt Nickel's interview with Vernon Boersma on 22 May 2003 deals almost exclusively with the polio epidemic in Holland.

CHAPTER 24

Politics

Democrats carried the city of Holland in the 2008 presidential election for the first time in 144 years, since the 1868 election after the Civil War. The margin was slim, 127 votes out of 14,500 ballots, but the outcome was cataclysmic (see appendix 7.1 for Holland City Presidential Elections, 1852-2012). Holland experienced a political revolution at the hands of Barack Obama, the junior senator from Illinois and a black (actually interracial) man. Obama defeated the Republican nominee, Arizona's senator John McCain, in a nationwide Democratic sweep. The growing Hispanic vote in Holland, boosted by a major voter registration drive, likely made the difference. Although Holland went Democratic in 2008 by .009 percent, in 2012 President Obama's re-election vote total dropped by one thousand, and he failed to carry the city a second time. The surrounding townships have remained rock-ribbed Republican, as always. McCain in 2008 won Ottawa County by 61 percent, down only 10 points from President George W. Bush's 71.5 percent margin in 2004. Mitt Romney, the 2012 Republican presidential candidate, captured 66 percent of the county vote and 53 percent in the city of Holland.[1]

1 *Holland Sentinel*, 9 Nov. 2008, 9 Nov. 2012.

Ottawa County is a conservative, Dutch Reformed center that has earned a national reputation as a Republican Party stronghold. That McCain and Romney lost the state by wide margins was not the fault of the Dutch Reformed, who take their politics seriously and dutifully cast straight Republican tickets.

The West Michigan Dutch were not always Republican. In the first twenty years, until after the Civil War, they identified with the Democratic Party, as did European immigrants generally and Dutch immigrants elsewhere. Democrats cast themselves as the party of the common people, in keeping with the social and economic ideals of their patron saints, Thomas Jefferson and Andrew Jackson. The Dutch immigrants, *kleine luijden* (literally, "little people") all, had suffered much at the hands of the aristocratic Dutch authorities, especially the Seceders who broke with the state church. They wanted no part of aristocracy in America. Democracy was a sweet word in their ears; it denoted that no one was better than any other in virtue and morality. That the chief architect of the Democratic Party was the Old Dutch politico, Martin Van Buren of New York, likely made the party even more attractive for the young Dutch. Van Buren, a second-generation immigrant, could still speak the native tongue.

In addition to its populist image, the Democratic Party took pro-immigrant positions on naturalization and suffrage laws, in sharp contrast to the xenophobia of many in the opposition Whig Party. Indeed, the pioneer Dutch considered *Whig* and *Republican* to be synonymous with *aristocratic*. One of their first impressions of a Whig politician came from Yankees in the town of Allegan, led by Flavius T. Littlejohn, a leading citizen who ran for governor on the Whig ticket in 1849. Littlejohn and his cronies, when they learned of the Dutch settlement nearby, "talked loud" against them and wished "that they should move away." Otherwise, there would be "such a lot of paupers" to support that it would raise the taxes.[2]

2 Jacob Van Hinte, *Netherlanders in America: A Study of Emigration and Settlement in the Nineteenth and Twentieth Centuries in the United States of America*, 2 vols. (Groningen, 1928, English edition, Robert P. Swierenga, ed., Adriaan de Wit, transl., Grand Rapids: Baker, 1985), 421, 263; Engbertus Vander Veen, *Life History and Reminiscences* (Holland, 1917), 11; D. C. Henderson's editorial in *Allegan Journal*, 23 May 1859. Littlejohn's view of the Hollanders changed completely in the 1850s, and he also switched to the Democratic Party. In 1856 he ran unsuccessfully for Congress on the Democratic ticket and won office as Circuit Court Judge in 1858. "No man ever stood higher in the estimation of the people of 'the colony' than did Judge Littlejohn," declared Gerrit Van Schelven in 1898. Van Schelven was then Holland's leading historian and a judge himself (Gerrit Van Schelven, "The Early Administration of Justice," in Peter T. Moerdyke Papers, box 15, Holland Museum Archives (HMA); *De Hollander*, 18 Mar. 1880.

Once the Dutch immigrants passed the desperate years and gained a foothold in America, political rhetoric based on class and race had less appeal. They had fled a rigidly structured society in the Netherlands controlled by royalty, landed nobility, and church officials, all of whom pinched the common people at every turn. The government taxed them mercilessly and licensed every craft and trade. Large landowners and businessmen hired and fired them at will, and social rules required that they show deference to those of higher status. Dominies (literally "Lords") ran the church, and kings ruled the state. Escaping such circumstances for a land famed for social, economic, and political freedom was their dream.

The political behavior and culture of the Dutch Reformed in America can best be explained as a refutation of Old Country hierarchy and an embrace of New World equality, freedom, and opportunity. As immigrants and the children of immigrants, the Dutch saw the promise of American life and went for it. America was a place where a man could make his own way, where individual initiative, self-reliance, and rugged individualism gained one a competence. In America farm laborers could climb the agricultural ladder to ownership; tradesmen could become capitalists, apprentices master craftsmen, and laborers entrepreneurs. Everything was possible. Less government was better than more, low taxes were a virtue, and churches and schools must be free from outside control.

The annual American Fourth of July celebration provided an ideal way for the Dutch to express their ideals and "connect" emotionally with their new country. Hendrik Van Eyck recorded in his diary the 1849 commemoration of Independence Day in Zeeland. With the Stars and Stripes waving over the Zeeland Hotel amid a sky alight with torches, Dominie Vander Meulen led an emotional civic memorial in a "religious fashion." He gave the immigrants a history lesson, recounting Columbus' discovery of America, the Declaration of Independence, and the Revolutionary War that the "brave" George Washington so "brilliantly" brought "to a glorious conclusion," after which "hearty prayers of thanksgiving were sent up to the Great Ruler of peoples and of states." The young people then "proclaimed their joy by shooting guns and pistols."[3]

With these values and aspirations, the Dutch initially found appealing the small government ideals of the Democratic Party of

3 Hendrik Van Eyck, "Diary," in Henry Lucas, ed., *Dutch Immigrant Memoirs and Related Writing*, 2 vols. (Assen: Kok, 1955; revised edition, Grand Rapids: Eerdmans, 1997), 1:479.

Jefferson, Jackson, and James Polk. After the Civil War, when that party became dominated by southern whites, northern Catholics, and socialists, and the Republicans took up the mantle of social freedom and economic growth, the Dutch switched allegiances and found a comfortable home in the Grand Old Party, with its ideology of free soil, free labor, and free men.

Van Raalte endorses the Democratic Party

Van Raalte had much to do with the early political persuasions of the Dutch, but he never considered himself a politician. Already before emigrating, he told his followers that Americans controlled community affairs through the political process of electing local officials, such as the justice of the peace. "[A]ll the land and business belongs to us, and we govern ourselves by way of our own smartest citizens." He also knew that the American two-party system required choosing sides, and the Democratic Party was the logical choice. It had a history of favoring immigrants and had been the dominant party in Ottawa County and the State of Michigan since the 1830s. Michigan Senator Lewis Cass, hero of the War of 1812 and secretary of war under President Andrew Jackson and James Buchanan, befriended Van Raalte in Detroit, and Judge John Kellogg of Allegan had directed him to Ottawa County for open land. Both were Democrats. Van Raalte's newspaper, *De Hollander*, the colony's first sheet in 1850, championed Democratic candidates from the outset. Henry D. Post was the English editor of the bilingual paper, which was printed in Allegan.[4]

Van Raalte took the lead because his followers were complete novices politically. None had been eligible to vote in the Old Country. As farm laborers, small farmers, mechanics, and artisans of all kinds, they had failed to meet the landed property requirements. The new constitution of 1848, instigated by the liberal thinker Johan Thorbecke, recognized a general right to vote in principle, but in practice only tax-paying males were granted the franchise. This gave voting rights to only seventy-three thousand men in a population of four million, less than 2 percent. Thorbecke intended a gradual extension over time, but almost seventy years passed before the Netherlands achieved full suffrage. Males won full voting rights in 1917 and women in 1919.[5]

4 Hans Krabbendam, *Freedom on the Horizon: Dutch Immigration to America, 1840-1960* (Grand Rapids: Eerdmans, 2010), 287; William O. Van Eyck, "Old History on Sheriff-ship in Ottawa County," *Holland City News*, 25 Sept. 1930; "When Holland Was Democratic," *Holland City News*, 23 Feb. 1911, Moerdyke Papers, box 15, HMA.

5 Ivo Schöffer, *A Short History of the Netherlands* (Amsterdam: Allert de Lange, 1973), 116-20, 135.

Conversely, in the United States, taxpayer suffrage, which had replaced property suffrage after 1789, gave way in the 1820s to universal male suffrage, although women had to wait for the vote until 1919, same as in the Netherlands. Thus, some two decades before Dutch immigration began in earnest in the 1840s, all adult male citizens had gained the franchise. In America the immigrants, therefore, could enjoy the full blessings of citizenship for the first time.

Besides being political neophytes, the immigrants needed Van Raalte to tutor them in American politics because it was so strange. The free-wheeling, boisterous style of politicking and the unusual two-party, winner-take-all system differed radically from the staid and deferential society in the Netherlands where "people of the lower sort" were still required to doff the hat or curtsy to "people of the better sort." In the United States, the only prerequisite for foreign-born residents was naturalization. Federal election law required a five-year residency before applying for citizenship. But immigrants could file a declaration of intent or "first papers" after two-and-a-half years, which indicated their intent and, more important, allowed them to vote in local elections. Van Raalte was anxious to reach this stage, since as aliens he and the colonists lived in a civic twilight zone.

The language barrier also kept most Hollanders in the dark about American political discourse and the points of difference between the two major parties. Immigrants had to gain political smarts mostly second hand from American neighbors, who flabbergasted them by their interest in politics during the perennial election cycles. It seemed that the Americans talked of little else. One Dutchman reported that an American "very seldom will . . . converse with you about the weather, your health or anything of that sort; a laborer doesn't speak to his fellows about work, but the subject of conversation is nearly always government and politics." The Hollanders did no better in public governance than in worship. "The prospect of making anything more than raw Dutchmen out of this generation is poor indeed," Post opined. "They have no idea of a government or of a people's capacity to govern themselves; they do not entertain that idea for an instant. Here they are right; they have blundered into the truth, for they are not fit to elect their public officers, being on those points entirely destitute of judgment."[6]

Until they obtained the right to vote, the Dutch had to depend on opinionated Americans like Hoyt and Henry Post to run local

6 Quoted in George S. May, "Politics–As Usual?," Holland Historical Trust *Review* (Spring 1994): 4.

government. At Hoyt Post's death in 1903, Holland postmaster Gerrit Van Schelven eulogized him: "Mr. Post was greatly admired by the early Holland colonists and had their universal esteem and regard." If this bit of hyperbole was true, Post had done well to mask his true feeling toward the Dutch.[7]

During the Civil War era, Van Raalte led his followers in the next step of their Americanization—switching from the Democratic to the Republican Party. This transition is a marker of the maturing of the colony, since the Republicans represented the dominant Yankee Protestant culture of the Union. This was for the Dutch a "positive reference group" that they looked up to and tried to emulate.

People's Assembly, board of trustees, and consistory

In the beginning, authority in the Holland colony was divided between two institutions—one old and one new. Familiar was Van Raalte's consistory in the Log Church, who managed not only religious life but also secular affairs. Besides directing congregational life and guarding the daily walk of church members, the consistory, by default, became a judicial court and had to settle disputes among members over land dealings, business contracts, wages, livestock and woodlands, schooling, and domestic troubles. The sword in the hands of the elders, the spiritual overseers, was the power to bar confessing members from the communion table or, even worse, to excommunicate them. With only one church in the village for the first fifteen years, the threat of spiritual discipline was severe.

Totally unfamiliar to the immigrants was the *volksvergadering*, or People's Assembly, a gathering of adult males who assumed administrative and legislative powers and managed civic matters. The Hollanders, like so many other frontiersmen, had to fend for themselves in the years before township government was organized. This New England-type, town hall gathering, which Van Raalte first convened in February 1847 with the vanguard of his followers, met weekly from seven to nine in the evening to discuss and act on everyday concerns of the settlement. Usually the body met in the large house of Jan Binnekant centrally located a mile east of Holland on the Statesland Road (now Eighth Street at Waverly Road). This crude form of local government continued until the organization of Holland Township in 1849.[8]

7 Hoyt G. Post, "Holland," a manuscript deposited in the cornerstone of the Ottawa County Courthouse; "Identified With Holland's History; Postmaster Van Schelven's Reminiscences of Deceased," clipping from *Holland City News*, 1903, both in Post Family Papers, HMA.

8 The minutes of the People's Assembly (*volksvergadering*) 1848-49 are available in the

The first officers included Van Raalte's right-hand man, Bernardus Grootenhuis, along with Jacobus Schrader, Jan Binnekant, Jan Slag, and Oswald Van der Sluis. In 1848 the body chose Johannes Terhorst to preside and Hermanus Doesburg to record the minutes—only part of which has survived. The meetings continued until the end of 1849, when the functions were taken over by legal bodies. (In 1852 Doesburg became the editor of the local newspaper, *De Hollander*.) In April 1849 the Zeelanders and Vrieslanders set up their own people's assembly.[9]

Jurisdictional lines between the consistory and the People's Assembly were fuzzy. Spiritual issues, of course, clearly came under the purview of the consistory, but the elders in the early years also dealt with cases of petty thievery, intemperance, and Sabbath desecration. For example, a woman who slandered another had to make a public confession, and a troubled teen who fled from her stepfather was admonished. An elder criticized a woman whose dress exposed her neck below the collar. A man whose son cut down a neighbor's tree was sent home and ordered to read the biblical account of Eli, the judge of Israel who failed to discipline his two wicked sons. When the circus came to town, two elders posted themselves at the entrance to the tent, which so inhibited traffic by the youth that the men folded their tents and left in frustration.[10]

The assembly, as an extra-legal body, had no governing power, yet it levied taxes and private subscriptions for projects, based on its moral authority as reflecting the will of the people. The assembly, "a Common Council of the whole," discussed and acted on matters of a material, political, educational, religious, and social nature. The body constructed and maintained roads, a school and a church, the River Avenue bridge, and a pier at the mouth of Black Lake (now Lake Macatawa); it drew up a plan for fire protection and elementary education; it opened the Colony Store on the corner of Seventh Street and River Avenue; it regulated livestock (for example, pigs had to be penned until November 1 to save the gardens); and it held a subscription for a town (and church) bell.

The body also forbade the importation of store merchandise on Sunday and tried to ban the sale of all liquor, including *Hollands jenever*

---

original and in translation in the Moerdyke Papers, box 10, HMA; Jan Binnekant obit., *Holland City News*, 12 Feb. 1876.

9 Van Hinte, *Netherlanders in America,* 240-41; Henry Lucas, *Netherlanders in America: Dutch Immigration to the United States and Canada, 1789-1950* (Ann Arbor: University of Michigan Press, 1955, reprinted Grand Rapids: Eerdmans, 1989), 96-97; Adrian Van Koevering, *Legends of the Dutch* (Zeeland, MI: Zeeland Record, 1960), 240-42.

10 Engbertus Vander Veen, "Life Reminiscences" [1915], in Lucas, *Dutch Immigrant Memoirs,* 1:504; Van Hinte, *Netherlanders in America*, 238-39.

(Dutch gin). This decision augmented the clause in most of Van Raalte's deeds on village lots that barred the sale on the premises of "wine and spirituous liquors, or any mixed liquors." Yet state law permitted a trade in alcoholic beverages, and even Van Raalte provided an "out"—settlers might use wines and liquors for "medicinal purposes." So complaints continued about public drunkenness in the village, but most cupboards included alcoholic beverages. Dutchmen could not be kept from their drinks, even by a "moral majority."[11]

Alongside these two bodies stood a third, the Board of Trustees, which was formed early in 1848 at a special meeting of the male settlers to manage the financial affairs of the colony, sell communal town lots, direct the colony store, and set priorities for public improvements. The trustees were led by Van Raalte and included Jacob Van Der Veen, Johannes "Jan" A. Verhorst, Jacobus Schrader, and Jan Slag. A major problem was that the trustees had no defined structure, lines of accountability, or terms of tenure. They were an unaccountable governing body. And they did not limit actions to lands and finances, but "meddled" in the legislative area. The trustees, for example, forbade selling liquor, butchering cattle, or erecting shoddy fences within the village. This followed the Netherlandic model of the *B. en W.—Burgemaster en Wethouders* (mayor and commissioners)—which comprised the *gemeente* (municipal) executive and judicial body.[12]

The People's Assembly raised questions about the trustees' competence and authority, and "heated discussions" took place, especially after communal ventures stumbled. In early 1850 the board of trustees dissolved itself and turned over the management of community property, including the debts and liens, exclusively to Van Raalte. That Van Raalte took title to all lands in his own name was judicious, because he could thereafter warrantee deeds of all town lots sold to the colonists, which removed threats of titles "clouded" by speculators that so often plagued frontier communities. But it opened the dominie to increasing criticism for his real estate dealings and other leadership functions.[13]

The People's Assembly proved to be cumbersome and unwieldy. So after two years, on April 2, 1849, Van Raalte convened a meeting in his cedar log home on Fairbanks Avenue to organize Holland

11 Aleida Pieters, *A Dutch Settlement in Michigan* (Grand Rapids: Eerdmans Sevensma, 1923), 150-56; Lucas, *Netherlanders in America*, 96-98.

12 Van Hinte, *Netherlanders in America*, 240, citing Gerrit Van Schelven, "Historical Sketches," *De Grondwet*, 15 June 1915.

13 Ibid.

Township. The Michigan legislature had carved the township out of Ottawa Township two years earlier, on March 16, 1847, but without a fixed date of organization. It comprised all of Township 5 North and Ranges 14, 15, and 16 West and covered what is now Holland and Park Townships and the city of Holland. Van Raalte waited several years because the colonists could not bear the additional tax burden until then. The step gave the *Kolonie* a greater measure of autonomy and efficiency in local affairs. And it eliminated the need for the People's Assembly. Van Raalte's consistory, however, continued to rule on secular problems until the 1860s when it began referring members with contract and property disputes to civil authorities. In the outlying villages, the consistories continued for many more years to act in the civil realm.[14]

Van Raalte was "The Man" in early Holland. Newspaperman Gerrit Van Schelven, the first historian of the colony, aptly described the situation: "The People's Assembly at Holland was Van Raalte, the consistory at Holland was Van Raalte, the Classis of Holland was Van Raalte." Given the circumstances, this concentration of power "was the best way," said Van Schelven. But, he added, "[T]he inevitable outcome was this: since there was no appeal for the dissatisfied, justly or unjustly, there was little recourse besides secession." Netherlands historian Jacob Van Hinte observed wryly that "not everyone was in favor of this theocracy and many saw in the 'democracy' of Van Raalte actually his 'autocracy.'"[15]

Township and local politics

In the second phase of development in the 1850s and 1860s, which might be viewed as a time of Holland's adolescence, the American legal structure rendered the founders no longer "undisputed lords in their own castle," as Van Hinte put it. The formation of Holland Township in 1849, for example, created a rival government for the consistory to deal with. Since neither body had clearly delineated authority, the township officials and consistory had to tread carefully so as not to walk on each other's turf. Fortunately, church members guided by Van Raalte served in both bodies, and they could maintain a measure of harmony.[16]

14 Consistory Minutes, First Reformed Church, 18 Jan. 1859.

15 Gerrit Van Schelven, "The Classis of Holland: Social Relations and the Schism Following in 1857," Feb. 1914, Van Schelven Papers, box 9, HMA; Van Hinte, *Netherlanders in America*, 241.

16 Van Hinte, *Netherlanders in America*, 242.

The major social upheaval broke out when new immigrants arrived who could not appreciate the founders' struggle for survival, which had bound them together so tightly. The newcomers challenged the founding clerics for economic and political power, and the dominies, willingly or not, had to step back. As early as 1852 Hermanus Doesburg, a maverick school teacher in Van Raalte's congregation, gained editorial control of Van Raalte's newspaper, *De Hollander*, and began criticizing the dominie in print, despite pressure from the consistory to desist. Doesburg published an anonymous article that referred to Van Raalte and his clerical allies as "the Pope and his Cardinals," and he titled another article "Playing Boss." The consistory closed the communion table to Doesburg until he repented, which he finally did. But Van Raalte was so hurt that he refused to preach and went to Kalamazoo, while threatening to seek a call from the Dutch colony at the Cape of Good Hope. The editor of the Grand Rapids *Argus* took great delight in washing this dirty linen about Holland in its pages (chapter 32).[17]

To organize the government of Holland Township was a two-step process, according to the law. First, on March 31, 1849, all legal voters were called to caucus at the Post & Co. store and nominate candidates for office. Nine of the ten registered voters came. The offices, as needs be, were divided among the few Americans in town. Henry D. Post, who Democratic President James K. Polk had named postmaster of Holland in July 1848, was to be supervisor, director of the poor, and commissioner of highways. Post, a Vermont native, settled in Holland at Van Raalte's urgings. William Bronson was nominated clerk and assessor, and Hoyt D. Post (Henry's younger brother) treasurer and school inspector. Also nominated were three justices (Josiah Martin, James Walker, and Asa Haynes), another school inspector (Ira Manley), two more highway commissioners (Alvan Benham and James Walker), another director of the poor (James Walker), and two constables (Alvin Benham and Benjamin Brist).

Step two, the election, was held two days later, on April 2 at Van Raalte's home, and the outcome was a foregone conclusion. The ten qualified voters polled were all Americans, because no Dutchman yet qualified for the franchise. Nine of the ten were candidates for office! Many voters, according to William O. Van Eyck, worked temporarily at Benham and Brist's steam sawmill (located on what later became Benjamin Van Raalte's farm on Sixteenth Street). The partners had been

17 Grand Rapids *Argus*, 9 Mar. 1852; Van Hinte, *Netherlanders in America*, 241-42; undated letter, "Pope and Cardinals," of Oswald Van der Sluis "to my dear Friend Hein" (Van der Haar), translated by Moerdyke in Moerdyke Papers, box 14, HMA.

elected constables, appropriately. The only voter not a candidate was C. D. Stenich; he had not attended the caucus and missed the gravy train. To fund operations, the new board levied real estate taxes for schools at the rate of 50¢ per pupil, and allocated $200 for operating expenses and $25 for a pound to contain stray cattle and hogs. Since cattle and hogs over six months of age were allowed to roam at will, one wonders why a public pound was needed.[18]

The board apparently had an informal understanding to act on behalf of the Dutch under Dominie Van Raalte's direction. Despite this seeming friendly gesture by the Americans, the fact that they held all the offices seemed to cause some bad blood. One wag wrote the following doggerel: "Supervisor—Old Sort [Henry Post], Clerk—Hop Yeast [Bronson], Treasurer—Fresh Brine [Hoyt Post], Assessor—Whiskey Pop [Bronson], Highway Comm.—Go-it-stiff [Henry Post], School Insp.—Epsom Salts [Hoyt Post], Justices—Ginger Pop and Sour Kraut [Josiah Martin and Asa Haynes], Dir of Poor—Alcohol and Tobacco [James Walker]."[19] Whether these labels fit the particular officials is difficult to say without knowing more about their lives and character.

So insignificant were the early local elections that in 1849 only four votes were cast and in 1850 three votes. The 1850 poll was held in the Old Groningen schoolhouse near Jan Rabbers' house (directly east of, and across the Black River, from the former country club). Hoyt Post described the April 1 election: "Held a town meeting, polled three votes, and Henry [Post], Mr. [William] Bronson, and myself voted ourselves into office with hardly enough opposition to make it interesting. Our townsmen took very little interest in town matters. But two or three were there, and they were too busy quarreling among themselves to give attention to town matters."[20]

To gain control of their own political destiny, the Dutch filed their first papers as soon as possible. It was just in time for the spring township contest of 1851, the third election and the most boisterous. Three hundred men in Holland, one hundred in Zeeland, and forty in Vriesland wished to apply for citizenship. Van Raalte and Vander Meulen,

18 "A Holland Election of 'Ye Old Days,'" *Holland City News*, 15 Mar. 1909; Randall P. Vande Water, "First Election Held in 1849," in *Holland Happenings, Heroes and Hot Shots*, 2:19-21.

19 List of Holland Township officials, 1849-76, Moerdyke Papers, box 15; anonymous undated 3-page memo (by Gerrit Van Schelven), "Early Historical Data," Moerdyke Papers, box 15; Hoyt G. Post, "Holland," undated reminiscences (ca. 1893) in Post Family Papers, all in HMA.

20 Quote in Hoyt G. Post Diary, 1 Apr. 1850, typescript, 27; *Holland City News*, 1903 clipping in Van Schelven Collection.

who emphasized the duty of the Dutch to become active citizens, asked Henry Griffin, the Ottawa County clerk, to come from Grand Haven for the wholesale naturalization. Griffin agreed and cut his normal 50¢ fee in half. He went home that day whistling through the forest with $70 jingling in his pockets and his ears ringing from the hundreds of Hollanders who had taken their oaths. Jannes Vande Luyster, the "banker of the forest" and proprietor of the village of Zeeland, paid the fee for his one hundred townsmen. These 340 men represent the first citizenship class among the 1847 immigrants in the Holland colony. Obtaining their legal rights fulfilled the "fundamental understanding" that Van Raalte had agreed to while still in the Netherlands, namely, that all colonists upon reaching their majority would have equal rights and a full voice in governance.[21]

Rev. Albertus C. Van Raalte filed his first papers at the Allegan County courthouse on April 6, 1847. The document, reprinted below, reads as follows:

> I, Albertus C. Van Raalte do declare on oath that it is bone fide my intention to become a Citizen of the United States and to renounce forever all allegiance and fidelity to all and every Foreign Prince, Potentate, or State and all sovereignty whatever, and particularly to William Second King of the Netherlands. Sworn and subscribed this 6th day of April, 1847, before Mr. N. Manson, Clerk of Allegan County Mich.

The oath was filed and certified by Eli P. Watson, clerk of Allegan County and of the circuit court, on October 11, 1847. Note that Van Raalte did not use the clerk's correct name, but the official filed the oath as is.

The Holland Township election of April 1851 was held in the log church in Zeeland, chaired by the pastor, Cornelius Vander Meulen. It was a typical American-style gathering, where politicos fought for the spoils of office and a fair share of tax dollars for local roads and bridges. In cash-starved settlements like Holland, government jobs were coveted because they paid a regular salary in hard currency. The low tax base meant that road funds were never enough, and the ones who set priorities had power. Zeelanders were frustrated from the outset that the township did not provide enough monies to finish the Black River Bridge at Groningen and extend the roads from Zeeland southeast to Vriesland and east to Grandville. The 1851 poll was unusual, even by

[21] Report, H. Griffin, Ottawa County Clerk, in Detroit *Daily Free Press*, 17 July 1848; Pieters, *Dutch Settlement in Michigan*, 157-58.

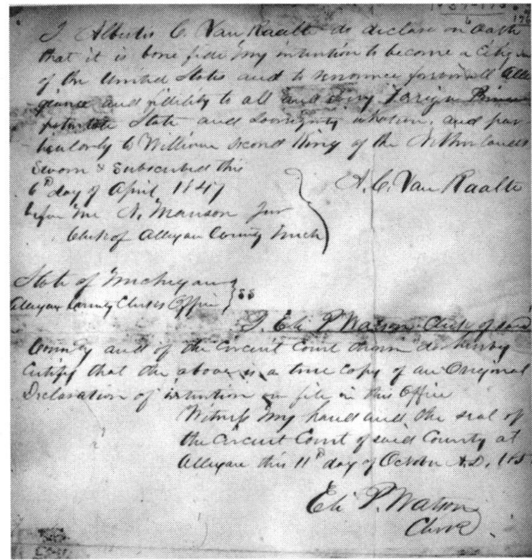

I Albertus C. Van Raalte do declare on oath that it is bona fide my intention to become a Citizen of the United States and to renounce forever all allegiance and fidelity to all and every Foreign Prince potentate State and Sovereignty whatever, and particularly to William Second King of the Netherlands

Sworn & Subscribed this 6th day of April, 1847 before me A. Manson Jun Clerk of Allegan County Mich

A. C. Van Raalte

State of Michigan Allegan County Clerks Office } ss

I, Eli P. Watson Clerk of said County and of the Circuit Court thereof do hereby Certify that the above is a true copy of an Original Declaration of intention on file in this Office

Witness my hand and the seal of the Circuit Court of said County at Allegan this 11th day of October A.D. 185

Eli P. Watson Clerk

First papers filed by Rev. Albertus C. Van Raalte, April 6, 1847, Allegan County Courthouse (*Joint Archives of Holland*)

American standards. Historian William Van Eyck claims it "was perhaps the most boisterous and disorderly ever held hereabout." A huge crowd of 264 voters came to cast ballots, and they became so raucous that a brawl broke out with shoving and some fisticuffs. The issue went deeper than jobs and dollars. The event aroused latent rivalries and animosities between the "city people" in *de stad* (Holland) and the "county people" in *het dorp* (Zeeland), which had age-old roots in the Old Country. Zeelanders and their compatriots from Drenthe–Staphorsters all–had reputations for being headstrong and stubborn. No wonder that these villagers often spit out the words "*de stad*" in a "venomous tone," as pioneer settler and local historian Engbertus Vander Veen (1828-1917) noted. The animosity between *stad* and *dorp*, like a "prickly little thorn," persisted for more than fifty years in the Holland settlement.[22] Besides the historic rivalry between the two peoples and towns, settlers in the outlying villages resented Van Raalte's perceived autocracy and theocracy.[23]

Vander Veen, an eyewitness and close friend of Van Raalte, recalled the scene vividly in his *Reminiscences*. The meeting clearly made an indelible impression on him:

> Early in the morning of the day of the caucus, Dominie Van Raalte, accompanied by such as had the right to vote and also by some

22 Vander Veen, *Life History*, 19-21; William O. Van Eyck, "The Three Town Halls," *Holland City News*, 23 Jan. 1930.

23 Van Hinte, *Netherlanders in America*, 243.

> friends and boys, went to Zeeland, walking the entire distance, climbing over fallen trees, and wading through water. They arrived in time for the meeting. Dominie Vander Meulen was in the pulpit, acting as chairman. Soon there was great excitement, and Dominie Van Raalte stood on the pews appealing to the men, saying 'Brothers! Brothers!' The Zeelanders, supported by their friends from Statesland [Drenthe], wanted all the offices to the exclusion of the men from Holland. The dominie's exhortations calmed the spirits just in time to prevent hard blows.
>
> After the caucus we went home in a body. Some of the office seekers were angry and jealous, complaining that the Zeelanders had captured the best offices. Pieter Van den Burg said: "Holland is ignored." Others said: "Well! Well! That old Jan Hulst from Statesland, justice of the peace. That man was such a rebellious character! He is more for war than peace!" [Hulst, a native of Staphorst, in June 8, 1847, was the first white settler in what became Zeeland.]

Vander Veen then explained the background of the conflict:

> The Zeelanders and Stateslanders were angry with the men from Holland. They declared that the Pope and his Cardinals of Holland [Dominie Van Raalte and his consistory] had come to Zeeland to impose their rule, and they were selfish. The expression "Pope and his Cardinals" was frequently employed by malcontented spirits, especially in the editorials of Giles Vande Wall in *De Nederlander*, a weekly newspaper published [in Kalamazoo] for a short time by men who gloried in publishing vicious articles.[24]

Although the men from Holland may have lost in the caucus, they did snag most of the township posts. These included Bernardus Grootenhuis as highway commissioner, Teunis Keppel director of the poor, Van Raalte as school inspector, Aldert Plugger and Hendrik Van Eijk (Van Eyck) assessors, and constables Hendrik Van Eijk and Fredrick Kieft. Two other Zeelanders triumphed besides Van Eijk, Robbertus De Bruyn as treasurer and Jacob Den Herder as one of the four constables. Another constable was Willem Kremers from Drenthe.[25]

24 Vander Veen, "Life Reminiscences," [1915] in Lucas, *Dutch Immigrant Memoirs,* 1:512; Lucas, *Netherlanders in America*, 241-42. Another eyewitness, Jacob Den Herder of Zeeland, in an 1876 address, referred obliquely to "the tricks of American [township] supervisors and voters at a warm gathering." Den Herder, "Brief History of the Township and Village of Zeeland," translated by Nella Kennedy, Jacob Den Herder Papers, JAH.

25 Van Schelven memo, undated, in Holland City Records, box 1, HMA.

Water color painting of brawl by Anneus J. Hillebrands (signed "JH"), school teacher in Old Groningen from 1848 to 1851. Those named are; *lower left*: Mulder & Zoon (Berend and Johannes); *left to right, center*: Henry Meengs, Sylvester L. Morris, Herman Verbeek, Jan Trimpe, James Koning, Jan (John) Roost (Roest), and Isaac Kapon (Cappon); *far right*: Cornelius Blom Sr. All were from Holland except the Mulders and Blom. Trimpe, Koning, and Blom were "star route" mail carriers, and Trimpe was the road overseer (*Archives, Holland Historical Trust*).

After this election Zeelanders decided to become the absolute masters of their fate. In 1849 Vande Luyster had platted the village of Zeeland (in the northern half of Section 19, Township 5 North, Range 14 West), and the next year the state legislature set off Zeeland Township from Holland Township. In the summer of 1851, some three months after the bitter spring caucus, on July 14, 1851, the Zeelanders assembled in their log church to organize themselves and elect township officials. This rendered the People's Assembly of Zeeland obsolete.[26]

Remarkably, as much as the Dutch fought among themselves over the offices, they did not claim them all, as their numbers would warrant. Rather, Van Raalte and Vander Meulen saw to it that their American friends retained posts that required special expertise. Henry Post continued as supervisor, justice of the peace, and highway

26 Journal of the Board of Supervisors, Ottawa County, 17 June 1851, in Moerdyke Papers, box 15, HMA. Elected were Robbertus De Bruyn of Zeeland, schoolteacher Elias G. Young of Vriesland, and Johannes Op't Holt of Drenthe.

Water color by Anneus J. Hillebrand, signed "JH," making sport of the fight for political spoils between Dutch and Americans (*Archives, Holland Historical Trust*)

commissioner; Hoyt Post was treasurer and Bronson clerk. The Dutch took as many of the other posts as they were capable of holding, given their limitations of language and civic knowledge. In the 1853 township elections, Hendrik Van Eijk became treasurer and justice of the peace, and Pieter Vanden Berg clerk, Jannes Vande Luyster director for the poor, and Jacob Liesveld, Jan Kolvoord, and Barend Van Lente constables. Homer Hudson, another American, received one of the four constable jobs. It was 1856 before Post stepped aside as county supervisor and Hendrik Van Eijk became the first Dutchman to hold this top administrative office. Van Raalte continued as director (trustee in 1860) of the Holland Township school until 1861, when he declined re-election, believing that the board needed some Americans.[27]

Anneus Hillebrands' water color, which portrays the fight for political spoils between Dutch and Americans, demonstrates that some degree of animosity existed between foreign-born and native-born citizens in the early 1850s. The water color shows four Dutchmen acting to "Replace!" (*Afgelost!*) the "ex"-Americans as director of the poorhouse, justice of the peace, clerk, and supervisor. At the top of the drawing are the words "time pass" and "one year," with the wind

[27] *De Hollander*, 6 Apr. 1853, 16 Apr. 1856; *Allegan Journal*, 20 Apr. 1857; "Our Pioneer School District," *Holland City News*, 15 Apr. 1893. The latter is a summary of official school board minutes that are no longer extant.

goddess blowing the Americans away. Above the heads of the Dutchmen is the word "majority" and the number of votes: 38, 62, 33, and 76²/₃. Over the heads of the Americans is the phrase "Nothing to do for us" and four zeroes, to show that they received not a single vote. Hoyt Post, the outgoing treasurer, is pictured with a moneybag on his shoulder containing $1,500. Bronson, the clerk, has an ink quill stuck between his ear and glass frame. The Americans look scruffy and the Dutchmen spiffy. The Dutchmen on the left hand are Henry D. Post (an "adopted" Dutchman), supervisor; Pieter Vanden Berg, township clerk; Hendrik Van Eijk, justice of the peace; and Jannes Vande Luyster, director of the poor.

National politics: nativism, prohibition, and abolition, 1852-60

In the 1851 gubernatorial vote in Holland Township, the last before the Dutch participated, there were thirty-one Democrat votes and only four Whig votes. This proves that the few Americans in Holland were Democrats, except for four or five Whigs. Understandably, in the 1850s, the Dutch also voted overwhelmingly Democratic, beginning with the 1852 presidential race, the first in which they could vote. In that election Holland Township voters cast 123 Democratic ballots for Franklin Pierce (96 percent) and five Whig ballots for Winfield Scott. Since the five Whig ballots were likely cast by Americans, one can conclude that the Dutch voted Democratic "to a man."[28] This could be expected, given Van Raalte's persuasion and their own proclivities. The elections from 1852 through 1854 took place in the Holland schoolhouse, and thereafter in the Orphan House, until the first town hall was erected in 1862. A constable stood by each time to prevent a repeat of the near riot of 1851 in Zeeland.[29]

Democrats dominated Michigan state government, and their leaders had befriended Van Raalte and helped the Dutch find a home here in 1847. Detroit attorney Theodore Romeyn "was brought up

[28] In Zeeland Township the outcome was 128 to 11 (92 percent) in favor of the Democrats. Grand Haven *Grand River Times,* 24 Apr. 1852; Van Eyck, "Old History of Sheriff-ship," *Holland City News*, 25 Sept. 1930; "When Holland was Democratic," *Holland City News*, 23 Feb. 1911, in Moerdyke Papers, box 15, HMA; report on "De Hollander" by *Sheboygan Nieuwsbode* correspondent "Argus," 12 Feb. 1852, in Moerdyke Papers, box 3, HMA; Larry Wagenaar, "The Early Political History of Holland, Michigan, 1847-1868" (MA Thesis, Kent State University, 1992), 13-17, 28-29, 45. Since 254 votes were cast in the spring 1851 local election in Holland Township, when the Hollanders participated for the first time, and only 128 votes were cast in the 1852 presidential election, it appears that many Dutch had still not completed the naturalization process. They could vote in local elections after filing first papers, but not in national elections.

[29] Van Eyck, "Three Town Halls."

in the Democratic school of politics," as was Kalamazoo postmaster and state senator Nathaniel Balch, and most important of all, Allegan Judge John Kellogg, who personally led Van Raalte to the mouth of Black Lake, Ottawa County sheriff Henry Pennoyer, and the Post brothers, Henry and Hoyt. All these close friends of Van Raalte in the early years indoctrinated him in the standard political doctrine that the Democrats befriended immigrants while the Whigs were tainted with nativism (antipathy to immigrants). Van Raalte was introduced to United States Senator Lewis Cass of Michigan, the former territorial governor and a dominant figure in national politics since the 1810s. The Dutch cleric also became friends with Judge Epaphroditus Ransom of Kalamazoo, whose policies as governor of Michigan in 1849-50 were "immigrant-friendly." The pioneer Dutch owed much to the Democrats and willingly joined the party.[30]

In contrast to Van Raalte, Hendrik P. Scholte in Pella relished the role of politician. An admirer of Henry Clay, Scholte induced his colonists to vote for Clay and the Whig ticket in 1852, which over 80 percent did. Only after nativism reared its ugly head in Iowa did Scholte switch to the Democrats by 1854. Democrats dominated in Iowa as they did in Michigan in the early years.[31]

Senator Cass took care to cultivate the Dutch vote by befriending them and giving the impression that he supported the river and harbor bill pending in Congress in 1851, which included monies for the Black Lake harbor improvement and a lighthouse. On the political stump in Grand Rapids, Cass spoke eloquently in favor of the bill, while he castigated "aristocracy" and defended "democracy." Such rhetoric played well in Holland. But when the harbor bill came to the floor of the Senate, Cass voted against it, much to the chagrin of the Dutch.[32]

Van Raalte and the colonial leaders had determined that a harbor on Lake Michigan was an absolute necessity for the future success of the settlement. That Whig President Millard Fillmore, in office since 1849, had failed to fund the Rivers and Harbors bill, after Congress had appropriated the monies, strongly displeased over two-thirds of the voters in Ottawa Country, according to the editor of *De Hollander*.[33]

30 Van Hinte, *Netherlanders in America,* 419; Willis F. Dunbar, *Michigan: A History of the Wolverine State* (Grand Rapids: Eerdmans, 1965), 356, 416-18, 420-21.

31 Robert P. Swierenga, "The Ethnic Voter and the First Lincoln Election," *Civil War History* 11 (Mar. 1965): 27-43, reprinted in Swierenga, *Faith and Family: Dutch Immigration and Settlement in the United States, 1820-1920* (New York: Holmes & Meier, 2000), 274-89.

32 Henry Lucas, *Netherlanders in America*, 543.

33 *Grand Rapids Enquirer*, 4 Aug. 1852, quoting De Hollander, 30 Apr. 1852; Grand Haven *Grand River Times*, 18 Aug., 1 Dec. 1852.

Nativism and a niggardly attitude toward harbor improvements extinguished the last spark of Whiggism among the Dutch, according to William Van Eyck. In a political parade in Grand Rapids in 1852, a wagon carried a banner in both Dutch and English that declared: "Oppressed in the Old World, protected by Democracy in the New World, we go for Pierce and [William R.] King [the vice-presidential candidate]." Beneath the banner hung a dead raccoon, head down. This vivid prop said it all; Whiggery was dead in Holland and Zeeland. Vander Meulen called on Hollanders to support Samuel Clark, the Democratic candidate for the House of Representatives, because "he had proven to be a reliable person . . . by his knowledge of our most precious interests which he . . . desires [to] endorse and promote."[34]

Another contentious issue was prohibition, which was considered a stalking horse for nativism. The Whig Party, especially its dominant New England Yankee Protestant wing, sought to ban the manufacture and sale of alcoholic beverages, both to reduce the social costs of alcoholism and to strike at the perceived licentious lifestyle of (mostly Catholic) immigrants. The state of Maine had accomplished this goal in 1851, and the crusade was spreading. In Zeeland, for example, Arie Van Bree, the state liquor agent (whose salary was $15 per year), could barely sell his $20 of inventory the first year, since so few accounts were permitted.[35]

In 1853 Whigs in the Michigan legislature managed to enact a prohibition law, but it was made contingent on a popular referendum. The act would ban the manufacture and sale of alcoholic beverages and levy heavy fines for possession; even communion wine was proscribed. This ballot issue further incensed the Hollanders in West Michigan, who despite an aversion to saloons, wanted no legal impediment to their glass of beer or communion wine. They and most new immigrants considered the law an infringement on personal and religious liberty and not a panacea for the nation's social and moral ills. As Scholte declared, it is misguided to "try to effect by law that which can only be effected by the Gospel." Worse, the Dutch detected nativist overtones among the proponents of the referendum. As a result, Holland voted down the proposal by a majority of more than three to one and Zeeland by more than five to one. But the referendum passed statewide by twenty thousand votes, only to be overturned by the courts on a technicality.[36]

34 *Sheboygan Nieuwsbode*, 2 Nov. 1852, cited in Lucas, *Netherlanders in America*, 543 (quote); *De Hollander*, 13 Oct. 1852 (quote).

35 Van Loo, "Zeeland Township and Village," in Lucas, *Dutch Immigrant Memoirs,* 1:246; *De Hollander*, 15 June 1853.

36 Van Hinte, *Netherlanders in America*, 239-40 (quote), 545; Dunbar, *Michigan*, 430; *De*

In the meantime, consistories had difficulty obtaining sacramental wine. Mattheus P. Naaije, an elder in the Graafschap Church, was turned away by the two Holland storekeepers, Aldert Plugger and Henry Post, with the same message: "I may not sell any wine without a doctor's prescription," and the doctor would only prescribe wine for sickness, since medicinal wine alone could be sold under the Maine Law. Naaije penned an angry letter of lament to *De Hollander*: "If this law prevails, will we ever be able to celebrate communion?" When the Republicans came to power in 1855, they passed a revised law that permitted communion wine and Michigan joined the "dry" states. Enforcement of the law, however, was so lax that it became a dead letter.[37]

The Dutch vote against teetotalers brought nativist attacks down on their heads. John Wilson, a Michigan Republican, charged in a speech that "not one single throb of patriotism" beats in the hearts of foreigners. "Some tell me that many foreigners are intelligent; yes intelligent," Wilson cried. "How in the name of Almighty God can they say it? Look at the Dutchman smoking his pipe, and if you can see a ray of intelligence in that dirty, idiotic face of his, show it to me."[38] "Dutch Cattle" was another epithet contemptuously hurled at the Hollanders. In 1854 and 1855 the stridently nativist and anti-Catholic Know Nothing (or American) Party captured many votes in the Midwest among Yankees who touted the slogan: "America for the Americans." The Know Nothings pushed for a naturalization law that would require twenty-one, rather than five, years before immigrants could apply for citizenship. The Dutch read this as a call for the repeal of all naturalization laws.[39]

Rhetoric and "reforms" such as these kept the Dutch in the Democratic camp, despite their growing disappointment with the party's refusal to support internal improvement grants and its increasingly southern, pro-slavery stance, especially on the controversial issue of the fugitive slave law and likely extension of slavery into Kansas Territory under the Kansas-Nebraska Act. The Dutch had always opposed

---

Hollander, 7, 14 Sept., 1 Dec. 1853, 2, 23 Feb., 20 Apr., 14 Sept. 1854. The vote in July 1853 in Ottawa County was 427 for and 321 against (*De Hollander*, 13 July 1853).

37 *De Hollander*, 22 Dec. 1853.

38 *Grand Haven News*, 12 Sept. 1860, quoted in Wagenaar, "Early Political History," 27; Van Hinte, *Netherlanders in America*, 239; *De Grondwet*, 22 Mar. 1887, quote translated by William Buursma. Wilson may have had Germans more than Dutch in his line of fire, because he made a reference to their love of "cabbage and lager beer." But Americans seldom differentiated between Germans and Hollanders (Duits and Dutch); all foreigners suffered from such stereotyping.

39 Swierenga, "Ethnic Voter."

slavery, even before emigrating, but they had no first hand experience with it, and slavery seemed a distant problem. President Pierce's veto in 1854 of the Whig-sponsored Rivers and Harbors appropriation bill, presumably as an economy measure, struck much closer to home and was a particularly bitter pill for the Dutch to swallow. Their man had failed to deliver. How blind the Dutch are, sneered the editor of the *Grand Rapids Eagle*, a Republican sheet, to support an "administration that gives 'millions to slavery' but not a cent to commerce."[40]

The Kansas-Nebraska Act also split the dysfunctional Whig Party and led to the emergence of a new free-soil party that attracted northern Whigs and also some disillusioned Democrats. The Republican Party was formed at Ripon, Wisconsin on February 28, 1854, and on July 6 some 1,500 people gathered in Jackson for the first Michigan Republican state convention. It is unlikely that any political leader from Holland participated, given their strong Democratic proclivities. Cornelius Van Loo of Zeeland, then sixteen years old, may have been the only Hollander present under "the Oaks" at Jackson, Michigan, and he boasted about it at every Republican gathering for the next fifty years. Editor Doesburg of *De Hollander*, a Democratic sheet, made no mention of the historic Jackson meeting until three months later, in late August, when Jacob Quintus, editor of the *Sheboygan* (Wisconsin) *Nieuwsbode* and a fresh convert to the Republicans, challenged him in an editorial to take a public stand for the new party and the candidates nominated in Jackson. The possibility of opening Kansas territory to slavery under a policy of squatter sovereignty would be the defining issue in the upcoming mid-term national elections, and Doesburg must let it be known "whether he be 'bone or fish.'... No one can serve two masters."[41]

Since the *Nieuwsbode* served as the national Dutch-language weekly and circulated widely in West Michigan, Doesburg had to respond. He did so in a lengthy rebuttal, charging Quintus with being a turncoat to Democratic principles; he and the Holland citizens would "prefer to abide in the ship" and stay with the Northern Democrats. The Republican Party was "merely the Whig Party under a new name" and could not be trusted. Moreover, Doesburg asked rhetorically, "Do you believe that Slavery will ever be abolished in the states by act of Congress?"[42]

40 *De Hollander*, 17 Aug. 1854, 12 Sept. 1855 (quote).

41 *Ottawa Register*, 23 Nov. 1857; *De Hollander*, 22 Aug. 1855; *Holland City News*, 23 Sept. 1926. Randall P. Vande Water hypothesized that John Roost might have attended the Jackson convention, given local concerns about federal funds for the harbor ("Holland Never Voted for Lincoln," in *Holland Happenings,* 4:15), but no evidence has been found to confirm this.

42 *De Hollander*, 24 Aug. 1854.

Despite Doesburg's brush off of the Nebraska bill as reason enough to switch parties, many in the Holland colony began to have second thoughts. By the 1854 November elections, Dutch dissatisfaction with the Democrats was growing; the 100 percent vote of 1852 declined by one-third to 64 percent. Whig-Republicans in Zeeland led the move away from the Democrats, much to the disapproval of Vander Meulen and Van Raalte. While Zeeland went Republican for the first time, Fillmore and Holland Townships remained in the Democratic column, "aided by the pastors, elders, and deacons of the *Gereformeerde* [Reformed] Church," according to *De Hollander*. George Boer, a Drenthe farmer who switched already in 1854, noted in 1859 how lonely it had been in the new party. "We have had hardly none that would advocate the principles of the Republican Party, so we lived here dead to its true and honorable principles." Old-timer Dirk Vyn recalled that Republicans were "as scarce as hen's teeth." But change was in the wind, Boer declared. "A good many around me seem to be aroused" and turn from the "Democratic, Slavocratic party" to "Liberty's rays." It was especially in the cities of Grand Rapids, Kalamazoo, and Grand Haven that the Dutch first showed Republican tendencies.[43]

The appeals of abolitionists notwithstanding, *De Hollander* held steadfast and endorsed Democratic Representative Clark for re-election, even though he had voted for the Kansas-Nebraska Act. Since Clark worked assiduously for a harbor improvements bill, Doesburg cut him some slack on Kansas. Slavery there or in any other territories would not thrive, he thought, because it was in violation of God's natural law. It would implode on its own. No need to place the Union in jeopardy over its expansion, as the radical Republicans risked doing. That Scholte of the *Pella Gazette* agreed with him gave added assurance. But Jacob Quintus, editor of the influential *Sheboygan Nieuwsbode*, thought otherwise; he deserted the Democratic Party over the Kansas-Nebraska bill. Quintus had many subscribers in Michigan. The Kansas bill fiasco perhaps prompted Senator Cass to make a campaign stop in Grand Haven in late September to shore up the Democratic base.[44]

43 Ibid., 9 Nov. 1854 (quote), translated by Simone Kennedy; Boer's letter in *Allegan Journal*, 23 May 1859; Cornelius Van Loo, "Zeeland Township and Village," in Lucas, *Dutch Immigrant Memoirs and Related Writings*, 1: 246-47.

44 In 1854 the vote was 107 Democrat and 60 Republican (Van Eyck, "Old History on Sheriff-ship, HMA"; *Sheboygan Nieuwsbode*, 9 Mar. 1853, 15, 22 Aug., 21, 28 Nov. 1854, 14 Apr. 1857 (cited in Lucas, *Netherlanders in America*, 545-47); *De Hollander*, 5 Oct. 1854, 28 May 1856. Doesburg's editorials in *De Hollander* include "Throw off your mask," 24 Aug. 1854; "American Slavery," 28 Sept. 1854; also 31 Aug., 21 Sept., 5 Oct. 1854.

A major loss for Holland was the defeat in 1854 of their townsman Hoyt Post as county clerk and registrar. Post spoke fluent Dutch and went out of his way to help the Dutch in court cases and other county business. He was a friend sorely to be missed at the courthouse. The editor of the *Grand River Eagle* thought otherwise: "We are glad to see, by the result of the last election, that this crooked Post is fast losing his boasted standing, as the political autocrat of the Holland colony."[45]

As the fall 1856 presidential election heated up between Democrat James Buchanan and Republican John C. Frémont, county Democrats held a mass rally in Grand Haven that attracted about two hundred Dutchmen. Pieter Vanden Berg of Grand Haven gave an eloquent speech on behalf of Buchanan, and stressed that the Democratic Party had always befriended immigrants. Jan Binnekant of Holland declared that Buchanan had to be elected "in order to preserve our liberties." Doesburg of *De Hollander* reported that the meeting "clearly demonstrated that our small band of Dutch people is firmly attached to the Democratic Party. Mr. Quintus may shout 'Frémont! Frémont!' but all his howling will help him not at all. The Know-Nothing Republicans are distributing *De Nieuwsbode* gratis, but it were better for them to keep their money in their pockets, because the simple Hollanders are slow to let themselves to be delivered even though people try to sell them."

Despite the Dutch support of the Democrats, not one Hollander was placed on the Ottawa County ticket in the November election. That party seemingly also harbored anti-immigrant Know Nothing sympathies. The Frémont Club in West Michigan attracted barely a half dozen men from Holland. In a meeting at Grand Rapids, Isaac Cappon was elected president and George Steketee secretary. Oswald Van der Sluis addressed the group, and John Roost likely also was there. These were among the first Republicans in Holland. Adrian J. Westveer, who was a student at the Holland Academy at the time, later wrote sarcastically that there were in Holland, "all told, about 6½ Republicans. In the surrounding settlements I doubt whether there could be found a single one."[46]

During the 1856 campaign, Doesburg looked to Scholte for rhetorical arguments against Republicans. He copied so many *Pella Gazette* editorials condemning "Know Nothing Abolition Republicanism" that a local critic, signed "Overisel," humorously

45 *De Hollander*, 23 Nov., 28 Dec. 1854.

46 *Allegan Journal*, 6 Aug., 17 Oct. 1856; *De Hollander*, 3 Sept. 1856, quoted and translated in Lucas, *Netherlanders in America*, 552; Adrian Westveer, "Some Memories of Ante-College Days," *Anchor* 10 (Sept. 1888): 152.

dubbed *De Hollander*'s editorial byline, "Doesburg, Scholte & Co."[47]

In September Scholte accepted an invitation to visit Michigan for the first time. He preached in Van Raalte's new church sanctuary and spoke at a Democratic campaign rally in the schoolhouse, where he was "received with much real enthusiasm." Before returning to Iowa, Scholte also stumped among the Dutch in Zeeland, Grand Haven, Grand Rapids, and Kalamazoo. He got a hero's welcome everywhere, both for his role in leading the Secession of 1834 in the Netherlands and for his American political savvy. But as a clergyman, he took some brickbats for entering the domain of politics.[48]

Dominie Scholte's energetic speeches and Doesburg's sharp editorial pen held the 1856 Democratic vote in Holland Township steady at 64 percent, as in 1854. Frémont and the Republicans would have done better if the Dutch had not feared that he and his cohorts were tainted with Know Nothingism. Some painted him black, instead of red, white, and blue. An editorial in *De Hollander* raised the question: "Is or was Colonel Frémont a Catholic?" In Holland these unproven "facts" about the colonel's nativism and Catholicism proved fatal.[49] Not so in Grand Haven, Ottawa County, and statewide, where Democrats "suffered a most disastrous defeat, a complete annihilation," while Republicans swept to victory for the first time. Doesburg was totally dejected.[50]

With Doesburg down, Republican politicos in Detroit, Lansing, Grand Rapids, and Grand Haven encouraged Holland Township clerk Jacob Bailey, a Republican, to offer to buy Doesburg's paper and turn it into a Republican sheet. Other rumors circulated that Doesburg was offered lucrative state printing contracts, including the county delinquent tax lists worth $300 a year, if he would switch party allegiances. He declined both offers, yet the so-called "Doesburg bribery case" caused much ink to flow in state newspapers for some weeks. Local Democratic leaders—postmaster Henry Post, Jan Trimpe, Manly Howard, and Kommer Schaddelee—all stood solidly behind Doesburg. But just in case the Dutchman caved, Post decided to establish an English-language paper in Holland, the *Ottawa Register*, the first issue of which appeared in August 1857. Post's paper strongly defended

47 Scholte editorials on "De Know Nothings," *De Hollander*, 25 Feb., 23 May 1855, 30 Apr., 4, 21 May, 27 Aug., 3 Sept. 1856; Doesburg, "Republican Consistency," *De Hollander*, 16 July 1856; *Allegan Journal*, 10 Sept. 1856.

48 "Mr. Scholte's Visit to Holland," *De Hollander*, 9 July (quote), 12, 24 Sept. 1856; Lucas, *Netherlanders in America*, 552.

49 *De Hollander*, 23 July 1856.

50 Holland Township in 1856 cast 129 Democrat and 74 Republican votes, ibid., 19 Nov. 1956.

Democrats as the party of national unity and the Republicans as the Negro party, whose abolitionist agenda is the "folly of our times."[51]

In the spring 1857 state and local election, Democrats carried Holland Township by a majority of ninety-five votes, although Republican Jacob Bailey won re-election as township clerk. Democrats again captured most state and local races in 1858, but John Roost defeated the incumbent Democrat, Hendrik Van Eijk, for Holland Township supervisor. Roost was the first prominent politician to switch parties; he founded the Republican Party in Holland, along with Cappon, George Steketee, and Van der Sluis. D. C. Henderson, editor of the *Allegan Journal*, a Republican paper, crowed: "We pity Doesburg, Post & Co. and as far as we are concerned, we say, let them rail on. The election of John Roost as Supervisor seems to give them considerable uneasiness. Well it may. What will they do about it?"[52]

In the 1857 state elections, the Democratic Party of Kent and Ottawa Counties nominated Vander Meulen to be a regent of the University of Michigan, which prompted their Republican counterparts to nominate Van Raalte for the same position under its banner. Both hoped to snare the Dutch vote. The two ministerial colleagues sidestepped this crass use of their positions by withdrawing their nomination and suggesting instead John Van Vleck, principal of the Holland Academy. Van Vleck easily won with 2,400 votes, but Van Raalte and Vander Meulen still received 34 and 157 votes, respectively. Their wise withdrawal shielded them from political intrigues and relieved their parishioners from having to make a difficult choice. Vander Meulen remained active in Democratic Party gatherings and attended a rally for US Senator Stephen Douglas of Illinois held in Chicago. But did Van Raalte's nomination by the state Republicans signal a change of heart on his part?[53]

In the 1858 fall national election campaign, Roost organized the first Republican meeting in Holland, and recruited Nicholas Vyn, Johannes Hoogesteger, Herman Verbeek, Anne Flietstra, Isaac Cappon,

51 *Allegan Journal*, 10 Sept., 1, 31 Oct. 1856; 3 Aug. 1857; *Ottawa Register*, 16 Nov. 1857.

52 Roost's controversial political career as a Republican began in late 1857 when Holland Township clerk Jacob Bailey moved to Allegan County and appointed Roost as his successor. The Democratic-controlled County Board of Supervisors deemed Roost's appointment illegal and named Democrat Cornelius Doesburg, Holland's school teacher, to the clerkship. Roost refused to give up the records, however, until Doesburg successfully sued in the county court and Sheriff Gray compelled him to hand them over (*Ottawa Register*, 14 Dec. 1857; *Allegan Journal*, 26 Apr. 1858).

53 Grand Rapids *Argus*, 31 Mar., 14 Apr. 1857; *Grand Rapids Daily Eagle*, 19, 27 Mar. 1857; *De Hollander*, 1, 15 Apr. 1857, 24 Oct. 1860; *Allegan Journal*, 23 Mar., 27 Apr. 1857.

Engbertus Vander Veen, and Pieter Zalsman, among others. All these men had been active Democrats. "The Hollanders Awake for Freedom," crowed the *Grand Rapids Daily Eagle* headline, and it seemed like the boasting was for real. Clearly, a political realignment was underway in Holland. Van Raalte very likely supported this movement but was not yet emboldened to do so openly. Doesburg kept the Democratic banner on the masthead of the *De Hollander*. During the campaign, Cornelius Steketee, deputy postmaster of Grand Rapids and a Democratic Party workhorse, labeled Roost a "black Republican," which carried racist overtones. The *Daily Eagle* published Roost's lengthy response to the "slander" under the title, "A Misstatement Exposed." In the election, Dutch support for the Democrats in Holland Township again climbed above 80 percent. But it was the last hurrah.[54]

In the spring 1859 election, Republican leader Roost won re-election for supervisor and highway commissioner by more than a one-hundred-vote majority for each office, but most local races and the governor's office again had solid Democratic majorities. Running a divided and very partisan township board made Roost's job difficult. Near the end of his first term in office, local Democrats attempted to unseat him with a dirty trick. On the very day of the township caucus, they had the county sheriff in Grand Haven arrest him on trumped up charges of embezzlement as agent of the Harbor loan fund bonds, so that Roost could not attend the meeting. Then the caucus nominated Henry Post, a Democrat, to run against him. The ruse backfired, and Roost was re-elected by a "handsome majority" (a margin of sixty-nine votes), along with the entire Republican slate. Local Democrats continued to charge Roost with chicanery and declare him guilty in the case of "The People vs. J. Roost," although he was never convicted and Van Raalte continued to defend him. The issue revolved around Roost's refusal to turn over to the township treasurer some $149 in harbor funds that he had received in a draft from Van Raalte.[55]

Hermanus Doesburg's son Jacob O. voiced the Democratic line in a March 1860 letter to his former classmate at the Holland

[54] *De Hollander*, 29 Apr. 1857, 7 Apr., 21 Oct. 1858, 14 Mar. 1860; *Allegan Journal*, 19 Apr. 1858; *Grand Rapids Daily Eagle*, 6, 14 Oct. 1858. Holland Township in 1858 voted for governor 143 Democrat and 32 Republican; Zeeland Township voted 62 Democrat and 9 Republican, *De Hollander*, 23 Dec. 1858.

[55] *De Hollander*, 7 Apr. 1859, 28 Mar. 1860; *Allegan Journal*, 11 Apr. 1859, 9 Apr. 1860; *Ottawa Register*, 18 Apr. 1860; *Grand Haven News*, 25 Apr. 1860, citing *Ottawa Clarion*, 12 Apr. 1860; Holland Township Board Minutes, 14 June 1859, MHA. Flavius J. Littlejohn of Allegan weighed in against Roost in a lengthy recital of "facts" in *De Hollander*, 18 July 1860.

Academy, Christian Van Der Veen, who was studying for the ministry at New Brunswick Theological Seminary. "John Roost was nominated candidate for Supervisor there by roguery and cheating. Some of them throwed [*sic*] but a handful of ballots in the chairman's cap at a time and so they gained the point." Doesburg then commented on the legal matter:

> As you probably know, John Roost, wouldn't settle with the Township Board, although several times kindly asked to, and is now sued and has to appear before the Circuit Court, and was there held to bail for the sum of $4,000, to await his trial in a few days. The Deputy Marshal just arrested him last Monday before the caucus, so you can imagine if any consternation or excitement prevailed in the Black Republican ranks. Henry D. Post is our candidate and stands a great chance of being elected.[56]

In a lame attempt to explain the Republican success in Holland Township in the spring of 1860, Doesburg opined that a political machine, organized by ministers who had always opposed political organization as "wicked and wrong," had used "mass manipulation." They drew the sword and struck the first blow. (Doesburg, as we shall see, had in mind Van Raalte and his associates.) But the victory, Doesburg predicted, would soon turn sour. "Coaxing Hollanders to uphold Republican principles is like compelling water to flow uphill. As long as you keep pumping and forcing, it goes up, but the moment you remove the strong hand of power, it goes down again in obedience to the laws of its Creator." Hollanders, with few exceptions, are "naturally Democrats. They have felt the strong hand of power too heavy upon them to desire to belong to the party that has heretofore advocated the doctrine that the government must take care of the rich, and let the rich take care of the poor."[57]

Political cataclysm of 1859-60

The growing political cataclysm struck with full force in Holland and Pella in the summer of 1859, when both Van Raalte and Scholte openly switched party allegiances and joined the Republicans. Van Raalte, who might well have been a closet Republican since 1857, changed

56 Jacob O. Doesburg, Holland, MI, to Christian Van Der Veen, 28 Mar. 1860, in Christian Van Der Veen Papers, box 1, Archives, Calvin College.

57 *Ottawa Register*, 18 Apr. 1860; *De Hollander*, 11 Apr. 1860, translated by Simone Kennedy.

rather quietly, as befitting a minister of the Gospel, although none could doubt his newfound political convictions.[58] Scholte, by contrast, defected from the Democratic party in such a dramatic fashion that his name appeared in Iowa newspapers statewide and far beyond. Although Scholte was elected a delegate to the state Democratic convention in Des Moines, he appeared one day earlier at the Republican convention in the capital at the head of the Marion County delegation! The convention then chose him as a delegate to the Republican national convention in Chicago, where he voted to nominate Lincoln for president.[59]

When Doesburg heard the shocking news about Scholte, he published in *De Hollander* a scathing condemnation, under the title "Scholte is a dishonest Republican." Most of the piece consisted of a lengthy letter of Hendrik Hospers, a Pella Democrat, which castigated Scholte for dishonest land dealings and dabbling in politics. Scholte, "the best minister" in town, "is able to sit Saturday on a Republican float surrounded by 30 young ladies in white, and preach a good biblical sermon on Sunday—yes, he mixes politics and religion." Hospers also ingratiated himself with Doesburg by noting that an "evil spirit" had come over Scholte when he called Doesburg a "'dwarf cock,' 'frog,' and other bad and dirty names" in a letter published in the *Sheboygan* (Wisconsin) *Nieuwsbode*.[60]

Political activities at that time often degenerated into street theater. Dirk Vyn recalled that in the 1860 campaign, Republicans put up a flagpole on the west side of River Avenue at Eighth Street in front of Pfanstiehl's store, adorned with a twenty-five-foot party flag provided by state Senator Thomas White Ferry of Grand Haven. Not to be outdone, the Democrats, led by Bernardus Ledeboer, a medical doctor, and Henry Post, erected their own pole, "larger and taller, and more beautiful," in the center of the intersection. The Democratic pole featured a colorful crosstree topped with a golden ball. In those days,

58 There is no poll list or political party document to prove that Van Raalte became a Republican, but his close association and positive support of Lincoln's policies during the Civil War, and comments in letters of opponents such as George Steketee in 1867, all make it certain that Van Raalte indeed aligned himself with the Republicans (Wagenaar, "Early Political History," 57-59). Van Hinte noted that William O. Van Eyck personally told him in 1922 that, according to Van Eyck's father, who was editor of *De Hollander* during the Civil War years, "Van Raalte became a Republican, especially after he came to Detroit" (Van Hinte, *Netherlanders in America*, 1058 n46); Henry E. Dosker, *Levenschets van Rev. A. C. Van Raalte, D.D.* (Nijkerk: Callenbach, 1893), 229.

59 Swierenga, "Ethnic Voter," 281-83.

60 "Scholte a dishonest Republican," *De Hollander*, 24 Oct. 1860, translated by Simone Kennedy.

said Vyn, the Democrats were "well heeled, while the Republicans were as poor as Job's turkey." But it so happened that one Saturday night high winds broke off the topmast of the Democratic pole and it fell, knocking off a piece of the cornice of Vander Veen's hardware store. At this the Republicans lowered their flag to half-mast "as an indication of mourning." This taunt, Vyn noted, "made the 'Demmies' boiling hot, after which a fist fight ensued." Carpenter Gerrit Jan Slenk repaired Vander Veen's store at the expense of the Democrats.[61]

The political shenanigans reached the consistory room at Van Raalte's church, when the brothers practiced *censura morum* (Latin for mutual censure), a routine practiced prior to the celebration of the Lord's Supper, in which church members state, in turn, "if they are able, in love and peace, to commune together." At the October 1860 meeting, Harm Broek and Pieter E. De Vries declared that they were offended that Teunis Keppel and Derk Te Roller had not "expressed more condemnation of certain music and torch lighting on the occasion of a recent Republican gathering." Presumably, the offending Republican brothers apologized to the offended Democratic brothers, because the communion service went forward as planned. But the fact that political shenanigans on the streets affected the celebration of the sacrament in the church showed the delicate social threads in the tight ethnoreligious community of Holland.[62]

Party pros assumed that Van Raalte and Scholte would carry their followers into the Republican camp. After all, the immigrants could barely read English or understand the nuances of American political rhetoric, and they would continue to need their dominies to explain and interpret the meaning of the ballot choices. Van Raalte, in the words of Van Hinte, "fired up popular enthusiasm; he saw in Lincoln the ideal American statesman. Van Raalte could be found everywhere," Van Hinte continued, "on the streets, at meetings, in homes, at assemblies, near the rolling drums which were encouraging men to sign up—working for the Union."[63] The race took on greater significance, because after Muskegon County was detached from Ottawa in 1859, Holland Township was by far the largest voting precinct in the county. As Holland went, so went the county.

As an enthusiastic convert to Republicanism, Van Raalte's activism caused some to complain that their dominie was a *knoeier* (a

61 Dirk Vyn, "When Holland Was Democratic," *Holland City News*, 23 Feb., 6 Apr. 1911.

62 Consistory Minutes, First Reformed Church of Holland, 26 Oct. 1860, Art. 9, translated by William Buursma, Van Raalte Institute, Hope College.

63 Van Hinte, *Netherlanders in America*, 435.

bungler) who was bringing politics into the pulpit. In reply Van Raalte told his consistory "that he was a citizen before he was a minister," and he would not separate his political beliefs from his faith. He must continue to defend the Union and condemn American slavery, with its vile practice of "breeding men," a practice that is "*absolutely* forbidden in the Bible." The complaints came before the consistory, but the body tabled the matter "because of the profound political changes in which NN (Latin *Nomen Nescis*, that is, anonymous) and others are so deeply involved." That the consistory would not come to Van Raalte's defense suggests that his political transformation and campaigning for the hitherto hated Republicans was not generally accepted in town. In the Eastern wing of the Reformed Protestant Dutch Church in America, however, Van Raalte's new political orientation was much appreciated. In 1858 both New York University in New York City and Rutgers College in New Brunswick, New Jersey, bestowed honorary doctorates on him.[64]

Theodore Romeyn, Van Raalte's friend who had likewise joined the Republicans, also stumped the state for Lincoln. Throughout 1859 and 1860, Romeyn made prolonged visits to Holland, often to attend board meetings of the Hope Preparatory School. But no one spoke out more strongly in support of Lincoln than Van Raalte, who "admired him with his whole heart."[65] Had either Lincoln or his running mate, Hannibal Hamlin, come to Holland during the campaign, the hands of Romeyn and Van Raalte would have been strengthened.

Van Raalte saw to it that the Dutch had a new weekly, *De Grondwet* (Constitution), to tutor them in the nascent Republican faith. Under editors Jan Roost and his understudy, the schoolmaster Marinus Hoogesteger, the inaugural issue, with columns in both Dutch and English, hit the streets on April 30, 1860. Holland had arrived; it was now a two-newspaper town, with the rival editors critiquing each other's writings. The choice of the name, *Constitution*, in contrast to the title, *The Hollander*, is significant. Instead of an ethnic identity, Van Raalte gave the Republican paper an American identity, even though most columns were written in the Dutch language. In editorial policy, Roost emulated Scholte's *Pella Gazette* and cloaked Republican ideology

64 First Reformed Church consistory minutes, 16 Apr. 1860, cited in Dosker, *Levenschets*, 228; and in J. A. Wormser, *Een Pilgrimsvader: Het leven van Albertus Christiaan Van Raalte* (Nijverdal: Bosch, 1915), 224, 227, English translation typescript by Henry ten Hoor. On 12 Aug. 1863, Van Raalte preached a powerful sermon from his pulpit that condemned slavery in the strongest terms. A copy is preserved at the Bentley Library, University of Michigan, Ann Arbor.

65 Gerrit Van Schelven, "Michigan and the Holland Immigration of 1847," *Michigan History* 1 (Oct. 1917): 72-96.

with the mantle of the Constitution, thereby implying that Democrats disregarded the revered document. *De Grondwet* soon became known far and wide as "the Republican Bible."[66]

The masthead of *De Grondwet* set off alarm bells for Doesburg, who launched Holland's first newspaper war with a sarcastic blast at the name *Constitution* as "hypocritical, simulated, sly, or a manipulation to attract the Dutch to their views." If the paper followed the radical Republican ideology, it would be anything but honoring of the Constitution and upholding of Union. "Can it be called 'aiming for Union' if the North attacks the South?" declared Doesburg. And how was attacking the Supreme Court decision in the Dred Scott case (that a Negro slave is property and not protected by Constitutional rights), anything but despising of the very body that under the Constitution must interpret the fundamental document?[67]

Doesburg's ultimate tactic was to tie Christianity and American patriotism. In a clever dialogue between two Hollanders, Klaas and Jan, printed in *De Hollander* just one week before the election, Doesburg repeated the Democratic campaign theme that Lincoln, as an abolitionist, would undermine the Union and the Constitution. If elected, Southerners would secede in order to safeguard slavery, which institution was protected by the Constitution. But Doesburg took this argument one step further by linking the Republicans to oath breaking and the antichrist. He reminded the Dutch of their citizenship oath to uphold the Constitution and the Union, and he linked abolitionists to the antichrist. By labeling Democratic policies as Christian and Republican as anti-Christian, Doesburg was indirectly accusing Van Raalte, the spiritual leader of Holland and erstwhile Republican, for allying with the devil. Van Raalte's support for the Union was merely Satan's "venom beautifully adorned. . . . [It is] terrible to us . . . that so many of our friends till now hear and abet" these errors. Such was hardball politics Doesburg's style. Little had changed since he castigated the Pope and his Cardinals in 1852.

Dialogue between Klaas and Jan:

Jan: Ja, Klaas, I'll be glad when the election is over.

Klaas: That I well believe. It's also a matter to be longed for. But have you decided yet who you will vote for?

Jan: I have. It's as clear to me as the sun, which party indeed loves the Union and the Constitution. And I'll stay with that party.

66 *Grand Rapids Democrat*, 5 Sept. 1896.

67 "De Grondwet," *De Hollander*, 9 (quotes), 23 May 1860, translated by Simone Kennedy.

I've sworn to do that and I'll keep my oath, as long as I live.

Klaas: Yes, me too, but which party must I chose? *De Grondwet* says that they love the Union and the Constitution and *De Hollander* says that too.

Jan: That's true, but doesn't that prove to you beyond a doubt that this involves lies and word twisting? *De Hollander*, as you know, for years has an entirely different character. *De Grondwet* works hand in hand with Opposition, Abolition, and Revolution. But *De Hollander* has pointed out that these three monsters, according to the Scriptures, belong to the Antichrist, and has warned you against them. This is upright and clear. If you follow the advice of *De Grondwet,* then you break your oath, for the party they stand for proclaims the entire Constitution as nothing. But the party that *De Hollander* stands for is safe and agrees with God's Word. The teaching of *De Grondwet* is to break the Union, and the teaching of *De Hollander* is to keep it safe. *De Grondwet* stands for Lincoln and the Republican Party, which calls the Constitution an alliance with Hell, and *De Hollander* urges you to stay with your oath. He who despises the Constitution cannot love the Union, for the Constitution is the foundation of the Union.

Klaas: I must agree with you. Now it is clear to me. I too will vote for the safekeeping of the Union and the Constitution. That's indeed the Douglas party.[68]

To the great joy of Doesburg and the consternation of Republican leaders, most Dutch voters in Holland and Zeeland in November 1860 agreed with him and again cast Democratic ballots, although by smaller margins than previously. Holland Township voted Democratic by only 53 percent (208 Democrat and 187 Republican) (appendix 7.1) and Zeeland by 51 percent (89 to 85). Overisel Township was especially pro-South in sentiment. Pella went Democratic by 66 percent. Abraham Lincoln was not their man; they preferred the "Little Giant," Stephen Douglas. Lincoln's election triumph prompted the Republicans in Holland to hang Douglas in effigy, which so infuriated Democrats that they stole Douglas away. The Republicans then made another Douglas effigy and ceremonially buried "him" in the swamp east of town. No wonder that someone threw a stone through the window of Roost's office at the *De Grondwet*, and editor Hoogesteger remained in his home

68 "Dialogue Between Klaas and Jan," *De Hollander*, 31 Oct. 1860, translated by Peter Moerdyke, in Moerdyke Papers, box 15, HMA.

after the polls closed on Election Day "out of fear that he would be attacked and mistreated."[69]

The election-day shenanigans of the Republicans disturbed Doesburg greatly. In an unduly alarmist and almost apocalyptic postmortem, Doesburg painted politics in Holland as over the edge:

> The day of the election turned out to be more peaceful than we had expected in the morning. . . . But when we received the news that there was a Republican majority in our County, our State, and our Republic, the quiet was gone. The victorious party wanted to bury a straw Douglas with a cross, in a manner that was offensive to Democrats. Tension built quickly, and bats and revolvers were drawn. We are fortunate that this did not lead to a fight. If the roots of bitterness in both parties grow any deeper, we will have to deal with murders and arson. . . . Now that the election is over, we have to stop our party fervor, and rest in the dispensation of the one Lord. Everyone should calm down and get over the heated debates, be sorry for the hot-tempered zeal and through forgiveness try to re-establish former relationships. Should a Christian people sink below the pagan state and follow the directions of a vengeful heart? Shame on us! We, people of influence, people from both parties, we call on you sincerely: Work on maintaining peace and encouraging love, so that the people will not be destroyed or consumed![70]

As a spokesman for the losing party, Doesburg failed to mention the fury of his own partisans directed at their opponents. Rather, he followed the time-honored tactic of losers and called for compromise and bipartisanship. But the triumphant Republicans were not about to oblige.

That Republicans won the 1860 election in Ottawa County by 197 votes signaled the winds of change. Democrats were converting to Republicans due to the course of national events and the editorial pages of the newspapers many locals read, notably the *Sheboygan Nieuwsbode* and Roost's *De Grondwet*. Roost won the newspaper war against Doesburg and subscriptions to *De Hollander* fell off dramatically. *De Grondwet*, as Henry Lucas noted, became the "most influential newspaper ever to be published for Dutch immigrants."[71]

69 Hoogesteger obit., *De Grondwet*, 3 June 1879.

70 *De Hollander*, 14 Nov. 1860.

71 Roost was an 1847 immigrant from Harderwijk, province of Overijssel, who settled in Grand Rapids until 1853, when he opened a wagon manufacturing business in Holland. He served as Holland Township supervisor (1858-60). In 1867 Roost sold

Doesburg continued to condemn Republican ideas, even with a bit of race baiting. He noted, for example, that in 1860 the Republican majority in the Michigan legislature passed a law giving Negro freedmen the right to vote if they owned goods worth at least $250, "while they denied this right to residents born in a foreign country." Thus, Doesburg argued, Republicans valued Negroes above Hollanders. "One finds their papers filled with nothing else than with human love toward the black people." At the same time, said Doesburg, Republican lawmakers would levy high taxes and then squander the money. The only goal of the Republicans, Doesburg concluded in strident tones, was "to brutally plant their dirty party principles here. . . . They will do anything they can to persuade voters, so they can empty our pockets." The day after the election, however, Doesburg titled his lead editorial simply, "No large Republican victory." There was little to crow about. Republicans had swept the county, state, and nation.[72]

One result of the political shift in 1860 and the growing Dutch population was to give Holland Township greater influence in Ottawa County governance. Dutchmen, for example, began a lengthy run as county sheriffs, led by Charles J. Pfaff, a general merchant in Holland and captain of Plugger's ship *Commencement*, who could speak Dutch, German, and English. The popular Pfaff ran eighty votes ahead of presidential candidate Stephen Douglas at the top of the Democratic ticket. According to William Van Eyck, Pfaff was considered a "great man for his time." He served as a draft and recruiting officer during the Civil War. John Roost, a member of the Radical Republican faction and township supervisor for three years, apparently won the race for Holland Township supervisor, but by only one vote. A recount resulted in a tie, which set off a war in Grand Haven for six months. The sitting treasurer, Democrat George Parks, possessed all the books and records, and he refused to relinquish his office.

So Roost took up another room at the courthouse pending the outcome of legal maneuverings. Eventually, the circuit court declared

---

the paper to his partner Hoogesteger and Leendert Mulder. The Mulder family in 1880 became sole owners and ran the paper until 1938 (Lucas, *Netherlanders in America*, 535). *De Grondwet* continued until 1938; *De Hollander* ceased publication in 1895.

72 *De Hollander*, 3 Oct., 7 Nov. 1860, translated by Simone Kennedy. Another race-baiting article, "Negroes vs. Foreigners," clipped from the *Detroit Free Press* by the *Ottawa Register* (27 Apr. 1859) reported that Republicans in the Massachusetts legislature passed a constitutional amendment that would allow freedmen and runaway slaves to vote after one year's residence but would make foreigners wait two years after naturalization. "How immeasurably above white foreigners do the black republicans place negroes!"

him the winner, but Parks still refused to vacate the office, even under the threat of arrest and imprisonment. In the end, Parks got the superior court to overrule the lower court, and Roost lost out. He had carried only 44 percent of the vote in Holland Township, six points behind his county total. Some countrymen had clearly disapproved of his being a political turncoat. As a consolation prize, the newly elected President Lincoln named Roost to the coveted job of postmaster at Holland, in place of Democrat Henry Post, who had held the position for thirteen years. In American politics before the era of the civil service reform in the 1880s, the adage applied: "To the victor go the spoils."[73]

During Lincoln's two administrations, partisan politics continued to rule in Holland. In the local elections in April 1861, tensions remained "strong" and a "warm fight" ensued, according to city historian William O. Van Eyck, a lifelong Democrat. The Democrats nominated Ledeboer for supervisor against Republican Derk Te Roller. Roost had held the post for "three years of storm and stress; and party lines were tight." In a virtual dead heat, Ledeboer won the race with 204 votes to 201 for Te Roller. Ledeboer held the post for six years, until 1866. Although he was born in the Netherlands and completed his medical training there, Ledeboer had lived in New York for more than twenty years (since 1834). There he mastered the English language and identified with the increasingly American Dutch Reformed Church. In 1857 he moved to Grand Rapids and two years later was recruited to practice in Holland, which desperately needed physicians fluent in Dutch. Ledeboer's political views were shaped during his decades in the East. He was one of the first elders in Hope Church in 1862, and Van Raalte appointed him a trustee of the Holland Academy. He was also elected a public school inspector.[74]

During the war years, Holland continued to vote Democratic. In the 1862 gubernatorial elections, the Democratic candidate for governor won 63 percent of the vote in Holland Township. In the 1864 presidential election, with General George "Little Mac" McClellan representing the Peace Democratic faction, and Lincoln seeking re-election in the midst

73 Van Eyck, "Old History of Sheriff-ship," HMA; Jan Roost to Messrs. J. and J. W. Burns, *Grand Haven News*, 29 Jan. 1861; "Roost vs. Parks," ibid., 30 Jan. 1861; George Parks to John Roost," ibid., 29 July 1861; *Grand Rapids Inquirer* 1, 12 Feb. 1861, all translated by Moerdyke, in Moerdyke Papers, box 15, HMA.

74 Coenraad Hofman was elected clerk and Hendrik Van Eijk and Engbertus Vander Veen justices of the peace. Wm. O. Van Eyck, "Holland Man Gives History of Old Town Hall," Jan. 1930, in Moerdyke Papers, box 15, HMA. For Ledeboer's career, see *Holland City News*, 25 Apr. 1874, and Michael Douma, comp., "Biographical Information for the Mayors of Holland, Michigan," Joint Archives of Holland (JAH).

of a floundering war effort, Holland again voted Democratic, by 58 percent. Besides winning handily in Holland, McClellan carried Ottawa County by 53 percent. Dutch votes also helped Doesburg capture the county clerkship.[75]

The Democratic triumph during the war was remarkable, since more than four hundred Dutch volunteers from western Michigan, including two of Van Raalte's sons, were putting their lives on the line in the Union army. This was a ratio of one soldier for every ten residents of Holland Township, and the soldiers in the field overwhelmingly voted for Lincoln.[76] Yet, nearly six out of ten voters supported a candidate President Lincoln had fired in 1862 after ignominiously losing the Battle of Antietam, and who, if elected president, would willingly acquiesce in the breakup of the Union and allow the Confederacy to form an independent nation. The 1864 poll testifies to the depth of the hurt inflicted on the Dutch in the mid-1850s by Whig and Republican nativists.

Lincoln's assassination in 1865 only days after the war ended had a tremendous emotional impact across the country. The news reached Holland on a Sunday morning and Van Raalte immediately dispatched messengers to the outlying villages, where they arrived during the afternoon worship services. The dastardly deed, which threatened the very survival of the Union, turned a number of Dutch Democrats into Republicans—but not in Overisel. When an elder relayed the message to Gerrit J. Nykerk in his pulpit at the Overisel Reformed Church, he reportedly interrupted the service to announce the news and then immediately asked the congregation to sing the Fifty-Fourth Psalm—one of King David's songs of thanksgiving![77]

The next Sunday service at Van Raalte's church stuck with nine-year-old Albert Pfanstiehl for a lifetime. Walking into the sanctuary, he saw black crepe hanging everywhere; the pulpit "was one black mass." More drama was yet to come. In the congregational prayer, the dominie "began to choke with emotion, and suddenly buried his head in his

75 Van Schelven, "Michigan and the Holland Immigration of 1847," *Michigan Historical Magazine* 1 (1917): 31; Van Koevering, *Legends of the Dutch*, 394-95; Wagenaar, "Early Political History," 34-35, 42, 45, 48-49; Van Eyck, "Old History on Sheriff-ship," 2, "Early Historical Data—Political," 3, HMA. Zeeland Township in 1860 voted Democratic by only a 51 percent majority, down from 92 percent support for Buchanan in 1856.

76 This is the report by Ben Van Raalte, serving with the 25th Michigan regiment in Tennessee, to his father: "*The Hollander* was wrong when it said that the company was all democrats. Thirty were for Lincoln, and nine for Mac," Ben Van Raalte, Johnsonville, TN, to Van Raalte, 11 Sept. 1864, translated by Clarence Jalving, HMA.

77 This comes from Arthur A. Visscher, "Recollections [of Arend Visscher]," typescript, 1959, section "Civil War," Visscher Family Papers, HMA.

hands and burst out sobbing." The entire congregation then "convulsed with grief!" "I cried as if my heart would break," Pfanstiehl recalled. "I felt as if some great catastrophe had come to overwhelm us all." A few days later, sadness gave way to joy with the news: "Lee had surrendered! We've won! The Union is saved"![78]

The 1864 national election victory was the last for the Democrats in Holland, although they continued to carry local races through the spring elections of 1866. Doesburg won a second term as county clerk, the only Hollander to win county office; three of his sons had fought in the war. Ledeboer won re-election as township supervisor, having held the chief executive post since 1861. In the mid-term national election of 1866, Holland went Republican for the first time, but by the slimmest of margins at 52 percent (235 to 217). And in the local election of 1867, Van Raalte's long-time friend Grootenhuis took the supervisor's seat from Ledeboer.[79]

The great reversal

In 1868 Ulysses S. Grant won Holland by 58 percent; it was the first local Republican triumph in the presidential race. Lincoln's martyrdom after saving the Union, and the votes of Civil War veterans, all strongly Republican, made a mark. The Hollanders also approved of the national economic program of the Republican—especially the Homestead Law of 1862—sound money and a national banking system and generous funding of internal improvements. The Dutch in the Holland colony were twelve years behind the rest of Michigan in joining the Republican crusade; the state had turned Republican already in 1855. The Dutch Reformed and the Republican Party were natural allies. The party was composed of men of New England Calvinist ancestry, Presbyterians and Congregationalists, and backers of denominational schools and a Christian society. They were fellow Reformed believers, although of an English and Scottish stripe, instead of the Low Countries and German Rhineland. Yet the Michigan Dutch lagged behind their compatriots elsewhere in the Midwest in switching political allegiances. In the 1868 presidential race, compared to Holland Township's 52 percent, Republicans carried Sheboygan, Wisconsin's Holland Township by 78

78 Albert A. Pfanstiehl, Deal Beach, NJ, to "My dear Grandchildren Cody & Alfred," 16 Dec. 1919, letter no. 9, in "Letters to my Grandchildren, A. A. Pfanstiehl, 1919-1920," Pfanstiehl Family Papers, HMA.

79 Van Eyck, "Old History on Sheriff-ship, HMA"; *Grand Haven News*, 28 Nov. 1866; *De Hope*, 4 Apr. 1866; *Historical and Business Compendium of Ottawa County*, 88; Van Eyck, "Early Historical Data—Political," 3.

percent, nearby Oostburg by 98 percent, and New Amsterdam in western Wisconsin by 91 percent. Pella, Iowa on the other hand, continued to vote Democratic.[80]

The vote in the city of Holland, which was carved out of Holland Township in 1867 (see below), is unknown, because the Holland Fire of 1871 destroyed city records, including voting records, and also the files of the two newspapers, *De Hollander* and *De Grondwet*, which always reported the results. But it can be assumed that the city went Republican, in sync with Holland Township.

Van Raalte's inability to carry Holland for the Republicans during the Civil War is remarkable. His grip on leadership clearly was slipping, and his people's time of dependency had passed. Van Raalte's correspondence reveals the depth of his despondency; he felt he was stabbed in the back. In a confidential letter to a friend in the Netherlands in 1862, Van Raalte poured out his heart: "It is impossible for me to continue my work amongst this dissention." In 1866 he went to the Netherlands for several months and upon his return, he resigned in 1867 as pastor of First Reformed (now Pillar) Church. He also declined an offer to become a professor of theology at Hope College. Van Raalte's waning political influence thus coincided with his decision to retire from his pulpit. The ministry was demanding, and he had led the congregation for twenty years, yet he was only fifty-six years of age. Did he step down out of chagrin that his leadership was spurned?

The next blow came in 1867 when, over the dominie's strenuous objections, the citizens of Holland, now numbering six thousand, approved carving the city of Holland out of Holland Township and electing a mayor and common council. The additional taxes on real estate to fund a second layer of government would fall heavily on Van Raalte, as Holland's largest landowner with three hundred city lots and many acres of farmland around town. Van Raalte had blocked incorporation for years, but he could no long prevail. On this issue, Van Raalte stood in an adversarial relationship with the local governing body of his colonial creation. As a concession to the father of the colony, the city boundary on the east was drawn to exclude his home and farm, thus making those properties subject to township, but not city, taxes.[81] With incorporation, the transformation of Holland from colony to city was complete.

Van Raalte's stand against creating a city government aroused bitter feelings. One member of the committee, George Steketee,

80 *Allegan Journal*, 23 Nov. 1868, clipping from the *Grand Rapids Eagle*.
81 Wagenaar, "Early Political History," 55-59.

complained in a letter to state representative Moses Hopkins of Grand Haven, that Van Raalte "has made him Self Rich out of us poor Dutchmen and therefore it is no more than Right that he should help bare [*sic*] the Expense of the City and in this way our taxes would be lower." In the same letter Steketee opined that the main reason for setting off the city was to create a Republican stronghold against the outlying areas of the township, the "majority of which are Copper Heads." Opponents of incorporation, he added, are "Seven Eighths of them Cops."[82]

Republicans had coined the pejorative label, Copperheads, to refer to Peace Democrats during the Civil War. Proof of Steketee's assertion is the fact that in the 1868 presidential election, Overisel Township, "a hitherto impregnable stronghold of the bogus Democracy," gave that party a fifty-three-vote majority. While this was much less than the usual one-hundred-vote majority, it showed that Dutch farmers east of Holland held to their Democratic allegiance. Farmers in Fillmore and Laketown went for the Republican Ulysses S. Grant.[83]

Holland became a city in three steps. First, in February 1867, advocates led by Ledeboer and Kommer Schaddelee convened a meeting of interested citizens in the town hall, which body voted to incorporate, and appointed a commission of seven community leaders to draft a city charter. Second, they circulated two petitions to determine the will of the public, one *for* and one *against*. This informal poll yielded 140 *yea* and 120 *nay* signatures. Third, they had state representative Hopkins introduce a bill in the legislature to approve incorporation, which passed both houses in March. The final step was to hold elections for city mayor and aldermen and to adopt an official seal. The seal portrayed a lion and crown in the center, surrounded by the phrases *Eendragt maakt macht* (Union is Strength) and *God zij met ons* (God Be With Us).

The first elections for city and state offices took place on Monday, April 1, 1867. Eligible voters had registered prior to the election, paying a small poll tax for the privilege. Polls opened at eight o'clock in the morning under the watchful eyes of election judges E. J. Harrington and Gerrit Van Schelven, with G. J. Hall appointed as election clerk and Willem Vorst as his assistant. The four men were duly sworn in

82 George G. Steketee, Holland, to Moses B. Hopkins, Grand Haven, 1 Mar. 1867, Gerrit Van Schelven Papers, box 1, HMA. The committee for incorporation included, besides Steketee, Bernardus Ledeboer, Teunis Keppel, Richard K. Heald, Isaac Cappon, Gerrit Van Schelven, and Jacob Van Putten.

83 *Allegan Journal*, 23 Nov. 1868. More than ten years later, Overisel Township retained its reputation as "*almost* 'solid Democratic,'" according to the *Holland City News*, 19 Oct. 1878.

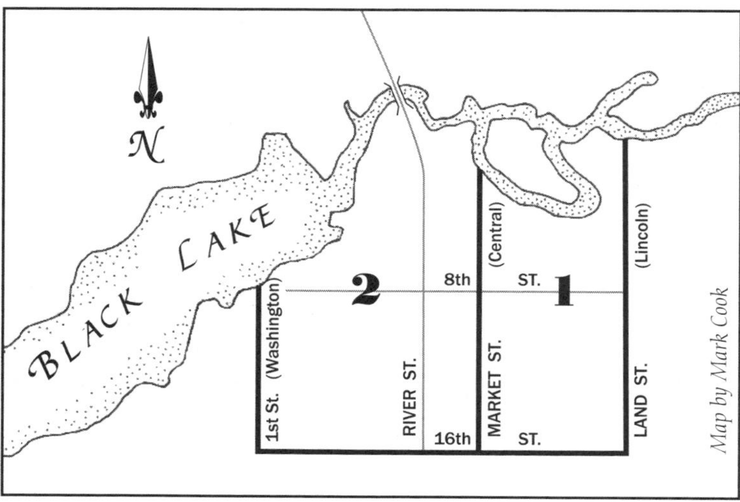

Fig. 24.1. Ward Map, 1867

by notary Marinus Hoogesteger. That two of the four officials were Americans and two were Hollanders was no accident; the politicos took care to maintain a balance of power. In all, 306 registered voters turned out. In the First Ward (east of Market Street [now Central Avenue]), held at the portrait galley of George Lauder on Eighth Street, 152 votes were cast, and in the Second Ward (west of Market Street), held at the Select School House, 156 votes were cast. Later, voters in the Second Ward marked their ballots at city clerk George Sipp's house at 229 West Twelfth Street. The imposing house, which resembled an old fortress, survived the 1871 fire and for years was the only structure west of Pine Avenue.[84]

Holland's seminal mayoralty race pitted the leading Republican, Isaac Cappon, against the old Democratic warhorse, Bernardus Ledeboer. Cappon, co-owner of the large Cappon & Bertsch tannery and a member of the charter commission, won in a close race by a plurality of eleven votes. He carried the Second Ward by a larger margin (94 to 62) than Ledeboer won the First Ward (86 to 65), which gave Cappon the victory 159 to 148. From the outset, Holland's west side had a solid Republican orientation, while the east side remained a Democratic base, although a weaker one. The strong west side showing by Republicans enabled their candidates to win every city office, despite losing the east side. Cappon's margin of victory held for the other offices

84 The George Sipp house, a landmark, was razed in 1922 to make way for Jacob Lokker's $9,000 mansion (*Holland City News*, 3 Aug. 1922).

Holland's first mayor, Isaac Cappon, 1867-68 (*Joint Archives of Holland*)

as well. According to the poll registers, the number of non-Dutch voters in the First Ward was thirty-five (22 percent), and the Second Ward was forty (26 percent). The parity between Dutch and non-Dutch voters in the two wards suggests that factors other than ethnicity determined the party differentials.[85] (See appendix 7.3 Holland City and Township Officials, 1867-2012, for a list of mayors and other local officials.)

The first officials of the city of Holland took office on April 4, 1867, in the original town hall, constructed in 1861, which stood on the northwest corner of Market Square (now Centennial Park). After the Rev. Abel T. Stewart opened with prayer, Mayor Cappon took up the gavel. Aldermen Jan Pauels and George Steketee, both Democrats, represented the First Ward, and Richard K. Heald and Engbertus Vander Veen, both Republicans, the Second Ward. Henry Post was recorder; George Lauder treasurer; Teunis Keppel marshal and street commissioner; John Roost supervisor; school inspectors, T. Romeyn Beck and Marinus Hoogesteger; directors of the poor, Conrad Hofman and Hendrik Meengs; justices of the peace, John Huizenga and E. J. Harrington; and George N. Smith Jr. attorney.[86]

Post, Harrington, and Smith had thrown in their lot with the Holland colony from the outset, mastered the Dutch language, and lent their considerable business acumen and legal expertise to help the settlement prosper. Romeyn Beck was a professor at Hope College.

85 The First Ward cast 150 votes and the Second Ward 156 votes, City Clerk Records, boxes 1, 2; HMA. On Cappon, see Elton J. Bruins, "Holland's Foremost Citizen," unpublished paper, 1987, JAH.

86 "Journal of the common council of the City of Holland," 1 (Apr. 4, 1867), 10, in Moerdyke Papers, box 10, HMA; *Holland City News*, 25 Apr. 1891.

Johannes Dykema defeated Lauder by one vote (151 to 150) but declined to accept the office. Keppel, an original follower of Scholte to Pella, arrived in Holland in the third contingent in the spring of 1847 and was a leading elder in Van Raalte's congregation. Roost led the local Republican Party through his mouthpiece *De Grondwet*, until selling the paper in 1867 to Hoogesteger.[87]

"Normal" politics after the turn to Republicanism

After the political reversal, a herd instinct seemed to keep Holland voters in the same rut for more than a hundred years. The majority voted Republican in national contests as a matter of course. Some attributed this to a "too low level of education, a too low phase of cultural development," or simply a "typical lack of judgment." More likely, fathers brought up their sons to be Republicans, just as they tutored them in the Reformed faith. It was a natural alliance, which made party loyalties as important as church loyalties. And the more that Democrats became identified as the Catholic party, the more Calvinistic Hollanders endorsed the Republicans.[88]

Although Republican victories were predictable after the postwar transition, political contests were hard fought and hotly contested. The Democrats never surrendered without a fight, and emotions ran high. Political campaigns were boisterous events that offered a diversion from the humdrum of everyday life. The rallies, parades, debates, songs, slogans, and stump speeches provided entertainment, street theater, and an education in issues of public policy and democracy.

Whether Holland or Zeeland had the more boisterous campaigns is open to debate. Cornelius "Case" Van Loo claimed that there was "more politics to the square foot in Zeeland, year in and year out, than any other locality in the state." Van Loo contributed to the torrid rhetoric more than anybody by waving the "bloody shirt" of the Rebellion in every campaign and calling Democrats Copperheads. In Holland, Van Raalte's son Dirk, the one-armed veteran of the Twenty-Fifth Michigan Infantry, was the ace political orator, that is, until fellow attorney Gerrit Diekema assumed that mantel.

Presidential campaigns were anything but staid. "Great enthusiasm manifested," read the headline in the *Holland City News*, reporting on a Republican rally in 1872 for President Grant's re-election bid. More than one thousand partisans turned out. Grant's opponent was

87 Van Hinte, *Netherlanders in America*, 441.
88 Ibid., 440-41.

the New York newspaperman, Horace Greeley, famed for his slogan: "Go West, Young Man, Go West." George McBride, one of the speakers, reportedly gave the Greeley followers some "good blows to the stomach." One tactic was to accuse them of being the party of saloonkeepers. This played on the stereotype of the Democrats as the Irish Catholic party, while the Republicans spoke for American Protestants. Grant carried both Holland Township and the city by more than 70 percent. But amazingly, the Democrat Ledeboer won the office of state senator.[89] (See appendix 7.2 Holland Township Presidential Elections, 1872-1896.)

Four years later, in the 1876 presidential campaign, both parties again staged torchlight parades and rallies late into the night, with candidates stumping for votes in both Dutch and English. Geesje Van der Haar Visscher noted: "There was activity every day until November 7th. . . . Tension had been rife and many had feared there might be some disturbances." Arthur A. Visscher tells about the famed torchlight parades in Holland during the life of his father Arend:

> Torchlight parades were very common just before elections; many hundreds of these torches, made in quantities for the purpose, were used. They were sticks about four feet long, at the end of which there would be a swinging can filled with kerosene from which a coarse wick protruded. When lit, there was a smelly large black flame. These torches were owned by someone in Grand Rapids who rented them locally for parades of both parties. It is probably just as well that they are no longer used, because the kerosene would leak out, getting on one's clothes, and when the excitement was at its height, they were used as weapons.[90]

The campaign between Democrat Samuel Tilden and Republican Rutherford Hayes was bitter, and the outcome was too close to call. But the death of Van Raalte at 7:45 a.m. on Election Day, announced by the mournful tolling of the church bell, cast the citizens into great sadness and the "day passed quietly." Van Raalte's death, his biographer Henry Dosker noted, dissipated the tension, and "voting took place as an inferior business." Predictably, the Republicans in Holland "won easily" with 57 percent of the votes, although the margin was considerably less than the 74 percent in 1872.[91] But the presidential race nationally was so

89 *De Hollander*, 14 Aug. 1872, translated by Simone Kennedy; *Holland City News*, 10 Aug., 9 Nov. 1872, 5 Apr. 1873, "Presidential Elections in Yester-year," 29 Oct. 1936.

90 Geesje Van der Haar Visscher, "Diary, HMA"; Visscher, "Recollections," section "Politics," HMA.

91 The election results are reported in *De Hollander*, 18 Nov. 1876. The First Ward again ran 10 points more Democratic than the city at large.

close that it ended up being decided by the US House of Representatives after a prolonged deadlock.

Two local men, Jacob Den Herder of Zeeland and Thomas W. Ferry of Grand Haven, were members of Michigan's Republican Electoral College, and both went to Washington, DC, to cast their votes. Den Herder, a naturalized citizen, was called to appear personally before the electoral commission that Congress had established to determine the victor. At question was his citizenship, which he had to prove by producing both his and his father's naturalization records. This was a dramatic moment. After examining the papers, the committee's reaction was emotional. "All at once the Republican side began to cheer and on the other side were long faces," Den Herder recalled. Despite further challenges from Democrats, Den Herder's vote was declared legal. The electoral commission gave Hayes all the disputed electoral votes, making him president by a one-vote margin, 185 to 184.[92]

Community tragedies tend to put politics in proper perspective and drive politicos to cooperate across party lines, at least in local elections. The Holland Fire of October 1871 had this effect. The two parties held Union caucuses for the city ticket and, irrespective of party, chose any candidate with majority support. In the spring of 1872, Democrat Gerrit Van Schelven was nominated as one of two justices of the peace and Democrat Kommer Schaddelee as First Ward alderman. The next year both Republicans and Democrats nominated Joos Ver Planke, a veteran of the Michigan Twenty-Fifth Infantry, for city marshal; he won hands-down. "Politics have been smothered during the canvas and no party lines are drawn," was the inference. But some Hollanders, led by Isaac Cappon, chafed at the bit, and there were reports that they caucused secretly and drew up a straight Republican ticket. No such ticket ever surfaced, however.[93] Further proof of the meaninglessness of party labels in local races is the fact that Ver Planke in 1876 ran successfully for county sheriff on the Democratic ticket, and two years later he won re-election on the Greenback ticket. Ver Planke was the only Greenback candidate who has ever held office in Holland. In 1880 the attempt at bipartisanship ended, and normal politics resumed.[94]

The Holland Fire prompted Sylvester Morris in February 1872 to make Holland a three-newspaper town again when he launched the

92 Aaron Bodbyl-Mast, "Local men had key roles in 1876 vote," *Grand Haven Tribune*, reprinted in *Holland Sentinel*, 24 Dec. 2000. The original account, "Het 'Des Herder' Geval," is in *De Grondwet*, 20 Feb. 1877.

93 *Holland City News*, 12 Apr. 1873.

94 Ibid., 30 Mar. 1872; Van Eyck, "Old History on Sheriff-Ship, HMA"; *Allegan Journal*, 3 Nov. 1876.

English-language *Holland City News* (chapter 32). It replaced the *Gazeteer*, which never reopened after its shop was destroyed in the fire. More than one-quarter of the population was native-born, and they needed a paper. Like *De Grondwet*, the *News* endorsed the Republican Party, which left *De Hollander*, published by Zeeland postmaster Willem Benjaminse, as the sole Democratic sheet. (Benjaminse belonged to the Methodist Church, and his son Anthony was ordained in that denomination.) In his inaugural issue Morris insisted that a large portion of the American reading public in Ottawa County and western Michigan wanted a newspaper that touted the commercial importance of Holland and to help the city "dig out from the ruins of the 9th of October last."[95]

Within a few weeks, Morris used his new mouthpiece to attack Hollanders who were deemed too narrow morally or ethnically. The morality issue came to the fore when *De Hop*e, the Hope College Dutch-language weekly and voice of the western wing of the Reformed Church in America, published an article by Rev. Nicholas Steffens, then a clergyman in western Illinois, which attacked the common council for permitting a circus to open in town. At Steffens' critique, Morris "got on his high horse" and denounced the professor roundly. When "in the purity of his heart [Steffens] . . . pronounced the Anathema Maranatha against those who then favored or would hereafter favor the public exhibition of any show, theatrical troop, or any thing of that character in this city, does he think he can enforce morality and bind the conscience of free citizens?" Further, Morris decried the "spirit of nativism" among some Dutch politicians, who in the party caucuses struck the names of Americans in favor of Hollanders, except for a token few. Any "idea of nationality" is wrong, lectured Morris.[96]

While Morris singled out Steffens for being narrow-minded, he somehow missed an editorial by Douwe Vander Werp in *De Wachter*, the denominational periodical of the Christian Reformed Church that was also published in Holland. Vander Werp, pastor of the Graafschap congregation, made opposition to Freemasons a litmus test. He declared in a strong editorial that in local elections his readers, on principle, must not vote for Freemasons or those "debtor to that order" (meaning one who had borrowed money), unless they are paired against one another for an office. Then one has no choice but to choose between the lesser of two evils. Vander Werp was very direct about the fall 1872 election slate. With five Dutch nominees, of whom four–all members of the Reformed Church–were Freemasons or its debtors, and one Seceder

95 *Holland City News*, 24 Feb. 1872; *De Hollander*, 2 Aug. 1876.

96 *Holland City News*, 6 Apr. 1872.

(that is, Christian Reformed) candidate, namely Cornelius Van Loo of Zeeland, Vander Werp declared that "every Hollander that desires to see his Reformed (orthodox) principles triumph must vote for C. Van Loo." The admonition bore fruit. Van Loo won with a majority of forty-eight votes in Holland Township and 110 votes in Zeeland Township. Van Loo was an elder in the flagship Seceder congregation, the Noordeloos Christian Reformed Church. In the early 1880s, he represented Ottawa County in the Michigan House of Representatives.[97]

Locally, Republicans and Democrats alternated in the mayor's chair between 1867 and 1882. Thereafter, Republicans predominated. Cappon served four terms (1867-68, 1870-71, 1874-75, and 1879-80), and E. J. Harrington three terms (1872-73, 1873-74, 1892-93). Four Democrats held the office in between: Bernardus Ledeboer three terms (1868-69, 1869-70, 1871-72), John Van Landegend two terms (1875-77), Kommer Schaddelee two terms (1877-79), and John Roost one term (1881-82). Except for Cappon's terms, Democrats carried the city ticket regularly from 1875 to 1882, due to the hard times nationally that followed the crash of 1873, which put three million people out of work. Tight finances did not keep the common council from proposing an annual stipend of fifty dollars in hard currency for the mayor and aldermen. Their timing was poor. Following a crusade against the proposal by *De Hollander*, former mayor Isaac Cappon organized a "No Salary" ticket that carried the day in the spring 1874 election. Another notable feature of local politics was the lack of ethnic chauvinism. The common council in 1877 included three Hollanders, two Americans, two Germans, and one Canadian. "Who says this is not a liberal place?" crowed editor Gerrit Van Schelven of the *Holland City News*.[98]

The city marshal was the second most contested local race because it became the stepping stone to the coveted position of county sheriff. For thirty-two years, beginning with Arie Woltman in 1871, the county sheriffs hailed from Holland and were groomed for the post by serving as city marshal. The list includes Joos Ver Planke, John and Edward Vaupell, Frank Van Ry, Henry J. Dykhuis, his son Hans Dykhuis, and Frederick H. "Fred" Kamferbeek. Ver Planke and Kamferbeek were the only two Democrats ever elected county sheriff. In those days, among

97 *De Wachter*, 18 Oct. 1872; in Holland City Records, box 1, HMA; Van Hinte, *Netherlanders in America*, 438.

98 This and the next paragraph rely on "Biographical Information for the Mayors of Holland," JAH; *Holland City News*, Apr. 8, 1876. On the stipend, see the resolution of Alderman D. Kamperman, 16 Sept. 1874, in Early City Records, box 1, HMA. The negative public reaction is noted in *De Hollander*, 18 Feb., 11 Mar., 1, 8 Apr. 1874.

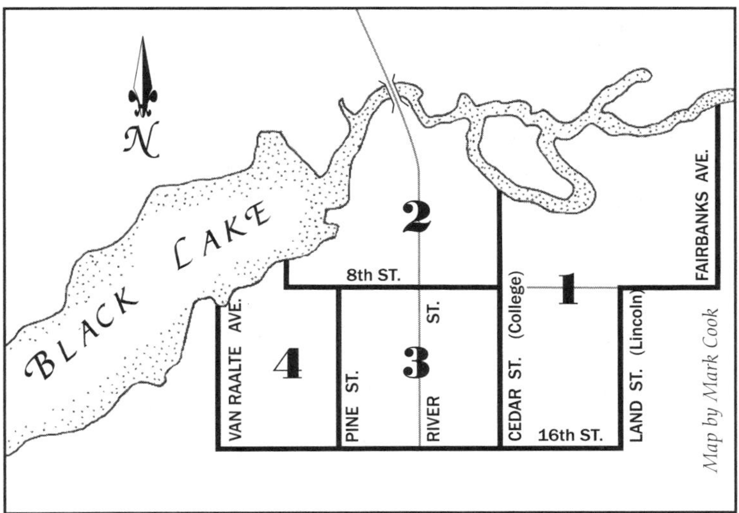

Fig. 24.2. Ward Map, 1871

the rank and file, the town marshal really was the "King Bee" of the town. He corralled the rowdies on the infamous market days, when men stood five deep in front of the bar at the saloons. As custodian of the town cannon in the public park, he set off the charge on the biggest public celebration of the year, the Fourth of July. To misfire was unthinkable. And on winter days at Union School, when the East Enders got into snowball fights with the West Enders, with Market Street (Central Avenue) as the dividing line of their respective turf, it was the marshal's job to keep the youngsters at bay. In the 1890s, when Bastian Keppel was marshal, Dick Vander Haar and Cy Rose led the East Enders, and the Vander Hills, Kuites, Borgmans, and Mulders directed the West Enders. Old timers recalled that the battles royal raged for hours, with the marshal in the thick of things taking his share of icy missiles and worse.[99]

"Politically, all is quiet," intoned *City News* editor Otto J. Doesburg in 1876. Otto, a son of Hermanus, had recently taken over as editor from Van Schelven and declared the paper Independent in politics. That Van Schelven and Doesburg were ardent Democrats in a rock-ribbed Republican town may explain their desire for nonpartisanship. When asked for endorsements by partisans, Doesburg replied: "My advice is for every man to come up and vote according to his own conviction, after mature reflection." Party labels had little meaning in city politics,

99 *Holland City News*, 23 Nov. 1922, 14 July 1932; "Joos Ver Planke," 5 June 1930.

ELECTION NOTICE!

Notice is hereby given, that the Annual Charter Election for the City of Holland will be held on Monday, the first day of April 1872, in the several wards respectively, to wit:
For the 1st ward at the Harness shop of H. Vaupell;
For the 2d ward at the office of H. D. Post;
For the 3d ward at the Common Council Room.
For the 4th ward at the Residence of L. D. Vissers.
The Polls will be opened at nine o'clock A. M.
By order of the Common Council,
C. HOFMAN, City Clerk.
Holland, Mich., March 21 1872.

Election Notice for the Annual Charter Election by city clerk Conrad Hofman, March 21, 1872 (*Donald van Reken Collection, Joint Archives of Holland*)

he averred. "When we know the persons, we discard political affiliation entirely."[100]

Most elected officials, regardless of party affiliation, ran tight ships and preached frugality, but partisanship was the order of the day, except for briefly in the 1870s. There was no middle of the road for Independents to stand. Party lines were so rigidly drawn that even weekly shopping trips became political, at least during campaigns. Ben Mulder of the *Holland City News* recalled that party banners bearing the likeness of the presidential candidate and his running mate were generally strung across the street where two Democratic or two Republican shopkeepers faced one another, and "Democrats traded with Democratic storeowners and the Republicans did likewise at Republican stores."[101]

Winning candidates were expected to treat supporters with a cigar. Arend Visscher, who touched no tobacco of any kind, had his wife bake hundreds of donuts for his expected victory party of coffee and donuts. When he narrowly lost the race to Cornelius J. De Roo, Visscher magnanimously thought to offer the donuts to De Roo for his victory party, but Mrs. Visscher adamantly refused. De Roo, apparently had made some "bitter" remarks about her husband in the heat of the campaign. The donuts went to family and friends over the next few days; the chickens enjoyed the rest.[102]

Reform politics has its day

The national economic depressions of 1873-77 and 1893-97 undermined Republican gains in Holland. From a high point of 74

100 *Holland City News*, 30 Oct. 1880.
101 Ibid., 2 Nov. 1878, "Fifty Years Ago Today," 1 Sept. 1939 (quote).
102 Visscher, "Recollections," section "Politics," HMA.

percent in the 1872 election, Republicans in presidential elections over the next thirty years only carried between 46 and 56 percent of the city electorate. Yet they won every race, three times by a plurality (rather than a majority), because Democrats split the opposition votes with reformist parties: Greenback, Granger, Socialist, Populist, and Prohibition. The decades of the 1870s, 1880s, and 1890s were an unsettled era of protest politics in America, brought on by economic dislocations due to rapid industrialization and the ups and downs of the business cycle. Industrial workers turned to socialist labor unions to deal with the vagaries of the market; farmers formed the Grange and Farmers Alliance movements. Socialists who preached class warfare, "soft money," and government regulation of railroads enjoyed their heyday.

Democrats in the 1870s tried to capitalize on the protest movements by dropping their party name in state and local elections in favor of more inclusive labels: Union Ticket (1872, 1874, 1875, 1877), Citizen's Ticket (1873, 1879, 1880), People's Ticket (1874), and Independent Ticket (1876, 1878). It was an effective public relations ploy by a threatened minority. Holland had become a Republican stronghold, the banner town in the county. Faced with this reality, Benjaminse of *De Hollander* announced in June 1880 that his paper no longer would carry a Democratic masthead, thus leaving Dutch Democrats with no paper in their native language and Ottawa County Democrats with no paper—period. *De Hollander* carried on for another fifteen years and gradually resumed its Democratic advocacy. But with a circulation of only five hundred, its influence was minimal. Calls for non-partisan local tickets, however, continued in the next years.[103]

The financial panic of 1873 and ensuing depression caused problems for the Republican administrations of Grant (1872-76) and Hayes (1876-80). As the party in power, they inevitably were blamed for rising unemployment and bank failures. When railroad companies cut wages in 1877, the American Railway Union called a strike that crippled the country and led to mob violence in Chicago and other cities that claimed dozens of lives. Troops were mobilized in Grand Rapids as a precaution. In rural America the Patrons of Husbandry, better known as the Grange, formed the Greenback Party with a platform of inflating the money supply by printing more paper dollars, called Greenbacks. This supposedly would restore prosperity. Some Dutch fell for the

[103] *Holland City News*, 22 July 1876, 4 Apr. 1885, 27 Feb. 1888; *De Hollander*, 13 Nov. 1872, 15 June 1880; *De Grondwet*, 6 Nov. 1872, 8 June 1880. See Holland City Records, box 1, HMA, for many examples of election tickets.

panacea of soft money. The Greenback Party found enough adherents in West Michigan to warrant publishing a Dutch-language newspaper, *De Standaard*, in Grand Rapids. Although the name mimicked that of Abraham Kuyper's mouthpiece in Amsterdam, the local Greenbackers did not share Kuyper's disdain for socialism in all its facets. A Holland resident, in a letter to *De Grondwet*, under the signature "Anti-Communist," declared: "No Christian may have such a newspaper [The Grand Rapids *Standaard*] in his house" (16 July 1878).

Dutch Calvinists saw in the Greenback movement the specter of European communism and its rhetoric of class warfare. Holland's Greenback Club counted only seventeen members in 1878; yet in the gubernatorial election that year their candidate got eighty-two votes (12 percent), almost all from soft money Democrats. Curiously, John Klyn, a son of Hendrik G. Klyn, the founding pastor of the Second Reformed Church of Grand Rapids, was a leading Greenbacker, as was Ottawa County Sheriff Joos Ver Planke and former Holland Mayor E. J. Harrington. Otto Doesburg's editorials in the *City News* gave cover to the radicals by condemning Republican "hard money" policies and their seeming allegiance to business tycoons like railroad magnate Jay Gould. Given the "prevailing dissatisfaction about the hard times in such a magnificent country," Doesburg noted, "who knows how large a Greenback vote may be rolled up here yet." In the municipal elections of 1879, when Republican clerics and professionals cried "Down with Greenbackers," Doesburg retorted that "all those zealous hard money men are people who draw a regular salary," not lowly wage earners. Yet the charge of Greenbacker was the kiss of death in Holland and no one on that ticket won except for Ver Planke.[104]

Holland's mayors during the hard times, Van Landegend and "Boss" Schaddelee, as he was known, kept a tight rein on city expenditures and raised revenues to cover welfare costs, such as a new office of the poor and a city library. Van Landegend welcomed saloons to town and instituted fees for the purchase of liquor licenses. But he failed in an effort to raise taxes in 1877; citizens voted this down decisively. Van Landegend's seemingly pro-saloon policies aroused temperance forces, led by Hope President Charles Scott, theology professor T. Romeyn Beck, and local Methodists, to organize the Holland City Temperance Society. This movement gained strength over the next decades (see below and chapter 20).[105]

104 *Holland City News*, 28 July, 1 Dec. 1877, 17 Aug., 21 Sept. 1878, 20 Mar. 1880; *De Grondwet*, 16, 30 July, 6, 13 Aug, 19 Nov. 1878, 8 Apr. 1879.

105 *Holland City News*, 28 Aug., 11 Sept., 2 Oct. 1875, 19 Apr. 1877.

Mayor Schaddelee launched a second crusade—sabbatarianism—when he urged the common council to enact a Sunday ordinance to close down excursion trains, pleasure boating, and "sporting and recreation parties" on the day of rest. But the popular outcry was so great that the council refused, even though many of Holland's 3,400 inhabitants were members of one of the seven Holland churches or were affiliated with Hope College. Leaders in the Reformed Church in America, acting through the Holland Ministerial Association, took up the crusade against Sabbath desecration again in 1883; specifically, they condemned the Sunday excursion boats running to Macatawa Park. The ministers blamed the federal postal service for the first public desecration of the Sabbath in 1810 and again in 1835 by requiring mail delivery, but that was water over the dam. The need now was to uphold "social order and public morals" locally. When the common council again put them off, the clerics in 1885 formed the Sabbath Law and Order League to keep the pressure on. Almost all the crusaders were Reformed Church leaders, except for Evert Bos of the Ninth Street (Pillar) Christian Reformed Church and elder Cornelius Van Loo of Zeeland, the group's secretary.[106]

John Roost was an unlikely Democratic mayor. He was the founder and for many years the leader of the Republican Party in Holland. But business losses of $30,000 in the Holland Fire and the hard times of the mid-1870s, together with the fiscal scandals of the Grant administration, turned him against the Republicans, and in 1876 he switched party allegiance and supported New York Governor Samuel Tilden in the presidential campaign. The next year Roost took another major step, and for the first time, at age fifty-three, he joined a Christian church, Grace Episcopal in Holland. In 1882 Roost ran for the state senate on the Democratic ticket in the Twenty-Third District (Ottawa and Muskegon Counties) and won by 390 votes.[107]

Dirk Van Raalte entered local politics in 1874 after his father had settled into his retirement from pulpit and politics. Dirk lost his right arm marching through Georgia with the Michigan Twenty-Fifth under General W. T. Sherman, and this fact was endlessly repeated and paid high political dividends. Young Van Raalte, "a good, healthy Republican," was elected to the Ottawa County board of commissioners to represent the First District (Holland Township and city). His

[106] *De Hollander*, 7 Aug. 1877, 26 Feb. 1878; *De Grondwet*, 7 Oct. 1884, 9 Aug. 1887; *Holland City News*, 6 Oct. 1883, 9, 20 Sept., 4 Oct. 1884, 28 Mar. 1885.

[107] "Biographical Information for the Mayors of Holland," JAH; Vande Water, "Holland Never Voted for Lincoln," in *Holland Happenings*, 4:19-20.

majority was the highest among six Republican candidates. Young Van Raalte had his father's business instincts and operated a boot and shoe store on Eighth Street. Two years later, in 1876, he ran successfully as the state representative from Ottawa County's First District, which included the city of Holland. That Hollanders, ten thousand strong and largely Republican, made up two-thirds of Ottawa County's population gave Van Raalte a decided advantage. As a member of the ways and means committee, Van Raalte helped supervise the construction of the state capitol building. He served in the 1875 and 1877 sessions, and then declined to serve again. But thirty years later, in 1909, party leaders induced him to run again, and he reclaimed his old seat.[108]

Local politics had its own drama and "lingo," especially during the tense wait for polling results to come in. In November 1885 editor William H. Rogers of the *Holland City News* described a typical scenario:

> Local politicians on Wednesday morning last were occupying the street corners waiting for news from the November election. Mac [attorney Patrick McBride], the doctor [Bernardus Ledeboer], and Van [Gerrit Van Schelven–all Democrats] looked as though they had suddenly been hit with something besides a club, while "Church" [perhaps Gerrit Diekema], Ald. [Martin] Rose, and L. T. [Kanters] looked happy in their sweet innocence and were only too ready to answer all questions as to the 'result.' The amount of cigars and rainwater [alcohol] consumed was greater on Wednesday than on any previous day of the week. Quiet now reigns in all political souls and the family is once more at rest.[109]

The issue of women's suffrage was on the ballot in Michigan in 1876 for the first time. Holland lacked a single public advocate for the change, except Sylvester Morris, editor of the *City News*, who gave the proposal his endorsement in a low-key editorial. City voters squashed the proposal overwhelmingly, 49 in favor (13 percent) and 321 against (87 percent). Only the Third and Fourth Wards showed a glimmer of interest; their votes in favor were 16 and 18 percent, respectively. The First and Second Wards gave the proposal *yes* votes by only 4 and 12 percent, respectively. "Woman suffrage has but few votaries here," declared Hope College student Walter C. Walsh in the student paper,

108 *Holland City News*, 7 Nov. 1874, 17 Feb. 1910; *Allegan Journal*, 31 Oct. 1874; *De Hollander*, 23 Sept. 1872, 7 Nov. 1876, translated by Simone Kennedy; Elton J. Bruins, et al., *Albertus and Christina Van Raalte: The Van Raalte Family, Home, and Roots* (Grand Rapids: Eerdmans, 2004), 129-30.

109 *Holland City News*, 7 Nov. 1885.

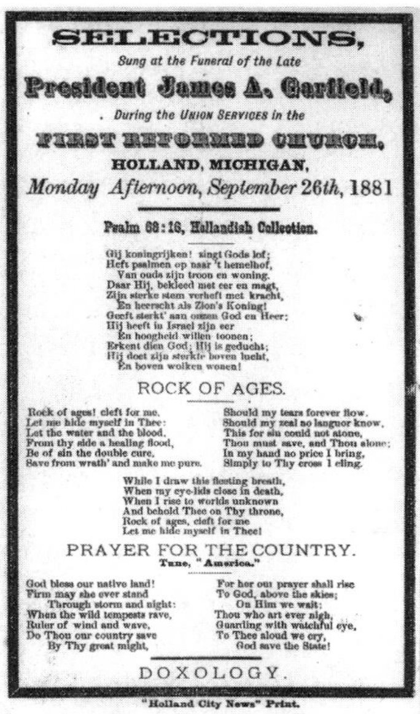

SELECTIONS,
Sung at the Funeral of the Late
President James A. Garfield,
During the UNION SERVICES *in the*
FIRST REFORMED CHURCH,
HOLLAND, MICHIGAN,
Monday Afternoon, September 26th, 1881

Psalm 68:16, Hollandish Collection.

Gij koningrijken! zingt Gods lof;
Heft psalmen op naar 't hemelhof,
Van ouds zijn troon en woning.
Daar Hij, bekleed met eer en magt,
Zijn sterke stem verheft met kracht,
En heerscht als Zion's Koning!
Geeft sterkt' aan onzen God en Heer;
Hij heeft in Israel zijn eer
En hoogheid willen toonen;
Erkent dien God; Hij is geducht;
Hij doet zijn sterkte boven lucht,
En boven wolken wonen!

ROCK OF AGES.

Rock of ages! cleft for me,
Let me hide myself in Thee:
Let the water and the blood,
From thy side a healing flood,
Be of sin the double cure,
Save from wrath' and make me pure.

Should my tears forever flow,
Should my zeal no languor know,
This for sin could not atone,
Thou must save, and Thou alone;
In my hand no price I bring,
Simply to Thy cross I cling.

While I draw this fleeting breath,
When my eye-lids close in death,
When I rise to worlds unknown
And behold Thee on Thy throne,
Rock of ages, cleft for me
Let me hide myself in Thee!

PRAYER FOR THE COUNTRY.
Tune, "America."

God bless our native land!
Firm may she ever stand
Through storm and night:
When the wild tempests rave,
Ruler of wind and wave,
Do Thou our country save
By Thy great might,

For her our prayer shall rise
To God, above the skies;
On Him we wait;
Thou who art ever nigh,
Guarding with watchful eye,
To Thee aloud we cry,
God save the State!

DOXOLOGY.

"Holland City News" Print.

First Reformed Church bulletin with songs selected for the "Union" memorial service of the late President James A. Garfield, September 26, 1881. Note Psalm 68:16 in Dutch and the English hymns "Rock of Ages," "Prayer for the Country," and the "Doxology" (*Joint Archives of Holland*)

Excelsiora. But he added, "there are strong minded women who say: '[I]t is only a question of time.'" Until that time, as another student declared, "idiots, lunatics, and females" are denied the right to vote. He might have added convicts and aliens to the list.[110]

Holland in the 1880s continued in the Republican column. In the presidential election of 1880 James A. Garfield won with a plurality of 49 percent in a four-way race. And when he died from an assassin's bullet in September 1881, both First Reformed (Pillar) and Hope Churches hosted citywide memorial services, the former in Dutch and the latter in English. The service at First Church included singing Psalter number 68, verse 16, "*Gij koninkrijken, zingt Gods lof*" ("Oh kingdoms! Sing God's Praise") and the hymns "Rock of Ages" and "America." Garfield's vice president, Chester A. Arthur, succeeded him. Republicans in Holland also gained victory in the 1882 state election.[111]

Locally, Republicans won most city races, beginning in 1882 when William H. Beach unseated mayor Roost. Significant too were the switches to the Republicans by long-time Democrats Gerrit Van Schelven and E. J. Harrington. Yet, Schaddelee continued his hold on the office of county supervisor; Roost won the state senate race in the

[110] Ibid., 9, 30 May, 7 Nov. 1874; *Excelsiora* (Hope College semi-monthly student paper, 1871-93), 4 Dec. 1874.

[111] *Holland City News*, 6 Nov. 1880, 8 Oct. 1881, 11 Nov. 1882; Church bulletin, Holland City Elections, box 1, HMA.

fall elections; newcomer Reinder E. Werkman, a member of the People's Party, won the alderman's seat in the Third Ward once in 1883; and Democratic candidates carried the First, Second, and Third Wards in 1884, leaving only the Fourth in Republican hands. Dark clouds seemed to appear on the horizon from the anti-Republican coalition of Democrats, Greenbackers, and the Workingmen's Party.

The 1884 presidential campaign of Grover Cleveland against James Blaine was long remembered as a nasty one, marked by anti-Catholic hysteria and charges of personal scandal against Cleveland for fathering an "illegitimate" child. Blaine harped on "Rum, Romanism, and Religion" as the hallmarks of the Democratic Party. Some one hundred of Holland's Republicans organized a Blaine and Logan Club (Logan being the "veep" nominee). The members were ecstatic when Blaine, a flamboyant congressman from Maine, nicknamed "the Plumed Knight," came to Holland to stump for votes, en route to Muskegon after a rally in Grand Rapids. The gathering came hard on the heels of a big Democratic rally staged by the Cleveland and Hendricks Club a week earlier. Blaine's Grand Rapids appearance attracted a huge crowd of thirty-five thousand people from all across West Michigan, including two hundred from Holland. Many, including Mayor Beach, Oscar Yates, and Hope professor Gerrit J. Kollen, Van Raalte's son-in-law, remained in Grand Rapids overnight so they could accompany their hero on the train to the lakeshore the next morning.[112]

Almost the whole town of Holland turned out the next morning to greet Blaine. While awaiting his belated arrival, former mayor Isaac Cappon and the young attorney and rising star, Gerrit J. Diekema, gave inspiring speeches to warm up the crowd. The Republican Martial Band, under Captain Peter Moose, provided rousing music. The band was part of a long tradition of marching clubs in Holland with uniformed men in red, white, and blue capes made of oilcloth, colorful caps, and torches in hand. At ten o'clock, as the train rolled into the station, the old cannon that had been towed from Centennial Park boomed out several salutes of welcome. Blaine addressed the throng of two thousand from a temporary platform on the back of the railcar. Everyone went home convinced that the 1884 contest was "one of [the] most spectacular and one of the most strenuous ever waged in Holland."[113]

With all the hoopla, Blaine won Holland by a slim margin of thirty-three votes. Cleveland carried only the traditional Democratic

112 *Holland City News*, 16 Aug., 11, 18 Oct., 8 Nov. 1884.
113 Ibid., 18 Oct. 1884, "Presidential Elections in Yester-Year," 29 Oct. 1936.

First Ward, but by a mere six votes. It was a cliffhanger locally as it was nationally. Political junkies stayed up late at the Lyceum Hall watching the telegraph dispatches come in with the latest results. Each report was hailed with cheers or jeers, depending on the numbers. "Old and young alike were fairly crazed with excitement and it was broad daylight before many sought their homes," after learning that Cleveland had garnered just enough electoral votes to win the presidency. It had been twenty-eight years since a Democrat—James Buchanan in 1856—had captured the White House, and the long-suffering party faithful in Holland finally could celebrate. They organized a victory parade, replete with two hundred "footmen bearing banners, brooms, and torches, and judging from the noise, each was armed with a tin horn."

The procession formed in front of the Cleveland and Hendricks Club on Eighth Street and proceeded to River Avenue, circled Centennial Park, and then followed Eighth Street west to Macatawa Bay. Steam whistles at local factories, including the stave factory, Phoenix Planing Mill, and Plugger Mill "belched forth steam and hideous noises at the rate of about sixteen ounces to the pound. . . . The canon at short intervals added its thunder to the occasion." Democratic homeowners and places of business along the parade route decorated their buildings and 254 candles shone from the windows of the Phoenix Hotel near the Chicago Depot. The Phoenix under proprietor J. McVicar boasted in its advertisements that it was the "only American hotel in town," thereby differentiating itself from its Dutch-owned and Republican competitors.[114]

The parade seemed innocuous enough, but a riot nearly erupted when young Democrats added an unofficial float at the tail end. It was made from two empty crockery crates that looked like a prison cage, adorned with an effigy of James Blaine on top. Enraged Republicans stopped the horse-drawn float, took down the cage and effigy, and burned them in a bonfire on the waterfront. Years later Ben Mulder recalled other incidents on that emotional night. His father Leendert's newspaper plant for *De Grondwet*, a rabid Republican sheet, was "the target of many brickbats in the hands of young obstreperous Democrats. . . . Many windows [were] broken [and] the printing office was thoroughly painted in red skull and bones." The mob also burned Blaine's body in effigy in the large swamp where the Holland Interurban freight depot was then located. "One can imagine the hatred for the red-headed editor [Isaac Verwey] with the sharp Republican pen." For the next fifty years, locals remembered the bitter hatred, the "seething

114 *Holland City News*, 5 Nov. 1884.

political turmoil," of this election, which poisoned politics for many years.[115]

The Knights of Labor for the first time in 1884 played a small part in the outcome of an election in Holland. This socialistic labor movement, founded as a secret society among Philadelphia garment cutters in 1860, evolved in the 1870s into a union of unskilled laborers, including, for the first time, women and blacks. The Knights reached a high point in 1886 with 730,000 members, and they placed a candidate, Henry George, on the presidential ballot. In Grand Rapids the organization was strong enough to publish its own periodical, *The Workman*, and "many" Dutch Reformed factory workers joined up.

Christian Reformed Church leaders became so concerned, that Cornelis Vorst of the First Church of Grand Rapids published a scathing indictment in *De Grondwet*, and editor Lammert Hulst of *De Wachter* followed up with a warning to members nationwide not to join this "*secret*" brotherhood and "dangerous enemy of the Church." It stood condemned for the same reason as freemasonry; both were secret societies that "unequally yoked" believers with unbelievers. Worse yet, the Knights included radical socialists and even anarchists "who resort to force." In 1885 Classis Grand Rapids of the Christian Reformed Church condemned the Knights and threatened church discipline against any members who joined. The next year, the church's synod, its highest assembly, at the behest of Classis Holland unanimously approved an "overture" (proposal), drawn up by the consistory of the Ninth Street Church (formerly First Reformed Church), that extended the ban against the Knights to church members nationwide. The Netherlands Anti-Revolutionary Party of Guillaume Groen van Prinsterer had for decades similarly militated against such ideologies, as all orthodox Reformed immigrants knew full well.[116]

In Holland, Gerrit Diekema ran successfully on the Republican ticket for the Michigan House of Representatives in 1884 representing the First District (Ottawa County). It was the first of four consecutive terms (1885-92), including being elected speaker in 1889. In his first re-election campaign in 1885, Diekema carried his district handily, but lost the city of Holland by twenty-nine votes to the Knight's candidate, John

115 "Presidential Elections in Yester-Year," ibid., 29 Oct. 1936 (quotes); Ben Mulder, untitled paper on the history of Holland newspapers (quotes), presented to the Holland Merchants Association, 1924, HMA.

116 *De Grondwet*, 14 Oct., 4, 25 Nov. 1884, 20 Jan., 3, 10, 17 Feb., 3, 17 Mar., 21 Apr., 23 June, 14 Sept., 22 Dec. 1885, 6 July 1886; Christian Reformed Church, *Acts of Synod*, 1886, Art. 90.

A. Roost, son of the political leader of the Republicans and later the Greenback Party. Roost won the populous Second and Fourth Wards, which were traditionally Republican. Editor Rogers of the *Holland City News* attributed this victory entirely to the support of the Land and Labor Club of Holland, the local arm of the Knights of Labor, who had raised $286 in the campaign. Roost's win was a shot across the bow for politicians and presaged class warfare in local politics.[117]

The Haymarket riot in Chicago on May 1, 1886, in which four policemen were killed, so discredited the Knights that they quickly died out, but radical ideologies continued to gain strength among Greenbackers, leading in the 1890s to the Populist or People's Party. In 1887 the Knights in Holland even celebrated the fifth of September as Labor Day. Since the day was not yet a national holiday, the event had to take place in the evening. It featured some seventy men marching around with torches ablaze, followed by a cleric from Lansing who recounted the history of the organization.[118]

The Knights were a flash in the pan locally. In the 1888 local elections, Republicans swept every office in Holland Township and city, except for Ottawa County supervisor, in which John Kerkhof of the Citizen's Ticket unseated Wiepke Diekema after eighteen years in office. Turnout was unusually light at 73 percent, and the day passed without the usual excitement. Remarkably, the Democrats did not field a single candidate, choosing instead to combine with the Knights and other dissidents on the Citizen's Ticket. Kerkhof won re-election as supervisor ten times in succession, in part because he transitioned himself into the Republican Party.[119]

The temperance movement also heated up in the 1880s, after a hiatus of thirty years. After a ten-year effort, the Republicans succeeded in placing a Prohibition Amendment on the state ballot in 1883, and after the initial effort failed, again in 1887. Religious and business leaders in Holland, both Reformed and Christian Reformed, met in 1887 to consider the issue in the Ninth Street Church, under the aegis of its pastor, Evert Bos. After many speeches, "almost all" favoring prohibition, the assembly resolved without a dissenting vote to support the amendment. Similar meetings were held in Zeeland and Grand Rapids. In contrast to the clerics and some businessmen, both Holland

117 C. Warren Vander Hill, *Gerrit J. Diekema* (Grand Rapids: Eerdmans, 1970), 17-23; *Holland City News*, 30 Oct., 6 Nov. 1886. The Greenback Party advocated a policy of the Treasury printing paper money to inflate the dollar.

118 *Holland City News*, 19 Feb., 2 July 1887; *De Grondwet*, 6, 13 Sept. 1887.

119 *Holland City News*, 7 Apr. 1888, John Roost Jr. obit., ibid., 30 July 1908.

newspaper editors came out strongly against the amendment. Leendert Mulder of *De Grondwet* and a member of Bos' congregation, warned that the amendment would limit personal freedom, ban sacramental wine, and make illegal the ownership of any alcoholic beverages in the home (except with a doctor's prescription for medicinal purposes). Editor Nick Whelan of the *Holland City News* declared the proposal the worst kind of "hypocrisy in politics." Moderation in all things, he declared—ban saloons, not alcohol. When Election Day came, it was apparent that the editors and not the clerics had their finger on the public pulse. Only 37 percent of Holland's electors cast *yes* votes; the amendment also failed in Ottawa County and statewide.[120]

Dutch Reformed and German Lutheran voters liked their beer just as much as Irish Democrats liked their whiskey. Prohibition was class warfare at its worst, and hyphenated Americans would have nothing to do with teetotalers. Further, every time Republicans endorsed prohibition, it proved disastrous at the polls. "Republicanism and prohibition do not mix," declared Whelan. "The prohibition question is a question in itself and should stand on its own bottom. It has no business in the Republican party."[121]

The experience in Kalamazoo in 1883 bore him out. Two weeks before the election, with a Republican Temperance ticket on the ballot, local WCTU ladies came out strongly for the referendum and "preached against strong drink and especially against smoking." This made Dutch and German voters, who were mostly loyal Republicans, so angry that three hundred refused to vote, and some "were so angry that out of pure cussedness, they voted for a Roman Catholic Democrat." They could not abide their party making alcohol and tobacco litmus tests of loyalty. "The rich have money, beautiful homes, horses, and carriages to ride in," said one, "but I have to stay home, and in the sweat of my brow eat my bread. If then I come home warm and tired, my wife says: 'Jan, here is a glass of beer,' then I smoke my pipe, and I am happy! If I have to quit all of this, America is no longer a free country for me."[122] The battle against "demon rum" would continue for many decades, led by the Prohibition Party. More than twenty years passed after the 1887 referendum before Holland faced another liquor vote, and saloons were then the flash point.

[120] *De Grondwet*, 4 Apr., 24 Oct., 21 Nov. 1882, 3 Apr. 1883, 8 Apr. 1884, 1, 19, 26 Mar., 3 May 1887; *Holland City News*, 29 Mar. 1879, 7, 28 Aug. 1880, 26 Feb. 1887; *Excelsiora*, 17 Mar. 1887.

[121] *Holland City News*, 5 Mar., 9 Apr. 1887.

[122] *De Grondwet*, 24 Apr. 1883, translated by William Buursma.

In the summer of 1888, the Democratic Party convention re-nominated President Cleveland. "A national scandal," cried Leendert Mulder, editor of *De Grondwet* and the *Holland City News*. His readers knew full well the sordid fact that Cleveland, a bachelor, in the 1884 campaign had admitted having an out-of-wedlock son. It was a scandalous situation. Redemption came in November when the telegraph reported that Republican Benjamin Harrison had won and turned Cleveland out of office. The *City News* proclaimed: "Hurrah for Harrison!!! We're All Right!"[123] Mulder could hardly have imagined that four years later Cleveland would run again and win!

Harrison carried all four wards in 1888, but he won the Second Ward by only two votes. This ward had replaced the First as the Democrat stronghold, and quickly earned the derogatory label, "the bloody Democratic second." Republicans swept all state and congressional races, except for Democrat Leendert Kanters' narrow win as county register of deeds. A week after the election, local Republicans celebrated with a great festival that featured a twenty-eight-gun salute at sunrise, a parade in the afternoon, and fireworks to cap off the evening. Harrison could count on committed Republicans like the Jan Rychel family of Vriesland who were among the 1847 immigrants. Two weeks before the election, Widow Rychel, the oldest inhabitant in Ottawa County, died at age ninety-nine, leaving eighty voters among her many descendents, all but one a Harrison supporter. Zeeland also consistently voted Republican by two-thirds and more in these years.[124]

On the local level, Democrats were far from finished. In 1889 a Fusion ticket of the Democratic and Single Tax (Socialist) parties, led by Mayor Henry Kremers, Isaac Fairbanks, Schaddelee, the Van Puttens (Jacob, Ben, and Marinus), the Kanters (Leendert and Abraham), Richard Vanden Berg, and Cornelius Ver Schure, captured the city offices of mayor, marshal, school inspectors, justice of the peace, and Second and Fourth Ward aldermen. Only the First Ward remained solidly in Republican hands. Kremers, a graduate of the University of Michigan Medical School, and Kanters, were unlikely socialists. Kanters was chief of the fire department and publisher of Hope College's newspaper, *De Hope*. Kremers served on the boards of a local bank and several companies and was a well-respected community leader.

As mayor, Kremers pushed for lower taxes, human rights, and new sewers. While in office, he had contractor George Dalman build

[123] *Holland City News*, 27 Oct., 10 Nov. 1888; *De Grondwet*, 13 Nov. 1888.

[124] *Holland City News*, 12 Apr., 15 Nov. 1890, 15 Mar. 1923.

a new house for his family at the corner of Twelfth Street and Central Avenue. It was one of the most extravagant homes in town and later became the city hospital, then the Netherlands Museum, and now the Centennial Inn Bed and Breakfast (chapter 25). The annual salary of marshal Richard Vanden Berg was raised to $480, the highest amount in fifteen years, but he was expected to "be on hand early and late." Kremers served only one year; Republican Oscar Yates succeeded him in 1890 and was re-elected in 1891.[125]

The 1889 and 1890 elections for school inspectors (that is, board members) reflected a fundamental change in public school governance. Beginning with Van Raalte in 1848, local voters customarily elected to the school board Reformed church leaders and their close allies. The schools reflected the constituency and essentially functioned as Christian schools, so it was most appropriate for clerics and church elders to control the curriculum and staffing. But in 1889 Fusion candidates George Ballard and James Mabes, both Americans, defeated the Dutch Reformed Republican nominees, Matthew Notier and Bernard J. De Vries. The next year, 1890, Republicans nominated two Reformed stalwarts, Nicholas M. Steffens of Western Seminary and Teunis Keppel, a close associate of Van Raalte since 1847 and former elder in First Reformed (Pillar) Church.

Just days before the 1890 election, the Democrats had caucused and nominated a Union ticket of dissidents. This move, said *City News* editor John C. Post, "was essentially aimed to defeat the [Republican] nominees for school inspectors," and thereby to take over the school board. The ploy succeeded, and the Fusionist candidates, David L. Boyd and George P. Hummer, won office. Hummer, a backer of the inflationary "free Silver" policy, had been superintendent of schools for seven years (1882-89) and had recently resigned to become the manager of the new West Michigan Furniture Company. He would serve as mayor during the economic crisis of the mid-1890s. Hummer, who held a graduate degree from Valparaiso University, apparently wanted a career change from education to business.[126]

John A. Roost, who helped engineer the revolt, expressed the thinking of the dissidents in an article in the Grand Rapids *Workman*, a socialist labor newspaper, under the title, "The Destruction of the Gods." Roost labeled Steffens and Keppel the "priest and the Levite"

125 Ibid., 23 Feb., 30 Mar., 6 Apr., 11 May 1889, 11 Apr. 1891, 1 May 1903; "Biographical Information for the Mayors of Holland," JAH.

126 *Holland City News*, 12 Apr. 1889; *Holland Daily Sentinel Semi-Centennial Supplement*, 1897.

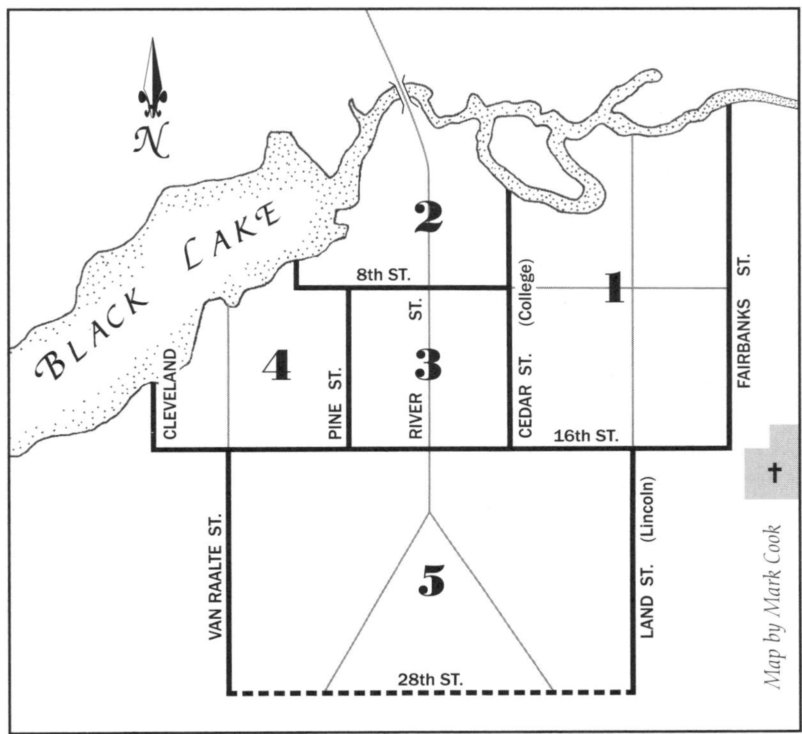

Fig. 24.3. Ward Map, 1893

and rejoiced that the election freed the city "from the rule of hypocrisy." Roost charged that Hope College faculty had run the public schools for too long as the "dominion of priests," with the aim to keep out Americans and other "strangers" who might "infect the good and true Hollanders. . . . But now the fight is over. We have killed the enemy of the public schools, the enemy of general freedom, the enemy of who believes in different social classes, the enemy of progress." Presumably, Hummer shared these views, which might explain his decision to resign as superintendent and run for supervisor. The secular winds of change gave Reformed parents pause, and within two years, they began planning for a Christian school, which came to fruition in 1901.[127]

Another notable change in city politics was the reorientation of the wards. From 1867 until the mid-1880s, Wards One and Three were Democratic and Wards Two and Four Republican. By the late 1880s

[127] *De Grondwet*, 15 Apr. 1890, translated by Michael Douma; Donald van Reken, *Changing Footprints: A Memory Book of the Holland Christian Schools* (Holland, 1984), 5-7.

this was reversed; the east side Wards One and Three voted Republican, and the west side Wards Two and Four voted Democratic, Greenback, Fusionist, or Union. The Prohibition Party base also was on the east side; in 1890, 7 percent in Ward One and 5 percent in Ward Three voted "dry." Most were Methodists and Reformed Church members from New York and the East, led by Hope College professors. Prohibition was always a Yankee Protestant crusade, and only immigrants well along the path of assimilation voted that ticket. Significantly, by 1892 there were enough drys in town to organize the Holland Prohibition Club.[128]

Holland Township in the 1880s developed a novel nomination system that resulted in a single ticket, known as a "double-header" or "double ticket." Only one caucus was called, and all interested voters balloted for each office until one person received a majority. His name and that of the man receiving the next highest votes were then printed on the ballot. On Election Day voters simply scratched off the name they rejected, leaving the man of their choice. This system required only one ticket, and no votes were lost from misspelling of names or "bogus" tickets.[129]

Populism

Populism arrived in Holland in the early 1890s, and the People's Crusade, a third party movement with socialist ideals, roiled local and national politics for several years. Americans, not Hollanders, led the way locally, and most of the support came from factory workers and not farmers. In 1891, at the first convention of the People's Party in Ottawa County, some forty delegates elected George Ballard of Holland as president and John A. Roost, David Bertsch, David Cronin, and Ballard to the county committee. Only Roost was of Dutch ancestry. The next year, James De Young, a Democratic sachem, chaired a newly formed city committee and two other Hollanders, John Elferdink Jr., and Martin Klyn, joined the county committee.[130] In the state gubernatorial election in 1891, both Holland Township and city went Democratic by a small majority, although the Republican candidate in the Fifth Congressional District, Charles Belknap of Grand Rapids, won easily in Ottawa County and statewide.

The Populists gained so little traction with the voters that to have any hope of defeating the Republicans they had to "fuse" with the

128 *Holland City News*, 8, 15 Nov. 1890, 27 Sept. 1892.

129 Ibid., 4 Apr. 1889, 5 Apr. 1890.

130 Howard Lubbers, "The History of the Populist Party in the City of Holland and the Dutch Reaction to It," seminar paper, Calvin College, 1968, 1-4, 14.

Democrats. In Holland the People's Party and Democrats formed a non-partisan Citizen's Caucus, which nominated George Ballard for mayor in 1892. The ploy nearly succeeded. E. J. Harrington, the Republican, won by only five votes (360 to 355) in the April election. Most opposition voters were Democrats, and Democrats carried Wards Two, Three, and Four. Only the "Solid First" saved the day for Harrington. Van Schelven won the office of supervisor on the Republican ticket. He had transformed himself from ardent Democrat to true Republican in the early 1880s.[131]

In the 1892 presidential race, the Populists insisted on running their own candidate, James Weaver, and the Democrats turned to ex-president Grover Cleveland. Cleveland won the presidency again, and local Republicans, like ex-mayor Isaac Cappon, had to swallow hard. As one of Cappon's Prohibitionist friends, William Crowley, reminded him, "Years ago you wrote me a Thanksgiving letter. You said you could not feel thankful over the election of Cleveland. Well, how do you feel now? I feel thankful and I hope you do too. . . . God knows best who should be President. . . . Is Boss Skadelee [ex-mayor Kommer Schaddelee] alive yet or did he explode over the great Democratic victory." Crowley knew how to rub it in.[132]

Cappon could take comfort that Republicans again gained a majority in Holland Township (56 percent) and a winning plurality in the city of Holland (46 percent), although the margins were down by ten points from the 1888 election. Only the Second Ward went Democratic. Populists nearly held the swing vote in Holland. They collected sixty-four votes (7 percent) in the presidential election that Harrison won by a plurality of sixty-five votes. Republicans won all eight county races, but in the city of Holland, they lost five seats in which Populists and Democrats supported the same candidate. So the impact of Populists locally far exceeded their small numbers.[133]

The apex for the Populists in Holland was the 1894 gubernatorial race in which they garnered 172 votes (15 percent). Hard times after the 1893 business panic brought out dissidents. Also, an internecine struggle among Ottawa County Democrats over Cleveland's hard money policies split the party. Many West Michigan Dutch were pro-silver men who favored the unlimited coinage of silver dollars. But Cleveland in

131 *Holland City News*, 11, 18 Feb. 1882, 7 Nov. 1891; "The Late Leendert Mulder," ibid., 18 Sept. 1897.

132 Wm. Cropley, Napa City, MI, to Isaac Cappon, Holland, MI, 24 Nov. 1892, in Cappon Family Papers, box 1, HMA.

133 Lubbers, "Populist Party," 4-8.

1893 called a special session of Congress to repeal the Sherman Silver Purchase Act of 1890, which was bankrupting the treasury. Many Democrats voted Populist in protest. But to no avail; Republicans swept every office. In the 1895 spring election, with M. Vander Heide as party secretary, Populists' strength in Holland dropped to 12 percent. A change in Michigan election law barred candidates from running on more than one ticket. Populists could no longer share candidates with Democrats; they had to fuse or die. They chose to fuse in the 1896 presidential race and lost their identity. In the end, the Democrats co-opted them.[134]

The Dutch Reformed rejected Populism and its free silver panacea, despite tutoring by *De Volksstem* (The Voice of the People), a Dutch Catholic weekly from De Pere, Wisconsin. Gold was God's money, and the Republican Party was God's voice. It was the non-Dutch who sang the song of socialism, although some Dutch factory workers joined them. Of the seven Populist county conventions in the 1890s for which names of delegates are known, only 41 percent from Holland were Dutch, who comprised two-thirds of the electorate. Most of Holland's Populists were loyal Democrats who voted the Fusion ticket. In the end, reformers did the crusading and the Dutch did the voting.[135]

Gerrit Van Schelven, editor of the *Holland City News*, lampooned Populist free silver nostrums in 1896 by using pidgin English:

> I also notis that most all the men who hev maid a faleyure in their own finansis want to do the finanseering fur the government by dubbling the bullyan value uv silver. This lets me into the gaim, so to speek. I am fur dubbling up awl the time. The moar a thing is dubbled the moar thair is fur me to git sum uv it without givin ennything in return.[136]

Holland's vote totals surpassed those of Grand Haven for the first time in the 1892 canvas. The county seat had slipped to second place in population. In 1893 the city of Holland doubled its territory by annexing all the platted additions south to the Allegan County line (Thirty-Second Street) and east to Lincoln Street. From then on, Holland was the dominant town in Ottawa County. No wonder that Holland's political leaders had believed for years that the city should become the seat of a new "Van Raalte County." In 1887 they spoke

134 Ibid., 10-11.

135 Statistics compiled by Lubbers, ibid., 20-21.

136 *Holland City News*, 11 July 1896.

Mayor Gerrit J. Diekema, 1895-96 (*Joint Archives of Holland*)

openly of a genuine ethnic county, in which the four Allegan townships of Fillmore, Laketown, Manlius, and Saugatuck would join Van Raalte County, while Grand Haven and several adjacent townships would be assigned to Muskegon County. The realignment proposal died quickly when the townships to be realigned showed no enthusiasm for it.[137]

The economic distress in the mid-1890s opened doors for Democrats to carry city races, if not state and national elections. Hummer, a Democrat, in 1893 defeated Republican E. J. Harrington, the incumbent, and in 1894 Hummer upset Isaac Cappon, the strongest possible candidate. This was quite a feat in the "staunch, rock-ribbed" Republican town, but Hummer's coattails were short and his tenure brief. Republicans won most of the other offices in 1893, except for aldermen in the Second, Third, and Fourth Wards, and in 1895 Gerrit Diekema wiped out the "disgrace of having a Democratic mayor" by winning the mayoralty by a huge 337-vote majority. Diekema's coattails were also long; he carried to victory every nominee on the Republican ticket–city, district, and ward. "Unprecedented!" crowed Van Schelven of the *City News*. But hard times stemming from the 1893 financial panic also limited Diekema to one term.[138]

The next year James De Young, the Democratic-Fusion candidate, turned Diekema out by twenty-six votes. Diekema lost to De Young again in 1897 by a slim twelve votes. Both elections were so close they required recounts. Diekema's support of public schools, a position he announced

137 Ibid., 19, 26 Nov. 1892, 4, 11 Mar. 1893; *De Grondwet*, 8 Dec. 1888, 15 Jan., 5 Feb. 1889. The total vote in the 1892 presidential election was Holland 996 and Grand Haven 957.

138 *Holland City News*, 8 Apr. 1893, 17 Apr. 1894, 6 Apr. 1895, 11 Apr. 1896.

already in 1895, likely cost him some Christian Reformed votes. De Young was the "father of the Holland BPW" (board of public works), having led the first board in 1893. In 1898 De Young lost the mayoral office to Germ Mokma, treasurer of the Holland Sugar Company and former Fourth Ward alderman. Mokma won again in 1899 by a huge two-to-one majority. He was succeeded by William Brusse (1900-1902), a fellow Republican and son-in-law of Isaac Cappon and former city clerk and treasurer. In local elections in the 1890s, the Second, Third, and Fourth Wards usually went Democratic; the First remained solidly Republican.[139]

Progressive era politics

William Jennings Bryan, William McKinley, and Theodore Roosevelt

While Holland was steadfast in its Republicanism, the city was not given to demagoguery, particularly not in the tolerant tides of the Progressive Era. Issues of proper morality and religion generally superseded those of political affiliation. Republicans increased their hold on Holland in the four presidential elections from 1896 through 1908. In the presidential elections of 1900, 1904, and 1908, the Republican Party received 61, 71, and 61 percent, respectively, of the vote in Holland.

William McKinley, the conservative congressman from Canton, Ohio who defended the gold standard, began the string by twice defeating the Democrat-Populist fusion candidate, William Jennings Bryan, the Christian socialist and silver-tongued orator who preached "free silver," that is, unlimited silver coinage, as a panacea for the national economic crisis of the mid-1890s. The Great Commoner campaigned in Holland in 1896, and four thousand people came to hear the eloquent young politician advocate the unlimited coinage of silver at a ratio of sixteen ounces of silver to one ounce of gold. It was the first of five appearances in the Holland area over the years. Supporters organized a Bryan Free Silver Club and launched a Dutch-language newspaper to tout free silver, but McKinley and his Honest Money Club of "gold bugs" won with 56 percent in 1896 and 60 percent in 1900. The *Volksstem* did not survive the election of 1900. McKinley apparently gained more votes in Holland by his hard money stand than he lost by siding with the British against the "freedom-loving" Dutch of the Transvaal in the Boer War (1899-1902). One group McKinley did lose was that of 250 workers at

[139] Ibid., 10 Apr. 1897, 8 Apr. 1898, 7 Apr. 1899, 6 Apr. 1900; "Biographical Information for the Mayors of Holland," JAH.

the Cappon & Bertsch tannery who voted during the campaign to take a half-day off to attend a Bryan rally at Battle Creek.[140]

Bryan supposedly had one big asset among Dutch American voters. He supported the Afrikaners. Abraham Kuyper, Prime Minister of the Netherlands and editor of the Anti-Revolutionary Party newspaper, *De Standaard*, in an address to "descendents of the Dutch race in America," printed in both Dutch and English, strongly condemned McKinley's pro-British policies and urged his American cousins to vote for Bryan, who stood by "our fellow kinsmen in Africa." The Dutch in Transvaal numbered about fifty thousand at the time. The *Ottawa County Times*, a Democratic sheet in Holland, happily reprinted Kuyper's position paper for every Hollander to read—which they did—and a number held a mass meeting to organize a local Bryan Club.[141]

Kuyper's pronouncement against McKinley did not sit well. Isaac Verwey, editor of *De Grondwet*, lambasted the good doctor for meddling in American politics. "America for Americans, and the Netherlands for the Netherlanders," Verwey declared. Verwey also printed a long letter of prominent Zeeland attorney Cornelis Van Loo, who charged that Kuyper's "thoughts do not move in American channels. He is aristocratic, not Democratic; patrician not plebian." Kuyper did not seem to understand that Bryan, as the candidate of the Democratic Party, was inevitably under the thumb of Tammany Hall and the Catholic Church, who together controlled the party. "No, we will not change over to Bryan. . . . We cannot tolerate free trade, free silver, and anarchistic principles." Rev. Johan Fles of the First Muskegon Christian Reformed Church, a graduate of the Reformed Seminary at Kampen in the Netherlands, similarly insisted that Dutch foreign policy was more to blame for the Boers' fate than any American action or inaction. After the election, Verwey crowed that Kuyper's support for Bryan was "superfluous"; it had only served to increase McKinley votes by 50 percent among the Dutch. Some Holland Republicans never forgave Kuyper for choosing Bryan over McKinley.[142]

In 1900 a correspondent of the *Detroit Evening News* reported that the Cappon & Bertsch Leather Company had refused to allow its

140 *Holland City News*, 5 Sept., 7 Nov. 1896, 31 Aug., 9 Nov. 1900, 13 Apr. 1922, 24 Mar. 1938; *De Grondwet*, 16 Oct. 1900. On the Dutch American reaction to the Boer War, see Lucas, *Netherlanders in America*, 565-70.

141 *Ottawa County Times*, 14 Sept. 1900; *De Grondwet*, 30 Oct. 1900; *Holland City News*, 28 Oct. 1898.

142 *De Grondwet*, 30 Oct., 13 Nov. 1900, translated by Nella Kennedy; Peter S. Heslan, *Creating a Christian Worldview: Abraham Kuyper's Lectures on Calvinism* (Grand Rapids: Eerdmans, 1998), 74-84.

William Jennings Bryan in Holland, 1900
(*Archives, Holland Historical Trust*)

workers a half-day off to attend a Bryan rally. George Hummer, owner and spokesman of the company clarified the situation. The company had taken a vote among its workers as to which of two Bryan gatherings they wanted to attend. One gathering was decided upon, and workers were then given the opportunity to attend. Hummer continued, "We can not run our factory on half power. We let everyone freely decide what their political or religious feelings are. The only reason for which we fire is drunkenness." Hummer, it should be noted, was a staunch Democrat who voted for Bryan.[143]

Although Bryan at first did not attract Dutch Reformed voters, in later years, after he had exchanged a political career for Christian apologetics and joined the fight against Darwinism, he won their hearts. He spoke in Holland and Grand Haven to admiring crowds, who relished his defense of the Bible against modernism more than his radical political ideas. At his death in 1925, the *Holland City News*, although a Republican sheet, published a number of favorable reminiscences of Bryan. One was an effusive eulogy to the Christian statesman by Rev. C. P. (Clarence) Dame of Trinity Reformed Church, delivered before a packed church on a Sunday evening. Another summarized a sermon by Hope College graduate, Rev. Joseph R. Sizoo of the New York Avenue Presbyterian Church in Washington, DC, who recounted how Bryan's address at the college on the subject, "The Value of an Ideal," had changed his life.[144]

143 *De Grondwet*, 16 Oct. 1900; Andrew M. Hyma, interview by Donald van Reken, 7 Aug. 1975, typescript, JAH .

144 *Holland City News*, 22 Nov. 1922, 30 July, 6, 13, 20 Aug. 1925.

Bryan's opponents were McKinley and Teddy Roosevelt. McKinley's foreign policy of support for the English in the Boer War angered many Hollanders in West Michigan (chapter 20). But he managed to defuse these emotions in 1900 by choosing as his running mate a man of Dutch ancestry. During the campaign, Diekema, chairman of the Republican State Central Committee, arranged for "T.R." to come to Holland. This was the first visit ever by a vice presidential candidate, and it signified that the Dutch colony had arrived on the national scene. Better yet, Roosevelt had Dutch blood coursing through his veins. The locals turned out three thousand strong to cheer him and listen to his tirade against Bryan and soft money Democrats. Mayor Brusse, former mayor Cappon, Diekema, Professor Kollen, and Michigan Republican Governor William Alden Smith welcomed Governor Roosevelt. The West Michigan Music Corps roused the crowd with patriotic songs and marches.[145]

So popular was the New York "cousin" that some local Democrats split their tickets to vote for McKinley and Roosevelt, and the pair garnered a majority of 60 percent. This despite the anti-Roosevelt flyer local Democrats distributed during his speech, which lambasted "T. R." (see below) as an imperialist marauder who boasted of shooting a man in the back. Teddy "showed his teeth" at the affront, blinked his eyeglasses, and then won the crowd over by reciting a Dutch ditty: "*Tripje, Trapje, Troontje, De Varkens in de Boontjes; De Koetjes in de Klaver, De Paardjes in de Haver.*" A literal translation that misses the rhyme is: "The pigs are in the beans, the cows are in the clover, the horses are in the hay." The 1900 election was considered at the time to be a watershed in local politics, but it was overshadowed by the 1904 presidential election.[146]

Roosevelt!

Volunteer Soldiers! Don't fail to hear the man who captured San Juan Hill and in his official report, for which he was rebuked by Gen. [Russell] Alger, said that each Rough Rider was equal to three of any of you.

Farmers and Mechanics of Holland and Vicinity! Don't fail to see this great man with his cowboy hat who in his book published in 1896, page 505, pays you this handsome compliment: "When drunk on the villainous whisky of the frontier towns, the cowboys are much better fellows and

145 *De Grondwet*, 11 Sept. 1900.

146 Ibid., 13 Nov. 1900; "Presidential Election," *Holland City News*, 29 Oct. 1936; Michael Douma, "The Reaction of Holland, Michigan to the Boer War," unpublished paper, 2003, JAH.

pleasanter companions than the small farmers and laborers. Nor are the mechanics of a great city to be mentioned in the same breath."

Democrats and Republicans! Don't fail to hear this great exponent of imperialism and high-minded statesmanship, who as in his recent St. Paul speech will tell you that "Every Democrat stands for lawlessness and disaster at home, and cowardice and dishonor abroad." This will amuse Democrats and disgust decent Republicans.

Hollanders! Hear this Hero who boasts that he shot a man in the back. He will appeal to your vanity by telling you that you are the most wonderful people in the world, expecting this silly taffy will offset his party's cruel indifference to the crushing out of the liberties of the South African brothers.[147]

Democratic anti-Roosevelt flyer (1900) by angry Boer War supporters who sarcastically call on "Hollanders" to come and "Hear This Hero who boasts that he shot a man in the back. He will appeal to your vanity."

After McKinley's assassination in 1901 and Roosevelt's ascendancy to the presidency, the Dutch were dumbfounded that American policy toward the Boers did not change one whit, and the Boers had to lay down their arms in defeat. Yet, the Dutch surprisingly did not abandon Roosevelt over his egregious policy, and when he ran for president in his own right in 1904, he took a whopping 71 percent of the vote in Holland. This was the largest margin of victory for any candidate in Holland's history to this time. Four years later, in 1908, William Howard Taft could do no better than McKinley in 1900, winning 61 percent of the vote. Roosevelt's popularity was so high that in 1912, when he defected from the Republicans to form the Bull Moose Progressive Party, he split the Republican vote and carried all five wards and outpolled the sitting President Taft three to one (1,102 to 371 votes). Democrat Woodrow Wilson, the victor nationally, gained only one-quarter of the total vote in Holland.

As the *Holland City News* noted, Roosevelt ran even stronger than expected: "There was hardly a precinct in the county in which he did not get a heavy vote." Indeed, Roosevelt won the entire state of Michigan, which gave his Progressive Party the top place on official election tickets for the next four years. Republicans, who had held this coveted spot

147 Holland City Records, box 1, HMA. Gen. Russell A. Alger, a Michigan lumber baron, commander of the Michigan Department of the GAR in 1888, secretary of war in McKinley's cabinet, governor of Michigan (1885-87), and US senator (1902-3), en.wikipedia.org/wiki/Russell_A._Alger.

Ninth Street Christian Reformed Church sanctuary draped in mourning for death of President William McKinley, September 19, 1901 (*Archives, Holland Historical Trust*)

since the party was formed fifty years earlier, dropped to third place on the ballots. Eugene Debs, the labor leader, orator, and perennial presidential candidate of the National Socialist Party, who had addressed a large audience in Holland in 1905, garnered 10 percent of the vote in 1912, primarily from factory workers who felt exploited and downtrodden. The Populist-Progressive era was the high tide of political activism in West Michigan. Yet, Roosevelt's third party was short-lived. By the fall gubernatorial election in 1914, Bull Moose was "vamoosed," as the *Holland City News*, a Taft organ, happily proclaimed.[148]

From 1900 until 1936, Holland was a Republican bastion, with 60 to 80 percent of the votes in presidential elections. Many citizens voted a straight ticket. In 1910 eighty-three-year-old Roelof Van Raalte entered the Second Ward polling place and called Alderman Art Drinkwater aside, and said: "For 60 years, I have voted the Republican ticket. I want you to go in the booth with me to see that I do not make a mistake as I am getting old."[149]

Teddy Roosevelt, the favorite son, increased the Republican vote in every Dutch city and hamlet, except in the 1912 race. Although he represented the reformist "liberal" wing of the party, every Bull Moose vote in 1912 was, in essence, a Republican vote. The strength of the Progressive Party was found in the city's Fifth Ward, where forty-seven men were enrolled party members. Population growth in the Fifth Ward

[148] *Holland City News*, 11 Nov. 1904, 30 June 1905, 5 Nov. 1908, 7, 14 Nov. 1912, 5 Nov. 1914.

[149] Ibid., 10 Nov. 1910.

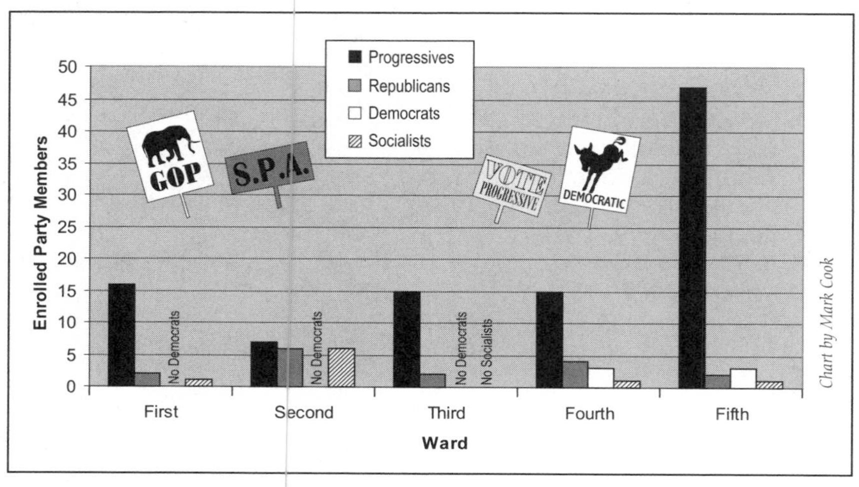

Fig. 24.4. Party Enrollment by Ward, 1912

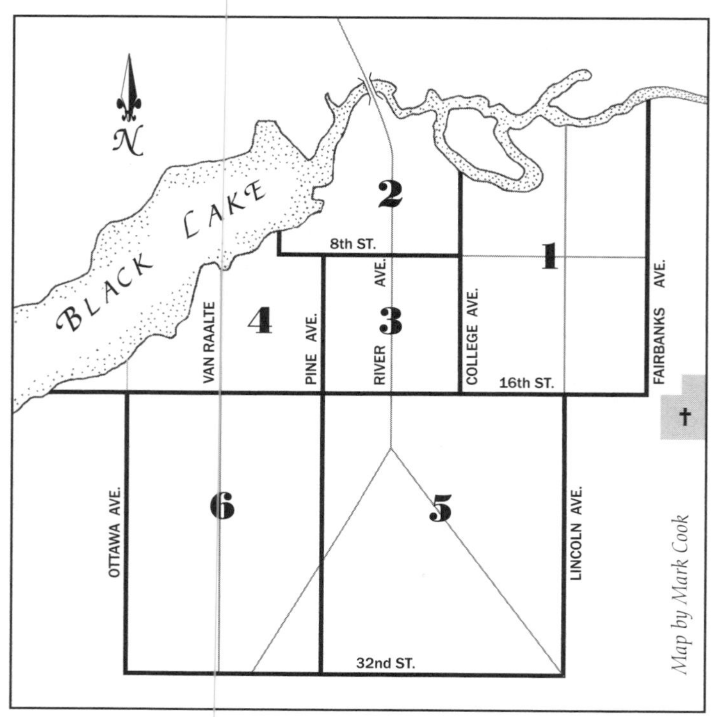

Fig. 24.5. Ward Map, 1915

Citizens took their politics seriously one hundred years ago, as is evident from the crowds awaiting their candidate at the Pere Marquette Railway station (*courtesy Randall P. Vande Water*)

led to a proposal for its division into two wards at the end of the year 1914. Political processes had to keep pace with the times.[150]

Gerrit J. Diekema, Holland's Mr. Republican

Gerrit J. Diekema was the leader of the local Republicans and their constant campaigner. Loyal to his hometown, Diekema returned to Holland to establish a law firm after earning his law degree at the University of Michigan in 1883. All the while, he remained active in politics. He served as the city's mayor (1895-96), chairman of the Michigan Republican State Central committee, (1901-7), a member of the US House of Representatives (1907-11), and US Minister to the Netherlands (1929-30).[151]

Diekema praised the Progressive reforms in Congress–the pure food law and legislation to regulate slaughterhouses and limit industrial kings, political bosses, and monopolies (chapter 20). He unapologetically equated Republicanism with Patriotism, and on most political issues, he stayed true to his party's platform. In economic policy, he supported "sound money," meaning the gold standard rather than "Free Silver," or unlimited silver coinage. He also advocated protective

150 *De Grondwet*, 11 Sept. 1900; *Holland City News*, 30 Jan. 1913.

151 A full-length biography is Vander Hill, *Diekema*.

tariffs rather than free trade. Diekema tolerated but eventually opposed popular measures to bring the government closer to the people—initiative, referendum, and recall.[152]

Diekema's political struggles and opinions were indicative of those of his voting base. Given to hyperbole, he saw McKinley as "the brightest star," a president who had initiated the greatest decade in the history of the world. Diekema equally admired as "the Man of the Hour" Theodore Roosevelt, McKinley's Vice President and successor in 1901. Hollanders had always liked the youthful Roosevelt. In 1900, when he was Governor of New York and the running mate of the incumbent McKinley, Roosevelt made a campaign visit to Holland where supporters were quick to point out that he had Dutch blood running through his veins.

In 1907 Diekema in his first try for national office won the Republican primary in the Fifth Congressional District against a sitting state senator. He carried Holland by a ten-to-one margin. His Democratic opponent in the general election was his Democratic friend George P. Hummer, former mayor of Holland and now a Grand Rapids resident, who had endorsed him in the Republican primary. Diekema easily defeated Hummer, a poor public speaker, and became the first son of Dutch immigrants to win a seat in the US Congress. His victory proved the slogan of the day: "You can turn the damper up, and you can turn the damper down, but Diekema goes to Congress just the same."[153]

Diekema was sent off to Washington by a procession of thousands, punctuated by fireworks. The festivities started on the Hope campus, where Mayor Jacob "Jaap" Van Putten gave a rousing speech in the jam-packed Carnegie Hall auditorium, and then the throng escorted him on the train to Grand Rapids for further celebrations. It was a gala day for Holland's favorite son. Although no local company had a labor union, Diekema adroitly portrayed himself as a friend of workingmen and secured the endorsement of the *Union Sentinel*, the mouthpiece of Grand Rapids labor unions. This was a rare coup for a Republican candidate and portended his victory in the fall. While Diekema did not win every contest, he often garnered 80 percent or more of the vote. Diekema's arrival in Washington in 1907 happily coincided with Teddy Roosevelt's national ascendancy.[154]

Diekema held the Fifth Congressional District for two terms (1907-11) and enjoyed many rousing public ovations in his hometown.

[152] For Diekema's political philosophy, see also William Schrier, *Gerrit J. Diekema: Orator* (Grand Rapids: Eerdmans, 1950), 32.

[153] *De Grondwet*, 7 Mar. 1907; Vander Hill, *Diekema*, 41-45.

[154] Vander Hill, *Diekema*, 45-49.

Holland Cornet Band regales Republican Senator William Alden Smith of Grand Rapids (*center right*), who came to support Holland's favorite son, Gerrit J. Diekema (*center left*), in his first run for Congress, 1907 (*Archives, Holland Historical Trust*)

The local boy had gained a national reputation and was even mentioned for vice president. But in 1910, Diekema unexpectedly lost his seat by a razor thin margin to Edwin Sweet, the leader of the Grand Rapids Democracy. The "public can be a fickle master," opined the *Holland City News* editor. According to his biographer, Warren Vander Hill, Diekema "found himself in a position where he was considered too conservative in his political views for Kent and Ionia and too liberal in his religious outlook for many of his home-town constituents." His support of Freemasonry, women's suffrage, public education, and hyper-Americanism, hurt him in West Michigan, especially among Christian Reformed voters. Regional rivalries played a part too. Some Grand Rapids ward heelers portrayed the election as pitting their native son against Holland's favorite son, with epithets such as "Beat the 'Hollicky'" (Hollander) and "Keep Grand Rapids on the Map."[155]

Early in the unsuccessful primary campaign, in March 1910, Diekema lost his beloved wife Mary E. Alcott, the toast of the Washington social scene and an accomplished soloist, after a brief illness. He remained a widower for ten years before marrying Leona Belser, a teacher at Holland High School who had taught his daughters. Diekema was sixty-one, the "energetic, bright" Leona thirty-five.[156]

155 *Holland City News*, 30 June, 10 Sept. 1910, 10, 17 Nov. 1911 (quotes); Andrew M. Hyma interview by Donald van Reken, 7 Aug. 1975, typescript, 3 (slogan quote), JAH. Vander Hill, *Diekema*, 42-53, 67 (quote), 65 (quote), 89-91.

156 Vander Hill, *Diekema*, 18, 60, 76 (quote).

Gerrit J. Diekema bids farewell at the Holland railroad station in 1929 to serve as US Envoy and Minister Plenipotentiary to the Netherlands (*Joint Archives of Holland*)

When Roosevelt held to his promise and did not seek a third presidential term in 1908, Diekema was quick to support the new Republican nominee, William Howard Taft, who, Diekema wrote, "combines the best qualities of McKinley and Roosevelt." Although in some respects more conservative than Roosevelt, Taft continued with progressive reform, especially in regard to large industries and monopolies. Diekema, no doubt, supported progressive reforms, but he was a loyal Republican above all, supporting Taft over Roosevelt and his Bull Moose Party in the 1912 election. All the city's major newspapers also sided with Taft, and a Taft Club formed in October 1912, a month before the election. But Diekema and the Taft supporters went against the current in Holland, where Roosevelt easily gained a majority, leaving Taft's Republican Party with only seventeen percent of the city's vote. The newly formed Woodrow Wilson Club sought to attract factory workers and workingmen but barely made a stir.[157]

Diekema spent the next decades practicing law in Holland, but he remained active in Lansing, serving as chair of the Republican State Central Committee. In 1916 he made a run for governor but failed to garner the necessary support downstate, even though in the primaries

[157] Kirk N. Slater, "Gerrit J. Diekema–Standpatter or Progressive," Hope College student paper, 1989, Diekema Collection, JAH; C. Warren Vander Hill, *Gerrit J. Diekema* (Grand Rapids: Eerdmans, 1970); *Holland City News*, 17 Oct. 1912; *Holland Sentinel*, 6 Aug. 1912.

Officials receive Minister Gerrit J. Diekema's remains at Holland railroad station after shipment by sea and rail from the Netherlands, January 3, 1931 (*Joint Archives of Holland*)

he carried Holland, Zeeland, and Ottawa County almost unanimously. The city of Holland honored him in 1923, when over four hundred people jammed into the Masonic Temple, which had the largest banquet hall in town, for a gala testimonial dinner. A dozen leading men, beginning with Mayor Stephan, sang their praises, and the honoree responded by likening his emotions to that of old Simeon when he held the Christ child in the temple. All in all, it was a celebration fit for Holland's leading citizen; Diekema received more accolades than anyone had a right to expect. Six years later, President Herbert Hoover in 1929 appointed Diekema US Envoy and Minister Plenipotentiary to the Netherlands in The Hague, where he died within a year "with his boots on." He died on December 20, 1930, at age seventy-one, having lived life to the full. When his remains arrived back home, Holland's foremost citizen received a funeral fit for a president, outdoing even that of Holland's founder, Rev. Albertus C. Van Raalte (chapter 2).[158]

Several sons of the Dutch represented Michigan in Congress after Diekema, including Bartel Jonkman of Grand Rapids (Fifth District, 1940-49), Guy Vander Jagt of Cadillac (Ninth District, 1963-93), Vernon Ehlers of Grand Rapids (Third District, 1993-2011), and Peter "Pete" Hoekstra of Holland (Second District, 1993-2011). Only

158 *Holland City News*, 16 Dec. 1915, 31 Aug. 1916, 22 Mar. 1923, 24 Aug. 1929, 25 Dec. 1930, 8 Jan. 1931.

Hoekstra was born in the Netherlands. Jonkman and Vander Jagt were attorneys; Ehlers had been a physics professor at Calvin College, and Hoekstra was a vice president at Zeeland-based furniture manufacturer Herman Miller Inc.

City politics

During the Progressive Era, from 1900 to 1918, Republicans and Democrats alternated in the mayor's office like revolving doors, with Democrats winning six out of the first eleven years, often after making alliances with the local Socialist Party. Yet Republican aldermen continued to hold sway in the common council. Party labels seemingly carried less weight in local affairs, and in 1914 a non-partisan charter went into effect that removed parties from any official role in local elections. It also set mayoral terms at two years instead of one.[159]

Republican William Brusse (1900-1902) was succeeded in turn by Republicans Cornelius J. De Roo (1902-4) and Henry Geerlings (1904-6) and Democrats Jacob "Jaap" Van Putten (1906-8) and Henry Brusse (1908-11). Then came Republicans Evert "Abe" Stephan (1911-12) and Nicodemus Bosch (1912-16). Bosch served a second time (1918-20) following Democrat John Vander Sluis (1916-18). The city's longest-serving mayor, Albert "Al" McGeehan (1993-2009), noted in his farewell address that national party identities have "no relevance, significance or importance" in the city council. "All of the baggage that comes with partisan politics we leave to the 'professionals' in Lansing and Washington."[160]

William Brusse owned a clothing store on the southwest corner of Eighth Street and River Avenue, De Roo co-owned the Walsh & De Roo Milling Company and was business manager of several prominent local companies, and Geerlings worked in a furniture factory. De Roo campaigned vigorously and ingeniously. He went through the factories shaking hands with the "boys," and telling them that though he did not expect to be elected, he would appreciate it if they would give him "a complementary vote." Lo and behold, he surprised everyone and won. In office, De Roo in 1903 raised the contentious issue of buying the Holland City Gas Company franchise and making it a municipal operation, to be financed by issuing $100,000 in bonds. Republicans charged that the city's indebtedness of $300,000 was high enough,

159 *Holland City News*, 30 Jan. 1913, 9 Apr., 10 Dec. 1914.

160 Charter of the City of Holland, Michigan, 5 May 1913 (Holland, MI: 1913), 7-9; "Biographical Information for the Mayors of Holland," *Holland Sentinel*, 2 Nov. 2009.

and the private companies should lay pipes and supply the gas, so that consumers and not taxpayers would pay for it. "Those entrusted with the public business must not step over the limit. Wise and intelligent economy must be exercised at all times."[161]

Some mayors were more ambitious than others. De Roo unsuccessfully sought a city-owned gas works; Henry Brusse dedicated a new city hall in 1911 and enlarged the electric plant and water system. Abe Stephan launched an initiative to pave nearly all the remaining dirt streets in the city and to install boulevard lighting on Eighth Street. A veteran city alderman and president for six years of the board of public works, Stephan worked his way up the ladder from sweeper in a furniture factory to general manager of the Bush & Lane Piano Company. Efficiency in spending the public's money was his watchword. He believed so strongly in public service as a citizen's duty that he gave his entire salary to charity. This civic gesture did not spare him in his last months in office from a bitter, though unsuccessful, fight by the socialists to reduce the workday of city employees from ten to eight hours with no reduction in pay.[162]

Earlier in his term, in 1911, Stephan also lost credibility when he led a referendum campaign to extend the private Holland City Gas Company franchise, then governed by a public contract, only to have it go down to defeat. The company, based in Niles, had operations in fifteen Michigan cities to provide natural gas for cook stoves and lighting through a system of underground pipes. The gas company had earned a poor reputation, which alderman Vernon King and his socialist allies exploited in the campaign. A rumor, never proven, that the company had bribed former mayor Brusse with $5,000 to support the referendum also cost some votes. King argued that a city-owned gas utility was far preferable. The city fathers might have agreed, but the huge cost to launch such a utility deterred them. Mayor Stephan finessed the situation by negotiating a more favorable contract with the private company, and this quieted the clamor for a municipal gas works for a time. This proved to be only the first round in a long-running conflict between the city and the gas company (chapter 25).[163]

Mayor Nicodemus "Nick" Bosch, a Roosevelt Republican who with John Boda founded the Western Machine Tool Works and led the firm for forty years, ran a tight ship of state. Bosch served three separate times (1912-16, 1918-20, 1932-36), for a total of ten years. A

161 *Holland City News*, 9 Jan. 1903, 21 Apr. 1905, 1 Apr. 1909, 23 Nov. 1922.
162 Ibid., 4, 18 Jan., 8 Feb. 1912.
163 Ibid., 12, 19, 26 Oct., 2, 9 Nov. 1911, 18 Apr. 1912.

Mayor Nicodemus Bosch, 1920s (*Archives, Holland Historical Trust*)

conservative in many ways, his motto was frugality and efficiency in government services. Yet Bosch was a progressive in T. R.'s mold. He led the charge, along with alderman King, against the contract extension of the private gas company in 1911, and he backed improvements in streets, parks, and public buildings that would "reflect credit upon the industry and civic pride" of the city. He also endorsed a nine-hour workday for all city employees with ten hours' pay. This agenda was in keeping with Bosch's education at Hope College, his membership in Hope Church, and his active role in the Century Club and the Social Progress Club.[164]

These progressive voices also instigated the non-partisan city charter in 1913, thinking that this would increase citizen participation and obviate the role of political parties. Nominations were open to any citizen to file on his own behalf for one dollar or to submit a petition with ten signatures of registered electors for aldermen and twenty-five signatures for citywide offices. Terms were extended to two years, with annual elections every April and half the offices at stake. Women who owned property singly or jointly could also vote in state and local elections involving the expenditure of public money, under an amendment to the Michigan constitution in 1909.[165]

In his first term Bosch and the common council had a stormy relationship. He was too progressive for the conservative establishment.

164 *Holland City News*, 18 Apr. 1912.

165 Ibid., 27 Mar., 10 Apr. 1913, 29 Jan. 1914. In Holland the 1913 suffrage amendment went down by more than two to one.

Bosch wielded his veto pen five times in 1913 and drove the aldermen to distraction. Often they passed laws over his veto, but not always wisely. The first flare up came over the perennial liquor question. In 1908, 1910, and 1911, citizens (except in the Second Ward) had voted to close saloons as dens of vice and drunkenness. But Hollanders were not teetotalers; they liked their beer and gin and rejected the local option alternative in 1909, which would ban alcohol sales entirely. The common council continued to license the Anton Seif Brewery, Holland's long-time brewery, and the three existing liquor stores, who could only sell beer by the keg and whiskey by the bottle for consumption off the premises. Finally, an April 1913 poll, which the drys won by a mere twenty-three votes, settled the matter until the Prohibition movement in 1918 extended the ban nationwide (chapter 20).[166]

Shortly after the liquor referendum, the council got into another controversy over street paving, of all things. It began when Mayor Bosch rejected a council decision to purchase for the street department a new paving machine, known as a "tandem roller," to replace a three-wheeled roller that was supposedly good for macadam roads but too heavy for the new asphalt surfaces. City engineer Henry Naberhuis and his crew of city employees insisted that they needed the $2,100 machine to carry on the long-term street improvement program, with several blocks of Twelfth Street next in line. The council, on the recommendation of its committee on streets and crossings, approved the expenditure, but Bosch vetoed the bill as an unnecessary expense.[167]

In anger the council met in a special session to resolve the "'dog gone' steam roller" matter, and again they overrode the mayor's veto. This turned out to be the "most exciting meeting that had taken place in years," according to the *Holland City News* reporter. "Harsh words and rhetoric were hurled right and left by the different council members, with the mayor as the hub of contention." When Bosch was slow to call the question, Fifth Ward Alderman Austin Harrington, president of the Holland Board of Trade, shouted at him: "You can't roll this steamroller over us." In the end, seven of ten council members voted to override. The "immortal seven" struck again, Bosch commented. After hours of

166 Ibid., 8 Apr. 1909, 7 Jan. 1910, 6 Apr. 1911, 27 Mar., 3, 10 Apr., 8 May 1913, "Fifty Years Ago Today" 30 Mar. 1935. The city was evenly divided in 1913: Wards 1, 2, and 4 voted for saloons and Wards 3 and 5 against. The three licensed wholesale liquor houses were those of Martin Vander Bie at 180 River Avenue, David Blom at 5 W. Eighth Street, and Walter Sutton at 122 E. Eighth Street.

167 *Holland City News*, 5 June, 3, 10 July 1913. The old Kelley-Springfield road roller had been purchased in 1910 for $2550, after Mayor Henry Brusse broke a tie council vote (ibid., 5 May 1910).

heated debate and calls for order, the stormy session mercifully came to an end. Little wonder that Harrington challenged Bosch for mayor in 1914, but Bosch outpolled him 2.5 to one.[168]

Interestingly, two of the immortal seven were members of the Socialist Party, including Vernon King of the Second Ward, who ran unsuccessfully for mayor in 1910, 1911, and 1912 (he garnered 23 percent of the vote in 1912 and carried his ward), and Olaf J. Hansen of the Fourth Ward, who it was charged, "fought the mayor on practically every question that pertains to the general welfare of the city." King often stood on a portable soapbox on Holland's street corners speaking about socialist doctrines. Everyone liked him but wrote off his theories as wild. Hansen ran for mayor in 1913 and captured only 14 percent of the vote. Both left office as aldermen in 1914; King stepped down, and Hansen was defeated. The rejection did not dissuade Hansen from making a futile run for state representative in the fall. Several of Holland's Socialists subscribed to the national paper, *Appeal to Reason*, but their reasoning did not resonate with local voters.[169]

Rather than buy the new roller, the council sought a compromise. "Something must be sacrificed to opinion, which is not well founded," the members groused. First, they took bids from private paving contractors, but the low bid came in $1,500 to $2,000 above what city crews could do the work for, and homeowners would thus bear higher assessments. This was deemed unfair. Next, the aldermen granted engineer Naberhuis permission to rent a tandem roller at a cost of $500. Remarkably, Bosch also vetoed this decision, claiming that the old roller was entirely adequate, and the expense was needless. Further, the rental cost of the new machine would over time "make the tax burden in this city rise to appalling figures." The council promptly passed the rental ordinance anyway by the same seven-to-three vote. The paving program went on thereafter with a rented machine. Within two years, Bosch made a complete about face and urged the council to buy a second roller because of the heavy demands for paved streets.[170]

Before the summer was over, Bosch and the council had another hot potato on their hands. This was the contract between the city and

[168] *Holland City News*, 12, 19 Feb., 3 Mar., 2 Apr., 29 Oct. 1914.

[169] The "immortal seven" aldermen were Frank Congleton, Art Drinkwater, Frank Dyke, Austin Harrington, Olaf Hansen, Vernon King, and Luman Van Drezer. Drinkwater, an iron molder from England, served the Second Ward for 28 years between 1908 and 1941 and earned the title "Dean of the Council" (ibid., 18 Apr. 1918, 7 July 1927, "Twenty-Five Years Ago Today" 30 Apr. 1936, 20 May 1948).

[170] Ibid., 2 Sept. 1915, 12, 19 July 1917. Mayor Bosch's three supporters were Peter Prins, Arie Vander Hill, and Henry Sterenberg.

the Holland City Gas Company, a licensed franchise based in Niles, to provide natural gas for cook stoves and lighting through a system of underground pipes. The company, with operations in fifteen Michigan cities, was losing money on the Holland contract, and they filed suit in an attempt to force the city fathers to make certain concessions, such as allowing the company to charge homeowners for hookups from the street to their homes. In return, the company would freeze the rate for three years and extend service to every homeowner who wanted it. The common council agreed to modify the contract, which had twenty-five years to run, provided that voters approve the amendments by a 60 percent majority. One key amendment allowed the city to buy the company for $300,000 and make gas delivery a municipal service. That the company would be happy to sell out was proof, said the editor of the *Holland City News*, that citizens were getting a good deal, and any city takeover would be a money pit. The editor strongly urged a *no* vote on this amendment, as did former mayor Henry Brusse. With many other community leaders voicing opposition, the proviso for municipal ownership was defeated by a two to one ratio. Within months the gas company was embroiled in further controversy as it pushed, successfully it turned out, to run gas lines eastward beyond the city limits to Zeeland.[171]

In 1916 Mayor Bosch sought re-election for a fourth term, but the rising Democratic tide under President Wilson and his crusade "to make the world safe for democracy" reached Holland, and a political novice, dry goods merchant John Vander Sluis, trounced Bosch mightily with a five-hundred-vote majority out of 1,800 votes cast. Vander Sluis' run for office began with a rumor among the "boys" at the morning *koffie kletch*, who announced his candidacy before he had given any thought to it. What began as a joke among friends became serious when the local newspaper picked up the story and a committee of progressive citizens persuaded "Van" to "do it for Holland." Vander Sluis had a well-earned reputation as a city booster and was widely known as the choral conductor at Third Reformed Church. He inherited Democratic genes from his father Oswald, who had been one of Van Raalte's closest political advisors and an official in the early People's Assembly, and from his uncle, mayor Kommer Schaddelee, a Democratic party warhorse, with whom John went to live at age ten after his father died. A towering figure, Vander Sluis had the distinction of being Holland's

171 Ibid., 7 Nov. 1912, 28 Aug., 11, 25 Sept., 2, 9, 16 Oct. 1913, 15 Jan. 1914. Joseph Brewer of Holland was vice president of the Holland franchise.

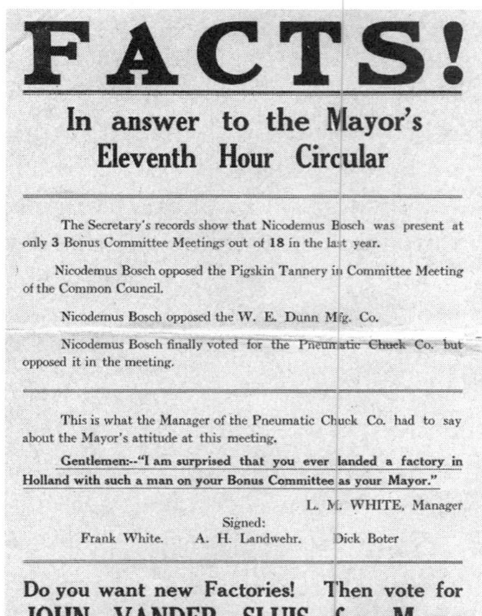

FACTS!

In answer to the Mayor's Eleventh Hour Circular

The Secretary's records show that Nicodemus Bosch was present at only 3 Bonus Committee Meetings out of 18 in the last year.

Nicodemus Bosch opposed the Pigskin Tannery in Committee Meeting of the Common Council.

Nicodemus Bosch opposed the W. E. Dunn Mfg. Co.

Nicodemus Bosch finally voted for the Pneumatic Chuck Co. but opposed it in the meeting.

This is what the Manager of the Pneumatic Chuck Co. had to say about the Mayor's attitude at this meeting.

Gentlemen:--"I am surprised that you ever landed a factory in Holland with such a man on your Bonus Committee as your Mayor."

L. M. WHITE, Manager

Signed:
Frank White. A. H. Landwehr. Dick Boter

Do you want new Factories! Then vote for
JOHN VANDER SLUIS for Mayor

"FACTS!" Anti-Bosch flyer by the John Vander Sluis campaign in the 1916 election, which Vander Sluis won in a landslide (*Archives, Holland Historical Trust*)

tallest mayor. The *Holland City News* story of his candidacy as a result of a joke made the rounds of newspapers nationally, as editors far and wide "clipped" the item.[172]

Vander Sluis led the city during the coal shortage and rationing of the First World War and the 1917 snowstorm—the worst Michigan had ever known—when the mayor enlisted a pick and shovel brigade of two hundred unemployed men to dig the city out from under five feet of snow dumped over three days. Despite his personal popularity, in 1918 Sluis lost his re-election campaign by a large margin, as voters returned Bosch to office for a fifth term (1918-20). Bosch then led a campaign to improve public health; he had the city take over the first hospital (chapter 27), and he pushed for a municipal gas works.[173]

In the November 1918 election campaign, the issue of women's suffrage came to a head in Michigan. An earlier attempt to extend full suffrage rights failed in 1913 by a narrow majority but succeeded handily in the Damon bill of 1917, which set in motion a state constitutional amendment. Some 535 women of voting age in Holland, 35 from Hope Church alone, signed a petition in 1918, addressed "To the Voters of Ottawa County," asking them to support the proposed state equal suffrage amendment. The *Holland City News* published the names in

172 *Holland City News*, 3 Feb., 16, 29 Mar., 8 June 1916.
173 Ibid., 14 Mar. 1918, 29 Apr. 1920; Dunbar, *Michigan*, 685.

Kate Ledeboer (Mrs. Dirk B. K.) Van Raalte adorned in her fox stole and feather-topped hat (*Archives, Holland Historical Trust*)

alphabetical order for all to read. It included wives and daughters of leaders from all walks of life—from Kate Ledeboer (Mrs. Dirk B. K.) Van Raalte and Katherine (Mrs. Arnold) Mulder to Martha (Mrs. George E.) Kollen and Lavina Cappon (Isaac's daughter). The Holland Equal Suffrage Club, an organization of prominent women in town, also took up the cause. But the activism had little impact; the amendment went down in the city by a resounding two to one majority in every ward, the same proportion as in Ottawa County as whole. Thus, one can assume that many husbands and fathers of the petitioners voted *no* on the women's suffrage amendment. Many believed women should not "be besmirched" by the rough and tumble of politics.[174]

Though the women lost the battle locally, they won the war. Voters state-wide approved the amendment, and in the next weeks nine hundred women trooped into the city hall to register under the new rules, about one-third of the 2,500 women who were eligible. This suggests that suffrage was not a burning issue among most women in Holland. Yet politicians quickly recruited women and chose them as delegates to party conventions. And the Woman's Club held seminars that "led the women through the maze of balloting" before the spring elections. Attorney Charles McBride, who had served two terms in the state legislature (1911-13), tutored the club members, and his wife Emily was the first woman in Holland chosen as a delegate to a county

[174] *Holland City News*, 31 Oct., 7, 14 Nov. 1918; *Holland Sentinel*, 19 Aug. 1924; Judy Tanis Parr, *Hope Church, Holland, Michigan, The First 150 Years, 1862-2012* (Grand Rapids: Dickenson Press, 2012), 165-66.

convention–the Republican one. Emily McBride later took a leading role in the local Women's Lincoln Republican Club, along with Leona (Mrs. Gerrit) Diekema, Estella (Mrs. Charles) M. McLean, and Evelyn (Mrs. Sears) McLean. Yet in the 1919 primaries, the first in which women could vote, only 173 women marked ballots out of 1,033 registered, a turnout of 17 percent.[175]

The question on the minds of the politicos was: "How will the women of Holland stack up in the next presidential election?" The answer, as we will see, is that they had no impact whatsoever, although women's suffrage pushed the normally high turnout down sharply, from the 90 percent range to the low 70s. Most women in Holland apparently agreed with the views of Peter P. Cheff, who told the local chapter of the WCTU that should women seek political power, it would undermine their natural moral influence. They should vote, but leave politics to the men. In the end, the Nineteenth Amendment to the US Constitution in 1920, which confirmed women's voting rights for all time, changed the political landscape forever. But eighteen years passed before the first woman ran for public office in Ottawa County. The pioneer was Cora Vande Water of Holland, sister of Coroner Gilbert Vande Water and for fifteen years the registrar of probate court. Cora Vande Water in 1938 announced her candidacy for probate court judge, and in November she won handily over five rivals. For the next eighty years, local women would generally eschew political office. A *Holland Sentinel* investigation in 2010 revealed that in the six largest municipalities in the Holland-Zeeland area, on the Ottawa and Allegan county boards, and among the five local state legislators, only ten of the eighty-one are female (12 percent). Nationally, women represented 17 percent of Congress, 24 percent of state legislatures, and 17 percent of mayors of cities over thirty thousand in population.[176]

Holland's favorite president, Theodore Roosevelt, died in 1919, and the city fathers led by Mayor Bosch responded to the call of the Roosevelt Memorial Committee for $5 million for a suitable national memorial. The council resolution asked "every man, woman, and child in the city, without regard to party affiliation" to contribute in a popular subscription. "Holland is not going to stand back as far as 'Teddy' is concerned," declared the *City News* editor. "Only $800 is required of Holland and then we have done our bit." All the schools and

[175] *Holland City News*, 3, 10 May, 14 June 1917, 1 Aug. 15 Dec. 1918, 30 Jan., 13 Feb., 18 Dec. 1919, "Twenty Years Ago Today," 6 Apr. 1939.

[176] *Holland City News*, 6 Apr. 1922, 26 July 1928, 11 Feb., 15 Sept. 1932; *Holland Sentinel*, 26 Aug. 2010.

many businesses got involved in the campaign, and the money came in quickly from rich and poor alike. Ten major companies bought a full-page advertisement in the *City News* showing a portrait of the president over the words "Above All, He Loved America!" Another thirty-six merchants and businessmen bought a second full-page spread showing Teddy on his horse charging up San Juan Hill in Cuba in 1898, with effusive words of praise for "a man whose spirit continues to lead the Nation on the long trail to progress."[177]

Gerrit Diekema, Holland's consummate politician and "No. 1 orator for 45 years," lectured around the area on the life and character of Teddy Roosevelt, including a talk at Holland High School at the unveiling of a bust of Roosevelt donated by the 1923 graduating class. A few months later, on Roosevelt's birthday, Diekema again spoke in tribute to the ideal American at a special service at Hope College for faculty and students. In death Roosevelt joined the pantheon of martyred presidents. As the local headline read: "The Party of Lincoln, Garfield, McKinley and Roosevelt is the Republican Party—Vote Next Tuesday."[178]

While the Republican Roosevelt was highly admired in Holland, his Democratic cousin Franklin D. Roosevelt was not. FDR came to town during the 1920 campaign as the vice-presidential nominee on the Democratic ticket of James Cox of Ohio. "It was a great day for Holland Democrats Monday," read the opening sentence of the *Holland Sentinel* report on the visit. The brief, 160-word account noted that a mixed political crowd packed the Knickerbocker Theatre to hear Roosevelt, who spoke earnestly but "quietly, almost devoid of gestures," in favor of President Wilson's demand for United States membership in the League of Nations. Though Franklin made a "fine impression," he was no Teddy, at least not in Holland. The masthead of the *News* pictured the Republican team of Warren Harding and Calvin Coolidge.[179]

The "Roaring Twenties"

Republican hegemony in Holland continued through the First World War and the prosperity decade of the Twenties. Warren Harding won in 1920 with 77 percent of the vote, Calvin Coolidge in 1924 with 78 percent, and the very popular Herbert Hoover in 1928 won a whopping 88 percent of the vote over the first Roman Catholic candidate for

177 *Holland City News*, 9, 23, 30 Oct. 1919.

178 Ibid., 7 Oct. 1920, 6 Jan. 1921, 6 Apr. 1922, 4 June, 1 Nov. 1923, 28 Oct. 1926; Vande Water, "Diekema—Minister Plenipotentiary," in *Holland Happenings* 1:103-5.

179 *Holland Sentinel*, 4, 16, 19 (quote), 1920; *Holland City News*, 7, 21 Oct. (quote) 1920.

president, Alfred E. Smith, governor of New York and an advocate of the repeal of the Prohibition Amendment. Smith benefited not a whit from a visit to Holland and an overnight stay at Lakewood Farm of his friend George Getz, the Chicago millionaire and prominent lakeshore socialite and promoter. Smith, the "Happy Warrior" and man with the "brown derby," attended Sunday Mass at St. Francis de Sales Church and mixed with the townsfolk afterward. Yet 88 percent of Holland's registered voters turned out to keep a "wet" out of the White House. His candidacy led to the largest voter registration in city history up to that time.[180]

The Great Depression tested Republican loyalties and substantially reduced their majorities. Yet Franklin Roosevelt could not carry Holland, even in the depths of despair. In 1932, when he swept Hoover in almost every state, FDR garnered only 26 percent of the vote in Holland. He did somewhat better in 1936 after six years of depression, taking 43 percent. In 1940 his margin dropped to 32 percent on a record turnout, and in 1944 it dropped again to 32 percent. Harry Truman did even worse in 1948, capturing only 31 percent of the vote. Hollanders preferred Hoover in 1928 and 1932, Alfred "Alf" Langdon in 1936, Wendell Wilkie in 1940, and Thomas Dewey in 1944 and again in 1948.

During the prosperous Twenties, three mayors served Holland: Abe Stephan, Nicholas Kammeraad, and Earnest Brooks. All had to deal with the fallout of the federal ban on the manufacture and sale of alcoholic beverages, known as Prohibition, and the "speakeasies" and backroom bars that sprang up. Stephan's tenure began on a light note. During his successful campaign against Bosch, a sitting mayor, Stephan's Third Ward boosters club boasted that they would out-hustle the Fourth Ward club, and the latter wagered a dinner on the outcome and won. Some months later Stephan heard grumbling that the losers had not paid their bet. So he told them, "I'll furnish the banquet hall in my home if you furnish the banquet." This prodded the Third Ward club, led by William Orr and Henry Geerlings, to issue a subpoena demanding that the winners appear at the mayor's home at 24 East Ninth Street. After a most enjoyable evening, the Fourth Warders "smiled benignly" as the Third Ward club paid the bill, all the while complaining lightheartedly about their neighbors who had failed to go to the polls. Supporters in these two wards gave Stephan a slim margin of victory in his re-election in 1922.[181]

180 *Holland City News*, 20 Sept., 25 Oct., 8 Nov. 1928, "Ten Years Ago Today" 12 Jan. 1939.
181 Ibid.,10 Mar. 1921 (quote).

As mayor, Stephan, an executive at the Holland Furnace Company, took to heart Andrew Carnegie's challenge to public officials to serve rather than be served. Each year Stephan donated his $100 salary to a worthy city cause: boulevard lighting in 1920, an all-expenses paid overnight outing to Grand Rapids for all aldermen in 1921, and the soldiers memorial project of the American Legion Women's Auxiliary in 1922 and 1923. Stephan also ended the long-standing practice of the common council meeting in secret session.[182]

In the 1920 election, voters unexpectedly approved a referendum to have the city buy the Holland City Gas Works and supply natural gas to city residents, as well as municipal light (electricity) and water. Eight years earlier, in 1912, voters had rejected a gas referendum, and Stephan lost his office to Bosch. Now Stephan defeated Bosch, and he had to work for a city-owned gas plant that he opposed. Fortunately for him, the gas project fizzled when voters learned it would cost at least $400,000 to buy the lines and equipment of the private gas company. This at a time when state health officials were prodding the city to build a sewage treatment plant to take the strain off Tannery Creek, when the city needed a new hospital, when they wanted to continue a five-year plan to pave all remaining streets and install "boulevard lighting" on Eighth and River Streets, and when veterans of the First World War were asking for $30 million for a "soldier's bonus," of which Holland must shoulder its share. At the 1921 spring election, the municipal gas works referendum, which required 60 percent to pass, failed by an even wider margin of 66 percent. Even the Fifth and Sixth Wards, which expected to be hooked up soon, opposed the plan. This vote was the coup de grace to this "football of politics" that had been kicked around for eight years. With two-thirds of the electorate opposed, city officials never again considered a municipal gas works (chapter 25).[183]

Stephan in his second stint as mayor (1920-24) valiantly strove to clean up illegal liquor trafficking and plan for a municipal sewage treatment plant to allay the pollution of Black Lake, a new hospital, and funding for the armory on Ninth Street. At the beginning of his term, he opened a discussion on Holland's charter, suggesting that a commission form of government, led by a professional city manager, might be a better way to do city business. (It was 1950 before the city adopted this idea.) Stephan also had the distinction in 1923 of introducing the first voting machines in Holland. With the machines,

182 Ibid., 3, 17 Apr. 1924.

183 Ibid., 8 Apr., 21 Oct. 1920, 31 Mar., 24 Apr. 1921, 20 Apr. 1922; "Frightened! An Open Letter to E. P. Stephan," by John G. Blok, Holland City Records, box 1, HMA.

the results of the special election on storm sewer bonds were tallied in thirty seconds! On the ideological level, Stephan perceived a rising tide of Bolshevism, and he repeatedly tried to eradicate class conflict demagoguery in Holland.[184]

During the 1922 campaign, John Blok, Socialist candidate for mayor, published a handbill charging that the Republican Party, which despite non-partisan city elections presumably included Stephan, "does not represent the interests of the working class and that no working man can vote the Republican ticket without voting directly against his class." Stephan replied in his inaugural address: "It is to be deplored that there are those in this city who persist in trying to arouse and promote a class feeling for political purposes. . . . There is no professional class, manufacturers' class, or laborers' class in this city. There is no room for any kind of group or class here. White-collared, blue-shirted, or blue-overalled should make no difference whatever at the ballot box, and it is un-American to think so," Stephan opined. His rhetoric resonated with Holland citizens, except for a small contingent of socialists and radical labor types.[185]

But when his ox was gored by big business, Stephan could "act the trustbuster" as well as Teddy Roosevelt. In 1921 the Holland & Lake Michigan Railway, operator of the Grand Rapids-Holland-Saugatuck Interurban line, announced a sharp fare increase within the city limits from 5¢ to 15¢, and out to Macatawa Park from 15¢ to 35¢ round trip. Stephan "put on his fighting clothes" at this unilateral move, which in his opinion not only violated the city contract with the railway but also threatened the city economy. He shot off an angry letter to the company, demanding that the increase be canceled, or he would have the common council retaliate by having the police enforce the contract to the letter, namely: that city cars run every fifteen minutes and observe a maximum speed of eight miles per hour on Eighth Street and fourteen miles per hour elsewhere; they stop at every street where passengers wished to get on or off, with no loading of freight or baggage on the street; they allow no switching of cars on Eighth and River; they have no more than three cars per train; and they install decent crosswalks everywhere and gravel all streets along the tracks.

But the Interurban owners had their ducks in a row: they had the state public utilities commission take fare-making authority to itself and thereby approve the increase. Stephan was livid, but helpless. The

[184] *Holland City News*, 16 Dec. 1920, 1 Nov. 1923, 9 Nov. 1950.

[185] *Holland City News*, 20 Apr. 1922. The Social Progress Club, known for its progressive thinking, advocated this change at its March 1920 meeting (ibid., 20 Mar. 1920).

Interurban, to make peace, unilaterally reduced the fare to 20¢, provided that customers bought a strip of five tickets. Mayor Stephan and the city fathers were mollified. Even so, the company could not compete with automobiles; it closed the Holland-Grand Rapids run four years later, in 1926, and the rest was shut down in 1933.[186]

When President Harding, whose administration was rife with scandals, died in office in 1923 of an apparent heart attack, Stephan had Holland join in President Coolidge's call for a national day of mourning for "the wise statesman, the devout Christian, the patriotic American, and the devoted husband" who was struck down in the prime of life. Stephan asked businesses, factories, and schools to close for the day at noon, so that residents could attend memorial services in their churches. The public service was held at Central Avenue Christian Reformed Church for the beloved president, who "died a martyr's death, and will ever live in our hearts as a spotless hero of American patriotism." Diekema was the featured speaker, as he always was at such occasions. He had the advantage of having known Harding "intimately thru life."[187]

Hollanders being both patriotic and Republican, the response was overwhelming. Two thousand people jammed into Central Avenue church—two hundred beyond its capacity—by standing in the aisles and hallways. The fire marshal must have looked the other way. So revered was Harding that citizens readily contributed several hundred dollars to the national Harding Memorial Drive, and several prominent men asked the common council to honor the president by renaming Columbia Avenue as Harding Avenue. Though several streets had already been renamed, this idea went nowhere.[188]

When the war president, Woodrow Wilson, died a few months after Harding, Mayor Stephan did not call for a local day of mourning, although some Democrats in the Second Ward living along First Avenue asked the common council to rename it Wilson Boulevard. This suggestion backfired on the petitioners. The council, led by alderman Kammeraad, chair of the street committee, decided instead to rename First Street as First *Boulevard* from Eighth to Sixteenth Streets, since it was extra wide. (First Boulevard was later renamed Washington Boulevard.)[189]

186 Ibid., 18 Aug., 8 Sept. 1921, 16 Feb., 15 June 1922; *Holland Sentinel*, 1 Jan. 2000; Donald van Reken, *The Interurban Era in Holland, Michigan* (Holland: privately printed, 1981).

187 *Holland City News*, 9, 16 (quote), 1923.

188 Ibid., 31 Jan., 2, 7, 14 Feb., 6 Mar. 1924.

189 Ibid., 24 Apr. 1924.

The 1924 spring election that brought Nicholas "Nick" Kammeraad (1924-28) to the mayor's office was the quietest in a dozen years, and less than half the electorate bothered to vote. Kammeraad, a humble shoemaker and alderman for twelve years, surprisingly led an activist city administration. Under his watch, the city fathers improved Kollen Park; erected a new railway depot, a $350,000 sewage disposal plant, and a new city hospital; and paved eight miles of roads, all while holding the line on taxes. Kammeraad at the urging of friends, "stood" for a third term in 1928, but he refused to campaign, allowing his record to speak for itself. Apparently, it did not, and he was defeated by the young and energetic Earnest Brooks, one of Holland's leading citizens. The council then elected Kammeraad president of the board of public works, which post he held until his death in 1935. Kammeraad served as an elder in both the Fourteenth Street and Central Avenue Christian Reformed congregations. He and Richard M. Smith were Holland's only mayors from that denomination.[190]

"Ernie" Brooks, a Democrat, broke the Republican string by winning office in 1928 and again in 1930. He carried all six wards in both elections. In background and in political ideology, he contrasted sharply with his mayoral predecessor. Brooks was an American, highly educated, a high-order Mason, a civic leader, and in favor of an activist government. A minister's son from Chicago, he first came to Holland with his parents to vacation at Macatawa Park. He attended Hope College (1908-10) and later graduated from the University of Chicago. After completing military service in World War I, Brooks returned to Hope to teach and coach football for a year before going into the insurance business with Arthur A. Visscher and the 7Up Bottling Company with his brother Phillip. Brooks served as treasurer of the chamber of commerce and contributed liberally to local improvement projects.[191]

On the social scene, Brooks was active in the Holland Country Club, the Century Club, the Exchange Club, the American Legion, and the Masonic Order. In his campaign flier, he promised to hold taxes "as low as possible, consistent with keeping Holland in the front of the finest cities to live in," and to appoint only qualified people to city posts. He held to those promises. And despite his outsider status in town, Brooks helped launch the Tulip Time festival in 1929, and his

190 Ibid., 20 May 1924, 8 Mar. 1928; "Biographical Information for the Mayors of Holland," JAH.

191 For this and the previous paragraph, see *Holland City News*, 4 Nov. 1926, 8, 15 Mar., 28 Oct. 1928, 8 Aug. 1929.

family planted ten thousand tulips in front of their home. The next year he had the city plant one hundred thousand bulbs along the streets and lanes, in a legacy that continues to the present. Under Brooks, in 1930 the common council purchased a dozen of the new-fangled voting machines for $128 apiece to make counting on election night quick and accurate. Another longtime Democrat, Fred Kamferbeek, city patrolman and chief of police, ran against the tide for Ottawa County sheriff in 1924 and 1926 and won election handily as the first Democrat in that office in fifty years, but Kamferbeek could not withstand the Republican tide in 1928 and lost to Cornelius Steketee.

The Great Depression

When the Great Depression brought rising hardship and unemployment in the early 1930s, Mayor Brooks was proactive. He instituted a "market basket plan," a make-work program for unemployed men to earn enough to feed their families, which won kudos in the statehouse in Lansing. President Roosevelt's New Deal program resonated with him and he "joined the team," becoming chair of the Michigan Welfare Commission (1930-34), secretary of the Michigan Emergency Relief Administration (1933-35), and director of the state Federal Surplus Foods Corp. (1933-35). Under the federal relief programs, Brooks started the school lunch program for needy pupils in the state. Later, Brooks served two terms as state senator (1937-41) and ran unsuccessfully in the Democratic gubernatorial primary in 1944. Former *Sentinel* editor Randall P. Vande Water aptly calls Brooks "Holland's best known Democrat" from the 1920s to the end of Governor G. Mennen "Soapy" Williams' twelve-year tenure in1961. The Brooks family has cut a wide swath in Holland and continues to do so. But Ernie's strong support of New Deal programs cut no ice with city voters.[192]

In April 1932 they turned him out in favor of former mayor Bosch, which must have been a hard blow. The Great Depression was in full swing, and the country was on the cusp of Roosevelt's smashing victory a few months later, yet the innate conservatism of the town's residents led them back to Bosch, who continued for another two terms, until 1936. In that year Democrat Nicholas Sprietsma, former city treasurer, ousted Republican John Den Herder by 169 votes for county treasurer. Sprietsma served only one term before Den Herder's son Fred defeated him in 1938. Sprietsma was the last Democrat to hold office in Ottawa County.

[192] *Holland Sentinel*, Earnest Brooks obit., 16 Apr. 1981; Vande Water, "Holland Never Voted for Lincoln," in *Holland Happenings,* 4:20.

Mayor Earnest C. Brooks, 1928-32 (*Archives, Holland Historical Trust*)

Holland voters in 1936 re-elected another former Republican mayor, Henry Geerlings, who had served thirty years earlier. Geerlings' second stint as mayor ran for eight years (1936-44), through the challenges of the Second New Deal and the Second World War. In the spring primaries of 1938, Democrats got only 12 percent of all votes cast. As the *City News* editor noted wryly: "It would appear that the WPA, PWA, and similar alphabet arrangements have not cut into the Republican ranks much." In that fall's general election, the entire Republican ticket swept the slate in the city of Holland and Ottawa County.[193] Since 1936 Holland has not elected a Democrat to any local or county office. Winning the GOP (Grand Old Party) primary is thus tantamount to victory in local races.

The repeal of the Eighteenth Amendment in 1933 brought back the bitter battles between wets and drys of the years 1908 to 1913, when citizens cast ballots on six liquor referenda and old friends on opposite sides of the issue broke off relationships. The city of Holland in 1933 again voted dry on the Twenty-First (Repeal) Amendment, as did Holland Township and the city of Zeeland. But the margin of 54 percent in the city of Holland was smaller than in the pre-war years, and it bode ill for the prohibitionists. Indeed, the next year Holland voted overwhelmingly wet by 64 percent on a state local option referendum. Never again would the saloons in Holland be shuttered by the ballot box. But the 1913 law against selling liquor by the glass remained in place,

193 *Holland City News*, 15 Sept. (quote), 10 Nov. 1938.

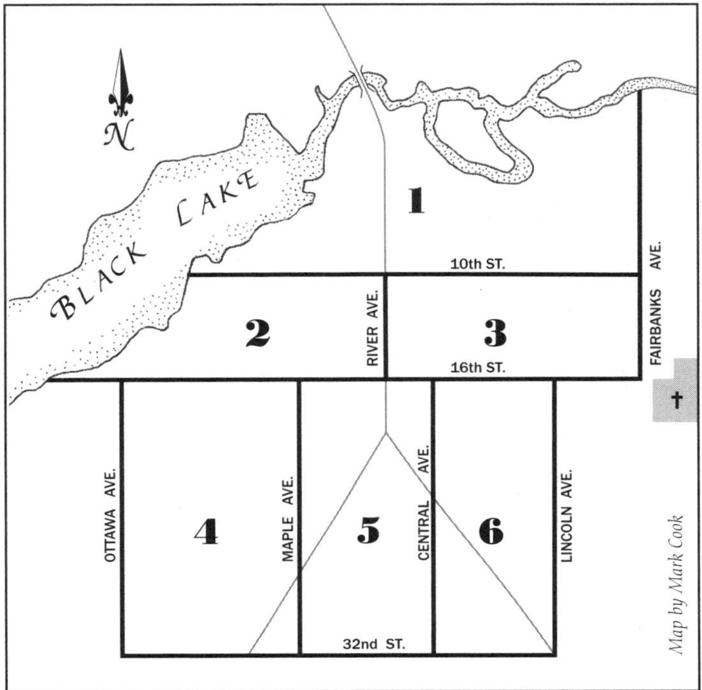

Fig. 24.6. Ward Map, 1941

and also the 1926 law banning Sunday sales of all alcoholic beverages. This followed a straw vote in a primary election that strongly endorsed a Sunday ban. In 1938 saloon interests in Holland got up a petition with more than 1,300 signatures to force the city to place on the ballot a liquor-by-the-glass referendum, but it went down in resounding defeat by a margin of nearly seven to one. Hollanders liked to drink, but at home—not in saloons. Ottawa County dry forces put a local option proposal back on the ballot in 1954, and again Holland voted it down, this time by 55 percent.[194]

After World War Two

In 1950 Holland voters adopted a new charter, which among other changes, vested executive authority in a city manager and made the mayor's role largely a ceremonial one, although the mayor remained a full voting member of the city council (the new name for the common council). In a referendum in June, the voters turned down the revised

194 Ibid., 6 Apr. 1933, 1, 8 Nov. 1934, 17 Sept. 1936, 17, 31 Mar., 7 Apr. 1938. 4 Nov. 1954.

City council with first councilwoman, 3 April 1951 (*l-r, seated*): John Beltman, Laverne Rudolph, Mayor Harry Harrington, Bernice Bishop, John Van Eerden (*standing*): Anthony Nienhuis, Rein Visscher, Robert Visscher, Raymond Holwerda (*courtesy Randall P. Vande Water*)

charter by two hundred votes, so the aldermen put the issue back on the ballot in November, and this time it passed by a mere forty-two votes. Clearly, citizens were ambiguous about giving control of the city to an un-elected official who was also an outsider. Harold C. McClintock was the first city manager, and in his four short years, he established the workings of the office and set a bar of excellence and responsibility for his successors.[195]

The Republican dominance in the city of Holland and Ottawa County increased after the death of the popular Franklin Roosevelt in 1945. With only two exceptions—1964 with Barry Goldwater and 1992 with George H. W. Bush's re-election bid—Republicans won presidential elections by majorities of two to one and often three to one. The Democratic low point was in 1960 when John F. Kennedy, the second Roman Catholic candidate, won a mere 17 percent against Richard Nixon. Other Democrats fared little better. Adlai Stevenson (1952, 1956), Hubert Humphrey (1968), George McGovern (1972), Jimmy Carter (1976, 1980), and Walter Mondale (1984) all gained only 20 to 25 percent against a string of popular Republicans: the war hero Dwight Eisenhower, the political warhorse Richard Nixon, and

195 *Holland Sentinel*, 8 Nov. 1950. See chapter 27, footnote 1, for a list of city managers.

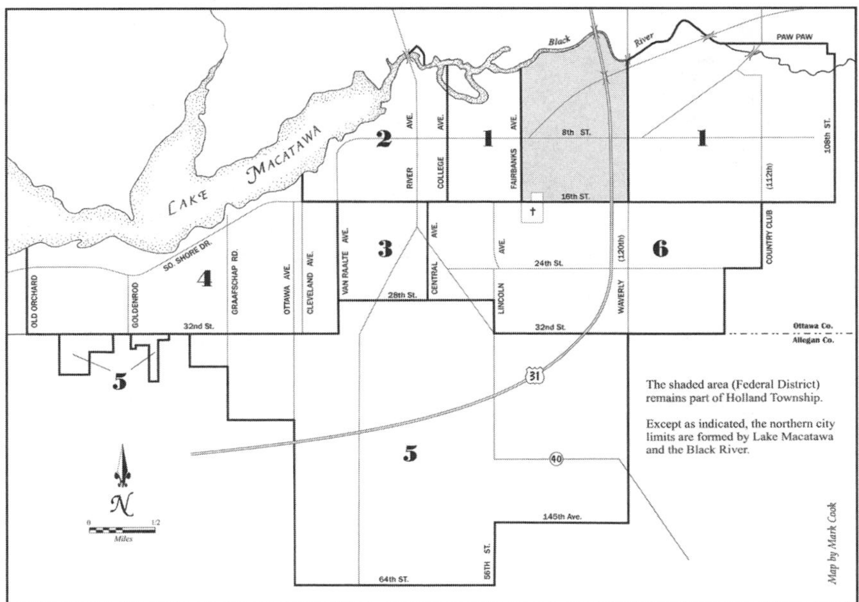

Fig. 24.7. Ward Map, 1961

the beloved Ronald Reagan. Reagan, while still a Hollywood film star, visited Holland in April 1960 at the invitation of the local General Electric plant; he was the TV host for GE. After a warm welcome at the Hotel Warm Friend, he went to the Civic Center to address three hundred business and political leaders on the topic, "Business, Ballots, and Bureaus." His hard-hitting talk warned against "socialistic trends in government" and called for smaller government, less bureaucracy, lower taxes, and the defense of freedom, all familiar themes in his political career. "Dutch" Reagan relished putting on a pair of wooden shoes.[196]

Another local favorite was Gerald R. Ford—Grand Rapids' native son and the nation's thirty-eighth president (1973-76)—who rode in the 1976 Tulip Time parade. Ford vacationed at an Ottawa Beach cottage as a youth, and his fondness for the area induced him to return as the first sitting president to visit Holland. He was "old hat" by then, having "pressed the flesh" already in 1948 during his first run for Congress. Ford was back to campaign for re-election in 1950, and to boost oilman William C. Vandenberg's unsuccessful run for lieutenant governor. Mayor Louis Hallacy II considered the hosting of President Ford the highlight of his mayoral career.

[196] *Holland City News*, 28 Apr. 1960.

Congressman Gerald R. Ford astride a circus elephant in Holland while campaigning for re-election in 1950 and to boost William C. Vandenberg's bid for Michigan lieutenant governor (*Joint Archives of Holland*)

Motorcade of President Gerald R. Ford with First Lady Betty Ford and Congressman Guy Vander Jagt at 1976 Tulip Time parade, surrounded by wary US Secret Service agents (*Joint Archives of Holland*)

Left to right: Hope College President Gordon Van Wylen, President Gerald R. Ford, Provost Jacob E. Nyenhuis, and Hope College Trustee Peter C. Cook, April 1987. President Ford was on campus to receive an honorary doctorate (*Joint Archives of Holland*)

Republican President George H. W. Bush campaigned at Hope College in his 1992 race against Bill Clinton, and his son George W. Bush came to Holland in his 2004 re-election campaign. Bush "45" purchased a Tommy Turtle at Captain Sundae on Douglas Avenue and met an enthusiastic crowd at the Ottawa County Fair Grounds. In 2010-11 Democratic President Barack Obama came to Holland twice within thirteen months, to break ground first for LG Chem and then the Johnson Controls-Saft battery plants, both to demonstrate his environmental bona fides (chapter 15). To have presidential visits two years in a row is unprecedented for a small town such as Holland, but it is fitting, since Obama in 2008 was the first Democratic presidential candidate to carry the city in 140 years, since 1868.

During the 2012 Republican primary, Mitt Romney, who grew up in Michigan as the son of former governor George Romney, came to Holland on a sunny June afternoon to address supporters at Holland State Park, with the lighthouse "Big Red," blue Lake Michigan, and a giant American flag as the backdrop. Romney carried Michigan in the primary, but although he won Holland and the surrounding townships handily, he lost the general election.[197]

[197] *Holland Sentinel*, 10 Nov. 1979, 14 June 1998, 13 Sept. 2004, 28 Dec. 2006, 10 July 2010, 5 Aug. 2011, 20 June, 8 Nov. 2012; *Grand Rapids Press*, 5 Aug. 2011.

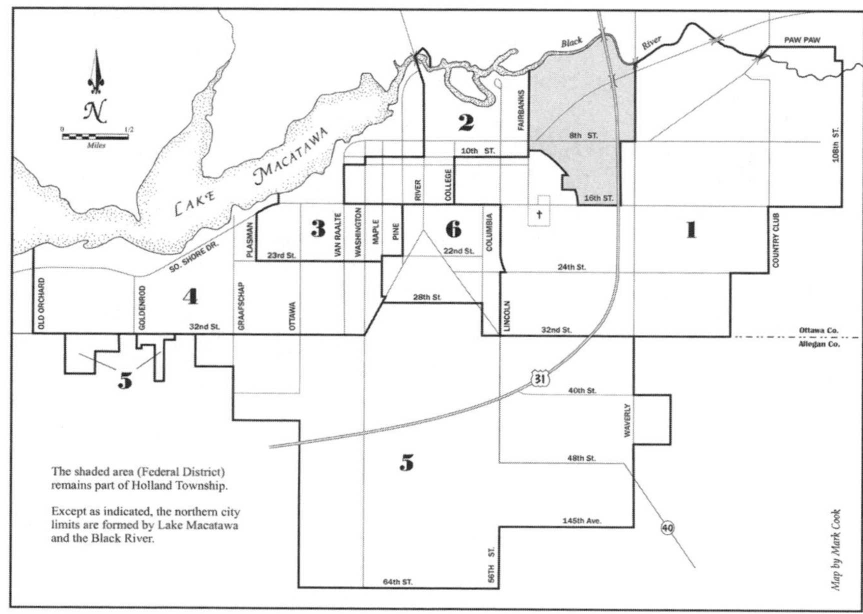

Fig. 24.8. Ward Map, 1972

Not only were the region's voters overwhelmingly Republican, but they also went to the polls in record numbers. Until the 1970s, turnouts of 85 to 90 percent of registered voters were common, as city newspapers boasted with bold headlines. In 1952, for example, 88 percent of registered voters went to the polls—92 percent in the Third Ward—despite waiting lines of more than an hour. Upon returning home, voters put on their porch lights as a sign they had done their duty as citizens. The city, it was reported, was "ablaze" with light in the early evening.[198]

Congressman Peter "Pete" Hoekstra in 1992 became the second Holland resident (Gerrit Diekema was the first) elected to Congress. An immigrant from the Netherlands in the 1950s, he rose to a top executive position at the Herman Miller Furniture Company before running against and unseating the long time incumbent Guy Vander Jagt, a native of Cadillac. Hoekstra shared the values of his conservative district, and his Dutch Reformed roots appealed to many voters. He won re-election five times by overwhelming numbers and chaired the powerful House Intelligence Committee in Washington. In the same election that launched Hoekstra's career in Congress, Luciano Hernandez became the first Hispanic American in Holland to win office;

198 *Holland City News*, 5 Nov. 1952.

namely, a seat on the Ottawa County Board of Commissioners, after serving on the Holland city council, representing the Second Ward. This victory was only possible because Hernandez ran as a Republican (chapter 32). His decision dashed the hopes of Holland's Democrats that the growing Hispanic vote would gain them a majority in the city, or at least level the playing field against a party that had dominated political life for 140 years (chapter 32). Hoekstra unsuccessfully ran for Michigan governor in 2010 and the US Senate in 2012.[199]

Conclusion

Since 1868 Holland Township and the city of Holland, as well as Ottawa County generally, have voted Republican in every state and national election. Neighboring Allegan County went Democratic only once in the twentieth century, and that was Franklin Roosevelt's second run in 1936. As the population of the city of Holland has become more diverse, however, with foreign-born residents making up nearly 40 percent, the Democratic vote has been increasing, and that party may soon become the new majority. The rising Democratic trend first became evident in the late 1980s when Michael Dukakis (1988) and Bill Clinton (1992, 1996) won nearly 30 percent. Al Gore in 2000 and John Kerry in 2004 pushed the Democratic vote to 32 and 37 percent, respectively. That was almost twice the historic level since 1952. The key for the Democrats in Holland is to get out the vote. Turnout was down to 64 percent in 2004. Park Township, in contrast, had a turnout of 79 percent; the city of Zeeland and Zeeland Township were at 76 percent, and they voted Republican by 84 and 85 percent, respectively. This pattern reflects the Holland of old.

In 2008 Obama brought the Democratic vote up to 49.6 percent, its apogee to this time. But in his re-election triumph in 2012, President Obama's support in Holland dropped by one thousand votes to 45.5 percent (appendix 7.1). The Democratic Party does not yet have a lock on the city in state and national elections, like they have in Grand Rapids. But a major voting realignment is clearly underway, thanks to the growing Hispanic and African American population, which nationwide in 2012 voted 71 percent and 93 percent Democratic, respectively. As these newer Holland residents assimilate, they may give the Republican Party a second look, provided candidates appeal to their moral values of family, traditional marriage, the protection of human life in the womb, and self reliance.

[199] May, "Politics—As Usual?," 4-6; *Grand Rapids Press*, 8 Nov. 2012.

Bearings of sailing courses are true. Distances in statute miles.

The sailing courses *begin at a point $1\frac{1}{2}$ miles W. $\frac{1}{4}$ S. (267° 15′) of* Holland Rear Range Light *and in range of* Front Light.

To Saugatuck	S. $\frac{1}{8}$ W.	8	Miles
" Michigan City	SSW. $\frac{5}{8}$ W.	79	"
" Calumet Harbor	SW. $\frac{1}{4}$ S.	96	"
" Chicago	SW. $\frac{1}{4}$ W.	$91\frac{1}{4}$	"
" Waukegan	WSW. $\frac{1}{4}$ W.	84	"
" Racine	W. $\frac{1}{8}$ S.	$75\frac{1}{2}$	"
" Milwaukee	WNW. $\frac{7}{8}$ W.	$82\frac{3}{4}$	"
" Port Washington	NW. by W. $\frac{5}{8}$ W.	$91\frac{3}{4}$	"
" Sheboygan	NW. $\frac{1}{8}$ W.	$98\frac{1}{2}$	"
" Manitowoc & Two Rivers	NW. $\frac{3}{4}$ N.	113	"
" Sturgeon Bay Canal	N. by W. $\frac{7}{8}$ W.	148	"
" Little Sable Point	N. by W. $\frac{1}{2}$ W.	$63\frac{1}{2}$	"
" Grand Haven	N. $\frac{3}{4}$ W.	20	"

The above distances of sailing courses *are to the points of departure shown on Coast and General Charts.*

For LAKE and HARBOR DESCRIPTIONS, &c.

Consult the latest annual Bulletin and Supplements of the Survey of Northern and Northwestern Lakes published under the direction of the Chief of Engineers, U.S. Army, by the U.S. Lake Survey Office, Detroit, Mich.

ABBREVIATIONS.

F.-fixed, *W.*-white, *R.*-red, RGE.-Range, LT.-Light, FOG W.-Fog Whistle, L. SAV. STA.-Life Saving Station, STO. SIG. STA.-Storm Signal Station.

The figures in brackets placed after the letters denoting character of light, indicate its visibility in statute miles when observer's eye is 15 feet above lake level.

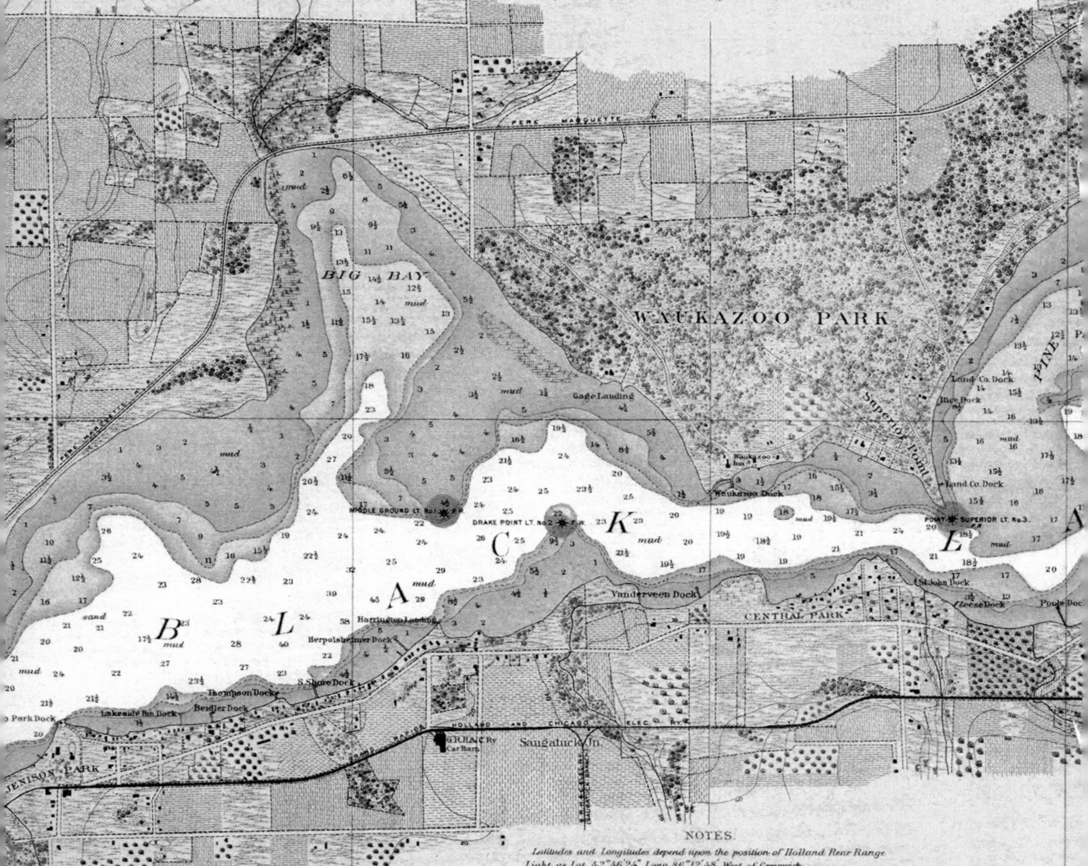

NOTES.

Latitudes and Longitudes depend upon the position of Holland Rear Range Light as Lat. 42° 46′ 24″, Long. 86° 12′ 48″, West of Greenwich.

Based on the newly adopted U.S. Standard datum the Latitude of this station is 42° 46′ 23.″771, Longitude 86° 12′ 45.″286, West of Greenwich.

Topographic contours are 10 feet apart, and the figures thereon indicate elevations in feet above mean lake level.

Soundings, in feet, *are reduced to Standard Low Water datum, which for Lake Michigan is 578.51 feet above mean tide at New York. See table of comparative elevations of water levels.*

Water areas with depths to 6, 12 and 18 feet are tinted in blue.

6 ft. contours
12 ft. "
18 ft. "

Comparative Elevations of Water Levels on Lake Michigan referred to Mean Tide at New York, (adjusted Levels of 1903.)

High Water of 1838	584.69 ft.
Plane of reference of General Chart	581.63 ft.
Mean stage 1860-1907 both inclusive,	581.32 ft.
Lowest recorded monthly mean (Dec. 1895)	578.98 ft.
Plane of reference of this Chart (Standard Low Water)	578.51 ft.

0.47 2.81 3.12 6.18

SCALE OF FEET.

SCALE OF METERS.